A Note From the Publisher

The Educational Book Division of Prentice-Hall, Inc., is committed to the publication of outstanding textbooks. One important measure of a book's excellence is how well it communicates with its readers. To insure a highly readable book, the content for this text was selected, organized, and written at a level appropriate for the intended audience. The Dale-Chall readability formula was used to control readability level. An inviting and meaningful design was created to enhance the book's visual appeal as well as to facilitate the reading process. We are confident that the students for whom this book is intended will read it, comprehend it, and learn from it.

The following features were incorporated into the content and design of this text. A page reference is given to provide an example of each feature.

- Major historical concepts and other important social studies terms are italicized and defined in the text. These terms also appear in the section reviews (page 87).

- Important historical terms are included in a glossary. Each glossary entry refers to the page on which the term is first discussed in the text (page 767).

- To aid pronunciation, difficult terms and names are phonetically respelled the first time they appear (page 42). A pronunciation key that explains the system of respelling is included in a special reference section at the end of the book (page 766).

- A chapter outline appears at the beginning of each chapter (page 610).

- A chronological list of major events appears near the end of each chapter (page 185).

- Each chapter ends with a chapter summary (page 498).

- Questions that help students check their comprehension of text material appear after every section of a chapter (page 273).

- Each chapter concludes with review questions, questions for further thought, and activities for developing basic skills (page 359).

- Instruction in such social studies skills as reading maps and graphs, comparing, classifying, and analyzing help the student read, interpret, and evaluate the content of the text. Such instruction appears at the end of each chapter (page 285) and in special skill lessons (page 89).

- Boxed features, including vignettes, biographies, diary excerpts, and extracts from government documents heighten student interest (page 537).

THE
UNITED
STATES

A HISTORY OF THE REPUBLIC

James West Davidson   Mark H. Lytle

PRENTICE-HALL, INC.,   Englewood Cliffs, New Jersey

THE UNITED STATES A HISTORY OF THE REPUBLIC

SECOND EDITION

Teacher's Edition

ISBN 0-13-938167-8   10 9 8 7 6 5 4 3 2 1

PRENTICE-HALL INTERNATIONAL, INC., London
PRENTICE-HALL OF AUSTRALIA, PTY, LTD., Sydney
PRENTICE-HALL CANADA INC., Toronto
PRENTICE-HALL OF INDIA PRIVATE LTD., New Delhi
PRENTICE-HALL OF JAPAN, INC., Tokyo
PRENTICE-HALL OF SOUTHEAST ASIA PTE. LTD., Singapore
WHITEHALL BOOKS LIMITED, Wellington, New Zealand
EDITORA PRENTICE-HALL DO BRASIL LTDA., Rio de Janeiro

Contents
To the Teacher
Answer Key

Contents

Answer Key

To the Teacher

The United States: A History of the Republic offers the student a chronological narrative treatment of American history. Within this framework the authors deal with several important themes that reappear throughout American history—such themes as the growth of national unity, the diversity of the population, and the development of democratic institutions. The authors have presented and interpreted the facts of history in light of these themes.

Great care has been taken to create a distinctly teachable text, one that will serve the needs of both teachers and students. With this aim in mind, each element of the program has been designed to contribute to the success of your lessons.

Three auxiliary components accompany the student edition of *The United States: A History of the Republic*—a Teacher's Edition, a Teacher's Resource Handbook, and a Test Bank. The Teacher's Edition consists of the complete student text and a comprehensive Answer Key to all questions posed in the text. The Teacher's Resource Handbook presents daily lesson suggestions, worksheets keyed directly to specific lesson suggestions and assignments, and a full program of chapter and unit tests. The Test Bank and a computerized testing service are also available. The service allows you to choose questions from the Test Bank for custom-made tests.

The Student Text

■ General Organization

The United States: A History of the Republic is divided into ten units. Chronologically organized, each unit covers a period in American history. The beginning of a unit coincides with a significant moment in the nation's growth and development. Thus students acquire a clear sense of the periods by which American history is often categorized.

Each unit is divided into chapters, which total 41 in all. Most chapters are between 16 and 20 pages long and represent about one week's worth of instructional time, sometimes less. The chapters are divided into sections that provide a sharply focused discussion of specific issues. In many cases a section forms the basis of a single lesson.

The Reference Section, pages 751–831, is designed to supplement the body of the text. It is intended for student use throughout the course of study.

■ Reading Aids

The United States: A History of the Republic is written in clean, uncluttered prose. Its easy-to-follow writing style will heighten students' interest in the material and further their understanding as well. The following features serve as special aids to readability:

Terms

Major historical concepts and other important social studies terms are italicized and defined when they first appear in the text.

Pronunciations

Difficult terms and names are phonetically respelled when they first appear in the text. The Pronunciation Key, which explains the system of respelling, can be found on text page 766.

Glossary

The Glossary in the Reference Section defines most of the key historical terms introduced in the text. Each entry in the glossary is cross-referenced to the page on which it first appears in the text.

Footnotes

In some cases further explanation of a term, idea, or event is important for student understanding of the material, yet such an explanation would be intrusive if placed within the narrative itself. In these instances, additional information is presented in a footnote.

■ Features of the Text

In addition to the reading aids, the student text contains many other carefully constructed pedagogical features:

Unit and Chapter Openings

Each unit opens with a contemporary painting that captures the spirit of the era. An outline of chapter titles and section headings is part of each unit opening. Thus the structure and overall content of each unit is clear at a glance. See text pages 16–17 for an example.

Each chapter also opens with an illustration from the period, usually a painting or a photograph. A written introduction to the chapter and an outline of section headings accompany the opening illustration. These features are designed to preview chapter content and arouse student curiosity about the forthcoming material.

Special Features

Interspersed throughout the text are vignettes, profiles, and primary source documents, including speeches, diary excerpts, and letters. These special features are boxed off against a light tan background. By enlivening the study of American history they offer an additional dimension to the text. Each chapter has at least one special feature. A full list of titles is provided in the table of contents to the student text.

Skill Lessons

Thirteen skill lessons teaching important social studies skills are integrated into the student text. The content of each skill lesson is directly related to the chapter and section in which it appears. Included among the skills are reading graphs, reading maps, analyzing primary sources, and synthesizing pieces of evidence. See the table of contents to the student text for a complete list of the skill lessons.

Visual Aids

The text contains many photographs, paintings, cartoons, maps, charts, and graphs, each accompanied by an explanatory caption. These visual aids reinforce and enrich the narrative. Several of the skill lessons instruct students how to read, interpret, and analyze these visual aids.

Metrics

The text introduces students to the metric system by providing metric equivalents in parentheses for each measurement presented in traditional form. Maps include both a scale of miles and a scale of kilometers.

Section Reviews

Each section concludes with several review questions. The opening questions in most Section Reviews ask students to identify important people, places, laws, and documents and to define the italicized historical terms in the section. The remaining questions ask students to discuss information they recall from the section.

Major Events

A time chart called "Major Events" is placed near the end of each chapter, to give students a clear chronological perspective when they have finished the chapter.

In Perspective

As a conclusion to the chapter narrative, this feature offers a brief summary of the chapter's most important points. Students can use this summary as a guide when studying for tests.

End-of-Chapter Questions

Each chapter ends with three sets of questions, entitled "Chapter Review," "For Further Thought," and "Developing Basic Skills." Chapter Review questions ask students to comprehend, analyze, and synthesize information from the chapter. For Further Thought questions ask students to draw inferences from information in the chapter or to defend a point of view. Developing Basic Skills questions ask students to apply such skills as comparing, interpreting visual evidence, reading maps and graphs, and undertaking library research. All Developing Basic Skills questions relate directly to the content covered in the chapters; many reinforce the skill lessons presented in the text.

Reference Section

This section, pages 751–831, contains a number of important elements, each designated by a colored tab at the right edge of the page. The elements are described below:

- Eight reference maps provide general information about the United States and the world (pages 752–761).
- The Chronology of American History traces developments in politics and government, exploration and innovation, society and economics, and culture and religion.

These parallel sections help students place major events and developments in perspective (pages 762–765).

- The Pronunciation Key explains the phonetic respelling of difficult terms and names used throughout the text (page 766).
- The Glossary defines key historical terms (pages 767–772).
- Suggested Readings supplement each chapter (pages 773–779). This student bibliography contains works of fiction and nonfiction, including biographies. Many of the suggested titles are standard historical works; many others were written especially for a high school audience.
- Two charts contain basic information about the 50 states and the Presidents and Vice-Presidents of the United States (pages 780–781).
- The text of the Declaration of Independence is reproduced in full (pages 782–783).
- The full text of the Constitution of the United States is accompanied by annotations explaining the substance of each clause (pages 784–814). The annotations define technical and archaic terms and explain how the courts have interpreted particular clauses. The annotations include cross-references to pertinent discussions in the text.
- A detailed index (pages 815–831) lists all the important names, events, subjects, terms, and places discussed in the text. Charts, maps, and pictures are included, each identified by an italicized letter (*c, m,* or *p*) preceding the page reference.

Teacher's Edition

The Teacher's Edition consists of the complete student text and an Answer Key to all questions contained in the text. On-page annotations in the Teacher's Edition key text questions to the page in the Answer Key on which the answers can be found.

Every effort has been made to provide a complete and comprehensive Teacher's Edition. To this end, answers have been provided for all Section Review questions and for those questions that appear at the end of each chapter. Questions posed in the skill lessons are also answered in the Answer Key, as are questions contained in captions. In many cases in which a question calls upon students to prepare a chart, the Answer Key supplies a completed sample chart. See page A 33 for an example of this feature.

Teacher's Resource Handbook

The Teacher's Resource Handbook is written to closely correspond with the student text. The Handbook contains three basic components: lesson suggestions, work sheets, and tests.

■ Lesson Suggestions

The lesson ideas in the Handbook are organized into chapters and sections that correspond to the chapters and sections in the text.

The lesson ideas for each chapter begin with an overview providing general planning suggestions for the chapter as a whole. Following the chapter overview are Suggested Procedures for each section: specific lesson ideas based on text material. A wide variety of learning strategies is used, and all of them encourage students to become actively involved in the lessons. After completing the steps in each set of Suggested Procedures, students will have accomplished several important knowledge and skills objectives.

The Suggested Procedures for each section are followed by Reinforcement and Enrichment Assignments. Reinforcement Assignments involve students in review and mastery of the text material. A wide variety of activities is presented. Students can be expected to enjoy as well as profit from such assignments as completing word puzzles, interpreting visual evidence, and writing historical fiction, to name a few.

Enrichment Assignments provide students of all ability levels with yet another kind of learning opportunity. Enrichment Assignments encourage students to extend their knowledge beyond the text by researching in greater depth some of the topics they have learned about or by investigating new ones.

■ Worksheets

The worksheet program ties in directly with the lesson suggestions. The worksheets are designed for use either with the Suggested Procedures for a given section or with a Reinforcement or Enrichment Assignment. Located following the lesson suggestions, the worksheets are intended for duplication and distribution to your classes.

The worksheets contain many different types of activities. For example, some ask students to analyze primary source material; others require students to interpret maps, graphs, or charts. Some are word games; others are completion exercises. Answers to the worksheets can be found in the Answer Key section of the Handbook.

■ Tests

The Teacher's Resource Handbook contains a comprehensive testing program consisting of chapter and unit tests. All tests are composed of objective and essay questions. All are designed for completion in one class period.

For your convenience, an Answer Key is provided in the Handbook. Like the worksheets, the tests are intended for duplication and distribution to your classes.

Test Bank

The Test Bank that accompanies *The United States: A History of the Republic* enables you to create tests tailored to the needs of your class. After selecting questions from the Test Bank, you can order a custom-made test from Prentice-Hall's Computerized Testing Service. The Test Bank contains over 1,200 questions—some with several parts—providing over 1,900 individual test items. A complete answer key is included.

Approximately 50 test items are provided for each of the 41 chapters of the student text. Each item is keyed to the section of the chapter in which the topic is discussed. The Test Bank includes both objective and essay questions divided into four categories: "Skills," such as map and graph reading, "Key People, Places, and Terms," "Chronology," and "Critical Thinking."

Unit One: The Americas

1 Two Worlds (Prehistory–1492)

Section Review, text page **20**

1. *prehistoric period:* the time before recorded history. *archaeologist:* scientist who studies the life and cultures of ancient people. *artifact:* object made by a human being. Tools and weapons are types of artifacts studied by archaeologists. *carbon-14 test:* a method for determining the age of plant and animal remains. *amino acid racemization:* another method for determining the age of plant and animal remains. Certain limitations of the carbon-14 method have been solved by amino acid racemization.

2. Archaeologists study skeletons to learn about the age and appearance of early people. They study artifacts to discover the kinds of tools and weapons that early people used.

3. (a) Land bridge theory: according to this theory, a land bridge, perhaps 1,000 miles wide, connected Asia and North America thousands of years ago. Experts who believe in this theory have suggested that people migrated from Asia to the Americas, tracking herds of animals westward across the land bridge. (b) The land bridge would have covered the area today known as the Bering Strait.

4. It is probable that about 10,000 years ago glaciers retreated, temperatures warmed, lakes dried up, lush vegetation died, and many large animal species became extinct. These environmental changes required people living in the Americas during this period to adapt their ways of life.

Section Review, text page **25**

1. *Dekanawidah:* Huron religious leader. It is believed that he encouraged the formation of a confederation of the Iroquois tribes. *Hiawatha:* Mohawk chief and disciple of Dekanawidah. He too worked toward an alliance of the Iroquois tribes. *Iroquois League:* political confederation, or alliance, of Iroquois tribes, established between 1570 and 1600. Its purpose was to end fighting among member tribes and to provide a defense against enemies.

2. *potlatch:* ceremonial feast to demonstrate prosperity, held by the early peoples of the northwest

Pacific coast. *pictogram:* picture drawn to convey an idea. The Anasazi of the Southwest drew pictograms on canyon walls. *adobe:* brick made of sun-dried clay, used to construct Pueblo buildings. *kiva:* religious ceremonial room located at the center of each Pueblo town. *hogan:* Navajo home fashioned as an earthen dome with a log frame. *nomadic:* representing a wandering way of life. *sachem:* Iroquois leader specially chosen to govern the Iroquois League.

3. People of the northwest Pacific coast had the most plentiful food supply.

4. (a) The Pueblo probably learned arts such as pottery making from the Anasazi. (b) The Navajo probably learned farming and weaving from the Pueblo. Navajo religion was also influenced by that of the Pueblo.

5. The travois made it easier for the Plains people to carry their possessions. The teepee provided the Plains people with portable shelters.

6. (a) "Matrilineal" refers to a system by which lines of descent are traced through the mother's family. (b) Pueblo and Iroquois societies were matrilineal.

Section Review, text page **27**

1. *People of the Sun:* name that the Aztecs called themselves. *Tenochtitlán:* Aztec capital city. *Huitzilopochtli:* chief god of the Aztecs. *Sapa Inca:* supreme Inca ruler.

2. The Mayas used their cities as religious centers where people gathered to worship.

3. (a) Maya scientific accomplishments: in the field of astronomy, the Mayas could predict eclipses of the sun and moon and could chart the movements of the planet Venus; they also developed exact calendars and a complex system of writing. (b) Aztec scientific accomplishments: technological advances in building, irrigation, and mathematics; advanced knowledge of star formations. (c) Inca scientific accomplishments: engineering and building. (Students should receive credit for listing two areas of achievement for each culture.)

Section Review, text page **32**

1. *Marco Polo:* son of a Venetian merchant. He traveled through China in the late 1200s and reported what he saw. *Henry the Navigator:* Portuguese prince who pioneered and fostered European explo-

ration of the world beyond Europe and the Mediterranean. *Sagres:* port and castle in Portugal where Prince Henry maintained a school of navigation. *Bartolomeu Dias:* explorer who sailed around the Cape of Good Hope in 1487. *Vasco da Gama:* explorer who made the trip around Africa to India in 1497.

2. *serf:* in the Middle Ages, a peasant bound to work on a lord's land. *vassal:* in the Middle Ages, a person who received land from a king or other superior in return for loyalty. *feudalism:* political and social system of the Middle Ages. *manor:* in the Middle Ages, a large estate owned by a lord. *compass:* instrument used to determine direction. *astrolabe:* instrument used to fix location by sighting the stars. *quadrant:* instrument used to take bearings from the sun or stars in order to plot a ship's position on a map. *caravel:* vessel with triangular sails, developed by Prince Henry to sail into the wind. *carrack:* vessel with square sails that preceded the development of the caravel.

3. (a) The Crusades were a series of wars waged by European Christians beginning in 1099 to recapture the city of Jerusalem from Muslims. The Crusades lasted for about 150 years. (b) Ways Crusades increased interest in world beyond Europe: accept all answers that describe new ideas and knowledge inspired by books or other items from the Arab world, such as spices and fabric.

4. (a) Marco Polo's explorations sparked interest in trade and travel to China. (b) The desire for spices sparked a search for faster and cheaper trade routes to China. (c) Through alliance, monarchs and merchants used their wealth to finance expeditions and hence increase their power and influence.

5. Technological innovations such as the astrolabe, quadrant, and caravel made sea travel safer and easier.

6. Reasons for Prince Henry's interest in exploring the west coast of Africa: belief that he had a duty to convert Africans to Christianity; concern for the commercial well-being of Portugal and legends of rich kingdoms and gold in western Africa; dream of finding a sea route around Africa to India.

7. (a) Scandinavian sailors known as Vikings visited the Americas around 1,000 A.D. Different theories hold that explorers from Ireland, China, Africa, Egypt, and Polynesia may also have visited the Americas before the 1490s. (b) These early explorers had little impact in the Americas, since they left no traces of their presence and did not develop lasting relationships with the people of the Americas.

Chapter Review, text page 33

1. (a) Archaeologists seal off an area, divide the ground into squares, map it out, and begin to dig. Digging is done with hand tools and screens. (b) Archaeologists seek skeletons and artifacts as evidence.

2. (a) Carbon-14 tests can date only those remains less than 40,000 years old and heavier than one pound. (b) Amino acid racemization is considered a better method because it can date objects up to a million years old and weighing less than one ounce.

3. (a) New evidence resulting from improved tests suggests that humans may have migrated to the Americas thousands of years earlier than originally believed. (b) Scientists use the results of racemization tests as evidence to support their argument.

4. Students should note that the people of the northwest Pacific coast had a more diverse society than either the Eskimos or the people of the Great Basin. Accept those answers that suggest that cultural diversity is in part dependent on the extent of a society's resources.

5. The Anasazi, Pueblo, and Navajo were able to establish civilizations in the desert by developing complex irrigation systems for farming and by building dwellings suitable to vast temperature changes.

6. (a) At the center of each Pueblo town was a room called a kiva, where religious ceremonies were held. The Pueblo held ceremonies to bring rain, cure the sick, please the gods, and ask for blessings. (b) The Navajo shared the Pueblo religious belief that a person's life should be in harmony with the universe. (c) The Plains culture emphasized the role of visions in religion; they believed that visions revealed their destinies. (d) The Mayas built cities as great religious centers.

7. (a) Mayan building achievements: built great cities with huge temple-pyramids containing carved picture walls. Aztec building achievements: floating artificial islands formed the foundations of cities connected by aqueducts, bridges, and causeways. Inca building achievements: moved massive stones from remote quarries to mountaintops; the stones, which were precision cut, shifted to accommodate shifts in the land such as those caused by earthquakes; no cement was required. (b) Accept any justifiable answer regarding which type of accomplishment was most difficult.

8. (a) Feudal system: social and political system in which kingdoms were broken into somewhat self-sufficient manors run by lords and worked by serfs. The lords offered the serfs protection in exchange for their service on the manor. (b) Each manor was largely self-sufficient economically. Under the feudal system there seemed to be no need to explore for new goods or new markets.

9. (a) The Renaissance was a time of intellectual revival. Attitudes toward life, learning, and religion changed greatly. European knowledge was stimu-

lated by the works of Arab scholars that were brought back by the Crusaders. Interest in one branch of knowledge stimulated curiosity about others. (b) As a result, people began to investigate their surroundings and question what they found. This new inquisitive attitude encouraged advances in science and technology. Both the new attitudes and the advances contributed to an age of discovery in Europe.

10. (a) Portugal was the first Euopean nation to begin systematic exploration of the world beyond Europe. (b) Prince Henry established a school of navigation to teach new methods of exploration and the use of new instruments of navigation.

For Further Thought, text page 33

1. Student responses should include the idea that environmental changes thousands of years ago required people to adapt their ways of life. Adaptation was necessary in order for people to survive (that is, in order for them to satisfy basic needs for food, clothing, and shelter). Different groups adapted in different ways, depending on the climate and natural environment in which they lived. Adaptation thus led to cultural diversity.

2. See chart below. Students should mention the following ideas in answering the second part of this question: differing environments can contribute to a diversity of cultures by requiring people to develop different skills of survival; varying methods of obtaining food, clothing, and shelter will create varying social and political organizations, as well as different religious beliefs and customs. Students should refer to the cultures discussed in the text for supporting examples.

3. (a) *Pueblo:* kiva societies controlled Pueblo life. They emphasized conformity and subordination of the individual to society. A warrior class enforced the rules of conduct. *Plains people:* the Plains cultures were governed by supreme chiefs and councils composed of the most prominent men in each community. Council decisions usually had to be unanimous. *Iroquois:* the Iroquois developed a league and a representative council consisting of the chiefs of each tribe and 50 specially chosen leaders (sachems) responsible for all matters involving relations among the tribes. (b), (c), (d) Accept all justifiable comparisons of similarities and differences.

4. (a) Pueblo women headed their families and held all property rights. In Ute and Shoshone societies

Culture	Examples of Resources From Environment	Use of Resources
Inhabitants of the Arctic region (Eskimo)	seals, walruses, whales, caribou	food, clothing, tools, weapons, household implements
Inhabitants of the northwest Pacific coast	salmon and other fish, seals, whales, otters, deer, moose, elk	food
	forests (wood)	totem poles, canoes, masks, furniture, utensils
Inhabitants of the Southwest (Anasazi, Pueblo, Navajo)	desert land	farming
	clay	pottery
	stone, adobe, mud, logs	houses
Inhabitants of the plains	grassland	farming
	logs, brush, sod	houses
	buffalo	food, teepees
Inhabitants of the eastern woodlands (Algonquin, Iroquois, Muskogeans)	forests (wood)	snowshoes, toboggans, canoes
		food
	deer, caribou, wild nuts, berries	
	land	farming

women held low-status positions. (b) Accept all justifiable reasons for this difference.

5. (a) There is no concrete evidence to prove several of the theories of exploration that have been proposed. If people from places such as Ireland, China, Africa, Egypt, and Polynesia did explore America before Columbus, they left no trace of their presence. (b) Students may suggest that evidence such as artifacts, building foundations, and written information would help historians and archaeologists reach more positive conclusions about early explorations.

Developing Basic Skills, text page 33

1. In column 1 the factors that inhibited European exploration prior to 1500 should include the feudal system and the prevailing religious ideas. In column 2 the factors that encouraged explorations should include the Crusades, a changing political scene, a growing middle class, new attitudes growing out of the Renaissance, and new inventions that aided travel. (a) Column 2 should be longer than column 1. (b) Accept all justifiable answers. Answers may focus on the fact that new developments sparked a growing interest in trade, travel, and exploration. The strength of this interest eventually outweighed the influence of factors that formerly had inhibited exploration. (c) Answers will vary.

2. (a) Answers should focus on Portugal's geographic proximity to Africa as well as its position on the Atlantic coast. (b) A water route would be desirable because the land route was long and difficult, across mountains and deserts.

2 Europe's Age of Discovery (1492–1608)

Section Review, text page 37

1. *King John II:* Portuguese king who refused to support Columbus in a westward voyage to Asia. *Queen Isabella:* Spanish queen who sponsored Columbus in his search for a westward route to Asia. *"Indians":* the people whom Columbus mistook for the inhabitants of India when he arrived in the New World. *Arawaks:* name of the people who greeted Columbus in the New World. *Hispaniola:* island in the Caribbean where Spain established its first settlement in the New World; the name means "Little Spain." *Pedro Álvares Cabral:* explorer who in 1500 claimed territory now part of Brazil for King John II of Portugal. *Amerigo Vespucci:* a merchant from Florence, Italy, who in 1501 scouted the North American continent, after whom it is named.

2. *circumnavigate:* to sail around.

3. (a) Portugal refused to sponsor Columbus in his search for a westward sea route to Asia because King John was more interested in scouting an eastern route around Africa. (b) Spain agreed to sponsor Columbus because Queen Isabella was interested in spreading the power of Spain and the influence of Christianity.

4. The Line of Demarcation divided all the undiscovered lands in the world between Spain and Portugal. It was located about 1,100 miles west of the Azores. Spain received the rights to territory west of the line, and Portugal was given the territory east of the line.

5. (a) Balboa discovered the shortest land route across the New World. In 1513 he journeyed across the Isthmus of Panama, the narrow strip of land connecting North and South America. He was the first European to see the Pacific Ocean. An expedition led by Magellan was the first to circumnavigate the globe. The expedition sailed westward from Spain in 1519; those who survived the journey returned to Spain in 1522. Magellan was not among the survivors. He died in a battle in the Philippine Islands. (b) The discoveries of both explorers contributed to Spain's position as a world power.

Section Review, text page 40

1. *Cortés:* Spanish conquistador who came to present-day Mexico in search of gold and riches. Through battle and starvation Cortés and his army defeated the Aztec empire in 1520. *Doña Marina:* Native American woman who served as a translator, speechmaker, and negotiator for Cortés. *Montezuma:* Aztec ruler defeated by Cortés. *Pizarro:* conquistador who conquered the Inca Empire in 1535. *Atahualpa:* Inca leader defeated by Pizarro. *Ponce de León:* Spaniard who explored Florida in search of a "fountain of youth" in 1513. *Pánfilo de Narváez:* Spaniard who explored deep into Florida in further search of a "fountain of youth" in 1513. *Appalachees:* Native American group that thwarted the Narváez expedition. *Cabeza de Vaca:* Spanish explorer of the Americas, one of four survivors of the Narváez expedition. *Estevanico:* African survivor of the Narváez expedition.

2. (a) Conquistadores were professional Spanish soldiers who explored lands in the New World. Each conquistador received permission from the Spanish government to establish settlements in America. In return, the conquistadores were to send to Spain one fifth of the gold or silver they mined. (b) The conquistadores came to the New World in search of riches and adventure. Many were also motivated by missionary zeal.

3. Cortés hoped to gain the riches of the Aztec Empire.

4. Efforts at finding a fountain of youth were unsuccessful. Ponce de León did not find this miraculous fountain, and the expedition led by Narváez was forced to retreat under attack by Native Americans.

5. (a) Coronado explored areas in what is now the southwestern United States. De Soto explored areas in what is now the southeastern United States. (b) Neither Coronado nor de Soto was successful in the search for gold.

Section Review, text page 43

1. *Santo Domingo:* the first permanent settlement in the New World, built on the island of Hispaniola. *New Spain:* the term used to refer to the North American part of the Spanish empire in the New World. *Antonio de Mendoza:* the first viceroy of New Spain. *Philip II:* Spanish king who proclaimed the Laws of the Indies in 1573. *Bartolomé de Las Casas:* Dominican priest who devoted his life to rescuing Native Americans from brutal treatment by the Spanish.

2. (a) One-man rule was inadequate in New Spain because rapid growth required a more formal system of government. (b) The Laws of the Indies represented an attempt to exert tighter control over Spain's New World colonies.

3. The three types of Spanish settlements in the New World were presidios, missions, and pueblos. Presidios were for military activities; missions were centers from which the Spanish could carry on the work of converting Native Americans to Christianity; pueblos, or villas, were for farming, trade, and town life.

4. (a) An encomienda was the right granted to successful conquistadores to demand a tribute or tax from Native Americans living on a given piece of land. (b) The encomiendas forced Native Americans to work for the conquistadores since they had no other way to pay the tax. Thus the Native Americans eventually became bound to the land.

5. By suggesting that the Spanish import slaves from Africa, Las Casas hoped to reduce the reliance on Native American slave labor.

A View of the New World: Using Visual Evidence, text page 46

1. (a) The people wearing loincloths and carrying bows and arrows probably lived in the territory shown. The people carrying spears and on horseback at the bottom left probably just arrived. They came by ships. (b) The territory had trees, rivers, wildlife, and mountains. The waters off the coast were thought to contain sea creatures. (c) Florida, Canada, and Mexico are at the top of the map. It seems that the map is upside down. (d) North America is shown.

2. (a) The artist probably did not see all the things shown because the area was largely unexplored at this time and many of the things, such as the sea creatures, did not exist. The picture should not be used as an accurate view of America. (b) One could infer that the artist was French since the detail centers around the area that the French explored. It would be best to use this picture to understand the viewpoint of the French. (c) Yes, the source is good for understanding French perception of the New World circa 1500.

3. (a) European activity should be described as exploratory. (b) People in the 1540s viewed the voyage to the Americas as dangerous, as evidenced by the creatures in the sea. (c) The picture is upside down because the perspective is that of the early French explorers, who were only tentatively aware of their whereabouts. A Spaniard might have drawn this map right side up with more detail in the areas of Florida and Mexico.

Section Review, text page 48

1. *Jacques Cartier:* explored the St. Lawrence River for France in 1534 in search of a northwest passage to Asia. *Samuel de Champlain:* explored eastern Canada and built the fortress around which the city of Quebec grew. *John Hawkins:* the first English sea captain to engage in the slave trade. *Sir Francis Drake:* English sea dog whose pirating activities preceded the British defeat of the Spanish Armada. *The Armada:* the huge Spanish fleet that King Philip sent to battle the English in 1588. *Sir Walter Raleigh:* English aristocrat who in 1585 made the first attempt to sponsor an English settlement in America. *John White:* a surveyor and artist who settled in Roanoke, the first English settlement in the New World.

2. (a) Early French and English explorers wanted to find as much gold as possible in the New World and to discover a fast, all-water route to Asia. (b) Their efforts were unsuccessful. As a result, England and France embarked on other ventures in the New World.

3. Fish and fur became the basis for French activity in the New World.

4. (a) Sea dogs were English sailors who pirated Spanish treasure ships and transported African slaves to the New World. (b) They wanted to make money through plunder and trade.

5. England defeated the Spanish Armada in 1588 and thereby ended Spanish dominance in Europe.

6. (a) Raleigh envisioned a colony that would raise crops and export raw materials to England. (b) Roanoke did not survive as a permanent settlement, although the reasons for its disappearance remain a mystery.

Chapter Review, text page 49

1. (a) Queen Isabella financed explorations to the New World because she was eager to spread the power of Spain and the influence of Christianity. (b) The explorations helped Spain become a world power.
2. (a) Each conquistador was permitted by the Spanish government to establish outputs and settlements in America. In return, the conquistadores were expected to send to Spain one fifth of the riches they found. (b) Spain gradually gained control of most of South and Central America and parts of North America.
3. (a) The Spanish explored much of the present-day southwestern United States. (b) The explorers had come in search of gold. (c) The Spanish were not successful in their search for gold.
4. (a) The three major activities of the Spanish in the Americas were military activity, religious work (converting Native Americans to Christianity), and the establishment of pueblos for farming, trade, and town life. (b) In the process, Native Americans were mistreated and enslaved.
5. Bartolomé de Las Casas, a Dominican priest, persuaded the Spanish government to place the Native Americans under the protection of the clergy and suggested the importation of slaves from Africa.
6. (a) Other European nations became interested in the New World for its gold and silver as well as for the discovery of an all-water route to Asia. (b) When it became clear that their original goals would not be fulfilled, they began to exploit the land for what it had to offer: fish, fur, and agricultural products.
7. (a) The sea dogs pirated Spanish treasure ships. Although England did not officially encourage their actions, an undeclared war gradually developed on the seas between Catholic Spain and Protestant England. (b) The sea dogs profited from their plunder. As further reward for his exploits, Drake was knighted by Queen Elizabeth.
8. (a) The first English colony at Roanoke disappeared within three years of its founding. (b) The attempt was important because it demonstrated that a colony could be started but that a new way to sponsor settlements had to be devised.

For Further Thought, text page 49

1. (a) All the explorers were probably adventuresome, courageous, and bold. (b) The explorers had to be ambitious, strong, and skilled in sailing the seas.

2. (a) Native American reaactions to early Europeans were varied. Some, like the Arawaks, welcomed the Europeans in friendship. The Aztecs in Mexico believed the Spanish had come to fulfill an ancient prophecy; they did not resist Cortés and his army when the Spanish first appeared. Other groups, such as the Appalachees and the Zuñi, attacked the Spanish conquistadores as they journeyed through Native American land. (b) As the previous answer shows, Native Americans reacted in different ways to the Europeans. (c) Answers will vary. Students may suggest that as news of the Spanish soldiers spread, Native Americans prepared themselves for resistance against the Europeans.

Developing Basic Skills, text page 49

1. Column 1 should include explorers, conquistadores, settlers, and missionaries. They came from Spain, Portugal, England, and France. Column 2 should include the following motives: riches, power, adventure, religious zeal, and trade. (a) Students should note that all groups were motivated by the desire for material wealth. (b) While the Spanish were primarily interested in discovering gold, the English wanted to establish permanent agricultural colonies. (c) Reasons included the desire to spread Christianity and the desire to gain material wealth.
2. Research will vary.

3 England's New World (1607–1732)

Caption, text page 51

The Mohegan, Wampanoag, Pequot, and Narraganset lived on land granted to the Plymouth Company. The Seneca, Susquehanna, Powhatan, and Tuscarora lived on land granted to the London Company.

Section Review, text page 54

1. *joint stock company:* a form of business organization used by the English in trading ventures and to finance the founding of colonies in America. Since a joint stock company pools the funds of many investors by selling shares in the company, the amount of risk and the amount of profit for an investor depends only on the number of shares that investor owns. *Plymouth Company:* the English joint stock company that acquired from King James I exclusive rights to settle land from present-day Maine to New York. *London Company:* the English joint stock company that acquired rights to territory stretching from the Potomac River south to present-

day North Carolina. *John Smith:* leader of the Jamestown colony who steered the settlement through its first years. *Pocahontas:* Native American who saved the life of John Smith. *"the starving time":* the winter after John Smith departed to England, when food was so scarce that the Jamestown settlers barely survived. *John Rolfe:* English settler who discovered in 1612 that Jamestown was an ideal place to grow tobacco. *Magna Carta:* English document signed by King John in 1215 guaranteeing certain rights and privileges to nobles and setting the precedent that the king's power was not absolute.

2. Advantages of the joint stock company over individual investors: joint stock companies were able to muster large amounts of capital, and each investor had only limited liability. In case of bankruptcy, each investor was liable only for the amount of his or her investment.

3. (a) Jamestown was built on a marshy peninsula, which created several problems: the drinking water was brackish, the damp air rotted the wooden buildings, and settlers were infected by malaria-carrying mosquitoes. (b) Other difficulties the settlers faced: (1) lack of skills needed to survive in the wilderness; (2) selfish desire to search for gold rather than work at farming or hunting; (3) low incentive to make Jamestown self-supporting; and (4) inability to govern themselves peacefully.

4. Smith's contributions to Jamestown's success: Smith governed sternly; he insured that all men reported to work each day, building shelters, clearing land, and planting crops. He also halted the search for gold.

5. (a) Native American contributions to Jamestown's success: Native Americans provided food in return for English beads and copper. (b) Relations worsened as the settlers demanded more food at their own price and infringed on Indian lands by clearing trees and planting crops. Better relations were gradually restored.

6. (a) The House of Burgesses was a representative assembly established in Virginia in 1619, consisting of 22 burgesses, or representatives, two from each of the 11 areas of the colony. (b) Eligible voters elected its members.

Section Review, text page 59

1. *Martin Luther:* German monk who in 1517 began the movement known as the Protestant Reformation. *Henry VIII:* English king who broke with the Catholic church. *Separatists:* those who believed the Church of England to be so "impure" (retaining too many Catholic practices and forms of organization) that they separated from it completely. *Pil-*

grims: Separatists who were granted permission by the London Company to settle in North America in 1620. The Pilgrims founded the Plymouth colony. *Mayflower Compact:* an agreement made by the Pilgrims before stepping ashore in the New World. It stated that they would consult one another about matters affecting the community and that they would abide by majority rule. *William Bradford:* first governor of the Plymouth colony. *Puritans:* dissenters from the Church of England who tried to reform it from within. When they were denied freedom of worship by King Charles I, the Puritans left England and established the Massachusetts Bay Colony. *Roger Williams:* a settler of Massachusetts Bay who was branded a heretic and expelled from the colony for his views on the separation of church and state. He established Rhode Island. *Anne Hutchinson:* settler who quarreled with Massachusetts leaders over theology and fled to Rhode Island. *Thomas Hooker:* minister and leader of a group that settled in Hartford, Connecticut, in 1636. He believed that government should rest on "the free consent of the people." *Fundamental Orders of Connecticut:* Connecticut's plan for a government based on self-government, not on the divine rule of kings.

2. Possible reasons for seeking a life in the New World: (a) second son of a wealthy family: he would find himself without gainful employment upon reaching adulthood. (b) tenant farmer: as wool became the staple of the English economy, English farmland disappeared and tenant farmers were evicted from their homes. (c) city worker: bad living and working conditions in English cities made America attractive.

3. (a) Under Queen Elizabeth, the Church of England retained the traditional hierarchy of bishops and archbishops and kept many Catholic practices. (b) The Separatists did not approve of these similarities to the Catholic Church.

4. The Pilgrims left the Netherlands for the New World in an effort to keep their English customs and to avoid possible rule by Catholic Spain.

5. (a) The Massachusetts Bay Company established self-government in the colony. (b) Only male church members were allowed to vote.

6. Both Rhode Island and Connecticut were founded on the basis of religious toleration.

Section Review, text page 64

1. *George Calvert:* established the first proprietary colony, Maryland. *Cecilius Calvert:* son of George Calvert who received the actual charter for Maryland in 1632. *Maryland Toleration Act:* law affirming religious toleration for all Christians in

Maryland. *Charles II:* king of England who provided land grants in America as rewards to English nobles who had remained loyal to the monarchy following the revolt against his father, Charles I. *New Netherlands:* territory originally established as a Dutch colony, also claimed by the English, who established a land grant in 1664. The area soon came under English control and was renamed New York. *William Berkeley:* one of eight men granted all the land between present-day Virginia and Florida. *James Oglethorpe:* led the establishment of Georgia as a place where debtors could get a new start in life. *William Penn:* established the colony of Pennsylvania as a religious refuge. *Society of Friends:* religious group also known as Quakers.

2. (a) A proprietary colony was a form of colonial organization in which a territory was granted to a person or group of persons by the king. (b) Proprietors ruled the territory in accordance with the laws of England, and they had the right to parcel out their land to tenants, who did not own the land but held it only as long as the proprietor wished. (c) In return for use of the land, tenants paid rent and taxes to the proprietors, who in turn made payment to the king.

3. (a) George Calvert wanted to establish a colony as a refuge for Roman Catholics and as a money-making real estate venture. (b) Both Protestants and Catholics settled in Maryland.

4. (a) Charles II's motive was to reward nobles who had remained loyal to the monarchy following a revolt against his father. (b) Charles II made the first grant to his brother James, the Duke of York.

5. The Fundamental Constitutions of Carolina specified that Carolina society would be set up along rigid class lines, with a heredity nobility at the top. Early settlers rejected most of the plan's provisions, and the plan was eventually replaced by a more democratic system of government.

6. (a) Oglethorpe wanted to establish Georgia as a place where people who had been imprisoned for debt could get a new start; he also wanted to provide a barrier between the other English colonies and the Spanish in Florida. (b) Georgia was unique among the English colonies because the other colonies were founded either as money-making ventures or as places of religious refuge.

7. (a) William Penn founded Pennsylvania as a refuge for himself and fellow Quakers. (b) Pennsylvania had a democratic form of government. (c) Every man who owned a small amount of land or paid taxes could vote.

8. (a) A royal colony was governed differently from a proprietary colony. It has a colonial governor and council appointed by the king. The eligible voters elected an assembly. (b) Colonists often preferred royal colonies to proprietary colonies because royal colonies seemed to receive better protection from the English army and navy, and because colonial representatives often enjoyed more political power than in a proprietary colony.

9. (a) Three attempts to undermine colonial governments: in New York, the Duke of York tried to continue the Dutch system; in the Carolinas, the Fundamental Constitutions violated the representative tradition; in the colonies north of New Jersey, the Duke of York tried to discard all representative assemblies. (b) None of these attempts was successful because of settlers's resistance.

Chapter Review, text page 65

1. (a) The London Company was interested in a site that would have good trade and defense advantages. It did not anticipate the environmental conditions that were the source of many of the colony's problems. Moreover, the London Company wanted settlers to search for gold and a northwest passage to China. Because settlers spent their time primarily searching for gold, they did little to help make Jamestown a self-supporting, growing settlement. (b) John Smith took control of Jamestown and insured that all colonists worked toward the settlement's survival. Local Native Americans helped the colonists by providing part of their food supply. John Rolfe discovered the crop (tobacco) that turned out to be a key to the colony's survival. The House of Burgesses was the representative assembly for the people of Jamestown.

2. (a) In contrast to Jamestown, the climate of Massachusetts was dry and healthy, with fresh water, fertile soil, different types of crops, and an abundance of fish and game. (b) The New England settlers did not come seeking instant fortune with hopes of returning to England. They came to settle down and begin new lives.

3. (a) The Pilgrims and the Puritans both came to the New World seeking refuge from religious persecution. (b) Whereas the Pilgrims wanted to separate from the Church of England, the Puritans wanted to reform it from within.

4. (a) The Puritans wanted a "Bible Commonwealth," run according to their interpretation of scripture. (b) Roger Williams was banished from Massachusetts because he believed in the separation of government and religion. Anne Hutchinson was banished because she differed with Massachusetts leaders over questions of religion. Thomas Hooker left because he believed that Massachusetts leaders had assumed too much power.

5. (a) In Massachusetts, the colonists ruled themselves with little regard for the crown. In Virginia, the London Company mismanaged its business. Both experiences prompted England to try a new method of establishing colonies. (b) The crown turned to proprietary colonies. (c) The proprietary method enabled the king to coordinate the settlement of the colonies and to establish uniform conditions for them.

6. Some proprietors established colonies because of religious motives or, in the case of Georgia, humanitarian motives.

7. The crown transformed most colonies to royal colonies so that it could exert greater control.

8. (a) In a royal colony the king appointed the colonial governor and council. The governor controlled trade, appointed judges, and served as the colony's chief executive. The council advised the governor, approved official appointments, and served as the colony's highest court. The assembly has to consent to all proposed laws before they could be passed. (b) Assemblies increased their influence as they gained the right to propose laws and exercised the right to approve the salaries of government officials.

For Further Thought, text page 65

1. (a) The English government did not play a role in the settlement of Jamestown, Plymouth, or Massachusetts Bay. Each of these colonies was founded through the sponsorship of English joint stock companies. (b) The Spanish government played a larger role initially than the English government in the settlement of America. (c) Students might explain this difference by referring to the Spanish monarchs' desires to gain wealth and world power and to spread Catholicism. (d) During the 1600s the English government began to exert greater influence over the colonies.

2. (a) Accept all answers that refer to the role of the people in government as originally conceived in the Magna Carta. (b) Students should discuss the representative assemblies that were formed in most of the other colonies, to show how English political traditions were continued there.

3. (a) The proprietary government of New York was under the absolute political power of the Duke of York, who at first did not permit any form of representative government in the colony. This was in contrast to other proprietary colonies, where democratic forms of government were permitted. (b) Students might indicate that the Duke of York's absolute rule in New York can be explained by the fact that under the Dutch the colony had been ruled

by a director-general who held complete authority. The Duke of York tried to continue this system. (c) King James II was opposed to representative government. Students should mention that after he succeeded to the throne James dismissed representative assemblies in those colonies north of New Jersey.

4. (a) Pennsylvania had the most democratic government. (b) Pennsylvania's form of government reflected William Penn's religious beliefs.

Developing Basic Skills, text page 65

1. (a) Delaware and New York were founded by people from nations other than England. (b) Thirteen colonies were founded before 1700. (c) New Hampshire, New York, Delaware, New Jersey, Pennsylvania, Maryland, the Carolinas, and Georgia were founded as proprietary colonies. (d) The most common reason for founding a colony was religious freedom. The second most common reason was trade.

2. For ready reference, see page 62. (a) Most colonies were founded between 1620 and 1640. (b) No colonies were founded between 1640 and 1660. (c) Georgia was the last colony to be founded. Students may suggest Georgia's location adjoining the territory of rival Spain as a major reason for its being founded so long after the other colonies.

4 Life in Colonial America (1650–1750)

Caption, text page 68

The New England colonies included New Hampshire, Massachusetts, Rhode Island, Connecticut, and Maine, which was part of Massachusetts. The Middle Colonies included New York, New Jersey, Pennsylvania, and Delaware. The Southern Colonies included Maryland, Virginia, North Carolina, South Carolina, and Georgia.

Section Review, text page 69

1. *subsistence farming:* a level of farming in which farmers produce just enough to feed their families. *self-sufficient:* capable of supporting itself. *town meeting:* a meeting of townspeople. At open town meetings in colonial New England, residents elected local representatives to the colonial assembly and discussed matters of importance to the community.

2. New England was a difficult area in which to settle because the winters were long and cold, the topsoil

was thin, and dense forests had to be cleared before the land could be farmed.

3. The New England farm family had the resources to get along without outside help. Men were responsible for the crops and animals; women made clothing, utensils, and other household necessities.

4. Many early towns were founded by congregations of a church. The elders of a congregation requested a tract of land from the colonial legislature. After approval of the request the tract was surveyed and divided into lots.

5. New England industries: timber, fishing, ship-building.

6. (a) New England society was less rigid than society in Europe. (b) Economic prosperity enabled members of the lower and middle classes to imitate the upper classes. Dress was one form of imitation. The social system grew more democratic as people became financially able to improve their status.

Caption, text page 70

The English settled in each of the 13 colonies. The Scotch-Irish settled in western Pennsylvania, Maryland, and Virginia. The Germans settled in New York, Pennsylvania, New Jersey, Maryland, Virginia, North Carolina, and Georgia. The Scottish settled in the Carolinas. The Dutch settled in New York. The French settled in New York and Maryland. The Swedes settled in Maryland. The Africans settled along the coast from Maryland south through Georgia.

Section Review, text page 72

1. *Scotch-Irish:* people from northern Ireland. *Pennsylvania Dutch:* Germans who settled in Pennsylvania. *Paxton boys:* band of Pennsylvania frontiersmen who led a violent revolt in Pennsylvania in 1763. Angry that the colonial government would not provide protection against Indians at war with them, these frontiersmen ended up destroying a peaceful Indian village.

2. *patroon:* a feudal-style Dutch lord who settled in New York. *fall line:* the area in which inland rivers begin dropping toward sea level.

3. (a) The Scotch-Irish and the Germans, who became known as Pennsylvania Dutch, were the two largest groups of non-English settlers in the Middle Colonies. (b) Each came to America seeking religious toleration and economic prosperity.

4. (a) The Middle Colonies contained some of the richest farmland on the Atlantic coast; farming thus became the basis of economic life. (b) Pennsylvania was the most productive colony. (c) New York was the least productive colony because of the patroon

system of landholding. Settlers preferred to settle in other colonies where they could own their own farms, and lower immigration to New York resulted in lower productivity.

5. (a) Most free blacks lived in the Middle Colonies and New England. (b) They did not have the same freedom as whites, since most of the colonies passed laws restricting their activities.

6. (a) The backcountry was the land west of the established areas of settlement. (b) Settlers survived through subsistence farming.

7. Isolated from others, settlers of the backcountry paid no taxes, were subject to few laws, and seldom mixed with others.

Caption, text page 76

The growth of slavery was most dramatic between 1760 and 1770.

Section Review, text page 77

1. *Regulators:* a Carolina group that revolted in 1771 against taxes and lack of representation in the colonial legislature. *Eliza Lucas Pinkney:* the settler who introduced indigo as a cash crop in the South in the 1740s. *Nathaniel Bacon:* a wealthy landowner who sympathized with the backcountry farmers. He led a revolt in 1676 against the Virginia legislature for not protecting the backcountry farmers from Indian attacks. *Royal African Company:* English company established in 1672 to promote the slave trade. *"middle passage":* the journey by ship endured by Africans taken as slaves to America.

2. *piedmont region:* region of rolling hills. *tidewater region:* flat coastal plain where the land is so low that rivers crossing it flow backwards with the incoming tides. *planter:* powerful plantation owner. *cash crop:* crop grown to be sold at a profit. *indigo:* a West Indian plant used to make dye. *indentured servant:* person from Europe or Africa who agreed to work for a planter in America for a specified period of time in return for the cost of passage to America. *slave codes:* laws regulating relations between slaves and their owners.

3. Farmers in the southern backcountry had to clear dense forests by hand in order to build their farms. As a result, farms were small, and families lived at a subsistence level. Most backcountry farmers were poor, and they resented the wealthy landowners along the coast.

4. Cash crops such as indigo and rice could be sold for large profits when planted on large tracts of land.

5. In coming to America, indentured servants hoped for an opportunity to eventually acquire land and become independent. Many also gained the opportunity to learn a trade and get an education.

6. The inability of indentured servants to meet labor demands, the need to teach skills to a new group every few years, and the presence of embittered former servants in the backcountry created a growing demand for slave labor among the planters.

7. (a) The slave codes prohibited slaves from leaving a plantation without permission and established rules of criminal justice for slaves that differed from those for whites. (b) Many slaves outwardly accepted their status while looking for ways to undermine the system. Some slaves purposely worked slowly or secretly damaged tools. Many tried to preserve their African culture by retaining African names or religous traditions.

The Growth of Colonial Cities: Reading Graphs, text page 81

1. (a) Growth of Colonial Port Cities, 1690–1730. (b) Population. (c) Years. (d) Cities. (e) The information on the graph shows population growth in New York, Philadelphia, Boston, and Charleston between 1690 and 1730.

2. (a) 3,900. (b) 3,500. (c) 1690–1700. (d) 3,500.

3. (a) Boston. (b) Boston. (c) 2,000. (d) Boston.

4. (a) All four cities experienced population growth. (b) Accept those answers that relate to trade, transportation, and immigration. (c) Boston was probably the largest port city because it had a good harbor and many shipyards. Students might list other industries that contributed to Boston's growth. (d) New York and Philadelphia: accept those answers that refer to manufactured goods. Charleston: accept those answers that refer to agricultural products.

Section Review, text page 82

1. *established church:* officially recognized and tax-supported church in colonial America. The Congregational church was the established church in New England; the Church of England, or the Anglican church, was the established church in Virginia, Maryland, New York, the Carolinas, and Georgia. *primer:* an illustrated textbook that taught children how to read and spell while they memorized the tenets of the Puritan faith. *dame schools:* classes held by women in their homes for girls and younger children. *literacy rate:* proportion of the population that can read and write.

2. Many colonies had originated as havens for religious freedom. This factor contributed to greater religious toleration among the colonists.

3. (a) Mutual toleration developed as a matter of necessity among the different denominations coexisting in the colonies. (b) Roman Catholic and Jewish people were often not tolerated.

4. (a) Massachusetts passed the first public school law. (b) Education was important to the Puritans because they believed it provided access to important truths found in the Bible.

5. (a) Girls were educated in dame schools, where they learned reading and writing as well as skills like sewing and embroidery. In the South some were educated by tutors. (b) In New England, boys were educated in public grammar schools, where their instruction prepared them for college. In the other colonies, private schools and tutors existed for those who could afford them.

6. As exchange centers for ideas as well as for goods, cities contributed to the development of colonial culture.

Chapter Review, text page 83

1. (a) The basis of the New England economy was timber, shipbuilding, and fishing. (b) The basis of the economy in the Middle Colonies was agriculture. (c) The basis of the economy in the Southern Colonies was agriculture. (d) Different climates and topography account for the different economic patterns.

2. (a) In New England, as in England, families belonging to the upper class occupied the top of the social structure, followed by the landowners and merchants. Beneath were the shopkeepers, artisans, and small landowners. Lowest stood city workers, tenant farmers, and agricultural laborers. (b) It became less rigid as the colonies became more prosperous, enabling people to improve their social status.

3. Large numbers of people who immigrated to the Middle Colonies came not only from England but also from Ireland, Germany, and other nations of Europe. Immigrants to New England and to the coastal region of the South came primarily from England. (b) The Middle Colonies, especially Pennsylvania, provided religious toleration and rich farmlands with low rents.

4. Free blacks lived primarily in the Middle Colonies and New England. They did not live as freely as whites, however, because laws restricted their activities.

5. (a) Backcountry farming was on a subsistence level, and the families were much more dependent on each other for survival. The backcountry people

had little political influence in colonial legislatures and often resented their coastal counterparts. (b) Isolation made life in the backcountry different from life along the coast.

6. (a) Slavery became a more viable way of meeting labor demands on the plantations than the system of indentured servants. (b) Eventually slaves were a preferred source of labor because they were permanent and, in the long run, cheaper.

7. There were fewer slaves in New England and the Middle Colonies than in the South because the economic structures in these regions did not require a large low-cost work force to survive.

8. (a) Greater religious tolerance existed in the colonies than in Europe for several reasons. No one church ever dominated religious life in the American colonies, and the diversity aided the toleration of various groups for one another. Also, many of the colonies had been founded as places of religious refuge, and this religious freedom was maintained. (b) Although most groups were tolerated, Jews and Roman Catholics were often discriminated against.

9. (a) The literacy rate was relatively high in the American colonies because of the existence of various types of schools, both public and private. Schooling was central to religion, especially in New England, where the Puritans believed that everyone should learn to read in order to study the Bible. (b), (c) The literacy rate was lower in the backcountry, where there were no public and few church-supported schools.

For Further Thought, text page 83

1. (a) Slavery was dehumanizing because it deprived the slave of freedom to make choices. Students might point out that it was the master who had the right to determine where a slave's spouse and children would live. All slaves, whether their masters were cruel or kind, knew that they were merely property. (b) Slaves tried to keep their humanity by preserving elements of their African culture. Students might point to examples of slave resistance to show that blacks were not content to regard themselves as docile property.

2. (a) An indentured servant was different from a slave in that the servant was required to work for a master only for a specified period of time. A slave, on the other hand, served for life. (b) A poor person might become an indentured servant if he or she wanted free passage to America in the hope of eventually becoming independent and acquiring land. Indentured servitude was also desirable to people who wanted to learn a trade.

3. (a) New England farm women made clothing, utensils, and other necessities. New England town and city women worked as tinkers and shipbuilders. Backcountry women hunted and practiced other frontier skills. Plantation women supervised work in the main house. (b) Students might indicate that all of the women described above had socially useful roles. (c) Students might point out that the New England farm woman and the planter's wife usually worked in the home while the other women described above worked outside it. (d) A student could suggest that labor was scarce in colonial America and therefore all women were needed for tasks in addition to housework. The role of the planter's wife was probably different from those of other women because most of the work on plantations was done by slaves. Accept all answers that explain the differences in women's roles in terms of regional differences in economic or social systems.

4. (a) Education for boys differed from education for girls in that boys could attend grammar school and go on to college, while girls were restricted to home instruction. (b) A student could answer that colonial Americans regarded females as intellectually incapable of profiting from anything but the most basic education, or that advanced education was not necessary for women in their most common roles as mothers and homemakers.

Developing Basic Skills, text page 83

1. From most rigid to least rigid: Southern Colonies coastal area, New England towns, Middle Colonies coastal area, Southern Colonies backcountry, Middle Colonies backcountry. (a) The Southern Colonies coastal area had the most rigid social system in that the slaves were absolutely barred from improving their status. Students could place the New England towns in the second rank because people in this area observed sharp distinctions among classes. The Middle Colonies coastal area could be ranked third because it contained manors worked by tenant farmers who could never own their own land. People in the backcountry of the Southern and Middle Colonies lived in the least socially rigid areas. Here nearly all farming was on a subsistence level and social distinctions were not important. (b) The Southern Colonies coastal area and the New England towns were most rigid. (c) The backcountry areas of the Southern and Middle Colonies were least rigid. (d) Students might suggest facts about the history and environment of each area which explain the extent of social rigidity.

2. (a) The graph shows the ethnic breakdown of the colonial population in 1775. (b) 48.7 percent (c)

African, Scotch-Irish, German, Scottish, Dutch, French, and Swedish. (d) English, African, and Scotch-Irish. (e) Dutch, French, and Swedish. (f) A student could suggest that most people in the colonies were of English origin.

5 A Struggle for Empire (1600–1763)

Section Review, text page 87

1. *Molasses Act:* act passed by Parliament requiring the colonists to pay a tax on all molasses or rum imported from the non-British West Indies.
2. *mercantilism:* an economic theory and system whereby each nation would attempt to sell more than it bought. *enumerated commodity:* a colonial product that Parliament ruled could be shipped only to England. *triangular trade:* pattern of trade existing between New England, Africa, and the West Indies.
3. Colonies could provide essential raw materials for the English and serve as a market for finished products.
4. (a) The Navigation Acts were designed to insure that the colonies traded with Britain only. (b) By prohibiting colonists from using foreign ships, Britain hoped to stop colonial trade with other nations, particularly the Netherlands.
5. (a) For the most part the trade laws worked. (b) Colonial benefits included bonuses for producing certain necessary goods and protection from French and Spanish competition.
6. (a) Opposition to trade regulations centered around the requirement that imported and exported goods pass through England and on the restrictions placed on the sale of enumerated commodities to Britain. (b) New England demonstrated the greatest resistance to the trade regulations because of restrictions placed on the rum trade.

Rival Claims in North America: Reading Maps, text page 89

1. (a) Land Claims in North America, 1753. (b) 1753. (c) British, French, Spanish, and Russian claims are shown. (d) Each country is represented by a different color. (e) The map shows the territorial claims of each nation.
2. (a) The distance between Quebec and Charleston is approximately 1,950 kilometers; between Quebec and New York, 800 kilometers. (b) France claimed land north and west of British territory. (c) The Appalachian Mountains bordered British claims. (d)

The Mississippi and Ohio rivers were part of French territory.
3. (a) France claimed the most territory. (b) The explorations of Narváez, Coronado, de Vaca, de Soto, and Ponce de León served as the basis for Spanish claims. (c) The explorations of Verrazano and Cartier served as the basis for French claims. (d) British settlement extended to the Appalachian Mountains. The mountains formed a natural barrier to further expansion. (e) Conflict between Spain and Britain would most likely occur at the border of present-day Florida. (f) Conflict between France and Britain would most likely occur west of the Appalachian Mountains in present-day Ohio.

Section Review, text page 92

1. *Louis XIV:* French king who assumed power in 1661 and launched an ambitious program of empire building in America. *Joliet:* French explorer who journeyed by canoe down the Fox, Wisconsin, and Mississippi Rivers in 1673. *Marquette:* French Jesuit priest who accompanied Joliet on his journey. *La Salle:* French explorer who in 1682 reached the Mississippi delta, claimed the surrounding area for France, and named it Louisiana in honor of the king. *coureur de bois:* French term meaning "runner of the woods," used in reference to Frenchmen who carried on a fur trade with Native Americans in New France. *Iroquois, Algonquin,* and *Huron:* Native American groups infringed upon by the fur trade; rivalries developed among these tribes as they were forced out of their native lands by the French and as they became involved in alliances with competing European powers. *Pequot War:* 1636 war between colonists and Native American groups in which over 600 Pequot men, women, and children were killed. *King Philip's War:* 1675 war between colonists and Native Americans in New England.
2. (a) Britain and Spain were in competition in the area of Georgia and Florida. (b) Competition in this area was part of a traditional rivalry between Britain and Spain.
3. (a) Louis XIV hoped to make New France a market for French exports and a food source for the French West Indies. (b) The plan was for the most part unsuccessful because the colonists were incapable of producing enough food for themselves, let alone for the West Indies.
4. (a) Exploration and fur trading proved successful for the French. (b) As a result of French activities in North America, Native American hunters in the Northeast competed with each other for hunting grounds and a role in the French trade. This com-

petition sometimes resulted in war between Native American groups.

5. As a result of British settlement, Native Americans were pushed out of their territories.

Section Review, text page 96

1. *Plan of Union:* a plan designed to unite the 13 colonies under a single government. It materialized out of the 1754 Albany conference. *Benjamin Franklin:* author of the Albany Plan of Union. *George Washington:* 22-year-old colonel of Virgina militia who led soldiers into western Pennsylvania to construct forts for the British as defense against the French; Washington and his soldiers surrendered to the French in July 1754. *William Pitt:* British secretary of state who reversed the string of British defeats in the French and Indian War. *Treaty of Paris:* 1763 treaty ending the French and Indian War.

2. Conflicting claims to the Ohio Valley triggered the hostilities between the French and the British.

3. The Albany Conference was in response to mounting fears of an attack by the French and their Native American allies. Its aim was to solidify friendship between the colonists and the Iroquois and to plan for a common defense.

4. Pitt united the previously divided colonies by guaranteeing colonial payment for services and supplies. He also dismissed incapable military leaders, replacing them with more capable ones.

5. (a) According to the Treaty of Paris, France lost Canada and land east of the Mississippi to Great Britain. (b) Spain gave up Florida to Britain.

Chapter Review, text page 97

1. The British government believed that by controlling trade in the colonies Britain would be one step closer to "commanding the riches of the world" and then "the world itself."

2. The Navigation Acts: colonial merchants were allowed to ship goods on British or colonial vessels only; three quarters of the crew had to be British or British colonists; enumerated commodities could be shipped only to Britain; imported products from countries other than Britain had to be routed through Britain first.

3. (a) New England merchants became more unhappy about the Navigation Acts in the 1700s because they interfered with the rum trade. (b) The Molasses Act actually had little impact on the triangular trade because it was not enforced.

4. (a) Britain competed with France over claims to the Ohio Valley. Control of Canada was also an issue between the two nations. Britain and Spain competed for control of Florida. (b) France was Britain's strongest competitor in North America because expanding French territorial claims threatened the British position in America.

5. (a) French fur trade created competition among Native Americans for control of rich hunting grounds and for a role in the French trade; sometimes the competition resulted in armed conflict. (b) British settlers encroached upon Native American territory, forcing Native Americans from their land. (c) Violent conflict was more likely to occur between Native Americans and the British colonists, because the growing number of British colonists caused a greater encroachment on Native American territory than the French caused.

6. William Pitt, as secretary of state, initiated policies that were instrumental in Britain's victory in the French and Indian War.

For Further Thought, text page 97

1. Answers may vary. Accept all justifiable answers that refer to mercantilism and colonialism. Students should note that colonialism gave Britain access to raw materials and markets, while the policy of mercantilism guaranteed that Britain would enjoy a favored position in its trade with the colonies.

2. Answers may vary. Accept all justifiable answers that refer to proximate land claims on the North American continent. Students should also refer to the historic antagonism between the British and the French and the Spanish.

Developing Basic Skills, text page 97

1. (a) The map describes territorial claims in North America in 1763. (b) British territory extends as far west as the Mississippi River. (c) Spanish territory extends as far east as the Mississippi River. (d) French territory is located in the Caribbean Sea. (e) Spain would probably be Britain's territorial rival in North America after 1763.

2. (a) Between 1753 and 1763 the British gained all territory in North America east of the Mississippi River and in French Canada. (b) France lost all claims to North America with the exception of some Caribbean islands. Spain lost Florida to Britain and gained all lands west of the Mississippi River from France. (c) Britain gained the most territory east of the Mississippi River. France lost the most.

Unit Two: Creating a Republic

6 The Road to Revolution (1763–1775)

Section Review, text page 105

1. *Pontiac:* Ottawa chief who led a rebellion of Native Americans against the British in 1763. *Proclamation of 1763:* British policy restricting colonial settlement west of the Appalachian Mountains. *George Grenville:* chancellor of the exchequer; began Britain's policy of taxing the colonies. *Sons of Liberty:* self-appointed colonial group who used violent means to stop the enforcement of the Stamp Act. *Stamp Act Congress:* representatives from nine colonies who met in 1765 to protest taxation and to demand repeal of the Stamp and Sugar acts. *Daughters of Liberty:* protest group of colonial women who aided the boycott of British cloth.

2. Developments leading to Pontiac's Rebellion: settling and fortifying land in violation of treaties with Native Americans; British General Amherst's refusal to pay Native Americans for land.

3. (a) The Proclamation of 1763 aimed to create a boundary between colonial and Indian lands. (b) The colonists reacted unfavorably to the proclamation. They wanted freedom to expand west of the Appalachian Mountains without the presence of British troops.

4. The primary purpose of the Sugar Act was to raise revenues as well as to regulate trade. This was a departure from previous British policy toward the colonies in that for the first time Britain had gone beyond the regulation of trade. The colonists interpreted the Sugar Act as a form of taxation.

5. (a) The Currency Act of 1764 forbade colonial governments from issuing their own paper money, demanded the recall of paper money in circulation, and required British money to be used to pay debts owed to British merchants. (b) The Quartering Act of 1765 passed the responsibility and expense of housing and providing for British troops on to the colonists. (c) The Stamp Act of 1765 required that a stamp, representing a paid tax, be placed on a large number of items, including legal documents and newspapers.

6. The colonists did not want representation in Parliament because of the difficulties arising from long-distance communication. They wanted to control their own tax laws.

7. Reactions to the Stamp Act: violent reactions included mob activities such as the ransacking and destruction of property; nonviolent reactions included the Stamp Act Congress, the boycott of British goods, and protests by the Daughters of Liberty.

8. Two important consequences of the Stamp Act were the creation of colonial unity over the tax issue and the emergence of spokespeople for the colonial position.

Section Review, text page 108

1. *Charles Townshend:* British chancellor of the exchequer who tried to raise revenues by taxing the colonies. *Townshend Acts:* series of acts passed in 1767 aimed at raising revenue in the colonies. *Boston Massacre:* open conflict between angry, taunting colonists and British troops at the Boston customs house in 1770 in which five colonists were shot to death. *John Adams:* defense attorney for the British soldiers accused of killing civilians during the Boston Massacre. *Lord North:* prime minister of Great Britain appointed by George III in 1770. He persuaded Parliament to repeal the Townshend Acts.

2. *nonimportation agreement:* agreement signed in 1768 by colonial merchants not to import certain British goods that carried a tax. *writs of assistance:* documents authorizing unrestricted searches.

3. (a) The Townshend Acts were supposed to raise revenue by placing moderate customs duties on imported items such as glass, tea, and paper. (b) They were unsuccessful because of the colonial reaction, which included the signing of a nonimportation agreement and the preference for colonial-made products.

4. (a) Townshend tried to enforce the Quartering Act by punishing one of its chief offenders, New York. All meetings of the New York assembly were suspended until the act was obeyed. (b) The colonial legislatures showed their support of New York by threatening to resist every tax put on them by Great Britain.

5. The stationing of troops in Boston to protect British customs commissioners sparked the Boston Massacre in 1770.

6. (a) The Townshend Acts were repealed for two basic reasons: the Boston Massacre revealed the gravity of colonial anger; colonial boycotts and manufacture of needed items were effectively hurting Britain. (b) Two reasons the tax on tea remained: guaranteed some revenue for Britain; served as a reminder to colonists of Parliament's authority.

Section Review, text page 112

1. *Gaspee:* British warship burned by Rhode Island colonists while on a customs patrol in 1772. *British East India Company:* private investment company granted special tax exemptions for its tea trade. *Boston Tea Party:* an incident created when members of the Sons of Liberty boarded East India Company ships and dumped tea into the Boston Harbor in 1773. *Intolerable Acts:* label given by the colonists to the Coercive Acts and the Quebec Act of 1774; these acts closed the post of Boston, revoked the Massachusetts charter, suspended the Massachusetts legislature, imposed military rule on the colony, and expanded Quebec's boundaries. *Committees of Correspondence:* organized colonial groups within each colony whose goal was to keep people informed about events in the struggle with Great Britain. *Samuel Adams:* organized first Committee of Correspondence in Massachusetts in 1772.
2. The *Gaspee* incident worried the colonists because the British bypassed Rhode Island's court system and set up a special commission to investigate the burning of the *Gaspee.* Colonists feared a permanent shutdown of their courts.
3. (a) The purpose of the 1773 Tea Act was to make tea sold by the British Each India Company in the colonies cheaper than Dutch tea, which was smuggled in. The Tea Act was an effort to increase the company's revenues. (b) Complaints by colonial tea merchants about a British monopoly led to a widespread tea boycott. When Governor Thomas Hutchinson tried to enforce the Tea Act in Massachusetts, colonists dumped the tea on British ships into Boston Harbor.
4. (a) The purpose of the Coercive Act was to punish Boston, the center of colonial resistance, and to make an example of Massachusetts, with the hope of forcing all colonies to obey British laws. (b) Measures taken against Boston: the port was closed, town meetings were forbidden, local government was put under military control, more soldiers were stationed in Boston.
5. Colonial unity grew as colonists learned about the issues involved in their struggle against Britain. They were further united as they read pamphlets calling for greater resistance against Britain.
6. The First Continental Congress met in 1774 to discuss a unified response to the Intolerable Acts.

Section Review, text page 115

1. *Joseph Galloway:* moderate representative from Pennsylvania at the First Continental Congress. *Thomas Jefferson:* represented the radical view at the First Continental Congress. The radicals did not believe that Parliament had the right to regulate trade or tax the colonists. *Declaration and Resolves:* most important document of the First Continental Congress. It attacked all British legislation since 1763 and demanded that Parliament repeal all oppressive laws. *Suffolk Resolves:* resolutions approved by the First Continental Congress recommending that the people of Massachusetts openly defy the Coercive Acts and prepare for their own defense against the British. *Association:* group of committees set up in every city to insure compliance with the First Continental Congress's decision ending all trade with Great Britain. *minutemen:* armed colonial militia formed in Massachusetts in 1774–1775; they stood ready to fight at a minute's warning.
2. (a) The moderates proposed a colonial union under British control. According to this plan Parliament would still be able to legislate for the colonies, but such acts of Parliament could be vetoed by a council of American representatives. (b) The plan was defeated, largely because of resistance to it by Samuel Adams, who represented a radical point of view.
3. The radicals, unlike most Americans in 1765, believed that Parliament did not have the right to regulate trade or tax the colonists.
4. (a) The Congress voted for an immediate and complete end to trade with Great Britain. (b) Committees were set up to insure that no colony traded with Britain.
5. After General Gage received word that minutemen had an arsenal of weapons, he decided to act against the colonists.

Lexington and Concord: Analyzing a Primary Source, text page 116

1. (a) Government document. (b) Lieutenant-Colonel Smith. He was closely involved in the event. (c) Written on April 22, 1775.
2. (a) He was probably expected to inform his supervisors of the results of the battles in which he was engaged. (b) He commanded British troops that marched on Concord and Lexington. His position could have affected the report's reliability. (c) He was British. From the context it is clear that he is commanding the "king's troops." He might be inclined to exaggerate the bravery of his troops or the numerical strength of the enemy. (d) This is a reliable source from a British eyewitness. However, one should take into account the author's need to justify his role to his commanding officer.
3. (a) Smith's troops moved in response to Gage's orders. Smith marched to Concord. The British fired the first shot. (b) He believed that the colonists

planned an attack on the British. He believed that the British intended no harm. (c) Yes. The colonists had dug in for an 18-mile stretch between Concord and Boston. This is probably a fact. (d) They seemed reluctant to engage the colonists in battle.

Chapter Review, text page 117

1. (a) Pontiac led a rebellion against the British because settlers had built forts in western lands in violation of Indian treaties and because the British had not paid Indians for confiscated land. (b) The Proclamation of 1763 was a direct result of Pontiac's Rebellion. The British created and tried to enforce a border between colonial and Indian lands.
2. Great Britain's attempts to ease its national debt and the colonial reaction to each measure: The Sugar Act cut taxes on molasses and added a tax on coffee, wine, sugar, and cloth; colonists objected to Parliament's attempt at taxation. The Currency Act prohibited colonies from issuing paper money, required the recall of paper money in circulation, and required British debts to be paid with British currency; colonists objected to the British attempts at controlling colonial finances. The Quartering Act required that the colonists provide room and board for British troops; colonists objected, maintaining that the close personal contact intensified ill feelings. The Stamp Act required that a stamp, representing a paid tax, be affixed to a long list of items; colonists objected, engaged in acts of physical violence, and convinced the Stamp Act Congress to protest Parliament's threat to their liberties.
3. (a) The Townshend Acts were revenue measures passed in 1767 by Parliament. The money collected from small customs duties on imported items was supposed to pay for colonial governmental functions. (b) The British tried to enforce the Townshend Acts by firing customs officials who accepted bribes, by issuing writs of assistance, and by stationing more troops in Boston. (c) The colonists reacted by bribing customs officials not to collect the tax, by manufacturing goods instead of importing them, by signing nonimportation agreements and by taunting British soldiers in Boston (leading to the Boston Massacre).
4. (a) The Tea Act was a symbol of British oppression because a tax imposed by Parliament was a reminder of British authority. Also, the act excluded American middlemen from the tea business. (b) The colonists opposed the Tea Act by boycotting tea. Also, the Sons of Liberty dumped tea into Boston Harbor during the "Tea Party."
5. (a) The Coercive Acts closed the port of Boston, suspended meetings of the Massachusetts courts and legislature, imposed military rule on the colony, and forbade town meetings. More troops were sent to Boston, and the Quartering Act was revived. (b) The Quebec Act threatened colonial western expansion because the British allowed Quebec's borders to extend to the Ohio and Mississippi Rivers. (c) Accept any justifiable answer that explains how the Intolerable Acts helped to unite the colonies (for example, a discussion of a common cause overcoming regional differences).
6. (a) The major question facing the First Continental Congress was how to respond to the Intolerable Acts. (b) Actions taken by the First Continental Congress include preparation of the *Declaration and Resolves,* approval of the Suffolk Resolves, a vote to end trade with Britain, and formation of an Association to monitor the cessation of trade.
7. (a) The moderates at the First Continental Congress sought a compromise with Great Britain. The radicals wanted to redefine the relationship of the colonies to Britain. For them the British Empire was a loose union of independent states, each with its own legislature and united by loyalty to the king. They did not seek compromise with Britain. Instead they insisted that their demands be met. (b) The radicals dominated by the end of the Congress.
8. The Suffolk Resolves urged the people of Massachusetts to disobey the Coercive Acts and prepare to defend themselves against British attack.

For Further Thought, text page 117

1. (a) Both the Sugar Act and Stamp Act were viewed as taxation without representation because they were imposed as revenue-raising measures on the colonies by Parliament, a body 3,000 miles away that had no colonial representatives. (b) The Sugar Act and the Stamp Act were passed as revenue-raising measures. The Molasses Act imposed tax on all molasses or rum imported from the West Indies, but its primary purpose was the regulation of trade. (c) The colonists felt that the colonial legislatures, as representative bodies of the people, had the authority to levy taxes.
2. "Massacre" is defined as the "indiscriminate merciless killing of a number of human beings." The incident in Boston was a massacre in that British fire was indiscriminately aimed at the crowd.

Developing Basic Skills, text page 117

1. (a) The nonimportation agreement made by the First Continental Congress was most effective. Trade dropped from almost 2.6 million pounds sterling in 1774 to 196,162 pounds in 1775. The least

effective nonimportation agreement occurred after the Stamp Act crisis in 1765. Here trade dropped from about 1.9 million pounds in 1765 to about 1.8 million pounds in 1766. (b) To explain this difference in effectiveness, students might point to the crisis that erupted during the intervening years. The Boston Massacre and Boston Tea Party might be mentioned as factors that promoted colonial unity.

2. (a) Appalachian Mountains. (b) Native Americans. (c) Spain. (d) Effectiveness of the Proclamation Line: answers may vary. Accept those answers that relate to its proven ineffectiveness.

7 A War for Independence (1775–1783)

Section Review, text page 122

1. *John Dickinson:* leader of the moderates at the Second Continental Congress. The moderates were in favor of negotiating an agreement with Britain. *Committees of Safety:* local organizations that recruited and trained men, collected supplies and money, gathered information, and disrupted the activities of British officials. *Ethan Allen:* captured a British garrison with his Green Mountain Boys at Fort Ticonderoga, New York, in 1775. *Israel Putnam:* commander of colonial troops at Breed's Hill and Bunker Hill. *Bunker Hill:* site of an early battle between American militia and British troops in Boston in June 1775. *William Howe:* British commander in Boston who withdrew his troops to Nova Scotia after the battle at Bunker Hill. *Benedict Arnold:* American colonel who led the advance on Quebec during the fall and winter of 1775. In December, he and General Richard Montgomery lost the siege.

2. (a) The most significant question facing the Second Continental Congress was whether to negotiate agreement with Great Britain or to declare independence for the 13 colonies. (b) The moderates wanted to compromise with Great Britain. (c) The radicals were in favor of independence.

3. Although the Americans lost to the British in the Battle of Bunker Hill, they learned that they could fight effectively against the better-equipped and better-trained British troops.

4. Soldiers respected George Washington's leadership abilities; delegates to the Continental Congress trusted his dedication to the colonial cause; his southern background broadened support for what southerners had seen as a New England war.

5. The Continental Congress learned that Canadian Governor Guy Carleton planned an invasion of the colonies, so the Congress decided to attack first. The invasion failed.

Section Review, text page 124

1. *Olive Branch Petition:* resolution prepared in 1775 by moderates of the Second Continental Congress. Aimed at compromise, the resolution called for the repeal of the Coercive Acts as a reconciliatory measure. *Prohibitory Act:* passed by Parliament in 1775 six weeks after the Olive Branch Petition. The act proclaimed that a state of rebellion existed in the colonies, and it authorized steps aimed at punishment. *Thomas Paine:* wrote the pamphlet *Common Sense* in January 1776. *Common Sense:* pamphlet written by Thomas Paine. It aroused patriotism by declaring that Americans did not owe allegiance to any monarchy.

2. (a) King George was not willing to repeal the Coercive Acts. (b) The Prohibitory Act and the hiring of Hessian mercenaries helped make the colonists more radical.

3. Thomas Paine convinced many colonists that they should not support a king who ruled simply because he inherited his position.

4. Two arguments that convinced hesitant delegates to declare independence: captured American fighters would be considered prisoners of war and not traitors; Britain's enemies might give financial aid to an independent country.

5. (a), (b) The first section of the Declaration of Independence is the preamble, which explains the reasons why the colonists wanted independence. The second section is a list of complaints against the king and Parliament; its purpose was to justify and bolster the call for independence. The third section is in effect the declaration of independence; it presents a new government and severs all ties with Great Britain.

Section Review, text page 129

1. *Loyalists:* name used by those colonists who maintained allegiance to King George III during the Revolutionary War. *Patriots:* name used by those who supported independence from Great Britain. *Tories:* name the Patriots called those loyal to Great Britain. *redcoats:* name given to British soldiers because of the color of their uniforms. *John Paul Jones:* naval commander who defeated the British in a hotly contested sea battle.

2. *localism:* the practice of each state or area acting independently and not as part of a unified nation.

3. Wealthier colonists tended to remain loyal to Great Britain. They included successful merchants, large

plantation owners, former royal government officers, and Church of England ministers.

4. (a) Members of the Continental Congress were concerned that if large numbers of blacks joined the army to fight for independence they would encourage slaves to revolt for their independence. (b) Once the British actively started recruiting blacks, offering to free any slave who joined the British army, the Continental Congress allowed blacks to enlist.

5. Contributions of women to the war effort: a few women dressed as men and fought in battles; others were successful spies; wives made camp life bearable for their soldier husbands; some women did the work the men had left to go to war.

6. (a) Advantages of the British forces: experienced generals, a well-trained and well-equipped army, and a large navy. (b) Major disadvantage: difficulty in obtaining supplies.

7. American advantages: love and knowledge of the land; superior accuracy of American rifles; leadership of Washington; and foreign aid, especially from France.

8. The single most difficult problem faced by leaders of the Continental Army was forming a united army from local militia units.

9. The Continental Congress printed paper money to buy supplies and pay troops.

Section Review, text page 132

1. *Sir William Howe:* commanded British forces to victory in the Battle of New York; also captured Philadelphia. *Lord Cornwallis:* British general who forced Washington to retreat across New Jersey into Pennsylvania after the American defeat in New York. *John Burgoyne:* commander of the British army in Canada who marched south and was defeated by the Americans at the Battle of Saratoga in October 1777. *Horatio Gates:* American general who captured Burgoyne's army at Saratoga in October 1777.

2. The defeat in New York greatly lowered American morale. Soldiers began deserting in large numbers.

3. The victory at Trenton and the capture of Princeton lifted American spirits at the end of 1776.

4. (a) The British developed a plan to split the colonies by capturing New York and isolating New England. (b) General Howe deviated from the plan by moving to capture Philadelphia. He thereby failed to support General Burgoyne in his march south from Canada. Burgoyne was captured during the Battle of Saratoga.

5. Americans won the Battle of Saratoga.

Section Review, text page 136

1. *Baron von Steuben:* former Prussian soldier who organized the Continental army into a trained fighting unit. *Thaddeus Kosciusko:* Polish engineer who built forts along the Delaware River and the first fortifications at West Point. *Casimir Pulaski:* Polish cavalry officer who fought with Americans during the Revolutionary War. *George Rogers Clark:* Virginia commander who defeated the British in western areas of Illinois and Ohio. *Sir Henry Clinton:* developed British strategy for an offensive in the South. *Nathanael Greene:* American commander who won battles in the South by using small units of soldiers against the British, who continued to mass for battle in large units. *Comte de Rochambeau:* French commander who marched with Washington to capture Cornwallis at Yorktown. *Marquis de Lafayette:* French general who helped defeat the British at the Battle of Yorktown.

2. The Battle of Saratoga convinced France to support the United States.

3. The French helped the Americans by sending supplies and military experts. Also, with Britain at war with France, British military pressure on the Americans was reduced.

4. The British expected victory in the South because they believed that they could easily move troops around by sea and that southern Loyalists would support them.

5. The major goals of the Americans were British recognition of the United States as an independent nation and acquisition of all land from the Atlantic Ocean to the Mississippi River between the Great Lakes and Florida.

Chapter Review, text page 137

1. At the Battle of Bunker Hill the Americans successfully repelled two British charges. Even though the British won the battle, the Americans learned they had a chance to defeat the better-trained and -equipped British troops.

2. The king's decision not to compromise with moderates in the Continental Congress angered the delegates. They saw independence as the only solution.

3. (a) The preamble established general principles of human rights. (b) These principles of human rights have shaped the work of those who believe in equal rights for all. (c) The declaration cited natural rights that cannot be violated as the major justification for independence. (d) The Continental Congress acted by adopting the Declaration of Independence.

4. (a) British advantages: experienced generals, a well-trained and well-equipped army, and a large navy. (b) British disadvantages: supplies could not reach troops; troops could not adapt to hit-and-run warfare.

5. (a) Many southern leaders owned slaves. They felt that the wide participation of blacks in the army might encourage slaves to revolt to gain their own independence. (b) Blacks were involved in many battles during the war. Rhode Island had an all-black battalion.

6. (a) In building an maintaining an army, Washington had to deal with desertion, supply shortages, and securing the soldiers' loyalties. (b) Washington did overcome these problems. (c) The most difficult problem was that of forming a truly American army from the various colonial militias.

7. Fears of a strong federal government limited the Congress' power to draft soldiers and issue money.

8. (a) Washington decided to attack Trenton and Princeton because he knew a bold plan was necessary to boost army morale and maintain military strength. (b) From these and other battles Washington learned that successes against the British were possible.

9. (a) The first treaty recognized the United States as an independent nation and granted special trading privileges to France. The second treaty specified that if France and Great Britain went to war, France would give up all land east of the Mississippi River and the United States would recognize any French claims in the West Indies. (b) Before entering the war, the French wanted to see if Americans could really defeat the British. (c) The American victory at Saratoga convinced the French to enter the war.

10. The British miscalculated in the following ways: they did not anticipate that the French would prevent the movement of British soldiers by sea; they overestimated the number of Loyalists in the South; they mistakenly continued to rely on traditional, European-style fighting methods; and Cornwallis made a disastrous decision to fortify Yorktown instead of marching to New York.

For Further Thought, text page 137

1. (a) According to Thomas Jefferson, natural rights were God-given rights that no government could take away. (b) Since Jefferson believed that the power to rule flowed from the people to the government, the king had no God-given power to rule. Thus, a government that trampled on the natural rights of its citizens could be overthrown.

2. (a) Generally the Loyalists were among the wealthier colonists, such as rich merchants, large plantation owners, former royal governmental officials, and Church of England ministers. (b) Many of these people probably remained loyal to Britain because it was in their personal interest to do so.

3. Students could suggest that some members of Parliament might have agreed with the political philosophy of John Locke, who maintained that the people were the source of government. This could have been the basis for their support of the Patriot cause.

4. (a) Black slaves might have enlisted in the Continental Army to win their freedom. (b) Free blacks might have joined because job and educational opportunities were limited for them in civilian life.

5. Factors contributing to the American victory: accept any justifiable answer that includes knowledge and love of the land, help from the French, Washington's able leadership, hit-and-run tactics, and mistakes by British generals.

Developing Basic Skills, text page 137

1. In column 1, the advantages of the British at the start of the war should include superior generals and a superior army and navy. In column 2 the disadvantages should include supply-line difficulties and an inappropriate fighting style. In column 3 the advantages of the Americans should include knowledge and love of the land, superior rifles, Washington's leadership, and foreign aid. Disadvantages of the Americans should include localism, a weak central government, and few supplies. (a), (b), (c) Accept all justifiable answers.

2. Boundary line changes between 1763 and 1783: in 1783 the United States boundary extended to the Mississippi River, and Great Britain claimed the lands north of the United States border; in 1763 British territory was restricted to the original 13 colonies, France had vast claims west of the Appalachian Mountains, and Spain controlled Florida and the lands north and northwest of present-day Mexico.

8 An Experimental Era (1777–1787)

Section Review, text page 143

1. *Cincinnati Society:* club formed in 1783 to voice concerns of army veterans, especially officers. Because membership was hereditary, many denounced it as an attempt to establish a new aristocracy.

Abigail Adams: wife of John Adams; she voiced concern over women's inequality during the time of the Continental Congress. *Noah Webster:* helped develop national pride by experimenting with the American language to make it more American.

2. *segregated:* set apart from. *manumission:* legal procedure that freed slaves.
3. (a) To qualify as a voter a person typically had to be male, white, Christian, and a property owner. (b) Some states extended the right to vote by lowering property requirements.
4. (a) The education system below the college level provided some new opportunities for women in the 1780s and 1790s. (b) Women continued to face discrimination in higher education.
5. (a) After the Revolutionary War, free blacks in some states gained more equality in the legal system, constitutional voting rights, and increased opportunities for jobs. (b) Free blacks did not gain equality with whites, since discrimination remained.
6. Vermont was the first state to abolish slavery.
7. Thomas Jefferson felt that established churches limited religious freedom because they had an unfair advantage over other churches.
8. Concerned Americans organized reform societies, charitable societies, volunteer fire departments, school fund organizations, and immigrant aid societies. (Students should receive credit for giving two examples.)
9. Examples of an emerging national consciousness: feelings of pride and predictions of greatness by citizens, written celebrations of the "birth" of a nation by authors and poets, changes in the language to distinguish it from the "King's English."

Section Review, text page 145

1. *veto:* to reject; for example, to reject a bill passed by a legislature. *bicameral:* referring to a legislature with two houses, a lower house and an upper house. *inalienable rights:* natural rights that governments cannot take away from citizens.
2. (a) Americans made few changes in their state governments because they were basically satisfied with them. (b) Changes constituted safeguards to keep the government from abusing its power.
3. (a) The three branches of state governments: executive, legislative, and judicial. (b) State legislatures were divided into upper and lower houses.
4. The British lacked a written constitution; Americans felt that a written statement of their rights would be harder to violate.
5. The people of Massachusetts took the writing of the constitution out of the state legislature and placed it in the hands of delegates to a special convention.

Legislators could not change the constitution without the people's consent.

Section Review, text page 150

1. *Articles of Confederation:* the nation's first constitution, ratified in 1781. *Northwest Territory:* large land area ceded to the national government by Virginia. *Land Ordinance of 1785:* law passed by Congress authorizing the survery and sale of land in the Northwest Territory. *Northwest Ordinance:* passed in 1787, this law concerned the political organization of the Northwest Territory and set guidelines for eventual statehood.
2. *confederation:* alliance of separate, equally independent states. *reserved powers clause:* clause in the Articles of Confederation stating that all powers not expressly given to the central government were retained by the states. *ratify:* approve. *squatters:* people who settle on land without right or title (for example, illegal settlers in the Northwest Territory).
3. (a) Under the Articles of Confederation Congress had the power to declare war, commission military officers, enter into treaties and alliances, receive and send envoys, establish post offices, borrow money, deal with Native Americans, fix weights and measures. (b) Congress could not collect taxes or order men to serve in the army.
4. (a) Delegates from states with heavier populations felt they should have greater representation and influence in Congress. (b) Delegates from less-populous states favored equal representation since it gave them power equal to that of more-populous states.
5. Ratification was delayed because of disputes over conflicting state claims to western territories.
6. Two problems complicated the enforcement of the Land Ordinance of 1785: wild terrain that could not easily be divided into squares, and squatters, who had settled illegally.
7. A territory could become a state when the adult male population reached 60,000.
8. New England shippers and southern planters were hurt economically by the Revolutionary War.

Section Review, text page 152

1. *Shays' Rebellion:* 1786–1787 uprising of Massachusetts farmers protesting low farm prices and high state taxes.
2. (a) Under the Articles of Confederation the states, not Congress, had the power to tax citizens. (b) Congress could raise money by asking states for funds, borrowing from foreign governments, printing money, and selling western lands.

3. Trade between states was difficult because states issued their own currencies, they often imposed tariffs on one another, and economic rivalry in general ran strong.
4. (a) King George III kept troops in the Northwest Territory, thereby violating the peace treaty. (b) Spain showed its lack of respect for the new nation by pressuring western settlers to break away from the United States and by closing the lower Mississippi River to American ships.
5. The original purpose of the Annapolis convention was to discuss new ways to regulate commerce.

Chapter Review, text page 153

1. (a) In the post-Revolutionary period Americans began to question all aspects of their life to see if things could be done differently. (b) Experiments in education: less emphasis on Latin and Greek, coeducation, general increase in knowledge through newspapers and books. Experiments in political equality: denunciation of clubs that seemed aristocratic, redistribution of large landholdings through changes in inheritance laws, easing of restrictions on free blacks, more religious equality. Experiments to improve people's lives: lesser criminal penalties, formation of charitable societies.
2. (a) A typical state government had executive, legislative, and judicial branches of government. (b) The legislative branch had the most power because it symbolized the power of the people. (c) Because the people feared giving too much power to any one governmental body, the legislature was divided into two branches to balance each other.
3. (a) Under the Articles of Confederation there were strict limits on congressional authority to protect states' rights. For example, Congress could not levy taxes or draft soldiers. In addition, all states had equal representation in Congress. (b) States were reluctant to grant Congress too much power because abuses of the British Parliament were fresh in their memories.
4. (a) Under the Articles of Confederation the national government was composed of a congress, which had a variety of powers. Nine of the 13 states had to approve a bill before it became law. There were no provisions for a national court or a chief executive. (b) All states were represented equally in Congress. (c) Even though states wtih large populations did not agree with the policy of equal representation, they followed it because they recognized the need for a central government.
5. (a) States that had no western land wanted profits from the sale of all western lands to benefit the entire country and not just a few states. (b) Ratification was held up until the problem was settled.

Jealousy over profits and fear that neighboring states with western lands would gain more power held up ratification.
6. (a) According to the Land Ordinance of 1785, land in the Northwest Territory would be divided into townships. Each township would be subdivided into 36 one-square-mile lots for settlement. One lot would be set aside for a public school. (b) According to the Northwest Ordinance, the entire area would be divided into three to five territories. When the adult male population of a territory reached 5,000, it could elect a legislature. Each territory would be governed by a governor, a secretary, and three judges. A territory could apply for statehood once its male population reached 60,000. Slavery was banned in the Northwest Territory.
7. Economic unity was difficult to achieve under the Articles of Confederation because Congress was weak and the national currency was worthless. State legislatures protected local interests by issuing their own currency and imposing tariffs on interstate commerce.
8. In response to signs of weakness in the United States, Spain renewed its interest in claiming western land, and England ordered military posts in the Northwest Territory to remain there, in violation of the peace treaty. Other nations were initially hesitant about entering into trade agreements with the United States.

For Further Thought, text page 153

1. Most Americans considered their state government more important than the national government. The organization of government under the Articles of Confederation is one indication of this view.
2. (a) Under the Articles of Confederation the national government lacked important powers, such as the power to levy taxes, raise an army, and regulate interstate commerce. All powers were reserved to the state if not expressly given to Congress. (b) Answers will vary.

Developing Basic Skills, text page 153

1. (a) The legislative branch. (b) Congress could declare war and make peace, raise an army and navy, make foreign treaties and alliances, coin and borrow money, regulate weights and measures, establish a post office, and regulate Native American affairs. (c) State governments had an executive, a legislative, and a judicial branch, whereas the national government had only a legislative branch. (d) Accept those answers that relate to the limitations placed on the national government's power.
2. Research will vary.

9 A More Perfect Union (1787–1791)

Section Review, text page 158

1. *Virginia Plan:* proposal presented at the Constitutional Convention by James Madison. It called for a bicameral Congress consisting of a House of Representatives and a Senate and for the popular election of representatives to the House, with representation based on population. Members of the House would select senators from candidates suggested by state legislatures. The House would also choose members of the judiciary and a President. Congress could override state laws as well as make state laws. *New Jersey Plan:* proposal presented at the Constitutional Convention by William Patterson. Each state would be represented equally in a unicameral Congress. Members would be elected by state legislatures. States would give the national government the power to levy taxes, regulate commerce, and enforce national laws; they would reserve powers not given to the national government for themselves. *The Great Compromise:* compromise submitted by Roger Sherman of Connecticut. It called for a two-house Congress consisting of a House of Representatives and a Senate. Members of the House of Representatives would be elected from each state for two-year terms; the number of representatives from a state would be proportional to its population. Each state, large or small, would have two senators, who would serve six-year terms.
2. John Adams and Thomas Jefferson did not attend the Constitutional Convention because they were serving abroad as foreign ambassadors. Patrick Henry and Samuel Adams did not attend because they did not want to be associated with a move toward strong central government.
3. Delegates to the convention agreed that the new government would: be a representative form of government; have the power to levy taxes, enforce laws, and provide for national defense; and be based on a written constitution.
4. (a) According to the Virginia Plan, the number of House representatives from each state would be based on the size of the state's population. The House would select members of the Senate from candidates suggested by state legislature. (b) According to the New Jersey Plan, Congress would consist of one house, in which each state, large or small, would be represented equally.
5. The Great Compromise resolved the issue of fair representation.
6. The delegates agreed that only three fifths of the slaves in a state would count toward determining its representation in the House.
7. To protect southern trade interests, delegates agreed to prohibit export taxes. They also required a two-thirds-majority vote in the Senate to ratify treaties, including trade agreements.
8. Nine of the 13 states had to ratify the Constitution before it went into effect.

Caption, text page 159

The Articles of Confederation established a national government that possessed little real power. Dissatisfied with the weaknesses of the national government, the framers of the Constitution delegated new powers to Congress.

Section Review, text page 160

1. *sovereignty:* the source of a government's power or authority. *federalism:* system of sovereignty whereby governmental authority is divided between national and state governments. *delegated powers:* powers given by the Constitution exclusively to the national government and forbidden to the states. *reserved powers:* powers that the Constitution did not grant to the national government that were therefore reserved for the states. *concurrent powers:* powers shared by the national and state governments.
2. Under the Virginia Plan the central government would have been sovereign. Under the New Jersey Plan state governments would have been sovereign.
3. The Constitution solved the conflict over sovereignty by establishing a system of shared sovereignty between the national and state governments.
4. Delegated powers include the power to declare war, coin money, regulate foreign and domestic trade, and establish a postal system. Reserved powers include the right to control intrastate trade, provide a militia, and establish voting qualifications. Concurrent powers include the right to support education and to enforce laws. (Students should receive credit for providing one example of each type of power.)
5. Under the Constitution there is a direct link between citizens and the national government. State governments do not serve as intermediaries, as they did under the Articles of Confederation.

Section Review, text page 162

1. *Montesquieu:* wrote *The Spirit of the Laws,* published in 1748. *The Spirit of the Laws:* written work presenting Montesquieu's views on government. Montesquieu believed that to prevent tyranny the powers of government should be divided among legislative, executive, and judicial branches.
2. *separation of powers:* system by which the functions of government are divided among its branches

to prevent one branch from becoming too powerful. *checks and balances:* system established by the Constitution by which each branch of government can check the power of the other branches. These checks create a balance of power among the branches. *impeach:* to bring charges of wrongdoing against a public official. The House of Representatives has the power to impeach a President for "treason, bribery, high crimes and misdemeanors." The Senate has the power to then hear the charges against the President and remove the President from office if convicted by a two-thirds vote. *unconstitutional:* in violation of the Constitution. *electoral college:* method established in the Constitution by which the President and Vice-President are elected. State legislatures choose electors (as a group the electors are called the electoral college). The number of electors for each state is equal to the total number of representatives to Congress from that state. Electors cast ballots for the President and Vice-President. Their voting determines the election results.

3. (a) The three branches of the new government were the legislative, executive, and judicial branches. (b) Functions: legislative branch passes laws; executive branch enforces laws; judicial branch interprets laws.

4. (a) The President can check the power of Congress by vetoing bills. (b) Congress can check the power of the President by refusing to approve presidential appointments. (c) The Supreme Court can check the power of Congress by declaring laws unconstitutional.

5. The delegates limited the direct power of the people in the national government by creating a republic in which the people would choose representatives to govern for them; by determining that state legislatures would elect members of the Senate; and by establishing the electoral college system.

Section Review, text page 165

1. *Federalists:* name given to people who supported the adoption of the Constitution and a strong central government. *Federalist Papers:* series of articles written by Alexander Hamilton, James Madison, and John Jay to gain support for the Constitution in New York State. *Antifederalists:* name given to people who opposed ratification of the proposed Constitution.

2. Federalists argued that a strong national government was needed to remedy the weaknesses of the Articles of Confederation, that controls on the states were necessary to insure survival of the new country, and that states' rights were still protected under the new Constitution.

3. (a) The main concern of the Antifederalists was that the new central government would be too strong and the state governments too weak. (b) The Antifederalists argued that the electoral college system removed the people too much from the process of electing the President and Vice-President. They also opposed the longer terms of office established in the Constitution for congressional representatives. Most importantly, they opposed the Constitution because it lacked a bill of rights to protect individual liberties.

4. (a) Delaware, New Jersey, and Connecticut ratified the Constitution most quickly. (b) Key ratification battles took place in Pennsylvania, Massachusetts, Virginia, and New York.

Section Review, text page 168

1. *amend:* to change. *writ of habeas corpus:* a court order granting prisoners the right to be released unless specific charges are filed. Habeas corpus is a protection provided by the Constitution against arbitrary imprisonment. *bill of attainder:* a law that fines or imprisons a person without a trial. The Constitution prohibits state and national governments from passing bills of attainder. *ex post facto law:* law that makes an act a crime after it has been committed. The Constitution prohibits ex post facto laws. *due process:* constitutional protection that guarantees individuals accused of crimes a fair, standardized, and open legal process.

2. (a) Constitutional amendments can be proposed by a two-thirds majority vote of Congress or by a special convention ordered by two thirds of the state legislatures. (b) Three fourths of the states are needed to ratify an amendment.

3. Madison opposed a specific bill of rights because he feared that those rights not listed in it might be unprotected.

4. (a) The Second Amendment allows state militia to keep and bear arms (insuring a means of protection). (b) The Third Amendment prohibits the quartering of soldiers in private homes. (The Americans had clear memories of the Quartering Act.) (c) The Fourth Amendment prevents unreasonable searches and seizures. (People bitterly remembered the writs of assistance used by the British.)

Chapter Review, text page 169

1. (a) Delegates held heated debate over the allocation of representatives in the national government because the issue of fair representation of states in Congress was at stake. (b) The Virginia Plan proposed a Congress divided into two houses: the House of Representatives and the Senate. The

number of House representatives allotted to each state would be based on the size of that state's population. The House would select Senate members from candidates proposed by the state legislatures. (c) The New Jersey Plan proposed a one-house Congress in which all states, large or small, would have the same number of representatives. (d) According to the resulting compromise, two houses of Congress were established: a House of Representatives based on proportional representation, and a Senate in which all states would be represented equally (two senators from each state).

2. Compromises were made relating to the slave trade, export taxes, treaty ratification, and the method for counting slaves when determining representation in the House.

3. (a) Federalism divided sovereignty between state and national governments by establishing a system of delegated, reserved, and concurrent powers. (b) The Articles of Confederation did not provide an effective system of shared powers between the national and state governments. The state governments exclusively held several important powers.

4. (a) Under the system of federalism neither the national government nor the states have absolute power. (b) Through the separation of powers, the three branches of national government divide power among one another. (c) The checks and balances method allows each of the three branches of national government to prevent any other branch from abusing its power. (d) The electoral college system is intended to place the election of President and Vice-President in the hands of informed representatives of the people.

5. (a) Checks on presidential power: appointments of cabinet officials, federal judges, and ambassadors are subject to Senate approval; two thirds of the Senate is needed to approve treaties negotiated by the President; Congress has the power to declare war, impeach the President, and override, by a two-thirds vote in each house, a presidential veto. (b) Remembering their experience with the British king, the delegates were concerned about how to distribute executive authority.

6. (a) Checks on congressional power: both houses must agree on bills; the President can veto bills; the Supreme Court can declare laws unconstitutional. (b) Checks by the legislative and executive branches on the judicial branch: the President appoints federal judges with the consent of the Senate; Congress can impeach and remove judges.

7. Arguments for ratification: a strong central government was needed to remedy the weaknesses of the Articles of Confederation; controls on the states were necessary to unite the country; states' rights would still be protected. Arguments against

ratification: the central government would become too strong; the people would be too far removed from the process of electing the President, Vice-President, and senators; congressional terms of office would be too long; no bill of rights.

8. (a) Delegates saw the need to be able to peacefully change the Constitution to adapt to future needs. (b) An amendment can be proposed by a two-thirds vote in Congress or by a special convention ordered by two thirds of the state legislatures. Approval by three fourths of the states is necessary for an amendment to be added to the Constitution.

9. (a) The Constitution protects individual liberties by guaranteeing the right to a writ of habeas corpus, by prohibiting the passage of bills of attainder, by outlawing ex post facto laws, and by insuring the right to a jury trial in criminal cases. (b) Antifederalists maintained that a specific bill of rights was needed to insure that the liberties won in the Revolution would be preserved.

10. The Bill of Rights guarantees freedom of speech, religion, and the press; the right of petition and peaceful assembly; the right to bear arms; protection against unreasonable searches and seizures; and the right to due process of the law. Other guarantees include the following: a person does not have to testify against him- or herself in a trial; a person accused of a crime has the right to a speedy and public trial by jury and the right to be represented by a lawyer; a person cannot be tried twice for the same crime; judges may not set excessive bail or inflict "cruel and unusual punishment" on those convicted.

For Further Thought, text page 169

1. (a) Answers may vary. Accept any justifiable answer that discusses the fear of establishing another monarchy. (b) Students may suggest that some delegates still preferred a monarchy because of their aristocratic backgrounds.

2. (a) The method of electing representatives to government and the electoral college system limit the direct power of the people. (b) Delegates wanted to limit the direct power of the people because they believed that the people might not be sufficiently informed to make wise decisions. The delegates also feared that the public would be influenced by emotional appeals. The delegates believed that representatives would be better educated, better informed, and capable of making more careful decisions. (c) Answers will vary.

3. (a), (b) Accept all justifiable answers that include leadership qualities, powers of reasoning, and the ability to compromise.

4. Although the author of this quotation could either be a Federalist or Antifederalist, students should recognize its Antifederalist tone. Students should mention that the Antifederalists distrusted government power and desired the imposition of restraints on that power.

Developing Basic Skills, text page 169

1. Under Delegated Powers: army, off-shore drilling rights, interstate trade regulations, postal service. Under Reserved Powers: voting age, fishing regulations, police protection, motor-vehicle regulations, intrastate trade regulations. Under Concurrent Powers: education, income tax, luxury tax.
2. Research: answers will vary.

Unit Three: An Emerging Nation

10 A Federalist Beginning (1789–1801)

Section Review, text page 177

1. *John Jay:* first Chief Justice of the Supreme Court. *James Madison:* leader of the House of Representatives who served as adviser to President Washington. *Thomas Jefferson:* appointed secretary of state by President Washington. *Henry Knox:* appointed secretary of war by President Washington. *Alexander Hamilton:* appointed secretary of the treasury by President Washington.
2. *funding:* the method that a government uses to raise or borrow money to pay off its debts. *assumption:* process whereby the federal government took over all state debts incurred during the Revolutionary War. *strict construction:* a literal interpretation of the Constitution that holds that the federal government has only those powers explicitly stated in the Constitution. *loose construction:* a broad interpretation of the Constitution that holds that the federal government has powers that are reasonably implied. *protective tariff:* a tax placed on imported products to encourage people to buy less expensive, domestically produced goods.

3. Washington brought to the presidency his popularity, prestige, and strength of character.
4. (a) The purpose of the original cabinet was to help the President handle the administrative duties of government. (b) Article II of the Constitution authorized the creation of several executive departments.
5. (a) The Judiciary Act of 1789 specified how the Supreme Court should be organized and described its jurisdiction. (b) The Judiciary Act provided for the creation of one Chief Justice and five associate justices. It gave the Supreme Court final jurisdiction over any dispute involving the Constitution, federal laws, and treaties. The act also established 13 district courts and three circuit courts.
6. (a) The most serious problem facing the United States in 1789 was how to pay off its huge war debt. (b) Hamilton proposed that the federal government issue new bonds, to be exchanged at face value for the bonds that had been circulated during the war. In addition to this full funding of the national debt, Hamilton proposed that the national government assume the state debts.
7. (a) Hamilton proposed a national bank in order to put the economy on sound footing. (b) The Bank would issue currency and serve as a depository for federal taxes. The Bank's directors would have the power to invest that money. Stock in the Bank would be owned jointly by the federal government and private citizens.
8. (a) The Whiskey Rebellion was sparked by the passage of an excise tax on whiskey. It enraged farmers in western Pennsylvania because whiskey was their source of income. (b) Washington suppressed the rebellion by bringing in the state militia, thereby showing the power of the federal government to enforce its laws.

Section Review, text page 179

1. *Edmond Genêt:* French ambassador to the United States; he encouraged Americans to undertake activities against nations that were at war with France. *Thomas Pinckney:* American diplomat who negotiated a treaty with Spain.
2. (a) Americans were at first enthusiastic about the French Revolution. (b) They became outraged when the revolutionaries executed the king and many nobles and when they turned against Christianity.
3. (a) Hamilton opposed American support of the French Revolution because the revolution attacked the aristocracy and because American support might mean risking war with Great Britain. War with Britain would threaten the economic prosperity of the United States. (b) Jefferson disagreed with

Hamilton because he was sympathetic to the idealistic goals of equality espoused by the French revolutionaries. (c) Washington decided on a course of neutrality by issuing a Proclamation of Neutrality in 1793.

4. Genêt outfitted American ships to attack English ships, he organized an attack by Americans on Spanish New Orleans, and he organized pro-French clubs that criticized Washington's policy of neutrality. Through these actions he risked bringing the United States into war against Great Britain and Spain.

5. (a) In the Jay Treaty Great Britain promised to evacuate military posts on United States soil and to pay damages for ships it had seized. (b) Most Americans were unhappy with the treaty because it seemed to represent a surrender to Britain. The British did not promise to stop seizing American ships or to stop arming Native Americans. Southern planters were especially unhappy because according to the treaty Americans had to pay debts owed to British merchants before the Revolutionary War. This provision primarily affected the southerners, while northerners benefitted from compensation for ships and cargoes that had been seized.

6. The Pinckney Treaty established a border between Spanish Florida and the United States at the 31st parallel. It also gave Americans the right to ship cargo down the Mississippi River and to deposit cargo at New Orleans.

7. Washington warned against permanent alliances because he was afraid they would involve the United States in European conflicts and threaten the development of the United States.

Section Review, text page 182

1. *Republican party:* the political party formed by Thomas Jefferson, James Madison, and their followers. *Federalist party:* the political party formed by Alexander Hamilton and his supporters.

2. *faction:* a group of people who hold similar beliefs and attempt to exercise those beliefs in politics.

3. (a) Hamilton believed that wealthy, well-educated people should control the government. (b) Jefferson believed that power should be spread among the common people.

4. Hamilton and Jefferson disagreed on how the nation's economy should develop. Hamilton believed that the nation's economy should depend on manufacturing, shipping, and commerce. Jefferson believed that it should be based on farming. They also disagreed in their interpretation of the Constitution. Hamilton believed in a strong central government and applied a loose interpretation to its list of powers in the Constitution. Jefferson, who be-

lieved that states should retain authority, was a strict constructionist.

5. (a) John Fenno's *Gazette of the United States* supported Hamilton. (b) Jefferson counteracted the influence of this paper by engaging Philip Freneau to start a new newspaper, *The National Gazette*. This paper published attacks on Hamilton and praised Jefferson.

6. The 1796 presidential election revealed that candidates with opposing views could be elected President and Vice-President.

Section Review, text page 186

1. *High Federalists:* Federalists who were loyal to Alexander Hamilton. *XYZ Affair:* incident in which secret representatives of the French government attempted to extort money from American representatives in return for an audience with French officials. This incident occurred when President Adams sent a mission to France to negotiate an end to France's seizing of American merchant ships sailing for England. *Napoleon Bonaparte:* leader of France who was willing to compromise with the United States because of his strong interest in conquering Europe. *Convention of 1800:* agreement between France and United States in which France promised to stop seizing American ships at sea; this agreement prevented war between the two countries. *Aaron Burr:* Republican nominee for Vice-President in 1800. He tied the election with Thomas Jefferson, thus throwing the vote into the House of Representatives. After many ballots Jefferson emerged as President, Burr as Vice-President. *Judiciary Act of 1801:* legislation that created 16 circuit courts and gave outgoing President John Adams the chance to appoint Federalist judges to these circuit courts; the Judiciary Act also reduced the number of justices on the Supreme Court to five.

2. *nullify:* to declare invalid. This term refers to the theory held by Jefferson, Madison, and others that states had the power to declare federal laws invalid.

3. (a) Adams decided to keep Washington's cabinet partly because he did not want to offend Washington and also because it was difficult to find people to fill positions in government. (b) Keeping Washington's cabinet proved to be a problem for Adams because the cabinet members were loyal to Hamilton, the man who had tried to sabotage Adams's election.

4. (a) French seizure of United States ships and the XYZ affair led to a demand for war with France. (b) To avoid war Adams tried one more attempt at negotiating with France. He appointed a new ambassador to France and submitted the nomination to

the Senate. When the Senate threatened to block his nominee, Adams threatened to resign. The Senate then agreed to a three-person delegation to France; the delegation negotiated successfully and thereby avoided war with France.

5. (a) The stated purpose of the Alien and Sedition Acts was to prepare the nation for war. (b) In reality, the Alien Act attempted to weaken the Republican party. It tried to reduce the political influence of immigrants, who usually voted for Republicans, by extending the residency requirement for citizenship and by permitting the President to deport or imprison foreigners during time of war. The Sedition Act also served to weaken the Republican party and at the same time to protect the Federalist party by providing for the fine or imprisonment of anyone who spoke out against the government (which was led by the Federalist party). (c) The Republicans tried to repeal the two laws by turning to the state governments. Kentucky and Virginia both passed resolutions nullifying the Alien and Sedition Acts.

Chapter Review, text page 187

1. (a) George Washington was a strong, popular leader respected by the American people. He held himself aloof from political strife. (b) The Judiciary Act of 1789 established how the Supreme Court should be organized and what its jurisdiction should be. (c) The creation of a cabinet helped the President establish major policies as well as handle administrative details.

2. (a) Hamilton proposed full funding of the national debt, the assumption of state debts, creation of a national bank, and a protective tariff. (b) All of the above except the protective tariff proposal were adopted.

3. (a) Madison objected to full funding of war bonds because most of the national debt was owed to northern speculators. Full funding seemed to reward northerners at the expense of southerners. (b) Hamilton believed it was important for the United States to pay its debts in full to restore its credit and reputation. He felt that those who had supported the government in time of war deserved whatever profit they might make. Also, he argued that the nation might have to turn to the wealthy speculators in the future for credit.

4. (a) Hamilton believed that a national bank would help put the economy on sound footing. (b) Jefferson argued that the national government did not have the authority to create a national bank because the Constitution did not specifically authorize it. (c) Hamilton justified his proposal by

arguing that the government had the power to make all laws "necessary and proper" to carry out the specific powers listed in the Constitution.

5. (a) The federal government summoned the state militia to subdue the Whiskey Rebellion. (b) This move demonstrated the government's authority to act within state borders and its ability to act decisively when necessary.

6. (a) Washington was concerned that Genêt's activities would threaten American neutrality. (b) Great Britain alienated pro-British Americans by maintaining forts in the United States, selling arms to Native Americans, and seizing American ships and sailors suspected of deserting British ships. (c) Most Americans were unhappy with the Jay Treaty. Although it avoided war, it appeared to be a surrender to Great Britain.

7. (a) Jefferson and Madison went to New York in 1791 to meet with political leaders. They struck a deal with Clinton and Burr that became the seed of formal opposition. They also sponsored a new newspaper, *The National Gazette,* which printed attacks on Hamilton and praise of Jefferson. (b) Jefferson and Madison had not planned to start an opposition political party.

8. (a) French attacks on American shipping, combined with cries for war within Federalist ranks, made it hard for Adams to continue Washington's policy of neutrality. (b) By successfully negotiating with France, Adams managed to appease those seeking war.

9. (a) Ostensibly, the High Federalists proposed the Alien and Sedition Acts in an effort to prepare for war. In reality, the acts represented attempts to weaken the opposition Republican party. (b) Republicans opposed the Alien and Sedition Acts because these laws seemed to be an abuse of governmental power intended to silence Republican criticism. In particular, the Sedition Act seemed to violate the First Amendment right of free speech.

10. (a) Resentment over the Alien and Sedition Acts, the Federalist image as warmongers, and unpopular tax legislation contributed to the Federalist defeat in 1800. (b) At that time the Constitution provided that each elector cast two ballots. The candidate receiving the most electoral votes became President; the runner-up would become Vice-President. In the election of 1800, Republican presidential candidate Thomas Jefferson and Republican vice-presidential candidate Aaron Burr tied on the first ballot with the same number of votes. The election was then decided by the House of Representatives, in accordance with the Constitution.

For Further Thought, text page 187

1. (a) Accept all justifiable answers that deal with Hamilton's background and his political beliefs. (b) Washington chose Hamilton as secretary of the treasury because of Hamilton's knowledge of economics and because Hamilton had gained Washington's confidence during the Revolutionary War. (c) Accept those answers that discuss Hamilton's economic programs in relation to his aristocratic leanings and attitude toward the common people.
2. (a) The Kentucky and Virginia resolutions would have given states the power to nullify federal laws. (b) Jefferson and Madison believed that the states were sovereign. (c) These resolutions revived discussion over whether the federal government or the states were sovereign. (d) The resolutions had little impact in 1798 because no other states adopted similar measures and because the Alien and Sedition Acts soon expired. (e) The resolutions might have had greater impact if they had been supported by other states or if the Alien and Sedition Acts had remained in effect longer.
3. (a) Newspapers helped communicate the positions of Jefferson and Hamilton and thereby helped convince people to support one political group or the other. (b) Accept all justifiable answers that discuss the absence of well-developed communication in the 1790s and the power of newspapers to shape public opinion.

Developing Basic Skills, text page 187

1. See the chart at right. Basis of differences between Hamilton and Jefferson: Answers may vary. Accept all answers that refer to their personal backgrounds and philosophies.
2. (a) This document was written by Washington. (b) The document is part of Washington's official papers. (c) He wanted to advise his country on its future course. (d) Washington was very careful to give the nation good advice. (e) Accept answers that refer to the themes in the speech. (f) Students should refer to the problems cited by Washington.

11 The Republicans in Office (1801–1815)

Section Review, text page 192

1. *"midnight appointments"*: series of appointments to the Supreme Court made by President Adams just before leaving office. Adams's hope was to leave the Federalists in control of the federal judiciary. *Marbury* v. *Madison*: Supreme Court case that challenged Jefferson's decision not to honor the

Issues	Hamilton's View	Jefferson's View
creation of a national bank	helpful to a sound economy	feared it would give bank directors too much control over nation's economy
interpretation of the Constitution	loose constructionist; federal government has more powers than specifically listed	strict constructionist; federal government limited to those powers listed
the French Revolution	perceived revolution as an attack on the upper class, whom he regarded as the mainstay of society	sympathized with idealistic goals of revolution
powers of the national and state governments	emphasized strong central government with implied powers	emphasized states' rights with federal government maintaining only the specific powers listed in the Constitution
belief in the people	common people not knowledgeable enough to make decisions regarding government	power should be dispersed among people, whom he regarded as the true representatives of democracy
manufacturing versus farming	supported manufacturing as basis of economy	supported agriculture as basis of economy

"midnight appointments" of President Adams. Part of this case rested on a section of the Judiciary Act of 1789 that had set up much of the federal court system. In this case the Supreme Court ruled the Judiciary Act of 1789 unconstitutional, thereby establishing the principle of judicial review.

2. *judicial review:* principle by which the Supreme Court has the authority to review laws passed by Congress and to decide whether they are constitutional. *laissez-faire:* policy of noninterference. *secede:* to withdraw from.

3. By avoiding pomp and ceremony in his duties, Jefferson made his approach to government informal.

4. (a) Jefferson tried to conciliate the Federalists by extending reassurance in his inaugural address, by allowing some Federalists to keep their government positions, and by retaining some important Federalist policies. (b) Jefferson quickly implemented his Republican principles by allowing the Alien and Sedition Acts to expire and refunding all fines that had been paid under those acts. He also restored the five-year residence requirement for naturalization (in place of the 14-year requirement established by the Alien Act).

5. Jefferson objected to the Supreme Court's decision in *Marbury* v. *Madison* because he thought the judiciary was assuming too much power through the principle of judicial review and because he feared that the balance of power among the three branches of government would be upset.

6. Jefferson believed that the government should play a limited role in people's lives. This is often referred to as a laissez-faire philosophy.

7. (a) The United States paid tribute to the Barbary Coast states to avoid the risk of having its merchant ships captured. (b) The piracy ceased after United States marines landed in Tripoli, captured a city, and forced the Barbary rulers to make peace.

Section Review, text page 195

1. *Napoleon Bonaparte:* French leader who decided to sell the area known as the Louisiana Territory to the United States. *Toussaint L'Ouverture:* leader of the successful slave rebellion that won Haiti's independence from France. *Meriwether Lewis, William Clark:* leaders of the expedition that explored the Louisiana Territory. *Sacajawea:* Shoshone woman who acted as translator and guide for the Lewis and Clark expedition.

2. (a) Jefferson wanted to buy the Louisiana Territory because he feared that Napoleon would close the port of New Orleans to American shipping and he hoped to avoid an alliance with Britain against France. Also, he worried that Napoleon might use the territory as a base to build a colonial empire in America. (b) Napoleon needed money for military campaigns in Europe. Also, with the revolt in Haiti, his dreams of an American empire had dissolved.

3. (a) The Constitution does not state specifically how new territory can be acquired. (b) Jefferson based the purchase on his constitutional power to make treaties with foreign nations.

4. Lewis and Clark were sent to gather information about the rivers, natural resources, climate, plant growth, and geology of the Louisiana Territory.

Section Review, text page 199

1. *Henry Clay:* Republican senator from Kentucky who led a faction in favor of war with Great Britain. *War Hawks:* group of prowar Republican congressmen from the West. *Battle of Fallen Timbers:* 1794 battle in which American forces defeated Native Americans. *Treaty of Greenville:* 1795 treaty in which Indian leaders ceded a large part of present-day Ohio to the United States. *Tecumseh:* Shawnee leader who organized a confederation of Indian nations that stretched from the Northwest Territory to Florida. His goal was to unite Indian nations in resistance to further settlement by whites. *the Prophet:* Shawnee leader who joined with Tecumseh in uniting Indian nations. He further called for the preservation of Indian culture and the rejection of white customs. *William Henry Harrison:* military general and governor of Indiana Territory; he led a battle at Tippecanoe Creek against Tecumseh in 1811; this battle marked doom for the Indian confederation.

2. *impressment:* British practice of forcing sailors to serve in their navy. *naturalized citizens:* people born in one country who become citizens of another country (by going through a process of naturalization). *embargo:* a halt to trade.

3. After 1806 the French and British violated American neutrality by searching, seizing, and in some instances firing upon American merchant ships. The British practice of impressment further angered Americans.

4. (a) To pressure France and Great Britain to recognize American neutrality, Jefferson imposed an embargo. (b) Many merchants who cooperated with the embargo were ruined. Many other merchants evaded the law, because their economic survival depended on trade.

5. (a) The Nonintercourse Act prohibited trade with Great Britain and France until they removed their restrictions on neutral shipping. In contrast to the Embargo Act, it allowed Americans to trade with other nations. (b) The Nonintercourse Act was as

unpopular as the Embargo Act, because most American trade was with France and Great Britain.

6. The War Hawks hoped to gain Canada by going to war against Britain.

7. (a) Tecumseh tried to organize the Indians into a united front against American expansion. (b) Tecumseh was successful in organizing a confederation of Indian nations. The confederation, however, was not successful in resisting the expansion of white settlers into Indian lands.

Section Review, text page 204

1. *Hartford Convention:* a gathering of 26 New England delegates to protest the war against Britain. The delegates issued a set of demands to protect New England's interests and threatened to secede if the demands were not met. The war was over, however, by the time these demands reached Washington, D.C. *Andrew Jackson:* victorious commander of American forces at the battle of New Orleans. *Creek War:* struggle between the Creeks and the Tennessee militia in 1813 and 1814. *Treaty of Ghent:* peace treaty ending the War of 1812; signed in 1814.

2. United States disadvantages at the outset of war: small army and small navy, incompetent military leaders, and ineffective strategy.

3. (a) Strong opposition to the war existed in New England. (b) New Englanders opposed the war because it disrupted trade and upset the shipbuilding industry. Also, they were wary of territorial expansion, because they feared the growing influence of new western states.

4. Perry's victory on Lake Erie, Harrison's victory at the Battle of the Thames, and Macdonough's victory on Lake Champlain were turning points for the Americans.

5. The Battle of New Orleans did not affect the outcome of the war, because a peace treaty had already been signed when the battle was fought.

6. Free blacks served as soldiers and sailors in the War of 1812. Many slaves also fought for the United States; others fought for the British.

Chapter Review, text page 205

1. (a) After his election, Jefferson tried to conciliate the Federalists by retaining some Federalist officials and programs. His inaugural speech extended a spirit of acceptance to the Federalists. (b) Jefferson implemented his own principles of government by acting in accordance with his laissez-faire philosophy.

2. (a) Jefferson tried to reduce Federalist influence on the judiciary by refusing to acknowledge the "midnight appointments" of President Adams and by convincing Congress to repeal the Federalist-sponsored Judiciary Act of 1801. (b) Jefferson objected to the principle of judicial review because he thought it gave the Supreme Court too much power and that it would upset the balance of power among the three branches of government.

3. (a) Jefferson reduced the military budget because of his belief in laissez-faire and because he believed that a large military in peacetime could be a threat to liberty. (b) This action hurt the United States in its conflict with the Barbary Coast states because more sailors and ships were needed than were available.

4. (a) The United States was interested in buying land in the Mississippi area because the Mississippi River and its tributaries served as major trade routes for the western region. New Orleans was an especially important port. The United States wanted to keep these trade areas open and also to avoid possible conflict with France. (b) American negotiators were able to purchase the entire Louisiana Territory because Napoleon wanted to sell the land. He needed money for his European wars; moreover, his goal of an American empire had been destroyed earlier.

5. (a) Jefferson believed in a strict interpretation of the Constitution. Purchase of the Louisiana Territory conflicted with strict interpretation because the Constitution did not explicitly provide for the purchase of new territory. (b) Jefferson ultimately acted on his power to make treaties with foreign nations.

6. (a) The purpose of the Lewis and Clark expedition was to explore the Louisiana Territory. Lewis and Clark were instructed to gather information about the rivers and natural resources of the area, primarily to aid in plans for future commercial development. They were also told to study the climate, plants, and geology of the region. (b) The information gathered by Lewis and Clark was used by fur traders, road builders, and settlers who entered the new frontier.

7. (a) After 1806 Britain and France challenged American neutrality by searching and seizing American merchant ships. (b) Jefferson responded by asking Congress to pass the Embargo Act. (c) The Embargo Act was not successful. Many merchants evaded it to avoid financial ruin; many who did obey the act eventually faced such disaster.

8. (a) To maintain neutrality, Madison encouraged Congress to pass the Nonintercourse Act. This act prohibited trade with Britain and France until each nation stopped violating neutral shipping. It did allow Americans to trade with other nations. Madison then added that if either Britain or

France would remove its restrictions on neutral shipping, the United States would halt its trade with the other nation. (b) President Madison was not successful in maintaining American neutrality. France repealed its decrees against American trade with the British, and the British did likewise regarding American trade with the French. The British action came too late, however. Impatient with the policy of neutrality, President Madison had already asked Congress to declare war on Great Britain by the time that news of the British repeal reached the United States.

9. Conflicts between Americans and Indians forged the Indians into an alliance with the British. This contributed to increased hostility between the Americans and the British prior to the War of 1812.

10. (a) Tecumseh and the Prophet saw white settlers as a threat because they encroached upon Indian land and pushed the Indians farther west. Also, Indian culture was weakened by the adoption of European customs. (b) In response to this threat, the two Shawnee leaders organized all Indians east of the Mississippi to resist white expansion. (c) They were successful in creating a confederation, but the confederation was not successful in resisting the expansion of white settlement.

11. (a) The War of 1812 began poorly for the United States because the army was small, there was a lack of competent leaders, and the strategy was not well planned. (b) By 1813 the United States cause became more hopeful as Americans started to win major battles.

12. (a) The Treaty of Ghent essentially restored prewar conditions. (b) Border disputes were not resolved in the treaty; they were to be settled later. The issue of impressment was not included either, because the British had already stopped this practice. (c) Americans felt they had won the war because the United States had held its own against a major European power.

For Further Thought, text page 205

1. Accept those answers that refer to impeachment proceedings held by Congress against members of the judicial branch accused of misconduct in office.

2. (a) The western War Hawks favored war with Great Britain in 1812 because they were desirous of controlling British Canada. Also, they believed that the British were supporting Native Americans who were resisting white settlement of the Northwest Territory. (b) New Englanders opposed the war because it would affect their trade and industry. (c) Since the Treaty of Ghent did little to change prewar conditions, the New Englanders probably thought they had been right in 1812.

3. (a), (b) Accept those answers that refer to American pride and nationalism.

Developing Basic Skills, text page 205

1. (a) The following states were part of the Louisiana Territory: Louisiana, Arkansas, Missouri, Iowa, North Dakota, South Dakota, Nebraska, Kansas, Oklahoma, Colorado, Wyoming, Montana. (b) Lewis and Clark passed through the following states: Missouri, Iowa, South Dakota, North Dakota, Montana, Idaho, Washington. (c) Oil, natural gas, iron ore, coal, gold, silver, lead, zinc, copper, and uranium have been found in the area that made up the Louisiana Territory. (d) Today the land is used for agriculture, livestock, forestry, and mining.

2. (a) The graph shows American foreign trade, 1800–1812. (b) 1807. (c) 1807. (d) 1808. (e) Accept those answers that refer to the threat of war and the Embargo Act.

12 A Growing Nation (1815–1824)

Section Review, text page 209

1. *Era of Good Feelings:* period during the early 1800s when good feelings, unity, and optimism prevailed in the United States. *James Monroe:* President of the United States (1817–1824) during the Era of Good Feelings; symbol of the nation's political unity. *John Marshall:* Chief Justice of the Supreme Court for 35 years (appointed by President Adams in 1801); a moderate Federalist; under Marshall the Supreme Court handed down rulings that strengthened the power of the national government.

2. During a goodwill tour by President Monroe, a newspaper noted the nation's political unity and dubbed the times the "Era of Good Feelings."

3. President Monroe believed that Congress should interpret the public will.

4. Before John Marshall became Chief Justice, the Supreme Court lacked both power and prestige. Its deliberations attracted little public attention.

5. (a) The Supreme Court upheld the rights of private property in *Fletcher* v. *Peck* (1810) and in *Dartmouth College* v. *Woodward* (1819). (b) The authority of the national government was strengthened through *McCulloch* v. *Maryland* (1819) and *Gibbons* v. *Ogden* (1824).

Section Review, text page 213

1. *James Watt:* Scottish inventor who patented a steam engine in 1769. *James Hargreaves:* English inventor of the spinning jenny. *John Fitch:* Ameri-

can inventor of the steam-powered boat (1787). *Robert Fulton:* proved the value of using the steam engine for transportation by traveling (in 1807) from New York City to Albany on the steam-powered *Clermont*. *Eli Whitney:* American inventor of the cotton gin in 1793; he also introduced the use of interchangeable parts. *Samuel Slater:* brought plans for textile machinery from Britain to the United States in 1789; built improved versions of this machinery to set up a textile mill. *Frances Cabot Lowell:* formed the Boston Manufacturing Company in 1813. *Boston Associates:* established the first textile factory that brought together all the tasks required to turn raw cotton into finished cloth.

2. *factory system:* a system for organizing labor by which all workers in the manufacturing process are brought together under one roof. *capital:* money used for investment. *limited liability:* liability in which the investor's personal responsibility for the debts of a corporation does not exceed that person's initial investment. *interchangeable parts:* identical component parts that can be used in place of one another in the manufacturing process.

3. (a) Important inventions in the late 1700s include the steam engine, spinning jenny, and the cotton gin. (Students should receive credit for naming two inventions.) (b) steam engine, used to provide power for factories and in transportation; spinning jenny, greatly speeded up the process of spinning cloth; cotton gin, greatly speeded the process of cleaning seeds from cotton.

4. American manufacturers acquired British industrial secrets through British mechanics who were willing to supply the necessary information. Several state legislatures offered rewards for such information.

5. (a) Textile factory employers sought to hire women and children as laborers because both worked for low wages. Also, children, because they were small, were agile around dangerous machinery. (b) The Boston Associates hired many young, unmarried women from farm families to work in their textile mills. They sought hard-working women with respectable backgrounds.

6. (a) Industrialization brought Americans closer by helping to create a pride in self-sufficiency. (b) Divisions were also created because industrialization developed primarily in the North, whereas the South continued to rely on agriculture. This difference contributed to different ways of life and economic interests.

Section Review, text page 215

1. *Henry Clay:* Republican from Kentucky who emerged as a dominant political figure after the War of 1812. *Daniel Webster:* Federalist from New Hampshire who also became an important leader after the War of 1812. *John C. Calhoun:* Republican from South Carolina who, along with Clay and Webster, became a major political figure.

2. *bank note:* paper money backed by bank reserves of gold or silver.

3. Although they came from different backgrounds, Clay, Webster, and Calhoun each supported nationalism at one time or another in their political careers.

4. The three main parts of Clay's American System were a protective tariff, a new national bank, and a federal program of internal improvements.

5. (a) The purpose of the Tariff of 1816 was to raise tariffs on foreign imports and thereby guard American industries from lower-priced competition. (b) Webster opposed the Tariff of 1816 because it threatened the shipping industry in New England.

6. Clay believed that a national bank would provide a stable means of issuing money and that it would serve as a safe depository for federal funds.

7. The national Bank encouraged land speculation by liberally extending credit.

Westward Movement: Using Statistics, text page 217

1. (a) 1790–1830. (b) 10 years. (c) The numbers represent the population of different states at various points in time. (d) The table shows population growth in the West between 1790 and 1830.

2. (a) 75,400. (b) 145,300. (c) 1820. (d) 3,671,000.

3. (a) Kentucky's population grew. (b) Between 1810 and 1820, Louisiana's population grew by 76,900. (c) Kentucky; Ohio. (d) Ohio. (e) Ohio grew more quickly.

4. (a) The region experienced significant population growth. (b) Students might indicate that better transportation encouraged population growth in the West. (c) Students might suggest that each state benefitted from good river transportation. (d) Ohio, 1803; Kentucky, 1792; Tennessee, 1796; Mississippi, 1817; Indiana, 1816; Michigan, 1837; Louisiana, 1812; Illinois, 1818; Missouri, 1821; Arkansas, 1836; Alabama, 1819. The more heavily populated territories seemed to achieve statehood sooner than the less-populated territories.

Section Review, text page 220

1. *National Road:* first government-supported road, authorized by Congress in 1806; it stretched from Cumberland, Maryland, to Wheeling, Virginia, and from there to Vandalia, Illinois. *Erie Canal:* waterway connecting New York City to Buffalo, completed in 1825; the canal was a great boon to trade

between New York City and the Ohio River Valley–Great Lakes region.

2. *corduroy roads:* roads made by lying tree trunks side by side; these served as early overland routes for people traveling west.

3. Western settlers needed good roads to send their farm products to the East and to bring manufactured goods back to the West.

4. (a) State governments or private investors paid for the construction of the earliest roads. (b) The federal government became involved during Jefferson's administration. (c) Madison curbed the role of the federal government by vetoing a congressional measure to allocate money to states for internal improvements.

5. The Erie Canal cut the cost of transportation and reduced the travel time between New York City and western markets.

6. Before steamboats could be used on western rivers they had to be adapted to shallow water. They also had to prove that they could travel upstream and carry heavy loads of cargo.

Section Review, text page 224

1. *John Quincy Adams:* secretary of state under President James Monroe; he played an important role in United States foreign affairs while serving in this office. *Convention of 1818:* set the border between the United States and Canada at the 49th parallel. *Rush-Bagot Treaty:* 1817 treaty between Great Britain and the United States in which the two nations agreed not to use military ships on the Great Lakes. *Adams-Onís Treaty:* 1819 treaty in which Spain ceded Florida to the United States; in return the United States dropped claims of about $5 million against Spain; the treaty also established the boundary between the Louisiana Purchase and Spanish territory.

2. (a) Spanish-owned Florida served as a haven for outlaws and as a refuge for escaped slaves. Also, some Native Americans raided United States settlements from there. (b) The Adams-Onís Treaty solved these problems for the United States by transferring control over Florida to the United States.

3. (a) Most American sympathized with the newly independent Latin American nations. (b) Americans feared that the alliance in Europe might lead to military intervention to restore Spanish control over its former colonies.

4. (a) The Monroe Doctrine proclaimed that the United States would not interfere in the internal affairs of Europe or of European colonies in the Americas. It declared that the United States would oppose European intervention in the affairs of independent nations in the Americas. The doctrine further stated the United States position that the Americas were not to be considered for future colonization by any European country. (b) British support of the Monroe Doctrine was important because the United States alone lacked the strength to back up its declaration.

Chapter Review, text page 225

1. (a) President Monroe rejected the idea of political parties and attempted to foster good relations between political opponents. In this way he symbolized the Era of Good Feelings. (b) In dress and mental outlook he reflected the perspective of the revolutionary generation.

2. (a) Under Marshall's leadership the Supreme Court acquired greater status and prestige. (b) Under Marshall the Court ruled that Congress did have power to create a national bank (*McCulloch* v. *Maryland*). In *Gibbons* v. *Ogden* the Court ruled that only Congress could control interstate commerce. Through this case the Court also reaffirmed its power to overrule a state law. (c) The Supreme Court under Marshall contributed to the spirit of national unity by clarifying and strengthening the powers of the federal government.

3. (a) Labor was scarce because skilled artisans, accustomed to working at home, had little interest in factory work. (b) Manufacturers turned to women and children as a labor source. (c) The Boston Associates required that their women laborers work long, hard hours, but they provided boarding, education, recreation, and religious facilities for them. In the early years of the company, workers earned relatively good wages.

4. Industrialization served as a unifying force because as Americans came to rely on local industries, they developed a sense of pride to accompany their newfound self-sufficiency. Divisions were also created as different ways of life and economic needs emerged between the industrialized and agricultural sections of the country.

5. (a) Henry Clay believed that by raising the price of imported goods, the Tariff of 1816 would eliminate lower-priced competition for domestic products. This protection would allow industries to grow and foster self-sufficiency for the United States. (b) Representatives from the West and Middle Atlantic states supported the tariff because they believed the revenues would help pay for roads and canals needed for trade. Calhoun, as a representative of the South, supported the tariff because he thought it was necessary to protect the cotton industry in the South.

6. (a) A national bank seemed necessary in 1816 because the absence of a uniform currency made commerce difficult and the federal government needed a secure place to deposit its funds. (b) The second Bank contributed to the Panic of 1819 by calling in its loans to state banks, which in turn recalled their loans to land speculators. (c) A declining European demand for textile and farm products and a resulting drop in southern cotton prices contributed to the Panic of 1819.

7. (a) As people moved west, they demanded better transportation links with eastern markets. (b) Better transportation speeded the flow of trade and improved communication among various parts of the country, thus helping to bind the nation together.

8. (a) Adams and Monroe supported the Monroe Doctrine because they wanted to check further European intervention in the western hemisphere. Adams in particular was further motivated by the hope of annexing new territory in the future and by the desire to show United States strength. (b) The doctrine provided Americans with the opportunity to demonstrate their pride.

For Further Thought, text page 225

1. Between 1816 and 1824 a sense of national unity was fostered by the following: President Monroe's desire to avoid struggles between political parties; Supreme Court decisions that strengthened the power of the national government; industrialization; the tariff; transportation improvements that linked East to West; the Monroe Doctrine.

2. (a) Leaders in Congress thought the national government should play an active role in supporting programs for economic development. (b) Clay's American System reflected this attitude by calling for the federal government to charter a national bank, provide a protective tariff, and finance internal improvements for more efficient interstate commerce.

3. Accept those answers that discuss the absence of political parties in the early years of federal government.

Developing Basic Skills, text page 225

1. *Marbury* v. *Madison:* Article III, Section 2a: "The judicial power shall extend to all cases, in law and equity, arising under this Constitution, the laws of the United States." *Fletcher* v. *Peck:* Article I, Section 10a: "No state shall . . . pass any . . . law impairing the obligation of contracts." *Dartmouth College* v. *Woodward:* See the clause cited for *Fletcher* v. *Peck. McCulloch* v. *Maryland:* Article I, Section 8r: "The Congress shall have the power

to make all laws which shall be necessary and proper for carrying into execution the foregoing powers." *Gibbons* v. *Ogden:* Article I, Section 8c: "The Congress shall have the power . . . to regulate commerce . . . among the several States."

2. (a) The United States, 1824. (b) Convention of 1818. (c) Adams-Onís Treaty. (d) Through the Adams-Onís Treaty, Spain ceded Florida to the United States. (e) United States territory increased.

3. Henry Clay: United States commissioner during peace talks with Great Britain after the War of 1812, member of the House of Representatives, member of the Senate. John C. Calhoun: secretary of war, Vice-President of the United States, member of the Senate, secretary of state. Daniel Webster: member of the House of Representatives, member of the Senate. These men held important positions and as such had an opportunity to influence national policy.

Unit Four:
An Era of Expansion

13 A Democracy for the People (1824–1844)

Caption, text page 231

The National Republican party was strongest in the Northeast.

Section Review, text page 231

1. *National Republicans:* branch of the Republican party that supported President Adams during the election of 1828; members believed in a strong national government. *Democratic-Republicans:* name given to the supporters of Andrew Jackson; they stressed ties to the common people. *"Old Hickory":* nickname given to Andrew Jackson during the War of 1812 because of his endurance and determination on the battlefield.

2. *party platform:* a declaration of a political party spelling out its principles and programs.

3. (a) Because no candidate won a majority in the electoral college, the President was selected by the House of Representatives. John Quincy Adams was

the choice of the House of Representatives. (b) Henry Clay persuaded his supporters in the House of Representatives to back Adams; afterwards Clay was appointed secretary of state. People suspected a "deal" had been made.

4. (a) President Adams believed the national government should actively encourage economic and intellectual growth. He proposed a national university and a national observatory. (b) Many people considered his proposals extravagant and impractical.

5. (a) In the 1828 election Adams won all the New England states, Delaware, and New Jersey. (b) Jackson took the South and West.

Section Review, text page 236

1. *Removal Act:* law passed in 1830 providing government funds to negotiate treaties that would force Native Americans to sell their land east of the Mississippi River and move to present-day Oklahoma. *Trail of Tears:* forced march of Choctaw, Creek, and Cherokee tribes to present-day Oklahoma in 1838. *Blackhawk:* Chief of Sac and Fox Indians who led a series of attacks to regain the homeland of his people east of the Mississippi River. *Osceola:* Seminole chief in Florida who led a struggle (1835–1838) for his people to remain in their homeland.

2. *white manhood suffrage:* the extension of voting rights to all white males; during the colonial period only property owners had the right to vote. *caucus:* political meeting in which select members of Congress chose presidential candidates.

3. All white males, propertied or not, gained the vote during the first half of the nineteenth century.

4. Originally presidential electors were chosen by state legislatures. By 1832 voters chose electors directly in every state but South Carolina.

5. Women, black Americans, and Native Americans continued to be denied political participation under Jacksonian democracy.

6. (a) In an attempt to safeguard their land, the Cherokee in 1828 wrote a constitution establishing themselves as an independent state within Georgia. (b) The state government refused to recognize the Cherokee's constitution, and though they won a favorable ruling from the Supreme Court, Jackson refused to enforce the Court's decision.

7. The Cherokee, Choctaw, and Creek nations were most affected by the Removal Act.

Section Review, text page 239

1. *Kitchen Cabinet:* unofficial advisers to President Jackson, including old Tennessee friends, editors, and officeholders. *Tariff of Abominations:* label given to 1828 law that placed a high tax on

manufactured goods from Europe; the tariff protected New England manufacturers but angered southern farmers who sold raw materials to Europe and resented having to pay more for the European products they bought in exchange. *Robert Hayne:* supporter of John Calhoun's states' rights position on nullification; he debated Daniel Webster in the Senate in 1830. *Nicholas Biddle:* director of the Second Bank of the United States, a powerful privately controlled bank. *pet banks:* Democrat-controlled state banks in which federal funds were deposited during Jackson's feud with the Second Bank.

2. *spoils system:* policy of removing from appointed office people who did not support the President and replacing them with loyal supporters. *nullify:* to declare a federal law unconstitutional.

3. Jackson believed the spoils system furthered democratic ideals by preventing bureaucrats from thinking of their jobs as personal property. Also, since jobs changed with each administration, the development of a government elite was discouraged.

4. Under the tariff of 1828, a tax of 45 to 50 percent was placed on manufactured goods imported from Europe. Since southerners imported manufactured goods and exported cotton and other raw goods, the tax hurt them financially.

5. (a) John C. Calhoun defended a state's right to be free of unwanted federal intervention; he said a state could nullify any federal law considered unconstitutional by the state. (b) Daniel Webster argued that the federal government had final constitutional power and was a direct agent of the people. He believed Calhoun's theory was illegal and unconstitutional.

6. (a) South Carolina called a convention in 1832 to nullify the tariff. (b) South Carolina's challenge to the federal government failed, but the maneuver did lead to a compromise that reduced duties to 20 percent over a nine-year period.

7. (a) President Jackson opposed the Second Bank because it represented private stockholders' interests and not those of the United States; the Bank's influence in government was strong, with bribes of officials common; he believed the bank charter was unconstitutional and viewed it as favoring the rich and powerful owners. (b) A wide variety of Americans also opposed the Bank, including business leaders, owners of state banks, speculators, southern farmers, and eastern factory workers.

Section Review, text page 242

1. *Whigs:* new name for the National Republicans taken during the 1835 election. *Specie Circular:* document issued by Jackson in 1836 to slow down land speculation; it stated that public land could be

bought only with gold or silver. *John Tyler:* elected Vice-President in 1840 on the Whig ticket; he succeeded to the presidency when William Henry Harrison died within one month of taking office; he was the first Vice-President to take over the presidency.

2. (a) By running three separate candidates the Whigs hoped to prevent any candidate from winning a majority of electoral votes, thereby throwing the vote into the House of Representatives, as in 1824. (b) The strategy failed, since Democratic candidate Martin Van Buren won a small majority of both the popular and electoral votes.

3. With the drop in cotton prices, farmers who had borrowed money for land purchases went broke and were unable to repay their loans. Banks failed, land sales stopped, factories closed, and unemployment climbed. Even some states went bankrupt.

4. The Whigs, using mass campaign methods that had worked for the Democrats, portrayed their candidate as a simple western farmer and attracted voter interest with rallies, parades, bonfires, and barbecues complete with bands and entertainment.

5. President Tyler was a states' rights advocate and did little to carry out Whig policies. He blocked legislation that would strengthen the national government at the expense of the states. He opposed using federal funds for internal improvements and vetoed bills to charter a new national bank.

Chapter Review, text page 243

1. The presidency of John Quincy Adams was weakened by bitterness over how he won the election, his extravagant spending proposals, his inability to develop a strong political party, and his reserved personality. He was not popular.

2. (a) The new political parties to emerge in the late 1820s were the National Republican and the Democratic-Republican. (b) The National Republicans supported the national programs of John Quincy Adams. The Democratic-Republicans opposed government elitism and stressed ties with common people. (c) In the 1828 election the National Republicans backed Adams for reelection, while the Democratic-Republicans supported Andrew Jackson. Both parties were vociferous in their attacks on the other side.

3. Great hordes of people came to cheer Jackson during his inauguration. Afterwards large numbers went to the White House to celebrate. Clearly the public believed Jackson was one of them.

4. (a) Several reforms in the electoral process increased the political participation of many Americans. The right to vote was extended to all white males; by 1832 all states except South Carolina allowed voters to choose presidential electors directly; and within the political parties, national nominating conventions replaced secret caucuses. (b) Women, black Americans, and Native Americans were still unable to vote.

5. (a) White settlers wanted southern Native Americans moved west to eliminate their valuable holdings east of the Mississippi River. (b) President Jackson and Congress passed the Removal Act of 1830 to further this goal. (c) Chief Blackhawk of the Sac and Fox tribes fought in Illinois in 1832; Chief Osceola led the Seminole War in Florida from 1835 to 1838. (d) These attempts at resistance were unsuccessful; by 1844 few Indians remained east of the Mississippi River.

6. (a) Since the Kitchen Cabinet was composed of unofficial advisers, its members seemed to be more in touch with the general public. (b) Within the spoils system, government positions were rotated, preventing officials from viewing their jobs as permanent and also preventing the development of a government elite. (c) Jackson believed a privately controlled bank was beholden to its stockholders, not to the people. Its power made it a corrupting influence in politics.

7. (a) Calhoun believed states should be free from federal interference. (b) Webster argued against nullification by maintaining that the federal government held the final power under the Constitution and was a direct agent of the people.

8. (a) South Carolina tried to nullify the tariff law because tariffs hurt southern farmers who were deeply involved in trade with Europe. (b) Jackson responded by urging Congress to pass a bill allowing him to use the military to enforce tariffs if necessary. (c) Jackson agreed to a compromise bill because he did not want an open conflict; South Carolina agreed because it did not have support from other southern states.

9. (a) The Second Bank of the United States was powerful because it held the resources of the federal government, controlled the currency, and paid no interest on federal fund deposits. It was not under federal control and often bribed federal officials. (b) Jackson tried to kill the Bank by vetoing renewal of its charter in 1832; by ordering federal deposits placed in "pet banks"; by refusing to back down when the Bank retaliated by calling in loans and refusing to issue new ones. Jackson's maneuvers proved successful. The Bank lost popularity and finally went out of business in 1841.

10. (a) The Panic of 1837 had its roots in land speculation. Lured by hopes of high profits, people rushed to buy land, some borrowing heavily to do so. Land prices skyrocketed. (b) Bank notes, many not backed by gold or silver, flooded the country as obtaining credit became easy. (c) Jack-

son tried to slow speculation with his Specie Circular, which stated that all public land had to be paid for in gold or silver. As a result, land sales dropped. (d) When cotton prices dropped, farmers who had borrowed heavily to buy land reneged on their loans. This caused many banks to fail.

11. (a) The Whigs nominated William Henry Harrison for President because, like Andrew Jackson, he was a popular military hero with western ties. (b) They nominated John Tyler for Vice-President to balance the ticket. (c) Their choice backfired because Harrison soon died, and Tyler, who succeeded him, would not support Whig policies.

For Further Thought, text page 243

1. (a) Accept those answers that include the idea that vague positions alienate the fewest people. (b) Accept those answers that include the idea that the President would not be "shackled" by a definite position. (c) Answers should include the idea that voters could not accurately differentiate between candidates on the issues.
2. From the Jackson defenders accept answers that refer to his trust in the people and his distrust of elitism. From the Jackson critics accept answers that mention his heavy-handed way of dealing with opposition and his authoritative manner.
3. Accept those answers that refer to Jackson's origin as a western farmer and his experience fighting Indians in Tennessee.
4. Accept those answers that relate to the suffering caused by being displaced from one's homeland or refer to the pain and hardship suffered during the long trek west.
5. (a) During his years as President, Jackson had opportunities to demonstrate the power of a strong President. His handling of the nullification dispute and the dispute over the constitutionality of the Second Bank strengthened the presidency, as did his refusal to enforce the Supreme Court's decision that granted sovereignty to the Cherokee nation. Of it he said, "John Marshall has made his decision. Now let him enforce it." In that brief statement he summed up the weakness of the Supreme Court. (b) Many of his actions also strengthened the national government. He championed the common people and asserted federal authority whenever it was needed.

Developing Basic Skills, text page 243

1. (a) The map shows the relocation of Indians, 1830–1842. (b) Before 1830 the southern Indian nations held land in Florida, Georgia, Alabama, Mississippi, Tennessee, and North Carolina. (c)

Their largest holdings were in Mississippi. (d) The Seminoles moved 1,125 miles (1,800 kilometers) from their homeland; the Choctaw 500 miles (800 kilometers); the Creek 750 miles (1,200 kilometers); the Chickasaw 500 miles (800 kilometers); and the Cherokee 750 miles (1,200 kilometers).
2. (a) Adams and Jackson. (b) 1824 electoral: Adams 32 percent, Jackson 38 percent; 1828 electoral: Adams 32 percent, Jackson 68 percent. 1824 popular: Adams 31 percent, Jackson 43 percent; 1828 popular: Adams 44 percent, Jackson 56 percent. (d) Jackson had reason to be upset with the outcome of the election of 1824 because he won more popular and electoral votes than any one of his opponents and yet he was not elected President. Jackson believed that John Quincy Adams's election by the House was the result of a "corrupt bargain" between Adams and Henry Clay.

14 From Sea to Sea (1820–1860)

Section Review, text page 247

1. *Don Gaspar de Portola:* led expedition in 1769 to reassert Spanish authority in upper California; discovered San Francisco Bay. *Father Junípero Serra:* accompanied Portola's expedition and established Catholic missions along the California coast, hoping to convert Indians to Christianity. *Secularization Act:* Mexican law passed in 1832 that opened church lands to settlement and removed Indians from church protection. *Stephen Austin:* founded an American colony in Mexican-controlled Texas in 1821.
2. *ranchero:* Mexican ranch owner. *mortality rate:* death rate.
3. In the mid-eighteenth century the Spanish took a renewed interest in northern New Spain to counteract the movement of Russian seal hunters and traders into the area.
4. The missions were of vital importance to the Spanish, serving as political and economic symbols of their control.
5. The Indians worked as farmhands or herders on mission lands and ranches; they had become a source of cheap labor.
6. (a) The Spanish established missions in Arizona, New Mexico, and Texas. (b) They were least successful in Arizona and Texas, where Indians were most hostile.
7. The joint-occupation agreement between the United States and Great Britain allowed people of both nations to settle the Oregon country.

Section Review, text page 250

1. *Oregon Trail:* well-known 2,000-mile route to Oregon that began at Independence, Missouri, followed the Missouri and Platt rivers, crossed Wyoming and the Rocky Mountains to the Columbia River, and ended in the Willamette Valley.
2. (a) Mountain men hoped to make a fortune selling pelts. (b) The fur trade declined because too much trapping reduced the beaver population and too many companies competed for pelts.
3. Most pioneers went to Oregon in search of rich land, some to bring Christianity to the Indians.
4. (a) The trip west held many dangers and uncertainties, among them the possibilities of Indian attack, summer drought, and shortages of food for livestock. (b) There is generally safety in numbers. Wagon trains gave people a sense of security, allowed them to pool resources, and deterred attack.
5. (a) The First Organic Law, drawn up by the Americans, outlined a temporary government for the Oregon country. (b) It provided a system of government until a more permanent form could be established.

Section Review, text page 254

1. *Antonio de Santa Anna:* Mexican revolutionary who became self-proclaimed dictator in 1834. *William B. Travis:* American who led a revolt against Mexico by capturing the Mexican garrison at Anahuac in 1835; he was also commander at the Alamo. *Declaration of Causes:* document issued in 1835 by American settlers in Texas explaining their reasons for armed rebellion against Mexico. *Sam Houston:* a popular figure in Texas, appointed commander of the rebel forces. *"Remember the Alamo":* rallying cry in the Texas struggle for independence from Mexico; the Alamo, an abandoned mission in San Antonio, was the scene of an heroic battle in which Americans were finally overwhelmed by superior Mexican forces.
2. (a) Culturally Americans and Mexicans differed in two important ways. Americans spoke English; Mexicans spoke Spanish. Americans were mainly Protestant; Mexicans were mainly Catholic. (b) There were political differences too. Americans had a strong democratic tradition and were accustomed to local rule; Mexicans were accustomed to being ruled by provincial officers and mayors appointed by the crown. The Mexican judicial system was less protective of individual rights than the American; a single judge decided on cases without a jury, and testimony by the parties involved was not customary. Slavery was abolished by Mexico in 1827; most American settlers in Texas were from the South and approved of slavery.

3. Santa Anna abolished the Mexican constitution and legislatures and set himself up as dictator. It was rumored that he also planned to disenfranchise American Texans, abolish local governments, and drive all Americans out of Texas. When he sent reinforcements into Texas, Americans reacted.
4. Sam Houston retreated in order to train recruits. Though Houston was outnumbered, this tactic proved successful, as he surprised Mexican troops at the San Jacinto River and won.
5. One of the treaties signed in 1836 granted independence to Texas; the other established the Rio Grande as its southern border.
6. (a) Jackson was reluctant to annex Texas because he feared war with Mexico. Many northerners were afraid annexation would increase the power of the southern states. (b) In the end he formally recognized Texan independence but refused to annex the territory.

Section Review, text page 258

1. *manifest destiny:* commonly held belief that it was the United States' mission to expand its borders to incorporate all land between the Atlantic and Pacific oceans. *James K. Polk:* President 1845-1849; he believed strongly in expansion of United States, divided Oregon with Great Britain, and served as President during the Mexican War. *"Fifty-four Forty or Fight":* campaign slogan of American expansionists who wanted the United States to claim all of the Oregon country jointly governed with Great Britain. *John C. Frémont:* known as the "Pathfinder" for his exploration of the Sierra Nevada mountain passes. *Zachary Taylor:* United States Army commander who led a series of victories against Mexico climaxing with the Battle of Buena Vista. *Stephen W. Kearny:* United States Army commander who captured Santa Fe during the Mexican War and helped the navy subdue the Mexicans in California. *Winfield Scott:* American general who captured Mexico City, ending the Mexican War in 1847. *Gadsden Purchase:* strip of land south of Gila River in Arizona and New Mexico, bought from Mexico in 1853; it provided a favorable route for the transcontinental railroad and seemed to represent the completion of American expansion across the continent.
2. (a) In 1844 the United States recognized the Rio Grande as the southern border of Texas. (b) Mexico recognized the Nueces River, 200 miles north, as the border.
3. In 1846 the United States and Great Britain agreed to divide the Oregon country at the 49th parallel.
4. President Polk ordered the army to cross the Nueces River and move toward the Rio Grande.

5. (a) Under the terms of the Treaty of Guadalupe-Hidalgo the United States gained control of California and the New Mexico territory, and Mexico recognized the Rio Grande as the southern border of Texas. (b) In return the United States was obliged to pay Mexico $15 million and assume all debts owed to United States citizens by Mexico.

Section Review, text page 262

1. *Joseph Smith:* in 1830 founded the religion that later was named the Church of Jesus Christ of the Latter Day Saints. *Brigham Young:* leader of the Mormons after Smith; he led the Mormon migration to Utah. *Sutter's Mill:* California location where the first large gold deposits were found in 1848.
2. Living in the territory acquired in the Mexican War were Native Americans with a wide variety of cultures and Mexicans with a combined Spanish and Native American heritage.
3. Following the gold rush the California Indians were driven off their lands and many fell ill or starved to death. Some were killed and whole villages were massacred. Their population fell from 250,000 in 1848 to 17,000 20 years later.
4. (a) The Chinese came to California expecting to make their fortune and take it back to their native land. (b) At first they were accepted but eventually they were met with jealousy, prejudice, discrimination, and denial of political rights.
5. Black Americans faced many problems in California, among them prejudice, discrimination, and denial of political rights.

Chapter Review, text page 263

1. (a) The Spanish brought Christianity to Native Americans in California and turned them into a source of cheap labor. (b) After Mexican independence the Secularization Act was passed, which changed Indians' lives. They were no longer under church protection. Large ranches replaced missions as economic centers, and Indians were forced to work on them.
2. (a) In the 1800s Spain claimed land as far north as Montana, as far west as California, and as far east as the Mississippi River. (b) The missions served as focal points or symbols of Spanish rule as well as the backbone of Spain's attempt to settle California.
3. (a) The mountain men contributed to the settling of Oregon by blazing trails and spreading word about its abundant resources. (b) The fur trading companies relayed stories about natural resources to the East and set up rudimentary governments.

(c) Based upon the mistaken belief that the Indians wanted to convert to Christianity, many missionaries took friends and families west and encouraged others to join them.
4. (a) Cultural, religious, political, and language differences led to tension between Americans and Mexicans. (b) Santa Anna's revolution spurred the Texans to push for independence, since they were worried that they would be disenfranchised or driven out of Texas.
5. (a) Most Americans in Texas favored annexation. (b) Most northerners opposed annexation because they feared the growing power of the South. (c) President Tyler annexed Texas in 1845 by a joint congressional resolution requiring only a simple majority of both houses. Texan voters approved the plan.
6. (a) "Manifest destiny" refers to the commonly held belief that all land between the Atlantic and Pacific oceans should belong to United States. (b) The term reflected both America's faith in its institutions and its desire for expansion by implying that expansion was destined. (c) This attitude was not new; Puritans and Quakers believed that God favored their type of settlements because they were superior models for government and living.
7. (a) According to the 1844 Democratic party platform, all of Oregon belonged to the United States. (b) The British had claims to Oregon. (c) President Polk negotiated a treaty that divided Oregon at the 49th parallel.
8. (a) The United States wanted to acquire California in order to fulfill its manifest destiny and complete its continental expansion. The fine harbors of San Diego and San Francisco offered further incentive. (b) President Polk sent Slidell to Mexico City with a purchase offer of $25 million in 1846. Other attempts at purchase had been made in other administrations. Failing to buy California, President Polk tried a little diplomacy. Eventually the United States resorted to war. (c) War resulted in the achievement of United States aims. (d) Answers may vary. Accept all answers that refer to Mexico's interests in the area and the tendency of all nations to maintain their holdings.
9. (a) The Mormons migrated to Utah so that they could practice their religion in peace without interference or persecution from those hostile to them. (b) Their plan proved successful. Safe from interference and hostility, they established cooperative communities and made the desert bloom with a remarkable system of irrigation.
10. (a) The discovery of gold at Sutter's Mill drew hordes of people to the area: 80,000 in 1849. Large mining companies soon followed. The influx of people increased tensions among the di-

verse cultures in the state. (b) The gold rush society was a lawless, unrestrained one. Drinking and gambling abounded along with racing, singing, and dancing. It was composed mainly of men who governed themselves informally, resulting in a crude form of justice. Rights of Native Americans and immigrants were often overlooked.

11. Competition between different culture groups increased prejudice and hostility. (a) English-speaking miners felt their ways were superior to others. Their land claims were upheld by miners' courts. (b) California Indians, basically peaceful people living in small clans, were easily conquered, driven off the land, or killed. The Indian population dropped by over 230,000 in 20 years. (c) Californians of Mexican origin were treated as a conquered people; they were discriminated against even though they had lived in California for generations. (d) Chinese immigrants were at first welcomed as a source of cheap labor, but their different cultural heritage eventually aroused suspicion. Many became prosperous, which caused jealousy. (e) Black Americans faced prejudice and discrimination as they did in other parts of the West, but many free blacks prospered, and some slaves were able to earn their freedom.

For Further Thought, text page 263

1. (a) Accept those answers that include loneliness, danger, adventure, setting traps, making money. (b) Accept answers that refer to harsh conditions, blazing trails over unexplored terrain, meeting unknown Indians, and the like. (c) Accept answers that focus on resourcefulness, daring, courage, backwoods skills, stamina, wilyness.

2. (2) Accept answers that reflect admiration for ruggedness, bravery, self-reliance, heroics, defense of freedom. (b) Accept answers that focus on heroes as reflections of who Americans are as a people and what they value. Through heroes Americans develop pride in their nation.

3. (a) Like the early colonists, Texans were treated as second-class citizens. They were not permitted to participate fully in directing their own destiny. They had little influence on the government of Mexico. Like the early colonists the Americans in Texas believed in democracy and local control. (b) Accept answers that point out there were no language differences or cultural differences behind the American Revolution. The American judicial system was borrowed in part from the English, whereas the Mexican system was completely alien to Americans. Texans were not taxed, as the early colonists were.

Developing Basic Skills, text page 263

1. (a) Mountains made the journey to California and Oregon difficult. (b) The Oregon Trail was planned to avoid high mountains.

2. See the following chart. (a) The United States first acquired the Louisiana Territory; parts of Arizona and New Mexico were acquired last. (b) Most territories were acquired by treaty or purchase. (c) The Louisiana Purchase was the largest territory; the smallest was the Gadsden Purchase. (d) The United States acquired the most territory from France. (e) This is a correct statement. During the period 1845–1848 the following areas became part of the United States: Texas, the Oregon territory, California, and the Southwest.

Territory Acquired	Date of Acquisition	Country Acquired From	Method of Acquisition
Louisiana	1803	France	purchase
Florida	1819	Spain	Adams-Onís Treaty
Texas	1845	Republic of Texas	admitted as a state by joint resolution of Congress
Oregon	1846	Britain	Oregon Treaty
southwestern United States, California	1848	Mexico	Treaty of Guadalupe-Hildago
parts of Arizona and New Mexico	1853	Mexico	Gadsden Purchase

15 The Different Worlds of North and South (1820–1860)

Caption, text page 266

According to the map, Chicago, Cleveland, Buffalo, and St. Louis were among the cities developing as major rail centers.

Section Review, text page 268

1. *Charles Goodyear:* in 1839 invented a process for vulcanizing rubber so it could withstand extremes of heat and cold. *Samuel F.B. Morse:* perfected the telegraph in 1844, speeding up communication. *Elias Howe:* invented the sewing machine in 1840, making the mass production of clothing possible. *John Stevens:* invented the steam locomotive in 1820. *Commodore Matthew Perry:* sailed to Japan in 1853 and convinced Japanese leaders to open commercial trade with the United States. *Donald McKay:* designed fast clipper ships like the *Flying Cloud*, which aided long-distance trading. *Cyrus McCormick:* in 1834 invented the first mechanical reaper for harvesting wheat. *John Deere:* invented the steel plow in 1837.
2. *feeder lines:* railroad lines that led to water transportation; later similar lines connected major lines. *trunk lines:* heavily traveled railroad routes between major cities. *clipper ship:* fast-sailing ship that aided America's foreign trade in the 1850s.
3. Before trains could be widely used, sturdier bridges and roadbeds had to be built, rails improved, and smoke and sparks kept from falling on passengers.
4. By 1860 the North and West had the most developed railroad network.
5. The term merchant marine refers to the nation's commercial shipping fleet. The major activity of the American merchant marine was to carry America's growing trade with Europe and Asia.
6. McCormick's reaper enabled farmers to harvest many more acres of wheat with much less labor.

Caption, text page 272

Between 1841 and 1860 the greatest number of immigrants came from Ireland.

Section Review, text page 273

1. *National Trades Union:* organization of workers formed in 1834 in response to the need to coordinate labor union efforts among cities. *Commonwealth v. Hunt:* 1842 Massachusetts Supreme Court ruling that recognized the legality of labor unions.
2. *strike:* organized employee work stoppages. *union:* association of workers. *workingmen's party:* political group of workingmen who campaigned to improve the status of workers. *nativist:* native-born American protesting the influx of immigrants in the 1850s and 1860s; nativists formed the Know-Nothing Party. *assimilate:* term referring to the process by which immigrants became Americanized.
3. The earnings of artisans such as hatmakers declined as efficient factories made competing goods that could be sold for a lower price.
4. (a) In the 1820s and 1830s skilled workers—craftsmen such as shoemakers, typesetters, carpenters—tried to organize unions. (b) Unskilled workers were unrepresented in the early labor movement.
5. The workingmen's parties hoped to achieve universal white male suffrage, free public education, and an end to imprisonment for failure to pay debts.
6. Immigrants were attracted to the North because its economy was expanding and jobs were plentiful; it seemed truly a land of opportunity.
7. Because immigrants were willing to work for less pay, would work as strikebreakers, and increased the competition in the job market, many Americans began to resent them.

Section Review, text page 276

1. *Eli Whitney:* invented cotton gin, which revolutionized southern cotton production in 1793. *William Gregg:* encouraged development of southern industry by establishing a textile mill patterned after the early Lowell mills.
2. (a) The cotton gin had a bigger impact on the southern economy than any other single invention. (b) The machine separated cotton seeds from cotton fibers. Before its invention this was a slow process done by hand.
3. An abundance of fertile, available land attracted cotton farmers to Alabama, Mississippi, and Louisiana.
4. Rice and sugar were expensive crops to grow; they required many laborers plus expensive irrigation and drainage systems and were therefore better suited to large plantations. In addition sugar growers needed machinery to grind the sugar cane.
5. During the first half of the nineteenth century northern banks loaned money to southern planters, northern factories made the tools and machines they needed, and the North provided a market for the South's agricultural products.

Section Review, text page 279

1. Most white southerners owned small farms.
2. The main source of income among poor whites was raising wild cattle or razorback hogs.

3. (a) Most free blacks lived in cities in the upper South. (b) Most worked as domestic servants or farm hands. Some held skilled jobs (shoemakers, blacksmiths, barbers); some were merchants; some were planters.

4. To be considered a planter, a farmer had to own 20 slaves or more, enabling him to buy a cotton gin and hire an overseer to supervise the slaves.

Two Views of Slavery: Analyzing Conflicting Sources, text page 282

1. (a) Lyell says the working conditions are not taxing, that slaves have free time, are able to fish and sell their produce. The whip is hardly used. Northup says they work in cotton fields from sunrise past sunset, are frequently flogged, and get little rest. (b) According to Lyell the slaves get Indian meal, rice, milk, and occasionally pork and soup. They raise chickens, buy molasses, and catch fish. According to Northup they get only cold bacon and corn cake, three and a half pounds of bacon per week, and a peck of meal. (c) Lyell says the whip is a threat rarely used; Northup says daily whippings occur for any offense.

2. (a) Both agree that a whip was present, that food was given out, and that work began early. (b) They disagree over the extent of flogging, the types of tasks, the length of the work day, and the types and amount of food given to the slaves.

3. (a) As Lyell was an aristocrat he was possibly sympathetic to the conduct of others in his social class. (b) As Northup had experienced first hand the bitterness and frustration of slavery, he was more likely to sympathize with the plight of the slaves.

4. (a) Answers may vary. Lyell could have been on a "task system" plantation, Northup on a "gang system" plantation; no one description could account for all plantations. (b) Answers may vary. Accept all justifiable answers that address the indignity of slavery, the principles of human rights that are part of the American tradition and written into the Constitution, and the economic reasons for slavery.

Section Review, text page 284

1. *"puttin' on old Massa":* slaves' term for their day-to-day resistance to slavery; involved such acts as slowing down work, breaking tools, and pretending to be sick. *Nat Turner:* slave who led a slave revolt in Virginia in 1831.

2. *task system:* system of assigning work on plantations; each slave had a specific job to do each day with free time after the job's completion. *gang system:* a more common system; slaves worked together in gangs under an overseer during all daylight hours with short lunch break.

3. (a) The task system was used on hemp and rice plantations. (b) The gang system was used on tobacco, sugar, and cotton plantations.

4. State governments in the South did not recognize the legality of slave marriages.

5. Slaves stressed Christian teachings on family life, marriage, and people's obligations to one another.

6. Turner's revolt shocked and frightened many southerners. It led to harsher slave laws and strengthened the conviction that slavery was good for slaves and nonslaves alike.

Chapter Review, text page 285

1. (a) Railroads were first used as feeder lines to major water routes. Later they linked major cities. Most development was in the North. (b) Stronger bridges and roadbeds, a uniform track gauge, and better equipment overcame early problems. (c) Railroads spurred on the growth of industrialization in the North; they transported goods to markets and natural resources to industry.

2. (a) During the 1840s and 1850s America began trading with Japan and China. (b) The clipper ships provided the fastest means of water transportation. (c) Steamships replaced clipper ships because they were faster and larger.

3. (a) Effect of industrialization on northern agriculture: farmers relied more on machines to harvest crops; subsistence farming gave way to the growing of cash crops; crops reached markets easily by railroad; farmers bought more manufactured goods. (b) By 1860 northern farmers (in contrast to southern farmers) used more machines for harvest, employed only nonslave labor, had access to a better system of railroad transportation, and concentrated on the production of food.

4. (a) During the 1830s factory owners were not greatly concerned with providing pleasant working conditions; workers were regarded as machinery; increased competition led owners to cut wages in order to lower prices. (b) Workers attempted to improve conditions through strikes, union organizing, political action, legal action. (c) Workers had mixed success. Three hundred thousand trained workers belonged to local labor organizations, but conditions remained poor and unskilled workers were unorganized.

5. (a) Immigration increased in the 1840s because Europeans viewed America as a land of opportunity and Europe was experiencing political upheavals and famines. (b) Most of the new immigrants came from Ireland and Germany. (c) Many Irish immigrants settled around Boston; most Germans settled in midwestern cities. (d) Some Americans protested the arrival of new immigrants because the newcomers would work for less pay, were used as strikebreakers, and maintained cultural and religious differences. Many people were alarmed by the poverty and high crime rate found in immigrant neighborhoods. Some feared the political power of immigrants as they gained the right to vote.

6. (a) After the invention of the cotton gin the cotton growing region expanded inland, more land was put under cultivation, and more cotton was profitably produced. (b) As the textile industry grew the demand for cotton increased. (c) The need for more cotton increased the need for a labor force and contributed to the spread of slavery.

7. (a) In an attempt to make the South more independent, some southerners tried to foster industry in the South in the 1840s. They believed the South was too dependent on the northern banks, factories, and shipping firms. (b) Textile mills, flour mills, and iron works were built.

8. (a) Small farmers grew their own food and produced a small amount of cash crops. They constituted 80 percent of southern white families. "Poor whites" represented 10 percent of the South's population. They lacked cash crops, and raised wild hogs or cattle. (b) Most planters owned 20 or more slaves, possessed large land holdings, and raised profitable crops. Their life was modeled after that of wealthy English landed gentry.

9. (a) On small plantations slaves were generally in everyday contact with the owner, sharing the same tasks and often the same food. Most slaves on large plantations worked as field hands. They were often under the supervision of an overseer. (b) On rice and hemp plantations slaves worked under the task system. On cotton, sugar, and tobacco plantations they usually worked in gangs. (c) The temperament of the slave owner greatly affected whether slaves were abused or treated humanely.

10. (a) To maintain their dignity slaves stressed family life and religion, developed a musical tradition, and tried to preserve African traditions. (b) Other reactions to slavery included work slowdowns, equipment sabotage, escape, and rebellion.

11. (a) The southern defense of slavery was intensified by Nat Turner's revolt of 1831. (b) Proponents of slavery argued that slavery worked well in ancient Greece and Rome, that slaves were property and the Constitution protects private property, and that the conditions for slaves in the South were better than those for factory workers in the North.

For Further Thought, text page 285

1. (a) Accept answers that bring out the economic

bonds between the East and West and the natural tendency for people and industry to move to the unsettled areas. (b) Railroads hastened the settlement of the West.

2. (a) Workers with a craft or skill actively organized in the early nineteenth century. (b) They were more successful than unskilled workers because they were more difficult to replace.

3. (a) Free blacks faced prejudice and job discrimination in the North. (b) In the South they faced resentment from white workers, laws restricting their movement and assembly, discrimination, and prejudice. (c) In neither area did they enjoy full citizenship, respect, or opportunities. (d) The degree of political restriction was less in the North and the fear of being sold into slavery was greater in the South.

4. Accept all answers that refer to the power the rich can wield in politics and economics and the status they hold in society. Large planters had time and money to promote their own ideas and way of life.

Developing Basic Skills, text page 285

1. (a) The map shows the growth of railroads, 1850–1860. (b) The number of miles of track laid increased (tripled). (c) The North had the most highly developed railroad network. It was in the North where the Industrial Revolution had its start. (d) Accept all answers that make a connection between increased industrialization and the increase in jobs and availability of manufactured goods.

2. (a) The map shows the distribution of major southern crops. (b) In 1840 cotton growing was most prevalent in South Carolina, North Carolina, Georgia, Alabama, Mississippi, and Louisiana. (c) It expanded to Texas and Arkansas. (d) Little cotton was grown in Virginia because the growing season there was too short.

3. Research: Answers may vary.

16 A Land of Idealism (1820–1860)

Section Review, text page 288

1. *Maine laws:* laws passed in the 1850s forbidding the sale of alcoholic beverages.

2. *revivals:* meetings led by preachers to revive or restore the religious spirit in people; they were quite popular in the early nineteenth century. *temperance movement:* early-nineteenth-century campaign against the consumption of alcohol. *abstinence:* doing without; in the context of the temperance movement, doing without alcoholic beverages.

3. Reformers believed that the rights delineated in the Constitution and the Bill of Rights were denied to some Americans.
4. Reformers shared the dream that one day the United States would be a Christian commonwealth. This encouraged them to found new churches and spread their beliefs.
5. Through revivals reformers hoped to influence people to change their habits and lead moral lives.
6. Because of pressure from the temperance movement some state legislatures imposed liquor taxes and passed Maine laws forbidding the sale of alcoholic beverages.

Section Review, text page 291

1. *Horace Mann:* reformer who traveled widely advocating free public education; he was appointed Massachusetts' first superintendent of education in 1837. *Dorothea Dix:* Massachusetts woman who campaigned for improved treatment of the mentally ill during the 1840s and 1850s.
2. *compulsory education:* a requirement that every child attend school until a certain age. *utopian:* ideal or perfect; movement in the United States in the 1830s and 1840s to establish model communities.
3. In the early nineteenth century public education lacked adequate public support. Schools were poorly equipped, facilities inadequate, and teachers untrained.
4. Horace Mann believed in a well-educated citizenry. He crusaded for better books, buildings, and trained teachers.
5. Some people opposed public education because they resented taxation, especially people without children and those who sent their children to private school; poor people opposed it because they needed their children to work.
6. Imprisonment replaced physical punishment for criminal offenders.
7. (a) In the early nineteenth century the mentally ill were usually treated as criminals. (b) Dorothea Dix brought national attention to the problem. Eventually 15 states established hospitals for the mentally ill.

Section Review, text page 294

1. *Emma Willard:* established Troy Female Seminary in 1821; her purpose was to train women teachers to teach other women and demonstrate their competence in fields traditionally closed to them. *Mary Lyon:* established Mount Holyoke, the first women's college in the United States. *Sarah and Angelina Grimké:* sisters from South Carolina who worked toward achieving equal participation for women in the antislavery movement. *Lucretia Mott:* co-organizer of the Seneca Falls Convention on women's rights in 1848; it was the first national meeting ever held to discuss the status of women. *Elizabeth Cady Stanton:* co-organizer of the Seneca Falls Convention; she wrote many resolutions adopted at the convention and began the women's suffrage movement. *Susan B. Anthony:* joined Stanton in women's suffrage movement, bringing tremendous energy and skills to the cause. *Elizabeth Blackwell:* became the first American woman doctor in 1850; founded first United States nursing school in New York City in 1857. *Margaret Fuller:* editor; her work *Women in the Nineteenth Century* (1845) played an important role in the women's rights movement; she argued that women were as capable as men of doing all types of work. *Louisa May Alcott:* wrote *Little Women* and other children's books. *Harriet Beecher Stowe:* wrote *Uncle Tom's Cabin,* which gave impetus to the antislavery movement.
2. Mary Lyon intended Mount Holyoke to be a permanent women's college, unlike other female seminaries.
3. Female reformers often faced rejection and ridicule from male reformers.
4. The purpose of the Seneca Falls Convention was to publicize the need for political and social equality for women and propose programs to achieve it.
5. As women's role in American life expanded, some entered the medical, teaching, and publishing professions.

Section Review, text page 298

1. *Benjamin Lundy:* abolitionist who published an antislavery newspaper in Ohio during the 1820s. *William Lloyd Garrison:* hired as an assistant editor by Lundy; became a leader of the antislavery movement; published his own antislavery paper, *The Liberator,* in the 1830s; formed the American Anti-Slavery Society. *Theodore Weld:* abolitionist who in 1834 led a revival at Lane Seminary in Cincinnati against the moral evils of slavery. *David Walker:* free black who advocated that slaves rise and free themselves in his 1829 book, *Appeal to the Colored Citizens of the World. Frederick Douglass:* best-known black leader in the antislavery movement; he published an antislavery newspaper, *North Star* (1847), and actively protested discrimination against free blacks. *Sojourner Truth:* black woman who lectured extensively and passionately about the need for equality between blacks and whites and men and women. *underground railroad:* network of men and women who helped

slaves escape to the North or to Canada. *Harriet Tubman:* escaped slave who, risking her own life, led many slaves to freedom via the "underground railroad"; known as "Black Moses" among abolitionists and slaves. *Elijah P. Lovejoy:* abolitionist newspaper publisher killed by mob in Illinois in 1837; regarded as a martyr in the North and created sympathy for the abolitionist cause.

2. Lundy proposed these steps for the gradual emancipation of slaves: stop slavery from spreading to new states, end slave trade within the United States, persuade slave states to free slaves.

3. The colonization movement finally came to an end because it was too costly, plantation owners could not be persuaded to release slaves, and most blacks wanted freedom in America, not Africa.

4. By the 1830s some abolitionists began to see a need for a more radical approach in part because slavery was actually spreading as a result of the cotton gin and Nat Turner's rebellion had hardened the position of many slave owners on slavery.

5. The role of women in the antislavery movement divided radical abolitionists, as did the question of whether political action should be a vehicle for achieving its goals.

6. (a) The goal of the Liberty party was to abolish slavery. (b) The Free Soil party called for a halt to the expansion of slavery into new territories.

7. (a) In reaction to radical abolitionist agitation many southerners became more vigorous in their defense of slavery. Postmasters did not deliver antislavery material; Georgia offered a reward for capturing William Lloyd Garrison. (b) Many northerners also reacted adversely. Many did not want free blacks in their towns; a Boston mob attacked Garrison; Elijah Lovejoy was killed by a mob in Illinois.

Section Review, text page 300

1. *George Caleb Bingham:* leading "genre" painter who painted scenes of everyday life in Missouri. *Hudson River School:* group of artists who painted idealized landscapes focusing on the area around the Hudson River and the Catskill Mountains. *Ralph Waldo Emerson:* philosopher who commented on the temper of the times through essays and lectures; he believed in self-reliance and progress, and his works inspired many reformers of the era. *Henry David Thoreau:* writer and proponent of individualism; he defended the principle of civil disobedience and lived a life that reflected his mistrust of the growing industrial society. *James Fenimore Cooper:* author who wrote tales of life on the American frontier. *Washington Irving:* another writer whose works focused on American themes;

wrote "The Legend of Sleepy Hollow" and "Rip Van Winkle." *Nathaniel Hawthorne:* used the history and culture of New England as the background for his novels *The Scarlet Letter* and *The House of Seven Gables. Herman Melville:* wrote *Moby-Dick,* which became an American classic. *Edgar Allan Poe:* poet who contributed to America's stature in the world literary community. *Henry Wadsworth Longfellow:* another famous American poet. *Walt Whitman:* American poet who, in *Leaves of Grass,* celebrated American energy and variety and captured the nation's idealistic spirit.

2. American landscape paintings glorified and idealized the rugged nature of the American landscape.

3. Accept any of the following: frontier, Cooper; New England culture, Hawthorne and Melville; New York, Irving; variety and greatness of America, Whitman.

Chapter Review, text page 301

1. The reform spirit of the early nineteenth century had its roots in the Revolutionary War, the Declaration of Independence, and the Bill of Rights, as well as in the nation's religious heritage. The early colonists hoped the young republic would be an example to the world of a society based on Christian principles and justice.

2. (a) Some reformers attempted to turn people away from bad habits and dishonesty. The temperance reformers influenced state legislatures to pass Maine laws outlawing drinking. (b) The reformers had mixed success. Revival meetings had high attendance; the temperance movement gained, then lost members.

3. (a) In New England every town was required by law to have a public school; however, laws regarding the support of such schools were unenforced. In the Middle Atlantic states free education existed for those who claimed poverty. In the South there was no support for public education. The West had only a few poorly equipped schools. (b) Other types of education available to American youth were private tutors, religious instruction, and private colleges.

4. (a) Horace Mann believed free public education was essential for well-educated citizens. (b) Opposition to free public education came from taxpayers who would not utilize public schools. (c) Opposition to compulsory education came from farmers and factory workers who needed their children's help to support their families.

5. (a) In the early nineteenth century, towns ignored the educational needs of black Americans or bar-

red them from public schools. New York and Boston segregated black children. (b) Women recieved little education beyond basic writing and reading. (c) Between 1820 and 1860 religious denominations began schools and states founded colleges; however, few colleges admitted blacks or women.

6. Reform efforts: (a) Inmates of prisons were isolated at night and were forbidden from talking during the day. Reform efforts were unsuccessful. (b) Reformers were more successful in seeing that the mentally ill were treated more as sick people and less as criminals. State hospitals were established in 15 states. (c) Several utopian communities were founded (for example, the Shakers in Ohio, New Harmony in Indiana); they failed to sustain themselves on a permanent basis.

7. (a) Women played an active role in the abolitionist movement. (b) Many male reformers tried to exclude women from the antislavery movement (1840 World Anti-Slavery Convention voted to keep women delegates out). (c) Frustrated by the restraints placed upon them, women began to organize and campaign for their own rights. (d) During the 1840s and 1850s, beginning with the Seneca Falls Convention, annual meetings were held and state legislatures were petitioned to grant women the vote. The movement remained small until after the Civil War.

8. (a) In the battle to abolish slavery Benjamin Lundy called for gradual emancipation; he suggested stopping slavery from spreading to new states, ending slave trade inside the United States, and persuading slave states to free slaves. (b) William Lloyd Garrison called for an immediate end to slavery with no compensation to slaveowners; he was against violence and political action. (c) David Walker urged slaves to revolt to free themselves. (d) Arthur and Lewis Tappan believed in political action; they formed the Liberty party.

9. (a) Radical abolitionists aroused resentment among southerners because they attacked slave owners and the South itself, as well as its institutions. (b) Northerners opposed radical abolitionists because many feared that free blacks would take jobs away from whites by working for less pay. (c) When abolitionists were denied free speech or when their other civil rights were violated, they often received sympathy even from ardent slavery advocates.

10. In the first half of the nineteenth century, American artists focused on the nation's unique heritage and natural landscape, giving the art of the time a distinctly American character.

For Further Thought, text page 301

1. (a) Many of the reform movements that began during and after the revolution flowered during the first half of the nineteenth century. Prison reform, for example, was born in the years after the revolution and continued to spread during the early nineteenth century. Similarly the movement against slavery, which reached its height during the 1830s and 1840s, had its roots in the antislavery feeling of the late 1700s. (b) Current examples of this tradition might include the civil rights movement, the women's rights movement, struggle of Native Americans to regain ancestral lands, antinuclear and other environmental movements, antismoking and antidrug campaigns, and the like (for example, American Cancer Society, Red Cross, National Organization for Women).

2. Individuals like Sojourner Truth and Frederick Douglass were effective because as former slaves they spoke from firsthand experience. They brought conviction and a good deal of passion to their cause. Their intelligence and fervor made them impressive models to follow. They inspired courage in others.

3. Whitman's boast that his joints are "the limberest joints on earth and the sternist joints on earth" suggests the optimism of the American people. His assertion that "in all people I see myself" represents American idealism.

Developing Basic Skills, text page 301

1. (a) In the early nineteenth century women could not vote, own property, write a will disposing of property, or sue someone in court. The husband controlled his wife's income. (b) Accept those answers that include the idea that barriers to equality between the sexes have decreased.

2. (a) Douglass' speech is a primary document. (b) The author was deeply involved with the events described; he was an escaped slave. (c) Douglass made this speech to persuade New Yorkers to support the antislavery movement and to fight the slave trade. His purpose probably encouraged him to deliver an emotional appeal. (d) The facts Douglass mentioned were these: slaves were taken to Baltimore for shipment to Mobile and New Orleans; he had been a slave as a child and had witnessed slaves being marched off in chain gangs. (e) In his opinion the slave trade was a terrible horror led by fleshmongers. (f) From the document one can learn something of the horror involved in the taking of blacks for sale as well as something of the fear felt by blacks.

Unit Five: A Nation Torn Apart

17 The Cords of Union Broken (1820–1861)

Section Review, text page 308

1. *David Wilmot:* representative from Pennsylvania who in 1846 introduced a resolution, known as the Wilmot Proviso, that would ban slavery forever from any territory acquired from Mexico; the Wilmot Proviso was defeated. *Stephen Douglas:* senator from Illinois who championed popular sovereignty. *Zachary Taylor:* wealthy slaveowner from Louisiana, hero of the Mexican War, and Whig candidate for President in 1848; Taylor won the election with support from the North and South.
2. *free state:* a state where slavery was not permitted. *slave state:* a state where slavery was permitted. *popular sovereignty:* method by which the voters of each territory would decide whether or not to allow slavery within the territory.
3. The Missouri Compromise of 1820 provided that Congress admit Missouri as a slave state and Maine as a free state. This preserved the balance between slave and free states in the Senate. The Missouri Compromise further prohibited slavery in the remaining portion of the Louisiana Purchase north of latitude 36°30′.
4. (a) The extreme northern position, as stated by David Wilmot, held that slavery should be excluded from all the territory gained from Mexico. (b) The extreme southern position, represented by John C. Calhoun, declared that slavery should be permitted in all of the territories. (c) One moderate position suggested that the Missouri Compromise line of 36°30′ be extended to the Pacific, with slavery prohibited to its north and allowed to its south. Another moderate position favored popular sovereignty in the territories.
5. The Free Soil party opposed the extension of slavery into the territories.
6. (a) Northerners would benefit from the admission of California as a free state and from the abolition of the slave trade in the District of Columbia. (b) Southerners would benefit from a strong fugitive slave law, from Congress' officially declaring it had no power to abolish the slave trade between states, and by a provision that the rest of the southwestern territory would be open to slavery by popular sovereignty.

Section Review, text page 312

1. *Uncle Tom's Cabin:* a novel by Harriet Beecher Stowe published in 1852; it depicted the plight of slaves and thus contributed to northern opposition to the Fugitive Slave Law. *Franklin Pierce:* Democrat from New Hampshire, elected President in 1852. *Ostend Manifesto:* declaration stating that if Spain refused to sell Cuba, the United States might be justified in seizing the island by force; northerners saw the declaration as an attempt to expand slavery into Cuba. *John Brown:* antislavery agitator who massacred innocent proslavery settlers in retaliation for a raid several days earlier at Lawrence, Kansas.
2. (a) Southerners thought the Fugitive Slave Law represented what was due them, because slaves were their property. (b) Northerners were angered because the law denied a person accused of being a fugitive slave the right to a jury trial and the right to testify on one's own behalf. In addition, the law obligated citizens in the North to assist in capturing fugitive slaves.
3. The Kansas-Nebraska Act divided the Nebraska territory into two territories, Kansas and Nebraska, and instituted popular sovereignty on the issue of slavery. Since these territories were located north of 36°30′, the Kansas-Nebraska Act repealed the Missouri Compromise.
4. (a) In the first territorial elections in Kansas thousands of Missouri "border ruffians" crossed into Kansas and voted illegally, giving a lopsided victory to the proslavery forces. (b) Since large numbers of citizens thought the election was illegal, and since many became angered by harsh proslavery laws passed by the new territorial legislature, antislavery settlers in Kansas refused to recognize the authority of the territorial government. They established a rival "free state" government at Lawrence.
5. Three events that brought the Kansas issue to the center of the nation's attention in 1856: the mob attack on Lawrence on May 21; Preston Brooks's attack on Charles Sumner on May 22; John Brown's raid at Pottawatomie Creek on May 24.

Section Review, text page 315

1. *Dred Scott:* A Missouri slave whose owner had taken him into the free states of Illinois and Minnesota; abolitionists filed suit on Scott's behalf, claiming he was free on the basis of having resided in a free state, but the Supreme Court ruled that he was not free. *Abraham Lincoln:* Illinois attorney who ran on the Republican ticket against Stephen Douglas for the U.S. Senate in 1858; challenged

Douglas to a series of debates; Lincoln opposed slavery; he lost to Douglas. *Freeport Doctrine:* Stephen Douglas's idea that since slavery could not be legally prohibited in the territories, the people could prevent its extension by refusing to enact a slave code to protect slavery.

2. *free soiler:* citizen who opposed the expansion of slavery into the territories; many free soilers joined the new Republican party.

3. The Republican party was formed in 1854 by conventions of free soilers who opposed the extension of slavery into the territories.

4. The election of 1856 demonstrated the divisions between North and South; the Democratic nominee, James Buchanan, carried every southern state except Maryland, while the Republican nominee, John Frémont, carried every northern state except Pennsylvania, Indiana, Illinois, New Jersey, and California.

5. (a) The Supreme Court ruled in 1856 as a part of the Dred Scott decision that persons of African descent, whether slave or free, could not be citizens of the United States and therefore had no right to sue in a federal court. (b) Scott was bound by Missouri law, and, therefore, still a slave. Furthermore, since under the Fifth Amendment Congress had no power to deprive anyone of property without due process of law, the Missouri Compromise was unconstitutional because it deprived people of property (slaves) north of 36°30'.

6. Lincoln argued that the main difference between Republicans and northern Democrats was the Republican belief that slavery was morally wrong.

Causes of the Civil War: Analyzing Interpretations, text page 319

1. (a) Owsley seems to think the basic cause of the war was economic: a commercial, industrial North in conflict with an agrarian South. (b) Schlesinger believes a major cause was slavery.

2. (a) Answers should reflect the idea that the Great Depression probably caused many people to think in terms of economics. (b) The slavery of the concentration camps focused thinking on moral questions and human rights.

3. (a) Answers might suggest that the North as an industrialized section favored a protective tariff; the South opposed high tariffs because tariffs made manufactured goods more expensive. Reference could also be made to other northern efforts to use the resources of the federal government to aid industry. (b) The moral aspects of slavery generated emotions that encouraged extremists on both sides. Students might indicate that the highly

charged emotional atmosphere made compromise difficult. (c) Mention should also be made of the territories that were added to the United States prior to the Civil War. The issue of whether the newly created states should be slave or free constantly aggravated tensions between the North and South.

Section Review, text page 320

1. *Harpers Ferry:* on October 15, 1859, abolitionist John Brown led a raid on the federal arsenal at Harpers Ferry, Virginia, and seized its weapons, hoping to start a slave rebellion; his plan failed and he was later hanged, winning sympathy for his cause from many northerners. *Constitutional Union party:* new political party founded in 1860 that denounced the sectionalism of the other parties; the party nominated John Bell of Tennessee as its candidate for President. *Confederate States of America:* new government formed by the seven states of the deep South that seceded from the Union: South Carolina, Georgia, Florida, Alabama, Mississippi, Louisiana, and Texas. *Jefferson Davis:* first President of the Confederate states; inaugurated February 18, 1861. *Fort Sumter:* Union fort on an island in Charleston Harbor, attacked by the Confederate forces on April 12, 1861; the attack marked the beginning of the war between the states.

2. *secede:* to withdraw, as in seceding from the Union. *lame duck:* official whose term is about to end.

3. (a) John Brown's death mobilized antislavery opinion, although many northern leaders dismissed him as a lunatic. (b) The North's sympathy for Brown convinced many southerners that their security could be maintained only by seceding from the Union.

4. Republicans nominated Abraham Lincoln as their presidential candidate in 1860 because they feared the leading contender, William H. Seward of New York, was too radical to win. Lincoln, on the other hand, a moderate, was acceptable to all factions of the party and came from Illinois, a key state in the upcoming election.

5. Lincoln's election convinced many southerners that the South had lost political power and should secede. Lincoln's name had not been on the ballot in the South and yet he had won. The North had outvoted the South. With only one third of the nation's white population, the South could no longer play an important role in national politics.

6. (a) The attack on Fort Sumter boosted the South's morale. (b) Because the South had fired the first shot, the North rallied behind Lincoln and the cause of the Union with a sense of moral outrage.

1. (a) A balance in the Senate was necessary so that each side could block legislation it considered detrimental. (b) A balance in the Senate was probably more important to southerners because in the House, southerners were outnumbered by northerners. The North, with its larger population, had more votes in the House of Representatives. (c) As new states were added the balance was carefully maintained. Under the Missouri Compromise (1820) Missouri was added as a slave state, Maine as a free state. In 1846 Arkansas was admitted as a slave state, Michigan free; Florida and Texas both were admitted as slave states (1845), but then Iowa (1846) and Wisconsin (1848) were admitted as free states.

2. (a) The territory acquired from Mexico complicated the problem of slavery because the vast new region lay outside the Louisiana Purchase and thus was not subject to the provisions of the Missouri Compromise. (b) Under the Wilmot Proviso slavery would have been outlawed in all territories acquired from Mexico. (c) Other proposals included allowing slavery in all the territories; extending the 36°30′ line to the Pacific, with slavery allowed below it and prohibited above it; popular sovereignty, or allowing residents to vote. (d) The most moderate proposals were extending the Missouri Compromise line and allowing the voters to decide. (e) Extreme positions were the Wilmot Proviso, prohibiting slavery in all the territories, and John C. Calhoun's proposal to allow slavery in all the territories.

3. (a) California's request for admission brought heated debate in Congress because as an additional free state, it would upset the slave-free state balance of 15 to 15 in the Senate. (b) The Compromise of 1850 tried to solve the question of extending slavery into the territories by admitting California as a free state but allowing slavery in the rest of the southwestern territory. (c) In addition, slave trading was prohibited in Washington, D.C., but allowed among states, and a strong fugitive slave law was enacted.

4. (a) A fugitive slave law was important to slave owners because it discouraged slaves from running away and empowered officials to return them as if they were lost or stolen property. (b) The new law increased sectional tensions because it affected northerners directly. Newspapers in the North denounced it as an "outrage to humanity." Many northerners resented the provisions that denied civil rights to those accused of being fugitive slaves; many also resented the law's requirement that all citizens assist in capturing fugitive slaves.

(c) Free blacks felt threatened because the law permitted retrieval of anyone who had ever escaped from slavery. They also feared the danger of being falsely claimed as fugitives by slave owners.

5. (a) Slavery in Kansas and Nebraska was to be decided by popular sovereignty. (b) It differed from the Missouri Compromise by leaving to the people rather than to Congress the question of whether slavery would be permitted. (c) Uncertainty over whether Kansas would become a slave state or a free state led to violence. Proslavery Missouri "border ruffians" entered Kansas and voted illegally. Antislavery forces responded by setting up a rival "free state" government at Lawrence. Chaos soon regined, with armed bands roaming the countryside, attacking each other and raiding towns.

6. (a) The Republican party was formed by former free soilers who wanted a major political party to oppose the extension of slavery. (b) The successes of the Republicans in the 1856 elections showed their strength and demonstrated just how divided the nation had become.

7. (a) In the Dred Scott decision the Supreme Court ruled that blacks could not be citizens and could not sue in a federal court. The Court also concluded that since Scott was a resident of Missouri, he was subject to its laws. (b) The Dred Scott decision nullified the Missouri Compromise by ruling that Congress could not outlaw slavery in any territory. (c) Republicans were outraged since the decision, in effect, made their party goals unconstitutional. (d) Northern Democrats too were shocked because the Court ruled against the doctrine of popular sovereignty, which many favored.

8. (a) The Lincoln-Douglas debates pitted two eloquent speakers against each other so that the issues of the day were discussed clearly. (b) Douglas's Freeport Doctrine stated that the people of a territory could exercise popular sovereignty and prohibit slavery by not enacting a slave code. (c) The Freeport Doctrine gained the Democrats' support and helped Douglas defeat Lincoln for the Senate.

9. Brown's raid at Harpers Ferry increased northern sympathy for his cause and convinced many southerners that their way of life was under attack.

10. (a) There were two Democratic candidates in 1860 because the party had split into regional factions; northerners supported Stephen Douglas and southerners supported John Breckinridge. (b) The Republicans tried to broaden their support by nominating a moderate, Abraham Lincoln, endorsing a protective tariff to appeal to the industrial

Northeast, and proposing a homestead law that would be popular in the West. (c) In the election voting followed sectional lines, with Lincoln winning by carrying the more populous North. The South was simply outvoted, further intensifying the region's sense of isolation.

11. (a) South Carolina decided to secede because Lincoln's election seemed to demonstrate that the only way the South could continue to play an important role in a national government was to form one of its own. (b) South Carolina seceded first. (c) Other seceding states: Georgia, Florida, Alabama, Mississippi, Louisiana, and Texas. (d) The new President moved cautiously because he did not want to provoke the South in such a delicate situation. He was determined to hold the Union together. Moreover, he did not want to lose the upper South or the border states.

For Further Thought, text page 321

1. (a) Political parties as a cord binding the Union together: answers may vary. Accept those answers that reflect the idea that the parties sought compromises that would please the greatest numbers of people in each section in order to gain votes. (b) Elections demonstrating the gradual breaking of the cord: in 1848, Democrats and Whigs sought to avoid the question of slavery in the territories, but their evasion gave rise to the Free Soil party, which won 10 percent of the popular vote, all in the North. In 1852, both Whigs and Democrats endorsed the Compromise of 1850, but Northern and Southern factions disrupted the Whigs, allowing the less-troubled Democrats to win, thus electing Franklin Pierce, who proved sympathetic to southern goals. In 1856, many former Whigs, Democrats, and Free Soilers joined the growing Republican party, and the vote divided along clear sectional lines, with the Republicans receiving support strictly from the North, while the Democratic candidate, James Buchanan, narrowly won on the basis of solid southern votes plus some in the northern and middle states. In 1860 southern Democrats walked out of the party's convention and nominated their own candidate, John C. Breckinridge; northern Democrats nominated Senator Stephen Douglas, who campaigned in the North and South; another party, the Constitutional Unionist party, sought support throughout the North and South but failed to get it; the Republican nominee, Abraham Lincoln, won on the basis of a northern vote.

2. Accept those answers that reflect the idea that armed proslavery mobs invaded Kansas from Missouri in response to rumors that abolitionists

were moving in. The two groups fought each other at various sites in what amounted to a small civil war. The violence spread even to the halls of Congress when a Massachusetts congressman was beaten for a speech he made condemning the violence in Kansas.

3. Answers should mention that the raids on Pottawatomie Creek and Harpers Ferry were violent and poorly executed but that Brown's conduct after capture seemed noble and dignified and made him a martyr.

4. (a) Like the Articles of Confederation the Confederate Constitution stressed the "sovereign and independent character" of each individual state. (b) Importance of states' rights: answers should include the idea that southerners feared oppression by a strong central government.

Developing Basic Skills, text page 321

1. (a) The Missouri Compromise line applied to the Louisiana Purchase. (b) It would have been difficult to apply a similar line in California because part of the state lay above the line, part below it. (c) The Missouri Compromise outlawed slavery above 36°30′. The Compromise of 1850 opened the southwestern region to slavery through popular sovereignty. The Kansas-Nebraska Act voided the Missouri Compromise and opened territory above 36°30′ to slavery through popular sovereignty.

2. (a) Most events contributing to the North-South split occurred in the 1850s. (b) Answers may vary, but the events of the 1850s point to a likely split. Require students to support conclusions with factual evidence.

18 Divided by War (1861–1865)

Section Review, text page 326

1. *National Bank Act:* act passed in 1863 for the purpose of raising capital for the northern war effort; new national banks were required to invest one third of their deposits in federal bonds, and state banks were required to stop issuing their own notes; the new requirements created the nation's first truly centralized banking system.

2. *habeas corpus:* the right not to be imprisoned without a trial. *bounty:* a sum paid to a recruit for signing up for military service. *bounty jumping:* enlisting to collect a bounty, then deserting and reenlisting somewhere else to collect another bounty.

3. (a) As the North and South prepared for war, border states had to decide on which side they

would fight. (b) Maryland, Missouri, and Kentucky sided with the Union.

4. Southerners were fighting for independence and to defend their homeland.

5. As the war began the North had the advantages of a larger population from which to recruit soldiers and greater industrial strength.

6. Jefferson Davis had served in the House of Representatives, in the Senate, and as President Pierce's secretary of war. He was a graduate of West Point and a veteran of the Mexican War.

7. (a) To raise its army the Union called for volunteers, offered bounties, and in 1863 passed a draft law. (b) The Confederacy called for volunteers and passed a draft law in 1862.

8. (a) To raise funds the Confederacy sold bonds and printed currency. (b) The Union levied an income tax. It also imposed new sales taxes, taxes on manufactured goods, and a direct tax on the states. In addition, it sold bonds and issued paper money.

9. Both the Union and Confederacy wanted Britain's support because of its strong navy and large industrial capacity. The North pinned its hopes on Britain's sympathy for a crusade against slavery. The South viewed its cotton trade with England as a solid diplomatic link.

Section Review, text page 331

1. *Stonewall Jackson:* Confederate General Thomas J. Jackson, who earned the nickname "Stonewall" when he and his men resisted a Union attack "like a stone wall" at the first battle of Bull Run on July 21, 1861. *the Virginia:* the first fully ironclad warship; actually an abandoned Union ship, reconditioned by the Confederacy and renamed *Virginia;* it entered combat on March 8, 1862, and devastated the wooden ships it encountered. *the Monitor:* the Union's ironclad, which met the *Virginia* in combat on March 9, 1862; neither was able to seriously damage the other. *Ulysses S. Grant:* Union general in command of the western theater. *George B. Mc-Clellan:* Union general in command of the Army of the Potomac; a good organizer, but too slow in his preparations; his attack on Richmond (March through May 1862) failed. *Robert E. Lee:* Confederate general in command of the Army of Northern Virginia; he defeated McClellan at Richmond.

2. In the Civil War larger numbers of soldiers were involved in each battle than in the battles of previous wars. Also, weapons were more efficient.

3. (a) Scott's strategy was to blockade Confederate ports, divide the Confederacy into three theaters of war, and use the Union's superior naval strength to strangle each weakened section. (b) The three theaters were the far west (west of the Mississippi River), the west (between the Mississippi and the Appalachian Mountains), and the east (area around Virginia and Maryland).

4. A blockade of the southern coast would cut off the Confederacy's supply of manufactured goods.

5. To keep Union forces from taking Richmond, Lee sent Stonewall Jackson's army on a series of diversionary attacks that kept McClellan from getting the reinforcements he needed to lead an attack on the city. Then Lee and Jackson kept McClellan off balance with a series of encounters. Finally, with the help of J.E.B. Stuart's cavalry, McClellan was forced back to the James River. A second Union attack on Richmond under General John Pope also failed when Lee and Jackson surrounded Pope's forces and made him retreat.

6. At Antietam, Lee's army, though not decisively defeated, had to retreat across the Potomac to Virginia.

Section Review, text page 334

1. *contraband:* item subject to seizure; fugitive slaves who entered Union camps were declared contraband of war and not returnable to their masters.

2. Lincoln's primary reason for the war was to preserve the Union, that is, to keep the United States together as one nation.

3. Pressure to end slavery came from abolitionists, fugitive slaves, and radical Republicans in Congress.

4. The Emancipation Proclamation applied only to Confederate states still at war. It did not free slaves in areas occupied by Union troops or slaves in border states still loyal to the Union.

5. (a) Before the war, blacks in the North faced discrimination in housing, employment, and civil rights. They could vote only in New York and New England; in New York blacks had to meet a property qualification not applied to whites. Only in New England could they attend the same schools as whites. In many major cities public transportation was segregated, or blacks were not allowed to ride at all. (b) In the army, the term of enlistment was longer for blacks than for whites, and they were paid less. They were assigned to all-black regiments under the command of white officers and were given inferior weapons and medical care.

Section Review, text page 337

1. *copperheads:* northerners who favored the Confederacy or protested the war. *Homestead Act:* act passed in 1862 that gave 160 acres of western land to any citizen who agreed to occupy and improve the land for five years. *Morrill Act:* legislation that

gave states land grants to endow colleges of agriculture. *Clara Barton:* former school teacher who organized care for the sick and wounded in the North, sometimes serving on the battlefield.

2. Many northern workers resented being drafted for what they considered a "rich man's war" because those who could afford to pay a $300 exemption fee were not drafted. Whites feared job competition from free blacks, so they had little interest in fighting a war to free the slaves.

3. Industry and agriculture were stimulated by the war.

4. As most of the fighting took place in the South, the destruction of property and crops was greater there.

5. The upper South, the mountain regions, and the poorer sections of the Confederacy were pro-Union. In 1861, the western section of Virginia broke away to form West Virginia and join the Union.

6. Women contributed to the war effort by forming aid societies to collect supplies. They gave food, drink, and medical care to soldiers passing through their towns. Some raised money to purchase military hardware. In the South, women harvested crops and supervised farms. They worked as clerks and secretaries in the North. In both sections, women became nurses.

Section Review, text page 341

1. *William Tecumseh Sherman:* Union general who marched from Chattanooga to Atlanta to Savannah, leaving a trail of destruction; his march dealt the South a devastating blow.

2. (a) The victories at Fredericksburg, Virginia, (November 1862) and Chancellorsville, Virginia, (May 1863) encouraged the Confederates. (b) Lee and President Davis hoped that a Confederate victory in Pennsylvania, which was Union territory, would break the Union's resolve to continue the war.

3. The capture of Vicksburg and Port Hudson placed the entire Mississippi River under Union control. This completely cut off the far western region from the rest of the Confederacy and prevented the Confederates from using any part of the Mississippi to resupply its armies.

4. Grant planned to lay waste to the Shenandoah Valley so that no crops could be grown until after the war, capture Atlanta, and take the Confederate capital, Richmond.

5. Sherman, under Grant's direction, waged total war, destroying farmland, homes, railroads, and cities, and leaving the civilian population unable to contribute to the war effort.

6. After Grant forced Lee to withdraw from Petersburg, Richmond fell to the Union. Lee, with his army surrounded, realized that resistance would lead to greater loss of life among his troops. He surrendered rather than sacrifice his soldiers.

Chapter Review, text page 343

1. (a) As the war began the Confederates were at an advantage because they were strongly motivated to defend their homeland. In addition, they were experienced in using firearms and horses and had better military leaders than their northern counterparts. (b) However, the fact that the Confederate government had strong constitutional limits to its authority meant that it had a limited ability to direct the course of the war. And as the South was defending slavery it had a limited ability to attract European aid. (c) The Union had these advantages: greater manpower, more plentiful supplies, a larger railroad network, a larger merchant marine, and a larger navy. (d) Counteracting these advantages, though, was the fact that northern industry had to be converted from peacetime to wartime production, a time-consuming process.

2. (a) Neither side received enough volunteers to carry out the war effort. (b) To get recruits bounties were offered in the North. (c) Because both sides exempted people who were wealthy, some people called the war "a rich man's war and a poor man's fight." In the North a man could pay a $300 exemption fee. In the South, one man on each plantation with 20 or more slaves could be exempted. During the early years of the war the Confederacy also allowed paid substitutes. (d) Resistance to the draft was especially strong in large northern cities because white workers feared job competition from freed blacks.

3. (a) British support was important to both the South and the North because of Great Britain's strong navy and large industrial capacity. (b) In Britain sympathy for the Union was strong among anti-slavery reformers. (c) Sympathy for the Confederacy was strong among the upper class, who identified with southern planters. (d) Great Britain's official policy was one of neutrality.

4. (a) Congress established a centralized banking system during the war in order to raise capital to finance the war. (b) Under the centralized banking system new national banks were required to invest one third of their deposits in federal bonds, and state banks were ordered to stop printing paper money. (c) The South raised money during the war mainly by printing paper money, even though there was no gold or silver to back it. (d) This led to runaway inflation.

5. (a) General Scott's strategy was to blockade the southern coast, divide the Confederacy into three

regions, and then attack and strangle each region separately. (b) Scott's plan was called the "anaconda," after the South American snake that encircles its prey and then crushes it. (c) The strategy worked best in the East, which was dependent on northern and European sources for manufactured supplies. (d) The blockade greatly reduced the number of ships entering southern ports, from 6,000 to 800 a year. The only supplies the South could receive by sea came from small ships that ran the blockade.

6. (a) Lee invaded the North twice in the hope that victories inside Union territory would undermine northern determination to fight. His plan was foiled. (b) At Antietam (September 18, 1862) the Union forced Lee back to Virginia. The Union victory bolstered northern morale and allowed President Lincoln to expand his war aims to include ending slavery. At Gettysburg (June through July 1863) the Confederates again suffered defeat, marking the turning point of the war, the beginning of the end for the South.

7. (a) Lincoln handled the slavery issue cautiously at the beginning of the war because he did not want to chance losing support of the border states. (b) As the war progressed the demand for abolition grew. The Union victory at Antietam spawned enough support to allow the President to issue the Emancipation Proclamation, which he hoped would frighten southern slaveholders into ending the war in order to keep their slaves. (c) Only slaves in Confederate states still at war with the Union were affected by the proclamation.

8. The Civil War made the abolitionist cause more respectable. New attention was given to instituting equal rights for blacks in the North and abolishing slavery in the South. New York integrated its public transportation. More public schools admitted black children. Blacks became entitled to citizenship.

9. (a) Throughout the war a certain number of northerners opposed the war and the draft. Workers in particular resented the draft because of provisions exempting the wealthy. And many opposed the war because they believed an end to slavery would put blacks in competition with them for jobs. (b) In the South the draft also evoked discontent, because of the exemption issue and because some people were pro-Union. (c) Both Presidents Lincoln and Davis suspended the right of *habeas corpus* to deal with dissenters.

10. (a) Demands for war supplies accelerated the industrialization of the North and increased agricultural production, especially of foodstuffs. But the war also brought inflation that outstripped wages. (b) As a result of the war much of the South's

industrial capacity was destroyed. Farmlands, too, were laid waste. Inflation in the South was astronomical. (c) Grant and Sherman deliberately sought to destroy the South's capacity to support a war effort, and thus they destroyed whole cities, farmlands, railroad tracks, and even homes. The effect was to disable the civilian population and deprive them of the ability to help the armed forces.

11. (a) Grant's plan was to destroy the farmlands of the Shenandoah Valley and capture Atlanta and Richmond. (b) The capture of Richmond proved most difficult. (c) Answers may vary. Accept answer that refer to Lee's exceptional leadership.

For Further Thought, text page 343

1. (a) Accept those answers that emphasize the existence of slavery in the border states as well as the geographic factor of having Union and Confederate neighbors. (b) The state of Maryland was important to the Union because if it aided the Confederacy, the Union capital would be surrounded by Confederate territory. Missouri and Kentucky had importance because of their proximity to the Mississippi River. (c) Answers may vary, but they should include reference to the strategic importance of the border states. (d) Answers may vary. Maryland was probably most crucial because of its position north of Washington D.C.

2. (a) Answers may vary. Accept answers that emphasize the military leadership in both regions. (b) Answers may vary. Accept answers that refer to the North's greater industrial strength, larger work force, and better transportation network.

3. (a) Answers may vary. Accept answers that emphasize that there were more soldiers involved in this war than in previous wars and that weaponry was more sophisticated. (b) Emphasize that new technology made war more "efficient," that is, more people were killed or wounded and more property was destroyed.

4. (a) Nursing was considered too unpleasant and difficult for women. (b) Answers may vary. Accept answers that refer to women's push for greater legal rights and their involvement in the antislavery movement.

Developing Basic Skills, text page 343

1. (a), (b), (c) Encourage students to prepare a worksheet with these headings: Leadership Strengths, Leadership Weaknesses, Importance to the War. Under each column they should note the characteristics that apply to each of the Civil War leaders listed. Answers will vary. In general both

	Western Theater	Eastern Theater
Confederate Victory	Chickamauga	First Bull Run
		Seven Days' Battle
		Richmond
		Second Bull Run
		Fredericksburg
		Chancellorsville
Union Victory	Fort Henry	Antietam
	Fort Donelson	Gettysburg
	Shiloh	Atlanta
	Vicksburg	Savannah
	Port Hudson	Petersburg
	Chattanooga	Appomattox
Neither	none	*Monitor* v. *Virginia*

strengths and weaknesses would have importance in a person's ability to lead in wartime. The ability to act quickly, of course, would be a definite advantage during a war.

2. See the chart above. (a) The Confederacy won the most battles in the eastern theater. (b) The Union won the most battles in the western theater. (c) The Union won the most in total. (d) Students might suggest that the chart explains the outcome of the war because it describes the progression of the battles. (e) A fuller treatment of the battles might more clearly reveal trends in the fighting.

19 A Difficult Reunion (1865–1877)

Section Review, text page 348

1. *Freedmen's Bureau:* government agency established in 1865 to aid former slaves and refugees. *Wade-Davis Bill:* bill supported by moderate as well as radical Republicans in Congress; this bill outlined conditions by which southern states could be re-admitted to the Union; President Lincoln vetoed the bill because he felt its restrictions on the seceded states were too severe. *John Wilkes Booth:* a former actor who assassinated President Lincoln. *Andrew Johnson:* Vice-President under Lincoln who succeeded to the presidency upon Lincoln's assassination; he had been governor of Tennessee and had represented the state in the House and Senate before becoming Vice-President. *Joint Committee on Reconstruction:* congressional committee set up in December 1865 to review the "reconstruction" of

the southern states; establishment of this committee was part of a move to wrest control of Reconstruction from the President.

2. *freedmen:* former slaves, freed as a result of the war; most were illiterate although skilled in farming, had no land and no way to buy any; their prospects for employment were slim.

3. Following the war there was widespread unemployment in the North as factories shut down. Veterans had difficulty finding work. In the South factories, railroads, and farmlands had been devastated, cities burned out, banks closed, and businesses disrupted. The South also experienced widespread unemployment. And in both regions thousands of veterans were permanently disabled.

4. The Freedmen's Bureau issued surplus army food, distributed clothing, organized schools, provided medical care, and sought work and job protection for former slaves and poverty-stricken whites.

5. Lincoln's 10-percent plan enabled a state to reorganize and rejoin the Union after it abolished slavery and after 10 percent of its citizens who had voted in the 1860 election subscribed to an oath to support Constitution and the Union.

6. Johnson required former Confederate states to disavow their acts of secession, repudiate their war debts, and ratify the Thirteenth Amendment.

Section Review, text page 351

1. *Thaddeus Stevens:* one of the most outspoken Radicals in the House of Representatives. *Black Codes:* laws passed in the South to limit the activities of freedmen. *Civil Rights Act:* passed in April 1866, it provided that blacks could become United States

citizens and possess all the legal rights of citizens. *Reconstruction Act:* radical new program for Reconstruction passed in March 1867; it was designed to make readmission tougher for southern states; it divided the South into five military districts, each to be governed by an army general. *Tenure of Office Act:* stated that any official appointed by the President, with the advice and consent of the Senate, could not be dismissed without the Senate's consent.

2. The Radical Republicans maintained a harsh position toward the former Confederate states for the following reasons: they believed these states had forfeited their statehood and were now no more than territories, subject to the control of Congress; they wanted to protect their commanding majority in Congress by preventing newly elected southern Democrats from being seated; they felt Johnson's plan was too lenient and that the South should be punished; some were deeply committed to winning civil rights for blacks.

3. (a) Under the Black Codes black Americans were given the right to sue and be sued, to buy and sell property, to marry legally, and to receive certain protections when working as apprentices. (b) Black Americans were forbidden to bear arms, to meet together after sunset, and to marry whites. In addition, they faced fines or imprisonment for being idle or unemployed.

4. (a) The major provision of the Fourteenth Amendment guaranteed citizenship to black Americans. (b) The Fifteenth Amendment gave black Americans the right to vote.

5. The 1867 provision for readmission stated that each state had to adopt a state constitution that forbade former Confederate officials from holding office and that granted black citizens the right to vote. In addition, the state had to ratify the Fourteenth Amendment.

6. President Johnson's dismissal of Secretary of War Edwin Stanton and of several Reconstruction district commanders prompted Congress to begin impeachment proceedings against him.

Section Review, text page 354

1. *Hiram R. Revels, Blanche K. Bruce:* the only blacks elected to the Senate during Reconstruction; both from Mississippi.

2. *tenants:* people who rented land from a large landowner and supplied their own seed and supplies; rent was paid either in cash or "in kind" (a portion of the crop). *sharecroppers:* people who farmed a piece of land and shared the crop with the landowner; usually one third went to each of the following: the sharecropper, the owner, and the

merchant who supplied the seed and equipment. *carpetbaggers:* northerners who settled in the South after the war and supported Radical Reconstruction. *scalawags:* white southerners who supported Radical Reconstruction.

3. Because Confederate money was worthless and U.S. currency did not filter into the South as rapidly as it was needed, the South experienced a shortage of cash.

4. After the war carpetbaggers, scalawags, and blacks became new forces in southern politics.

5. During Radical Reconstruction southern state governments gave blacks civil and political rights, established free public education for all children, improved prisons, and established centers for the care of mentally and physically handicapped people.

6. Reconstruction governments were sometimes plagued by inexperienced and incompetent leadership and corruption.

Section Review, text page 358

1. *Ku Klux Klan:* a secret organization dedicated to ending Radical Republican rule in the South and preventing blacks from acquiring civil rights. *Force Act, Ku Klux Klan Act:* passed in 1870 and 1871, they outlawed the use of force to prevent people from voting and authorized the use of federal troops to enforce the laws. *Rutherford B. Hayes:* Republican who won the presidential election in 1876 by the decision of an electoral commission. *Samuel Tilden:* Democratic presidential candidate in 1876.

2. The death of Stevens in 1868 and the defeat of Wade in 1869, combined with the retirement of other Radicals, weakened the influence of Radical Reconstruction.

3. Corruption among carpetbaggers and scalawags and the involvement of some black officials in scandals disillusioned many northerners and convinced them that southerners should be allowed to run their own governments.

4. Northern business leaders concluded that the Radical Republican governments were preventing the South from expanding economically. They wanted to invest in the South, but only if they could count on stable governments.

5. (a) Pressure and intimidation were used to prevent blacks from voting. Some people resorted to force or the threat of it. In some areas armed pickets prevented blacks from registering to vote. Secret organizations such as the Klan and the Knights of the White Camelia burned houses and whipped, shot, or hanged blacks and sympathetic whites. (b) The campaign of intimidation was successful in keeping

many blacks and potential Republicans away from the polls.

6. In exchange for support from conservative southerners, Hayes promised federal aid to construct new railroads and to control floods along the Mississippi River, as well as the removal of all federal troops from the South and a speedy end to Reconstruction.

Chapter Review, text page 359

1. Bitterness and resentment over the war, southern fears of northern retribution, and the new status of blacks, plus widespread unemployment and other grave economic problems in both regions, made reunion of the North and South especially difficult.

2. (a) After the war former slaves faced poverty and unemployment. Whites feared them and were not willing to accept them as equals. Most blacks were illiterate and few had skills beyond those of farming. Most had no land or money so they were unable to take up farming. (b) The Freedmen's Bureau distributed food and clothing, set up schools, sought jobs for blacks, and tried to prevent exploitation by employers.

3. (a) Lincoln contended that the southern rebellion was an insurrection, not a secession. The Constitution gave the President power to quell insurrections; thus Lincoln believed he should restore harmonious relations with the South as soon as possible. (b) Lincoln's plan for Reconstruction was to pardon Confederates who swore an oath to support the Constitution and the Union. When 10 percent of a state's citizens who had voted in the 1860 election subscribed to the oath and the state abolished slavery, the state would be readmitted. (c) President Lincoln favored a moderate approach because he believed the process of Reconstruction had to work gradually.

4. (a) The Radical Republicans thought Johnson would be sympathetic to their plan because, although a southerner, he had little love for the rich planter class. Also, he had opposed secession. (b) The Radical Republicans misjudged Johnson, however. Johnson did not have such a harsh attitude after all, and he continued to honor Lincoln's moderate plan. His own Reconstruction steps were more moderate than those proposed by the Radical Republicans.

5. (a) All the southern states except Texas moved to obtain recognition, but South Carolina refused to condemn its act of secession, and several others refused to repudiate their war debts. Most indicated that they had no intention of giving freedmen equal rights. (b) Johnson recognized them anyway because he wanted the states back in the Union as quickly as possible. (c) When Congress reconvened in December 1865, it refused to seat the former Confederate states' representatives. It then set up a Joint Committee on Reconstruction for the purpose of carrying out Reconstruction on its own terms.

6. (a) Radical Republicans believed the former Confederate states had forfeited their statehood and returned to the status of territories. (b) The Radical Republicans favored harsher requirements for readmission because they thought Congress should have exclusive jurisdiction over the territories. Also, they wanted to retain their majority in Congress by refusing to seat Democrats elected by the South, and some simply felt Johnson's plan was too lenient. They felt the South deserved to be punished. Some Radical Republicans were deeply concerned about the treatment of blacks in the South.

7. (a) The Black Codes were laws passed in the South to limit the activities of freedmen. (b) They were passed to maintain white supremacy, to prevent black revolts, and to provide for those blacks who were unable to adapt quickly to freedom. (c) Reacting to the Black Codes, Congress attempted to protect the rights of freedmen by increasing the authority of the Freedmen's Bureau and by passing the Civil Rights Act.

8. (a) Congress proposed the Fourteenth Amendment because it feared the Supreme Court might declare the Civil Rights Act unconstitutional. (b) In the main the amendment guaranteed citizenship to blacks. (c) It also denied participation in government to former Confederate officeholders, canceled all Confederate debts, and prohibited reimbursement by any government for loss of slaves. (d) The Fifteenth Amendment guaranteed blacks the right to vote.

9. (a) The 1866 congressional elections were important for Radical Republicans because they won over a two-thirds majority in both houses of Congress. They were thus assured of enough votes to pass their own program of Reconstruction. (b) Johnson's political power was undermined by the impeachment proceedings, while the power of the Radicals was increased.

10. (a) A severe shortage of cash in the South, combined with the region's general impoverishment after the war, made planters and farmers mortgage their future crops in order to pay for seed and supplied. (b) After the war many poor whites and freedmen worked as tenants or sharecroppers.

11. (a) Before the war politics in the South was dominated by the planter aristrocracy. In the Reconstruction South carpetbaggers, scalawags, and blacks dominated government. (b) White conser-

vatives tried to regain political influence by pointing out the inexperience, incompetence, and corruption of the Reconstruction governments and by appealing to northern businesspeople who would stand to gain from a more stable South. (c) The conservatives eventually succeeded in 1877, when in exchange for their support of Rutherford B. Hayes they won from him a promise of federal troop withdrawal from the South as well as aid for internal improvements.

12. (a) The Reconstruction governments increased civil rights for blacks, established free public schools, and improved prisons and institutions for the mentally and physically handicapped. (b) Inexperienced and incompetent leadership, corruption, and the resentment of the South's former ruling class constantly plagued these governments.

13. (a) The retirement of Radical Republican leaders reduced support for Radical Reconstruction in Congress and thus undercut the authority of the Radical state governments. (b) Corruption in the Grant administration brought dissension within the Republican party and undercut Grant's political influence. (c) Corruption in southern state governments reduced nationwide support for Radical Reconstruction and curtailed business expansion. (d) Desiring to expand their businesses in the South, many northern businesspeople sought an end to Radical Republican rule in the hope that greater economic stability could be achieved. (e) The violence against blacks and sympathetic whites kept many potential Republican voters away from the polls in spite of federal laws against intimidation, thus bringing about the election of a conservative government. (f) The Hayes-Tilden Compromise ended Reconstruction when Hayes agreed to withdraw all federal troops from the South in return for southern conservative support of his bid for the presidency.

For Further Thought, text page 359

1. The Radical Republicans believed in a loose interpretation of the Constitution. Students could suggest that the Constitution does not specifically empower the Congress to establish racial equality, yet the Radical Republicans worked for the passage of the Civil Rights Act of 1866, which tried to secure equal rights for blacks. A strict interpretation of the Constitution would not permit this exercise of federal power.

2. (a) The House can impeach a President by a majority vote. Thus accused, the President must stand trial in the Senate. If two thirds of the senators find that the President is guilty of the charge made against him or her in the House, the President is removed from office. (b) Answers may vary. Accept all answers that reflect the understanding that removing a President is a serious matter not to be done hastily or without due cause. (c) Answers may vary. Accept answers that acknowledge that his accusers could give no evidence of any crimes committeed by him and that he was not convicted.

3. Answers may vary. Accept all answers that acknowledge Lincoln's great skills as a leader as well as the many serious problems with which any President would have had to contend.

Developing Basic Skills, text page 359

1. See the following chart. (a) Lincoln proposed the least severe policy. (b) Radical Republicans proposed the most severe policy. (c) Johnson's southern roots may have softened his policy toward the former Confederate states. The Radicals, on the other hand, were northerners who wanted to punish the South.

Lincoln's Policy	Johnson's Policy	Radical Republican Policy
10 percent of citizens voting in the election of 1860 would have to subscribe to an oath declaring their loyalty to the Union and the Constitution	disavow secession legislation	all of Johnson's requirements
	repudiate war debts	disqualify former Confederate officeholders from holding office
abolish slavery	ratify Thirteenth Amendment	grant blacks the right to vote
		ratify Fourteenth Amendment

2. (a) Hayes emerged with a majority of electoral votes (185) after the electoral commission awarded him the electoral votes in the disputed states. (b) Tilden received the most popular votes. (c) Votes were disputed in Florida, Louisiana, South Carolina, and Oregon. (d) Accept all answers that point out that the Republicans were responsible for Reconstruction.

Unit Six: Transforming a Nation

20 The Western Frontier (1865–1900)

Section Review, text page 364

1. *William Gilpin:* first territorial governor of Colorado; booster of western development who believed the West had unlimited resources. *John Wesley Powell:* geologist who led an expedition down the Grand Canyon of the Colorado River; challenged Gilpin's vision of western development and suggested careful regulation of its water.
2. The Great Plains is a virtually treeless area with an annual rainfall of less than 20 inches (50 centimeters).
3. Buffalo was a source of food, shelter, clothing, thread, bowstrings, tools, eating implements, and fuel.
4. The Plains Indians disturbed the land as little as possible. They revered nature and believed it was important to remain in harmony with it. Any wasteful or harmful use of the natural environment disturbed their vision of a world in balance.
5. (a) Native Americans of the plains believed the land and its creatures should exist in harmony with the spiritual world. They sought to maintain a balance between nature and the spirits who governed it. (b) Gilpin thought that the West's resources were unlimited, that the West would eventually support over a billion people, and that the climate would become more humid after crops were planted. (c) Powell realized water was scarce and needed to be conserved. He foresaw the need for western settlers to regulate and share the West's water.

Section Review, text page 368

1. *Comstock Lode:* site of the richest mining strike in history, near Virginia City, Nevada; it yielded over $300 million in gold and silver. *Pony Express:* mail service established in 1860; used 80 riders to relay the mail along a 2,000-mile route across the West. *Union Pacific Railroad:* one of two companies involved in the building of the first transcontinental railroad; laid the track from Nebraska west. *Central Pacific Railroad:* the other company to help build the transcontinental railroad; laid the track from Sacramento east.
2. *vigilante:* self-appointed enforcer of the law; in the West vigilante groups frequently tried and lynched outlaws. *public domain:* land that belongs to the nation, not to individuals.
3. In the late 1850s and early 1860s new discoveries of gold and silver were made in California and western Nevada, in the Columbia and Fraser river valleys, in Idaho and Montana along the Bitter Root and Salmon River mountain ranges, and in Colorado.
4. Travel by stagecoach was cramped, exhausting, and bumpy; in comparison to travel by train, it was slow and restricting as only limited luggage could be carried.
5. As an incentive for laying tracks in the West the federal government offered railroad companies 20 square miles plus a 400-foot right-of-way for every mile of track the company laid. The federal government also loaned money to the railroad companies.
6. Chinese laborers helped in laying track for the Central Pacific; Irish laborers worked for the Union Pacific.

Section Review, text page 372

1. *Little Big Horn:* battle between the Sioux Indians and U.S. army led by General Custer in which all U.S. troops were killed. *Chief Joseph:* leader of the Nez Percé Indians who led a brilliant defensive campaign through Oregon and Idaho before he was finally forced to surrender in Montana. *Geronimo:* determined chief of the Apaches of Arizona who held out against the U.S. until 1886. *Susette La Flesche:* Omaha Indian woman who wrote and lectured about Indian grievances. *Helen Hunt Jackson:* author of *Century of Dishonor,* a book outlining the history of broken treaties between the United States and the Indians. *Dawes Act:* act passed in 1887 that sought to bring Indians into the mainstream of

American life by breaking up old tribal organizations. *Ghost Dance:* Sioux religious ritual celebrating the sacred customs of the past and looking to a return of freedom. *Wounded Knee:* site in South Dakota where over 290 Indian men, women, and children were killed by the U.S. cavalry.
2. *reservation:* an area of land specifically set aside for Indians.
3. (a) The Fort Laramie agreement was an attempt to find a way for the Indians and the new settlers to live peacefully. In return for promises of yearly payments and gifts, Indian leaders promised to confine their hunting to separate areas with definite borders. (b) The agreement worked poorly because neither side could enforce it. Indians continued hunting where they wished and settlers continued claiming Indian land.
4. (a) The gold rush of 1859 brought thousands of miners into Colorado and eventually led to war as government agents forced Indians to give up more land. (b) New fighting broke out in 1874 when gold was discovered in the Black Hills and thousands of miners moved into Indian reservations in the area.
5. The buffalo herds were decimated by railroad crews who took them for food, by wealthy easterners who hunted them for sport, and by merchants who used their hides for robes or belts for machinery.
6. (a) The purpose of the Dawes Act was to bring Indians into the mainstream of American life by breaking up old tribal organizations. (b) Its provisions: reservation land was parceled out in 160-acre lots to families and individuals. Those who accepted land were made full citizens. Congress appropriated funds to support schools that would teach Indian children "the white man's way of life."

Section Review, text page 375

1. *Texas longhorn:* type of cattle that could survive untended on prairie grass. *long drives:* drives in which large herds of cattle were moved across hundreds or thousands of miles to the railheads, where they could be shipped to market.
2. (a) Railroads contributed to the growth of cattle ranching by opening new markets for Texas beef. (b) Cattle were moved to the railhead by long drives.
3. The competition for grazing land led to overgrazing, quarrels over water rights and land boundaries, and the fencing in of land, all of which contributed to an end to the cattle bonanza.
4. Two harsh winters in the late 1880s followed by drought killed 80 to 90 percent of the herds and had a devastating effect on the cattle business.

Section Review, text page 378

1. (a) The purpose of the Homestead Act was to encourage farmers to settle the West. (b) It provided that any citizen or immigrant who intended to become a citizen could purchase 160 acres of public land for a small registration fee.
2. Railroad companies attracted settlers to the plains through advertising and by selling land and providing transportation west.
3. Among the new techniques and inventions that made farming easier and more profitable were deep wells, dry farming, steel-tipped plows, threshing machines, and mechanical binders.
4. Schools and churches provided education for children. They also served as community centers where farm families could gather and find relief from the isolation and hard work of life on the plains.

Chapter Review, text page 379

1. (a) The Great Plains is a dry, virtually treeless region stretching from about the 98th meridian to the Rocky Mountains. (b) With the introduction of horses in the 1700s Indians became expert riders and were thus able to roam hundreds of miles on their nomadic hunts. Their population tripled. (c) Buffalo provided the Indians with all the necessities of life: meat, shelter, clothing, thread, tools, eating implements.
2. (a) Native Americans believed the natural world was in close harmony with the supernatural spirits who governed it. People had to maintain harmony in order to be rewarded with success in hunting and war. (b) They performed religious rituals to bring their lives into harmony with the natural world, and disturbed nature as little as possible.
3. (a) Gilpin viewed the West as a place of unlimited resources. He believed it would eventually support over a billion people. Artesian wells would supply water, and crops would create a more humid climate, which would encourage new vegetation. (b) Powell believed rainfall shaped the natural environment of each locality. As water was scarce throughout the West, western farms would have to be larger than those in the East. Irrigation and cooperation among farmers would be necessary to insure an adequate supply of water. (c) Powell recognized the limitations imposed by the region's small water supply; Gilpin did not. (d) Neither Powell nor Gilpin emphasized the need for people to live in harmony with nature as the Indians did, although Powell's view was closer to theirs than Gilpin's.
4. (a) The new mining frontier of the 1850s and 1860s was located in the Sierra Nevadas and the

Rockies. (b) The discovery of new mineral deposits in this frontier brought thousands of people into the region, causing towns to spring up overnight. Some farsighted people began developing towns in anticipation of a big mining strike.

5. (a) Before the West could be settled a transportation system was needed to move people and goods into the area. (b) During the 1850s and early 1860s the stagecoach, pony express, telegraph, and transcontinental railroad contributed to improved transportaion and communication in the West.

6. (a) Building a transcontinental railroad was expensive, and crossing the mountains posed difficult engineering problems. (b) To overcome the difficulties Chinese and Irish laborers were brought in to to do the work largely by hand. The had to cut through the mountains, sometimes through solid granite, and cart the rubble away in wheelbarrows. (c) The transcontinental railroad both sped up and influenced the pattern of the West's settlement. Towns grew along the tracks. The largest towns and citites developed at intersections of railroad lines. The railroad allowed the movement of products to markets in the East and thus stimulated population growth.

7. (a) In 1851 representatives of the United States government met with Indian spokespersons at Fort Laramie, Wyoming, and offered to give the Indians payments and gifts if they agreed to confine their hunting to separate areas with definite borders. (b) The attempt failed because neither side could enforce the agreement. Indians continued to hunt according to their customary patterns, and new settlers arriving in the wake of gold strikes moved on Indian land. (c) In 1867 and 1868 government agents demanded that the Plains nations give up even more land and live on reservations. (d) This action failed, too. Though the major tribes agreed, other did not and fighting continued. When gold was discovered on some of the reservations, thousands of miners moved in and staked claims, and war broke out again.

8. (a) In an effort to improve the treatment of Indians on reservations, land was parceled out to individual Indians rather than to tribes as a whole. Those who accepted were made citizens of the United States. Congress provided additional funds to support schools designed to teach Indian children the "white man's way of life." (b) The efforts failed because customs violated Indian traditions, whites tricked Indians into selling their land for cheap prices, and the Indians resisted giving up their religion.

9. (a) The development of the railroads opened up eastern markets and led to the cattle boom of the 1860s and 1870s. (b) The long drive allowed cattle ranchers to move large herds across open plains to railheads where the cattle could be shipped to market.

10. The following contributed to the end of the cattle bonanza: (a) The increase in the number of cattle led to overgrazing and quarrels over land. (b) Barbed wire allowed ranchers to fence in ranges. It helped create conflict over boundaries between cattlemen and sheep ranchers, especially when the conflict involved water rights. (c) Sheep cropped the grass so close to the ground that cattle could not eat it; bitter range wars erupted between cattlemen and sheep ranchers. (d) When farmers fenced in former grazing land for crops, conflict developed with cattlemen. (e) Two harsh winters (1885–1887), followed by dry summers, killed 80 to 90 percent of all cattle.

For Further Thought, text page 379

1. Students should emphasize that the Plains Indians depended on the buffalo for many of their needs.
2. (a) The Indians were struggling to defend their homeland and maintain a way of life that was on the verge of extinction. (b) Earlier conflicts involved territory, while in the plains, an entire culture (or what remained of it) was at stake. In addition, the Indians had already experienced too many broken promises in the past to be willing to believe white negotiators. (c) As in past conflicts, land was still a central issue.
3. The mining and cattle bonanzas were similar in that both stimulated population growth and the growth of towns in the West. Also, both the cattle and mining industries were greatly dependent on transportation, especially railroads.

Developing Basic Skills, text page 379

1. (a) Abilene, Ellsworth, Dodge City, San Antonio, Los Angeles, San Francisco, Seattle, Butte, Duluth, St. Paul, Omaha, Kansas City, St. Louis, New Orleans, Chicago, and Santa Fe developed along railroad lines. (b) Abilene, Ellsworth, and Dodge City developed as cattle centers along the railroad lines. (c) The Shawnee Trail, Western Trail, Goodnight-Loving Trail, and Chisholm Trail led to the cattle centers. (d) Accept answers that discuss the role of railroads in transporting goods and cattle to market and in stimulating the growth of towns.
2. New states that entered the Union between 1860 and 1900: Kansas, Nevada, Nebraska, New Mexico, Colorado, Washington, Montana, North Dakota, South Dakota, Wyoming, Idaho. (a) Kansas,

Nebraska, North Dakota, and South Dakota are located on the Great Plains. (b) Gold and silver were discovered in Colorado, Nevada, Wyoming, Montana, Idaho, and North Dakota. (c) Cattle trails crossed Kansas, Nebraska, New Mexico, and Colorado. (d) Transcontinental railroads crossed Nevada, Utah, and Wyoming. (e) As the railroads made it easier to reach the West, the population of the West increased and the territories sought admission to the Union.

3. (a) Between 1850 and 1870, Indians ceded lands in the far western, northern, central, and southern sections of the territory west of the Mississippi River. (b) Between 1870 and 1890, Indians ceded the remaining land west of the Mississippi River. (c) In these years the Indians lost their native land to the United States government, and they were moved onto reservations.

21 An Age of Industry (1865–1900)

Section Review, text page 384

1. *Samuel Morse:* perfected invention of the telegraph in 1844. *Alexander Graham Bell:* invented the telephone in 1876, then established the Bell Telephone Company. *Cornelius Vanderbilt:* made a fortune with a steamship line on the Hudson River, then set out to consolidate railroads between New York and Chicago in 1866.

2. *consolidate:* to combine smaller companies into a larger one. *bonds:* certificates that earn interest and are redeemed on a given date. *stock certificates:* shares of ownership in a company. *assets:* all of a company's property and cash. *watered stock:* stock certificates that were not backed by a company's assets. *rebates:* discounts; to attract more business the railroads offered rebates on normal shipping charges to their largest customers. *pooling:* agreements among managers that each railroad line would carry a certain portion of the total volume of freight.

3. The telegraph greatly speeded the pace of American business by speeding up the communication of orders and messages. It also provided employment opportunities for women.

4. Before 1860 most of the American rail system was in the East. No railroad bridge crossed the Mississippi, the Ohio, or the Hudson rivers. A large number of small companies controlled various sections of track that often were not interconnected and not of a standard gauge.

5. To consolidate the railroads connecting New York City and the Great Lakes region Vanderbilt bought up the smaller lines that were willing to sell to him. When one line, New York Central, refused to sell, Vanderbilt counteracted by refusing to let passengers and freight transfer from his lines to theirs. New York Central had to surrender, and Vanderbilt was then able to buy up all the feeder lines.

6. Railroads improved after the Civil War by adopting a standard gauge, decreasing rates, allowing freight cars of one line to use another line's tracks, replacing iron rails with steel rails, installing a second set of tracks so that traffic could move in two directions, and by consolidating. (Students should receive credit for listing four improvements.)

7. (a) Railroad companies raised money by issuing bonds, selling stock certificates, and watering stock. (b) They attracted business by offering rebates, pooling, and reducing rates for long hauls.

Section Review, text page 387

1. *Gustavus Swift, Philip Armour:* introduced refrigeration in the meatpacking industry in the late 1800s; each established firms in Chicago, midway between the cattle ranges of the Great Plains and the cities of the East. *George Pullman:* designed a railroad car for sleeping. *George Westinghouse:* invented an air brake for trains that gave engineers the ability to stop all cars simultaneously. *Thomas Edison:* invented the light bulb and other electrical items; his generators supplied power to buildings in Manhattan. *Gospel of Wealth:* Andrew Carnegie's idea that the rich should donate their money to worthy causes. *social Darwinism:* the application of Darwin's "survival of the fittest" concept to business and society; believers in social Darwinism argued that since only the "fittest" would survive in business and society, government regulation was wrong and that the natural talent of society should be allowed to lead.

2. *Bessemer process:* a method of manufacturing steel that involved heating iron in a large furnace, then blasting cold air through the heated iron to burn off the impurities. *laissez-faire economics:* school of economic thought that rejected government involvement in the economy.

3. The Bessemer process of steel production reduced the amount of coal needed to produce steel. It also speeded up the manufacture of steel, increasing output from 2,000 tons per year in 1867 to 7 million tons in 1899.

4. Refrigerated warehouses and rail cars made possible the marketing of the most perishable goods and increased the availability of foods.

5. Refrigeration, the sleeping car, air brake, typewriter, elevator, light bulb, generator, electric car,

and trolley were all inventions that helped create new industries. (Students should receive credit for listing four inventions.)

6. Carnegie believed that the millionaire should be a "trustee to his poorer brethren," that he should use his experience, wisdom, and ability to work on their behalf, and donate money to worthy causes.

Section Review, text page 391

1. *John D. Rockefeller:* formed the Standard Oil Company, which by 1879 controlled over 90 percent of the American refining capacity.

2. *capital:* money invested in a business. *vertical integration:* the control of all the industries required to turn a raw material into a finished product. *horizontal integration:* acquisition of a large number of businesses in one area of production to eliminate competition. *trust:* system by which stockholders in small companies exchange their stock certificates for trust certificates in a giant company; the holders of trust certificates receive dividends but lose the right to participate in the management of the firm. *dividend:* a share of a company's profit. *monopoly:* system by which one firm has almost total control of the market. *free enterprise:* system in which private individuals make economic decisions such as what products to make, how much to produce, and what the price should be.

3. A corporation has these advantages over individual proprietorships and partnerships: it has limited liability, is legally permanent, can act as a person in its own right, and usually is able to attract capital more easily.

4. In the latter nineteenth century businesspeople could obtain capital from commercial and savings banks, life insurance companies, and the sale of stock.

5. Through vertical integration Carnegie did not have to depend on owners of independent mines, railroads, and shipping lines for supplies and transportation.

6. To eliminate competition in the oil industry Rockefeller demanded rebates from railroad companies. He cut prices to capture a competitor's customers and then raised them again when the competition had been driven out of business.

7. (a) Critics of big business in the late nineteenth century say that big business administrators ruthlessly drove competitors out of business, exploited labor, discouraged technological change, polluted the environment, and wasted raw materials. (Students should receive credit for listing one criticism.) (b) Defenders of big business say that big business administrators supported schools, libraries, and museums, financed technological

breakthroughs, provided jobs allowing Americans to better their economic condition, and brought lower production costs and prices, higher wages, and a better quality of life to the American family. (Students should receive credit for listing one defense.)

Section Review, text page 394

1. *Henry Grady:* editor of the Atlanta *Constitution* who advocated southern industrialization. *Washington Duke:* using innovative advertising techniques and machines to roll cigarettes, he revolutionized the tobacco industry; formed the American Tobacco Company.

2. After the Civil War southern states encouraged northern financiers to invest in southern lines by offering free land as well as access to the South's natural resources. As a result, southern railroads grew at a pace that was faster than the national average.

3. Southern industries used cotton to manufacture thread, cottonseed oil for soap and cosmetics, tobacco for cigarettes, and timber for shingles and furniture.

4. Northern railroad owners charged higher rates to southern factories, making it difficult for southern products to compete with those made in the North. Furthermore, the rates for shipping raw materials to northern factories were deliberately set low.

Caption, text page 396

The most prosperous periods occurred during the early 1870s and early and late 1880s. Severe depression struck in 1865, between 1875 and 1878, and between 1883 and 1885.

Section Review, text page 400

1. *Knights of Labor:* organization for skilled workers that began in secrecy and later opened up to all workers; advocated social and economic reforms. *Terence Powderly:* elected president of the Knights of Labor in 1879; he lifted its veil of secrecy and expanded its membership to include all workers. *American Federation of Labor:* federation of self-governing national unions founded in 1881; its membership was restricted to skilled white male workers; it favored an eight-hour work day and collective bargaining. *Samuel Gompers:* London-born cigar maker who was the first president of the American Federation of Labor.

2. *anarchists:* people who oppose all organized government. *craft union:* a union whose members prac-

tice the same occupation. *collective bargaining:* the right of a union to represent workers as a group. *injunction:* a court order prohibiting a given action.

3. (a) Workers faced a host of dangers in the late 1800s: factories were badly lighted and poorly ventilated; in some excessive heat, explosions, and cave-ins were a constant threat. (b) During the depression many workers lost their jobs.

4. (a) The Knights of Labor campaigned for the eight-hour work day, improved safety in factories, compensation for on-the-job injuries, and equal pay for men and women. (b) At first only skilled workers could join.

5. The Haymarket riot turned the public against labor organizations.

6. (a) The American Federation of Labor campaigned for an eight-hour work day and collective bargaining. (b) Only skilled white male workers could join; recent immigrants were excluded.

7. In the late 1800s much of the public opposed unions. They were considered radical organizations by many people.

Chapter Review, text page 401

1. The telegraph and telephone helped stimulate industrial growth.

2. (a) The post–Civil War railroads were too highly concentrated in the East, and no bridges crossed the Mississippi, Ohio, or Hudson rivers. Further, tracks were not always interconnected, and gauges were not standard. (b) To improve the situation small lines consolidated, gauges were standardized, iron rails were replaced with steel rails, and second sets of tracks were installed to allow traffic in two directions at once.

3. (a) As companies expanded between 1860 and 1900 they often took on heavy debts, which they had difficulty paying off. (b) Attempts to solve the problems led to cutthroat competition. Many lines resorted to illegal means: rebates, pooling, charging unfair rates for small and short-haul shippers.

4. Each of the following helped stimulate American industry: (a) The Bessemer process enabled manufacturers to increase production of steel from 2,000 tons in 1867 to over 7 million tons in 1900. (b) Refrigeration allowed companies to store meat in warehouses and transport it from the West to the East, even in warm weather. (c) Air brakes gave locomotive engineers the ability to stop all cars on a train simultaneously, thus eliminating the need for individual brakemen on each car and allowing longer and faster trains. (d) The typewriter improved business communication. (e) The incandescent light bulb opened the way for new industries and made it possible to light large buildings.

5. Each of the following contributed a new philosophy for business: (a) Carnegie's Gospel of Wealth directed the wealthy to donate money to worthy causes. (b) Social Darwinism applied the idea of survival of the fittest in the business world; government regulation was viewed as interference with a natural process and thus as wrong. (c) Laissez-faire economics rejected government involvement in the economy. (d) Horatio Alger's stories reinforced the rags-to-riches theme that through talent and hard work an American could rise to the top.

6. (a) Corporations had less difficulty raising capital than proprietorships and partnerships because investors incur limited liability when investing in a corporation. In addition a corporation has a special, permanent legal status, and its survival does not hinge on the life of its owner. (b) Corporations raised capital by borrowing from commercial banks, savings institutions, and insurance companies and by selling stocks.

7. (a) Vertical integration is the taking control of all industries involved in the process of turning raw materials into a finished product. (b) It improved efficiency by eliminating a company's dependence on other companies. (c) Horizontal integration is the taking control of all companies in a single area of production. (d) By eliminating companies in the same business, horizontal integration reduces competition.

8. (a) Free enterprise is a system in which key economic decisions are made by private investors. (b) Critics of giant corporations pointed to ruthless competitive practices and unsatisfactory labor conditions. (c) Business leaders were sometimes referred to as robber barons because of the questionable methods they employed to acquire their wealth. Other people referred to business leaders as industrial statesmen because of their positive contributions to American life.

9. (a) Southern industries took advantage of the region's natural resources by concentrating on the manufacture of products related to agriculture, such as cotton, timber, and tobacco. (b) Southern industry remained dependent on the north, and thus the southern economy lagged behind that of the North. Northern bankers exerted control over southern industries, and northern railroad owners charged them high rates. Southern factories were discouraged from producing final goods, which yielded the greatest profits; they were instead encouraged to produce raw materials for shipment to northern factories.

10. (a) Long hours and hazardous working conditions convinced many American workers to join unions in the late 1800s. (b) Attempts to create a national labor organization: the Knights of Labor in 1869

	Knights of Labor	American Federation of Labor
Date Founded	1869	1881
Goals	unite all labor in one organization; eight-hour work day; equal pay for men and women	eight-hour work day; collective bargaining
Types of Members	skilled workers only at first; later all workers of any race, nationality, or sex	skilled workers only
Approved Tactics	campaigns for social and economic reform; opposed strikes	strikes

and the American Federation of Labor in 1881. (c) The Knights of Labor achieved gains in the mid-1880s; by 1886 its membership reached 700,000. Its success was weakened, however, by the Haymarket riot and violence during a railroad strike. By 1890 its membership had dropped to 100,000. The AFL achieved longer-lasting success as a labor organization, despite setbacks and negative public attitudes toward unions in the late 1800s.

11. (a) Industrialists reacted to labor unions with open hostility because they felt they had a right to bargain with each worker individually. (b) The courts, too, were generally hostile; many issued injunctions against the unions or held that strikers could be held liable to the company for losses incurred due to a strike. (c) The public associated labor unions with radicalism and they were suspicious of collective bargaining. The tradition of individualism was strong, and people believed that individual effort was the way to advancement.

For Further Thought, text page 401

1. Answers may vary. Students should recognize that Rockefeller himself was involved in activities that upheld his observation.
2. (a) Grady emphasized industrialization, whereas the South before the Civil War was overwhelmingly agricultural and dominated by a planter aristocracy. (b) Grady envisioned agriculture as a foundation for future development. The prewar South was indeed rich in natural resources and agricultural products that could be the basis of industrial growth. (c) and (d) Accept answers that describe the South's attempts to industrialize.
3. Answer will vary. Students should be aware of the tremendous impact of the railroad.

Developing Basic Skills, text page 401

1. See the chart above. (a) The Knights of Labor was founded earlier. (b) The Knights admitted all workers; the American Federation of Labor admitted skilled workers only, no blacks, women, or recent immigrants. (c) An eight-hour work day. (d) The AFL opposed social reform as a union goal. (e) The AFL approved of strikes; the Knights did not. (f) Accept reasonable answers. Students should understand the AFL had a moderate policy on labor relations and social reform.

2. (a) When a company is vertically integrated, it controls all steps in the process required to turn a raw material into a finished product. (b) When a company is horizontally integrated, it controls many businesses in one area of production. (c) Vertical integration might make a company more efficient by eliminating bottlenecks in production resulting from undependable supplies of raw materials. Horizontal integration might make a company more efficient by affording it economies of scale resulting from use of large-capacity production equipment. (d) A vertically integrated firm can control its costs more easily than a firm using a wide range of independent suppliers. A horizontally integrated firm is often able to buy supplies at a lower price than its smaller competitors.

22 Politics and Reform (1867–1896)

Caption, test page 403

The speech being parodied is Lincoln's Gettysburg Address, in which he spoke of "government of the people, by the people, for the people."

Section Review, text page 405

1. *Crédit Mobilier:* dummy construction company owned by the Union Pacific railroad that raised money by selling high-dividend stock; members of Congress were often recipients of these stocks and dividends. *Whiskey Ring:* people involved in a scandal in which hundreds of distillers bribed treasury officials to avoid paying taxes on their whiskey.
2. Some wealthy industrialists thought bribery made sense. They thought their wealth and power placed them above the law.
3. (a) In the years following Reconstruction congressional leaders thought it was their responsibility to propose and make the laws. (b) They believed the President's job was to enforce the laws passed by the legislative branch.
4. Presidents during the Gilded Age were prevented from leading vigorously in part because they themselves agreed that the Presidency was second to the legislative branch. In addition the executive staffs were small; none of the presidents of the period enjoyed the advantage of having their own parties in control of Congress. Also, widespread political corruption thwarted what they tried to do.
5. The scandals during Grant's administration tarnished and weakened the Presidency; at the same time they inspired some people to work for political reform.

Section Review, text page 409

1. *Mugwumps:* group of reformers within the Republican party who crusaded to clean up American politics. *Civil Service Act:* act passed in 1883 that classified approximately 15,000 federal jobs as civil service positions to be given only after competitive examination; civil service officeholders were not subject to dismissal on political grounds. *Munn* v. *Illinois:* 1877 Supreme Court ruling that upheld the constitutionality of state regulation of railroads. *Wabash, St. Louis, & Pacific Railway Company* v. *Illinois:* 1886 Supreme Court ruling that reversed the *Munn* v. *Illinois* decision and stated that only Congress could regulate commerce between the states; any railroad freight crossing state lines could not, therefore, be regulated by state commissions. *Interstate Commerce Act:* act passed in 1887 that outlawed rebating and pooling and established a commission to investigate complaints. *Sherman Antitrust Act:* act passed in 1890 that outlawed monopolies. *United States* v. *E.C. Knight Company:* 1895 Supreme Court ruling that weakened the Sherman Antitrust Act; said the law applied only to companies engaged in trade or commerce, not to those that operated exclusively within one state.
2. *patronage system:* the practice of giving out government jobs as favors to political friends. *holding company:* a company that gained control of other companies by buying their stock; used by corporations to sidestep the Sherman Antitrust Act.
3. The Mugwumps advocated testing job applicants to determine their fitness for positions in the federal government.
4. Under the Civil Service Act a potential government employee had to pass a test and could not be appointed merely as a political favor. In addition, an employee could not be fired for political reasons.
5. (a) The railroads discriminated against small shippers by giving larger shippers cheaper rates. (b) They discriminated against short-haul shippers by charging higher rates for hauling freight short distances than they did for long distances.
6. The Interstate Commerce Act set the important precedent that federal agencies could regulate large industries in interstate commerce.
7. To sidestep the law, corporations created holding companies.

Section Review, text page 413

1. *Conservatives:* Democrats who came to dominate southern politics after Reconstruction; many were industrialists. *"solid South":* refers to the domination of the South's political affairs by Democrats. *Jim Crow laws:* segregation codes passed in the South during the 1890s. *Plessy* v. *Ferguson:* 1896 Supreme Court ruling stating that blacks could be required to use separate facilities if those facilities were equal to the ones maintained for whites. *Booker T. Washington:* prominent black leader who advocated that blacks focus on achieving economic success rather than social equality; founded Tuskegee Institute in Alabama, a school for blacks with a curriculum that emphasized vocational training. *Atlanta Compromise:* refers to Booker T. Washington's speech in which he abandoned his pleas for social and political equality for blacks and asked for their economic success instead. *W.E.B. Du Bois:* black educator who insisted that blacks fight for social and political equality.
2. *disenfranchise:* to take away the right to vote. *poll tax:* a fee that had to be paid in order to vote. *grandfather clause:* voting regulation adopted by a number of southern states that allowed a person to satisfy voting requirements if his father or grandfather had been eligible to vote in 1867; it discriminated against blacks.
3. Southerners were especially supportive of laissez-faire because they had experienced what they con-

sidered the height of government interference under Radical Reconstruction.

4. Rigid residency requirements, literacy tests, and poll taxes discouraged blacks from voting.

5. Under Jim Crow laws blacks were forbidden to mingle with whites in railroad cars, buses, trolleys, passenger terminals, and other public facilities; they were forbidden to drink from the same public water fountains as whites, or to sit in the same section of a theater.

6. Tuskegee Institute offered vocational training.

7. W.E.B. Du Bois thought the right to vote and the right to enjoy equal economic opportunity were rights worth fighting for.

Section Review, text page 416

1. *Grangers:* members of an organization of farmers founded in 1867 for social reasons; later served political purposes. *National Farmers' Alliance:* farmers' organization formed in 1889 out of the joining of the Northwestern Farmers' Alliance and the Southern Alliance; worked for political reforms. *Ocala Platform:* set forth demands of the National Farmers' Alliance; chief among these was a call for the creation of subtreasuries to lend farmers money to get them through times of deflation. *Populist party:* a national third party founded in 1892 dedicated to agrarian reform.

2. *deflation:* economic condition in which the price of goods and services drops. *graduated personal income tax:* a tax system in which the tax rate is proportional to a person's income; people with higher incomes pay higher taxes.

3. During the last half of the nineteenth century American farmers faced a number of problems. Prices for their goods were declining, goods were being overproduced, credit was hard to get, they were paying back debts with deflated currency, railroads were charging unfair prices for shipping, and they were hit by a series of natural disasters in the 1880s.

4. To aid farmers Grangers campaigned for political reforms, formed cooperatives that stored grain, marketed farm products, and sold farm machinery without attempting to make a profit.

5. The Ocala Platform called for these reforms: creation of government subtreasuries to help farmers out of their credit bind; minting of silver coins to increase the money supply and fight deflation; reduction of high tariffs; and creation of a graduated personal income tax.

6. In the 1892 election the Populists did surprisingly well for a new party, receiving over a million votes for their national ticket and raising hopes that their influence would continue to grow.

Section Review, text page 420

1. *Coinage Act:* act passed in 1873 that declared that henceforth gold alone would be minted to back paper money. *Bland-Allison Act:* required the government to buy a set amount of silver each year to be minted into coins. *Sherman Silver Purchase Act:* increased the amount of silver that had to be purchased yearly and allowed the treasury to issue paper money based on silver. *Coxey's Army:* marchers led by Jacob Coxey; this group traveled from Ohio to Washington, D.C., to protest unemployment and to urge that the government undertake a massive road-building campaign to relieve unemployment. *William Jennings Bryan:* dramatic orator from Nebraska; strong supporter of the Populist cause; presidential nominee of both the Democratic and Populist parties in 1896. *William McKinley:* Ohio Republican who defeated Bryan in 1896. *Mark Hanna:* McKinley's campaign manager.

2. *gold standard:* system by which the value of currency is based on the value of gold.

3. Cleveland thought the depression had been caused by allowing silver to circulate as part of the currency.

4. Farmers and silver miners favored the coinage of silver.

5. Both the Populists and Democrats nominated William Jennings Bryan for President in 1896.

6. Hanna helped McKinley's campaign by raising campaign contributions. These were used to send speakers around the country on McKinley's behalf and to print campaign literature.

7. After Bryan's defeat in 1896 the Populist party lost morale and declined. In addition, improved economic conditions robbed the movement of some of its appeal.

Chapter Review, text page 421

1. In the late 1800s many industrialists achieved so much power and wealth that they felt contempt for the law. Since they were able to buy whatever they wanted, they thought they should be able to buy votes, political offices, and political favors.

2. (a) During the Gilded Age the reputation of the Senate and the House of Representatives reached a low point. Congress was thought to be corrupt and interested only in enjoying the spoils of victory. (b) Congress was able to dominate the presidency because many legislators had been in office for several decades and had accumulated much power and influence. Many Senators were wealthy as well. Besides, the presidency itself had experienced a declining reputation. The impeachment of

Andrew Johnson weakened the presidency, and the corruption of subsequent administrations put its authority in doubt.

3. (a) Before the Civil Service Act government jobs were given to people as awards for political support. (b) Demand for change arose after the assassination of President Garfield by a dissatisfied office seeker. (c) Under the Civil Service Act competitive examinations were used to determine an applicant's qualifications for a civil service job.

4. (a) In the 1870s the states created regulatory commissions of varying power to regulate the railroads. (b) They were trying to control rebates, pooling, and price discrimination, especially against short-haul shippers. (c) In 1875 the Supreme Court ruled in *Munn* v. *Illinois* that the Constitution permitted state regulation of railroads; in 1886 it ruled in *Wabash, St. Louis, & Pacific Railway Company* v. *Illinois* that only Congress had the power to regulate commerce between the states. (d) In the main the Interstate Commerce Act outlawed rebating and pooling; ordered railroads to establish reasonable and just rates and to refrain from charging short-haul customers higher rates than long-haul customers; and established an Interstate Commerce Commission to investigate complaints and take action by filing suit in the courts.

5. (a) Large corporations were able to become monopolies by lowering prices to drive out their competition and by then raising prices again. (b) The Sherman Antitrust Act outlawed monopolies. (c) Corporations were able to sidestep the law by forming holding companies, or companies that owned other companies. (d) In *United States* v. *E.C. Knight Company* the Supreme Court ruled that the Sherman Antitrust Act applied only to companies engaged in shipping across state lines.

6. (a) To disenfranchise black voters southern states instituted residency requirements, literacy tests, and poll taxes. (b) The Jim Crow laws were segregation codes passed in the 1890s. (c) *Plessy* v. *Ferguson* strengthened Jim Crow laws by allowing "separate but equal" facilties for blacks and whites.

7. (a) Booker T. Washington urged southern blacks to abandon political and social equality as a cause and concentrate on achieving economic success as a goal, because conditions in the South made social and political equality impossible. (b) W.E.B. Du Bois said blacks should demand the right to vote and the right to enjoy equality of opportunity. He believed that the right to vote was necessary to human dignity, that color discrimination was barbaric, and that black children needed education as well as white children.

8. (a) In the late 1800s declining prices, crop overproduction, difficult credit conditions, and unfair railroad rates made it difficult for farmers to make a living. (b) To deal with their problems they formed the Grange and the Farmers' Alliance. (c) To help farmers, these organizations formed cooperatives to build grain elevators, market grain, and sell farm equipment; lectured or published pamphlets on farm problems; and engaged in political action.

9. (a) The Ocala Platform called for the federal government to do the following: set up regional subtreasuries that would lend farmers up to 80 percent of the local value of their crops; increase the amount of money in circulation by minting silver coins; reduce high tariffs, and institute a graduated personal income tax. (b) The subtreasury system would allow farmers to hold their products until market conditions favored selling. Increasing the money supply would discourage deflation. Reducing high tariffs would lower the prices of manufactured goods. A graduated personal income tax would force the wealthy to assume a greater share of the tax burden.

10. (a) Tom Watson decided to form a "People's Party" because none of the other reform candidates elected in 1890 continued to support agrarian reforms after they were elected. (b) In the election of 1892 the Populist party received over a million votes.

11. (a) Farmers favored the coinage of silver because they believed it would increase the money supply. Miners favored the coinage of silver because they believed it would increase the price of the metal. (b) In response to pressure from the two groups Congress passed the Bland-Allison Act in 1878, requiring the government to buy a set amount of silver each year for minting into coins. Congress also passed the Sherman Silver Purchase Act in 1890, increasing the amount of silver to be purchased and allowing the treasury to issue paper money based on silver. (c) Cleveland favored a gold standard because he believed other standards weakened the value of gold. He felt this in turn weakened the confidence of the business community, discouraging new investment and creating unemployment.

12. (a) The Democratic platform in 1896 reflected several Populist goals, including unlimited coinage of silver, a lower tariff, and an income tax. (b) The defeat of Bryan in the presidential election of 1896 undermined Populist morale. Then as conditions improved in the country people lost interest in the reforms they advocated.

For Further Thought, text page 421

1. (a) The Gilded Age label reflected Twain's belief that the political corruption of the era was like the brass under a layer of gold. (b) Answers will vary.

Accept answers that refer to the ostentatious displays of wealth of the time, the wielding of power, and the undercurrent of poverty and want on the part of farmers, blacks, and others.
2. Students should recognize that Washington's views allowed discrimination to continue and would cause little social disruption.

Developing Basic Skills, text page 421

1. (a) The cartoon illustrates the development of corporate trusts. (b) The cartoonist believes the people are losing liberty and control of the country, as portrayed by the sinking ship. (c) Accept all justifiable reasons for why the cartoonist opposes trusts. Students should make reference to the enormous political and economic power wielded by the trusts.
2. See the following chart. (a) Reformers tried to end political corruption and make the economic system fairer for all groups. (b) Reformers were able to weaken the spoils system and pass legislation that curbed some economic abuses. (c) Muckraking journalists contributed to the success of the movement to root out political corruption. Organized pressure groups, such as the farmers, contributed to the movement for economic reform. Judges who believed that Congress lacked the power to enact broad regulatory legislation retarded the success of the movement for economic reform.

23 Toward an Urban Age (1865–1900)

Urban Growth: Interpreting Thematic Maps, text page 424

1. (a) The two maps deal with the growth of industries and cities. (b) The circles represent the populations of urban areas. (c) The shading represents major industrial areas.
2. (a) Eight cities appear on the 1860 map. (b) Thirty-one cities appear on the 1900 map. (c) In 1860 New York had a population between 1 and 5 million. (d) In 1900 Chicago, New York, and Philadelphia had a population between 1 and 5 million. (e) Chicago, Philadelphia, Boston, and St. Louis grew in population between 1860 and 1900. (f) The northeast coast was industrialized in 1860. (g) By 1900 industry had spread to the Great Lakes region and St. Louis. (h) St. Louis, Chicago, Detroit, Buffalo, and Rochester are located on important waterways.
3. (a) The maps show that industrial development and urban growth are interrelated. (b) Cities develop around waterways. (c) Cities developed in the Great Lakes region and the Midwest between 1860 and 1900. (d) There was little urban growth in the South. This was because the South lacked industry.

Reform Actions	Purpose	Degree of Success
Civil Service Act	eliminate spoils system	over half of all federal employees in civil service jobs by 1897
President Hayes's investigation of New York customs house	eliminate corruption in hiring practices and tariff collection	two senior customs house employees dismissed
Interstate Commerce Act	eliminate rebating and pooling	difficult to enforce in the courts
Sherman Antitrust Act	prohibit monopolistic practices	scope narrowed by Supreme Court in *United States* v. *E. C. Knight Company*
Sherman Silver Purchase Act	increase the supply of money	limited impact on money supply

Section Review, text page 426

1. Large numbers of workers and transportation facilities encouraged manufacturers to build plants in cities.
2. Urban growth was fastest in the Northeast.
3. Excellent rail and water transportation facilities made Chicago a transportation hub.
4. As Chicago grew it faced problems such as slums, overcrowding, lack of basic facilities, insufficient paved streets, filth, pollution of the Chicago River, and corruption in politics.

Section Review, text page 430

1. *pogrom:* violent attack on a Jewish neighborhood in Russia or Poland.
2. Wars, famines, religious persecution, overpopulation, and a lack of available jobs and land prompted many Europeans to immigrate to the United States in the years after the Civil War.
3. (a) The largest group of immigrants came from Italy. (b) The second largest group were Jews from eastern Europe, mainly Russia.
4. Most immigrants settled in cities, especially in industrial centers and ports such as Boston, New York, Philadelphia, and Chicago.
5. (a) Some Americans began to resent foreigners because the new immigrants competed for jobs and were often willing to accept lower wages and inferior working conditions. (b) In addition their languages, religions, and customs seemed strange to Americans.
6. The immigrants contributed to the cultural life of cities by forming choral groups, literary societies, and theater groups; by playing in or supporting symphony orchestras and opera companies; and by bringing to America the traditions of their homelands.

Section Review, text page 433

1. *F. W. Woolworth:* pioneer of the "five and ten" department store. *Joseph Pulitzer:* publisher of the New York *World*, a flamboyant mass-circulation newspaper. *Louis Sullivan:* Chicago architect who designed some of the first skyscrapers. *Winslow Homer:* painter who specialized in Maine coastal scenes. *Thomas Eakins:* taught at the Pennsylvania Academy of Art and painted realistic, often harsh, portraits and landscapes. *American Realists:* school of American artists consisting of Eakins and his followers; they painted the harsh life they saw around them. *Abner Doubleday:* credited with the invention of baseball in 1839. *James Naismith:* inventor of basketball.

2. Because of the trolley and the electrified railways, cities could expand. These new forms of transportation allowed settlement farther from the center of town. They increased the speed of travel and offered greater mobility to city dwellers.
3. In department stores people were offered a wider variety of merchandise—all on display—than in shops. Prices were lower in department stores and were marked on all items. Department stores offered free delivery and credit.
4. Newspapers like the New York *World* tried to attract readers by emphasizing news of crime, sports, and gossip. In addition they might devise stunts such as sending a reporter on a race around the world and giving readers a chance to guess how long it would take.
5. Attending symphonies, operas, the theater, vaudeville, museums, sporting events, and the like became popular leisure activities of the late nineteenth century.

Section Review, text page 438

1. *Jacob Riis:* author of *How the Other Half Lives,* a description of life in the slums. *Jane Addams:* founder of Hull House, a settlement house that offered services to help the poor. *John Dewey:* educational theorist; leader of the progressive education movement. *Social Gospel:* philosophy of some clergymen who believed that churches should become actively committed to social reform. *Frances Xavier Cabrini:* Italian nun who founded hospitals in North and South America. *William Booth:* a Methodist minister who established the Salvation Army in London in 1878. *Marcy Tweed:* the "boss" of New York City's Democratic political machine.
2. Reformers like Jacob Riis helped bring to light urban problems such as high infant mortality, overcrowding, lack of fire protection, filth, inadequate educational facilities, and lack of medical care.
3. Hull House provided a nursery and kindergarten for children of working mothers; adult education classes in English, nutrition, and health; a gymnasium for young people; a theater; and medical services.
4. (a) In the late nineteenth century many women moved into teaching, social work, clerical and sales jobs. (b) Women could vote in Wyoming, Colorado, Utah, and Idaho.
5. The major goals of progressive education were to widen school programs to include teaching about health, jobs, and family and community life; to apply new discoveries in science and psychology to classroom teaching; and to adapt teaching techniques to suit the needs of children being taught.

6. (a) The political machine might give a poor person aid in finding a job, or a loan to pay the rent. Sometimes the machine offered free English lessons, legal advice, and baskets of free food on holidays. (b) Because the political machines stole money from the cities, offered jobs and contracts to their supporters, and accepted bribes in return for building contracts, reformers demanded a better form of urban government.

Chapter Review, text page 439

1. In the last half of the nineteenth century the growth of industry in American cities created additional jobs, which drew increasing numbers of people to the cities. The increased number of people attracted more industries to the cities, and the growth spiral continued. In addition, the influx of huge numbers of immigrants contributed to urban growth.

2. (a) Chicago's central geographic location, its importance as a center of transportation for railroads and water traffic, its proximity to sources of raw materials, and its growing population made it attractive to industry. (b) As a rapidly growing city Chicago faced such problems as overcrowding; development of slums; lack of running water and sanitation facilities; insufficient, dirty, and obsolete streets; polluted water; and corruption in politics.

3. (a) In the late 1800s immigrants were attracted to the United States by the prospects of finding employment and the chance for a better life. (b) On the journey over immigrants were often cheated by transportation or hotel officials. Their cheap accommodations were overcrowded, dirty, and hot, and outbreaks of disease were common.

4. (a) The "new" immigrants of the 1880s and 1890s were mostly from southern and eastern Europe, especially Italy, Poland, Russia, Hungary, and Bohemia; earlier immigrants had been from Canada and northern Europe, especially the British Isles, Germany, and Scandinavia. (b) The fact that many new immigrants did not speak English and that their customs and languages seemed strange to some Americans contributed to antiforeign feeling.

5. Each of the following affected life in the cities: (a) Electric trolleys improved transportation, allowing people greater mobility and influencing the expansion of cities outward. (b) Department stores sold larger quantities of goods at lower prices than smaller shops, so more people could buy more things. (c) Mass-circulation newspapers attracted readers with news of crime, sports, and gossip.

6. (a) Illiteracy, unsanitary conditions, crime, fire hazards, high infant mortality, and overcrowding were problems that arose in the new urban areas. (b) Set-

tlement houses such as Jane Addams' Hull House offered a wide range of services to slum residents. These services included education, medical help, and recreation. Reformers also crusaded for health and industrial legislation.

7. (a) The need for clerical workers, teachers, social workers, and sales people created new opportunities for women. (b) In some states women had won the right to vote; in a number of states laws were passed giving women control over their own property.

8. (a) Political machines often controlled the governments of American cities. The machines offered city jobs and contracts to those who had the right connections. The machines often paid for their activities with city funds. (b) Because city governments were corrupt, inefficient, costly, and unresponsive to the needs of the people, reformers wanted to see changes in the way they were run.

For Further Thought, text page 439

1. (a) Answers may vary. Accept answers that refer to the excitement and diversity of city life and the opportunities for employment. (b) Students should recognize that these aspects of city life still exist.

2. (a) Humanitarian groups tried to improve the lives of city residents by helping feed and house the poor and by offering free or inexpensive medical and social services. (b) Early in American history volunteer groups, such as the abolitionists, formed to make social reforms.

Developing Basic Skills, text page 439

1. Students should include in their lists the following problems: unemployment, overcrowding, crime, illiteracy, unsanitary conditions. Research will vary.

2. Research will vary.

24 Becoming a World Power (1865–1900)

Section Review, text page 444

1. *William H. Seward:* secretary of state under Presidents Abraham Lincoln and Andrew Johnson; negotiated the purchase of Alaska from Russia. *Alabama Claims:* a demand that England compensate the United States for damages caused by the *Alabama*, a Confederate warship built in Britain; the British agreed to pay $15.5 million. *Frederick Jackson Turner:* a professor of history at the University of Wisconsin during the 1890s; he advocated expanding trade abroad as a substitute for the loss of economic opportunities caused by a shrinking frontier. *Alfred Thayer Mahan:* naval officer who believed that the expanding industrial capacity of the United States required new markets abroad; he urged the government to build a strong navy to protect trade routes. *Josiah Strong:* Congregationalist minister who envisioned an American Christian empire that would spread across the Pacific to Asia. *Queen Liliuokalani:* queen of Hawaii who came to the throne in 1891; a strong nationalist.

2. *empire:* a system of territories governed by one nation.

3. Seward ended Russian influence in North America by buying Alaska from that nation in 1867 for $7.2 million.

4. Admiral Mahan believed a strong navy was essential to protect trade.

5. Josiah Strong believed the United States had been divinely chosen to civilize the rest of the world.

6. (a) Germany, Great Britain, and the United States wanted to control Samoa. (b) The three nations agreed to share control of Samoa, with the United States obtaining the harbor at Pago Pago.

7. Before Queen Liliuokalani came to the throne, Hawaii was dominated by sugar growers.

8. By using a canal across Central America, ships would be able to pass between the Atlantic and Pacific oceans without circling South America.

Sinking of the Maine: Recognizing Propaganda, text page **448**

1. Facts in Sigsbee's message: (a) The *Maine* exploded in Havana Harbor and was destroyed. Many people were killed. The injured were put aboard a Spanish warship and a Ward Line steamer. Representatives of the Spanish armed forces expressed their sympathy to Captain Sigsbee. (b) Opinions in Sigsbee's message: the *Maine* was "blown up." Efforts to shape public opinion should be suspended. (c) Facts in *World* report: there is doubt as to the cause of the explosion. The *World* is conducting an inquiry. (d) Yes. It is the opinion of the *World* that the explosion was caused by a bomb or torpedo.

2. (a) Captain Sigsbee says the *Maine* was blown up. (b) The *World* implies that Captain Sigsbee's opinion of the cause of the explosion is correct. (c) Captain Sigsbee says the Spanish were sympathetic to the American loss. (d) No. (e) The *World* suggests that Captain Sigsbee is suspicious of Spain.

3. (a) No. On the contrary he wants to restrain public opinion until the facts are discovered. (b) The picture would arouse the public because it clearly shows the damage that resulted from the explosion. (c) The term "enemy" would stir up public opinion against Spain. (d) Suspicions, plot, and torpedo all have emotional appeal. The first two would generate suspicion of Spain while the third term would heighten the public's sense of horror.

4. (a) The overall message conveyed by the *World* report is that the *Maine* was deliberately blown up and that Spain is probably to blame. (b) Anger against Spain was aroused by the headlines featured in the *World*. The Sigsbee report, on the other hand, would leave the reader uncertain as to the cause and the culprit. (c) The author of the headlines featured in the *World* may have wanted to heighten reader interest in the story to increase newspaper sales. (d) Newspaper treatment of the sinking of the *Maine* encouraged prowar feeling in the United States.

Section Review, text page **450**

1. *Valeriano Weyler:* Spanish governor of Cuba whose actions fanned anti-Spanish feelings in the United States. *William Randolph Hearst:* publisher of the New York *Journal,* which printed sensational stories about conditions in Cuba in the late 1890s. *the Maine:* U.S. battleship whose sinking in Havana harbor increased the war fervor in the United States. *George Dewey:* commander of a U.S. Naval fleet based in Hong Kong; after the United States and Spain declared war on one another, he destroyed the Spanish fleet at Manila Bay in the Philippines. *Theodore Roosevelt:* assistant secretary of the navy under McKinley who resigned his position to command the Rough Riders.

2. *jingoism:* intense national pride with warlike overtones. *reconcentration:* policy imposed by Weyler in Cuba whereby people were marched into detention camps. *yellow journalism:* form of newspaper writing designed to stir up the emotions of readers.

3. The yellow press stirred up hatred against Spain with screaming headlines and sensational stories that pictured Spain as a villain.

4. The sinking of the *Maine* enraged the American public and created a call for war with Spain.

5. Dewey's victory in Manila Bay thrilled expansionists, who believed they were seeing the dawn of a new age of American expansion.

6. The battle of Santiago Harbor on July 3, 1898, ended Spanish resistance in Cuba.

7. (a) As a result of the Spanish-American War the United States acquired Puerto Rico, Guam, and the Philippines. (b) Cuba achieved independence as a result of the war.

1. *Platt Amendment:* an amendment to the Cuban constitution, added at the insistence of the United States; it stated that Cuba would not make treaties or loans threatening its independence, that the United States would be given two naval bases in Cuba, and that the United States had the right to send troops to Cuba if security was threatened. *William McKinley:* President of the United States during the Spanish-American War. *Emilio Aguinaldo:* led a rebellion against the United States to win Philippine independence. *John Hay:* secretary of state under McKinley; author of the Open Door notes. *Open Door notes:* letters written by Hay to the European powers with spheres of influence in China; the letters asked for cooperation in maintaining open trade with China. *Boxer Rebellion:* a Chinese nationalist revolt against Europeans in 1900.
2. *spheres of influence:* areas of control.
3. The Platt Amendment gave the United States the right to maintain two naval stations on the island and the right to send troops to Cuba in order to preserve life, liberty, or property.
4. (a) Aguinaldo and his rebels tried to win Philippine independence. (b) Aguinaldo held out for three years, but the United States eventually crushed the revolt in 1901.
5. (a) Russia, Japan, Britain, and Germany all had spheres of influence in China. (b) The spheres of influence restricted United States participation in the China market.
6. Hay's second Open Door notes were intended to prevent European nations from colonizing China.

Chapter Review, text page 455

1. (a) Few Americans had interest in foreign affairs after the Civil War. (b) By the 1880s many Americans had begun to dream of overseas expansion. (c) Economic growth and the closing of the frontier inspired these dreams.
2. (a) France in Mexico (1866): the French had established a puppet government in Mexico. The United States moved 50,000 troops to the Mexican border, making its opposition to French intentions clear. (b) France in Panama (1878): President Hayes condemned the French attempt to build a canal across Panama, but malaria actually pushed them out. (c) Great Britain in Venezuela (1895): during a border dispute between Venezuela and the British colony of Guiana, Britain dismissed the United States' offer of mediation. In doing so Britain rejected the United States' position that the Monroe Doctrine

gave it the right to intervene in Latin American affairs. To avoid conflict, Britain agreed to have an independent commission settle the border dispute.
3. (a) Turner believed that the United States should expand overseas markets because the frontier was shrinking and Americans needed new outlets for economic expansion. (b) Mahan favored expansion because he thought the expanding industrial capacity of the United States required markets abroad. Strong favored expansion because he believed the white race had been divinely chosen to civilize the world.
4. (a) In the 1800s the United States was particularly interested in the Hawaiian Islands as a stopover point in trade with China. (b) Events leading to the American annexation of Hawaii: Americans organized the overthrow of Queen Liliuokalani in January 1893. Then with the help of the U.S. Marines, they set up a new government. Cleveland opposed the annexation, but it was finally completed during McKinley's administration. (c) President Cleveland opposed the annexation because he was outraged at the actions of the American sugar growers and the role of the marines in the revolt.
5. Each of the following contributed to the outbreak of the Spanish-American War: (a) Jingoism created popular support for a warlike foreign policy. (b) General Weyler's policies and actions in Cuba fanned anti-Spanish feeling in the United States. (c) Some newspapers tried to increase circulation by printing sensational stories that depicted Spain as a villain. Yellow journalism, as this style of newspaper writing has come to be called, stirred up reader emotions and encouraged the clamor for war. (d) sinking of the *Maine:* this act outraged the American public and created a call for war.
6. (a) McKinley installed an American governor in Cuba after the Spanish-American War because the island was in a state of chaos, with government at a standstill, sanitation almost nonexistent, and disease widespread. (b) Under the Platt Amendment, Cuba had to agree not to make treaties or loans that would endanger its independence, to give the United States two naval stations on the island, and to recognize the right of the United States to send in troops to protect life, liberty, or property.
7. (a) In the late 1800s missionaries were interested in converting the Chinese to Christianity, and merchants wanted to take part in the China trade. (b) European governments with influence in China kept the Americans out. (c) In reaction Hay wrote a series of letters urging acceptance of three principles: European governments would allow other nations to trade within their spheres of influence; tariffs in China would be collected by the Chinese,

not by foreign powers; European powers would refrain from charging harbor or railroad duties in their spheres that discriminated against other powers.

8. (a) The Boxer Rebellion was a Chinese nationalist rebellion against Europeans. (b) The Boxer Rebellion was not successful. Military reinforcements sent by the United States and the European powers repressed the Boxers.

For Further Thought, text page 455

1. Developments confirmed Sumner's argument. Students should discuss the fact that the United States was involved militarily for three years in an attempt to crush the Filipino revolt.
2. (a) McKinley believed that the Filipinos "were unfit for self-government" and that the United States had a responsibility to Christianize them. (b) Answers may vary, but students should note that most Filipinos were already Christians.

Developing Basic Skills, text page 455

1. Territories acquired by the United States between 1865 and 1901: Hawaii, Alaska, Midway Island, Guam, Wake, the Philippines, part of Samoa, Puerto Rico. (a) Hawaii and Alaska are states. The Midway Islands, Puerto Rico, Guam, Wake, and part of Samoa are United States possessions. The Philippines are independent. (b) In the late 1800s all of these were U.S. territories. (c) Research will vary.
2. Answers will vary. Students should recognize these causes of the Spanish-American War: American jingoism, Cuban revolution and Weyler's atrocities, yellow journalism, sinking of the *Maine*, expansionist sentiment, reform sentiment.

Unit Seven: Entering a Modern Age

25 The Progressives (1900–1909)

Section Review, text page 463

1. *muckraker:* journalist intent on reforming society through the reporting of corruption or health hazards in government, business, or factory conditions.

Lincoln Steffens: writer whose book *The Shame of Cities* called attention to corruption in city government. *John Spargo:* journalist whose book *The Bitter Cry of Children* exposed the abuses of child labor in the coal mines. *Ray Stannard Baker:* writer for McClure's magazine whose articles exposed abuses in railroads and the terror of lynchings. *Ida Tarbell:* writer who focused on the ruthless tactics used by John D. Rockefeller against his competitors in her book *The History of the Standard Oil Company*. *NAACP:* National Association for the Advancement of Colored People, an organization founded in 1909 by black and white progressives to provide legal counsel and aid to black people. *Florence Kelley:* successful progressive reformer who led the National Consumers League in its campaign for better working conditions for women and children.

2. Urban, college-educated, middle-class people, including reporters, professors, teachers, doctors, nurses, and business people, formed the core of the progressive movement.
3. Progressive reformers were concerned with corruption in government, making local government more responsive to the needs of the people, unsafe working conditions, health hazards such as spoiled food, slum housing, and regulation of the business practices of the country's monopolies. (Students should receive credit for listing three concerns.)
4. In its early years the NAACP provided legal aid to black citizens, fought for passage of a federal anti-lynching law, and investigated race riots and lynchings.
5. Four types of legislation passed to protect working people included minimum wage laws for women, state-sponsored industrial accident insurance plans, laws prohibiting children from working at night, and improved factory safety regulations.
6. The National Consumers League favored boycotting companies with unsafe working conditions and purchasing only those products that carried the Consumers League label.

Section Review, text page 465

1. *Robert La Follette:* Wisconsin governor elected in 1900; he instituted many progressive reforms to make state government more democratic and efficient; nicknamed "Battlin' Bob." *Wisconsin Idea:* La Follette's program for the reform of state government; became a national model, a so-called "laboratory for democracy." *Woodrow Wilson:* New Jersey governor who instituted such reforms as the state regulation of railroads and utilities, the direct primary, and a system of industrial accident insurance.

2. *primary election:* election held before the general elections to pick a political party's candidate. *initiative:* a measure that allows citizens to propose a bill by collecting a required number of signatures from registered voters. *referendum:* the practice of allowing voters to vote directly on a measure proposed by the legislature or by popular initiative. *recall election:* a special election that allows voters to vote on the removal of elected officials before completion of their terms. *city manager:* a professional administrator hired by an elected board of trustees of a city to manage the city government.
3. Greater efficiency and democracy were two main pillars of progressive reform.
4. Governor La Follette hired economists, engineers, and social workers from the University of Wisconsin faculty to draft legislation and sit on government commissions, such as his railroad rate commissions.

Section Review, text page 467

1. *Northern Securities Company* v. *United States:* 1907 case in which the Supreme Court ruled that Northern Securities had violated the Sherman Antitrust Act; the Court ordered that the company be broken up.
2. Before becoming President, Theodore Roosevelt had served in the New York state legislature, as a commissioner of the U.S. Civil Service Commission and of the New York City police force, and as an assistant secretary of the navy. He had also been governor of New York and Vice-President of the United States.
3. Roosevelt did not oppose all big businesses, only those he felt acted irresponsibly, such as those that endangered public safety or failed to accept negotiation.
4. When coal mine owners refused to negotiate with striking workers in 1902, Roosevelt threatened to send in troops to run the mines. The owners then agreed to negotiate.
5. The first task undertaken by the Department of Commerce and Labor was gathering facts about American business and publicizing information about industry through its Bureau of Corporations.

Section Review, text page 470

1. *Upton Sinclair:* muckraking writer whose book *The Jungle* exposed unsanitary conditions in the meatpacking industry. *Meat Inspection Act:* federal law that provided for the hiring of federal inspectors to enforce health and sanitation standards in the interstate meatpacking industry. *Pure Food and Drug Act:* federal law prohibiting use of harmful additives in foods and use of misleading statements in drug advertisements. *Hepburn Act:* federal act giving the Interstate Commerce Commission (ICC) the power to set maximum shipping rates for the railroads and placing such transportation, facilities as ferries and oil pipelines under ICC supervision. *John Muir:* conservationist who helped convince Roosevelt of the need for a national conservation program. *Gifford Pinchot:* chief of the United States Forest Service under Roosevelt; believed in multiple uses for forest land and planned harvests of trees. *William Howard Taft:* secretary of war under Roosevelt, then Republican nominee for President who succeeded Roosevelt in the White House.
2. After reading *The Jungle* Roosevelt pressed Congress to pass a meat inspection law. He stirred public interest in the bill's passage and encouraged the Republican leadership of the House and Senate to work out a compromise bill when the two houses disagreed.
3. By threatening to lower import tariffs, Roosevelt convinced Senate conservatives to vote for the Hepburn Act.
4. Pinchot believed that forests could have many uses, including recreational and planned industrial uses, while Muir felt strongly that the wilderness should be left alone.
5. Roosevelt's calls for inheritance and income taxes, workers' compensation, more regulation of interstate commerce and of stock sales, federal investigation of labor disputes, and other progressive reforms deepened the split within the Republican party.

Chapter Review, text page 471

1. (a) Typically, progressives were middle-class city dwellers and college-educated professionals. (b) Most progressives shared the belief that the United States needed to be reformed and the confidence that it could be. (c) Not all progressives pursued the same reform goals. Some fought government corruption; others sought regulation of powerful monopolies or legislation against unsafe working conditions, spoiled food, and slum housing.
2. (a) Muckrakers were crusading journalists who sought to reform society by exposing unsafe or unfair practices in government, business, and industry. (b) Muckrakers contributed to reform efforts by raising public awareness of urgent social and economic problems.
3. (a) Some progressives, believing in the superiority of the white race, ignored segregation and discrimination or worked to strengthen Jim Crow laws. Others, shocked by racial discrimination, felt the

rights of blacks should be protected. (b) Concerned progressives formed the NAACP to protect the rights of blacks through legal services and through investigation of race riots and lynchings.

4. (a) Progressives fought for legislation to improve conditions for workers and to protect workers' rights. (b) The progressives were successful in getting minimum wage laws for women passed in 12 states between 1912 and 1917. In addition, by 1917, 30 states had industrial accident insurance plans and several states had passed laws prohibiting employment of children at night.

5. (a) Progressives believed primary elections would make the electoral process more democratic by allowing voters to choose among several candidates for a political party nomination. (b) They believed the initiative would give voters more say in law making by allowing voters to propose a bill. (c) Progressives believed the referendum made government more responsive by allowing voters to vote directly on an issue. (d) Progressives believed the recall election made the electoral process more responsive by allowing voters to express their dissatisfaction with elected officials before the completion of their terms.

6. (a) Roosevelt believed in the government's right to control business abuses and supervise business practices, particularly when he felt big business had not acted in the public interest. (b) By ordering his attorney general to prosecute the Northern Securities Company as a violator of the Sherman Antitrust Act, Roosevelt renewed judicial action against the trusts. The government prosecuted the beef, oil, and tobacco trusts during his administration. In the coal miners' strike of 1902, Roosevelt threatened the use of troops to run the mines when coal mine owners refused to negotiate. This ended the strike. By establishing the Department of Commerce and Labor to gather facts about American business and bring them to the attention of the public, Roosevelt also facilitated government supervision of business practices.

7. (a) The publication of Upton Sinclair's book *The Jungle*, exposing the unsanitary conditions in the meatpacking industry, generated public support for federal inspection of meatpacking plants. Dr. Harvey Wiley of the Department of Agriculture exposed the dangers of chemical additives in canned foods, while muckraker Samuel Hopkins publicized misleading and fraudulent claims in the nonprescription drug industry. (b) The Meat Inspection Act and the Pure Food and Drug Act were passed in 1906 to deal with these problems. The Meat Inspection Act provided for the enforcement of health and sanitary standards in the interstate meatpacking industry. The Pure Food and Drug Act banned the

use of harmful additives in foods and forbade misleading drug advertising.

8. (a) Roosevelt favored multiple uses of natural resources, believing for example that trees could be harvested without destroying the forests. Roosevelt favored a balanced conservation program. (b) He supported not only the 1906 Forest Homestead Act, which opened up certain forest land for agricultural use, but also a 1907 act that prevented the cutting of government timberland. He also created five national wilderness areas.

For Further Thought, text page 471

1. (a) Roosevelt's trustbusting activities against the Northern Securities Company and the beef, oil, and tobacco trusts, his creation of the Department of Commerce and Labor, and his fight for passage of laws on food, drugs, and railroad rates all increased the role of the federal government in the national economy. His threat to use force against the coal owners during the coal strike of 1902 demonstrated the power the federal government could exercise over business. (b) Answers relating to the wisdom of Roosevelt's policies should refer to their impact on specific problems.

2. (a) People whose business practices were likely to be affected by muckraker publicity were angry about the muckrakers' activities. (b) Answers will vary. Students might mention the television program *Sixty Minutes*, which features the work of investigative journalists. In the early 1970s Bob Woodward and Carl Bernstein of the Washington *Post* worked to expose the Watergate scandal.

Developing Basic Skills, text page 471

1. Research will vary.
2. See the chart on page A 81. (a) All of the new laws reflected the concerns of progressives. (b) Progressives were not entirely happy with the Meat Inspection Act of 1906 because the government had to pay the salaries of meat inspectors. The Forest Homestead Act may have caused concern to strict conservationists.

26 Reform Continues (1909–1919)

Section Review, text page 475

1. *Payne-Aldrich Tariff:* a tariff reduction bill sponsored by Sereno Payne in 1909 and amended by Nelson Aldrich; the bill actually raised the tariff on

Legislation	Problem	Solution
Meat Inspection Act (1906)	unsanitary conditions in meatpacking plants	government enforcement of sanitary and health standards in meatpacking plants
Pure Food and Drug Act (1906)	misleading advertising and harmul additives in canned foods	barred false advertising and harmful additives in foods
Hepburn Act (1906)	excessive railroad shipping rates	gave the Interstate Commerce Commission the power to set maximum freight rates
Forest Homestead Act (1906)	controversy over conservation of natural resources	opened up forest lands for agricultural use

500 frequently used items. *Joseph Cannon:* powerful and conservative Republican representative from Illinois who served as speaker of the house in the early twentieth century. *Richard Ballinger:* secretary of the interior under President Taft; allowed the government to sell certain wilderness areas over the objections of conservationists. *Mann-Elkins Act:* 1910 legislative act that gave the Interstate Commerce Commission the power to regulate telegraph and railroad company rates even without complaints from customers. *New Nationalism:* phrase used by Roosevelt in a 1910 speech to describe a program of reforms advocated by progressive Republicans.

2. (a) Progressives opposed high tariffs because they believed tariffs were unfair to American consumers. (b) Progressives were dismayed by Taft's support of the Payne-Aldrich Tariff.

3. Joe Cannon's position as speaker of the house made him a powerful figure in the House of Representatives.

4. Taft continued progressive reform in several ways: (1) by continuing to set aside public lands for conservation and by supporting new conservation laws; (2) by continuing prosecution of the trusts; (3) by supporting the Mann-Elkins Act; (4) by creating a new Children's Bureau in the Labor Department; (5) by approving new safety regulations for mines and railroads; (6) by establishing an eight-hour work day for government workers and an increased number of Civil Service positions. (Students should receive credit for listing three of the ways mentioned above.)

5. Theodore Roosevelt's call for a program of progressive reform called the "New Nationalism" helped split the Republican party in 1910.

Section Review, text page 477

1. *Progressive party:* new political party launched by Theodore Roosevelt and his supporters in the 1912 presidential election. *New Freedom:* phrase used by Democratic presidential candidate Woodrow Wilson to describe his political platform in the 1912 election. *Eugene V. Debs:* one of the founders of the Socialist party and its presidential nominee in the 1912 election. *Socialist party:* political party founded in 1901 that favored government ownership of business and supported rights of workers to join unions.

2. Theodore Roosevelt's disappointment with Taft's performance in office and his own failure to gain the Republican nomination for President led him to leave the Republican party in 1912.

3. Wilson believed that trusts should be broken up because they strangled competition and could not be regulated successfully by government. Roosevelt disagreed, believing the federal government could be given the power to successfully regulate trusts rather than disband them.

4. Eugene V. Debs believed that businesses should be publicly rather than privately run and favored government ownership of all large businesses.

Section Review, text page 480

1. *Underwood-Simmons Tariff Act:* 1913 law that substantially lowered the duty on imports and enacted a graduated income tax. *Federal Reserve Act:* 1913 law that transformed the nation's banking system; it divided the nation into 12 districts with a federal reserve bank in each district and a Federal Reserve

Board in Washington, D.C., supervising the banking system. *Federal Trade Commission:* commission created by the Federal Trade Commission Act (1914) to preserve competition by preventing one firm from destroying another through unfair business practices. *Clayton Antitrust Act:* 1914 law that prohibited pricing policies that might destroy competition, outlawed the purchase of stock in competing firms, and made the use of interlocking directorates illegal; the law was designed to strengthen the Sherman Antitrust Act.

2. *graduated income tax:* a form of income tax whereby people with higher incomes pay higher taxes. *interlocking directorate:* a monopolistic system, made illegal by the Clayton Antitrust Act, in which the same people could serve on the boards of directors of several firms within the same industry.

3. Woodrow Wilson believed that competition from foreign firms through lower tariffs would force American industry to become more efficient, to improve its products, and to lower prices. Wilson believed this would benefit the economy.

4. To increase the money supply the Federal Reserve Board could lower interest rates on loans made by federal reserve banks to private banks.

5. The Clayton Antitrust Act outlawed the following: pricing policies destructive to competition, the purchase of stock in competing firms, the use of interlocking directorates to stifle competition, and the prosecution of labor unions under antitrust laws. (Students should receive credit for listing two practices.)

6. Examples of social reform legislation passed during the Wilson administration include the Seaman Act (1915), establishing minimum standards for treatment of merchant sailors; the Adamson Act (1916), setting an eight-hour work day for railroad workers; the Workingmen's Compensation Act (1916), providing financial assistance to disabled federal civil service employees; the Child Labor Act (1916), prohibiting interstate sale of goods produced by child labor; and the Farm Loan Act (1916), making it easier for farmers to get loans. (Students should receive credit for listing three examples.)

Section Review, text page 484

1. *Women's Christian Temperance Union:* group led by Francis Willard that fought for the prohibition of liquor. *Anti-Saloon League:* along with the Women's Christian Temperance Union, led the drive for prohibition. *Carrie Chapman Catt:* leader of the National American Woman Suffrage Association. *Alice Paul:* founder and leader of the Women's party; introduced militant tactics to the campaign for women's suffrage.

2. *prohibition:* ban on the sale and manufacture of alcoholic beverages.

3. Progressives favored an income tax for two reasons: (1) it provided revenue to pay for progressive reforms, and (2) a graduated income tax placed greater tax burdens on the wealthy than on the poor.

4. Progressives believed that direct election of senators would reduce political corruption by ending the possibility of special interest groups bribing legislators to elect favored candidates and by reducing the control of political machines over the election of senators.

5. (a) Advocates of prohibition believed excessive drinking ruined families, caused industrial accidents, and attracted people to saloons, which were seen as centers of immorality and corruption. (b) The United States entry into World War I gave prohibitionists a patriotic rationale for their cause. They argued that a ban on alcohol would help the war effort by increasing industrial efficiency and by insuring that grain was used to feed soldiers rather than make alcohol.

6. To call attention to the suffrage movement Alice Paul organized a large march through Washington, D.C., on Wilson's inauguration day. This was followed by daily picketing of the White House and hunger strikes while Paul and other pickets were in prison.

Chapter Review, text page 485

1. (a) Taft alienated progressives by calling the Payne-Aldrich Tariff "the best bill that the Republican party ever passed." (b) In addition, after first agreeing to aid progressives, Taft changed his mind and supported Cannon's reelection as speaker of the house when conservatives promised to cooperate with him on other issues. (c) In the Ballinger-Pinchot controversy, Taft fired Gifford Pinchot, who had attacked the administration's position on conservation; Taft thus alienated progressives who supported Pinchot.

2. Taft continued progressive reform in several ways: by initiating 90 antitrust suits against such companies as Standard Oil and the American Tobacco Company, by supporting the Mann-Elkins Act, by creating a Children's Bureau within the Labor Department, and by approving legislation to improve conditions for workers.

3. (a) Theodore Roosevelt decided to become involved in politics again when progressive Republicans asked for his support in the congressional elections of 1910. (b) Roosevelt proposed a program of progressive reforms called the New Nationalism. (c) Roosevelt's actions divided the Republican party.

4. (a) The Progressive party was founded to provide a voice for progressives dissatisfied with the Republican party and to nominate Theodore Roosevelt for President. (b) The Progressive platform called for such reform measures as initiative and referendum legislation, women's suffrage, direct presidential primaries, government regulation of large businesses, passage of a minimum wage law, unemployment insurance, and worker's compensation insurance.

5. (a) President Wilson favored a reduction of tariffs because he believed American businesses would be more efficient and creative when faced with foreign competition and because he believed reduced tariffs would lead to lower prices. (b) Representatives of such industries as lumber, steel, and wool opposed tariff reductions, fearing greater competition from abroad. (c) The Underwood-Simmons Tariff Act substantially lowered the duty on imports for the first time since the Civil War and provided for a graduated income tax.

6. (a) The financial panic of 1907 made many Americans feel that to insure a reliable credit supply the banking system needed reform. (b) The system established by the Federal Reserve Act divided the nation into 12 districts, with a federal reserve bank for each district. The national banks in each district deposited their monetary reserves in the district federal reserve bank. The Federal Reserve Board in Washington, D.C., controlled this system by setting interest rates on loans made by federal reserve banks to private banks. (c) By lowering or raising interest rates the Federal Reserve Board could control the amount of money in circulation.

7. (a) The two laws supported by Woodrow Wilson to control monopolies were the Federal Trade Commission Act (1914) and the Clayton Antitrust Act (1914). (b) The Federal Trade Commission Act created the Federal Trade Commission, which sought to preserve competition by preventing unfair business practices. The Clayton Antitrust Act prohibited noncompetitive pricing policies and the use of interlocking directorates. It also recognized the rights of workers to strike and picket, and barred the prosecution of labor unions under antitrust laws.

8. (a) Woodrow Wilson's interest in economic fairness made him hesitant to support social legislation that benefited only certain groups of people. (b) Reform measures passed during Wilson's administration included the Seaman Act (1915), the Workingmen's Compensation Act (1916), the Child Labor Act (1916), and the Farm Loan Act (1916). (c) Because of his attitude toward segregation, black leaders were especially disappointed by Wilson.

9. (a) Between 1913 and 1920 the Sixteenth through Nineteenth Amendments were ratified. (b) The Sixteenth Amendment gave Congress the power to authorize and collect income taxes. The Seventeenth Amendment required the direct election of senators. The Eighteenth Amendment banned the sale or manufacture of alcoholic beverages, and the Nineteenth Amendment gave women the right to vote.

10. (a) Progressives supported an income tax because it provided revenue to pay for progressive reforms and would be fair, they thought, since it placed the heaviest tax burden on the rich. (b) Many Americans were opposed to an income tax because they did not feel the government was entitled to the money they earned or because they did not favor the programs tax revenues would finance.

For Further Thought, text page 485

1. Students should recognize that during the progressive era a larger number of people than ever before favored the kinds of reforms called for by the Progressive party platform. Theodore Roosevelt's popularity and record as a former President may have added to its appeal.

2. As women entered the work force in large numbers, gaining some economic independence, they became more willing to organize and fight for their political rights. Increased interest in and acceptance of reform in many areas of social life during the progressive era also helped the suffrage movement succeed. Finally, the widespread acceptance of women's suffrage at the state and local level in the West and Midwest made its eventual ratification as a constitutional amendment more likely.

3. Supporters of the New Freedom wanted to break up trusts, while supporters of the New Nationalism wanted to put them under government supervision. Students might argue that the New Freedom approach was impractical in that the break-up of trusts would dismantle efficient business organizations and thus disrupt the economy. Critics of the New Nationalism might suggest that government regulation of the scope envisioned by Roosevelt would stifle private initiative.

Developing Basic Skills, text page 485

1. (a) The Seventeenth Amendment changed part of the original Constitution. (b) The clause "chosen by legislatures thereof" was altered. (c) The Eighteenth Amendment was eventually repealed. Reasons as to why may vary. Students might discuss how difficult it is to control people's personal lives.

President Roosevelt	President Taft	President Wilson
prosecution of Northern Securities Company	Mann-Elkins Act	Underwood-Simmons Tariff Act
Department of Commerce and Labor	Children's Bureau, Department of Labor	Federal Reserve Act
Meat Inspection Act	prosecution of Standard Oil and American Tobacco Company	Federal Trade Commission Act
Pure Food and Drug Act		Clayton Antitrust Act
Hepburn Act		Workingmen's Compensation Act
restrictions on lumbering on some government land		Child Labor Act

2. See the chart above. Answers may differ concerning which President best represented the progressive era. Accept answers students can support with evidence.

27 The United States in World Affairs (1900–1916)

Caption, text page 488

The cartoonist probably agreed with Roosevelt. The title suggests that Roosevelt is playing the part of the world's policeman. Roosevelt seems to be protecting Latin America from greedy Europeans.

Section Review, text page 489

1. *Roosevelt Corollary:* corollary to the Monroe Doctrine formulated by Theodore Roosevelt; it asserted the rights of the United States to exercise "international police power" in Latin America.
2. American merchant ships carrying goods abroad were protected by United States navy warships.
3. (a) In his role as mediator, President Roosevelt helped resolve the 1902 Venezuelan crisis by guaranteeing United States protection of Venezuelan territory against German seizure and by suggesting arbitration of the dispute by the Hague Court. (b) In 1905 President Roosevelt persuaded Dominican Republic officials to allow American supervision of their nation's debt repayment to Germany, Italy, and France.
4. The Roosevelt Corollary changed the Monroe Doctrine from a policy designed solely to protect the Americas from European intervention to one justifying United States intervention in Latin America.
5. During the 1906 rebellion in Cuba the United States sent Secretary of War William Howard Taft to Cuba to stop the fighting and set up a temporary government of American civilians. Backed by 5,000 troops, this government remained in power for 28 months.

Section Review, text page 492

1. *Clayton-Bulwer Treaty:* 1850 treaty between the United States and England providing for joint control of a future canal in Panama or Nicaragua. *Hay-Pauncefote Treaty:* 1901 treaty between Great Britain and the United States giving the United States sole right to build, operate, and fortify a canal across Panama or Nicaragua. *Philippe Bunau-Varilla:* French citizen who, with United States support, led the successful revolt of Panamanian rebels against Colombia in 1903.
2. The construction of a canal across the Isthmus of Panama would link the Pacific and Atlantic coasts of the United States, shortening the distance by sea between New York and San Francisco by over 7,500 miles. The canal would thus reduce shipping costs and allow the United States to maintain a single navy rather than two separate navies in the Atlantic and Pacific oceans.
3. The Colombian government was interested in the American offer to buy land for a canal but asked for more money than President Roosevelt was willing to pay.
4. The United States government supported the Panamanian revolt and sent troops to block the Colombian army's advance. The United States officially recognized Panama two days after the new nation declared independence.
5. Colonel William C. Gorgas prepared the way for the digging of the Panama Canal by draining swamps, cutting down brush, and destroying marshes where mosquitoes that carried yellow fever or malaria and rats carrying bubonic plague might breed.

Section Review, text page **495**

1. *Treaty of Portsmouth:* 1905 agreement between Japan and Russia recognizing Japan's victory in the Russo-Japanese war and giving Japan Port Arthur in Manchuria, the southern half of Sakhalin Island, and control of the Manchurian railroads. *"dollar diplomacy":* term describing Taft's foreign policy of encouraging financial investments in Asia as a means of increasing American power in the area.
2. (a) In Manchuria Japan hoped to find raw materials to aid its industrial growth. (b) Russia wanted to claim and use Manchuria's resources.
3. At President Roosevelt's invitation, Russian and Japanese representatives attended a peace conference in Portsmouth, New Hampshire, where, through Roosevelt's efforts, the Treaty of Portsmouth was negotiated.
4. Harassment of Japanese immigrants and segregation of San Francisco's Asian students in a special school led to increased friction between Japan and the United States.
5. President Taft hoped to further American interests in Asia through so-called dollar diplomacy, the use of financial investments, and increased commerce to heighten American influence in the area.

Section Review, text page **498**

1. *"moral diplomacy":* term describing Woodrow Wilson's approach to foreign policy, which emphasized the use of negotiation and arbitration rather than force to settle disputes. *Victoriano Huerta:* Mexican general who seized control of the Mexican government in 1913, starting a civil war. *Venustiano Carranza:* General Huerta's opponent and the eventual victor in the Mexican civil war; he assumed control of the Mexican government in 1914. *Francisco "Pancho" Villa:* Mexican opponent of Carranza whose anti-American raids led President Wilson to send American troops into Mexico. *John Pershing:* brigadier general who led American troops into Mexico to capture Pancho Villa.
2. The purpose of the "cooling-off" treaties negotiated by Secretary of State Bryan was to foster world peace by encouraging disputants to refrain from acts of war or arms build-ups for one year while an international committee investigated their disputes.
3. Bryan and Wilson used troops in Haiti in 1915 and in the Dominican Republic in 1916.
4. (a) In 1914 the United States and Mexico avoided war by agreeing to let Argentina, Brazil, and Chile mediate their differences. (b) Pancho Villa's shooting of 17 Americans in Mexico and his raid on Columbus, New Mexico, led to American intervention in Mexico in 1916.

Chapter Review, text page **499**

1. (a) President Roosevelt believed that the United States had a "mission" as a "superior country" to carry out an international police duty. (b) Roosevelt performed that "duty" in Venezuela by warning Germany that he would use force to protect Venezuelan territory from seizure. (c) He performed that "duty" in the Dominican Republic by supervising Dominican finances to insure repayment of that country's debts to Germany, Italy, and France.
2. (a) The Roosevelt Corollary to the Monroe Doctrine asserted the right of the United States to intervene in Latin American affairs. (b) Applying his corollary in Cuba, Roosevelt sent American troops to stop a Cuban rebellion and support a temporary government led by American civilians. (c) President Taft used the Roosevelt Corollary to justify sending American troops into Nicaragua and Honduras to impose order.
3. (a) The United States wanted to construct a canal across the Isthmus of Panama to reduce the cost of shipping, enable the United States to maintain a single navy for the Atlantic and Pacific oceans, and shorten the distance from New York to San Francisco by sea. (b) To gain control of the canal zone for the United States, President Roosevelt negotiated the Hay-Pauncefote treaty with Great Britain and offered to purchase the land for the canal from Colombia. When his offer was rejected, he supported the Panamanians in their revolt against Colombian rule. (c) United States support of the Panamanian revolt and its rapid recognition of Panamanian independence led the new Panamanian government to grant the United States control of the canal zone on favorable terms.
4. (a) Before work on the Panama Canal could begin, the United States had to rid the canal zone of such diseases as yellow fever, malaria, and bubonic plague. (b) The problem of disease was solved by exterminating rats, which were carriers of the plague, draining swamps, cutting down brush, and destroying grassy marshes where mosquitoes carrying yellow fever or malaria bred.
5. (a) In 1905 Russian and Japan went to war over control of Manchuria. (b) The war was won by Japan, who by treaty received Port Arthur, the southern half of Sakhalin Island, and control of the Manchurian railroads. (c) The United States invited Russia and Japan to a peace conference in Portsmouth, New Hampshire. Through President Roosevelt's efforts, the two nations agreed to the Treaty of Portsmouth, which ended the war. (d) As a result of the peace treaty, the United States

was assured that China would be kept open to trade with all nations.

6. (a) After the Russo-Japanese War United States relations with both countries were strained because the Russians blamed Roosevelt for their losses in the Treaty of Portsmouth and the Japanese feared that the Open Door policy would decrease their supply of Manchurian raw materials. (b) To ease tensions with Japan, President Roosevelt sent Secretary of War Taft to Japan to negotiate an agreement that acknowledged Japanese control over Korea. (c) Threats and discrimination against Japanese Americans on the west coast and the 1906 San Francisco Board of Education decision to segregate Asian students created strains in United States–Japanese relations. (d) President Roosevelt denounced the school board's action and negotiated an agreement with the board to return the Japanese children to their regular schools. Further Japanese immigration was restricted.

7. (a) The term "dollar diplomacy" referred to President Taft's foreign policy of encouraging financial investments and commercial ventures abroad as a means of fostering United States interests. (b) Dollar diplomacy had little effect on Asian affairs. (c) President Taft was able to use dollar diplomacy in Latin America.

8. (a) The goals of Woodrow Wilson's "moral diplomacy" were to support democracy, maintain peace, and secure American economic interests abroad. (b) To put this diplomacy into action President Wilson and Secretary of State Bryan initiated a series of "cooling off" treaties. According to these treaties 29 nations agreed to refrain from acts of war or arms build-ups for one year while their disputes were submitted to an international committee for arbitration. In Asia they pursued this policy by ending American participation in a China railway consortium that Wilson feared would endanger Chinese independence. (c) The policy faltered in Japan when Wilson failed to enforce America's treaty obligations to treat Japanese immigrants fairly.

9. (a) Wilson's and Bryans's ideas of "moral diplomacy" were not carried out in Nicaragua, the Dominican Republic, and Haiti. (b) In Nicaragua, Bryan agreed to a treaty that authorized United States intervention in Nicaraguan internal affairs. In the Dominican Republic, he sent U.S. Marines to end a civil war. In Haiti, internal turmoil in 1915 prompted the United States to send in marines to restore order and protect American property and banking interests. To end the bloodshed the Haitian government agreed to a treaty establishing a United States protectorate over Haiti.

10. (a) By "watchful waiting" Wilson hoped to see the Mexican civil war lead to a constitutional government that would meet the needs of all Mexicans and establish friendly relations with the United States. (b) Wilson first tried to influence the outcome of the war by banning arms shipments to Mexico after Huerta proclaimed himself dictator. He then offered to mediate the dispute between Carranza and Huerta and somewhat indiscreetly offered to support the Carranza faction if it agreed to establish a constitutional government. (c) The United States sent troops into Mexico in 1916 to capture Pancho Villa and his followers.

For Further Thought, text page 499

1. (a) *"big stick" policy:* President Roosevelt believed a powerful military force was the best means of assuring American interests and security abroad. *"dollar diplomacy":* President Taft sought to avoid military conflicts, believing American financial and commercial investments would do more to further American foreign policy. *"moral diplomacy":* President Wilson believed in the use of negotiation and arbitration rather than force or finance as the basis of foreign policy. (b) Answers may vary. Students should recognize that each President did become militarily involved in the affairs of other countries, whether he wanted to or not. (c) Answers will vary but should examine the goals of each policy and the methods employed to achieve them. (d) Students should note that since the Vietnam War there has been a decrease in the willingness of the United States to send troops to other nations. This should be contrasted with the frequent dispatch of troops in the early 1900s.

2. The construction of the Panama Canal and the harassment of Japanese immigrants are two examples.

3. Students should make reference to United States construction of the Panama Canal, the application of the "big stick" policy in Latin America, the enforcement of the Open Door Policy in China, and the United States' growing foreign commerce. Accept answers that are supported by relevant data.

4. (a) Answers should refer to Wilson's inexperience in foreign affairs. The governorship of New Jersey, not diplomatic experience, was Wilson's steppingstone to the presidency. (b) Wilson thought of himself as a progressive reformer who would tackle domestic problems.

Developing Basic Skills text page 499

1. Actions to include in time line: purchase of Alaska (1867); the *Alabama* Claims (1879); U.S. shares control of Samoa with Great Britain and Germany (1889); Spanish-American War begins (1898); annexation of Hawaii (1898); Hay-Pauncefonte Treaty (1901); U.S. granted canal zone (1903); Roosevelt

Corollary to Monroe Doctrine (1904); U.S. supervises finances of Dominican Republic, initiates Treaty of Portsmouth (1905); U.S. restores order in Cuba (1906); U.S. Marines sent to Haiti (1915); U.S. troops enter Mexico to search for Pancho Villa, U.S. troops sent to Dominican Republic (1916). (a) There was little activity in the 1860s and 1870s. (b) The United States acquired new territory in the 1860s, 1880s, and 1890s. (c) The United States intervened militarily in other nations in the 1900s and 1910s. (d) Accept all answers that refer to the nation's ability to use force, money, and diplomacy to shape world affairs.

2. (a) Russia, Japan, Germany, France, and Great Britain all claimed spheres of influence in China. (b) Great Britain, France, the Netherlands, the United States, and Japan claimed territories in Asia. (c) The United States claimed the Philippine Islands. (d) Conflict could be expected to occur along the China coast and in Manchuria.

28 The World at War (1914–1919)

Caption, text page 501

Spain, the Netherlands, Switzerland, Albania, Denmark, Norway, Sweden, and Spanish Morocco remained neutral during World War I.

Section Review, text page 505

1. *Central Powers:* the alliance of Austria-Hungary and Germany. *Allies:* the alliance of Great Britain, France, and Russia. *Lusitania:* British passenger ship sunk by a German submarine in 1915. *Charles Evans Hughes:* Supreme Court justice and Republican nominee for President in the 1916 election. *Zimmerman Telegram:* secret note from German Foreign Minister Arthur Zimmerman to German minister in Mexico, urging Mexico and Japan to join the Central Powers if the United States entered the war in Europe.
2. When war first broke out, President Wilson followed a policy of neutrality.
3. (a) Both the Central Powers and the Allies tried to influence American public opinion through propaganda in American newspapers. (b) The propaganda effort of the Allies was more successful.
4. After an initial slump, the war in Europe created a boom for the United States economy.
5. (a) International law, which required that a ship give warning before attacking, was difficult for submarines to follow because submarines were slow-moving on the surface and could not risk surfacing to warn their targets. (b) President Wilson reacted to the German attacks on unarmed ships by

issuing protests to the German government. (c) After the sinking of the *Sussex* in March 1916 Germany agreed to suspend unannounced attacks.
6. The three events that eventually led to American entry into the war were the sinking of ships by submarines, the publication of the "Zimmerman Telegram," and the Russian Revolution.

Section Review, text page 509

1. *War Industries Board:* board created by President Wilson in 1917 to spur industrial production and coordinate wartime activities. *Bernard Baruch:* chairman of the War Industries Board. *William Gibbs McAdoo:* appointed by President Wilson (his father-in-law) to head the United States Railroad Administration; he organized all the nation's rail lines into a single network. *National War Labor Board:* board created by President Wilson in 1918 to unify labor policies; the board served as arbitrator of disputes between management and labor. *Herbert Hoover:* engineer and self-made millionaire appointed by President Wilson to head the Food Administration; through his efforts food production tripled. *Committee on Public Information:* committee created by President Wilson to solidify public support for the war effort. *George Creel:* head of the Committee on Public Information.
2. To raise an army to fight in Europe the United States instituted a draft and launched a patriotic appeal for voluntary enlistments.
3. To mobilize industry the War Industries Board established controls over scarce materials like steel, set prices, and standardized production.
4. The government improved conditions for workers by insisting on an eight-hour work day in some industries, setting standards for employment of women and children, and demanding decent wages for workers.
5. During the war the American public contributed to increased food production by observing meatless and breadless days and by planting "victory" gardens in their backyards.
6. The purpose of the Committee on Public Information was to increase public support for the war.

Section Review, text page 512

1. *Fourteen Points:* document describing President Wilson's program for peace.
2. *convoy:* protective escort for merchant ships crossing the ocean during wartime, consisting of warships and destroyers. *reparations:* payment of monetary penalties by countries defeated in war. *territorial integrity:* guarantee of protection of a country's boundaries. *self-determination:* freedom of a country to determine its own form of government.

3. (a) Admiral Sims advocated the use of convoys to reduce the danger of submarine attacks. (b) His tactic was successful. Convoys transported American soldiers to Europe without the loss of a single American and delivered supplies to Allied and American forces more quickly than expected.

4. The arrival of American troops and supplies in 1918 helped turn the tide of the war.

5. President Wilson proposed a "liberal" peace that guaranteed the territorial integrity of nations and the right of nations to self-determination, freedom of the seas, and protection from aggression. He called for disarmament and public diplomacy. He urged rejection of reparations.

An American Experience in the World War: Analyzing Fiction as Historical Evidence, text page 514

1. (a) The document is an excerpt from a novel. (b) The novel, *Three Soldiers*, was written by John Dos Passos. (c) *Three Soldiers* was written in 1919.

2. (a) Dos Passos was disillusioned about the war. (b) Yes. His account of the war suggests a sense of futility and impending doom. (c) This document was not intended to describe the experience of all American soldiers during World War I. While an historian or sociologist might make a systematic survey of the experiences of combat troops, a novelist seeks to raise broad questions while relying on a relatively narrow field of evidence.

3. (a) One can learn that the war was a terrifying experience for those who fought in it. Dos Passos conveys this message in a particularly convincing way. (b) The excerpt is not based on a study of large numbers of combat troops. (c) Yes. Both Chrisfield and the soldiers in the picture experienced heavy enemy fire. Notice the shattered trees in the picture. Dos Passos makes this point in *Three Soldiers*.

Section Review, text page 516

1. *Treaty of Versailles:* 1919 peace treaty ending World War I. *League of Nations:* an international organization formed after World War I to prevent wars. *Henry Cabot Lodge:* Republican senator who led the Senate attempt to "Republicanize" the Treaty of Versailles. *Article 10:* article of the League of Nations constitution, guaranteeing the territorial integrity of member states and calling for possible sanctions against violators.

2. President Wilson's attempt to make the 1918 congressional elections a referendum on his policies, his failure to appoint any influential Republicans to the Paris negotiating team, and his decision to personally lead the delegation to Paris stirred up opposition to his peace plans.

3. The idea of the League of Nations and especially Article 10 of the Covenant disturbed Republican senators.

4. To gain public support for the treaty, Wilson went on a crosscountry speaking tour to explain it.

5. The Senate rejected the Treaty of Versailles.

Chapter Review, text page 517

1. (a) At the outbreak of the war, the United States government followed a policy of neutrality. (b) The strong cultural and language ties of many Americans with Great Britain and traditional feelings of friendship for France made many Americans side with the Allies. Effective propaganda by the Allies in major American newspapers also worked against neutrality. German Americans, Irish Americans, and American Jews tended to sympathize with the Central Powers for various reasons, and effective propaganda in foreign-language presses helped the German cause.

2. (a) During the early years of the war, the United States traded more with Great Britain than with Germany because a British naval blockade disrupted American trade with the Germans and the Allies deluged the United States with orders for war supplies. (b) This trade created an economic boom in the United States.

3. (a) The German use of submarines complicated the question of neutral rights because international law required a ship to give warning before an attack and it was impractical for a submarine to do this. (b) When the German submarines sank ships, Wilson demanded that the Germans end this practice. (c) The Germans agreed in 1916 to stop unannounced attacks because they did not want the United States to enter the war on the side of the Allies.

4. (a) German resumption of submarine attacks with the resulting loss of American lives and ships angered many Americans and moved the United States closer to war. (b) The Zimmerman Telegram, urging Mexico and Japan to join the Central Powers if the United States entered the war, was a direct threat to American security. (c) The overthrow of the Russian czar and the establishment of a constitutional government made Russia a more honorable ally in Wilson's eyes and allowed him to claim that the Allied cause was more just.

5. (a) To support the war effort the government tried to mobilize industry by creating the War Industries Board. This board spurred industrial production and coordinated activities. In addition the government attempted to improve the railroad and shipping industries and build an adequate merchant marine. (b) To win the support of American workers the government created the National War Labor Board to act as arbitrator in disputes between management and labor. The government also gave full support to improvements in working conditions for American workers.

6. (a) Increased food production was important to the war effort because the Allies and their armies were facing starvation at the time the United States entered the war. (b) The United States was able to nearly triple the amount of food sent to the Allies through voluntary restraints on meat and bread consumption and through the planting of "victory" gardens.

7. (a) The government tried to solidify public support for the war effort through the efforts of the Committee on Public Information (CPI), which enlisted writers, lecturers, actors, artists, and scholars in a propaganda campaign. (b) The CPI, with its warnings that disloyalty, spying, and sabotage threatened the war effort, stirred up suspicion and fear, especially of German Americans.

8. The arrival of American troops gave the Allies a numerical advantage and raised the morale of French and British soldiers.

9. (a) The first five of President Wilson's Fourteen Points called for open treaties, freedom of the seas, free trade, arms reductions, and impartial adjustment of colonial claims. Points six through thirteen called for national self-determination and the realignment of borders that had been changed during or before the war. Point fourteen called for the establishment of the League of Nations. (b) The Treaty of Versailles was negotiated secretly; this secrecy violated one of the Fourteen Points. In addition, the treaty recognized new nations created out of the old Austria-Hungary empire and gave France the formerly German province of Alsace-Lorraine, mining rights in the Saar Valley, and the right to occupy the Rhineland for 15 years. Along with the reparations clause and the addition of a clause blaming Germany for the war, these aspects of the treaty violated the spirit as well as some of the stated goals of the Fourteen Points. (c) Wilson was willing to accept the treaty despite such violations because it included the Covenant for the League of Nations.

10. (a) Wilson alienated many Americans even before the peace conference began by trying to make the 1918 congressional elections a referendum on his policies, by failing to appoint influential Republicans to the negotiating team, and by leading the delegation to Paris himself. (b) Most Republican senators opposed the treaty because Republicans had not participated in the negotiations and because they believed Wilson was using it to win a third term as President. (c) The purpose of Senator Lodge's amendments was to protect United States sovereignty, prevent American involvement in other nations' internal affairs, and protect the authority of the Congress to declare war. He also wanted to "Republicanize" the treaty so that Democrats would not use it to political advantage.

For Further Thought, text page 517

1. (a) Black Americans and women found new job opportunities during the war. However, once the war ended, many members of these groups lost their jobs or had to accept lower-paying ones. For workers in general, working conditions improved during the war and many of these changes were long-lasting. (b) Because workers were so vital to the war effort and because they were in short supply, the government made every attempt to satisfy and recruit them.

2. (a) Students should understand that the union official meant that soldiers returning from the battlefields would need jobs and that he thought it would be patriotic for American women to relinquish their jobs to the returning soldiers. (b) Answers may vary, but students may suggest that some women needed their jobs to support their families.

3. (a) President Wilson was able to keep the United States neutral until 1917 because he refused to declare war over German submarine attacks on neutral ships and attempted to use diplomatic negotiations to end the war. (b), (c) Answers may vary. Students should recognize that in the end all attempts at neutrality failed.

Developing Basic Skills, text page 517

1. (a) After World War I Estonia, Latvia, Lithuania, Poland, Czechoslovakia, Yugoslavia, Austria, and Hungary became independent countries. (b) Austria-Hungary no longer existed after the war. (c) Russia, Austria-Hungary, Germany, Bulgaria, and Turkey lost territory as a result of the war. (d) France gained territory after the war. (e) Students should discuss boundary changes in explaining this statement.

2. (a) Wilson's foreign policy speech is a document written during World War I by a person directly involved and is thus a primary source. (b) By reading the speech, one can learn that Wilson's goal was to effect a just and nonpunitive peace. (c) A diary account is a personal record of a time or an event; President Wilson's foreign policy speech is a public statement.

3. (a) The purpose of the poster was to advertise the sale of war bonds. (b) The poster was an attempt to generate patriotic emotions. (c) The list of names represents a broad crossection of ethnic groups in the United States. (d) Answers should reflect the significance of patriotic feeling during wartime.

Unit Eight: The Roaring Twenties

29 A Search for Peace and Prosperity (1919–1928)

Section Review, text page 525

1. *A. Mitchell Palmer:* United States Attorney General in the early 1920s who organized raids to arrest suspected communists. *Calvin Coolidge:* governor of Massachusetts who in 1919 called in the National Guard when Boston police went on strike. *Bolsheviks:* group of radical communists who led a revolution in Russia in 1917. *Red Scare:* term for American fears in the 1920s that communists were trying to cause a revolution in the United States; labor unrest and terrorist incidents were seen as evidence of communist plots.
2. *general strike:* a strike of the members of all unions. *company union:* employee association sponsored by management.
3. Because of the general strike in Seattle and the police strike in Boston, many Americans were convinced that radicals were behind labor unrest.
4. Southeastern Europeans (Italians, Slavs, and other), Africans, and Japanese were virtually barred by the restrictive immigration legislation.
5. Black veterans were disillusioned because they did not receive the jobs and treatment they thought they deserved.
6. The post–Civil War Klan had been primarily opposed to blacks and their white sympathizers. The new Klan opposed these groups and, in addition, Jews, Catholics, and immigrants.

Section Review, text page 528

1. *Warren G. Harding:* President of the United States from 1921 to 1923; he had been a small-town politician, newspaper editor, and a United States senator prior to his election. *Andrew Mellon:* millionaire secretary of the treasury under Harding and the dominant figure in the Harding administra-tion; he favored a high tariff to protect American business from foreign competition and a reduction of taxes on the wealthy. *Harry Dougherty:* attorney general under President Harding who sold government favors, immunities from prosecutions, and pardons. *Albert Fall:* Harding's secretary of the interior who masterminded the illegal oil deal known as the Teapot Dome Scandal.
2. *normalcy:* term used by Harding to describe the American desire to return to a time of peace and quiet.
3. Andrew Mellon believed that if the taxes of the wealthy were cut, the wealthy would have more money to invest. This would create more jobs, which in turn would mean more income for middle- and lower-income people.
4. Mellon tried to effect businesslike efficiency and economy in government by instituting a budgeting process for government departments and by reducing the national debt and balancing the budget.
5. Albert Fall leased government oil reserves to two oil men, Harry Sinclair and Edward Doheny, in exchange for $400,000. This led to Fall's conviction for bribery.

Section Review, text page 530

1. *McNary-Haugen Bill:* bill supported by the "farm bloc" and vetoed by Coolidge that would have provided a government-supported two-price system for some farm products such as wheat and corn; the bill proposed to assure farmers of the purchase of their produce at a parity price, regardless of the market price.
2. *parity:* government-supported price for farm products.
3. Farmers, social reformers, and socialists supported the Progressive party in the 1924 election.
4. Spiraling railroad shipping rates, taxes, seed prices, and interest rates plus the purchase of expensive machinery and chemical fertilizers increased farmers' expenses during the 1920s.

Chapter Review, text page 531

1. (a) Many Americans were unemployed after World War I ended. Prices rose as consumer demand increased for products that had been unavailable during the war. (b) Because of these problems workers demanded higher wages to meet the increasing cost of living; their demands were often rejected by employers who wanted to keep costs down.
2. (a) The steel strike in 1919 resulted in 20 deaths, the loss of $100 million in wages, but no concessions from employers. (b) The coal strike resulted in a 14 percent wage increase. (c) The tactics used

in the Seattle general strike and in the Boston police strike were regarded as radical by many Americans.

3. (a) Terrorists who sent bombs through the mail frightened Americans and convinced them that communists were a real threat to the country. (b) Responding to public concern, Attorney General Palmer organized a series of raids to arrest suspected communists.

4. (a) Antiforeign feeling increased after the war because many foreigners immigrated to the United States and competed for jobs. In addition, terrorist activities were blamed on foreigners. (b) Congress responded to the antiforeign feeling by passing restrictive immigration laws. (c) Both laws decreased the flow of immigrants. (d) This legislation reduced the number of immigrants from southern and eastern Europe. (e) Because the quota system did not count black Americans, it effectively barred immigration from Africa.

5. (a) Because they had served their country in war or had worked in factories producing war equipment, many black Americans expected and believed they deserved a better life after the war. (b) Instead they faced discrimination in northern cities and unemployment. In some cities tensions between blacks and whites erupted into riots.

6. Reflecting the probusiness policies of the Harding administration, Andrew Mellon favored a high tariff to protect American business from foreign competition. Toward this end Congress passed the Fordney-McCumber Act in 1922, which raised tariffs to a new high. Mellon also believed that taxes on large incomes should be reduced. The Revenue Act of 1921 was one among a number of laws passed during the 1920s that cut taxes on higher incomes.

7. (a) Some major scandals during Harding's presidency included the selling of government favors, immunities from prosecution, and pardons; the stealing and selling of medical supplies; and in the Teapot Dome Scandal, the worst scandal of all, the receipt of kickbacks by Albert Fall from the leasing of government oil reserves. (b) Harding was spared full knowledge of the scandals because he died before the extent of the scandals became well known.

8. (a) Coolidge helped business by appointing men who favored business to head regulatory agencies and by signing in 1926 the Revenue Act, which cut tax rates on higher incomes. (b) George Norris claimed that Coolidge's appointments had set the country back more than 25 years and that they served the purpose of nullifying federal law from within.

9. (a) The 1920s were a difficult time for farmers because they faced high expenses and depressed prices for their products. (b) To improve their situation farmers banded together in farm bureaus, formed cooperatives, and sought assistance from the federal government. (c) Farmers were not successful because overproduction continued and President Coolidge vetoed the McNary-Haugen Bill, which would have provided for price parity.

For Further Thought, text page 531

1. Answers may vary. Students should recognize that Harding and Coolidge appointed people who favored business to government positions. Because some of these people headed regulatory agencies, they turned a blind eye to business operations that might have bordered on the illegal. They favored high tariffs to protect American goods from the competition of foreign products. Taxes on the wealthy were slashed. This was intended to give businesspeople more money to invest.

2. The Republicans nominated Coolidge without difficulty, but it took 17 days for the Democrats to nominate James W. Davis. The Progressives selected Robert La Follette. The Republican and Democratic candidates had a business orientation, while the Progressives wanted social reform. The Progressive party won only one state, La Follette's home state of Wisconsin. Because of the probusiness orientation in the 1920s, the Progressives had little chance of winning.

Developing Basic Skills, text page 531

1. (a) Between 1900 and 1920 the largest percentage of immigrants came from southern and eastern Europe. (b) Southern and eastern Europe showed the largest increase since the 1840s. (c) Northern and western Europe experienced a decrease in immigration to the United States whereas southern and eastern Europe and Asia experienced an increase.

2. (a) In the 1840s Chinese and Irish immigrants were subject to antiforeign feeling. In the 1880s and 1920s eastern and southern Europeans were subject to similar sentiments. (b) Job competition caused resentment among native-born Americans in each period. (c) General restrictions on immigration did not become government policy until the 1920s. (d) In each period antiforeign sentiment was fed by fears that immigrants, desperate for work at any wage, would take the jobs held by American-born working people. (e) During the 1840s Congress did not pass anti-immigrant legislation. Except for the Chinese Exclusion Act of 1882 Congress did not restrict the number of immigrants entering the United States during the 1880s. But during the 1920s Congress passed several restrictive immigration laws. Another difference among the three periods is that during the 1920s immigrants became

linked in the popular mind with radicalism. Few Americans during the 1840s and 1880s associated immigrants with radicalism. (f) Students might explain the similarities in the antiforeign impulse by suggesting that the prospect of unemployment or lowered wages is always terrifying to working people. Differences could be explained by noting that communists had not seized power in any action during the nineteenth century. Their seizure of power in Russia in 1917 made the danger of communism seem more real.

30 Life in the 1920s (1920–1929)

Section Review, text page 535

1. *Frederick W. Taylor:* engineer and leading advocate of scientific management. *Henry Ford:* founded Ford Motor Company in 1903 and revolutionized the automobile industry by introducing the electrically powered assembly line.
2. *scientific management:* systematic study of the performance of workers and machines for the purpose of finding ways to increase efficiency. *assembly line:* the grouping of machines and workers so that work passes from worker to worker, each performing one task, until the product is assembled. *synthetics:* chemically produced fibers. *telephoto:* the process of sending pictures by wire.
3. Frederick Taylor's studies at the Midvale Steel plant led to an increase in output of 300 percent.
4. Ford was able to keep the price of the Model T low by employing the assembly line method of production.
5. As a result of the growth of the automobile industry, the rubber, steel, and glass industries grew.
6. Three scientific breakthroughs made during the 1920s were the development of synthetics and telephotos and the discovery of penicillin.

Section Review, text page 541

1. *Harlem Renaissance:* flowering of black creativity in the arts during the 1920s in the area of New York City known as Harlem. *Langston Hughes:* black poet of the 1920s who reminded readers of America's African heritage. *Marcus Garvey:* black leader of the 1920s who urged black Americans to return to Africa to establish a nation there; publisher of the *Negro World*. *Gertrude Ederle:* first woman to swim the English Channel, 1926.

Charles Lindbergh: first person to make a solo non-stop air flight across the Atlantic, 1927. *Museum of Modern Art:* a New York City Museum, opened in 1929, that exhibited a wide variety of visual art.
2. American jazz had its roots in West African rhythms, black work songs and spirituals, minstrel songs, the harmonies of European music, ragtime, and the "blues."
3. During the 1920s movies and radio became popular.
4. His bravery, flying skill, courage, and modesty made Lindbergh a hero to most Americans.
5. The Armory Show in 1913 was the first major exhibition of modern art in the United States.

Section Review, text page 544

1. *Sinclair Lewis:* author of the novels *Main Street* and *Babbitt*; winner of the Nobel Prize for Literature in 1930. *Willa Cather:* author of novels that stressed moral values; winner of Pulitzer Prize in 1922 for *One of Ours*. *F. Scott Fitzgerald:* author of *The Great Gatsby* and *This Side of Paradise*, novels that epitomized the glitter of the 1920s. *Ernest Hemingway:* expatriate author who in his novels explored the disillusionment that followed the idealism of World War I. *T. S. Eliot:* a poet; author of *The Waste Land*.
2. *migrant worker:* worker who travels from farm to farm as the seasons change looking for work. *expatriate:* person who leaves his or her homeland to live in another country.
3. Achieving the right to vote did not usher in an age of equality for women. They continued to face discrimination in the job market and in education and they were excluded from management positions in business and industry.
4. Farmers, black Americans, Native Americans, and Mexican Americans all missed the prosperity of the 1920s.
5. The name Babbitt came to refer to people who were boorish, smug, and determined to make everyone else think and act as they did.

Chapter Review, text page 545

1. (a) Great changes in the use of electricity took place between 1900 and 1930. Domestic use grew dramatically, with 70 percent of homes having electric power by the end of the 1920s. This percentage was equaled in American industry. (b) The increased use of electricity made home life more enjoyable. Americans could use such consumer goods as refrigerators, vacuum cleaners, and radios. (c) Electricity contributed significantly to increases in industrial production. Factory output increased by

25 percent from 1921 to 1928 and output per work hour increased by 35 percent from 1920 to 1929.

2. (a) Frederick W. Taylor tried to make industry more efficient by applying the techniques of scientific management. This involved the study of productivity of workers and machines and the planning of ways to increase their efficiency. (b) Taylor was successful; he increased the output of the Midvale Steel plant by 300 percent. Many others used his methods to increase industrial production.

3. (a) Henry Ford revolutionized the automobile industry by using electrically powered machines and the assembly line. (b) Ford's techniques caused auto production to soar and the industry to prosper. The year 1900 had seen the production of 4,000 cars; with the use of Ford's methods a record 4.8 million cars were produced in 1929.

4. (a) With the growth of the automobile industry more and better roads were needed and built. With better roads workers no longer needed to live in the city close to their jobs. There was a dramatic exodus from the city and a rapid growth of suburbs. (b) The automobile industry gave rise to the growth of the rubber, steel, and glass industries, all of which supplied materials used to build cars.

5. Much of the writing of the Harlem Renaissance focused on such themes as black pride and the problems of prejudice and discrimination faced by blacks in our society.

6. (a) Motion pictures became a very popular form of entertainment during the 1920s as the talking movies were introduced and the age of the movie star began. (b) A new style of life developed in America as people clustered around the radio after dinner to listen to their favorite programs.

7. (a) The "modern art" shown in the Armory Show in 1913 differed from traditional art in that it did not try to represent reality in a photographic way. Much of the art was abstract, using cubes, spheres, and cones. (b) The Museum of Modern Art helped the public understand that architecture, photography, and films were forms of art.

8. (a) Women still faced job discrimination. (b) Electric appliances made housework easier. (c) Women generally held jobs with low pay and little prestige.

9. (a) Black Americans missed the prosperity of the 1920s because segregation and prejudice continued to plague them in both the North and South. (b) Native Americans had lost most of their land, and much of what they still owned was unsuitable for farming. Their culture and traditions had been weakened and a majority of these people were poor, uneducated, and in poor health. They had little opportunity to prosper in the 1920s. (c) Mexican Americans, like most blacks and Native Americans, tended to be stricken by poverty.

For Further Thought, text page 545

1. (a) The writers of the Lost Generation were critical of the obsession Americans had with material wealth and conformity. (b) Students might suggest that the tremendous number of casualties and the unfulfilled ideals of the war made some writers cynical about American society. Students might also note that the persistence of traditional values in small towns and rural areas offended writers who thought of themselves as individuals who had outgrown the old ways. (c) Answers may vary. Students should understand that many Americans enjoyed the prosperity of the time.

2. (a) Radio made the world more accessible to millions of Americans. Listeners in rural America could follow prize fights in New York City's Madison Square Garden and catch the presidential election returns as they came into a newsroom a thousand miles away. Radio established an electronic link between personal lives and world events. (b) Evidence of the popularity of radio can be seen in some of the statistics of the time. In 1922, only two years after the first radio broadcast, sales reached $60 million. By 1929 people had spent $843 million on radios.

Developing Basic Skills, text page 545

1. Research will vary.

2. (a) Answers may vary. Accept answers that refer to the entertainment and informational functions of both radio and television. (b) Answers may vary. Students should recognize that listening to the radio is no longer likely to be a family activity. People tend to listen to the radio alone, while they are traveling, or while they are doing other things.

31 From Prosperity to Despair (1928–1932)

Section Review, text page 549

1. *Al Smith:* Roman Catholic governor of New York who was the Democratic nominee for President in 1928; a supporter of public ownership of some companies and of government aid for farmers, he was defeated by Herbert Hoover.

2. *on margin:* refers to a system of buying stock in which buyers use a specified amount of their own money and borrow the remainder from a broker. *margin calls:* demands made by brokers that investors who have purchased stock on margin put up extra money to cover their loans.

3. Signs of economic slowdown in the 1920s: industries like coal and textiles were in decline; agriculture was laden with economic problems; rising unemployment; prices and profits began to level off; construction leveled off.
4. Hoover's popularity rested on his image as a self-made man, an efficiency expert, and a humanitarian.
5. Hoover believed that farmers should cooperate to solve their problems. Smith urged government action.
6. Speculators bought land and stocks in the 1920s.

Section Review, text page 553

1. *durable goods:* manufactured items meant to last for several years, such as cars, radios, and refrigerators. *business inventories:* the manufactured, but unsold, goods kept on hand.
2: Supply greatly exceeded demand by the late 1920s. Workers were not making enough to buy the products industry was making.
3. When the stock market crashed, banks that had loaned large sums tried to collect on their loans. Speculators were unable to recoup their money to repay the banks, and many banks then went bankrupt.
4. At the onset of depression many people lost their jobs and their savings. With no money they began losing items they had bought on credit, and some even lost their homes. People who couldn't pay rent were evicted. Many people became so impoverished they couldn't buy food or clothing.

The Economy of the Roaring Twenties: Synthesizing Pieces of Evidence, text page 554

1. (a) 11.15. (b) The index rose to 26.02 in 1929. (c) The average yearly income of farmers increased from $551 in 1922 to $651 in 1929. (d) Manufacturing workers enjoyed the largest increase in yearly wages between 1921 and 1929. (e) This picture depicts the results of wild speculation in Florida land. (f) Ayres believed that changes in the business cycle were a thing of the past.
2. (a) One would conclude that the economy was becoming more prosperous. (b) Data about farm wages would confirm the conclusion stated in (a). (c) No. The quotation represents an optimistic view of the economy while the picture presents a somewhat gloomy assessment. (d) Both the picture and the text suggest that Americans were seized with "get-rich-quick" fever. This fever encouraged speculation, which in turn pushed stock prices to artifi-

cially high levels. Pumped up by speculation, the bubble burst in late October 1929.
3. (a) The 1920s was a prosperous period. During most of the decade wages in farming, manufacturing, and government service increased. Sales of consumer goods soared while stock market prices reached new highs. (b) Several problems beset the economy during the 1920s. While the farm economy improved during the decade, conditions in some cases were far from good. Cotton prices, for example, stayed low during the 1920s. Minority groups—black Americans, Native Americans, and Mexican Americans—generally missed the prosperity of the 1920s. Finally, the gap between industrial wages and consumer prices caused a decline in sales and ultimately a slowdown in production. (c) In this essay students should refer to the increased use of new products, new techniques of production and management, the stock market boom and collapse, and the groups that did not share in the general prosperity.

Section Review, text page 558

1. *Reconstruction Finance Corporation:* government agency set up in 1932 to stop bank failures and business closings by loaning money to banks, railroads, and insurance companies. The RFC was not successful because it was reluctant to loan the money Congress had given it and because many of the banks it did give money to used the money improperly. *Bonus Army:* group of World War I veterans who marched on Washington, D.C., demanding early receipt of their promised bonuses. *Franklin Delano Roosevelt:* New York governor and 1932 Democratic candidate for President who promised a pragmatic and active program to deal with the depression; Roosevelt and his New Deal were victorious over Hoover.
2. Hoover believed that depression, like recovery, was an inevitable part of the economic cycle. He thought that his duty was to provide moral leadership during the crisis.
3. Congress went beyond Hoover's initial intentions when it gave the RFC the right to lend money to communities for public-works programs.
4. During the early years of the depression far too many people were unemployed for local relief agencies to handle the problem successfully. Furthermore, tax revenues shrank, leaving too little money available.
5. The Bonus Army wanted early payment of their promised World War I bonuses.
6. As the 1932 election campaign neared, Hoover was dreary and pessimistic.

1. Signs of economic problems during the 1920s: wages did not keep pace with prices; decline in demand for goods; increasing unemployment; poor state of coal mines, textiles, and agriculture; a slowdown in housing construction and automobile production; large industrial inventories; over-speculation to "get rich quick."
2. Hoover, a man of considerable experience, was the Republican nominee. He was wealthy, efficient, and a humanitarian. He believed that economic problems, such as those of the farmers, would correct themselves with time and effort in the private sector. He believed in the philosophy of "rugged individualism." Smith, the Democrat, was governor of New York, a Catholic, more middle class, and the son of immigrant parents. Smith believed that the government should take a more active role in economic problems. He favored government ownership of some electric companies and direct aid to farmers.
3. (a) By investing money in the Florida land boom and in the stock market, speculators during the 1920s tried to "get rich quick." (b) A very severe hurricane in 1926 ended the Florida land boom. (c) Investors bought stock without paying the full price by using a small down payment and borrowing the remainder on margin from their brokers.
4. (a) The imbalance of supply over demand slowed production, created layoffs, and lowered wages, each of which contributed to the onset of the depression. (b) As durable goods are expensive and long-lasting, they tend not to be purchased when money is tight. (c) Faced with increasing inventories, industries had to reduce production and lay off workers. (d) Each bank closing shook the confidence of depositors in other banks. As people withdrew their money, the money supply decreased.
5. (a) With the onset of depression people bought only the necessities of life. Rents and mortgages went unpaid, and people became homeless. Life savings were lost through bank closings. Many people became destitute. (b) The Great Depression seemed worse than earlier depressions because for the first time mass-communications media, through photographs, could make the general public aware of the misery that existed. Also, the nation was more industrial than ever before, and most people could not grow their own food, as they had in the past.
6. (a) Hoover's advisers favored a hands-off policy. They believed the business cycle would run its course and the depression would end. (b) Hoover tried to restore the public's confidence and boost morale by making public pronouncements and sponsoring economic conferences. (c) Hoover supported public-works programs that had cash to back them.
7. (a) The Reconstruction Finance Corporation (RFC) had the power to make loans to troubled banks, railroads, and insurance companies. It could also make loans to local communities to fund public-works programs. (b) The RFC was supposed to work according to the "trickle-down" theory. By spending money to solve the problems of business and industry, the money would "trickle down" to ordinary people. The trickle was too slow to counteract the worsening conditions.
8. (a) Hoover believed that relief agencies, both private and voluntary, should provide the necessary relief. Some would be sponsored by local governments. (b) Because incomes were shrinking, taxes and charitable contributions dropped. Thus, private agencies and local governments could not provide enough relief.
9. (a) The Bonus Army was a group of World War I veterans who marched on Washington, D.C. (b) They wanted early payment of their bonuses.

For Further Thought, text page 559

1. (a) If the RFC had worked the way it was intended and had solved the problems of business and industry, according to Mellon's theory, then benefits would have "trickled down" to ordinary people. (b) Answers may vary. Students should recognize that Hoover, a self-made man, became wealthy through his own efforts. He therefore believed that other people could take care of themselves, as he had.
2. Poor morale, lack of confidence, and despair under Hoover led most people to seek a change. Roosevelt offered hope, while Hoover represented the bleakness of the Great Depression.

Developing Basic Skills, text page 559

1. Research will vary. Students should find evidence that the stock market was unstable and that there was a downward movement of stock prices preceding the crash.
2. (a) The Democratic candidate received 472 electoral votes in 1932. (b) Roosevelt received 22,809,-638 popular votes. (c) Hoover received 5,633,092 more popular votes in 1928 than in 1932. (d) The Democratic candidate received 7,793,522 more electoral votes in 1932 than in 1928. (e) Based on these statistics it seems that the public lost its confidence in Hoover. Accept answers that discuss events between 1929 and 1932.

Unit Nine: A Time of Trial

32 A New Deal (1933–1935)

Section Review, text page 564

1. *brain trust:* group of Roosevelt's advisers, several of whom had taught at universities. *Harold Ickes:* Roosevelt's secretary of the interior, formerly a progressive Republican from Chicago. *Henry A. Wallace:* Roosevelt's secretary of agriculture; publisher of an important farm magazine; a former progressive Republican. *Frances Perkins:* Roosevelt's secretary of labor; first woman to hold a cabinet position; a labor-relations expert.
2. From his bout with polio Roosevelt learned that through courage and determination he could succeed against adversity.
3. The ideas upon which the New Deal were based came from the progressive movement, lessons learned during the World War, the brain trust, and Roosevelt's cabinet.
4. On inauguration day in 1933 Hoover was glum before the crowd. Roosevelt, on the other hand, waved gaily, feeling confident and optimistic.

Section Review, text page 570

1. *Harry Hopkins:* appointed by Roosevelt to administer the Federal Emergency Relief Act and the Civil Works Administration. *Blue Eagle:* symbol of the National Recovery Administration (NRA); Americans stamped this symbol on their products and posted it where they worked to show that they followed NRA codes.
2. *fireside chat:* one of a series of informal radio talks President Roosevelt made to the American people to bolster their faith in the future.
3. To relieve the banking crisis Roosevelt declared a national "bank holiday," closing all banks to prevent further bank failures. He also proposed the Emergency Banking Relief Act, which allowed banks to reopen if they had sufficient funds on hand to meet depositors' withdrawals; permitted sound banks to borrow federal funds; and closed unsound banks.
4. The dual aims of the Civilian Conservation Reforestation Relief Act were to conserve natural resources and put young people to work.
5. (a) The purpose of the Federal Emergency Relief Act was to provide immediate relief payments to the unemployed. (b) The Civil Works Administration offered jobs rather than relief.

6. The Agricultural Adjustment Act tried to reduce farm surpluses by paying farmers to destroy part of their crops.
7. (a) The main provision of the National Industrial Recovery Act permitted trade associations to draft codes that would regulate production, prices, and working conditions. (b) The Public Works Administration tried to stimulate employment by spending large sums of money on public works projects.
8. The Tennessee Valley Authority built dams, constructed hydroelectric power plants, made fertilizer and sold it to farmers at cost, planted trees to stop erosion, and introduced educational and health services.

Caption, text page 572

CCC, Civilian Conservation Corps; CWA, Civil Works Administration; AAA, Agricultural Adjustment Administration; NRA, National Recovery Administration; FDIC, Federal Deposit Insurance Corporation; PWA, Public Works Administration; FERA, Federal Emergency Relief Act.

Section Review, text page 573

1. *Huey Long:* senator from Louisiana who thought Roosevelt's New Deal was too conservative; his alternative to the New Deal was called "Share Our Wealth." *Charles Coughlin:* priest who told his radio listeners that the Great Depression was the fault of an international conspiracy of bankers; at first he supported Roosevelt, but later he lost his enthusiasm for the New Deal. *Francis E. Townshend:* retired California physician who was concerned about the condition of the elderly poor; proposed a retirement pension for people over 60. *American Liberty League:* organization that believed the government should encourage private enterprise and protect private property; its members felt that New Deal programs were undermining private enterprise. *Schechter* v. *United States:* Supreme Court decision that declared the National Industrial Recovery Act unconstitutional, based on the principle that the federal government has no power to regulate commerce that takes place exclusively within a state.
2. Huey Long thought the government should use the tax money it collected from the rich to provide every American family with a house, a car, education for children, a pension for the elderly, and an income of $2,000 to $3,000 a year.
3. Francis Townshend was concerned about the elderly poor.
4. Conservatives thought excessive taxes and government regulation were a threat to private enterprise.

5. The Supreme Court declared the New Deal's National Industrial Recovery Act and Agricultural Adjustment Act unconstitutional.

Section Review, text page 576

1. *Robert F. Wagner:* senator from New York who championed organized labor and sponsored the National Labor Relations Act, also known as the Wagner Act.

2. *utility company:* company that distributes gas and electricity.

3. (a) Widespread unemployment led to the creation of the Works Progress Administration in 1935. (b) The WPA tried to solve the problem of unemployment by putting people to work on a wide variety of construction projects.

4. The National Youth Administration offered part-time jobs to young people so they could stay in school and earn money as well.

5. The Wagner Act guaranteed workers the right to organize and bargain collectively.

6. (a) The purpose of the Public Utilities Holding Company Act was to give the government the power to restrict the activities of monopolistic holding companies. (b) The act dissolved most of the large utility empires and put the industry under federal supervision.

7. (a) The Social Security Act of 1935 aided the elderly, people who had lost their jobs, the handicapped, and certain dependent children. (b) The Social Security Act created a national system of pensions for retired people and a system of unemployment insurance.

Chapter Review, text page 577

1. Roosevelt's philosophy was shaped by several experiences: his early training that his position of wealth and privilege obliged him to help others; his belief, developed as governor of New York during the stock market crash, that government should actively help those in trouble; and his bout with polio, which showed him that adversity can strike anyone.

2. Each of the following contributed to the ideas of the New Deal. (a) Progressivism had stressed conserving natural resources, breaking up monopolies, regulating the way business was conducted, and improving working conditions. (b) The world war had demonstrated that government planning agencies could work with business and agriculture to produce the right goods in the right quantities. (c) The brain trust provided ideas on how to fight the depression. (d) Cabinet members provided ideas and plans for experimentation.

3. (a) When Roosevelt took office people were withdrawing their money from banks and hoarding it at home. As the money flowed out, the banks collapsed. (b) To solve the banking crisis Roosevelt declared a bank holiday, closing all banks. Then he had Congress pass the Emergency Banking Relief Act, which allowed the reopening of banks that had sufficient funds on hand to meet depositors' withdrawal requests; permitted essentially sound banks to borrow federal funds to reopen; and closed those banks judged unsound.

4. (a) During the first hundred days Congress passed the Civilian Conservation Reforestation Act and the Federal Emergency Relief Act, both of which provided immediate relief to the unemployed. (b) The Civilian Conservation Reforestation Relief Act set up the Civilian Conservation Corps (CCC), which enlisted single men, aged from 18 to 25, and sent them to CCC camps. At these camps they planted trees, made reservoirs, built bridges, and developed parks. The FERA made relief payments to the unemployed through local and state welfare agencies. (c) Roosevelt agreed to the Civil Works Administration because he felt that the major task of government was to get Americans back to work.

5. (a) The purpose of the Agricultural Adjustment Act was to limit farm production. (b) To achieve its goals the AAA would pay farmers not to plant crops. (c) In 1933 the government encouraged farmers to plow under part of their crops. (d) Ironically this meant that sources of food and clothing were destroyed while thousands of Americans were hungry and poorly clothed.

6. (a) The National Industrial Recovery Act tried to stop the downward spiral of industry by encouraging trade associations in each industry to cooperate in regulating production, prices, and working conditions. It established the NRA and the PWA. (b) The NRA faced a number of problems. It overextended itself, many businesses ignored NRA codes, and labor leaders thought the NRA kept wages too low.

7. (a) The purpose of the Tennessee Valley Authority was to transform the Tennessee River Valley from a backwater of poor farms into a rich and productive region. (b) Power companies opposed the TVA because they objected to government competition; other critics objected to TVA's social planning.

8. (a) Huey Long criticized the New Deal because he thought it was too conservative. He wanted government to embark on his "Share Our Wealth" program. (b) Charles Coughlin believed that Roosevelt did not act strongly enough against "banking and money interests." (c) Francis E.

Townshend wanted government to do more for the elderly poor. (d) Raymond Moley charged that the New Deal was undermining the free enterprise system. (e) The American Liberty League believed that government should promote private enterprise and protect private property.

9. (a) The Supreme Court declared the National Industrial Recovery Act unconstitutional on the grounds that the federal government had no power to regulate commerce that takes place exclusively within a state. (b) The Agricultural Adjustment Act was ruled unconstitutional on the grounds that the tax levied to pay farmers for cutting back on production was an unfair use of the congressional power to tax.

10. (a) Legislation passed during the "second hundred days": the Emergency Relief Appropriations Act, which created the Works Progress Administration and the National Youth Administration; the Wagner Act; the Public Utilities Holding Company Act; and the Social Security Act. (b) The main purpose of this legislation was to remove the causes of the depression.

For Further Thought, text page 577

1. (a) Answers may vary. Emphasize Roosevelt's "the only thing we have to fear is fear itself" attitude, coupled with his concrete action in the form of government programs. (b) Answers may vary. Point out that many Americans had lost hope, that they had given up, and that many had reached a point of desperation.

2. (a) During the New Deal workers were guaranteed the right to organize and to bargain collectively with management under the Wagner Act. (b) During the 1920s management-sponsored company unions became more prevalent, union membership dropped, and collective bargaining was practiced less often. (c) Accept answers that refer to the New Deal's sympathetic stance toward organized labor.

3. (a) Many critics of the New Deal believed that the federal government had imposed too many regulations on private industry. (b) Students might suggest that the New Deal transformed the federal government's role in the economy and changed the rules under which the free enterprise economy operated.

Developing Basic Skills, text page 577

1. See the chart on page A 99. (a) The largest number of laws were generated by unemployment. (b) Industrial workers, employers, farmers, retired people, bank depositors, unemployed people, and residents of the Tennessee Valley were among those affected by New Deal legislation. (c) Answers may vary, but students should explain the impact of a particular piece of legislation on a given group. (d) Again answers may vary, but students should note that New Deal legislation was aimed at alleviating the suffering caused by the Great Depression.

2. Research will vary.

33 The New Deal Continues (1936–1939)

Caption, text page 581

World War II reduced unemployment to 9.9 percent of the labor force in 1941 and 1.2 percent in 1944.

Section Review, text page 582

1. *Alfred M. Landon:* Republican candidate who ran against Róosevelt in 1936.
2. *deficit spending:* a spending plan whereby government spends more money than it takes in.
3. In his original message about the New Deal Landon argued that he could manage New Deal programs more efficiently, waste less money, and achieve longer-lasting results.
4. Roosevelt's coalition was made up of the "solid South," big-city "machines," organized labor, and blacks.
5. Roosevelt wanted to increase the size of the Supreme Court by adding one Justice for every justice aged 70 or over who refused to retire, thus increasing the Court's size to 15.
6. In the fall and winter of 1937–1938 the economy suffered a severe recession.

Section Review, text page 587

1. *John L. Lewis:* president of the United Mine Workers; a founder of the Congress of Industrial Organizations. *Congress of Industrial Organizations:* groups of unions that rivaled the AFL; the CIO organized workers into industrial unions. *Farm Security Administration:* extended loans to help tenants and sharecroppers buy farms and equipment. *second Agricultural Adjustment Act:* passed in 1938, this law gave government the right to call on farmers to limit their crops; payments for such limitations came from congressional appropriations.

New Deal Laws	Problem(s)	People Affected
a. Emergency Banking Relief Act	failing banks	banks and depositors
b. Civilian Conservation Reforestation Relief Act	unemployment; dwindling national resources	unemployed young people
c. Federal Emergency Relief Act	poverty of the unemployed	unemployed
d. Civil Works Administration	unemployment	unemployed
e. Agricultural Adjustment Act	overproduction; low farm prices	farmers
f. National Industrial Recovery Act	price cutting and destructive competition	industry
g. Tennessee Valley Authority	regional underdevelopment; unproductive lands; floods	people in the Tennessee Valley
h. Truth in Securities Act	wild stock market speculation	stock market investors
i. Glass-Steagall Banking Act	bank failures	depositors
j. Farm Credit Administration	farm foreclosures and bankruptcies	farmers
k. Home Owners' Loan Corproration	foreclosures on homes	homeowners
l. Wagner Act	management interference with union organizing	industrial workers
m. Public Utilities Holding Company Act	utility monopolies	utilities owners
n. Social Security Act	poverty and unemployment	retired and unemployed

2. *industrial union:* a union that represents every worker in an entire industry, not just members of skilled crafts. *sitdown strike:* strike in which workers sit down on the job and refuse to work.
3. John L. Lewis wanted to organize every worker in an entire industry, not just skilled workers.
4. The Fair Labor Standards Act established minimum wages and maximum hours of work in a number of industries whose products entered interstate commerce.
5. During the 1930s the farmers of the Midwest were hit by the Great Depression and a disastrous drought, lasting from 1932 to 1936.

6. The second Agricultural Adjustment Act differed from the first by using congressional appropriations, rather than a tax, to pay farmers for limiting production.

A View of the New Deal: Analyzing Oral Evidence, text page 591

1. (a) David Kennedy was interviewed. (b) The interview took place during the late 1960s.
2. (a) Kennedy was a member of the Federal Reserve Board during the New Deal. As a government official he might have been biased in favor of the Roo-

sevelt administration's policies. (b) The interview took place about 30 years after the Great Depression. The intervening years may have changed his perception of events. (c) At the time of the interview Kennedy was the chairman of the board of a major corporation. This experience may have given him an anti–New Deal perspective.
3. (a) Kennedy stated that Roosevelt saved the nation from complete collapse by giving it hope at the beginning of the Great Depression. (b) Kennedy grew disenchanted with Roosevelt when he found that the nation was not making as much progress under the New Deal as he had hoped. (c) This document suggests that while the New Deal generated much hope, it did not always fully implement its programs.

Section Review, text page 592

1. *John Steinbeck:* author of *The Grapes of Wrath,* a book that dealt with the migration of farmers westward to California. *Dorothea Lange:* photographer who captured Dust Bowl scenes, later published in *An American Exodus. Margaret Bourke-White:* photographer who portrayed rural poverty in the South in *You Have Seen Their Faces. Walker Evans* and *James Agee:* photographer (Evans) and writer (Agee) team who portrayed southern poverty in *Let Us Now Praise Famous Men. Richard Wright:* novelist who wrote *Uncle Tom's Children* and *Native Son*, both depicting what it meant to be black during the Great Depression. *John Collier:* director of the Bureau of Indian Affairs during the 1930s who worked to extend New Deal benefits to Native Americans. *Mary Dewson:* coordinator of women's activities in Roosevelt's campaign and, later, in his administration.
2. During the Great Depression Americans listened to radio and went to view talking pictures to forget their troubles.
3. Under the New Deal blacks were included in relief and job programs partly because of the efforts of Eleanor Roosevelt and Harry Hopkins. Thousands of black teenagers were employed by the CCC, and more blacks than ever before were appointed to important government positions.
4. The Indian Emergency Conservation Work group employed Indians in soil erosion control, irrigation, and tribal land development programs.
5. As a result of the depression thousands of Mexican workers were deported, along with their children, to make room for American workers.
6. During Roosevelt's administration Frances Perkins was named secretary of labor. Women were also appointed to various other posts, including minister to a foreign nation, director of the U.S. Mint, and

judge on the Circuit Court of Appeals. Mary Dewson coordinated women's activities. Eleanor Roosevelt championed women's rights.

Chapter Review, text page 593

1. (a) At the start of the 1936 election campaign Landon claimed he could manage New Deal programs better than Roosevelt. Later he denounced them altogether. (b) Roosevelt met anti-New Deal feelings head on, saying he welcomed the opposition.
2. (a) Roosevelt's coalition in the 1936 election included the solid South, big-city machines, blacks, and organized labor. (b) Democrats had won the support of organized labor and blacks by giving labor the right to organize and by taking an active interest in living conditions in the black community.
3. (a) By redesigning the Supreme Court Roosevelt hoped to keep the Court from striking down other New Deal legislation, especially the Social Security and Wagner acts. (b) He failed to redesign the Court because there was almost universal opposition to his efforts, but the Court did not strike down the legislation as he had feared.
4. (a) Reduced government spending and the inability of private business to take up the slack led to recession in 1937–1938. (b) Roosevelt hesitated to increase government spending because he hoped private business could reverse the downward trend of the economy.
5. (a) All workers in an industry, not just skilled workers, were represented by the Congress of Industrial Organizations. (b) The CIO developed the sitdown strike as a new tactic. (c) The tactic worked because industries could not find ways to remove the workers without risking damage to the plant or other violence. (d) The Fair Labor Standards Act established minimum wages and maximum hours.
6. (a) The drought from 1932 to 1936 destroyed soil and crops and led to bankruptcies, foreclosures, and a mass exodus from the Midwest. (b) To alleviate the problems of farmers the Resettlement Administration attempted to resettle farmers on more productive land, the Farm Security Administration extended loans, the Forest Service promoted conservation, the Soil Conservation and Domestic Allotment Act encouraged farmers to stop growing soil-depleting crops and stimulated soil restoration, and the second Agricultural Adjustment Act regulated production and provided for storage in granaries.
7. (a) During the Great Depression blacks were often the first to be fired, black tenant farmers and sharecroppers often lost their land when production was

reduced, and lynchings increased. (b) Under the New Deal Eleanor Roosevelt and Harry Hopkins worked to prevent discrimination in New Deal programs, black teenagers were employed by the CCC, and blacks were appointed to important positions in the administration.

8. (a) Collier tried to improve the lot of Native Americans by extending the benefits of New Deal relief and job programs to them. He stopped the sale of Indian land. He also saw to it that Indians received jobs as well as help in improving their farms. (b) The Indian Reorganization Act offered scholarship money to Indian students and funds with which Indians could start their own businesses.

9. (a) During the Great Depression women were forced out of jobs, which were given to men. (b) Mary Dewson tried to improve the position of women by persuading Roosevelt to appoint women to important posts in his administration and by insisting on equal treatment of women in New Deal programs.

For Further Thought, text page 593

1. (a) Movies and radio helped Americans temporarily escape the reality of the Great Depression. (b) Movies reinforced the values of hard work, honesty, and cooperation among people to overcome life's difficulties. (c) Answers may vary. Students might discuss how movies have shaped the students' own thinking.

2. (a) The New Deal permanently increased the size of the federal government, its role in the economy, and people's expectations from government. (b) Answers may vary. (c) Student answers should refer to the programs established by the New Deal and to changes in business activity during the 1930s. (d) Answers may vary but should point to New Deal programs that are still in effect.

3. Students could note that Roosevelt's plan might have weakened the independence of the Supreme Court. The contrary position could suggest that the Court's independence would be preserved by the constitutional provision granting lifetime tenure to the justices.

Developing Basic Skills, text page 593

1. (a) The painting shows the construction of a dam. (b) By showing people at work, the picture reflects the goals of the New Deal. (c) The artist was trying to convey hope. (d) Students might suggest that the picture reflects the New Deal's efforts to stimulate economic activity. The painting celebrates work and thus reveals America's hope to eliminate unemployment.

2. Research will vary.

34 Prelude to Another World Conflict (1920–1941)

Section Review, text page 597

1. *Kellogg-Briand Pact:* contained a pledge by 62 nations that they would never resort to war. *Dawes Plan:* agreement by the United States to loan money to Germany so Germany could pay its reparations to France and other allies. *Clark Memorandum:* U.S. declaration drawn up in 1928 stating that the United States did not have the right to intervene militarily in the affairs of Latin American nations. *Stimson Doctrine:* declaration issued in 1932 stating that the United States would not recognize Japan's territorial gains in China.

2. *isolationist:* person who believes that the United States should avoid alliances and agreements with other nations. *internationalist:* person who supports an active role for the United States in international affairs.

3. President Harding dismissed any suggestion that the United States join the League of Nations.

4. The Dawes Plan rescued Germany from economic ruin and enabled the Allies to fulfill their obligations to the United States.

5. In the agreement Dwight Morrow worked out with the Mexican government, United States corporations were allowed to permanently hold all oil properties acquired before 1917.

Section Review, text page 600

1. *Benito Mussolini:* became dictator of Italy in 1922. *Adolf Hitler:* leader of the Nazi party in Germany; he came to power in 1933. *Nye committee:* Senate committee headed by Senator Nye of North Dakota that investigated United States entry into the war in 1917. *"good neighbor" policy:* Roosevelt's nonintervention policy toward Latin America.

2. *totalitarian state:* country in which the government is supreme and individuals have few rights. *devalue:* to reduce the value of.

3. Bitterness over the Treaty of Versailles helped Hitler gain power in Germany.

4. Roosevelt hoped to stimulate foreign trade by devaluing the American dollar.

5. The Nye Committee claimed that bankers and munitions manufacturers had tried to push the United States into World War I.

6. President Roosevelt implemented the "good neighbor" policy by withdrawing United States Marines from Haiti and by nullifying the Platt Amendment, which had restricted Cuban independence by making Cuba a United States protectorate.

Section Review, text page 604

1. *Panay incident:* the 1937 Japanese bomber attack on the American gunboat *Panay*, on patrol in the Yangtze River; the United States accepted Japan's apology and $2 million for damages. *Ludlow Amendment:* proposed amendment to the Constitution that would have required a national vote before the United States could enter a war, except in case of invasion; the amendment failed in Congress. *Neville Chamberlain:* prime minister of Britain who appeased Hitler's territorial ambitions. *Winston Churchill:* succeeded Chamberlain as prime minister; a long-time critic of appeasement.
2. *appeasement:* policy of not resisting Hitler's demands in order to avoid war. *Blitzkrieg:* lightning warfare; method that Germany used against Poland in 1939.
3. The United States continued to ship weapons to China after the Japanese attack in 1937.
4. (a) At the Munich Conference Hitler promised Britain and France that he had no interest in additional territory in Czechoslovakia or anywhere else in Europe. (b) Hitler did not keep his promise. In 1939 he invaded and annexed the rest of Czechoslovakia.
5. Preparing for the possibility of war, Congress authorized cash sales of arms to the Allies. In 1940 it appropriated over $17 billion for modernizing the U.S. army and navy. In June 1940 Roosevelt sold 50 destroyers to England in return for 99-year leases on naval and air bases in Newfoundland and the Caribbean.

Section Review, text page 608

1. *Wendell Willkie:* Roosevelt's Republican opponent in 1940. *Lend-Lease Act:* act passed in early 1941 that authorized the President to sell, exchange, lend, or lease war materials to any country whose defense he deemed to be vital to the defense of the United States. *Atlantic Charter:* agreement between the United States and Britain; both nations promised to seek no territorial gain and to support "the right of all peoples to choose the form of government under which they will live."
2. Both Roosevelt and Willkie supported the Selective Service Act and increased aid to Britain, including the destroyer deal.
3. Roosevelt proposed the "lend-lease" policy because Britain was running out of money and could not pay cash for arms purchases.
4. When Germany invaded the Soviet Union in 1941 the United States extended the Lend-Lease Act to include the Soviet Union.
5. Trade with the United States was important to Japan because the latter received 90 percent of its scrap metal and 60 percent of its oil from the United States.
6. Americans thought the Japanese would attack in Southeast Asia.

Chapter Review, text page 609

1. (a) President Harding's hostility to American involvement in the League of Nations reflected the isolationist mood of the 1920s. (b) Increased tariffs also reflected the isolationist sentiment of the time.
2. (a) By sending representatives to several conferences, supporting the Kellogg-Briand Pact, instituting the Dawes Plan, and participating in international trade, the United States demonstrated its willingness to support world cooperation in the 1920s. (b) By instituting the Dawes Plan in 1924 the United States became directly involved in the world economy.
3. (a) United States policy toward Latin America was not isolationist, as the United States sent in troops to restore order there on several occasions during the 1920s. (b) This policy changed under Coolidge and Hoover as both refrained from military intervention in Latin America. (c) Roosevelt instituted the "good neighbor" policy of nonintervention in Latin America.
4. (a) World-wide depression drastically reduced international trade. (b) Roosevelt tried to improve American foreign trade by devaluing the dollar and pressing for lower tariffs. (c) He failed because demand for American goods increased only modestly; other countries just could not afford to buy the goods.
5. (a) Nye's committee investigations contributed to feelings of isolationism because Nye told the American people they had been tricked into war by bankers and munitions manufacturers. (b) Isolationist legislation included the Neutrality Act of 1935, authorizing the President to ban arms sales to nations at war, and the Neutrality Act of 1936, prohibiting loans to nations at war. The Neutrality Act of 1937 further extended the President's authority to bar shipments to nations at war.
6. (a) Japan's attacks on China between 1930 and 1937 alarmed the United States. (b) The Hoover administration opposed Japanese aggression but took no actions to preserve China's independence. (c) Roosevelt reacted by continuing arms shipments to China. (d) Roosevelt was not able to counter the isolationist mood of the country, as evidenced by the *Panay* incident and the near passage of the Ludlow Amendment.
7. (a) Rather than resisting the Nazi occupation of the Rhineland, Britain and France tried to appease Hitler. (b) In 1938 Germany took over Austria

and the Sudetenland. (c) War began in 1939 when Germany invaded Poland.

8. (a) At the outbreak of war Americans overwhelmingly sympathized with the Allies. (b) Initially the government issued a proclamation of neutrality. At the same time it pushed for a repeal of restrictions on arms sales.

9. (a) The Lend-Lease Act gave the President authority to sell, exchange, lend, or lease war materials to any country whose defense was deemed vital to the defense of the United States. (b) It allowed the United States to lend Britain whatever supplies it needed to resist the Nazis.

10. (a) To stop Japanese aggression the United States placed an embargo on the export of scrap metal, oil, and aviation fuel to Japan. Also, all Japanese bank accounts in the United States were blocked. (b) The United States finally declared war on Japan when the Japanese attacked Pearl Harbor.

For Further Thought, text page 609

1. Answers may vary. Accept justifiable answers, but emphasize the threat of war and the tendency to stay with a President in time of crisis.

2. Students should refer to the desire to avoid getting into another world war in explaining the prevalence of isolationist sentiment during the 1920s and 1930s.

Developing Basic Skills, text page 609

1. In discussing the differences between America's entry into the two world wars students should discuss the question of neutrality legislation as well as the immediate cause of each war. A discussion of similarities should refer to American reluctance to become entangled in a foreign conflict. The role of America's commitments to its allies should also be examined.

2. (a) The subject of the cartoon is the threat of war in Europe. (b) Uncle Sam is reflecting about the cost of World War I in American lives and money. (c) Answers may vary, but they should reflect an isolationist theme. (d) This is an isolationist cartoon because it presents only the arguments against American intervention in European affairs.

3. During the 1920s isolationist events included the United States' refusal to join the League of Nations. Internationalist events included the establishment of the Dawes Plan and the signing of the Kellogg-Briand Pact. During the 1930s isolationist events included the Nye committee investigation, the enactment of neutrality legislation, and the refusal of the United States to declare war on Germany when World War II began. Internationalist

events included increased military preparedness and legislation that provided for the sale of arms to the Allies on a cash-and-carry basis. Accept factually based answers on the extent of isolationism in the 1920s and 1930s.

35 The Second World War (1941–1945)

Section Review, text page 613

1. *Allies:* 26 nations, later expanded to 49, headed by the United States, Great Britain, and the Soviet Union, that opposed the Axis powers. *Axis powers:* Germany, Italy, Japan, and four other nations that fought the Allies during World War II. *Operation Torch:* plan to invade North Africa proposed by Churchill. *Dwight D. Eisenhower:* commander of the combined British and American forces in North Africa. *Douglas MacArthur:* commander of United States forces in the Pacific.

2. Most of World War II was fought in the Pacific and in Europe.

3. In 1942 the Allied situation in the Pacific was desperate. The United States was short of critical military supplies, and Japanese submarines were sinking ships faster than the Allies could build them. Also, the Japanese had conquered many of the islands in the western Pacific as well as the nations of eastern and southern Asia, and they threatened India and Australia.

4. Allied victory in North Africa opened the Mediterranean Sea to Allied shipping and made an invasion of southern Europe possible.

5. Victories in the Coral Sea near Java, at Midway Island, and at Guadalcanal Island helped stop the Japanese advance in the Pacific.

Section Review, text page 617

1. *War Production Board:* took charge of the national production system, which had to be converted from a peacetime to a wartime economy. *Office of Price Administration:* attempted to control inflation by setting price ceilings on most items; it also set up a system of rationing. *Office of War Mobilization:* coordinated the activities of all the wartime agencies. *War Manpower Commission:* determined where in the economy workers were most needed. *War Labor Board:* worked out problems between labor and management; it contributed to the growth of union membership by enforcing the Wagner Act, and it allowed wage increases to offset rising prices while at the same time trying to limit inflation. *A. Philip Randolph:* head of the Brotherhood of Sleep-

ing Car Porters; he threatened to lead a march on Washington, D.C. to protest discrimination against black workers. *Executive Order 8802:* banned racial discrimination in all government agencies, in job training programs, and in all companies doing business with the federal government.
2. Examples of how industry was converted from peacetime to wartime production: shirt factories were converted to the production of mosquito netting; model train producers made bomb fuses; metal weather stripping factories made mortar shells; kitchen sink assembly lines produced ammunition cartridge cases; and automobile factories manufactured tanks, trucks, personnel carriers, and aircraft.
3. During the war workers' wages increased and unemployment dropped.
4. As a result of the war women for the first time piloted airplanes, repaired airplanes and vehicles, drove trucks, operated radios, did clerical and technical work of all kinds, and found employment in steel mills, shipyards, and other industries.
5. (a) Employment opportunities for blacks increased because of the increased demand for workers due to war production. (b) Blacks continued to face segregation, housing shortages, and hostility in the job market.
6. Fear of sabotage led to the relocation of Japanese Americans.

Section Review, text page 622

1. *Joseph Stalin:* premier of the Soviet Union during World War II. *Operation Overlord:* code name for the Allied invasion of Europe in 1944. *Cherbourg:* French port captured by the Allies in 1944; served as a receiving point for supplies for the rest of the war. *Chester Nimitz:* U.S. Admiral in cocommand with MacArthur of the Allied effort in the Pacific.
2. *leapfrogging:* term for the invasion of a few strategically placed Pacific islands.
3. The Allied successes in Sicily and Italy led to the overthrow of Mussolini.
4. The Russians began an offensive against the Germans in the summer of 1943.
5. For Operation Overlord to succeed, the Allies needed a huge reserve of supplies, secrecy had to be maintained, and the weather had to be clear.
6. In 1943–1944 the Allies followed the policy of leapfrogging the Japanese-held islands in the Pacific.

Section Review, text page 624

1. *Chiang Kai-shek:* Chinese leader during World War II. *the Big Three:* name given to the leaders of the United States, Britain, and the Soviet Union.

United Nations: international peacekeeping organization conceived at the Dumbarton Oaks conference. *Harry S. Truman:* senator from Missouri; Roosevelt's vice-presidential running mate in 1944. *Thomas E. Dewey:* governor of New York; Roosevelt's Republican opponent in 1944.
2. At Teheran in 1943 the Big Three discussed the strategy for final defeat of the Axis powers, plans for a new international peacekeeping organization, and the postwar fate of Germany.
3. In the election of 1944 Dewey emphasized the failure of Democratic economic policies.
4. At Yalta the Big Three decided to divide Germany into four zones of occupation governed by American, British, French, and Russian forces.

Section Review, text page 628

1. *Manhattan Project:* massive research effort that led to the development of the atomic bomb.
2. *genocide:* total destruction of a race of human beings. *kamikaze:* practice of Japanese fighter pilots of committing suicide by crashing their planes into Allied ships.
3. At the Battle of the Bulge the Germans broke through Allied lines and surrounded American soldiers at Bastogne.
4. In 1945 Eisenhower thought the most important Allied goal was to defeat Germany as quickly as possible.
5. Joy over German surrender was clouded upon learning about the Nazi concentration camps and the policy of genocide that had been carried out at these camps against European Jews. Many Americans were also saddened by the death of President Roosevelt.

Chapter Review, text page 629

1. (a) The year 1942 was a dark time for the Allies because Japan had conquered many Pacific islands and the nations of eastern and southern Asia. Japan had also crippled China and threatened India and Australia. In addition, Germany had conquered most of eastern and western Europe. (b) Operation Torch improved the Allied situation in Europe because capture of North Africa allowed use of the Mediterranean Sea and facilitated the invasion of southern Europe. (c) The situation of the Allies in the Pacific was more hopeful by 1943 because of Allied victories there.
2. (a) The War Production Board helped mobilize American industry by supervising conversion from peacetime to wartime production. (b) The Office of Price Administration set price ceilings on most items and supervised rationing. (c) The Office of

War Mobilization coordinated the activities of all wartime production agencies. (d) The War Manpower Commission determined where in the economy workers were most needed. (e) The War Labor Board handled problems between labor and management.

3. The war dramatically affected the American economy. Wages and employment increased. Taxes, especially on high incomes, increased, and war bonds were sold. Between 1939 and 1945 the gross national product rose from $91.3 billion to $166.6 billion.

4. (a) During the war union membership increased. (b) Many job opportunities opened up for women. (c) Job opportunities for blacks increased and some gains were made in the fight against discrimination. Racial tension did not disappear, however, and blacks still faced segregation and hostility. (d) Mexican Americans continued to face discrimination and were sometimes attacked. (e) Italian Americans and German Americans faced some discrimination during the war, but they were not treated as severely as Japanese Americans. (f) Japanese Americans were evacuated from their homes and interned in camps.

5. (a) The Allies decided to invade Italy because Italy appeared to be the weakest point in the Axis empire. (b) The attack succeeded. The Allies first took Sicily and then Italy. The success of this invasion led to the overthrow of Mussolini.

6. (a) Operation Overlord, the plan for the Allied invasion of Europe, called for attacking beachheads in northern France. It depended on a buildup of supplies, as well as on secrecy and favorable weather. (b) Operation Overlord succeeded. The beachheads were secured in six weeks, the French port of Cherbourg was captured, and from there the Allies were able to move into western Europe.

7. (a) To defeat Japan MacArthur preferred a South Pacific route, pushing northward from Australia through New Guinea. Nimitz favored an advance toward Japan via the islands of the central Pacific. (b) The technique of leapfrogging enabled the Allies to isolate Pacific islands and cut off Japanese forces from their supplies. (c) Also important to the attacks on Pacific islands was the use of amphibious landings, which required close coordination among air bombings, naval support, and troop movements.

8. (a) During the war diplomatic conferences among Allied leaders took place at Moscow, Cairo, Teheran, Bretton Woods, Dumbarton Oaks, and Yalta. (b) At these conferences the Big Three discussed plans for creating an organization of nations to maintain world peace and security, the strategy for defeating the Axis powers, postwar

economic recovery, and the fate of Germany. (c) At Yalta they agreed that Russia would declare war on Japan three months after Germany surrendered. In return Russia would control the Kurile Islands and the southern portion of Sakhalin Island, as well as Outer Mongolia. Russia would also maintain shipping rights through Port Arthur and control of the railroads in Manchuria. As for Europe, free elections would be held in countries that Germany had occupied during the war. Germany was to be divided into four zones of occupation, which would be governed by the United States, Britain, France, and Russia.

9. (a) The Battle of the Bulge was a German offensive in December 1944 along the border of Belgium and Luxembourg that broke through Allied lines. The Germans surrounded American forces at Bastogne. (b) German success at the Battle of the Bulge slowed the invasion of Germany.

10. (a) American leaders believed the final assault on Japan would be costly because the Japanese had demonstrated their willingness to fight to the death. (b) For this reason, the United States thought Russia's help would be needed in the invasion of Japan. Therefore the United States had tried to compromise with Stalin.

For Further Thought, text page 629

1. In discussing how the Second World War was more worldwide than the First World War, emphasize the number of nations that fought in this war and the many parts of the world in which battles took place.

2. (a) Japanese Americans were interned at special relocation camps. (b) During World War I German Americans were harassed by some Americans but they were not placed in detention centers by the federal authorities. (c) Students might suggest that race is a factor that explains the different treatment received by each group.

Developing Basic Skills, text page 629

1. During World War I the War Industries Board established controls over scarce materials, set prices, and coordinated war production. The War Labor Board supervised labor-management relations. Students should note that during World War II the War Production Board coordinated war production. Another War Labor Board regulated labor-management relations. Similarities can be explained by noting the need to coordinate all phases of the economy to support the war effort. One difference between government's economic role in the two world wars is that only during World War II did

the government attempt to control the prices of most items. Students might suggest that this difference can be explained by the New Deal's redefinition of the government's economic role.
2. Research will vary.

Unit Ten: The United States in a Changing World

36 The Postwar International Scene (1945–1960)

Section Review, text page 636

1. *United Nations:* international peacekeeping organization founded in 1945. *Security Council:* United Nations body most directly responsible for maintaining world peace; it investigates conflicts between nations and recommends solutions. *General Assembly:* UN body that considers world problems and makes recommendations to other UN agencies. *Syngman Rhee:* president of South Korea. *Mao Tse-tung:* leader of the Chinese communist forces that opposed the nationalist government of Chiang Kai-shek.
2. After the war, the Allies agreed to divide both Germany and Berlin into four zones, each administered by one of the Allies.
3. The United States, Great Britain, France, the Soviet Union, and China received permanent seats on the United Nations Security Council.
4. The UN recommended that Palestine be divided into an Arab and a Jewish state.
5. The defeat and demilitarization of Japan left a power vacuum in East Asia after the war.
6. The nationalist and the communist forces were involved in the civil war in China.

Caption, text page 640

Lithuania, Latvia, and Estonia were independent nations after World War I but were later absorbed by the Soviet Union.

Section Review, text page 640

1. *Truman Doctrine:* foreign policy announced by President Truman in March 1947, committing the United States to the support of "free peoples who are resisting attempted subjugation by armed minorities or by outside pressures." *Marshall Plan:* mas-

sive four-year economic aid program proposed by Secretary of State George C. Marshall and approved by Congress in 1948 to finance European economic recovery. *NATO:* North Atlantic Treaty Organization; peacetime allliance created in 1949 and committed to the defense of Europe; membership includes the United States, Canada, Iceland, and their European allies.
2. *containment:* foreign policy first outlined by State Department official George Kennan in July 1947, stating that the United States would contain, or hold, Soviet influence within its present limits.
3. President Truman decided to aid Greece after the British government announced discontinuation of military aid to the Greek government. He realized that the loss of British aid was likely to lead to a communist victory in the Greek civil war.
4. According to General Marshall the main purpose of the Marshall Plan was to preserve "free institutions" in Europe.
5. When the Soviets blockaded Berlin, the United States ordered a massive airlift of supplies to West Berlin. The airlift continued until the blockade ended.
6. The communist takeover of mainland China in 1949 and the news that the Soviets possessed an atomic bomb increased cold war tension.

Section Review, text page 643

1. *38th parallel:* the boundary between North and South Korea.
2. *limited war:* war in which specific objectives rather than total victory over the enemy are sought; weaponry is limited.
3. When North Korea invaded South Korea, the United Nations Security Council condemned the invasion, demanded withdrawal of North Korean forces, and voted to provide military aid to South Korea.
4. (a) The original goal of the United Nations and the United States in the Korean War was to drive the North Koreans out of South Korea. (b) With MacArthur's successes in October 1950, the goal changed to "the establishment of a unified, independent, and democratic Korea."
5. The issue of how the Korean War should be fought led to conflict between President Truman and General MacArthur.

Section Review, text page 645

1. *Nikita Khrushchev:* premier of the Soviet Union after the death of Joseph Stalin. *John Foster Dulles:* secretary of state in the Eisenhower administration.
2. *massive retaliation:* military strategy, proposed by Secretary of State Dulles, to fight Soviet or Chinese

aggression directly with nuclear weapons if necessary. *arms race:* Soviet-American competition to accumulate nuclear weapons.
3. Dulles thought the United States should use political pressure and propaganda to encourage the people of eastern Europe to revolt against the Soviet Union.
4. Nikita Khrushchev's two-week visit to the United States in the summer of 1959 was the high point of the thaw in the cold war.
5. The "U-2 incident" temporarily ended the thaw in Soviet-American relations.

Section Review, text page 648

1. *Ho Chi Minh:* leader of the Vietnamese forces in their war for independence from France. *Dien Bien Phu:* place where French forces surrendered to Vietnamese forces in May 1954. *domino theory:* belief that if one nation fell to communism, neighboring nations would follow. *SEATO:* Southeast Asia Treaty Organization; alliance sponsored by the United States to protect Asia from communist expansion; under its terms the United States pledged to aid Asian nations threatened by communism. *Gamal Abdel Nasser:* nationalist leader of Egypt in the 1950s. *Eisenhower Doctrine:* foreign policy formulated by President Eisenhower that offered United States military aid to Middle Eastern countries requesting help against communist aggression. *Fidel Castro:* Cuban revolutionary who led a successful revolt against the regime of Fulgencio Batista and became the leader of Cuba in 1959.
2. In their 1956 revolt Hungarian nationalists demanded removal of pro-Soviet Hungarian officials, withdrawal of Soviet troops, and legalization of anticommunist political parties.
3. The United States encouraged the French to stay in Vietnam because Ho Chi Minh, the leader of the Vietnamese forces, was a communist.
4. When Israel invaded Egypt in 1956, Britain and France began bombing Egyptian targets, claiming that they were protecting the Suez Canal. The canal was important to the West for economic and military reasons.
5. Castro's seizure of American-owned oil refineries and other businesses disrupted relations between the United States and Cuba.

Chapter Review, text page 649

1. (a) Soviet resentment over the delay in the cross-channel invasion of Europe and American suspicion that Stalin meant to spread communism throughout Europe contributed to postwar tensions between the United States and the Soviet Union. (b) In defending its actions in eastern Europe the Soviet Union argued that it needed friendly states near its borders to act as a buffer against future German attack. (c) The Americans rejected this argument, charging that Soviet domination of eastern Europe was part of the Soviet Union's larger plan for world rule.
2. (a) The goals of the United Nations were peaceful solutions to international conflicts, the prevention of wars, and cooperation to eliminate hunger, disease, and illiteracy. (b) The Security Council was mostly concerned with seeking peaceful solutions to international conflicts. (c) To achieve this goal, the Security Council was given the power to investigate conflicts between nations and recommend solutions. It could also organize a peacekeeping force composed of troops from member nations. (d) Its actions were limited by the fact that the council was not given power to enforce its decisions. Also, any permanent member of the council could veto that body's actions.
3. The following postwar conditions contributed to the cold war. (a) Civil war raged in Greece, the Greek economy was in ruin, and starvation was widespread. In addition, many opponents of the Greek monarchy were communists and received aid from Yugoslavia, a communist nation. (b) In Italy, difficult economic conditions made many Italians desperate for reform, and they turned to the Communist party for help, electing 104 communists to the 1946 parliament. (c) The Soviet Union installed a communist government in the northern zone of Korea and then refused to cooperate in national elections. (d) In China both the nationalists and the communists refused to accept a truce or agree on a government acceptable to both sides, and the civil war resumed.
4. (a) The Truman Doctrine declared that the United States would support "free peoples who are resisting attempted subjugation by armed minorities or by outside pressures." (b) President Truman implemented this doctrine to block communist expansion. (c) The doctrine was successful in Greece and Turkey. With American aid the Greek government crushed the communist revolt in October 1947; Turkey resisted Soviet territorial demands.
5. (a) The Marshall Plan called for the United States to provide massive economic aid to Europe to finance European economic recovery. (b) The designers of the Marshall Plan hoped that by helping with the economic recovery of European nations they would make the people of these countries immune to the promises of communist politicians. (c) The plan worked. Industrial growth in western Europe returned to its prewar level, with the result that the appeal of communist political parties in these countries declined.

6. (a) The Soviets hoped that a blockade would drive Great Britain, France, and the United States out of Berlin and would allow them to unify Germany under communist rule. (b) The United States broke the blockade with a massive airlift to West Berlin. The airlift supplied West Berlin with 13,000 tons of supplies daily.

7. (a) After Mao's victory in China, President Truman refused to recognize the communist government on mainland China. Instead, he recognized the nationalists on Taiwan as the legitimate Chinese government. (b) Following the Soviet test of an atomic bomb the United States authorized the development of a hydrogen bomb and gave more attention to rebuilding its conventional forces.

8. (a) Following the North Korean invasion of South Korea, the United States ordered its planes and ships to back up the South Korean army and sent its own troops into the conflict. (b) The goal of the United Nations and the United States changed in October 1950 because of General MacArthur's successes in overcoming North Korean forces. (c) Reacting to the invasion of North Korea, Communist Chinese forces entered the war and forced the United Nations troops to retreat with heavy losses across the 38th parallel.

9. (a) New directions in Soviet policy such as concentration on internal affairs and statements that war between the Soviet Union and the West was unnecessary led to a "thaw" in the cold war during the late 1950s. (b) The 1955 summit conference between Khrushchev and Eisenhower opened the way for further discussions of disarmament and the banning of nuclear testing. (c) The thaw ended with the "U-2 incident" and the collapse of the Paris summit in 1960.

10. (a) Nasser seized the Suez Canal in 1956 after the United States offered and then withdrew its support for the construction of a dam in Egypt. (b) Britain and France threatened military action against Egypt because the canal was crucial to Western economic and military interests. (c) Although not directly involved in the war, the Soviet Union offered military and economic aid to Egypt.

11. (a) At first the United States reacted positively to Fidel Castro's revolution in Cuba. President Eisenhower recognized the Castro government one week after it took power. (b) The American attitude toward Cuba changed after American businesses there were seized.

For Further Thought, text page 649

1. Students might suggest that Vandenberg was right because the explosion of the first Soviet atomic weapon broke America's nuclear monopoly. The atomic bomb gave the Soviets the leverage to act assertively in a series of postwar crises.

2. (a) The expansion of communist power in the postwar world forced the United States to abandon its historical policy of isolationism. In answering this question students should refer to Soviet military occupation of eastern Europe and the growth of communist movements in western Europe. (b) Acceptable answers may refer to the Soviet domination of eastern Europe or to the Soviet explosion of a nuclear weapon.

3. (a) American industry and agriculture were not damaged by enemy attack during the war. (b) Students should mention those countries in which the possibility of communists' coming to power was strongest. (c) In the absence of postwar American aid, communism would have spread more easily.

4. The blockage of Soviet expansion in eastern Europe and the defeat of North Korean aggression indicate the success of the policy of containment between 1947 and 1960. Castro's seizure of power in Cuba represents a setback for the policy of containment.

Developing Basic Skills, text page 649

1. (a) Most of the NATO nations are located in western Europe. Note that the United States and Canada are NATO members. (b) The Warsaw Pact nations are located in eastern Europe. (c) Students should suggest that this terminology originated in the postwar military alignment.

2. (a) The photograph shows MacArthur being welcomed by a large crowd. (b) A supporter of MacArthur might argue that the photo suggests that the American people backed MacArthur in his dispute with President Truman. (c) MacArthur publicly differed with Truman's military goals in the Korean War. (d) Truman relieved MacArthur of his command. (e) The principle of civilian control of the armed forces was reinforced by Truman's dismissal of MacArthur.

37 A Search for Stability (1945–1960)

Section Review, text page 654

1. *Taft-Hartley Act:* bill passed in 1946 over Truman's veto; it gave the attorney general the power to apply for a court order that would delay a strike for 80 days if national health or safety were threatened; it also banned the closed shop and union contributions to political campaigns. *Thomas E. Dewey:*

governor of New York and Republican nominee for President in the 1948 election. *States' Rights party:* political party formed by southern Democrats, which nominated Strom Thurmond for President in the 1948 election. *Progressive party:* political party that nominated Henry Wallace for President in the 1948 election; opposed Truman's containment policy.

2. *closed shop:* a business in which all workers are required to be union members. *de facto segregation:* segregation that exists in fact, although not in law.

3. Reacting to postwar inflation, workers demanded higher wages to keep up with the rising cost of living. In January 1946, strikes took place in the steel, automobile, meatpacking, and electrical appliance industries.

4. The GI Bill of Rights provided a year of unemployment insurance to jobless veterans, gave financial aid to veterans who attended college, and entitled veterans to government loans for home building and business.

5. Most members of the Eightieth Congress opposed social welfare legislation.

6. The National Housing Act of 1949, which helped finance low-income housing; a rise in the minimum hourly wage under the Fair Labor Standards Act; and the Social Security Act of 1950, which increased the number of people covered by old age insurance, were all part of Truman's Fair Deal.

7. To reduce discrimination in employment, Truman reaffirmed Franklin Roosevelt's executive order banning discrimination in firms doing business with the federal government. He also created the Committee on Contract Compliance to investigate firms that might have violated the order.

Section Review, text page 656

1. *House Un-American Activities Committee:* a committee created by the House of Representatives in 1938 to investigate subversive activity in the United States. *Joseph R. McCarthy:* Wisconsin senator who rose to power in the early 1950s by accusing government employees of having communist affiliations. *McCarthyism:* term used to describe the technique made famous by Joseph McCarthy of ruining someone's reputation by making numerous charges, often without any evidence to support them.

2. The purpose of the Loyalty Review Board was to guarantee the "unswerving loyalty" of all federal government employees.

3. Contributing to the increased public concern about communist activity in the United States were the HUAC hearings on alleged communist activity in the movie industry, the Whittaker Chambers–Alger Hiss investigation, and the conviction and execution of Ethel and Julius Rosenberg on spy charges.

4. Joseph McCarthy rose to national prominence by playing on American fears about disloyalty and communist infiltration of government.

5. The televised Army-McCarthy hearings showed McCarthy as a bully, not a hero, and led to a decline in his popularity.

Section Review, text page 658

1. *Adlai E. Stevenson:* Illinois governor and Democratic party nominee for President in the 1952 election.

2. In the 1952 election Dwight Eisenhower was seen as a down-to-earth person, while Adlai Stevenson was considered too intellectual. Eisenhower was also a national hero because of his service in World War II, while Stevenson was practically unknown outside of Illinois.

3. President Eisenhower believed in reducing the government's role in the economy and made it clear that he did not favor additional social welfare programs.

4. Suburbs grew after World War II because a "baby boom" created a demand for new housing. Also, prosperity and the GI Bill enabled many people to buy their own homes, and a massive road-building program had made commuting from city jobs to suburban areas easier.

5. During the 1950s managing a home in the suburbs and raising a family became the ideal of many American women.

Section Review, text page 664

1. *Rosa Parks:* black woman who started the Montgomery bus boycott in December 1955 by refusing to move from the "white" section of a bus. *Martin Luther King:* leader of the Montgomery bus boycott and advocate of civil disobedience. *Sputnik:* satellite launched by the Soviet Union in October 1957. *rock 'n' roll:* new type of music in the early 1950s that blended elements of country and western music with elements of rhythm and blues. *beatniks:* critics of American society in the 1950s who expressed their discontent by refusing to conform to accepted ways of dressing, thinking, and acting. *Richard M. Nixon:* Vice-President under Eisenhower and Republican nominee for President in the 1960 elections. *John F. Kennedy:* Democratic senator from Massachusetts who in 1960 became the youngest man and first Catholic to be elected President.

2. *civil disobedience:* illegal nonviolent protest.

3. (a) In the case of *Brown* v. *Board of Education of Topeka*, the Supreme Court ruled that "separate educational facilities are inherently unequal," and that the doctrine of "separate but equal" had no place in public education. (b) To enforce the Court's ruling in Little Rock, Arkansas, President Eisenhower sent federal troops in 1957 to assist a group of black students in entering Little Rock Central High School.

4. Boycotts and sit-ins were two tactics used by black Americans against segregation in the 1950s.

5. In reaction to the public outcry about the launching of Sputnik by the Soviet Union, Congress passed the National Defense Education Act in 1958. This legislation provided federal aid for schools and colleges. It also increased the budget of the National Science Foundation, which provided research grants for scientists and curriculum-improvement projects.

6. Two new art forms that developed during the 1950s were abstract expressionism and pop art.

7. (a) In 1960 John Kennedy declared that the nation seemed to be drifting, and he promised to get it "moving again." He also used the "missile gap" between the Soviet Union and the United States as a campaign issue. (b) Richard Nixon campaigned on Eisenhower's record, boasting of the years of peace and prosperity under the Republicans.

Chapter Review, text page 665

1. (a) Problems of unemployment and inflation confronted the nation after World War II. (b) The return of American soldiers to civilian life, the cancelation of government war contracts, and the end of wartime price controls were the basic causes of these problems. (c) To solve these problems Congress passed the GI Bill of Rights, a tax cut in 1945, and the Employment Act of 1946.

2. (a) The Republicans won a majority in both houses of Congress in 1948 because many voters blamed President Truman for the inflation, shortages, and strikes that plagued the nation. (b) The Eightieth Congress opposed Truman's legislative program and rejected many bills. (c) After the 1948 election the Congress passed the National Housing Act of 1949, an amendment to the Fair Labor Standards Act, and the Social Security Act of 1950. (d) Congress defeated several parts of the Fair Deal, including bills to provide federal aid to education, to establish federally financed health insurance, and to ban the poll tax and discrimination in employment. It also refused to repeal the Taft-Hartley Act.

3. (a) In the North segregation was largely *de facto*, existing in fact if not in law, while in the South Jim Crow laws required segregation. (b) President

Truman advanced the civil rights of black Americans by placing the weight of the presidency on the side of civil rights. He condemned lynchings, created the President's Committee on Civil Rights, issued a directive banning segregation in the armed forces in 1948, and attempted to reduce discrimination in employment.

4. The American public became increasingly concerned about the danger of communist activity at home because of the spread of communism abroad and the intensification of the cold war. Investigations that uncovered a few cases of disloyal activity at home heightened these fears. The investigations included the work of the Loyalty Review Board, the hearings of the House Un-American Activities Committee on the movie industry, the Whittaker Chambers–Alger Hiss affair, and the trial of Ethel and Julius Rosenberg for passing atomic secrets to Soviet agents. Public support of Joseph McCarthy's activities showed how frightened the public had become.

5. (a) Senator Joseph McCarthy charged that employees of the federal government were Communist party members or "bad security risks." (b) He persuaded thousands of Americans that he was protecting American security, and he succeeded in ruining the reputations and careers of many scholars and other public figures. (c) He ceased to be a political force after the televised Army–McCarthy hearings revealed him as a bully and a 1954 Senate censure resolution further reduced his popular appeal.

6. (a) During President Eisenhower's administration economic conditions were generally good. Unemployment remained near a relatively low 5 percent, factory wages climbed, labor's share of the national income increased, and the rate of inflation was lower than it had been under Truman. (b) Eisenhower refused to increase federal spending during the recession of 1957–1958 because he believed government should play a limited role in the economy. He said increasing federal spending would lead to inflation.

7. (a) Suburbs grew dramatically during the 1950s because a postwar "baby boom" created a need for new housing, while the prosperity of the period and the GI Bill of Rights enabled many people to buy their own homes. In addition, a postwar road-building program linked city jobs and suburban homes. (b) The suburbs of the 1920s lacked entertainment and shopping facilities, while the suburbs of the 1950s were increasingly self-contained.

8. (a) The 1896 decision had ruled that "separate but equal" facilities for blacks and whites were constitutional. The Supreme Court's decision in

Brown v. *Board of Education of Topeka* ruled that "separate educational facilities are inherently unequal." (b) The NAACP lawyers argued that public school segregation violated the "equal protection" clause of the Fourteenth Amendment, that it deprived black children of equal educational opportunity, and that it lowered the morale and motivation of black students. (c) President Eisenhower decided to send troops to Little Rock to integrate the city high school.

9. (a) The launching of Sputnik by the Soviet Union shocked most Americans because they had long believed that the United States was technologically superior to the Soviet Union. (b) Americans blamed weaknesses in education for that development.

10. Beatniks were disillusioned with American society because in their eyes it overvalued material success and emphasized conformity at the expense of individuality. Social scientist William Whyte criticized bureaucratic organizations for discouraging creativity and individualism. David Riesman charged that Americans cared too much about pleasing others, and economist John Kenneth Galbraith argued that unplanned economic growth had resulted in great private fortunes but had left the public sector impoverished. Others were disillusioned because of television quiz show scandals that were seen as signs of a breakdown of moral values.

For Further Thought, text page 665

1. Students should point out that the cold war and fear of Soviet expansion affected domestic politics in many ways. As the cold war intensified, many Americans became less tolerant of any sympathy toward communism or the Soviet Union. The creation of the Loyalty Review Board, the investigations of the House Un-American Activities Committee, the execution of Ethel and Julius Rosenberg, and Joseph McCarthy's great influence in the early 1950s are related to attitudes toward the Soviet Union.

2. (a) Students should suggest that during both the Red Scare of the 1920s and the McCarthy era the public became acutely aware of the dangers presented by communism. In both instances the government moved to counter the communist threat by limiting freedom of expression. (b) Senator McCarthy frequently charged that communists and communist sympathizers occupied high government positions. Such charges were not made during the Red Scare of the 1920s.

3. President Eisenhower tried to reduce the government's role in the economy, while President Tru-

man in his Fair Deal programs favored a strong role for government and supported social welfare legislation. Under Eisenhower, Congress limited federal aid for public housing and dropped wage and price controls established by the Truman administration.

4. Answers may vary. Point out that some parents worried that rock music would contribute to juvenile delinquency.

Developing Basic Skills, text page 665

1. (a) From a distance the houses appear to be look-alike "little boxes." (b) A closer view, however, would reveal that these houses are different in important respects. A walk through the neighborhood might show that the owners have made their homes quite distinctive. Answers may vary, but students should point to specific features of the community they describe.

2. (a) Students might note that today some commercials depict women as business executives. This is a new development in television advertising. (b) The similarity that remains between 1950s and current advertising is that women are typically shown doing household chores. Often women are seen learning about a household product from a man.

3. Results of research will vary.

38 A Turbulent Decade (1960–1969)

Section Review, text page 670

1. *Robert McNamara:* former president of Ford Motor Company who became secretary of defense under President Kennedy. *Peace Corps:* foreign-aid organization proposed by President Kennedy; composed of American volunteers who would teach in, or give technical aid to, developing countries. *Alliance for Progress:* alliance composed of the United States and Latin American nations pledged to improving economic development in Latin America; the United States pledged approximately $20 billion in aid over a ten-year period.

2. *strategic forces:* specially trained American armed forces units that could be moved quickly to any part of the world.

3. (a) The purpose of the Peace Corps was to build friendship with countries in Africa, Asia, and South America and to persuade neutral nations that western-style democracy offered the best way to achieve peace, stability, and growth. (b) The purpose of the Alliance for Progress was to improve relations with Latin American countries.

4. The Kennedy administration's attempt to overthrow Castro's government in Cuba undermined the goodwill of the United States in Latin America.
5. The Berlin wall proved to be a valuable propaganda weapon for the Western powers because they were able to say that the communist governments of eastern Europe had to use force to keep their people from fleeing.
6. In response to Khrushchev's decision to build missile bases in Cuba, President Kennedy's advisers proposed either a naval blockade of Cuba or an air strike against the missile sites.

Section Review, text page 672

1. *Alan Shepard:* American astronaut who in 1961 made a suborbital flight. *John Glenn:* American astronaut who orbited the earth three times on February 20, 1962. *Telstar:* commercial communications satellite that orbited the earth transmitting live television broadcasts over long distances. *James Meredith:* black Air Force veteran who enrolled in classes at the all-white University of Mississippi with the aid of federal marshals and the National Guard. *George Wallace:* governor of Alabama who attempted to stop a black student, Autherine Lucy, from registering at the all-white University of Alabama.
2. President Kennedy pledged the United States to the goal of putting an American on the moon before 1970.
3. (a) In an attempt to control inflation, President Kennedy established an informal standard of "wage-price guideposts" for business and labor. (b) He was especially concerned about the steel industry.
4. In support of civil rights President Kennedy backed the voting rights bill and the Twenty-fourth Amendment to the Constitution, and he appointed blacks to key positions in government.

Section Review, text page 674

1. *VISTA:* Volunteers in Service to America; domestic version of the Peace Corps. *Hubert H. Humphrey:* Minnesota senator and Democratic party vice-presidential candidate in the election of 1964. *Barry Goldwater:* Arizona senator and Republican party presidential candidate in the election of 1964.
2. Lyndon Johnson's political rise can be attributed to his shrewd political sense and his ability to convince fellow senators to vote his way.
3. The Economic Opportunity Act of 1964 provided job training programs for the poor, loans to encourage rural farm cooperatives and urban businesses, and aid to migrant laborers.

4. The Medicare Act provided hospital coverage for citizens over 65 and allowed them to participate in a program that shared other medical costs.
5. The enforcement of the Voting Rights Act of 1965 resulted in the registration of one million new black voters by the 1968 election.

Section Review, text page 677

1. *Black Muslims:* black organization led by Elijah Muhammed that believed that blacks would achieve personal and economic success only if they separated completely from white society. *Malcolm X:* former black Muslim minister who rejected Elijah Muhammed's separatist ideas in favor of a new philosophy that envisioned "a society in which there could exist honest white-black brotherhood." *Kerner Commission:* commission appointed by President Johnson to study causes and consequences of the civil disorder that had swept the nation.
2. In the early 1960s black Americans used a number of tactics to fight segregation including sit-ins, protest marches, and "freedom rides." "Freedom riders" refused to be segregated on buses and trains and in depots, stations, and rest rooms.
3. Some black leaders were particularly concerned about the plight of northern blacks and demanded more radical political action to overcome the *de facto* segregation, high unemployment, and low average income that existed for blacks there.
4. Before his death Malcolm X supported the goal of creating "a society in which there could exist honest white-black brotherhood."
5. Moderate black leaders believed black power should be expressed as self-reliance and pride, not as violence.

Section Review, text page 680

1. *Cesar Chavez:* Mexican American who began the movement to unionize California grape pickers. *National Congress of American Indians:* organization founded in 1940 to fight discrimination against Native Americans and to lobby for greater congressional recognition of Indian rights. *Dennis Banks, Clyde Bellecourt:* organizers of the American Indian Movement. *American Indian Movement:* militant Indian group organized in the 1960s. *Betty Friedan:* author of *The Feminine Mystique* and founder of the National Organization for Women. *National Organization for Women:* organization founded in 1966 to press for legislation guaranteeing women their civil rights. *Equal Rights Amendment:* proposed constitutional amendment passed by Congress in 1972 forbidding discrimination based on sex.

2. *bracero:* a term applied to a Mexican worker who, under a government program started in the 1950s, obtained a temporary permit to work in the United States; a bracero typically received low wages.

3. After 1952 Puerto Rico received commonwealth status.

4. To gain support for his union, Cesar Chavez organized sit-ins, protest demonstrations, and a nationwide boycott of table grapes.

5. Indian groups sharply protested the government's decision to turn its Indian programs over to the states.

6. The Equal Pay Act of 1963 and the Civil Rights Act of 1964 provided a legal basis for greater economic equality between men and women.

Section Review, text page 686

1. *Third World:* the developing nations of Asia, Africa, and Latin America. *Viet Cong:* anti-Diem rebels also known as the National Liberation Front who used guerrilla warfare to attack village officials supporting Diem. *Rolling Thunder:* bombing campaign over North Vietnam begun in February 1965. *William Westmoreland:* commander of the United States forces in Vietnam. *Eugene McCarthy:* Democratic senator and a leading opponent of the Vietnam War; ran against Johnson in the 1968 Democratic presidential primary in New Hampshire.

2. *apartheid:* policy of legal racial separation.

3. The United States publicly condemned apartheid while continuing to trade with South Africa and Rhodesia for strategic materials.

4. After the Gulf of Tonkin incident Johnson asked for authority to take "all necessary steps" to "prevent further aggression" by the North Vietnamese.

5. The main purpose of the Rolling Thunder campaign was to cut the flow of supplies from North Vietnam to the Viet Cong.

6. Reacting to growing opposition to the war, President Johnson announced in March 1968 that he was suspending bombing of North Vietnam and that he would not run for reelection.

Chapter Review, text page 687

1. (a) In reaction to Khrushchev's pledge to support anti-American "wars of liberation," President Kennedy developed strategic forces, specially trained units that could be moved quickly to any part of the world. In addition, the armed forces set up jungle warfare schools to teach guerrilla fighting techniques. (b) To win the friendship of developing nations, he set up the Peace Corps and the Alliance for Progress.

2. (a) The purpose of the Bay of Pigs invasion was to overthrow Castro's government in Cuba. (b) The Bay of Pigs invasion was a disaster. The United States did not deliver its promised air strike against the Cuban air force, and the Cuban people failed to join the anti-Castro invaders.

3. (a) Khrushchev's threat to sign a defense treaty with East Germany if NATO troops were not withdrawn from West Berlin, construction of a wall between East and West Berlin by the East Germans, and the Soviet resumption of aboveground nuclear testing after a three-year moratorium increased tensions between the Soviet Union and the United States in 1961 and 1962. (b) The Soviet Union was willing to limit nuclear tests by 1963 because it wanted to devote more of its resources to improvement of its domestic economy. Americans were interested in reducing the radioactive fallout from the testing.

4. (a) John Kennedy's New Frontier goal in the area of space exploration was to put an American on the moon before 1970. He moved toward this goal by supporting the NASA space program. (b) In the area of economic policy Kennedy hoped to stimulate economic growth while controlling inflation. In support of his economic policies, he attempted to increase government spending and persuade Congress to pass a tax cut. He also pushed Congress to pass several programs designed to reduce poverty. To control inflation, he established informal "wage-price guideposts." (c) In the area of civil rights John Kennedy pushed for passage of a comprehensive civil rights legislative package that would ban discrimination in employment and voting and in state programs receiving federal aid. It would also guarantee all Americans access to public accommodations.

5. (a) According to President Johnson, the Great Society "asks not only how much, but how good; not only how to create wealth, but how to use it; not only how fast we are going, but where we are headed." To achieve it, Johnson urged Congress to pass the major bills of the Kennedy administration. (b) The major pieces of legislation passed by Congress as part of the Great Society were the Civil Rights Act of 1964, the Economic Opportunity Act of 1964, the Medicare Act, the Voting Rights Act of 1965, the Immigration Act, the Housing Act, plus legislation creating VISTA, expanding social security benefits, providing aid to higher education, and creating the National Foundation for Arts and Humanities.

6. (a) In the early 1960s black Americans used sit-ins, "freedom rides," protest marches, and boycotts to fight segregation. (b) Some black leaders demanded more radical tactics because they be-

lieved that nonviolent tactics were not bringing full equality quickly enough. (c) To militant blacks, "black power" meant blacks taking control of the economic and political aspects of their lives, even if this required a violent revolution. (d) To moderate black leaders, "black power" meant black self-reliance and pride, not violence.

7. (a) By the 1960s hispanic Americans faced problems of discrimination in education and employment. Since few schools had programs to teach English to students whose first language was Spanish, hispanic students fell behind academically. Lack of a good education made it more difficult to obtain good jobs. (b) Cesar Chavez tried to improve conditions for migrant workers by unionizing California grape pickers. He believed a strong union would help the migrant workers gain higher wages and better working conditions. (c) Joseph Angel Gutierrez and his political party, La Raza Unida, called for bilingual education in the public school systems, improved public services in Chicano neighborhoods, and an end to job discrimination. The Brown Berets and La Communidad Latin advocated militant self-defense to fight discrimination.

8. (a) Since the 1880s government policy toward Native Americans had shifted several times. In 1934 the Indian Reorganization Act encouraged Native Americans to govern themselves through tribal organizations. During the 1950s government officials favored turning federal government programs over to the states. In the 1960s the federal government again encouraged a return to the tribal system. (b) In reaction to the weakening of traditional tribal ties and customs, some Indians began to take greater pride in their heritage and make more militant demands for Indian rights.

9. (a) In her book *The Feminine Mystique*, Betty Friedan described women as victims of discrimination. Most were working in the home. Those working in the job market were restricted primarily to a few professions, such as nursing, teaching, and secretarial positions. The few who did perform the same jobs as men were paid consistently lower wages. (b) In the 1960s women began to assume more diverse roles, entering the work force in record numbers. In addition, the Equal Pay Act of 1963 guaranteed equal pay for equal work and the Civil Rights Act of 1964 banned job discrimination on the basis of sex. (c) Inequalities remained in the areas of income and types of jobs open to women. A 1974 study showed that while more women were employed in 1974 than in 1960, their salaries were even further behind men's salaries than they had been in 1960. In 1970 only 2.8 percent of all lawyers and 9 percent of medical students were women.

10. (a) President Kennedy supplied the South Vietnamese army with United States military advisers. (b) After the North Vietnamese attacked the United States destroyers *Maddox* and *Turner Joy* in the Gulf of Tonkin in 1964, President Johnson asked Congress for the authority to take "all necessary steps" to "prevent further aggression" by the North Vietnamese. This authority, granted the President in the Gulf of Tonkin Resolution, led to a dramatic increase in American involvement.

11. (a) Factors that contributed to growing opposition to the war included troop escalation, the costs of the war, the deaths of over 25,000 Americans by 1968, and the media coverage of the devastation of the Vietnamese people and countryside. (b) Opposition to the war had great impact on the 1968 presidential election. Opponents of the war put pressure on President Johnson not to run for reelection. After Johnson's withdrawal from the race, Vice-President Humphrey's support of administration policies led to violent antiwar demonstrations and confrontations with police at the Democratic nominating convention, dividing the Democratic party. Opposition to the antiwar movement led Alabama Governor George Wallace to run as a third-party candidate for President, campaigning on a pledge to restore "law and order."

For Further Thought, text page 687

1. Answers may vary. Emphasize that President Truman had to work with a heavily Republican Congress, while President Johnson enjoyed a Democratic congressional majority during his years in office.

2. The Kerner Commission Report warned that "our nation is moving toward two societies, one black, one white—separate but unequal." However, it also noted that black Americans had made significant progress in some areas and that the move toward two societies could be reversed.

3. (a) Johnson was a skilled legislative leader who had the support and the goodwill of the nation after the assassination of President Kennedy. (b) Students might argue that by outlawing segregation in public accommodations the Civil Rights Act of 1964 transformed race relations in the South during the mid-1960s. (c) Several pieces of legislation might be mentioned. Students could suggest, for example, that the Medicare Act had an important impact on the financing of medical expenses. (d) Accept reasonable answers; students should be able to list the benefits and disadvantages of the program.

4. (a) During the Korean War the United States fought as part of a United Nations effort to stop North

Korean aggression. In the Vietnam conflict, on the other hand, the United States did not fight under the UN banner. (b) In World War II the United States declared war on Japan after Japan attacked Pearl Harbor. The Vietnam War was not rooted in an attack on United States territory. (c) The participation of United Nations troops in the Korean War meant that the United States was fighting in a struggle that had the support of the noncommunist world. United States efforts in Vietnam, however, were not actively supported by the noncommunist world. Lack of UN support may have weakened popular acceptance of the war. The attack on Pearl Harbor presented a clear issue to the American public, while the causes of the Vietnam War were less immediately apparent. (d) The Vietnam War eroded Presient Johnson's popularity. The stalemate in Korea also decreased public confidence in President Truman. Eisenhower, however, gained from the settlement of the Korean War, which was reached during his first term in office. President Roosevelt enjoyed great popularity as a result of the United States' successful struggle against the Axis powers. (e) Students might suggest that presidential popularity often hinges on the attainment of military and diplomatic goals.

Developing Basic Skills, text page 687

1. Students' time lines may vary, but they should include these events: 1941, President Roosevelt issues Executive Order 8802, barring discrimination in businesses having defense contracts; 1948, President Truman orders desegregation of armed forces; 1954, *Brown* v. *Board of Education*; 1957, President Eisenhower sends troops to Little Rock, Arkansas; 1960, sit-ins begin in the South; 1963, civil rights march on Washington, D.C.; 1964, Civil Rights Act; 1968, assassination of Martin Luther King, Jr. (a) The most important civil rights activity occurred during the 1960s. Students might suggest that the federal government supported the goals of the civil rights movement during this period. (b) Students could argue that the Civil Rights Act of 1964 was the most important federal action on behalf of integration. (c) Students might note that the legislative branch was a relative latecomer to the civil rights struggle.
2. (a) The income of women has increased. (b) The income of men has also increased. (c) The dollar difference between the income of men and women increased between 1950 and 1970. Note that when 1950 and 1970 are compared, the income of women as a percentage of the income of men remains essentially unchanged (about 55 percent). (d) Women did not gain economic equality during that period.

39 Challenges at Home and Abroad (1969–1976)

Section Review, text page 691

1. *Henry Kissinger:* Harvard professor who became national security adviser to President Nixon. *SALT:* Strategic Arms Limitation Talks; arms control agreement between the United States and the Soviet Union.
2. *détente:* relaxation of tension between the United States and the Soviet Union.
3. Kissinger identified Europe, Japan, the People's Republic of China, the Soviet Union, the Middle East, and the United States as centers of world power.
4. The aim of Vietnamization was to give South Vietnam increased responsibility for the war.
5. Both sides signed a cease-fire agreement in January 1973. Over the next few months American troops withdrew from Vietnam.
6. The major provision of the War Powers Act stated that a President could not send United States military forces into action for longer than 60 days without the approval of Congress.
7. President Nixon and Chinese leaders agreed to allow scientific, cultural, and journalistic exchanges between the two countries.

Section Review, text page 696

1. *Neil Armstrong:* leader of the first manned lunar landing. *Earl Warren:* Chief Justice of the Supreme Court during the 1960s. *Warren Burger:* Minnesota judge who succeeded Earl Warren as Chief Justice in 1969. *George McGovern:* South Dakota senator nominated for President by the Democratic party in 1972.
2. *impound:* to refuse to spend funds appropriated by Congress. *stagflation:* economic slump combining stagnation and inflation.
3. Answers will vary. Students might mention improvements in communications, navigation, and weather forecasting and the development of microelectronics, solar energy devices, and freeze-dried foods.
4. In *Miranda* v. *Arizona* the Supreme Court ruled that before questioning accused persons police were required to inform them of their rights to remain silent and to be represented by a lawyer.
5. Students might mention that President Nixon closed the Office of Economic Opportunity, vetoed bills providing funds for social programs, and impounded funds appropriated by Congress.
6. Phase I was a 90-day freeze on all wages, prices, and rents.
7. Students might note the stabilization of the economy, the popularity of Nixon's trips to China and

the Soviet Union, Kissinger's announcement of a breakthrough in the Paris peace talks, the promise of stricter law enforcement, or the well-organized and well-financed campaign based on Nixon's image as a statesman in the White House.

8. Kissinger successfully negotiated a cease-fire agreement between Egypt and Israel.

Section Review, text page 700

1. *John Sirica:* judge in the trial of the Watergate burglars. *Sam Ervin:* North Carolina senator who chaired the Senate Select Committee on Presidential Campaign Activities. *John Mitchell:* attorney general under Nixon who was linked to the Watergate cover-up. *John Dean:* former White House counsel who testified before the Ervin committee that Nixon and his staff had tried to suppress information linking the Watergate burglary to the White House. *Archibald Cox:* Harvard law professor who served as the first Watergate prosecutor. *Leon Jaworski:* Texas lawyer who was appointed special Watergate prosecutor after the firing of Archibald Cox.

2. McCord charged that witnesses in the trial of the Watergate burglars had committed perjury and that certain high officials had pressured the burglars to plead guilty so that the trial would be concluded quickly.

3. A strong prosecution case aimed at proving that Agnew had accepted bribes while governor of Maryland and the prospect of a prison sentence led to Agnew's resignation.

4. The phrase "Saturday Night Massacre" was used to describe Nixon's order to fire Watergate special prosecutor Archibald Cox and the consequent resignations of Attorney General Elliot Richardson and his assistant William Ruckelshaus.

5. The House Judiciary Committee charged that the President had obstructed justice, misused his presidential powers, and refused to comply with the committee's request for evidence.

Section Review, text page 706

1. *Nelson Rockefeller:* former New York governor appointed Vice-President by President Ford. *WIN:* Whip Inflation Now, President Ford's voluntary program to control wages and prices. *Helsinki Accords:* agreement in which 32 western and eastern European nations accepted human rights standards and post–World War II borders. *Jimmy Carter:* former Democratic governor of Georgia who was elected President in 1976.

2. Some Americans agreed with Ford that former President Nixon had suffered enough; others questioned the justice of allowing him to escape punishment.

3. Press reports revealed that the CIA had violated its charter by keeping files on American citizens and that J. Edgar Hoover, longtime head of the FBI, had kept secret files on prominent Americans.

4. (a) President Ford tried to stimulate the economy by convincing Congress to pass a tax cut. (b) This action sparked a modest recovery, but it also caused inflation to worsen.

5. Some criticized détente on the grounds that the Soviet Union had violated nuclear arms pacts, built up its arsenal of weapons, encouraged Egypt to attack Israel in 1973, and was arming other Third World countries.

6. (a) The cease-fire agreement broke down, and the war resumed. (b) The South Vietnamese army was defeated in April 1975 and surrendered to the North Vietnamese.

7. President Ford sent a naval force and 2,000 Marines to free the 39-man crew of the *Mayaguez.*

8. Inflation, unemployment, and energy shortages were the main concerns in the 1976 election.

Chapter Review, text page 707

1. During most of the 1950s and 1960s the United States took a hard-line approach to communism, viewing the world as divided between communist and anticommunist nations. Kissinger and President Nixon believed there were many centers of world power and that a successful foreign policy should aim for a balance of world power.

2. (a) Vietnamization increased South Vietnamese responsibility for the fighting. (b) President Nixon ordered 32,000 American troops to join the South Vietnamese in an invasion of Cambodia. (c) Congress passed the War Powers Act.

3. To ease tensions with the People's Republic of China, President Nixon visited China in 1972 and agreed to allow scientific, cultural, and journalistic exchanges between the two countries. He also visited the Soviet Union and signed an arms control agreement with that country.

4. (a) In *Gideon* v. *Wainwright* (1963) the Supreme Court held that states were obligated to provide legal representation for defendants who could not afford to hire their own lawyers. In *Miranda* v. *Arizona* (1966) the Supreme Court held that before questioning accused persons police were required to inform them of their rights to remain silent and to be represented by a lawyer. In *Mapp* v. *Ohio* (1961) the Supreme Court held that items illegally seized by police could not be used as evidence against the accused. (b) They felt such rulings unreasonably restricted the power of the police and protected the rights of accused persons at the ex-

pense of crime victims and society as a whole. (c) The Burger Court held that pretrial confessions obtained in violation of the *Miranda* rule could be used to discredit the trial testimony of the defendant. It also narrowed the scope of the *Mapp* decision by ruling that questions based on illegally seized evidence could be asked at a grand jury hearing.

5. (a) They resented United States aid to Israel during the October War. (b) The boycott disrupted American life. It caused long lines at gas stations; increased the price of fuel and other petroleum-based products, such as plastics, synthetic fibers, medicines, and fertilizers; and, as a result, aggravated inflation.

6. (a) The House Judiciary Committee began impeachment hearings in response to 16 bills calling for the impeachment of the President. These bills were introduced after the Saturday Night Massacre. (b) The committee passed three articles of impeachment against the President, claiming that he had obstructed justice, misused his presidential powers, and refused to comply with the committee's request for evidence. (c) President Nixon released transcripts of taped conversations recorded only a few days after the Watergate burglary. On August 8, 1974, he resigned.

7. (a) "Imperial presidency" refers to a presidency in which the President becomes too powerful. (b) Critics charged that Nixon refused to give frequent press conferences, impounded funds appropriated by Congress, and refused to allow members of the executive branch to testify before Congress. (c) Congress passed a law prohibiting a President from impounding funds appropriated by Congress. Amendments to the 1966 Freedom of Information Act tried to check the growing power of the presidency by giving the public greater access to government information.

8. (a) Gerald Ford brought to the office of the presidency a reputation for hard work and dependability. He was regarded by his colleagues in the House of Representatives as open, outgoing, and scrupulously honest. (b) President Ford's candor and goodwill drew the nation together and helped it recover from the crisis atmosphere of Watergate.

9. (a) Inflation, unemployment, and energy shortages faced the nation during the Nixon-Ford years. (b) President Nixon tried to combat inflation first by freezing prices and then by imposing price controls. President Ford hoped to limit price increases by calling for a policy of voluntary restraint. Both President Nixon and President Ford tried to lower unemployment by cutting taxes. President Nixon worked to ease the energy crisis by asking the states to lower speed limits and by signing a bill

authorizing the construction of an oil pipeline across Alaska and Canada. (c) President Nixon's policies restrained price increases in the short run, but after government controls were lifted, inflation again became a serious problem. Although President Ford's tax cut reduced unemployment, it also aggravated inflation. President Nixon's energy policies made the nation more sensitive to the need to conserve energy.

For Further Thought, text page 707

1. Answers may vary. Emphasize that a person without a strong anticommunist background may have been labeled "soft on communism" by some Americans.

2. (a) Opponents of the Vietnam War condemned President Nixon's order to resume the bombing of North Vietnam, his intervention in Cambodia, and his conduct of the war without a clear legal basis. (b) Opponents of the communist government in China resented President Nixon's encouragement of closer ties betweeen the United States and China. (c) Supporters of the Great Society opposed President Nixon's elimination of the Office of Economic Opportunity and his veto of several social spending bills. (d) Critics of the "imperial presidency" resented President Nixon's impoundment of funds appropriated by Congress and his refusal to allow members of the executive branch to testify before Congress.

3. (a) Congress reviewed the President's activities and was thus able to check his abuse of power. The investigations of the Senate and House committees led to impeachment proceedings against President Nixon and to his eventual resignation. The ruling of the Supreme Court forced the President to produce the tapes needed by the special prosecutor and the Judiciary Committee for their investigations. (b), (c), Answers may vary. Accept all answers that students can document with examples.

4. (a) A trial of Richard Nixon after he resigned as President would have revived the issue of Watergate and divided the nation. (b) Trial of the former President might have disclosed more facts about Watergate and would have underscored the nation's commitment to the principle that no person is above the law. (c) Accept answers that show an understanding of the results of President Ford's pardon of Richard Nixon.

Developing Basic Skills, text page 707

1. Encourage students to investigate additional products developed as a result of the space program.

2. (a) About $80; about $235. (b) About $91; about $98. (c) Income in current dollars rose sharply, but

income in constant dollars rose more slowly be-tween 1960 and 1965 and fell slightly between 1970 and 1980. (d) Although the salary of the aver-age worker grew rapidly, the actual value of that salary increased very little.

40 Beginning the Nation's Third Century (1977–Present)

Section Review, text page 715

1. *Anwar el-Sadat:* president of Egypt and first Arab head of state to visit Israel. *Menachem Begin:* Is-raeli prime minister who worked out a peace for-mula with Sadat and President Carter at Camp David. *Mohammed Reza Pahlavi:* shah of Iran who was overthrown in 1979.
2. (a) Carter's plan was to lower income taxes for the poor and close loopholes in tax laws that allowed people to avoid paying taxes. (b) Congress's tax bill lowered some taxes, but it raised the social se-curity tax and reduced taxes of some high-income people by cutting rates for capital gains.
3. President Carter required the State Department to use human rights as a criterion for receiving United States aid and suspended military aid to nations guilty of human rights violations.
4. Carter, Sadat, and Begin signed the "Framework for Peace in the Middle East," which proposed a five-year plan for developing Palestinian self-rule and laid the foundation of a peace treaty by which Israel would return the Sinai Peninsula to Egypt.
5. (a) Carter and Brezhnev signed Salt II. (b) The So-viet invasion of Afghanistan destroyed any chance that the Senate would ratify Salt II.
6. Ronald Reagan was elected President in 1980 on a platform charging that Carter did not have a sound economic program. Reagan promised to lower taxes and reduce government spending.

Section Review, text page 719

1. *Sandra Day O'Connor:* first woman justice of the United States Supreme Court. *Reaganomics:* Presi-dent Reagan's economic program, involving lower taxes and reduced government spending. *Solidarity:* independent Polish trade union outlawed by the Pol-ish government.
2. (a) Reagan blamed excessive spending by the federal government, which created large deficits that fueled inflation. (b) Congress enacted a three-year cut in income taxes and a $35-billion cut in funds budgeted for social programs.
3. The economy moved into deep recession, and the unemployment rate was the highest since the Great Depression.

4. The marines joined an international peacekeeping force that was organized to help the government of Lebanon keep order.
5. High unemployment, the recession, and the sharp increase in military spending were central issues in the 1982 mid-term elections.

Section Review, text page 723

1. *Columbia:* the first reusable space shuttle. *Voyager 1:* unmanned spacecraft that sent back pictures of Sat-urn in 1980. *Voyager 2:* unmanned spacecraft that sent back pictures of Saturn in 1981 and will fly past Uranus and Neptune. *laser:* Light Amplifica-tion by Stimulated Emission of Radiation, an in-tense light of a narrow range of wavelengths.
2. Answers will vary. Students might mention the arti-ficial production of insulin; development of pace-makers and dialysis machines; creation of artificial body parts; and reattachment of severed limbs by means of microsurgery.
3. Computers can perform many office tasks, includ-ing record keeping, inventory control, payroll ac-counting, and billing.
4. Private companies have booked space on future flights of *Columbia* to launch communications sat-ellites.
5. News organizations can send information in-stantaneously around the world. Satellite discs can be used to pick up television transmissions, and newspapers and magazines can be received on home computer screens.

Section Review, text page 728

1. *OPEC:* Organization of Petroleum Exporting Coun-tries, formed in 1960 to control price of oil and amount of oil produced. *Project Independence:* President Nixon's plan to make the United States self-sufficient in energy by encouraging conserva-tion and increasing domestic production.
2. Some OPEC members imposed an embargo on oil that resulted in shortages and soaring oil prices.
3. Rising oil prices forced some developing nations to borrow huge sums of money to pay for oil. High prices also contributed to inflation and a slowdown of production in industrialized nations. These de-velopments resulted in a worldwide recession in the late 1970s.
4. Oil prices fell during the early 1980s because a world surplus of oil developed.
5. (a) Carter proposed to levy high taxes on petroleum products and to use the resulting revenues for mass public transportation. (b) Reagan abolished price controls on most domestic crude oil and its by-products because he believed that higher oil prices would encourage more domestic production.

6. Heavy use of fossil fuels results in acid rain, which harms agriculture, forests, and water supplies.

Chapter Review, text page 729

1. (a) President Carter had a difficult relationship with Congress. (b) His difficulties stemmed in part from the fact that he and his advisers had little experience in Washington politics. In addition the President was not always effective in building support for his programs. (c) Carter's legislative program ran into strong congressional opposition. None of the bills he proposed was passed without major alterations.

2. (a) Critics charged that Carter used a double standard in enforcing his policy on human rights. They said he was lenient with the nation's important allies and strict with those considered less important. (b) Although Carter saw the Panama Canal treaties as a step toward improving relations with Latin America, his critics charged that he was giving away American property. (c) As part of the agreements establishing formal diplomatic relations with the People's Republic of China, the United States had to withdraw its recognition of the nationalist Chinese government on Taiwan as the official government of China. Conservative Republicans accused Carter of abandoning a long-time ally of the United States. (d) Critics of the SALT II agreement argued that the treaty would give the Soviet Union an advantage in nuclear weapons since the Soviets had been outspending the United States on defense for ten years. Carter's supporters recognized that the treaty posed some risks but felt it was a necessary step toward reducing the threat of nuclear war.

3. The revolution in Iran resulted in the taking of more than 50 Americans as hostages, the death of eight American soldiers during a failed attempt to rescue the hostages, and a steep increase in oil prices as Iran's oil exports dropped to virtually nothing. Furthermore, President Carter's image was damaged because many Americans felt he had shown neither sound judgment nor strong leadership during the crisis.

4. Ronald Reagan was a more effective public speaker than Jimmy Carter, as a result of his long career as a film actor. He also appeared less involved in the details of daily administration than Carter had been, delegating many tasks to his aides that Carter would have handled himself.

5. (a) Reagan faced problems of excessive government spending, high taxes, inflation, high interest rates, and severe unemployment. (b) Carter had faced similar problems at the end of his term in office. (c) Reagan's solution included a cut in personal income taxes, which, he maintained, would spur economic growth by giving people more money to spend and invest. He argued that the resulting increase in business activity would produce enough revenue to make up for money lost through the tax cuts. He also proposed to cut government spending.

6. (a) Reagan was disturbed by the Soviet Union's continuing occupation of Afghanistan, by its policies of repression at home, and by the pressure it had exerted on the Polish government to impose martial law and outlaw Solidarity. (b) The Reagan administration sharply criticized Soviet actions. It also imposed trade and political sanctions against the Soviet Union as a result of events in Poland.

7. Medical advances have controlled or prevented many diseases, made it possible to replace and repair damaged organs, improved diagnosis and detection of diseases, and produced devices that assist or substitute for the body's own organs.

8. The 1980s are called the computer age because computers are being used so widely and for so many activities that they have come to influence many aspects of modern life.

9. Voyager and *Columbia* spacecraft are the two main components of the 1980s space program. *Columbia* is a reusable space shuttle from which satellites can be launched and damaged satellites can be repaired. Voyager spacecraft provide glimpses of the outer reaches of our solar system by sending back pictures of the outer planets. *Voyager 2* will go beyond our solar system to more remote parts of the universe.

10. The United States became less vulnerable to OPEC policies in the 1980s because it relied less on imported oil and because oil consumption by individuals and industries had declined.

For Further Thought, text page 729

1. Students should note such factors as nationwide dissatisfaction with Carter's handling of economic problems; the fact that Carter did little active campaigning and that Reagan campaigned vigorously and was able to project a more vivid public image; the role played by John Anderson in the election; the feeling among many Americans that Carter had been responsible for precipitating the hostage crisis in Iran.

2. (a) Roosevelt responded to the Great Depression of the early 1930s by dramatically increasing the involvement of the federal government in all aspects of the American economy in order to provide jobs and to stimulate economic recovery. Reagan, on the other hand, felt that the recession of the early 1980s had been caused, in large measure, by exces-

sive involvement of the federal government in the national economy. He proposed measures to decrease such involvement, including reduced government spending and less regulation of business and industry. (b) In the period between the beginning of the New Deal in 1933 and the early 1980s, the role of the federal government in American economic life had expanded enormously. In the early 1980s many people felt that the government's role had become too large and its activities too all-encompassing.
3. Answers will vary, but students should note how computers could affect their homes, their work, their recreation, and their health.

Developing Basic Skills, text page 729

1. (a) About 5.5 percent. (b) 1973. (c) 1980. (d) Both inflation and unemployment rose between 1973 and 1974 and between 1979 and 1980. (e) Inflation declined between 1980 and 1982, but unemployment rose.
2. Students should list problems such as the end of the Vietnam War, human rights, relations with China and Soviet Union, conflict in the Middle East, arms control, and unrest in Latin America. Many of these areas were also of concern after World War II. Students should cite specific examples, such as the policy of containment toward the Soviet Union.
3. (a) The Soviet invasion of Afghanistan. (b) The names represent countries that became Soviet satellites after World War II. (c) Iran and Pakistan. (d) The cartoonist is saying that the Soviet Union has an aggressive foreign policy.

41 The United States: Yesterday and Tomorrow

Caption, text page 733

Through age 19, males outnumber females. As the number of older people increases, the pyramid will widen at the top.

Caption, text page 736

Rhode Island and New York lost population during the 1970s. Since 1970 population growth has shifted to states in the South and Southwest, thus the title "Move to the Sunbelt." Alaska's population increase can be attributed to energy resources, which attract many workers and investors to the state.

Section Review, text page 737

1. *sunbelt:* region of the United States, including the states of the Southeast and Southwest, known for its warm, sunny weather.

2. Immigrants of the 1840s and 1850s were mostly Catholic, whereas earlier immigrants were predominantly Protestant.
3. During the 1970s an increasing number of immigrants came to the United States from Latin America and Asia.
4. A melting pot is a culture in which different cultures merge into one; a pluralistic society is one in which many different cultures exist side by side.
5. (a) Because Americans are marrying later and having fewer children, population growth has slowed. (b) The population is also growing older. As fewer babies are born, there are fewer young people in the population.
6. (a) The automobile sparked the growth of suburbs. (b) During the late 1970s suburban growth slowed. (c) Unemployment and crime contributed to a population decline in some major cities.
7. People are moving to the sunbelt in search of good jobs and mild winters.

Section Review, text page 740

1. The Twenty-sixth Amendment guaranteed the right to vote to persons 18 years of age and older.
2. Since 1964 the percentage of eligible voters who vote in presidential elections has declined from 62 percent to 53 percent.
3. Voters gained a more direct role in government through ratification of the Seventeenth Amendment, which called for the direct election of senators by the voters of each state. In some states citizens can propose legislation and vote on it directly in a referendum and remove officials from office by a recall election.
4. The Interstate Commerce Commission was created to prevent abuses of power in the railroad industry.
5. Answers will vary. Students might mention unemployment insurance, Social Security, road and transit maintenance, water purification plants, and airports.

Section Review, text page 747

1. *productivity:* output per hour of work.
2. Answers will vary. Students might mention coal, iron ore, navigable rivers, and oil and gas supplies.
3. The professional and service sectors have grown the fastest over the past 50 years.
4. Between 1950 and 1980 the percentage of women working outside the home rose 17 percent.
5. The value of the dollar has declined steadily since 1945.
6. (a) American productivity is increasing, but the rate of increase has been slower than that of Japan, France, and West Germany. (b) Companies have invested in new plants and equipment, have given workers a greater role in solving on-the-job prob-

lems, and are experimenting with more flexible working arrangements, such as job sharing, longer vacations, and a four-day work week.

7. (a) The abundance of American life has contributed to such environmental problems as air pollution, waste disposal, diseases caused by newly created chemicals, and contamination of water and food supplies. (b) Plant owners charge that additional regulations will not significantly improve the environment but will increase both operating expenses and the prices of products. As a result, they conclude, plants will be forced to close and jobs will be lost.

Trends in American History: Forecasting Alternative Futures, text page 749

1. Students might mention the rise of government spending as a future trend. Students should cite examples that illustrate such an increase.
2. (a) Accept answers that refer to movements to limit taxes and government spending. (b) Continued inflation might slow the trend toward increased government spending. (c) Because government spending is generally regarded as inflationary, continued inflation may generate a strong movement to limit government expenditures.
3. Students should consult data that describes changes in the consumer price index and government spending. Reference should be made to what economists say about the relationship between government spending and inflation.

Section Review, text page 749

1. *balance of trade:* the difference in value between imports and exports. *trade deficit:* condition under which the value of imports exceeds the value of exports. *trade surplus:* condition under which the value of exports exceeds the value of imports.
2. (a) The United States exported raw materials in the early 1800s. (b) The value of exports rose from $845 million to $2.3 billion.
3. The primary concern was containing the power of the Soviet Union.
4. Today policy makers can less easily classify nations as pro-Soviet or pro-American, and traditional American allies such as France and West Germany do not automatically support American positions.
5. In 1960 the United States had a trade surplus of $4.6 billion, but in 1982 the trade deficit had grown to about $44 billion.

Chapter Review, text page 750

1. (a) In the 1840s and 1850s most immigrants came from Germany and Ireland. (b) From 1880 to 1920 a growing number of immigrants came from south-

ern and eastern Europe. (c) The 1960s and 1970s witnessed a dramatic increase in immigrants from Asia and Latin America.

2. (a) Immigration shifts added to religious and cultural diversity in the United States. The first settlers had been predominantly Protestant. Large numbers of later settlers were Catholic or Jewish. Each group brought a rich ethnic heritage that was reflected in its language, customs, foods, and dress. (b) Earlier generations of Americans looked with suspicion at the varied cultural traditions brought by new immigrants. Immigrants feared that they would lose their cultural heritage. Overcoming these fears and suspicions was a challenge.
3. (a) From an historical perspective, Americans have always been on the move. The westward movement is a continuation of an historical trend. (b) The move south is a new trend. In the past, the South had experienced a decline in population.
4. (a) Since colonial times, religious and property qualifications for voting have been removed, as have race and sex qualifications. (b) Americans can elect senators directly, remove officials from office, and initiate legislation.
5. (a) Government has played a more direct role in people's lives since the 1800s. (b) Some Americans believe government has overextended its authority. Many are concerned about the size of government and the cost of running it. (c) Reagan has attempted to cut back the size of the federal government by trimming the federal budget, with many of the cuts coming from federal benefit programs.
6. (a) Before the late 1800s a majority of Americans were employed in farming. (b) Over the last 50 years the professional and service occupations have experienced dramatic growth.
7. (a) Inflation reduces the buying power of people's salaries as it diminishes the value of the dollar. (b) A limit to natural resources challenges Americans to use resources more efficiently and to search for alternatives to resources in short supply.
8. Rising oil prices in the 1970s contributed to high inflation and created a deficit in foreign trade. Foreign competition has hurt some American industries, as has a worldwide recession.

For Further Thought, text page 750

1. (a) Answers will vary. Examples could include the foods Americans eat and the prices they pay for goods. (b) Answers may vary; students should refer to the benefits, problems, and costs associated with government programs.
2. (a) Students should note that since pollutants adversely affect the environment and all living things, some people insist on antipollution regulations. (b) Students should point out that some people oppose

such regulation because they think the amount of improvement in the environment is too small to justify the costs of enforcing and obeying antipollution laws. (c) Answers will vary.

Developing Basic Skills, text page 750

1. (a) The graph shows the percentage of women and men holding various occupations. (b) 35.1 percent. (c) 6.4 percent. (d) A slightly higher proportion of women hold professional positions than men. (e) The underrepresentation of women in managerial positions helps explain the lower salaries of women.
2. The local historical society might be able to help students find the origins of the names of rivers, lakes, and streets. Consult the local library for published histories of the community.
3. Answers may vary. Encourage students to provide specific information to support their ranking.

Unveiling, by Edward Moran. The Statue of Liberty, which was unveiled in New York Harbor on October 28, 1886, had a special meaning for Edward Moran because he had immigrated to the United States at the age of 15. The statue, by French sculptor Frédéric Auguste Bartholdi, was a gift from the people of France to the people of the United States. It symbolized America's role as a beacon of liberty, and after its unveiling it became a sign of welcome to millions of immigrants. At the unveiling ceremony President Grover Cleveland proclaimed, "We will not forget that Liberty has here made her home; nor shall her chosen altar be neglected. Willing votaries [devoted supporters] shall keep its fires alive, and they shall gleam upon the shores of our sister Republic in the East [France]. Reflected thence and joined with answering rays, a stream of light shall pierce the darkness of ignorance and man's oppression until liberty shall enlighten the world."

THE
UNITED STATES

A HISTORY OF THE REPUBLIC

THE UNITED STATES

A HISTORY OF THE REPUBLIC

James West Davidson   Mark H. Lytle

PRENTICE-HALL, INC., Englewood Cliffs, New Jersey

James West Davidson

James West Davidson has authored books and papers on a wide range of American history topics including *After the Fact: The Art of Historical Detection* with Mark H. Lytle. With teaching experience at both the college and high school levels, Dr. Davidson consults on curriculum design for American history courses. While completing his Ph.D. at Yale University, he participated in the History Education Project sponsored by the National Endowment for the Humanities and the American Historical Association.

Mark H. Lytle

Mark H. Lytle is chairperson of American Studies at Bard College, where he also serves on the Women's Studies faculty. Author of numerous articles on the United States and Iran, Dr. Lytle has taught high school social studies, including Black History, in the Buffalo public schools. Dr. Lytle wrote *After the Fact: The Art of Historical Detection* with James West Davidson. He also participated in the History Education Project at Yale University.

SECOND EDITION

SUPPLEMENTARY MATERIALS
Teacher's Edition
Teacher's Resource Handbook
Test Bank

ISBN 0-13-938027-2   10 9 8 7 6 5 4 3 2 1

PRENTICE-HALL INTERNATIONAL, INC., London
PRENTICE-HALL OF AUSTRALIA, PTY. LTD., Sydney
PRENTICE-HALL CANADA INC., Toronto
PRENTICE-HALL OF INDIA PRIVATE LTD., New Delhi
PRENTICE-HALL OF JAPAN, INC., Tokyo
PRENTICE-HALL OF SOUTHEAST ASIA PTE. LTD., Singapore
WHITEHALL BOOKS LIMITED, Wellington, New Zealand
EDITORA PRENTICE-HALL DO BRASIL LTDA., Rio de Janeiro

Unit Opening Illustrations

Unit One: *1590 View of Roanoke Island, New World,* by Theodore De Bry (detail).
Unit Two: *Congress Voting Independence,* by Robert Edge Pine (detail).
Unit Three: *A View of New Orleans Taken From the Plantation of Marigny,* by Boqueto de Woiseri (detail).
Unit Four: *View of St. Louis 1835,* by Leon Pomarede (detail).
Unit Five: *Capture of Fort Fisher,* by Currier and Ives (detail).
Unit Six: *Song of the Talking Wire,* by Henry F. Farney (detail).
Unit Seven: *The Bowery at Night,* by W. Louis Sonntag, Jr. (detail).
Unit Eight: *City Activities,* by Thomas Hart Benton (detail).
Unit Nine: *Steel Mill,* by Ben Shahn (detail).
Unit Ten: *Golden Gate,* by Charles Sheeler (detail).

Illustration Credits

Frequently cited sources are abbreviated as follows: AMNH, American Museum of Natural History; LC, Library of Congress; MCNY, Museum of the City of New York; MFA, Museum of Fine Arts, Boston; MMA, Metropolitan Museum of Art, New York; NA, National Archives; NASA, National Aeronautics and Space Administration; NG, National Gallery of Art, Washington, D.C.; NYHS, courtesy of the New York Historical Society, New York; NYPL, New York Public Library; NYSHA, New York State Historical Association, Cooperstown; SI, Smithsonian Institution; UPI, United Press International; WW, Wide World; Yale, Yale University Art Gallery.

Key to position of illustrations:
b, bottom; *l,* left; *r,* right; *t,* top.

Cover David Christensen, from a photograph by Steve Allen/Black Star; **Page 1** MCNY; **5** *t* Arizona State Museum, University of Arizona, silkscreen print by Robert Spray for Margaret Schevill Link, *b* MFA; **6** *t* Independence National Historic Park, *b* NG, gift of Edgar William and Bernice Chrysler Garbisch; **7** Mystic Seaport Museum, Mystic, Conn.; **8** LC; **9** *t* Chicago Historical Society, *b* MCNY, J. Clarence Davies Collection; **10** LC; **11** National Aeronautics and Space Administration.

UNIT ONE Pages 16–17 NYPL; **18** British Museum; **19** Arizona State Museum, University of Arizona, silkscreen print by Robert Spray for Margaret Schevill Link; **22** AMNH; **26** AMNH; **28** Bibliotheque Nationale; **29** Bibliotheque Nationale; **30** British Museum; **34** MMA; **38** AMNH; **40** AMNH; **42** Hispanic Society of America; **44** British Museum; **45** National Portrait Gallery, London; **47** Public Archives of Canada, Map Division; **50** Pilgrim Society; **53** National Portrait Gallery, Washington, D.C.; **57** Mansell Collection; **60** Enoch Pratt Free Library, Baltimore, Md.; **66** MFA; **74** Colonial Williamsburg Foundation; **77** *t* National Maritime Museum, Greenwich, England, *b* NYPL; **78** Historical Society of Pennsylvania; **79** LC; **80** Colonial Williamsburg Foundation; **84** Anne S.K. Brown Military Collection, Brown University Library; **85** NYHS; **90** NYPL; **91** National Gallery of Canada, Ottawa; **92** Public Archives of Canada; **95** Royal Ontario Museum, Canadiana Gallery.

UNIT TWO Pages 98–99 Historical Society of Pennsylvania; **100** Patrick Henry Memorial Foundation; **104** Brown University Library; **106** LC; **107** LC; **109** LC; **111** *t* LC, *b* MFA; **112** MFA; **114** Connecticut Historical Society; **118** Yale (detail); **124** WW; **125** LC; **126**

(continued on page 832)

Contents

Unit Seven
Entering a Modern Age 456

Unit Ten
The United States in a Changing World 630

Special Features

Skill Lessons

Maps

Reference Section Maps

13

Charts and Graphs

To the Student

Through a study of the history of the United States, you will become familiar with the common experiences that bring Americans together as well as the diverse experiences that make American life rich and varied. You will learn about the development of a national spirit and the preservation of local traditions. As you study the nation's past, you will begin to better understand the challenges of the present and the major issues of the future.

Many features have been included in this book to assist you during your course of study:

1. **Outline.** Each chapter begins with an outline of the contents to give you an overview of the chapter.

2. **Introduction.** The chapter introduction provides a setting for the material in the chapter.

3. **Important Terms.** Historical terms and vocabulary words are italicized and clearly defined the first time they appear in the text. You will be asked to define each term in a section review question. Important historical terms also appear in a glossary at the end of the book.

4. **Maps, Graphs, Charts.** Numerous maps, graphs, and charts appear throughout the book to help you understand major historical developments and events. Their clarity makes them useful additions to the narrative. Captions provide background information and relate the maps, graphs, and charts to what you are reading.

5. **Illustrations.** The text contains many historic paintings, photographs, cartoons, and posters to enliven the study of each historical period. The captions contain useful information about the illustration and the people or events pictured.

6. **Special Features.** Boxed features give you a close look at people and events in American history. They include vignettes, biographies, selections from diaries and other contemporary sources, and excerpts from government documents.

7. **Skill Lessons.** Special boxed lessons help you understand and practice important skills, such as reading maps and graphs, using visual evidence and statistics, recognizing propaganda, and analyzing conflicting sources.

8. **Section Reviews.** Each section ends with a set of review questions including identifications and vocabulary definitions to test your understanding of what you have read.

9. **Major Events.** Near the end of each chapter you will find a chronological list of major events. This will help you review what you have learned and place the flow of historical developments in proper time sequence.

10. **In Perspective.** The chapter summary, called "In Perspective," reviews the developments you read about in the chapter and puts them in perspective.

11. **End-of-Chapter Materials.** Three sets of questions end each chapter. Chapter review questions guide your review of the basic content of the chapter. The questions labeled "For Further Thought" ask you to consider historical issues and to offer your interpretations of them. In "Developing Basic Skills" you will learn and practice such basic skills as classifying, comparing, map and graph reading, researching, analyzing cartoons, interpreting source material, and relating past to present.

12. **Reference Section.** At the back of the book you will find a special section of material to be used throughout the course. The reference section includes important maps, a chronology of American history, a pronunciation key, a glossary, a list of suggested readings for each chapter, information about the 50 states and the Presidents and Vice-Presidents of the United States, the Declaration of Independence, and the Constitution of the United States of America. The Constitution has been carefully annotated to help you understand its historical roots and its enduring significance in American life.

James West Davidson
Mark H. Lytle

SECOTAN

Dasamonquepeuc

Roanoac

Hatorasck

Unit One

The Americas

1

Two Worlds

(Prehistory–1492)

Mayan corn god.

Chapter Outline

1 *The First Americans*

2 *Many Cultures Among the First Americans*

3 *Great Empires*

4 *Europe Awakens*

In the late 1400s two worlds met, and the destinies of both were changed forever. For most of human history the continents now known as North and South America were isolated from the rest of the world. There was probably some contact between the original Americans and individuals from other parts of the world. But generally Europeans, Asians, and Africans did not know of the existence of the American continents until the late fifteenth century.

In this chapter you will read about the original Americans and learn about some of the hundreds of cultures existing in North and South America by the 1400s. You will also read about developments in Europe that led explorers farther and farther into the open sea. By the late 1400s the two worlds were on the verge of an encounter that would alter the course of human history.

1 The First Americans

Fifty thousand years ago huge herds of animals roamed across what is now known as North and South America. Wild horses, bison, and camels grazed in vast fields. Jaguars stalked their prey. Woolly mammoths—large, shaggy-haired elephants with long, sweeping tusks—wandered from present-day Alaska to Texas.

Just when and how people came to be a part of this landscape is uncertain. Although scientists have attempted to answer these questions, no one theory has been conclusively proven. Moreover, discoveries made during the 1970s have served to intensify the controversy rather than to settle it. Therefore, questions still remain: How long have men and women inhabited the Americas? Did these people come from another continent? How did these first Americans live?

Studying Early People

The first Americans belong to the *prehistoric period*, the time before recorded history. Cultural groups in the prehistoric period had not developed a system of writing so they could not keep records. The lack of records makes the study of early cultures difficult.

Scientists who study the life and culture of ancient peoples are called *archaeologists*. In making educated guesses about the lives of early groups of people, archaeologists examine skeletons and *artifacts*, objects the people made. Skeletons provide information about the age and appearance of early people, while artifacts reveal the kinds of tools and weapons they used.

Whenever archaeologists discover an area where prehistoric people might have lived, they seal it off. Then they divide the ground into squares and carefully reproduce each square on a map. Next the digging begins. Using hand tools and screens, the diggers sift away the soil. Whenever they locate a significant object, workers use smaller tools such as dental picks and brushes. They mark on the map the location of each stone tool, bone chip, or skeletal piece that is found. In this way archaeologists get a clear picture of the site.

After artifacts and skeletons have been gathered, scientists test them for age. With the results of this analysis they can develop theories about the prehistoric people who lived on a given site. Using such procedures, archaeologists have drawn some conclusions about the first Americans.

Archaeological Theories

For decades many archaeologists have held that people first arrived in this hemisphere from 12,000 to 20,000 years ago. During this period the earth underwent one of its periodic ice ages. Vast amounts of water froze into glaciers, and as a result the depth of oceans dropped as much as 200 to 300 feet (about 60 to 90 meters). Underwater ridges were exposed and formed land bridges, linking some continents and islands. As the glaciers advanced southward, ice covered large areas of North America, Europe, and Asia. People and animals were then forced to migrate in search of food and warmer climates.

Experts who adhere to this theory believe that a land bridge perhaps 1,000 miles (about 1,600 kilometers) wide connected Asia and North America during this period. According to these experts, herds of animals moved eastward across the bridge and Asian hunters followed, tracking them throughout North and South America. When

Some early Americans drew sand paintings as part of religious ceremonies or to heal the sick. After the ceremonies, the paintings were brushed away. In this copy of a Navajo sand painting, a bright arc of pollen links Father Sky and Mother Earth. Symbols of four sacred plants—corn, squash, beans, and tobacco—are pictured on Mother Earth's body.

the climate warmed again, the glaciers melted and the oceans rose. Water that today forms the Bering Strait then covered the land bridge, ending the migration. To prove this theory, scientists have traditionally used the *carbon-14 test*, a method for determining the age of plant and animal remains.

In the 1970s, however, a small group of scientists challenged the earlier theories. They asserted that the carbon-14 test had a limited use in studying prehistory. First, the test can date only those remains that are less than 40,000 years old; second, it works only on large objects as much as a pound (454 grams) in weight. Few archaeologists find bone fragments that large, and those who do are usually unwilling to destroy them, as is necessary to run the procedure. Therefore, the challengers of the theory argue, the carbon-14 test provides only an incomplete view of the first Americans.

To solve these problems a young California chemist developed a new method of testing, *amino acid racemization* (ras eh mih ZAY shuhn). With this method archaeologists can determine the age of remains up to a million years old, and they can test objects weighing less than an ounce (28 grams).

In the late 1970s racemization tests on pieces of bone found in a California dig indicated that people might have lived on the site over 48,000 years ago. Some scientists suggest that humans may have come to the Americas as long as 70,000 years ago, when another ice age had exposed the land bridge across the Bering Strait. Over thousands of years, these hunting peoples would have migrated southward until they reached recently examined sites in California.

Although racemization has led to some important discoveries, the controversy remains. Most archaeologists are reluctant to accept the new theories without further investigation. However, in spite of disagreements over these theories, archaeologists can agree on certain features of prehistoric cultures. As a result of studies done to date, a partial picture of the earliest Americans has begun to emerge.

Climate Change and Culture Change

Although scientists do not agree on the origins of the earliest Americans, most agree that about 10,000 years ago certain environmental changes took place in the Americas. The glaciers retreated, temperatures warmed, lakes dried up, lush vegetation died, and many large animal species became extinct.

These changes forced prehistoric peoples living in the Americas to alter their way of life. As the climate became more diverse, people living in different parts of the Americas developed the skills needed to survive in their new environments. When the huge game animals disappeared, people turned to hunting smaller game. Groups who lived close to the sea usually depended on fishing for a livelihood. Many organized their daily lives, their holidays, even their religions around fishing.

Other people followed similar patterns. For example, groups living in the present-day San Francisco Bay area found vast supplies of acorns. Although they fished to supplement their diet, they spent much time collecting and storing acorns. The acorn was the main ingredient of their meals.

During this period, people not only adapted their lives to their surroundings, they also changed their natural environment to meet their needs. Instead of following herds of animals or gathering wild foods, some groups learned how to grow such plants as beans, squash, and maize, or corn. With the emergence of agriculture, people no longer had to move from place to place in search of food. They were able to settle in permanent communities.

Over the centuries a wide variety of cultures developed in North and South America. Some people lived in small hunting and gathering bands, while others lived in larger, more permanent communities. Each had its own forms of government, religion, and art, reflecting and expressing its culture.

For answers, see p. A 5.

Section Review

1. Define the following terms: prehistoric period, archaeologist, artifact, carbon-14 test, amino acid racemization.

2. How do archaeologists use skeletons and artifacts to learn about prehistoric cultures?

3. (a) What is the land bridge theory of how people came to the Americas? (b) Where would the land bridge have been located?

4. What environmental changes probably occurred about 10,000 years ago, changing the way many prehistoric peoples lived?

2 Many Cultures Among the First Americans

Most early American peoples did not have names that you would recognize. They referred to themselves as "the people," "the ancient ones," or "the genuine people." Such names illustrated the pride they had in themselves and in their long-felt association with the land on which they lived. The map on this page and the discussion in this section and the next give some idea of the rich and diverse cultures that existed in the Americas by the fifteenth century.

Life in the West

Many of the early Americans who lived in the western region extending from the Arctic Circle to the warm Pacific coast of California lived by hunting, fishing, or gathering plants. Within the region, diverse cultures developed. Among them were the Eskimo, the Northwest Coast, and the Great Basin cultures.

The Eskimos inhabited the plains and seacoasts of the Arctic region. For most of the year they faced bitter cold and heavy snows. Because few plants grew in the frigid climate, the lives of the Eskimos revolved around hunting and fishing. Animals such as the seal, walrus, whale, and caribou were a source not only of food, but also of clothing, tools, weapons, boats, household implements, and other necessities. The crucial

■ This map shows the distribution of American cultures in the 1500s. Groups that had similar styles of living are shown within culture regions, indicated by color.

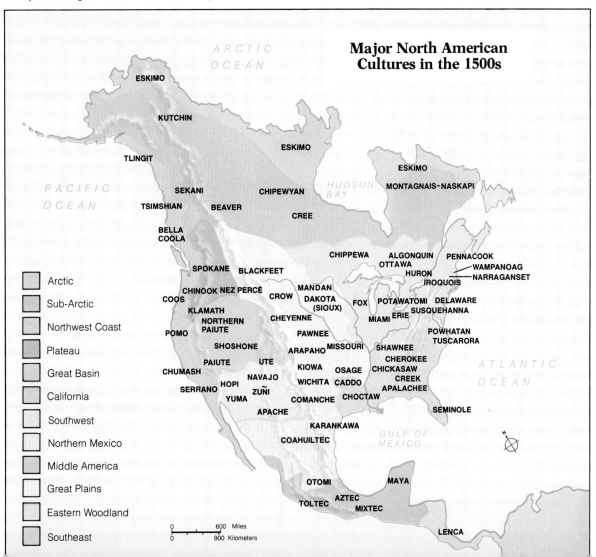

Food, especially salmon, was so abundant along the northwest Pacific coast that early Americans there had leisure time to develop the decorative arts. The elaborately carved and painted cedar canoe in this painting by A. A. Jansson is typical of the designs used on totem poles, clothing, and other items. Cedar trees provided wood for canoes and houses, and the soft inner bark was used for woven cloth and baskets.

importance of these animals to the Eskimos is shown by the prominent part they played in Arctic folklore, religion, and art.

The first Americans who settled along the northwest Pacific coast, with its mild climate and abundant food, had a much easier life. Salmon and other fishes thrived in the many streams and rivers. Offshore the seas teemed with seals, whales, and otters, while on land herds of deer, moose, and elk roamed the thick forests. The food supply of these people was plentiful.

These favorable conditions left the people of the northwest Pacific free to engage in other, more diversified activities. They built huge, elaborately decorated houses, fashioned handsome copper shields, carved great totem poles and canoes, and made beautiful wooden masks, furniture, and utensils of all kinds.

Gradually, they developed a complex society based on wealth. Each person's status depended on the possessions he or she owned. To demonstrate their prosperity people held feasts called *potlatches* (PAHT latch ehz). At these ceremonies, which lasted several days, the host family entertained guests lavishly and gave away valuable possessions. Those who received gifts held their own potlatches in return. Anyone who could not do this lost status in the social hierarchy of the community.

The groups living in the Great Basin had a more difficult life. The Great Basin is a dry, bleak region between the Sierra Nevadas and the Rocky Mountains. It supports few animals or edible plants. Peoples such as the Ute and Shoshone had difficulty finding food, so they were forced to move about in small bands often no larger than a single family. Family members spent most of their time searching for scarce food. The adult men dominated the bands, and women and children held low status.

The Desert Tradition

The environment of much of the region that now comprises part of Arizona, New Mexico, southern Utah, and northern Mexico was also harsh for people who lived there. In the north, rapidly flowing rivers had carved steep-walled canyons into the land or washed away the soil to form huge mesas* thousands of feet high. In the south, foothills and mountains gave way to flat stretches of desert. There, summer temperatures reached over 100° Fahrenheit (38° Celsius) and winter temperatures dropped well below 0° Fahrenheit (-18° Celsius).

Despite these extreme conditions, several imposing civilizations emerged in the area. One of the earliest groups was the Anasazi (ah nah SAH zee). An ingenious people, they turned the desert into productive farming land with a system of dams and irrigation canals. Within the remote canyons of much of today's Southwest, they built cliff dwellings resembling modern high-rise apartments. On the rock walls of the canyons they drew *pictograms*, pictures conveying their ideas about life. The Anasazi were also skilled weavers, basketmakers, and potters.

The Anasazi disappeared mysteriously; however, several later groups traced their origins to the Anasazi. One group, the Pueblo†, lived in the area of present-day Arizona and New Mexico. The Pueblo were a farming people who grew beans, cotton, tobacco, squash, and gourds—a difficult task in a region that received so little rain.

Like the Anasazi, the Pueblo often built their dwellings on the summits of mesas or along the sides of steep cliffs. With stone and *adobe*, sun-dried clay brick, they constructed oval, square, or rectangular structures several stories high. They grouped the buildings around a broad, open space, forming a kind of town with a main square.

At the center of each town lay a room called the *kiva*. Within the kiva, Pueblo men met to conduct religious ceremonies. The purpose of the rites varied. The Pueblo held some to bring rain, others to cure the sick, and still others to please the gods or to ask

*mesa: a high, flat plateau or tableland with steep sides.

†The name "pueblo" (PWEHB loh), which means "town" in Spanish, was given to these people by Spanish explorers in the 1500s. These explorers thought the settlements looked like European towns.

for a blessing. The kiva societies controlled Pueblo life. They emphasized conformity and the importance of society over the individual. A warrior class enforced the rules of conduct.

The Pueblo were a matrilineal society. In other words, they traced descent within a family through the mother's line. Women headed the families and held all property rights. A wife who wanted to divorce her husband just put his belongings outside her door—a signal that the husband had to go back to his mother's house. Pueblo women were also exceptionally skilled potters and basketweavers—crafts the Pueblo probably learned from the Anasazi.

During the sixteenth century, another important southwestern group, the Navajo (NAV uh HOH), migrated into what is now northern New Mexico. There, the Navajo came under the influence of their Pueblo neighbors, from whom they learned farming and weaving.

The early Navajo lived in settlements consisting of "forked stick" homes, made by piling logs against three poles joined together at their tops, then covering the outside with mud. Later, they fashioned *hogans*, earthen domes with log frames.

Navajo religion, which was influenced heavily by that of the Pueblo, centered on the idea that a person's life should be in harmony with the universe. Immortal beings called Holy People, who had to be pleased through strict rituals, could affect the lives of mortals, called Earth Surface People. To the Navajo illness indicated disharmony. Harmony and health returned when the Holy People were satisfied.

On the Great Plains

Between the Rocky Mountains and the Mississippi River lies a large area of relatively flat grasslands known today as the Great Plains. For thousands of years, most inhabitants of the Great Plains lived near rivers so they could be sure of a water supply for farming. Women were responsible for the farming and plowed their garden plots with digging sticks and hoes made from large animal bones. Maize, squash, beans, and sunflowers were the principal crops.

For most of the year, the Plains people lived in fairly permanent villages. There they built lodges by covering log frames with brush and sod. But during the summer, the men often left the villages for weeks at a time to hunt buffalo.

Sometime in the mid-sixteenth century most of the Plains people became more *nomadic*. Instead of living in permanent villages all year long, they moved from place to place, building temporary settlements near water and food supplies. Migrations were carried out on foot. Dogs dragged travois* carrying the owners' possessions. The change may have been caused by drought or by enemy attacks.

The nomadic settlements still relied on farming for much of their food, but the men engaged in many more hunting expeditions. On the hunt they lived in portable teepees made from buffalo hides. Farther to the west, Americans who were completely nomadic lived in teepees year-round.

The semiagricultural, seminomadic groups of the Plains included the Osage, Missouri, Omaha, Kansas, Iowa, Wichita, and Mandan, as well as the Pawnee. The Blackfeet achieved the greatest power in the western part of the Great Plains. The Crows hunted the land between the Missouri and Yellowstone rivers, and the Comanche, Kiowa, and Apache dominated the southern plains.

Each of the Plains groups had a well-developed religion. In most of them visions played an important role because people believed that visions revealed their destinies. To intensify their visions and thus to get a clearer picture of their destinies, young men and women would go out into the wilderness and fast.

Supreme status in the Plains communities belonged to the chief. He achieved this honor by demonstrating bravery, good judgment, skill in public speaking, or some other outstanding quality. A council made up of the most prominent men ruled each group. The council's decisions usually had to be unanimous.

In the Eastern Woodlands

Three major groups of people lived in the woodlands east of the Mississippi River: the Algonquin (al GAHN kwihn), the Iroquois (IHR uh kwoi), and the Muskogean (muhs KOH gee ehn).

---

*travois (trah VOI): two poles with an animal skin mounted between them. After the Spanish reintroduced horses to the Americas, the Plains people used horses rather than dogs during their migrations.

The Algonquins inhabited the forests that covered the Northeast from present-day Labrador and Quebec as far south as Maryland and Virginia. They lived in small bands, hunting deer and caribou or gathering wild nuts and berries. The Algonquins also used the resources of the forest to build efficient transportation: snowshoes and toboggans in the winter, canoes in the summer.

Algonquin society was relatively simple. Each band shared the major food resources of the territory. Although families within the band hunted primarily in one area they regarded as theirs, they willingly shared their catch with others. Food was often scarce during the harsh winters, and every family knew that one day it might have to depend on another's support.

The Iroquois were several related tribes that originally lived in southeastern North America. Around 1300 they migrated north to the area of present-day New York State and drove out the Algonquins. However, not long after the departure of the Algonquins, the Iroquois began to feud among themselves. During the sixteenth century, the warfare became especially bitter. The waste of tribal energies on fruitless conflict threatened to undermine the Iroquois people.

According to legend, two reformers, Dekanawidah, a Huron religious leader, and his disciple Hiawatha, a Mohawk chief, responded to the situation by preaching the idea of a political confederation, or alliance, of the Iroquois tribes. They believed that such a union would not only end the bloodshed among the tribes but would also provide a strong defense against the Iroquois' enemies.

The goal of the two reformers was finally achieved during the 1500s. Five tribes—the Mohawk, the Seneca (SEHN ih kuh), the Cayuga (kay YOO gah), the Oneida (oh NĪ duh), and the Onondaga (ahn uhn DAH guh)—gradually joined together to form a confederation known as the Iroquois League.

The league, whose values were based on those of traditional Iroquois culture, proved successful. A representative council, consisting of the chiefs of each tribe and 50 specially chosen leaders called *sachems* (SAY chehms), governed the league. The sachems were responsible for all matters involving relations among the tribes.

Iroquois society, like that of the Pueblo, was matrilineal. All property passed from generation to generation on the female side of the family. Thus, women owned the gardens of the settlements and the spacious longhouses in which several related families lived. Although they did not serve on the league council, women who headed the clans appointed the male sachems.

Other eastern woodlands groups also had complex social and political systems— the Muskogeans, for example. These farming people had a highly structured class system based on worship of the sun. At the top of the system was the chief, called the Great Sun. Just below him in status were the nobles, known as Suns. Below them were the Honored People, and lowest of all was the class known as the Stinkards.

The reigning Great Sun had the power of life and death over the Muskogeans, who worshiped him as a god. The group's complicated marriage rules insured that membership in each class changed over time, however, so that no one family could hold the position of Great Sun indefinitely. In the space of several generations, a Great Sun's descendants would become Stinkards.

For answers, see p. A 5.

Section Review

1. Identify the following: Dekanawidah, Hiawatha, Iroquois League.
2. Define the following terms: potlatch, pictogram, adobe, kiva, hogan, nomadic, sachem.
3. Which of the following cultures had the most abundant food supply: Eskimos, people of the northwest Pacific coast, people of the Great Plains?
4. The cultures of the desert peoples influenced each other in many ways. (a) Name one thing the Pueblo probably learned from the Anasazi. (b) Name one thing the Navajo probably learned from the Pueblo.
5. How did the travois and the teepee contribute to the way of life of the Plains peoples?
6. (a) What is the meaning of the word "matrilineal"? (b) Which early American societies were matrilineal?

3 Great Empires

Many scientists believe that the Muskogeans and other southeastern peoples were influenced by cultures that had developed to the southwest of them, in present-day Mexico. There the Mayas and later the Aztecs built great empires, sophisticated civilizations that influenced many early American societies. In South America the Incas also established a powerful empire.

The Mayas

Mayan civilization flourished on the Yucatan peninsula of Mexico and in present-day Guatemala from about 300 to 900 A.D. The Mayas built great cities, but few people actually lived in them, used them as fortresses, or even used them as the headquarters of government. Instead, the cities were religious centers where the people gathered to worship at huge temple-pyramids, whose walls were covered with carved pictures. The pyramids demonstrate the Mayas' great engineering skills.

The Mayas were skilled in many sciences. Mayan priests were excellent astronomers. They could predict eclipses of the sun and moon and could chart the movements of the planet Venus. Their knowledge enabled them to work out exact calendars, an important part of their religion. The Mayas also developed a complex system of writing that is still not completely understood.

Rise of the Aztecs

Farther to the north, in the Valley of Mexico, a people known as the Toltecs rose to power around 900 A.D. Unlike the peaceful Mayas, the warlike Toltecs extended their influence through conquests. They conquered tribes around them with well-organized armies and new weapons such as the atl-atl, a hand-held catapult that increased the force of a thrown spear. The Toltecs in turn were conquered sometime after 1200 A.D. by the even more warlike Aztecs, who adopted many Toltec customs.

Aztecs called themselves the People of the Sun. As their power grew, they forced their neighbors to pay tributes of food and labor. They erected a spectacular capital city, Tenochtitlán (tay NOHCH tee TLAHN), in the middle of a large saltwater lake. An

Mayan Ideograms

The Mayas developed a sophisticated system of writing. Their writing was hieroglyphic in form; that is, they used pictures or symbols rather than letters to represent sounds and ideas. For example, if a Mayan scribe wanted to convey the idea of travel, he or she would draw two parallel lines, the symbol for road, and then add the outline of a human footprint between them to show travel. In this way the scribe created an ideogram, or picture expressing an idea.

The Mayas carved ideograms onto large stone shafts known as stelae and onto altars, doorways, and wall panels. The Mayas also had books consisting of large sheets of bark paper doubled and enclosed between boards. Some of their books contained records of important events; others concerned religion and science, especially astronomy.

enormous pyramid now called the Pyramid of the Sun dominated the other structures in the city. Here Aztec priests sacrificed humans to Huitzilopochtli (WEE tsee loh POHCH tlee), the chief god.

Floating artificial islands, made by piling dirt on log rafts, surrounded Tenochtitlán. Some formed the foundations for homes; others were cultivated as vegetable gardens. Fresh water flowed into the city through aqueducts. Several long causeways connected the island-city to the mainland. Inside the city, paved streets led to the elaborate homes of the wealthy, to beautiful temples, and to zoos, orchards, and public gathering places.

The construction of Tenochtitlán, as well as the Aztec irrigation systems, bridges, causeways, and amphitheaters, indicates an advanced technology. The Aztec calendar reflects a knowledge of star formations precise enough to predict certain stellar locations on a 52-year cycle. The Aztec system of mathematics probably was better than European systems of the time.

The Incas

Other imposing civilizations developed along the western coast of South America and in the highlands of the Andes Mountains. By 1400 A.D. one group, the Incas, dominated settlements along a band 1,500 miles (about 2,400 kilometers) long, from what is today southern Ecuador to Chile.

Incan engineering achievements surpassed even those of the Aztecs. Sometimes the Incas constructed cities on the tops of mountains or along the faces of steep cliffs. Although no one can be sure how they accomplished it, the Incas moved massive stones from remote quarries, then cut them so precisely that they fit together like pieces of a puzzle. No cementing was required. Even today Incan structures survive earthquakes that demolish modern buildings; the stones move apart under stress, then slide back together.

The Sapa Inca, or supreme ruler, possessed absolute power over his subjects. He ruled a highly efficient economy based on diversified agriculture, with goods transported over an impressive system of roads, footpaths, and floating bridges. The Incas, like the Aztecs, worshiped the sun, and religious leaders performed various rituals to prepare the way for life after death.

The Mayas, the Aztecs, and the Incas were among the first Americans who would feel the impact of European exploration in the late fifteenth century. One by one their complex civilizations would fall to the invading newcomers. In the process, many valuable traces of their cultures would be destroyed—sometimes deliberately, sometimes out of carelessness. What is known of them today comes largely from the remains of their huge stone temples and public buildings. Through these, all three groups have left an indelible imprint on the imagination of the world.

For answers, see p. A 5.

Section Review

1. Identify the following: People of the Sun, Tenochtitlán, Huitzilopochtli, Sapa Inca.
2. What did the Mayas use their cities for?
3. List two examples of the scientific accomplishments of each of the following cultures: (a) Maya, (b) Aztec, (c) Inca.

4 Europe Awakens

Until the late fifteenth century, people in the Americas remained largely isolated from the rest of the world. In Europe, however, an age of discovery was beginning that would soon end that isolation. The new spirit of discovery had its roots in developments that had been under way for many years.

Europe in the Middle Ages

During the Middle Ages (500–1500 A.D.) people in Europe focused largely on local affairs. Since the fall of the Roman Empire in the fifth century, the continent of Europe had been split into hundreds of small, independent states, each ruled by a lord.

Most of the people, peasants called *serfs*, were bound by custom to the lord's land. They gave the lord part of their crop in return for protection against bandits or invaders. Serfs could not leave the land to take up another kind of work, nor could they travel even short distances without the lord's permission.

Theoretically, the lord also owed allegiance and services to a superior: a king, an emperor, or a higher lord. He was the king's *vassal*, or tenant. According to the law of the time, a lord received lands from his superior in return for loyalty. For the most part, however, lords ruled their territories absolutely and independently of one another. This political and social system is known as *feudalism*.

Most medieval states were divided economically into *manors*, or large estates owned by lords. Peasants grew food for everyone on the manor and produced most of life's other necessities. A manor would have, for example, a cobbler who made shoes, a blacksmith who forged tools, a brewer who made beverages, and a miller who ground grain into flour. As a result, few goods had to be traded between manors.

The religious ideas of the Middle Ages further contributed to a lack of interest in the wider world. Christians learned that their life on earth was merely a preparation for life after death. They saw this world as a place of suffering and sadness, or of riches and corruption, but they believed that their station in life was God's will and did not question it.

A New Age Dawns

Around 1100 A.D. life in Europe began to change. People's horizons gradually widened, and they became more curious about the world beyond their own localities.

The Crusades were a major cause of the new atmosphere in Europe. Beginning in 1099, European Christians conducted a series of holy wars, or crusades, with the aim of recapturing the city of Jerusalem and the Holy Land from the Muslims.*

The Holy Land had fallen into the hands of the Muslims in the seventh century. Until around 1000 A.D., however, Muslim rulers allowed Christians to come and go as they wished. At that time, the Seljuk (sehl JOOK) Turks, Muslims not as tolerant of Christianity as their predecessors, conquered the Holy Land. Pilgrims returning to Europe from the Holy Land claimed that the Turks were killing and torturing Christians and turning Christian churches into Muslim temples.

---

*Muslim: a believer in the Muslim religion, in which the supreme deity is Allah and the chief prophet and founder is Mohammed. The Muslim religion is also known as Islam and the Muslims are sometimes known as Moslems.

Europeans quickly developed a taste for the spices Crusaders brought back from Asia. At first only the rich could afford the scarce cinnamon, pepper, and cloves sold by merchants such as the man at right. The search for a less costly way to transport precious spices helped spur sea exploration.

The Crusades against the Turks lasted for about 150 years. At first the Christian armies were successful, but by the end of the thirteenth century all the territory they had won was again under Muslim control.

Although the Crusaders did not achieve their goal, they did affect life in Europe. For example, they brought back books written by Arabic scholars. The new ideas and knowledge the books contained sparked curiosity about the world beyond local borders.

The spices, perfumes, fabrics, and other items the returning Crusaders introduced to Europe also gave people new tastes in foods, new fashions in clothing, and new ideas of comfort in their homes. Soon, a profitable trade arose between the countries of Europe and Asia.

Expanding Horizons Eastward

At first, Europeans traded only with the countries of the Middle East; however, merchants eventually became curious about what lay beyond that area. In 1271 Venetian merchants Maffeo and Niccolo Polo and Niccolo's 17-year-old son Marco set off from Venice. Their destination was Cathay, as China was called, a land celebrated for its fabulous wealth.

The Polos traveled over sea and land for three years, reaching the court of Kublai Khan (KOO blī KAHN), China's emperor, around 1275. They remained in China as guests of the Khan for 17 years. During that time, Marco Polo traveled far and wide throughout the vast empire of China. Little escaped his notice, and in 1295, three years after the Polos had returned to Venice, he dictated the story of his travels to a scribe.* Marco Polo's account of the wonders he had seen revealed to Europeans a civilization beyond anything they had dreamed of.

In addition to describing the wonders of China, Polo provided some very practical information. He told readers that Asian goods were much cheaper in China than they were in Europe. Furthermore, he noted that China was bordered by oceans, not by huge, impassable swamps as had been thought. Therefore, a sea route to Asia would be possible if one could be found.

Over the next 200 years, interest in trade with China and with India, China's neighbor to the southwest, grew. Fine silks, gold, and jewels attracted mainly the wealthy, but nearly all Europeans wanted to buy Asian spices.

In the years since the Crusades, Europeans had discovered that cloves, ginger,

*In the Middle Ages, few men and women could write, so they hired professional writers called scribes.

cinnamon, and pepper did wonders for food. Without these spices, food had a bland, flat taste. Furthermore, many foods were extremely perishable and could be preserved only by heavy, often unpalatable, salting. It was not unusual for a medieval cook to have to pick worms out of meat before cooking it. Sauces made with Asian spices covered up the taste of rotten meat and other spoiled foods.

Because of the growing demand for products from Asia, merchants and adventurers began to search for faster and cheaper routes to Asia. They hoped to avoid paying extremely high taxes charged by rulers along the land routes, so they looked to the sea.

Exploration and Politics

A changing political scene in Europe further contributed to a growing interest in exploration. During the Middle Ages kings and queens for the most part had ruled in name only. Real power lay in the hands of the feudal lords.

As a new middle class grew and prospered, merchants, bankers, and other well-to-do commoners began to wish for the kind of power and status that the nobility had. Kings and queens discovered that they could increase their own power by taking advantage of the merchants' aspirations. Over a period of a hundred years or so, they allied themselves with the merchants and bankers, using their wealth to help create strong monarchies and powerful nations.

Merchants and bankers also profited from the alliance. With the backing of a strong nation, merchants could compete with the city-states* of Italy, which had a virtual monopoly on the Asian trade. Such a monopoly could not be broken by one merchant, or a group of merchants, no matter how powerful. But it could be broken by the combined power of a country's merchants and its government. A city-state like Venice, no matter how wealthy, was no match for the might of a united nation.

Changes in Outlook

Politics and economics were not the only areas in which significant changes took place. During the period of intellectual revi-

*city-state: a governmental unit made up of an independent city and the surrounding territory it controlled.

val known as the Renaissance (REHN uh sahns), which began in the 1300s, attitudes toward life, learning, and religion also changed profoundly.

The work of Arabic scholars brought back by the Crusaders made a deep impression on European learning. Arabic translations reintroduced European scholars to the writings of many classical Greek and Roman thinkers whose works had been lost to Europe since the fall of Rome. Europeans also studied Arabic science, especially advances made by Arab mathematicians.

Interest in one branch of knowledge stimulated curiosity about others. Increasingly, people wanted to learn more about the world in which they lived. They began to investigate their surroundings and to question what they found.

This new inquisitive attitude toward the world sparked advances in science and technology, including new inventions in sea travel. For example, a ship's captain could

At age 17 Marco Polo left home with his father and uncle to journey beyond the limits of the known world in 1271. His destination was the splendid court of Kublai Khan at the site of present-day Peking, China. This illustration from a fourteenth-century manuscript shows the wedding of Ghazan Khan, son of Kublai Khan, to Princess Cocachin. Polo's tales of the wealth and luxury of the Khan's court heightened European interest in trade with Asia.

use a *compass* to tell direction, even when neither land nor the sun was visible. With the *astrolabe* (AS truh layb), the captain was able to fix the ship's location by sighting the stars. With the *quadrant* the captain could take bearings from the sun or the stars in order to plot the ship's position on a map.

By making more precise measurements of distance and location possible, new inventions also advanced the art of map making. Another invention, the printing press, made the improved maps more widely available. All these developments contributed to a growing interest in travel and exploration.

Prince Henry the Navigator

Of course, mariners had to be taught to use new instruments. One person more than any other was responsible for doing this—Prince Henry of Portugal, known as the Navigator.

Portugal was the first European nation to begin systematic exploration of the world beyond Europe and the Mediterranean Sea. Prince Henry played the leading part in this effort. In 1418 Henry established a school of navigation in his castle at Sagres (SAH grehs) on the southwestern tip of Portugal. From there he sent expeditions to Africa.

Realms of Wealth and Culture

The Portuguese were first attracted to West Africa by reports of great wealth. The wealth they sought had grown over many centuries as great African empires rose and fell. The ancient West African empire of Ghana began to develop in size and importance around 700 A.D. Most people of Ghana were farmers, but it was commerce rather than agriculture that accounted for Ghana's remarkable prosperity. Because of its location midway between the salt mines in the Sahara and the gold mines in the tropics, Ghana controlled the highly profitable trade in gold and salt.

At its peak around 1100 A.D., Ghana's capital, Kumbi (KOOM bee), consisted of two connected cities with a magnificent palace for the king, a merchants' trading center, a prison, and several mosques where scholars and priests met.

The kingdom of Mali assumed a prominent position in the thirteenth and fourteenth centuries. Like Ghana, Mali had a well-run government and drew much of its wealth from the gold and salt trade. Its flourishing cities attracted many scholars as well as merchants. In particular, the city of Timbuktu (tihm buhk TOO) became a major center of learning for the Islamic world. Many who studied at its university went on to distinguished careers at universities in the Middle East.

Stories about the fabulous riches of West Africa began to thrill Europeans around the fourteenth century. One such story centered on the hajj (haj), or pilgrimage to Mecca, made by Mansa Musa (MAN suh MOO sah), the ruler of Mali from about 1312 to 1332. Mansa Musa traveled in an extraordinarily lavish manner. Twelve thousand slaves accompanied him. Five hundred slaves carried six-pound staffs of gold, while each of 80 camels bore a 300-pound load of gold dust. Throughout Africa people marveled at the spectacle of Mansa Musa's great wealth and power.

Having reached the height of its power under Mansa Musa, Mali was eventually absorbed into the empire of Songhai in the fifteenth century. The rulers of this third empire continued the tradition of stable and effective government established by their predecessors. They created a civil service, a system of courts, a professional standing army, and even a navy.

The West African kingdoms of Ashanti, Dahomey, Benin, and Oyo also developed sophisticated cultures expressed in their beautifully woven fabrics, elaborate jewelry, carvings in wood and ivory, and bronze sculpture. It was little wonder that Europeans who learned of these civilizations were eager to make contact with them.

Prince Henry had several reasons for sending explorers to investigate the western shores of Africa. Like other European princes, Henry felt that his nation had the duty to convert people to Christianity. He had heard the popular tale of Prester John, who was said to rule a Christian empire in the heart of Africa, and he hoped to be the first to find this legendary kingdom.

A concern for the commercial well-being of his country further heightened Henry's interest. Legends of rich kingdoms in western Africa had been circulating in Europe for years. In fact, gold from these kingdoms had reached Europe as early as the tenth century. However, it had come to Mediterranean ports by a long and costly route across the Sahara. Prince Henry hoped to find a quicker, cheaper route to the source of this gold by sea. Finally, Prince Henry, like other Europeans of his time, dreamed of finding a sea route to India, a place that symbolized riches.

For many years Henry could not convince his sailors to dare a trip beyond Cape Bojador (boh huh DOHR) on the African coast. At that time ships had difficulty sailing into the wind. Since the prevailing winds blew from the north, the sailors wondered how a ship could turn around once it headed due south. The sailors worried that if they passed Cape Bojador, they would not be able to sail back to Portugal. In addition, many sailors had heard that the water of the southern oceans was so hot it boiled.

At Sagres Henry encouraged his shipbuilders to experiment with new model ships. Eventually, they developed a vessel called the *caravel* (KAR uh vehl), which could sail into the wind. It had sleeker lines than the older *carracks* (KAR ukz), which looked like squat wooden tubs, and it used triangular rather than square sails. Henry also showed his captains how to use the quadrant so that they could sail out of sight of land and still be confident of getting back. In 1434 one of Henry's ships finally sailed beyond Cape Bojador. The crew found that it was able to turn around and sail back home. And the sailors discovered that the southern seas really did not boil.

Prince Henry died in 1460, but Portuguese explorers continued to push farther and farther down the African coast, building stone pillars on the shore to mark their progress. Gradually, they established a profitable trade with West African kingdoms. The bulk of their trade was in gold, but they also bought some African slaves. The explorers took the slaves back to Portugal to work as domestic servants. Some were eventually freed, took Portuguese names, and within generations became assimilated into the population.

In 1487 Bartolomeu Dias sailed around the Cape of Good Hope, the southernmost tip of Africa. He had planned to go on to India, but his crew mutinied and forced him to return to Portugal. Ten years later, in 1497, Vasco da Gama made the complete trip to India. Europeans had finally reached Asia by water, and Portugal was well on its way to becoming a powerful trading empire.

Early Contacts

By 1490 Europeans were on the verge of discovering the Americas. Yet this would not be the first contact between American cultures and people from other parts of the world. The first European visitors to the Americas were the Vikings. Sometime around 1000 A.D., Scandinavian sailors led by Leif Ericson reached the northern tip of North America.

Major Events	
300–900	Mayan civilization flourishes
1000	Leif Ericson lands in North America
1099	Crusades begin
1100	Height of Ghana's empire in West Africa
1200	Aztecs conquer Toltecs
1275	Polos reach China
1312–1332	Rule of Mansa Musa in Mali
1400	Incas establish dominance on west coast of South America
1418	Prince Henry founds navigation school at Sagres
1487	Dias sails around Cape of Good Hope
1497	Vasco da Gama reaches India

Throughout the winter of their arrival, they roamed up and down the rough Atlantic coast exploring present-day Labrador and Newfoundland. Then they went home.

Twenty years later, another group of Scandinavians arrived. Their settlement, built in a sheltered Newfoundland bay, lasted little more than two years and was abandoned. The only trace of these early visitors are the half-buried foundations of their houses and a few stone objects.

According to legend, a few Irish fishermen crossed the Atlantic to North America. But if they did, they left no evidence of it. Some maintain that a group of Chinese sailors reached Mexico around 450 A.D., and others claim that Africans explored parts of the Americas several hundred years before Columbus. Present-day Norwegian explorer Thor Heyerdahl believes that ancient Egyptians and Polynesians may have piloted large reed boats to the Americas long before European exploration.

None of these Europeans, Africans, or Asians left lasting traces of their presence in the Americas, nor did they develop any lasting relationships with the first Americans. America continued to go its own way until the late fifteenth century, when the new spirit of discovery that was infecting Europe ended its isolation.

For answers, see p. A 5.

Section Review

1. Identify the following: Marco Polo, Henry the Navigator, Sagres, Bartolomeu Dias, Vasco da Gama.

2. Define the following terms: serf, vassal, feudalism, manor, compass, astrolabe, quadrant, caravel, carrack.

3. (a) What were the Crusades? (b) List two ways the Crusades increased people's interest in the world beyond local borders.

4. How did each of the following contribute to an age of discovery in Europe: (a) Marco Polo's explorations; (b) desire for spices; (c) alliance between monarchs and merchants?

5. What technological innovations made sea travel safer and easier?

6. List three reasons Prince Henry of Portugal was interested in exploration of the west coast of Africa.

7. (a) What groups may have visited the Americas before the 1490s? (b) What impact did they have?

★ ★ ★ ★ ★ ★ ★ ★ ★ ★ ★ ★ ★ ★ ★ ★ ★ ★ ★ ★

IN PERSPECTIVE Although scientists debate the origins of America's first inhabitants, most agree that people lived in the Americas as many as 20,000 years ago. Over thousands of years, people learned to use the resources available to them to survive and then to build diverse cultures throughout North and South America. Some groups hunted and fished or gathered plants. Others planted crops, even in harsh desert climates.

Each culture had its own religious traditions, art forms, and ways of life. These produced the monuments that survive today, from the totem poles of the northwest coast to the cliff dwellings of the Pueblo and the mighty cities of the Mayas, Aztecs, and Incas. The first Americans governed themselves in different ways and developed a variety of social systems.

While hundreds of cultures were developing in the Americas, many other cultures were developing in Africa, Asia, and Europe. Changes in Europe, especially, would eventually bring together the Americas and the rest of the world. During the 1300s and 1400s, the localism of the Middle Ages was giving way to the unification of strong nations that would sponsor explorations of unknown parts of the world. The Crusades and Marco Polo's travels sparked curiosity about the world, and technological developments made travel across the world's oceans safer and more practical. The eventual meeting of the two worlds seemed to be only a matter of time.

For answers, see p. A 6.

Chapter Review

1. (a) Summarize the methods archaeologists use to study a site where prehistoric people may have lived. (b) What types of evidence do they use?

2. (a) What are the weaknesses of the carbon-14 test for determining the age of plant or animal remains? (b) Why do some scientists consider amino acid racemization an improvement over the carbon-14 test?

3. (a) Why have some scientists challenged earlier theories of when the first people came to America? (b) What evidence do they use to support their argument?

4. The Eskimos, the people of the northwest Pacific coast, and the people of the Great Basin all lived by hunting, fishing, or gathering plants, but their lives were very different. (a) How were they different? (b) How might you explain the differences?

5. How were the Anasazi, the Pueblo, and the Navajo able to build their civilizations in the harsh environment of the desert?

6. What role did religion play in each of the following cultures: (a) Pueblo, (b) Navajo, (c) Plains, (d) Maya?

7. (a) Describe the building achievements of the Mayas, the Aztecs, and the Incas. (b) Who probably had the most difficult task? Why?

8. (a) Describe the feudal system. (b) How did it inhibit European exploration?

9. (a) How did the intellectual climate of Europe change after the beginning of the Renaissance? (b) How did this contribute to an age of discovery in Europe?

10. (a) Describe the role Portugal played in the exploration of the world beyond Europe. (b) Why were the activities of Prince Henry so important to that exploration?

For answers, see p. A 7.

For Further Thought

1. How did the environmental changes about 10,000 years ago probably contribute to the diversity among early cultures in America?

2. Early American cultures, like all cultures, were influenced by their environment and also made special use of the natural resources they found. For each of the cultures you read about, make a list of the ways they were able to use local resources. How do you think differing environments can contribute to a diversity of cultures? Explain.

3. (a) Describe how the Pueblo, the Plains people, and the Iroquois governed themselves. (b) How did these systems of government differ from one another? (c) How were they similar? (d) What factors do you think could account for the similarities and differences?

4. (a) How did the status of Pueblo women differ from the status of Ute and Shoshone women? (b) Can you suggest any possible reasons for this difference?

5. (a) Why are historians and archaeologists uncertain about the nature of explorations of the Americas before Columbus? (b) What type of information would they need to reach more positive conclusions about these explorations?

For answers, see p. A 8.

Developing Basic Skills

1. *Classifying* Make a chart with two columns. In column 1 list the factors that inhibited European exploration before 1500. In column 2 list the factors or developments that encouraged exploration. (a) Which column has the most items? (b) Why do you think the developments that encouraged exploration became more important than those that inhibited it? (c) Would you agree with the statement "The European discovery of the Americas was inevitable"? Explain.

2. *Map Reading* Locate the following on the world map (pp. 754–755): Mediterranean Sea, Atlantic Ocean, Europe, Africa, Asia, Portugal, India, Cape of Good Hope, and China. (a) Why might Portugal have been more likely than other European nations to lead in the exploration of the West African coast? (b) What geographical features shown on the map help you explain why Europeans wanted to find a water route to Asia rather than continue to use the land route?

See page 773 for suggested readings.

2

Europe's Age of Discovery

(1492–1608)

Christopher Columbus, *by Sebastiano del Piombo.*

European sailors and adventurers were not looking for a new world in the 1400s. They were searching for the fastest route to Asia. The governments that financed their voyages planned to set up trading posts where European goods could be exchanged for the fabled riches of Asia. However, things did not turn out as planned.

Instead of finding a new route to Asia, Christopher Columbus and the explorers who followed him found two continents whose existence no one had predicted. Instead of meeting the Asians Marco Polo had described, they met people who were not mentioned in any of the books they had read.

In this chapter you will read about the meeting of the Old World and the New World as Europeans discovered the wealth of great American empires and the attraction of establishing colonies in the Americas.

1 A New World for Europeans

As Portuguese sailors were sailing along the African coast, other adventurers sought still faster routes to the wealth of Asia. Among them was Christopher Columbus, a tall, stubborn, and well-seasoned sailor from the Italian port of Genoa.

Columbus: A Determined Explorer

Columbus had sailed much of the then-known world in the service of the Portuguese. An insatiably curious man, he had studied geography and had read and reread Marco Polo's account of his travels.

Scholars had believed for hundreds of years that the world was round, and Columbus accepted their conclusions. He was also convinced, on the basis of his own calculations, that the earth was much smaller than people thought it was. Thus, he maintained, the distance between Europe and China, sailing west, could be navigated in "a very few days" if winds were favorable.

Armed with these convictions, Columbus tried to persuade King John II of Portugal to support a westward voyage to Asia. Portugal was a logical choice, but King John remained unconvinced. He preferred to concentrate his energies on an eastern route around Africa. Columbus spent the next ten years pleading his case at the courts of Europe. He approached the French, then the English. Rebuffed by both, he turned to Spain as a last resort.

The Spanish were not a seafaring people by tradition. However, they were a venturesome, ambitious nation, eager to spread the power of Spain and the influence of Christianity. Against the advice of cautious counselors, Queen Isabella agreed to back Columbus's venture. She outfitted him with three ships, the *Niña*, the *Pinta*, and the *Santa María*, and a crew of 90 sailors.

Columbus paid for part of the voyage himself. However, he demanded and received important concessions from the Spanish crown. Queen Isabella agreed to make him an admiral, to name him ruler of all the "islands and the mainlands" he discovered, and to give him one tenth of all the riches he "bought, bartered, discovered, acquired, or obtained."

Arriving in the Americas

Admiral Columbus set sail from Palos, Spain, on August 3, 1492. Two months later, on October 7, sailors spotted great flocks of birds flying southwest. Suspecting that the birds were heading for land, Columbus altered his course to follow them. Four days later the crew saw tree branches and flowers floating in the water.

Finally at two o'clock in the morning on October 12, the *Pinta*'s lookout spotted white cliffs on the horizon and raised a shout. Columbus and his crew had discovered a world unknown to Europeans, though no one on board the ships knew it yet.

Columbus, convinced that he had reached India, called the friendly people who greeted him Indians. "They invite you to share anything that they possess," he reported, "and show as much love as if their hearts went with it."

The Europeans saw no evidence of the fine silks or large buildings Marco Polo had described. The inhabitants of the island, the Arawaks (AR uh WAHKS), seemed to lead a simple life. The Arawaks did produce enough gold ornaments, however, to convince Columbus that he was not far from the Asian mainland.

Three months later, after exploring neighboring islands, including present-day Haiti and Cuba, the expedition sailed home to Spain. Columbus's success gained him immediate popularity in Spain. Queen Isabella and her husband Ferdinand were impressed by the "Indians" whom Columbus brought back to the Spanish court as evidence that he had found a western route to Asia. Consequently, the queen financed a more extensive expedition by Columbus in 1493. Columbus made two further voyages for the Spanish crown, one in 1498 and another in 1502.

Thirty women went along on the third expedition. By that time the Spanish had decided to establish settlements in the West Indies, as the Caribbean islands came to be called. The island of Hispaniola, or Little Spain, was chosen for the first settlement and a colony was organized. Eventually, the settlers established outposts on other islands.

Rivals for the New World

Word of Columbus's discoveries spread rapidly. Portugal's King John refused to believe the news that Columbus had reached India or China, nor would he recognize Spain's claim to the Caribbean islands. He argued that they were actually part of the Azores, islands in the Atlantic already owned by Portugal, and he claimed them for himself.

The two neighboring kingdoms were suddenly embroiled in a bitter dispute. Worried that the rivalry would lead to war and weaken European Christianity, the Pope offered to mediate. After months of negotiation papal ambassadors convinced Spain and Portugal to agree to the Treaty of Tordesillas (taw day SEE yahs). The treaty, signed in 1494, established the Line of Demarcation. Drawn on a map of the world about 1,100 miles (1,770 kilometers) west of the Azores, the line divided all undiscovered lands between Spain and Portugal.

The treaty granted Spain the right to the territory west of the line and Portugal the territory east of it. What neither Spain nor Portugal knew in 1494 was that the eastern part of South America extended across the line. When a storm blew Portugal's Pedro Álvares Cabral (AHL vah rehz kuh BRAHL) off his course in 1500, he landed in this part of the Americas and promptly claimed it for King John. The territory is now part of Brazil.

A Western Route to Asia

Although Spain and Portugal showed some interest in settling what came to be known as the New World, discovery of a fast route to Asia remained the top priority for most explorers. After Columbus's voyages, many believed that Asia lay just beyond the western coast of North America. To reach it a person only had to find a water passage through the continent.

In the early 1500s hundreds of people joined expeditions sailing from the ports of Spain and Portugal in search of this passage. These included sailors from many European nations as well as a number of Africans, who had been brought to Europe originally by Portuguese and Spanish traders.

Vasco Nuñez de Balboa (NOO nyehth day bal BOH uh), a Spanish explorer, discovered the shortest route across the New World. In 1513, Balboa made a grueling journey across what is now called the Isthmus of Panama, the narrow strip of land connecting North and South America. His route cut through rain forest so thick that an explorer who followed the same trail 350 years later could not see the sky for 11 days.

Balboa's courage and stamina were rewarded at the end of the trek. Emerging from the rain forest onto the top of a mountain, the explorer gazed down on the vast ocean now known as the Pacific. He named it the South Sea, assuming that it was south of Asia.

Balboa was the first European to see the Pacific Ocean, but he had no idea of its great size. It remained for Ferdinand Magellan (muh JEHL uhn) to discover its immensity by sailing across it.

Magellan's expedition sailed from Spain in 1519, made its way around the stormy southern tip of South America, and then crossed the Pacific to the Philippine Islands. There Magellan died in a battle with the island's inhabitants.

What was left of Magellan's fleet continued the eastward journey. In 1522 the one remaining ship limped back to Spain. Of the 237 men who had set sail three years earlier, only 18 survived. Those 18 sailors were the first to have *circumnavigated*, or sailed around, the globe.

The discoveries of Balboa and Magellan added to Europe's store of knowledge about the world and to Spain's position as a world power. Spain now possessed the key both to the largest ocean on earth and to the lands on the western side of the vast American continent.

The Fate of Columbus

And what became of Columbus, the original discoverer? After three voyages he still believed he had found India, although in fact, he succeeded only in exploring the eastern coast of Central America.

Eventually, Columbus was hauled home in chains by Spanish authorities. Some Spaniards who had come to the Americas had begun to enslave and kill the original Americans. Authorities in Spain held Columbus responsible for the atrocities. Furthermore, when the promised gold and riches

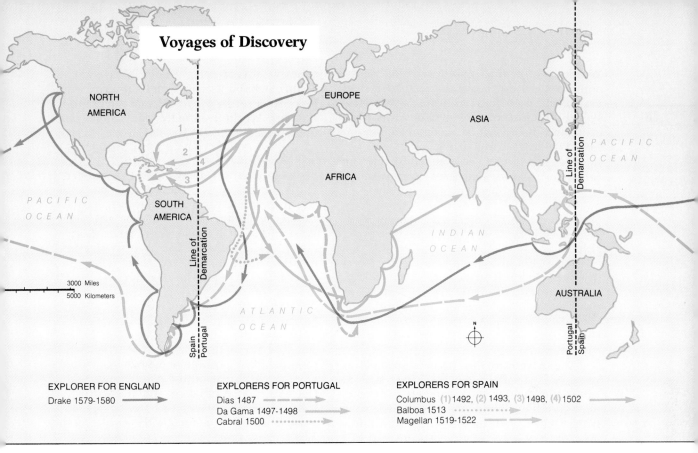

Voyages of Discovery

NORTH AMERICA

EUROPE

ASIA

AFRICA

SOUTH AMERICA

PACIFIC OCEAN

PACIFIC OCEAN

ATLANTIC OCEAN

INDIAN OCEAN

AUSTRALIA

Line of Demarcation

Spain | Portugal

Portugal | Spain

3000 Miles
5000 Kilometers

EXPLORER FOR ENGLAND
Drake 1579-1580

EXPLORERS FOR PORTUGAL
Dias 1487
Da Gama 1497-1498
Cabral 1500

EXPLORERS FOR SPAIN
Columbus (1) 1492, (2) 1493, (3) 1498, (4) 1502
Balboa 1513
Magellan 1519-1522

■ *The hope of discovering a fast route to Asia led European explorers far out into the world's oceans, as this map shows.*

did not appear, complainers at the Spanish court began calling him "Admiral of the Mosquitoes."

Even more insulting to Columbus, the new continent was not even named after him. Instead it was called America after Amerigo Vespucci (ah may REE goh veh SPOO chee), a merchant from Florence, Italy, who realized that the coast he had scouted on a voyage in 1501 was "a very great continent, until hitherto unknown."

Although Columbus did not get the fame or riches he had dreamed of, his skill as a sailor and his grand visions earned him a lasting place in history.

For answers, see p. A 8.
Section Review

1. Identify the following: King John II, Queen Isabella, "Indians," Arawaks, Hispaniola, Pedro Álvares Cabral, Amerigo Vespucci.
2. Define the following term: circumnavigate.
3. (a) Why did Portugal refuse to support Columbus's plan for a westward voyage to Asia? (b) Why did Spain agree?
4. What land rights were granted to Spain and Portugal by the Line of Demarcation?
5. (a) What roles did Balboa and Magellan play in the exploration of the world? (b) How did their discoveries benefit Spain?

2 Exploration and Conquest

Even though Columbus had not discovered a western route to Asia, his voyages led the way to further exploration of two vast continents. Spanish adventurers were soon exploring North and South America.

The Conquistadores

To gain a strong foothold in the Americas, Spain originally relied on *conquistadores* (kohn KEES tah DOH rehs), or conquerors.

37

Well-known for their boldness, ruthlessness, and daring, these professional soldiers had various motives for venturing to the New World. The lure of fabled riches was powerful, and the appeal of adventure in an untamed wilderness was strong.

Many, however, were also drawn to the Americas by a missionary zeal to convert the continents' inhabitants to Christianity. Bernal Díaz (DEE ahs), one of the conquistadores, aptly described their motives: "We came here to serve God, and also to get rich."

Each conquistador received permission from the Spanish crown to establish outposts and settlements in America. In return for a license to colonize the New World, the conquistadores agreed to send one fifth of any gold or silver they mined back to the royal treasury.

The adventure, as the conquistadores knew, was a calculated risk. They had to equip and finance their expeditions, taking the risk of huge losses or even complete ruin. If they succeeded, they stood to gain a fortune. If they were shipwrecked or suffered other accidents, they stood to lose everything—including their lives.

For many years the Spanish government was content to leave colonization to these military adventurers. Under this system Spain extended its power and authority with little expense. In fact, gold and silver from the New World eventually made Spain one of the wealthiest countries in Europe.

Great Empires Fall

Spain gradually gained control of most of South and Central America and parts of North America. Until 1519, however, colonization was limited to small settlements in the West Indies. In that year Hernando Cortés (kawr TEHZ) gathered a small army and prepared to look for the gold and riches rumored to exist in present-day Mexico.

An unusually intelligent leader, Cortés understood the value of psychological warfare as well as physical combat. When he discovered the skill of Aztec warriors, he decided to ally himself with other tribes who resented paying tribute to the Aztecs.

Cortés also acquired the services of a translator, speechmaker, and negotiator, a Native American woman whom the Spanish named Doña Marina (DOH nyah mah REEN ah). Doña Marina "possessed such manly valor," reported one soldier, "that . . . [she] never allowed us to see any sign of fear in her."

Cortés then made one of the most daring—some might say the most foolhardy—moves in military history. He marched 400 heavily armored soldiers into Tenochtitlán, the Aztec capital city of 250,000 people, and confronted the Aztec ruler, Montezuma (MAHN tee ZOO muh).

Tenochtitlán, as you will remember, was located on an island. At any time the Aztecs might have trapped Cortés and his army simply by raising their bridges. But, as Cortés knew, Montezuma believed that the Spanish had come to fulfill an ancient Aztec prophecy. According to the prophecy, the Aztec god, Quetzalcoatl (keht SAHL koh AH tuhl), would return to Mexico from the east, the direction of the rising sun. So Montezuma allowed Cortés and his army to enter the city unharmed.

In a tense game of diplomacy lasting over six months, Cortés held Montezuma a virtual captive in his own city. Then the Spanish fought their way out, losing half their number in the process. With their Native American allies, they surrounded Tenochtitlán. Through battle and starvation they destroyed the city, and with it the Aztec empire.

Aztec artists recorded history through detailed pictures. An Aztec artist-historian recorded this meeting between the emperor Montezuma (seated at left) and Cortés at Tenochtitlán. Doña Marina, a Native American, translated for them.

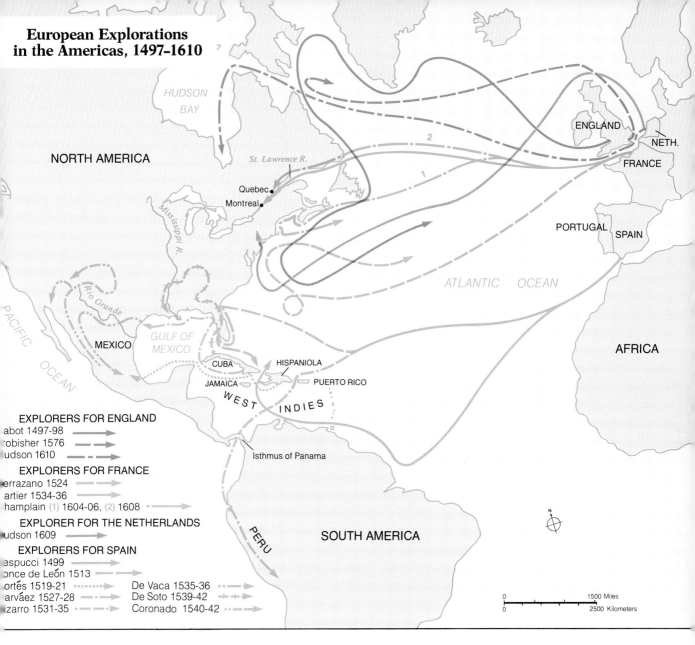

European Explorations in the Americas, 1497–1610

HUDSON BAY

NORTH AMERICA

St. Lawrence R.

Quebec
Montreal

Mississippi R.

Rio Grande

PACIFIC OCEAN

MEXICO

GULF OF MEXICO

CUBA
JAMAICA
HISPANIOLA
PUERTO RICO

WEST INDIES

Isthmus of Panama

PERU

SOUTH AMERICA

ATLANTIC OCEAN

ENGLAND
NETH.
FRANCE

PORTUGAL   SPAIN

AFRICA

EXPLORERS FOR ENGLAND
Cabot 1497-98
Frobisher 1576
Hudson 1610

EXPLORERS FOR FRANCE
Verrazano 1524
Cartier 1534-36
Champlain (1) 1604-06, (2) 1608

EXPLORER FOR THE NETHERLANDS
Hudson 1609

EXPLORERS FOR SPAIN
Vespucci 1499
Ponce de León 1513
Cortés 1519-21   De Vaca 1535-36
Narváez 1527-28   De Soto 1539-42
Pizarro 1531-35   Coronado 1540-42

0   1500 Miles
0   2500 Kilometers

■ *After the first voyages of discovery, the race to explore and claim sections of the New World intensified. English, French, and Dutch adventurers explored parts of North America. (See page 44.) The more numerous Spanish explorers claimed most of Central and South America as well as large areas of North America.*

Ten years later, in 1530, Francisco Pizarro (pee ZAHR oh), another conquistador, received permission to conquer the Inca empire of present-day Peru. With 180 metal-clad soldiers—less than half of Cortés' force—Pizarro marched into the Andean kingdom. Luck was with him. When he arrived, the Incas were embroiled in a civil war.

Pizarro launched a surprise attack, imprisoned the Inca leader, Atahualpa (AH tah WAHL pah), and killed most of his attend-

ants. The attack stunned the Incas, weakening their resistance to the Spanish. By 1535 Pizarro had captured Cuzco, the Inca capital, and crushed nearly all opposition.

Exploration to the North

Legends of great wealth drew Spanish adventurers to the northern regions of the Americas as well as to the south. However, these expeditions were much less profitable to Spain than those of Cortés and Pizarro.

The Spanish showed little appreciation for the work of Inca silversmiths. Instead, the conquistadores melted down vast quantities of jewelry and sculpture for shipment as pure metal to Spain. Some of the surviving work, such as this silver alpaca from Peru, offers glimpses of the talents of Inca artists.

In 1513 Juan Ponce de León (PAWN say day lay AWN) journeyed north to Florida in search of a miraculous fountain whose water reportedly kept people young forever. His search was in vain, but Pánfilo de Narváez (nahr VAH ehz) tried again in 1527.

Determined to find the legendary "fountain of youth," Narváez marched deep into Florida, all the while under attack from the Appalachees (a pah LAH chees), the best archers in the area. They strung their six-foot oak bows so tightly that no Spaniard could pull them. And their precisely aimed arrows could pierce the cracks between the soldiers' armored fittings.

Unable to withstand the Appalachees' attack, the Spanish retreated to the coast. There they rigged makeshift boats—their ships had been destroyed by a hurricane—and sailed across the Gulf of Mexico to present-day Texas.

Only four of the original expedition of 260 soldiers survived. The rest perished at sea. The two most famous survivors were Cabeza de Vaca (kah BAY sah day VAH kah), a Spanish conquistador, and Estevanico (ehs tay vahn EE koh), an African.

For six years the four lived as the slaves of Native Americans, gradually gaining reputations as medicine men. After they were freed, Cabeza de Vaca, Estevanico, and the other two explorers made their way on foot across the hot, dry plains of present-day

western Texas. Finally after two years they met another Spanish expedition.

Cabeza de Vaca returned to Spain, but Estevanico stayed in the New World to join a new expedition organized by Francisco Coronado (KOH roh NAH doh). Coronado hoped to find the legendary "seven cities of gold" reportedly nestled in the hills of present-day New Mexico. Because of Estevanico's experience with the Native Americans of the Southwest, Coronado chose him to head the scouting party.

When the expedition reached the first of the Zuñi pueblos, the villages named in the exaggerated tales, the inhabitants launched an attack. Refusing to retreat with his companions, the "Black Mexican," as Zuñi legend later called Estevanico, was killed by a hail of arrows.

The next year, in 1540, Coronado himself led a full-scale expedition in search of the seven cities. He found the Zuñi pueblos but not the gold. In the process, however, he explored much of the future southwestern United States. One of his lieutenants was the first European to see the Grand Canyon.

While Coronado was looking for gold in the west, Hernando de Soto (day SOH toh) led another gold-hunting expedition into the Southeast. From 1539 to 1542 his army wandered as far north as the Carolinas and as far west as present-day Oklahoma. When de Soto died, the expedition returned without finding any large supplies of gold. Even before de Soto's death, however, the Spanish had begun to concentrate on settling the area to the south, in present-day Mexico, the Caribbean, and South America.

For answers, see p. A 8.

Section Review

1. Identify the following: Cortés, Doña Marina, Montezuma, Pizarro, Atahualpa, Ponce de León, Pánfilo de Narváez, Appalachees, Cabeza de Vaca, Estevanico.

2. (a) Who were the conquistadores? (b) What motives did they have for going to the New World?

3. What did Cortés hope to gain by conquering the Aztec empire?

4. Were the Spanish efforts to find a fountain of youth successful? Explain.

5. (a) What areas did Coronado and de Soto explore in search of gold? (b) Were they successful? Explain.

3 Spanish Settlement of the Americas

In December 1492 Columbus and his crew constructed the first Spanish settlement in the New World, a crude fortress built from the timbers of the *Santa María*, which had been wrecked on a reef on Christmas Eve. That first settlement, called La Navidad, or "the birth," in honor of Christmas, and a second, called Isabella, were only temporary outposts, however.

The first permanent settlement, Santo Domingo, was built on the southern side of Hispaniola in 1496. When a tropical storm destroyed Santo Domingo in 1502, the Spanish lost no time rebuilding it.

Designed to resemble a Spanish town, Santo Domingo grew rapidly and became an important base for explorations. Within a few decades, other towns sprang up on Hispaniola, on the islands of Puerto Rico and Cuba, and on the mainland of the Americas.

Governing New Spain

Soon the Spanish faced the task of managing a huge empire. They not only had to oversee explorations, but they also had to find ways to choose sites for towns, transport colonists from Europe to America, distribute land, and organize an economy based on farming and mining as well as trade.

It quickly became apparent that the informal, one-man rule of the conquistadores was inadequate. The rapid growth of New Spain, as the North American part of the empire was called, demanded a more formal system of government. In 1535 Emperor Charles V appointed Antonio de Mendoza (mehn DOH sah) the first viceroy* of New Spain. Mendoza was an able administrator, and the Spanish colony prospered, as did the South American part of Spanish America.

By the middle of the sixteenth century, Mexico City, the capital of New Spain, boasted paved and lighted streets, as well as a police department and public water system. By 1551, universities had opened in the Indies, Mexico, Ecuador, and Peru. Theaters and printing presses were thriving in Spanish America before England began colonizing.

In 1573 Charles's successor Philip II proclaimed the Laws of the Indies in an attempt to exert tighter control over Spain's New World colonies. This royal legislation outlined the way in which Spain intended to govern its New World empire.

The Laws of the Indies dealt with New Spain's political organization and with all other details of colonial life as well. One of the laws indicated, for example, that a town should be built on high ground, surrounded by good farming land, with an abundant supply of water, fuel, and wood. Another told town planners to leave enough open space so that when a town grew it could spread evenly. The laws even contained regulations for planting seeds and raising cattle.

A Plan for Settlement

The Laws of the Indies reveal much about the goals of the Spanish in the New World. They specified that separate settlements be constructed for three main activities: *presidios* (pray SIH dee ohs) for military activities, missions for religious work, and *pueblos* or *villas* for farming, trade, and town life.

The presidios, designed in the shape of a rectangle, were surrounded by high, thick walls. Within the walls were barracks, storehouses, stables, shops, and a few houses for the families of married soldiers.

In time, houses and farms grew up outside the walls of the presidio as colonists moved there for security. Gradually the military communities developed into towns much like the civilian pueblos.

The missions were meant to be centers from which the Spanish could carry on the work of converting the Native Americans to Christianity. Roman Catholic priests ran the missions, and many Native Americans were either persuaded or forced to live there. Usually, the mission community also included a few Spanish settlers and a small garrison of soldiers.

Each of the missions was a self-supporting settlement. Most were farming communities. Many combined farming with the manufacture of pottery, woven blankets, leather, wine, or olive oil, all goods that the mission exported to Spain or sold to other colonists.

Pueblos were usually situated in the middle of a huge tract of farm land. The

---

*viceroy: a person who rules a country or province as the deputy of a king or queen.

buildings found in the towns of New Spain were far from simple "frontier" structures. The Laws of the Indies stated clearly that settlers were to build with "the beauty of the town" in mind. Thus, churches, private homes, shops, and other buildings equaled the finest examples of Spanish architecture.

Impact on Native Americans

Many Spaniards migrated to the Americas because of the promise of free or cheap land for farming. They raised crops that were much in demand in Europe: bananas, rice, melons, and wheat. They also began to cultivate crops native to the Americas such as potatoes, tomatoes, maize, beans, pumpkins, squash, and tobacco.

Although farming was a profitable occupation for many Spanish colonists, ranching brought even higher income. Many settlers thus turned to raising horses, pigs, cattle, burros, and sheep on the broad expanses of American land. The vastness of many of these ranches, however, required back-breaking work, usually done by Native Americans.

An early policy of the Spanish government had effectively forced many Native Americans to work on Spanish estates. Successful conquistadores had been granted *encomiendas* (ehn koh mee EHN dahs), the right to demand a tribute or tax from Native Americans living on a given piece of land. Often the conquistador would force the Native Americans to work for him as payment. Eventually they became bound to the land because they had no other way of paying the tax. Work on the encomiendas amounted to a form of slavery. Once a Native American had been enticed or forced to become a laborer, he or she had little chance of becoming anything else.

In those areas of the Americas where gold and silver had been discovered, the

An unknown artist sketched this scene around 1584 at a silver mine and processing plant in South America. The Spanish forced conquered Indians to work incredibly long hours in their gold and silver mines. The pack animals partway up the mountain are llamas.

Spanish put Native Americans to work in the mines. If labor on the encomiendas was grueling, working in the mines was even more deadly. The dust, dirt, darkness, and disastrous cave-ins combined to produce staggering rates of injury and death among Native American miners.

To make matters worse, the Native Americans proved extremely susceptible to European diseases carried over by the colonists. Smallpox spread like wildfire through the Americas, killing millions of people. The original population of Mexico, for instance, dropped from over 5 million in 1492 to only one million a century later.

A Misguided Proposal

Eventually, word of the brutal treatment of Native Americans reached Spain. Many Spaniards reacted with concern. Bartolomé de Las Casas (day lahs KAH sahs), a Dominican priest, devoted his life to rescuing the Native Americans. He pleaded the cause of the oppressed to Spanish officials and convinced them to place Native Americans under the protection of the clergy. De Las Casas and other priests were not able to end the Native Americans' enslavement throughout all the colonies, but they did try to relieve some suffering. For example, they allowed many Native Americans to own cattle and raise their own crops. They also replaced some Spanish overseers in the mines with Native Americans.

Although de Las Casas's suggestions may have improved the lot of the Native Americans, they led to the subjugation of another people. To reduce the reliance on Native American labor, de Las Casas suggested that the Spanish import slaves from Africa.

Africans, he reasoned, had demonstrated their ability to live in the New World on the early voyages of exploration, and they had developed immunity to many European diseases. Furthermore, because their own societies were mainly agricultural, they were skilled farmers.

The implementation of de Las Casas's proposal inaugurated the African slave trade in the New World. The Spanish were soon buying slaves by the shipload from Portuguese traders, who had established contacts years before with African kingdoms.

De Las Casas later realized that his efforts to free one group from slavery had resulted in the equally cruel bondage of another and he bitterly regretted his mistake. To other Spaniards, however, the solution seemed worth the brutal price. American gold and silver, mined by both Native Americans and newly enslaved Africans, catapulted Spain to unprecedented riches. By the mid-sixteenth century, Spain's overseas empire was the most powerful in the world.

For answers, see p. A 9.

Section Review

1. Identify the following: Santo Domingo, New Spain, Antonio de Mendoza, Philip II, Bartolomé de Las Casas.

2. (a) Why was the one-man rule of the conquistadores inadequate in New Spain? (b) What was the aim of the Laws of the Indies?

3. Name the three types of Spanish settlements in the New World. What was the main activity of each?

4. (a) What was an encomienda? (b) How did the Spanish use encomiendas to force Native Americans to work for them?

5. What problem did de Las Casas hope to solve by suggesting that the Spanish import slaves from Africa?

4 The French and English Look North

By the middle of the sixteenth century, Spain had become the strongest nation in Europe. King Philip II ruled not only Spain but also Portugal, the Netherlands, and parts of Italy. Without colonial competitors, Spain dominated the Americas, and its ships monopolized their coastal waters.

The enormous wealth that Spain reaped from North and South America aroused the curiosity and envy of other European nations. The governments of France and England, in particular, began to wonder what the New World might have to offer other enterprising people.

Some Native Americans resisted the instrusion of European explorers. This drawing by John White shows a skirmish between Eskimos and an English exploring party headed by Martin Frobisher. White made detailed sketches of Frobisher's expedition and later of the English colony at Roanoke. (See page 46.)

An Empire of Fish and Fur

In 1504 fishermen from France sailed into what is today known as the Gulf of St. Lawrence looking for cod. Each year after that they returned. Gradually they realized that they could increase their profits by trading with the Americans they encountered there. In exchange for furs, they supplied the Indians with hatchets, kettles, muskets, and other European goods.

In 1534 the French explorer Jacques Cartier (kahr tee YAY) sailed up the river now called the St. Lawrence. Cartier, like other explorers, was looking for the fabled northwest passage to Asia and hoped that the St. Lawrence River would be that passage. Furthermore, local inhabitants had told him that great golden cities lay "just beyond" the horizon. Cartier explored the St. Lawrence as far as present-day Montreal, where he founded an outpost. But the northwest passage and the gold always seemed to stay just beyond the horizon.

Political and religious strife in France prevented the French government from devoting much further attention to colonizing activities until 1560. In that year the head of the French navy sent an expedition to Florida, where he hoped to establish bases from which the French could prey on Spanish commerce. The Spanish, however, retaliated in 1565 when they dispatched an army to the French outpost. The army slaughtered most of the inhabitants.

During the 1590s, when the French government took a renewed interest in North America, it directed its efforts primarily to encouraging the lucrative fur trade. The government granted fur-trading rights to a select few, including Pierre du Guast (doo GAWST). In 1604 du Guast hired Samuel de Champlain (sham PLAYN) to explore lands he had been granted by the king and to establish a few trading settlements.

Limited French Settlement

Champlain was a knowledgeable sailor, geographer, and superb map maker. His maps, most of which have survived to this day, showed not only the features of the areas he explored but also details of the settlements he founded.

Champlain established one settlement on the Île de Sainte Croix (eel duh saynt KROI), now in the state of Maine. Settlers

At first, neither the French nor the English had any carefully thought-out plans for exploration or colonization. Their goals were simple: to find as much gold and silver as possible and to discover a fast sea route to Asia.

During the late 1400s and early 1500s explorers employed by England and France, including John Cabot, Giovanni da Verrazano, and Martin Frobisher among others, sailed along the North American coast looking for a likely waterway to the East. (See the map, page 39.) They gathered valuable information about the geography of the area, but found no passage to the Pacific. The only gold and silver they found was on Spanish treasure ships, which they pirated on the high seas.

When it became apparent that their original goals were not to be accomplished, both nations embarked on other, more realistic ventures. Each organized colonies in the northern part of North America and began to exploit what the land had to offer.

found the climate so inhospitable, however, that they abandoned it in less than a year. He founded a second settlement, Port Royal, the next year on a sheltered bay in present-day Nova Scotia. Here Champlain left forty-five people to establish a permanent colony.

Champlain himself continued to explore the region, charting the Atlantic coast as far south as Cape Cod. In 1608 he sailed up the St. Lawrence River as far as present-day Quebec (kwee BEHK). There, on a shelf of land overlooking the river, he constructed a massive wooden fortress, which he called the Habitation (ah bee tah SYOHN). Slowly, the city of Quebec grew up around the fortress.

The French government's interest lay primarily in trading furs, not in establishing populous settlements. Thus, they did little or nothing to encourage immigration to New France, as the region was called. Instead, they devoted their efforts to building up trade along the St. Lawrence into the interior of North America.

Over the next hundred years, settlers did trickle in, but there were never enough to sustain a thriving colony. The wealth and success of New France lay not in towns and cities but in the packets of furs from the interior, paddled down the St. Lawrence in 36-foot (11 meter) birchbark canoes.

The Sea Dogs

Relations among the nations of Europe during the sixteenth century were tense. Religious disputes pitted Catholic countries against Protestant countries, as each struggled to win people and lands to its cause.

At the time, Spain was the most powerful Catholic nation in the world. Its resounding success in the New World and subsequent expansion of power heightened existing tensions. England, the leading Protestant nation, was Spain's natural foe.

Gradually, an undeclared war developed between the two. Into the fray stepped the "sea dogs." Eager for plunder and also fiercely loyal to England and its Queen, Elizabeth I, the sea dogs scoured the Atlantic Ocean, pirating Spanish treasure ships. The English government did not officially employ them; nonetheless the crown encouraged their exploits and took a share of the booty.

Sea dogs were involved not only in pirating, but also in transporting slaves to the

As war between Protestant England and Catholic Spain loomed, Queen Elizabeth I stalled for time while England built ships. In the meantime English captains known as "sea dogs" preyed on treasure-filled Spanish vessels returning from the New World. Although the queen did not officially sanction the piracy, she expected a generous share of the booty—preferably in the form of magnificent jewelry.

Americas. One, an adventurer named John Hawkins, was the first English sea captain to engage in the slave trade. In the 1560s Hawkins sailed to Africa several times, picked up slaves from the Portuguese, and transported them to the West Indies. There he exchanged them for gold or rum, which he brought back to England. His days as a slave trader ended when the Spanish scattered his fleet.

Sir Francis Drake, one of the boldest sea dogs, pulled off an especially daring and profitable exploit in 1573. Aided by black slaves who had escaped from the Spanish, he and his crew stole the yearly silver shipment being carried from Peru to Spain over the Isthmus of Panama. Four years later Sir Francis followed Magellan's route around the world, raiding Spanish settlements along the way on the Pacific coast of South America. Because no English ship had sailed those waters before, Drake caught the Spaniards by surprise.

Drake returned to England in 1580 with millions in stolen treasure. King Philip II of Spain demanded that the booty be returned, but Queen Elizabeth saw the matter in a different light. She knighted Drake right on the

For answers, see p. A 9.

A View of the New World: Using Visual Evidence

You are probably familiar with the expression, "A picture is worth a thousand words." This can be true in a history book as well as in a newspaper or magazine. The pictures in this American history textbook include drawings, paintings, and photographs. All are forms of visual evidence.

Pieces of visual evidence provide valuable information about people, places, and events in history. They can show you what people and places looked like as well as give you a glimpse of what was happening at a given time and place. Thus they can help you understand the past.

Pictures do not present a complete story, however. They can only show you a part of what was happening. Furthermore, the people who take the photograph or do the drawing or painting influence what you see. In order to make the best use of visual evidence, therefore, it is important to carefully analyze what you see.

Follow the steps below, using the picture on page 47, to practice using visual evidence.

1. **Study the visual evidence to decide what you are seeing.** Look both at the details and at the picture as a whole. Answer the following questions about the picture on page 47: (a) Locate the people in the picture. Which people probably lived in the territory shown? Which seem to have arrived recently? How did they come? (b) What does the picture tell you about the territory itself? What does it tell you about the waters off the coast? (c) Where are Florida, Canada, and Mexico located in this picture? What seems unusual about their location? (d) What area is being shown in this picture?

2. **Analyze the reliability of the visual evidence as a source.** In other words, you need to decide if it is a good source. You also need to decide the *best* way to use the source. The questions below will help you analyze the value of this picture as a source: (a) Do you think the artist actually saw all the things shown? Why or why not? Should you use the picture as an accurate view of what America was really like in the 1500s? Why or why not? (b) Can you tell from the picture where the artist was from? What hints can you find? Would it be best to use the picture to help you understand the viewpoint of the Spanish, the English, or the French? Why? (c) Is this a good source?

3. **Study the visual evidence to learn more about an historical event or period.** Refer to the picture and what you have read in your text to answer the following questions: (a) Describe European activity in the Americas in the 1540s. (b) How did people at that time view the voyage to the Americas? Do you think they considered it safe or dangerous? Why? (c) Why do you think the picture appears to be upside down? Why might this view seem natural to a French artist? How might a Spaniard have drawn this picture?

deck of his ship as a reward. Spain responded to the insult by preparing for war.

In 1588 Philip sent a huge fleet, known as the Armada, against England. The English navy was outnumbered two to one, but Drake and other captains made good use of their smaller, more maneuverable ships. With the help of a storm that scattered the Spanish fleet, the English won a stunning victory. Spain's dominance of Europe was shattered.

The First English Colonies

The English did not long limit themselves to piracy and slave trading. Once their interest in the New World had been aroused, they began to think of more permanent ways to exploit the Americas for England's benefit.

Sir Walter Raleigh, an aristocrat high in the queen's favor, sponsored the first English attempt to found a settlement in North America. He spent much of his personal fortune on the venture and also received support from other wealthy investors.

Raleigh envisioned the settlement as more than a way station for pirates and gold diggers. The colonists, in Raleigh's vision, would raise bananas, sugar, and other crops impossible to grow in England's cold climate. They would ship these products back to England along with valuable raw materials such as lumber.

An expedition sponsored by the Virginia Company, as Raleigh and his associates called themselves, sailed from England in 1585. Months later the seven ships, carrying over a hundred men, women, and children, landed on Roanoke (ROH uh NOHK)

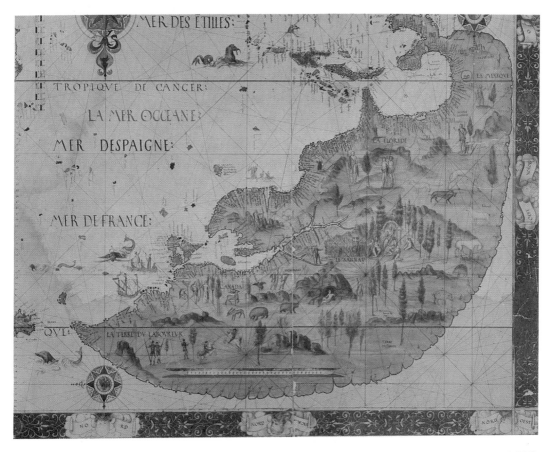

North America in the Desceliers world map of 1546.

Island, off the coast of what is today North Carolina.

Roanoke was an appealing location for a settlement because a chain of long, narrow, sandy islands sheltered it from the Atlantic Ocean. The colonists included Joachim Ganz (yoh AH ihm GAHNZ), a mineral expert, and John White, a surveyor and artist, who painted watercolors of the new land and its inhabitants. Thomas Hariot, another member of the expedition, was an English scholar and friend of Raleigh. He may have gone as an interpreter, having learned the language of the local people from Indians who had journeyed back to England with earlier explorers.

The 1585 expedition returned to England, but another, including 100 men and 17 women, set out for Roanoke in 1587. Later that year John White returned to England for supplies, leaving behind a prospering colony as well as a granddaughter, Virginia Dare, the first English child born in America. Unfortunately, John White did not

Major Events

1492	Columbus's ships land in Americas
1494	Line of Demarcation established
1513	Balboa discovers Pacific Ocean
1517	Protestant Reformation begins
1519	Cortés begins conquest of Aztecs
1534	Cartier explores St. Lawrence River
1535	Charles V appoints first viceroy of New Spain
1585	First English settlement at Roanoke
1588	English fleet sinks the Spanish Armada
1608	Champlain founds Quebec

Henry Hudson and Dutch Claims in the New World

By 1600 both Spain and Portugal had established bases for thriving empires. England and France had made tentative efforts at colonization. But all four countries were to feel the competition of a fifth energetic nation, the Netherlands, which had revolted against Spain in the late 1500s.

The seventeenth century was a time of high achievement for the Dutch. Rembrandt and Jan Vermeer (YAHN vuhr MEER) established their reputations as great painters; Christian Huygens (HĪ guhnz) contributed to astronomy and mathematics; Spinoza to philosophy. The Dutch were no less energetic in matters of trade. The Dutch East India Company was formed in 1602, and soon Dutch vessels of all kinds were sailing the world's waters. By 1650 the Dutch owned 16,000 ships out of some 20,000 that engaged in European trade.

At the beginning of the century, Europeans still hoped to find a water route to Asia around the top of the Americas. To that end the Dutch East India Company sent Henry Hudson and a crew of 20 westward in his ship, the *Half Moon*. This was Hudson's third voyage. Earlier he had sought a passage directly over the North Pole, but the solid ice of the polar seas had proved impossible to navigate. On this third voyage, in 1609, Hudson reached Newfoundland, then sailed south as far as Virginia.

Frustrated in his search, Hudson swung north again. On September 2, he sailed into the fine, deep harbor of present-day New York. "This is a very good land to fall in with," reported his mate, "and a pleasant land to see." After spending a few days fishing, picking huckleberries, and trading with the local inhabitants, Hudson journeyed up the broad river that was later named after him.

The *Half Moon* sailed as far north as the site of present-day Albany. On the way Hudson was escorted ashore to visit a prosperous Indian village. He was impressed: the village was stocked with "a great quantity of maize or Indian corn, and beans of last year's growth . . . enough to load three ships, besides what was growing in the fields." But he realized, soon enough, that what he had hoped was a strait leading to the Pacific was simply an inland river. Disappointed, he returned home.

His journey was not in vain, though. While Henry Hudson had not found a way through the continent, his explorations laid the foundation for the Dutch colony of New Netherland, whose settlements were to line the banks of the Hudson River in the years to come.

---

return with fresh provisions until 1590, nearly three years later.

In the place where he had left a small but thriving colony, his relief expedition found deserted buildings, rusty armor, grass choking the lanes and paths, and the word "CROATOAN" carved on the door post of the crumbling fort. They saw no sign of the cross, which had been designated as a sign of distress. White also found food buried in the ground, suggesting that the colonists had left willingly, intending to return.

Had the colonists, threatened with hunger and privation, joined the friendly Croatoan tribe nearby? White never found the answer. A storm prevented him from staying to search for the settlers and, to this day, the mystery of the "lost colony" persists.

Roanoke failed as a permanent settlement, but the experience proved to be valuable. Raleigh and his friends realized that a colony could be started with private funds. But they saw that its continued existence depended on more financial support than an informally organized group of investors could provide. Permanent English settlements would have to depend on a different form of sponsorship.

For answers, see p. A 9.

Section Review

1. Identify the following: Jacques Cartier, Samuel de Champlain, John Hawkins, Sir Francis Drake, the Armada, Sir Walter Raleigh, John White.

2. (a) What two goals did most of the early French and English explorers have? (b) Were they successful? Explain.

3. What two products became the basis for French activity in the New World?

4. (a) Who were the sea dogs? (b) What did they want to accomplish in the New World?

5. How did England break Spain's dominance of Europe?

6. (a) Why did Sir Walter Raleigh sponsor the founding of an English colony in America? (b) Did it succeed? Explain.

IN PERSPECTIVE Columbus's voyage in search of a western route to Asia ended the isolation of American cultures and brought two worlds together. European explorers were soon searching the coast of the Americas for a passage to Asia and searching the interior for gold and silver.

Spanish conquistadores found great wealth among the Aztecs and Incas but found little precious metal north of present-day Mexico. Spanish soldiers, missionaries, and settlers followed the adventurers to the New World and began to establish a permanent home. Spanish accomplishments, however, came at the expense of Native Americans.

Spain's growing wealth and power aroused the envy of its European rivals, particularly France and England. French attempts to find a passage through North America and to find gold and silver were futile. But during the 1500s the French developed a prosperous trade with Native Americans.

Early English explorers also sought precious metals and a northwest passage. However, most English activity in the New World was limited at first to pirating Spanish ships. The sea dogs were able to enrich themselves while weakening their country's chief rival. In the late 1580s the first group of English settlers arrived in North America. Although their attempt to settle on Roanoke Island failed, they led the way for more permanent English settlement in the 1600s.

49

For answers, see p. A 10.

Chapter Review

1. (a) Why did Queen Isabella finance exploration of the New World by Columbus and other explorers? (b) How did Spain benefit from their activities?

2. (a) What role did the conquistadores play in the colonization of the Americas? (b) What parts of the continents could Spain claim as a result of their activities?

3. (a) Describe the Spanish exploration of the area north of present-day Mexico. (b) What were the goals of the explorers? (c) Were they successful? Explain.

4. (a) What were the three major activities of the Spanish who settled in the Americas? (b) What impact did the settlers have on Native Americans?

5. How did concern about the treatment of Native Americans lead to the introduction of African slavery into the Americas?

6. (a) Why did other European nations like France, England, and the Netherlands first become interested in the New World? (b) How did their goals change? Why?

7. (a) How did Sir Francis Drake and other sea dogs help England in its struggle with Spain? (b) What was their reward?

8. (a) What was the fate of the first English colony at Roanoke? (b) Why was it important?

For answers, see p. A 10.

For Further Thought

1. (a) What personal characteristics did people like Columbus, Cortés, Narváez, Estevanico, Hudson, Cartier, and Drake probably have in common? (b) What skills and attitudes would have been most important to them?

2. (a) How did Native Americans react to the early groups of Europeans that landed in the New World? (b) Did they all react the same? (c) How might you explain their reactions?

Developing Basic Skills
For answers, see p. A 10.

1. *Classifying* Make a chart with two columns. In column one, list the groups and individuals you read about in this chapter who ventured to the New World. In column two, list the motives of each. (a) What similarities do you see? (b) What differences do you see? (c) What were the most common reasons people set sail for the New World during the late 1400s and early 1500s?

2. *Researching* Choose one of the explorers of the New World. Research his personal background in order to answer the following questions: (a) Where was the person born and raised? (b) What training and experience contributed to his abilities as an explorer? (c) Why do you think he became an explorer?

See page 773 for suggested readings.

3

England's New World

(1607–1732)

Signing the Mayflower Compact

The failure of the colony at Roanoke did not end English interest in settling North America. On the contrary, less than 25 years later, in 1607, a group of English men and boys landed at Jamestown. Other men and women soon followed, and by 1732, 13 thriving colonies had been established along the eastern coast of North America.

European settlers came to America for many reasons. Some came in search of wealth, some to start a new life, some to find religious freedom. All took a chance coming to a new land far from the life they had known, and most faced great hardships.

As you will read in this chapter, the founders had a variety of reasons for sponsoring the 13 colonies. In addition, the role of the English government changed during the 1600s as the crown took a growing interest in the New World.

Regardless of how the American colonies were founded and who settled them, all proved to be fertile soil for the growth of a strong tradition of representative government that resisted any attempt to deny it.

1 A Gamble in Virginia

Sponsoring a colony in an untamed, unknown country thousands of miles from England was a difficult, risky business. The sponsor had to buy ships, pay sailors to transport colonists, persuade settlers—especially laborers and skilled workers—to migrate to America, and outfit an expensive expedition. Raleigh's experience with the colony of Roanoke had shown that individuals, no matter how wealthy, could not do this alone.

Financing the Colonies

The English devised a form of business organization that helped them solve the problem of financing colonies. This organization was known as a *joint stock company.* English merchants had used the joint stock company successfully in trading ventures to Russia, Persia, and the East Indies.

A joint stock company pooled the funds of many investors by selling stock or shares in the company. The amount of risk investors took, as well as the amount of profit they made, depended on the number of shares they owned. In case of bankruptcy, the investors were liable only for the amount of their investment. With the joint stock company, creditors could not seize the investor's personal property as payment for a debt as they could with private individuals or other forms of business organization.

Their ability to muster large amounts of capital and their limited liability permitted joint stock companies to undertake ventures both expensive and risky. Among these ventures was the founding of colonies in the American wilderness.

The Fort on the James

In 1606, 15 years after John White had returned from England to the ghostly emptiness of Roanoke, King James I granted a charter to two companies of English investors. The charter authorized the companies to found colonies in the New World.

One group, the Plymouth Company, included merchants from the port of Plymouth, England. For many years they had sponsored expeditions to the rich Atlantic fishing grounds off Newfoundland. The Plymouth Company's charter gave it the exclusive right to settle land from present-day Maine to New York. (See map below.)

■ *King James I of England gave two companies of English investors the right to found New World colonies. Land between the two grants could be claimed by the company that settled it first. Which Native American groups lived on land granted to the Plymouth Company? Which groups lived on land granted to the London Company?* For answers, see p. A 10.

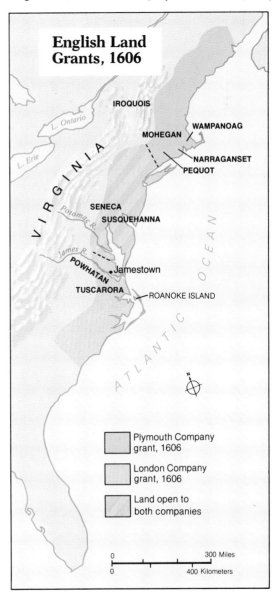

English Land Grants, 1606

IROQUOIS

L. Ontario

L. Erie

VIRGINIA

WAMPANOAG

MOHEGAN

NARRAGANSET

PEQUOT

SENECA

Potomac R.

SUSQUEHANNA

James R.

POWHATAN • Jamestown

TUSCARORA

ROANOKE ISLAND

ATLANTIC OCEAN

☐ Plymouth Company grant, 1606

☐ London Company grant, 1606

☐ Land open to both companies

0   300 Miles

0   400 Kilometers

The London Company acquired rights to the territory stretching from the Potomac River south to what is now North Carolina. According to the agreement between the crown and the investors, the land between the two grants could be claimed by the company that settled it first.

In December 1606, 120 men and boys left London with instructions from the London Company to establish a settlement in what is now Virginia. Four months later 104 survivors landed in North America. After a two-week search for a suitable site, the colonists chose a low, swampy peninsula 30 miles (49 kilometers) upstream from the mouth of the James River.

Their orders from the London Company stated that they were to look for a place well inland on a navigable river. Such a site was thought to have advantages for trade and yet be easier to protect from attack than a location on the coast. The instructions, prepared by men who had never laid eyes on the New World, proved to be disastrous.

The colonists built a fort on the James River and called their settlement Jamestown after the king. The location was easy to defend from attack by local inhabitants, but the marshy peninsula provided a breeding ground for malaria-carrying mosquitoes. Furthermore, the drinking water was brackish, and the unusually damp air rotted the wooden buildings.

Soon Jamestown residents were beset by disease. To make matters worse, most colonists were soldiers or aristocrats unaccustomed to physical work of any kind. Others knew how to make glass, do brickwork, or fashion implements of iron, but virtually no one had the skills needed to survive in the wilderness.

The London Company's goals for the settlement made the shortage of labor for such tasks as growing and hunting food even more acute. They wanted the settlers to continue the search for the northwest passage to China and to look for gold in America.

When the settlers realized that a northwest passage did not exist in that area, they gave top priority to the search for gold. They spent most of their waking hours hunting the precious metal. "No talk, no hope, nor work," recalled Captain John Smith, Jamestown's military expert, "but dig gold, wash gold, refine gold, load gold."

The Jamestown settlers themselves had little incentive to try to make their settlement independent and self-supporting. According to the charter, the London Company owned all the land and was supposed to provide all necessities. Thus, colonists often demanded food from the common food supply while refusing to do any farm work or hunting.

Conditions deteriorated rapidly. The London Company had appointed a council of 13 men to govern the settlement, but the council members quarreled among themselves and seemed incapable of acting. By the end of the first year at Jamestown nearly half of the original 104 settlers had died, and the future of the only English outpost in the New World looked very bleak.

Jamestown Survives

The experiment on the James River might well have ended in its first year if John Smith had not been a member of the colony. Smith, an experienced soldier and intensely independent man, was appalled by the apathy, selfishness, and disorganization he saw around him.

Smith had been expelled from the colony's governing council for fighting with its aristocratic leaders. However, when those who remained could not halt the colony's march toward destruction, they recalled him—this time as president of the council.

He responded to the chaos by taking control of what was left of the colony. He governed sternly, refusing to allow anyone the privilege of not working. Under Smith's leadership, the men of Jamestown marched to work each day as if they were members of a military battalion. They built shelters, cleared the land, and began planting crops. Furthermore, Smith put a stop to the hunt for gold, which had wasted so much of the colony's energy.

From the beginning, Jamestown's residents obtained part of their food supply from the original inhabitants of the area in exchange for English beads and copper. These friendly relations began to cool, however, when Smith demanded more food at his own price. Moreover, the Indians regarded the settlers' clearing of land and planting crops as an invasion of their hunting grounds. The growing hostility sometimes erupted into violence.

Once, a group of Indians seized Smith and threatened his life. Only the intervention of Pocahontas (poh kuh HAHN tuhs), the chief's young daughter, saved Smith. After this incident friendly relations between the English and the Native Americans gradually resumed.

John Smith steered the settlement through its first years, but his efforts alone were not enough to save the colony. The winter after he departed for England, the colonists experienced "the starving time." Food was so scarce that they had to eat shoes, rats, horses, frogs, roots, and insects.

Because of such conditions, the London Company had to resort to extraordinary measures to keep Jamestown populated. At one time company employees kidnapped 100 English orphans and shipped them to the colony. The company gave some English prisoners the opportunity to serve out their sentences in Jamestown, and convinced some settlers to come voluntarily. But by 1617 only 400 of more than 2,000 people who had come survived.

The London Company realized that if the settlement were to last, some family life would have to develop. In 1620 and 1621, two ships brought groups of unmarried women to Jamestown. The company auctioned them off as wives for a product that was beginning to provide the solid economic base the colony needed, tobacco.

Tobacco: The Key to Survival

Ultimately, Virginia's survival depended on two things: its ability to make a profit for the London Company and its ability to attract new settlers. In 1612 a settler named John Rolfe found the key to both when he discovered that Jamestown was an ideal place to grow West Indian tobacco.

The Spanish had first introduced Europeans to tobacco, a native American plant. In the early 1600s the market for tobacco grew as the use of snuff and the habit of smoking spread. The West Indian tobacco that Rolfe adapted to Virginia soil became a favorite with Europeans. Within a few years, tobacco farms dotted the banks of the James River, and the settlers were soon shipping large quantities of tobacco to England at a handsome profit.

Tobacco not only guaranteed the survival of Jamestown, it also encouraged the growth of slavery in the English colonies. Raising tobacco involved back-breaking, unskilled hand labor, the kind of labor the Jamestown settlers found distasteful.

The daughter of an Indian chief, Pocahontas brought food to hungry Jamestown settlers during "the starving time." Said John Smith, "she . . . was . . . the instrument to preserve this Colony from death, famine, and utter confusion." Later Pocahontas married John Rolfe, and the two of them took Virginia's first tobacco crop to London, where a portrait of her in English costume was painted.

In 1619, just as tobacco cultivation was expanding rapidly, a Portuguese ship arrived at Jamestown with 20 Africans, who were sold either as servants or slaves. Since the Africans came from agricultural societies, they proved to be a boon to the colony.

Slavery did not take hold immediately, though. Until 1670 some blacks and whites worked side by side as servants, and some blacks were free laborers. By the close of the seventeenth century, however, slavery had become entrenched in Virginia.

The First Representative Assembly

Originally, a council of 13 men, each with an equal vote, governed the Jamestown colony. The London Company appointed the council by sending their names to Virginia in a sealed box that was to be opened only upon arrival. However, the council members could not find a competent council leader after John Smith returned to England so the London Company disbanded the council. A governor who had the power to rule in both military and civilian affairs was appointed.

In 1619 the London Company again revised the colony's system of government. When the new governor arrived in Virginia, he instructed the eligible voters to elect 22 burgesses, or representatives, two from each of the 11 areas of the colony. The burgesses, meeting with a council appointed by the governor, would make laws and help administer the colony.

As a representative assembly, the House of Burgesses was part of an English tradition of limiting royal authority and increasing citizen participation in government. In 1215 a group of English nobles forced King John to guarantee them certain rights and privileges, set down in a document known as the Magna Carta, or Great Charter. These rights and privileges benefited mainly the nobles, not the common people, but having the rights listed on paper set a precedent, or tradition, that the king's power was not absolute.

In 1265 the English established a parliament that further limited the power of the monarchy. Parliament consisted of two groups who represented their interests to the king: the House of Lords, made up of nobles and high church leaders; and the House of Commons, a group of gentlemen* elected to represent English counties and boroughs.

Parliament was far from representative of all English people. Yet its existence guar-

anteed that monarchs could not rule without obtaining the consent of at least some of their subjects.

The London Company's order establishing Virginia's new government in 1619 also came to be called the Great Charter, a Magna Carta in its own right—and with good reason. The House of Burgesses, as the first representative assembly in the New World, established a pattern of government that other English colonies would follow.

For answers, see p. A 10.

Section Review

1. Identify the following: joint stock company, Plymouth Company, London Company, John Smith, Pocahontas, "the starving time," John Rolfe, Magna Carta.
2. List two ways a joint stock company worked better than individual investors for sponsoring colonies.
3. (a) How did their choice of location create problems for the first settlers at Jamestown? (b) Name two other difficulties they faced.
4. What steps did John Smith take to help Jamestown survive?
5. (a) How did Native Americans contribute to the success of Jamestown? (b) Were relations between the local inhabitants and the English at Jamestown always friendly? Explain.
6. (a) What was the House of Burgesses? (b) Who elected its members?

2 The New England Way

Thirteen years after the first English settlers arrived in Virginia, another group of English men and women put down roots on the continent, but this time farther north along the coast. The path followed by these colonists, however, differed from that followed by the Jamestown settlers.

For one thing, the environment of Massachusetts, where the first New England colonists landed, was much more favorable for settlement than the environment of James-

town. The climate was dry and healthy. Pure, clear brooks provided a supply of fresh water. Fish and game abounded. Winters were harsh, but just a few years after they arrived, New England colonists were living longer than people in either Virginia or England.

People also had different reasons for migrating to Massachusetts. Most early Jamestown settlers hoped to "get rich quick" and return to England. As a result, early Jamestown had the feel of a frontier "boom town." Flimsy houses of unseasoned wood were thrown up quickly. Ships anchored off shore as floating taverns where colonists all too quickly spent the riches gained from tobacco.

*The title "gentleman" referred to any man who was rich enough to support himself without working. Most often a gentleman's wealth came from land. However, university students, members of the clergy, and army commanders could call themselves gentlemen.

Eventually, the London Company sent women to Virginia, but for years male colonists outnumbered the females. On the other hand, more families with children settled in New England. Furthermore, they came not to make instant fortunes and return to England, but to settle down and begin new lives in the New World.

Search for a More Comfortable Life

Many families migrated to the New World because they were dissatisfied with their lives in England. There a person's social class and place of birth often determined the quality of his or her life.

Among the upper classes, the eldest son inherited family wealth. Younger sons often found themselves without gainful employment upon reaching adulthood. Traditionally, these young men entered the church or the army, or competed for posts at the royal court. With the opening of America, they had other, better prospects.

Lower classes from the rural areas and the cities also found reasons to search for a better life in the New World. As wool became a staple of the English economy, acre upon acre of English farmland was fenced in for sheep pastures. Peasants who had tilled the land for centuries as tenant farmers suddenly found themselves evicted from their homes. Some found employment in rural industries, but most could find no satisfactory work at all.

A middle class of merchants and artisans lived prosperously in England's cities. But life for most city dwellers was characterized by cramped housing, filthy streets with open sewers, frequent fires, water shortages, rampant crime, epidemics, and chronic unemployment.

These conditions influenced many people's decision to make the long and risky journey to the New World. Even more important to earliest immigrants, however, was the New World's promise of the chance to worship in their own way.

The Protestant Reformation

Throughout the Middle Ages, the Roman Catholic Church united Christian believers under the spiritual leadership of the Pope. On the local level, the church was led by priests, who in turn were responsible to their superiors, the bishops and archbishops.

At the beginning of the sixteenth century, Martin Luther, a young German monk, became increasingly distressed by conditions in the church. He was dismayed by the corruption and worldliness that had crept into it, especially the clergy's preoccupation with power and wealth. Most of all, Luther disapproved of certain aspects of Roman Catholic theology. He particularly opposed the church's strong emphasis on good works as a means to eternal salvation. Good works could never save a Christian, Luther argued; faith alone had the power to do that. Luther tried to convince others within the church, but he remained unsatisfied and left the church in 1517.

Martin Luther's actions inaugurated a movement that came to be known as the Protestant Reformation. Soon it spread throughout Europe. John Calvin established a strict version of the new faith in Geneva, Switzerland, and new churches also formed in France and in the Netherlands.

In England Henry VIII declared himself, rather than the Pope, head of the church, provoking a split with Rome. Henry, unlike Luther and Calvin, did not oppose the beliefs of the church. He simply wanted to govern his nation's branch of the church himself—without interference from the Pope. After Henry's death, however, Protestantism flourished in England. Elizabeth, who became queen in 1558, was a Protestant, as were many of her subjects.

But what did being a Protestant mean? Leaders of the reformed churches could not always agree. Luther wanted to base all theology on the Bible, allowing the church to keep only those customs that were specifically permitted by Holy Scripture.

All Protestants agreed, in one degree or another, with Luther's emphasis on scripture, but they often parted company there. Some felt that all church hierarchies should be abolished because the Bible made no mention of them. Others disagreed and felt that the offices of bishop and archbishop should be continued. Still others argued that the only spiritual leaders should be local ministers.

Under Elizabeth, the Church of England felt it was proper to retain the traditional hierarchy of bishops and archbishops. Furthermore, the English church kept many of the Catholic practices, such as not eating meat at certain times.

Some English people believed, however, that the English church had not reformed enough. They objected to church services that incorporated Catholic practices. And they claimed that English priests were still too worldly, superstitious, and ignorant. One Protestant called them "Dumme Doggs, Unskilful sacrificing priestes, Destroyeing Drones." From these strongly dissenting groups came many of New England's colonists.

The Pilgrims of Plymouth Colony

Some dissenters believed that the Church of England remained so impure that true believers should separate from it completely. Those who held this radical position were called Separatists.

When James I succeeded Elizabeth in 1603, the Separatists became alarmed, for the king had vowed to "harry them out of the land." Fearing for their safety and their freedom, many moved to the Netherlands. There the Dutch, known in Europe for their tolerance, allowed the Separatists to worship as they pleased. Yet the Separatists were not satisfied with their new home. They missed their familiar English neighborhoods and customs. When Catholic Spain threatened to seize the Netherlands, which it had ruled earlier, the English Separatist community looked for another haven.

Along with other English people, the Separatists obtained permission from the London Company to start a new settlement in the company's North American territory. In September 1620, 102 men, women, and children, later called Pilgrims, set sail from Plymouth, England, on a small ship, the *Mayflower*.

When they reached the coast of North America, the Pilgrims realized that their course had taken them north of the London Company's lands and, hence, outside its authority. The colonists were thus responsible for governing themselves.

While still on shipboard, the Pilgrims gathered together and drafted an agreement that formed the basis of their community in the New World. Forty-one colonists signed this agreement, called the Mayflower Compact. The compact was not intended to establish a formal government. Rather it was a simple agreement that the settlers would consult each other about matters affecting the community and abide by majority rule.

The first winter at the colony was hard, for the Pilgrims had arrived in December, much too late to plant crops. By the following spring, almost half the settlers had died from cold, hunger, and disease. That more did not perish was due partly to the firm leadership of the young William Bradford. He assumed the governorship of the Plymouth colony during that first winter and led it for many years.

The colony also received invaluable aid from Native Americans, who befriended the

The Mayflower Compact

The Pilgrims knew they would need some type of government when they left the *Mayflower*. Although it is a short document, the Mayflower Compact helped establish the principle of self-government in America.

In the name of God, Amen. We, whose names are underwritten, the loyal subjects of our dread [awesome] Sovereign Lord King James by the Grace of God, of Great Britain, France, and Ireland, King defender of the faith, etc.

Having undertaken for the glory of God, and the advancement of the christian faith, and the honour of our king and country, a voyage to plant the first colony in the Northern parts of Virginia. Do by these presents, solemnly and mutually, in the presence of God, and one another, covenant [contract] and combine ourselves together into a Civil body politick, for our better ordering and preservation and furtherance of the ends aforesaid; and by Virtue hereof do enact, constitute, and frame such just and equal laws, ordinances, Acts, constitution, and officers, from time to time, as shall be thought most meet [suitable] and convenient for the general good of the Colony; unto which we promise all due submission and obedience. In witness whereof we have hereunto subscribed our names at Cape-Cod the eleventh of November, in the year of the reign of our sovereign Lord King James, of England, France, and Ireland, the eighteenth, and of Scotland, the fifty-fourth, Anno Domini, 1620.

Pilgrims and showed them how to raise corn. When the colonists harvested their first crop in October 1621, they gratefully proclaimed a day of thanksgiving.

The Puritans

While the Pilgrims separated themselves completely from the Church of England, other dissenters, called Puritans, hoped to reform it from within. For a while the Puritans achieved modest successes. Many English congregations simplified their forms of worship. And quite a few Puritans attained positions of power within the English government and universities.

When King James's son, Charles I, assumed the throne, the Puritans found themselves threatened. Charles's religious beliefs had more in common with the Catholic church of Rome than with a "purified" and simplified English church. Also, he felt that the Puritans' objection to a hierarchy threatened not only the church but his own power as well.

In retaliation, Charles and his government denied Puritans the freedom to worship as they pleased and deprived them of leadership positions in the church and the universities. As a result, some Puritans began to look toward the New World.

After much negotiation, a group of Puritans obtained a charter from King Charles to establish a colony in America under the auspices of the Massachusetts Bay Company, a joint stock company Puritans had formed. In 1630 an impressive fleet of 11 ships carrying over 900 colonists arrived in Massachusetts, where an exploratory party had established a beachhead the year before. Under the leadership of John Winthrop, the colony soon began to prosper.

Government at Massachusetts Bay

Meanwhile, persecution of English Puritans continued unabated. The government's hostility to their beliefs led the members of the Massachusetts Bay Company to take an unusual step. Instead of governing from England, as other joint stock companies had, the company moved its headquarters to Boston, its new American settlement.

The company retained the right, under its charter, to make laws for its settlers and to govern them without giving anyone but

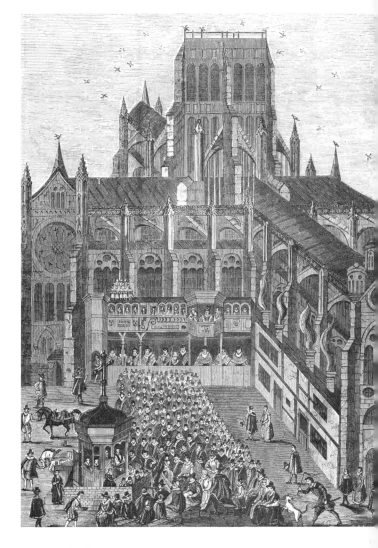

Although the Church of England separated from the Roman Catholic Church in 1534, its services retained a good deal of pomp and ritual. This engraving of a service at St. Paul's Cathedral in London around 1618 shows the type of elaborate ceremony the Puritans hoped to escape in the New World.

shareholders a voice in deliberations. But Winthrop and the other leaders did not follow this course of action. They turned the government of the company into a true government of the colony by allowing settlers, not just shareholders, to elect the colony's officers.

Voters chose a legislature, called the General Court, and a governor to direct affairs. In order to preserve the religious character of the colony, however, only male church members were allowed to vote.

Even with this requirement, though, many more citizens could vote in Massachusetts than in England, where only men who owned or rented property worth 40 shillings could vote. As long as a Massachusetts settler was a free man and a church member, he could vote no matter how much his property was worth. Thus, at an early stage, Massachusetts governed itself with a representative assembly.

Despite this genuine advance, Puritans did not believe in democracy. Free men elected leaders, but the leaders' duty was to do God's bidding. Puritans wanted their colony to be a "Bible Commonwealth," run according to their interpretation of scripture. They did not want other religious groups tainting the settlement with "impure" notions. Any such heretics were expelled.

A Search for Tolerance

One of the most prominent "heretics" was Roger Williams, who arrived in Massachusetts Bay in 1630. Williams, like the Puritans, believed that spiritual leaders of the church should keep themselves separate from the worldly affairs of the state. He agreed that ministers should not hold political offices. But Williams went a step further and claimed that the state should have nothing to do with religious matters either. It should not force people to worship in a particular way, as the Puritans were doing in Massachusetts Bay.

In 1635 Massachusetts banished Williams for these opinions, as well as for his belief that the king had no right to grant the settlers lands that already belonged to Native Americans. Williams fled into the wilderness and established what later became the colony of Rhode Island. There he tolerated all forms of religious worship.

Rhode Island soon became a haven for religious dissenters. Among them was Anne Hutchinson, an intellectual and forceful woman who quarreled with Massachusetts leaders over theology and was subsequently banished.

Another group of settlers from Massachusetts Bay founded a town at Hartford, Connecticut, in 1636. Their minister and leader, Thomas Hooker, agreed with the Puritans' theology but felt that John Winthrop and the other magistrates had assumed too much power. Government, Hooker believed, should rest on "the free consent of the people."

Accordingly, in 1639 the settlers in the Hartford area adopted the Fundamental Orders of Connecticut as their new plan of gov-

Anne Hutchinson: A Voice of Religious Dissent

In March of 1638 the Massachusetts Bay Colony was shaken by a religious scandal. Anne Hutchinson a strong-minded woman whose religious teaching had won her the support of some of the most influential members of the colony, was brought to trial. The charge was a serious one. She was accused of nothing less than an attempt to destroy the very foundations of the Puritan Church.

The wife of a prosperous merchant and mother of fourteen children, Anne Hutchinson had come from England to the colony a few years earlier. She had followed her minister, John Cotton. Shortly after her arrival, she began to hold weekly meetings at which she discussed Cotton's sermons with other colonists.

Cotton preached that individuals could know intuitively whether or not they were chosen as God's elect. But he held that this knowledge did not free the individual from the responsibility of leading a godly life.

Anne Hutchinson, however, went much further than Cotton. According to her, the saints, or people who had received the gift of God's grace, were not necessarily bound by the laws that bound other people. Such revolutionary ideas created a serious rift in the colony. Over seventy men and women sided with Hutchinson against the orthodox Puritan authorities. When her followers refused to fight in a war against the Pequot Indians, the very existence of the colony seemed dangerously threatened.

Anne Hutchinson was hauled before the Massachusetts General Court and charged with heresy. Although she defended herself ably, the court declared her guilty and banished her from the colony. Together with her husband and family, she fled first to Rhode Island and later moved to New York, near Long Island Sound, where she died in an Indian attack. The idea of religious freedom, however, continued to develop and grow in the American colonies.

ernment. While the Fundamental Orders resembled the Massachusetts system closely, they differed significantly in basing their authority on self-government by the people rather than on the divine rule of kings.

While neither Rhode Island nor Connecticut was democratic in the modern sense, both established representative governments of some kind. Both also adopted positions of tolerance and respect for differing religious beliefs.

Section Review

For answers, see p. A 11.

1. Identify the following: Martin Luther, Henry VIII, Separatists, Pilgrims, Mayflower Compact, William Bradford, Puritans, Roger Williams, Anne Hutchinson, Thomas Hooker, Fundamental Orders of Connecticut.

2. Explain why each of the following English subjects might have decided to try a life in the New World: (a) the second son of a wealthy family; (b) a tenant farmer; (c) a city worker.

3. (a) List two ways the Church of England under Queen Elizabeth was still like the Roman Catholic church. (b) Which English Protestants did not approve of these similarities?

4. Why did the Pilgrims decide to leave the Netherlands and establish a colony in the New World?

5. (a) What type of government did the Massachusetts Bay Company establish for the colony? (b) Who was qualified to vote?

6. In what way was the founding of Rhode Island similar to the founding of Connecticut?

3 Developing a Colonial System

England's first New World colonies were established by joint stock companies in Virginia and Massachusetts. At first, this method of colonization seemed to hold the solution to the problem of organizing and managing settlements thousands of miles from England.

A company of profit-minded investors could provide the money needed to get the colony off to a good start. Furthermore, because the crown authorized the enterprise by granting the company its charter, the government seemed assured of having some control over colonial affairs. In reality, however, things did not work this smoothly.

A New Approach to Colonization

Although the colony of Virginia thrived, the London Company failed as a profit-making venture. The company mismanaged its business, and the members fought among themselves. Furthermore, as you read, the early colonists, lacking most of the necessities of life, barely survived until tobacco proved to be a profitable crop. In 1624 James I took matters into his own hands. He revoked the company's charter and placed the colony under his personal control.

Massachusetts posed other problems for England. After a few uncertain years the colony thrived, making a profit for the Massachusetts Bay Company. But it acted with more independence than the English government felt a colony should.

Believing that their authority came directly from God, the leaders of Massachusetts ruled church and state with little regard for the king or his ministers. The crown, in turn, found it nearly impossible to impose its will on a settlement of dissenters 3,000 miles away.

With the lessons of Virginia and Massachusetts before them, the English government began to see the need for a more systematic approach to colonization. In an effort to coordinate the settlement of the colonies and to establish uniform standards for them, the crown created a new form of colonial organization, the proprietary colony.

With this method, the king granted territory to a person or small group of persons called *proprietors*. Like feudal lords, proprietors held their domains as absolute and sole owners and acknowledged the sovereignty of the king by making an annual payment of some sort. Proprietors had the right to parcel out their land to other individuals. These tenants did not own the land but held it only as long as the proprietor wished. They also paid rent and taxes to the proprietors, an important source of income.

In most cases the king did limit the authority of the proprietors however. They could institute only those laws that were in accord with the laws of England. And in making laws they usually had to have the consent of the free men of the colony or their chosen representatives.

Maryland: The First Proprietary Colony

George Calvert, Lord Baltimore, established the first proprietary colony. One of the original stockholders of the London Company, Calvert envisioned his colony as a refuge for Roman Catholics and as a money-making real estate venture.

Calvert first obtained a grant of land in Newfoundland from James I. When the cold, rough territory proved unsuited for settlement, Calvert moved south. From James's son, Charles I, he acquired the right to 10 million acres (4 million hectares) of Virginia territory around the Chesapeake Bay.

George Calvert died before the grant could be issued, but his son, Cecilius, accepted it in 1632. The Calverts named the new colony Maryland in honor of King Charles's wife, Queen Henrietta Maria.

The first 200 settlers arrived in March 1634. Their only early troubles resulted from border disputes with their Virginia neighbors, which the king brought to a quick end by deciding in Maryland's favor. Relations with neighboring Indians who supplied them with corn were generally friendly.

In this detail from a portrait of his grandfather, Lord Baltimore, young Cecil Calvert points to a map of Maryland, his family's proprietary colony in the New World.

If their colony was to be profitable, the Calverts knew they had to attract thousands of settlers. Thus, they welcomed Protestants as well as Roman Catholics. In 1649 the colonial assembly passed the Maryland Toleration Act, affirming religious freedom for all Christians.

Land Grants Under Charles II

Charles II made land grants in America primarily as rewards to English nobles who had remained loyal to the monarchy following a revolt against his father, Charles I, in 1642. The leaders of the revolt had executed Charles I in 1649 and abolished the monarchy. Charles II then spent the next 11 years in exile in France until he was restored to the throne in 1660.

The king made an early land grant to his brother James, the Duke of York, in 1664. This grant, stretching from Connecticut to the Delaware Bay, was a bold move on the part of the king because the territory had been settled by the Dutch, who called it New Netherlands. Soon after English forces appeared at the mouth of the Hudson River the inhabitants of New Netherlands, dissatisfied with Dutch rule, surrendered, and the colony was renamed New York. The Dutch retaliated by declaring war on England and harassing English shipping, but New York remained in English hands.

The Duke, who had absolute political power in the colony, appointed a governor and council to administer it rather than go to America himself. He allowed wealthy Dutch landowners to retain their huge estates and gave away equally large tracts of land to his English followers. In matters of religion, James was broad minded. A Roman Catholic himself, he allowed colonists to worship as they pleased.

The area adjoining New York, renamed New Jersey, was originally a part of the Duke of York's grant. He in turn granted the rights to this land to two friends, Sir George Carteret and Lord John Berkeley. Unfortunately, the governor of New York did not hear about the new owners until after he had assigned governmental authority over the area to a group of Puritans. The ensuing legal tangle lasted almost 50 years. The territory was divided into two colonies in 1676 and was not united as New Jersey until 1702.

The Carolinas and Georgia

Charles II made a second gift of land to a group of eight nobles including Sir William Berkeley, the governor of Virginia. In 1663 the group requested and received all the land between present-day Virginia and Florida, bounded on the east by the Atlantic Ocean and on the west by the Pacific.

Settlement of the territory, which was named Carolina after the king and his father, centered around Albemarle Sound, the mouth of the Cape Fear River, and the area that soon came to be known as Charles Towne. Though themselves Anglican, the lords proprietors, as they became known, welcomed colonists of all denominations.

Like the Calverts in Maryland, the lords proprietors of Carolina had the powers of feudal lords. They kept huge estates for themselves and parceled the rest of the land out to tenants, collecting annual rents in return. The proprietors hoped to earn an enormous profit as landlords. Their plan nearly misfired, however, when they tried to impose a strange social and governmental plan on their territory.

Their plan, known as the Fundamental Constitutions of Carolina, was drawn up by the English political philosopher John Locke. The constitution specified that Carolina's society was to be set up along rigid class lines with a hereditary nobility at the top. The proprietors themselves would have titles like Lord Palatine and Lord High Chamberlain.

The first settlers were appalled by the Fundamental Constitutions and rejected all but a few of its provisions. When word of it reached England, immigration to the colony nearly came to a standstill, threatening the proprietors' profit. Eventually a more democratic and realistic government developed.

In 1712 the proprietors divided Carolina into northern and southern parts and gave each its own government. Most settlers in North Carolina moved there from other colonies, especially New England and Virginia, while the first colonists of South Carolina came largely from England or from the plantations of the West Indies. A few were Protestant refugees from France.

Georgia was a third part of the original Carolina grant, and was finally separated from South Carolina in 1732. It was unique among the colonies in being founded neither as a money-making venture nor as a refuge for religious dissenters. A group of proprietors, led by James Oglethorpe (OH gehl thorp), wanted the colony to provide a place where people imprisoned for debt could get a new start in life. Second, they wanted to provide a barrier against the Spanish in Florida.

No more than a few debtors actually migrated to Georgia. But the colony did become a haven for poor shopkeepers and artisans from England and Scotland. Protestant refugees from Switzerland and Germany also found a home there. Roman Catholics, however, were forbidden to settle in Georgia. The proprietors feared that they would side with Catholic Spain in the event of a war.

A Haven in Penn's Woods

When Charles II was in exile, Admiral William Penn had loaned him a substantial sum of money. After Penn died, the king, chronically short of cash, paid the debt in land to Penn's son William.

As a young man, Penn had joined the Society of Friends. Members of the Society were also known as Quakers because their founder, George Fox, directed them to "tremble at the name of the Lord."

The Quakers were a thorn in the side of English authorities. They had no church hierarchy, no regular church building, and no paid clergy. Furthermore, they showed their contempt for the English class system by treating everyone as an equal, and they refused either to take oaths or to fight in wars.

With the Church of England stepping up its persecution of dissenting religious groups, Penn sought a refuge for himself and his fellow Quakers. Pennsylvania, literally "Penn's woods," seemed the ideal place. Penn eventually added more land to his proprietorship by purchasing neighboring territory that would become Delaware.

William Penn, unlike most proprietors, lived in America himself for a while and administered the colony. When he had to be away, he appointed a deputy governor to take charge.

Penn's plan of government was the most democratic in the colonies. Until 1701, it consisted of a legislature with upper and lower houses elected by the freemen of the colony. The upper house proposed laws, and the lower house accepted or rejected

Founding of the Colonies

Colony/Date Founded	Leader	Reasons Founded	Type of Government
New England Colonies			
Massachusetts Plymouth/1620 Massachusetts Bay/1630	William Bradford John Winthrop	Religious freedom Religious freedom	Corporate 1620-1691 Corporate 1630-1691 Both colonies merged 1691; royal 1691-1776
New Hampshire/1622	Ferdinando Gorges John Mason	Profit from trade and fishing	Proprietary 1622-1641; corporate (part of Mass.) 1641-1680; royal 1680-1776
Connecticut Hartford/1636 New Haven/1639	Thomas Hooker	Extend trade; religious and political freedom	Self-governing 1636-1662 Self-governing 1639-1662; royal 1662-65 Both colonies merged 1665; royal 1665-1776
Rhode Island/1636	Roger Williams	Religious freedom	Self-governing 1636-44; corporate 1644-1776
Middle Colonies			
*New York/1624	Peter Minuet	Expand trade	Colony of Dutch West India Co. 1624-1664; proprietary (Eng.) 1664-1685; royal 1685-1776
**Delaware/1638	Swedish settlers	Expand trade	Proprietary 1638-1682; part of Pa. (proprietary) 1682-1704; royal 1704-1776
New Jersey/1664	John Berkeley George Carteret	Profit for founders from land sales; religious and political freedom	Proprietary 1664-1702; royal 1702-1776
Pennsylvania/1682	William Penn	Profit for founders from land sales; religious and political freedom	Proprietary 1682-1776
Southern Colonies			
Virginia/1607	John Smith	Trade and agriculture	Corporate 1607-24; royal 1624-1776
Maryland/1632	Lord Baltimore	Profit for founders from land sales; religious and political freedom	Proprietary 1632-1691; royal 1691-1715 proprietary 1715-1776
The Carolinas/1663 North Carolina/1712 South Carolina/1712	Group of eight proprietors	Profit from trade and agriculture; religious freedom	Proprietary 1663-1712; self-governing until 1719; king buys back North 1719; king buys back South 1729; both royal 1730-1776
Georgia/1732	James Oglethorpe	Profit; haven for debtors; buffer against Spanish Florida	Proprietary 1732-1752; royal 1752-1776

*New York was settled by the Dutch in 1624 and named New Netherlands. It surrendered to the English in 1664.

**Delaware was settled by the Swedes in 1638 and named New Sweden. It was captured and incorporated into New Netherlands by the Dutch in 1655. It was then captured by the English in 1664.

them. Every man who owned a small amount of land or paid taxes was entitled to vote, so a large number of colonists participated in choosing the government.

The Movement Toward Royal Colonies

As the colonies grew and prospered, the English crown became increasingly interested in their development. Gradually the king assumed control, creating royal colonies. By 1730 only Pennsylvania and Maryland remained as proprietary colonies.

Colonists usually found royal control preferable to government by the proprietors. For one thing, royal colonies seemed to receive better protection from the English army and navy. Secondly, colonial representatives often had more political power in a royal colony than in a proprietary one.

In a royal colony the king appointed the colony's governor and council, and the eligible voters elected an assembly. The governor controlled trade, appointed judges and other officials, and served as the colony's chief executive.

The council, usually composed of leading colonists, advised the governor and approved official appointments. Furthermore, the governor had to consult the council before he called the assembly into session, issued paper money, or declared martial law. The council functioned as the highest court and as the upper house of the assembly.

The colonial assembly considered itself the guardian of colonial interests. Legislation could not become law until the assembly consented to it. This continued the tradition of representative government that was common to all colonies. The original charters for Massachusetts and Virginia had guaranteed settlers a voice in the colony's government, a tradition that persisted when men and women from Massachusetts founded Rhode Island and Connecticut. Furthermore, the grants to all proprietors, except for the Duke of York, had required them to make laws with the consent of the colonists.

Gradually, the people's right to consent to laws through their representatives grew into the right to initiate, or propose, laws, a trend that continued in royal colonies.

Colonial assemblies also increased their influence in the government because they had to approve the salaries of other officials,

Major Events

1607	English settlers arrive at Jamestown
1619	House of Burgesses established in Virginia
1620	Pilgrims arrive in North America
1630	Puritans establish Massachusetts Bay
1632	Maryland becomes first proprietary colony
1649	Maryland Toleration Act affirms religious freedom for all Christians in colony
1660	Charles II restored to throne in England
1685	James II establishes Dominion of New England
1688	Glorious Revolution in England

including the governor. They considered this an especially important power, as you will see in Chapter 6.

Persistence of the Representative Tradition

The strength of the representative tradition in the English colonies is most evident in light of the failure of three attempts to bypass it. The first of these was in New York.

Under the Dutch, a director-general had held complete authority in the colony. He ruled without any representative assembly. When the Duke of York assumed control of the colony, he tried to continue the Dutch system. The settlers, however, resisted vigorously and finally forced him to grant them an assembly.

The Fundamental Constitutions of the Carolinas also violated the representative tradition and failed as a result. A third attempt in the 1680s, like the first, involved the Duke of York.

When Charles II died in 1685, his brother, the Duke of York, succeeded to the throne as James II. The new king promptly revoked Massachusetts's original charter. Next, he tightened royal control and discarded the representative assemblies in all colonies north of New Jersey. Then he renamed the area the Dominion of New England.

The American colonists greatly resented the action and threatened rebellion, but the English beat them to it. In 1688, the English deposed James II in a revolt called the Glorious Revolution. The New England colonies promptly reinstated the representative assemblies, showing England and the world that, in America at least, representative government would endure.

For answers, see p. A 11.

Section Review

1. Identify the following: George Calvert, Cecilius Calvert, Maryland Toleration Act, Charles II, New Netherlands, William Berkeley, James Oglethorpe, William Penn, Society of Friends.

2. (a) What was a proprietary colony? (b) What role did a proprietor play? (c) What did the tenants have to do in return for use of the land?

3. (a) Why did George Calvert want to establish a colony? (b) Who settled in Maryland?

4. (a) What was Charles II's motive for granting land in America? (b) Who received the first grant?

5. What were the Fundamental Constitutions of Carolina?

6. (a) What two goals did Oglethorpe have for founding Georgia? (b) How was this unique among the English colonies?

7. (a) Why did William Penn found Pennsylvania? (b) What kind of government did it have? (c) Who was entitled to vote?

8. (a) What is a royal colony? (b) Give two reasons why colonists often preferred royal colonies to proprietary colonies.

9. (a) What three attempts were made to undermine representative government in the colonies? (b) Were they successful? Explain.

★ ★

IN PERSPECTIVE   English settlement in North America began in earnest in the 1600s. The colony at Jamestown was the first. It was founded by a group of private investors who had formed a joint stock company. Joint stock companies also sponsored the founding of Plymouth and Massachusetts Bay. But the first settlers to New England differed from the early Virginians because most came in search of freedom from religious persecution. Religious freedom was also the main motive of the founders of Connecticut and Rhode Island, although they were fleeing persecution in Massachusetts, not Europe.

Most of the remaining colonies began as proprietary colonies. Proprietors wanted to use their land grants in the New World to make a profit, but most had other reasons as well. These included religious freedom for Catholics in Maryland and for Quakers in Pennsylvania. The proprietors of the Carolinas tried but failed to establish a rigid social and political system in their colony. Georgia was originally founded as a refuge for debtors and a buffer against the Spanish in Florida.

In spite of the variety of ways the colonies were founded and settled, they all eventually developed a representative form of government. The belief in representative government had deep roots in English political traditions, and it was to be the basis for the movement toward independence, as you will see in later chapters.

For answers, see p. A 12.

Chapter Review

1. (a) How did the goals and actions of the London Company itself create problems for the colony at Jamestown? (b) How did each of the following contribute to the survival of the colony: John Smith, local Native Americans, John Rolfe, the House of Burgesses?

2. (a) In what ways was the environment of Massachusetts better suited for settlement than Jamestown? (b) How did the people who first settled in New England differ from those who first settled in Jamestown?

3. (a) Why did the Pilgrims and Puritans immigrate to the New World? (b) How did their attitudes toward the Church of England differ?

4. (a) What type of society did the Puritans want to create in America? (b) Why did Roger Williams, Anne Hutchinson, and Thomas Hooker leave Massachusetts?

5. (a) How did developments in Virginia and Massachusetts convince the English crown to try a new way of establishing colonies? (b) What method did they turn to? (c) What advantages did it have?

6. Most proprietors hoped to make a profit from their land in America. What other motives did the proprietors have?

7. Why did the English crown eventually transform most colonies to royal colonies?

8. (a) Describe the role of each of the following in the government of a royal colony: the king, the governor, the council, the assembly. (b) How did the assemblies increase their political influence?

For answers, see p. A 13.

For Further Thought

1. Review what you learned in Chapter 2 about the role of the Spanish government in the settlement of America. (a) What was the role of the English government in the settlement of Jamestown, Plymouth, and Massachusetts Bay? (b) Which government played the larger role? (c) How might you explain the difference? (d) How did the role of the English government change during the 1600s?

2. (a) How did the Virginia House of Burgesses and the Massachusetts General Court reflect English political traditions? (b) How were the traditions continued in other colonies?

3. (a) How did the proprietary government of New York differ from the governments of other proprietary colonies? (b) Why do you think this was the case? (c) What was James's attitude toward representative government? What evidence can you cite to support your answer?

4. (a) Which colony had the most democratic government? (b) What factors might explain that?

For answers, see p. A 13.

Developing Basic Skills

1. *Reading a Chart* A chart can summarize a large amount of information in a small space. This often makes it easier to compare data and to trace developments. Answer the following questions about the chart on page 62: (a) Which colonies were originally founded by people from nations other than England? (b) How many colonies were founded before 1700? (c) Which colonies were founded as proprietary colonies? (d) What was the most common reason for founding a colony? What was the second most common reason?

2. *Placing Events in Time* A time line allows you to see the relationship between events as they happened over time. Make a time line of the founding of the American colonies. To construct a time line, draw a long vertical line on a blank sheet of paper. Make one end 1600 and the other 1740. Divide the line into seven equal parts, each representing 20 years. Using the information from your text and the chart on page 62, write in the name of each colony by the date it was founded. Then answer the following questions: (a) In which 20-year period were the most colonies founded? (b) Are there any 20-year periods when no colonies were founded? (c) What was the last colony founded? Why do you think it was founded so long after the other colonies?

See page 773 for suggested readings.

4

Life in Colonial America

(1650–1750)

Pat Lyon at the Forge, *by J. Neagle.*

Chapter Outline

1 *The New England Colonies*

2 *The Middle Colonies*

3 *The Southern Colonies*

4 *Colonial Culture*

As colonists put down roots in the New World, they developed ways of life that differed from those in Europe and in other parts of the colonies. Between 1650 and 1750 three distinct styles of life emerged in the New England Colonies of Massachusetts, Connecticut, Rhode Island, and New Hampshire; the Middle Colonies of New York, Pennsylvania, New Jersey, and Delaware; and the Southern Colonies of Maryland, Virginia, North Carolina, South Carolina, and Georgia.

Colonists in each area faced different challenges as a result of varied climates and topographies. As you will read in this chapter, their responses to these challenges affected the types of society and economy that evolved in each region.

In spite of the regional differences, however, certain American traditions were growing. These included a belief in representative government, as you read in the last chapter, the growth of religious tolerance, and a concern for education. By the 1750s a distinctive new American culture was beginning to emerge.

1 The New England Colonies

The weather was harsh in New England. Winters were long and cold, with howling winds, violent storms, and heavy snowfalls. The topsoil was thin, and rocks dropped by ice age glaciers studded the landscape. Inland, dense forests had to be painstakingly cleared before the land could be farmed, while along the coast lay long stretches of barren sand dunes and salt marshes.

One settler wrote to relatives back in England that Massachusetts was "builded upon rocks, sand, and salt marshes." His fellow colonists so resented his bitter remark that they took him to court for slandering a place they believed was next to the promised land.

Rural Life and the New England Town

Despite the generally poor soil of the region, many New Englanders earned a living as farmers. Most farmed at a *subsistence* level, producing just enough to feed their families but little more. Some worked the land with the help of slaves, but few farms were large enough to make slave labor profitable.

Running a farm in New England depended largely on cooperative effort. Each member of the family, including the children, had assigned duties, and survival depended on their regular performance. Men were largely responsible for cultivating crops and raising animals, and the women of the household made clothes, utensils, candles, and other necessities, rendering the New England farm largely *self-sufficient*. In other words, a farm family had the resources to get along without help. In spite of this self-sufficiency, families did not live in isolation. Farmers settled in clusters around a town.

Because religion was so important to New England settlers, many of these early towns were founded by the congregations of single churches. The elders of a congregation requested a tract of land from the colonial legislature. If the request was approved, the tract was surveyed and divided into lots. Each family in the community received land on which to build a house, to pasture animals, and to grow crops. In addition, families had the right to cut wood in the communal forest land.

At the center of the settlement stood the meeting house, a plain building used for *town meetings* as well as worship. During a settlement's early years, the elders who planned the town served as its leaders and supervised its expansion. At open town meetings the residents of the town discussed matters of importance such as hiring a new schoolteacher, building or repairing streets, or regulating livestock. They also elected local representatives to the colonial assembly.

A Diverse Economy

While many farm families in New England produced most of their necessities, a large number of residents were less self-sufficient. City dwellers, in particular, depended on trade with other colonies or with England for food, clothing, and other supplies. To pay for such purchases, colonists needed to find a product that could be traded at a profit.

At first furs seemed a likely answer. The forests abounded with raccoon, beaver, and otter, whose pelts were in great demand. However, New England trappers proved to be too skilled for their own good and soon depleted the local fur supply.

The New England forest also provided timber that colonists could ship to England or to other colonies. Gradually the timber industry developed into a major source of income for the region.

In addition to exporting timber, New Englanders used it to build ships. Shipbuilding grew rapidly as fishing became the area's most important commercial activity. Over 5,000 fishermen worked the coastal waters, and New England ports boasted of more than 900 oceangoing vessels. The city of Boston alone had 12 shipyards.

Yet fishing was not the only enterprise that employed New England's ships. The burgeoning shipping industry rapidly took the lead in trade between the colonies, England, and the West Indies.

Shipping could be very profitable, but it was a risky business. Communication was slow, so by the time a cargo arrived at its destination, the product might no longer be needed. The success of New England merchants in this competitive business earned them a reputation as shrewd "Yankee traders."

Women as well as men played an important economic role in New England's towns and cities. They worked as shopkeepers, printers, tavern and hotel keepers, merchants, tinkers, midwives, and shipbuilders. Colonial women often learned new occupations from a male relative, since most colonial businesses operated out of the home. Frequently women would take over the family business when a male relative died.

■ *Between 1650 and 1750 North American colonies developed in three regions: the New England Colonies, the Middle Colonies, and the Southern Colonies. Life in each area was distinctive. According to this map, which colonies made up each section?* For answers, see p. A 13.

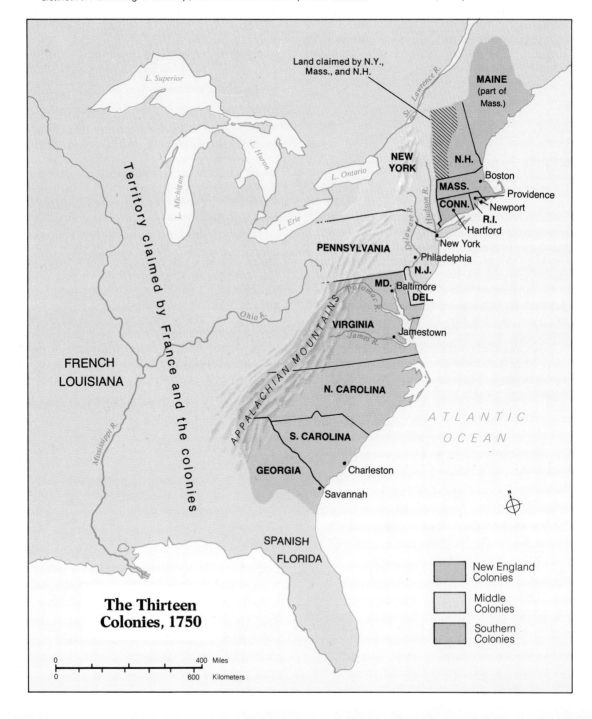

The Thirteen Colonies, 1750

Social Classes in New England Society

A rigid class system existed in England, as in the rest of Europe. The royal family and the aristocracy occupied the top, followed by landowners and merchants. Beneath them were shopkeepers, artisans, and small landowners. Lowest on the social scale stood city workers, tenant farmers, and agricultural laborers. These class lines were firm, and movement from one class to another was virtually impossible.

New England society reflected the orderliness of the English class system but not its rigid inflexibility. In colonial New England a person could improve his or her status. Still, most people continued to observe sharp distinctions between classes.

In 1651, for example, the Massachusetts General Court passed a law that officially divided the colony's inhabitants into three classes: "the better class," "those above the ordinary degree," and "those of mean condition." Members of each class were expected to keep to their places and to behave as befitted their station.

As the New England colonies grew, a more democratic spirit began to infiltrate the social system. Members of the lower and middle classes, especially the skilled artisans, grew increasingly prosperous. And with their prosperity came a desire to imitate the upper classes.

Since a person's clothing indicated his or her place in society, dressing like the upper classes was the most popular and widespread form of imitation. Alarmed by such behavior on the part of the lower classes, the Massachusetts General Court expressed its

> utter detestation ... that men and women of mean condition should take upon them the garb of gentlemen, by wearing gold or silver lace, or buttons ... or to walk in great boots, or women of the same rank to wear silk or tiffany hoods or scarves which, though allowable to persons of greater estates ... yet we cannot but judge it intolerable in persons of such like condition.

To stamp out such "intolerable" behavior the court promptly passed a law specifying how much property a family had to own in order to wear "any gold or silver lace, or gold and silver buttons, or any bone lace above two shillings per yard, or silk hoods, or scarfs." The penalty for violating the law was ingenious. A person not only had to pay a fine, but his or her property would be taxed at the rate for the social level being imitated.

Despite such attitudes, social mobility soon became the norm rather than the exception in New England. Everyone except slaves could aspire to and often attain a place in society higher than the one he or she had been born into.

For answers, see p. A 13.

Section Review

1. Define the following terms: subsistence farming, self-sufficient, town meeting.
2. What environmental conditions made New England a difficult area in which to settle?
3. How were New England farms self-sufficient?
4. How did local congregations establish towns in New England?
5. What three industries played a leading role in the New England economy?
6. (a) Was New England society more or less rigid than society in Europe? (b) How did economic prosperity make the social system more democratic?

2 The Middle Colonies

The largest wave of immigration to New England took place in the 1600s, with most new settlers arriving from England. However, the Middle Colonies did not really begin to grow until the 1700s. People who migrated to this part of North America came not only from England but also from Ireland, Scotland, and the nations of continental Europe.

A Diverse Population

The largest number of non-English settlers came from northern Ireland and Germany. The Scotch-Irish, as those from northern Ireland were known, were the most numerous of the new wave of immigrants. Of Scottish origin, their families had settled in the north of Ireland in the sixteenth century.

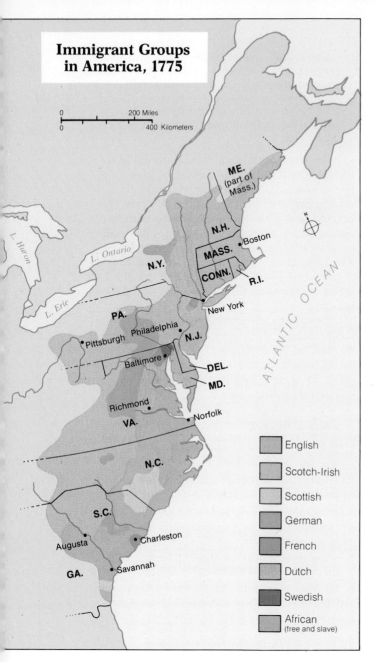

Immigrant Groups in America, 1775

0 _____ 200 Miles
0 _____ 400 Kilometers

L. Huron
L. Ontario
L. Erie

ME. (part of Mass.)
N.H.
MASS. • Boston
N.Y.
CONN.
R.I.
• New York
PA.
• Pittsburgh   Philadelphia •
N.J.
Baltimore •
DEL.
MD.
Richmond •
VA.   • Norfolk
N.C.
S.C.
• Augusta   • Charleston
GA.   • Savannah

ATLANTIC OCEAN

Legend:
- English
- Scotch-Irish
- Scottish
- German
- French
- Dutch
- Swedish
- African (free and slave)

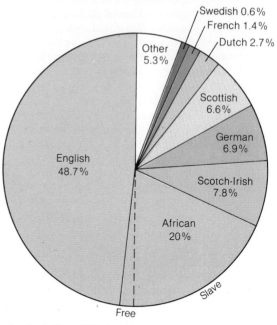

Ethnic Division of Colonial Population, 1775*

- Swedish 0.6%
- French 1.4%
- Dutch 2.7%
- Other 5.3%
- Scottish 6.6%
- English 48.7%
- German 6.9%
- Scotch-Irish 7.8%
- African 20%
- Slave
- Free

* estimated from 1790 census

■ By the mid-1770s, only about half the population of the 13 colonies was of English background. New immigrants brought their own cultures, which added to the richness and diversity of colonial America. According to the map, where did each group mainly settle? For answers, see p. A 14.

During the eighteenth century, about 250,000 Scotch-Irish migrated to the Middle Colonies, especially to Pennsylvania. They left northern Ireland because the policies of the English government and the Anglican church had destroyed their economic well-being and virtually outlawed their Presbyterian religion. Their hatred of England had a profound influence on the future of the colonies.

The second largest group of settlers, the Germans, had been pushed out of their homeland by a series of brutal religious wars between Protestants and Catholics. Invading armies had devastated their homeland, the Rhineland of southwestern Germany. Furthermore, successive crop failures had brought dire poverty and famine to the Rhineland area.

Pennsylvania, with its rich lands, low rents, and widespread toleration, seemed a haven to these immigrants. Eventually, the Rhineland Germans came to be known as Pennsylvania Dutch, from a misuse of the word *Deutsch* (doich), meaning German. These two new groups, when combined with the Swedish colonists in Delaware and the Dutch in New York, made the population of the Middle Colonies the most diverse of English-ruled America.

An Agricultural Economy

The Middle Colonies contained some of the richest farmland on the Atlantic coast of North America. Thus, agriculture became the foundation of the region's economic life. As in other colonies, farmers either adapted European plants and animals to the American environment or used European farming methods to cultivate native American crops.

Although the soil was fertile and capable of yielding abundant harvests, farming was back-breaking work. Farmers used crude wooden plows drawn by teams of oxen to till the soil or did it by hand with a hoe. Harvesting was a grueling task performed by hand with sickle or scythe.

Pennsylvania farms were the pride of the Middle Colonies. On the rich farmlands of the Delaware River Valley, German farmers turned agriculture into a thriving commercial enterprise. These farms produced such large surpluses of wheat, rye, and corn that they were able to feed not only their own people but many people in New England and the Southern Colonies as well. They even shipped some of their products to Europe.

New York's soil was as rich as that of Pennsylvania, but its farms produced considerably less because of the colony's system of landholding. The original Dutch settlers of the area had established an agricultural system based on feudal-style manors.

Some of these manors consisted of hundreds of thousands of acres. Each was owned by one man, called a *patroon*. The patroon divided the lands among tenant farmers who worked their farms but could never own them outright. Furthermore, each year they had to pay the patroon rent and taxes as well as spend time farming his lands.

Few European settlers were willing to put up with such oppressive conditions when they could obtain their own farms in other colonies. Thus, New York's rate of immigration and, consequently, its agricultural productivity, lagged behind that of the other colonies.

Blacks in the North

Although slavery existed legally in the Middle Colonies and in New England, there were far fewer slaves in those colonies than in the South. Farms were smaller and required much less labor. Thus, most northern slaves worked as household servants, and a

few worked at skilled and unskilled trades in the towns.

One observer even complained that there was much too much social equality between slaves and their masters in the North. A French traveler remarked that slaves in Pennsylvania "were regarded as being part of the family. They are assiduously cared for when they are sick. They are well fed and clothed."

Free blacks lived primarily in the Middle Colonies and New England; however, their freedom was not complete. Most of the colonies passed laws restricting their activities. In some places, laws limited the number of free black residents. In others, free blacks were allowed to work only at certain occupations. Many free blacks joined the movement to the frontier, where they found more equality and freedom than elsewhere in colonial America.

The Backcountry Frontier

The population of the Middle Colonies grew rapidly and soon expanded westward beyond the established areas of settlement into the backcountry. Pioneers moved beyond the *fall line*, the area in which inland rivers begin dropping toward sea level, and carved farms out of the wilderness.

Expansion continued westward through Pennsylvania to the Appalachian Mountains. The settlers then turned south, following a wide Indian trail that became known as the Great Wagon Road.

In the backcountry nearly all farming was on a subsistence level. Farmers planted crops in small patches between the stumps of newly felled trees rather than on broad, well-plowed fields. When the fertility of one patch was exhausted, the farmers simply cleared another. They supplemented the meager harvests with wild game and plants from surrounding forests.

Separated from the coastal settlements, the people of the backcountry frontier developed a unique way of life. The settlers could often live as they saw fit. They paid no taxes, were subject to few laws, and seldom mixed with others.

Under such conditions, family members depended heavily on one another for basic survival. Although the men generally did

■ *Before 1700 settlements clustered along the Atlantic coastline and spread inland along navigable rivers or bays. By 1770 the English colonies had established outposts in the Appalachians and beyond.*

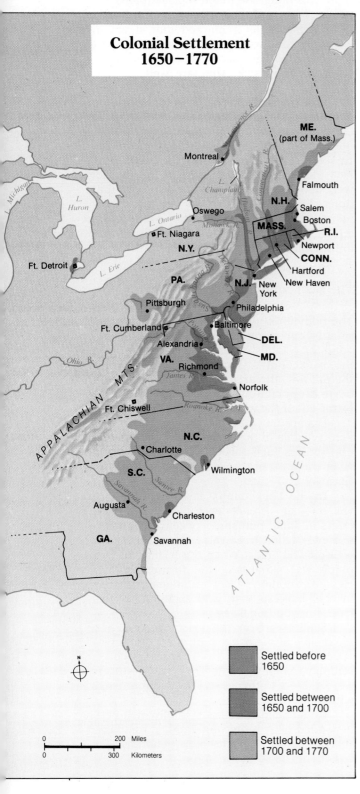

Colonial Settlement 1650–1770

Settled before 1650

Settled between 1650 and 1700

Settled between 1700 and 1770

0   200   Miles
0   300   Kilometers

most of the hunting, trapping, and farming, the women were proficient in frontier skills, too. Philip Ludwell, one of the first colonists to leave a full record of rural life, had great admiration for the frontier woman in 1710.

> She is a very civil woman and shews nothing of ruggedness or Immodesty in her carriage, yett she will carry a gunn in the woods and kill deer, turkeys &c., shoot down wild cattle, catch and tye hoggs, knock down beeves [domestic cattle] with an ax, and perform the most manfull Exercises as well as most men in those parts.

Politically, the backcountry settlers were among the most independent in the colonies. They deeply resented the colonial governments, which seemed to be dominated by easterners who ignored their interests. Frustrated by their lack of political influence, these pioneers occasionally resorted to violent revolt.

In 1763, for example, a band of Pennsylvania frontiersmen known as the Paxton boys took matters into their own hands after the colonial government refused to provide protection against Indians who were at war with the settlers. But the Paxton boys ended up destroying a peaceful Indian village instead of fighting the Indians who were actually at war. The woodsmen then stormed off to Philadelphia demanding further protection. They intended to attack the city, but a delegation of city leaders talked them out of it.

In time, conditions in the backcountry improved. Social conditions came more and more to resemble those in the coastal regions. As the pioneers became more prosperous, neat farmhouses replaced rough log cabins. Yet the pioneers did not give up their independence. They continued their tradition of self-sufficiency and repeatedly demonstrated their willingness to take matters into their own hands if necessary.

For answers, see p. A 14.

Section Review

1. Identify the following: Scotch-Irish, Pennsylvania Dutch, Paxton boys.
2. Define the following terms: patroon, fall line.
3. (a) What were the two largest groups of non-English settlers in the Middle Colonies? (b) Why did each choose to come to America?

4. (a) Why was farming the basis of economic life in the Middle Colonies? (b) Which colony was the most productive? (c) Which colony was the least productive? Why?

5. (a) In what areas did most free blacks live? (b) Did they have the same freedom as whites? Explain.

6. (a) What was the backcountry? (b) How did settlers make a living there?

7. List three ways the isolation of the backcountry made life there different from life in the coastal region.

3 The Southern Colonies

Perhaps more than any other area, the South was a region of sharp contrasts. Geographically, it had three distinct areas: the mountainous highlands that formed the western boundary; the rolling hills of the *piedmont region;* and the *tidewater region,* a flat coastal plain with land so low in places that the rivers crossing it flowed backwards with the incoming tides.

The people and ways of life in the South contrasted almost as sharply as its geographical features. While mostly English settlers inhabited the coastal plain, many Germans and Scotch-Irish, a few English, and some French Protestants settled the interior.

Small Farmers of the Southern Backcountry

In many ways the southern backcountry was an extension of the backcountry of the Middle Colonies, and the farmers who settled there had similar problems. In spite of the rich soil, dense forest that had to be cleared by hand made farming a demanding task.

As a result, the farms tended to be small, and families usually lived at a subsistence level. Farmers produced what they needed to live on, with just enough left to trade at the local market for tools and other necessities.

Many farmers, chronically in debt, bitterly resented the wealthy landowners along the coast. As it did in the Middle Colonies, such resentment occasionally erupted into violence. For example, in 1771 a Carolina group calling themselves the Regulators revolted against taxes and their general lack of representation in the colonial legislature. The revolt was put down, but bitterness only increased.

Growth of the Plantation System

The wealthy, aristocratic landowners, who were the objects of backcountry anger, controlled the colonial governments of the South. These powerful magnates, or *planters,* owned the huge plantations that became the region's distinctive type of farm.

The roots of the plantation system went all the way back to the Virginia tobacco boom of the early 1600s. When settlers discovered that tobacco cultivation was most profitable if done on a large scale, they planted huge tracts of land. To tend the crop, planters employed work crews of up to thirty people each.

As the market for tobacco grew, the plantations multiplied. Eventually, planters experimented with other *cash crops,* those grown to be sold at a profit. Along the coasts of Georgia and South Carolina, for example, rice was cultivated.

In the 1740s a woman named Eliza Lucas Pinckney successfully grew *indigo,* a West Indian plant used to make dye. Planters soon began to cultivate this valuable crop. Southerners also started growing some cotton in the eighteenth century. These cash crops produced the largest profit when grown on large plantations.

Life on the Plantation

Plantations usually developed into self-sufficient communities as a result of their large size. Along with one or more cash crops, indentured servants or slaves grew food for all residents of the plantation. Skilled artisans also produced many of the tools and other necessities for the plantation.

New England Puritans may have disapproved of dancing, but plantation families in Virginia did not. As this painting of a family group in Virginia shows, dancing was considered an important social grace for young ladies and gentlemen.

Life for the planter family centered around the great house, or mansion. Besides gracious and elegant quarters for the family, the mansion usually contained numerous guest rooms, a wine cellar, a large dining room, a variety of parlors, and often a library and music room. Such rooms played an important part in the plantation's social life of elaborate parties and extended formal visits from neighbors and relatives.

Other buildings found on the plantation contributed to its self-sufficiency. These might include a coach house, stables, a dairy, a bakehouse, and a schoolhouse, which often provided quarters for a teacher. A separate workhouse might contain a blacksmith's shop, brickworks, or smokehouses.

The landowner presided over the many plantation activities. He decided what lands would be planted each season and what crops would be grown. He arranged for the shipment and sale of harvested crops, and he purchased items not manufactured on the plantation. Together with his wife, the planter supervised the servants, clerks, overseers, skilled artisans, and slaves.

Although women's legal rights to land ownership were limited, the planter's wife, who was called the plantation mistress, often played a key role on the estate. She organized household activities and supervised the people who worked in the house.

Some women also assumed more direct control of the operations of the plantation.

74

Eliza Lucas Pinckney, for example, managed both her father's and her husband's plantations in South Carolina when the men were away on business.

Indentured Servants

Because cash crops such as tobacco, rice, indigo, and cotton had to be cultivated on a large scale to be profitable, a plantation's prosperity depended on a correspondingly large supply of labor. At first, such labor was supplied by men, women, and children who came to the colonies as *indentured servants.** Indentured servants agreed to work for a specified period of time in return for the cost of their passage to America. The period of service varied from place to place, ranging from four to seven years. When the term of service was completed, the workers received "freedom dues": clothing, tools, a rifle, and occasionally a parcel of land.

Most of the servants came to the colonies willingly, even eagerly. However, some did not. Throughout the colonial period, the English government sent shiploads of convicts and prisoners of war to the colonies. Orphans, vagrants, poor people, and those considered a nuisance to society were also shipped to America as servants. In some cases, the English government used this method to exile political troublemakers.

Although the life of the indentured servant was hard, the system had its advantages. It often gave men and women the chance to learn a trade or get an education. Indentured servitude also provided an opportunity, not otherwise available, for a poor person to eventually acquire land and become independent.

In the South, however, the planters had claimed most of the good land along the coast. Thus, when an indentured servant became free, the only available land lay in the backcountry. Like other backcountry farmers, the former indentured servants resented the wealth and political power of the planters.

In 1676, the friction between backcountry farmers and coastal planters ex-

ploded in open warfare. A group of farmers from Virginia felt that the colonial government controlled by planters had not adequately protected them from local Indians, so they marched on the capital. Led by Nathaniel Bacon, a wealthy landowner who sympathized with their cause, the rebels burned the capital at Jamestown and attempted to redistribute large tracts of land. In the middle of the revolt, Bacon died. The uprising, known as Bacon's Rebellion, fell apart, and the governor hanged its leaders, but the friction between planter and farmer remained.

The Growth of Slavery

As plantations expanded, planters found it increasingly difficult to meet their labor needs with indentured servants. The supply of servants rarely met the planters' demand for them. Furthermore, every few years a new group of workers had to be taught the skills needed to run the estate efficiently. And, last but not least, the presence of embittered former servants in the backcountry constantly posed the threat of another Bacon's Rebellion.

Under these conditions, the demand for slave labor grew. As you read in Chapter 3, the first Africans arrived in Jamestown in 1619. Some were probably bought by the local planters as indentured servants, not as slaves. And like white servants, they were freed when their term of servitude had ended.

Gradually, however, temporary servitude became permanent bondage for blacks. There were several reasons for this change. First, slaves provided a constant supply of workers. Moreover, the owner had complete control over this labor force. Because of their color, black slaves found it nearly impossible to run away and blend into the free population.

Slaves did not pose the same social problems as indentured servants because they could never rise out of their bondage and compete with their former masters for wealth and power. The cost of buying a slave was higher than that of purchasing a servant's contract. In the long run, however, slaves came to be cheaper than servants. Servants worked for a limited term, but a slave's bondage to the master was lifelong.

---

*The term "indentured" came to be used because the papers that recorded the agreement were cut or torn with an indentured, or indented, edge so that the two copies, one going to the servant and one to the master, would correspond.

The English government responded quickly to the colonial planters' demand for more slaves. In 1672 it established the Royal African Company to carry on the slave trade. Soon, slave trading developed into a profitable colonial business. Colonists continued to import black Africans as slaves throughout the seventeenth and eighteenth centuries.

The Life of a Slave

The life of bondage for an African slave began on the notorious "middle passage" from Africa to America. On the slave ships, men, women, and children were crammed below deck in spaces sometimes less than five feet high. One observer said they were packed together "like books upon a shelf . . . so close that the shelf would not easily contain one more."

For most of the trip they were chained to each other, making it difficult for one to turn or move without hurting another. In rough seas, the confinement was torturing. With air holes closed off, the heat below deck became so intense as to be intolerable. At such times, large numbers of the slaves

■ Between what years was the growth of slavery most dramatic? For answer, see p. A 14.

Slave Population in the Colonies 1650–1770

YEAR	North	South	Total
1650	880	720	1,600
1660	1,162	1,758	2,920
1670	1,125	3,410	4,535
1680	1,895	5,076	6,971
1690	3,340	13,389	16,729
1700	5,206	22,611	27,817
1710	8,303	36,563	44,866
1720	14,091	54,748	68,839
1730	17,323	73,698	91,021
1740	23,958	126,066	150,024
1750	30,222	206,198	236,420
1760	40,033	285,773	325,806
1770	48,460	411,362	459,822

Source: *Historical Statistics of the United States*

would die. Others would contract debilitating, if not fatal, diseases.

Most new slaves worked in the fields, where they performed the tiring, repetitious tasks involved in cultivating tobacco, rice, indigo, and cotton. Some were trained as skilled artisans, becoming carpenters, blacksmiths, sailors, barrelmakers, and millers. A few slaves worked in the great house as cooks, maids, butlers, and nursemaids.

Few slave owners were purposefully brutal to their slaves. But even with the most humane treatment, life as a slave was oppressive and dehumanizing. This was especially true for Africans, who found themselves taken out of their familiar surroundings, deprived of their freedom, subjected to a horrifying trip, and thrust into a totally foreign environment.

All slaves, whether originally from Africa or born in the colonies, had no legal rights, since to most colonists they were merely property—no different from a horse or a plow. An owner had immense power over the lives of his slaves. He could break up a family, selling the members to other planters, or he could force slaves to perform life-endangering work.

As the number of slaves in the South grew, colonial assemblies passed laws to regulate relations between slaves and their owners. Eventually each colony had its own *slave code*. Regulations differed from place to place, but their purpose and effect were the same: to control slaves and prevent uprisings.

Slave codes typically prohibited slaves from leaving a plantation without written permission. A slave accused of a crime could be arrested, tried, and condemned on the testimony of only one witness. While slaves could testify against each other, they could not bear witness against whites. A slave who killed his or her owner—even if the owner had a reputation for exceptional brutality—was hanged, beheaded, or drawn and quartered. But the killing of a slave by a white person was not always a punishable offense.

Resistance to Slavery

The slave codes limited open resistance to slavery by slaves themselves. Running away was seldom successful, since there was nowhere to run, and organized rebellion was rare.

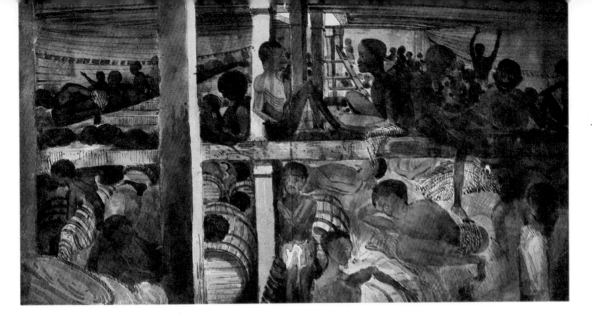

Millions of Africans were shipped unwillingly to the Americas in slave ships, shown here in two views. The diagram above shows the "loading plan" for jamming as many chained humans into the least space possible. The painting at top, by a British naval officer, is the only surviving sketch from life of the inhuman conditions aboard slave ships.

Some slaves, however, outwardly accepted their status while looking for ways to undermine the system. This might include purposefully working slowly to spite the planter or secretly damaging tools. For some slaves, trying to keep elements of their African cultures, such as names, songs, and religious traditions, and passing them on to their children made life more bearable.

While the vast majority of white colonists accepted slavery, a few protested. Quakers were well known for their opposition to slavery, but others also objected. Samuel Sewall, a New England merchant, commented on the "horrible ... Uncleanness, Mortality, if not Murder, that the Ships are guilty of that bring great crowds of these miserable Men and women."

As a result of protests, some people freed their slaves, and the law provided that their free status be passed on to their descendants. On the whole, however, the infrequent antislavery protests had little effect.

For answers, see p. A 14.

Section Review

1. Identify the following: Regulators, Eliza Lucas Pinckney, Nathaniel Bacon, Royal African Company, "middle passage."

2. Define the following terms: piedmont region, tidewater region, planter, cash crop, indigo, indentured servant, slave codes.

3. What problems were faced by farmers in the southern backcountry?

4. What was the advantage of growing crops such as indigo and rice on a large plantation rather than on a small farm?

5. What did indentured servants hope to gain by coming to America?

6. List three conditions that created a growing demand for slave labor.

7. (a) How did slave codes limit the slaves' open resistance to slavery? (b) How did some slaves try to undermine the system?

4 Colonial Culture

With the exception of African slaves, the colonists who first settled on the Atlantic coast of North America were European. They came to America with European ideas, customs, beliefs, and values. During their first grueling and often frightening years in America, they clung firmly to their European ways. To make themselves feel at home in their New World, nearly all the colonists tried to recreate the life they had known in the Old World.

Though the colonists were Europeans, the land in which they settled was not Europe. It was a completely new environment, offering different challenges and opportunities. Gradually, the settlers began to adapt their European ways to their new situation.

By the middle of the eighteenth century, the colonists were developing a distinctively American culture.

Religious Tolerance

The religious denominations of the colonies originated in Europe, but the resemblance ended there. Each European nation had an official, state-supported church to which responsible citizens were expected to belong. Other churches, if not officially outlawed, were nonetheless considered undesirable, and their members often suffered discrimination. Thus toleration of religious diversity in Europe was the exception, not the rule.

Benjamin Franklin: A Pioneer in Medicine

Medicine in colonial America was different from medicine today. Few physicians had any formal training. Some served an apprenticeship under an established doctor, but it was quite common for a person simply to declare entrance into the practice of "physick."

Benjamin Franklin's many and varied pursuits included a lifelong interest in medicine and health. Although most physicians in colonial times based their treatments on theology or philosophy, Franklin insisted on observing actual results, thus establishing a more scientific approach to medicine. And he did not mind admitting when experiments proved one of his theories unsound. For example, he tried applying electricity to stiff or paralyzed joints but stopped such treatments when he found little or no improvement.

One of Benjamin Franklin's contributions to good health would be called preventive medicine today. When he was only sixteen years old, he convinced his fellow printing apprentices that they should not drink beer with breakfast.

In an age when the idea of personal cleanliness did not even occur to most people, Franklin urged regular bathing by immersing the entire body, nude, in a tub of water. The idea shocked many. He designed and constructed his own copper bathtub, including a special provision for resting a book so that he could read while bathing.

In *Poor Richard's Almanac* he counseled moderation: "He that drinks fast pays slow," and "Early to bed and early to rise makes a man healthy, wealthy, and wise." He considered exercise, especially swimming, important to maintaining vigorous health. Franklin also championed inoculation against smallpox, especially after his son died from the disease.

Franklin maintained his health practices throughout his long life. But when he fell ill at age 84, he recognized the seriousness of his condition. His daughter, sitting by his bed, wished him many more years of life. "I hope not," commented Franklin. As usual, he was right.

No single church dominated all the colonies. The Puritans' Congregational church was the official, or *established*, church in New England. The Church of England, or the Anglican church, was the established church in Virginia, Maryland, New York, the Carolinas, and Georgia. Regardless of their personal beliefs, citizens paid taxes to support the established church in their colony.

Furthermore, many colonies originated as havens for religious dissenters who resisted any attempt by either the Anglicans or the Puritans to impose their beliefs on the community. Massachusetts, which had managed for so many years to smother dissent within its borders, eventually granted religious freedoms. In 1691 a new charter specified that all religious groups in the colony were free to worship.

Although Protestant denominations gradually extended toleration to each other, they tended to discriminate against Roman Catholics. Even Maryland, which had been founded as a refuge for English Catholics, persecuted them. Laws passed there at the end of the seventeenth century deprived Catholics of political rights and forbade them to hold religious services anywhere but in the privacy of their homes.

Jewish settlers also suffered discrimination, although less than they had in Europe. Most colonies, for example, did not allow Jews to vote.

Still, when compared to Europe at the time, the American colonies practiced a relatively high degree of religious tolerance. This toleration developed mainly out of necessity. With so many different denominations coexisting in the communities, mutual toleration seemed to be the easiest way to get along.

The Importance of Education

Education was often closely connected with religion in colonial America, especially in New England. The early Puritan colonists had emphasized the importance of schooling. They believed that everyone should have access to the "divine truth" found in the Bible. Thus everyone should know how to read. To achieve this goal, the Puritans created a *primer*, an illustrated textbook that taught children how to read and spell while they memorized the tenets of the Puritan faith.

In 1647 Massachusetts passed the earliest public school law in America. It

Black men and women had little opportunity for a formal education in colonial America, but some individuals overcame the obstacles. Phillis Wheatley was brought from Africa and sold as a slave at age eight. She taught herself English and Latin and began writing poetry. Her verse was widely admired, especially in London, where she visited after she was freed at age 20.

stipulated that towns of 50 or more families should maintain a grammar school to prepare young men for college by instructing them in Latin and other classical subjects. Other New England colonies passed similar laws.

Although the Middle Colonies had no tax-supported schools, religious groups founded schools for poor children. Some private schools, mainly for boys, also existed for those who could afford them. In the Southern Colonies tutors who lived with the planters' families customarily taught their children. Others had little access to education.

Although most colonial education was limited to boys, women frequently held classes in their homes for girls and the younger children. At these so-called "dame schools," pupils learned reading and writing, as well as skills like sewing and embroidery. In some colonial cities, artisans also set up evening schools for their workers.

As a result of such efforts, the *literacy rate*, or the proportion of people who could read and write, in the colonies was relatively high, especially in towns and in New England in general. In frontier areas fewer

The Arts in the Colonies: A Practical Approach

In Europe only the wealthy had much opportunity to enjoy art, music, and literature. Greater opportunity existed in colonial America, but there the arts themselves took on a different expression. Mere decoration and frivolous entertainment had little place, because people were concerned with the practical needs of living in the New World. Creative expression in the colonies, therefore, usually meant enhancing everyday products.

Women made colorful quilts and embroidered or printed designs on the fabric, thus providing warmth for cold evenings as well as decoration. Colonial artists often painted glassware or china. The Pennsylvania Dutch region became especially well known for its stenciled designs.

Stonecarvers and blacksmiths decorated objects such as gravestones and weathervanes. Smiths wrought designs out of various metals. They made lanterns and candleholders from tin, pewter, silver, or brass. Silversmiths created tea- and coffeepots, tankards, and serving trays. Paul Revere designed a bowl whose pattern still bears his name.

Furniture was usually made from locally available woods. Oak and pine were popular during the early years when most furniture had bare wood surfaces—durable, but not very comfortable. Later those who could afford them demanded mahogany, walnut, and other more costly woods, as well as upholstered furniture. Vegetable dyes colored wood and fabric.

Colonial architecture began to develop around the end of the seventeenth century. Northerners built wooden houses from locally available timber. They could get brick, but the lime used to make mortar was in short supply. Brickwork had to be reserved for large fireplaces, used for cooking as well as heating. Extremely high glass prices necessitated small windows. Southerners, on the other hand, used more brick and stone, since clay and lime were not as scarce in their region. Wealthy plantation owners sometimes copied grand English manor houses.

Literature followed practical lines too. People read mostly history, diaries, political essays, and sermons. Poetry also had a place. Anne Bradstreet was one of the earliest colonial poets. Married at 16, she came with her husband to New England, "where," she wrote, "I found a new world and new manners, at which my heart rose."

people could read. People who could not write signed legal documents with an *X*.

Soon after their arrival in the New World, colonists had also turned their attention to higher education for young men, primarily to educate ministers and preachers. Settlers in Massachusetts established the first colonial college in 1636, naming it Harvard after a wealthy colonist who donated land and money to build it. The College of William and Mary was founded in Virginia in 1693, and in 1701 a group of Congregationalists founded Yale.

Boys as young as fourteen could enter college by passing an entrance exam in Greek and Latin. Once there, they studied more Greek and Latin, as well as logic, Hebrew, rhetoric, mathematics, geography, theology, and philosophy. Small amounts of history and botany rounded out the college curriculum.

Cities: Centers of Culture

Although the towns and cities of mid-eighteenth-century America contained less than 10 percent of the population, they significantly influenced colonial life. Through the great ports of Philadelphia, New York, Boston, and Charleston, merchants shipped the products of America to England and the West Indies. Towns and cities also served as the focus of a busy trade between the coast and the rapidly growing backcountry.

Cities were the exchange points not only for goods but also for ideas. In Boston, colonists founded the first regular weekly

The Growth of Colonial Cities: Reading Graphs

Graphs are one way to present information visually rather than describing it with words and numbers. Three types of graphs—line graphs, bar graphs, and circle graphs—are frequently used in American history textbooks, as well as in many newspapers and magazines.

A single graph can condense a large amount of data. Graphs allow you to see the relationship between two or more sets of data. In a line or bar graph you might also be able to trace changes over time. A circle graph illustrates the relationship of various parts to a whole.

The steps outlined below will help you learn more from graphs. Follow the steps and answer the questions about the accompanying graph.

1. **Identify the type of information presented on the graph.** You can do this by asking yourself a few basic questions. Answer the following questions for this line graph: (a) What is the title of the graph? (b) What do the numbers on the vertical axis represent? (c) What do the numbers on the horizontal axis represent? (d) What items are included in the legend, or key? (e) In your own words describe the type of information shown on the graph.

2. **Practice reading the data shown on the graph.** Use the following questions to practice reading the line graph at right: (a) What was the population of New York in 1690? (b) What was the population of Charleston in 1720? (c) In what decade did the population of Boston decline? (d) How much did the population of Philadelphia grow between 1710 and 1720?

3. **Look for relationships among the data presented.** Use the following questions to practice this step: (a) Which city had the largest population in 1690? (b) Which city grew most rapidly between 1700 and 1710? (c) How many more people lived in Boston than in Philadelphia in 1720? (d) Which city grew the least between 1690 and 1700?

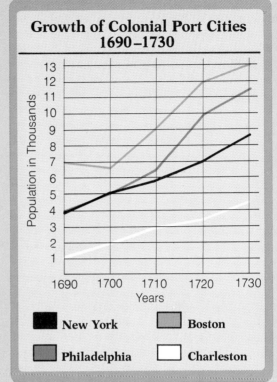

Growth of Colonial Port Cities 1690–1730

Legend:
- New York
- Boston
- Philadelphia
- Charleston

The figures above are estimates, except the New York population for 1730, which is from an actual census.

4. **Use the graph to draw conclusions about a topic.** Study the line graph and what you learned about colonial America in this chapter to answer the following questions: (a) What statement can you make about the population of all four cities between 1690 and 1730? (b) Why do you think port cities were the largest cities in the 1700s? (c) What factors probably contributed to Boston's being the largest port city during this period? (d) Which products were probably shipped out of New York and Philadelphia? Which products were probably shipped out of Charleston?

newspaper in the colonies in 1704. Fifty years later, each of the 13 colonies except New Jersey and Delaware had at least one weekly paper.

The growth of colonial newspapers led to a dispute over freedom of the press. In 1734 John Peter Zenger, publisher of the *Weekly Journal* in New York City, was arrested for libel.* Zenger, who often criticized government officials in his paper, had attacked the governor of New York. Zenger's lawyer argued that his client had not libeled the governor because what he printed had

---

*libel: the act of publishing a statement that unjustly damages a person's reputation.

Major Events	
1636	Harvard founded as first institution of higher learning
1647	First public school law passed in colonies
1676	Bacon's rebellion
1734	John Peter Zenger arrested
1763	Paxton boys revolt

been the truth. The court agreed and freed Zenger.

At the time this seemed like a revolutionary idea, since criticism of the government was generally considered a crime. The principle of freedom of the press was upheld in this case, but years would pass before it was firmly established in America.

Culture also flourished in the cities. By the middle of the eighteenth century, all the major colonial cities had their own theaters. City dwellers also found entertainment at singing societies, traveling circuses, carnivals, and horse races. Here and there public libraries were established, stocked with books imported from abroad or printed on new colonial presses.

The lives of city dwellers were not typical of most colonists. But the cities served as a focal point for new products and ideas that eventually spread throughout the colonies.

For answers, see p. A 15.

Section Review

1. Define the following terms: established church, primer, dame school, literacy rate.
2. How did the origin of many colonies contribute to greater religious toleration?
3. (a) How did the variety of churches in the colonies contribute to religious toleration? (b) Which religious groups were often not tolerated in the colonies?
4. (a) Which colony passed the first public school law? (b) Why did the Puritans think that education was important?
5. (a) What education existed for girls in colonial America? (b) What education existed for boys?
6. How did cities contribute to the development of colonial culture?

★ ★

IN PERSPECTIVE   By the 1700s most of the American colonies had become royal colonies with representative governments. Yet the colonists' way of life differed in the New England Colonies, the Middle Colonies, and the Southern Colonies. In New England a profitable shipping and fishing industry became the mainstay of a thriving economy, which gradually made it easier for people to aspire to a higher place in society.

A diverse group of settlers made their homes on the fertile farmland of the Middle Colonies. Agriculture was also the basis of the Southern economy, but there the plantation system flourished. Wealthy planters who dominated political and economic life grew cash crops that required a large amount of land and labor. Increasingly, they came to rely on slaves rather than indentured servants. In the Middle and Southern Colonies a different way of life emerged in the backcountry. Socially and politically isolated, the pioneers resented the farmers and planters of the coastal regions.

Despite the differences among the colonists, by 1750 they differed more from Europeans than from each other. Religious toleration was more prevalent in the colonies, and the emphasis on education yielded a relatively literate society. Growing cities provided an arena for the exchange of news and ideas. These shared ideas and values provided the basis for greater unity, as you will read in later chapters. Yet the diversity of beliefs and experience also contributed to the richness of the emerging American culture.

For answers, see p. A 15.

Chapter Review

1. (a) What was the basis of the economy in New England? (b) What was the basis of the economy in the Middle Colonies? (c) What was the basis of the economy in the Southern Colonies? (d) What factors help account for the different patterns?

2. (a) Describe the social class system in New England. (b) Why did it gradually become less rigid?

3. (a) How was the ethnic composition of settlers in the Middle Colonies more diverse than that of settlers in New England or in the coastal region of the South? (b) Why did the Middle Colonies seem attractive to these settlers?

4. What was the position of free blacks in colonial America?

5. (a) How did life in the backcountry differ from life along the coast? (b) How can you explain this difference?

6. (a) Why did slavery replace the use of indentured servants on southern plantations? (b) Why did planters come to prefer buying slaves to employing indentured servants?

7. Why were there fewer slaves in the Middle Colonies and New England than in the South?

8. (a) What conditions led to greater religious tolerance in the colonies than in Europe? (b) Were all groups tolerated? Explain.

9. (a) Why did the American colonies have a relatively high literacy rate? (b) In what part of the colonies was the literacy rate lower? (c) How would you account for this?

For answers, see p. A 16.

For Further Thought

1. (a) Why was slavery a dehumanizing experience regardless of how a slave was treated? (b) How did slaves try to keep their humanity?

2. (a) How did the position of an indentured servant differ from the position of a slave? (b) Why do you think a person would decide to become an indentured servant?

3. (a) What roles did women play in each of the following areas: New England farms, New England cities, backcountry farms, southern plantations? (b) In what ways were their roles similar? (c) In what ways were they different? (d) How might you explain the similarities and differences?

4. (a) How did education for boys differ from education for girls? (b) Why do you think there was a difference?

For answers, see p. A 16.

Developing Basic Skills

1. *Ranking*   Rank the social systems of each of the following regions from the most rigid to the least rigid: New England towns, Middle Colonies coastal area, Middle Colonies backcountry, Southern Colonies backcountry, Southern Colonies coastal area. (a) Why did you rank them in the order you did? (b) Which areas of the colonies probably had the most rigid class system? (c) Which areas probably had the least rigid class system? (d) How would you account for the different patterns?

2. *Graph Reading*   Use the steps you learned on page 81 to read the circle graph on page 70. A circle graph, which is sometimes called a pie graph, shows the relationship of the parts to a whole. Study the graph and answer the following questions: (a) What information is shown on this graph? (b) Which portion of the colonial population in 1775 was English? (c) What other ethnic groups are represented on the graph? (d) Which are the three largest ethnic groups? (e) Which are the three smallest? (f) Based on the graph, what general statements would you make about the ethnic composition of the American colonies?

See page 773 for suggested readings.

5

A Struggle for Empire

(1600–1763)

Battle of Louisbourg.

Chapter Outline

1 *The American Colonies: A Vital Part of the British Empire*

2 *Rivalry in North America*

3 *The French and Indian War*

By the first decades of the 1700s, Europeans had made their presence felt not only in the Americas but also around the world. European merchants were trading with Asian nations, as they had dreamed since the 1400s. Missionaries, fur traders, and settlers often followed.

Having discovered the world beyond their doorsteps, the nations of Europe were soon embroiled in a struggle to control it and to obtain a lion's share of its riches. Chief among the competitors for power, wealth, and land were Great Britain, France, and Spain. Each hoped to establish an empire of global proportions.

Although originally valued far below the fabled lands of Asia, by the 1700s America came to occupy an important position in European imperial designs. As you will read in this chapter, the three European powers claimed large parts of North America in spite of the Native Americans already living there. As American colonies became more important to the British Empire, conflict between the British, French, and Spanish became more likely.

1 The American Colonies: A Vital Part of the British Empire

The rivalry among European nations involved more than the struggle for political control of far-flung parts of the world. During the late 1600s and the 1700s, commerce also became an arena of fierce, sometimes violent, competition. Colonies became increasingly important in this competition, especially for the British Empire.*

Mercantilism

Behind this fierce rivalry lay an economic theory that has come to be called *mercantilism,* from the word merchant. Under the mercantilist system, each nation attempted to sell more than it bought. In this way, it would preserve or even increase its precious and limited supply of gold. Furthermore, a nation that did not rely on other nations for necessary goods would be less vulnerable in time of war.

A nation could achieve economic independence in several ways. One of the best ways was to have overseas colonies and trading posts. These would increase a nation's self-sufficiency by providing essential raw materials such as precious metals, lumber, agricultural products, cotton, and wool that would otherwise have to be bought from rival nations.

Colonies played a second vital role in the mercantilist system, since they served as markets for goods produced at home. Without colonies, a nation could manufacture only what it could reasonably expect to sell at home and to a few foreign customers. Unsold goods would have to be counted as a loss. With colonial outlets, however, surplus goods could be exported, and manufacturers would have fewer losses and greater profits.

Early in the age of exploration, Sir Walter Raleigh had foreseen the value of mercantilism to a nation. "Whoever commands the trade of the world," he said, "commands the riches of the world and consequently the

Ships like the ones in this 1760 painting of New York Harbor carried valuable cargo between England and the colonies. Such trade was a vital part of mercantilism.

world itself." In the late seventeenth century, the crown began to act on Raleigh's advice.

First, as you learned in the preceding chapter, the crown tightened its political control over the colonies. Next, it strengthened its hold on colonial trade. Charles II worked with his ministers to design a strong mercantilist colonial policy that would allow the empire to "command the riches of the world" and then "the world itself."

Regulating Trade

Before the mid-1600s colonial merchants had enjoyed a measure of economic independence. England provided a profitable market for many of their goods. What they could not sell profitably there they traded in the English, French, Dutch, and Spanish islands of the Caribbean, often for an even larger profit.

From the king's point of view, such practices were dangerous. By trading with other nations and their colonies, a colonial merchant deprived the crown of valuable revenues. If such activities occurred on a large scale, England's mercantilist economy, and its status as a world power, would be threatened.

---

*One part of England's transformation into a world power was the unification of England and Scotland into the nation of Great Britain in 1707. After that date, "Great Britain" and "British" were the official terms used to describe the new nation and its residents. Throughout the 1700s, however, these new terms were used interchangeably with "England" and "English."

Unless the American colonies were forced to play their appointed role in the mercantilist system, England's chances of commanding "the world itself" were slim. In 1660 and 1663, therefore, Parliament passed a series of trade regulations called the Navigation Acts. Their purpose was to make sure the colonies traded with England and only with England.

First, colonial merchants were allowed to ship goods only on colonial or English-owned vessels. Three quarters of the crew of such a vessel had to consist of colonial or English sailors.

This regulation was aimed primarily at the Netherlands, England's chief commercial competitor. The Dutch possessed the world's largest merchant fleet, and their ships regularly transported products to and from the English colonies. Every Dutch ship trading with the colonies meant profits for the Dutch and losses for the crown. By prohibiting colonists from using foreign ships, Charles II intended to stop this drain on his nation's economy.

Next, Parliament drew up a list of colonial products, called *enumerated commodities*, that could be shipped only to England. Enumerated articles included sugar, cotton, indigo, ginger, tobacco, and woods used for dye. In later years, the list of enumerated goods was expanded to include other items, such as rice, furs, and naval supplies.

The Navigation Acts also prohibited the colonies from importing products from other European nations unless those products were sent first to England and shipped from there to the colonies. The only exceptions to this rule were slaves, wines, horses, and salt.

This provision guaranteed the crown income from taxes on all products going to and from the colonies, even if the products had been manufactured elsewhere. The taxes imposed on European products would also raise their prices in the colonies. Thus, English industries would be protected from cheap competition. Furthermore, jobs would be created in England to process imports and exports.

Impact on England and the Colonies

For the most part, the trade laws worked, and the mercantile system benefited both England and the colonies. American merchants benefited from laws that excluded foreigners from colonial trade. To compensate the colonists for any profits that might be lost, the crown granted them bonuses for producing certain essential goods. Furthermore, colonial traders welcomed the protection from French and Spanish competitors provided by British forces.

Although most colonists took the trade laws in stride, resistance to the regulations did exist. Some merchants resented the law

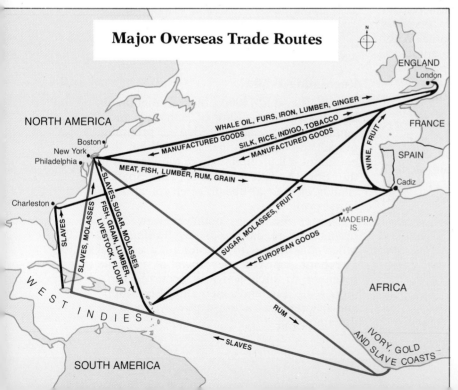

Major Overseas Trade Routes

■ Overseas trade was an important part of mercantilism. Much of the colonial trade was with England, but colonial merchants also traded with other European nations, Africa, and the West Indies. The slave trade was part of a triangular route (shown on this map in red) between the colonies, the West Indies, and the west coast of Africa.

requiring that goods they imported and exported pass through England. They claimed that it cut into their profits and consumed precious shipping time.

Others were angered by the regulation forcing them to sell enumerated articles only to England. They knew that they could get higher prices for their products in other European countries. Merchants also found that, on occasion, it was cheaper to bribe customs officials than to pay British import and export duties.

The biggest problem with the Navigation Acts arose in the eighteenth century. Increasingly, New England had come to rely on the production of rum, made from molasses, to support its trade. Merchants would ship grain, barrel staves, horses, and fish to the West Indies and bring back molasses.

New England merchants could use the profits from rum to buy English manufactured goods. Or they could ship rum to Africa, buy slaves with it, sail to the West Indies and sell the slaves for more molasses, then return home and make more rum. These patterns of exchange, outlined on the map on page 86, came to be known as the *triangular trade*.

Under the mercantilist system, colonists were supposed to import molasses only from the British West Indies. But the islands there could supply only a small amount of the molasses needed. New England merchants thus made up the difference by importing large amounts from the French, Spanish, and Dutch West Indies.

In 1733, however, the rich sugar planters of the British West Indies convinced Parliament to pass the Molasses Act. The Molasses Act required colonists to pay a stiff duty on all molasses or rum imported from the foreign West Indies. If the duty had been enforced, it would have ruined New England's economy, but New England merchants usually ignored the law or else paid customs officials a small bribe to overlook the foreign molasses. Consequently, the triangular trade routes flourished as much as ever.

By and large the mercantile system worked well—so well, in fact, that, as you will read in the next section, it brought the prospering English colonies into conflict with the two rival empires on the continent, Spain and France.

For answers, see p. A 17.

Section Review

1. Identify the following: Molasses Act.
2. Define the following terms: mercantilism, enumerated commodity, triangular trade.
3. In what two ways were colonies an important part of the English mercantilist system?
4. (a) What was the main purpose of the Navigation Acts? (b) What did England want to gain by prohibiting colonists from using foreign ships?
5. (a) Did the trade laws work? (b) In what ways could colonists benefit from them?
6. (a) Why were some colonists opposed to the trade regulations? (b) Where was resistance the greatest?

2 Rivalry in North America

England's aggressive mercantilist policies helped transform it from a tiny, self-contained nation into a major world power in less than a century. Step by step, the British strengthened their hold on lands as far from each other as India and North America.

Although British possessions in America were much smaller than those of Spain or France, the British presence grew much more rapidly. At the end of the seventeenth century, 200,000 people lived in British America. By the mid-eighteenth century, the population reached 1,500,000 and was still growing. At the same time, barely 70,000 colonists lived in New France, a territory more than twice the size of the British colonies.

As English settlements expanded, they ran the risk of encroaching on French or Spanish territory. From the start, friction seemed inevitable.

The Spanish Empire

Spain, as you will recall, had established its American colonies years before either France or England and had realized a far greater profit from them. By the eighteenth century, the Spanish empire in America included most of Central and South America, plus what is now Mexico, Florida, the southwestern United States, and California.

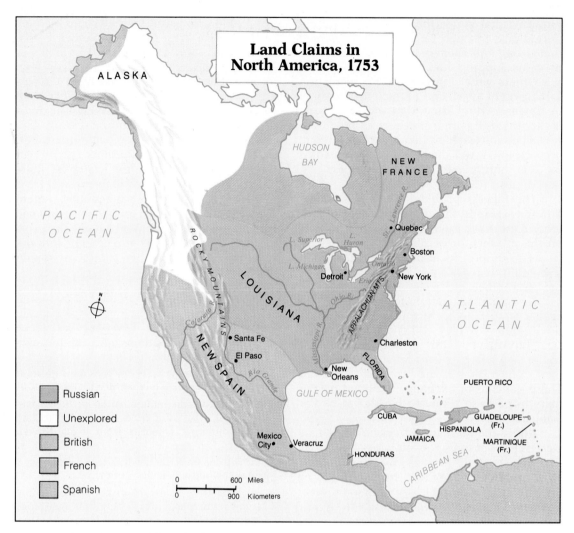

Land Claims in North America, 1753

ALASKA

HUDSON BAY

NEW FRANCE

PACIFIC OCEAN

ROCKY MOUNTAINS

L. Superior

L. Michigan

L. Huron

L. Ontario

L. Erie

St. Lawrence R.

•Quebec

•Boston

Detroit•

New York

LOUISIANA

APPALACHIAN MTS.

Ohio R.

•Charleston

ATLANTIC OCEAN

Colorado R.

•Santa Fe

El Paso•

NEW SPAIN

Rio Grande

Mississippi R.

•New Orleans

FLORIDA

GULF OF MEXICO

PUERTO RICO

CUBA

HISPANIOLA

GUADELOUPE (Fr.)

JAMAICA

MARTINIQUE (Fr.)

Mexico City•

•Veracruz

HONDURAS

CARIBBEAN SEA

Russian
Unexplored
British
French
Spanish

0   600 Miles
0   900 Kilometers

■ *France, Spain, Russia, and Great Britain all claimed parts of North America. However, only the English established colonies with rapidly growing populations. As English colonists moved westward, conflicts with other European nations and with Native Americans increased.*

Since the defeat of the Armada in 1588, however, Spanish power had been declining, and active control of the American colonies had slackened. The amount of money invested by the home country in the New World dwindled, and fewer Spaniards were encouraged to immigrate to America. As a result, the colonies were left to develop largely on their own.

Spanish ships brought fewer soldiers, fewer missionaries, and fewer settlers. Gradually, American-born settlers began to replace Spanish immigrants in positions of authority in the colonies.

The Spanish did continue some explorations of the southwest and Pacific coast during the seventeenth and early eighteenth centuries. Sebastián Vizcaíno (VEES kah EE noh) explored the northern coast of California as early as 1602. He paved the way for later Spanish settlement of the area and gave many places their present names, including San Diego, Santa Barbara, Monterey, and Carmel.

The Spanish founded Santa Fe in present-day New Mexico in 1609, and almost fifty years later established several missions near El Paso. During the 1690s Father Eusebio Francisco Kino helped establish missions in present-day Arizona and California.

Since English settlement was confined to the east coast of North America, however,

For answers, see p. A 17.

Rival Claims in North America: Reading Maps

With the exception of the written word, maps tell you more about historical events than any other social studies tool. They can provide geographic, social, political, and economic information. Knowing how to understand and interpret maps is important to your understanding of American history.

Certain features are found on most maps. These include a title, legend, scale, directional indicator, and topographical features. By using these features to read a map, you can draw conclusions about events or developments in American history.

Follow the steps below, using the map on page 88 to practice using maps.

1. **Decide what is shown on the map.** The title and legend usually provide this information. The *title* tells you the subject of the map. The *legend*, or key, tells you what the symbols and colors on the map represent. Answer the following questions for the map on page 88: (a) What is title of the map? (b) What is the date of the information? (c) What countries' claims are shown on the map? (d) How is each country represented? (e) What information is shown on the map?

2. **Practice reading the information on the map.** In addition to the legend, the scale, directional indicator, and topographical features help you read a map. The *scale* tells you the actual distances that are represented on the map. The

maps in this textbook show the distance in both kilometers and miles. *Direction* is usually shown by an arrow or compass needle indicating which way is north. *Topographical features* are surface land characteristics such as mountains or rivers. Mountains on maps in this textbook are shaded to indicate height. Answer the questions below about the map on page 88 to practice reading a map: (a) What is the distance in kilometers between Quebec and Charleston? between Quebec and New York? (b) Which country claimed the territory north and west of British territory? (c) Which mountains bordered British claims? (d) Which two major rivers were part of French territory?

3. **Use the information on the map to draw conclusions about the historical period being studied.** Answer the following questions based on the map and what you have read in your text: (a) Which nation claimed the most territory? (b) What explorations were the basis for Spanish claims? (See Chapter 2.) (c) What explorations were the basis for French claims? (d) How far west did British settlement extend? Why do you think it stopped there? (e) Where would conflict between the Spanish and British be most likely to occur? (f) Where would conflict between the French and British be most likely to occur?

contacts between the two empires were limited to skirmishes between trading vessels at sea and to friction between Spanish Florida and its English neighbors to the north.

Settlers in Georgia accused Spain of permitting outlaws to cross the Florida border and harass them. Their anxieties were further aggravated in 1738 when the Spanish governor declared that slaves who escaped from servitude in the English colonies could live in freedom in Florida. And the British had always suspected that Spain had its eye on more territory in the area.

New France

Friction with Spain was an irritation, but only a minor one. France, on the other hand, posed the threat of a major conflict.

During its first years, New France grew slowly. Few French men or women wanted

to leave their homeland for the dangers and uncertainties of a wilderness thousands of miles away. Those who wanted to leave, Protestants trying to escape religious persecution, were forbidden to settle in New France.

After 1661, the situation changed. Louis XIV assumed complete control of the French government and launched an ambitious program of empire building. He hoped to make New France into a market for French exports and a source of food for the French West Indies.

Without more French colonists, however, the imperial design would not work. So, for the first time, the French government took steps to encourage people to migrate to North America. It granted large tracts of the best land in New France to army officers and other gentlemen, who in turn rented parts of their land to merchants or peasants.

The Spanish built Mexico City, the colonial capital of Mexico, on the ruins of the Aztec capital of Tenochtitlán. This detail from a 1728 painting of Mexico City shows the city and part of the surrounding lake.

The land grants improved the rate of immigration to North America somewhat. But the gentlemen-landlords, unused to manual labor, made little or no effort to cultivate their land. Although some of their tenants made farming pay, most resented working land they did not own.

As a result, New France was never able to play the role Louis XIV had envisioned for it in his empire. In addition to failing to grow food for the West Indies, the colonies proved incapable of producing enough to feed their own population. The people of New France were forced to depend on the farmers of either the home country or neighboring New England for provisions.

Expanding French Claims

Although farming failed, two other enterprises succeeded: exploration and fur trading.

In 1673 Louis Joliet (zhoh LYEH) and Jacques Marquette (mahr KEHT), a Jesuit priest, journeyed by canoe down the Fox, Wisconsin, and Mississippi rivers, as far south as the mouth of the Arkansas River. There they encountered Indians who told them that the Mississippi emptied into the Gulf of Mexico, not into the Gulf of California to the west or the Atlantic Ocean to the east, as previously thought. Armed with this information, the explorers decided to turn back rather than to push on to the gulf and risk capture by the Spanish who controlled the territory to the south.

In following years René-Robert Cavelier, Sieur de La Salle (suhr duh lah SAHL), continued the explorations of Marquette and Joliet. By 1682 he had reached the delta* of the Mississippi, just north of present-day New Orleans. There he claimed the surrounding area for the king, naming it Louisiana in his honor.

*delta: a deposit of soil at the mouth of some rivers, usually forming a triangular shape.

Coosaponakeesa: Mary Musgrove

Coosaponakeesa, born around 1700, was the daughter of a Creek woman and an English trader. As a young child, she went with her father to South Carolina to begin her education. Her ability to speak both English and Creek served her well throughout her life.

When Coosaponakeesa was about 18 years old, she married John Musgrove, a fur trader from South Carolina, and became known as Mary Musgrove. In the 1730s the Musgroves opened a trading post on the Savannah River.

At this time James Oglethorpe was trying to establish the colony of Georgia. He knew that the continued friendship between the English and the Creeks was crucial to the survival of Georgia because the Creeks provided rich trade and a vital buffer against the Spanish in Florida.

From the 1730s until her death in 1760 Mary Musgrove served Oglethorpe as a translator and negotiator between the American colonists and the Creeks. She promoted the trading interests of the Creeks among the colonists and rallied the Creeks in support of Oglethorpe against the Spanish. She also successfully countered French efforts to woo the Creeks. Mary Musgrove played an important part in the history of Georgia by supporting British colonial interests during the crucial years of the struggle for empire in North America.

French and Indian fur traders often traveled by water through the wooded wilderness of North America. In this painting by Paul Kane, the Indians portage, or carry, their canoes around some rapids.

To consolidate their claims in the New World the French built a string of settlements, missions, forts, and trading posts. From the trading posts, *coureurs de bois* (koo RUHR duh BWAH), literally "runners of the woods," fanned out into the thick forests of New France to trade metal axes, knives, hoes, kettles, woolen blankets, textiles, and weapons to Indian hunters for the furs so valuable to French merchants. To the trading posts came fleets of canoes to take heavy loads of fur over the northern rivers to Quebec and then to Europe.

Impact of the Fur Trade on Native Americans

The fur trade, so lucrative to the French, proved disastrous to many Native American hunters of the northeast. Some tribes competed fiercely with each other for control of rich hunting grounds and for a role in the French trade.

Often, peoples were forced out of lands they had inhabited for centuries. The Iroquois, for instance, drove the Algonquins out of their hunting grounds, forcing them eastward to the Atlantic coast. There the displaced Algonquins vented their anger on New England villages and settlements.

As they were drawn into alliances with European powers, Native Americans also became embroiled in European efforts to dominate the North American continent. Frequently, Europeans manipulated existing rivalries between Native American groups to their advantage.

The Huron and the Iroquois, for example, were traditional rivals. The Huron, who had established friendly relations with the French, served as middlemen between other tribes and French traders. The Dutch, eager for a share of the rich fur trade, encouraged their Iroquois allies to attack the Huron. Although the Huron responded forcefully, they were no match for the more numerous and better-armed Iroquois. The Iroquois forced the surviving Hurons to flee westward toward the Mississippi.

The English who replaced the Dutch in present-day New York State also profited from the warfare. By pitting the Iroquois

One of four Iroquois chiefs invited to London in 1710 to meet Queen Anne was Ho Nee Yeath Taw No Row, a name the English shortened to John Wolf Clan. The Dutch artist John Verelst painted this portrait during the visit.

against Indian nations that were friendly with the French, they struck a blow at French power in North America. Native Americans would eventually be drawn in on both sides when war broke out between the French and the British in 1754.

British Relations With Native Americans

Because New France was so sparsely populated, French settlers did not encroach heavily on Indian lands. The British, in contrast, were more numerous and their numbers were growing each year. In addition, the British built permanent settlements rather than temporary trading outposts.

Furthermore, as farmers rather than fur traders, English settlers wanted as much land as possible. More often than not, this involved pushing the Native Americans out of their territory. Sometimes this was done by treaty, but often settlers simply moved into Indian lands and began clearing the forest

for planting. Indian reaction to this threat produced recurring violence along the frontier.

In 1636 the Pequot (PEE kwaht) resisted English settlement in the Connecticut Valley. In the so-called Pequot War that followed, colonists attacked and burned a major Pequot town, killing 600 men, women, and children.

Almost 40 years later, in 1675, another war, known as King Philip's War, broke out between Native Americans and colonists in New England. The Indians inflicted heavy losses on the New England militia and destroyed 13 frontier towns, but the Indians were ultimately defeated. After that, settlers in New England generally met little resistance.

Some early English settlers had established harmonious relations with Native Americans. Roger Williams and William Penn, for example, were known for negotiating fair treaties and paying for their land. South Carolina fur traders were as successful as the French in their dealings with the original inhabitants of the territory. But in general the competition for land between Native Americans and English settlers led to conflict.

Although individual Indian nations often successfully resisted English expansion for a while, the cultural diversity among tribes made a united effort difficult. As a result, the settlers steadily pushed the Native Americans farther west.

For answers, see p. A 17.
Section Review

1. Identify the following: Louis XIV, Joliet, Marquette, La Salle, coureur de bois, Iroquois, Algonquin, Huron, Pequot War, King Philip's War.
2. (a) In what area of North America did the English and Spanish compete? (b) What was the basis for the competition?
3. (a) What role was New France to serve in Louis XIV's design for his empire? (b) Did his plan succeed? Explain.
4. (a) What two French activities in North America were successful? (b) What impact did their activities have on Native Americans in the area?
5. What impact did English settlement have on Native Americans?

3 The French and Indian War

The English, French, and Spanish colonies in North America were all extensions of their European governments. Therefore, it was probably inevitable that they would be caught up in conflicts among the great powers. Eventually, these conflicts exploded in a war that determined which nation would control much of North America.

European Conflict Spreads to America

Competition for North American territory was part of a larger struggle between Great Britain, France, and Spain for dominance of Europe. Since the defeat of the Armada in 1588, Spain had been the least powerful of the three nations. The power of Britain and France, on the other hand, steadily increased, and a showdown between the two was simply a matter of time.

France and Britain had gone to war in Europe three times since the late 1680s: the War of the League of Augsburg (1689–1697), the War of the Spanish Succession (1702–1713), and the War of the Austrian Succession (1740–1748). Beyond some border skirmishes, colonists were little affected by these wars. However, a fourth war, which came to be known as the French and Indian War, began in North America.

The initial conflict occurred in the Ohio Valley. France claimed the region, but the British colonies had been expanding toward the valley for more than a decade. In fact, Virginia considered the Ohio Valley part of its territory. Several prominent Virginians had formed the Ohio Company to promote settlement in the area. In 1749 the Ohio Company obtained a 200,000-acre grant (81,000 hectares) from the British government. As settlers moved into the valley, however, they found themselves face to face with the French.

The Albany Congress

In June 1754 representatives from New Hampshire, Massachusetts, Connecticut, Rhode Island, Pennsylvania, Maryland, and New York met in Albany, New York, with

■ *In the French and Indian War control of key western forts was a major objective of both sides. An arc of French forts in the Northwest guarded the approaches to Canada and was not broken by colonial and British forces until late in the war.*

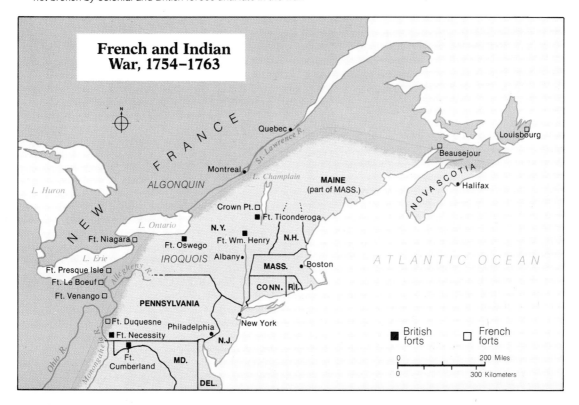

French and Indian War, 1754–1763

representatives from the Iroquois League. Fearing attack by the French and their Indian allies, the colonists wanted to solidify their friendship with the Iroquois and plan a common defense.

In addition to questions about the best way to defend the colonies, the delegates also discussed the possibility of an intercolonial union. They drew up a plan, called the Albany Plan of Union, which was designed to unite the 13 colonies under a single government.

When the Plan of Union was submitted to the individual colonial governments, however, none of them approved it. In the opinion of most colonial legislators, it called for too much control by a central government. Benjamin Franklin, author of the original plan, lamented, "Everyone cries a union is necessary, but when they come to the manner and form of the union, their weak noodles are perfectly distracted."

Early French Victories

While the representatives argued at Albany, the French finished building their forts along the Ohio River. At the same time George Washington, a 22-year-old officer in the Virginia militia, led 150 soldiers into western Pennsylvania to construct forts for the British.

On March 28, 1754, Washington's troops fired on a small party of French soldiers and took them prisoner. Learning from the prisoners that the French were about to move against them, the colonists hastily built a stockade and dubbed it Fort Necessity.

The fort was quickly besieged by a combined force of almost 1,000 French soldiers and their Indian allies. Washington and his small party could not withstand the siege and surrendered on July 3. This was the first of a series of French victories.

The following year, General Edward Braddock took command of British colonial forces. With 2,500 soldiers Braddock began cutting a road through the wilderness of western Pennsylvania to Fort Duquesne (doo KAYN), a French stronghold at the junction of the Allegheny and Monongahela (muh NAHN guh HEE luh) rivers.

When Braddock was within ten miles of the fort, the French launched an ambush. On July 9, just after the red-coated British soldiers had crossed the Monongahela, they were mowed down by musket fire from 100 French troops, 150 Canadian militia, and 800 Indians. Braddock and 900 soldiers perished. The surviving British troops destroyed their supplies and retreated as fast as they could to the safety of Philadelphia.

That same year an expedition under Governor William Shirley of Massachusetts tried and failed to capture Fort Niagara. A campaign against Crown Point, led by William Johnson, ended in a virtual draw. The British, however, desperately in need of success, proclaimed Johnson the victor and knighted him.

Pitt and British Victories

In 1756 William Pitt became the British secretary of state. He moved quickly to reverse the string of British defeats. Pitt was a vigorous, uncompromising man, confident of his ability to win the war. "I am sure that I can save the country, and that no one else can," he remarked, and he promptly set out to do just that.

Pitt united the previously divided colonies by guaranteeing the colonists payment for military service and supplies. He also dismissed older military commanders and installed more capable young officers. Two of these, General Jeffrey Amherst and General James Wolfe, captured Louisbourg, the most important French Canadian fortress, in 1758. General John Forbes, another Pitt appointee, led an advance on Fort Duquesne. He forced the French to abandon and burn the fort, later rebuilt by the British as Fort Pitt.

In 1759 Pitt planned a three-pronged attack on the French: first, capture Fort Niagara and thus cut off the Great Lakes from the east; second, clear Lake Champlain of French forts; and, third, strike at Quebec itself.

Pitt's plan succeeded. British troops captured strategic French forts, and in early September 1759 General Wolfe and his fleet sailed up the St. Lawrence to Quebec. Fifteen thousand French troops were quartered in the city. At first, Wolfe bombarded the city from the land and the water. When this failed to draw the French into open battle, he boldly ordered his troops to mount a sur-

One of the turning points of the French and Indian War was the British victory at Quebec. When bombardment by British ships failed to draw the French into open battle, the British secretly scaled the cliffs by a little-known path, shown at left in this painting by Sigmund Samuel. The surprised French troops poured out of the fort to defend the city but were soundly defeated by the invaders.

prise attack by scaling the cliffs below Quebec during the dead of night.

On September 13, the French commander, Louis Joseph de Montcalm, awoke to find 5,000 British troops arrayed for battle on the Plains of Abraham outside the city. The French marched out to engage them. In the ensuing battle, both Montcalm and Wolfe were killed. On September 17, Quebec surrendered to the British.

Return of Peace in North America

Fighting continued between the major powers and their allies in Europe, but the fall of Quebec signaled the end of the war in North America and the fall of France's New World empire.

According to the Treaty of Paris of 1763, France granted Canada and lands east of the Mississippi River to Great Britain. Spain,

Major Events	
1602	Vizcaíno explores California
1609	Spanish found Santa Fe
1660, 1663	English Parliament passes Navigation Acts
1673	Joliet and Marquette explore Mississippi River
1682	La Salle reaches Mississippi delta
1733	Parliament passes Molasses Act
1754	Albany Congress
1754–1763	French and Indian War

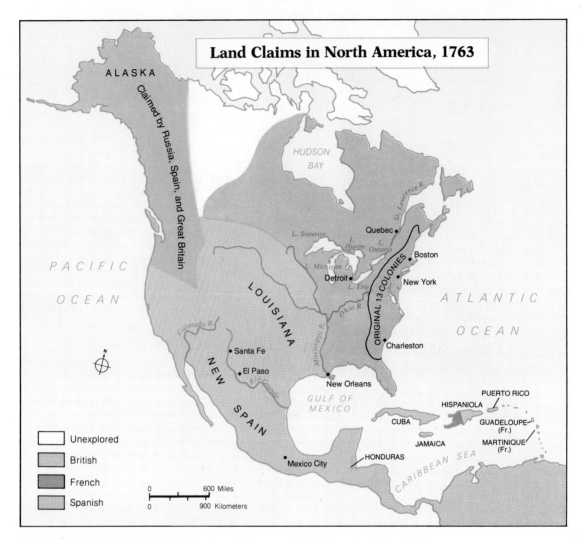

Land Claims in North America, 1763

ALASKA

Claimed by Russia, Spain, and Great Britain

HUDSON BAY

PACIFIC OCEAN

ATLANTIC OCEAN

L. Superior

L. Huron

L. Ontario

L. Michigan

L. Erie

Quebec

Boston

Detroit

New York

ORIGINAL 13 COLONIES

St. Lawrence R.

Ohio R.

Mississippi R.

LOUISIANA

Charleston

Colorado R.

NEW

Santa Fe

El Paso

Rio Grande

SPAIN

New Orleans

GULF OF MEXICO

Mexico City

HONDURAS

CUBA

JAMAICA

HISPANIOLA

PUERTO RICO

GUADELOUPE (Fr.)

MARTINIQUE (Fr.)

CARIBBEAN SEA

☐ Unexplored

☐ British

☐ French

☐ Spanish

0   600 Miles
0   900 Kilometers

■ *The Treaty of Paris (1763) drastically changed the areas in North America claimed by the British, French, and Spanish.*

which had entered the war against England in 1762 in alarm at British success, gave up Florida to Britain. In return, Spain received French lands west of the Mississippi. France retained two islands in the Gulf of St. Lawrence and the prosperous sugar-producing islands of Guadeloupe and Martinique in the Caribbean.

The English colonies, which had been confined to the Atlantic coast until 1763, now stretched as far west as the Mississippi River. With the French and the Spanish removed from their flanks, the colonists looked toward a new frontier. Wagons were soon rolling westward.

For answers, see p. A 18.

Section Review

1. Identify the following: Plan of Union, Benjamin Franklin, George Washington, William Pitt, Treaty of Paris.

2. What incident led to the outbreak of hostilities between the French and the British in North America?

3. Why was the Albany Conference held?

4. What two actions did William Pitt take to help turn the tide of war in Britain's favor?

5. (a) What territories did France lose to Great Britain according to the Treaty of Paris? (b) What territory did Spain lose to Britain?

IN PERSPECTIVE   During the 1600s European nations were engaged in fierce competition with one another for power in Europe and for empires overseas. Commerce became another area of competition as monarchs turned to the economic theory of mercantilism.

The American colonies played an important role in England's mercantilist system both as a source of raw materials and as a market for English goods. The system seemed to benefit both England and the colonies until the early 1700s, when it came to threaten the profitable triangular trade of New England merchants.

The growth and development of the colonies also brought the British into conflict with the Spanish and, especially, the French. When war broke out between Great Britain and France in 1754, both nations allied with Native Americans by exploiting traditional rivalries. The British and colonists defeated the French by 1763, and the colonists looked forward to unchecked growth and expansion.

For answers, see p. A 18.

Chapter Review

1. Why did the English government want to control trade in the colonies?

2. Describe the major provisions of the Navigation Acts.

3. (a) Why did New England merchants become more unhappy about the Navigation Acts in the 1700s? (b) What impact did the Molasses Act have on the triangular trade?

4. (a) In what areas in the Americas did the British empire compete with the French? with the Spanish? (b) Which nation was Britain's strongest competitor in North America? Why?

5. (a) What impact did the French fur trade have on Native Americans? (b) What impact did English settlement have? (c) Which was most likely to lead to violent conflict? Why?

6. What development helped Britain and the colonists win the French and Indian War?

For answers, see p. A 18.

For Further Thought

1. Sir Walter Raleigh said, "Whoever commands the trade of the world commands the riches of the world and consequently the world itself." Did this seem to be true for Great Britain in 1763?

2. Some people have argued that conflict in North America between the English and the French and Spanish was inevitable. Do you agree? Explain.

For answers, see p. A 18.

Developing Basic Skills

1. *Map Reading*   Use the map-reading steps you learned in this chapter (page 89) to study the map on page 96. Then answer the following questions: (a) What information does the map provide? (b) How far west does British territory extend? (c) How far east does Spanish territory extend? (d) Where is French territory located? (e) Which nation would probably be Britain's main territorial rival in North America after 1763?

2. *Map Reading*   One map can provide much information about an historical event or period. However, if you compare maps, you can often gain important insight into historical developments. Compare the maps on pages 88 and 96, and answer the following questions: (a) How did the extent of British territory change between 1753 and 1763? (b) How did the extent of French and Spanish claims change? (c) Which nation gained the most territory east of the Mississippi River? Which lost the most?

See page 774 for suggested readings.

Unit Two

Creating a Republic

6

The Road to Revolution

(1763–1775)

Detail from Patrick Henry Before the House of Burgesses.

Chapter Outline

1 *Problems of Britain's New Empire*

2 *The Quarrel Widens*

3 *The Roots of Independence*

4 *From Protest to Revolution*

As a result of its victory in the French and Indian War, Great Britain emerged as the unchallenged ruler of the entire North American continent east of the Mississippi River. Spain controlled the western part of the continent. The French, however, were limited to a few islands in the Caribbean Sea.

Never before had the British Empire been so large. Never before had it seemed so secure. Yet less than two years after the signing of the Treaty of Paris in 1763, many American colonists were openly challenging British authority.

The extent of the empire itself and the British attempts to support it contributed to growing colonial resentment. By 1775 American colonists were exchanging gunfire with British soldiers. Some colonists were even ready to consider a declaration of independence from Great Britain.

1 Problems of Britain's New Empire

Britain's victory over France won vast new territories, but it also brought a host of new problems. British officials had to come to terms with France's Native American allies. They also had to decide whether to allow settlement of the new lands. Furthermore, if settlers were permitted to move into the area, they would have to be protected from the anger of Native Americans defending their lands. Finally, the crown had to cope with the staggering national debt left by the war.

Each of these problems had to be confronted and solved. Ironically, British attempts to do so created new and potentially more disastrous troubles. Inch by inch the problems drove a wedge between the home country and its American colonies that would eventually split the two apart.

An Uneasy Frontier

The question of settlement of lands west of the 13 British colonies demanded an immediate response. At the end of the war, the region was inhabited by many Indian nations, including the Seneca, Delaware, Shawnee, Huron, Ottawa, and Miami. A small number of French farmers and traders also remained. Neither group had heard of the Treaty of Paris, but they were aware that settlers from the British colonies had begun to filter into the area.

Friction between the newcomers and the older inhabitants developed quickly. And, as if this were not enough, several colonies added fuel to the fire by claiming that their boundaries extended all the way to the Pacific. To back up their claims they promptly built a road over the Appalachian Mountains into the Ohio Valley.

Britain tried to head off open conflict by stationing troops under the command of General Jeffrey Amherst in the disputed territory. General Amherst, however, only provoked the Indians when he allowed settlers to build forts in western New York and present-day Ohio, a violation of treaties with the local tribes.

Amherst also infuriated the Indians by refusing to pay them for their land. The French had long cultivated friendly relations with Native Americans by trading supplies and offering gifts and credit. Amherst had no such intentions. He was determined to force the Indians into submission.

In spring 1763 Amherst harvested the fruits of his efforts, but they were hardly what he expected. Pontiac, an Ottawa chief, led the combined forces of the Seneca, the Delaware, the Shawnee, and other western nations in a rebellion against the British. In May and June, Pontiac's alliance captured British forts in various parts of present-day Michigan, Indiana, Wisconsin, and Pennsylvania. Amherst's forces were able to hold Fort Pitt, Fort Detroit, and Fort Niagara.

For a while the uprising, known as Pontiac's Rebellion, was remarkably successful. But Pontiac's coalition eventually faltered when the Native Americans learned they could expect no more help from the French. By December peace had been restored.

A New Approach to Western Settlement

Although the uprising failed, the threat forced the British to review their western land policy. The new policy, issued in the Proclamation of 1763, established a boundary between Native American and colonial lands. The boundary line followed the crest of the Appalachian Mountains. According to the proclamation, no colonists were to settle west of the line. Furthermore, colonists already living there were ordered "forthwith to remove themselves." In the future no one could enter the area without permission from British authorities.

The British government had three goals in attempting to control the settlement of the West. First, it wanted to reduce the cost of protecting settlers by eliminating the major source of friction. Next, it hoped to control the colonists more easily by keeping the majority of them between the Atlantic coast and the Appalachians. Finally, the crown wanted to keep revenue from the western fur trade and land speculation in British rather than in colonial hands. To achieve these aims the British stationed 6,000 troops in the western region.

The colonists welcomed reduction of conflict with the Indians but were annoyed

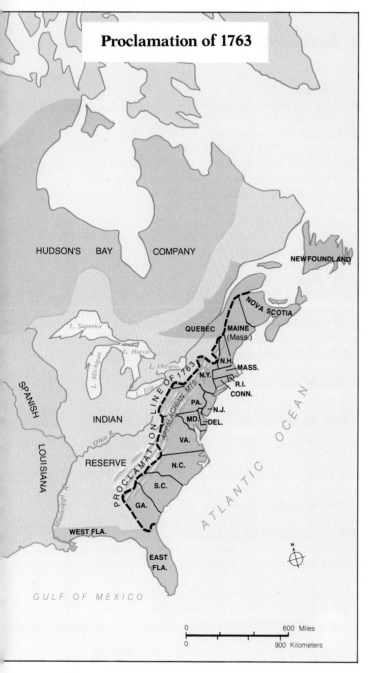

Proclamation of 1763

HUDSON'S   BAY   COMPANY

NEWFOUNDLAND

L. Superior

QUEBEC

NOVA SCOTIA

MAINE (Mass.)

L. Huron

N.H.

L. Ontario

MASS.

L. Erie

PROCLAMATION LINE OF 1763

N.Y.

APPALACHIAN MTS.

R.I.
CONN.

L. Michigan

PA.

N.J.

SPANISH

INDIAN

MD.
DEL.

Ohio R.

VA.

LOUISIANA

RESERVE

N.C.

ATLANTIC OCEAN

S.C.

Mississippi R.

GA.

WEST FLA.

EAST
FLA.

GULF OF MEXICO

N

0   600 Miles

0   900 Kilometers

■ *To reduce friction with Native Americans, the British issued the Proclamation of 1763, which prohibited settlement west of a line along the crest of the Appalachians. Settlers already living in the area were told to abandon their claims and move out of the region.*

with the rest of the western policy. With the French pushed out of the West, many had looked forward to unchecked expansion into the forests of the frontier. Now, the colonists

learned, their movements were to be tightly controlled.

Furthermore, the colonists grew to resent the presence of so many British troops in America. Successes in the French and Indian War had given the colonists a new sense of confidence. And in 1763 most Americans were convinced that they could do with less, not more, supervision by the crown. The colonists' annoyance increased when they discovered that the British expected them to make a larger contribution to the empire's finances.

The Empire's Empty Treasury

When George Grenville became the British chancellor of the exchequer in April 1763, he encountered a national debt that had grown to staggering proportions during the war with France. Before the war, a normal budget had amounted to about 8 million pounds.* Grenville now faced a figure nearly twenty times that much, around 140 million pounds.

Moreover, Grenville discovered that the American colonies were costing Britain more than they brought in. By smuggling, bribery, or both, the colonists managed to evade British customs duties. Yet salaries for colonial customs officials cost the treasury more than 8,000 pounds a year, four times what the officials collected. Grenville was determined that the colonies would be profitable for the crown. He especially wanted colonists to shoulder some of the burden of Britain's war debt. In cooperation with Parliament he designed a series of measures to bring this about.

In April 1764 Parliament passed the Sugar Act, which cut the molasses duty in half. Grenville thus hoped that the colonists would pay the duty rather than evade it. The Sugar Act, however, also levied new duties on indigo, coffee, wine, cloth, and sugar.

The Sugar Act represented an important departure from previous British policy. For years colonists had accepted Parliament's right to regulate colonial trade for the benefit of the parent country. The Sugar Act, however, was intended not only to regulate trade but also to raise revenue. The colonists interpreted this as a form of taxation, and

---

*pound: British monetary unit.

they objected even though their taxes were much lower than taxes in England. (The average tax per person in Massachusetts, for example, was one shilling,* while in England it was 26 shillings.)

The colonists objected not because the tax was a burden but because it came from Parliament. None of the colonies sent representatives to Parliament, and Americans firmly believed that British subjects could not be taxed without the consent of their representatives. American representatives sat in colonial legislatures, they argued. If Britain wanted revenue, it should ask those legislatures to raise it.

By raising revenue through taxes passed by Parliament the British threatened their tradition of "no taxation without representation." If such actions went unchallenged, the colonists realized that participation in colonial government might become meaningless.

Growing Pressures

Grenville and Parliament further irritated the colonists with the Currency Act in 1764 and the Quartering Act in 1765. The Currency Act struck another blow at colonial control of public finance. It prohibited the colonial governments from issuing any more paper money and demanded that they recall immediately all the paper money they had issued during the war. Furthermore, the act stated that all taxes and all debts owed to British merchants be paid only in British currency.

Before the act was passed the Americans had always suffered a shortage of silver currency. Trade restrictions, coupled with the need to import many expensive manufactured goods, forced the colonists to pay out more to Great Britain than they received for their products.

The colonists had eased their situation somewhat by printing their own money and paying debts and taxes with it. Colonial currency, however, was valued at much less than British silver coins and was not worth as much in international trade. While the colonists were getting, in effect, a discount on goods, debts, and taxes, the British were losing money. The Currency Act put a stop to this.

---

*shilling: British coin, equal to ⅟₂₀ of a pound.

The Quartering Act angered the colonists as much as, if not more than, the Currency Act. The measure required the colonists themselves to help support the several thousand British troops stationed in the colonies. Upon demand, Americans were to provide barracks, candles, bedding, and beverages to any soldiers stationed in their area. Such close personal contact with the army intensified the general ill will the colonists felt toward Britain.

The Stamp Act

When Grenville introduced the Sugar Act, he announced that he planned to institute a stamp tax in the colonies similar to one already in effect in Great Britain. He gave the colonists one year to react to the proposal for a stamp tax and to suggest alternative methods of raising money. Both he and Parliament ignored the colonists' complaints, however, and on November 1, 1765, the Stamp Act went into effect.

The act specified that a stamp be affixed to a wide variety of items. The stamp showed that a tax had been paid on an item. All legal documents were taxed, as well as such things as almanacs, newspapers, pamphlets, playing cards, and dice. The tax on newspapers was a half-penny, that on diplomas two pounds.

The Stamp Act aroused intense anger because of its high visibility. Unlike the duties levied by the Sugar and Molasses acts, the stamp impression could not be overlooked, and there seemed to be no way to avoid paying it.

Adding insult to injury, Grenville planned to try offenses involving the Stamp Act in the Vice-Admiralty Courts, denying violators a trial by jury in regular colonial courts. Furthermore, Admiralty Courts were used mainly for cases involving maritime laws. Using them to try other cases appeared to threaten the colonists' cherished liberties.

A Question of Representation

Perhaps most important, the Stamp Act again raised the issue of "taxation without representation." Unlike the Sugar Act, which at least claimed to regulate trade, the Stamp Act was an outright tax. The British government had assumed powers that the colonists felt belonged to their assemblies. Colonists resented being taxed by a legislative body in which they had no representatives.

British officials replied to the colonists' complaints by claiming that all members of Parliament represented all British subjects. Even though the colonists had not elected specific members of Parliament, their interests were represented there. Thus Parliament could tax them.

Although Americans complained loudly, they did not really want to be represented in Parliament. They knew that at a distance of 3,000 miles (4,800 kilometers), necessary communication between representatives and constituents would be impossible. Americans wanted colonial legislatures to continue to be responsible for tax laws, as they always had been. An editorial in the Providence, Rhode Island, *Gazette* summed up the American position.

> It is really a piece of mockery to tell us that a country, detached from Britain by an ocean of immense breadth, and which is so extensive and populous, should be represented by the British members, or that we can have any interest in the House of Commons.

American Reaction

Before the Stamp Act could even take effect, colonists demonstrated that they would back their principles with action. From Massachusetts to South Carolina, mobs often calling themselves the Sons of Liberty stopped stamped papers from being unloaded. Stamp tax collectors all over the colonies began to wonder if their positions were worth the price of the hot tar and feathers the colonists threatened them with.

On the morning of August 14, 1765, a Boston mob hanged the Massachusetts stamp distributor in effigy. Later they destroyed the stamp tax collector's warehouse, tearing it apart board by board. They chopped off the effigy's head, "stamped" its body, and burned the remains in a bonfire made from the timbers of the collector's building. Next they attacked the stamp collector's house and ransacked the rooms. When the Massachusetts lieutenant governor tried to disperse the crowd, they stoned him and chased him off into the night. Satisfied, the mob finally dispersed at midnight.

As this British cartoon made shortly after the repeal of the Stamp Act shows, many people in Great Britain considered the Stamp Act an unwise law. Here British Prime Minister George Grenville (fourth from left) carries a ''coffin'' for the Stamp Act's burial.

Colonists also took more responsible action against the Stamp Act. In October 1765 representatives from nine colonies convened a Stamp Act Congress in New York. They drew up a petition to King George and Parliament, stating their position on Parliament's recent actions.

They granted that the colonies were legally subordinate to Parliament and that the British government had the power to regulate colonial trade. They denied, however, that Britain's legislature had the right to tax the colonists; only the colonial assemblies could rightfully do that. Finally, they asked the king and Parliament to repeal the Stamp and Sugar acts.

Colonial merchants backed up the appeal by resolving to boycott British goods. The Daughters of Liberty, a protest group formed by colonial women, aided the boycott by promoting home cloth manufacturing and signing protest petitions.

The boycott did disrupt the British economy, producing the desired effect. In March 1766 Parliament repealed the Stamp Act. Yet stung by colonial insubordination and fearful that repeal might be interpreted as weakness, Parliament passed the Declaratory Act. This legislation denied the claims of the Stamp Act Congress and in effect reasserted Parliament's authority to tax the colonies.

Consequences of the Stamp Act

The Stamp Act had far-reaching consequences. It created colonial unity where dissension had been the rule. The same colonists who had been unable to agree to a plan of union at the Albany Congress in the 1750s stood together against king and Parliament in the 1760s. While accepting Parliament's right to regulate trade, they firmly rejected its right to tax them.

Perhaps even more important, colonial opposition to the Stamp Act brought to the public arena men whose names would haunt the British in the years to come. Among them were cousins Samuel Adams and John Adams in Massachusetts and Patrick Henry and George Washington in Virginia.

One other Virginian would not emerge into the public eye for some time, but he was present during the Stamp Act debates in the House of Burgesses. A young law student, aged 22, he stood outside the legislature, thrilled by what he called Patrick Henry's "torrents of sublime eloquence." Although he was too young in 1765 to participate in politics, 11 years later his own words would stir the people to revolution. His name was Thomas Jefferson.

For answers, see p. A 19.
Section Review

1. Identify the following: Pontiac, Proclamation of 1763, George Grenville, Sons of Liberty, Stamp Act Congress, Daughters of Liberty.

2. What developments led to Pontiac's Rebellion?

3. (a) How was the Proclamation of 1763 supposed to prevent further conflict in the West? (b) How did the colonists react to the British land policy?

4. In what way was the Sugar Act a departure from Britain's former policy toward the colonies?

5. (a) What were the provisions of the Currency Act? (b) of the Quartering Act? (c) of the Stamp Act?

6. Did Americans want representation in Parliament? Explain.

7. How did the colonists react to the Stamp Act?

8. What were two important consequences of the Stamp Act?

2 The Quarrel Widens

The repeal of the Stamp Act brought universal rejoicing in America, but the same could not be said for Great Britain. The nobility there grumbled that the government had "sacrificed ... gentlemen to the interests of traders and colonists." And the British treasury needed revenue as much as ever. Consequently, the newly appointed chancellor of the exchequer, Charles Townshend, faced the same problems that George Grenville had faced in 1763: making the colonies more profitable and reducing the national debt.

A cartoonist spread the story of the "Patriotick Barber" who, on discovering that his half-shaven customer was a British officer, ejected the officer from his New York shop, shaving cream and all. Such cartoons encouraged American colonists to defy British authority.

The Townshend Acts

Townshend's task was even more difficult than Grenville's because by 1767 the British economy had plunged into a sharp depression. The depression had bred outbursts of violence and demands that taxes be reduced. Townshend allowed Parliament to cut taxes at home, but this made him even more determined to gain additional revenue from the colonies.

In 1767 Parliament passed new revenue measures, which soon became known as the Townshend Acts. Ultimately, they met the same fate as Grenville's legislation—disastrous failure and repeal.

The Townshend Acts placed small customs duties on glass, tea, silk, paper, paint, and lead, all items that the colonists imported from Britain. The revenues from these duties were to be used to pay the expenses of colonial administration, including governors' and judges' salaries. Because the colonial assemblies traditionally paid these expenses, Townshend's measures looked to them like another attack on their authority.

Townshend thought he could convince opponents of the measures by claiming that the duties were merely regulations of trade. After all, he argued, the colonists agreed that Parliament had the right to control trade.

Townshend convinced no one. Americans saw the acts for what they were: taxes to raise money, not duties to encourage trade. In fact the measures even hurt British trade because they encouraged the colonists to manufacture goods rather than to import them from England.

As a protest against the Townshend Acts, merchants from Philadelphia, New York, and Boston signed a *nonimportation agreement* in 1768, vowing not to import certain articles rather than pay the tax. Later they were joined by southern merchants and planters. Colonial-made goods suddenly became fashionable, and colonists scorned English luxury items.

Asserting British Authority

Townshend tried to enforce his measures by firing the customs collectors who had been taking bribes. But to no one's surprise, the new officials turned out to be as corrupt as their predecessors. Customs jobs could be quite profitable. Collectors would frequently seize ships and cargoes and sell them at exorbitant prices. The customs official could then pocket a commission amounting to one third the value of the vessel and its contents. The other two thirds of the sale was divided between the governor and the British treasury.

John Hancock, one of Boston's most prominent merchants, experienced typical treatment at the hands of customs officials. After he threw two customs officials off one of his ships for boarding it illegally, they sought revenge. Hancock's sloop *Liberty* carried a cargo of whale oil and tar. The law required that Hancock post a bond as the ship was being loaded, but officials had been allowing the bond to be paid when the ship sailed.

Using one of the hated *writs of assistance*, documents authorizing unrestricted searches, customs officers boarded the *Liberty*, searched the holds, then ordered ship and cargo seized because the bond had not been posted. The incident demonstrated to many colonists the kind of justice Americans could expect from the British government.

Townshend also tried to enforce the irritating Quartering Act, which the colonial legislatures had largely ignored. Since New York was one of the chief offenders, Townshend decided to single it out as an example to the rest of the colonies. He suspended all meetings of the New York assembly until the Quartering Act was obeyed there.

To the rest of the colonies this threat to the political liberty of New York appeared to be a threat to all. They rallied immediately to the support of New York by drafting letters announcing that they would resist every tax imposed by the crown.

Faced with such hostility, Townshend modified the Quartering Act. Instead of requiring the colonists to open their homes to soldiers, he allowed them to provide barracks, unoccupied dwellings, or barns. Even a weakened Quartering Act, however, demanded a greater British presence than the colonists were ready to tolerate.

The Boston Massacre

In response to repeated pleas from Boston customs commissioners for assistance, the British government agreed to send two regiments of troops to Boston. In September 1768 a sullen town watched as the troops came ashore and set up camp on the Boston

common. For the next year and a half, the citizens of the city did all in their power short of violence to make the soldiers' lives miserable. They shunned them and taunted them behind their backs.

On March 5, 1770, the friction turned to open conflict. A crowd of several hundred colonists gathered in front of the Boston customs house, where ten British soldiers stood guard. The crowd began jeering and cursing the soldiers, pelting them with oyster shells, snowballs, sticks, and slivers of ice. At least one member of the mob had a cutlass, and another carried a pistol.

Captain Thomas Preston, the commander of the guard, ordered his men to hold steady and not to fire. Unfortunately, someone—whether a soldier or a member of the crowd is unknown—fired a gun, and a volley of shots from British muskets followed. When the shooting stopped, five of the crowd lay dead or mortally wounded on the street. The first to die was Crispus Attucks, a black sailor active in the Sons of Liberty. His wounds killed him almost immediately. The colonial press called the incident the Boston Massacre.

Preston and his troops stood trial in Boston later that year. John Adams accepted the

Boston silversmith Paul Revere made this famous propaganda engraving of the Boston Massacre. The engraving was widely circulated in the colonies as evidence of British arrogance. The first colonist to be killed was Crispus Attucks, a black sailor, who is not shown in Revere's engraving.

unpleasant duty of defending them in court, in the belief that British soldiers as well as American colonists had the right to a legal defense. Just as crucial was his feeling that the American cause would lose its moral advantage if the soldiers could not get a fair trial in Boston.

Adams obtained deathbed testimony from one of the five men who had been mortally wounded by the British soldiers. The dying man swore that the crowd, not the troops, had been to blame for the Boston Massacre. As a result of this testimony, the worst penalty any of the soldiers received was a branding on the hand.

Repeal at Last

News of the Boston Massacre soon reached Britain, where it contributed to growing concern about the colonies. Clearly, the Townshend Acts were not working. Little tax money flowed to British coffers, and by 1769 the nonimportation agreements had reduced trade at least to some degree. Americans themselves had begun to manufacture paint, glass, paper, and lead products. This new American economic independence represented one of the least desirable developments possible.

Ironically, Charles Townshend had died in 1767 and never saw the problems his taxes had created. In 1770 George III appointed Lord North as prime minister. Both men agreed completely about how to run the colonies. Thus, for the next 12 years, King George would stand firmly behind his prime minister.

Upon taking office, Lord North convinced Parliament to allow the unpopular Quartering Act to expire. Parliament also repealed all the Townshend taxes, except the one on tea, guessing correctly that the repeal would end the American boycott of British goods. The remaining tax on tea guaranteed that at least some money would come into the government's treasury, since the colonists consumed a lot of tea. The tax also served as a reminder that Parliament claimed the right to tax the colonists.

Resistance to Parliamentary measures broke down in America. On the surface, the colonies were calmer than they had been at any time since 1764. Nevertheless, the colonists had been shaken. They had begun, for the first time, to think more clearly about their political rights.

For answers, see p. A 19.

Section Review

1. Identify the following: Charles Townshend, the Townshend Acts, the Boston Massacre, John Adams, Lord North.
2. Define the following terms: nonimportation agreement, writs of assistance.
3. (a) How were the Townshend Acts supposed to raise revenue? (b) Did they work? Explain.
4. (a) How did Townshend try to enforce the Quartering Act? (b) What was the colonists' reaction?
5. What incident sparked the Boston Massacre?
6. (a) What developments convinced the British to repeal the Townshend Acts? (b) What two reasons did they have for keeping the tax on tea?

3 The Roots of Independence

The 1770s began in an atmosphere of deceptive calm. Although Lord North's repeal of the Townshend Acts had taken the edge off colonial anger, suspicion and mistrust remained. For the time being, those feelings were quiet. If new conflicts occurred, however, those suspicions would be awakened and passions would become inflamed once again.

Beginning in 1772, a disturbing series of events convinced Americans that the British were conspiring to take away their rights.

Looking back on these events years later, George Washington would conclude that the evidence of British tyranny had been "as clear as the sun in its meridian brightness."

Tensions Renewed

Early in 1772 the British government renewed its challenge to colonial self-rule. Parliament passed an act stating that the crown would henceforth pay the salaries of royal governors and judges in the colonies, formerly the responsibility of the colonial assemblies. Throughout the 1760s the colonies had staunchly resisted attempts like Townshend's to curtail or remove the responsibility. The colonists realized that the assemblies would have little control over governors and judges who no longer depended on them for their salaries. When Governor Thomas Hutchinson of Massachusetts announced the new law, the reaction was swift and unfavorable.

That same month another incident further heightened tensions. A British warship, the *Gaspee*, patrolled Rhode Island's Narragansett Bay to enforce customs regulations. The *Gaspee* also harassed the local inhabitants. Its captain and crew frequently seized small boats engaged in local trade, cut down orchards for firewood, and stole farmers' livestock. One day, while on a routine patrolling mission near Providence, the *Gaspee* ran aground. That night, the people of Providence burned the ship.

The British government quite correctly believed that the Rhode Island officials would do nothing to round up the offenders, so it appointed a special investigative commission of its own. The commission found no Rhode Islanders willing to testify, and the investigation failed. Nevertheless, the very existence of such a commission made the colonists edgy. They feared that if Britain could bypass the colonial courts, it might shut them down permanently.

These and other incidents (for example, the tarring and feathering of a customs officer on Boston's streets and the seizing of a revenue ship on the Delaware River) increased friction between the British and the colonists. Until 1773, however, there was no clear-cut renewal of old hostilities. In that year, the lull broke once and for all.

The Tea Act

The British East India Company, a private investment company similar to the London and Plymouth companies of the seventeenth century, managed British interests in India. Among these interests was the exporting and marketing of Indian tea.

During the 1760s the European economy had been depressed and the East India Company's business had declined. This left the company with substantial stocks of un-

Respectable colonial merchants routinely smuggled goods past British tax collectors, even though British warships like the Gaspee *patrolled the coastal waters. When the* Gaspee *went aground off Providence, Rhode Island, gleeful colonists in Indian disguises rowed out and burned it.*

sold tea, much of it originally designated for the American market.

In part, the company's problems resulted from British trade restrictions. The East India Company could sell its tea only to British wholesalers, not on the open market. The wholesalers, in turn, sold the tea to American distributors who then resold it to retail merchants. By the time the tea had reached the colonial market it had been marked up four times.

Dutch tea, on the other hand, was smuggled into the colonies directly from the East Indies. Wholesalers and customs officials were bypassed, making the tea much cheaper than that sold by the East India Company. Needless to say, the colonists preferred it.

In 1773 Parliament tried to boost the company's fortunes by passing the Tea Act. The measure allowed the East India Company to sell its tea directly to American retailers. In addition, the act eliminated Britain's own import tax on tea. When the tea arrived in the colonies, only one duty had to be paid on it, the small tax remaining from the original Townshend Acts. (See page 108.) As a result, East India Company tea would cost no more than Dutch tea.

A Tempest Over Tea

The solution looked good to Parliament. Americans would get cheaper tea and pay more taxes, and the crown would gain revenue. The plan, however, cut most American merchants out of the tea trade.

Soon, colonial tea merchants began to complain about losing business. They warned that other merchants might suffer the same fate before long. All over the colonies the tea tax became a symbol of British oppression. The American spirit of independence had been aroused again.

The enraged colonists acted as quickly as they complained. For the third time since 1763, a colonial boycott went into effect. East India tea rotted on the waterfronts up and down the American coast. Women brewed "liberty teas" from local plants, signed anti-tea declarations, and formed anti-tea leagues.

In Boston, Governor Thomas Hutchinson decided to force the issue. He believed that unless the Tea Act were enforced, British control over the American colonies would end. In December 1773 he ordered East India tea ships in Boston harbor to tie up along the wharves and unload their cargoes.

The Sons of Liberty responded immediately. On the night of December 16, a gang of 30 to 60 men thinly disguised as Indians boarded the East India ships and dumped the tea into the harbor. The incident became known as the Boston Tea Party.

The Intolerable Acts

When Lord North received news of Boston's defiance, he lost all patience. He felt that "New England fanatics," as he called them, were undermining all British authority in the colonies. Both North and George III agreed that the time had come to force the colonists to obey.

Since Boston was the center of colonial resistance, Lord North and the king decided to make an example of Massachusetts. In 1774 they imposed the Coercive Acts, hoping that the retaliation would spread fear throughout the colonies and force them into submission.

First, the acts closed the port of Boston. Second, they revoked the Massachusetts charter, prohibiting the Massachusetts legislature and courts from holding sessions. Military rule was imposed on the colony, and General Thomas Gage, commander of all British troops in North America, became governor of the colony. The acts also forbade town meetings, placing even local government under military control.

More troops arrived in Boston to reinforce the existing garrison. By the time the new arrivals stopped coming, the Boston contingent totaled 4,000 men, one British soldier for every four Bostonians.

Finally, the Coercive Acts revived the old Quartering Act, giving General Gage the authority to house all his troops in Boston, in private residences if need be. Furthermore, any British officials who committed crimes while enforcing the acts would be tried in Britain, not in America. The colonials saw that last provision in particular as a mockery of justice.

The Quebec Act, an attempt to secure the loyalty of the French-Canadians to Britain, soon followed. This act gave the French-Canadians freedom to practice their Catholic faith and expanded the boundaries of Quebec west and south to the Mississippi and Ohio rivers.

The act was not intended to punish the colonies, but the colonists east of the Appalachians regarded the expansion of Quebec's borders as an insult. They felt that Britain had deliberately created an obstacle to westward expansion.

Ultimately, the Intolerable Acts, as the colonists labeled the Coercive Acts and the Quebec Act, helped forge the colonies into a united front. Before a workable alliance between the colonies could be created, however, major differences had to be overcome.

To Submit or Unite?

Thirteen separate and often disparate governments found it difficult to work together, as the Albany Congress of 1754 had demonstrated. Furthermore, the colonies occupied a vast region with varied climate and geography. The economies and social systems of the colonies differed, too, ranging from the sprawling plantations of the South to the compact farms of New England.

Yet, the forces for unity were stronger than the differences that set the colonies apart. Up and down a territory 1,500 miles long and several hundred miles wide, most colonists spoke a common language and shared common traditions of government.

When Parliament and the crown acted to deny what the colonists saw as their "English liberties," Americans began to recognize how much the thirteen colonies had in common.

This sense of unity grew as colonists learned more about the issues of the day. Communication increased as newspapers spread reports of events from colony to colony. In pamphlets writers examined vital issues in depth and called for greater resistance to British tyranny.

Committees of Correspondence

The most effective means of developing a united colonial front proved to be the Committees of Correspondence. First organized by Samuel Adams in 1772 to connect Boston

Considered by some the first political cartoon in America, this sketch urged the 13 colonies to unite or be pulled apart by the British. Colonial leaders such as Benjamin Franklin felt that only if the colonies worked together could they stand up to British power.

The Local Tavern: A Communication Center

Colonists read handbills, pamphlets, and local newspapers for news about developments between Great Britain and the colonies during the crucial years of the early 1770s. But casual gatherings at local taverns were often even more important. Not only could people hear the latest news, they could also discuss events with one another and plan possible actions to take. In the excerpt below John Adams describes one conversation he heard at a tavern in Shrewsbury, Massachusetts, in 1774.

> Within the course of the year, before the meeting of Congress in 1774, on a journey to some of our circuit courts in Massachusetts, I stopped one night at a tavern in Shrewsbury about forty miles from Boston, and as I was cold and wet, I sat down at a good fire in the bar-room to dry my great-coat and saddle-bags, till a fire could be made in my chamber. There presently came in, one after another, half a dozen, or half a score substantial yeomen of the neighborhood, who, sitting down to the fire after lighting their pipes, began a lively conversation on politics. As I believed I was unknown to all of them, I sat in total silence to hear them. One said, "The people of Boston are distracted." Another answered, "No wonder the people of Boston are distracted. Oppression will make wise men mad." A third said, "What would you say if a fellow should come to your house and tell you he was come to take a list of your cattle, that Parliament might tax you for them at so much a head? And how should you feel if he was to go and break open your barn or take down your oxen, cows, horses, and sheep?" "What should I say?" replied the first. "I would knock him in the head." "Well," said a fourth, "if Parliament can take away Mr. Hancock's wharf and Mr. Rowe's wharf, they can take away your barn and my house." After much more reasoning in this style, a fifth, who had as yet been silent, broke out: "Well, it's high time for us to rebel; we must rebel some time or other, and we had better rebel now than at any time to come. If we put it off for ten or twenty years, and let them go on as they have begun, they will get a strong party among us, and plague us a great deal more than they can now."

Among the most effective American propagandists was Mercy Otis Warren of Plymouth, Massachusetts. She wrote and published many political satires and plays, all anonymously, although her close friends Abigail and John Adams knew of her authorship. This 1763 painting is by John Singleton Copley.

A decisive step toward unity came in 1774. After the royal governor of Virginia dissolved the House of Burgesses, members of the assembly met in a Williamsburg tavern. They declared that the Intolerable Acts threatened the liberty of all the colonies, and they called for a meeting of delegates from each colony to discuss the legislation. The Committees of Correspondence quickly communicated Virginia's declaration to the rest of the colonies. Soon, colonial assemblies were at work electing delegates to the First Continental Congress.

When the meeting convened in Carpenters' Hall at Philadelphia in September 1774, all 13 colonies except Georgia were represented. As the delegates assembled, they knew their first task was to decide on a response to the Intolerable Acts. Yet another more unsettling question probably lingered in the back of their minds. At some future date, would the colonies have only one recourse left—independence?

For answers, see p. A 20.
Section Review

1. Identify the following: *Gaspee*, British East India Company, Boston Tea Party, Intolerable Acts, Committees of Correspondence, Samuel Adams.
2. How did the *Gaspee* incident worry the colonists?
3. (a) What was the purpose of the Tea Act? (b) How did the colonists react?
4. (a) What was the purpose of the Coercive Acts? (b) What measures were taken against Boston?
5. How did effective communication contribute to colonial unity?
6. Why did the First Continental Congress meet?

to the rural towns of Massachusetts, committees existed in every colony by 1774.

The Committees of Correspondence kept colonists from north to south and east to west continuously informed of developments in the struggle with Britain. For instance, when the Committees of Correspondence spread the word that the Coercive Acts had closed the port of Boston, the response was instantaneous and supportive. South Carolina sent rice to the beleaguered colony, and Pennsylvania sent flour.

All along, the committees made sure that every incident was reported as an attack on American liberty. One British sympathizer called the committees "the foulest, subtlest, and most venomous serpent ever issued from the egg of sedition."

4 From Protest to Revolution

What could be done about the Intolerable Acts? This question was the first order of business before the Continental Congress, and the delegates had different answers.

The moderates, led by Joseph Galloway and John Dickinson of Pennsylvania, wanted to patch up the quarrel with Great Britain. The radicals, following Samuel and John Adams of Massachusetts, Charles Thomson of Pennsylvania, and Patrick Henry of Vir-

ginia, felt the time had come to take a stronger stand. They wanted either to force Britain to agree completely with their demands or to declare total independence.

Defining Relations With Britain

At first the moderates seemed to be making headway at the Congress. Under Galloway's leadership they proposed a union of the colonies under British authority. Colonial legislatures would retain the powers they had before 1763, but Parliament still would be able to pass legislation affecting the colonies. Galloway proposed, however, that Parliament's acts could be vetoed by a "grand council" of American representatives.

Galloway's plan was defeated in a close vote, in large part because of the hard work of Samuel Adams. Adams, complained Galloway, was a man who "eats little, sleeps little, thinks much, and is most decisive . . . in the pursuit of his objects."

With the defeat of Galloway's plan, the radicals increasingly dominated the Congress. They no longer accepted the American position of 1765 that Parliament had the right to regulate the trade of the colonies. Instead they accepted a new theory outlined in a pamphlet written by Thomas Jefferson, *A Summary View of the Rights of British America.*

Jefferson argued that just as Parliament had no right to tax the colonies, so it could not legislate for them either. The only connection between the colonies and Great Britain, he asserted, was the king. For Jefferson and the radicals, the British empire was not a single, undivided whole. Rather it was a loose union of more or less independent states. Each had its own legislature, which acted as a little parliament, and all were united by a shared loyalty to the king.

The Congress's most significant document, *Declaration and Resolves,* attacked the Coercive Acts and the Quebec Act as well as all revenue measures passed by Parliament since 1763. Citing both "the immutable laws of nature," "the principles of the English constitution," and the original colonial charters, the *Declaration and Resolves* demanded the repeal of all oppressive legislation.

A Step Toward Economic Independence

The First Continental Congress also took other decisive actions. Urged on by Samuel Adams, the delegates approved a set of resolutions that had been adopted in Suffolk County, Massachusetts. These resolutions, known as the Suffolk Resolves, called upon the people of Massachusetts to openly disobey the Coercive Acts because they were illegal. The resolutions also recommended that the colonists prepare to defend themselves against possible attack by the British at Boston.

The Congress further voted for an immediate and complete end to trade with Great Britain. To see that this was carried

■ *Colonists boycotted British goods in 1765 and 1766 to protest the Stamp Act, in late 1768 and 1769 to protest the Townshend Acts, and again in 1775 and 1776. This graph shows the effects of these boycotts on the value of colonial imports from Great Britain.*

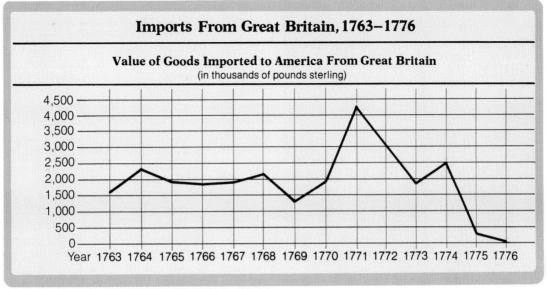

Imports From Great Britain, 1763–1776

Value of Goods Imported to America From Great Britain
(in thousands of pounds sterling)

Source: *Historical Statistics of the United States*

out, the delegates formed a continental Association. Committees were to be set up in every city, county, and town to insure that no colony imported or consumed British goods or exported American goods to Britain. By April 1775 committees were operating in 12 colonies.

Before adjourning on October 26, 1774, the delegates agreed to meet again the following spring. Little did they know that by that time an incident in Massachusetts would set forces in motion that would sever the colonies from Great Britain forever.

Lexington and Concord

Over the winter of 1774–1775, Massachusetts protestors formed a militia, calling themselves *minutemen* because they would be

Minuteman Amos Doolittle made detailed engravings of the first skirmish of the Revolution. In this drawing, two British commanders scout the terrain around the Concord cemetery as their brilliantly clad troops march toward the center of the village—where colonial minutemen awaited them.

ready to fight on a moment's notice. The minutemen took seriously the Continental Congress's commitment to colonial self-defense. They did not have long to wait for a hostile move by the British troops.

As winter turned into spring, General Thomas Gage, commander of the British forces in Boston, received orders to round up the leaders of the colonial resistance. At first he hesitated, unwilling to provoke open conflict. However, when news arrived that the colonists had an arsenal of weapons and powder at Concord, Gage acted. On April 18 he sent nearly 1,000 soldiers under Major John Pitcairn to seize the arsenal. Pitcairn, who believed that the resistance movement could be smothered easily with a "small action" and the burning of a few towns, looked forward to doing the job.

Pitcairn and his men set out from Boston at night, hoping to surprise the colonists at daybreak. But as the soldiers tramped over the countryside, William Dawes and Paul Revere galloped to villages and farms to warn the minutemen. At sunrise, when the British reached Lexington, 70 minutemen commanded by Captain John Parker waited on the village green. Pitcairn ordered the minutemen to disperse, and Parker gave the order to retreat. Then someone—no one knows who—fired a shot. After a brief skirmish, eight Americans lay dead and ten more lay wounded on the new spring grass. Only one British soldier received a wound, and that was slight.

Delayed no more than 15 minutes, Pitcairn pushed on to Concord. He entered the village without resistance at eight o'clock but found few of the military supplies he had been sent to seize. To protect his main body of troops while they searched, Pitcairn ordered a covering party to North Bridge, just outside the village center. There, the British met 300 minutemen, and a British trooper fired "the shot heard 'round the world."

After a five-minute exchange of fire, Pitcairn began his retreat. By then, over 3,000 minutemen lined the woods, fields, and stone fences along the road to Boston. Pitcairn's command barely made it back to Lexington. There 1,200 British reinforcements, wisely sent by General Gage, rescued them. By the time the British ran the entire "bloody chute" back to Boston, 73 of their men had been killed, with

Give Me Liberty or Give Me Death

On March 28, 1775, Patrick Henry rose to address the Virginia Convention of Delegates. For almost ten years Henry had actively opposed Britain's attempts to impose taxation without representation on the American colonists. As the excerpt from his speech clearly shows, by 1775 he had lost patience with words and was demanding action.

Let us not deceive ourselves, sir. These are the implements of war and subjugation; the last arguments to which kings resort. I ask gentlemen, sir, what means this martial array, if its purpose be not to force us to submission? Can gentlemen assign any other possible motives for it? Has Great Britain any enemy, in this quarter of the world, to call for all this accumulation of navies and armies? No, sir, she has none. They are meant for us; they can be meant for no other. They are sent over to bind and rivet upon us those chains which the British ministry have been so long forging. And what have we to oppose to them? Shall we try argument? Sir, we have been trying that for the last ten years. . . . Sir, we have done everything that could be done . . . and we have been spurned, with contempt, from the foot of the throne. . . . We must fight! I repeat it, sir, we must fight! . . .

Gentlemen may cry peace, peace—but there is no peace. The war is actually begun! The next gale that sweeps from the north will bring to our ears the clash of resounding arms! Our brethren are already in the field. Why stand we here idle? . . . Is life so dear, or peace so sweet, as to be purchased at the price of chains and slavery? Forbid it, Almighty God! I know not what course others may take; but as for me, give me liberty, or give me death!

---

another 200 wounded or missing. In contrast, the Americans had only 93 casualties.

On April 22 the Massachusetts provincial congress voted to raise 13,600 troops, to be commanded by Artemas Ward. Within a week, Boston was a city under seige. When the Continental Congress gathered again in Philadelphia on May 10, 1775, it had a fight on its hands.

For answers, see p. A 20.
Section Review

1. Identify the following: Joseph Galloway, Thomas Jefferson, *Declaration and Resolves*, Suffolk Resolves, Association, minutemen.

2. (a) What plan did the moderates propose to the Continental Congress? (b) Did the plan succeed? Explain.

3. How did the radicals' attitude toward Parliament differ from that of most colonists?

4. (a) What action did the First Continental Congress take to establish greater economic independence? (b) How was this to be carried out?

5. What information convinced General Gage to act against the colonists?

Major Events

1763	Pontiac's Rebellion; Proclamation of 1763
1764	Parliament passes Sugar Act and Currency Act
1765	Quartering Act passed; Stamp Act goes into effect; colonists hold Stamp Act Congress
1766	Parliament repeals Stamp Act
1767	Parliament passes Townshend Acts
1770	Boston Massacre; repeal of Townshend Acts except tax on tea
1772	Rhode Island residents burn the *Gaspee*
1773	Parliament passes Tea Act; Boston Tea Party
1774	Parliament passes Coercive Acts; First Continental Congress meets
1775	First military conflict between British and colonists at Lexington and Concord

115

For answers, see p. A 20.

Lexington and Concord: Analyzing a Primary Source

Two types of written sources can be used to learn about historical events: primary sources and secondary sources. *Primary sources* are first-hand accounts usually written by a person who was closely involved in the event being described. They include government documents, letters, diaries, and eyewitness newspaper accounts. *Secondary sources* are second-hand accounts of historical events based on a study of primary sources and other secondary sources. Most history books, including this textbook, are secondary sources.

Both types of sources provide factual information about an historical event, but primary sources also provide insight into the feelings, attitudes, and motives of the people involved in the event. Because the author is closely involved in the event, however, he or she may not give a totally objective or accurate account of the event. Thus when using a primary source it is important to analyze its reliability.

Carefully read the document at right. Then use the steps described below to analyze it.

1. **Identify the nature of the document by asking yourself the following questions.** (a) What type of document is it? For example, is it a letter, a diary entry, or a government document? (b) Who wrote the document? Was he or she closely involved in the event? (c) When was it written?

2. **Decide how reliable the source is.** To do this you need to analyze several other characteristics of the document and of the author. The following questions will help you judge the reliability of this document. (a) Why did the author write the document? (b) What was the author's role in the event described? Could that have affected what was reported? Explain. (c) Was the author British or American? How can you tell? How could that have affected what was reported? (d) Would you say this is a reliable source? What should you watch out for when you use it?

3. **Study the source to learn more about an historical event.** As you study the document for information, distinguish between facts and opinions. A *fact* is something that is true and that can be proven. An *opinion* is a judgment that reflects a person's feelings, beliefs, or attitudes. Use the report of Lieutenant-Colonel Smith to Governor Gage and your textbook to answer the following questions. (a) What facts about the fighting at Lexington and Concord can you learn from this document? (b) What was the author's opinion of the colonists' actions at Lexington?

What was the author's opinion of British intentions? (c) Did the author think the colonists had planned the attacks on the British as they marched back to Boston? Why or why not? Is this a fact or an opinion? (d) How would you describe the British feelings toward the fighting based on this document?

Report of Lieutenant-Colonel Smith to Governor Gage, April 22, 1775

SIR,—In obedience to your Excellency's commands, I marched on the evening of the 18th with the corps of grenadiers and light infantry for Concord, to execute your Excellency's orders with respect to destroying all ammunition, artillery, tents, &c, collected there. . . . When I had got some miles on the march from Boston, I detached six light infantry companies. . . . On these companies' arrival at Lexington, I understand, from the report of Major Pitcairn, who was with them, and from many officers, that they found on a green close to the road a body of the country people drawn up in military order, with arms. . . . Our troops advanced towards them, without any intention of injuring them, further than to inquire the reason of their being thus assembled, and, if not satisfactory, to have secured their arms; but they in confusion went off, principally to the left, only one of them fired before he went off, and three or four more jumped over a wall and fired from behind it among the soldiers; on which the troops returned it, and killed several of them. . . .

While at Concord we saw vast numbers assembling in many parts; at one of the bridges they marched down, with a very considerable body, on the light infantry posted there. On their coming pretty near, one of our men fired on them, which they returned; on which an action ensued and some few were killed. . . .

On our leaving Concord to return to Boston, they began to fire on us from behind the walls, ditches, trees, &c which as we marched, increased to a very great degree, and continued . . . for, I believe, upwards of eighteen miles; so that I can't think but it must have been a preconcerted scheme in them, to attack the King's troops the first favorable opportunity that offered, otherwise, I think they could not, in so short a time from our marching out, have raised such a numerous body, and for so great a space of ground.

I have the honor, &c,
F. Smith, Lieutenant-Colonel 10th Foot.

IN PERSPECTIVE   In 1763, after its victory in the French and Indian War, Great Britain was the undisputed ruler of North America east of the Mississippi River. The British as well as the American colonists looked forward to a prosperous future. Yet the problems of governing the new empire gradually drove a wedge between the British and the colonists.

Britain's land policy prohibiting settlement in the West irritated some colonists, as did the arrival of more British troops to police the area. But the most serious problem was the need for money to support the empire. Attempts through the Sugar Act, the Stamp Act, and the Townshend Acts to impose taxes to raise money rather than to control trade met with growing resistance in the colonies.

In the early 1770s tensions increased further as the British government tried to enforce its legislation. After Parliament passed the Coercive Acts, colonial representatives met at the First Continental Congress to protest the acts and to take the first steps toward economic independence from Great Britain. The first military clash between British troops and colonial militia took place soon afterward at Lexington and Concord. The step of declaring total independence seemed to be only a matter of time.

For answers, see p. A 21.

Chapter Review

1. (a) Why did Pontiac lead the western Indian nations in a rebellion against the British? (b) What impact did the rebellion have on British policy?

2. (a) Describe the measures George Grenville and Parliament took to ease Britain's national debt. (b) How did the colonists react to each measure? (c) Why did they react that way?

3. (a) What were the Townshend Acts? (b) How did the British try to enforce them? (c) How did the colonists react?

4. (a) Why did the Tea Act symbolize British oppression to the colonists? (b) What actions did they take to oppose this act?

5. (a) Describe the Coercive Acts. (b) Why did the colonists consider the Quebec Act a threat? (c) How did these so-called Intolerable Acts help unify the colonies?

6. (a) What was the major question facing the First Continental Congress? (b) What actions did it take?

7. (a) How did the position of the moderates at the First Continental Congress differ from the position of the radicals? (b) Which position seemed to dominate by the end of the Congress?

8. How did the Suffolk Resolves probably help set the stage for the outbreak of fighting at Lexington and Concord?

For answers, see p. A 21.

For Further Thought

1. (a) Why did the colonists consider the Sugar Act (1764) and the Stamp Act (1765) to be taxation without representation? (b) How did these acts differ from the Molasses Act (1733)? (c) What body did the colonists think had authority to tax them? Why?

2. Look up a definition of the word "massacre" in a dictionary. Why do you think the incident in Boston was called a massacre in the colonial press when only five people were killed?

For answers, see p. A 21.

Developing Basic Skills

1. *Graph Reading*   Study the graph on page 113. Then answer the following questions: (a) During what years were the nonimportation agreements most effective? Least effective? (b) What might explain this difference?

2. *Map Reading*   Study the map on page 102. Then answer the following questions: (a) What served as a natural boundary for the Proclamation Line of 1763? (b) For whom was the land west of the Proclamation Line intended? (c) What country claimed the territory west of the Mississippi River? (d) How effective do you think the Proclamation Line would be?

See page 774 for suggested readings.

7

A War for Independence

(1775–1783)

Detail from *The Battle of Bunker Hill.*

Relations between Britain and its American colonies grew steadily worse during the 1770s. The British seemed determined to maintain their authority, while the colonists vigorously defended their rights. Yet even when fighting broke out at Lexington and Concord, few expected it to evolve into a war for complete independence.

The decision to declare independence came at the Second Continental Congress, as you will read in this chapter. The Declaration of Independence adopted by the Congress outlasted the struggle at hand. It articulated political and social ideals that would play a major role in shaping the new nation.

Before the American colonies could become truly independent, however, they had to fight a long and often bitter war. These years of sacrifice and determination resulted in victory and the creation of a new republic.

1 The Revolution Begins

Once fighting had broken out between American colonists and British soldiers, colonial leaders realized the need for a unified and coordinated plan of action. Meeting once again in Philadelphia in 1775, the delegates to the Second Continental Congress took a step far more radical than skirmishing with British troops. The following year they would declare independence from Great Britain.

Declaring independence, however, did not make the colonies independent. The crown was prepared to fight for its American possessions. To achieve their goal, the colonies would have to fight as well. That step demanded that the Americans meet the British with a real army.

The Opening of the Second Continental Congress

On May 10, 1775, less than a month after the outbreak of fighting at Lexington and Concord, the Second Continental Congress convened in Philadelphia. Delegates from each of the colonies except Georgia, who joined the rest a few months later, assembled in the Pennsylvania statehouse, a simple impressive brick building with a white steeple.

The inscription on the steeple's bell reflected the feelings of many delegates: "Proclaim liberty throughout all the land unto all the inhabitants thereof." Over the main entrance to the building, however, was King George III's coat of arms. As the delegates walked into the statehouse, few could have avoided noticing this visible reminder of other sentiments—the colonies' past loyalty to the crown.

The Liberty Bell and the king's coat of arms symbolized the most significant question facing the delegates: where did their loyalties lie? The moderates, led by John Dickinson of Pennsylvania, still wanted to negotiate an agreement with Britain. The radicals, following John and Samuel Adams, clamored for independence.

The radicals had public opinion on their side. Throughout the colonies citizens were forming Committees of Safety to recruit and train local militia, collect funds and supplies, gather information, and disrupt the activities of the king's representatives. One traveler reported, "Wherever you go, you see the inhabitants training, making firelocks, [and] casting mortars, shells and shot."

The radicals also benefited from the superb political skills of Samuel and John Adams. Both worked tirelessly and skillfully to prod the moderates ever closer to independence. In private John Adams complained about the Congress's lengthy debates, but in public he was more than willing to argue, cajole, and then wait. At one point he described America as "a great unwieldy body. It is like a large fleet sailing under convoy. The fleetest sailors must wait for the dullest and the slowest."

The Colonists Take Action

Adams did not have to wait long. Events rapidly drove most of the delegates toward a decision for independence. On the morning of May 10, the same day that the Second Continental Congress convened, Ethan Allen and his band of 83 volunteers, called the Green Mountain Boys, surprised and captured a sleepy British garrison at Fort Ticonderoga in New York. Within a few days, the news reached Philadelphia.

A little over a month later, fighting broke out again. For weeks both the British and the Americans had been pouring troops and supplies into the Boston area, the center of radical agitation. On June 12 the British declared that the city and surrounding area were under military command. When the local Committee of Safety discovered that British troops planned to move onto the heights overlooking the city, they devised a countermove. On the night of June 16, American General Israel Putnam occupied and fortified Breed's Hill and Bunker Hill.

The next morning more than 1,500 British troops launched a frontal attack on the heights, with each soldier carrying a full pack of almost 125 pounds. Positioned securely on the hills, Putnam cautioned his inexperienced troops to conserve their ammunition. "Don't fire until you see the whites of their eyes!" he warned them.

Withering fire from American guns forced the British back twice. Reinforced with fresh troops, the British prepared for a third attack. They threw off their heavy packs, fixed their bayonets, and stormed the heights. But this time they met only sporadic fire. The Americans, with dwindling supplies of powder and no bayonets, had held their ground as long as they could. They were unable to withstand a third British assault.

The British captured the entire area around Charlestown, but they paid a high price for it. Over 1,000 soldiers were killed or wounded, including a number of officers. The Americans lost only 397 soldiers.

The Battle of Bunker Hill was a technical victory for the British but a moral victory for the Americans. Colonial forces had proved they could hold their own against better trained and better equipped troops. Now they could enter the struggle in earnest—and with some hope of winning.

Beginnings of a Continental Army

Two weeks after the battle at Bunker Hill, Massachusetts asked the Continental Congress to take control of the army that had begun to form in the Boston area. Congress then established an army of 20,000 men and unanimously appointed George Washington commander in chief.

Although the forty-three-year-old Washington had limited military experience, he brought a valuable combination of qualities to the job. As a southerner, he broadened colonial support for what had been seen as a New England war. As a natural leader, he knew how to command the respect of the officers and soldiers in the army. And as an early supporter of independence, he had the trust of the delegates to the Continental Congress.

Shortly after his appointment, Washington left Philadelphia for Cambridge, Massachusetts, to take command of an undisciplined force of about 14,000 men. The task he faced would have overwhelmed a lesser man. From a motley group of local militia and volunteers, Washington had to build a continental army. Fortunately, the British, troubled by their heavy casualties at Bunker Hill, remained inactive and gave him time.

Washington also had much to learn. He knew little about directing large groups of soldiers, less about military strategy, and virtually nothing about the use of artillery.

The Sword of Bunker Hill

The showing of the American troops at Bunker Hill was important for the colonists' morale, and the Battle of Bunker Hill became a source of great pride, as you can see in this Revolutionary War song.

He lay upon his dying bed;
His eye was growing dim,
When with a feeble voice he call'd
His weeping son to him:
"Weep not, my boy!" the vet'ran said,
"I bow to Heav'n's high will,—
But quickly from yon antlers bring
The Sword of Bunker Hill;
But quickly from yon antlers bring
The Sword of Bunker Hill."

The sword was bro't, the soldier's eye
Lit with a sudden flame;
And as he grasp'd the ancient blade,
He murmured Warren's name:
Then said, "My boy, I leave you gold,—
But what is richer still,
I leave you, mark me, mark me now—

The Sword of Bunker Hill;
I leave you, mark me, mark me now—
The Sword of Bunker Hill.

"'Twas on that dread, immortal day,
I dared the Briton's band,
A captain raised this blade on me—
I tore it from his hand;
And while the glorious battle raged,
It lightened freedom's will—
For boy, the God of freedom blessed
The Sword of Bunker Hill;
For, boy the God of freedom blessed
The Sword of Bunker Hill.

"Oh, keep the sword!"—his accents broke—
A smile—and he was dead!
His wrinkled hand still grasped the blade
Upon that dying bed.
The son remains; the sword remains—
Its glory growing still—
And twenty millions bless the sire,
And Sword of Bunker Hill;
And twenty millions bless the sire,
And sword of Bunker Hill.

Furthermore, his staff, appointed by the Continental Congress, consisted of a few well-meaning but poorly qualified officers. Israel Putnam, or Old Put, as he was known, had Bunker Hill behind him as well as some combat experience during the French and Indian War. But another officer, Artemas Ward, reportedly "had no acquaintance whatever with military affairs."

Two generals, Horatio Gates and Charles Lee, resisted Washington's command because they had had wider military experience as officers in the British Army. In time Washington developed a corps of capable officers: Nathanael Greene, Anthony Wayne, Daniel Morgan, and Henry Knox, among others. At the start, however, poor leadership hampered American efforts.

Military Action in Canada

With their forces and supplies depleted by the battle at Bunker Hill, the British stayed in their Boston quarters during the summer of 1775. While the British waited for reinforcements from across the Atlantic, Washington mounted a siege, placing cannons on Dorchester Heights, strategically located above Boston's harbor. General William Howe, the new British commander, realized that he could no longer defend Boston. In March 1776 he withdrew the British garrison north to Halifax, Nova Scotia.

Meanwhile, the Continental Congress, which was beginning to function as a government for the colonies, learned that Canada's governor, Guy Carleton, was preparing to invade the colonies. Rather than wait for the attack, the Congress decided to act. It ordered American troops to invade Canada.

Marching at a brutal pace through rough northern country, Colonel Benedict Arnold reached Quebec in September 1775. His troops menaced the Canadians throughout the autumn and early winter. In mid-December General Richard Montgomery brought reinforcements, and the troops launched an attack on Quebec.

The Canadians fought valiantly. Montgomery was killed and Arnold wounded. But, instead of withdrawing, Arnold laid siege to the walled city. Hunger, smallpox, and bitter Canadian weather took their toll on his troops. The Canadians, equipped with ample food and supplies, simply bided their time, and the siege, a desperate gamble, ended in failure and frustration.

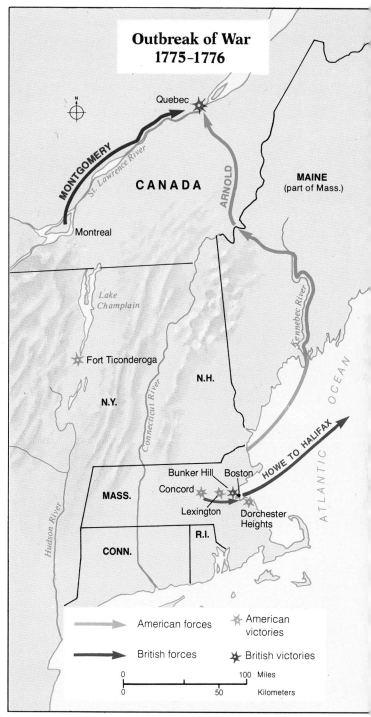

■ The first skirmishes between American colonists and the British took place in the northern colonies and Canada even before the colonies declared their independence. Ethan Allen's "Green Mountain Boys" gave Patriot confidence an important boost when they captured Fort Ticonderoga in 1775. The Battle of Bunker Hill was also a moral victory for Americans, but the siege of Quebec during the winter of 1775–1776 failed.

121

For answers, see p. A 22.

Section Review

1. Identify the following: John Dickinson, Committees of Safety, Ethan Allen, Israel Putnam, Bunker Hill, William Howe, Benedict Arnold.
2. (a) What was the most significant question facing the Second Continental Congress? (b) What was the goal of the moderates? (c) What was the goal of the radicals?
3. In what way was the Battle of Bunker Hill a moral victory for the Americans?
4. What three qualities made George Washington a good choice for commander in chief of the Continental Army?
5. What news convinced the Continental Congress to order an invasion of Canada?

2 The Road to Independence

The Americans' attempt to capture Canada enraged the British. To punish the rebels, they adopted harsher policies. But such tactics only served to swell the radicals' following. The final break came on July 4, 1776. Until that time, the colonists had not really thought of the military actions as a war for independence.

A Harsher British Position

Colonial radicals, favoring independence, found unexpected allies in King George and his ministers. Infuriated by colonial resistance, George III repeatedly refused to make concessions that might have strengthened the position of the moderates. As early as November 1774, he had concluded that "blows must decide whether they are to be subject to the Country or Independent."

In a final attempt to mend the rift, the Continental Congress adopted the Olive Branch Petition on July 8, 1775. Written by John Dickinson, the resolution urged the king to pressure Parliament to repeal the Coercive Acts and to bring about "a happy and permanent reconciliation." Six weeks later George III responded with the Prohibitory Act. In it the king and Parliament proclaimed that a general rebellion existed in the colonies and authorized steps "to bring the traitors to justice." These measures included cutting off all American trade, seizing American ships, and demanding that the rebels formally and publicly repent.

When news of the Prohibitory Act reached the Continental Congress on February 27, 1776, John Adams declared that it was an "Act of Independency, for the King, Lords and Commons have united in sundering this country from that I think forever."

To make matters worse, information soon reached the Continental Congress that the king had hired 10,000 Hessian mercenaries* to suppress the rebellion. The news stunned the delegates, who knew that such troops usually brought looting, plundering, arson, and uncontrolled violence in their wake. Benjamin Franklin remarked with bitter irony on the British need to use German soldiers to crush colonists who were British subjects.

Thomas Paine's *Common Sense*

If George III's harsh statements inflamed Americans, another Briton's words kindled colonial patriotism even more. With the publication of his pamphlet *Common Sense* in January 1776, Thomas Paine helped colonists define their position more sharply and clearly than ever.

Paine, the son of a poor English corset maker, had drifted from one job to another before immigrating to America in late 1774. Over the years, however, Paine had educated himself and had learned to write better than most university-trained men of the day. Using direct and forceful language that aroused his readers, Paine argued that common sense showed that Americans owed allegiance neither to the king of Great Britain nor to any monarchy.

> For all men being originally equals, no one by birth could have a right to set up his own family in perpetual preference to all others for ever. ... [A monarch is] nothing better than

---

*mercenary: a soldier who fights for pay in a foreign army. The Hessians were from the German state of Hesse.

the principle ruffian of some restless gang. Of more worth is one honest man to society and in the sight of God, than all the crowned ruffians that ever lived.

Declaring Independence

By the spring of 1776 the Continental Congress had begun to adopt resolutions as if it were making laws for an independent nation. Although sentiment in the Middle Colonies still seemed to favor compromise, a decisive break had already been made in New England and the South. Following the lead of these colonies, the Continental Congress approved privateering against British ships, outlawed the importation of slaves, entered into relations with foreign nations, and cut off all trade with Great Britain.

Congress also organized a committee to draft a formal declaration of colonial independence from Britain. Declaring independence seemed a good idea for several reasons. As citizens of an independent nation, captured Americans could demand to be treated as prisoners of war rather than as traitors, subject to the death penalty. Moreover, an independent nation would probably be able to obtain aid from Britain's enemies. Eventually, arguments like these won over all but the most reluctant moderates.

Supported by a congressional resolution stating that "these United States are, and of right ought to be, Independent States," John Adams, Benjamin Franklin, Robert Livingston, Roger Sherman, and Thomas Jefferson set to work on the declaration. Jefferson, who was responsible for most of the draft, later commented, "I turned to neither book nor pamphlet while writing the Declaration."

On July 2, 1776, the committee presented the completed declaration to the Continental Congress. Two days later the delegates adopted it. No opposing votes were cast. Three delegates from Pennsylvania, however, absented themselves, and the New York delegation abstained. Congress then sent the document to the printer.

The Declaration

The Declaration of Independence contained three major sections. The preamble explained the philosophical principles behind the act of declaring independence. The middle section listed specific grievances against the king. The Declaration concluded by stating that the United States of America had severed its ties to the crown and had formed an independent government. (See the Declaration, pages 782–783.)

The preamble had the greatest impact on American society because it established general principles of human rights that applied to all people, not just to the colonists. The beliefs about human rights set forth in the Declaration of Independence were ideals rather than realities in late eighteenth-century America. Yet they helped lay the foundation for a future society based on equal rights for all. Over the years, these ideals encouraged a greater regard for human dignity in nations around the world, stimulating reform movements and political revolutions.

The preamble also justified colonial resistance to Britain in a new way. Earlier, during the Stamp Act crisis, for example, colonists had emphasized the rights they possessed as British subjects, rights guaranteed them by the unwritten British constitution. Now they spoke of natural rights that no human power could take away. Jefferson wrote that people were "endowed by their Creator with certain unalienable rights" and that "among these are life, liberty, and the pursuit of happiness."

People "secure these rights" by forming governments for their protection. Jefferson was guided in his thoughts on this subject by John Locke, a seventeenth-century English political philosopher. Jefferson, like Locke, believed that "governments . . . [derive] their just powers from the consent of the governed." Thus, he argued, the people are the fundamental source of power in any state. This claim ran directly counter to the European theory that kings were the source of power in a state with a God-given right to rule over their subjects.

If the people were the source of government, it followed that they had the right "to alter or to abolish it." However, Jefferson wrote, such a change should be made only when the circumstances truly warranted it, not for "light and transient causes."

The second section of the Declaration of Independence then listed the causes that justified American revolt against British rule. To make the argument as forceful as possible and to cut the ties once and for all,

Jefferson blamed everything on the king. The king, he stated, had refused to allow laws "necessary for the public good" unless the people gave up their "right of representation in the legislature."

The third section of the Declaration officially established a new independent nation. It said that the states had the power to make war, establish alliances, trade with whomever they wanted, and sever all connections with Great Britain. With the adoption of the Declaration of Independence on July 4, 1776, the 13 British colonies ceased to exist. The United States of America were at war.

For answers, see p. A 22.

Section Review

1. Identify the following: Olive Branch Petition, Prohibitory Act, Thomas Paine, *Common Sense*.
2. (a) Was King George willing to repeal the Coercive Acts? (b) What two actions by the king helped make the colonists more radical?
3. What argument did Thomas Paine make in support of an American revolt against Britain?
4. What two arguments won over some delegates reluctant to declare independence?
5. (a) What were the three major sections of the Declaration of Independence? (b) What was the purpose of each?

3 The Balance of Forces

Early in 1776, John Adams had predicted that Americans would "have a long, obstinate, and bloody war to go through." But few believed that the fighting that had erupted at Lexington in April 1775 would continue for six and a half years. Even fewer realized that it would be the first of over eighty major battles.

The identity of this free black American sailor is not known. The portrait, done in 1779, was discovered in Newport, Rhode Island.

Choosing Sides

The crowd outside the Philadelphia state-house rejoiced when a representative of Congress read them the Declaration of Independence a few days after its passage. People rang bells and lighted bonfires. In New York City, an enthusiastic crowd threw ropes around a statue of King George and pulled it to the ground.

Not all Americans felt the same about independence, though. A significant minority—estimates range from 10 to 20 percent—remained loyal to the crown. They called themselves Loyalists; the Patriots* called them Tories.

Loyalists tended to be among the more well-to-do Americans. They included wealthy merchants, most former officials of the royal government, and ministers of the Church of England. Many farmers and artisans remained "loyal" too, and some large planters sided with the British. Harassed by Patriots, many Loyalists fled to Canada or

---

*Patriot: the name by which colonists who wanted independence called themselves.

Paul Cuffe: Another View of Taxation Without Representation

During the Revolutionary War, Paul Cuffe, a free black from Massachusetts, learned that the colonists' persistent cries for "no taxation without representation" had ironic implications for black property owners. Cuffe grew up on an island off the Massachusetts coast, where his father, an African slave who had bought his freedom, owned a farm. Fascinated by the sea and tutored in navigation, Cuffe decided at age 16 to try his hand on a whaling ship.

On his third whaling voyage the Revolutionary War broke out, and Cuffe was held by the British for three months as a prisoner of war. After his release, Cuffe bought a farm in Westport, Massachusetts, and settled there with his brother. As a Westport property owner Cuffe got his first real taste of "taxation without representation."

Though Cuffe and his brother were required to pay property taxes on their land, they found that they did not have the same rights as white property owners. "We are not allowed the Privilege of freemen of the State, having no vote or influence in the Election of those that Tax us," Cuffe wrote in a petition to the Massachusetts state legislature. "We have not an equal chance with the White people neither by sea nor by land." Cuffe's petition was signed by seven other free blacks. As a further protest, the Cuffe brothers stopped pay-

ing taxes on their land. In 1780 the Cuffes were jailed for these activities.

Behind bars, they continued their fight for representation and finally succeeded in forcing the issue before a local town meeting. Although the Cuffes lost the case, the issue was brought out in the open. Through such efforts free blacks would eventually win the right to vote in Massachusetts.

Paul Cuffe returned to the sea when the war ended and became a successful trader with his own small fleet of ships. He continued the struggle for equal rights for black Americans throughout his lifetime.

Britain. Others found shelter in cities controlled by the British, such as New York. Most, however, remained in their homes as inconspicuously as possible.

While nearly half of the American people actively participated in the Patriot cause, almost as many—perhaps about 30 to 50 percent—remained neutral. Among them were religious groups such as the Moravians, Quakers, and Mennonites, whose beliefs emphasized pacifism, opposition to the use of force for any reason. Although most managed to stay out of the fighting, the tide of battle sometimes forced them to supply aid to one side or the other.

As a result of such divided loyalties, America found itself in a state of civil war. Many prominent families had members on opposing sides. For example, Benjamin Franklin's son, the governor of New Jersey, sided with the British, causing his father much anguish.

The British population itself was split on the American question. Some prominent members of Parliament publicly supported the Patriot cause. Several leading generals refused to fight in the war and resigned their commissions.

Many Native Americans saw the war as an opportunity to oust colonial intruders. The Iroquois in the North, the Shawnee and Delaware in the western part of the Middle Colonies, and the Cherokee in the South formed key alliances with the British.

The Role of American Blacks

Blacks, both slave and free, tended to support the Patriot cause. A reservoir of black veterans remained from the French and Indian War, and some had already enrolled as minutemen. Black soldiers had also fought at Fort Ticonderoga, Bunker Hill, and Lexington and Concord.

Some of the women who accompanied their husbands to war shared in the freezing winter at Valley Forge and the savage heat of battle. Among them was Mary Ludwig Hays, nicknamed Molly Pitcher. She became a legend in the Battle of Monmouth when she took her fallen husband's place to keep a Patriot cannon firing.

an entirely black battalion, made up of soldiers both slave and free. Ultimately about 5,000 black soldiers fought for the Patriot cause.

Women's Contribution to the War Effort

Although men were expected to do the fighting, women fought too. Sally St. Clair of South Carolina and Deborah Sampson of Massachusetts disguised themselves as men and enlisted in the Continental Army. When Molly Pitcher's husband fell next to his artillery piece, legend has it that she took his place. Women were also among the most skilled spies in the colonial intelligence network.

Wives often accompanied their husbands' regiments. In camp they cooked, laundered, or sewed during lulls in combat. They collected or prepared medicines and nursed sick and wounded soldiers. Benjamin Franklin's daughter, Sarah Franklin Bache, organized a Daughters of Liberty chapter to make clothing and handle hospital shipments. With many men away fighting, women often had to take over traditionally male jobs. They maintained farms, ran businesses, and worked as blacksmiths, manufacturing the cannons, guns, and shot needed to keep the Continental Army going.

The British Position

Great Britain, the strongest military power in the world at the time, began the war with several distinct advantages. Generals Thomas Gage, William Howe, Henry Clinton, and John Burgoyne had wide-ranging experience in large-scale European wars. They understood military strategy and how to transport and deploy regiments effectively.

For years the British had maintained a huge standing army in the colonies. Redcoats, as British soldiers were called because of their bright red uniforms, were well drilled and fully disciplined. They followed the orders of superior officers unquestioningly, unlike the freewheeling amateur colonial militia. Moreover, the redcoats were fully equipped with artillery, firearms, powder, tents, uniforms, blankets, and the many other necessities of war.

The British regulars were supported by a navy that commanded the seas. The Royal

As much as they welcomed the support of able-bodied soliders, members of the Continental Congress saw that the participation of blacks posed problems. They worried that blacks would take the idea of freedom too seriously and wondered if such thinking might encourage slaves to revolt.

In November 1775 George Washington, acting with the advice of other generals, recommended that black soldiers be barred from enlisting in the Continental Army. The Continental Congress agreed. In the same month, the British stepped up their efforts to recruit blacks, offering freedom to any slave or indentured servant who would join the British Army.

The British action forced the Americans to reconsider their position, and in January 1777 the Continental Army began enlisting free blacks. A year later Rhode Island raised

Navy placed 28 warships equipped with over 500 guns in ports from New York to Halifax, Nova Scotia. Vessels could transport fresh troops from Europe, usually without interference, and shift armies in the colonies by sea, a method considerably more efficient than marching men along dangerous country roads. In contrast, the Americans had no real navy but only privateers.

The British faced disadvantages too, and these ultimately contributed to their undoing. Their chief drawback was the problem of supply, a disadvantage for all foreign-based armies. Fighting in a hostile country, the British had to transport war material 3,000 miles (4,800 kilometers) from ports in England. It took weeks and sometimes months for needed materials and reinforcements to arrive in the colonies. Campaigns often stalled while generals waited for supplies. The farther British troops pushed into the interior, the more problems they faced in transporting supplies.

The British also found it difficult to adapt to the new kind of war being fought in America. Following European custom, the well-trained redcoats lined up in three straight rows, loaded their muskets, and fired across a field at an enemy that was expected to line up in a similar formation. At Lexington, Concord, and other early battles, however, they faced rebel militia who shot at them from behind stone walls and trees.

The British Army could conquer, occupy, and hold cities like Boston, New York, or Philadelphia without difficulty, but in the countryside it was at the mercy of colonial forces. The extent of the land permitted the colonial militia to fall back and vanish into the woods, only to reappear in unexpected locations to ambush British soldiers and supply units. As they gained experience, American officers used this hit-and-run tactic often. These and other guerrilla tactics wore down the British until the Continental Army grew strong enough to defeat them.

The American Position

The colonies began the war with several advantages. As a besieged nation they benefitted from the love of a people for their own land. Patriots defending their own farms and cities responded with a fervor that often inspired heroism. Most Americans also knew how to use guns, and in battle American hunting rifles proved more accurate than British muskets. Furthermore, George Washington turned out to be a superb leader. Finally, several foreign countries, especially France, provided valuable aid, as did private citizens from other nations.

The Americans faced problems too. Few soldiers had regular army experience, and volunteers enlisted for short terms. No navy of any significant size existed. And while Americans did not have to transport supplies across an ocean, as the British did, the Continental Army could never get enough food, ammunition, or clothing. The Continental Congress lacked the authority to require states or citizens to provide funds or military service. And most of all, the Americans had to overcome the problem of *localism*, thirteen states going their separate ways instead of acting as one nation.

Maintaining American Military Forces

The development of a navy posed a serious problem for the Americans. Six states owned ships suitable for patrolling inland waterways, but none had vessels like the seagoing British men-of-war. On October 13, 1775, the Continental Congress authorized the construction of a Continental Navy, but one hardship after another befell the effort. For instance, four frigates had to be destroyed before they were finished in order to prevent capture by the British.

Despite these and other problems, the United States did achieve a few notable naval successes. In 1779 Captain John Paul Jones, commanding the *Bonhomme Richard*, named after Benjamin Franklin's book *Poor Richard's Almanac*, engaged the British ship *Serapis* in one of the most savage naval battles of the war. When the British captain called on Jones to surrender his leaking ship, Jones retorted, "I have not yet begun to fight!" Two hours later the British captain surrendered. Jones's feat, however, represented the exception, not the rule. At the end of the war, the American navy consisted of one ship.

Creating the Continental Army was also difficult. The single greatest task faced by Washington and his staff was that of molding a truly American army from the various colonial militias. Most soldiers' loyalties were to their own states. Few if any felt loyalty to the nation as a whole. If war threatened their home ground, they flocked to its defense. But as soon as the scene of battle shifted, the war became someone else's problem. Soldiers returned immediately to their farms, shops, and families. Those who remained often refused to serve under officers from other colonies.

Generally, each colony took care of its own fighting forces. Colonial governments supplied powder, tents, uniforms, and blankets to their soldiers. Contributing such supplies to the Continental Army was unheard of. It was not unusual for one state militia to refuse to share its provisions and equipment with another—even when it had a surplus.

Washington did everything in his power to discourage the individual colonies from operating as though they were fighting private wars with Britain, but it was an uphill struggle and rarely successful. "I have laboured," he wrote, "to discourage all kinds of local attachments and distinctions of country . . . but I have found it impossible to overcome prejudices."

Political and Financial Localism

Washington's problem with the state militias paralleled the political problems facing Congress. Originally, the Continental Congress had met to deal with a specific threat: the Coercive Acts. By the time it had approved the Declaration of Independence, the Congress had become a national government. But what powers did it have? How could it enforce its acts? In the beginning no one knew, so the Continental Congress had to move cautiously.

Individual states repeatedly demonstrated concern with local matters and indifference to those affecting the nation as a whole. For example, only states had the authority to draft men into the army. Yet when the Continental Congress requested troops, few states regularly filled their quotas. Early in the war, several states even seemed willing to negotiate separate treaties with foreign nations.

Raising money to finance the war created the worst problems. The states would not surrender power to a central government or grant the Continental Congress authority to tax. The Congress assessed each state a certain sum, but the states either refused to pay or refused to levy the necessary taxes for fear of alienating their people.

Finally Congress authorized a national currency, known as the Continental dollar, but this only contributed to the nation's difficulties. The Continental Congress did not have gold and silver to back up the currency it printed, yet it needed money to support

Both the British and the colonists sometimes found it hard to recruit enough men for their armies. At left is an American recruiting poster. The 1779 British cartoon at right mocks the difficulty British recruiting sergeants had enlisting soldiers. The British Army was forced to hire German mercenaries to fill its ranks.

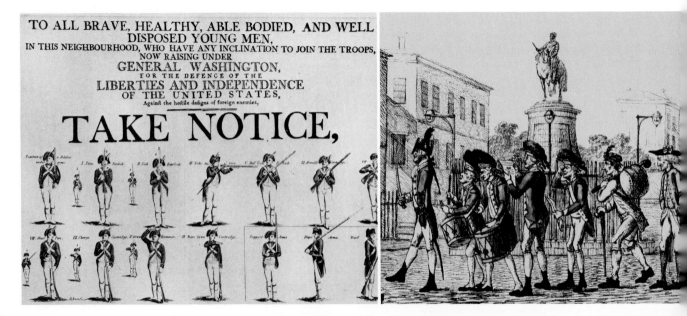

the war—to buy supplies and pay soldiers. Consequently, Congress simply began to print the money it needed.

Inflation was the result. As more money was printed, its value declined. Eventually even Patriots objected to being paid for supplies in Continental dollars, and the phrase "not worth a Continental" soon became popular. To make matters worse, each of the thirteen states continued to print its own paper money. As a result, 14 different currencies circulated during the war, leading to unavoidable confusion.

For answers, see p. A 22.

Section Review

1. Identify the following: Loyalists, Patriots, Tories, redcoats, John Paul Jones.
2. Define the following term: localism.

129

3. Which groups of colonists often remained loyal to Great Britain?
4. (a) What problem did members of the Continental Congress foresee if American blacks joined the army? (b) What development caused them to reconsider their position?
5. How did women contribute to the war effort?
6. (a) List three advantages the British forces had at the beginning of the war. (b) What was their major disadvantage?
7. What four advantages did the Americans have?
8. What was the single most difficult problem in the creation of the Continental Army?
9. What did the Continental Congress do in order to raise money for the war?

4 Fighting a Colonial War

The first real test of the newly formed Continental Army came in the months following the Declaration of Independence. Washington had to thrust his hastily trained and poorly armed band of Patriots into combat against the largest military force Britain had ever sent across the seas.

During the last months of 1776, more than 30,000 well-armed British regulars opposed no more than 18,000 Continentals in a series of battles throughout the Middle States. American victories were few and defeats were many, but valuable lessons were learned.

The Continental Army gained both experience and confidence in its powers of survival. Furthermore, Washington and his staff realized that the British were far from being the invulnerable war machine everyone feared they would be. Though their army won skirmish after skirmish, a decisive military victory was always just out of reach.

The New York Campaign

After the British had withdrawn from Boston to Halifax, they decided to strike at New York City. In the summer of 1776, 32,000 British soldiers, led by General Sir William Howe, poured into the city.

Howe, who was sympathetic toward the Americans, believed that the mere sight of such a formidable array of troops would terrify the rebels into surrender. He hoped, if possible, to avoid an armed confrontation and even went so far as to offer the Continental Congress a royal pardon if it would surrender.

To Howe's regret the Congress chose to fight rather than submit. Though he was able to muster a force little more than half as large as Howe's, Washington marched resolutely into battle. War, even with the threat of crushing defeat, seemed preferable to a humiliating surrender.

Despite valiant fighting and skillful maneuvering, Washington's troops could not hold New York and the surrounding area. The British chased them out of Long Island, forced them to abandon strategic positions on Manhattan Island, and pushed them across the Hudson River into New Jersey. Pursued by Lord Cornwallis, Washington beat a hasty retreat southward over the New Jersey plains, finally crossing the Delaware River into Pennsylvania.

As the year drew to a close American morale reached a low point. Thousands of militiamen began to desert the Continental Army. Others, whose one-year enlistments

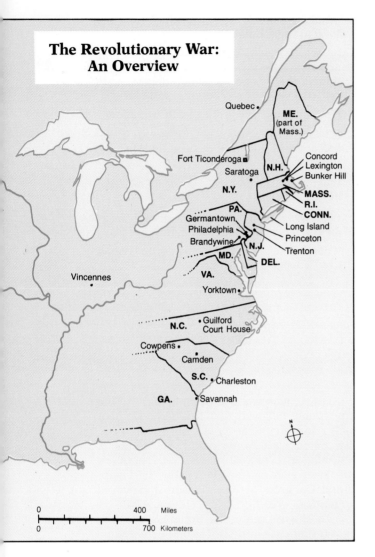

The Revolutionary War: An Overview

■ *For nearly eight years, the Revolutionary War raged over an enormous land area: from Quebec south to Georgia and from the Atlantic coastline west to the Mississippi River. This map shows the location of the major battles you will read about in this chapter.*

were to expire on January 1, 1777, counted the days before they could rejoin their families. For Washington the situation could not have been bleaker.

Success at Trenton and Princeton

In that desperate hour Washington conceived a bold plan. On the night of December 25, just days before his soldiers' enlistments expired, Washington recrossed the Delaware into New Jersey with 2,400 men.

The British, as was customary in eighteenth-century warfare, had settled in for the winter. Their troops occupied various New Jersey towns, including Trenton, just across the river from Pennsylvania.

There a contingent of Hessian mercenaries was celebrating the holidays when Washington pounced on them under cover of night. Groggy with drink, the mercenaries were beaten in forty-five minutes. Washington recrossed the river with 900 prisoners in tow. Four days later, American troops, flushed with success, forged the river again with an army of 5,000.

Although their path was blocked by Cornwallis with an even larger force, the Americans managed to outfox the British and capture Princeton. Had Washington possessed the necessary supplies and equipment, he would have been able to hold the town. Without them, and with an exhausted army, he was forced to relinquish Princeton and take refuge for the rest of the winter in the Morristown hills.

As 1776 drew to a close, the Americans settled into winter quarters with renewed hope. They had suffered defeat, but they had also accomplished one of their principal objectives: to push the British 60 miles (96 kilometers) back from Philadelphia. An Englishman took note of the fact, commenting sadly, "A few days ago they had given up the cause for lost. Their late successes have turned the scale and now they are all liberty mad again."

Saratoga and Philadelphia

During the winter of 1777, the British secretary of war approved a plan to conquer New York and isolate New England. Had the strategy succeeded it would probably have split the United States in two and paved the way for a British victory. Through a combination of chance, poor coordination by British generals, and American persistence, the plan failed. This failure turned the tide of the war firmly in the Patriots' favor.

According to the plan, Lieutenant Colonel Barry St. Leger was to lead a force down the St. Lawrence and then east to the Hudson River. General Howe was to move up the Hudson River to Albany, New York, while another British force, commanded by General John Burgoyne, moved south from Canada to meet him. Instead, Howe decided to

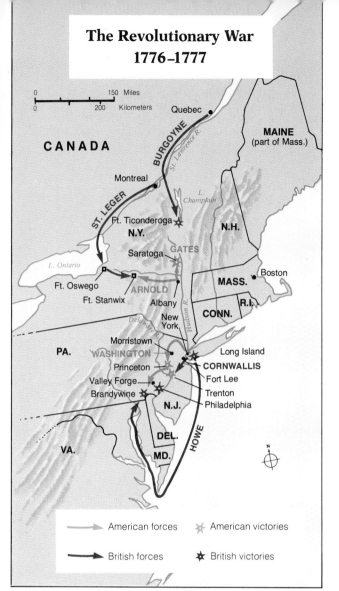

The Revolutionary War 1776–1777

150 Miles
200 Kilometers

CANADA

Quebec

MAINE (part of Mass.)

BURGOYNE

St. Lawrence R.

Montreal

ST. LEGER

L. Champlain

Ft. Ticonderoga

N.Y.

N.H.

Saratoga

GATES

L. Ontario

Ft. Oswego

ARNOLD

Ft. Stanwix

MASS.

Boston

Albany

R.I.

New York

CONN.

Morristown

PA.

WASHINGTON

Long Island

Princeton

CORNWALLIS

Valley Forge

Fort Lee

Brandywine

Trenton

N.J.

Philadelphia

DEL.

HOWE

VA.

MD.

N

→ American forces ✦ American victories

→ British forces ★ British victories

■ By the end of 1776 Washington's troops had retreated through New York and New Jersey into Pennsylvania. In late December, Washington led a small force across the Delaware River for a surprise attack on Trenton. Victory there and at Princeton gave new heart to the Patriot cause. The following year the Continental Army won a stunning victory over the British at Saratoga, which was a turning point in the war.

At the start of the war, Washington's poorly equipped and untrained army was no match for the well-drilled British forces. British troops drove the colonials first from one position, then another. A British officer painted this watercolor of the successful British assault on Fort Lee, on the New Jersey side of the Hudson River.

seize Philadelphia, the Patriots' capital city. He hoped the move would both demoralize the Americans and encourage the dispirited Loyalists.

Howe successfully occupied Philadelphia, disrupted Congress, and trounced Washington at the Battle of Brandywine. But in the long run his maneuver proved disastrous to the British cause.

St. Leger's forces reached Fort Stanwix, but they retreated when they received word that a large American army led by Benedict Arnold was approaching. General Burgoyne got off to a more promising start. He captured strategically placed Fort Ticonderoga, with its huge arsenal of gunpowder and supplies. But without help from Howe, Burgoyne could not keep up the pace, and a string of crushing defeats followed. Marching south from Ticonderoga, Burgoyne's large, unwieldy army was constantly harassed by the hit-and-run guerrilla tactics of the smaller, more agile American forces. Short of supplies and with no reinforcements in sight, Burgoyne finally withdrew to Saratoga.

The move was ill-advised and Burgoyne knew it, but he had no choice. At Saratoga he was besieged by a crack force under the command of General Horatio Gates and some of the finest officers of the Continental Army. Realizing that he had no alternative but to surrender, Burgoyne ordered his entire army of 6,000 men to lay down their arms on October 17, 1777.

For answers, see p. A 23.

Section Review

1. Identify the following: Sir William Howe, Lord Cornwallis, John Burgoyne, Horatio Gates.

2. What impact did the defeat in New York have on American morale?

3. What event gave the American forces renewed hope at the end of 1776?

4. (a) What new plan did the British devise during the winter of 1777? (b) How did General Howe's actions lead to failure of the plan?

5. Who won the battle at Saratoga?

5 Victory for the Americans

The victory at Saratoga proved to be a major turning point of the war. It wiped out the British threat from the north and destroyed an entire British army. Even more important, it brought France into the war on the American side.

The French Alliance

France, as a traditional rival of Britain, had decided early in the struggle that support for the Americans was in its own best interest. Before making a commitment, however, French leaders adopted a wait-and-see policy. Knowing that an American alliance would mean war with Britain, the French wanted to be assured of American chances of success before they acted. Saratoga gave them that assurance.

In February 1778 Benjamin Franklin, who had spent more than a year at the French court trying to win friends for the American colonies, negotiated two treaties with France. The first recognized the United States as an independent nation and granted France special trading privileges with it. The second agreement, which was to go into effect only if France and Great Britain went to war, announced that France would give up claims to land in North America east of the Mississippi. The Americans, in turn, agreed to recognize the French right to any lands in the West Indies captured during the war.

The French alliance offered the United States substantial benefits. French naval vessels soon appeared along the American coast, and the new ally dispatched large quantities of supplies and military experts. Even more important, the alliance reduced British pressure on America. When war broke out with France in June 1778, and later with Spain, Great Britain could no longer devote all its military strength to suppressing the American revolution.

Individuals from foreign nations also aided the Patriot cause. After spending a bitter, hungry, and demoralizing winter (1777–1778) camped at Valley Forge, Penn-

■ During the Revolutionary War, several Indian nations allied with the British and attacked western settlements. George Rogers Clark led a Patriot force down the Ohio River to defeat the British and their Indian allies.

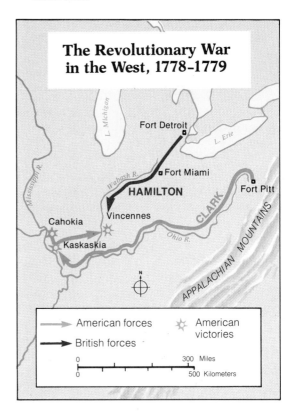

The Revolutionary War in the West, 1778–1779

American forces
British forces
American victories

0   300 Miles
0   500 Kilometers

sylvania, Washington's ragged troops were whipped into fighting shape by Friedrich von Steuben. An experienced veteran of the Prussian Army, Baron von Steuben taught the Continentals how to drill, maneuver, and use bayonets like professional soldiers.

From Poland came Thaddeus Kosciusko (kahs ee UHS koh) and Casimir Pulaski (poo LAHS kee). Kosciusko, an able engineer, designed forts along the Delaware River and the first fortifications at West Point. Pulaski served as a cavalry officer.

The War in the West

Although most of the crucial battles of the war took place along the Atlantic coast, significant developments occurred in the area of present-day Ohio, Illinois, and Kentucky. From time to time, Washington sent troops to fight the Shawnee and other western tribes who, as allies of the British, had been attacking frontier settlements.

British power in the West was finally broken by 25-year-old George Rogers Clark, a Virginian who led 175 volunteer frontiersmen against the British and their Native American allies. Clark and his party rescued the Illinois and Ohio settlements.

The War in the South

Having failed in 1777 to crush the revolution by conquering New York and New England, the British developed another battle plan a year later. This time the target was the South rather than the North. The goal, however, remained the same: to crush American resistance once and for all.

Sir Henry Clinton, a cautious strategist, designed the offensive. To execute it he chose Lord Cornwallis, a capable but hotheaded general. Cornwallis, like Howe before him, tended to follow his own instincts even when it meant disobeying orders and changing battle plans in mid-course.

The British based their hope of success on two factors. First, they believed that they could use troop ships to move soldiers from place to place in the South. In this way they would be able to travel more rapidly and efficiently than the Americans, who had to march overland. Second, the British counted on extensive support from southern Loyalists.

On both points, Clinton and his fellow strategists guessed wrong. The British wildly overestimated the number of Loyalists in the South. Most southerners ardently supported the Patriot cause and provided American forces with constant aid as they trekked over the countryside. The southerners supplied the army not only with food, but also with vital intelligence about British maneuvers. Furthermore, the British had not anticipated the presence of French warships. Although the French could not patrol every inch of the coast, they prevented the British navy from having a completely free hand.

The British captured Savannah, Georgia, in December 1778, and for a year American forces tried to regain it without success. In May 1780 the British won a stunning victory at Charleston, South Carolina. Then, working their way inland, they crushed a Continental force under Horatio Gates at Camden. (See the map on page 134.)

Although the British had won three major victories in the South, they would see few more. Washington relieved Gates of his command and replaced him with the abler General Nathanael Greene. By the time Greene assumed command of the Continental forces, the British had begun to make mistakes that would cost them the war.

Final Victory

Despite mounting evidence that traditional European battle tactics did not work, Lord Cornwallis continued to use them. While Greene harassed the British with small units, Cornwallis massed his troops for a showdown in open battle. Thus, although the redcoats had superior numbers and artillery, they often found themselves standing in battle as stationary targets.

As a result of his devotion to such tactics, Cornwallis received a "very unexpected and severe blow" at Cowpens, South Carolina, on January 17, 1781. Three months later more than a quarter of his army was destroyed by Greene at Guilford Court House, North Carolina. Cornwallis claimed victory at Guilford because Greene withdrew his troops from the field before the close of the battle, but a British observer, hearing of the victory, accurately evaluated its significance. "Another such victory," he commented, "would destroy the British army."

After the "victory" at Guilford Court House, Cornwallis withdrew to Wilmington

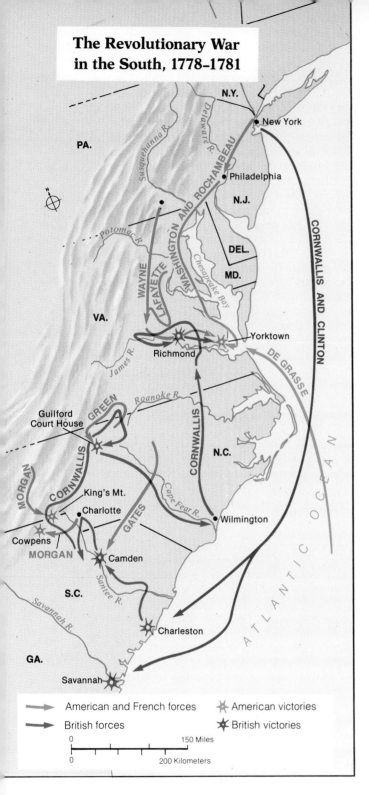

The Revolutionary War in the South, 1778–1781

Legend:
- → American and French forces
- → British forces
- ✶ American victories
- ✶ British victories

0 _____ 150 Miles

0 _____ 200 Kilometers

■ *The final stages of the Revolutionary War were fought in the South. Despite British victories at Savannah, Charleston, and Camden, Patriot troops continually harried the British Army. After battles at Cowpens and Guilford Court House, General Cornwallis retreated first to Wilmington, then to Yorktown. There American and French troops forced him to surrender on October 17, 1781.*

on the North Carolina coast. Battle-weary and discouraged, he wrote to Clinton.

> My present undertaking sits heavy on my mind. I have experienced the distresses and dangers of marching some hundreds of miles, in a country chiefly hostile, without one active or useful friend; without intelligence, and without communication with any part of the country.

For a while Cornwallis's situation seemed to improve. Benedict Arnold, who had deserted to the British, captured and burned Richmond, Virginia. Areas of the state succumbed to isolated British raids, and reinforcements brought Cornwallis's army up to 7,000 men.

Once again, however, Cornwallis erred disastrously. He refused an order by Clinton to send part of his army to New York. Instead, he retreated to the Yorktown peninsula in Virginia and began building fortifications.

Washington, who had just received 5,000 French reinforcements led by the Comte de Rochambeau (roh shahm BOH), immediately recognized Cornwallis's mistake. He realized that the British general had given him the chance he had been waiting for: an opportunity to stage a combined land and sea attack on the major British force.

Rochambeau and Washington marched a French and American force overland from New York to join the Marquis de Lafayette (lah fay EHT) in Virginia. At the same time Admiral de Grasse sailed with thirty ships and 3,000 French marines to Chesapeake Bay. Cut off by land and sea, Cornwallis held out for three weeks. Then, realizing that rescue was impossible, he surrendered his entire army on October 17, 1781.

The battlefield presented an imposing spectacle. The French and the Americans lined up in two facing columns a half mile long. As the British army marched between the victorious troops, the British band played "The World Turned Upside Down." Cornwallis, unwilling to appear, sent his deputy, General Charles O'Hara, who turned his sword over to Washington's deputy, General Benjamin Lincoln. The British soldiers then marched to an open field, where they stacked their muskets.

Clinton still had 16,000 troops in New York, but Yorktown and several French victories in the West Indies brought the war to a close. The defeated British sued for peace.

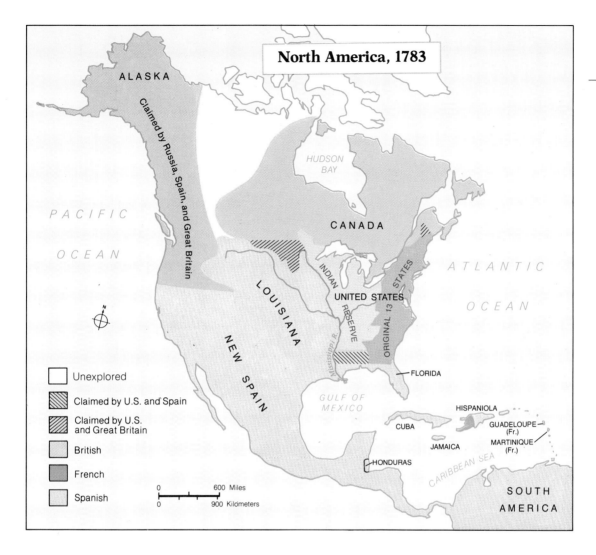

North America, 1783

ALASKA

Claimed by Russia, Spain, and Great Britain

PACIFIC OCEAN

HUDSON BAY

CANADA

LOUISIANA

INDIAN RESERVE

UNITED STATES

ORIGINAL 13 STATES

ATLANTIC OCEAN

MISSISSIPPI R.

NEW SPAIN

FLORIDA

GULF OF MEXICO

HISPANIOLA

CUBA

GUADELOUPE (Fr.)

JAMAICA

MARTINIQUE (Fr.)

HONDURAS

CARIBBEAN SEA

SOUTH AMERICA

Unexplored

Claimed by U.S. and Spain

Claimed by U.S. and Great Britain

British

French

Spanish

0   600 Miles
0   900 Kilometers

■ *The Treaty of Paris (1783) ceded to the United States all British land between the Atlantic coast and the Mississippi River as far north as the Great Lakes and as far south as Florida.*

The Peace Treaty

Congress ordered Benjamin Franklin to hold no peace talks without the French, but Franklin began informal, secret talks with the British anyway. When the other peace commissioners, John Adams, John Jay, and Henry Laurens, arrived, formal talks began. In the course of negotiations, the Americans achieved their major goals: British recognition of American independence, and acquisition of all the land from the Atlantic coast to the Mississippi River between the Great Lakes and Florida.

Great Britain also agreed to evacuate military posts in several areas, and the United States won fishing rights off New-foundland. Britain asked for compensation for the property losses of Loyalists. Although Congress agreed to "recommend" payment, the Loyalists never received compensation from the American government.

Both sides signed the treaty on November 30, 1782. It went into effect two months later and was ratified by Congress on April 19, 1783, eight years to the day after the first shot at Lexington.

How did it all happen? Washington later marveled at the achievement. Who would believe, he said, "that such a force as Great Britain has employed for eight years in this country could be baffled in their plans of subjugating it by numbers infinitely less, composed of men sometimes half-starved, always in rags, without pay, and experiencing every species of distress, which human nature is capable of undergoing." But happen it did!

The Patriots straggled home, one way or another, to neglected farms and happy families. Now there were 13 free states. What kind of nation would they form? Would they be able to work together for the common good of all?

For answers, see p. A 23.

Section Review

1. Identify the following: Baron von Steuben, Thaddeus Kosciusko, Casimir Pulaski, George Rogers Clark, Sir Henry Clinton, Nathanael Greene, Comte de Rochambeau, Marquis de Lafayette.

2. What battle convinced the French to openly support the Americans?

3. In what three ways did the French alliance help the American cause?

4. What two beliefs led the British to think they would succeed in the South?

5. What were the two major goals of the Americans at the peace treaty?

Major Events

1775	British pass Prohibitory Act; Second Continental Congress convenes; Ethan Allen and Green Mountain Boys capture Fort Ticonderoga; battle at Bunker Hill; Continental Army formed under Washington's command; American attack on Quebec
1776	*Common Sense* published; Declaration of Independence signed; New York campaign; Battles of Trenton, Princeton
1777	Battles of Philadelphia, Brandywine, Saratoga
1778	French alliance; British capture Savannah
1780	British victories at Charleston, Camden
1781	Battles of Cowpens, Guilford Court House, Yorktown; British surrender
1783	Treaty of Paris ratified by Congress

★ ★

IN PERSPECTIVE After the Second Continental Congress opened in May 1775, fighting between the British and the colonists broke out in New York, Massachusetts, and Canada. The British reacted to colonial resistance by imposing harsh measures in the Prohibitory Act. Such actions only helped convince delegates to the Congress to declare independence in July 1776.

The Americans had to fight a long and difficult war in order to gain the independence they had claimed. Not all former colonists supported the war, however. Many remained loyal to Great Britain, and others were neutral. The colonists also had to overcome localism, which hampered the war effort.

The British had many advantages at the beginning of the war, including a large, well-trained army and navy. Yet the colonists were defending their homeland, and they had excellent leadership in George Washington. Furthermore, the aid of other European nations, especially France, helped counter British advantages. Tactical errors by British commanders led to final American victory at Yorktown in 1781. When the peace treaty was ratified in 1783, the American states were finally independent. Now they faced the challenge of surviving as a new republic.

For answers, see p. A 23.

Chapter Review

For answers, see p. A 24.

For Further Thought

1. What was the significance of the Battle of Bunker Hill?

2. How did Britain's harsh position toward the colonies help convince many delegates to the Congress that independence was necessary?

3. (a) What important principle was established in the preamble to the Declaration of Independence? (b) Why has this continued to be significant? (c) What major justifications did the declaration give for independence? (d) What actions did the Continental Congress take to put the principles of the declaration into effect?

4. (a) What advantages did the British have as war began? (b) What disadvantages did they face?

5. (a) Why did the participation of black soldiers in the war pose serious problems for American leaders? (b) What role did American blacks play in the war?

6. (a) Describe the problems that George Washington faced in building and maintaining a continental army. (b) Was he able to overcome these problems? Explain. (c) Which proved most difficult? Why?

7. How did localism handicap the Continental Congress during the war?

8. (a) Why did Washington decide to attack Trenton? Princeton? (b) What did he and his staff learn from these and other battles throughout the Middle States?

9. (a) What were the terms of the treaties Benjamin Franklin negotiated with the French? (b) Why were the French originally reluctant to form a formal alliance with the United States? (c) Why did they change their minds?

10. How did miscalculations on the part of the British in the South contribute to an American victory?

1. (a) According to Thomas Jefferson, what are natural rights? (b) Explain how the theory of natural rights could be used as a justification for independence from Britain.

2. (a) What was the professional and financial status of many Loyalists? (b) Why might such characteristics have influenced these people to remain loyal to Britain?

3. Some members of Parliament supported the Patriot cause. What reasons might they have had for this?

4. (a) Why do you think slaves might have decided to enlist in the Continental Army? (b) Why might free blacks have joined?

5. Despite many disadvantages faced by Americans entering the war, they were victorious. List and explain the factors that contributed to their victory.

For answers, see p. A 24.

Developing Basic Skills

1. *Comparing* Make a chart with four columns. In column one list the advantages of the British at the start of the war. In column two list the disadvantages. In columns three and four do the same for the Americans. (a) Who would seem to have the most advantages? (b) Who would seem to have the most disadvantages? (c) Which advantages or disadvantages do you think were the most important to the outcome of the war? Explain.

2. *Map Reading* Study the map on page 135 and compare it with the map on page 96. Describe how the boundary lines changed between 1763 and 1783.

See page 774 for suggested readings.

8

An Experimental Era

(1777–1787)

Detail from Exhuming the First American Mastadon, *by Charles Willson Peale.*

Chapter Outline

1 *Making a New Start*

2 *The New American States*

3 *The First National Government*

4 *A Need for Further Experimentation*

As the newly formed Continental Army struggled against the well-trained British forces, an independent American government took shape. States drafted constitutions and elected legislatures, and they took steps to create a national government. Strong state loyalties made that a difficult task, but by the end of the war the nation's first constitution had been ratified.

As you will read in this chapter, the new government faced difficult challenges boldly. An experimental mood characterized government as it did many other areas of American life. If one idea did not work, people were willing to try another. The new central government had weaknesses that prevented it from solving important political, economic, and foreign policy problems. When the weakness of the central government became obvious, Americans showed that they were willing to experiment again.

1 Making a New Start

The Revolutionary War was a far-reaching event that affected more than the nation's government. It jolted Americans out of their everyday habits. Things that they had taken for granted changed drastically. By the 1780s Americans were ready to experiment in many facets of their lives.

An Experimental Mood

Following the hard-fought struggle for independence, Americans sought practical ways to use their heritage. More Americans began to think that there might be better ways of doing things. As Benjamin Franklin observed, "We are, I think, on the right road to improvement, for we are making experiments." Not only political experiments, he might have added, but experiments that affected all aspects of life.

In education, for example, Americans began to question the teaching of ancient languages such as Latin and Greek. Parents began to demand that their children receive useful, practical educations. Some educators questioned the practice of providing separate schools for boys and girls. Soon the first coeducational schools were founded, and some girls and boys began to go to school together.

Overall, Americans sought to increase their knowledge. They established newspapers and magazines and published more books than ever before. Scientific societies such as the American Academy of Arts and Sciences were founded, and the American Philosophical Society grew in stature.

But behind all the ferment and change was a belief in liberty. And perhaps the most significant American experiments were in the search for liberty and equality.

Steps Toward Greater Political and Social Equality

Political equality became a major goal in the young republic. The newly created constitutions of the state governments seemed to echo Jefferson's words in the Declaration of Independence that "all men are created equal." Most significant, some states extended the right to vote by lowering or eliminating property requirements.

But the echo of political equality was less than perfect. Only "qualified" citizens could vote in elections. To qualify, a person typically had to be male, white, Christian, and a property owner. Despite some criticism of these qualifications, state governments did little to amend them in the early years.

The concern for equality did lead citizens of the new nation to suspect any privilege that made some people seem superior to others. In 1783, for example, a group of former Continental Army officers founded the Cincinnati Society. The society's primary goal was to make the government aware of the needs and wants of veterans, especially officers. Membership was hereditary; only officers and their descendants could belong.

Many people feared that the founders of the Cincinnati Society wanted to establish a new aristocracy. The society was denounced throughout the nation, even though George Washington was its president. The Massachusetts legislature claimed that the society "may be dangerous to the peace, liberty, and safety of the United States." Such intense opposition caused the Cincinnati Society to drop its political activities and become a social club.

Americans greeted other organizations that hinted of aristocracy with similar though less powerful reactions. Such reactions showed that Americans were beginning to think of equality in a social as well as a political context. A popular magazine commented, "The idea of equality breathes through the whole and every individual feels ambitious, to be in a situation not inferior to his neighbor." A Boston newspaper added that the phrase *the better sort of people* became thoroughly contemptible and odious in the estimation of the people."

Some efforts to dissolve social-class barriers proved successful. Changes in inheritance laws broke up large landholdings and redistributed property. In addition, the government sold millions of pounds worth of property confiscated from Loyalists during the revolution. The creation of new opportunities for land ownership accelerated the breakdown of old social barriers.

Limited Opportunities for Women

Although theories and experiments in equality abounded in the United States, inequality for women persisted. Yet some people hoped to remedy the situation. Abigail Adams denounced the lack of female equality, and she warned her husband, John, when he was attending the Continental Congress, "Do not put such unlimited power in the hands of husbands. Remember all men would be tyrants if they could."

Abigail Adams was not the only person who believed that the phrase "all men are created equal" meant "all humans are created equal." Nonetheless, the laws did not provide for such equality. Women had few property rights and no voting rights, in spite of a brief period in New Jersey when they were entitled to vote. The political system was legally restricted to men and remained that way until the twentieth century.

Unlike the political system, the educational system provided some limited new opportunities for women in the 1780s and

Until 1806 women in New Jersey could vote, a right not enjoyed by most American women until the twentieth century.

1790s. A number of New England academies began to admit female students and to allow women to study the same subjects as men. But women continued to face discrimination in higher education.

Lucinda Foote's experience is just one example. At age twelve, Foote proved to a board of examiners that she could do college work, but the report came back saying that she appeared "fully qualified except in her sex, to be received as a pupil of the freshman class of Yale University." Hence, her admission was denied.

Limited Advances for Free Blacks

The revolutionary idea that "all men are created equal" had an impact on black as well as white Americans. Over 50,000 free blacks lived in the United States in the 1780s, most of them in the Middle Atlantic states. Courts in several states began to look more favorably on lawsuits filed by black slaves seeking freedom. North Carolina, Maryland, Kentucky, and Tennessee extended to free blacks the right to trial by jury, the right to compel the appearance of witnesses, and the right to legal counsel.

Furthermore, the first state constitutions in the Northeast did not generally discriminate against blacks in voting rights. In the years following the revolution, free blacks living in the North tended to improve their standard of living due to the high demand for workers. In addition, some formerly all-white churches admitted blacks, although not always with equal membership rights.

In spite of these advances, free blacks in the new nation still suffered discrimination. Most northern states passed laws discouraging black immigration into the region, and areas where free blacks could live were *segregated*, or set apart from others. In some states in the northern part of the South, the danger of being kidnapped back into slavery remained a reality. States in the deep South, if they allowed free blacks at all, usually deprived them of most civil rights.

Early Actions Against Slavery

Try to picture Thomas Jefferson, sitting at his desk, reviewing the words he wrote in the Declaration of Independence. As his eyes once again scan the phrase "all men are created equal," he turns and looks out the

Folk artists captured many vignettes from American life, like the scene on this tea tray. It shows Congregational minister Lemuel Haynes with one of his congregations. A Revolutionary War veteran, the Reverend Haynes preached in Connecticut, Vermont, and New York.

window at some of the people working on his estate. These people are his slaves. The dilemma did not escape him. Jefferson struggled with the problem of slavery all of his life.

Jefferson was not alone in his concern about slavery. The Continental Congress had banned the slave trade during the Revolutionary War, and all states except Georgia and South Carolina outlawed it by the war's end. Such actions did not end the slave trade however. As you will see in the next chapter, the Constitution protected the slave trade until 1808.

Vermont's constitution, written in 1777, was the first to provide for the complete abolition of slavery. Over the next 20 years, all the northern states either outlawed slavery or devised plans to gradually free slaves within individual state borders, but these changes came slowly.

In the South the problem of slavery proved more difficult. While Jefferson and his fellow Virginians, George Washington and James Madison, opposed slavery in principle, in practice they could not run their plantations without slave labor. Slavery was too important to Southern agriculture. The Virginia legislature, among others, did make the freeing of slaves, called *manumission*, easier. However, sentiment for the abolition of slavery did not gain a strong foothold in the South.

In some states, especially New York and Pennsylvania, groups of citizens banded together to oppose slavery and promote equality. Together with the Quakers, who steadfastly opposed slavery, such societies formed the base from which a strong abolitionist movement would eventually grow. (See Chapter 16.)

The Separation of Church and State

Before the Revolutionary War, most colonies officially recognized and supported only one established church. All citizens, whether they belonged to the church or not, had to pay taxes to support it. The Congregational Church was often an established church in the Northeast, and the Church of England, renamed the Episcopal Church after the war, was the established church in the South.

Thomas Jefferson, among others, thought that such partnerships of church and state restricted religious freedom and gave the established church an unfair advantage over others. In 1786 the Virginia legislature passed a bill, sponsored by Jefferson, that effectively separated church and state. "Almighty God hath created the mind free," argued Jefferson. The Virginia law stated that "no man shall be compelled to frequent or support any religious worship, place, or ministry whatsoever." Other southern states also disestablished the Episcopal Church, but in New England, Puritan descendants maintained a favored status for the Congregational Church.

Helping Humanity

During the eighteenth century, many Americans came to believe that society could be improved by human effort. Even before independence, Americans had organized groups to solve problems that individuals could not handle on their own. The large number of volunteer fire departments was one example. In this way the colonists had provided services that their governments had not.

The idealism of the revolution further encouraged Americans to try to improve the lives of their fellow human beings. For example, the treatment of criminals bothered many people. Harsh penalties for crimes, such as execution for robbery, and the appalling conditions in prisons led to the formation of many reform societies. Concerned citizens also formed charitable societies to help the poor, raise money for schools, and

provide aid to new immigrants. One society even existed especially to assist sea captains' widows.

Still other societies were devoted to the economic development of the new nation through transportation and land-use projects. Some encouraged bridge construction and road improvement. Others worked to make rivers passable. George Washington was a member of the Great Dismal Swamp Company, for example, which planned to drain the swamp south of Norfolk, Virginia, and develop the land. The formation of voluntary societies devoted to improving the human condition seemed to encompass all aspects of early American life.

Beginnings of a National Consciousness

The revolution forced Americans in the 1780s to change the way they thought about themselves. No longer British subjects, they were citizens of a new nation, and they were proud of that fact.

Politicians, philosophers, and ordinary citizens predicted that America would become "a great and mighty empire." According to one New England minister, it would be "the largest the World ever saw, to be founded on such principles of Liberty and Freedom, both civil and religious, as never before took place in the world." Historians wrote about the revolution and the birth of a country. Poets offered lofty praise to their newborn republic.

Assertions of American inferiority by European philosophers brought quick denials. Thomas Jefferson once wrote a scholarly defense of Americans, but not all reactions were so formal. Benjamin Franklin, for example, gave a dinner party in Paris at which a Frenchman, the Abbé Raynal (ray NAHL), argued that the American environment caused plants, animals, and even humans to grow smaller than those found in Europe. Franklin, noticing the height of his dinner guests, asked everyone to stand. The Abbé, who had been so eager to make his point, stood nearly a head shorter than the American guests.

Noah Webster, who would later gain fame for his dictionary, contributed to the new national awareness by experimenting with the American language. Some of his changes survived—"labour" became "labor"—but not all of them caught on. Efforts

Noah Webster: Creating an American Language

Noah Webster studied to be a lawyer, but fees were so low during the 1780s that he decided to become a teacher instead. The real goal of his life, however, was to promote the adoption of an American language. He wanted to free Americans from British English as they had freed themselves from the British crown. To this end he published a series of three textbooks: a speller in 1783, a grammar in 1784, and a reader in 1785.

Webster objected to the way certain words had been borrowed from other languages but had not been respelled. The result, he claimed, was a confusing mixture of letters, many of which were not pronounced the way they looked, and others of which were not pronounced at all.

Webster urged Americans to simplify their spelling. For example, he argued that "head" should be spelled "hed"; "bread" should be spelled "bred"; "friend" should be spelled "frend"; "laugh" should be spelled "laf"; and "machine" should be spelled "masheen". Most of Webster's suggestions did not catch on, but his textbooks sold millions of copies during the century after they were first published.

Webster continued to work for a national language, publishing the first edition of *An American Dictionary of the English Language* in 1828. "A *national language,*" he wrote, "is a band of *national union.* Every engine [means] should be employed to render the people of this country *national;* to call their attachments home to their own country; and to inspire them with the pride of national character."

by individuals like Webster, along with the pride of creating a nation, helped the people of the United States to begin thinking of themselves as Americans.

For answers, see p. A 24.

Section Review

1. Identify the following: Cincinnati Society, Abigail Adams, Noah Webster.
2. Define the following terms: segregated, manumission.
3. (a) What were the typical qualifications for voting in state elections? (b) How had some states extended the right to vote?
4. (a) What new opportunity did some women have in the 1780s and 1790s? (b) How was it limited?
5. (a) List three ways the position of free blacks improved after the Revolutionary War. (b) Did they gain equality with white Americans? Explain.
6. Which state was the first to abolish slavery?
7. How did established churches limit religious freedom, according to Thomas Jefferson?
8. Give two examples of ways Americans organized to try to improve society.
9. List three examples of the emerging national consciousness.

2 The New American States

Although former British subjects were beginning to think of themselves as citizens of a new nation, their chief loyalty was still to their individual states. Even leaders of the struggle for independence felt that way. John Adams referred to Massachusetts as "our country" and called the Massachusetts delegation to the Continental Congress "our embassy." For Thomas Jefferson, "my country" meant Virginia for many years to come. With their own sense of identity and pride,

the 13 former colonies assumed their status as independent states and clearly viewed their state governments as more important than the new national government.

Preserving Traditions

The English philosopher John Locke had theorized that when a people overthrow one government, they have to design a new one from the ground up. Yet nothing of that sort happened in the America of 1776.

Instead Americans built on English traditions and their own experiences. Colonial assemblies became state legislatures, many prewar laws remained in effect, and in a few cases the old royal charters became the new state constitutions. By the end of 1776 independent governments were functioning in every state except Georgia and New York.

So few changes were made largely because Americans in general were not displeased with the unwritten English constitution or with the local colonial governments. Their anger had been directed at the king, his representatives, and Parliament for violating English political traditions. The changes they did make were usually to insure that power could not be abused by the new governments as it had been by the old.

State Governments

Each new state government had three branches: an executive branch, a legislature, and a court system. Colonial governors had been the symbol of the British monarchy, and Americans remained suspicious of the office. Accordingly, state constitutions limited the governors' powers.

In most states the governor was elected by the legislature, often for only a one-year term. Usually the governor could not *veto*, or reject, a bill passed by the legislature. Pennsylvania eliminated the position of governor entirely and substituted a council of twelve men as the executive. State judges, like governors, had limited authority. The legislatures, on the other hand, had rather extensive powers, including the power to declare war and conduct foreign affairs.

This faith in representative assemblies had deep roots. Americans had depended on their colonial assemblies to represent their interests since the establishment of the Virginia House of Burgesses in 1619. Not only did the assemblies symbolize the authority of the people, they actively resisted numerous attempts by the king and Parliament to diminish that authority, as you read in Chapter 6. Furthermore, delegates selected by those assemblies had written and signed the Declaration of Independence and had organized the military struggle against the British.

Yet the former colonists did not intend to grant unlimited power to the state legislatures. With the exception of Pennsylvania, each state had a *bicameral* legislature, or one with two houses, a lower house and an upper house. In this way legislative power was divided between two groups that balanced each other.

The lower house was the larger, and voters elected its members directly, usually every year. It generally possessed greater power than the upper house because people believed that it was most responsive to their needs and wishes. Out of tradition, the smaller upper house was intended to be a more cautious body. Accordingly, its members were elected for longer terms, ranging from two to four years.

Some people feared that the upper house might be composed of persons with aristocratic leanings, like the members of the British House of Lords. As a result, some states provided that the lower house elect the upper house. Other states called for direct elections. No longer would governors appoint the upper house as they had in many colonies.

John Adams strongly argued that an upper house should include people of great talent and prestige, an aristocracy based on merit rather than heredity. Adams thought that such people would temper the wilder ideas that the lower houses might receive from the people.

Most state constitutions protected the people from possible abuse by their government by including a bill of rights. This guaranteed certain *inalienable rights* that governments could not take away, including freedom of the press, freedom of religion, and the right to trial by jury.

A Written Constitution Drawn From the People

The content of the new state constitutions reflected colonial experiences under British rule, and so did the actual work of drafting the constitutions. During the colonial period, American rights had been based on the English constitution, but that was not a written document. It consisted of centuries of accumulated laws, judicial decisions, and traditions subject to many interpretations. Americans sought to guarantee their freedoms by putting them in writing, thus hoping to make violations of those rights more difficult.

In most states a provincial congress elected during the Revolutionary War simply wrote a constitution and passed it. Although vague dissatisfaction with this method existed, no one faced the problem squarely until 1778. That year the people of Massachusetts rejected the constitution written by their state legislature. Massachusetts citizens argued that if a legislature could write a constitution, it could also change it whenever it pleased. As a result, nothing could stop a legislature from being as tyrannical as a king.

Instead, Massachusetts devised a system whereby the constitution came from the people. In 1779 its voters elected delegates to a special constitutional convention. The document they drafted was approved the following year by a vote of the people. This system put the constitution beyond the reach of the legislature. The state legislature could not change the constitution without the consent of the people it represented.

Thus Massachusetts helped formulate an important principle of American government: constitutions were to be written by special conventions. The principle gained wide acceptance during the 1780s and was followed in 1787 when a special convention wrote the national constitution in use today.

For answers, see p. A 25.
Section Review

1. Define the following terms: veto, bicameral, inalienable rights.

2. (a) State one reason why Americans made few changes in their new state governments. (b) What was the purpose of the changes they did make?

3. (a) What were the three branches of the new state governments? (b) Into what two groups were the state legislatures divided?

4. Why did Americans want to put a constitution into writing?

5. How did Massachusetts protect its constitution from changes by the legislature?

3 The First National Government

When the delegates to the Continental Congress declared American independence in 1776, they had to decide what sort of national government would bind the 13 states together. Their task was formidable. The former colonists were staunchly loyal to their own states, and most feared a powerful national government. Yet the delegates knew the new nation needed a government to act for it. A committee, appointed by the Continental Congress, quickly went to work on a constitution.

The Articles of Confederation

The committee completed a draft in a month. But because of fighting on the battlefields, not to mention disputes among delegates trying to protect the rights of their individual states, almost a year and a half passed before the Continental Congress agreed on a final draft of the nation's first constitution. This constitution, known as the Articles of Confederation, was not ratified until 1781. (See page 147.)

The Articles of Confederation proposed a *confederation*, or alliance of independent states. The central government of the confederation was to be composed of a congress. Not surprisingly, the new Congress was much like the existing Continental Congress. On paper, it appeared to be a powerful national government. Congress could declare war and appoint military officers. In foreign affairs it could receive and send ambassadors, sign treaties and alliances, and regulate dealings with Native Americans. In the domestic sphere it could establish post offices, borrow money, and fix weights and measures.

In spite of these specific powers, the Articles of Confederation placed strict limits on the authority of Congress. For example, it could not collect taxes or draft men into the Continental Army. Congress could only request soldiers and money from the states.

With abuses by the British Parliament fresh in their memories, the states were wary of giving too much power to a central authority. To ease this concern, a clause in the

Articles guaranteed that each state would retain its "sovereignty, freedom, and independence" and keep "every power, jurisdiction, and right" not given directly to Congress. This strong *reserved powers* clause protected the rights of the states and made it more likely that the state legislatures would approve the document.

A Question of Fair Representation

The question of representation in the new Congress had caused heated debate in the Continental Congress before it approved the Articles of Confederation. In the Continental Congress each state had one vote regardless of its area or population. The proposed Articles of Confederation contained the same provision. Since the United States was to be a confederation of states, many delegates said, states must have equal representation.

Delegates from states with larger populations strongly objected. They insisted that states with more people deserved more influence and hence more votes. Delegates from less populous states, on the other hand, favored one vote per state, since it gave them equal power.

The majority of delegates eventually accepted the principle of equal representation for each state, with every state having one vote in Congress. Nine of the 13 states had to approve a measure before it became law. Although the representatives of the larger states were not completely satisfied, they recognized the urgent need for a national government because of the ongoing war with Great Britain.

Before the Articles of Confederation could take effect they had to be *ratified*, or approved by the state legislatures of all thirteen states. The Continental Congress submitted the finished document to the states in November 1777, expecting rapid ratification. However, disputes over conflicting state claims to western territories delayed approval until March 1781.

■ *The Articles of Confederation created a loose confederation of states. The national government had very limited powers, while the states kept important powers such as the right to tax.*

The Articles of Confederation

No chief executive
No national court system
Laws need approval of 9 of the 13 states
All other powers reserved to the states

Congress could	Congress could not
Declare war and make peace	Levy taxes
Raise an army and navy	Regulate foreign or domestic trade
Make foreign treaties and alliances	Settle disputes among states
Coin and borrow money	Collect state debts owed the central government
Regulate weights and measures	Enforce any of its powers
Establish a post office	
Regulate Indian affairs	

Dispute Over Western Lands

The boundaries of the new states were not clearly defined. Two or more states often claimed the same territory, and a few states claimed land all the way to the Pacific. Some states refused to ratify the Articles of Confederation until their claims were settled. States that had no claim to lands in the West also balked at ratifying the new constitution until the land issue was resolved.

Legislators from Maryland, for example, thought that the vast claims of some states, particularly Virginia, gave them an unfair advantage. What if Virginia sold its western lands to provide income for the state? Then it would not need to tax its citizens. What would prevent people and businesses located in Maryland, which did levy taxes, from flocking to Virginia? Such a situation could rob Maryland of population and revenue. Other states with fixed boundaries, particularly Pennsylvania and New Jersey, urged that all western lands be ceded to the national government. Then, as the land was sold, the revenue would benefit the entire nation and not just a few privileged states.

Such rational arguments, however, were not the only reasons some state legislators wanted the western lands ceded to the national government. A group of individuals, mostly from Maryland, Pennsylvania, and New Jersey, had "purchased" vast stretches of western territory from Native Americans, often illegally.

These land speculators hoped to sell the land to settlers and make a big profit. But first their claims had to be validated. The speculators believed that a national congress would be more cooperative than legislatures outside their own states. Therefore, they pressured their state legislators to refuse to ratify the Articles until the states ceded all western territory to the national government.

Recognizing the need to establish a national government, Thomas Jefferson and other Virginians urged their legislature to cede Virginia's land to the United States. They argued that with all its western lands, Virginia would be too large to govern properly. Virginia agreed to cede its land, but the agreement would take effect only when the government voided all purchases of Native American land. In effect, this action destroyed the speculators' hopes for profits. In

As more and more settlers occupied the lands of Native Americans, Indian leaders had to decide whether to fight or try to bargain to keep the settlers out. The Iroquois chief Ki-on-twog-ky, called Cornplanter, wrote several letters to General Washington complaining about the newcomers to his lands.

February 1781 Maryland finally approved the Articles of Confederation, the last state to do so.

A New Land Policy

After the Revolutionary War ended in 1783, Congress had to decide how to settle and govern the western lands. Representatives were particularly worried about the vast area ceded by Virginia known as the Northwest Territory. (See the map on page 148.)

Congress passed the Land Ordinance of 1785 in the hopes of raising money. The ordinance provided for the survey and sale of the land. The territory was to be divided into townships. Each township would be subdivided into 36 lots, each one measuring one square mile (2.6 square kilometers), with one

147

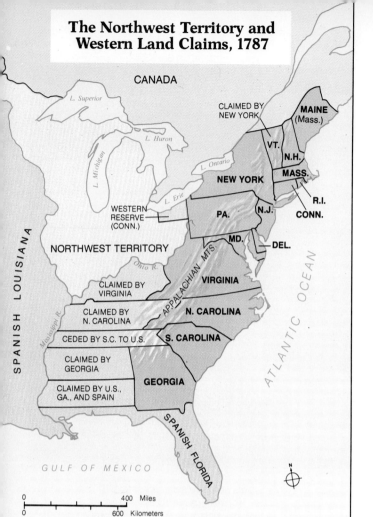

The Northwest Territory and Western Land Claims, 1787

CANADA

L. Superior

L. Huron

L. Michigan

L. Ontario

L. Erie

CLAIMED BY NEW YORK

MAINE (Mass.)

VT.

N.H.

NEW YORK

MASS.

R.I.

CONN.

PA.

N.J.

WESTERN RESERVE (CONN.)

NORTHWEST TERRITORY

Ohio R.

MD.

DEL.

CLAIMED BY VIRGINIA

VIRGINIA

APPALACHIAN MTS.

CLAIMED BY N. CAROLINA

N. CAROLINA

CEDED BY S.C. TO U.S.

S. CAROLINA

CLAIMED BY GEORGIA

GEORGIA

CLAIMED BY U.S., GA., AND SPAIN

SPANISH LOUISIANA

Mississippi R.

SPANISH FLORIDA

ATLANTIC OCEAN

GULF OF MEXICO

N

| 0 | 400 Miles |
| 0 | 600 Kilometers |

■ *Land claims west of the Alleghenies had created friction between American states since they declared their independence. Land ceded to the national government by Virginia and New York became the Northwest Territory.*

lot set aside to support a public school. One provision called for honoring Indian claims, but it was largely ignored.

On paper the plan appeared sound, but in actuality surveyors encountered many difficulties. The terrain was basically uncharted wilderness, with rivers, mountains, and swamps that did not lend themselves to perfect squares. Thus the work progressed slowly and allowed land speculators time to revive their efforts.

One group of New England speculators, calling themselves the Ohio Company, pressed for the suspension of the Ordinance of 1785 so they could purchase a large tract of unsurveyed land. Because Congress desperately needed the additional revenue, it sold over a million acres (about 400,000 hectares) of land to the Ohio Company for less than ten cents per acre.

The plan was further complicated by *squatters* who had moved into the new territory and established homesteads without complying with the ordinance or any of its provisions. Congress unsuccessfully tried to clear the Northwest Territory of these unauthorized settlers.

Squatters also presented a problem to land speculators. The Ohio Company, fearing the loss of its legally purchased territory, urged Congress to pass new legislation dealing with the territory. Other eastern interests, viewing the squatters as violent and dangerous, supported the Ohio Company's urgings. As a result, in 1787 Congress passed a second land bill: the Northwest Ordinance.

The Northwest Ordinance

Under the new ordinance Congress would appoint a governor, secretary, and three judges to govern the territory. Residents could elect a representative legislature when the adult male population reached 5,000, but the governor had the power to veto legislative action.

The ordinance gave Congress the authority to divide the entire area into three to five separate territories based on settlement patterns. Once a territory had a population of 60,000 free inhabitants, it could be admitted as a state with all the rights and obligations of existing states. Until such time, the ordinance guaranteed protection of residents' property rights as well as other rights such as trial by jury and religious freedom. The ordinance also prohibited slavery throughout the territory.

Despite continued wheeling and dealing by land speculators, the land ordinance experiment succeeded. Congress had created an orderly system that extended republican government westward with the settlers. New states would be admitted as equals of the original states. The pattern established by the Northwest Ordinance continued to work well for over a hundred years.

Economic Recovery

As with all wars, the American War for Independence had a disruptive impact on the nation's economy. The impact was particularly dramatic because the United States had waged this war against its principal trading partner, Great Britain. Merchants were hard hit by the separation from Britain. Some profiteers managed to continue trading during the war and made huge profits, but they were the exceptions.

In New England especially, the merchants suffered terribly. Massachusetts shipyards, turning out 125 ships per year before the war, built only 25 ships per year after the war. The whaling industry was reduced from 150 whaling ships to a mere 24. Some shippers took to privateering and robbed British vessels, but the risks were great and the income sporadic.

After the war foreign trade resumed, but it was not immediately profitable. France expected to gain a large segment of American trade after its wartime alliance with the United States, but it did not. Americans still had a taste for the British products they had traditionally used.

Independence did provide American merchants with the freedom to seek world markets outside the British empire. Merchants pursued these markets with great enthusiasm, taking their trade as far as China. In May 1785 the sailing ship *Empress of China* returned from Canton carrying a highly profitable cargo of tea and silks. Before long, ships from Boston, Philadelphia, and Providence began plotting new routes to Asia.

American industry also profited as a result of the war. The fighting itself created a demand for munitions, guns, clothing, and other supplies. In addition, during the war Americans created new industries to manufacture goods they formerly had imported from Great Britain.

Southern planters survived the war, but not without taking great losses. Exports of tobacco and indigo dropped sharply, while Britain's high import duty prevented South Carolina from selling as much rice as before. Furthermore, Loyalists and British invaders had kidnapped many slaves during the war (almost 25,000 in South Carolina). That meant many southern plantations lacked the

Freed of British restrictions on their trade, American merchants opened up new markets in Asia. In this scene, traders deal with tea merchants in Canton, China. Yankee captains also brought back fine Chinese porcelains, silks, and new kinds of trees, shrubs, and flowers.

labor needed to continue production at prewar levels.

Small farmers were in a better position. Many grew wealthy providing food for the armies. Farmers who had borrowed large sums of money before the war—and there were many of them—also benefitted from the inflation of the war years. The same was true of debtors who, after the war, paid back their debts with nearly worthless Continentals. These economic dislocations caused a depression in the years following the war, but by 1787 economic recovery was clearly evident. Americans were beginning to build a sound economy.

For answers, see p. A 25.

Section Review

1. Identify the following: Articles of Confederation, Northwest Territory, Land Ordinance of 1785, Northwest Ordinance.

2. Define the following terms: confederation, reserved powers clause, ratify, squatters.

3. (a) List the powers given to Congress under the Articles of Confederation. (b) What two important powers did it not have?

4. (a) Why did delegates from more populous states object to equal representation in Congress? (b) Why did delegates from less populous states favor it?

5. What unsettled dispute delayed the ratification of the Articles of Confederation?

6. What two problems complicated the enforcement of the Land Ordinance of 1785?

7. When could a territory become a state according to the Northwest Ordinance?

8. Which of the following groups were hurt economically by the Revolutionary War: New England shippers, southern planters, small farmers?

4 A Need for Further Experimentation

The willingness of Americans to experiment continued even after the formation of the first national government. The problems facing the new republic quickly revealed the weakness of the national government and convinced Americans they had to seek better solutions.

Raising Revenue for the New Government

Since "taxation without representation" had been the major charge against the British Parliament, the authors of the Articles of Confederation tried to guarantee that history would not repeat itself. Consequently, raising money proved to be one of the most serious problems the new national government confronted.

Under the Articles, state legislatures, not the people, elected members of Congress. Thus Congress did not directly represent the people and could not tax them. It could ask the states for money, but only the representatives of the people—the state legislatures—could grant such requests. If the states turned down the request, as they usually did, Congress could do nothing.

Still, the young nation desperately needed money. Without the power to tax, Congress began looking elsewhere. It could continue printing paper money as it had done to help finance the war, but inflation had made the paper Continentals virtually worthless. Dutch bankers loaned some money to the new government. But the sale of western lands turned out to be the best source of revenue.

Yet these sources of income were not nearly enough. On two occasions Congress tried to levy tariffs but failed. Both times the vote was just one short of the number needed for passage. Congress seemed powerless to raise the money it needed.

Economic Disunity

Congress also had little authority to promote economic cooperation among the states. State legislatures protected their economic independence as strongly as they did their political independence.

As the only national currency, the Continental dollar, continued to decline in value, states issued their own money. Businesses and individuals preferred their own state currency to others. Furthermore, states often refused to accept other state currencies at face value. The resulting confusion made trade between states difficult.

Economic rivalry among the states further compounded the difficulty. State legislatures tried to regulate trade with other states, often imposing tariffs. Sometimes one state hoped to make a handsome profit from trade between two other states. New York, for example, taxed goods transported between New Jersey and Connecticut.

Actions like these stifled economic cooperation and unity in the new nation. The Articles of Confederation did not give Congress the power to regulate trade or settle disputes between states. The continuing rivalry seriously threatened the nation's economic development.

Foreign Pressures and Western Intrigues

The lack of unity also threatened the new nation's reputation among European nations. Observing the lack of unity, foreign countries initially refused to enter into trade agreements with the United States. Congress's inability to raise an army—it could only "request troops" from the states according to the Articles—also made the new nation appear weak in the eyes of many Europeans, including the British.

Even though the colonists had defeated Great Britain, King George III was not impressed with American power. He ordered troops in military posts in the Northwest Territory to remain, thus violating the peace treaty. The king knew that the French troops were gone and that the weak central government could not raise or support an army. Ambassador John Adams's heated protests moved neither the British monarch nor the British troops.

Spain renewed its interest in western American lands after the war. Although many Americans had flocked into the areas that would eventually become Tennessee and Kentucky, the situation there was unstable. Some settlers were squatters with no deeds to their lands. Eastern speculators also claimed vast areas granted to them years before by states like Virginia and North Carolina. Congress had to resolve many conflicting claims, but it made little progress.

In the confusion a group of settlers in the area organized a new state called Franklin in honor of Benjamin Franklin. They petitioned Congress to admit the state to the Union but were refused. At the same time, Spain was trying to separate Franklin from

Of all the backwoodsmen who helped open the frontier, none was more famous or more likely to spin tall tales about his exploits than Daniel Boone. Boone led a group of settlers who carved the Wilderness Road through the Cumberland Gap in Kentucky and opened the western frontier to settlement.

Major Events

1777	Vermont constitution first to abolish slavery within state; Articles of Confederation submitted to states
1781	Articles of Confederation ratified; American victory at Yorktown
1783	Treaty of Paris ratified
1785	Land Ordinance passed by Congress to organize western lands
1786	Virginia legislature passes bill separating church and state; Shays' Rebellion begins
1787	Northwest Ordinance passed

151

the United States and bring it under Spanish rule. Spain paid secret agents (identified with code numbers) to promote its interests. Among the agents was the famous frontiersman Daniel Boone, who apparently took the money but did nothing to earn it.

Spain discovered still another way to pressure the westerners. Spanish forts flanked both sides of the lower Mississippi River, the only practical route for western settlers to ship products to New Orleans and points east. Realizing the river's importance, Spain closed it to American navigators in 1784. If people in the West wanted to use the river, the Spanish declared, they had only to agree to become part of New Spain. Such foreign challenges to American integrity underscored the weakness of the national government.

Weakness at the Center

In the years following the war, the prestige of Congress among Americans steadily declined. The most experienced leaders of the war years were busy elsewhere. George Washington had returned to his Mount Vernon plantation. Thomas Jefferson served as ambassador to France and John Adams as ambassador to Britain. Others, such as Patrick Henry, remained active in state government. Those states that bothered sending representatives to Congress sent poor substitutes for the leaders of the Revolutionary War. It was not unusual for representatives of fewer than nine states to be present, fewer than necessary to act on important matters.

George Washington showed great foresight in 1780 when he warned, "I see one head gradually changing into thirteen. ... I see the powers of Congress declining too fast for the consequence and respect which is due to them as a grand representative body of America." Others such as James Madison, Alexander Hamilton, and John Adams saw the nation they had worked so hard to create seemingly break up into 13 stubbornly independent nations.

They saw Congress, the symbol of the national government, becoming a subject of ridicule in the world community and being scorned by state legislatures. They saw a central government so weakened by its inability to raise money that it could not even dislodge troops of the very country that the Americans had defeated in war.

They saw speculators, whose concern was money and not the welfare of the new nation, influencing territorial land policies. They saw the possibility of losing territory in the West to Spain because of jealous bickering among states. These leaders saw many faults in their first experiment. They needed little prompting to try again.

Toward a Constitutional Convention

The opportunity to act came in the fall of 1786. Convinced that the nation was falling into a state of economic anarchy, leaders in Virginia called on the other states to meet in Annapolis, Maryland, to discuss new ways of regulating commerce. Representatives from only five states showed up, but they decided to call another meeting the next year to discuss the broader problem of government under the Articles of Confederation.

If any of the other states doubted that action was needed, they became convinced during the winter when a group of disgruntled farmers from western Massachusetts rebelled against the state government. The farmers had been especially hard hit by a combination of low farm prices and high state taxes. Under the leadership of Daniel Shays, they closed many county courthouses and nearly captured an arsenal at Springfield.

The Massachusetts militia finally quelled the uprising, but it convinced many Americans that they needed a stronger, more effective government. With the reality of rebellion and the threat of anarchy in their thoughts, state delegates began arriving in Philadalphia in the spring of 1787. A new experiment was under way.

For answers, see p. A 25.

Section Review

1. Identify the following: Shays' Rebellion.
2. (a) According to the Articles of Confederation, who had the power to tax? (b) How could Congress raise money?
3. List three factors that made trade between states difficult.
4. (a) What action did George III take that showed his lack of respect for the new nation? (b) What action did Spain take that showed its lack of respect?
5. What was the original purpose of the convention that met in Annapolis in the fall of 1786?

IN PERSPECTIVE   The idealism of the revolutionary period sparked an experimental age in America. The first small steps were taken toward broader political and social equality although some Americans were aware that much remained to be done. The most significant experiments took place in government.

Once Americans declared their independence from Great Britain in 1776, they were responsible for governing themselves. The newly independent states quickly adopted state constitutions that reflected American belief in a representative government with limited powers. Creating a national government proved more difficult. Throughout most of the Revolutionary War, the nation was without an official government because not all state legislatures had ratified the Articles of Confederation. The major stumbling block was the dispute over control of land in the West.

The Articles were finally ratified in 1781. When the war was over, the new government established its land policy through ordinances in 1785 and 1787. Yet the weakness of the central government prevented it from solving crucial economic, political, and foreign policy problems. By 1787 many Americans were ready to experiment again.

For answers, see p. A 26.

Chapter Review

1. (a) How was the period after the Revolutionary War an experimental era? (b) What type of experiments took place?

2. (a) Describe a typical state government. (b) What branch had the most power? Why? (c) Why was the legislature divided into two branches?

3. (a) How were states' rights protected under the Articles of Confederation? (b) Why did the delegates think this was necessary?

4. (a) Describe the national government under the Articles of Confederation. (b) How were representatives allocated among the states? (c) Did everyone agree with this system? Explain.

5. (a) Why were claims to land in the West a problem for states that had none? (b) What effect did such claims have on the ratification of the Articles of Confederation? Why?

6. (a) According to the Land Ordinance of 1785, how was land in the Northwest Territory to be settled? (b) According to the Northwest Ordinance, how was this territory to be governed?

7. Why was economic unity difficult to achieve under the Articles of Confederation?

8. How did foreign nations react to signs of weakness in the United States?

For answers, see p. A 26.

For Further Thought

1. Did Americans during the 1770s and 1780s consider their state government or national government more important? What evidence can you give to support your answer?

2. (a) What weaknesses did the national government have under the Articles of Confederation? (b) Which of these weaknesses do you think was most serious? Why?

Developing Basic Skills

For answers, see p. A 26.

1. *Using Diagrams*   Study the diagram on page 146. Then answer the following questions: (a) What branches of government existed under the Articles of Confederation? (b) What powers did Congress have? (c) How did the structure of the national government differ from most state governments? (d) How did the powers of the national government reflect Americans' suspicion of a strong central government?

2. *Researching*   Visit a local library or write to your state's secretary of state for information to answer the following questions about your state constitution. (a) When was the constitution ratified? (b) Was the constitution written at a specially elected convention? If not, how was it written? (c) How do the powers of the governor of your state differ from the powers of most governors during the 1780s?

See page 774 for suggested readings.

9

A More Perfect Union

(1787–1791)

Chapter Outline

1 *Producing a New Constitution*

2 *Federalism*

3 *Limits to Power*

4 *Ratifying the Constitution*

5 *Insuring Individual Rights*

The powerful bald eagle, with its ability to soar high above other birds, was chosen as the symbol of the new republic.

By the spring of 1787, many Americans realized that the Articles of Confederation needed to be changed if the young republic was to survive. The threat of foreign intrigue, economic disruptions, and armed rebellion revealed the weaknesses of the Articles of Confederation.

The decision to revise the Articles was a bold one. Thomas Jefferson, observing events from his post as ambassador to France, approved. "This example of changing [the Articles] by assembling the wise men of the state, instead of assembling armies, will be worth as much to the world as the former examples we have given it."

The delegates to the Constitutional Convention faced a difficult task. Many Americans feared a strong central government, yet they realized that a weak government could not survive. The states wanted to protect their rights, but the delegates knew that the states would have to relinquish some power. Compromise would be necessary. When the delegates completed their work, they had produced a new Constitution, one that would provide a solid and enduring foundation for the new nation.

1 Producing a New Constitution

Twelve states responded to Congress's call of February 21, 1787, to send delegates to a convention for "the sole and express purpose of revising the Articles of Confederation." Only Rhode Island declined. Altogether, 55 men journeyed to Philadelphia, where the convention was to be held.

Once gathered, the delegates soon realized that their task would have to go well beyond that of simply revising the Articles of Confederation. They spent much of their time examining and discussing alternatives to the kind of government the Articles had established.

The Delegates

Many of the men who came to Philadelphia had extensive experience in government. Probably the best known and most respected were George Washington and Benjamin Franklin, who was 81 when the convention opened. Other familiar names belonged to younger men, like Alexander Hamilton of New York and James Madison of Virginia, both in their thirties. Madison in particular was exceptionally well educated in history and political theory. He would emerge as one of the chief architects of the Constitution.

Many delegates were surprisingly young. Five men were only in their twenties; another five were in their early or mid-thirties. Despite their relative youth, however, the delegates included two college presidents, three professors, and 28 men who had served in the Continental Congress.

But several well-known and respected Americans were absent from the convention. John Adams and Thomas Jefferson did not attend because both were serving as American ambassadors, Adams in Great Britain and Jefferson in France.

Patrick Henry, an ardent champion of states' rights, suspected that the convention planned to establish a strong central government at the expense of state power. Although named a delegate, Henry stayed away because, as he put it, he "smelt a rat." Samuel Adams, who also declined to attend the convention, shared Henry's suspicions.

The Constitutional Convention Opens

The delegates convened on Friday, May 25, 1787, and elected George Washington as convention president. His presence, as one delegate noted, helped give the proceedings a "national complexion." When the delegates adopted the rules of the convention, they decided that all debates and discussion should be kept secret so that delegates could speak their minds freely.*

For the next six weeks, through a hot and humid Philadelphia summer, the delegates sat cooped up five or six days a week in a closed and stifling room in the Pennsylvania statehouse. Discussion centered on the disrupted state of affairs within the country. Nearly all present agreed that the nation was heading for disaster under the Articles of Confederation. "Something should be done immediately," argued Gunning Bedford of Delaware. Caleb Strong of Massachusetts agreed that under the Articles, Congress was "nearly at an end. If no Accommodation takes place the Union itself must be dissolved."

The delegates generally agreed as well that the new government must be given clear power to raise taxes, enforce laws, and provide for national defense. It should be a republic, in which citizens elected representatives to make and enforce laws. Finally, the delegates believed that the government of the United States should be based on a written constitution, which they set about drafting.

Within the framework of these principles, however, the delegates faced seemingly countless choices about the nature of the new government. For example, when the debates began, few delegates had a clear idea of what the office of chief executive would be like, although nearly everyone agreed that the nation needed one.

Numerous questions arose. Should the chief executive be an elected president or a monarch chosen for life? Some delegates,

---

*The record of the Constitutional Convention is based on notes taken by delegates. Extracts from James Madison's notes appear on page 158.

The men who gathered in Philadelphia in 1787 to write a constitution for the United States created a document that has stood the test of two centuries with remarkably few changes. Among those at the convention were George Washington, presiding, and Benjamin Franklin, seated, second from left.

such as Alexander Hamilton and John Dickinson, favored a monarchy. George Washington also expressed a somewhat monarchist view when he proposed that the executive be called "His High Mightiness, the President of the United States and Protector of their Liberties." The delegates finally agreed, however, that the nation should have an elected president.

But this decision only raised more questions. Who should elect the President—the people, the state legislatures, or the Congress? How long should the term of office be? Delegates debated and agreed on answers to dozens of detailed questions like these.

The Virginia and New Jersey Plans

Early in the convention, the Virginia delegation presented a plan for the new government. The Virginia Plan, written by James Madison, proposed a national legislature, or Congress, to be divided into two houses, the House of Representatives and the Senate. Voters in each state would elect members of the House of Representatives. The number of House representatives allotted to each state would be proportional to the size of its population. Larger states would have more representatives than smaller ones.

According to the Virginia Plan, the House of Representatives would select the members of the Senate from candidates suggested by state legislatures. The House would also choose members of the judiciary and a President, who would serve for seven years. Congress would have the power to override state laws and, when necessary, make laws for the states.

Delegates who feared excessive central power objected to the authority that the Virginia Plan gave Congress over state legislatures. The main subject of debate, however, was proportional representation. Delegates from small states like New Jersey protested that such a system would give larger states too much power in the national government. Pennsylvania delegate James Wilson only aggravated the small states' fears when he exclaimed with annoyance, "Shall New Jersey have the same right or influence in the councils of the nation with Pennsylvania? I say no. It is unjust."

After two weeks of debate, William Paterson of New Jersey proposed an alternative plan. The New Jersey Plan suggested that each state, large or small, have an equal voice in Congress. Congress would consist of only one house, to be elected by the state legislatures, not directly by the people.

The New Jersey Plan allowed the central government the authority to raise taxes, regulate commerce, and enforce national laws. But the plan also specified that the states would retain powers not expressly given to the national legislature. This plan, in effect, maintained the major features of the Articles of Confederation, making only minor revisions.

The Great Compromise

The delegates rejected both the New Jersey and Virginia plans. Finally Roger Sherman of Connecticut offered a compromise proposal, which became known as the Great Compromise.

The compromise, like the Virginia Plan, provided that Congress have two houses. Voters in each state would elect members of the House of Representatives for two-year terms. The number of representatives from a state would be proportional to its population. This satisfied the larger states. Each state, regardless of size, would have two representatives in the Senate. As in the New Jersey Plan, this stipulation gave all states an equal voice, at least in one house. This pleased the small states. State legislatures would choose senators for six-year terms.

The Great Compromise marked a turning point. No state wanted to give up some of its power to a national government if its voice in that government would be weak. Sherman's compromise proposal attempted to satisfy both sides in the long dispute over fair representation. Had each side steadfastly held its ground, the convention might have broken up. The willingness to compromise on this crucial issue opened the door for other compromises.

Compromise Between Northern and Southern States

The Great Compromise itself raised another question, one that split northern and southern states. If representation was to be based on the number of people living in the state, should slaves be counted as part of the population? Southern delegates, who wanted to increase their representation in the House, said yes. Northerners, however, argued that because slaves were considered property they should not be counted. Again the delegates compromised. They agreed that only three fifths of the slaves in a state would count toward determining its representation in the House.

Another conflict between northern and southern states involved the slave trade. Many northerners wished to abolish it completely. Southerners objected, claiming that slavery was a necessary part of the southern economy. The delegates finally agreed that Congress could not interfere with the slave trade for 20 years after the Constitution went into effect.

Southern delegates also sought to protect their interest in foreign trade. The South's economy was more dependent on the export of agricultural products than the North's. Southern delegates wanted assurance that northern congressmen would not band together to tax southern exports. Such export taxes would place their tobacco, rice, and cotton at a disadvantage in world trade.

As a consequence, the delegates agreed to prohibit export taxes. Moreover, they required that two thirds of the Senate ratify treaties of any kind, which meant that southern states would have enough power to block unfavorable trade agreements made with foreign countries.

The Convention Ends

By August 6 the delegates had placed most of the fruits of their labor in the hands of a five-member Committee of Detail. Assembling the resolutions, this group produced a document of 23 clauses. Finally, on September 12, the Committee on Style went to work to polish the language.

Five days later, 39 of 42 delegates remaining in Philadelphia signed the document. Two Virginians, Edmund Randolph and George Mason, along with Elbridge Gerry of Massachusetts, abstained. They had concluded that the new Constitution vested too much power in the national government. Alexander Hamilton left the convention early for the opposite reason. He thought the states had retained too much power.

The Question of Slavery in the Constitution

Delegates to the Constitutional Convention hotly debated whether the Constitution should abolish the importation of slaves. As you can see in this excerpt from James Madison's *Journal of the Constitutional Convention* from August 21, 1787, many views were presented as delegates wrestled with the moral, economic, and political issues involved.

Mr. L. Martin [of Md.] proposed to vary article 7, sect. 4 so as to allow a prohibition or tax on the importation of slaves. First, as five slaves are to be counted as three freemen in the apportionment of representatives, such a clause would leave an encouragement to this traffic. Second, slaves [through danger of insurrection] weakened one part of the Union, which the other parts were bound to protect; the privilege of importing them was therefore unreasonable. Third, it was inconsistent with the principles of the Revolution, and dishonorable to the American character, to have such a feature in the Constitution. . . .

Mr. Sherman [of Conn.] . . . disapproved of the slave trade; yet, as the states were now possessed of the right to import slaves, as the public good did not require it to be taken from them, and as it was expedient to have as few objections as possible to the proposed scheme of government, he thought it best to leave the matter as we find it. He observed that the abolition of slavery seemed to be going on in the United States, and that the good sense of the several states would probably by degrees complete it. . . .

Col. Mason [of Va.]. This infernal traffic originated in the avarice of British merchants. The British government constantly checked the attempts of Virginia to put a stop to it. . . . Maryland and Virginia, he said, had already prohibited the importation of slaves expressly. North Carolina had done the same in substance. All this would be in vain if South Carolina and Georgia be at liberty to import. The Western people are already calling out for slaves for their new lands, and will fill that country with slaves, if they can be got through South Carolina and Georgia. . . . He held it essential, in every point of view, that the general government should have power to prevent the increase of slavery.

Gen. [Charles C.] Pinckney [of S.C.] declared it to be his firm opinion that if himself and all his colleagues were to sign the Constitution, and use their personal influence, it would be of no avail towards obtaining the assent of their constituents [to a slave-trade prohibition]. South Carolina and Georgia cannot do without slaves. . . . He contended that the importation of slaves would be for the interest of the whole Union. The more slaves, the more produce to employ the carrying trade; the more consumption also; and the more of this, the more of revenue for the common treasury.

The Constitution required that the voters of each state choose delegates to special state conventions that would meet to decide whether the states should accept the plan for the new government. Once nine out of the 13 states accepted it, the Constitution would go into effect. Before considering the ratification struggle, it is important to look in detail at the new government the convention proposed. (See the Constitution, pages 784–814.)

For answers, see p. A 27.

Section Review

1. Identify the following: Virginia Plan, New Jersey Plan, the Great Compromise.
2. (a) Which well-known Americans did not attend the Constitutional Convention? (b) What were their reasons for staying away?
3. List three principles of government that the delegates to the convention generally agreed upon.
4. (a) How would representation have been allocated among the states according to the Virginia Plan? (b) How would it have been allocated according to the New Jersey Plan?
5. What major issue did the Great Compromise resolve?
6. How were slaves to be counted in determining representation for a state?
7. How did the delegates protect the South's interest in foreign trade?
8. How many states had to ratify the Constitution before it could go into effect?

2 Federalism

Central to any government is the question of *sovereignty*, the source of the government's power or authority. The opening words of the Constitution, "We, the people of the United States," suggest that the delegates to the convention in Philadelphia believed that sovereignty in the new government of the United States lay with the people. Yet they disagreed whether this meant the people of the individual states or the people of the nation as a whole. Should ultimate power be given to the states or to the national government?

Debate Over Sovereignty

Many delegates to the Philadelphia Convention considered sovereignty indivisible. It must, they believed, lie completely in one place or another, either with the states or with the national government.

Under the Virginia Plan, the people would have delegated power to the central government, which could veto state legislation. This arrangement satisfied men like Governeur Morris of Pennsylvania, who favored the establishment of "a supreme Legislative, Executive, and Judiciary" because he believed "that in all Communities there must be one supreme power and only one."

Under the New Jersey Plan, on the other hand, the states would have remained sovereign, as they had been under the Articles of Confederation. Although the Articles had provided for a national legislature, that body had not been sovereign. It had to depend on state governments to carry out national laws, raise money through taxation, and regulate trade.

A Division of Power

The Constitution solved the conflict over whether sovereignty belonged to the national government or to the states by designing a system of dual, or shared, sovereignty. Under this system, known as *federalism*, governmental authority was divided between national and state governments.

The Constitution gave certain powers exclusively to the national government. These *delegated powers* include the right to coin money, regulate foreign and interstate trade, declare war on another country, and establish a postal system. States were forbidden by the Constitution to do any of these things.

Powers that the Constitution did not specifically grant to the national government were reserved for the states. *Reserved powers* include the right to control trade within a

■ *The federal system created by the Constitution delegated some powers to the federal government and reserved others to the states. Some powers were to be concurrent, or shared by both the states and the federal government. How do you think experiences under the Articles of Confederation helped shape the way powers were divided?* For answer, see p. A 27.

System of Federalism

Examples of Delegated Powers

Regulate laws of immigration and naturalization
Regulate interstate and foreign commerce
Set standard weights and measures
Create and maintain armed forces
Make copyright and patent laws
Establish postal system
Establish foreign policy
Create lower courts
Print money
Declare war

Examples of Concurrent Powers

Borrow money
Provide for health, safety, and welfare
Administer criminal justice
Set minimum wage
Charter banks
Levy taxes

Examples of Reserved Powers

Create corporation laws
Regulate intrastate commerce
Establish and maintain schools
Establish and maintain local governments
Determine eligibility requirements for elected state officials
Determine and regulate laws of marriage, divorce, and professional licenses

state, to create local governments, and to establish qualifications for voting.

The Constitution granted a third set of powers to both the national and the state governments. Among these *concurrent powers* are the right to support education, enforce laws, and spend money on internal improvements, such as roads, dams, and parks. Finally the Constitution stated that in cases of a disputed claim to authority by states and the national government, federal courts would resolve the conflict.

A True Union

The system of federalism established a new relationship between the states and the national government and between the people and the national government. The Constitution stated that the Constitution and any national laws passed under it were the supreme law of the land. All people had to abide by them, and state legislatures could not change or violate them.

Under the Articles of Confederation, as you know, the people had no direct influence on the national government, nor could the government deal directly with the people. It could only act through the states.

The new Constitution established a direct link between the people and the national government. Voters elected members of the House of Representatives. Moreover, the laws passed by the national government affected the people directly. State legislatures no longer served as intermediaries.

Federalism is the central characteristic of the American political system. The delegates at Philadelphia created a stronger national government because they saw that a true union was necessary. At the same time, they retained significant powers for the state governments, to guarantee that the national government would not become too strong.

For answers, see p. A 27.

Section Review

1. Define the following terms: sovereignty, federalism, delegated powers, reserved powers, concurrent powers.
2. Would the central government or state governments have been sovereign under the Virginia Plan? under the New Jersey Plan?
3. How did the Constitution solve the conflict over sovereignty?
4. Give one example each of a delegated power, a reserved power, a concurrent power.
5. What was the relationship between people and the national government according to the Constitution?

3 Limits to Power

The long and difficult struggle against British tyranny had ended just four years before the Constitutional Convention opened. The delegates wanted to prevent such tyranny in the new government of the United States. Thus they tried to limit the concentration of power in any part of the government. As you read in the previous section, federalism divided power between the states and the central government to prevent either from becoming too powerful. The delegates further sought to define and limit the power of each branch of the national government.

Separation of Powers

The idea of establishing separate branches of government, each with well-defined and limited powers, was not a new one in America. Elected colonial legislatures had existed alongside governors and judges appointed by the king. Furthermore, as you read in Chapter 8, the state constitutions had specified separate executive, legislative, and judicial branches. But the state constitutions usually favored the legislative branch over the executive.

The Articles of Confederation had created a legislature but not a court system or an executive. The experiences of the preceding four years convinced many Americans of the weakness of that system. They also realized that legislatures, as well as executives, could become too powerful. Consequently, the delegates to the Constitutional Convention revived the idea of the *separation of powers*.

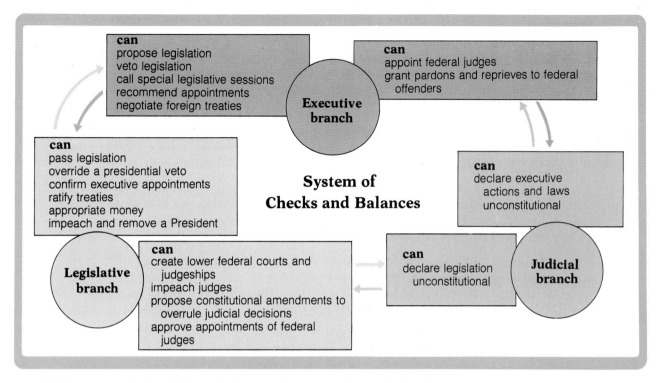

System of
Checks and Balances

Executive branch

can
propose legislation
veto legislation
call special legislative sessions
recommend appointments
negotiate foreign treaties

can
appoint federal judges
grant pardons and reprieves to federal
offenders

Legislative branch

can
pass legislation
override a presidential veto
confirm executive appointments
ratify treaties
appropriate money
impeach and remove a President

can
create lower federal courts and
judgeships
impeach judges
propose constitutional amendments to
overrule judicial decisions
approve appointments of federal
judges

Judicial branch

can
declare executive
actions and laws
unconstitutional

can
declare legislation
unconstitutional

■ *The framers of the Constitution wanted to prevent government tyranny. To do so they separated the powers of government among three branches: the legislature, the executive, and the judiciary. Then they established a system of checks and balances to keep any one branch from becoming too powerful.*

In so doing, they drew on the ideas of Baron de Montesquieu (mahn tuhs KYOO). Montesquieu's views on government, especially those he published in 1748 in *The Spirit of the Laws*, were well known to convention delegates, who often quoted him during the debates.

Montesquieu argued that to function properly a government had to possess legislative, executive, and judicial authority. In other words, the government had to be able to make, enforce, and interpret the laws of the land. To prevent tyranny, Montesquieu continued, these functions should be divided among three branches of government. The powers and duties of each branch should be carefully defined and separated so no branch could gain too much power.

The delegates built Montesquieu's ideas into the Constitution. Legislative, executive, and judicial powers of government were to be kept separate. The main function of the legislature, Congress, would be to make laws. The executive branch, headed by the President, would enforce the laws. The judiciary, or the courts, would interpret the laws and insure that they be applied on a fair and equal basis.

Checks and Balances

To reinforce the separation of powers, the Constitution established a system of *checks and balances* in which each branch of government could check the power of the others. This was based on another of Montesquieu's ideas, designed to prevent any one branch from exceeding its specified powers.

Remembering their quarrel with the king, the delegates in Philadelphia worried especially about the possible abuse of power by the chief executive. Some delegates considered distributing executive authority among several Presidents from different parts of the country. Although they quickly abandoned this plan, the delegates carefully built checks on presidential power into the new government.

The President was given the power to appoint cabinet officers, federal judges, and ambassadors. Such appointments, however, were to be approved by the Senate. The Senate also had to approve any treaties the President negotiated with foreign governments. Congress's sole authority to declare war would limit the President's power as commander in chief of the armed forces.

161

Congress could further check presidential authority by its power to remove a President from office. The House of Representatives could *impeach*, or accuse, a President of "treason, bribery, or other high crimes and misdemeanors." The Senate could then try the President and, upon conviction by a two-thirds majority, remove him or her from office.

Checks on the power of Congress were equally important. Both houses had to agree on a bill before it could be sent to the President. The President could check Congress by vetoing, or rejecting, measures it passed. Congress could override a veto, but both houses had to pass the bill again by a two-thirds majority.

The Supreme Court, with its authority to interpret the laws of the land, could check both the President and Congress by ruling their actions *unconstitutional*, that is, in violation of the Constitution. The President, in turn, appointed judges upon approval by the Senate. Moreover, Congress could impeach and remove judges from office, since the Constitution specified that they "hold their offices during good behavior."

The system of checks and balances resulted from compromises among the delegates, although nearly all agreed on the necessity of curbing excess power. In the end they were satisfied that the combination of federalism, separation of powers, and checks and balances would prevent tyranny by the national government. However, many delegates also feared tyranny by the people. The finished Constitution reflected this concern as well.

Limiting the Direct Power of the People

Several factors underlay the belief that the people's direct participation in the national government should be limited. Many delegates argued that representatives whose main business was to run the government were likely to be better educated and informed about issues than the people.

In addition the delegates believed that the people would have a hard time selecting national leaders wisely. Communication was slow and often unreliable. Voters could not possibly be familiar with national candidates and their views. Some delegates feared that large groups of people might be won over by rabble rousers and inflamed by emotional issues. Representatives, they thought, would be more likely to act slowly, deliberately, and intelligently.

Consequently, the Constitution created a republic in which voters elected representatives to govern the country. Further, as you have seen, voters were to choose only the members of the House of Representatives directly. State legislatures would select members of the Senate.*

The delegates also devised an indirect method of electing the President and Vice-President that is still in effect today. According to the Constitution, states were to choose electors who would vote for President and Vice-President. As a group the electors were called the *electoral college*. The number of electors for each state would equal the state's total number of representatives in Congress.

When the convention adjourned, most delegates felt that they had created a document that balanced the powers of the national government properly. The new government could act with firmness and vigor when needed, but the systems of separation of powers and checks and balances insured that the government would not abuse its power.

For answers, see p. A 27.

Section Review

1. Identify the following: Montesquieu, *The Spirit of the Laws.*
2. Define the following terms: separation of powers, checks and balances, impeach, unconstitutional, electoral college.
3. (a) What were the three branches of the new government? (b) What was to be the function of each?
4. Name (a) one way the President can check the power of Congress; (b) one way Congress can check the power of the President; (c) one way the Supreme Court can check the power of Congress.
5. In what three ways did the delegates limit the direct power of the people in the national government?

---

*The Seventeenth Amendment to the Constitution (1913) changed the method of electing senators. After that date, they were to be elected by popular vote rather than by state legislatures.

4 Ratifying the Constitution

Most delegates at Philadelphia were pleased with the government they proposed, but before the Constitution became law it had to be accepted by the people back home. Both supporters and opponents of the new Constitution gathered their forces and planned their arguments for the debates in the state conventions that lay ahead.

Arguments in Favor of the Constitution

Supporters of the Constitution, known as Federalists, argued that the United States needed a strong national government to overcome the clear weaknesses of the Articles of Confederation. The nation, in their opinion, had been in grave danger largely because individual states could reject national policy. According to the Federalists, the new Constitution gave enough authority to the national government to permit it to function effectively. Yet it still protected the rights of the individual states.

Three of the most able Federalists were Alexander Hamilton, James Madison, and John Jay. These men wrote a series of newspaper articles designed to win support for the Constitution in New York State. These articles, known as the *Federalist Papers*, summarized the advantages of a federal union under the Constitution. They remain one of the best discussions of the political theory behind the American system of government.

Opponents of the Constitution

The chief concern of the Antifederalists, or opponents of ratification, was that the new national government would be too powerful. Most thought the states should have retained more authority.

A Farmer Argues for the Constitution

Many Antifederalists were concerned that the proposed national Constitution did not adequately protect the country from tyranny. However, a farmer named Jonathan Smith urged the Massachusetts convention to ratify the Constitution precisely because he believed it was the only way to prevent tyranny.

Mr. President, I am a plain man, and get my living by the plough. I am not used to speak in public, but I beg your leave to say a few words to my brother plough-joggers in this house.

I have lived in a part of the country where I have known the worth of good government by the want of it. There was a black cloud [Shays' Rebellion] that rose in the east last winter, and spread over the west. . . . It brought on a state of anarchy and that led to tyranny. I say, it brought anarchy. People that used to live peaceably, and were before good neighbors, got distracted, and took up arms against government. . . .

Our distress was so great that we should have been glad to snatch at anything that looked like a government. Had any person that was able to protect us come and set up his standard, we should all have flocked to it, even if it had been a monarch, and that monarch might have proved a tyrant. So that you see that anarchy leads to tyranny; and better have one tyrant than so many at once.

Now, Mr. President, when I saw this Constitution, I found that it was a cure for these disorders. It was just such a thing as we wanted. I got a copy of it and read it over and over. I had been a member of the convention to form our own state constitution, and had learnt something of the checks and balances of power; and I found them all here. I did not go to any lawyer, to ask his opinion—we have no lawyer in our town, and do well enough without. I formed my own opinion, and was pleased with this Constitution. . . .

Some gentlemen say, don't be in a hurry; take time to consider; and don't take a leap in the dark. I say, take things in time—gather fruit when it is ripe. There is a time to sow, and a time to reap. We sowed our seed when we sent men to the federal convention. Now is the harvest; now is the time to reap the fruit of our labor. And if we won't do it now, I am afraid we never shall have another opportunity.

Source: Jonathan Elliot, *The Debates on the Federal Constitution* (1836), vol. 2, pp. 102–4.

The Antifederalists further believed that the indirect method of electing the President and the Senate removed government too far from the people. They opposed the longer terms of office proposed in the Constitution for similar reasons. Under the Articles of Confederation, congressional elections had been held every year. A longer term of office, argued the Antifederalists, would make representatives less responsible to the voters.

Even more serious in the eyes of many opponents was the lack of a specific bill of rights to protect individual liberties. Antifederalists worried that the new government might become one of tyranny, destroying everything that the colonists had won through the revolution. They urged delegates to state conventions to reject the Constitution.

Battles Over Ratification

State conventions in smaller states like Delaware, New Jersey, and Connecticut quickly ratified the Constitution. Antifederalist forces were weakest in small states, whose interests seemed to be well protected under the Constitution. The key ratification battles came in the more populous states of Pennsylvania, Massachusetts, Virginia, and New York.

In Pennsylvania Federalists showed that they could support their political arguments with tough political tactics. On November 30, 1787, Federalist legislators in the Pennsylvania assembly moved to form a ratifying convention, but before voting the assembly broke for lunch. When Antifederalist legislators refused to return for the vote, the assembly was two votes short of the quorum, or minimum number, needed to conduct business. The speaker of the assembly then sent the sergeant-at-arms out into the streets to find at least two more members and bring them back in. With the doors barred to prevent anyone from escaping, the assembly passed the motion for a convention, which ratified the Constitution on December 12.

Massachusetts delegates convened the next month. There, the Federalists avoided the political shenanigans used in Pennsylva-

This silk banner was carried by the Society of Pewterers in a huge New York City parade celebrating the ratification of the Constitution.

nia. Instead, they hinted to John Hancock, an influential delegate who wavered in his support of the Constitution, that he might win the post of Vice-President in the new government. Hancock's subsequent support helped Massachusetts ratify by a narrow margin in February 1788.

Maryland and South Carolina ratified later that spring. Then all eyes turned toward Virginia, where people expected a lively debate. Virginia delegates included prestigious figures like George Washington and James Madison, who supported the Constitution. On the Antifederalist side, however, stood Patrick Henry, George Mason, and Edmund Randolph, all names well known and respected in Virginia politics.

A real battle loomed until Randolph suddenly announced he would support ratification. His move weakened opposition, and Virginia ratified the Constitution at the end of June. Once news of the Virginia vote reached the New York convention, that state also ratified. New Hampshire's approval had already come in.

With more than the nine votes needed for ratification, Congress, in its last act under the Articles, ordered national elections to be held in January 1789. North Carolina did not ratify the Constitution until December 1789, and Rhode Island not until 1790. But by then the new government was already at work.

For answers, see p. A 28.

Section Review

1. Identify the following: Federalists, *Federalist Papers*, Antifederalists.

2. What arguments did the Federalists make in favor of ratification?

3. (a) What was the main concern of the Antifederalists? (b) What two other arguments did the Antifederalists make against ratification of the Constitution?

4. (a) Which states ratified the Constitution most quickly? (b) In what states did the key ratification battles take place?

5 Insuring Individual Rights

No sooner had the Constitution been ratified and the first Congress begun its work than changes were made in the document to insure individual rights. These and future changes were possible because the delegates to the Constitutional Convention had incorporated an amendment process into the final document.

Amending the Constitution

The delegates realized that a method of *amending,* or changing, the Constitution was necessary. They knew the document had to be flexible enough to adjust to conditions they could not foresee. Yet at the same time they wanted to guarantee that any changes would be well considered. Thus the amendment process they devised was a difficult one.

The Constitution provided that an amendment could be proposed at any time by either a two-thirds majority vote of Congress or by a special convention called by two thirds of the state legislatures. That amendment would become part of the Constitution when it had been ratified by three fourths of the states.

It is a testimony to the farsightedness of the men at Philadelphia that in nearly two centuries the Constitution has been amended only 26 times. The first ten amendments were adopted during the first years of the new government, and only 16 changes have been made since 1791.

The Debate Over a Bill of Rights

The first series of amendments involved individual liberties. The question of whether to include a guarantee of citizens' rights in the Constitution had surfaced many times during the convention. Several delegates wanted to clearly specify a list of rights that the government could not violate.

Others, led by Alexander Hamilton and James Madison, replied that there was no need for a bill of rights. The Constitution already protected individual liberties, they argued. One such protection was the right of

This painting, Stump Speaking, *by George Caleb Bingham, captures a typically American event: the campaign speech. The Bill of Rights in the new Constitution guaranteed Americans fundamental liberties such as the right to free speech and assembly.*

citizens to obtain a *writ of habeas corpus* (HAY bee uhs KOR puhs), a court order releasing a person arrested without specific charges. Habeas corpus thus protected a person against arbitrary imprisonment.

In addition, the Constitution prohibited state and national governments from passing a *bill of attainder,* a law allowing a person charged with treason or another serious crime to be fined or imprisoned without trial. Such laws had been common in Great Britain. The Constitution also outlawed *ex post facto laws,* or laws that made an act a crime after it had been committed. Finally, the document provided for jury trials in criminal cases.

Madison argued further that listing a set of guaranteed liberties might actually prove restrictive. To specify one set of rights might imply that only those rights and no others

deserved protection. Madison agreed that a bill of rights might be necessary in a government ruled by a king, but not in one, like the United States, in which sovereignty lay with the people.

Despite these arguments, pressure for a bill of rights persisted throughout the ratification struggle. Several states, including Massachusetts and Virginia, ratified the Constitution with the understanding that the new Congress would propose amendments incorporating a bill of rights into the Constitution. Madison, who served in the first Congress as a representative from Virginia, now decided that if there were to be a separate bill of rights, he should draft the document himself.

Congress took Madison's draft and passed it as the first ten amendments to the Constitution. These amendments, known as the Bill of Rights, were then submitted to the states for ratification. Over the next two years, the necessary three-fourths majority of the states accepted the amendments, and the Bill of Rights became part of the Constitution in December 1791.

The Bill of Rights

The ten amendments that make up the Bill of Rights insure the basic freedoms of American citizens. The First Amendment guarantees individual liberties, including freedom of speech and of religion, the right to peaceful assembly, and the right to petition the government. It also protects freedom of the press.

The next three amendments grew out of memories of British rule. The Second Amendment guarantees the right of people to keep and bear arms and thus assured the continued existence of local and state militias. The Third Amendment prohibits the quartering of troops in private homes during peacetime without the owner's consent. Ever since the Boston Massacre, Americans had feared the presence of soldiers in their cities. The Fourth Amendment, recalling the hated writs of assistance used by British customs officials during the 1760s, protects citizens from "unreasonable" searches of their homes or persons and seizure of their possessions.

The Fifth Amendment guarantees *due process* of law. This means that the government cannot act arbitrarily against a person. It must follow a specific open process in which the accused is notified of the charge and is given the opportunity to present a defense in court. Under the Fifth Amendment the government cannot require self-incriminating testimony nor may it try a defendant twice for the same crime.

The Sixth Amendment guarantees a jury trial in criminal cases and the right to be represented by a lawyer. Jury trials in civil cases are required by the Seventh Amendment. The Eighth Amendment forbids judges to set "excessive bail" or to prescribe "cruel and unusual punishments."

The Ninth Amendment assures citizens that the listing of rights in the Constitution does not deny the existence of others not named in that document. This answered the Federalist argument that such a list might restrict individual rights.

The Tenth Amendment was designed to reassure Antifederalists that the power of the national government would be limited. It states that all powers not given by the Constitution to the national government or specifically denied to the states are reserved for the states or for the people.

A Rising Sun

With the addition of the Bill of Rights, the Constitution seemed complete. Yet, the document's flexibility contributed to its greatness. The delegates foresaw that the framework of government would have to accommodate new circumstances. No one, perhaps, knew this better than Benjamin Franklin, who had seen his country grow and change so much over his long career.

When Franklin had first arrived in Philadelphia as a runaway boy many years earlier, the colonies were little more than local settlements along the Atlantic coast. Each colony observed its own customs and tended to go its own way. The colonies were, of course, able to unite on certain things because of a common English heritage and constant trade. Franklin himself had helped to bring the colonies together by improving communication in his post as deputy postmaster. But the colonies had been unable to unite in

167

Major Events	
1787	Constitutional Convention convenes in Philadelphia; Delaware, Pennsylvania, and New Jersey ratify Constitution
1788	Georgia, Connecticut, Massachusetts, Maryland, South Carolina, New Hampshire, Virginia, and New York ratify Constitution; Constitution goes into effect
1789	North Carolina ratifies Constitution
1790	Rhode Island ratifies Constitution
1791	Bill of Rights ratified as first ten amendments to Constitution

a common cause when Franklin had proposed his Plan of Union in 1754.

Yet Franklin had seen the colonies come together to fight a revolution and later to form a new government under the Articles of Confederation. Finally, at eighty-one, when the infirmities of old age required that he be carried by sedan chair to the convention, he witnessed Americans joining to create a new government.

As the finishing touches were put on the document, Franklin must have thought back over all of the obstacles to unity that he had watched the thirteen colonies overcome. While the delegates were signing the final draft of the new Constitution, Franklin called attention to the presiding officer's high-backed chair. On it was carved a sun.

Artists, he observed, often found it difficult to distinguish in their work a rising from a setting sun. "I have often in the course of the Session ... looked at that sun behind the President without being able to tell whether it was rising or setting. But now at length I have the happiness to know that it is a rising and not a setting sun." (See the picture on page 156.)

For answers, see p. A 28.

Section Review

1. Define the following terms: amend, writ of habeas corpus, bill of attainder, ex post facto law, due process.
2. (a) What are the two ways a constitutional amendment can be proposed? (b) What proportion of the states need to ratify an amendment?
3. In what way did Madison believe that a specific list of individual rights would be restrictive?
4. (a) How did memories of British rule affect the adoption of the Second Amendment to the Constitution? (b) of the Third Amendment? (c) of the Fourth Amendment?

★ ★

IN PERSPECTIVE When delegates from 12 states arrived in Philadelphia in February 1787, few realized that over the next seven months they would produce a new constitution. When they had completed their work, however, most felt confident that they had created a fair and workable system of government.

During the convention, the delegates successfully worked out compromises between large and small states and between northern and southern states. The federal system they created was designed to balance power between the national government and the state governments. Within the national government they divided powers among three separate branches and provided careful checks and balances to prevent any branch from becoming too powerful.

The first amendments to the Constitution, the Bill of Rights, were passed soon after the new government took office. These guarantees of individual liberties assured many opponents of the Constitution that the powers of the national government would be limited.

After its ratification, the Constitution remained a plan on paper. The challenge of making it work remained. As you will read in the next chapter, the next 12 years would witness a successful start of that process.

For answers, see p. A 28.

Chapter Review

1. (a) Why was the method of allocating representation in the national government such a hotly debated question? (b) How did the Virginia Plan propose to solve the question? (c) How did the New Jersey Plan propose to solve it? (d) What compromise was finally reached?

2. What compromises were made between the interests of the northern and southern states?

3. (a) How did federalism divide sovereignty between state and national governments? (b) How did this differ from government under the Articles of Confederation?

4. How was each of the following designed to prevent the abuse of power in the new republic: (a) federalism; (b) separation of powers; (c) checks and balances; (d) electoral college?

5. (a) What checks were to be placed on presidential power in the new government? (b) Why were the delegates especially concerned about the authority of the President?

6. (a) What checks were to be placed on the powers of Congress? (b) What checks do the legislative and executive branches have on the judicial branch?

7. Describe the arguments for and against ratification of the Constitution.

8. (a) Why did the delegates believe that a process for amending the Constitution was necessary? (b) Describe the process that was included in the Constitution.

9. (a) How were individual liberties protected in the Constitution? (b) Why did many Antifederalists believe that this was not enough protection?

10. List the individual liberties guaranteed by the Bill of Rights.

For answers, see p. A 29.

For Further Thought

1. (a) Why do you think the delegates to the Constitutional Convention decided to make the chief executive a President elected for a limited term of office rather than a monarch chosen for life? (b) Why do you think some delegates still seemed to favor a monarch?

2. Review the limits on the direct power of the people in the Constitution. (a) Which are still in effect today? (b) Why did the delegates want to limit the direct power of the people? (c) Do you think their reasons are still valid today?

3. (a) What personal characteristics did the delegates to the Constitutional Convention probably have in common? (b) What skills and attitudes would have been most important to them?

4. "Who are a free people? Not those whose government is reasonable and just, but those whose government is so checked and controlled that it cannot be anything but reasonable and just." Do you think the author of this quotation was probably a Federalist or an Antifederalist? Explain.

For answers, see p. A 30.

Developing Basic Skills

1. *Classifying* Make a chart with three columns. Title the columns Delegated Powers, Reserved Powers, and Concurrent Powers. Using the Constitution, your textbook, and other sources you may have, place each of the following in its appropriate column: voting age, education, an army, fishing regulations, off-shore drilling rights, income tax, luxury tax, police protection, motor-vehicle regulations, interstate trade regulations, intrastate trade regulations, postal service.

2. *Researching* Choose any two of the delegates to the Constitutional Convention. Research their personal backgrounds. In an essay, answer the following questions: (a) What similarities do you see in their lives? (b) What differences? (c) Was each a Federalist or an Antifederalist? Why?

See page 774 for suggested readings.

1803.

Unit Three

An Emerging Nation

10

A Federalist Beginning

(1789–1801)

Salute to General Washington, *by C. M. Cooke.*

Chapter Outline

1 *Challenges of the New Government*

2 *A Question of Entangling Alliances*

3 *The Birth of Political Parties*

4 *John Adams's Sacrifice*

To some, the most important question facing the new government of the United States seemed to be what to call the chief executive. The newly elected Senate spent almost three weeks debating the proper form of address.

Although many senators wanted to avoid the traditional titles of royalty, they thought that the President would need an impressive title when dealing with European heads of state. In the end they decided on the democratic-sounding "President of the United States."

The officials of the new government were well aware, however, that they faced greater challenges. They had the Constitution as a guide, but many details of government remained to be worked out. They knew that the decisions they made and the actions they took would set precedents, or examples, for the future. Presidents George Washington and John Adams were also to face unexpected challenges, among them the development of political parties and the threat of war with France.

1 Challenges of the New Government

Several serious problems faced the nation in 1789. Following election of the Congress and a President, other offices in the government had to be created and filled. President Washington could not handle all the executive duties by himself, so he would have to select advisers. He also had to choose justices for the Supreme Court.

The nation's income was small, its debt large. Paper money issued during the Revolutionary War was virtually worthless. The new nation would have to be put on a firm financial footing. Settlers on the western frontier were demanding that the national government protect them from attacks by Native Americans whose land the settlers had occupied. Finally, the new nation would have to establish credibility with foreign governments.

The First President

When the members of the electoral college unanimously chose George Washington as the nation's first President, they recognized that his popularity and prestige would give the new government much needed respectability. The strength of character Washington had exhibited as commander of colonial forces during the Revolutionary War had earned him the unreserved confidence of the American people.

Washington himself had hoped to retire from public life after the war, preferring the planter's life at Mount Vernon to a political career. However, the organizers of the Constitutional Convention had recalled him in 1787 to preside over the convention. And now he was being called upon again to lead the new government.

As President, Washington was a leader who stood above political conflict and intrigue. He saw himself as an arbiter, or a person who decides disputes, among the various interests within the government and within the nation. To fulfill this role, the President held himself aloof from others. He did not allow this air of dignity to be broken by familiarity. Once when Gouverneur Morris, acting on a wager, slapped the President on the back, the icy stare Washington gave him froze Morris in his tracks.

Setting Up the National Government

The First Congress of the United States, composed of 26 senators and 59 representatives, met in New York City, then the nation's capital. One of its first acts was the organization of the judiciary.

Although the Constitution stated that there would be a Supreme Court, it did not specify how the court should be organized. In the Judiciary Act of 1789 Congress provided that the Supreme Court would consist of a chief justice and five associate justices. President Washington appointed John Jay, who had been head of the Department of Foreign Affairs under the Articles of Confederation, as the first Chief Justice. The Judiciary Act also gave the Supreme Court final jurisdiction over disputes involving the Constitution, federal law, and treaties. Finally, it created thirteen district courts, one in each state, and three circuit courts.

A presidential cabinet also began to take form in 1789. Obviously, the President could not handle all the government's administrative duties by himself, but the Constitution was silent on the details of how to set up the executive branch. Washington frequently sought the advice of members of Congress, especially James Madison, a leader in the House of Representatives. But Presidents would need more formal assistance within the executive branch.

Article II of the Constitution authorized the creation of several unspecified executive departments. In 1789 these included an attorney general, a postmaster general, and secretaries of state, treasury, and war. Washington chose experienced advisers to head them. For example, he selected Thomas Jefferson, former governor of Virginia and author of the Declaration of Independence, as secretary of state. The secretary of war was 39-year-old Henry Knox, chief of artillery during the Revolutionary War.

The most important appointment in Washington's first administration was Alexander Hamilton as secretary of the treasury. As an expert in economics, Hamilton greatly influenced President Washington's policies on important financial questions. The President had personal confidence in Hamilton, since Hamilton had served on his staff during the Revolutionary War.

Only 34 at the time he accepted the treasury position, Hamilton was a man of rare genius and ambition. Born in the British West Indies, he had never developed the intense loyalty to a particular state that characterized so many Americans at that time. Thus he found it easier to think in terms of the nation as a whole.

Yet Alexander Hamilton held some strange opinions for a leader in a democratic republic. An admirer of Great Britain, he had little faith in the principle of equality, as he demonstrated in a speech at the Constitutional Convention when he said,

> All communities divide themselves into the few and the many. The first are the rich and well-born; the other the mass of the people. . . . Turbulent and changing, they seldom judge or determine right. Give therefore to the first class a distinct, permanent share in government.

Hamilton's aristocratic leanings influenced his proposals for solving the economic problems of the new nation, as you will see.

Restoring Public Credit

The most serious problem facing the United States was a huge debt from the war. The government had issued millions of dollars in bonds to support the war effort, and they had not yet been redeemed. Hamilton proposed funding the national debt at its full value of approximately $40 million. *Funding* is a process whereby a government raises or borrows money to pay off a debt. Hamilton planned to raise the money by issuing new bonds. These new bonds would be exchanged at face value for the bonds that had been circulated during the war.

People generally agreed that the debt owed to foreign banks or investors would have to be paid, but disagreement arose over what to do about bonds sold to American

The Creation of a National Capital

When the delegates to the Constitutional Convention met in Philadelphia in 1787 to draft a new constitution, they included a provision to set aside an area "10 miles square" to serve as the permanent capital of the republic. Never before had any nation created a totally new capital city.

Offers to host the "Federal Town" poured in from all parts of the country. The choice of a site on the Potomac River was made in 1790 when Jefferson and Madison convinced southern congressmen to support Hamilton's Assumption Bill in exchange for locating the nation's capital in the South. (See page 175.)

Pierre L'Enfant, a French engineer who had fought in the Revolutionary War, begged for "a

share in the undertaking." And his offer to help create a capital "magnificient enough to grace a great nation" was accepted. Andrew Ellicot and Benjamin Banneker were hired to survey the boundaries of the district.

L'Enfant enthusiastically laid out the plans for a city whose broad avenues would radiate out from the "Grand Edifices." He envisioned a "Congress House," a "Presidential Palace," and a monument that would pay tribute to Washington. Each structure was to be placed on ground that would command the greatest view. Upon seeing Jenkins Hill, L'Enfant proclaimed that it was "a pedestal waiting for a monument," and he chose it as the site for the Washington Monument.

Completing the grand design, however, was not easy. L'Enfant clashed with local landowners over sale of land for the capital and eventually quit in anger, taking his plans with him. But work could continue because Banneker had memorized the original plans.

Finally on June 15, 1800, the long-awaited public offices opened, and the national government moved from Philadelphia to its permanent home, the District of Columbia. Even then the main buildings were far from complete, and there were few places for government officials to live. Yet Washington, D.C., soon emerged as a symbol of American independence and national unity.

citizens. Most of the soldiers, widows, and other citizens who originally bought the bonds had sold them to speculators, in many cases for only ten to fifteen cents on the dollar. Was it fair, some asked, for the speculators to make a huge profit on the bonds they had purchased for such a low price?

James Madison, for one, objected to full funding. He felt the bonds should be paid off at a reduced rate to speculators, at full value only to the original holders. Madison's position in part reflected the sectional strain that was already developing between the North and the South. Over four fifths of the national debt was owed to northern investors and speculators. Full funding would seem to reward these northern interests at the expense of southerners.

Hamilton disagreed. He believed that purchasers of the bonds deserved a profit since they had supported the government in its darkest times. Besides, the purpose of funding was to restore the nation's credit and reputation. The United States could only do so if it paid its debts in full. Furthermore, Hamilton argued, many of the speculators were wealthy individuals whom the nation would have to depend on for future credit.

Congress passed Hamilton's proposal in February 1790. Some members of Congress who supported Hamilton may have been influenced by their own speculation in war bonds. They stood to make a profit if the bonds were funded in full.

As another step toward putting the new nation on a sound economic foundation, Hamilton proposed that the federal government assume, or take over, all state debts from the Revolutionary War. These totaled over $25 million. Such an action, he argued, would equalize the financial burden of the war. It would also bind the states more firmly to the national government, thus strengthening national unity.

Some states had already paid off their debts, however, so they opposed the *assumption* of state debts. Citizens in Virginia, Maryland, Georgia, and North Carolina did not want to be taxed to pay the debts of another state when they had already paid their own.

Hamilton, Madison, and Jefferson finally worked out a compromise, and Congress passed it. Since southerners owed a proportionately lower debt than northerners, Hamilton offered to appease them by moving the nation's capital from New York to a site on the Potomac River. The prestige and

Philadelphia mathematician and astronomer Benjamin Banneker published highly popular almanacs in the 1790s. At the urging of Thomas Jefferson, President Washington appointed Banneker to the commission that helped design the new capital city of Washington, D.C.

commercial advantages of having the nation's capital in the South appealed to Madison and Jefferson. Thus they agreed to full funding of the national debt and assumption of state debts.

The Bank of the United States

As a second part of his program to build a sound economy, Hamilton proposed the creation of a national bank. The bank would issue United States currency and would help carry out the nation's financial affairs. All federal taxes would be deposited in the bank, whose directors in turn could invest that money.

The government would own one fifth of the stock in the bank, and private citizens could buy the rest. Since stockholders would elect the bank officers, the management of the national bank would be in private hands. Hamilton's goal was to cement the loyalty of wealthy investors to the national government.

In February 1791 Congress passed a bill creating the national bank with little debate. Opponents of the bill, however, fervently urged President Washington to veto it. Madison and Jefferson strongly objected to the bank. They feared that the bank's directors would have too much power over the nation's economy. Together with Attorney General Edmund Randolph, they attempted to convince the President that the bank was unconstitutional.

Jefferson argued that the national government did not have the authority to create such a bank because the Constitution did not specifically authorize it. He cited the Tenth Amendment to the Constitution, which states that "all powers not delegated to the United States . . . are reserved to the states, or to the people." Thus, he concluded, the government had *only* those powers specifically listed in the Constitution. This literal interpretation of the Constitution has become known as *strict construction*.

Alexander Hamilton, on the other hand, favored a *loose construction* of the Constitution. He argued that the government had more powers than were actually listed. He cited Section 8, Clause 18 of the Constitution, which gives Congress the power to make all laws "necessary and proper" to carry out the specific powers listed in the Constitution.* Since the United States had the power to tax, according to Hamilton, it also had the power to create a bank to receive the taxes collected. Hamilton's arguments won the support of the President, who signed the bill into law.

Protecting the Nation's Industries

A third part of Hamilton's economic plan was not so successful. Hamilton wanted to see the nation's manufacturing grow, and he believed that the government should help. He therefore proposed that Congress pass a *protective tariff*. This would place a tax on imported products in order to raise their prices higher than prices on products made in the United States. People would then buy domestic goods. Such a tariff would thereby protect American manufacturers from European competition.

---
*This clause is often called the "elastic clause."

Congress did pass a tariff bill in 1792. However, the tariffs imposed were primarily for revenue, to raise money for the national government, and were lower than protective tariffs would have been.

Much of the opposition to Hamilton's tariff proposals came from the South. Since their economy was mainly agricultural, southerners had to buy more imported manufactured goods than northerners. They felt a protective tariff that raised the prices of those goods was unfair to them.

The Whiskey Rebellion

Finally, Hamilton proposed an excise tax on distilled liquors as another money-raising measure. Congress adopted such a tax in 1791. This measure eventually led to a rebellion in Pennsylvania that threatened the stability of the new nation.

Farmers in the Pennsylvania back country usually distilled their grain into whiskey, because whiskey was less bulky to transport by wagon and brought a higher price. They actually used the whiskey as money, since no stable currency existed yet. Resentment of the excise tax grew steadily as farmers saw their profits dwindle. The farmers finally rebelled in 1794 with cries of "liberty and no excise." They refused to pay any further tax, and some of them tarred and feathered revenue officials.

Although Pennsylvania's governor thought that the state could handle the situation, Alexander Hamilton saw a chance to demonstrate the power of the federal government. President Washington, taking Hamilton's advice, summoned a force of state militia. This show of federal force was overpowering, and the rebellion ended without a shot being fired. Hamilton wanted to punish the leaders, but Washington, with a cooler head, pardoned them.

Alexander Hamilton's economic program contributed to a strong start for the new government by restoring the confidence of both foreign and domestic investors and by building a firm foundation for future economic growth. President Washington's vigorous action against the Whiskey Rebellion also strengthened the national government. It demonstrated the government's authority to act within the borders of a state and clearly showed that the new government would act decisively in times of crisis.

When Pennsylvania farmers rioted against new taxes, President Washington called up the militia to put down the Whiskey Rebellion. Nearly 15,000 troops showed up, eager to fight. The President, mounted as usual on a magnificent white horse, personally rode out to review the troops at Fort Cumberland, Maryland, as depicted in this painting by James Peale.

For answers, see p. A 30.

Section Review

1. Identify the following: John Jay, James Madison, Thomas Jefferson, Henry Knox, Alexander Hamilton.

2. Define the following terms: funding, assumption, strict construction, loose construction, protective tariff.

3. What important attributes did George Washington bring to the presidency?

4. (a) What was the purpose of the original cabinet? (b) What was the source of the President's power to appoint a cabinet?

5. (a) What was the purpose of the Judiciary Act of 1789? (b) What were the major provisions of the act?

6. (a) What was the most serious problem facing the new nation? (b) What was Hamilton's solution to this problem?

7. (a) Why did Hamilton propose the creation of a national bank? (b) How would it operate?

8. (a) What sparked the Whiskey Rebellion? (b) What action did President Washington take?

2 A Question of Entangling Alliances

When they were part of the British Empire, the colonies had been drawn into European conflicts such as the French and Indian War. Now, even though the nation had achieved independence, it found it was still not totally separated from Europe. During the early years of the republic, Americans faced the danger of being drawn into yet another war.

Divisions Over Foreign Policy

The French people revolted against their king and aristocracy in 1789, the same year the United States adopted the Constitution. Most Americans reacted enthusiastically to the initial news of the French Revolution and the creation of a French republic.

In 1793, however, the French Revolution took a brutal turn. King Louis XVI was beheaded on the guillotine, as were many French nobles. The revolutionaries also replaced Catholicism with the worship of what they called the Supreme Being. This rejection of Christianity outraged pious Americans, and many people were shocked by the violence and bloodshed. Much of the early admiration turned into bitter opposition.

Alexander Hamilton was one person who abhorred the course of the French Revolution. In his opinion, by attacking the upper classes, the revolutionaries were eliminating the very people who were the mainstays of society.

Hamilton also feared that if the United States supported the French Revolution, it would risk war with Great Britain.* Such a development would mean economic disaster. About 90 percent of the nation's revenue came from customs duties, and 75 percent of its imports came from Great Britain. War with Britain would virtually wipe out this major source of income.

Other Americans were less disturbed by the turn of events in France. They believed that liberty often demanded great sacrifice. Thomas Jefferson had been ambassador to France before his appointment as secretary of state. Like many Americans, Jefferson deplored the violence, but he sympathized with the idealistic goals of the revolution. Indeed the French revolutionaries themselves had used Jefferson's ideas in their Declaration of the Rights of Man.

Hamilton and Jefferson tried to convince President Washington to take opposite sides in the war between France and Great Britain. But Washington decided on a more moderate course of action. In April 1793 he issued the Proclamation of Neutrality.

Citizen Genêt

About the same time Washington issued his proclamation, a new French ambassador, Citizen Edmond Genêt (zhuh NAY), arrived in Charleston, South Carolina. Genêt was an arrogant man. Even before he presented his credentials to the President, the Frenchman began outfitting American ships as privateers against England, setting up courts to deal with the ships they captured, and organizing an attack by American frontiersmen on Spanish New Orleans.

Genêt did not bother to consult the American government before undertaking these activities. Yet many Americans found him fascinating and cheered him on his journey to the nation's capital. This popular reception led Genêt to overestimate his influence. He began to believe he was better liked than the President. He told his government, "I live in a round of parties. Old Man Washington can't forgive my success."

When Genêt began organizing pro-French clubs that loudly criticized American neutrality, Washington decided to take action. Even Jefferson, always friendly to the French cause, agreed that Genêt's conduct had become intolerable. President Washington demanded that France recall their ambassador immediately. Genêt might have protested, but he learned that another revolution in France had removed his friends from power and that the new French government had ordered his arrest. Rather than face the guillotine, Genêt retired from public life, married the daughter of New York Governor George Clinton, and lived quietly in New York until his death in 1836.

The Jay Treaty

If Genêt's activities alienated many of France's friends in the United States, the British government was also alienating some of its supporters. Britain still had not withdrawn from its northernmost forts in the United States, although it had agreed to do so ten years earlier. British officials in those outposts reportedly sold firearms to Native Americans who were fighting an effective war against further intrusion into their lands.

Furthermore Britain's navy had begun stopping ships from the United States bound for the West Indies and seizing sailors whom they suspected of having deserted British ships. They then forced these sailors into service in the Royal Navy. In anger many Americans clamored for war with Great Britain.

In 1794 Washington sent Chief Justice John Jay, an experienced diplomat, to London to try to work out the dispute. Conditions did not favor successful negotiations. The British felt they were winning their war with France, so they were not in a con-

*By 1793 Great Britain had joined other European nations in a war against France. The British government considered the revolution in France a threat to all monarchies.

ciliatory mood. Jay himself could not negotiate from a position of strength since the United States lacked any real military power. Alexander Hamilton had further weakened Jay's position by telling the British minister about Washington's decision not to enter into an alliance with other European nations.

After learning that it did not have to worry about an American-French alliance, Britain could afford to drive a harder bargain. As a result, the Jay Treaty did not achieve what the United States had hoped for. The British did promise to evacuate their posts on United States soil and to pay damages for the ships they had recently seized. But they made no promises about future seizures or about their relations with Native Americans. Jay had to pledge payment of debts owed to British merchants before the American Revolutionary War.

Although the Jay Treaty avoided war, most Americans were unhappy with it. The pact seemed to be a surrender to Great Britain. The treaty especially offended southerners. Southern planters owed most of the debts outstanding to British merchants. They would have to pay, while northern shipping interests would collect compensation for ships and cargoes that had been seized.

President Washington was not happy with the treaty, but he recognized that the terms were probably the best Jay could negotiate. He recommended that it be ratified, and the Senate consented—barely—with exactly the two-thirds majority required by the Constitution.

A Treaty With Spain

The United States fared better when it negotiated a treaty with Spain shortly thereafter. The Spanish too were at war with France, but the war was not going well for them. Furthermore the Spanish government worried that the Jay Treaty might foreshadow a British-American alliance that one day could be directed against it. Thus when diplomat Thomas Pinckney arrived in Spain to begin negotiations for the Americans, he found the government quite willing to deal with him.

The United States wanted to settle two long-standing disputes with Spain. The border between the United States and Spanish Florida had never been firmly established. In addition Americans wanted to ship cargo down the Mississippi River and deposit it in New Orleans until it could be picked up by larger, oceangoing ships.

Pinckney negotiated solutions to both problems. Spain allowed the United States access to the Mississippi River as well as the right to deposit cargo in New Orleans. It further agreed to fix the boundary between the United States and Florida at the thirty-first parallel, exactly what Pinckney had been instructed to seek.

A Warning Against Permanent Alliances

When President Washington decided not to run for a third term in 1796, he was convinced that his policy of neutrality had been best for the nation. So important was the policy, in fact, that he devoted a lengthy portion of his Farewell Address to it. In the address, which newspapers published in September 1796, Washington warned the nation not to form "permanent alliances." The United States as a young nation would be better off, he said, if allowed to develop on its own.

Washington's warning referred to long-term political alliances that might embroil the United States in European conflicts. He did not oppose economic agreements that would build trade and promote economic growth. His successors would try to maintain a policy of political neutrality but would find it a difficult task.

For answers, see p. A 30.
Section Review

1. Identify the following: Edmond Genêt, Thomas Pinckney.

2. (a) How did Americans first react to the French Revolution? (b) What developments changed their attitude?

3. (a) What reasons did Alexander Hamilton have for opposing American support of the French Revolution? (b) Why did Thomas Jefferson disagree? (c) What action did President Washington take?

4. How did the actions of Edmond Genêt threaten American neutrality?

5. (a) What two promises did Great Britain make in the Jay Treaty? (b) Were most Americans happy with the treaty? Explain.

6. What two problems did Pinckney solve in the treaty he negotiated with Spain?

7. What reason did President Washington give for his warning against permanent alliances in his farewell address?

Washington's Farewell Address

President Washington's Farewell Address is probably best known for its warning against permanent foreign alliances. However, as you can see in the extracts below, Washington spoke about many challenges facing the young republic.

National Unity

The unity of government which constitutes you one people is also now dear to you. It is justly so, for it is a main pillar . . . of your real independence, the support of your tranquillity at home, your peace abroad, of your safety, of your prosperity, of that very liberty which you so highly prize. . . . It is of infinite moment [importance] that you properly estimate the immense value of your national union. . . . You have, in a common cause, fought and triumphed together; the independence and liberty you possess are the work of joint councils and joint efforts, of common dangers, sufferings, and successes.

The Constitution

The basis of our political systems is the right of the people to make and to alter the constitutions of government. But the constitution, which at any time exists, until changed by an explicit and authentic act of the whole people is sacredly obligatory upon all. The very idea of the power and the right of the people to establish a government presupposes the duty of every individual to obey the established government.

Political Parties

I have already intimated to you the danger of parties in the State. . . . Let me now . . . warn you, in the most solemn manner, against the baneful effects of the spirit of party generally. . . . It serves always to distract the public councils, and enfeeble [weaken] the public administration. It agitates the community with ill-founded jealousies and false alarms; kindles the animosity of one part against another.

The National Government

And remember especially, that for the efficient management of your common interests, in a country so extensive as ours; a government of as much vigor as is consistent with the perfect security of liberty, is indispensable. Liberty itself will find in such a government, with powers properly distributed and adjusted, its surest guardian. It is, indeed, little else than a name, where the government is too feeble . . . to maintain all in the secure . . . enjoyment of the rights of person and property.

3 The Birth of Political Parties

Political parties have become such a familiar part of the American scene that people often assume they have always existed. In the early years of the United States government, however, parties did not exist. In fact, people regarded them as evils to be avoided.

What you know as political parties today were called *factions* in the eighteenth century. The term described a group of people organized to pursue their own private advantages in politics. Faction members in British politics rarely concerned themselves with the interests of the community as a whole.

Thomas Jefferson expressed the general American attitude toward parties when he said, "If I could not go to heaven but with a party, I would not go at all." Even though most Americans shared Jefferson's views, the seeds of political parties were planted during the years of Washington's presidency.

Beginnings of Formal Opposition

James Madison, impressed with Alexander Hamilton's knowledge of economics, had recommended him highly to head the Treasury Department. Yet as the details of Hamilton's economic program emerged, Madison and Thomas Jefferson found themselves disagreeing with many of its main points, as you have seen. Both men tried to persuade President Washington to modify Hamilton's plans, but they were largely unsuccessful.

Jefferson and Hamilton, who came to symbolize opposing sides in the new government, were a study in contrasts. Hamilton dressed well; he was energetic and charming. He had married a woman from a wealthy New York family, and her aristocratic attitude influenced his thinking. Hamilton was knowledgeable and had a well-disciplined mind, yet he wrote in a heavy style that most people could not understand.

In contrast, Jefferson's clothes seldom fit well. He seemed awkward and shy and did not look people in the eye when he talked. His mind seemed less organized than Hamilton's when he spoke, but it was active and curious. His writing, in the Declaration of Independence, for example, had stirred the people to revolution.

Hamilton and Jefferson's political differences were even more significant than their personal ones. Hamilton felt the nation needed a strong central government with its power in the hands of wealthy, well-educated men rather than in the hands of the people. According to Hamilton, the nation's economy should depend less on farming and more on manufacturing, shipping, and commerce.

Jefferson, on the other hand, believed power should be dispersed. He favored democracy because he believed the people were the safest and most virtuous storehouse for power. He believed that universal education would increase the people's ability to govern. Jefferson thought the nation's economy should be based on agriculture.

While Hamilton emphasized a strong central government, Jefferson thought the states should retain authority. Since Hamilton's main concern was that government possess sufficient power to govern, he interpreted the Constitution and its list of governmental powers loosely. As he demonstrated during the debate over the national bank, he felt the Constitution implied powers that it did not specify.

Jefferson, in contrast, was a strict constructionist. He believed the Constitution granted only those powers that it specifically listed. The first two American political parties grew out of the differences between supporters of Hamilton and Jefferson.

Creation of a Party Machinery

In 1791 Jefferson and Madison went to New York, claiming they were going to study botany. The claim was not too preposterous since Jefferson was a well-known naturalist. But their real purpose was to meet with people in New York who also opposed Hamilton.

A small number of families competed for control of New York politics. Governor George Clinton and Aaron Burr led one side. The Schuylers, who were related to Hamilton by marriage, controlled the other.

While Jefferson and Madison were in New York, they struck a deal with the Clinton-Burr faction. This action marked a turning point in national politics. Previously, Jefferson and Madison had opposed Hamilton only on specific policy issues. Now they were taking the first tentative step toward establishing a national party of opposition.

A second step in setting up a party machinery was finding a way to inform the public of the party's point of view. In 1791 the only influential newspaper in Philadelphia, the nation's capital at the time, was John Fenno's *Gazette of the United States*, which consistently praised Hamilton and his economic program. Furthermore Fenno had received printing contracts from the Treasury Department and personal loans from Hamilton himself.

Jefferson had a plan for counteracting Fenno's newspaper. Shortly after returning from New York, he appointed Philip Freneau, a popular poet, to a clerk's position in the State Department. The job, which paid only $250 per year, required little work. But Freneau knew how he was expected to fill his time. He started a newspaper, *The National Gazette*, which published biting attacks on Hamilton. Its praise of Jefferson outdid Fenno's praise of Hamilton.

Madison, Jefferson, and their followers had not originally intended to start a political party, but by 1792 they were consciously referring to themselves as "the Republican party." When the Hamiltonians took the name "Federalists," their action marked the beginning of the two-party system in American politics.

Choosing a New President in 1796

The dispute between Hamilton and Jefferson greatly distressed President Washington since both men were valuable members of his cabinet. The dispute had, in fact, been one of the major factors in Washington's decision to seek reelection in 1792. He hoped that by running he could prevent the split between the supporters of his two cabinet members from developing further. Washington's continued popularity did eliminate the chance of much party activity in that election.

Four years later conditions had changed. Despite Washington's warning against political parties in his Farewell Address, the parties could not be kept out of the election in 1796. When Washington announced his decision not to run for a third term, the two parties became visible and active.

Although both Hamilton and Madison were influential among members of the government, neither had enough support among the people in 1796 to make a serious try for the presidency. The Federalists chose John Adams as their candidate; the Republicans chose Thomas Jefferson. Hamilton, who wanted to continue his influence in the government, feared that John Adams would be too independent if elected. So Hamilton devised a scheme to defeat Adams. First he arranged for Thomas Pinckney of South Carolina to be the Federalist candidate for Vice-President.

In the 1796 election the two parties specifically designated one candidate for President and one for Vice-President. The Constitution, however, did not recognize this distinction. It provided that each elector in the electoral college simply vote for two persons. The candidate receiving the largest number of electoral votes would become President; the one receiving the second largest number would become Vice-President.

Aware of this fact, Hamilton tried to persuade electors from both parties to cast one of their votes for Pinckney for Vice-President. He hoped that Pinckney would thus receive more electoral votes than either Adams or Jefferson. Then Pinckney, the Federalist candidate for Vice-President, would be elected President.

Hamilton's scheme did not work. Adams's supporters recognized the danger and cast their votes for Vice-President almost at random. As a result, Pinckney received only 59 votes. The Federalist John Adams became the second President of the United States with 71 electoral votes. Thomas Jefferson, a Republican, was elected Vice-President with 68 votes.

The outcome of the election had disclosed a flaw in the election process as originally defined in the Constitution. Candidates with opposing views could be elected President and Vice-President. This fact became all the more significant now that the opposing views were represented by distinct political parties.

For answers, see p. A 31.

Section Review

1. Identify the following: Republican party, Federalist party.

2. Define the term: faction.

3. (a) According to Hamilton, what group should control the government? (b) Who did Jefferson think should control the government?

4. List two other ways in which Hamilton's and Jefferson's views differed.

5. (a) Which Philadelphia newspaper supported Hamilton? (b) How did Jefferson counteract the influence of the paper?

6. What major flaw in the election process did the 1796 election reveal?

4 John Adams's Sacrifice

John Adams knew he would face difficult problems when he took office. First, he followed in the shadow of George Washington, already revered as the father of his country. Second, he inherited Washington's neutral foreign policy, which was becoming increasingly difficult to uphold. France had begun to attack American shipping, and members of Adams's own Federalist party were clamoring for war. The President, however, was committed to preventing just such an event.

Adams and the Federalists

Sixty-one years old at the time of his election as President, John Adams already had a distinguished political career behind him. As a lawyer, patriot, delegate to the Continental Congress, and Vice-President under Washington, Adams commanded the respect of all, especially for his fairness and honesty.

Yet honesty did not always serve Adams well in politics. He often told friend and foe alike what he thought, sometimes tactlessly. As a result, he neither commanded great personal loyalty from his subordinates nor encouraged close political friendships.

Nor did Adams and his wife, Abigail, particularly enjoy the cosmopolitan whirl of Philadelphia, the nation's capital from 1790 to 1800. They preferred the simple life on their farm in Quincy, Massachusetts. Adams left for home whenever he could and actually stayed there for 385 days during his four-year term as President. Consequently, he did not control his Federalist party as closely as he might have.

As President, John Adams retained Washington's cabinet, in part because he did not want to slight the former President. But he was also motivated by the difficulty of finding people willing to serve in government. The pay was low, the jobs were hard, and government officials were increasingly subject to personal criticism.

Unfortunately for Adams, Washington's cabinet members were loyal to Alexander Hamilton, the very man who had tried to sabotage Adams's election. The split between President Adams and Hamilton's followers, known as High Federalists, grew as the new administration faced worsening relations with France.

Pressure for War

The French government deeply resented the Jay Treaty (see page 178) because to the French it indicated that the United States favored Great Britain. In reaction France began to seize American merchant vessels sailing for England—300 by the middle of 1797. President Adams sent a mission of three men to France to negotiate an end to this activity.

When the Americans arrived, they were contacted by three secret representatives of the French government, called X, Y, and Z in published reports. X, Y, and Z demanded a loan of several million dollars to the French government, plus a bribe of $250,000 merely for allowing the Americans to talk to the French foreign minister. "Not a sixpence!" cried one of the Americans.

A war fever erupted in the United States at the news of the so-called XYZ Affair. The popular slogan was, "Millions for defense, but not one cent for tribute!" The pro-British Federalists led the cry.

American poets, cartoonists, and painters tried to find symbols for the vibrant patriotism of the new nation. This painting contains several such symbols, including the laurel leaf of victory being placed on George Washington's head, the new flag, the American eagle, and Miss Liberty. Washington's position as a symbol of the new nation made it difficult for his successor, John Adams, to establish his own independence.

The High Federalists saw the crisis with France as an opportunity to crush their Republican opponents. Arguing that the country had to prepare in case of war, they proposed that the United States raise a navy and an army—this in spite of the fact that all the fighting had been at sea. Republicans feared that an army might be used against opponents of the Federalists at home.

The President was under tremendous pressure to declare war, but John Adams had always been an independent man. In this crisis he acted in a way that surprised many people—not the least, the members of his own Federalist party.

Adams wanted to avoid war if possible, but he realized that the country must be prepared in case it came. He resisted the pleas of the High Federalists for an army because concentrating on land forces would leave the American merchant fleet defenseless. Instead he proposed the creation of an American navy.

As of March 1798, the United States had no warships. The small navy of the Revolutionary War had ceased to exist once the war ended. Congress now appropriated money to complete three frigates it had authorized earlier, and in July it issued bonds to pay for 24 more warships. During the summer the first three—the *Constitution*, the *United States*, and the *Constellation*—set sail. The new American ships, larger than comparable vessels in the British and French navies, performed well in skirmishes over the next two years.

As the United States and France teetered on the edge of war in the 1790s, the United States rushed to build warships. This print by William Birch shows construction of the frigate Philadelphia.

Avoiding War With France

In the meantime, the High Federalists continued to push for an army and a declaration of war. They persuaded George Washington to return to military duty, but he did so only on the condition that Alexander Hamilton be his second in command. President Adams resisted Hamilton's appointment, but he had to give in when Washington insisted. Adams realized that a declaration of war would increase the Federalists' popularity and perhaps win him a second term. But he knew the country was weak, and he would not gamble with its survival.

After receiving reports that the French might be willing to reopen negotiations, the President decided to make one more attempt. He appointed a new ambassador to France, and, as the Constitution required, submitted the nomination to the Senate.

The High Federalists, who wanted war, not negotiation, brusquely threatened to block Adams's nomination. Adams promptly threatened to resign and leave the presidency to the Republican Vice-President, Thomas Jefferson, if his own party blocked him. The High Federalist senators then agreed to compromise on a three-man delegation to France.

When the delegation arrived in Paris, it found a new French government, headed by Napoleon Bonaparte. Napoleon was more interested in European conquest than in conflict with the United States, so he was willing to compromise. In the Convention of 1800 the French promised that the seas would be free to American shipping. They refused, however, to pay for the American ships and cargoes they had already seized. Still, John Adams had saved the country from expanding a skirmish into a major war.

The Alien and Sedition Acts

Back home the High Federalists were creating another crisis. They introduced a series of acts in Congress, supposedly to prepare the nation for war. When passed by Congress, these laws were among the most repressive ever adopted in the United States.

One law, the Alien Act, attempted to reduce the political influence that foreigners or recent immigrants could have in the United States. It increased the residency requirement for citizenship from five to fourteen years and authorized the President to deport or imprison foreigners during war time. Most recent immigrants voted for Republican candidates when they became citizens. By delaying their citizenship the Federalists hoped to weaken the Republican party.

The Sedition Act had an even more directly political purpose. It provided for the fining or imprisonment of anyone who impeded the progress of the government or defamed its officials. To many people, especially the Republicans, this seemed to be a direct violation of the right of free speech so recently guaranteed in the First Amendment to the Constitution.

The expiration date of the Sedition Act was further evidence of its political nature— March 3, 1801—the day of the next presidential inauguration. The High Federalists hoped that the law would curb Republican criticism over the next three years and thereby guarantee a Federalist election victory in 1800. If the Federalists still lost the election, the law would expire and allow them to attack the new Republican President. While the Sedition Act was in effect the government indicted fifteen Republican newspaper editors, convicting ten.

Republican Resistance

To the Republicans, the Alien and Sedition acts seemed to be a clear abuse of governmental power. Since Federalists controlled the federal courts, Republicans turned to state governments in an attempt to end the persecution stemming from the acts.

In 1798 the Kentucky legislature acted against the Alien and Sedition acts by adopting a series of resolutions written by Thomas Jefferson. In the resolutions Jefferson theorized that since the states had created the federal government, they could *nullify,* or declare invalid, any law it passed. James Madison prepared similar resolutions that were passed by the Virginia legislature.

These resolutions revived the argument about whether the federal government or the states were sovereign. At the time the resolutions had little effect because no other states were willing to adopt such measures. The Alien and Sedition acts eventually expired. The idea of state nullification of federal laws would surface again, however, as you will see in Chapter 13.

Federalist Defeat in 1800

The Federalists faced many problems as the election of 1800 neared. Resentment over the Alien and Sedition acts lingered. The Federalists' agitation against France made them appear to be warmongers, and government preparations for a war that did not occur brought unpopular new taxes.

The taxes sparked violent resistance. In Pennsylvania federal tax assessors were attacked, and an armed band set two tax dodgers free. President Adams sent federal troops and state militia into Pennsylvania to restore order. Although Adams later pardoned all those arrested, the use of federal troops increased resentment.

The Federalists knew they faced a difficult election. They tried to persuade George

Major Events	
1789	Washington elected first President of United States; French Revolution begins
1790	Assumption Bill passed
1791	Bill of Rights ratified; Bank of the United States created
1793	Great Britain declares war on France; Proclamation of Neutrality
1794	Jay Treaty; Whiskey Rebellion
1795	Pinckney Treaty negotiated with Spain
1796	John Adams elected President
1797	XYZ Affair
1798	Alien and Sedition acts passed
1798–1799	Kentucky and Virginia resolutions passed
1800	Thomas Jefferson elected President
1801	John Marshall appointed Chief Justice of Supreme Court

Washington to reenter public life but he refused. The party finally decided to support John Adams for reelection. The Republicans nominated Thomas Jefferson for President and Aaron Burr for Vice-President.

During the bitter campaign, wild charges flowed from both sides. Federalists accused Thomas Jefferson of being an agent of French revolutionaries and atheists. Republicans, in turn, claimed that John Adams was a monarchist who wanted his daughter to marry Britain's King George III.

Tabulation of the electoral vote found Jefferson and his running mate, Aaron Burr, in a tie, each with more votes than Adams. Every Republican elector had cast one of his two votes for Jefferson as President and the other for Burr as Vice-President. In such an event the Constitution stated that the House of Representatives would select the President. The selection was complicated because Federalists had a majority in the House, and many tried to prevent Jefferson's election by voting for Burr. After 35 ballots in over a week's time, the House finally elected Thomas Jefferson.*

---

*Congress later took steps to prevent the situation from recurring. In 1804 the states ratified the Twelfth Amendment, which required electors to cast their ballots separately for President and Vice-President.

The Adams administration's last major accomplishment was passage of the Judiciary Act of 1801. It created a new system of sixteen circuit courts and reduced the number of justices on the Supreme Court from six to five. President Adams quickly appointed circuit judges to fill the new posts, rather than allow the incoming Republican President to select them. Adams also appointed a Federalist, John Marshall, as the new Chief Justice of the Supreme Court. Marshall was to become one of the most influential persons ever to hold that office.

For answers, see p. A 31.

Section Review

1. Identify the following: High Federalists, XYZ Affair, Napoleon Bonaparte, Convention of 1800, Aaron Burr, Judiciary Act of 1801.

2. Define the following term: nullify.

3. (a) What factors influenced John Adams to keep Washington's cabinet? (b) Why did that prove to be a problem?

4. (a) What two French actions led to demands for war by many Americans? (b) What steps did President Adams take to avoid a war?

5. (a) What was the stated purpose of the Alien and Sedition acts? (b) What political purpose did each also serve? (c) How did the Republicans try to repeal the two laws?

★ ★ ★ ★ ★ ★ ★ ★ ★ ★ ★ ★ ★ ★ ★ ★ ★ ★ ★ ★

IN PERSPECTIVE   The Federalists' defeat in 1800 marked the end of their era. Although they continued to be a strong opposing voice for a number of years, they never elected another President. Their own political philosophy led to their downfall. In thinking that an elite group of wealthy and talented men should run the country, they were out of step with the democratic sentiment of most Americans.

Their subsequent decline, however, does not diminish their accomplishments. In just twelve years the Federalists had established a vigorous and strong national government. Alexander Hamilton's ambitious economic program had returned prosperity to the nation and had earned it at least some respect abroad.

The creation of political parties was an unexpected development. Yet the two-party system has remained one of the major characteristics of politics to this day.

Perhaps most important, Presidents Washington and Adams kept the United States free from foreign entanglements during the first crucial years when the nation needed its strength to grow and develop. Yet this task became increasingly difficult for their successors.

For answers, see p. A 32.

Chapter Review

1. How did each of the following contribute to a strong beginning for the new government: (a) election of George Washington as President; (b) Judiciary Act of 1789; (c) creation of a cabinet?

2. (a) What measures did Alexander Hamilton propose to build a sound economy for the United States? (b) Which of these measures were adopted?

3. (a) Why did James Madison object to full funding of the war bonds? (b) What was Alexander Hamilton's position on the issue of funding war bonds?

4. (a) Why did Hamilton think the creation of a national bank was important? (b) Why did Thomas Jefferson believe that such a bank was unconstitutional? (c) How did Hamilton justifyflhis proposal?

5. (a) What was the American government's response to the Whiskey Rebellion? (b) How did this response demonstrate the strength of the national government?

6. (a) Why did the actions of Edmond Genêt concern George Washington? (b) What actions of the British government alienated even pro-British Americans? (c) Did the Jay Treaty satisfy most Americans? Explain.

7. (a) What actions did Jefferson and Madison take in 1791 that led to the creation of political parties? (b) Had they planned to start an opposition political party? Explain.

8. (a) What developments made it difficult for President Adams to continue Washington's foreign policy of neutrality? (b) What steps did Adams take to avoid war?

9. (a) Why did the High Federalists propose the Alien and Sedition acts? (b) Why did the Republicans object to the Alien and Seditions acts?

10. (a) What factors contributed to the Federalist defeat in the election of 1800? (b) How did the Constitution's provisions for electing a President and Vice-President complicate the election?

For answers, see p. A 33.

For Further Thought

1. (a) Why was Alexander Hamilton an unlikely choice for a position in the government of the United States? (b) Why do you think Washington probably chose him to be secretary of the treasury? (c) How did Hamilton's economic program reflect his political and social views?

2. (a) How would the Kentucky and Virginia resolutions have repealed the Alien and Sedition acts? (b) Based on these resolutions, did Jefferson and Madison think the federal government or the states were sovereign? (c) How did this revive the debate over sovereignty that had been so important at the Constitutional Convention? (See page 159.) (d) Why did the two resolutions have little impact in 1798? (e) Under what circumstances might they have had a greater impact?

3. (a) What role did newspapers play in the origin of the first two political parties? (b) Why were the newspapers so important?

For answers, see p. A 33.

Developing Basic Skills

1. *Comparing* Make a chart with three columns. In the first column list the following issues: creation of a national bank, interpretation of the Constitution, the French Revolution, powers of the national and state governments, belief in the people, manufacturing versus farming. In column 2 describe Hamilton's view on each issue. In column 3 describe Jefferson's view on each issue. Based on what you have learned about each man, how might you explain the differences between them?

2. *Using a Primary Source* Study the extracts from George Washington's Farewell Address on page 180 and answer the following questions: (a) Why is this document a primary source? (b) What type of document is it? (c) Why did the author write the document? (d) How might that affect what he said? (e) What does the document tell you about Washington's concerns for the new nation? (f) What can you learn from the document about the United States in 1796?

See page 775 for suggested readings.

The Republicans in Office

(1801–1815)

Thomas Jefferson, *by Rembrandt Peale.*

Chapter Outline

1 *Jefferson's Imprint on the National Government*

2 *Expanding the Nation's Boundaries by Treaty*

3 *The Coming of Another War*

4 *A Complex War*

When Thomas Jefferson became President in 1801, he was already well known to most Americans. He had designed the government and educational system of Virginia and had written the Declaration of Independence. His ideas had been incorporated into the Constitution, although a diplomatic assignment in Europe had prevented him from attending the Constitutional Convention.

Jefferson had served as George Washington's first secretary of state and as Vice-President under John Adams. As a defender of states' rights and limited government, he had become the most prominent Republican and the Federalists' chief rival.

During his administration, Thomas Jefferson was to preside over the most significant territorial expansion in United States history. He steered the nation along the edge of another European conflict, but his successor, James Madison, would not be able to avoid American involvement. Ironically, the young nation would emerge from that war with reaffirmed vitality and independence.

1 Jefferson's Imprint on the National Government

In his spare time Thomas Jefferson conducted scientific farming in Virginia, designed one of the most beautiful homes in the South at Monticello, filled it with intriguing inventions, and played the violin. But his ideas on government concerned Americans most as they awaited the inauguration of their third President. Federalists feared that his election would bring an end to stable and respectable government as they conceived it.

The New President's Style

Jefferson's inauguration was the first to be held in the new national capital, Washington, D.C. Despite this distinction, Jefferson deliberately made the event a low-keyed, almost casual affair. Rather than use the presidential coach, he walked from the boardinghouse where he had been living to the still unfinished Capitol building.

After taking the oath of office he read his inaugural speech in a voice so low that hardly anyone in the chamber could hear him. Then the new President walked back to his boardinghouse for a quiet dinner. When he entered the room, only one of his fellow diners even rose to offer him a chair.

Jefferson consciously made informality a part of his approach to government. The presidency, he felt, should not glorify the person who held the office. Consequently, the new President avoided pomp and ceremony in his duties. People in Washington grew accustomed to seeing the head of their government walking along the street or riding on an old horse as he went about the business of government. Instead of delivering rousing speeches to Congress, he had a clerk read his messages. Instead of holding formal meetings, he conducted as much business as he could at small dinners.

A Policy of Conciliation

Printed copies of Jefferson's inaugural speech quickly found their way into newspapers around the country, and most people liked what they read. This was as Jefferson intended, for he was determined, after the bitter election campaign, to unite the country, not divide it further. In particular, the President wished to assure his opponents that the new administration would not follow a wild course similar to that of the turbulent French Revolution.

To the embittered and defeated Federalists, Jefferson extended a conciliatory, reassuring hand, noting, "We are all Republicans, we are all Federalists." This spirit of acceptance ran throughout the speech.

Jefferson's early actions as President also eased Federalists' fears of an abrupt change in government. The new cabinet appointees, including James Madison as secretary of state and Albert Gallatin as secretary of the treasury, were Republicans, but Jefferson did not routinely dismiss Federalists holding government positions.

The new administration also retained some important Federalist policies. For example, the national government continued to pay off the states' war debts, as Alexander Hamilton had insisted it should do. Jefferson also allowed the Bank of the United States, another of Hamilton's economic measures, to remain in operation.

After his initial gestures of conciliation toward the departed Federalists, Jefferson moved quickly to implement his own Republican principles of government. In doing so he had the support of Republicans in Congress, who had won a majority in both the House and the Senate. He allowed the Alien and Sedition acts to expire and refunded all fines that had been paid under those acts. Under Jefferson's leadership, Congress also restored the former requirements for naturalization that allowed immigrants to become citizens after five years residence.

Conflict With the Judicial Branch

President Jefferson next turned to the task of dismantling the Federalist party's control of the judicial branch of the national government. As one of his last acts in office, President Adams had appointed a number of judges. He hoped this action would leave the Federalists in control of the federal judiciary during the new Republican administration.

Jefferson refused to be bound by these "midnight appointments," as he called them. He instructed the secretary of state, James Madison, not to deliver the official letters of appointment to any of the "midnight judges." The President further convinced Congress to repeal the Federalist-sponsored Judiciary Act of 1801, which had permitted a large number of new appointments to the judiciary.

Jefferson's decision not to honor the "midnight appointments" led to an important decision by the Supreme Court. William Marbury, one of the "midnight judges" appointed by Adams, sued Madison for refusing to deliver his letter of appointment. Part of Marbury's claim rested on a section of the Judiciary Act of 1789 that had set up much of the federal court system.

In the case of *Marbury* v. *Madison* the Supreme Court ruled that the Judiciary Act of 1789 was unconstitutional. Chief Justice John Marshall, a Federalist appointed by John Adams, stated that Congress had exceeded its constitutional authority when it passed the bill. In his decision, the Chief Justice firmly established the principle of *judicial review*, under which the Supreme Court has the power to review a law passed by Congress and reject it if it is considered unconstitutional.

This decision greatly angered Republicans, who thought Marshall was assuming too much power for the judiciary. To them it looked as if the Court could simply veto any legislation by declaring it unconstitutional. The justices had turned the Constitution into "a mere thing of wax," Jefferson complained, which they could shape any way they pleased. He believed this was unacceptable, not just because Federalists controlled the judiciary, but because he feared that Marshall might be upsetting the constitutional balance between the three branches of government.

Yet if the judiciary threatened to become too powerful, Congress itself had power it could use, the impeachment of judges.* Jefferson urged the House of Representatives to impeach certain judges who

he believed were unfit. The House impeached one federal judge for drunkenness, and the Senate convicted him.

The House of Representatives also began impeachment proceedings against Samuel Chase, a Supreme Court justice. Chase, a Federalist who openly denounced Jefferson's administration in court sessions, was accused of misconduct in office. The Senate, however, refused to convict Chase, arguing that his actions were not within the constitutional meaning of misconduct. In spite of Jefferson's efforts, the Federalists remained strong in the federal judiciary.

Jefferson's Philosophy of Government: Laissez-Faire

In his inaugural speech Thomas Jefferson suggested that the key to a "happy and a prosperous" future for America lay in a "wise and frugal [thrifty] government." The role of that government, Jefferson went on, should be confined to preventing people "from injuring one another" and "shall leave them otherwise free to regulate their own pursuits of industry and improvement." The philosophy that Jefferson described has become known by the French term *laissez-faire* (LEHS ay FEHR), meaning noninterference.

As President, Jefferson tried to limit the government's role in people's lives. He reduced the number of positions in the Departments of State and Treasury and cut the federal budget. Congress also repealed the unpopular excise tax on whiskey.

Jefferson took special aim at the military budget, partly because of his belief in laissez-faire, partly because he believed that a large army or navy in peacetime posed a threat to liberty. Consequently, he reduced the armed forces budget to half of what it had been under the Federalists. He confined the navy's role to coastal defense, using small, inexpensive gunboats. Thus the government canceled contracts to build several large oceangoing warships.

Conflict on the Barbary Coast

Cutting the navy proved too hasty an action, however, for its sailors and ships were soon needed against pirates off the coast of North Africa. For years the rulers of the Barbary Coast states of Morocco, Algiers, Tunis, and Tripoli had forced many nations, including

*According to the Constitution, the House of Representatives can impeach, or accuse, federal judges of "treason, bribery, or other high crimes." If a two-thirds majority of the Senate votes to convict the judge, he or she is removed from office.

the United States, to pay them an annual sum or risk the capture of merchant ships that ventured into the Mediterranean Sea.

Paying tribute irritated the American sense of honor. It was also expensive, since the United States trade in the area was extensive. When the pirates increased their demands in 1801, President Jefferson sent a squadron of eight naval vessels to the Mediterranean to enforce a blockade of Tripoli. When one of the ships, the *Philadelphia*, ran aground, the pirates threw its crew into prison and converted the ship to their own use. Lieutenant Stephen Decatur then sailed another United States ship into Tripoli harbor and burned the *Philadelphia*, depriving the pirates of its use.

Meanwhile, a small force of American marines landed in Tripoli, captured a city, and forced the Barbary leaders to make peace. The United States concluded a victorious treaty with Tripoli in 1805. The Barbary Coast action demonstrated the need to maintain a navy of reasonable size to protect American shipping around the world.

Threats to the Nation's Unity

Throughout his first term, Jefferson worked to conciliate Federalists and to smooth over disputes within the Republican party. He built Republican strength in the former Federalist strongholds of New York and New England. The President also won over some Federalists through his careful appointment policy, removing mostly High Federalists and replacing them with moderate Republicans. As a result, Jefferson won reelection in 1804, with George Clinton as Vice-President, replacing Aaron Burr.

Not everyone had been willing to come under Jefferson's banner during his first administration. Bitter at the resounding defeat of their party in 1800, a small group of High Federalists devised a scheme whereby New England and New York would unite in an independent confederation and *secede*, or withdraw, from the union. They approached Vice-President Aaron Burr. Burr, who had been out of favor with the Republicans since 1800, when he had allowed the Federalists to back his candidacy for President, agreed to join the scheme. (See page 186.) In return he expected the Federalists to support him as a candidate for governor of New York.

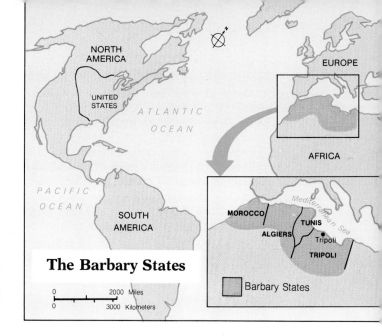

The Barbary States

■ For years the Barbary states on the coast of North Africa had forced other countries to pay an annual tribute or have their ships captured by pirates. When the Barbary states demanded more money from the United States, President Jefferson sent the small U.S. Navy to blockade the port of Tripoli.

Before the plot could get very far, Alexander Hamilton exposed Burr's role and called him unfit for public office. Burr responded by challenging Hamilton to a duel. Dueling was illegal, and Alexander Hamilton had publicly opposed the practice, but this time he decided to fight. Hamilton wrote to his wife and eight children that if he backed down from the challenge, he feared people would consider him a coward. Hamilton paid for his decision with his life. In Weehawken, New Jersey, at dawn on July 11, 1804, Vice-President Aaron Burr shot and killed Alexander Hamilton.

Soundly defeated in his bid for the New York governorship and liable for arrest on a charge of murder as a result of the duel, Burr next became involved in a wild conspiracy to take control of land west of the Mississippi River. In 1806 Burr plotted with General James Wilkinson, the commander of American troops in the Louisiana territory, to carve their own country out of Spanish territory in the Southwest.

The details of their scheme were probably no clearer in 1806 than they are to historians today. After a year of plotting, Wilkinson suddenly betrayed Burr and informed Jefferson of the scheme. Burr was arrested, charged with treason, and brought to Virginia to stand trial. But Chief Justice John Marshall, who presided, insisted there was not enough evidence of treason to convict Burr, so he was freed.

In spite of such dramatic dissension, the overall mood of the early years of Jefferson's presidency was one of cooperation and conciliation. His conscious efforts to bring Federalists into his following paid off. But perhaps Jefferson's most popular move came to him unexpectedly. With one stroke of his pen, President Jefferson almost doubled the size of the United States.

For answers, see p. A 33.

Section Review

1. Identify the following: "midnight appointments," *Marbury* v. *Madison*.

2. Define the following terms: judicial review, laissez-faire, secede.

3. In what ways was Thomas Jefferson's approach to government informal?

4. (a) List three ways Jefferson tried to conciliate the Federalists after he became President. (b) What early action did he take to implement his Republican principles?

5. What two reasons did Jefferson have for objecting to the Supreme Court's decision in *Marbury* v. *Madison?*

6. What role did Jefferson believe the government should play in people's lives?

7. (a) Why did the United States pay tribute to the rulers of the Barbary Coast states? (b) How did the American government finally end this piracy?

2 Expanding the Nation's Boundaries by Treaty

On April 12, 1803, representatives from the United States and France concluded an agreement in which the United States purchased the vast tract of French-owned lands west of the Mississippi River. For this immense territory, the United States paid about $15 million, or less than three cents an acre.

The Louisiana Purchase

Although few Europeans or Americans had explored the Louisiana territory, it had already changed hands several times before it became part of the United States. France, which had originally claimed the area, had given it to Spain as part of the treaty ending the French and Indian War. Then in 1800 Napoleon Bonaparte* secretly arranged for the territory to be transferred back to France.

At about the same time the press of American settlers west of the Appalachian Mountains increased the United States government's interest in the territory. As the number of new settlements in the area of present-day Ohio, Indiana, Kentucky, and Tennessee grew, the question of who owned the territories around the Mississippi River became especially crucial.

Roads in the western territories barely existed, so the Mississippi River and its tributaries served as the main route for trade into and out of the West. The port of New Orleans at the mouth of the river was especially important and, as you will recall, in 1795 Spain had granted American traders the right to use the port for overseas shipment. (See page 179.)

When President Jefferson learned of Spain's secret transfer of Louisiana back to France, he worried that Napoleon might attempt to use the territory as a base to build his own colonial empire in the West. Moreover, the French were again at war with Great Britain. Jefferson feared that if Napoleon closed New Orleans to American shipping, the United States would be forced to join an alliance with Britain against France. Jefferson, like Presidents Washington and Adams before him, wanted to avoid such entangling alliances. The President thus decided to try to gain control of New Orleans for the United States.

He sent Robert Livingston and James Monroe to France with instructions to offer to buy New Orleans and western Florida. Congress appropriated $2 million for the purchase. When Livingston and Monroe made their offer to the French government, its representative, Talleyrand, unexpectedly asked how much the United States would be

---

*At this time Napoleon was known as the first consul of France. In 1804 he became emperor.

willing to pay for the entire Louisiana territory, stretching from the Mississippi to the Rocky Mountains.

Although the American ambassadors had instructions only to purchase New Orleans, they quickly decided that this was an opportunity they could not pass up. So they agreed on behalf of the United States to buy Louisiana for about $15 million.

Napoleon had decided to sell the whole territory for several reasons. For one thing, he needed money to finance military campaigns in Europe, which he was trying to dominate. Furthermore, his aim of building an American empire had been shattered.

Napoleon had wanted to build this empire around a secure sea base in the Caribbean and had chosen the island of Haiti, a former French possession. In 1791, during the French Revolution, Toussaint L'Ouverture (too SAN loo vehr TYOOR) had led a successful slave rebellion and won Haiti's independence. Napoleon's attempt to reconquer Haiti in 1800 had failed. A combination of Haitian resistance and the devastating impact of yellow fever on the French troops successfully repelled the invasion. Once he had given up his goal of an American empire, Napoleon had little interest in keeping Louisiana.

Throughout the negotiations neither the French nor the United States government had considered the rights of the Native Americans living in the territory. Jefferson had assumed the problem could be resolved later. Napoleon did obtain from the United States the guarantee that French Catholics residing in the area would be given citizenship and the right to worship freely.

A Constitutional Dispute

When President Jefferson received word of the agreement, he faced a dilemma. He favored the purchase, but the Constitution did not specify how the country could acquire new territory or who had the authority to do it. As you know, Jefferson had long argued for a strict construction of the Constitution. His Federalist opponents, on the other hand, had endorsed a loose construction. (See page 176.)

The President first thought about submitting an amendment to the Constitution that would specify how new territory was to be purchased. But that procedure would take time, and the administration was afraid that Napoleon might change his mind and refuse to sell. Jefferson finally decided to base the purchase on his constitutional power to make treaties with foreign nations. He then sent the agreement with France to the Senate for ratification.

Federalists opposed the purchase, arguing that it was a waste of money and would add unreasonably to the national debt. Ironically, the Federalists also reversed their position on interpreting the Constitution. In this case they asserted that because the Constitution did not specifically authorize the President to buy land, he could not do so. Nevertheless, after a brief debate the Senate overwhelmingly approved the treaty. In December 1803 the United States took possession of its new territory.

Exploring the New Frontier

No one in the United States really knew how much land had been bought from France. The treaty that transferred title of the Louisiana Purchase to the United States stated its boundaries in vague terms. Jefferson believed that the United States could now claim all the land draining into the Mississippi River and its tributaries.

Even before the purchase, Jefferson had secretly planned an expedition to explore the territory. Soon after the Senate approved the treaty, he authorized the expedition to begin. Meriwether Lewis, Jefferson's private secretary, and William Clark, younger brother of Revolutionary War General George Rogers Clark, led the exploring party.

The President instructed Lewis and Clark to gather information about the flow of rivers and the availability of natural resources, information that could be used to plan the future commercial development of the region. But Jefferson's natural curiosity and interest in science inspired additional instructions to study the climate, plant growth, and geology of the area.

The Lewis and Clark expedition, consisting of about thirty soldiers and ten civilians, left St. Louis in May 1804. For the next two years they journeyed up the Missouri River to the Great Falls, crossed the Rocky Mountains, and canoed down the Snake and Columbia rivers toward the Pacific.

Along the route Sacajawea (SAHK uh juh WEE uh), a Shoshone woman married to a

French-Canadian explorer, assisted Lewis and Clark as a translator and guide. Her ability to locate edible wild plants fascinated Lewis, who referred to her in his journal as the "snake woman." Sacajawea proved especially helpful when the expedition reached what is now Idaho, the region of the Shoshone nation.

In general, Lewis and Clark dealt cautiously and fairly with Native Americans during their journey. They traveled through the territory of many Indian nations and spent the winter of 1804–1805 in a Mandan village near what is now Bismarck, North Dakota.

In November 1805 the expedition reached the Pacific Ocean, where Clark carved on a tree, "By Land from the U. States in 1804 & 5." The group returned by the same route to St. Louis the following year. Their expedition was an enormous success, and the publication of their journals several years later provided detailed knowledge about the territory.

For decades fur traders, road builders, and settlers referred to the records of the Lewis and Clark expedition as they ventured into the new frontier. Other expeditions that Jefferson organized, especially those led by Zebulon Pike up the Mississippi River and up the Arkansas River to the Rockies, provided further valuable information about the new lands.

■ After the United States bought the vast, uncharted Louisiana territory for $15 million, Jefferson was eager to have it thoroughly explored and mapped. A two-year expedition headed by Meriwether Lewis and William Clark explored northern parts of the territory as far west as the Pacific coast. Farther south, Zebulon Pike explored the Southwest to the Rockies.

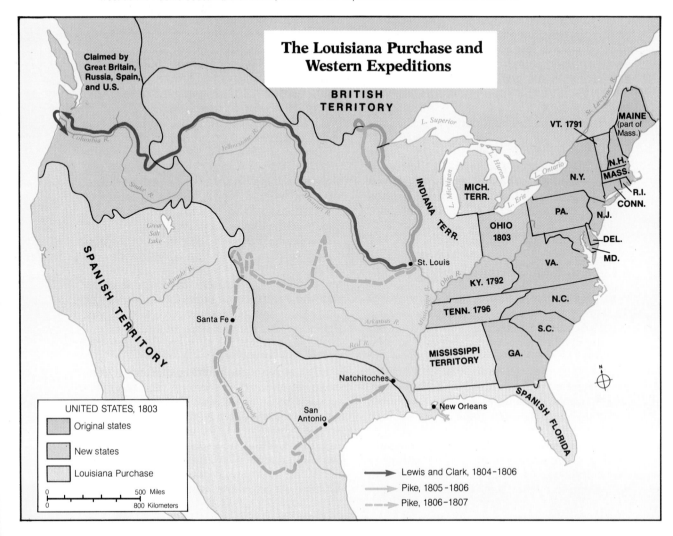

The Louisiana Purchase and Western Expeditions

Claimed by Great Britain, Russia, Spain, and U.S.

BRITISH TERRITORY

SPANISH TERRITORY

VT. 1791
MAINE (part of Mass.)
N.H.
MASS.
N.Y.
R.I.
CONN.
N.J.
MICH. TERR.
INDIANA TERR.
OHIO 1803
PA.
DEL.
MD.
VA.
St. Louis
KY. 1792
N.C.
TENN. 1796
S.C.
Santa Fe
MISSISSIPPI TERRITORY
GA.
Natchitoches
New Orleans
San Antonio
SPANISH FLORIDA

L. Superior
L. Michigan
L. Huron
L. Erie
L. Ontario
St. Lawrence R.
Columbia R.
Snake R.
Yellowstone R.
Missouri R.
Great Salt Lake
Colorado R.
Arkansas R.
Red R.
Rio Grande
Ohio R.
Mississippi R.

UNITED STATES, 1803
Original states
New states
Louisiana Purchase

0   500 Miles
0   800 Kilometers

Lewis and Clark, 1804–1806
Pike, 1805–1806
Pike, 1806–1807

The Lewis and Clark expedition spent a winter with the Mandan people, who built villages on bluffs above the Missouri River. The women in the foreground of this painting are using bullboats made of buffalo hide stretched over willow frames. The tail was left on the buffalo hide, and a piece of wood was attached to it to keep the round boats from spinning.

For answers, see p. A 34.

Section Review

1. Identify the following: Napoleon Bonaparte, Toussaint L'Ouverture, Meriwether Lewis, William Clark, Sacajawea.

2. (a) List two reasons Jefferson wanted to buy Louisiana from France. (b) What were Napoleon's reasons for wanting to sell the territory?

3. (a) What provisions did the Constitution make for acquiring new territory? (b) How did Jefferson justify his action?

4. What type of information were Lewis and Clark to gather on their exploration of the Louisiana Territory?

3 The Coming of Another War

Like his predecessors, President Jefferson wanted to avoid European entanglements that might push the nation into war. He had stated in his inaugural address that the United States had no interest in what happened in Europe.

The President hoped to devote the full attention of his administration to developing the economic, educational, and cultural institutions that would suit the new nation. But events in Europe dashed his hopes. Jefferson spent much of his second term in office trying to maintain American neutrality. James Madison continued the effort, but it was in vain.

Challenges to Neutrality

During the first decade of the nineteenth century, Europe was caught up in yet another war. Under Napoleon Bonaparte, France conquered nearly all of the continent between 1803 and 1807. Napoleon then turned his sights toward Great Britain. Although France was the undisputed master of the land in Europe, Great Britain ruled the seas.

Both nations used economic as well as military tactics in the struggle. In 1806 and 1807 Napoleon devised what came to be known as the Continental System. He closed

195

In this 1805 cartoon, King George III of Great Britain and the Emperor Napoleon of France carve up the world between their two nations. Napoleon's army controlled much of Europe, but England's navy dominated the seas.

all European ports to goods from Great Britain and ordered the seizure of all ships carrying such goods, even if they were the ships of neutral nations. The British government responded by issuing the Orders in Council, which prohibited neutral nations from trading with France or its allies. Violators of the orders risked seizure by the British navy.

The United States found itself caught in the middle. France would not allow American ships to trade with Britain, and Great Britain objected to United States trade with France. After 1806 ships bound for European ports were often stopped by the French or the British navies, or sometimes by both, and searched for cargoes destined for the enemy.

By 1807 France had seized five hundred United States ships and Britain had seized nearly one thousand. Such seizures were costly because by the early 1800s the United States had become the largest neutral carrier of goods in the world.

The British practice of *impressment*, or forcing sailors to serve in the Royal Navy, further angered Americans. Many sailors had deserted the British navy because of notoriously bad conditions. The British claimed the right to search American ships for these deserters. Indeed, since conditions on American ships were better than those in the British navy, many British deserters were serving with the Americans.

As the war with France continued, British impressment gangs became increasingly belligerent in their searches. Often they seized *naturalized* American citizens off the ships. These were former British subjects who had become American citizens. By 1811 nearly ten thousand American sailors had been illegally "pressed" into service for Great Britain.

American ships that resisted search and seizure risked damage. In 1807, for example, the British warship *Leopard* fired on the *Chesapeake* when it refused to allow an impressment gang to board. Badly damaged, the *Chesapeake* suffered 21 casualties.

The Embargo

Despite these violations of American rights, President Jefferson tried to find a peaceful way to show France and Great Britain that the United States would insist on respect for its neutrality. He decided to impose an *embargo*, or a complete halt to trade.

Britain and France each wanted to retain United States trade, but only for itself. Thus Jefferson thought that he could pressure the two governments into recognizing the new nation's neutrality by withholding trade benefits from both. Congress agreed and in 1807 passed the Embargo Act, which prohibited virtually all commerce with foreign nations.

The embargo did hurt both Britain and France. Unfortunately, it hurt American merchants too, especially in New England, where many sea captains had been willing to risk the seizure of their vessels for the high profits of wartime trading. The combination of the Embargo Act and the earlier French and British seizures of American ships had a devasting impact on United States exports. (See the graph below.)

President Jefferson had hoped to rely largely on voluntary cooperation from merchants to enforce the embargo, and some merchants did cooperate. Many, however, sought to evade the law. This evasion was most prevalent in New England, where economic survival depended on commerce. The West and South did not feel the effects of the embargo as much since they relied more on domestic trade. Yet some farmers did have a problem with grain surpluses because they could not export their products.

Many merchants who did not violate the embargo were ruined, and pressure mounted for its repeal. In 1809 Congress voted to end the embargo, and Jefferson reluctantly agreed that it had been a failure.

One positive effect of the embargo was not immediately apparent. While the United States was cut off from Europe, American manufacturers began to produce goods that were formerly imported. The embargo thus helped stimulate the development of American industry.

Outbreak of War

Thomas Jefferson decided not to run for a third term in 1808. He chose instead to return to the quiet life of Monticello. His secretary of state, James Madison, easily won election as President over Charles Pinckney, the Federalist candidate. Madison, one of the architects of the Constitution, wanted to continue Jefferson's policy of firm American neutrality.

When the new President took office in 1809, he encouraged Congress to devise a less severe alternative to the embargo, which it did in the Nonintercourse Act. This act prohibited trade with Great Britain and France as long as they continued to enforce their orders against neutral shipping, but it allowed Americans to trade with all other nations. The Nonintercourse Act proved to be as unpopular as the embargo because most American trade was with Britain and France.

Madison then announced that if either England or France would remove its restrictions on neutral shipping, the United States would halt its trade with the other nation. Napoleon saw this as an opportunity to trap the United States into siding with France. In November 1810 he announced that France would repeal its decrees against American trade with the British.

Napoleon probably had no intention of following through with his promise, but Madison believed him and did exactly what Napoleon had hoped. In February 1811 the President declared that the United States would continue trading with France but stop all shipments to Great Britain.

The interruption of trade with the United States severely damaged the British economy. In June 1812, following a difficult winter, the British government agreed to repeal the Orders in Council, but it was too late. By the time news of the repeal reached the United States, President Madison had

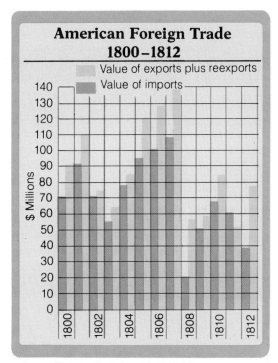

■ *French and British seizure of American ships plus a trade embargo in 1807 dramatically affected American foreign trade. President Jefferson imposed the embargo in hopes of keeping the United States out of the war between Great Britain and France.*

Source: *Historical Statistics of the United States*

lost patience with the policy of neutrality and had asked Congress to declare war on Great Britain.

The declaration passed with overwhelming support from the South and West. Federalists strongly opposed it because they had always been more sympathetic to Great Britain than to France. Representatives from New England and other trading centers—New York, New Jersey, and Delaware—also voted against the war. Despite the disruptions of trade since 1807, many merchants thought a war would be even more damaging to trade. For the second time in thirty years, the United States was at war with Great Britain.

Why War?

Historians have long debated why the United States went to war with Great Britain in 1812. The question is a difficult one since no single incident touched off hostilities. The attack on the *Chesapeake* was the sort of incident that could have started a war, but that happened in 1807, and war was not declared until 1812.

In his war message to Congress President Madison stated that the United States would fight to maintain freedom of the seas. Undoubtedly, Great Britain had violated that freedom. France had also seized American ships, but Madison and a majority of the members of Congress were Republicans, who traditionally sympathized with France.

One factor that contributed to the movement toward war with Great Britain was a growing sense of national pride, particularly strong among westerners. Although the British impressment of American sailors and the seizure of American ships had little direct impact on them, they considered such actions an attack on all Americans, and they clamored for war.

Senator Henry Clay of Kentucky led an especially belligerent group of Republican congressmen from the West, called War Hawks because of their prowar agitation. As intense nationalists, the War Hawks saw war with Great Britain as an opportunity to expand the territory of the United States. They made no secret of their desire to win Canada from Britain and, as one of them put it, "to drive the British from our Continent." The War Hawks also wanted war with Britain because they believed that the British

were supporting Native Americans who had been resisting settlement of the Northwest Territory.

Western Conflicts

American settlers had encountered resistance from Native Americans in the area west of the Allegheny Mountains since the mid-1700s. As you read in Chapter 6, in 1763 the British had tried to prevent such conflicts by restricting settlement beyond the mountains. After independence, the movement westward grew. Attempts to control settlement such as the Northwest Ordinance had little effect.

In theory the United States government was to obtain Native American land by treaties, then allow settlement. In actuality settlers pushed into whatever region they wanted. When they had taken up the best land in one tract, they expanded farther west without regard for the Indians' rights of possession. Furthermore, many of the treaties the United States did obtain were of dubious validity. Native Americans who signed the treaties often did not represent their nations or did not own the land in question.

Resistance to settlement increased in the late 1780s, especially in the area north of the Ohio River. In 1791 the Shawnee, led by Little Turtle, soundly defeated a force of militia under General Arthur St. Clair. But three years later an army expedition commanded by General Anthony Wayne defeated the Indians in the Battle of Fallen Timbers. The following year in the Treaty of Greenville, Indian leaders ceded a large part of present-day Ohio to the United States. This opened the way for greater settlement of the Northwest Territory, which also meant the acquisition of more Native American land, a total of about 48 million acres (about 20 million hectares) between 1795 and 1809.

Tecumseh and the Prophet

The continued movement of settlers into the Northwest Territory threatened the survival of the Native American nations that inhabited the area. Not only was their land being taken, often by deceit or violence, but their culture was being weakened by the adoption of alien customs.

The anger and frustration produced by this situation led to the emergence of two

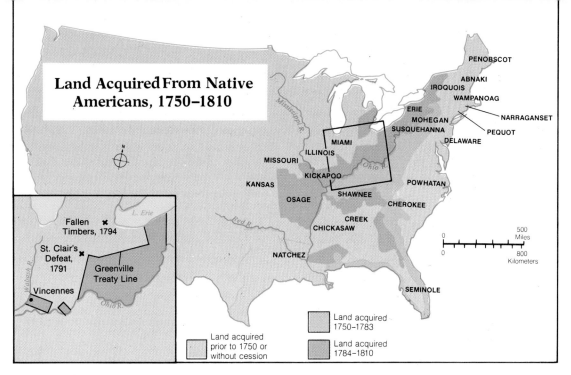

Land Acquired From Native Americans, 1750–1810

PENOBSCOT
ABNAKI
IROQUOIS
WAMPANOAG
ERIE
MOHEGAN
SUSQUEHANNA
NARRAGANSET
PEQUOT
DELAWARE
MIAMI
ILLINOIS
MISSOURI
KICKAPOO
POWHATAN
KANSAS
OSAGE
SHAWNEE
CHEROKEE
CREEK
CHICKASAW
NATCHEZ
SEMINOLE

Mississippi R.
Ohio R.
Red R.
L. Erie

Fallen Timbers, 1794
St. Clair's Defeat, 1791
Greenville Treaty Line
Vincennes
Wabash R.
Ohio R.

500 Miles
800 Kilometers

Land acquired prior to 1750 or without cession

Land acquired 1750–1783

Land acquired 1784–1810

■ As settlers moved westward, the United States took control of more and more Indian land. Indian attempts to resist the expansion ultimately failed. In the Treaty of Greenville (1795), Indian nations ceded much of present-day Ohio to the United States.

powerful Shawnee leaders, Tecumseh (tih KUHM suh) and his brother, who was called the Prophet. Their goal was to unite all Indian nations east of the Mississippi to resist further settlement. The Prophet further called on Indians to revitalize their own culture and to give up customs they had adopted from the new settlers.

By 1811 Tecumseh, a skillful orator, had organized a confederation that stretched from the Northwest Territory to Florida. A battle fought at Tippecanoe Creek in Indiana doomed the confederation, however. In November 1811 General William Henry Harrison, the governor of Indiana Territory, led a force of a thousand soldiers against Tecumseh's headquarters by the creek. The battle was a draw, but Harrison's forces destroyed the Indian camp. Westerners considered the battle a great victory, and many Indians became disillusioned with the confederation.

Tecumseh's activities further aggravated the anti-British feelings of westerners, who were convinced that the British were supporting him. When war did break out between the United States and Great Britain in 1812, Tecumseh announced his support for the British. During the war he led his Indian allies against United States forces in the Northwest Territory.

The alliance of the British and the Indians, however, did not dim the War Hawks' enthusiasm. Henry Clay boasted that "the militia of Kentucky alone" could beat the British. Clay would discover that winning another war was not that easy.

For answers, see p. A 34.
Section Review

1. Identify the following: Henry Clay, War Hawks, Battle of Fallen Timbers, Treaty of Greenville, Tecumseh, the Prophet, William Henry Harrison.

2. Define the following terms: impressment, naturalized citizens, embargo.

3. What actions did the French and the British take against American merchant ships after 1806?

4. (a) What step did President Jefferson take to pressure France and Great Britain into recognizing American neutrality? (b) What effect did the action have on American merchants?

5. (a) What was the purpose of the Nonintercourse Act? (b) Was it effective? Explain.

6. What did the War Hawks hope to gain from a war with Great Britain?

7. (a) How did Tecumseh try to halt the westward movement of settlers? (b) What was the result of his action?

Tecumseh: Who Has a Right to the Land?

Tecumseh tried to convince Indian nations living east of the Mississippi to stop selling land to the United States government. He argued that the land, like the air and the water of the rivers and lakes, belonged to everyone and could not be sold unless all residents agreed. In the following speech he protests the Treaty of Fort Wayne (1809) in which two Indian nations sold 3 million acres (1.2 million hectares) of land for a small amount of money.

The Being within, communing with past ages, tells me that . . . until lately there was no white man on this continent; that it then all belonged to red men, children of the same parents, placed on it by the Great Spirit that made them, to keep it, to traverse it, to enjoy its productions, and to fill it with the same race—once a happy race, since made miserable by the white people, who are never contented, but always encroaching. The way—and the only way—to check and to stop this evil is for all the red men to unite in claiming a common equal right in the land, as it was at first, and should be yet. For it never was divided, but belongs to all for the use of each. That no part has a right to sell, even to each other, much less to strangers; those who want all, and will not do with less.

The white people have no right to take the land from the Indians, because they had it first.

It is theirs. They may sell, but all must join. Any sale not made by all is not valid. The late sale is bad. It was made by a part only. Part do not know how to sell. It requires all to make a bargain for all. All red men have equal rights to the unoccupied land. The right of occupancy is as good in one place as in another. There cannot be two occupations in the same place. The first excludes all others. It is not so in hunting or traveling; for there the same ground will serve many, as they may follow each other all day. But the camp is stationary, and that is occupancy. It belongs to the first who sits down on his blanket or skins which he has thrown upon the ground; and till he leaves it no other has a right.

Source: Chauncey M. Depew, ed., *The Library of Oratory: Ancient and Modern* (New York: Globe, 1902).

4 A Complex War

At first, neither Britain nor the United States seemed to take the war very seriously. The British, preoccupied by their fight with Napoleon, tended to view military campaigns in the former colonies as a secondary venture. In the United States opposition to the war continued, especially in the Federalist stronghold of New England. Nearly two years would slip by before the United States could even organize its army into a major fighting force.

A Slow Start

The regular army of the United States numbered fewer than 7,000 soldiers when the nation declared war. Another 690,000 men made up the state militias. Although available for service, the militias were still under state and local control, and many were reluctant to leave their states. Bringing these units under federal authority required an act of Congress, but Congress moved very slowly.

In addition, the army suffered from an almost total lack of competent leaders. Most of its generals had participated in the Revolutionary War almost 30 years before. It took time and, unfortunately, some defeats in battle to identify promising junior officers and appoint them to command positions.

The navy was in slightly better shape; a number of its officers had gained experience in battles in Tripoli. Still the American fleet remained pitifully small, comprising only 16 vessels when the war began. Again Congress wasted valuable months arguing before it approved the construction of warships. And by the time these were completed, the war had ended.

Ineffective strategy further marred the initial military campaigns of the war. A quick American victory depended on conquering Canada, the center of British power in North America. That objective could most likely have been accomplished with an attack on Montreal to cut off British access to the sea, the same strategy that the British had employed successfully against the French in 1763. However, United States leaders, especially War Hawks, were preoccupied with western Canada and Indian activity on the frontier near Lake Erie. As a result, they never mobilized for a full-scale attack on Canada.

Not surprisingly, the war began with a series of reverses for the United States. In August 1812 General William Hull, a former commander in the Revolutionary War, moved his forces along Lake Erie to Detroit. At Detroit the British tricked Hull into believing that he faced a much larger force of British soldiers and Indian allies than was actually the case. Hull abruptly surrendered his army without firing a shot.

Closer to Montreal, another American campaign failed when the New York state militia refused to cross into Canada to fight. Only at sea were the Americans victorious, when the USS *Constitution* sank the British ship *Guerrière*.

Opposition to the War

The early defeats on land further convinced the Federalists in New England that the war was a mistake and could not be won. Moreover the British navy blockaded the Atlantic coast, which disrupted American trade. This further angered New England merchants. By 1814 foreign trade had fallen over 90 percent from its peak in 1807. Shipbuilding, a major New England industry, dropped 80 percent during the war.

New Englanders were also uneasy about the growing power of the western states. Territorial expansion would mean additional western states, and New England would have even less influence in national affairs.

■ *Much of the fighting in the War of 1812 took place in the West. Several Indian nations allied with the British in the hope of stopping further settlement.*

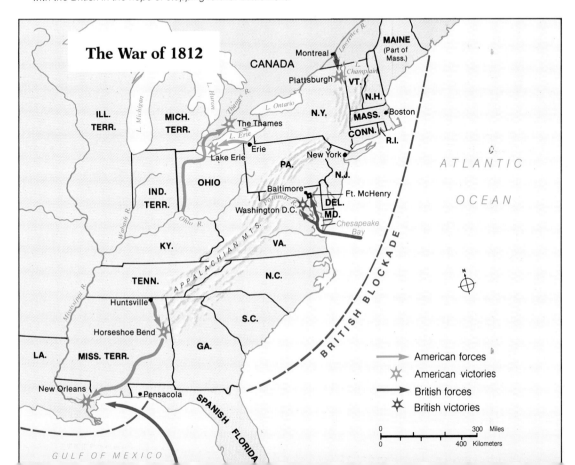

Opposition to the war peaked in the fall of 1814 at the Hartford Convention. Twenty-six delegates from the New England states gathered in Hartford, Connecticut, to protest President Madison's conduct of the war. The delegates issued a long series of demands designed to protect the interests of New England against the South and the West. They threatened to secede and form an independent federation if their demands were not met. However, by the time the results of the Hartford Convention reached Washington, the war was over, and the convention's demands became a dead issue.

The Tide Begins to Turn

By 1813 the American cause appeared more hopeful. In September Captain Oliver Hazard Perry won the first major American victory when his squadron of naval ships defeated a British fleet on Lake Erie. "We have met the enemy and they are ours," Perry reported to General Harrison. Perry's victory gave the United States control of Lake Erie.

Next General Harrison moved a force of recently recruited troops north of Lake Ontario into Canada. A month after Perry's victory, Harrison's troops defeated a combined British and Indian force at the Battle of the Thames. The Shawnee leader Tecumseh died during this battle. Without his leadership, the Indian confederation collapsed and ended its alliance with the British.

The following year the British planned an invasion of the United States from Canada. To repel the invasion, the Americans had to win control of Lake Champlain from the 16 British ships that patrolled it. The task fell to Captain Thomas Macdonough.

Macdonough recruited a force of Vermont shipbuilders who constructed ten ships in just 30 days. In September the American force won a decisive victory on Lake Champlain and forced the British to abandon their invasion from the north.

The British, however, had already launched another invasion farther south. This one proved more successful, at least initially. A large British force landed at the mouth of the Patuxent River on Chesapeake Bay and marched toward Washington, D.C. American defenders decided against a fight, and the British entered the city.

Dolly Madison, the President's wife, left the White House hastily, with dinner still on the table, and fled to Virginia. President Madison himself had ridden to the battle front to evaluate the British position, but he soon followed his wife and the cabinet members. After eating the dinner left behind in the White House, British troops burned most of the city and withdrew. Only the quick thinking of Dolly Madison and the efforts of White House servants saved a portrait of George Washington and several important government documents from destruction.

The British then moved up the Chesapeake Bay toward Baltimore. They met strong resistance from a force of volunteers manning Fort McHenry in Baltimore harbor. Despite a three-day bombardment, the British could not take the city.

The heroic defense of Baltimore disheartened the British and inspired the Americans. One person so inspired was Francis Scott Key. A prisoner on a British ship during the bombardment, Key wrote "The Star-Spangled Banner" when he saw that the American flag continued to wave after the bombardment.

Battle of New Orleans

The last battle of the war took place in the South. A British army planned to land at New Orleans, capture the city, and move up the Mississippi River. General Andrew Jackson commanded the United States forces. Jackson already had a reputation as a talented soldier. As major general of the Tennessee militia, he had been fighting against the Creeks in the Southwest since 1813. The so-called Creek War ended in March 1814 when Jackson and 2,000 militia won a decisive victory at Horseshoe Bend. In the resulting Treaty of Fort Jackson, the Creeks ceded two thirds of their land to the United States.

At New Orleans Jackson's men dug trenches for defense and crouched behind bales of cotton for protection. In January 1815 British forces landed and marched forward, expecting the entrenched soldiers to leave their defenses and run. Although far outnumbered, the Americans held their ground and slaughtered the advancing army, inflicting over 2,000 casualties while losing only 21 of their own troops.

It was a great victory for Jackson and his forces, which included the local militia, Kentucky riflemen, the militia from Jack-

Word of the 1814 peace treaty reached the United States too late to prevent the war's bloodiest battle. Vastly outnumbered American troops in well-fortified positions at left mowed down the advancing British near New Orleans. The American commander, Andrew Jackson, is shown near the United States flag in this painting by Hyacinthe de Lacotte.

son's home state of Tennessee, and two battalions of black soldiers. Many of the latter were veterans of L'Ouverture's revolt in Haiti. (See page 193.) After the battle Jackson congratulated his troops, singling out the black soldiers for special praise.

> I expected much from you but you have surpassed my hopes. . . . Soldiers, the President of the United States shall be informed of your conduct on the present occasion; and the voice of the Representatives of the American nation shall applaud your valor, as your General now praises your ardor.

Free blacks made other contributions to the war effort. Two thousand black men constructed fortifications for the defense of Philadelphia. Free black sailors fought in the Great Lakes battles under the command of Oliver Perry, and two regiments of black volunteers from New York served in the army.

Many slaves also fought for the United States in the war. Others fought for the British, who promised them freedom after the war. Some did win their freedom, but many were returned to their owners or sold in the West Indies.

A Tentative Victory

Jackson's victory at New Orleans actually came after a peace treaty, the Treaty of Ghent, had been signed in December 1814. But word of the treaty did not arrive in time to prevent the battle. News of the victory added a joyous note to the reading of the treaty in Congress, which quickly approved its terms.

The Treaty of Ghent itself did little more than restore prewar conditions. By late 1814 the British had dropped earlier demands, including the creation of a self-governing Indian nation in the area of Ohio. Furthermore, the war between Britain and France had ended, so the British had already stopped the impressment of American sailors and the search of American ships. The negotiators left other issues, such as border disputes, to be settled later.

203

Major Events	
1795	Treaty of Greenville
1803	*Marbury* v. *Madison;* Louisiana Purchase
1804–1806	Lewis and Clark expedition
1806–1807	Napoleon enforces Continental System; British enact Orders of Council
1807	Embargo Act passed
1808	James Madison elected President
1809	Embargo Act repealed; Nonintercourse Act passed
1811	Battle of Tippecanoe
1812	War breaks out with Great Britain
1813–1814	Creek War
1814	Treaty of Ghent
1815	Battle of New Orleans

Even though the treaty changed little, many citizens considered the War of 1812 a victory for the United States. The new nation had held its own in a war against a major European power. The final victory in the Battle of New Orleans further stimulated national pride and convinced many Americans that they had won the war.

The war also contributed to the nation's territorial and economic growth. The defeat of powerful Indian nations in the Northwest Territory and the South opened new land for settlement. And the British blockade of American ports encouraged many manufacturers to begin producing items that had been imported earlier.

For answers, see p. A 35.

Section Review

1. Identify the following: Hartford Convention, Andrew Jackson, Creek War, Treaty of Ghent.
2. List three disadvantages the United States faced at the beginning of the war.
3. (a) In which region of the country was there strong opposition to the war? (b) List three reasons for the opposition.
4. What two events in 1813 marked a turning point in the war for the Americans?
5. What impact did the Battle of New Orleans have on the outcome of the War of 1812?
6. What role did black Americans play in the war?

★ ★

IN PERSPECTIVE Thomas Jefferson began his term as the first Republican President by trying to unite the nation. While he did not abandon many Federalist programs, he did try to implement his own Republican principles, especially the idea of laissez-faire. Jefferson's most important single act was probably the purchase of the Louisiana Territory, which nearly doubled the size of the nation.

The threat of war dominated the last years of Jefferson's presidency. His attempt to force Great Britain and France to recognize American neutrality by imposing an embargo failed, largely because it hurt United States merchants. His successor, James Madison, also failed to maintain American neutrality, and in 1812 the United States was at war with Great Britain.

The war began with American defeats, but United States forces soon won important battles on the Great Lakes and in Canada. The heroic defense of Baltimore and the Battle of New Orleans inspired many Americans and convinced them that the United States had won the war. This spirit of nationalism continued to grow over the following decades.

For answers, see p. A 35.

Chapter Review

1. (a) What gestures of conciliation did Jefferson make toward the Federalists after his election? (b) How did he try to implement his own principles of government?

2. (a) What steps did President Jefferson take to reduce Federalist influence over the judicial branch of the government? (b) Why did he object to the principle of judicial review?

3. (a) Why did Jefferson reduce the military budget? (b) How did this decision affect the American conflict with Barbary Coast pirates? Explain.

4. (a) Why was the United States interested in buying land in the Mississippi River area, especially New Orleans? (b) How were the United States negotiators able to buy all of Louisiana?

5. (a) How did the purchase of the Louisiana territory conflict with Jefferson's interpretation of the Constitution? (b) On what presidential power did he ultimately base his action?

6. (a) What was the purpose of the Lewis and Clark expedition? (b) How was the information they gathered used?

7. (a) How did the British and the French challenge American neutrality after 1806? (b) How did President Jefferson react to the challenge? (c) Was he successful? Explain.

8. (a) What actions did President Madison take to maintain American neutrality? (b) Was he successful? Explain.

9. How did conflicts between American settlers and Indian nations in the Northwest Territory contribute to the beginning of the War of 1812?

10. (a) Why did Tecumseh and the Prophet believe that settlers threatened the Indian nations? (b) What actions did they take to counteract that threat? (c) Were they successful? Explain.

11. (a) Why did the War of 1812 begin poorly for the United States? (b) How did the American cause become more hopeful by 1813?

12. (a) What were the provisions of the Treaty of Ghent? (b) What issues were not included in the treaty? Why? (c) Why did many Americans feel that the United States had won the war?

For answers, see p. A 36.

For Further Thought

1. How did the principle of checks and balances operate during the dispute between President Jefferson and the Federalists in the judiciary?

2. (a) Who favored war with Great Britain in 1812? Why? (b) Who opposed the war? Why? (c) Based on the outcome of the war and the Treaty of Ghent, which group probably thought they had been right in 1812? Explain.

3. (a) Why do you think the Battle of New Orleans has been the subject of many popular songs and stories since 1815? (b) What impact did it have on Americans at the time?

For answers, see p. A 36.

Developing Basic Skills

1. *Map Reading* Study the map on page 194 and the maps of the United States on pages 759 and 760. Then answer the following questions: (a) Which present-day states were part of the Louisiana Purchase? (b) Which present-day states did the Louis and Clark expedition travel through? (c) What mineral resources have been found in the area that made up the Louisiana Territory? (d) How is the land used today, according to the map on 759?

2. *Graph Reading* Study the graph on page 197 and answer the following questions: (a) What information is shown on the graph? (b) In what year was the value of American exports the highest? (c) In what year was the value of American imports the highest? (d) In what year did the value of imports and exports drop sharply? (e) Based on what you read in this chapter, how would you explain the change in American foreign trade between 1807 and 1812?

See page 775 for suggested readings.

A Growing Nation

(1815–1824)

Deck Life on the Paragon, *by Pavel Petrovich Svinin.*

Chapter Outline

1 *A Sense of National Unity*

2 *The Industrial Revolution*

3 *Henry Clay's American System*

4 *Building Pathways to the West*

5 *James Monroe and Foreign Affairs*

The War of 1812, climaxed by Andrew Jackson's victory at New Orleans, stirred a new sense of national pride and unity among Americans. After the war, nationalism burst forth with a fervor never before experienced in the nation's short history. "The War," wrote Albert Gallatin, secretary of the treasury under Presidents Jefferson and Madison, "has renewed and reinstated the national feelings which the Revolution had given.... The people ... are more American, they feel and act more like a nation."

The growing spirit of nationalism took many forms. Love of country and patriotism were among them, but the new nationalism showed itself in more concrete ways as well. Supreme Court decisions were to strengthen the power of the national government. Industrial development bolstered a sense of national self-sufficiency at a time when better roads, canals, and river transportation were drawing the nation together. In foreign affairs, national pride was to manifest itself in President James Monroe's proclamation to the nations of the world, known as the Monroe Doctrine.

1 A Sense of National Unity

Political developments after the War of 1812 contributed to America's sense of national identity. For a brief period, the earlier competition between political parties seemed forgotten. Disagreement, however, still lay beneath the surface.

An Era of Good Feelings

As President Madison neared the end of his second term, he took great care to see that the Republicans nominated James Monroe, his secretary of state and fellow Virginian, to succeed him. Despite the objections of some Republican representatives and much grumbling about the "Virginia Dynasty" controlling the presidency, Monroe received the nomination. With the Federalist party now weak and breaking apart, he easily defeated his opponent, Rufus King of New York.

When Monroe was inaugurated in 1817, the nation seemed more united and optimistic than it had ever been. A presidential goodwill tour, which took Monroe to the former Federalist stronghold of New England, demonstrated this change in the American mood. Citizens of Boston warmly received him. One newspaper, the *Columbian Sentinel,* referring to the way in which old political foes greeted each other, called the times the "Era of Good Feelings."

Good feelings seemed to prevail all over the country. Four years later, in 1820 when President Monroe ran for reelection, no one opposed him. Only one electoral vote was cast against him. Monroe's reelection marked the end of the Federalist party. The Federalists, in decline since 1800, had lost most of their remaining support with the American victory in the War of 1812. During the Era of Good Feelings, only a few scattered supporters remained. The country seemed united under one party. the Republican party.

James Monroe: Symbol of Unity

As President, James Monroe became a symbol of the nation's political unity. Over sixty years old when he took office, Monroe was the last President of the Revolutionary War generation. To be sure, men such as Andrew Jackson and John Quincy Adams had been born before 1776, but they were children during the war. Monroe, in contrast, was a young man when Cornwallis surrendered in 1781.

Monroe's perspective was that of the earlier generation, as his quaint attire showed. He dressed in the fashion of decades past, from white-topped boots and knee-length pantaloons to cocked hat. He even powdered his hair and tied it in a queue at the back. To the postwar generation he was, as one historian observed, "a last nostalgic look at the eighteenth century."

Monroe's mental outlook was equally rooted in the past. Except in the area of foreign affairs, he thought the President had little responsibility for policy making. Monroe believed that the Congress should interpret and enact the public will, and the President should follow.

Nor had he ever fully accepted the idea of political parties. Calling them "the curse of the country," he rejoiced that an era of no parties seemed at last at hand. "The existence of parties," Monroe declared "is not necessary to free government." But political unity turned out to be only an illusion. A new and stronger opposition party would eventually grow out of the ruins of the Federalists.

John Marshall and the Supreme Court

Even while the Federalist party was in decline, a leading Federalist, John Marshall, was contributing to the growing sense of national unity.

President John Adams had appointed Marshall as Chief Justice of the Supreme Court in 1801. When Marshall assumed his duties, the Supreme Court lacked both power and prestige. Indeed, John Jay, the first Chief Justice, had resigned because he felt that he had too little to do.

The Supreme Court in the early 1800s rarely met in Washington longer than six weeks a year, and its proceedings attracted little attention. For part of the year, Marshall, like the other justices, rode a federal circuit.

The justices maintained a low public profile. They met in the basement of the Capitol, boarded together, and rarely went

Under the strong leadership of Chief Justice John Marshall, the Supreme Court gained new prestige and authority. This portrait is by Chester Harding.

out socially. In fact, Justice William Paterson once traveled a full day on the same stagecoach as Thomas Jefferson without either recognizing the other.

Chief Justice John Marshall was a simple man. He was not a legal scholar, but his keen mind helped him get to the heart of legal problems and write clear, forceful decisions. Seldom has a person so dominated the nation's highest court. During his 35 years as Chief Justice, he wrote almost half of the Court's decisions and dissented from the majority opinion only eight times. Even Republican justices appointed by Presidents Jefferson, Madison, and Monroe came under the sway of his forceful personality.

The Supreme Court and National Unity

John Marshall was a moderate Federalist who favored strengthening the power of the national government. As Chief Justice from 1801 to 1835, he was able to influence the nation's developing political system.

As early as 1803, in *Marbury* v. *Madison,* the Supreme Court had confirmed the principle of judicial review, the Court's power to decide if a law violated the Constitution. (See page 190.)

In *Fletcher* v. *Peck* (1810) the Court ruled a state law unconstitutional for the first time. The case involved land grants that the Georgia legislature had made to the Yazoo Land Company. The grants had been obtained by bribery and fraud, and a later session of the legislature had tried to invalidate them. In his decision Marshall ruled that the state could not repudiate the grants because they were contracts and the Constitution forbade states to "impair the obligation of contracts."

Nine years later in *Dartmouth College* v. *Woodward* (1819), the Supreme Court again upheld the sanctity of contracts. It overturned an attempt by the New Hampshire legislature to revise Dartmouth's charter, which had been granted during the colonial period. In so doing, Marshall asserted that a contract could not be changed without the consent of both parties, even if one of the parties was a state government. Through these rulings the Court made contractual obligations nearly unbreakable.

In two rulings that increased the authority of the national government, Marshall based his decisions on a loose construction of the Constitution. In the case of *McCulloch* v. *Maryland* (1819), the Court upheld the constitutionality of the second Bank of the United States, which Congress had chartered in 1816. While admitting that the Constitution did not specifically authorize a national bank, Marshall asserted that Congress had to have some leeway in exercising its powers.

> Let the end be legitimate, let it be within the scope of the Constitution, and all means which are appropriate, which are plainly adapted to that end, which are not prohibited, but consistent with the letter and spirit of the constitution, are constitutional.

In *Gibbons* v. *Ogden* (1824) the Supreme Court struck down a New York state law that had awarded a steamboat company a monopoly on passenger service across the Hudson River between New Jersey and New York. The ruling stated that a state can regulate commerce only within its borders. Marshall declared that only Congress could control interstate commerce. In this case the Court reaffirmed its power to overrule a state law. It also guaranteed that the nation would have a unified interstate trade policy. Individual states would not be able to interfere with interstate trade as they had under the Articles of Confederation.

The Supreme Court under John Marshall thus contributed to the growing sense of national unity. Its rulings clarified and affirmed important powers of the national government, especially of the Supreme Court and Congress.

For answers, see p. A 36.

Section Review

1. Identify the following: Era of Good Feelings, James Monroe, John Marshall.

2. What incident resulted in the name the "Era of Good Feelings?"

3. According to President Monroe, which branch of government should interpret the public will?

4. Was the Supreme Court powerful or prestigious before John Marshall became Chief Justice? Explain.

5. (a) In what two cases did the Supreme Court uphold the sanctity of contracts? (b) Name two court decisions that strengthened the authority of the national government.

2 The Industrial Revolution

A period of industrial growth began in Great Britain during the eighteenth century, but it was slow in coming to America. The colonies had depended on Britain for manufactured goods until the Revolutionary War. Local industries finally began to develop after independence and their growth was spurred on by the War of 1812. The British blockade of the Atlantic shore meant that the nation had to rely on itself for many products formerly imported.

The Needs of Industry

Historians often use the term "Industrial Revolution" to describe the economic shift from farming and commerce to manufacturing. The term "revolution" suggests that the changes brought about by the development of manufacturing were so far-reaching that they seemed like a complete overthrow of the old way of life.

In fact, however, the growth of industry was neither violent nor abrupt. It involved many gradual changes. These changes were most evident in three areas crucial to the development of industry: technology, labor, and capital. In the area of technology, inventors found ways to replace manual labor with mechanical devices, which helped speed up the production process.

A new way of organizing labor, known as the *factory system*, developed in Great Britain by the 1770s. Rather than spreading the manufacturing process out over several locations, factories brought workers together under one roof. In textiles, for example, early producers had farmed out wool for women to spin in their homes. Weaving took place in another location and sewing in still another. Textile factories brought the workers to the mill, rather than take wool to individual homes.

Capital, or money for investment, was required for industry to develop. As early as the sixteenth century joint stock companies had worked out fairly simple ways to pool money and lessen the risks of commercial ventures. (See page 51.) But the high cost of new machinery required even larger sums of money.

In Europe corporations had developed to raise the needed capital. Corporations could raise large amounts of money from many small investors. Each investor's personal responsibility for the debts of the corporation did not exceed the initial investment. This idea of *limited liability* made corporations attractive to people who might not otherwise be willing to invest their money.

In spite of these advantages Americans adopted the use of corporations slowly. At first they were formed only for public projects like bridges. Only after the Civil War did the corporation become a dominant business form in the United States. Until then family-owned firms and partnerships were most common.

Technology at Work

The development of the steam engine is an important example of how changes in technology reshaped the manufacturing process. In 1769 James Watt, from Scotland, patented a steam engine. Before the introduction of this new source of power, gristmills were turned by water. But by the 1790s millers had begun using more efficient steam engines to power mills.

A number of other significant inventions came out of Great Britain in the decades after 1760. Advances in the smelting process made iron purer and more durable. James Hargreaves devised the spinning jenny, a means of connecting several spinning wheels together so that they spun eight threads at a time. Improvements on his design soon enabled spinners to produce a hundred threads at once. Other inventions mechanized the process of weaving cloth.

Before long the excitement of the Industrial Revolution began to be felt in the United States. Improved versions of the steam engine appeared. In 1787 John Fitch launched the first steam-powered boat on the Delaware River in Philadelphia. Twenty years later, in August 1807, Robert Fulton traveled up the Hudson River from New York City to Albany in 32 hours aboard the steam-powered *Clermont*, proving to skeptics the practical value of using the steam engine to power new means of transportation.

Another American, Eli Whitney, revolutionized cotton-cloth production with the invention of the cotton gin in 1793. By hand, the average worker could clean the seeds out of one to three pounds of cotton per day. Using Whitney's power-driven cotton gin, the same worker could clean 1,000 pounds a day.

Whitney was the first inventor to introduce *interchangeable parts*, which he originally used in the production of firearms. Traditionally, gunsmiths made each gun by hand, slowly honing the various parts until they fit. Whenever a part broke, a new one had to be custom made. Whitney built a large number of each component part, all exactly alike. Guns could thus be manufactured rapidly by assembling the various interchangeable parts. Repairs could be made just as quickly. As the concept of interchangeable parts spread to other industries,

Early textile mills and factories often developed alongside waterfalls, which provided power to run machinery. The tall building in this painting of Pawtucket Falls on the Blackstone River in Rhode Island is thought to be the first American textile mill to use water-powered machinery.

it provided the basis for further industrial development in the United States.

The Spread of Industry to the United States

Not surprisingly, Great Britain, the first country to begin to industrialize, was eager to protect the competitive advantage British goods enjoyed. For this reason it banned the export of industrial secrets and prohibited skilled mechanics who had worked in its more advanced factories from moving to other nations. Initially this slowed American industrial development, but, as you have read, American inventors were at work themselves.

Furthermore, Americans tried to learn the secrets of the British textile industry. Several state legislatures offered large rewards to British mechanics who would supply technical information. In 1789 twenty-one-year-old Samuel Slater, attracted by such offers, slipped away to the United States. He had served as an apprentice in a cotton-spinning factory, and he carried in his head detailed plans of textile machinery.

A wealthy manufacturer, Moses Brown of Providence, Rhode Island, hired Slater to reproduce the machinery and set up a factory. Slater built several improved versions of the machinery he had used in Britain, and in a year he had a factory producing cotton thread. Slater's ideas spread. Seven similar mills were operating by 1800, and by 1815 there were 213 in operation.

In 1813 a group of merchants led by Francis Cabot Lowell formed the Boston Manufacturing Company. With about half a million dollars in capital, these men, known as the Boston Associates, established the first textile factory that combined all the tasks required to turn raw cotton into finished cloth. Like Slater, they relied to a large extent on British technology, for Lowell had smuggled the plans for a power loom into the country. In the following decades, the Boston Associates set up other centers of textile manufacturing in New England. A factory in Lowell, Massachusetts, became the center of their operations.

Labor for the New Factories

Scarcity of labor had been a factor in the economy of the United States from its beginning. With the nation's vast territory, Ameri-

With the growth of industry in the United States, women began to take jobs in textile mills and factories. The women in this drawing work in a book bindery.

cans had found it relatively easy to acquire land for farming, so few were interested in factory work at first. Yet factory owners needed workers. They could not turn to artisans, who had little interest in factory work. Artisans in the United States, like their counterparts in Europe, were used to working at home or in small shops, making quality products by hand. Indeed in the 1820s most products were still made that way. Thus early factory owners looked elsewhere for labor.

In the textile industry, especially, factory owners found most of their workers among women and children. Children held special appeal as textile workers because their small size enabled them to move nimbly around dangerous machinery. Women and children also worked for low wages. One reason was their relative lack of skills compared to artisans who had trained for many years.

Rules at a Mill Boardinghouse

Young women who worked at the textile mills lived in boardinghouses operated by the company. The rules of one early boardinghouse, reproduced below, are an example of how the mill owners tried to provide an orderly, protected environment for their workers.

Rules and Regulations to be attended to and followed by the Young Persons who come to Board in this House:

Rule first: Each one to enter the house without unnecessary noise or confusion, and hang up their bonnet, shawl, coat, etc., etc., in the entry.

Rule second: Each one to have their place at the table during meals, the two which have worked the greatest length of time in the Factory, to sit on each side of the head of the table, so that all new hands will of course take their seats lower down, according to the length of time they have been here.

Rule third: It is expected that order and good manners will be preserved at table during meals—and at all times either upstairs or down.

Rule fourth: There is no unnecessary dirt to be brought into the house by the Boarders, such as apple cores or peels, or nut shells, etc.

Rule fifth: Each boarder is to take her turn in making the bed and sweeping the chamber in which she sleeps.

Rule sixth: Those who have worked the longest in the Factory are to sleep in the North Chamber and the new hands will sleep in the South Chamber.

Rule seventh: As a lamp will be lighted every night upstairs and placed in a lanthorn, it is expected that no boarder will take a light into the chambers.

Rule eighth: The doors will be closed at ten o'clock at night, winter and summer, at which time each boarder will be expected to retire to bed.

Rule ninth: Sunday being appointed by our Creator as a Day of Rest and Religious Exercises, it is expected that all boarders will have sufficient discretion as to pay suitable attention to the day, and if they cannot attend to some place of Public Worship they will keep within doors and improve their time in reading, writing; and in other valuable and harmless employment.

Source: Edith Abbott, *Women in Industry* (New York : D. Appleton, 1910).

The Boston Associates, for example, recruited many young, unmarried women from farm families to work in their textile factories. The women usually worked for a few years before they married. Because the company wanted to attract hard-working women from respectable families, it closely supervised their lives. The company provided boardinghouses, educational and recreational facilities, religious instruction, and land for gardening. The workers even published their own monthly magazine.

The women in the Lowell mills worked long hours but, at least in the early years of the company, they were basically well treated. They earned relatively good wages because the company needed to attract workers. The textile mills gave many young women their first chance to work outside the home. Although some observers reported that the Lowell workers were oppressed or unhappy, the women themselves denied it. As their magazine, the *Lowell Offering*, declared, "We are not generally miserable, either in point of fact, or in the prospect of a dreadful future."

Over time, as the factory system spread, factory life became increasingly harsh. When the arrival of large numbers of immigrants provided a cheap labor supply, wages dropped. Those who needed jobs were forced to accept worsening working conditions. Such changes, however, were in the future. At the start, Lowell seemed a symbol of the benefits to be gained by transplanting the Industrial Revolution to America.

A Force for Unity and Division

The growth of industry enabled the United States to free itself from some of its Old World ties. The nation had grown up with an economy based on agriculture and exports. The colonies had exported raw materials to Britain, which in turn had produced manufactured goods and sold them back to the colonies. But by the early 1800s, the United States relied increasingly on local industries to supply manufactured goods. Americans took pride in this growing self-sufficiency, and the development of domestic industry enhanced their sense of national identity.

Industrialization produced divisions as well. Most manufacturing developed in the North, especially New England. The South and the sparsely populated West lagged behind. Northern industrial development did not necessarily hurt the South. The cotton gin, for example, brought major improvements in the South's cotton production. But the North's growing industrialization did foster different ways of life and economic interests among the nation's citizens. Thus the development of industry acted as a force for both unity and division. It nourished a sense of national pride, and at the same time sowed seeds of sectional discord.

For answers, see p. A 36.

Section Review

1. Identify the following: James Watt, James Hargreaves, John Fitch, Robert Fulton, Eli Whitney, Samuel Slater, Francis Cabot Lowell, Boston Associates.

2. Define the following terms: factory system, capital, limited liability, interchangeable parts.

3. (a) Name two important inventions of the late 1700s. (b) How did each affect the way products were manufactured?

4. How did American manufacturers learn British industrial secrets?

5. (a) List two reasons why owners of textile factories were anxious to hire women and children as workers. (b) Who did the Boston Associates hire to work in their textile mills?

6. (a) Give one example of how industrialization brought the people of the United States closer together. (b) Give one example of how it also created divisions.

3 Henry Clay's American System

During the War of 1812, a group of young men emerged in Congress who challenged the leadership of the older generation. After the war, these younger leaders sought a greater voice in public policy. They were impatient with what they saw as the old-fashioned ideas of Jefferson and Madison. In particular they wanted the federal government to take a greater role in national economic development. With their limitless faith in the country's future, they became the advocates of an economic program for the nation that put national rather than sectional needs first.

Three Dominant Political Figures

Three of these young leaders remained powerful figures in American politics in the coming decades. Daniel Webster was a Federalist from New Hampshire. Henry Clay of Kentucky and John C. Calhoun of South Carolina were Republicans. Clay and Calhoun had first attracted notice as War Hawks during the crisis that led to war with Britain in 1812.

Despite their different backgrounds, all three men championed nationalism at one time or another in their careers. Of the three, Clay was the most consistently nationalistic in his outlook. Webster and Calhoun spoke for nationalism when it benefited their section of the country but opposed it when it did not.

Daniel Webster's dark hair and brows had earned him the nickname "Black Dan." His stocky build helped lend forcefulness to a speaking style that was among the most powerful in the land.

Slim and handsome, John C. Calhoun was an intelligent and eloquent speaker. His knowledge of political theory served him well as a nationalist and as the eventual champion of the South.

Henry Clay was a tall, dashing Kentuckian, full of charm and swagger. His powerful personality enabled him to influence people and mold them into loyal political followers. At times pushy and overbearing, at other times cheerful and accommodating, he quickly set himself up as one of the most powerful political leaders in the nation.

Henry Clay's Design

The Republican party had traditionally opposed strengthening the national government at the expense of state or local governments. In fact, the party had developed out of opposition to Alexander Hamilton's

Daniel Webster was one of three rising congressional leaders to challenge the leadership of the earlier generation. Along with Henry Clay and John C. Calhoun, he urged the government to take a larger role in developing the national economy. This portrait of Webster was painted by Francis Alexander.

economic policies, by which the national government had taken an active role in the nation's economic development. Furthermore, Republicans had favored a rural economy rather than an industrial one. But the British blockade during the War of 1812 reduced America's supply of manufactured goods and revealed the danger of relying too heavily on foreign imports. Consequently, many Republicans began to change their thinking and accept some of Hamilton's original economic policies.

Henry Clay brought these ideas together in what he called his American System. Coming from the isolated and less developed West, Clay enthusiastically supported government programs for economic development. He believed that the recent war had shown the United States to be too dependent on foreign imports. The American economy had to become more self-sufficient.

Hence, the cornerstone of Clay's program was a protective tariff to keep American manufacturing growing. Second, Clay proposed that the government charter a new national bank to provide a sound and uniform currency, necessary for the smooth operation of business and trade. Finally, he urged a federal program of internal improvements such as better canals and roadways that would aid interstate commerce.

The Tariff of 1816

During the War of 1812 Americans began to manufacture products previously imported from Great Britain. Once peace returned in 1815, quick extinction threatened many new industries. Manufacturers in the United States, lacking the capital and skill of their British counterparts, could not compete with cheaper imported goods.

Clay, like Hamilton earlier, proposed guarding these new industries from foreign competition by means of a protective tariff. By raising the price of imported goods, a protective tariff would make the more expensive American-made products competitive.

Cries for protection from British goods increased when British manufacturers began dumping low-priced goods on the American market in order to get rid of surpluses built up during the European war. This seriously hurt American industry, putting many smaller factories out of business.

Congress finally responded by passing the Tariff of 1816, which raised tariffs on foreign imports by an average of 20 percent. This was enough to protect new and developing American industries from lower-priced competition.

Clay's followers in the Middle Atlantic and western states voiced the strongest support for the tariff. They believed that flourishing commerce as well as tariff revenues would help pay for the roads and canals they needed for trade with the Northeast and the South.

Calhoun also spoke eloquently in favor of the tariff. He thought it was necessary to protect the South's growing cotton industry, and he believed that the South would soon develop its own industrial strength.

Of the three young leaders only Daniel Webster spoke against the tariff. Although some New Englanders wanted it, Webster thundered out his opposition to it. His constituents in New Hampshire still relied on shipping from Great Britain, which the tariff would hurt. Over the years Calhoun and Webster would reverse their views on the tariff.

The Second Bank of the United States

Republicans in Congress had always been suspicious of the first Bank of the United States, which Hamilton had created, so they let its charter expire in 1811. As a result, state banks took charge of issuing *bank notes*, paper money that was supposed to be backed by gold or silver held by the bank.

The bank notes did not remain a stable currency, however. The number of state banks issuing them increased greatly. Since each bank issued its own notes, a wide variety of notes circulated at all times. Whenever the demand for credit rose, as farmers needed to buy land or manufacturers wanted to buy equipment for new factories, the situation worsened. Banks began issuing notes whose value exceeded the amount of gold or silver on deposit. In addition, during the War of 1812, most state banks had stopped redeeming their bank notes for gold and silver at all, and they showed no sign of resuming such payments after the war.

No one could be sure, therefore, exactly how much the various bank notes were worth. Businesses often did not know if the notes they accepted in payment actually matched the price of their goods. The lack of a uniform national currency made interstate commerce extremely difficult.

Clay and others argued that a new national bank was needed. It would provide a more stable means of issuing money and would offer a safe place for the federal government to deposit its funds. Recognizing the problems created by the state banks, President Madison overcame his qualms about expanding the power of the national government. In 1816 he recommended the creation of a new national bank.

In response, Congress chartered the second Bank of the United States for a twenty-year period. Like the first national Bank, its purpose was to serve as a depository for government funds and to stabilize the currency. The Bank soon had a chance to show whether or not it could do its job.

The Panic of 1819

The Bank's charter gave it enough power to regulate the state banking and currency system. Such regulation was badly needed during the period of economic boom after the war as speculation in western land became increasingly popular. But instead of restraining land speculators, the Bank recklessly encouraged them by eagerly extending credit.

In 1819 the national Bank, under a new and more conservative management, began to call in its loans and to demand gold or silver from state banks in exchange for their notes. State banks, in turn, called in their loans. Since prospective buyers could no longer obtain loans to buy land, speculators could not sell the land in which they had so heavily invested. Speculators could not repay their loans, and as a result, western land prices plummeted.

At the same time, European demand for American farm products and textiles began to decline. Southern cotton prices fell. Many planters, already unhappy because of the drop in demand for their products, found their problems compounded because they had speculated in western land.

These events brought on an economic panic that ended postwar prosperity. During the Panic of 1819, banks foreclosed on mortgaged farms, business firms went bankrupt, and people lost their jobs, especially in the South and West.

Americans tried to figure out what had caused their troubles, and they blamed the badly managed Bank of the United States. Right or wrong, their choice would have important political consequences in later years.

Section Review

For answers, see p. A 37.

1. Identify the following: Henry Clay, Daniel Webster, John C. Calhoun.

2. Define the following term: bank note.

3. What did Henry Clay, Daniel Webster, and John C. Calhoun have in common?

4. What were the three main parts of Henry Clay's American System?

5. (a) What was the purpose of the Tariff of 1816? (b) Why did Webster oppose it?

6. What two purposes did Clay think a national Bank would serve?

7. What action of the national Bank encouraged land speculation?

4 Building Pathways to the West

A major part of Clay's American System was a program of internal improvements paid for by the federal government. Transportation was difficult and costly in much of the United States, especially in the West. Better roads and canals needed to be built and obstacles cleared from rivers and lakes before further economic growth could take place.

Such economic growth was a vital part of the spirit of national unity and pride. John C. Calhoun argued that the lack of adequate transportation weakened the nation. He called on the Congress to "bind the republic together with a perfect system of roads and canals."

Westward Expansion

The postwar wave of migration into the area west of the Appalachian Mountains stimulated the demand for better transportation.

■ *The lure of land drew increasing numbers of pioneers westward. In 1810 only one in seven Americans lived west of the Appalachians, but by 1830 the population of the West was slightly larger than that of the South.*

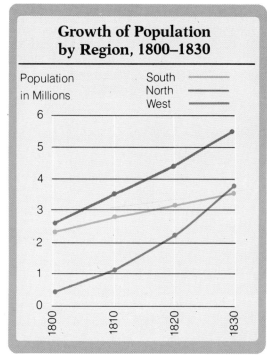

Growth of Population by Region, 1800–1830

Population in Millions

South
North
West

Source: *Historical Statistics of the United States*

High food prices in the East and the availability of rich western farmlands attracted new settlers. As you read in the last chapter, the United States government and individual settlers had used both legal and illegal treaties as well as armed force to push most of the Indian nations out of the area.

Even visitors sensed the size of the migration. "Old America seems to be breaking up and moving westwards," an English visitor observed in 1817. While the pace of westward movement slackened during the Panic of 1819, it picked up again in the economic recovery that followed and reached a peak in the 1830s. By 1840 more than a third of the United States population lived west of the Appalachians. In 1810 only one seventh had.

Most of the migrants came from the older eastern states. Families from New England and the Middle Atlantic region settled around the Great Lakes. Settlers from Kentucky and Tennessee turned to the lands of the old Northwest and the old Southwest. From the southern seaboard states, pioneers poured into the old Southwest and the Ohio River Valley.

The admission of new states to the nation reflected the steady growth of westward expansion. Ohio was admitted as a state in 1803 and Louisiana in 1812. Indiana (1816), Mississippi (1817), Illinois (1818), Alabama (1819), Missouri (1821), Arkansas (1836), and Michigan (1837) followed.

Demand for Better Transportation

As people moved westward the urgent need for better connections with the East and access to its markets became apparent. The difficulty, or in some cases the near impossibility, of transportation plagued the new settlers. In most areas no roads existed at all. In some places the traveler had to go on horseback or on foot.

Where roads did exist, they were crude at best. Following old Indian trails, most roads were too narrow for wagon passage. From winter through spring, the hard-packed dirt turned to mud, and stumps and ruts stood ready to break a wagon's axles.

For answers, see p. A 37.

Westward Movement: Using Statistics

Statistics, or numbers, are frequently used in American history. They provide factual information that helps you understand past events. Statistics presented in a table such as the one below can reveal important patterns or trends. Yet you must use statistics cautiously. As with any single piece of evidence, statistics present only a partial picture of what happened. The table below, for example, presents data about population growth in several western states. The population statistics, however, do not include Native Americans who lived in those states during the period. If you had not learned previously about the Indian nations in the region you might assume that the lands were uninhabited before white settlers arrived.

To use statistics most effectively, you should follow a few basic steps. Use the following steps to interpret the statistics below.

1. **Identify the type of information presented in the table.** Begin by asking yourself questions about the different categories of information and how they relate to one another. Answer the following questions about the table below: (a) What time period is covered by this table? (b) What is the interval between years? (c) What do the numbers represent? (d) Describe in your own words the type of information presented in the table.

2. **Practice reading the statistics.** Answer the following questions for this table: (a) What was the population of Mississippi in 1820? (b) What was the population of Ohio in 1800? (c) By what year did the population of Indiana total more than 100,000 people? (d) What was the total population of these western states in 1830?

3. **Look for relationships among the numbers.** With this table, for example, you can trace the population growth of each state. You can also compare the population growth of different states. Use the table to answer the following questions: (a) How did Kentucky's population change between 1810 and 1820? (b) How much did Louisiana's population grow between 1810 and 1820? (c) Which state had the largest population in 1810? Which had the largest population in 1830? (d) Which state's population grew the most between 1820 and 1830? (e) How does the population growth in Ohio between 1810 and 1830 compare with the population growth in Tennessee in the same period?

4. **Draw conclusions about an historical event or period by applying what you have learned from the statistics.** Use the table and your textbook to draw conclusions about developments in the West between 1790 and 1830. Answer the following questions: (a) How would you describe the population change in the region between 1790 and 1830? (b) Based on what you have learned, how might you explain the reasons for the change? (c) Why do you think Ohio, Kentucky, and Tennessee had the largest populations? (d) When did each state join the Union? (See page 748.) (e) Do you see a relationship between the date of statehood and population growth in the state?

Population Growth in the West, 1790–1830

	1790	1800	1810	1820	1830
Ohio	73,600	145,300	230,700	581,400	937,900
Kentucky	35,690	220,900	406,500	564,300	687,400
Tennessee	*	105,600	261,700	422,800	681,900
Mississippi	*	8,800	40,300	75,400	136,600
Indiana	*	5,600	24,500	148,100	343,000
Michigan	*	*	4,760	8,900	31,600
Louisiana	*	*	76,500	153,400	215,700
Illinois	*	*	12,200	55,200	157,400
Missouri	*	*	19,700	66,500	140,400
Arkansas	*	*	1,060	14,200	30,300
Alabama	*	*	*	127,900	309,500

*no data available

The expression, "I'm stumped," is said to have originated from travelers whose vehicles broke down on roads like the one pictured in George Tattersall's painting Roads to the West. *Such roads were only partially cleared of tree stumps. At right is a stretch of "corduroy road," with logs laid side by side over a rough or soggy stretch. The jolting ride made travel by boat the choice of those who had an option.*

Corduroy roads, made by laying tree trunks side by side, offered the best overland route. Yet even on good roads, travel was not easy. One uncomfortable traveler complained about "the noise of the wheels, the rumble of a coach ... the jerking of the bad roads," and "the most detestable stagecoach that ever a Christian built to dislocate the joints of his fellow man."

Most existing transportation simply did not meet western needs. Settlers wanted a way to send their farm products to the East and bring manufactured goods back to the West. In many cases, the cheapest way for residents of western towns to ship their products to eastern buyers was to float them down the Ohio and Mississippi rivers, around the Florida peninsula, and up the coast. Eager for more direct trade routes, settlers recognized that improved canals and roads could provide faster transportation of bulky goods.

The National Road

Either state governments or private investors paid for the construction of the earliest roads. They then charged a toll to pay for the investment. The federal government first supported construction of a major road during Thomas Jefferson's administration. Authorized by Congress in 1806, the National Road eventually stretched westward from Cumberland, Maryland, to Wheeling, Virginia, and from there through Ohio and Indiana to Vandalia, Illinois.

By the standards of the time, the National Road was of high quality. It was built to withstand the weight of wagons jammed with people moving West. One observant traveler counted 42 children in three wagons during one day's journey and testified to seeing a wagon with 20 passengers on another day.

Yet by modern standards the National Road, like other early roads, was crude and often impassable. In Indiana, for example, where nine tenths of the National Road ran through dense forest, construction plans permitted "rounded and trimmed" tree stumps 9 to 15 inches (about 23 to 38 centimeters) high to remain on the road.

Although President Madison had his doubts about the constitutionality of roads paid for by the federal government, he continued the construction of the National Road. But when Congress tried to distribute money to the states for their own internal improvements, Madison vetoed the measure. Thereafter, local roads and other local improvements became the responsibility of the states.

Canals and Steamboats

The completion of the Erie Canal in 1825, after eight years of construction, opened a new era in transportation. Built by the state of

New York with public funds, the Erie Canal stretched about 350 miles (560 kilometers) from Buffalo to Albany. Goods could then be shipped down the Hudson River to New York City.

The canal allowed New York City to tap the markets of the Ohio River Valley and the Great Lakes region. By using the canal, shippers could cut the cost of transportation from nearly $100 to $5 a ton. Travel time was reduced from 20 days to 8. The success of the Erie Canal made New York City the country's major commercial center.

Shippers used the Erie Canal so heavily that the state recovered its construction costs from tolls in just seven years. The canal's financial success prompted other states to fund ambitious canal-building projects. None, however, matched the Erie's success. The Erie Canal heralded the beginning of the nation's Canal Age.

The adaptation of steamboats to western rivers marked an important advance in American transportation and a new stage in the nation's industrial development. As you read earlier, inventors had improved upon

■ Westward expansion created an urgent need for better transportation to move people and goods. Private companies, state governments, and the federal government all built new roads in the first half of the 1800s. The construction of canals linking major river systems sharply reduced the cost of shipping goods to market and helped spur agriculture and industry.

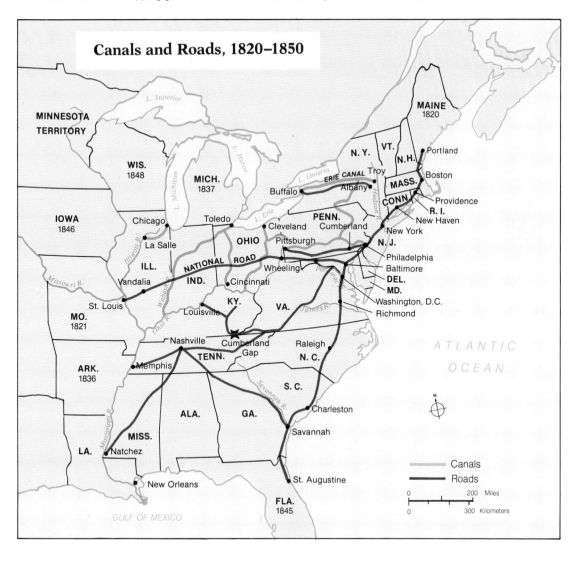

Canals and Roads, 1820–1850

The Erie Canal opened the way to ship goods from the Midwest via the Great Lakes, along the canal to the Hudson River, and then to the port of New York City. Boats had to pass through 82 locks like the one shown in this painting by John Hill on the 350-mile (560-kilometer) journey through the canal.

James Watt's early steam-engine design. In 1811 Robert Fulton and Robert Livingston built a boat in Pittsburgh and sent it down the Ohio and Mississippi rivers to New Orleans. This trip demonstrated that steamboats could be used in western waters.

Five years later Henry M. Shreve built a steamboat specifically designed to meet the needs of western commerce. Below its towering decks, Shreve's boat had a shallow draft and hull. Designed to operate in shallow water, it could navigate the numerous sandbars and snags of the Mississippi, Missouri, and Ohio rivers. Shreve's boat could also travel at great speeds and carry heavy loads of cargo. When several of his vessels successfully made upstream journeys to Pittsburgh, all doubts about the practicality of his design ended. Steamboats, which cut western freight and passenger rates in half, soon crowded the waters.

Improvements in technology quickened the flow of trade in all directions. Farm products could move eastward along the canals. Manufactured goods bound for the West

could come up the Mississippi in steamboats instead of taking the slower route over the mountains. As Calhoun had predicted, internal improvements led to better communications, helping to bind the republic together. This phase of Clay's American System seemed to be working.

For answers, see p. A 37.

Section Review

1. Identify the following: National Road, Erie Canal.

2. Define the following term: corduroy roads.

3. List two ways in which good roads were important to western settlers.

4. (a) Who paid for the earliest roads? (b) When did the federal government become involved? (c) How did Madison limit its role?

5. How did the Erie Canal improve trade between New York City and the West?

6. What special problems had to be overcome before steamboats could be used successfully on western rivers?

5 James Monroe and Foreign Affairs

Although he tended to follow Congress on domestic issues, President Monroe believed that the President should make foreign policy. In practice, Monroe delegated much of this responsibility to Secretary of State John Quincy Adams.

The choice of Adams as secretary of state was particularly fortunate for the nation. The son of former President John Adams, John Quincy Adams was a skillful and experienced diplomat. An enthusiastic expansionist, he was eager to extend the country's boundaries. And his shrewd grasp of diplomacy enabled him to accomplish many of his goals for the nation.

Foreign Affairs After 1812

Before Adams's appointment, Richard Rush, the acting secretary of state, concluded negotiations with Great Britain concerning the boundary between the Louisiana Purchase and Canada. The Convention of 1818 set the border at the 49th parallel. In the Rush-Bagot Treaty of 1817 the two nations had agreed not to use military ships on the Great Lakes.

Spanish-owned Florida posed another border problem for the United States. Outlaws frequently used it as a haven. Slaves escaping from southern plantations also sought refuge there. In addition, some

■ *By 1824, treaties and purchases had expanded the nation's territory to the south and west, and 11 new states had joined the original 13.*

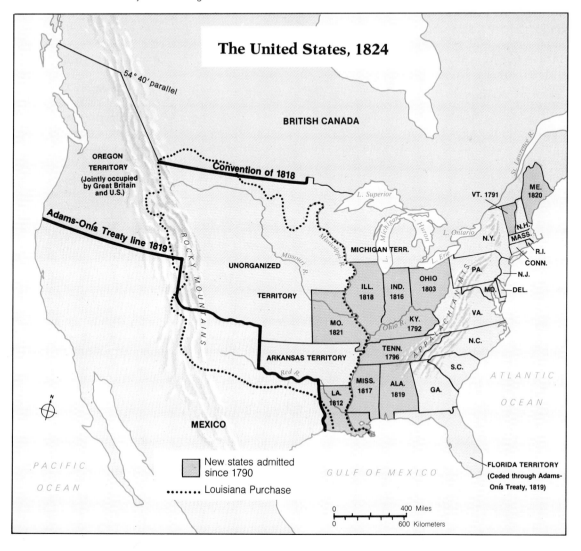

The United States, 1824

groups of Native Americans raided United States settlements from Florida. The Spanish government seemed unable to control these activities.

In 1818 President Monroe sent a military party under the command of Andrew Jackson into Florida to fight the Seminoles who had made raids into Georgia. Jackson, exceeding his instructions, captured two towns, hanged two British subjects for encouraging Indian attacks, and arrested the Spanish governor.

Although John Quincy Adams knew Jackson had no authority for his actions, the secretary was not displeased. Adams recognized that Jackson's raid had given the United States a stronger bargaining position with Spain. When the Spanish government protested the action, Adams replied that Florida had turned into "a derelict, open to the occupancy of every enemy . . . of the United States, and serving no other earthly purpose than as a post of annoyance."

Plagued by revolts among their own colonies, the Spanish wanted a way out of a difficult situation. In the Adams-Onís Treaty of 1819, negotiated by Adams and the Spanish minister to the United States, Don Luis de Onís, Spain agreed to cede Florida to the United States. In return, the United States dropped its claims of about $5 million against Spain. (See the map on page 221.)

The treaty also formally established the boundary between the Louisiana Purchase and Spanish territory. The western portion of the boundary would extend along the 42nd parallel from the Rockies all the way to the Pacific. This cleared the way for the nation to span the continent.

Other Concerns in the Western Hemisphere

In addition to the trouble in Florida, the Spanish confronted even more serious problems in other parts of their empire. Between 1810 and 1821 most of Spain's colonies in the Western Hemisphere revolted and declared their independence.

Henry Clay had grand visions of trade with these new countries and pressed Congress for immediate recognition of the revolutionary governments. However, President Monroe and Secretary of State Adams feared that such a rash move would endanger negotiations about Florida with Spain.

Consequently, they opposed Clay's efforts in Congress. The United States eventually granted official recognition to the Latin American republics in 1822, when it was clear that they would remain independent.

Most Americans sympathized with the new nations, but most European governments did not. After the defeat of Napoleon in 1812 the governments of Russia, Prussia, Austria, and France formed an alliance. Fearing that revolutionary activity abroad might spread to restless citizens in their own countries, they pledged to suppress any revolutionary movements in Europe. Americans feared that the alliance would not restrict its police efforts to Europe, but that it would try to intervene militarily to restore Spanish control over its former colonies in Latin America as well.

American diplomats also worried about Russian expansion down the coast of Alaska toward Oregon. Secretary Adams told Russia "that the American continents are no longer subjects for any new European colonial establishments." Russia agreed to retract its territorial claims south of the 54° 40' line.

The British government shared the United States's concern that other European countries might try to seize Spain's former American colonies. In 1823 the British foreign minister proposed that the two countries issue a joint declaration guaranteeing the independence of the new nations.

President Monroe considered the British proposal, but Secretary of State Adams strongly objected. He opposed any agreement that might prevent the United States from annexing new territory. Adams had tried to acquire Texas from Spain earlier, and he still had visions of expansion in that direction.

Furthermore, the intensely patriotic Adams wanted the United States to make a declaration of its own. A joint statement with Britain, he explained, would make the United States appear "to come in as a cockboat in the wake of the British man-of-war." The cabinet finally agreed with Adams's view.

The Monroe Doctrine

With his advisers in agreement, Monroe decided to issue a statement of United States policy concerning European influence in the New World. He chose to make his announce-

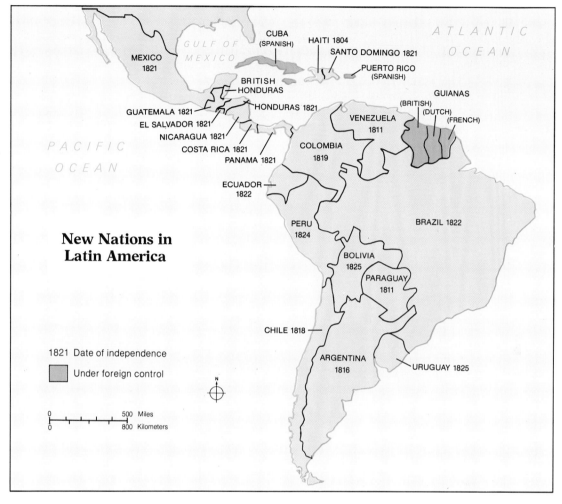

- Between 1800 and 1822, most Latin American countries won independence from Spain and Portugal. A few areas, however, remained European colonies. The Monroe Doctrine warned European powers not to intervene in the newly independent nations.

ment during his annual message to Congress in December 1823.

Monroe proclaimed that the United States would not interfere in the internal concerns of European countries or in existing European colonies in the New World. It would also oppose all European intervention in the affairs of the independent countries in the Americas. The United States, Monroe warned, would view such intervention as an unfriendly act toward itself. "The American continents," Monroe declared in conclusion, "are henceforth not to be considered as subjects for future colonization by any European powers."

Monroe's message marked the high point of a long period of United States diplo-

macy. Beginning with George Washington, Presidents had followed a policy of nonintervention in European affairs. In addition, Americans had always viewed European designs on the New World with suspicion. Monroe's declaration in effect united these principles in a single declaration that Europe and the New World would henceforth refrain from interfering in each others' internal affairs.

Impact of the Doctrine

Monroe's independent actions naturally annoyed the British government. It had wanted a joint declaration, and the President's course denied the British any outward role in setting the policy. Despite their annoyance, the British quietly informed other European governments that they agreed with Monroe's policy.

Without British support, the American declaration would have meant little. The young nation lacked the might to back up its strong words. The British navy, as the European nations well knew, made Monroe's doctrine a reality.

Monroe's message was in tune with the strong nationalist feeling of the time. It showed once again America's pride as a nation. Americans throughout the country warmly applauded and endorsed it. Despite this favorable response, the people soon forgot the Monroe Doctrine. Its greatest significance lay in the future, when a new generation of leaders would unearth it and reestablish it as the country's most basic diplomatic policy.

Major Events

1801	John Marshall appointed Chief Justice of Supreme Court
1803	*Marbury* v. *Madison*
1810	*Fletcher* v. *Peck*
1811	First national Bank charter expires
1816	Congress passes Tariff of 1816; Congress charters second Bank of the United States; James Monroe elected President
1819	*Dartmouth College* v. *Woodward; McCulloch* v. *Maryland;* first major banking crisis
1823	Monroe Doctrine
1824	*Gibbons* v. *Ogden*
1825	Erie Canal completed

For answers, see p. A 38.

Section Review

1. Identify the following: John Quincy Adams, Convention of 1818, Rush-Bagot Treaty, Adams-Onís Treaty.

2. (a) What three problems did Spanish-owned Florida pose for the United States? (b) How did the Adams-Onís treaty solve the problems?

3. (a) How did most Americans feel about the newly independent nations in Latin America? (b) Why were Americans concerned about the new alliance in Europe?

4. (a) What were the main provisions of the Monroe Doctrine? (b) Why was British support of the doctrine important?

IN PERSPECTIVE To President James Monroe, as to many Americans, the years after the War of 1812 were years of national pride and national unity. The country finally seemed to be truly united. Decisions by the Supreme Court under John Marshall contributed to the sense of unity by strengthening the national government. The Industrial Revolution brought greater economic independence, which enhanced national identity.

The American System, proposed by Henry Clay and supported by a new generation of political leaders, reflected the nationalism of the period. Improved transportation strengthened the ties between regions. Finally, in the Monroe Doctrine, President Monroe confirmed American independence and pride.

Yet, as you will read in later chapters, the forces of division as well as unity were at work. Industrialization and westward expansion would eventually contribute to a growing sectional split between North and South, a split that would threaten to tear the nation apart.

Chapter Review

1. (a) How did President James Monroe symbolize the Era of Good Feelings? (b) In what ways was he a part of the Revolutionary War generation?

2. (a) How did the status of the Supreme Court change while John Marshall was Chief Justice? (b) How did the Marshall Court increase the authority of the national government? (c) Why did this Court's decisions contribute to the spirit of national unity?

3. (a) Why was labor scarce in the United States in the early 1800s? (b) What groups of people did manufacturers rely on as a result? (c) How did the Boston Associates treat their workers at the Lowell mills?

4. How was industrialization both a force for unity and a force for division in the United States?

5. (a) Explain how, according to Henry Clay, the Tariff of 1816 would help the United States become more self-sufficient. (b) Why did representatives from the West, the South, and the Middle Atlantic states tend to support the tariff?

6. (a) Why did a national bank seem necessary in 1816? (b) How did the second Bank of the United States contribute to the onset of panic in 1819? (c) What other factors contributed to the panic?

7. (a) Why did westward movement lead to demands for better transportation? (b) How did better roads, canals, and steamboats help bind the nation together?

8. (a) Why did Secretary of State Adams and President Monroe believe that the President should issue the Monroe Doctrine? (b) How did the doctrine reflect the nationalism of the period?

For Further Thought

1. Which political, social, and economic developments contributed to the growing sense of nationalism and national unity between 1816 and 1824?

2. (a) What role did young leaders in Congress, such as Clay, Calhoun, and Webster, think the national government should play in the economy? (b) How did Clay's American System reflect this attitude?

3. President Monroe stated, "The existence of parties is not necessary to free government." How was his statement a reflection of American political traditions up to that time?

For answers, see p. A 39.

Developing Basic Skills

1. *Inferring* Review the Supreme Court cases described on pages 208–209. Study the Constitution and decide which clause or clauses the Court might have used to defend its actions.

2. *Map Reading* Study the map on page 221 and answer the following questions: (a) What is the topic of the map? (b) Trace the northern boundary of the Louisiana Purchase. What treaty established that border? (c) Trace the southern boundary of the Louisiana Purchase. What treaty established that border? (d) How did the Adams-Onís treaty change the status of Florida? (e) How was the size of the United States affected by the treaties?

3. *Researching* Using library resources, make a list of the government positions held by Henry Clay, John C. Calhoun, and Daniel Webster during their careers. Based on what you learn, why do you think these three men had such an important impact on American politics in the years during and after the War of 1812?

See page 775 for suggested readings.

Unit Four

An Era of Expansion

227

A Democracy for the People

13

(1824–1844)

Andrew Jackson, *by Thomas Sully.*

Chapter Outline

1 *Emergence of a New Party System*

2 *Rise of the Common People*

3 *Strengthening the National Government*

4 *Hard Times*

The first half of the nineteenth century was a period of growth and expansion for the United States. The nation expanded westward, and its economy grew dramatically. It was also a time of important political developments. New political parties evolved, and a growing number of people took an active role in government. Such participation, however, was restricted to white males.

Five Presidents served between 1824 and 1844. Among them, Andrew Jackson, the hero of New Orleans, had the greatest influence. For many Americans, he symbolized the rise of the common people, and he brought increased power and prestige to the office of President and to the national government.

As you will read in this chapter, Jackson's successors would have little opportunity to continue his traditions. A severe economic depression handicapped Martin Van Buren. William Henry Harrison died soon after taking office, and his successor, John Tyler, had little in common with Harrison's party or with Congress.

1 Emergence of a New Party System

As the Federalist party dwindled and finally disappeared during the Era of Good Feelings, President Monroe had looked forward to a period when the country would no longer be divided by political parties. Yet the young nation, which had grown from 13 colonies with many different peoples and interests, remained too diverse to be fully represented by one political party. By the end of Monroe's second term, a new party system had begun to take shape, one that would allow more people to participate in the government of their nation than ever before.

The Election of 1824

As the election of 1824 approached, the large number of presidential hopefuls revealed the divisions in Thomas Jefferson's old Republican party. Four major candidates emerged, and each of them tended to draw strength from a different section of the country.

Henry Clay, the Kentuckian who was speaker of the House, had support from many westerners. William Crawford, Monroe's secretary of the treasury, drew his following from his native Georgia and other southeastern states. John Quincy Adams, Monroe's able secretary of state, was popular in New England. Andrew Jackson, hero of the battle of New Orleans, was particulary strong in the states of the old Southwest.

The four-way race for the White House, between Jackson, Clay, Crawford, and Adams, resulted in a deadlock. Jackson won more popular votes than any other candidate, but no candidate received the necessary majority of the 261 votes in the electoral college. Jackson had 99 votes; Adams, 84; Crawford, 41; and Clay, 37. Therefore, as provided by the Constitution, the election was to be decided by the House of Representatives, which would choose from among the top three candidates. (See page 773.)

Henry Clay was eliminated; however, he had enough power and influence in the House to determine which of his rivals would be finally chosen. He decided to endorse Adams, whose principles were closest to his own. With Clay's endorsement the House elected John Quincy Adams on the first ballot. Adams then appointed Clay his secretary of state, a position that had often been a stepping stone to the presidency.

Jackson and his supporters were furious. They charged that Adams had been elected by a "corrupt bargain" that placed Adams in the presidency, with Clay set up as his successor. In fact, nothing so dishonest had happened, but the charge proved to be very damaging to both Adams and Clay.

No one believed the "corrupt bargain" charge more fervently than Andrew Jackson. Indignant at the result of the House vote, he resigned from the Senate and returned to Tennessee, where the legislature promptly nominated him for President. The 1828 campaign thus began almost with Adams's inauguration.

■ Andrew Jackson won the most popular votes in the 1824 election, but he did not receive enough electoral votes to be elected President. Under the Constitution, the House of Representatives chose a President from among the top three candidates.

Election of 1824

Candidate*	Popular Vote	Electoral Vote
Jackson	153,544	99
Adams	108,740	84
Clay	47,136	37
Crawford	46,618	41

Percent Popular Vote

13%, 13%, 43%, 31%

Percent Electoral Vote

16%, 14%, 38%, 32%

*No political parties

Source: *Historical Statistics of the United States*

John Quincy Adams: Unfulfilled Plans

John Quincy Adams's presidency never recovered from the cloud of suspicion surrounding his election. This was unfortunate, for President Adams was a man of considerable talent and vision. A nationalist, he took a broad view of the national government's powers. He wanted the federal government to actively encourage economic growth. He even proposed a program to foster the arts, literature, and science by establishing a national university and a national observatory.

Those who wished a more limited role for the federal government were aghast at these proposals. Jefferson accused Adams of trying to establish an aristocracy by plundering the treasury. Even the President's friends considered his proposals impractical. Adams weakened himself more by refusing to use his authority as President to build a strong party. Finally, his cold, reserved personality undercut his leadership still further. He lacked the skill, tact, and warmth necessary to develop a personal following among either politicians or the people.

Parties in the Campaign of 1828

Jackson's great popularity as well as his conviction that Clay and Adams had stolen the election from him, made it certain that he would run again in 1828. Four years earlier all four candidates had called themselves Republicans, but by 1828 the split in the Republican party had taken more definite shape. President Adams's supporters called themselves National Republicans, in order to emphasize the President's commitment to a national program.

Andrew Jackson and his followers wanted to stress their ties to the common people in opposition to the "aristocratic" Adams, so they called themselves Democratic-Republicans. In the next few years these names would undergo further change as party lines became more distinct. The National Republicans renamed themselves the Whigs and Jackson's party became the Democrats. This marked the beginning of the present-day Democratic party.

Party principles, like party names, were not firmly established in 1828. *Party platforms*, or declarations of principles and programs, remained quite vague, and a wide range of opinion existed within each party.

Jackson's political advisers hoped to attract as many voters as possible during the 1828 election campaign. They made few specific promises about what their candidate would do if elected. Instead, they ran Jackson on his popular reputation as "Old Hickory," a nickname acquired for his endurance and determination during the War of 1812.

All across the country, campaign managers used new methods to interest Americans in the election. They held barbecues, served roast ox, organized torchlight parades and bonfires, and provided fireworks displays. Old Hickory, man of the people, was celebrated everywhere.

The campaign of 1828 contained more than the usual amount of mudslinging, even by the standards of the time. Jackson's supporters accused the President of buying "gaming tables and gambling furniture" with government funds. (Actually Adams had installed a chess set and billiard table in the White House basement—with his own money.)

The Adams forces claimed Jackson was an ignoramus from the backwoods who could not spell "more than about one word in four." Even worse, they accused him of murder, circulating handbills with pictures of the coffins of twelve men supposedly executed by Old Hickory.

Jackson Triumphant

The campaign was rough, but it excited Americans as no presidential election had before. Jackson won handily, receiving 56 percent of the popular vote and 178 electoral votes to Adams's 83. In part the victory demonstrated that sectional differences continued to play a major role in American life. Adams won all the New England states but only Delaware and New Jersey outside of New England. Jackson took the South and West.

Although Jackson ran as the candidate of the "common people," many "common people" voted for Adams and many rich men voted for Jackson. Old Hickory received strong support from southern planters and small farmers in the South and West, the sort of people who shared his background and might be expected to favor him. But he also received the votes of many small busi-

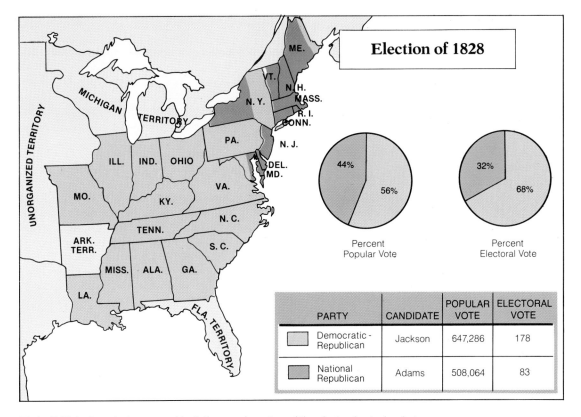

Election of 1828

PARTY	CANDIDATE	POPULAR VOTE	ELECTORAL VOTE
Democratic-Republican	Jackson	647,286	178
National Republican	Adams	508,064	83

Percent Popular Vote

Percent Electoral Vote

■ In 1828 Andrew Jackson swept both the popular vote and the electoral vote. In what section of the country was the National Republican party strongest? For answer, see p. A 39.

ness leaders, factory workers, and artisans in the large cities. He won Pennsylvania's electoral votes and a majority of New York's. He was, therefore, not simply the candidate of the rural South and West.

Andrew Jackson's inauguration was unlike that of any of his predecessors. Great crowds cheered the general as he slowly journeyed to Washington to assume his new duties. Days before he took the oath of office, people from all over the country began pouring into the capital to witness the event.

A cheering throng witnessed their hero take the oath of office and quietly deliver his inaugural address. After the ceremony, they flocked to the White House to greet the new President. Wild disorder resulted as men, women, and children scrambled for refreshments. Ann Royall, a journalist, commented on the scene.

They clambered upon the satin furniture with their muddy boots. . . . Only after disgraceful scenes in the parlors, in which even women got bloody noses, was the situation relieved by

the device of setting tubs of punch on the lawn to lure the new "democracy" out of the house.

To a horrified Supreme Court justice who was present, it seemed the beginning of "the reign of King 'Mob.' " In appearance, anyway, democracy reigned in the White House, and the people had come to power.

For answers, see p. A 39.

Section Review

1. Identify the following: National Republicans, Democratic-Republicans, Old Hickory.
2. Define the following term: party platform.
3. (a) How did John Quincy Adams win the presidency? (b) Why did some people claim that his election was the result of a "corrupt bargain"?
4. (a) What role did President Adams believe the national government should play in the economic and intellectual growth of the country? (b) How did people react to his proposals?
5. (a) Which region of the country voted for Adams in the 1828 election? (b) Which regions voted for Jackson?

2 Rise of the Common People

Jackson's election and administration have frequently been viewed as the triumph of democracy. His noisy and chaotic inauguration, as well as much of the rhetoric of his supporters, seemed to indicate a victory for the common people. But did Jackson's election mean that the average citizen had achieved power? To what extent did the new political system reflect the emerging power of the people, and to what extent did it remain unchanged?

Old Hickory

Andrew Jackson seemed to personify the aspirations of his era. Of humble origins, he had become a wealthy landowner who owned more than 150 slaves by the time he became President at age 62. He was the first President to rise from a log cabin to the White House, a process that eventually became an American dream.

Jackson lacked formal schooling, yet he was not, as his opponents sometimes claimed, an ignorant, crude frontiersman. He could write forceful, if simple, English, had practiced law, and had wide experience in Tennessee politics.

Old Hickory was an imposing figure. A handsome man with white flowing hair, he stood tall, lean, and erect. His drive and determination impressed everyone who met him. As a former military man, he was used to giving orders and being obeyed. Jackson's quick temper and great self-confidence made him prone to impulsive, energetic action, and he tended to take political disputes personally.

Throughout his life Andrew Jackson endured great pain. When he became President, he carried two bullets in him from frontier duels, and while in office he suffered several major illnesses. Yet he seemed able by sheer force of will to overcome these physical ailments, just as he had overcome other obstacles throughout his career. President Andrew Jackson was not exactly a common man, but he always thought of himself as the champion of the common people.

Political Reform

Political changes during Jackson's administration reflected the popular enthusiasm for democracy. The right to vote was extended to more Americans. During the colonial period, most political thinkers had believed that the right to vote should be given only to property owners, those who had a permanent stake in society. Most states eliminated property requirements during the first half of the nineteenth century and permitted *white manhood suffrage*, that is, voting by all white males.

Democratic changes were also made in the selection of the President. The framers of

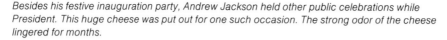

Besides his festive inauguration party, Andrew Jackson held other public celebrations while President. This huge cheese was put out for one such occasion. The strong odor of the cheese lingered for months.

The courtrooms of rural America provided more than a glimpse of the American system of justice. They also offered entertainment for spectators. This drawing shows the informality typical of many country courtrooms. While the jury hears a lawyer make his point, children play in the haylofts at the rear.

the Constitution had originally adopted the idea of presidential electors because they believed that the people themselves would not know enough about the candidates to make a wise choice. (See page 162.) In many states electors had been chosen by the state legislatures, not by the voters directly. However, states gradually moved toward more direct participation by voters. By 1832 every state except South Carolina allowed its voters to choose presidential electors directly.

Political parties, too, became more democratic. Formerly, a party's presidential candidate was usually chosen by a secret party *caucus,* a meeting in which only a few members of Congress had a voice in the decision. By the mid-1830s political parties were holding national nominating conventions in which delegates from all states could participate in the decision. Conventions could still be controlled by party leaders but were now more open and, it was hoped, subject to the voice of the people.

These reforms had an important impact on American politics. All white males were eligible to vote for the first time, and as voters, they had a greater opportunity to influence their government. Furthermore, voters seemed more anxious to use their power. Voting rose from 26 percent of eligible voters in 1824 to 56 percent in 1828 to 78 percent in 1840. Such widespread participation was new in national politics.

Limits to Jacksonian Democracy

Although white men took a greater part in government, other people did not. Women still had no direct political role. Nor did most black Americans. Some states had allowed free blacks to vote, but a number of those states repealed that right during the 1820s and 1830s. Slaves possessed no political rights at all.

Developments in industry and education, some already beginning in the 1820s, would eventually encourage more women to demand a voice in politics. The idea of greater equality for black Americans also gained wider acceptance as the abolitionist movement grew, but such changes evolved slowly. (You will read about these developments later in this unit.) To most white Americans in the first half of the nineteenth century, limiting political activity to white men seemed normal and proper.

A Continuing Policy of Indian Removal

Native Americans also had no part in Jacksonian democracy. In fact, by 1840 most Indian nations had been forced to move to land west of the Mississippi River. As you read earlier, attempts by Native Americans to resist the westward movement of settlers had largely failed. Tecumseh's confederation of Indian nations had collapsed when he was killed during the War of 1812. (See page 202.)

The British had insisted in the Treaty of Ghent, signed after the War of 1812, that the United States "restore to such tribes . . . all possessions . . . which they have enjoyed or been entitled to in [1811] previous to such hostilities." The provision was ignored, however, and settlers continued to push Indian nations westward.

By the mid 1820s about 125,000 Native Americans still lived east of the Mississippi. Chief among them were five southern nations, the Cherokee, Creek, Choctaw, Chicasaw, and Seminole. These were known as the "civilized tribes" because they had adopted many customs of the white settlers. Many were prosperous farmers, and some owned large plantations.

As settlers pressed westward in search of land, however, they eyed the fertile land owned by Indians in parts of western Georgia, North Carolina, Tennessee, Florida, Alabama, and Mississippi. These settlers found an ally in President Jackson.

One of Jackson's goals as President was to complete the removal of Indian nations from east of the Mississippi. His first opportunity to act came soon after he took office. In 1828 the Cherokee living in Georgia tried to safeguard their land by writing a constitution establishing an independent state within the boundaries of Georgia. Stating that the Cherokee were subject to the laws of Georgia, the state government refused to recognize the Cherokee constitution.

The Cherokee appealed to the Supreme Court, which ruled in their favor. Chief Justice Marshall held that the "laws of Georgia can have no force" in Cherokee lands. The Indian nations, he ruled, were "distinct political communities, having political boundaries, within which their authority is exclusive."

President Jackson refused to enforce the Court's decision. "John Marshall has made his decision," Jackson is reported to have said. "Now let him enforce it." The Cherokee were left without legal protection.

Sequoyah: Creating a Written Language

Before 1821 none of the languages of the Indian nations in the United States had a written form. Traditions were passed from generation to generation through oral stories or pictures. In 1809 a Cherokee named Sequoyah decided that his people needed a written language. Many Cherokee lived in the Southeast, but a growing number of settlers were moving into that area during the early nineteenth century. Sequoyah believed that a written language would help the Cherokee preserve their culture and independence.

Sequoyah, who was born about 1760 in the eastern region of present-day Tennessee, had been a skilled hunter and trapper before he was crippled in an accident. He worked on an alphabet for 12 years, eventually devising 86 symbols based on English, Greek, and Hebrew letters. In 1821 the leaders of the Cherokee nation accepted Sequoyah's alphabet. Soon Cherokee children were learning to read and write using his system. The Cherokee used the language to publish books as well as a weekly newspaper, *The Cherokee Phoenix*.

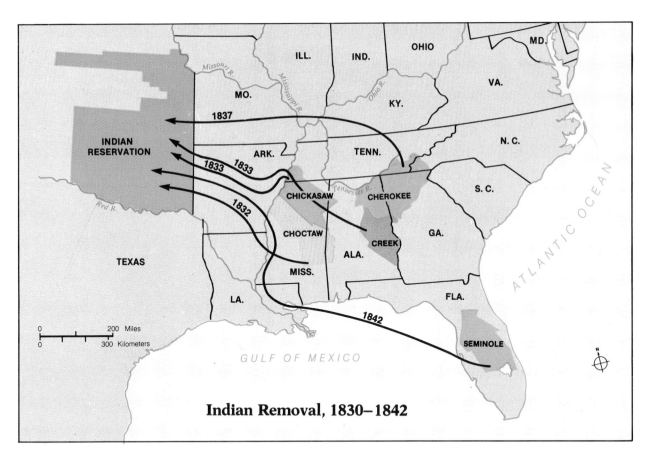

Indian Removal, 1830–1842

■ The Removal Act of 1830 forced many Indians living east of the Mississippi to leave their land and move to less fertile lands in the West. The five tribes most affected were the Chickasaw, Creek, Choctaw, Seminole, and Cherokee. The area shown in brown on the map was set aside as reservation land.

The Trail of Tears

In 1830 Congress passed the Removal Act. This legislation provided funds to negotiate treaties that would force Indians still living in the East to sell their lands and move west. Government officials used these funds to purchase fertile Indian lands in exchange for barren and desolate territory in what is today Oklahoma. White speculators cheated many Indians, buying up their land titles and then reselling them to the government.

With the scales of justice thus tipped against them, southern Indians were forced to embark on what came to be known as the Trail of Tears. In 1838 soldiers drove the remnants of the Choctaw, Creek, and other tribes, as well as over 15,000 Cherokee, west to Oklahoma. An eyewitness, the Reverend Evan Jones, described the scene in the *Baptist Missionary Magazine.*

The Cherokees are nearly all prisoners. They had been dragged from their homes and en-camped at the forts and military places, all over the nation. In Georgia especially, multi-tudes were allowed no time to take anything with them except the clothes they had on. . . . It is a painful sight. The property of many has been taken and sold before their eyes for al-most nothing—the sellers and buyers, in many cases, having combined to cheat the poor Indians.

Provided with little or no clothing or shelter, sick, and suffering emotionally after being wrenched from their homes, thousands of Indians died along the way.

Some Indian nations forcibly resisted removal. In the North the Sac and Fox Indians, unhappy with their new lands, crossed the Mississippi River in 1832 and returned to Illinois. Led by Chief Blackhawk, they launched a series of attacks to regain their homelands. But in the Blackhawk War, which followed, United States Army troops and the state militia defeated Indian forces and opened the way for the settlement of the rest of the state.

235

Under Andrew Jackson the United States government forced Native Americans to vacate most of their lands east of the Mississippi River. Groups that resisted, such as the Cherokee, were driven out by the army. This painting by Mary Ann Thompson shows a group of Cherokee moving westward along what they called the Trail of Tears. Thousands died along the way.

A larger war broke out in Florida, where the Seminole, led by Chief Osceola, refused to leave their homeland. Fugitive slaves who lived with the Seminole aided them in the struggle. The resulting war lasted from 1835 until 1838, when the army finally defeated and removed the Seminole. By 1844 only a few scattered groups of Native Americans remained east of the Mississippi.

For answers, see p. A 40.

Section Review

1. Identify the following: Removal Act, Trail of Tears, Blackhawk, Osceola.

2. Define the following terms: white manhood suffrage, caucus.

3. What group of people gained the vote during the first half of the nineteenth century?

4. How had the selection of presidential electors changed by 1832?

5. Which groups of Americans continued to be denied political participation under Jacksonian democracy?

6. (a) How did the Cherokee attempt to safeguard their lands? (b) Were they successful? Explain.

7. Which Indian nations were most affected by the Removal Act of 1830?

3 Strengthening the National Government

Because Jackson had made no specific campaign promises, no one could be sure of the policies he would pursue as President. Old Hickory soon indicated, however, that he intended to lead as firmly in the White House as he did on the battlefield. His actions had far-reaching consequences in two areas especially.

First, because Jackson saw himself as the protector of the common people, he vigorously opposed government policies that protected privileged groups. Second, because he saw himself as the leader of a truly united nation, he asserted federal authority whenever he believed it was needed. Although Jackson did support states' rights, he never allowed them to threaten national unity. Old Hickory was not afraid to challenge state governments on behalf of the federal union.

Jackson's Democratic Approach

The steps Jackson took to organize his administration reflected his democratic temperament. Like other Presidents, he appointed a cabinet, but these men proved to be generally undistinguished. For advice the President turned instead to a small group of editors, officeholders, and old Tennessee associates known as the Kitchen Cabinet.

In filling lower governmental positions President Jackson adopted a policy of removing people who opposed him politically and replacing them with faithful supporters. His political friends naturally approved of this plan, for it opened up many well-paying positions to them. As one Jacksonian leader explained it, "to the victors belong the spoils." This policy became known as the *spoils system.*

The spoils system made good political sense because it strengthened Jackson's party by rewarding party workers. But the President initiated the spoils system for another reason as well. He believed it furthered the ideals of democracy. Jackson believed that officeholders had begun to think of their jobs as personal property rather than as a public trust. Rotation in office would prevent such thinking. He also was convinced that most government jobs were simple enough that any intelligent man could perform them without special training. Thus Jackson attacked the idea of government workers as a special group set apart from the people.

Despite Jackson's promotion of the spoils system, he actually replaced only about one fifth of the federal officeholders. And some of those replacements were for misbehavior rather than for political reasons. Still, his actions set an unfortunate precedent for the future. Government jobs often became simply rewards for faithful political support, having no connection to public service. As you will read in Chapter 22, this frequently led to government corruption.

The Tariff of Abominations

A controversy that arose over tariffs soon put Jackson's democratic approach and his decisive style to a test. Ever since the nation's founding, Congress had placed tariffs on goods imported into the United States, originally to raise revenue. Over the years manufacturers had successfully convinced Congress to raise tariffs repeatedly. These protective tariffs benefited young American industries by raising the price of cheaper European products higher than American-manufactured goods.

In 1828, before Jackson's election, a new law raised tariffs on some items as high as 45 percent and 50 percent of the original European price. Opponents labeled the legislation of 1828 the Tariff of Abominations. Southern planters in particular bitterly objected to this protection for New England manufacturers. Southerners, after all, exported cotton and other raw materials to Europe and in exchange bought many European manufactured goods for their own use. Because the tariff raised the price of the items they bought, southerners protested that it was in effect an indirect tax on their region of the country.

A Controversy Over States' Rights

John C. Calhoun of South Carolina, Jackson's Vice-President, was the leading opponent of the tariff and a vigorous one at that. Calhoun had abandoned his earlier nationalistic views and by 1828 had begun to defend a state's right to be free from unwanted national control.

In an unsigned essay called the "South Carolina Exposition and Protest," Calhoun argued that the people of any state could *nullify,* or declare illegal, any federal law they believed to be unconstitutional. If a state convention declared a law null and void within the state, its citizens did not have to obey that law. Calhoun and his supporters were aware that this doctrine could be used to defend slavery from federal interference.

Calhoun had raised an important and familiar issue that had been debated since the Revolutionary War. Was the United States one nation indivisible, with the federal government supreme? Or did the states have final say on how much national authority they would accept, as Jefferson and Madison had suggested in the Virginia and Kentucky resolutions of 1798? The issue had been left unresolved because the Constitution was not specific on the question of sovereignty.

In 1830 Senator Daniel Webster of Massachusetts and Senator Robert Hayne of South Carolina debated whether the states or the federal government had ultimate authority. Hayne supported Calhoun's argument that states had the right to nullify federal laws. Webster replied for the nationalists. An impressive man with booming voice and piercing black eyes, he brought all his debating skills to bear against Hayne.

Webster argued that the federal government, not the states, held final authority under the Constitution and that Calhoun's theory of nullification was illegal and unconstitutional. If any state could disregard a law whenever it wished, chaos would reign and the nation would collapse. The federal government was not the agent of the states, Webster continued, but the agent of the people directly. "It is the people's Constitution, the people's government, made for the people, made by the people, and answerable to the people." His final ringing plea was, "Liberty *and* Union, now and forever, one and inseparable!"

The Nullification Crisis

The dispute over nullification simmered for two years, until Congress passed a tariff bill in 1832 that kept rates high and granted southerners little relief. Voters in South Carolina reacted angrily. A popularly elected convention met in November 1832 and declared the tariff null and void in the state.

This was too much for an old military man like Jackson. He blazed in fury at such defiance of federal authority. "If one drop of blood be shed there in defiance of the laws of the United States," he warned privately, "I will hang the first man of them I can get my hands on to the first tree I can find." Publicly he vowed to uphold the tariff law, and in 1833 he asked Congress to pass a "force bill" allowing him, if need be, to use the military to enforce the new measures.

Despite these threats, Jackson moved cautiously. He did not want to push South Carolina into open rebellion. Consequently he welcomed a compromise tariff bill, proposed by Henry Clay, that would reduce duties to 20 percent over a nine-year period. Since the compromise bill did lower tariffs

and since no other southern state supported South Carolina in this dispute, the state's leaders accepted the compromise.

On March 1, 1833, Congress passed Clay's tariff bill, and Jackson signed it. The South Carolina convention then repealed the act nullifying the earlier tariff law. South Carolina's challenge to the national government had failed, and the crisis passed. President Jackson's vigorous actions strengthened both the presidency and the federal government.

Jackson Against the Bank

Another major dispute in Jackson's administration erupted over the Second Bank of the United States. The Bank, originally chartered in 1816, was privately controlled, yet it had immense power. The federal government deposited all its revenue in the Bank, which could then use the money without paying interest. The Bank also issued the only national currency, in the form of bank notes, so it could control how much paper money was in circulation. If the Bank issued large numbers of notes, loans were easier to obtain.

No one was more hostile to the Bank than President Andrew Jackson. To him it was the epitome of special privilege. As a private business, it was responsible, not to the government, but to a small group of stockholders who, he believed, grew rich with public funds. Jackson also argued that the Bank's power made it a corrupting influence in politics. Indeed, the Bank had dispensed favors to government officials, some of whom were even on its payroll.

The Supreme Court had ruled in *McCulloch* v. *Maryland* (1819) that a national bank was constitutional, but President Jackson disagreed. He concluded that Congress had no constitutional power to charter such a bank.

The President was not alone in his opposition. A wide variety of Americans agreed with him, although their reasons differed. Many business leaders, state bankers, and speculators felt that the Bank did not issue enough currency in the form of paper money. They believed that a large supply of money was crucial for rapid economic growth and development.

In contrast, farmers in the South and West along with factory workers in the East thought that the Bank issued too much paper money. They favored a "hard" currency of gold and silver coins. Although some bank notes were backed by gold and silver reserves, some were not. The farmers argued that ordinary citizens had no way of knowing whether the bank notes they received in wages were really worth the amount printed on them. Like Jackson, both groups wanted to see the Bank destroyed.

Victory for the President

The Bank's charter was scheduled to expire in 1836, but the renewal of the charter became an issue in 1832. At that time the Bank's director, Nicholas Biddle, acting on advice from Henry Clay and Daniel Webster, decided to seek an earlier renewal. Clay and Webster felt sure they could get the renewal bill through Congress. If Jackson vetoed it, they would have a ready-made issue for the upcoming presidential election campaign.

Congress granted a new bank charter in March 1832. But President Jackson vetoed the bill, affirming, "The Bank is trying to kill me, but I will kill it!" His veto message attacked the Bank's constitutionality, its size and power, and its tendency to aid "the rich and powerful."

Later that summer, the National Republican party nominated Henry Clay as its candidate for President. As planned, Clay campaigned against Jackson's veto of the Bank. The voters, however, decisively backed Jackson. He won by an electoral college vote of 219 to 49. Taking his victory as a mandate against the Bank, Old Hickory resolved to kill the Bank immediately rather than wait until its charter expired.

First the President ordered all government deposits removed from the Bank. When the secretary of the treasury refused, Jackson fired him and appointed an old supporter, Attorney General Roger B. Taney, to the office. Taney continued to withdraw government funds for normal Treasury Department matters but stopped making deposits. Instead, he began depositing federal revenues in state banks controlled by fellow Democrats. Opponents angrily called them "pet banks."

Biddle responded by refusing to grant new loans and by demanding that existing loans be paid back immediately. With credit unavailable, businesses began to fail, and unemployment rose. Shocked business lead-

President Jackson opposed the Bank of the United States because he considered it undemocratic. This cartoon shows the Bank as a stumbling block to Jackson. The President is wielding a presidential veto against Henry Clay's plans to renew the Bank charter.

ers begged Jackson to end his opposition to the Bank in order to restore public confidence. Jackson refused, blaming the uncertain economic situation on Biddle.

President Jackson eventually won this economic war of nerves. The Bank lost popularity, and Jackson's support grew. After 1836, when its federal charter expired, the Bank continued to operate under a Pennsylvania charter. But the Panic of 1837 (see page 240) weakened it still further, and in 1841 it went out of business.

For answers, see p. A 40.

Section Review

1. Identify the following: Kitchen Cabinet, Tariff of Abominations, Robert Hayne, Nicholas Biddle, pet banks.

2. Define the following terms: spoils system, nullify.

3. According to Jackson, how did the spoils system further the ideals of democracy?

4. Why were southerners in particular opposed to the tariff legislation of 1828?

5. (a) What was John C. Calhoun's position on states' rights? (b) What was Daniel Webster's position?

6. (a) What action did South Carolina take against high tariffs? (b) Was it successful? Explain.

7. (a) Why was President Jackson opposed to the Second Bank of the United States? (b) What groups of citizens also opposed the Bank?

4 Hard Times

As Andrew Jackson neared the end of his second term, he remained as popular as ever. Although he might have used his popularity to run for a third term, Jackson decided to honor the two-term tradition that began with Washington. But he made sure that his influence was felt in the choice of his party's next presidential candidate.

The Election of 1836

The Democrats held their first national nominating convention in 1836, and Jackson took great pains to ensure that his Vice-President, Martin Van Buren, would be the nominee. Van Buren faced bitter opposition from the National Republicans, who renamed themselves the Whigs. *

Whigs agreed on their opposition to Jackson's policies, but they found it difficult to unite on a platform of positive principles. In general, they shared John Quincy Adams's faith that the United States could become a great nation through its wealth and growing industry. Many Whigs supported the goals of Henry Clay's American System and thought federal and state governments should take a more active role in promoting canals, roads, and other internal improvements.

In the North, many merchants and manufacturers supported the Whigs, as did educators, reformers, and commercial farmers. Many southerners also joined the Whigs, including merchants, bankers, and planters who believed that southern prosperity was linked with the expanding commerce of the North.

In 1836, however, the Whigs did not believe they were strong enough to run a single candidate for President. Instead, they decided to run three separate candidates, one popular in each section of the country: Henry Harrison in the West, Daniel Webster in New England, and Hugh Lawson White in the South. They hoped to prevent Van Buren from winning a majority in the electoral col-

---

*They named themselves after the British Whigs, who had opposed King George III during the Revolutionary War, because they claimed that Jackson acted like "King Andrew I."

lege and thus, as in 1824, throw the election into the House of Representatives.

The strategy failed. Van Buren won a small majority of both the popular and the electoral vote. Unfortunately for Van Buren, he soon encountered a situation he could not control.

Depression Strikes

As President, Van Buren intended to follow the policies of his popular predecessor, but disaster struck almost immediately. Two months after his inauguration, a severe financial panic soon known as the Panic of 1837, began.

The panic had its roots in land speculation. The prosperity of the previous decade had stimulated the purchase of western land more than ever before. The government held most of the region in public domain and sold it to farmers and investors, over 12 million acres (4.8 million hectares) in 1835 and over 20 million acres (8 million hectares) in 1836. The prospect of high profits brought speculators as well as farmers into the market. Soon speculators were purchasing huge tracts, sometimes by clearly illegal means.

Many of the new landowners in the Southwest grew cotton. For a time this expanded the cotton supply and opened new markets for eastern merchants and manufacturers. Land prices skyrocketed.

Without a powerful national bank to control the money supply, state bank notes flooded the country, many of them not backed by gold or silver. Because of the large amount of money in circulation, state governments began extensive canal and railroad building projects. Banks, merchants, and farmers borrowed money, and banks in turn gave easy credit terms to others.

Shortly before Van Buren's election, President Jackson had tried to slow speculation by issuing a Specie Circular. It stated that public land could be paid for only in gold or silver. The circular convinced prospective land buyers that the boom economy would not last forever. In the climate of economic uncertainty, land sales slowed.

In early 1837 the price of cotton on the international market dropped sharply because of a surplus. For cotton farmers who had mortgaged their farms to buy more land, this drop in prices meant disaster. Without adequate profits from their cotton sales, farmers could not repay their loans. The sagging land market then collapsed.

The resulting depression was one of the most severe in the nation's history. Banks failed by the hundreds, and even some states went bankrupt because of overambitious internal improvement schemes. Unemployment climbed as factories closed.

Many Americans blamed the Democratic administration for the economic hard times, although the administration was not directly responsible for the overspeculation that had caused the panic. Like most citizens, Van Buren did not really understand what caused the crisis. He attributed it to "overbanking" and urged Congress to restructure the Treasury. Congress complied in 1840, but the government did little else to combat the depression.

A Missed Opportunity for the Whigs

The Democrats renominated President Van Buren in 1840, but the continuing economic depression filled the party faithful with gloom. The Whigs, on the other hand, were enthusiastic. They believed that hard times and a popular candidate would insure their victory. They chose General William Henry Harrison of Ohio, a military hero still basking in his victory over Tecumseh at the Battle of Tippecanoe in 1811. To balance the ticket, they nominated John Tyler, a conservative Virginia Whig who favored states' rights, for Vice-President.

The campaign of 1840 was one of the most colorful in the nation's history. With the slogan "Tippecanoe and Tyler Too," the Whigs conducted a spirited and exciting campaign. Having learned the art of mass campaigning from the Democrats, they portrayed Harrison as a simple western farmer, a man of the people who lived in a log cabin and loved hard cider. (Actually, he came from one of Virginia's most distinguished families and lived in a rather elegant house.) People flocked to political rallies, parades, bonfires, and barbecues, where bands and other entertainment helped arouse popular interest.

The Whigs carefully avoided discussing any real issues and made sure that Harrison said nothing of substance. "Let him say not one single word about his principles, or his creed," Nicholas Biddle once advised. "Let him say nothing—promise nothing."

The Democrats sarcastically dubbed Harrison "General Mum," but the Whig strategy paid off. In a large turnout of voters, Harrison won 234 electoral votes to Van Buren's 60. The popular vote was much closer, but the Whigs had elected their first President after 12 years of Democratic control.

The Whigs optimistically looked forward to implementing a vigorous program of economic growth and development based on Clay's American System. But only a month after taking office, the 68-year-old Harrison died of pneumonia. The Whigs were thunderstruck. For the first time, a Vice-President succeeded to the presidency.

As President, Tyler blocked legislation that would have strengthened the national

The 1840 Whig candidate, General William Henry Harrison of Ohio, was nicknamed Tippecanoe for his victory over Tecumseh in 1811. (See page 199.) Harrison's campaign pictured him as a simple farmer living in a log cabin, as you can see in this campaign banner. Actually, he came from a distinguished Virginia family and lived in a fine house. By 1840 image building had become important in presidential campaigns.

Major Events

1825	John Quincy Adams elected President
1828	Tariff of Abominations passed; Andrew Jackson elected President
1830	Indian Removal Act
1832	Jackson vetoes new Bank charter; South Carolina "nullifies" tariff
1833	Nullification crisis ends
1836	Martin Van Buren elected President
1837	Panic of 1837 begins
1838	Army drives thousands of southern Indians to Oklahoma
1840	William Henry Harrison elected President
1841	After Harrison's death, John Tyler becomes first Vice-President to succeed to presidency

government at the expense of the states. He opposed federal funding for internal improvement projects and twice vetoed a bill to charter a new national bank.

The Whigs quickly realized that nominating as Vice-President a man so out of sympathy with their policies had been a mistake. For the last years of his presidency, Tyler was literally a President without a party, and Democrats gleefully encouraged his feud with the Whigs. Without effective leadership, national affairs drifted.

For answers, see p. A 40.

Section Review

1. Identify the following: Whigs, Specie Circular, John Tyler.
2. (a) What did the Whigs hope to gain by running three separate candidates for President in 1836? (b) Were they successful? Explain.
3. How did the drop in cotton prices in 1837 contribute to the depression?
4. What campaign strategies did the Whigs learn from the Democrats?
5. Did President Tyler carry out Whig policies? Explain.

IN PERSPECTIVE During the late 1820s two new political parties, the Democrats and the Whigs, gradually evolved from the Republican party of the Era of Good Feelings. Campaign techniques first used by the Democrats in 1828 added new excitement to presidential elections.

Andrew Jackson campaigned as the candidate of the common people in 1828, and for some people his election began an era of increased democracy. Political reforms led to greater political participation by white males and gave the average voter a stronger voice in the election process. However, women were denied the right to vote and lacked any voice in government, and most black Americans were denied even the most basic human rights. For many thousands of southern Native Americans the period was marked by heartbreak and horror as they were forced to leave their homelands.

President Jackson's determined actions against the national Bank and his strong position in the nullification crisis strengthened the office of the presidency. The Panic of 1837 resulted in a severe economic depression, which handicapped President Van Buren, who lost to William Henry Harrison in 1840. The Whigs' hopes of implementing their program of national development died with Harrison. His successor, John Tyler, had little sympathy with most Whig goals. Tyler, however, was a strong supporter of expanding the national boundaries, a process that reached a high point in the mid-1840s, as you will read in the next chapter.

For answers, see p. A 41.

Chapter Review

1. What factors contributed to the weakness of John Quincy Adams's presidency?

2. (a) What two new political parties emerged during the late 1820s? (b) How did the parties differ? (c) What role did they play in the election of 1828?

3. How was Jackson's inauguration evidence that the common people had come to power?

4. (a) What reforms increased the political participation of some Americans? (b) Which groups did not participate?

5. (a) Why did settlers want the southern Native Americans moved west of the Mississippi? (b) How did President Jackson and Congress contribute to this goal? (c) How did the Indian nations try to resist removal? (d) Were they successful? Explain.

6. Explain how each of the following reflected Andrew Jackson's democratic approach to government: (a) the Kitchen Cabinet; (b) the spoils system; (c) his opposition to the Second Bank of the United States.

7. (a) Why did John C. Calhoun support a state's right to nullify a federal law? (b) What argument did Daniel Webster use against the principle of nullification?

8. (a) Why did South Carolina try to nullify the tariff law? (b) What was President Jackson's reaction? (c) Why were Jackson and South Carolina both willing to accept Clay's compromise bill?

9. (a) Why was the Second Bank of the United States a powerful institution? (b) What steps did President Jackson take to try to "kill" the Bank? Was he successful? Explain.

10. Explain how each of the following contributed to the Panic of 1837: (a) land speculation; (b) the availability of large amounts of money; (c) Jackson's Specie Circular; (d) the drop in cotton prices.

11. (a) Why did the Whigs nominate William Henry Harrison for President? (b) Why did they nominate John Tyler for Vice-President? (c) How did their choices backfire?

For answers, see p. A 42.

For Further Thought

1. Political parties since the Jackson campaign have often taken vague positions on issues in order to gain the support of diverse groups. (a) How might a political party benefit from this strategy? (b) How might the presidential candidate benefit from this once he or she is in office? (c) What difficulty might this present for the voter?

2. People who supported Jackson saw his presidency as the embodiment of democratic ideals. His opponents viewed his administration as "the reign of King Andrew." With which view do you agree? Give evidence to support your answer.

3. From what you learned about Andrew Jackson in this chapter and in previous chapters, why do you think he was sympathetic to the settlers who wanted the Native Americans removed?

4. Why was the final removal of Indian nations to land west of the Mississippi called the Trail of Tears?

5. (a) How did Andrew Jackson's actions as President strengthen the presidency? (b) How did he strengthen the national government? Give examples to support your answers.

For answers, see p. A 42.

Developing Basic Skills

1. *Map Reading* Study the map on page 235 and answer the following questions: (a) What information is shown on this map? (b) In what states did the southern Indian nations hold land before 1830? (c) In which state did they hold the largest amount of land? (d) How far did each nation have to move from its homeland?

2. *Graph Reading* Study the circle graphs of the 1824 and 1828 presidential elections. (See pages 229 and 231.) Then answer the following questions: (a) Which two candidates ran in both elections? (b) What percentage of the electoral vote did each candidate receive in 1824? in 1828? (c) What percentage of the popular vote did each candidate receive in 1824? in 1828? (d) Based on the election results in 1824, do you think Andrew Jackson had reason to object when John Quincy Adams was elected by the House of Representatives? Why or why not?

See page 775 for suggested readings.

14

From Sea to Sea

(1820–1860)

Detail of Oregon Trail, *by Oscar Berninghaus.*

Chapter Outline

1 *The View From West to East*

2 *Oregon and the Fur Trade*

3 *The Republic of Texas*

4 *Surge to the Pacific*

5 *The Challenge of Greater Diversity*

By 1825 the United States had expanded far beyond its original borders, and settlers were moving into the Mississippi River Valley. Although the Louisiana Purchase had extended the nation's boundaries to the Rocky Mountains and beyond, there seemed to be little interest in the territory west of the Mississippi.

Yet within the next 25 years, the United States acquired vast new territory in the West, much of it through war with Mexico. Fur trappers and missionaries opened up the Oregon territory, prospectors streamed to California, and settlers moved into Texas and other parts of the Southwest.

The new territories added to the geographic diversity of the nation, ranging from rugged mountains to deserts and rain forests. The people who lived in the newly acquired areas, especially Native Americans and Mexicans, contributed to the ethnic diversity of the United States, as you will read in this chapter.

1 The View From West to East

Because the United States evolved from the English colonies along the Atlantic seaboard, thinking of the nation's growth as westward expansion to the Pacific Ocean may seem quite natural. Yet Native Americans had been living in the West, as they had in the East, for thousands of years. Their perspective was bound to differ from that of settlers from the east coast.

Spain's perspective also differed. The Spanish had established a claim to vast areas of North America almost 100 years before the first English settlers arrived in Jamestown. By the time settlers from the former English colonies became interested in the western part of North America, Spanish culture and institutions flourished in many areas there.

The Spanish in California

In 1800 New Spain, the northernmost Spanish province in the Americas, extended as far north as present-day Montana and as far east as the Mississippi River. Spain, however, paid little attention to its lands north and east of the Gila River and the Rio Grande. For the most part, only small settlements were established in order to prevent other European nations from claiming territory too close to Spanish lands.

In the mid-eighteenth century Spanish authorities took a renewed interest in the northern part of New Spain. They learned that Russian seal hunters and traders were moving south from Alaska into California. In 1769 the Spanish sent an expedition under Don Gaspar de Portola (POR TOH lah) to reassert Spanish authority in Upper California, the area north of the California peninsula.

Portola marched first to San Diego, where he built a stockade. Then he continued north to Monterey. On November 2, 1769, while exploring this area, he discovered San Francisco Bay. (Ships had passed the entrance to the bay for years without sailors realizing that it was the opening to a great inland harbor.)

A group of Franciscan friars led by Father Junípero Serra (SEHR rah) accompanied Portola's expedition. They intended to establish missions to convert the California Indians to Christianity. From San Diego northward a chain of missions was set up along the California coast, where they prospered, forming the backbone of the Spanish government's attempt to settle California. In 1776, the same year that the English colonies declared their independence from Great Britain, Misión Dolores was founded where San Francisco now stands.

The Mission System

The missions claimed virtually all the land in California. The friars who ran the missions either convinced or compelled local Indians to live on mission land, where they worked as farmhands or herders and were converted to Christianity. By 1830 approximately one tenth of the 300,000 California Indians lived on mission lands. They raised cattle, horses, and sheep, cultivated grapes and wheat, and built irrigation facilities. As a result of Indian labor, many of the missions were self-sufficient.

In return for Indian labor, the friars offered food, clothing, and shelter. In the Spaniards' eyes, their greatest contribution to the local Indians was the gift of Christianity. Many Indians accepted conversion, and over the years their own customs and traditions faded. Furthermore, even though the missionaries started with good intentions, many eventually came to view the Indians mainly as a pool of cheap labor. Working conditions then became harsher.

Although the Spanish established a few forts in California, the missions remained the main political and economic symbol of Spanish control until 1821. In that year revolutionaries in New Spain successfully threw off Spanish rule and declared Mexico an independent nation. California remained isolated from the fighting but accepted the authority of the new Mexican nation.

Impact of Mexican Independence

In 1833 the Mexican Congress passed the Secularization Act, which altered the economic and political administration of California. It opened church lands to settlement by other Mexicans and decreed that Indians were no longer under the protection or control of the church. Any semblance of real

Wealthy landowners in New Spain often controlled vast tracts of land. In this painting, a hacendado (landowner) and his wife are pictured at the center. Their elaborate clothing reflects the traditions of Spain. Spanish language and customs left a permanent stamp on the American Southwest.

freedom for the Indians, however, was short-lived.

The Mexican government granted large portions of valuable mission land to Mexican citizens, who were eager to exploit the profits to be made from farming and ranching. Vast ranches quickly replaced the missions as the main economic unit in California.

For manual labor, the *rancheros,* or ranch owners, turned to the local Indian populations, just as the missionaries had earlier. Although technically the Indians were free, most rancheros forced them to work and hunted them down if they tried to escape.

Hard work and alien customs took a tremendous toll. The *mortality rate,* or death rate, among Indians working on California ranches was four times as high as among Mexicans in California and twice as high as the mortality rate among slaves in the southern United States. By 1848 about 20 percent of the California Indians had died.

The independence of Mexico opened up the territory to traders from the United States for the first time. The ranches of California, with their vast cattle herds, offered a new market for enterprising Yankee merchants, who soon dominated the lucrative cattle-hide trade in California. In 20 years one Boston firm alone exported half a million hides. Still, until the mid-1840s, developments on the east coast of North America had little impact on life in California.

Arizona and New Mexico

The Spanish made several attempts during the eighteenth century to establish settlements in the area of present-day Arizona. The Yuma and Apache Indians of the area, however, defended their homelands fiercely, and by 1830 the Spanish had abandoned several mines and missions, leaving only a few outposts.

Farther east, in New Mexico, the Spanish established more permanent settlements. About 44,000 Spanish settlers lived along the Rio Grande from El Paso to Taos as sheep ranchers. As in California, a few rich families owned vast herds, numbering as many as a million sheep, which were tended by local Indians.

The Spanish also founded more missions in New Mexico than in Arizona, partly because the Pueblo and Zuni offered less open resistance than the Apache and Yuma. Yet many Indians in New Mexico did resent Spanish attempts to impose an alien religion and way of life on them.

Traders from the United States appeared in Santa Fe, the capital of New Mexico, as early as 1804, but the Spanish threw them in jail and confiscated their goods. Spain wanted to discourage foreign interest in its territory. But when Mexico declared its independence in 1821, the new government welcomed American traders as a way of increasing its own prosperity. The first successful trading expedition from Missouri reached Santa Fe the same year. The traders returned home triumphant; they dumped bags full of Spanish dollars on the sidewalks while onlookers watched in amazement. Soon the Santa Fe trade flourished.

Texas

In the 1720s the Spanish had claimed all of present-day Texas and had driven out the few French colonists living there. Yet a hundred years later only 4,000 Spanish settlers resided in Texas, making a living primarily by cattle ranching. Although the Catholic church established a few missions in Texas, the Indians there, such as the Comanche and Apache, were nomadic and resisted any attempts to force them to adopt Spanish ways.

Here and there, a few farmers from the United States had crossed the Sabine River into eastern Texas. But the area remained sparsely settled. In the 1820s the newly independent Republic of Mexico wanted to make its northern province, Texas, more prosperous and secure. To do that, the Mexican government knew it would have to attract many new settlers.

In 1820 an American named Moses Austin requested and received permission to found a colony of 300 people in Texas. Austin died before he could begin the trip, but his son Stephen took over the project. Stephen Austin appeared particularly ill suited for the task. He was sensitive and well educated and might have seemed more at home in a university than on the frontier. But he was tolerant, fair, and honest and displayed careful judgment and considerable diplomatic talent.

Austin founded his new colony in December 1821. Each family received about 250 acres (about 100 hectares) for farming and stock raising. Austin's colony thrived in large part because of his skill in choosing people. By 1824 he had settled 2,021 persons in his colony, the center of which was the little town of Austin. This marked the beginning of an ever-increasing flood of American settlers into Texas.

Oregon

The land north of Upper California extending to Vancouver Island and the coast of present-day British Columbia had been claimed not only by Spain but by Russia, Great Britain, and the United States as well.

In 1818 the United States and Great Britain agreed to a joint occupation of the Oregon country, the area north of the 42nd parallel and south of latitude 54° 40′. The British and the Americans would be free to settle and trade there. Both, however, generally ignored the rights and interests of the territory's original inhabitants, as Europeans had done since they first landed in the Americas. By 1825 Spain and Russia withdrew their claims to these lands.

For many years only a few Europeans or Americans came to settle in Oregon, and their main interest was the fur trade. Since furs bought from the Indians could be sold at tremendous profits in China, Yankee traders from New England stopped along the Oregon coast frequently—so frequently, in fact, that the Indian name for white man in many areas was "Boston."

The Yankee traders in Oregon were among a small number of Americans who lived in the West. Up until the mid-1820s, if you had viewed the history of North America from the west coast looking east, the conflicts and trials of the United States would have played a minor role. Soon, very soon, that situation would change.

For answers, see p. A 42.

Section Review

1. Identify the following: Don Gaspar de Portola, Father Junípero Serra, Secularization Act, Stephen Austin.

2. Define the following terms: ranchero, mortality rate.

3. What development led the Spanish to take a renewed interest in northern New Spain?

4. What political function did the missions serve for the Spanish in California?

5. What did California Indians do on mission lands and on Spanish ranches?

6. (a) In what areas of the Southwest did the Spanish establish missions and settlements? (b) In which area was this most difficult?

7. What was the joint-occupation agreement between the United States and Great Britain?

2 Oregon and the Fur Trade

The role of the United States in the far West changed partly because Americans began to learn more about the country beyond the Mississippi River. Before 1820, Americans knew little about the area except for information reported by the Lewis and Clark expedition. During the 1820s, however, word began to trickle back about the vast and fertile lands of Oregon, beyond the Rocky Mountains. Those who spread the word and blazed the trails that later pioneers would follow were enterprising fur traders known popularly as "mountain men."

The Mountain Men

Rocky Mountain streams abounded in beaver, and the resourceful and hardy mountain men could make a fortune trapping the animals and trading their pelts. Yet they led a lonely, often dangerous existence. Grizzly bears and other potentially dangerous animals populated the forests; an accident could strand a mountain man far from help. Furthermore, many of the Native Americans

in the territory, particularly the Blackfeet, resented the trapping on their hunting grounds and frequently attacked the outsiders.

These outsiders were a diverse group. French-Canadian trappers had begun to probe the Rockies as early as the 1770s. By the 1820s the mountain men included not only French-Canadians but also British, Irish, and Mexicans as well as white and black trappers from the United States. James Beckworth, a black mountain man from the United States, became a chief of the Crow Indians. Louis Vasquez, half French and half Spanish, became a mountain man in 1822 and was one of the founders of Denver, Colorado. At least one "mountain man" was a woman. Marie Dorion, an Iowa Indian, became famous throughout the United States for her feats of survival.

While the trappers made money from their labor, the traders who bought the furs and sold them in the East made the biggest profits. Two of the largest trading companies were John Jacob Astor's American Fur Company and the Rocky Mountain Fur Com-

Forts doubled as trading posts in the Northwest. In this painting, a fur buyer deals with several trappers, including Native Americans, at Fort Walla Walla in Oregon country. The heavy demand for beaver pelts led to overtrapping, and by the 1830s beaver were becoming scarce. Settlers began to arrive in greater numbers, signaling the end of the era of mountain men and trappers.

pany. In its 12 years of operation, the latter alone purchased furs worth nearly $500,000, an enormous sum at that time. Other smaller companies eagerly joined the search for furs, competed with each other, and recruited their own mountain men.

The competition between the companies, however, led to drastic overtrapping of streams and rivers. After 1832, with the beaver population greatly reduced, the fur trade fell into serious decline.

Early Settlers in Oregon

As the heyday of the mountain man ended, the day of the pioneer began. Former mountain men and employees of fur companies told of the beautiful and rich land that lay beyond the Rockies, in Oregon country.

Tales of rich land were not all that lured settlers westward. Easterners heard rumors that Indians in the West wanted to learn about Christianity and the Bible. The Indian tribes actually had their own rich religious traditions, and few had even heard of Christianity. But churches sent missionaries to Oregon in response to the reports.

The best-known missionaries were Jason Lee, sent by the Methodists in 1834; Marcus and Narcissa Whitman, Presbyterians who led a band of settlers west in 1836; and Henry and Eliza Spalding, who accompanied the Whitmans. None of the missionaries had much success converting Native Americans to the Christian religion, but they nevertheless wrote home urging friends to join them.

Gradually more and more Americans made their way to Oregon, settling in the Willamette Valley near the missionaries' homes. Families wrote descriptive letters back East, which newspapers often published.

Booklets appeared extolling the virtues of Oregon, often exaggerating wildly. Many Americans spoke the way one Missouri farmer did to his family when he announced his decision to move West.

> Out in Oregon I can get me a square mile of land. And a quarter section for each of you all. Dad burn me, I am done with this country. Winters its frost and snow freeze the body; summers the overflow from Old Muddy drowns half my acres; taxes take the yield of them that's left. What say, Maw, it's God's country.

The Way West

The Oregon Trail, developed by earlier traders and trappers, became the most famous route to Oregon country. It began at Independence, Missouri, followed the Missouri and the Platte rivers to southern Wyoming, crossed the Rockies at South Pass, and took a northern cutoff to the Columbia River, which it followed to the Willamette Valley. In all, the trail stretched for about 2,000 miles (about 3,200 kilometers), and the journey took four to six months.

In the early 1840s growing numbers of people responded to the publicity about Oregon. The pioneers traveled along the trails to Oregon in caravans of covered wagons. Safety and prudence required such organization. One danger was Indian attack. Indians did not often attack the wagon trains that crossed their lands, but the settlers wanted to be prepared in any case.

Another problem was the land itself. Beyond central Nebraska, streams ran dry in the summer, and the grass grew thin where it grew at all. For pioneers used to wooded, well-watered country, the experience was frightening. When the wagon trains drew into a circle for the night, it was as much to keep the precious livestock from wandering away to find more grass as it was for protection.

Each wagon train winding westward established its own government, complete with a code of laws and officials to enforce them. The experience of literally forming their own government proved valuable preparation for the settlers once they arrived on the Pacific coast, where government was limited, at times even nonexistent.

Self-Government: The First Organic Law

As you read earlier, Great Britain and the United States had agreed to a joint occupation of the Oregon country in 1818. But when the settlers arrived in the Willamette Valley, the only government authority they found was the British Hudson's Bay Company, which was hardly equipped to deal with a flood of permanent settlers. Americans thus grew dissatisfied with the vague arrangement of joint occupation.

After 1842, when Americans began to outnumber the British, they drew up their

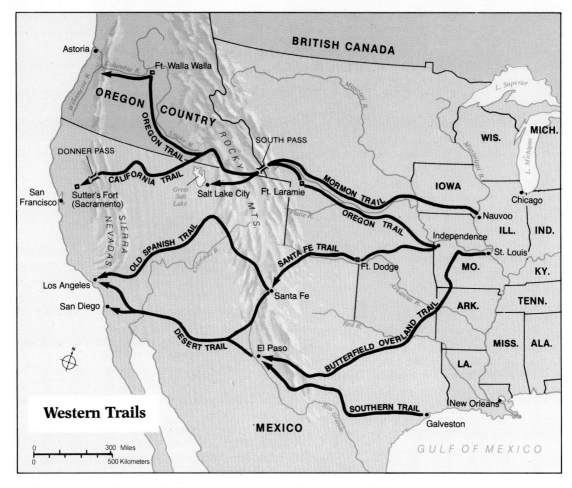

■ *The way west to Oregon and California stretched some 2,000 miles (about 3,200 kilometers) from Missouri and Illinois. Much of the land was arid or mountainous or both. Prudent pioneers, therefore, traveled with an experienced guide over one of the trails shown on this map.*

own framework of government, the First Organic Law. It outlined a temporary government for the Oregon Territory, which continued in force for the next few years.

By 1845 about 5,000 Americans had settled in Oregon, most of them from northern states. They opposed the introduction of slavery in Oregon, but many also objected to the immigration of free blacks. In an effort to discourage such immigration the First Organic Law provided that any black entering Oregon would be whipped.

Even under such harsh conditions, a few blacks did arrive and some prospered. George Washington Bush, for one, led a company of black settlers to Oregon. He and his family became wealthy wheat farmers, known for their kindness toward poorer white settlers. Bush and his company were also known for their willingness to shoot in

self-defense, so the antiblack provisions of the Oregon law were never enforced.

The American settlers, both black and white, looked forward to the day when Oregon would become first a territory of the United States and eventually a state.

For answers, see p. A 43.

Section Review

1. Identify the following: Oregon Trail.
2. (a) What did the mountain men hope to gain by their activities? (b) What development caused a decline in the fur trade?
3. List two reasons pioneers settled in Oregon.
4. (a) What dangers did Americans face on the trip to Oregon? (b) How did wagon trains provide protection?
5. (a) What was the First Organic Law? (b) What purpose was it to serve?

3 The Republic of Texas

Just as the increasing number of immigrants from the United States into Oregon caused problems for the Hudson's Bay Company, so the tide of settlers in Texas caused problems for Mexico. By the end of the 1820s about 20,000 Americans lived in Texas, compared to only about 4,000 Mexicans. Furthermore, the potential for conflict was high. Many differences existed between Mexican and American ways of life.

Clash of Two Cultures

Natural tensions arose between Mexicans and Americans because of basic cultural differences. Most Mexicans spoke Spanish; most Americans spoke English. The American settlers were overwhelmingly Protestant, while most Mexicans were Catholic. And the Mexican government permitted public worship only in Roman Catholic churches.

Political differences also contributed to the conflict. Settlers from the United States had strong democratic traditions. The background of the Mexicans was quite different. Under the old Spanish empire, government had been undemocratic. Provincial officials and local mayors were appointed by the crown, not elected by the people.

When Mexico became independent, its government did adopt a constitution and formed legislatures in each of its states. However, Texas was part of a larger state, and Texans sent only one representative to the legislature. Consequently they had little influence on the government of Mexico.

Furthermore, Americans found it difficult to become accustomed to the Mexican judicial system. A single judge sitting in Saltillo, the state capital, ruled on court cases. The plaintiff and defendant did not testify personally before the judge, nor was a jury present. A system that depended so heavily on one person's opinion did not seem just to Americans.

A further point of friction was slavery. Most Americans who settled in Texas were southerners. Some brought slaves along, and others expected to acquire them there. The Mexican government had abolished slavery in Texas in 1827 and later throughout Mexico. Yet since enforcement was lax, American settlers continued to bring slaves. Even though Mexican authorities revoked the ban on slavery in Texas a few years later, the American colonists still believed slavery would not be secure as long as Texas remained under Mexican rule.

Beginning of Conflict

The Mexican government had its own reasons for distrusting the American colonists. It suspected that the settlers wanted to bring Texas into the United States. The United States government, after all, had already attempted to purchase Texas twice, in 1826 and 1829.

To strengthen its hold on Texas, the Mexican government established new military garrisons in the province and fortified already existing ones. To American-born Texans, those actions looked like the beginning of military rule. Then, in the summer of 1832, a revolution in Mexico brought to power a new and vigorous leader, General Antonio de Santa Anna. Many American settlers had supported Santa Anna's struggle. They hoped that he would grant them a greater role in the government of Texas. Most were willing to remain loyal to Mexico despite their foreign background as long as the Mexican government allowed them a measure of freedom.

Santa Anna, however, proved to be less liberal than he had first appeared. In October 1834 he abolished the Mexican constitution and legislatures and set himself up as dictator of all Mexico. Rumors spread north from Mexico City: Santa Anna, some said, intended to disenfranchise American Texans, abolish local governments, and drive all Americans out of Texas. Santa Anna was sending troops north, said others.

When Santa Anna, hearing of discontent in Texas, actually did send reinforcements to the Mexican garrisons, a group of Americans led by the fiery William B. Travis decided to act. They captured a Mexican garrison at Anahuac (AHN ah wahk) on June 30, 1835.

The Struggle for Texan Independence

Stephen Austin rallied the American settlers behind the goal of independence for Texas. When a Mexican force reached Gonzales,

Americans from all over the countryside rushed to the town, fiercely attacked the Mexicans, and forced them to withdraw.

A convention representing all American settlements met in November 1835 at Austin. The delegates issued a Declaration of Causes justifying their decision to take up arms. They appointed Sam Houston, a popular figure in Texas, as commander of their forces, and they established a provisional government. The following year, on March 2, 1836, Texas declared its independence as the Republic of Texas.

True independence, however, would come only with military victory. During February and March of 1836, the Mexican army pushed northward, laying siege to a small Texas garrison of less than 200 men in the Alamo, an abandoned mission in San Antonio. The defenders of the Alamo included William B. Travis, commander; Jim Bowie, second in command; and Davy Crockett, the best known of a large number of United States volunteers who had come to Texas to join the fight. All of the defenders were killed when the fort fell to the Mexicans on March 6. Their heroic actions had given the Texas revolutionaries time to form an army and had provided the rallying cry, "Remember the Alamo."

With the Americans now aroused and united, volunteers flocked to Sam Houston's army. Houston, however, realized that his new recruits were too inexperienced to fight. So despite the criticism of rasher men, he temporarily retreated in order to get his army into fighting shape before challenging Santa Anna.

On April 21, 1836, Houston ended his retreat. Although outnumbered two to one, he led an attack on Santa Anna's army near the San Jacinto (SAHN jah SEEN toh) River. Catching the Mexicans by surprise, the Texans routed their foes in 15 minutes and cap-

The Siege at the Alamo

Fewer than 200 Americans held the Alamo for 12 days against almost 4,000 Mexican troops. The strength of this heroic defense can be seen in the following message from Commander William B. Travis.

Fellow Citizens and Compatriots:

I am besieged by a thousand or more of the Mexicans under Santa Anna. I have sustained a continued bombardment for twenty-four hours and have not lost a man. The enemy have demanded a surrender at discretion; otherwise the garrison is to be put to the sword if the place is taken. I have answered the summons with a cannon shot, and our flag still waves proudly from the walls.

I shall never surrender or retreat.

Then, I call on you in the name of liberty, patriotism, and of everything dear to the American character to come to our aid with all dispatch. The enemy are receiving reinforcements daily and will no doubt increase to three or four thousand in four or five days. Though this call may be neglected, I am determined to sustain myself as long as possible and die like a soldier who never forgets what is due to his own honor and that of his country. *Victory or death.*

William B. Travis

Source: Henderson Yoakum, *History of Texas* (New York: 1856).

tured Santa Anna. While a prisoner, Santa Anna signed two treaties, one granting Texas its independence and another setting the Rio Grande as its southern boundary.

Texas: An Independent Republic

In the fall of 1836 the Republic of Texas held its first presidential election, choosing Sam Houston by an overwhelming majority. But for most Texans independence was not the ultimate goal. In this same election, all but 61 of 6,000 voters voted in favor of annexation to the United States. President Sam Houston ardently shared their desire.

In the United States feelings were mixed. President Andrew Jackson favored annexation, but he shrewdly recognized the grave difficulties of such a move. Annexing Texas would mean war with Mexico. Furthermore, many northerners feared what they saw as the growing power of the South. Texas had been settled mostly by southerners. If it were admitted as a state, the northerners argued, the South would be strengthened. In the end, Jackson refused to support the annexation of Texas, but he did formally recognize its independence.

Heavy American immigration to the new republic during the late 1830s continued to swell its population. The Texas government encouraged this immigration by offering free land to settlers. It also granted land to speculators who agreed to establish settlements. The economic depression that began in 1837 brought hard times to the United States (see page 240), and many people pulled up stakes and moved to Texas.

Although most of the settlers were white southerners, other Americans moved to Texas. Among them were free blacks who were also attracted by the offer of land. Some, such as Greenburg Logan, came in the early 1830s and fought valiantly for Texan independence. But Logan found life difficult after independence. Severely wounded in the war, he applied to the legislature for tax relief but was refused. Aaron Ashworth, another free black who moved to Texas in the early 1830s, became a successful rancher. By 1850 he owned over 2,500 head of cattle.

The population of Texas soared from 30,000 in 1836 to 142,000 ten years later. Cotton was the major cash crop, and the economy flourished. The city of Houston, in 1838

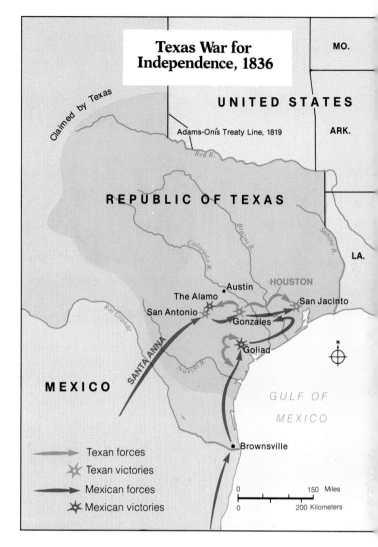

Texas won independence from Mexico in a short but bitter war. Massacres of small groups of Texans defending the Alamo and Goliad became rallying cries against Mexico. Texan forces eventually overwhelmed the Mexican Army near the San Jacinto River and took Santa Anna prisoner.

a small village with tree stumps blocking the main streets, grew in typical fashion. Only a year later it included a courthouse, a jail, two theaters, a statehouse, 12 stores, and 47 saloons. Five years later it had 40 stores, three hotels, several newspapers, schools, four churches, a cotton press, an iron foundry, grist- and sawmills, and two packing houses.

Texas continued to grow and to press for annexation. But the United States government remained reluctant to take the step until 1845.

253

This painting shows an early farm in Texas a few years after the family had settled there. The covered wagon beside the log house may have been the one in which the family traveled west. Work on a fancier house often had to wait while barns were built, corrals made, crops planted, and livestock tended.

For answers, see p. A 43.

Section Review

1. Identify the following: Antonio de Santa Anna, William B. Travis, Declaration of Causes, Sam Houston, "Remember the Alamo."

2. (a) What were two cultural differences between Mexicans and the Americans in Texas? (b) List three political differences that existed between the two peoples.

3. What action by Santa Anna led to military conflict between Mexicans and Americans?

4. What tactic did Sam Houston use to train his new recruits?

5. What were the provisions of the two treaties signed by Santa Anna in 1836?

6. (a) Why was President Jackson reluctant to annex Texas? (b) What action did he finally take?

4 Surge to the Pacific

The American movement to the far West, which had begun in the 1820s and had gathered momentum in the 1830s and early 1840s, reached a peak between 1844 and 1846. Americans had settled in areas beyond the territorial limits of the United States, and this situation was bound to give rise to tensions, as the story of Texas shows. Although most of the immigrants liked the new land they had moved to, they still thought of themselves as Americans. Many hoped that their territory would eventually be incorporated into the United States.

Manifest Destiny

From the days of the first English settlements, American colonists had felt a deep sense of mission about their society and its future. The New England Puritans, for example, tried to establish a society that would set an example for the world. In Pennsylvania the Quakers called their colony the Holy Experiment. Those people who carved farms and villages out of the wilderness were often sustained by a strong sense of the rightness of their actions. And they were moving ever westward.

The American Revolution added a strong political element to this sense of mission. The United States, many Americans believed, had become the torchbearer of liberty in the world. Its system of government was a shining example of how a republic ought to conduct its affairs. Americans in the nineteenth century continued to believe in the superiority of their way of life. When they heard tales of mountain men or listened to accounts of Yankee merchants in California or read letters from pioneers in Oregon and Texas, many naturally assumed that one day all those lands would become part of the United States.

In 1845 a New York editor, John O'Sullivan, neatly summarized those ideas. He wrote that it was America's "manifest destiny to overspread and to possess the whole of the continent which Providence has given us for the development of the great experiment of liberty and federated self-government entrusted to us." Americans quickly took up the new phrase "manifest destiny." It stood for both their faith in American institutions and their desire for expansion. In the 1840s the attitude of the United States government, led by President John Tyler, reflected those widely held sentiments.

Annexation of Texas

When their first efforts to join the United States failed, Texans decided that the next best thing would be to strengthen their independent republic. Mirabeau Bonaparte Lamar, who followed Sam Houston as president, hoped to extend the boundaries of Texas to the Pacific. The British government, seeing a chance to erect a powerful barrier against further United States expansion, actively encouraged Texas to maintain its independence.

In 1841 Sam Houston was reelected president. Two years later he opened negotiations with American officials about the possibility of annexation to the United States. President Tyler eagerly welcomed Houston's overture. As you read in Chapter 13, Tyler had lost most of his political authority because of disagreements with his party, and he hoped to regain his popularity by expanding the nation's boundaries.

The President signed a treaty of annexation with the Texans in April 1844. Many senators were uncertain of public support for the treaty and feared that war with Mexico would result. Consequently, the Senate refused to ratify the treaty.

The supporters of expansion, however, were undaunted. In 1844 the Democrats nominated James K. Polk of Tennessee, an enthusiastic expansionist, as their presidential candidate. Polk soundly defeated Henry Clay, his Whig opponent. Interpreting the results as a victory for expansionist sympathies, President Tyler decided to try again to annex Texas before he left office. He urged Congress to admit Texas by a joint resolution rather than a treaty.*

The Democrats mustered enough votes in Congress to approve annexation, and Tyler signed the joint resolution on March 1, 1845. In December 1845, after Texas voters had approved the proposal, Texas joined the United States as the twenty-eighth state.

The annexation brought new problems. Texas claimed that its borders extended south to the Rio Grande, as specified in the treaty that Santa Anna had signed in 1836. The Mexican government strongly disagreed. It argued that the Texas border should be the Nueces (noo AY says) River, some 200 miles (320 kilometers) to the north. The Mexicans claimed that virtually no Americans lived south of the Nueces and that the Republic of Texas had not previously tried to govern that territory. But the United States insisted that the Rio Grande was the border. Mexico broke off diplomatic relations with the United States in March 1845. Further troubles appeared likely.

The Division of Oregon

For a time war threatened in Oregon as well. Although the United States had agreed with Great Britain to a joint occupation of Oregon Territory north to latitude 54° 40', the expansionists who wrote the Democratic party platform of 1844 brushed Britain's claims aside. "Our title to the whole of the Territory of Oregon is clear and unquestionable," their platform proclaimed. They ignored a previous offer by the United States to divide the territory along the 49th parallel. "Fifty-four Forty or Fight!" became a rousing slogan.

The British government was alarmed by that slogan, and its alarm increased when Polk won the election. The British knew that in Oregon itself the 5,000 American settlers

---

*A joint resolution would require only a simple majority in both houses rather than the two-thirds vote in the Senate needed to ratify a treaty.

greatly outnumbered the 750 British. Furthermore, heavy American immigration and depleted fur catches had already convinced the Hudson's Bay Company to move its headquarters away from the Columbia River north to Vancouver Island. The American settlements were left to flourish unchecked.

Despite his expansionist beliefs and his party's slogan, President Polk did not want to fight Great Britain. He secretly renewed the earlier American offer to divide the territory. The British government decided that the disputed territory was not worth a war and agreed to divide the Oregon country at the 49th parallel. The United States Senate approved the treaty in June 1846.

Attempts to Acquire California

Like most believers in the manifest destiny of the United States, President Polk had a vision of the country stretching from the Atlantic to the Pacific Ocean. From the beginning, his ultimate aim had been the acquisition of California, with its excellent harbors at San Diego and San Francisco.

By 1845 only about 700 United States citizens lived in California, a small number compared to the 5,000 in Oregon. Most of the settlers had traveled along the same overland trails as the Oregon settlers, splitting off once the Rockies had been crossed and moving into the Sacramento and San Joaquin river valleys.

During the 1830s and early 1840s, under Presidents Jackson and Tyler, the United States had tried unsuccessfully to purchase California from Mexico. President Polk tried again in 1845. As you read, Mexico broke off relations with the United States in March 1845 over the issue of the southern border of Texas. When Polk sent diplomat John Slidell to Mexico City to try to continue discussions about the Texas border, he authorized Slidell to offer to buy California for $25 million and New Mexico for $5 million. However, the Mexicans adamantly opposed the further division of their country. The government refused to receive Slidell and he returned home.

The Bear Flag Revolt

Having failed to buy California, President Polk decided to try other methods of acquiring the territory. He encouraged Thomas Larkin, the American consul at Monterey, California, to quietly support those Mexican Californians who desired annexation to the United States.

Before Larkin could proceed, an extravagant and swashbuckling American named John C. Frémont arrived in California with plans of his own. Frémont, a United States Army captain, had become famous as the "Pathfinder" for his earlier exploration of the Sierra Nevada mountain passes. He claimed to be in California on a simple mission of scientific exploration for the United States. But he had brought with him a band of 60 frontiersmen, which made the Mexican government suspicious.

Before Frémont could take any action, another group of Americans impulsively attacked the unprepared town of Sonoma. On June 15, 1846, the rebels proclaimed the formation of the California Republic and raised their new flag over the plaza in Sonoma. The flag featured a grizzly bear and a lone star. This so-called Bear Flag Revolt signaled the beginning of the struggle to seize control of California from Mexico.

Frémont rushed to the support of the revolt. Taking command of the rebel forces, he drove the Mexican governor's troops out of northern California. He soon learned, however, that war had broken out between the United States and Mexico. The final conquest of California was to be the responsibility of United States military forces, not of the Bear Flag insurgents alone.

The War With Mexico

The spark that had finally touched off war between the United States and Mexico was ignited by the continuing dispute over the southern border of Texas. After the Slidell mission had failed, President Polk ordered General Zachary Taylor and an army of 1,500 troops to cross the Nueces River and take up a position along the Rio Grande. Tensions between Taylor's army and the Mexican authorities, who viewed his act as nothing less than an invasion of their country, remained high.

In the spring of 1846 Polk decided that if the United States was to acquire the territory it wanted and settle the Texas border dispute, a fight with Mexico was inevitable. As he was working on a war message to Congress, word arrived that on April 25, Mexican troops had crossed the Rio Grande and clashed with Taylor's force. Sixteen Ameri-

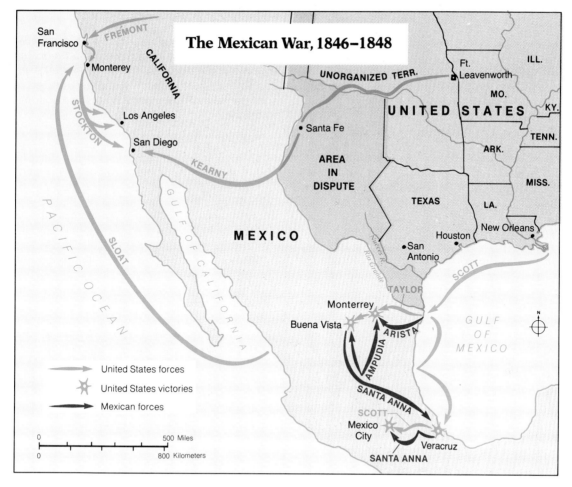

The Mexican War, 1846–1848

- United States forces
- United States victories
- Mexican forces

0   500 Miles
0   800 Kilometers

■ *To many Americans in the 1840s, it seemed inevitable that the United States would eventually span the continent. A dispute between the United States and Mexico over land claimed by Texas helped trigger the Mexican War in 1846. United States naval forces, led by John Sloat and Robert Stockton, contributed to the American victory.*

can soldiers were killed or wounded in the skirmish. In response to this news, Polk finished his message and sent it to Congress. Asserting that Mexico had "shed American blood on American soil," he asked for a declaration of war, which Congress quickly passed.

Mexico eagerly accepted war. It was confident that its army could defeat the Americans and end what it considered aggressive designs on its territory. Sentiment among Americans was by no means unanimous. Since the territory to be gained from Mexico lay to the south and west, most Americans in southern and western states enthusiastically supported the conflict. Northeasterners, on the other hand, tended to view the fighting as merely another way for southerners to extend the institution of slavery westward.

President Polk's plan was to attack on several fronts at the same time in hopes of winning a quick victory. In the summer of 1846 General Stephen W. Kearny marched from Fort Leavenworth to establish one front at Santa Fe, which he captured without firing a shot. Leaving part of his army behind, he then marched to California. There, in conjunction with American naval forces, he subdued scattered Mexican resistance. By January 1847 the United States controlled New Mexico and California.

General Taylor in the meantime had carried the war into Mexico. He crossed the Rio Grande and won a series of victories climaxing with the Battle of Buena Vista. Taylor's victory in this battle ended the war in northern Mexico.

The final offensive against Mexico was led by Major General Winfield Scott. Under

Scott, American forces landed near Veracruz and began a slow and difficult march toward the capital, Mexico City. On September 14, 1847, they successfully captured the city, ending Mexican resistance.

The Treaty of Guadalupe-Hidalgo

With their armies defeated and their capital occupied, Mexico's leaders had no choice but to agree to American terms. Under the Treaty of Guadalupe-Hidalgo (GWAH duh LOOP ay ih DAHL goh), the United States acquired California and the New Mexico territory. Mexico also recognized the Rio Grande as the border of Texas. In return for this territory, the United States paid Mexico $15 million and assumed responsibility for existing Mexican debts to United States citizens.

The treaty almost completed American expansion across the continent. In 1853 the United States paid Mexico $10 million for a strip of land south of the Gila River in Arizona and New Mexico. Known as the Gadsden Purchase, this land provided a favorable route for a southern transcontinental railroad. With the Gadsden Purchase, the great struggle to realize manifest destiny seemed to be over.

For answers, see p. A 43.

Section Review

1. Identify the following: manifest destiny, James K. Polk, "Fifty-four Forty or Fight," John C. Frémont, Zachary Taylor, Stephen W. Kearny, Winfield Scott, Gadsden Purchase.

2. (a) What did the United States recognize as the southern border of Texas in 1844? (b) What did Mexico recognize as the border?

3. What compromise did the United States and Great Britain reach over Oregon?

4. What action did President Polk take after the failure of the Slidell mission?

5. (a) Under the terms of the Treaty of Guadalupe-Hidalgo, what territory did the United States acquire? (b) What was its obligation to Mexico?

■ The growth of the United States from a cluster of 13 states on the Atlantic seaboard to a continental nation is shown on this map. Although present-day state boundaries appear on the map, Iowa, Texas, and California were the only states west of the Mississippi in 1853.

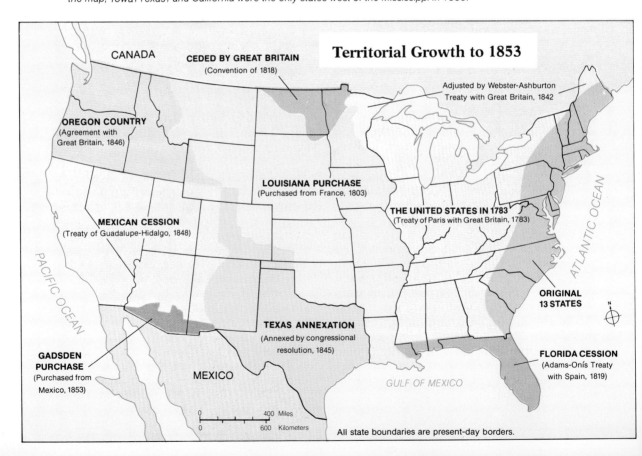

Territorial Growth to 1853

CANADA

CEDED BY GREAT BRITAIN
(Convention of 1818)

Adjusted by Webster-Ashburton
Treaty with Great Britain, 1842

OREGON COUNTRY
(Agreement with
Great Britain, 1846)

LOUISIANA PURCHASE
(Purchased from France, 1803)

THE UNITED STATES IN 1783
(Treaty of Paris with Great Britain, 1783)

MEXICAN CESSION
(Treaty of Guadalupe-Hidalgo, 1848)

ATLANTIC OCEAN

PACIFIC OCEAN

ORIGINAL
13 STATES

TEXAS ANNEXATION
(Annexed by congressional
resolution, 1845)

GADSDEN
PURCHASE
(Purchased from
Mexico, 1853)

MEXICO

FLORIDA CESSION
(Adams-Onís Treaty
with Spain, 1819)

GULF OF MEXICO

0   400 Miles
0   600 Kilometers

All state boundaries are present-day borders.

5 The Challenge of Greater Diversity

One of the central features of the United States since its founding has been the diversity of cultural groups living within a single nation. With the expansion of the nation to the Pacific, the United States acquired not only new territory but also hundreds of thousands of new residents to whom English culture and customs were foreign. These residents formed two major groups: Native Americans with a wide variety of cultures and Mexicans who shared a combined Spanish and Native American heritage.

Continuing Tensions

As you read earlier, the differences between Mexican and American cultures had created friction when Texas had been part of Mexico. This friction continued in the newly annexed areas. Many Americans, imbued with the spirit of manifest destiny, assumed that any inhabitants already living in an area would benefit from the government of the American republic.

Yet Mexicans, without moving an inch, suddenly found themselves living in a nation that was foreign to them, a nation that considered them "foreigners." Residents of New Mexico, for example, remained suspicious of American intentions. "The Americans say they have come for our good," one irate New Mexican declared. "Yes, for all our goods." Such resentment flared up in a rebellion at Taos, New Mexico, in 1847, which the United States Army subdued.

In California the wealthier Mexican landowners, desiring order and stability, generally welcomed United States rule. Other residents, however, shared the resentment of the New Mexicans and organized a rebellion of a thousand people. American forces defeated the rebels and offered generous terms of surrender, which were accepted.

The situation for Native Americans remained complex. The Mexican government had regarded the California Indians as Mexican citizens. When it surrendered territory to the United States, Mexico insisted on guarantees of the land rights of all Indians living there. The United States agreed to the guarantees in the Treaty of Guadalupe-Hidalgo. But there were no provisions to allow Native Americans full rights as United States citizens, and the nation's previous record of keeping promises to Indians had been poor.

A Sanctuary for the Mormons in Utah

While people with different cultures had to learn to live side by side in the new territories of California and New Mexico, a religious group from the East known as the Mormons developed another way of coping with diversity. They used the spaciousness of the land to evolve their own way of life in isolation.

In 1830 a farmer named Joseph Smith founded a new religion in Palmyra, a village in western New York. He based its teachings on a revelation that he claimed was given him through a set of golden tablets. Smith's followers assumed the name still used: The Church of Jesus Christ of the Latter Day Saints.

Joseph Smith was an energetic man who convinced many people to adopt his new religion. But some of the doctrines of the religion, such as the communal ownership of property, angered local residents. Such opposition forced Smith and his followers to move first to Ohio, then to Missouri, and finally to Illinois.

Everywhere the Mormons went, they met hostility. The situation worsened in 1843, when Smith officially revealed a teaching that permitted men to marry more than one woman. Tensions mounted near the Mormon settlement in Nauvoo, Illinois, until in 1844 a mob killed Smith and his brother.

Leadership of the Mormons fell to Brigham Young. A year after the murders, Young decided that his flock should move to the Great Salt Lake Basin, in present-day Utah, a sparsely populated area that was then still Mexican. Under Young's capable leadership, the final migration began in the summer of 1847. Wave after wave of faithful recruits followed, swelling the population of Utah. At last they seemed safe from interference.

In Utah they established a church-centered government that emphasized community and cooperation more than individual effort. Families were assigned land and not permitted to abandon it. They made the desert bloom with a remarkable system of irrigation. By moving to an isolated location, the Mormons were relatively free to develop a different life away from the conflicts of their earlier history.

Gold in California

The discovery of gold in the foothills of the Sierra Nevadas complicated life in California. The influx of large numbers of people increased tensions among the diverse cultures of the state. The result in the early days was frequently one of conflict. This "gold rush" was to be an early test of the nation's ability to accommodate different cultures and rapid change.

The first discovery of gold occurred at Sutter's Mill in January 1848. Soon gold fever gripped California, Oregon, and other western areas, and the rush was on. Sailors deserted their ships and flocked to the diggings. As many as two thirds of the able-bodied men in Oregon left for California.

Soon others joined the rush to California's gold fields. Beginning in 1849, men and women poured into California from all parts of the United States, as well as from Europe, Australia, South America, and China. About 80,000 people came to California that year, many by sea, more by overland trail.

The first miners to arrive found considerable deposits of gold. Moreover, they found them in places easy to mine, like dry gulches and former creek beds. In those early days some did, indeed, strike it rich, but few made large fortunes.

Deposits that could be dug up easily in dry gulches or shallow streams were soon picked clean. Then heavy machinery, which required a large capital investment and a large labor force, became necessary. Thus individual frontier prospectors gradually gave way to large mining companies. The miners became simply workers, toiling long hours for a wage.

Gold Rush Society

Society in early mining camps was unique. Towns sprang up overnight with names like Wildcat Bar, Skunk Gulch, Git-up-and-Git, and Ground Hog Glory. Without accepted social restraints, life went on at a hectic pace. Drinking and gambling abounded, along with racing, singing, and dancing.

Though the population of the mining camps consisted chiefly of young men, women were not absent. They came as workers and as shopkeepers. They laundered, cooked, entertained in saloons, ran boardinghouses, and sold food supplies. Those women who were merchants and landladies often prospered because of high California prices. Supplies were scarce, and demand was so great that shopkeepers in San Francisco could charge 50 to 75 cents for a loaf of bread that cost 5 cents in New York.

The miners governed themselves informally. They drew up codes, held their own trials, and carried out the punishments, including whipping, branding, and even ear cropping. Such crude justice was perhaps inevitable, since camps and towns grew so quickly. But it often had undesirable consequences. In a rough-and-tumble world where fortunes were at stake, it was easy for the majority of Yankees from the United States to overlook the rights of other immigrants as well as the rights of Californians of Mexican or Indian origin.

The "Conquered" Californians

Whatever the intentions of the United States government, the California miners ignored the rights of the Indians as spelled out in the Treaty of Guadalupe-Hidalgo. As far as the miners were concerned, the Native Americans were in the way and had to be removed.

The timeless lure of gold drew thousands of prospectors to California. The men in this early photo are using a sluice to separate the heavier gold from the lighter materials carried away by the water.

The California Indians were generally peaceful and lived in small groups, often numbering only a few dozen people. Consequently they could offer little resistance. They were driven off their lands and many fell ill or starved to death. Individual Indians were casually murdered; whole villages were massacred. The California Indian population, which had numbered over 200,000 in 1848, plunged to roughly 17,000 by the 1870s.

English-speaking miners generally regarded the Mexicans in California as a conquered people and treated them as such. If a dispute arose over land rights, miners' courts customarily ruled against Mexican claims. To make the court rulings stick, vigilante groups drove Mexicans from the gold fields. When California became a state in 1850, its legislature passed a law taxing foreign miners; "foreigners" included Mexicans, no matter how long they had lived in California.

Chinese Arrive in California

Like many other immigrants, the Chinese arrived in California expecting to make their fortune and then return to their native land. The first Chinese immigrants, who came after 1847, were treated with respect. California needed laborers, and the Chinese were hardworking and honest. But as their numbers increased, they encountered bitter hostility.

English-speaking miners found Chinese customs foreign and unsettling. Because

Major Events	
1818	United States and Great Britain agree to joint occupation of Oregon
1821	Mexico declares independence from Spain; Stephen Austin founds American colony in Texas
1830	Joseph Smith founds Church of Jesus Christ of the Latter Day Saints
1836	Texas wins independence
1843	First Organic Law drawn up by Americans in Oregon
1845	Polk becomes President; Texas admitted as twenty-eighth state
1846	Oregon divided along 49th parallel; Bear Flag Revolt; Mexican War begins
1848	Treaty of Guadalupe-Hidalgo; gold discovered at Sutter's Mill
1853	Gadsden Purchase

their appearance and behavior seemed so different, the Chinese became easy targets of mockery and abuse. Perhaps more important, their economic success aroused some

Fatt Hing: A Chinese Pioneer

Fatt Hing was an aspiring 19-year-old who helped support his family as a fish peddler on the wharves of Kwanghai, China, when he first heard tales of the "mountains of gold" on the other side of the ocean. Feeling compelled to seek out such fortunes, Fatt Hing had to find a way to California. This was not easy because leaving China was illegal. Fatt Hing finally raised the money he needed to bribe officials, a common practice at the time. Amidst a tearful farewell from his family, he was smuggled aboard a Spanish ship destined for San Francisco.

After a strenuous journey lasting three months, the California coast became visible on the horizon. Fatt Hing and hundreds of others watched anxiously as their ship approached the dock. Weary but happy, Fatt Hing was greeted by a group of fellow Chinese who had arrived earlier.

Well acquainted with the fears, problems, and purpose of their mission, these earlier Chinese pioneers had set up a company that served as an orientation center for more recent arrivals. Fatt Hing was assured of food, shelter, friendship, and work. If lucky, he was told, he would not have to remain in California long.

Fatt Hing was lucky. He quickly found a job in the mines, and he was permitted to keep half of the gold he mined. After two years Fatt Hing returned to his home in China. His family watched breathlessly as he opened the parcels of gold. In the short time that Fatt Hing had combed the hills of California, he earned enough money to marry and buy land for a farm. Fatt Hing eventually returned to California and like many Chinese made it his home.

Based on material in B. L. Sung, *Mountain of Gold: The Chinese in America* (New York: Macmillan, 1967).

resentment. By patience and hard work, the Chinese were often able to make mining claims profitable after more wasteful miners had abandoned them.

Faced with prejudice and hostility, the Chinese relied on one another for aid and protection. They regulated their own affairs, often transferring traditional Chinese institutions to America. Frequently forced out of the mines, the Chinese often did the back-breaking work scorned by other groups. Their contributions to the developing California economy were vitally important. They farmed, irrigated, and reclaimed vast stretches of land, and, in the 1860s, built the western part of the first transcontinental railroad, as you will read later.

Black Americans in California

Before 1850 it was unclear whether slavery would be allowed in California once it became a state. Consequently many slaveholders brought slaves to California. Some slaves later earned their freedom by working in the gold fields. Free blacks also came to the gold fields to make their fortunes. They numbered 1,000 by 1850 and were soon the wealthiest black community in the country.

Black Americans faced prejudice and discrimination in California, as they did in many other parts of the West. One law, for example, denied free blacks the right to testify in trials involving whites, but black Californians organized against that law and won its repeal in 1863.

The rapid influx of people to California made it essential that the issue of statehood be settled quickly. By 1850, California had passed the peak of its gold rush, and Californians looked forward to becoming a state. Yet the diverse groups in California still needed to learn how to live together.

For answers, see p. A 44.

Section Review

1. Identify the following: Joseph Smith, Brigham Young, Sutter's Mill.
2. What people lived in the area the United States acquired in the Mexican War?
3. What impact did the gold rush have on California Indians?
4. (a) What goal brought Chinese pioneers to California after 1847? (b) How did English-speaking miners react to the Chinese?
5. What problems did black Americans face in California?

IN PERSPECTIVE

Between 1825 and 1850, the United States expanded its territory from Texas and the Rocky Mountains to the Pacific Ocean. Responding to stories of the area's wealth brought east by trappers and missionaries, the United States negotiated with Great Britain for half of the Oregon country and conquered nearly half of Mexico.

In the process, the United States became a transcontinental nation and the strongest power in the Western Hemisphere. Its new domains were spectacular, rugged, and varied. They also contained valuable resources, as the California Gold Rush showed.

The new territories were also diverse in their people. In addition to the Indians and Mexicans already living there, the California Gold Rush attracted a variety of Americans and immigrants from around the world. Significant among these immigrants were the Chinese, the first large group of Asians to enter the United States.

Magnificent as the territorial gains were, they were accompanied by serious problems. After the Mexican War, Latin Americans viewed the United States with suspicion. It was unclear whether the diverse groups of people in the West could live together without open conflict. Furthermore, as you will read in Chapter 17, the acquisition of territory contributed to the bitter quarrel between North and South over whether slavery would be allowed in the new lands.

For answers, see p. A 44.

Chapter Review

1. (a) How did the arrival of the Spanish affect Native Americans in California? (b) Did their lives change much after Mexican independence? Explain.

2. (a) Which areas in North America were claimed by Spain in the early 1800s? (b) What role did missions play in the Spanish attempt to settle these areas?

3. Describe the role each of the following played in the American settlement of Oregon: (a) mountain men; (b) fur-trading companies; (c) missionaries.

4. (a) Why did tensions exist between Mexican and American settlers in Texas? (b) How did Santa Anna's revolution affect the American settlers?

5. (a) What was the attitude of most Americans in Texas toward annexation by the United States? (b) Which Americans in the United States opposed annexation? Why? (c) How did Texas finally become a state?

6. (a) What is the meaning of the phrase "manifest destiny"? (b) How did the term reflect Americans' attitude toward expansion during the first half of the nineteenth century? (c) Was this attitude a new one among Americans? Explain.

7. (a) What claims did the 1844 Democratic party platform make about Oregon? (b) Why did those claims alarm the British? (c) What agreement did President Polk make with the British?

8. (a) Why did the United States want to acquire California? (b) What methods did it try? (c) Which was finally successful? (d) Why did the others fail?

9. (a) Why did Mormons decide to start a new life in Utah? (b) Were they successful? Explain.

10. (a) Describe the impact of the discovery of gold at Sutter's Mill. (b) How was the gold-rush society unique?

11. Why did the discovery of gold in California increase cultural tensions there? Explain how each of the following groups of people were affected by the tension: (a) English-speaking miners; (b) California Indians; (c) Californians of Mexican origin; (d) Chinese immigrants; (e) black Americans.

For answers, see p. A 45.

For Further Thought

1. (a) Describe the life of a mountain man. (b) What challenges did mountain men face that most people in the early nineteenth century did not? (c) What personal characteristics would probably have been important in that type of life?

2. (a) Why do you think people such as Davy Crockett and Jim Bowie have been popularized in songs, movies, and stories? (b) What impact did such people have on the history of the United States?

3. Some Texans saw a parallel between their struggle for independence and the American Revolution. (a) In what ways were the struggles similar? (b) In what ways were they different?

For answers, see p. A 45.

Developing Basic Skills

1. *Map Reading* Study the map on page 250 and answer the following questions: (a) Based on the topographical features shown, why was the journey to Oregon and California difficult? (b) How might you explain the route of the Oregon Trail?

2. *Comparing* Make a chart with four columns. In the first column write the names of the following territories: Louisiana, Florida, Texas, Oregon, Mexican Cession, Gadsden Purchase. In the second column write the date each territory was acquired. In the third column write the name of the country or countries from which it was acquired. In the fourth column describe how each territory was acquired. To complete this chart you will need to refer to earlier chapters in this book.

   Use your chart and the map on page 258 to answer the following questions: (a) Which territory did the United States acquire first? Which did it acquire last? (b) Based on the chart, which method of acquiring territory was most common? (c) Which territory was the largest? the smallest? (d) From which country did the United States acquire the most territory? (e) Based on the chart and map, would you agree or disagree with the statement: The greatest expansion of the borders of the United States took place between 1845 and 1848.

See page 775 for suggested readings.

The Different Worlds of North and South

15

(1820–1860)

Camden and Amboy Railroad With the Engine Planet in 1834, *by Edward Henry.*

Chapter Outline

1 *The Growth of Industry in the North*

2 *Life in the Industrializing North*

3 *Economic Growth in the South*

4 *Life in the South*

5 *The Slaves' World*

By the middle of the nineteenth century, many people believed that the North and the South were two different worlds. The North seemed to be a world of factories, machines, and industrial workers, while the South seemed to be a world of large plantations, poor white farmers, and slaves. Such views reflected only the surface of life in the North and South, but they did represent important aspects of each region's economic development.

As you will read in this chapter, industry continued to expand in the North, and a railroad network emerged. Growing industry attracted large numbers of European immigrants, especially from Ireland and Germany. Workers' attempts to organize were to have limited success.

Industrialization also changed the southern economy. The invention of the cotton gin, in particular, greatly expanded cotton production. Although most white southerners did not own slaves or work on plantations, the "cotton kingdom" affected daily life in the South.

1 The Growth of Industry in the North

One of the most important developments that contributed to the growing differences between North and South was the Industrial Revolution. The first manufacturing firms had established themselves in the North, and new industries and factories continued to grow there. The North improved its transportation network by leading the way in railroad development and construction. Technological innovations also changed the shape of agriculture in the North, making commercial farming much more common.

The Spread of Industry

Early industries, such as textile manufacturing, continued to expand during the first half of the nineteenth century. In 1800 seven textile mills operated about 2,000 cotton spindles. By 1830 over 2 million spindles were operating, and by 1860 there were more than 5 million, most in New England.

The machinery for textile mills and other factories was made from iron, and the iron industry grew with the increased demand. In the 1820s iron foundries in Pittsburgh began using new techniques to refine the impurities out of iron. The switch from charcoal to anthracite coal for fuel after 1840 further improved the production of iron. The increased use of anthracite coal in turn stimulated the growth of mining operations in Pennsylvania and elsewhere.

Technology developed in other areas as well. In 1839 Charles Goodyear developed a method for vulcanizing rubber so it could withstand extremes of heat and cold. This allowed the manufacture of heavy-duty drive belts to help run machinery. In 1844 Samuel F. B. Morse perfected the telegraph. Messages that had taken days to deliver now took seconds, and the speed of American life and work increased to meet the change. Elias Howe's sewing machine, invented in 1846, made the mass production of clothing possible.

By 1860 over 74,000 manufacturing facilities employed almost one million people in the North. In contrast, in the South 20,000 factories employed only 110,000 workers. In 1859, for the first time, the value of the products of American industry exceeded the value of the products of American agriculture. Manufacturing would continue to grow most rapidly in the North, and it would affect the quality and style of life there.

Improved Transportation

As you read in Chapter 12, advances in transportation had encouraged the growth of trade and industry, especially the use of steamboats on western rivers and the construction of canals like the Erie Canal. Although the use of steamboats increased in the period before 1860, canal construction was slowed by the Panic of 1837. The depression forced many northern states to reduce their support for internal improvements, including canals. By that time also, railroads were becoming an alternative to water transportation.

The principles of railroad technology—the steam engine and carts drawn on rails—had been available since the beginning of the nineteenth century. Experiments using steam engines to tow cars on rails began soon after 1800 in both Great Britain and the United States. In 1820 a steam locomotive invented by John Stevens of New Jersey successfully pulled five cars over a short stretch of track.

Despite Stevens's work, government officials continued to favor canals because of the problems early railroads experienced. The first wood-burning locomotives belched great quantities of smoke and sparks into the air and onto the passengers. The first rails, which were made of wood covered with a strip of iron, frequently broke under heavy loads. Soft roadbeds and weak bridges added further hazards to railroad travel.

Still, promoters believed in the future of railroads. "The time will come," one boasted, "when people will travel in stages moved by steam engines . . . almost as fast as birds fly, fifteen or twenty miles an hour."

Gradually engineering skills caught up with this optimism. Engineers learned to construct sturdier bridges and solid roadbeds. They replaced the wooden rail with a T-shaped cast-iron rail. Such improvements made railroad travel safer, faster, and more efficient. Soon Americans looked as hopefully to the railroad as they had to the canal.

Expanding the Railroad Network

The first commercial railroads in the United States went into service in the 1830s. By 1840 the nation had 2,818 miles (4,509 kilometers) of railroad track. In the next decade, railroad construction rapidly expanded, so that by 1850 there were over 9,000 miles (14,400 kilometers) of track. The 1850s witnessed an even more startling increase to 30,626 miles (49,003 kilometers) by the end of 1860. In less than two decades, the railroads had gone from a novelty to a major means of transportation. (See the map below.)

At first railroads acted as *feeder lines* to the water transportation system. Trains hauled freight to a river or canal, where the load was transferred and transported by water to its final destination. Shipments by water still dominated the country's transportation network in 1850.

As railroads continued to expand, however, *trunk lines* developed. These were heavily traveled routes that linked major cities. Shorter side roads along the route served as feeder lines, just as smaller rail-roads had fed into canals and rivers. Merging railroads into great trunk lines was difficult. Varying gauges, or widths, of track, different equipment, and rivalry between competing lines all slowed the process of consolidation. But once established, the trunk lines cut shipping costs and time. By 1860 the nation, particularly the North and the West, was crisscrossed by a series of major lines and affiliated branch lines.

The South made enormous strides in the 1850s toward building a railroad network. Richmond, Charleston, and New Orleans were linked to Memphis, and Atlanta was rapidly emerging as a railroad center. But despite this progress, the North had much more track and many more trunk lines than the South. New York and Chicago were major railroad centers, and all the major northern cities were linked by one or more trunk lines. Thus the railroad joined the Northwest with the Northeast, while the South tended to remain isolated.

The railroads encouraged the growth of industry in the North by making it possible to distribute goods cheaply and quickly from a central point of manufacturing. Raw materials could also be moved to factories more easily.

■ *A flurry of railroad building in the 1850s greatly expanded train service. According to this map, which cities were developing as major rail centers?* For answers, see p. A 46.

America's Merchant Marine

Steam power came to dominate land transportation with the railroad and river transportation with the steamboat. Ultimately it would dominate ocean commerce as well, but not before Yankee ingenuity had enjoyed a triumphant "golden age" of sail.

You read earlier about American sailors and merchants traveling all over the world, buying hides in Spanish California, trading for furs with coastal Indians in Oregon, and sailing across the Pacific to Asia for tea, silk, and other luxuries. New England merchants had controlled shipping in the colonies, and the northern section of the United States continued to dominate foreign trade in the nineteenth century.

Trade with China grew in the 1840s and 1850s. When the British forced China to grant them special trading privileges in 1844, the United States was able to win the same guarantees. By 1860 Americans carried more than half the trade going to and from Shanghai.

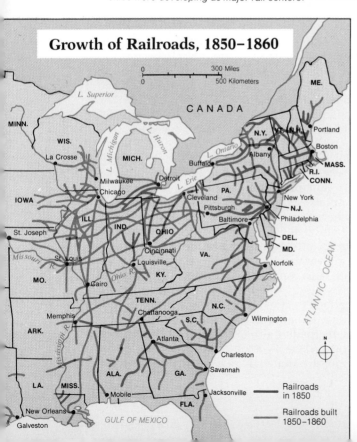

Growth of Railroads, 1850–1860

Railroads in 1850

Railroads built 1850–1860

Japan was closed to American trade until Commodore Matthew Perry sailed to Japan with a fleet of United States warships in 1853. Perry won Japanese agreement for limited trade. The commodore is shown here in Yokohama, Japan, with some of the gifts (including a miniature train) the United States sent to the Japanese government.

Japan remained closed to American merchants until 1853 when President Millard Fillmore sent Commodore Matthew Perry to Japan with a fleet of warships. Through a combination of vague threats of war and diplomatic skill, Perry secured commercial privileges for the United States in Japan.

In foreign trade speed was a considerable advantage. American merchants began designing sleek sailing vessels known as *clipper ships*. The ships were long and narrow, with tall masts towering almost 200 feet (60 meters) into the air and great canvas sails that strained to catch every gust of wind.

And race the clipper ships did! In 1851 Donald McKay, their most well-known designer, built the *Flying Cloud*, which sailed from New York to San Francisco in 89 days; another ship made the trip from Boston to Liverpool, England, in 12 days. With the advantage of speed, America's merchant marine prospered.

By the mid-1850s, however, steam power finally caught up with the clipper ships. On the heavily traveled routes to Europe, English steamships proved to be superior in both speed and cargo capacity. The construction of a railroad across Panama ended the need for long trips around South America for the California trade.

Impact on Northern Agriculture

You have already read that many of the railroads and canals linked the West and the East. Improved transportation made it more profitable for western farmers to ship their cash crops, such as wheat, to the East. In turn, farmers could afford to buy more manufactured goods, which stimulated eastern industry. Industrial innovations changed life for northern farmers in other ways as new inventions made farming more efficient.

A Virginia farmer, Cyrus McCormick, had worked for some time on a mechanical reaper to harvest wheat. In 1834 he finally solved the difficulties that made earlier versions impractical. The reaper was not an elegant-looking machine. When it was exhibited in England, the London *Times* ridiculed it as a "cross between an Astley chariot, a wheelbarrow, and a flying machine." Still, it worked. With a reaper, farmers could harvest many more acres of wheat with much less labor than before.

Another important invention was John Deere's steel plow, introduced in 1837. The deep root system of the midwestern prairie was almost impossible to plow with the traditional cast-iron plow. Deere's plow solved this problem and allowed farmers to put many more acres into production at less cost.

The impact of these inventions was not felt immediately. Farmers only gradually adopted new methods, and many could not afford expensive machinery. McCormick patented his reaper in 1834. Yet 13 years passed before he produced 100 machines for trial marketing. And it was not until the 1850s that the reaper came into general use.

The new machines offered northern farmers the opportunity to increase profits, but they needed money to buy the machines in the first place. As a result, subsistence farming gradually gave way to more specialized farming, by which farmers raised cash crops for sale in distant markets.

With continued improvements in transportation and farming equipment, northern agriculture developed a distinct character. Wheat production increased in the West, with its fabulously fertile black soil. Farmers in eastern states such as New York concentrated more on fruits and vegetables, which could be shipped swiftly to cities. By the end of the 1850s agriculture in the North differed from that in the South. As you will read later in this chapter, in the South, the main focus remained either on subsistence farming or on cotton planting.

For answers, see p. A 46.

Section Review

1. Identify the following: Charles Goodyear, Samuel F. B. Morse, Elias Howe, John Stevens, Commodore Matthew Perry, Donald McKay, Cyrus McCormick, John Deere.

2. Define the following terms: feeder lines, trunk lines, clipper ships.

3. What improvements were necessary on early trains before they could be widely used?

4. Which regions of the country had the most developed railroad network by 1860?

5. What was the major activity of the merchant marine?

6. How did McCormick's reaper increase wheat production?

2 Life in the Industrializing North

The coming of industry to the United States and its continuing development after 1820 changed not only the way the country organized its economy but also the way people lived and worked. This change was most visible in the North, which was turning out 90 percent of the country's manufactured goods by 1860. The expansion of industry brought increased demand for labor, and many of the workers came from Europe. By the 1840s immigration was as important a factor in the North's development as factories and industrial technology.

The New Factory as a Work Place

You read earlier how the factory system developed in the 1820s. (See page 209.) At first, factory work seemed to be an improvement over farm life. Farm work was toilsome and difficult, and the typical work day ran from dawn to sunset. This was especially true in New England, where the soil was thin and rocky and farms were unprofitable. Therefore women and children frequently worked in factories to help support their families.

Factory owners such as the Boston Associates had tried to provide good working conditions for their workers. However, the expense of programs like that at the Lowell Mills and increased competition from new factories eventually led manufacturers to try to cut costs by lowering wages.

Working conditions also worsened during the 1830s as the attitude toward workers changed. One factory manager remarked, "I regard my workpeople just as I regard my machinery. So long as they can do my work for what I choose to pay them, I keep them, getting out of them all I can."

When the reputation for bad working conditions spread around a New England town, mill owners had to try to recruit more workers from the countryside. This often meant describing an idyllic but false picture of factory life to farm women, promising "that the work is so very neat, and the wages such, that they can dress in silks and spend half their time in reading." "Now is this

In small towns and rural areas across the nation, one of the most welcome visitors was the traveling peddler, shown in this 1853 painting by John Whetton Ehninger. A peddler brought not only goods but also news and gossip. Many peddlers eventually established shops or warehouses as factories began turning out more and more products.

true?" fumed one angry woman. "Let those girls who have been thus grossly . . . deceived answer."

Artisans were also affected by the development of new industries. Shoemakers, for example, sewed their boots by hand, but now manufacturers could cut costs by stitching with the new sewing machines. Factory-made boots were cheaper, and shoemakers lost business, as did many other artisans. A hatmaker who could earn $12 a week in 1835 earned only $8 a week ten years later.

Worker Attempts to Organize

As early as the 1790s, workers in the United States had tried to organize to protect their rights. Their early efforts had limited success. The courts ruled that *strikes*, or work stoppages, were illegal because they were conspiracies to do economic harm to manufacturers and the public.

During the 1820s, however, as industry grew in the North, workers in major cities of the Northeast made further attempts to band together. Most of these workers were artisans who practiced skilled crafts, such as shoemaking, typography, carpentry, or cabinetmaking.

Workers' associations, or *unions*, as they began to be called, objected first and foremost to the long work hours. They proposed a ten-hour day, working from 6:00 A.M. to 6:00 P.M. with two hours off for meals. Workers called strikes in several cities to achieve their goal, but only in New York City were they successful. Elsewhere, employers either forced workers back to their jobs through court action or hired nonunion workers to take the places of the strikers.

Still the movement gradually expanded. Workers from different cities recognized the benefits of coordinating their efforts and in 1834 organized the National Trades Union. Other representatives of labor held a national convention in the same year. By this time about 300,000 workers belonged to some sort of labor organization, although most of them had not banded together on a national level.

Early Political Action

Workers also tried to improve their position through political action. Beginning in the late 1820s, they organized local *workingmen's parties*, which campaigned to improve the status of workers. Since most workers could not fulfill property requirements for voting, the parties demanded universal white manhood suffrage. To provide their children with better opportunities, they advocated free public education.

Workers had economic grievances too. In most states in the 1820s, a person could be thrown into jail for not paying a debt. Naturally such debtor laws worked primarily against the poor. In 1830 five sixths of the persons in the jails of northern states were debtors, most of them owing less than $20. Workingmen's parties campaigned to abolish all debtor imprisonment laws.

For all their efforts, the early unions and workingmen's parties were unable to gain the leverage they wished. The Panic of 1837, in particular, seriously weakened the early workers' movement. The depression threw thousands of people out of work. The jobs that remained were eagerly sought by workers desperate to make a living. Under such conditions employers easily found people willing to work for lower wages. The workingmen's parties disappeared and the unions were virtually destroyed.

Still, many of the political reforms succeeded even though the workingmen's parties did not. By the mid-1840s, virtually all states had abolished debtor imprisonment laws and provided for universal white male suffrage. Other reformers joined with labor to create or improve the state public school systems, as you will read in Chapter 16.

Workers also won an important legal victory in 1842 in *Commonwealth* v. *Hunt.* That case arose when a group of Boston bootmakers banded together to try to hire only union men. The employers took the workers to court, where union members were convicted of having formed a "criminal conspiracy" to injure their employers and the public. The Massachusetts supreme court overturned the conviction and for the first time ruled that labor organizations were not illegal. Yet the movement to organize workers grew slowly. In 1860 less than one percent of the nation's labor force was organized.

Other Workers

Only a small number of American workers, mostly skilled artisans, were involved in the early labor movement. Workers in the new factories, including women textile workers, generally did not participate. Attempts by these workers to organize were seldom successful. For example, in 1834, when the owners of the Lowell factories cut women's wages by 15 percent, a thousand women walked off the job. One of the leaders, reported a Boston newspaper, "mounted a stump, and made a flaming . . . speech on the rights of women," but the strike failed and the women returned to work.

Another group of laborers who remained outside the early labor movement were free blacks. Northern states had eliminated virtually all slavery by 1820,* but much prejudice remained against free blacks, and jobs were difficult to find. For example, Frederick Douglass, who had escaped from slavery in Maryland, was a skilled ship's caulker. Nevertheless he could not find work at his trade in the shipyards of New Bedford, Massachusetts. When he searched for a job there, he was told that if he was hired, he would drive white workers away. Turned away from his trade, Douglass supported himself by working as an unskilled laborer, a coachman, and a waiter.

Under such circumstances, free blacks were willing to work almost anywhere, often for very low wages. Consequently white workers feared that black laborers would undercut wages and take their jobs. In many cases blacks worked as strikebreakers and often had to fight striking white laborers to stay at work.

Though most black workers were unskilled, some became doctors, lawyers, ministers, and undertakers who served the needs of the black community. Frederick Douglass, in fact, complained that his son could more easily find work in a lawyer's office than in a blacksmith's shop.

An Increase in Immigration

One group of workers who helped make life in the North distinct from life in the South were European immigrants. There had al-

---

*All northern states had passed emancipation laws by 1804, but some of these laws called for gradual emancipation, so there were still slaves in the North after 1804.

ways been a steady flow of immigrants to the United States, but beginning in the mid-1840s the number increased dramatically. The South, with its system of slave labor, was generally unattractive to these immigrants, but the North, with its expanding economy and need for workers, seemed truly a land of opportunity.

Steamship companies, which could load their vessels with immigrants for the return voyage to the United States, and manufacturers, who were looking for cheap labor for their factories, actively promoted this image of America. This promotion was effective. Between 1845 and 1854 almost 3 million people from northwestern Europe migrated to the United States. However, the immigrants were not told about the competition for jobs and housing they would find in the United States.

Immigrants came for many reasons. In the British Isles, Scandinavia, and southwestern Germany, the enclosure system had converted peasant farms into pastures to raise wool for textile mills. Deprived of their homes, many peasants sought a better life in America. Miners left the coal pits of Wales for higher wages in the mines of Pennsylvania.

Roughly three fourths of the new immigrants came from Germany and Ireland. One cause of immigration from Germany was a revolution that swept the continent of Europe in 1848. Revolutionaries wanted to replace the European monarchies with demo-cratic governments, but they failed. Many German supporters of the revolution were forced to flee. They were attracted to the United States by the American traditions of freedom and republican government.

The main cause of the Irish exodus to America was a famine caused by a blight that wiped out the potato crop. For the two thirds of the Irish population affected by the famine between 1845 and 1850, the choice was stark: move or starve. Ireland was part of Great Britain, and support of the starving Irish peasants would have been a heavy public expense to the British government. So it was relieved at the massive exodus.

The Irish needed great courage to leave their homeland. Because of the famine, many began the trip in poor health and suffered greatly during the voyage. Hundreds died en route, and many arrived penniless in eastern cities. In fact, Boston became a major destination for the Irish precisely because the fare from Liverpool was cheaper than to any other American city. Although most Irish had been farm workers back home, few could buy land in America. Instead, they tended to take manual jobs, working on canals or railroads or in New England factories.

German farmers were often luckier. Many had been able to save money before they left Europe. When they arrived in the United States, they could move west and buy good farm land. German immigrants also

Carl Schurz: Crusader for Democracy

Carl Schurz was a German who immigrated to the United States in 1852. His life both in Germany and in the United States reveals him as a courageous, intelligent, and eloquent crusader for democratic ideals.

As a young man in Germany, Schurz's first dream was to be a history professor. While a student at the University of Bonn, he emerged as a leader in Germany's student movement and as a champion of political democracy. During the Revolution of 1848, Schurz fought as an officer in the revolutionary army.

When this struggle met with defeat, Schurz sought political asylum in Switzerland. He might have remained there forever but for his loyalty to an old friend and university professor imprisoned in Germany. Risking his own life, Schurz reentered Germany and liberated his friend. From there he sought sanctuary in France but was soon expelled because of his political background. After a brief interlude in England, where he met and married Margarethe Meyer, the hope and promise of the American republic beckoned him.

Carl and Margarethe Schurz set sail for the United States in August 1852. He soon mastered the English language and became a noted speaker against slavery. Schurz embraced the American political system and served his new country well. He would take an active role in the Civil War and would be elected to the United States Senate in 1868. The dynamic fervor with which Carl Schurz approached his life stands as a reminder of the dedication and devotion that drove many immigrants to the United States in their search for freedom.

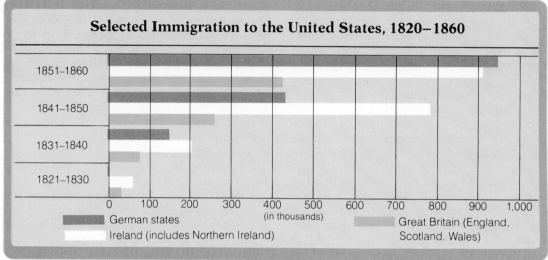

Selected Immigration to the United States, 1820–1860

1851–1860	
1841–1850	
1831–1840	
1821–1830	

0   100   200   300   400   500   600   700   800   900   1,000
(in thousands)

■ German states   ■ Great Britain (England, Scotland. Wales)
□ Ireland (includes Northern Ireland)

Source: *Historical Statistics of the United States*

■ *Immigration increased sharply after 1830. From what country did the greatest number of immigrants arrive between 1841 and 1860?* For answer, see p. A 46.

included merchants, artisans, and intellectuals, many of whom settled in midwestern cities such as Cincinnati, St. Paul, St. Louis, Chicago, and Milwaukee.

Like the earliest settlers in the American colonies, most immigrants of the 1840s and 1850s arrived from Europe in search of freedom and a better life. They worked hard to achieve their goals, and most became United States citizens as soon as they legally could.

Negative Reaction to Immigrants

Some Americans viewed the large influx of immigrants with alarm. They began to campaign against what they considered to be harmful consequences of immigration. These people were known as *nativists* because they championed the virtues of native-born Americans and their way of life.

Much of the nativist dissatisfaction sprang from economic causes. Immigrants competed for jobs and, with the increase in the labor supply, wages declined. Furthermore, when native-born workers went on strike for higher pay, immigrants were often hired as strikebreakers.

Also important were social, religious, and political tensions between new immigrants and persons born in the United States. Nativists resented the immigrants' tendency to cluster together. Immigrants

settled in areas where other people from their homeland lived. In these ethnic neighborhoods they continued to value old customs. They worshiped in their own churches, formed their own social institutions, and continued to speak their native language. As a result, immigrants did not always *assimilate* quickly into American society. That is, they did not merge into society by adopting American cultural standards and values. They continued to seem "foreign" rather than "American."

Furthermore, most of the Irish immigrants and many of the Germans were Catholics. This aroused concern among some Americans because the United States had been a predominantly Protestant country since its founding.

Nativists also pointed with alarm to the high rate of poverty and crime among new immigrants, especially in eastern cities. They blamed these conditions on the nature of the immigrants without considering the difficult circumstances immigrants faced.

The new immigrants seemed to be a political threat to nativists. After five years, immigrants could become naturalized citizens and be eligible to vote. And they began to vote in significant numbers. By the 1850s, immigrants outnumbered people born in the United States in several cities, including New York, Chicago, Milwaukee, and St. Louis.

Immigrants were a sizable minority in many other cities, such as Philadelphia and Cincinnati. As both major political parties appealed increasingly to the new voters, nativists began to put forward their own political candidates.

The Know-Nothings

During the 1840s in many areas of the North, nativists organized secret societies. Members pledged to oppose foreign influence by voting for candidates who were sympathetic to nativist beliefs and by refusing to vote for an immigrant or a Catholic. In a few cities these secret societies enjoyed some success.

Nativism became a national movement in the mid-1850s with the emergence of the Know-Nothings, who were so named because they were sworn to answer inquiries about the order by saying, "I know nothing." The Know-Nothings began in 1845 as a secret organization called the Supreme Order of the Star-Spangled Banner. The order rapidly spread through the North and showed considerable strength in the South. It soon dropped its secrecy and became a political party.

Calling themselves the American party, the former Know-Nothings nominated Millard Fillmore for President in 1856. But the party lacked sectional balance. Nativism was most popular in the North, where most immigrants had settled. As you will read in Chapter 17, the issue of slavery in the territories flared in the 1850s. The Know-Nothings in the North split over whether to take an antislavery stand, and the party rapidly lost support.

Nativism itself was soon overshadowed by the growing conflict between the North and the South. However, the underlying hostility toward immigrants, on which the Know-Nothings had built their strength, did not disappear. In future years it would surface again. Immigration and the tensions between immigrants and the native born had become a significant feature of northern society.

For answers, see p. A 46.

Section Review

1. Identify the following: National Trades Union, *Commonwealth* v. *Hunt.*

2. Define the following terms: strike, union, workingmen's party, nativist, assimilate.

3. How did the growth of industry affect the earnings of artisans?

4. (a) What types of workers tried to organize unions in the 1820s and 1830s? (b) Which workers were unrepresented in the early labor movement?

5. List three goals of workingmen's parties.

6. What attracted many new immigrants to the North?

7. What economic conditions created resentment by some Americans toward immigrants?

3 Economic Growth in the South

Although the impact of early industrialization was greatest in the North, it also affected the economy of the South. As you will read, some industries developed in southern cities, but for the most part new factories were located in the North. In the South the Industrial Revolution had the greatest impact on agriculture.

Changes in Southern Agriculture

Such improvements in transportation as the steamboat and the railroad affected the South as well as the North. Since the South had an extensive system of navigable rivers, the steamboat provided cheap, convenient transportation. This enabled farmers in the interior to ship products to the coast. After 1850 railroads developed in the South, but, as you read, the railroad network grew more slowly in the South than in the North.

The most significant development for the southern economy was the invention of the cotton gin. Eli Whitney invented the cotton gin in 1793 while working as a tutor on a Georgia plantation. This machine, which separated cotton seeds from fibers, transformed cotton production.

Before the introduction of the cotton gin, workers had to separate the seeds from the fiber by hand. This was a slow process, often requiring one worker a whole day to separate one pound (about .45 kilogram) of cotton. For cotton production to be profitable, planters needed to grow a strain of cotton with long fibers that could be separated fairly easily from the seeds. This type of cotton would grow only on the Sea Islands, off the coast of Georgia and South Carolina.

Cotton grown inland was a short-fiber variety, called short-staple cotton, that was more difficult to separate by hand. Because it required more labor, it was less profitable. Consequently most cotton production had been confined to the coastal region. The cotton gin, however, made it much easier to separate the seeds from the fiber whether the fiber was long or short. With the improved cotton gins available in the early nineteenth century, a worker could separate up to 1,000 pounds (about 450 kilograms) of cotton a day. This development greatly expanded the area where cotton could be grown profitably.

At the same time, the growth of the textile industry in the North and in Great Britain stimulated the demand for cotton. Southern farmers rushed to fill the demand by cultivating more land for cotton production.

Rise of the Cotton Kingdom

Gradually, the soil in the southern states along the Atlantic coast became depleted and farmers looked westward.* The large tracts of fertile unused lands in Alabama, Mississippi, and Louisiana appeared increasingly attractive. After the War of 1812, farmers flocked to those areas. By 1860 cotton production had expanded westward into Texas. Large portions of the South had become part of a cotton kingdom.

The map on page 275 shows the expansion of the cotton kingdom to the new states of the South. Since cotton required a growing season of at least 200 frost-free days a year, cotton growing was limited to the southernmost portion of the region.

The cotton boom had human dimensions too. Cotton was picked by hand, and the chance to make big profits depended on having a large labor force. As a result, slavery spread westward along with the cultivation of cotton.

By the 1840s cotton was a central part of the economy of the South. In the late 1790s, only about 10,000 bales of cotton were produced each year; in 1840 a million and a half bales were produced. That amounted to over 60 percent of all the cotton produced in the world and over 60 percent of the value of all American exports, from both North and South. Clearly cotton had become king.

Other Southern Crops

Because cotton could not be grown in the northern sections of the South, farmers there often depended on other cash crops. Tobacco had been exported since 1619, and it continued to be planted in Virginia, North Carolina, and Kentucky. However, the large plantations of colonial days gradually gave way to smaller tobacco farms.

■ *These two graphs show the relationship between cotton and slavery in the first half of the nineteenth century. As the production of cotton became more profitable, the demand for slaves increased.*

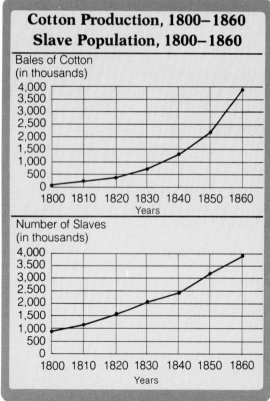

Cotton Production, 1800–1860
Slave Population, 1800–1860

Bales of Cotton
(in thousands)

Years

Number of Slaves
(in thousands)

Years

Source: *Historical Statistics of the United States*

---
*With land plentiful and cheap, Americans in both the North and the South had traditionally used land wastefully. Once minerals in the soil were depleted, a farmer could move on to new land.

274

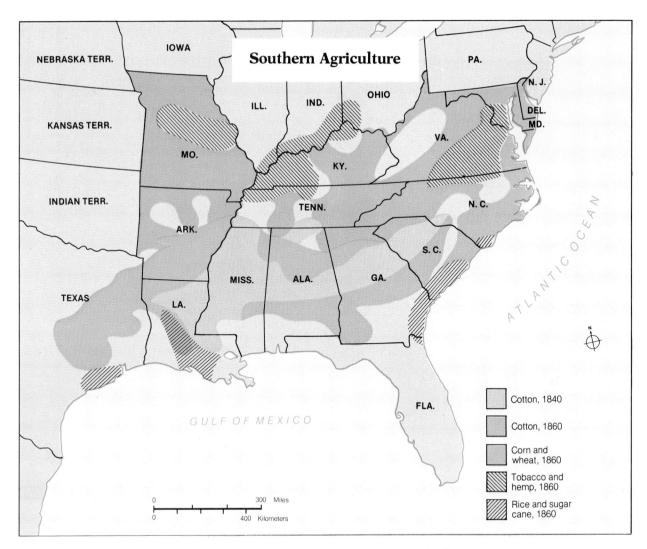

Southern Agriculture

Legend:
- Cotton, 1840
- Cotton, 1860
- Corn and wheat, 1860
- Tobacco and hemp, 1860
- Rice and sugar cane, 1860

■ The southern economy was predominantly agricultural. Although cotton was "king," other crops were also important to the economy—notably rice, tobacco, and sugar cane.

While the typical tobacco farm in Virginia or North Carolina needed only two field hands to raise five and a half acres of tobacco, other southern crops required large plantations if they were to make a profit. The rice growers along the South Carolina and Georgia coasts and the sugar growers of Louisiana and Texas needed many workers to raise their crops. They also used expensive irrigation and drainage systems, and sugar growers needed machinery to grind the sugar cane. Since small farmers simply could not afford the costs, the plantation system dominated the sugar- and rice-growing areas.

In addition to the major cash crops of cotton, rice, and sugar, the South led the nation in livestock production, including hogs, oxen, horses, mules, and beef cattle. Much of this livestock was raised in areas that were unsuitable for growing crops, such as the pine woods of North Carolina.

Early Industry in the South

As cotton became increasingly important to the economy of the South, many southerners began to realize how much they depended on the banks and factories of the North. Southern planters often borrowed money from northern banks to expand their plantations, and many of their farm tools and machines came from northern factories. Northern textile firms bought the cotton and wove it into cloth; northern shippers often hauled the raw cotton from the South to the

275

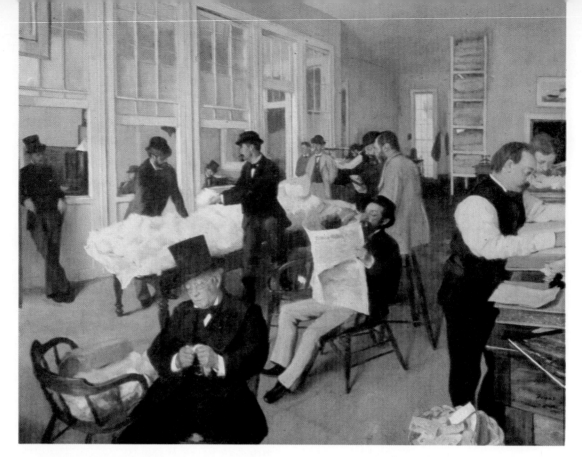

The great French artist Edgar Degas left this record of the gentlemen who controlled the New Orleans cotton market. Cotton dominated the economy of the South and was the nation's single largest export by the 1840s.

North or to Europe. When the price of cotton fell in the 1840s, some southerners began to establish factories in order to make the South more independent.

William Gregg of South Carolina led the movement to bring industry to the South. He built a successful textile mill in Graniteville, South Carolina, and operated it in the same benevolent manner that had characterized the early Lowell mills.

Gregg landscaped the grounds with shrubbery and flowers and set up cottages for working families, each with a large garden for the workers' children. He began the first compulsory school in the South and personally punished any boy or girl he caught playing hooky. In his more cheerful moments he held picnics for students. Wages for workers were low but compared favorably with wages in northern mills.

Manufacturers in Richmond, Virginia, made good use of the coal and iron ore in the area. The Tredegar Iron Works led production in the South, making railroad equipment, cannons for the United States Navy,

and steam machinery for Louisiana sugar plantations. The milling of flour was another leading form of southern manufacturing.

Yet by and large the South remained dependent on the North for industrial goods. Industrialization changed the South in the first half of the nineteenth century, but it did so chiefly by making cotton king.

For answers, see p. A 46.

Section Review

1. Identify the following: Eli Whitney, William Gregg.

2. (a) Which single invention had the biggest impact on the southern economy? (b) What was its function?

3. What attracted many southern farmers to Alabama, Mississippi, and Louisiana?

4. What factors help explain why rice and sugar were most often raised on plantations rather than small farms?

5. List two ways the southern economy depended on the North during the first half of the nineteenth century.

4 Life in the South

Although the southern economy revolved around farming, the daily lives of southerners varied. Few southerners lived in the grand style of wealthy planters. For most people, life meant hard work and simple joys.

Small Farmers

The great majority of white southerners, perhaps 75 percent, were small, independent farming families who owned their own land and possibly a few slaves. A description of a Virginia county in 1838 would apply to the whole South: "If we have very few rich men, we have, on the other hand, not many that are poor: the great mass is composed of the 'middle interest,' the bone and sinew of every country."

Such farmers could be found throughout the South but especially in the hilly regions of eastern Tennessee, northern Georgia, Alabama, and Mississippi and on the poorer soils of the coastal regions. Most were subsistence farmers who raised corn, oats, wheat, or sweet potatoes for food. They also sometimes planted an acre or two of cotton or tobacco to sell for cash.

In many ways these men and women were frontier people. Proud and hardworking, they lived simply. They learned to overcome their isolation by gathering together whenever they could, and they had a genius for turning work into play. Routine, time-consuming jobs, such as corn shucking, quilting, log rolling, and house raising became occasions for games and parties. For example, log rolling involved lifting logs off fields that were to be planted in the spring. A farmer's neighbors would gather from nearby farms and turn the job into a weight-lifting contest, followed by a cookout and a square dance.

Poor Whites

About 10 percent of the southern population consisted of "poor whites." They lived on land that for the most part could not support cash crops: backwoods, hills and mountains, sandy-soiled pine-barrens forests. Occasional travelers passing a backwoods cabin might well be deceived by seeing only a few acres of corn, a patch of sweet potatoes and other vegetables, perhaps a cow or two, three small horses, and a pack of hounds.

Yet this scene hid the family's greatest source of income: the herds of wild cattle or razorback hogs that fed off grass and forest land. Some poor whites were content to manage a small herd only large enough to sustain their families. Others tended several hundred head of cattle or hogs and drove them to market for a tidy profit.

Herdsmen usually considered it beneath them to farm. As a result, women not only had to do such household chores as weaving and making lye soap, but they also had to tend the vegetable patch and perhaps a small field of tobacco. Life in these areas was hardest for the women.

A monotonous diet and lack of medical care meant that the poorest of these people suffered from malnutrition. Furthermore, the hookworm parasite, which could be easily picked up in these areas, often sapped their energy.

Free Blacks

By 1860 about 260,000 free blacks lived in the South. Many of them were the descendants of slaves freed during the revolutionary era. Most free blacks lived in or around the cities and towns of the northern sections of the South, over one third residing in Maryland alone.

Most blacks worked as domestic servants or hired themselves out as agricultural laborers. Some were skilled workers, such as shoemakers and blacksmiths. They had a virtual monopoly on certain occupations, including barbering. A handful were merchants, hotel keepers, and planters who owned their own black slaves.

The life of a free black in the South was not easy. In the towns and cities, white workers and artisans resented them for competing for jobs, just as white laborers did in the North. Planters generally suspected free blacks of being potential leaders of slave insurrections. Moreover, the mere presence of blacks who were free and prospering struck many white southerners as a threat to the institution of slavery.

As a result of these fears, southern legislatures severely restricted the rights of free blacks. Though they had to pay taxes, as did other free persons, they could not vote, just as they were denied the ballot in most northern states.* Blacks normally could not testify in court, were sometimes required to have a white guardian, and were subject to curfew laws. Their rights of movement and assembly were severely curtailed, and they lived in constant danger of being illegally kidnaped and sold into slavery. Yet many of the harsh laws against free blacks were not enforced; and the status of free blacks in the South was in fact little worse than in the North.

The Planters

At the top of southern society were the planters, with their often elegant homes, gracious manners, and huge landholdings worked by slaves. Southern planters set the social style of the region, and they dominated its politics as well. Small farmers envied them, sometimes resented them for their power, but almost always hoped some

*After 1822 free blacks could vote only in Massachusetts, New Hampshire, and Vermont.

day to gain enough land and slaves to join them.

To be considered a planter, a farmer had to own at least 20 slaves, for then one could purchase a cotton gin and hire an overseer to supervise the slaves. Few achieved this goal. Out of 8 million southerners, fewer than 50,000 families owned more than 20 slaves, and only 10,000 owned more than 50 slaves.

Many planters tried to recreate the lifestyle of English country gentlemen. They built airy, spacious brick mansions faced with white columns, purchased elegant furniture and imported silver tea sets and other luxuries from Great Britain. They usually hired tutors to teach their children. The wealthiest planters also maintained town houses in cities like Charleston. Farther to the west in the newer farming regions, plantation life was much less refined, even among prosperous planters.

Planters had to work hard in order to succeed. A plantation was a large and difficult business. Planters had to make critical decisions about planting, harvesting, and marketing their crops. They had to be acquainted with the world market for cotton, sugar, or rice. A planter's wife often helped

Wealthy southern planters built elaborate country homes such as this one in Louisiana. The red building at right is the sugar refinery on the Olivier Plantation. Strolling peacocks (at left) were perhaps not standard scenery, but the elegant clothing of the family and their guests typified the lives of many plantation owners.

in the management of the business. She supervised the household servants, cared for the sick, both black and white, and supervised such domestic industries as weaving cloth, making soap, and sewing clothes.

Planters with large landholdings preferred to break them down into smaller plantations, since it was impractical for fields to be more than an hour's walk from the slave quarters. In such cases, the planters hired overseers to supervise the day-to-day operations of their individual plantations. Most of the overseers were ambitious small farmers and younger sons of planters who hoped to gain sufficient capital to enter the planter class themselves. Occasionally trusted slaves were made overseers, but this was the exception rather than the rule.

Though planters remained a minority among white southerners, they left an indelible stamp on the sectional character of the South. The elegant life of the rich set the standard for the region. Perhaps more important, their aggressive economic development of southern lands established cotton as king and commercial agriculture as a way of life.

For answers, see p. A 46.

Section Review

1. How did most white southerners make a living?

2. What was the main source of income among poor whites?

3. (a) Where did most free blacks live in the South? (b) What types of work did they do?

4. What distinguished planters from other farmers?

5 The Slaves' World

By 1860 slaves made up over one third of the population of the South. Slaves worked at many jobs and under a variety of conditions. Life on one plantation might differ greatly from life on a neighboring plantation. A slave who worked in the main house would have different experiences than one who worked in the cotton fields or the blacksmith shop. Yet slaves were united by the fact that they were another person's property. They could be bought and sold, and they were denied even the most basic human rights.

Work

The vast majority of slaves, both men and women, worked in the fields, cultivating, planting, and harvesting crops. Slaves also worked as servants in the plantation houses and as skilled artisans. The conditions under which they worked varied greatly. If slaves worked for a small landowner, they might be in close daily contact with their owner, working side by side, sharing the same tasks and often the same food. Most slaves, however, worked as field hands on large plantations.

On many rice and hemp plantations and on the Sea Island cotton plantations, slaves worked under the *task system*. Slaves had specific jobs or tasks to complete each day. If they completed their jobs before the end of the day, they had free time to devote to personal pursuits.

The *gang system*, used on tobacco, sugar, and short-staple-cotton plantations, was more common. Under this system slaves worked together as gangs in the field under the supervision of an overseer, sometimes aided by a black driver who helped maintain discipline. These slaves normally worked from sunrise to sunset, with a two-hour rest period in the middle of the day.

Slavery could be physically harsh and brutal or relatively mild, depending on the type of plantation and especially on the temperament of the owner. But regardless of their attitudes toward their slaves, most planters believed that slaves needed the threat of physical punishment to force them to work long hours for limited rewards.

Living Conditions

Large-scale planters typically grouped their slave quarters together not far from the main house. Southern farm magazines frequently advised planters to provide slaves with good housing. Some of the planters

This young mother and her baby are being auctioned from the steps of a Missouri courthouse. Members of a slave family could be sold to different owners. Another great fear among slaves was being sold "down the river" to a rice or sugar plantation. Working conditions "down the river" were reported to be the worst of all.

holiday feast, the usual slave diet was "hog and hominy," pork and corn. Seafood, dairy products, and other meats were rare but fruits and vegetables were often provided in season.

Importance of Family Life

Nothing provided critics of slavery with a more compelling case than the breaking up of slave families. State governments in the South did not recognize the legality of slave marriages. Although some planters tried to maintain slave families, it was by no means uncommon for families to be broken up and individual members sold, often to planters hundreds of miles away.

Family life was of great importance to slaves. By providing badly needed emotional support, the family could help make life under slavery bearable. Slaves who were sold to new owners often ran away from their new plantations in an attempt to rejoin their kin.

On some plantations, slaves used their garden plots and free time to hold their families together. By growing their own vegetables or hunting their own food, slave families quietly but firmly asserted their competence. By providing for their children's needs without the planter's direction, slave parents showed themselves worthy of their children's respect.

Preserving Human Dignity

Equally important to the slaves' sense of dignity were religion, holiday celebrations, and the remnants of African culture they managed to preserve. For slaves, Christianity proved to be sometimes a comfort, sometimes a hindrance. On one hand, planters often supervised the slaves' religious life, making sure the sermons they heard emphasized meekness and obedience.

On the other hand, slaves used Christianity to hold their community together. While masters emphasized Christian teachings of obedience, slaves stressed the importance Jesus attached to marriage, the family, and people's obligations to one another. In addition, they developed an important body of music, the spirituals, which protested slavery as much as it provided comfort.

Christmas was an important time for slaves. It provided them with a rare good

responded by building decent brick or frame cabins for their slaves and by providing ample firewood for fuel. However, most planters ignored the advice of the farm journals. Typically, slave cabins had one room and dirt floors and were crudely built. An Alabama doctor concluded, "One of the most prolific sources of disease among negroes is the condition of their houses. . . . Small, low, tight, and filthy, their houses can be but laboratories of disease."

Clothing and food were hardly better. Slaves commonly received a regular allotment of clothing that was too scanty to carry them through the year, and cases of frostbitten feet were fairly common in the colder areas of the South. Despite an occasional

meal and important free time. They used this time to celebrate another year's endurance and to visit each other. The holiday thereby reinforced their sense of community.

Many slaves relied on traditions from their African homelands to shape their distinctive culture. Because slave importation had been prohibited in the United States after 1808, few slaves had direct ties or contacts with Africa. Yet some African customs were passed down by word of mouth from older slaves to their children and grandchildren.

Such oral traditions played an important part in slave life. For example, slaves often followed the West African custom of naming children after their grandparents. The tradition of extended families, by which parents, grandparents, aunts, uncles, and other relatives were considered part of the immediate family, also had roots in Africa.

Most important, the oral traditions kept alive the memory of an African past when their ancestors had been free. This historial sense held out the hope that it was possible to resist slavery and that someday slavery would end.

The Slaves' Reaction to Slavery

Trying to preserve human dignity through family life, religion, holidays, and cultural traditions was one way slaves learned to live in a society that denied them their most basic rights. But there were other reactions to slavery.

Many slaves adopted an outwardly cheerful and carefree manner, professing loyalty to their masters. For some, especially house servants, that loyalty may have been sincere, especially when a master treated them kindly. But many slaves used this carefree face as a mask to hide their resentment. By pretending to be happy they developed countless ways to exasperate their masters and escape punishment.

Some slaves became adept at a sort of day-to-day resistance to slavery: slowing down work, stealing extra food, breaking tools, destroying crops, and pretending sickness or disability. Slaves aptly called this type of resistance "puttin' on old Massa."

Escape was another, more extreme reaction to slavery. The chances of success were slim. Runaways were tracked with

Despite the fact that laws usually did not recognize slave marriages, family ties remained strong and deep among slaves. The family in this early photograph worked on a South Carolina plantation.

For answers, see p. A 47.

Two Views of Slavery: Analyzing Conflicting Sources

As you learned earlier, primary sources provide important information about historical events and developments. (Review "Analyzing a Primary Source," p. 116.) But even two eyewitnesses can provide very different pictures of what happened.

Two descriptions of slavery are presented below. The first was written by Sir Charles Lyell, a British traveler who visited a plantation in Georgia in the 1840s. The second was written by Solomon Northup, a free black who was kidnapped in New York and sold into slavery on a Louisiana plantation. Read both sources. Then use the steps below to analyze their value as historical sources.

1. **Review the contents of each source.** Answer the following questions about the accounts below: (a) What does the writer say about the working conditions of slaves? (b) What does the writer say about the type of food given slaves? (c) What does the writer say about the use of whippings by slave owners?

2. **Compare the sources.** Answer the following questions about these two accounts: (a) On what aspects of slave life do the accounts seem to agree? (b) On what aspects do they disagree?

3. **Evaluate the reliability of the sources.** Begin with the same questions you would ask about any primary source. (See page 116.) Then answer the following questions: (a) How might the aristocratic background of Sir Charles Lyell affect his attitude toward southern planters and toward slavery? (b) How might the fact that Solomon Northup was kidnapped and sold into slavery affect his description of slavery?

4. **Study the sources to draw conclusions about an historical event or development.** (a) Based on what you read in your textbook, would you consider either account an accurate description of slavery on all southern plantations? Why or why not? (b) What conclusions would you make about slavery based on the two accounts and on what you have read in your text?

Sir Charles Lyell

The laborers begin work at six o'clock in the morning, have an hour's rest at nine for breakfast, and many have finished their assigned task by two o'clock, all of them by three o'clock. In summer they divide their work differently, going to bed in the middle of the day, then rising to finish their task, and afterward spending a great part of the night in chatting, merry-making, preaching, and psalm-singing. . . . The laborers are allowed Indian meal, rice, and milk, and occasionally pork and soup. As their rations are more than they can eat, they either return part of it at the end of the week, or they keep it to feed their fowls, which they usually sell, as well as their eggs, for cash, to buy molasses, tobacco, and other luxuries. When disposed to exert themselves, they get through the day's task in five hours, and then amuse themselves in fishing, and sell the fish they take. . . . The sight of the whip was painful to me as a mark of degradation, reminding me that the lower orders of slaves are kept to their work by mere bodily fear, and that their treatment must depend on the individual character of the owner or overseer. That the whip is rarely used, and often held for weeks over them, merely in terror, is, I have no doubt, true on all well governed estates.

Solomon Northup

An hour before day light the horn is blown. Then the slaves arouse, prepare their breakfast, fill a gourd with water, in another deposit their dinner of cold bacon and corn cake, and hurry to the field again. It is an offense invariable followed by a flogging, to be found at the quarters after daybreak. Then the fears and labors of another day begin; and until its close there is no such thing as rest. . . . The hands are required to be in the cotton field as soon as it is light in the morning, and, with the exception of ten or fifteen minutes, which is given them at noon to swallow their allowance of cold bacon, they are not permitted to be a moment idle until it is too dark to see, and when the moon is full, they often times labor till the middle of the night. They do not dare to stop even at dinner time, nor return to the quarters, however late it be, until the order to halt is given by the driver. . . . Finally, at a late hour, they reach the quarters, sleepy and overcome with the long day's toil. All that is allowed them is corn and bacon, which is given out at the corn-crib and smoke-house every Sunday morning. Each one receives, as his weekly allowance, three and a half pounds of bacon, and corn enough to make a peck of meal. That is all.

dogs, and slaves knew little about the countryside beyond their own plantation. Yet in the 1850s perhaps as many as 1,000 slaves tried to run away each year.

Sometimes slaves would run away as a temporary protest. They would hide in swamps or woods and often not return for months. This was one of the few means of active protest available to slaves in the deep South, where the great distances from the free states made successful flight all but impossible.

Slave Revolts

The slave's ultimate protest was violent revolt, something whites constantly feared. Rumors of slave conspiracies surfaced periodically, yet in reality few slaves revolted. This is hardly surprising, since the odds were overwhelmingly against the slaves. Slaves had few weapons and were under constant surveillance. The threat of discovery by whites or betrayal by slaves loyal to their masters was always present. As a result, only a handful of slaves ever participated in a revolt.

Nevertheless, there were several important slave revolts in the nineteenth century. The revolt of 1791 in Haiti, where Toussaint L'Ouverture successfully established a black republic (see page 193), served as an inspiration for many slaves, some of whom had come from Haiti.

In 1800 Gabriel Prosser was caught leading a conspiracy to make Virginia a black republic. In 1811 between 300 and 500 slaves marched on New Orleans in well-organized companies, but they were easily defeated by the militia. Denmark Vesey, a free black carpenter in Charleston, was plotting a major uprising when he and his associates were betrayed by a slave and arrested in 1822.

In 1831 Nat Turner, a slave preacher, led a full-scale revolt in Southhampton County, Virginia. Inspired by reading the Bible and by his vision of black and white angels fighting, he led a group of about 70 armed slaves in a bloody revolt. By the time the authorities had crushed the uprising, the rebels had killed over 60 whites. The state militia responded by killing scores of blacks, including many who had no part in the revolt. Turner himself was captured and executed.

The Defense of Slavery

The Turner revolt sent shock waves of fear throughout the South. As you will read in the next chapter, that anxiety, as well as the rise of abolitionist activity in the North, led many white southerners to change their attitudes toward slavery.

At the time of the Revolutionary War, many considered slavery a "necessary evil." They felt guilty about owning slaves and sometimes freed them in their wills. But following Nat Turner's rebellion in 1831, southern legislatures began to enact harsher slave codes that limited the actions of free blacks as well as slaves even further. The codes also made it more difficult for planters to free their slaves.

These attempts to strengthen the institution of slavery accompanied a growing conviction among many southerners that slavery was a positive good. They noted that the ancient civilizations of Greece and Rome had been based on slavery. Many slave

Major Events	
1793	Eli Whitney invents cotton gin
1825	Opening of Erie Canal
1831	Nat Turner's rebellion
1834	Cyrus McCormick patents the mechanical reaper; National Trades Union organized
1837	John Deere introduces steel plow
1839	Charles Goodyear develops method to vulcanize rubber
1844	Samuel Morse perfects telegraph; China grants United States special trading privileges
1845	Famine begins in Ireland
1846	Elias Howe invents sewing machine
1848	Revolutions in Europe
1853	Commodore Perry secures trading privileges for United States in Japan

owners pointed out that the Constitution protected a person's property. Furthermore, some argued, slavery was an economic necessity in the South, where planters depended on large labor forces. The defenders of slavery also insisted that slavery benefited the slaves.

Some writers defended slavery by comparing the lives of slaves with the lives of workers in northern factories. One of those writers was George Fitzhugh, a Virginia planter. He claimed that slaves received better treatment than northern workers because slave owners formed a genuine bond of affection with their slaves much like that between parents and children. A plantation, Fitzhugh asserted, was like a little community in which each person had certain responsibilities that contributed to the good of the entire community. Northern factory owners, on the other hand, felt no responsibility for workers who became sick, disabled, or aged.

While writers like Fitzhugh wrote perceptive critiques of northern society, they generally compared the luckiest of the slaves with the most unfortunate workers in the North. The supporters of slavery failed to recognize the cruel indignity of one person's being owned by another. That many slaves managed to retain their dignity and humanity in the face of such an institution is a tribute to their strength and perseverance.

For answers, see p. A 47.

Section Review

1. Identify the following: "puttin' on old Massa," Nat Turner.

2. Define the following terms: task system, gang system.

3. (a) What types of plantations used the task system? (b) What types used the gang system?

4. What was the legal status of slave marriages?

5. What Christian teachings were most important to slaves?

6. How did Nat Turner's revolt change the attitude of many southerners toward slavery?

IN PERSPECTIVE   The early nineteenth century was a period of economic growth for both the North and the South. Industrial expansion was greatest in the North, as was the development of railroad systems. The spread of industry in the 1830s contributed to a worsening of working conditions. Skilled workers tried to improve conditions by organizing unions and workingmen's parties but with limited success. The influx of European immigrants in the 1840s greatly expanded the labor supply in the North, which contributed to antiimmigrant sentiment among some Americans.

In the South the invention of the cotton gin and increased demand for cotton resulted in the expansion of cotton production. Large plantations dominated cotton growing and the production of other crops, such as sugar and rice. While the vast majority of southerners were small subsistence farmers, planters influenced much of southern life.

Most slaves lived on plantations, but their working and living conditions varied. Even under the best conditions, however, slaves were still the property of others. They often relied on family life, religion, holidays, and cultural traditions to retain a sense of human dignity.

The diverging economic development of the North and South contributed to growing sectional differences. The existence of slavery and especially its westward expansion became an increasingly divisive issue in the nation, as you will read in the next two chapters.

Chapter Review

For Further Thought

1. (a) Describe the development of the railroad network. (b) How were early problems overcome? (c) What impact did railroads have on the economy of the North?

2. (a) How did America's foreign trade expand during the 1840s and 1850s? (b) What was the role of the clipper ships? (c) Why were they replaced by steamships?

3. (a) How did industrialization affect northern agriculture? (b) How did farming in the North differ from farming in the South by 1860?

4. (a) How did factory work change during the 1830s? (b) How did workers try to improve conditions? (c) Were they successful? Explain.

5. (a) Why did an increasing number of people immigrate to the United States beginning in the 1840s? (b) Where did the new immigrants come from? (c) Where did they settle? (d) Why did some Americans protest the influx of immigrants?

6. (a) How did the invention of the cotton gin affect the nature of cotton growing in the South? (b) What impact did expanding textile mills in the North and Great Britain have? (c) What impact did the rise of the cotton kingdom have on slavery?

7. (a) Why did some southerners try to promote industry in the South in the 1840s? (b) What types of industries were established?

8. (a) How did the life of small farmers in the South differ from that of poor whites? (b) How did the life of planters differ from that of other southern farmers?

9. Explain how each of the following affected the conditions under which slaves worked: (a) the size of a plantation; (b) the crop grown; (c) the temperament of the slave owner.

10. (a) How did slaves try to maintain their sense of human dignity? (b) In what other ways did they react against slavery?

11. (a) Why did some southerners begin to defend slavery as a positive good in the 1830s? (b) What arguments did they make?

1. (a) Why do you think most railroads in the beginning of the nineteenth century ran east and west rather than north and south? (b) What effect do you think this had on the settlement of the West?

2. (a) What types of workers tried to organize most actively in the early nineteenth century? (b) Why do you think they had a better chance of success than other workers?

3. (a) What problems did free blacks face in the North? (b) What problems did they face in the South? (c) In what way were the problems similar? (d) In what way were they different?

4. Large planters were a very small portion of the southern population. Why do you think they had such a major impact on southern society, politics, and economics?

For answers, see p. A 48.

Developing Basic Skills

1. *Map Reading* Study the map on page 266 and answer the following questions: (a) What information is shown on the map? (b) How did the extent of railroads change between 1850 and 1860? (c) Which region of the country had the most highly developed railroad network? How can you explain this? (d) What impact would that development have on the economy of that region?

2. *Map Reading* Study the map on page 275 and answer the following questions: (a) What information is shown on this map? (b) In what areas was cotton growing most prevalent in 1840? (c) To what states did it expand? (d) In what part of the South was cotton not grown? How might you explain that?

3. *Researching* Find out more about the life of one of the inventors you read about in this chapter. Study the person's personal background and the circumstances surrounding his invention. What other devices did the person invent? Did he become successful as a result of his inventions?

See page 775 for suggested readings.

16

A Land of Idealism

(1820–1860)

The Country School, *by Winslow Homer.*

In 1840 the American writer and philosopher Ralph Waldo Emerson rode to Boston to satisfy his curiosity about a meeting of people who called themselves the Friends of Universal Reform. He found an unusual crowd—not just one group of reformers, but many different organizations, some with strange names and a wide variety of goals.

"If the assembly was disorderly, it was picturesque," remarked Emerson. "Madmen, madwomen, men with beards, Dunkers, Muggletonians, Come-outers, Groaners, Agrarians, Seventh-Day Baptists, Quakers, Abolitionists, Calvinists, Unitarians, and Philosophers—all came successively to the top, and seized their moment, if not their hour, wherein to chide, or pray, or preach, or protect."

During the mid-nineteenth century the United States seemed to be filled with reformers ready to change the world. They banded together to improve American life. "Everything is done now by Societies," noted one observer. "You can scarcely name an object for which some institution has not been formed." Women's rights, the abolition of slavery, better education for all Americans, humane treatment of the mentally ill—all these problems and more the reformers set out to conquer.

1 The Reforming Impulse

Although agitation for reform was especially strong in the period between the War of 1812 and the Civil War, the idea of remaking society for the better had strong roots in the political and religious heritage of the nation.

Political Ideals

The United States began its history with a revolution, one that freed Americans from British rule and proclaimed that all men were created equal. The Constitution of the new country, especially the Bill of Rights, established that an individual had certain rights under the law that could not be violated.

Reformers believed that those principles of individual liberty and equality had not been fully carried out. If all people were created equal, why did slavery continue to exist? And why did women have fewer rights than men? Reformers who were concerned with applying the principles of individual liberty and equality saw many areas in which to work.

Some reformers worked for the improvement of the public school system. How could a republic function properly, they argued, if its citizens were not well educated? How might prisons rehabilitate inmates so they would return to society as productive members of their community? What sort of treatment did the mentally ill deserve? Reformers believed they were moving the country closer to its ideals.

Religious Influence

When settlers first arrived in Massachusetts Bay during the 1630s, John Winthrop reminded them that they would be "as a city upon a hill" with the "eyes of all people . . . upon us." He encouraged the new colony to conduct itself as a shining example to the rest of the world. It had a mission to demonstrate how a "godly community" ought to live.

This religious vision of America persisted over the years. It inspired many of the Revolutionary War generation to believe that the young republic would be an example to the world, not just in politics but also in religion.

In the nineteenth century the religious community continued to grow just as the nation did. Many different denominations, such as the Congregationalists, Presbyterians, Baptists, and Methodists, founded churches in the new settlements and spread their own religious beliefs. All shared the dream that one day the United States would be a Christian commonwealth, where sin was unknown and virtue reigned. Combined with the political ideals of equality, liberty, and democracy, this religious conviction spurred many reformers.

Reforming Personal Lives

Some reformers tried to improve American life by convincing individuals to lead holy and upright lives. By changing personal habits, religious leaders hoped to improve the nation as a whole. Frequently they tried to achieve this goal by holding *revivals,* so called because these meetings attempted to revive a religious spirit in people who were not taking their religion seriously. Revivals had been held in America as early as the 1740s, but it was in the nineteenth century that they became more frequent.

Revivals often took place in the countryside. Several thousand people would come from miles around to a clearing in the woods, set up tents, and listen to preachers for several days.

At a large "camp meeting," six or seven ministers might preach at the same time to different crowds of people. "The noise was like the roar of Niagara," recalled one preacher. "The vast sea of human beings seemed to be agitated as if by a storm. . . . Some of the people were singing, others praying, some crying for mercy. . . ." On the frontier, where churches had not yet been established, revivals proved to be an effective method of spreading religion and exhorting people to reform their lives.

The effort to reform personal lives took many forms. For example, different Protestant denominations put aside their differences and formed organizations to promote Christianity. The American Bible Society made Bibles available at very low cost. Other societies published inexpensive religious pamphlets designed to reform personal morals. In 1836 alone, one such society sold over 3 million copies of their publications.

The Temperance Movement

One of the most widespread movements to improve individual lives was the campaign against alcoholic beverages, which came to be known as the *temperance movement*. For many Americans during the early nineteenth century, no social event—from dances and house raisings to weddings and funerals—was complete without a large amount of alcohol.

At first reformers in the temperance movement urged only that Americans reduce the amount of liquor they consumed. But beginning in the late 1820s, more and more reformers advocated total *abstinence*, refraining from all alcohol. They convinced some state legislatures to impose taxes on liquor and to allow local communities to prohibit the sale of alcoholic beverages.

The movement eventually led, in the early 1850s, to the passage of *Maine laws*, so named because Maine was the first state to enact one. These laws prohibited the sale of all alcoholic beverages. Many people opposed such drastic measures, however, so most states that adopted such laws soon repealed them.

Whatever the results, many reformers continued their efforts to improve personal morals. And their efforts soon extended to the area of social reform, where they tried to change not only personal behavior but also social institutions.

For answers, see p. A 48.
Section Review

1. Identify the following: Maine laws.
2. Define the following terms: revivals, temperance movement, abstinence.
3. What did reformers believe about individual liberties and equality?
4. How did the vision of America as a "Christian commonwealth" affect reformers?
5. According to some reformers, how would revivals contribute to a better nation?
6. What impact did the reformers of the temperance movement have on some state legislatures?

2 Social Reform

Reformers gradually came to believe that they needed to do more than change personal behavior. Even if citizens were virtuous and upright, reformers argued, the public could not vote intelligently if there were few schools to provide them with a proper education. Prisoners could not be expected to reform themselves if they were treated viciously and kept in filthy, cramped surroundings. Reformers decided that some of the institutions of American society also needed reforming.

Educating the Young

Colonial Americans, especially in New England, had placed great emphasis on educating the young. Those influenced by Puritan beliefs thought a person should be able at least to read the Bible. Therefore, New England colonial legislatures required each town to maintain a public school, with all families but the poorest paying fees to support it. Although similar laws still existed in the nineteenth century, public support for town schools had decreased. Buildings had fallen into disrepair, and teachers were not as well trained.

In other areas of the country the situation was worse. Free education did exist in the Middle Atlantic states but only for those who declared themselves paupers. Geography contributed to educational problems in the South. Because of isolated farms and poor roads, the community effort needed to support public schools was slow to materialize. Large plantation owners, who had the influence to make changes, had little interest in public education because they generally hired tutors for their children.

In the West residents of new communities faced a variety of problems that slowed the establishment of schools. Even when towns set up schoolhouses, they were often crude, desolate buildings, poorly ventilated, and inadequately heated. They were frequently located on the most worthless site in the town. "For the sheepfold and cow-house, sheltered situations are carefully selected," complained one reformer, "but a bleak hill-top, swept by the winter blast, or a sandy plain, scorched by a dogday sun, will do for a school." Inside, schools were equally unappealing, with a few rough benches and desks, bare walls, no blackboards, and few windows.

The quality of teachers around the country varied, but almost all were poorly paid and had received little education themselves. Even good teachers faced difficult conditions. Sometimes as many as 80 children of all ages crowded into a gloomy room. Some students were learning to read, some were studying arithmetic, others geography—all at the same time. Students who got too rowdy received a crack on the knuckles from the teacher's rod, or worse.

The Beginnings of Educational Reform

The lack of good public education concerned many reformers, chief among them, Horace Mann. Mann gave up a promising career as a lawyer to become Massachusetts' first superintendent of education in 1837. For 12 years he pleaded, argued, lectured, and goaded the state government into improving the schools. Every year he issued an annual report demanding better school buildings, better textbooks, and less physical punishment of students.

A dedicated reformer, Mann was enthusiastic about his work. He even devoted his vacations to work as he toured the country visiting schools. But Mann believed that the effort was worth the price. In his opinion a democratic republic needed well-educated citizens. "If we do not prepare children to become good citizens," he declared, "then our republic must go down to destruction, as others have gone before it."

During Mann's term as superintendent, education made important strides in Massachusetts. State appropriations for education doubled, teachers' salaries increased, and the school year was lengthened by one month. The state also established three schools to train teachers.

Public Education

In other states, reformers followed Mann's lead as they struggled to establish free public education for all students. This movement met with strong opposition, however. For one thing, all taxpayers would have to contribute to state-supported schools. Some taxpayers asked, "Why should we have to pay school taxes even if we have no children?" Parents who sent their children to private schools, a common practice, wondered why they should have to pay both tuition at a private school and taxes to support a public one.

Some parents also objected to the fact that reformers wanted education to be *compulsory*, that is, all children would have to attend until a certain age. They argued that this deprived parents of control of their own children. Furthermore, farm families as well as many factory workers depended on their children's labor to help support the family. If the government required children to attend school, they would not be able to work.

In spite of such opposition, most northern states followed the lead of Massachusetts and established free public elementary schools by the 1850s. In the South public education grew slowly although some people worked to improve conditions there.

Fewer high schools existed, partly because young people usually began work at an early age. Again Massachusetts led the way. By 1860 there were nearly 100 public high schools in that state, compared to about 200 in the rest of the nation. Private high schools continued to provide education for many young people.

Even with these achievements, much remained to be done. For example, although the Constitution guaranteed the separation of church and state, many public school teachers openly promoted Protestant Christianity, and schools often used textbooks written with an anti-Catholic bias. As a result, many Catholics hoped to establish their own parochial schools in which the education would include instruction in the Catholic faith as well as other subjects.

Black children found even less opportunity for public education. Most towns simply ignored the educational needs of black Americans or emphatically barred black students from the public schools. Where public schools existed for blacks, as in New York City and Boston, they remained segregated and were less well financed than schools for whites.

Women who wanted to continue their education beyond the basics of reading and writing met with little success at the beginning of the nineteenth century. "We don't pretend to teach the female part of the town anything more than dancing, or a little music perhaps," commented one New Hampshire resident.

Higher Education

Private colleges dominated the field of higher education. At first they offered few courses, but as the desire for wider and better education grew, the colleges responded by broadening their curriculums. Instead of studying only the classics, college students of the 1820s and 1830s learned about literature, history, political science, economics, and, increasingly, science. The number of colleges also grew as many religious denominations established their own schools and as more states supported colleges. By 1860, 16 states financed some type of higher education.

Colleges, like most elementary and high schools, were primarily for white males. A few private colleges, such as Oberlin, Harvard, and Dartmouth, did admit a small number of black students, and three colleges especially for black students were founded. For example, in 1856 the African Methodist Episcopal church founded Wilberforce College in Ohio, named after William Wilberforce, a noted English abolitionist.

Oberlin College admitted women in 1837, becoming the first coeducational college. For the most part, however, higher education for women was limited to a few academies or seminaries. (See page 292.)

Reforming the Prisons

Punishment for criminal offenses had been severe in the colonial period. The death penalty was generally imposed for serious offenses, and some form of pain or humiliation for minor ones. Virginia's colonial legislature made 27 offenses capital crimes, punishable by death. Other states designated fewer capital crimes, but listing 10 or more such offenses was common. As late as 1817, public floggings took place in Philadelphia.

In the early nineteenth century imprisonment gradually replaced physical punishment, but this created new problems. The first prisons were makeshift. Prisoners often ran short of clothing. Prison officials crowded men, women, and children together in small rooms, giving them poor and insufficient food. Prisons even charged inmates fees during their stay in jail, while jailers made extra money by selling rum to the prisoners.

These wretched conditions led reformers to press for change. In the 1820s, New York and Pennsylvania led the way by establishing new penitentiary systems based on isolation. In New York's Auburn system, for example, prisoners slept alone in a cell. They worked together during the day, but they could not talk to other prisoners or even exchange glances. Reformers hoped that if criminals were isolated from their old environment and given a regular occupation and a strict schedule, they would develop good habits. Yet the system placed a severe psychological strain on prisoners since it denied them the normal benefits of society. For all the changes, the new systems succeeded in "reforming" few of their inmates.

Helping the Mentally Ill

Most people understood little about mental illness in the nineteenth century. Men, women, and children who suffered from mental illnesses were locked up, sometimes in jails or poorhouses. They often received inadequate care and little medical attention. The condition of these people went largely unnoticed until the 1840s when Dorothea Lynde Dix, a Boston school teacher, began to campaign for better treatment of the mentally ill.

In 1841 Dix was invited to teach a Sunday-school class at a jail in Cambridge, Massachusetts. Among the inmates at the jail were mentally ill people dressed in rags and housed in unheated quarters. Dix was shocked at what she saw. She then visited every institution in the state where the mentally ill were housed and wrote a report detailing the mistreatment she discovered. She urged that such people be treated as patients who were ill, not as criminals.

Dix convinced the Massachusetts lawmakers to improve care for the mentally ill. She also carried her crusade to the rest of the nation, finding success among other state legislatures. In response to her appeals, 15 states established special hospitals for the mentally ill. Dix failed to win support from the national government, however. In 1854 she campaigned for federal land grants to support hospitals. Congress passed such a bill, but President Franklin Pierce vetoed it. Still, Dorothea Dix had called the public's attention to a long-ignored problem.

From the day Dorothea Dix first saw mentally ill people penned up in an unheated jail, she crusaded for better medical care and proper facilities for them. Her campaign led 15 states to establish hospitals for the care of the mentally ill.

Creating an Ideal Society

Some reformers were not content to reorganize or improve one particular institution, such as prisons or schools. Rather, they wanted to remake society entirely. Since they could not make over the entire country, these reformers founded their own *utopian*, or ideal, communities as a demonstration of how a new system might work.

Some groups based their utopian communities on religious principles. One such group, the Shakers, hoped to isolate themselves from what they considered a corrupt society, supporting themselves by farming while working to attain perfection. Other communities, such as Robert Owen's New Harmony in Indiana, were more concerned with economic principles. In New Harmony, Owen hoped to eliminate many of the harsh conditions he saw in the growing industrial society.

Most of these utopian communities ultimately failed to reach their goals. Often a strong leader organized and ran the community in its early days. Then, when the leader departed, the remaining members split into factions and the community dissolved. Furthermore, founding entire communities took a large amount of money, and many groups failed to find substantial support, especially in the first crucial years of existence.

It is perhaps the nature of utopians, and all reformers, that their dreams and hopes often exceed the concrete results of their efforts. Yet even if reforms in the areas of prisons, treatment for the mentally ill, and education had not perfected American society, at least reformers had forced Americans to ask questions about their society. They had held up to the public the political and religious ideals of the nation and demanded that their fellow citizens come closer to fulfilling those ideals.

For answers, see p. A 49.

Section Review

1. Identify the following: Horace Mann, Dorothea Dix.
2. Define the following terms: compulsory education, utopian.
3. List three problems of public education in the early nineteenth century.
4. What were Horace Mann's goals for education in Massachusetts?
5. What are two reasons some people opposed free public education?
6. What gradually replaced the physical punishment of criminal offenders?
7. (a) How were the mentally ill usually treated in the early nineteenth century? (b) What did Dorothea Dix accomplish on their behalf?

3 A Campaign for Women's Rights

During the 1840s and 1850s women took an increasingly active part in reform movements. Yet women themselves suffered many forms of legal discrimination. They could not vote, and in many states they could not own property, make a will, or file a lawsuit. If a woman worked outside the home, the law gave her husband the wages she brought home. Consequently, some reformers gradually turned their attention to rights for women.

Early Strides in Education

As you read earlier, women had limited educational opportunities in the early nineteenth century. Early attempts to establish college-level education for women widened these opportunities and contributed to growing demands for full legal rights.

As early as 1821, Emma Willard, a pioneer in the field of education, established the Troy Female Seminary in Troy, New York. Her father had given her a good basic education, but like other intelligent women, she had been unable to continue her education because no college would admit women. Her seminary successfully instructed students in mathematics, physics, history, and geography, proving that women could master such subjects as easily as men. Willard's goal was to train women teachers who in turn could teach others.

For many years seminaries were the only institutions in which women could attain a higher education. Many of the seminaries were small and existed only as long as their benefactors lived. Mary Lyon, however, dreamed of establishing a permanent college for women. During the 1830s she began a campaign to raise funds for such a college. Her work was slow and contributions were small, but she prevailed. In 1836 the cornerstone of Mount Holyoke Female Seminary was laid in South Hadley, Massachusetts. The name of the school hid Lyon's true intent. She realized that many people opposed a college education for women, so she carefully avoided calling the school a col-

Sojourner Truth: Equality for Women

Sojourner Truth was born a slave in New York State in 1797. She ran away in 1826 just one year before she would have been freed according to New York law. Originally named Isabelle Baumfree, she took the name Sojourner Truth about 1843 because she believed her calling was to journey around the country, boldly speaking the truth about slavery, women's rights, and other causes. At a women's rights convention in 1851, she responded with powerful words to a man who claimed that women were inferior to men.

Well, children, where there is so much racket there must be something out of kilter. . . . What's all this here talking about?

That man over there says that women need to be helped into carriages, and lifted over ditches, and to have the best place everywhere. Nobody ever helps me into carriages, or over mud-puddles, or gives me any best place! And ain't I a woman? Look at me! Look at my arm! I have ploughed, and planted, and gathered into barns, and no man could head me! And ain't I a woman? I could work as much and eat as much as a man—when I could get it—and bear the lash as well! And ain't I a woman? I have borne thirteen children, and seen them most all sold off to slavery, and when I cried out with my mother's grief, none but Jesus heard me! And ain't I a woman?

Then they talk about this thing in the head; what's this they call it? That's it, honey [in-

tellect]. What's that got to do with women's rights? . . . If my cup won't hold but a pint and yours hold a quart, wouldn't you be mean not to let me have my little half measure full?

Then that little man in black there, he says women can't have as much rights as men, 'cause Christ wasn't a woman! Where did your Christ come from? *Where did your Christ come from?* From God and a woman! Man had nothing to do with Him.

If the first woman God ever made was strong enough to turn the world upside down all alone, these women together [here] ought to be able to turn it back, and get it right side up again! And now they are asking to do it, the men better let 'em. Obliged to you for hearing on me; and now old Sojourner Truth ain't got nothing more to say.

lege. Despite its name, Mount Holyoke was the first women's college in the United States.

Resistance to Women Reformers

Many women shared in the general reforming spirit of the age. But women who tried to campaign for such causes, especially when they tried to speak in public, discovered that most male reformers did not want their help. Reforming, the men felt, was not a woman's occupation. "The power of woman is her dependence," lectured one group of Massachusetts ministers. A woman who gives up that dependence on men to become a reformer "yields the power God has given her for her protection, and her character becomes unnatural."

Some women vigorously rejected the status of "second-class" reformers. Sarah and Angelina Grimké, for example, led the fight for full female participation in the antislavery reform movement. The two sisters were from South Carolina, where their father was a slave owner. They left home because of their opposition to slavery. At first they lectured only to other women, but soon they began speaking to mixed audiences. To their dismay they found that the men would often boo and shout them down.

The Grimkés persisted, however. "To me," said Sarah Grimké, "it is perfectly clear that whatsoever it is morally right for a man to do, it is morally right for a woman to do." When some abolitionists asked them to give up the cause of women's rights, Angelina asked, "What *then* can *woman* do for the slave, when she herself is under the feet of man and shamed into *silence?*"

In 1840 the antislavery movement in the United States split into two groups. One of the issues was whether women should be allowed to participate in movement activities. Later that year in London, the World Anti-Slavery Convention voted to exclude the female delegates from the United States.

The Seneca Falls Convention

Frustrated by such restraints, women reformers began to see the need to campaign for their own rights as well as for the rights of others. In 1848 Lucretia Mott and Elizabeth Cady Stanton, two of the delegates who

Throughout her adult life Elizabeth Cady Stanton worked to gain for women such fundamental rights as legal ownership of their own property. Stanton helped found the women's movement in the United States. She is shown in this photograph with one of her seven children.

had been rejected by the London antislavery conference, called a convention for women's rights in Stanton's home town, Seneca Falls, New York. Stanton and Mott wanted to publicize the need for women's rights and to create a program for action.

In calling the meeting, Stanton drafted a proclamation modeled after the Declaration of Independence. "We hold these truths to be self-evident: that all men and women are created equal," it began. And it continued, "The history of mankind is a history of repeated injuries and usurpations on the part of man toward woman, having in direct object the establishment of an absolute tyranny over her."

Over 250 women and about 40 men attended the meeting. Stanton introduced nine resolutions. All passed unanimously except one calling for women's suffrage, which won a small majority. So began the long struggle for women's rights, which Stanton led throughout her lifetime.

Stanton was soon joined by Susan B. Anthony, who brought tremendous energy and organizational skills to the struggle for women's rights. In the years after the Seneca Falls Convention, advocates of women's rights held annual meetings and petitioned state legislatures to try to change laws. Despite such activity, the movement remained small until after the Civil War.

293

Overcoming limited opportunities for higher education for women, Maria Mitchell taught herself astronomy. She gained fame in 1847 by discovering a comet. Later she taught astronomy at Vassar, a college for women.

Advances of American Women

Slowly women's role in American life expanded. As schools such as the Troy Female Seminary and Mount Holyoke graduated qualified teachers, women were accepted into the teaching profession.

Elizabeth Blackwell applied to medical school at Geneva College, New York, and was voted in almost as a joke. But she surprised her male classmates and graduated at the head of the class. In 1850 she began practicing medicine in New York City as the first woman doctor. Blackwell founded the first school of nursing in the United States in 1857, to teach a profession that women would enter in increasing numbers.

Americans also accepted women as authors and editors. Margaret Fuller edited a

noted philosophical magazine and wrote several books. Her work, *Woman in the Nineteenth Century,* published in 1845, played an important part in the women's rights movement. Fuller argued that women were as capable as men and were able to do the same type of work.

Louisa May Alcott enjoyed considerable success with her children's books, including *Little Women.* Harriet Beecher Stowe excited nationwide controversy with her anti-slavery book, *Uncle Tom's Cabin,* as you will read later. (See page 309.) Many other women wrote essays and poetry for local newspapers or published tracts on popular moral crusades of the day.

However, despite the accomplishments of individual women, the legal status of women changed little. In some states women did gain the right to control their own property after they married, but the women's suffrage movement gained no headway. Women still remained outside the political process. Yet the reformers had publicized their cause well and did not abandon it. The questions of women's rights would be debated but could no longer be ignored.

For answers, see p. A 49.

Section Review

1. Identify the following: Emma Willard, Mary Lyon, Sarah and Angelina Grimké, Lucretia Mott, Elizabeth Cady Stanton, Susan B. Anthony, Elizabeth Blackwell, Margaret Fuller, Louisa May Alcott, Harriet Beecher Stowe.
2. How did Mary Lyon intend Mount Holyoke to be different from other female seminaries?
3. What reaction did women involved in reform movements often face?
4. What was the purpose of the Seneca Falls Convention?
5. List two examples of professions that gradually opened up to women.

4 The Battle Against Slavery

Many problems captured the attention of reformers during the first half of the nineteenth century, but the most far-reaching reform movement of the period was the crusade to abolish slavery. But Americans, both black and white, who opposed slavery did not agree on how it should be abolished.

A Gradual Approach

Opposition to slavery did not suddenly appear in the early nineteenth century. Some Americans from both northern and southern states had long opposed slavery and favored emancipation of the slaves. When the nation abolished the slave trade in 1808, many believed that slavery would soon die out. Others worked actively to abolish it. Such activity took many forms. One was to stimulate public discussion of the subject. Newspapers concerned with ending slavery sprang up in the North and in parts of the South, such as Tennessee and North Carolina.

During the 1820s Benjamin Lundy published the *Genius of Universal Emancipation* in Ohio. It became one of the most influential antislavery newspapers. Through his newspaper, Lundy proposed a program of gradual emancipation that included stopping the spread of slavery to new states, abolishing the slave trade within the borders of the United States, and urging slave states to free their slaves gradually. In 1829 Lundy hired an assistant editor, William Lloyd Garrison, a man who held a more radical viewpoint and who would eventually become a leader in the drive to abolish slavery.

The Colonization Movement

Even though many white Americans in both North and South admitted the evils of slavery, few could imagine blacks assuming a full and equal part in American society. As a result of such feelings, some abolitionists endorsed a program in which freed slaves would move to Liberia, a country in Africa founded in 1822 by former American slaves.

The American Colonization Society, established in 1817, tried to carry out the program but found it impractical. The society could afford to send only a small number of blacks to Liberia each year. In 1830, for example, the society sent only 259 free blacks to Liberia, bringing the total to about 1,400. Furthermore, the society failed to convince many plantation owners to free their slaves. Slave owners claimed that such a move would create too great an economic hardship.

Opposition from many free blacks eventually doomed the colonization movement. A free black, Paul Cuffe (see page 125), had been one of the originators of the idea. He thought that blacks would have a better chance of making a good life for themselves if they lived where they did not face discrimination. Cuffe personally took 38 black settlers to Africa in 1815. But many black Americans became disillusioned with the idea of colonization. In 1831 a convention of free blacks meeting in New York City declared that the United States, not Africa, was their home.

> The time must come when the Declaration of Independence will be felt in the heart, as well as uttered from the mouth, and when the rights of all shall be properly acknowledged and appreciated. God hasten that time. This is our home, and this is our country. Beneath its sod lie the bones of our fathers; for it, some of them fought, bled, and died. Here we are born, and here we will die.

Radical Abolitionism

By the 1830s some opponents of slavery believed that a more radical approach was needed. Gradual abolition seemed less and less likely. Whitney's cotton gin had enlarged the cotton kingdom in the South, and the planters' dependence on slave labor seemed greater than ever. Furthermore, as you read in Chapter 15, the fear created by Nat Turner's rebellion in 1831 hardened many southerners' attitude about slavery. Some who had once apologized for owning slaves now praised the institution. Abolitionists saw little hope that slave owners would voluntarily free their slaves.

William Lloyd Garrison symbolized the change within the abolitionist movement. While he worked with Lundy, Garrison tried to tone down his more radical ideas. But in 1831 he established his own antislavery paper, *The Liberator*, in Boston.

In *The Liberator* Garrison proclaimed his doctrine with vigor: slavery was a sin, and the nation had to be purged of this evil immediately and without compensation to slave owners. The first issue of the paper testified to Garrison's fierce unwillingness to compromise. "I *will be* as harsh as truth, and as uncompromising as justice. ... I am in earnest—I will not equivocate—I will not excuse—I will not retreat a single inch—*and I will be heard.*"

Yet even Garrison recognized that immediate emancipation was unlikely. "We have never said that slavery would be overthrown by a single blow," Garrison admitted privately, "that it ought to be, we shall always contend."

Garrison enjoyed support among many free blacks in the North and great notoriety in the South. In 1832 he organized the New England Anti-Slavery Society and helped found the American Anti-Slavery Society. Although he favored immediate emancipation,

Garrison opposed the use of violence to end slavery.

Other abolitionists contributed to the growing radicalism of the movement. Theodore Weld, an intensely religious young man, spoke eloquently about the moral evils of slavery. In 1834 Weld led a revival among the students at Lane Seminary in Cincinnati. When most of the students eagerly converted to the doctrine of immediate emancipation, the more conservative trustees of the seminary suppressed all antislavery agitation on campus. Weld and many of his students then began traveling from town to town, effectively organizing abolitionist sentiment.

David Walker's *Appeal to the Colored Citizens of the World*, published in 1829, advocated a more radical position than Garrison or Weld. A free black born in North Carolina and living in Boston, Walker appealed to slaves to rise up and free themselves. Walker's *Appeal* did not lead to revolts among slaves, but it created a sensation among many slave owners and among moderate and conservative whites in the North.

Division Among Abolitionists

Although radical abolitionists united in their desire to see slavery ended immediately, they did not agree on tactics. One dispute arose over whether women should participate in the movement. As you read earlier in this chapter, abolitionists split over this issue in 1840. William Lloyd Garrison's outspoken support for women's participation alienated many abolitionists.

Garrison's position on political action also divided the radical abolitionists. He opposed all political activity as a way to achieve emancipation. Garrison argued that the Constitution favored slavery and that political institutions were corrupt. Consequently, he believed nothing could be gained by trying to work within the system.

Instead Garrison sought to expose the evils of slavery in his newspaper, in lectures and public discussions, and through letter-writing campaigns. In this way he believed the American people would be convinced to support the abolition of slavery.

Many abolitionists supported this approach, including the Grimké sisters, Theodore Weld, Sojourner Truth, and Frederick Douglass. Sojourner Truth, who became well known as an antislavery speaker, greatly aided the abolitionist movement with her impassioned pleas for equality. Frederick Douglass emerged as the most important black leader of the abolitionist movement. Tall and broad-shouldered, his commanding presence was matched by a keen intelligence and powerful speaking voice. During the 1840s Douglass lectured in the United States and Great Britain against American slavery. In 1847 he began publishing an antislavery newspaper, the *North Star*, in Rochester, New York. Douglass also actively protested discrimination against free black Americans.

Black abolitionist groups generally supported Garrison's approach to abolitionism. Black Americans had actively opposed slavery long before most white reformers became involved. By 1830, 50 black antislavery groups existed, and they became increasingly important over the next three decades.

Political Opposition to Slavery

Those who disagreed with Garrison found leadership in Arthur and Lewis Tappan, two wealthy New York City merchants who first broke with Garrison over the inclusion of women in the movement. The Tappans concentrated on achieving change through political activity and found that many radical abolitionists had similar views. In 1839 the Tappans and James Birney, a former Kentucky slave owner converted to abolitionism by Theodore Weld, helped found the Liberty party. In 1840 and again in 1844 Birney ran for President on the Liberty party ticket.

In 1848 the Free Soil party replaced the Liberty party as the nation's most important antislavery political party. The support enjoyed by the Free Soil party among both politicians and voters resulted largely from its more moderate platform. Instead of demanding the abolition of slavery in the South, Free Soilers wanted to stop the expansion of slavery into new territories. Most Free Soilers demonstrated little concern for the rights of blacks. Many, in fact, wanted to keep all blacks, free as well as slave, out of the territories.

The Underground Railroad

Some abolitionists took direct action against slavery by working for the "underground railroad." This was not an actual railroad but rather a network of men and women who

Frederick Douglass: A Denunciation of the Slave Trade

The slave trade was one of the most important targets of abolitionists. Although the importation of slaves was banned after 1808, smugglers continued to bring Africans into the United States. Furthermore, the slave trade within the United States increased as the cotton kingdom pushed westward. (See page 274.) Frederick Douglass had known the degradation of slavery for 21 years in Maryland. After his escape in 1838, he became a noted abolitionist speaker. Below is an excerpt from a speech Douglass made in New York in 1852.

To me the American slave trade is a terrible reality. When a child, my soul was often pierced with a sense of its horrors. . . .

The flesh-mongers gather up their victims by dozens, and drive them chained, to the general depot at Baltimore. When a sufficient number has been collected here, a ship is chartered for the purpose of conveying the forlorn crew to Mobile, or to New Orleans. . . .

In the deep, still darkness of midnight, I have been often aroused by the dead, heavy footsteps, and the piteous cries of the chained gangs that passed our door. . . .

Fellow-citizens, this murderous traffic is, today, in active operation in this boasted republic. In the solitude of my spirit . . . I see the bleeding footsteps; I hear the doleful wail of fettered humanity on the way to the slave-markets where the victims are to be sold like horses, sheep, and swine. . . . My soul sickens at the sight.

---

helped slaves escape to the North or to Canada. These "conductors" led slaves, or "passengers," along back-country roads called "tracks." Farm wagons often served as "trains." Homes along the way where slaves could find food and shelter were called "stations."

The success of the railroad depended on the cooperation of many blacks and whites and on the heroic actions of such individuals as Harriet Tubman. An escaped slave herself, Tubman risked her life time after time, returning South to lead 300 fugitive slaves to the North. Her courage made her a legend among abolitionists and slaves, who called her the "Black Moses." Slave owners also knew her, and they offered a $40,000 reward for her capture.

Reaction to Abolitionism

The arguments of the radical abolitionists attracted only a small number of supporters to the abolitionist cause. In fact, their uncompromising attitudes and fiery rhetoric aroused opposition in both the South and the North.

Abolitionist agitation led more southerners to actively defend slavery. For one thing, Garrison began publishing his newspaper in 1831, the same year as Nat Turner's rebellion. Furthermore, his critique of slavery included strident attacks on the South and southerners. Southern postmasters struck against abolitionism by refusing to deliver abolitionist material. The state of Georgia even offered a reward of $5,000 to anyone who brought Garrison to the state for trial.

In the North more moderate abolitionists feared the consequence of the "immediate emancipation" advocated by Garrison. Moreover, although white northerners might abhor the institution of slavery, most did not want free blacks living in their communities. Many white workers feared that free blacks might take their jobs by working for lower salaries.

When abolitionists spoke throughout the North, they were frequently booed and treated roughly. In 1835 a Boston mob dragged Garrison through the streets with a rope around him. Authorities probably saved his life by throwing him in jail. Two years later Elijah P. Lovejoy, a New England abolitionist, established an antislavery newspaper at Alton, Illinois. A mob, aided by local authorities as well as "gentlemen of property and standing," destroyed the press and killed Lovejoy. Even people who were not abolitionists were shocked by the suppression of free speech and free press. Lovejoy became a martyr all across the North, and sympathy for the abolitionist cause grew.

Despite the antislavery agitation of the 1830s and 1840s, black Americans saw scant hope that they would be freed. More to their dismay, they found that even abolitionists were patronizing. "Too many," noted one black reformer, ". . . best love the colored man at a distance."

More and more black leaders began to heed David Walker's early call for stronger action. Henry Highland Garnet, a former Maryland slave, had seconded Walker's appeal in 1843. "Brethren, Arise, Arise! . . . Rather die like free men than live as slaves." In 1851 Frederick Douglass openly broke with Garrison's pacifism, and many others joined him. "The time is come," announced a group of blacks in 1854, "when our people must assume . . . the battle against caste and Slavery; it is emphatically our battle; no one else can fight it for us. . . ."

The calls for abolition continued through the 1850s, and increasingly Americans saw that the question of slavery seemed to be approaching a crisis. It highlighted the many social and economic differences between the North and South. The nation would soon find itself engulfed in a controversy that would test its ideals and reforming spirit as well as its identity as a nation.

For answers, see p. A 49.

Section Review

1. Identify the following: Benjamin Lundy, William Lloyd Garrison, Theodore Weld, David Walker, Frederick Douglass, Sojourner Truth, underground railroad, Harriet Tubman, Elijah P. Lovejoy.

2. What three steps did Benjamin Lundy propose for the gradual emancipation of slaves?

3. What three factors contributed to the end of the colonization movement?

4. What developments by the 1830s led some abolitionists to believe a more radical approach was needed?

5. What two disputes created divisions among radical abolitionists?

6. (a) What was the goal of the Liberty party? (b) In what way was the goal of the Free Soil party more moderate?

7. (a) **What** was the reaction of many southerners to radical abolitionist agitation? (b) How did many northerners react?

5 Flowering of an American Culture

The efforts of reformers in the first half of the nineteenth century reflected the tradition of idealism in American society. Most looked optimistically toward the future. While they argued that American society was far from perfect, they believed in the possibility of changing life for the better, of aspiring toward the ideal. Many American artists and writers also believed in the idealism of the period, and through their art they helped create a truly unique American culture.

Discovering the American Landscape

During the early 1800s American painters became increasingly interested in the wild, natural beauty of the land. Many painted lavish landscapes that glorified the rugged grandeur of American lakes, rivers, forests, and canyons. The nationalism of these painters is seen in their ideal portrayals of America.

George Caleb Bingham grew up in Missouri and painted scenes of everyday life there, known as genre paintings. His paintings of river life captured the harmony of nature on the American frontier.

Artists in the East also found beauty in the American landscape. Their view was often more nostalgic than that of western painters because in much of the East, settlement and growing industrialization were beginning to infringe on nature. A group of painters including Thomas Cole and Asher Durand became known as the Hudson River

Painters in the early nineteenth century tried to capture the beauty of the rugged American landscape. One group of landscape painters was called the Hudson River School because they so frequently depicted that river. This painting, The Oxbow *by Thomas Cole, shows another northeastern river, the Connecticut.*

School. Their landscapes of the Catskill Mountains and Hudson River area revealed a love of nature and a confidence felt by many Americans during the early 1800s. Such characteristics were also found in much American literature.

Reflections on Life in a Changing America

Ralph Waldo Emerson and Henry David Thoreau greatly influenced American writers, thinkers, and reformers during the period before the Civil War. Emerson himself did not join reform organizations, but he acted as a philosophic observer, commenting on the spirit of the times in essays and lectures. His optimism and belief in progress encouraged reformers.

Thoreau absorbed many of Emerson's ideas and developed them further. Emerson, like many Americans, believed in the self-reliance of the individual. Thoreau became a proponent of this individualism, refusing to be associated with institutions of government and industry that he considered corrupt. In 1845 his distaste for the artificial

Major Events	
1817	American Colonization Society founded
1821	Troy Female Seminary established
1829	David Walker's *Appeal to the Colored Citizens of the World* published
1831	Antislavery paper *The Liberator* established; Nat Turner's revolt
1836	Mary Lyon founds Mount Holyoke Female Seminary
1837	Horace Mann becomes first superintendent of education in Massachusetts
1839	Liberty party founded
1848	Seneca Falls Convention
1856	Wilberforce College founded

and complex nature of the growing industrial society led him to retreat to a cabin at Walden Pond outside Boston, where he lived alone for two years.

His refusal to conform to "corrupt" society led Thoreau to a principle of civil disobedience. He refused to pay taxes during the war with Mexico because he believed the war was immoral, arguing that individuals must be guided by their own conscience.

A Flourishing American Literature

The works of Emerson and Thoreau were part of a growing volume of American literature. Many writers of the period shared the reformers' vision of what America should be like, although they were often less optimistic about the chances of improving society. Literature also reflected the nationalism of the first half of the nineteenth century. This nationalism was most obvious in the increasing use of American themes. James Fenimore Cooper's tales of life on the American frontier and Washington Irving's "Rip Van Winkle" and "The Legend of Sleepy Hollow" are among the earliest examples.

Nathaniel Hawthorne used the history and culture of New England as the background for his novels *The Scarlet Letter* and *The House of Seven Gables.* Hawthorne's works and Herman Melville's *Moby-Dick,* dedicated to Hawthorne, became American classics and earned American authors a place in world literature. The poetry of Edgar Allan Poe and Henry Wadsworth Longfellow earned respect for American verse.

More than any other writer, the poet Walt Whitman captured the idealistic spirit and hopefulness of the early nineteenth century. His vibrant and visionary language virtually bursts from the page. Whitman's lines in *Leaves of Grass* take in every sort of scene, every kind of American.

> A southerner soon as a northerner, a planter nonchalant and hospitable
> A Yankee bound my own way . . . ready for trade . . . my joints the limberest joints on earth and the sternest joints on earth,
> A Kentuckian walking the vale of the Elkhorn in my deerskin leggings
> A boatman over the bays or along coasts . . . a Hoosier, a Badger, a Buckeye . . .
> In all people I see myself, none more and not one barleycorn less,
> And the good or bad I say of myself I say of them.

For answers, see p. A 50.

Section Review

1. Identify the following: George Caleb Bingham, Hudson River School, Ralph Waldo Emerson, Henry David Thoreau, James Fenimore Cooper, Washington Irving, Nathaniel Hawthorne, Herman Melville, Edgar Allan Poe, Henry Wadsworth Longfellow, Walt Whitman.

2. How did American landscape paintings reflect a sense of nationalism?

3. Give one example of the use of American themes in literature.

IN PERSPECTIVE The years between 1820 and 1860 were ones of intense reforming activity. Reformers had a vision of what they thought the nation should be like, and they tried to convince Americans to change in order to reach that ideal.

Horace Mann led the movement to improve public education in the United States, and Dorothea Dix campaigned for better treatment of the mentally ill. Reformers also tried to improve the prison system. Women played an important role in many reform movements and eventually began to demand their own rights.

The campaign to abolish slavery became increasingly important during this period. Abolitionists frequently disagreed among themselves, and their agitation created great resentment in the South as well as frequent opposition in the North. However, their efforts helped keep the issue before the public. Although few artists or writers actively participated in reform movements, many shared the idealistic vision of America.

For answers, see p. A 50.

Chapter Review

1. Describe the political and religious roots of the reform spirit of the early nineteenth century.

2. (a) How did reformers try to change the personal lives of Americans? (b) How successful were they?

3. (a) Describe the state of public education in New England, the Middle Atlantic states, the South, and the West. (b) What other types of education existed for America's youth?

4. (a) Why did Horace Mann believe so strongly in the need for public education? (b) Why did some Americans oppose free public education? (c) Why did some oppose compulsory education?

5. (a) What type of education existed for black Americans in the early nineteenth century? (b) What type of education existed for women? (c) How did the opportunities for higher education increase between 1820 and 1860?

6. Describe efforts of reformers in each of the following areas and note how successful each was: (a) prisons; (b) care of the mentally ill; (c) utopian communities.

7. (a) What role did women play in the abolitionist movement? (b) How did many male reformers react to their activities? (c) How did the male reaction contribute to the beginning of a movement for women's rights? (d) How successful was that movement during the 1840s and 1850s?

8. What tactics did each of the following propose for the abolition of slavery: (a) Benjamin Lundy; (b) William Lloyd Garrison; (c) David Walker; (d) Arthur and Lewis Tappan?

9. (a) Why did the agitation of radical abolitionists arouse resentment among southerners? (b) Why did many northerners oppose the radical abolitionists? (c) How did the reaction against abolitionists create more sympathy for them?

10. How did literature and painting assume a unique American character in the first half of the nineteenth century?

For answers, see p. A 51.

For Further Thought

1. (a) How do the reform movements of the first half of the nineteenth century reflect the American tradition of voluntary action to improve society, which you read about in Chapter 8? (See page 142.) (b) What current examples of this tradition can you identify?

2. Why do you think it was effective for individuals like Sojourner Truth and Frederick Douglass to speak out against slavery?

3. Reread the extract from Walt Whitman's poem on page 300. How does the poem reflect the idealism and optimism of many Americans during this period?

For answers, see p. A 51.

Developing Basic Skills

1. *Relating Past to Present* (a) Describe the legal position of women in the early nineteenth century. (b) How is woman's legal position different today?

2. *Using a Primary Source* Reread Frederick Douglass's speech about the slave trade on page 297 and answer the following questions: (a) What type of document is it? (b) Was the author closely involved with the events described? Explain. (c) Why did Douglass make this speech? How might that have affected what he reported? (d) What facts can you identify? (e) What opinions can you identify? (f) What can you learn about the slave trade from this document?

See page 775 for suggested readings.

Unit Five

A Nation Torn Apart

17

The Cords of Union Broken

(1820–1861)

Detail from The Underground Railroad.

In 1850 Senator Daniel Webster of New Hampshire predicted, "Secession! Peaceable secession! Sir, your eyes and mine are never destined to see that miracle." Webster knew Americans well. By 1860 the nation stood on the brink of civil war.

Strong sectional jealousies pitted North against South. The institution of slavery was a major source of disagreement. Abolitionists wanted to end slavery in the South. Other citizens saw little hope of total abolition but sought to restrict the spread of slavery into territories acquired through the war with Mexico. Southerners saw each attempt to control slavery as a threat to their way of life.

Violence in Kansas, a controversial Supreme Court decision, and an attempt to start a slave rebellion in Virginia all added fuel to the growing flames. Southern states eventually concluded that they had no future within the Union. But the newly elected President, Abraham Lincoln, saw the preservation of the nation as his duty. So Webster's prediction came true. Peaceable secession proved impossible as the flames quickly grew into the inferno of civil war.

1 Attempts to Resolve Conflicts Between North and South

During the first half of the nineteenth century, debates in Congress reflected the growing strain between the North and the South. Much of the tension arose from disagreements over western territories that wanted to join the nation as new states. Should Congress prohibit slavery within the territories and later admit them as *free states*, states in which slavery was prohibited? Or should Congress allow slavery within the territories and admit them as *slave states*, states in which slavery was permitted?

How Congress answered these questions could determine the balance of political power between North and South. The North, with its larger population, had more votes in the House of Representatives, since the number of representatives from each state depended on its population. But in the Senate each state had two senators. By 1819 there were 11 free states and 11 slave states. Thus, while southerners did not control the Senate, they could usually block legislation detrimental to their region. Neither the South nor the North wanted the balance in the Senate to tip in favor of the other.

The Missouri Compromise

In December 1818 Missouri, which had been part of the Louisiana Purchase, sought admission to the Union as a slave state. This request threatened the balance of power in the Senate. Northern members of Congress offered a counterproposal: admit Missouri as a slave state on the condition that no more slaves be brought into the state, and that all children of slaves be freed when they reached age 25. That way, Missouri would eventually become a free state.

Debate flared as northerners and southerners accused each other of trying to seize additional power and influence. Seventy-six-year-old Thomas Jefferson, observing the crisis from his plantation in Virginia, foresaw great danger to the Union: "This momentous question, like a firebell in the night, awakened and filled me with terror."

Henry Clay exercised his talents as a compromiser and, after long hours of negotiating, persuaded Congress to adopt a measure known as the Missouri Compromise. By admitting Missouri as a slave state and admitting

Maine, formerly part of Massachusetts, as a free state, Congress preserved the balance between free and slave states. The Missouri Compromise further provided that in the remaining portion of the Louisiana Purchase slavery would be prohibited forever north of latitude 36°30′, the southern boundary of Missouri, and would be permitted south of that line. Southerners accepted this limitation since plantation agriculture was unlikely to develop north of that line, and there would be less need for slaves. (See the map on page 306.)

Most Americans breathed a sigh of relief when Congress adopted the Missouri Compromise in 1820. Concerned citizens hoped that the slavery question had been settled to everyone's satisfaction and that it would gradually disappear. But the question persisted, and rivalry between North and South increased.

A Delicate Balance

Whenever a new state requested admission to the Union, the problem of maintaining a balance between the North and the South resurfaced. In 1836 and 1837 Arkansas and Michigan joined, the former a slave state, the latter a free state. But in 1845 Florida and Texas both entered as slave states. Additional free states (Iowa in 1846 and Wisconsin in 1848) soon restored the balance.

The outbreak of war with Mexico in 1846 raised a new problem, however. A victory over Mexico would add extensive territory to the United States. Since the Missouri Compromise applied only to territories in the Louisiana Purchase, a disturbing question arose: what would the status of slavery be in the new territories?

On a steamy Washington night in August 1846 Representative David Wilmot of Pennsylvania proposed an answer to the question. Congress was debating an appropriation for the purchase of land in the Southwest in connection with negotiations with Mexico. In a surprise move, Wilmot added a provision that would ban slavery forever from any territory acquired from Mexico.

Suddenly the congressmen, who had been wearily fanning themselves, plunged

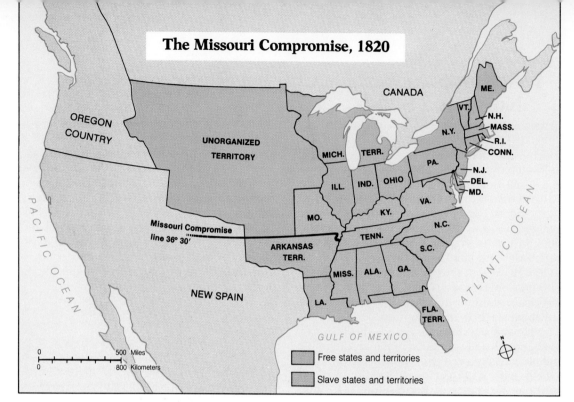

The Missouri Compromise, 1820

OREGON COUNTRY

UNORGANIZED TERRITORY

NEW SPAIN

Missouri Compromise line 36° 30'

Free states and territories

Slave states and territories

■ *The Missouri Compromise proposed by Henry Clay admitted Missouri as a slave state and Maine as a free state, thus maintaining a balance between slave and free states. The compromise also prohibited slavery in the Louisiana Purchase north of 36° 30' latitude.*

into a heated debate that threatened the long history of sectional compromise. The House passed the amendment, known as the Wilmot Proviso, but two days later the Senate defeated the measure. When the United States finally acquired the southwestern territory from Mexico in 1848, the peace treaty said nothing about slavery. The unsuccessful Wilmot Proviso had reopened the question of slavery in the new territories.

Positions on the Slavery Issue

As debate over the issue of slavery in the territories continued, various groups proposed remedies to the problem. David Wilmot's solution, which sought to exclude slavery from all territory gained from Mexico, represented the extreme northern position. Moderates from both North and South had long argued that slavery would eventually die out, but many northerners saw that slavery was spreading. In their opinion only firm legislative action would control it, so they supported the Wilmot Proviso.

John C. Calhoun, now a grizzled and gaunt old man, represented the extreme southern position. Slaves were personal property, he declared. The Fifth Amendment

to the Constitution specified that no person could be deprived of "life, liberty, or property without due process of law." Yet slave owners could be deprived of their property if they moved to a territory where slavery was forbidden. Therefore, Calhoun concluded, slavery should be permitted in all territories.

Between the extreme positions lay two moderate solutions. One group of moderates proposed that the Missouri Compromise line of 36°30' be extended west to the Pacific Ocean. Slavery would be prohibited north of the line but allowed south of it. President James Polk supported this solution. Senator Stephen Douglas of Illinois championed the idea of *popular sovereignty*. He proposed that the voters of each territory decide whether or not to allow slavery within the territory, regardless of where it was located.

Over the years the two moderate positions gradually lost support, and by the end of the 1850s the more extreme positions had become dominant.

Emergence of the Free Soil Party

During the election campaign of 1848, both the Democratic and Whig parties wanted to avoid the question of slavery in the territories, but many Democrats and Whigs in the North demanded a vigorous position against the expansion of slavery. Consequently they joined with members of the Liberty party (see page 296) and formed the Free Soil party. As you read in Chapter 16, the basis of the Free Soil party was its opposition to slavery in the territories. Despite some abolitionist and free black membership, the party did not advocate the abolition of slavery in existing states, North or South. In fact, many Free Soilers did not want any blacks, slave or free, in the territories.

In 1848 the Free Soilers nominated former President Martin Van Buren for President. The Democrats nominated Lewis Cass, a senator from Michigan who advocated popular sovereignty. The Whigs nominated Zachary Taylor, a hero of the Mexican War and a wealthy slave owner from Louisiana. Taylor had not taken a stand on the slavery question, but many assumed that he would support the South's position.

Taylor won the election in both the northern and the southern states. The Democrats and the Whigs had maintained their positions as national parties in 1848, but Van Buren won nearly 10 percent of the popular vote, receiving all his support from the North. The emergence of a political party whose strength lay in only one section of the nation showed that the issue of slavery in the territories was widening the split between South and North.

The Compromise of 1850

Although in 1848 the Democrats and Whigs had evaded the question of slavery in the southwestern territories, they were soon forced to address the issue. The discovery of gold had brought thousands of people to California, and in 1849 Californians requested admission to the Union as a free state. Since there were now 15 free states and 15 slave states, southerners opposed the admission, but northerners favored it.

When Congress convened in December 1849, the question of California's statehood was the subject of heated debate. Other issues also contributed to a bitter mood. Many northerners objected to the selling and buying of slaves in the nation's capital and wanted it ended. Southerners, in turn, demanded a more effective fugitive slave law to prevent abolitionists from helping slaves escape.

As the debate continued, tempers flared and the very existence of the Union seemed to be at stake. Henry Clay, who had earned the nickname "The Great Compromiser" during his long career, stepped forward to propose a solution that he hoped would satisfy both sides. Clay suggested that California be admitted as a free state but that the rest of the southwestern territory be open to slavery by popular sovereignty. Slave trade would be abolished in the District of Columbia, but Congress would officially declare that it had no power to abolish the slave trade between existing slave states. Finally, Congress would pass a strong fugitive slave law.

For six months Clay used all the bargaining skills and persuasive eloquence at his command to win support for the compromise. He received important support from Daniel Webster, his long-time rival, who believed that without a compromise the United States would be torn apart. When he addressed the Senate, Webster began, "I wish to speak today, not as a Massachusetts man, nor a northern man, but as an American. . . . I speak today for the preservation of the Union."

But John C. Calhoun, while strongly advocating the South's position, made the most dramatic warning about danger to the Union. Gravely ill, with only a month to live, Calhoun sat one last time in his Senate seat, staring fiercely ahead, too sick to read his speech, while Senator James Mason of Virginia read it for him.

"It is a great mistake to suppose that disunion can be effected at a single blow," Calhoun argued. "The cords which bind these states together in one common Union are far too numerous and powerful for that." Yet one by one these cords were being broken. "Already the agitation of the slavery question has snapped some of the most important, and has greatly weakened all the others. . . ." If controversy continued, he warned, the break-up of the United States would be inevitable.

Calhoun's stern warning, combined with the pleas of Webster and Clay, persuaded many members of Congress that the threat to the Union was real and that they should compromise once again. President Taylor vigorously opposed Clay's plan, but in the summer of 1850 he died suddenly. His successor, Millard Fillmore, supported the compromise, and in September Congress passed

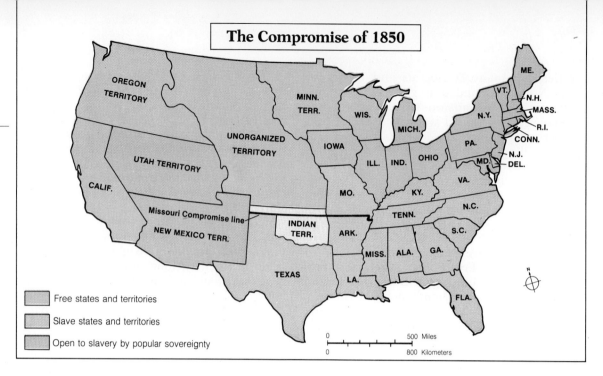

The Compromise of 1850

ME.
OREGON TERRITORY
MINN. TERR.
VT.
N.H.
MASS.
N.Y.
WIS.
MICH.
R.I.
CONN.
UNORGANIZED TERRITORY
IOWA
PA.
N.J.
UTAH TERRITORY
ILL. IND. OHIO
MD. DEL.
CALIF.
VA.
MO.
KY.
Missouri Compromise line
N.C.
TENN.
INDIAN TERR.
NEW MEXICO TERR.
ARK.
S.C.
MISS. ALA. GA.
TEXAS
LA.
FLA.

Free states and territories

Slave states and territories

Open to slavery by popular sovereignty

| 0 | | 500 Miles |
| 0 | | 800 Kilometers |

■ *According to the Compromise of 1850, California was to be admitted to the Union as a free state. The remainder of the southwestern territory acquired from Mexico, however, could be opened to slavery by popular sovereignty, that is, residents could decide whether to allow slavery.*

it. For the moment it appeared that compromise had succeeded one more time.

For answers, see p. A 52.

Section Review

1. Identify the following: David Wilmot, Stephen Douglas, Zachary Taylor.

2. Define the following terms: free state, slave state, popular sovereignty.

3. What were the two major provisions of the Missouri Compromise?

4. (a) What was the extreme northern position on slavery in the new territories? (b) What was the extreme southern position? (c) What were the two moderate positions?

5. What was the position of the Free Soil party on the issue of slavery in the territories?

6. (a) In what two ways would northerners benefit from the Compromise of 1850? (b) In what three ways would southerners benefit?

2 A Faltering Compromise

Most Americans hoped that the Compromise of 1850 would settle the questions dividing the North and the South. Yet portions of the compromise weakened it, and developments in Kansas soon revived the issue of slavery in the territories.

The Fugitive Slave Law

To southerners the new Fugitive Slave Law, part of the Compromise of 1850, represented only what was due them. They claimed that the Constitution permitted them to hold

slaves as property and that fugitive slaves were either runaways or stolen property and should be returned.

But many northerners bitterly resented certain provisions of the Fugitive Slave Law. For example, a person accused of being a fugitive slave had to stand trial before a special commissioner, not a judge. No jury heard the case, and the accused could not even testify in his or her own behalf. Furthermore, the commissioner received a $10 fee if he sent the accused fugitive back to slavery and only $5 if he freed the person.

This, angry northerners pointed out, amounted to little less than a bribe to insure that the accused was declared a runaway slave. Finally, the law required all citizens to assist in capturing a fugitive slave.

The new law terrified free blacks in the North. It permitted the retrieval not only of newly escaped slaves but of anyone who had ever fled from slavery. Thus a slave who had escaped many years earlier faced the prospect of being thrown in jail and returned to a former master in the South. Furthermore, the flimsy protections against incorrect identification meant that free blacks were in danger of being falsely claimed by slave owners as fugitives.

Newspapers throughout the North denounced the Fugitive Slave Law as "an outrage to humanity," "a hateful statute of kidnappers," and something that should be "resisted, disobeyed at all hazards." When slave owners from the South sent agents north in search of escaped slaves, abolitionists organized open resistance. Free blacks also set up vigilance committees to protect themselves against kidnappers.

Hatred of the Fugitive Slave Law was one reason for the immense popularity of Harriet Beecher Stowe's novel *Uncle Tom's Cabin,* published in 1852. With a brilliant grasp of the tensions slavery produced in American society, Stowe created scenes and images that haunted the imagination: the desperate flight to freedom of fugitive slaves,

Antislavery forces in the North printed posters such as this one to warn free blacks and fugitive slaves about the danger of being captured under the new Fugitive Slave Law.

the break-up of slave families and marriages, the cruel effects of slavery on blacks and whites alike. Southern leaders protested that slaves were treated much better than *Uncle Tom's Cabin* suggested, but thousands of

The Republic

Politicians were not the only Americans who feared for the fate of the United States in 1850. Henry Wadsworth Longfellow, one of the nation's most popular poets, expressed his faith in the republic in the following excerpt from the poem entitled *The Building of the Ship.*

Thou, too, sail on, O Ship of State!
Sail on, O UNION, strong and great!
Humanity with all its fears,
With all the hopes of future years,
Is hanging breathless on thy fate!
We know what Master laid thy keel,
What Workmen wrought thy ribs of steel,
Who made each mast, and sail, and rope,

What anvils rang, what hammers beat,
In what a forge and what a heat
Were shaped the anchors of thy hope!
Fear not each sudden sound and shock,
'Tis of the wave and not the rock;
'Tis but the flapping of the sail,
And not a rent made by the gale!
In spite of rock and tempest's roar,
In spite of false lights on the shore,
Sail on, nor fear to breast the sea!
Our hearts, our hopes, are all with thee,
Our hearts, our hopes, our prayers, our tears,
Our faith triumphant o'er our fears,
Are all with thee—are all with thee!

Source: Henry Wadsworth Longfellow, *Complete Poetical Works* (Boston: 1893).

northerners who read the book or saw the play came away determined to oppose the Fugitive Slave Law.

The Fugitive Slave Law increased sectional tensions because it affected northerners directly. Confronted with the plight of a slave seeking freedom, more and more northerners, even those previously immune to abolitionist appeals, sympathized with the fugitive. Nothing else stirred northern sensibilities in quite the same way.

Growing Political Division

Despite controversy over the Fugitive Slave Law, political leaders tried to minimize tensions during the presidential election of 1852. Both Whigs and Democrats accepted the Compromise of 1850, but the superficial similarities of the party platforms hid serious disagreements.

Disputes between northern and southern factions severely disrupted the Whig party, but northern Whigs finally pushed through the nomination of another war hero, General Winfield Scott, for President. Southern and northern Democrats quarreled too but avoided a split by nominating a little-known New Hampshire politician, Franklin Pierce. With the Whigs badly divided, Pierce won the election easily.

Northerners soon discovered, however, that President Pierce sympathized with many southern goals. In particular, Pierce hoped to obtain Cuba from Spain. If Cuba joined the United States, it would surely be as a slave territory and ultimately as a slave state.

In 1854 three of Pierce's diplomatic ministers, meeting in Ostend, Belgium, issued a manifesto, or declaration, in which they suggested that the United States try to buy Cuba from Spain. If that failed, the so-called Ostend Manifesto proclaimed boldly, Americans might be justified in seizing the island by force. President Pierce repudiated the statement, but northerners branded the act another attempt to expand slavery.

The Kansas-Nebraska Act

The question of slavery in the territories became an issue again in 1854 when Senator Stephen Douglas of Illinois introduced a bill in Congress to organize the vast Nebraska territory west of Iowa and Missouri. Douglas wanted to establish a transcontinental rail-

road by extending the existing lines from Chicago to the Pacific. The senator felt that such a route would be possible only if the Nebraska territory was organized.

According to the Missouri Compromise of 1820, slavery was prohibited in the Nebraska lands. But by 1854 a number of prominent southern senators had come to support John C. Calhoun's position that slavery ought to be permitted in all territories. Those senators refused to support Douglas's bill unless it allowed slavery within the Nebraska territory.

Douglas then proposed, and Congress passed, a compromise bill that divided the area into a Nebraska and a Kansas territory. The Kansas-Nebraska Act repealed the Missouri Compromise and in its place applied the doctrine of popular sovereignty. The people of each territory, rather than Congress, would decide whether to permit slavery.

Senator Douglas believed that popular sovereignty was the only democratic solution to the slavery question, but many northerners vehemently protested the repeal of the Missouri Compromise. They argued that the act created the possibility that any territory could be opened up to slavery.

Conflict Over Kansas

Most Americans assumed Nebraska would eventually become a free state because it was too far north for plantation agriculture. In addition, many thought Kansas would become a slave state because it was located directly west of Missouri, which was a slave state. But since the question of slavery would be decided by the voters, the final result remained uncertain.

Some abolitionist groups encouraged antislavery settlers to move to Kansas, hoping that the vote would go against slavery. The New England Emigrant Aid Society, for example, sent about 650 settlers to Kansas in 1854. Although the numbers were small, Missourians heard rumors that "mobs" of abolitionists were moving to Kansas. They feared that if slavery was not permitted in Kansas, their own slaves could easily escape across the border. Consequently proslavery elements encouraged settlers from Missouri to move to Kansas.

When the first elections to the territorial legislature were held in March 1855, about

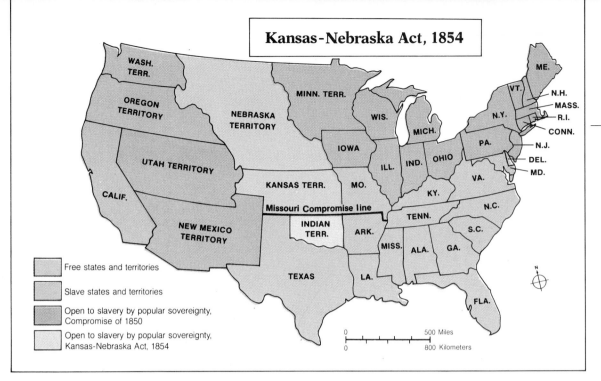

Kansas-Nebraska Act, 1854

WASH. TERR.

OREGON TERRITORY

ME.

VT.
N.H.
MASS.
R.I.
CONN.
N.J.
DEL.
MD.

MINN. TERR.

NEBRASKA TERRITORY

WIS.

N.Y.

PA.

UTAH TERRITORY

IOWA

MICH.

CALIF.

KANSAS TERR.

MO.

ILL.

IND.

OHIO

VA.

KY.

Missouri Compromise line

NEW MEXICO TERRITORY

INDIAN TERR.

ARK.

TENN.

N.C.

S.C.

MISS.

ALA.

GA.

TEXAS

LA.

FLA.

Free states and territories

Slave states and territories

Open to slavery by popular sovereignty, Compromise of 1850

Open to slavery by popular sovereignty, Kansas-Nebraska Act, 1854

0   500 Miles

0   800 Kilometers

■ The Kansas-Nebraska Act applied the principle of popular sovereignty in the Nebraska and Kansas territories. The act repealed the Missouri Compromise by allowing slavery in territories north of the Missouri Compromise line if the voters wanted it.

8,000 settlers lived in Kansas. Proslavery voters outnumbered antislavery voters by more than a thousand and could have won the election fairly. But several thousand angry Missouri "border ruffians" crossed into Kansas and voted illegally, giving the proslavery forces a lopsided victory.

Northerners promptly claimed the election had been stolen. They became even more incensed when the territorial legislature passed harsh proslavery laws. One law made it a crime to declare slavery illegal in Kansas; another ordered the death penalty for anyone who helped an escaped slave. In response to these actions antislavery settlers in Kansas refused to recognize the authority of the territorial government and established a rival free-state government at Lawrence, Kansas.

Chaos soon reigned throughout the territory, with two separate governments proclaiming authority and armed bands roaming the countryside. Finally, in May 1856 three events made the Kansas issue the focus of national attention. On May 21 a mob of Missourians acting as a sheriff's posse charged into Lawrence, looted and burned several houses, threw two printing presses into the river, and bombarded the Free State Hotel with cannon.

On May 22 Senator Charles Sumner of Massachusetts delivered a speech denouncing the violence in Kansas. Sumner charged that slave owners, including some of his colleagues in the Senate, were responsible. The next day Congressman Preston Brooks of South Carolina, a cousin of one of South Carolina's senators, attacked Sumner with a cane as he sat at his Senate desk. The injured Massachusetts senator was unable to resume his duties in the Senate for three years, and he never fully recovered.

On the night of May 24 a little-known Kansas antislavery agitator named John Brown took vengeance for the Lawrence attack into his own hands. Brown and a group of followers massacred five southern men and boys at a proslavery settlement at Pottawatomie Creek, Kansas, even though the victims had had nothing to do with the Lawrence raid.

The three violent events, following one another so closely, demonstrated how badly the Compromise of 1850 had failed. One of its major elements, the Fugitive Slave Law, had outraged the North. The question of extending slavery to the territories, which the compromise was supposed to settle, had been raised more violently than ever on the battleground of "Bleeding Kansas."

For answers, see p. A 52.

Section Review

1. Identify the following: *Uncle Tom's Cabin*, Franklin Pierce, Ostend Manifesto, John Brown.

2. (a) How did southerners justify the Fugitive Slave Law? (b) What aspects of the law especially angered northerners?

3. What were the provisions of the Kansas-Nebraska Act?

4. (a) What was the outcome of the first territorial elections in Kansas? (b) What led to the establishment of a free-state government?

5. What three events caused the Kansas issue to become the center of national attention?

3 Rise of Sectional Politics

The Whigs and Democrats as national political parties had been important "cords" binding the Union together since the mid-1830s. They had traditionally received support from both southern and northern states. However, growing sectional strains, aggravated by events in Kansas, divided the national parties and gave rise to a new political party.

Birth of the Republican Party

Citizens who opposed the expansion of slavery into the territories, known as *free soilers*, could find little hope in either the Whig or the Democratic party.* By the mid-1850s the Whigs had been seriously weakened by disputes between northern and southern factions; and the Democratic President, Franklin Pierce, had shown that he was sympathetic to the South.

During the summer of 1854, conventions of free soilers met in several northern states, hoping to form a new political party. At one such convention in Jackson, Michigan, the delegates for the first time called themselves Republicans. In the course of the next year, a sizable number of former Whigs, Democrats, and Free Soilers joined the Republicans, who were convinced that they could become a major party opposing the extension of slavery into the territories.

The Republican party grew rapidly. By 1856 they had elected some of their candidates to Congress and won several state elections. That same year they made their first bid for the presidency, nominating John Frémont, the impulsive, swashbuckling military leader who had encouraged the Bear Flag Revolt in California.

The Democrats chose James Buchanan of Pennsylvania. Buchanan supported the Kansas-Nebraska Act and popular sovereignty, but he remained vague about how or when the people of Kansas and Nebraska would decide the question of slavery. The remnants of the Whig and Know-Nothing parties both nominated former President Millard Fillmore in separate conventions, but the contest was between Frémont and Buchanan.

Republicans knew they had no chance in the South; most southern states did not even allow the names of Republican candidates on the ballot. But because the North had a majority of the electoral votes, the Republicans thought Frémont could win. When the ballots were counted, Buchanan had won—but only by a narrow margin.

The 1856 election demonstrated just how divided the nation had become. Buchanan carried every southern state except Maryland. Frémont carried every free state except Pennsylvania, Indiana, Illinois, New Jersey, and California. Increasingly, the Democrats spoke for the South, the Republicans for the North.

The Dred Scott Decision

A few months after Buchanan's victory, the Supreme Court rocked the nation with a major proslavery decision in the case of *Dred Scott* v. *Sandford.* Dred Scott had been a slave in Missouri. His owner served in the army for several years and took Scott with him to Illinois, a free state, and to Minnesota, a free territory. Eventually Scott's owner returned to Missouri.

---

*Both the Liberty and Free Soil parties had remained active for only a short period of time.

When Scott's owner died, some abolitionists aided Scott in suing for his freedom, claiming that he was free by virtue of his residence in Illinois and Minnesota. After a series of trials and conflicting judgments in the lower courts, the case finally went to the United States Supreme Court.

The Supreme Court faced two major questions in this decision. First, was Scott entitled to bring suit in a federal court? Slaves had no right to sue, and it was not even clear whether free blacks were United States citizens and as such had the right to sue. The Constitution itself did not specifically define the qualifications for citizenship. The second question was whether Scott's residence in a free state and a free territory had made him a free man.

The Court ruled that persons of African descent, whether slave or free, could not be citizens of the United States, and therefore Scott could not sue in a federal court. Missouri law, it concluded, should determine Scott's status, and according to Missouri law Scott was a slave.

The Court went further, ruling that the Missouri Compromise was unconstitutional because it had prohibited slavery north of 36°30′. Under the Fifth Amendment, the Court declared, Congress had no power to deprive anyone of property without due process of law. Because slaves were property, Congress could not forbid owners to take them into free territories—which was, in effect, what the Missouri Compromise had done.

The Dred Scott decision shocked a great many northerners, even moderates. First, it affirmed the most extreme southern position, that slavery could not be outlawed in any territory. Second, the decision marked the first time the Supreme Court had ruled a major piece of federal legislation unconstitutional. Only once before (*Marbury* v. *Madison,* see page 190) had it ruled any law unconstitutional.

Republicans were especially incensed. Above all, their party stood for the principle that Congress had the right to keep slavery out of the territories. And now the Supreme Court had, in effect, ruled that the party's goals were unconstitutional.

Northern Democrats, led by Stephen Douglas, also felt the shock. The Court by implication had ruled against the doctrine of popular sovereignty. If Congress had no power to prohibit slavery in the territories, then neither could it delegate that power to a territorial legislature.

A Senate Race With National Implications

As controversy enveloped the country, national attention focused on the 1858 Senate race in Illinois, in which the Democratic and Republican candidates skillfully debated the issues that divided the country.

The Democratic candidate, Senator Stephen Douglas, was the more well known of the two men. Douglas was just over five feet tall, with a large head and broad shoulders. A scrapper who loved an argument, he had a burning, energetic drive. Few could match his debating skills on the Senate floor, where he had helped Henry Clay push through the Compromise of 1850 and had vigorously defended the doctrine of popular sovereignty.

Dred Scott v. *Sandford*

The text of the Dred Scott decision, as expressed in the following opinion by Chief Justice Roger B. Taney, affirmed the position argued by John C. Calhoun that the Constitution protected a citizen's property, including slaves.

[T]he rights of property are united with the rights of person, and placed on the same ground by the fifth amendment to the Constitution, which provides that no person shall be deprived of life, liberty and property, without due process of law. And an Act of Congress which deprives a citizen of the United States of his liberty or property, merely because he came himself or brought his property into a particular Territory of the United States, and who had committed no offense against the laws, could hardly be dignified with the name of due process of law. . . .

And no word can be found in the Constitution which gives Congress a greater power over slave property, or which entitles property of that kind to less protection than property of any other description. The only power conferred is the power coupled with the duty of guarding and protecting the owner in his rights.

313

Stephen Douglas (left) was a nationally known leader of the Democratic party in 1856. His opponent for a seat in the United States Senate was the little-known Abraham Lincoln (right). Lincoln became a national figure as a result of a series of debates with Douglas.

Douglas's Republican opponent was a respected lawyer named Abraham Lincoln. Born in Kentucky, Lincoln had moved with his family to Indiana and then to Illinois, where he combined his law practice with a career in politics, first as a Whig and then as a Republican.

At six feet four inches, Lincoln was as tall and lanky as Douglas was short and stocky. Self-educated and unpretentious, the Republican ·candidate combined a folksy, backwoods manner with a keen legal mind that instinctively sought out the logic of a situation in its clearest, simplest terms. Lincoln appeared awkward and homely and lacked a polished speaking style, but he had a sharp sense of humor, an easy manner with all sorts of people, and a compelling eloquence.

He had sounded his campaign theme in his speech accepting the nomination for senator. Beginning with the biblical observation that "a house divided against itself cannot stand," Lincoln stated his case:

> I believe this government cannot endure, permanently half slave and half free. I do not expect the Union to be dissolved; I do not expect the house to fall; but I do expect it will cease to be divided. It will become all one thing, or all the other.

The Lincoln-Douglas Debates

As the lesser-known of the two candidates, Lincoln challenged Douglas to a series of debates during the campaign. In seven memorable appearances the "Little Giant," as people called Douglas, squared off against "Honest Abe." Cheering crowds, bands, and torchlight parades accompanied their appearances, and the debaters faced the controversial issue of slavery squarely and directly. Newspapers across the country reprinted the candidates' words, and citizens argued over who was more persuasive.

Lincoln argued that the major philosophical difference between Republicans and northern Democrats like Douglas was the Republican belief that the institution of slavery was morally wrong. Douglas, Lincoln pointed out, had said he did not care whether slavery was accepted or rejected in the territories. Although Lincoln believed that blacks and whites might not be equal, he maintained that blacks were entitled to "all the natural rights enumerated in the Declaration of Independence, the right to life, liberty, and the pursuit of happiness."

Douglas sought to defend the doctrine of popular sovereignty as fair and workable. At a debate in Freeport, Illinois, Lincoln pressed Douglas to reconcile his doctrine of popular sovereignty with the Dred Scott decision. The Supreme Court had ruled that slavery must be allowed in every territory. Was there any legal way, Lincoln asked, that the residents of a territory could exercise popular sovereignty and prohibit slavery?

Douglas replied that since slavery could not exist without a slave code to protect it, the people of a territory could simply refuse to enact a slave code. Douglas's solution, soon known as the Freeport Doctrine, gained him the support of many voters. In the election, he defeated Lincoln by a narrow margin.

The senator's victory cost his party dearly. The Freeport Doctrine impressed northern Democrats, but southerners considered it an act of treachery. From their point of view, Douglas was encouraging settlers in the territories to stop slavery from spreading. This drove a deeper wedge between northern and southern Democrats and further weakened the Democrats as a national party.

For answers, see p. A 52.
Section Review ▓▓▓▓▓▓▓▓▓▓▓

1. Identify the following: Dred Scott, Abraham Lincoln, Freeport Doctrine.

2. Define the following term: free soiler.

3. What issue led to the creation of the Republican party?

4. How did the election of 1856 demonstrate the divisions in the nation?

5. (a) How did the Supreme Court rule regarding Dred Scott's right to sue? (b) In the Court's opinion, why was Scott still a slave?

6. What did Lincoln consider the main philosophical difference between Republicans and northern Democrats?

4 The House Divided

The 1850s had begun with a concerted effort to put aside the differences that separated North and South. Yet by 1859 the country had been split apart in many ways. At the center of the conflict was slavery, the issue that would not go away. As the presidential election of 1860 approached, the nation resembled a powder keg waiting for a spark to ignite it.

Harpers Ferry

John Brown struck the spark. Brown, a Kansas abolitionist, had shocked the South and much of the rest of the nation by leading the massacre at Pottawatomie Creek. He seemed to be a strange, violent man with a flair for the dramatic. After his raids in Kansas, Brown returned east and began raising money for a mysterious mission. Concealing the details, he would only hint at his plan.

Some of the more radical abolitionists financed Brown's activities, knowing that he planned a raid on southern plantations to free slaves and begin a rebellion. When Frederick Douglass heard about the plan, he warned that it would not succeed. As an escaped slave, Douglass knew conditions in the South firsthand and recognized that the plan was impractical, but Brown would not change his mind.

On the night of October 15, 1859, Brown led a band of 18 men to the federal arsenal at Harpers Ferry, Virginia, seized its weapons, and waited for slaves to rise in rebellion and join him. But Brown had made several mistakes. Few slaves lived in the area of Harpers Ferry, and they were unlikely to stake their lives on the leadership of a man they

had never heard of. Furthermore, Brown lingered at Harpers Ferry until all avenues of escape were cut off. A day after the attack, United States troops led by Colonel Robert E. Lee easily subdued the raiders.

Brown's military conduct was amateurish, but he carried himself with dignity and calm when he was brought to trial for treason. Even his southern jailer and guards were impressed. Brown's dignity also won him sympathy in the North—and he knew the strategic value of martyrdom. On December 2, state authorities hanged Brown from a scaffold in Charlestown, Virginia, following his conviction.

A Charged Atmosphere

In the North church bells tolled in mourning. Black bunting hung on windows, and sympathizers held mass prayer meetings in New York, Boston, and Philadelphia. John Brown's death proved more effective in mobilizing antislavery opinion than his actions had. Despite the show of sympathy, however, many northern leaders, including Republican party members, repudiated Brown's actions and dismissed him as a lunatic.

In the South, however, such words had little effect. Southerners heard about the church bells and prayer meetings and read some abolitionist speeches calling for slave insurrections. Increasingly they came to believe that their security could be maintained only by *seceding,* or withdrawing, from the Union. One Virginia newspaper noted that there were "thousands of men in our midst who, a month ago, scoffed at the idea of a

In this painting by the black artist Horace Pippin, the fierce abolitionist John Brown is hauled to his execution in 1859. At right, a black woman turns away in despair as Brown rides his own coffin to the gallows. Pippin's mother told him she had watched Brown's execution.

dissolution of the Union as a madman's dream, but who now hold the opinion that its days are numbered."

In Washington tensions had grown so high that senators and representatives often went to legislative sessions armed, and some claimed that spectators in the galleries carried weapons too. When a pistol accidentally fell from the pocket of a New York congressman during one heated debate, a shooting fray nearly erupted. "The only persons who do not have a revolver and a knife," reported one South Carolina senator, "are those who have two revolvers."

The 1860 Conventions

In this atmosphere of increasing suspicion and distrust, the presidential nominating conventions assembled. The Democrats met in Charleston, South Carolina. Some southerners, determined to defeat Stephen Douglas and the northern Democrats, demanded that the party endorse a federal code to protect slavery in all territories. When the convention rejected this platform, those delegates walked out.

Unable to agree on a nominee, the convention finally adjourned, to reassemble six weeks later in Baltimore, Maryland. There the delegates quickly nominated Douglas. A group of southern Democrats then held their own convention, adopted the original southern platform, and nominated John Breckinridge of Kentucky to head their ticket.

A new party, the Constitutional Union party, also held a convention in 1860 and nominated John Bell of Tennessee for President. The Constitutional Unionists denounced the sectionalism of the other parties. They hoped to rally conservatives in both South and North around a vague platform that supported the Constitution and one Union.

The Republican convention met in Chicago in the Wigwam, a building specially constructed for the event. Hundreds of enthusiastic Republicans squeezed inside while a crowd of as many as 20,000 people cheered outside.

The leading contender for the nomination as the convention opened was William H. Seward of New York. Seward, however, had a reputation as a radical, and party leaders worried that he could not win. As they searched for a more moderate candidate, their attention focused on Abraham Lincoln, whom all factions of the party found acceptable. In addition, Lincoln came from Illinois, a state Republicans needed to carry in 1860. He received the nomination on the third ballot.

In 1860 the Republicans sought to broaden their platform. They endorsed a protective tariff, which was popular in the industrial areas of the Northeast, and a homestead law, granting free land to settlers, which was popular throughout the West. Moreover, their statements about slavery were less shrill than in 1856, although the party continued to insist that Congress ban slavery from all territories.

The Election of 1860

The presidential campaign of 1860 revealed just how close to disunion the country was. Lincoln's supporters did not campaign in the South, and his name was not even on the ballot in ten southern states. Breckinridge, on the other hand, had virtually no support in the North. Only Douglas, weary but determined, campaigned actively in both northern and southern states, warning of the dire consequences of disunion. A month before the election, Douglas knew his chances were lost, and he predicted that Lincoln would be elected.

On November 6, the voters confirmed Douglas's prediction. Lincoln received 39 percent of the popular vote and carried every northern state except New Jersey. Breckinridge swept the deep South and divided the border states with Bell and Douglas. Although Douglas finished last in the electoral college, he received more popular votes than anyone except Lincoln.

Lincoln's election marked a dramatic change in American politics. He was the first President to be elected by a sectional party with its strength entirely in the North. To southerners the future was particularly alarming. A man had been elected President who was not even on the ballot in their part of the country. The North had simply outvoted them. Since the South now had only one third of the total white male population of the United States, many southerners concluded that the only way they could continue to play a role in any national government was to secede and form a government of their own. (See map on page 318.)

(See map on page 318.)

The Secession Crisis

South Carolina, which had threatened to secede during the nullification crisis of 1832 (see page 238), again took the strongest action. Its legislature called a convention and, on December 20, 1860, the convention adopted an ordinance of secession, stating that South Carolina was no longer part of the Union but was now a free and independent state. By the end of February 1861, the seven states of the deep South had followed South Carolina's lead. (See map on page 324.)

In February delegates from the seceded states met in Montgomery, Alabama, and formed the Confederate States of America. As their frame of government they adopted most features of the United States Constitution, making only a few changes. They stressed the "sovereign and independent character" of each individual state, and they made it clear that slaves could be held as property.

On February 18 Jefferson Davis of Mississippi was inaugurated as the President of the Confederate States. Davis, a former United States senator, read his inaugural address while new military companies clad in red, green, and gray battle jackets paraded with new bayonets on their rifles.

In the North, meanwhile, James Buchanan watched these developments with an increasing feeling of powerlessness. He was a *lame duck* President, serving until his successor's inauguration. The Democrats had not renominated him, and the voters had rejected his policies by electing Lincoln. So Buchanan did little.

In December 1860 Congress made one last attempt to hold the Union together. Senator John Crittenden of Kentucky proposed that the Missouri Compromise line be restored and applied to all territory then part of or later acquired by the United States. He also suggested that an "unamendable"

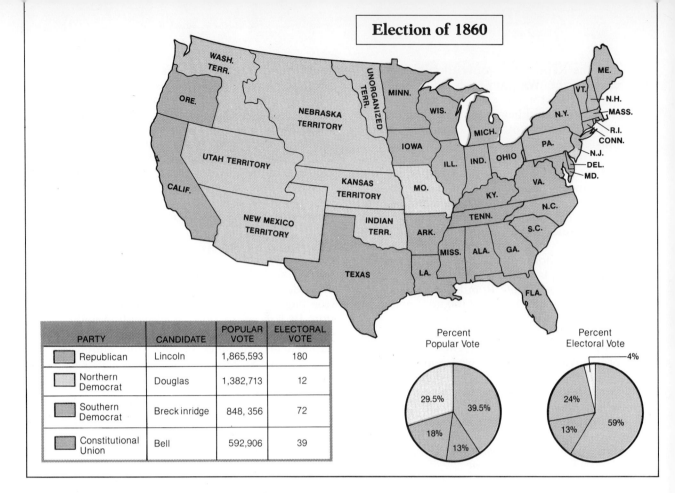

Election of 1860

PARTY	CANDIDATE	POPULAR VOTE	ELECTORAL VOTE
Republican	Lincoln	1,865,593	180
Northern Democrat	Douglas	1,382,713	12
Southern Democrat	Breck inridge	848, 356	72
Constitutional Union	Bell	592,906	39

Percent Popular Vote

39.5%
29.5%
18%
13%

Percent Electoral Vote

4%
59%
24%
13%

 The deep divisions of the nation in 1860 were shown vividly in the results of the presidential election. Lincoln carried every northern state except New Jersey, while Breckinridge swept the deep South. Border states were split between Bell, Douglas, and Breckinridge.

amendment be added to the Constitution to forever guarantee the right of slavery in states south of the compromise line. But Republicans refused to support these or any other compromise proposals, so Crittenden held no hope of getting them passed. The breach between North and South had become too wide for compromise.

Fort Sumter

When Abraham Lincoln became President in March 1861, the seceded states hoped that the North would allow them to depart in peace. Across the South, Confederate forces seized federal arsenals and forts. Only Fort Sumter, on an island outside Charleston Harbor, and three forts in Florida remained in federal hands.

Lincoln was determined to hold the Union together. Yet he faced a delicate situation. The northern section of the South, including the key state of Virginia, had rejected secession and remained in the Union.

If Lincoln used force rashly, he would risk losing the border states.

Events finally forced Lincoln to act. Major Robert Anderson, the commander of Fort Sumter, reported that his supplies were running low. Confederate forces were ready to take the fort, and he could not hold out much longer unless resupplied. Lincoln was determined not to surrender federal authority without a fight, yet he did not want the North to be guilty of starting a civil war. After much deliberation, he notified Confederate officials that he would not reinforce the fort with either arms or men. He promised to send only food.

In Charleston, Confederate General P.G.T. Beauregard demanded that Major Anderson surrender Fort Sumter. Anderson told the Confederates that he would withdraw on April 15 if he did not receive supplies or other orders.

But southern suspicion of northern intentions ran high. At four-thirty on the morn-

For answers, see p. A 53.

Causes of the Civil War: Analyzing Interpretations

As you know, eyewitness accounts of the same event often vary. Historians also interpret events differently even if they study the same sources. Their environment, especially the mood and events of the time in which they live, is one factor that can influence their *frame of reference*, or the way they view an historical event.

Historians have long disagreed about the causes of the Civil War. Excerpts from the works of two historians are presented at right. The first account was written by Frank Owsley in 1930, the second by Arthur Schlesinger, Jr., in 1949. Follow the steps below to analyze their interpretations of the causes of the Civil War.

1. **Identify the interpretation.** Answer the following questions about the accounts at right: (a) What does Owsley seem to think was the basic cause of the Civil War? (b) What does Schlesinger seem to think was a major cause?

2. **Decide how a person's frame of reference affects his or her interpretation.** To complete this step, you need to know about the time period in which the historian lived. The years after 1929 were ones of severe economic depression in the United States, and many people were trying to understand the reasons for the depression. After the Allies had defeated Germany in 1945, Americans were shocked and horrified to learn about the Nazi concentration camps in which millions of people were treated inhumanely and killed. Use this brief background information to answer the following questions: (a) Can you find any evidence that concern about the nation's economy after 1929 may have influenced Owsley's interpretation of the causes of the Civil War? (b) How might the discovery of the existence of Nazi concentration camps have affected Schlesinger's interpretation of the causes of the Civil War?

3. **Decide which interpretation you think is most accurate.** Use what you have learned about the history of the United States during the first half of the nineteenth century to answer the following questions: (a) What role do you think the economic relationship between the industrial North and the agricultural South played in the growing sectional splits and the outbreak of war? (b) What impact do you think the moral aspects of the slavery issue had on the growing sectional splits and the outbreak of war? (c) Based on all you have read, what other factors do you think were important in the eventual outbreak of war between the North and the South?

Frank Owsley

[S]lavery as a moral issue is too simple an explanation. . . . Complex though the factors were which finally caused war, they all grew out of two fundamental differences which existed between the two sections: the North was commercial and industrial, and the South was agrarian. . . . Herein lies the irrepressible conflict, the eternal struggle between the agrarian South and the commercial and industrial North to control the government either in its own interest or, negatively, to prevent the other section from controlling it in its interests. . . . The irrepressible conflict, then, was not between slavery and freedom, but between the industrial and commercial civilization of the North and the agrarian civilization of the South.

Arthur Schlesinger, Jr.

It was the moral issue of slavery, for example, that gave the struggles over slavery in the territories or over the enforcement of the fugitive slave laws their significance. . . . To say that the Civil War was fought over the "unreal" issue of slavery in the territories is like saying that the Second World War was fought over the "unreal" issue of the invasion of Poland. The democracies could not challenge fascism inside Germany any more than opponents of slavery could challenge slavery inside the South; but the extension of slavery, like the extension of fascism, was an act of aggression which made a moral choice inescapable. . . . Human slavery is certainly one of the few issues of whose evil we can be sure. It is not just "a very ancient labor system," it is also a betrayal of the basic values of our Christian and democratic tradition. No historian can understand the circumstances which led to its abolition until he writes about it in its fundamental moral context.

ing of April 12, Confederate batteries opened fire on the fort. All day long the Confederates kept up the bombardment while fashionable ladies and gentlemen of Charleston watched from the shore. On April 13, his ammunition gone, Anderson accepted Beauregard's terms of evacuation and marched out of the fort.

The tension of waiting was broken. Both sides had chosen war to achieve their goals. The attack on Fort Sumter boosted morale in the South, and because Lincoln's cautious

Major Events	
1820	Missouri Compromise
1846	Wilmot Proviso proposed
1849	California seeks admission to Union
1850	Compromise of 1850
1852	*Uncle Tom's Cabin* published; Franklin Pierce elected President
1854	Kansas-Nebraska Act
1856	James Buchanan elected President
1859	John Brown leads raid at Harpers Ferry
1860	Abraham Lincoln elected President; South Carolina secedes from Union
1861	Confederate States of America formed; Fort Sumter falls

diplomacy had forced the South to fire the first shot, the North rallied behind the cause of Union with a sense of moral outrage.

For answers, see p. A 53.

Section Review

1. Identify the following: Harpers Ferry, Constitutional Union party, Confederate States of America, Jefferson Davis, Fort Sumter.

2. Define the following terms: secede, lame duck.

3. (a) What effect did John Brown's death have in the North? (b) What effect did it have in the South?

4. Why did Republican party leaders choose Abraham Lincoln as their presidential candidate in 1860?

5. How did the election of 1860 convince many southerners that the southern states should secede from the Union?

6. (a) What effect did the attack on Fort Sumter have on the South's morale? (b) How did it affect the North?

★ ★ ★ ★ ★ ★ ★ ★ ★ ★ ★ ★ ★ ★ ★ ★ ★ ★ ★ ★

IN PERSPECTIVE   From the 1820s through the 1850s attempts were made to resolve conflicts between the North and the South. The Missouri Compromise, which prohibited slavery in the Louisiana Purchase north of latitude 36°30′, worked as long as the balance between slave and free states was maintained in the Senate. In 1848 vast new territories were added to the nation, and the question of slavery in the territories became a major issue.

The Compromise of 1850 was an attempt to solve the problem by admitting California as a free state but allowing slavery in the rest of the Southwest. The compromise included a strong fugitive slave law that was opposed by many northerners. When the Kansas and Nebraska territories were organized, the status of slavery there was to be decided by popular vote. This led to violent conflict in Kansas, which further divided the nation.

The two national political parties, the Whigs and the Democrats, were also divided by sectional strains, and the Republican party emerged in opposition to the extension of slavery to the territories. John Brown's raid at Harpers Ferry in 1859 contributed to an already charged political atmosphere. When Abraham Lincoln was elected in 1860, many southerners thought they had no choice but to secede from the Union. The bombardment of Fort Sumter marked the beginning of war between North and South.

John C. Calhoun's stern prophecy of 1850 had been tragically fulfilled. One by one the cords of Union had broken, and in 1861 one nation became two. Whether they would remain separated would be decided by four years of bitter fighting and heroic sacrifice.

For answers, see p. A 54.

Chapter Review

1. (a) Why was a balance between North and South in the Senate important? (b) Why was it probably more important to southerners than to northerners? (c) How was the balance maintained between 1820 and 1848?

2. (a) Why did the acquisition of territory from Mexico in 1848 complicate the problem of slavery in the territories? (b) What solution was proposed in the Wilmot Proviso? (c) Describe the other three proposed solutions. (d) Which two solutions were most moderate? (e) Which were most extreme?

3. (a) Why did California's request for admission to the Union cause heated debate in Congress? (b) How did the Compromise of 1850 try to solve the question raised by California's request for admission? (c) What other problems did the Compromise of 1850 try to solve?

4. (a) Why was a strong fugitive slave law important to slave owners? (b) Why did the new Fugitive Slave Law increase sectional tensions? (c) Why did free blacks feel threatened by it?

5. (a) How was the question of slavery to be decided in the Kansas and Nebraska territories? (b) How did that method differ from the one established by the Missouri Compromise? (c) Why did it lead to violent conflict in Kansas?

6. (a) Why was the Republican party formed? (b) What was the significance of its showing in the 1856 election?

7. (a) What did the Supreme Court rule in the Dred Scott decision? (b) How did the decision affect the status of slavery in the territories? (c) Why were Republicans especially shocked by the decision? (d) How did it affect northern Democrats?

8. (a) Why were the Lincoln-Douglas debates important? (b) What was Douglas's Freeport Doctrine? (c) What impact did the doctrine have on the Democratic party?

9. How did John Brown's raid at Harpers Ferry contribute to the tense atmosphere of 1860?

10. (a) Why were there two Democratic candidates for President in 1860? (b) How did the Republicans try to broaden their support? (c) How did the results of the election demonstrate the seriousness of the sectional split?

11. (a) Why did Lincoln's election lead southerners to seriously consider secession? (b) Which state seceded first? (c) Which other states followed? (d) Why did President Lincoln want to react cautiously?

For answers, see p. A 55.

For Further Thought

1. (a) How had the national political parties, the Whigs and Democrats, been a cord binding the Union together? (b) How did the presidential elections of 1848, 1852, 1856, and 1860 show the gradual breaking of this cord?

2. Why was the term Bleeding Kansas used to describe the territory after passage of the Kansas-Nebraska Act?

3. Why did John Brown's death probably create more sympathy for abolitionism than his actions at Pottawatomie Creek and Harpers Ferry?

4. (a) In what way was the Constitution of the Confederate States of America similar to the Articles of Confederation. (See page 145.) (b) Why do you think the principle of states' rights was so important to the Confederate states?

For answers, see p. A 55.

Developing Basic Skills

1. *Map Reading* Study the map on page 306 and answer the following questions: (a) To what territory did the Missouri Compromise line apply? (b) Why would it have been difficult to apply the Missouri Compromise line to California? (c) Based on that map and the maps on pages 308 and 311, how did each of the following change the status of slavery in the territory west of Iowa and Missouri: Missouri Compromise, Compromise of 1850, Kansas-Nebraska Act.

2. *Placing Events in Time* Construct a time line with 1820 as the starting date and 1861 as the end date. Write in the events that contributed to the growing split between South and North. (Review Chapters 13 through 17 for possible events.) When you have completed your time line, answer the following questions: (a) In which decade did most events occur? (b) Does the time line provide evidence to support the belief that a division of the nation was becoming increasingly likely?

See page 776 for suggested readings.

Divided by War

(1861–1865)

Confederate soldier, Private Edwin Francis Jenson.

Chapter Outline

1 *Preparing for War*

2 *War Begins*

3 *Freedom*

4 *Behind the Lines*

5 *An End to the War*

With the fall of Fort Sumter, a war fever swept the divided nation. Throughout North and South a similar scene repeated itself: wives, sweethearts, and children cheered as volunteers marched down the streets carrying an assortment of weapons, extra clothes, cooking utensils, and 'perhaps some cakes or cookies from home. "So impatient did I become for starting," wrote one eager Arkansas youth, "that I felt like a thousand pins were pricking me . . . and I started off a week in advance of my brothers."

Most Americans thought the conflict would be brief and decisive, but it stretched into four years of bloody combat. In the end more Americans died in the Civil War than in any war the nation has fought before or since.

That the war was a civil war, fought between two regions of one nation, made it particularly painful. While General Robert E. Lee led Confederate troops, his cousin Samuel Lee was an officer in the Union navy. Three grandsons of Henry Clay fought for the North, four grandsons fought for the South.

The war also produced dramatic political, economic, and social changes that were to have a more enduring effect on the nation than all the battles, hardships, triumphs, and tragedies.

322

1 Preparing for War

The guns at Fort Sumter began the war, but it took a great while for the North and the South to prepare for military conflict. The Union had just inaugurated a new President, Abraham Lincoln, who held responsibility for pursuing the war. He had to oversee the calling of troops, the organizing of supplies, and the raising of money.

The South faced similar problems, with the added disadvantage that their Confederate government was only a month old. For President Jefferson Davis and his administration, the tasks of organization and preparation were even greater.

The Border States

As the two sides prepared for war, one major question loomed above all others. On whose side would the unaligned states fight? Seven states had not yet committed themselves to either the Union or the Confederacy.

President Lincoln forced a decision on the question three days after the attack on Fort Sumter. On April 15, 1861, he issued a call to the state governors for 75,000 militiamen. Those states that had not seceded had to decide whether to send soldiers to fight the Confederacy or join it. Virginia, Arkansas, Tennessee, and North Carolina seceded; Maryland, Missouri, and Kentucky wavered.

The situation in Maryland was tense. If Maryland joined the Confederacy, the Union capital, Washington, D.C., would be surrounded by Confederate territory. After Confederate sympathizers attacked Union troops in Baltimore, President Lincoln decided to act. On April 27 he sent federal troops to occupy the city, proclaimed martial law in Maryland, and suspended *habeas corpus*, the right not to be imprisoned without a trial. He then jailed the most blatant Confederate supporters, including some state legislators.

With the major opposition in prison, the Maryland legislature defeated a resolution to secede. Although the state remained in the Union, many of its citizens continued to sympathize with the Confederate cause.

At first Kentucky tried to remain neutral, but Lincoln's careful personal diplomacy toward his home state fostered sympathy there for the federal government. A Confederate invasion of the state in September 1861 gave Kentucky's pro-Union legislature an excuse to throw its support to Lincoln, ending the state's neutrality.

In Missouri sporadic fighting occurred between groups favoring opposing sides until a decisive battle in 1862 secured the state for the Union. Three critical states had sided with the Union. (See the map on page 324.)

The South's Position

When the war began, each side was confident of victory. Southerners believed they were fighting a war for independence similar to the Revolutionary War. They did not intend to carry the war to the North. Their aim was to defend their homeland. The North faced the difficult task of invading. Northern lines of supply would have to be much longer than Confederate supply lines and would thus be more open to attack.

Soldiers from the rural South had the additional advantage of being generally more experienced than many northerners in the use of firearms and horses. The southerners often hunted game and felt at home in the outdoors. Furthermore, Confederate military leaders were among the best in the nation. Many had been trained at the United States Military Academy at West Point, including talented men like Robert E. Lee, Thomas "Stonewall" Jackson, and Joseph Johnston.

Despite these advantages the South faced major problems. The Confederate Constitution limited the authority of the central government over individual states. Governor Joseph Brown of Georgia, for example, insisted that Georgia troops be commanded only by Georgia officers. Moreover, the South carried the burden of defending slavery, which made it more difficult to enlist European nations as allies.

The North's Position

The North had a larger population, providing almost four times as many potential soldiers, and many more factories than the

On the Eve of War, 1861

Free states

Slave states loyal to Union
*separated from Va. 1861, admitted to Union 1863

The Confederate States of America

Seceded after April 14, 1861

Seceded before April 14, 1861

0 500 Miles
0 800 Kilometers

■ *In early 1861, seven states had not yet chosen sides in the struggle. Arkansas, Tennessee, North Carolina, and Virginia did not leave the Union until after the fall of Fort Sumter. Three border states remained in the Union: Maryland, Kentucky, and Missouri.*

South. Massachusetts alone produced more manufactured goods than the entire Confederacy. A good railroad network and control of the country's navy and almost all its merchant marine added to the strength of the North.

Before the impact of superior numbers and greater supplies could be felt on the battlefield, however, the North had to convert its industries from peace- to wartime production. The North put its superior resources to use slowly and thus lost some of its advantage.

President Lincoln first offered the command of the Union army to Robert E. Lee, a Virginian, but Lee chose to serve with the Confederacy. Like the South, the North had many able military men trained at West Point, but Lincoln and his advisers knew little of their abilities and made several false starts before finding a commander able to win the war.

Civil Leadership

Civil leaders as well as military commanders played a vital role in the war effort. When the Civil War began, few people in Washington knew Abraham Lincoln well. Many suspected he was not up to the job of commander-in-chief. Lincoln's own attorney general wrote that the President "lacks will and purpose, and, I greatly fear, he has not the power to command."

But Lincoln proved his critics wrong. He extracted the best from his cabinet and demonstrated exceptional political skills. For example, he had the ability to maintain public morale through regular contact with the citizens. Several days a week, he opened the White House to the public and talked with anyone who wanted to see him.

Jefferson Davis, the Confederate President, appeared more distinguished and more experienced than Lincoln. He had served in the House of Representatives, the Senate, and as secretary of war under President Pierce. He was hard working and dedicated. As a graduate of West Point and a veteran officer of the Mexican War, he seemed well equipped to lead the Confederacy.

Yet precisely because of his devotion, President Davis often overworked. He labored over details of military strategy best left to others. He quarreled often with the Confederate Congress and vetoed 38 bills. (All but one of the vetoes were overridden by the Congress.) Lincoln, in contrast, vetoed only three bills.

Mobilizing for War

At the beginning of the war, each side hoped to raise an army of volunteers, but responses were inadequate. The Union army tried to encourage enlistment by offering *bounties,* sums paid to recruits signing up for service. Bounties were especially appealing to the poor, but some unscrupulous men took advantage of the system by *bounty jumping.* They would enlist, collect a bounty, then desert and reenlist somewhere else, collecting another bounty.

In 1863 the United States passed its first national draft law, requiring military service of males between the ages of 20 and 45. A person with money, however, could hire a substitute or pay a fee of $300 to exempt himself from military service.

The Confederacy had passed its draft law earlier, in 1862. At first, men between the ages of 18 and 35 were eligible for the draft; the range was later extended to age 45. The Confederate law allowed paid substitutes until 1863, when that provision was repealed. The most hated provision of the Confederate draft law exempted one man from each plantation that had 20 or more slaves.

Disillusioned participants on both sides soon came to feel that the Civil War was "a rich man's war and a poor man's fight." Such dissatisfaction was one cause of desertion, a problem that plagued both the Union and the Confederate armies.

Paying for the War

Southern leaders did not levy taxes to support the war because they feared that heavy taxation would erode popular support. Instead, they raised two fifths of their income by selling bonds that could be cashed in after the war. The remaining source of income for the Confederacy was the printing press. The Confederate government simply printed money, even though there was no gold or silver to back it. Eventually that practice led to runaway inflation.

Like the South, the North was reluctant to raise money by imposing taxes. In August 1861, however, it levied the first income tax in the nation's history and imposed new sales taxes and taxes on manufactured goods. Only the tax on manufacturers raised much money, but the sales and income taxes established precedents for future legislation. The North also raised money by selling bonds.

By 1862 the war was costing the North almost $1.75 million a day. To raise further funds, Congress passed the Legal Tender Act, which authorized the government to issue paper money. Since the new bills were printed in green ink, people soon came to call them greenbacks.

The most significant change in northern finance came with the passage of the National Bank Act in 1863. The act raised additional war bonds by requiring new national banks to invest one third of their deposits in federal bonds. At the same time, it forced state banks to stop printing their own notes, allowing only national banks to issue paper money.

The new requirements created the nation's first truly centralized banking system. Since they wanted to continue issuing bank notes, over 800 state banks became national banks and invested their deposits in United States war bonds.

Diplomacy During the War

When the war began, both the Union and the Confederacy hoped for foreign assistance. Because of Great Britain's strong navy and large industrial capacity, both sides were especially eager to win its support.

British opinion about the war was divided. Despite President Lincoln's refusal to interfere with slavery where it already existed, many British reformers and ordinary citizens supported the North because of the slavery issue. On the other hand, many people in Britain supported the Confederacy's wish to be recognized as an independent state. Much of the British nobility, especially, identified more with southern planters than with northern factory workers.

Early in the war, Jefferson Davis banned cotton shipments to England, hoping that shortages would force the British to recognize the Confederacy. British textile mills, however, had a surplus of cotton when the war began, and the ploy failed. In the end, Great Britain chose to remain officially neutral, refusing to commit itself to either South or North. As the war continued and neither side gained a clear upper hand, Europeans generally decided to stay neutral. The war between North and South remained a civil war.

For answers, see p. A 55.

Section Review

1. Identify the following: National Bank Act.
2. Define the following terms: habeas corpus, bounty, bounty jumping.
3. (a) What decision did border states have to make while the North and South were preparing for war? (b) Which border states sided with the Union?
4. What goal were southerners fighting for?
5. What two major advantages did the North have over the South as the war began?
6. What were Jefferson Davis's qualifications as President of the Confederacy?
7. (a) What methods did the Union use to raise an army? (b) What methods did the Confederacy use?
8. (a) What methods did the Confederacy use to raise funds during the war? (b) What methods did the Union use?
9. Why did both the Union and the Confederacy want support from Great Britain?

2 War Begins

As both sides mobilized for war, few leaders realized how long or how devastating the conflict would be. Northerners thought that victory would be theirs once they captured Richmond, Virginia, the capital of the Confederacy. Southerners believed that if they pushed back northern invasion attempts often enough, the North would give up. In fact, the struggle would be a turning point in the history of combat, foreshadowing the more deadly warfare of the twentieth century.

The New Shape of War

The large number of soldiers involved in any given battle distinguished this war from previous American conflicts. In the War of 1812 and the Mexican War, there were never more than 14,000 or 15,000 soldiers opposing each other in a single battle. In the war between the Union and the Confederacy, battles involving more than 100,000 soldiers were not uncommon, and the number of casualties was correspondingly high. At least 540,000 Americans lost their lives.

More efficient weaponry was responsible for many of the deaths. Old rifle balls were replaced by cone-shaped Minié bullets, which were about twice as accurate. Thus trenches became necessary for defense. Bayonets lost much of their usefulness because soldiers could shoot one another from a distance long before they could get close enough for hand-to-hand combat. The Union manufactured artillery pieces that could fire projectiles weighing up to 300 pounds (135 kilograms). With few factories, the Confederacy had to import or capture most of its field artillery. Nevertheless it was able to bring these deadly weapons to bear.

Medical practices amidst difficult battlefield conditions were also responsible for much suffering and death. Sanitation was poor, and water was often contaminated. Doctors were in short supply. Antiseptics were unknown, so wounds and incisions often became infected. Painkillers were neither easy to come by nor particularly effective. One Confederate officer wrote that his men had as much to fear from their own doctors as they did from Union troops.

Northern Strategy

At the outbreak of war General Winfield Scott, a hero of the Mexican War, supervised all Union forces. Old and in ill health, Scott nonetheless retained a keen mind. Unlike most people, he realized that the war would not be over in 90 days.

Scott suggested a grand war strategy to President Lincoln. The navy should set up a complete blockade of Confederate ports from Norfolk, Virginia, to Galveston, Texas. Union forces should split the Confederacy into three parts at the Appalachian Mountains and the Mississippi River and then use Union naval superiority to isolate and strangle each weakened section.

People ridiculed Scott's scheme, calling it the "anaconda," after a huge South American snake that kills its prey by crushing, but the course of events would prove the value of Scott's strategy. The Appalachians and the Mississippi did divide the Confederate States into three regions, which became the theaters of the war.

West of the Mississippi, in Louisiana, Arkansas, and Texas, Confederate defenders under the command of Edmund Kirby-Smith kept northern forces at bay. But this far-western theater remained isolated from the main conflicts and influenced the final outcome of the war very little. Most of the action centered in the western theater (the area between the Appalachians and the Mississippi) and in the eastern theater (the area around Virginia and Maryland).

The First Battle of Bull Run

Implementing Scott's plan would take time, and northerners were demanding bold action to end the war quickly. To satisfy this demand President Lincoln sent Union troops to fight a Confederate army camped in northern Virginia near Washington. On a pleasant afternoon on July 21, 1861, northern picnickers and newspaper reporters settled on a hill overlooking a small stream called Bull Run. They waited for Union troops to advance, expecting to see a decisive Union victory.

The battle did not go according to expectations. Both Union and Confederate troops were inexperienced and poorly prepared. Furthermore, neither Union General Irvin McDowell nor Confederate General P.G.T. Beauregard was accustomed to commanding large forces.

At first Union troops fought well. But their advance was blocked by men under the command of General Thomas J. Jackson, who stood "like a stone wall" awaiting relief. (It was for this brave stand that Jackson earned the nickname "Stonewall.") When

Neither side expected a long struggle at the beginning of the war, and some families joined the soldiers in camp. You can see some of the daily routines of camp life in this photo of a Pennsylvania soldier and his family.

Confederate reinforcements arrived, General McDowell tried an orderly retreat, but his men bolted and ran. The green southern troops, in turn, were too surprised to press their advantage.

When the nation learned of the Confederate success, dismayed northerners realized that an easy victory was not in sight. Southerners rejoiced and felt confident about the war's eventual outcome.

War at Sea

Because the South was primarily an agricultural region, it had always depended on northern and European sources for manufactured goods. With the start of the war,

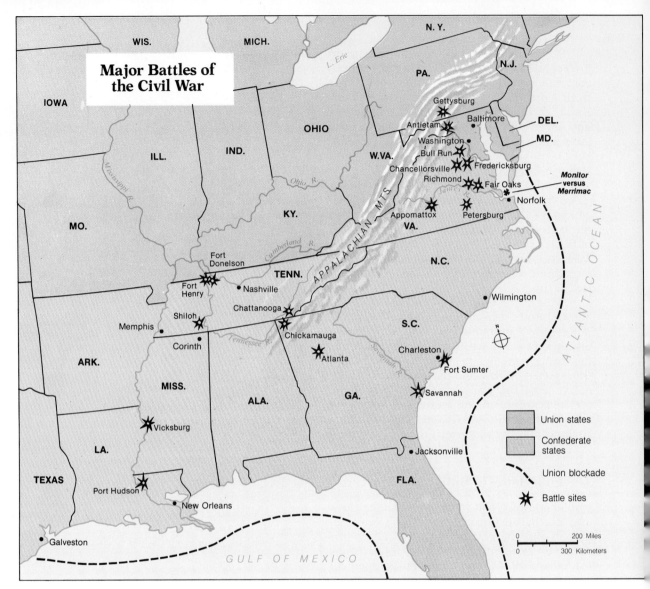

Major Battles of the Civil War

WIS.

MICH.

N.Y.

N.J.

IOWA

OHIO

PA.

Gettysburg

Baltimore

DEL.

Antietam

MD.

ILL.

IND.

W.VA.

Washington

Bull Run

Chancellorsville

Fredericksburg

Monitor versus Merrimac

Richmond

Fair Oaks

MO.

KY.

Appomattox

Petersburg

Norfolk

VA.

Fort Donelson

N.C.

TENN.

Nashville

Fort Henry

Chattanooga

Wilmington

Shiloh

Memphis

Chickamauga

S.C.

Corinth

Atlanta

Charleston

ARK.

Savannah

Fort Sumter

MISS.

ALA.

GA.

Vicksburg

LA.

Jacksonville

Port Hudson

TEXAS

FLA.

New Orleans

ATLANTIC OCEAN

Galveston

GULF OF MEXICO

Union states

Confederate states

Union blockade

Battle sites

0   200 Miles

0   300 Kilometers

■ *This map shows the broad extent of the Civil War, while the smaller maps on the following pages show details of individual campaigns. Most of the battles of the war were fought on southern ground.*

trade with Europe became even more crucial because the North was no longer a source of supply. Consequently the North began to implement Scott's anaconda strategy by blockading the southern coast. The Union navy tried to cut off all imports by patrolling major southern ports and wherever possible capturing the ports themselves.

Before the war, approximately 6,000 ships a year entered southern ports; in the first year of the blockade, the number dropped to 800. As the war continued, the Union blockade became even more effec-

tive. Still, loopholes existed. Enterprising southerners living along the coast sometimes successfully "ran" the blockade.

The small Confederate fleet of seagoing cruisers also damaged Union trade. In less than four years the *Alabama* and the *Florida*, built for the Confederacy in Great Britain, destroyed 257 northern ships.

Both sides recognized the importance of the navy in the war, and both worked to produce the newest and strongest ships possible. This led to the use of armorplating to strengthen ship hulls. The Confederacy was first to put a fully ironclad ship into service: the reconditioned *Merrimac*, a 40-gun warship abandoned by Union forces near Portsmouth, Virginia.

Armed with iron plate 4 inches (10 centimeters) thick and renamed the *Virginia*, the ironclad quickly proved superior to wooden warships. On March 8, 1862, it sank one Union ship at Hampton Roads, drove another aground, and forced a third to surrender. The *Virginia* seemed capable of defeating the entire Union navy.

The Union countered with its own ironclad, the *Monitor*. It did battle with the *Virginia* on March 9. When neither ship could seriously damage the other, they disengaged and the battle was a draw. Eventually Confederates were forced to destroy the *Virginia* before it fell into enemy hands. The *Monitor* later sank in heavy seas off the North Carolina coast.

General Grant in the Western Theater

While the Union blockade pressured the southern coast, a little-known Union general, Ulysses S. Grant, carried out another part of Scott's anaconda plan in the western theater. The plan called for Union forces to take control of the Mississippi River, but the Confederates had fortified it well. Grant saw that he could reach the heart of the Confederacy by pushing south along the Cumberland and Tennessee rivers. (See the map at right.)

Two Confederate forts stood in Grant's way: Fort Henry on the Tennessee and Fort Donelson on the Cumberland. President Jefferson Davis, recognizing Grant's intentions, dispatched General Albert Johnston to coordinate Confederate defenses. In early February 1862 Grant captured Fort Henry with a flotilla of Union gunboats. Johnston was forced to withdraw to Nashville, leaving 15,000 troops to guard Fort Donelson.

Grant sent gunboats against Fort Donelson, but the Confederates withstood the attack. Grant then surrounded the fort and prepared for a siege, correctly gauging that the Confederates were low on supplies. When the Confederates tried to break out and rejoin Johnston's army, Grant pushed them back into the fort, demanded unconditional surrender, and got it.

General Grant next pushed south along the Tennessee River but was surprised on April 6 by Confederate forces under Generals Johnston and Beauregard. The ensuing melee, which took place near a country meetinghouse called Shiloh, was the largest battle to date in North America. Johnston and Beauregard nearly routed the Union forces, but Grant held on until reinforcements arrived on April 7. The outnumbered Confederates, who had lost General Johnston in the battle, retreated to Corinth, Mississippi. By the end of May, Union forces had driven the Confederates out of Corinth.

The anaconda plan was having its effect in the West. Grant had penetrated south along the Tennessee River. Flag Officer David Farragut took New Orleans in April and continued up the Mississippi. Union gunboats also captured Memphis, leaving Vicksburg the only remaining Confederate stronghold on the river.

■ *Part of the Union's strategy was to gain control of the Mississippi River. A first step was to seize Fort Henry and Fort Donelson, shown on this map. By the spring of 1863, Vicksburg was the only remaining Confederate stronghold on the Mississippi.*

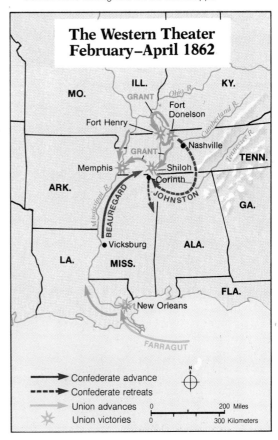

The Eastern Peninsular Campaign

The Union's eastern campaign did not go as well. After the defeat at Bull Run, Lincoln appointed General George B. McClellan commander of the Army of the Potomac. McClellan's first task was to transform raw recruits into able soldiers. This he did well. Discipline and organization replaced the confusion of Bull Run, and the troops respected McClellan. But the general seemed reluctant to engage in battle. "If McClellan does not want to use the army," said President Lincoln, "I would like to *borrow* it."

In March 1862, after almost a year of training, McClellan decided that his men were ready for combat, and he began to plan an attack on Richmond. He intended to move most of his army by steamboat down the Potomac River to the Chesapeake Bay, put them ashore on the peninsula between the York and James rivers, and move up the peninsula to attack the Confederate capital from the southeast. (See the map on page 331.) The success of the operation depended on surprise and speed. But after he landed McClellan moved cautiously, giving Confederate forces ample time to prepare.

On May 31 General Joseph E. Johnston attacked McClellan at Fair Oaks Station. When Johnston was wounded in the indecisive battle, Jefferson Davis ordered Robert E. Lee to take command of Johnston's forces, the Army of Northern Virginia. Lee would keep that command until the end of the war.

Robert E. Lee and George B. McClellan had attended West Point together. Remembering McClellan's caution, Lee devised a brilliant plan to keep the Union general from pressing too quickly toward Richmond. He sent Stonewall Jackson on a series of rapid marches against Union troops in the Shenandoah Valley of Virginia. Jackson's diversions were so successful that President Lincoln believed that Washington, D.C., was threatened. As a result, troops earmarked for McClellan were sent instead to deal with Jackson, and McClellan never received the reinforcements he had ordered.

Confederate General Robert E. Lee (right), in a photograph taken by Mathew Brady, was a military genius admired by soldiers on both sides. The son of a Revolutionary War hero, General Lee grew up in a wealthy Virginia family. General Ulysses S. Grant (left), with his stubby beard and casual dress, seemed the opposite of the aristocratic Lee. Yet he was the man President Lincoln would choose to lead the faltering Union armies.

Between June 26 and July 2, 1862, Lee and Jackson kept McClellan off balance in a series of encounters known as the Seven Days' Battles. With the help of the dashing cavalry of J.E.B. "Jeb" Stuart, the Confederates not only prevented McClellan from taking Richmond, but forced him to withdraw to the James River. By taking the offensive, Lee had saved Richmond. Disgusted by McClellan's failure to take the Confederate capital, President Lincoln ordered him back to Washington and temporarily relieved him of his command.

Union generals planned another attack on Richmond in August, but once again Lee and Jackson outwitted them, at the Second Battle of Bull Run on August 28 and 29. Union General John Pope found his forces surrounded, and he retreated in defeat. Reluctantly Lincoln allowed McClellan to resume his command.

Antietam

President Lincoln had reason to be concerned. In September General Lee crossed the Potomac on a bold offensive into Maryland. The Confederates knew that a successful campaign in enemy territory would be a great blow to northern morale.

Expecting McClellan to be slow, as before, Lee divided his army. He sent Stonewall Jackson to capture the federal arsenal at Harpers Ferry, Virginia, while he marched into western Maryland. But McClellan had an incredible stroke of luck. One of his men stumbled upon three cigars dropped by an unknown Confederate messenger. They were wrapped in a dispatch containing Lee's battle plan.

This time McClellan did not delay. He mobilized his forces and attacked Lee at Antietam Creek on September 17, hoping to defeat him before Jackson returned. Reinforcements arrived from Harpers Ferry in time to prevent a complete Confederate rout, but Lee was forced to retreat across the Potomac into Virginia.

The battle of Antietam may have marked the bloodiest single day of the war. Lee lost 11,000 men, McClellan, 13,000. The Union army had not decisively defeated Lee, but it had forced him back to Virginia. Limited though it was, the Union victory had more than just military importance, as you will read later.

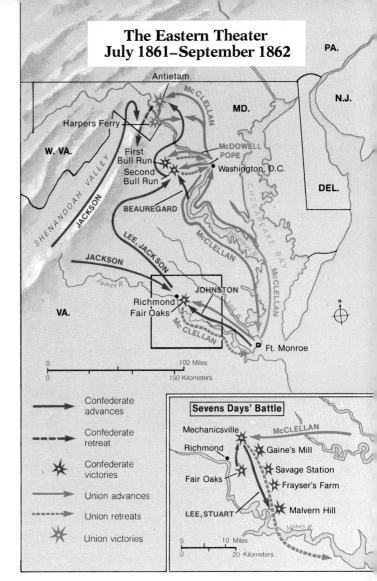

■ *During the early Virginia campaigns, Confederate forces under General Robert E. Lee outmaneuvered and outfought Union forces until the Battle of Antietam.*

For answers, see p. A 56.

Section Review

1. Identify the following: Stonewall Jackson, the *Virginia*, the *Monitor*, Ulysses S. Grant, George B. McClellan, Robert E. Lee.

2. List two ways in which warfare in the Civil War differed from warfare in earlier wars.

3. (a) What was General Scott's strategy for winning the war? (b) What were the three theaters of the war?

4. How would a blockade of the southern coast hurt the Confederacy?

5. How did General Lee prevent Union forces from taking Richmond?

6. What was the outcome of the battle at Antietam?

331

3 Freedom

As the battles raged and the soldiers died, many people questioned why the war was being fought. Southerners justified their resistance as a war for independence. They were fighting to preserve the southern way of life, which included slavery. Northerners remained less sure of their goals. First and foremost, they were fighting to preserve the Union; that seemed clear enough. But were they preserving a union that would continue with or without slavery?

Pressure for Emancipation

President Lincoln argued that union, not slavery, was the war's primary issue. "If I could save the union without freeing any slave I would do it," he announced in August 1862, "and if I could save it by freeing all the slaves I would do it; and if I could save it by freeing some and leaving others alone I would also do that."

Early in the war Lincoln handled the slavery issue cautiously, in part because he did not want to lose the support of the border states. As the war continued, however, more and more northerners began to favor an end to slavery. Pressure for emancipation came from several sources: abolitionists, fugitive slaves, and radical Republicans in Congress.

Abolitionists found increasing support in the North. "It is hard to realize the wondrous change which has befallen us abolitionists," wrote a reformer named Mary Grew. "After thirty years of persecution . . . abolitionists read with wonder . . . respectful tributes to men whose names had hitherto been used as a cry wherewith to rally a mob."

The question of what to do about fugitive slaves led the President to reconsider his policy. After the war began, thousands of slaves left southern plantations and fled behind Union lines. At first, in an attempt to conciliate the border states, Lincoln urged military commanders to return runaway slaves to their masters. But public sentiment in the North opposed such action.

In the spring of 1861 General Benjamin Butler declared fugitive slaves who had come into his camp to be *contraband* of war and not returnable to their masters. Thereafter Lincoln allowed Union generals to use their discretion in dealing with fugitive slaves.

Although the President still proceeded cautiously, Congress passed antislavery measures in the spring and summer of 1862. One law abolished slavery in Washington, D. C., and the territories. Another made Butler's contraband policy legal and forbade Union officers to return fugitive slaves. The bill also allowed the President to recruit blacks for the army. The most vocal support for these laws came from a group of radicals in the Republican party led by Senator Charles Sumner of Massachusetts and Congressman Thaddeus Stevens of Pennsylvania.

The Emancipation Proclamation

Lincoln recognized the growing call for abolition and was willing to respond. But he hesitated to act until Union forces had won a victory, so that emancipation would be seen as a bold, new policy. The Union showing at Antietam gave Lincoln the opportunity he had been waiting for. On September 22, 1862, he issued a preliminary proclamation that all slaves in territories still in a state of rebellion on January 1, 1863, would be freed.

On January 1, 1863, the Emancipation Proclamation was issued. It applied only to Confederate states still at war. It did not affect slaves in areas occupied by Union troops or slaves in border states still loyal to the Union. In effect, it did not apply to any slaves within the immediate reach of the Union.*

The President had hoped that the threat of emancipation would pressure southern slave owners to surrender in order to safeguard slavery. Although that goal was not realized, the proclamation dramatically changed the character of the war. The war had become a battle for freedom as well as for union.

Rights of Black Americans

The Emancipation Proclamation did not free any slaves in the Union, nor did it have any direct influence on free blacks in the North.

---

*Slavery was abolished completely by the Thirteenth Amendment to the Constitution, ratified in December 1865.

However, the President's decision to issue the proclamation did advance the struggle for equal rights for black Americans.

When war began in 1861, free blacks suffered severe discrimination in northern states. Only in New York and most of New England could black males vote, and in New York they had to meet a property requirement not applied to whites. Only in New England could black and white children attend the same schools. In many major cities, including Philadelphia and New York City, blacks rode on segregated public transportation, if they were allowed to ride at all. Black Americans everywhere faced discrimination in housing and employment.

With the outbreak of the Civil War, many abolitionists turned their attention to securing equal rights for blacks in the North. Advances were slow but meaningful. Even in New York City, where workers feared an influx of black labor from the South, reformers made progress. Increased support from social and political leaders led to the integration of public transportation in New York City before the end of the war. Reformers throughout the North also succeeded in opening many more public schools to black children.

After the war, several actions effectively nullified the Dred Scott case's denial of citizenship to black Americans. For example, in 1865 John Rock, a black attorney from Boston, was admitted to practice before the Supreme Court. Both the State and Justice departments established rules clearly stating that blacks were entitled to citizenship. The movement for black rights continued, gaining strength because of blacks' participation in the war.

Black Soldiers

From the onset of the war, many blacks volunteered as cooks, drivers, carpenters, and scouts for the Union army, not only out of patriotism but also to be recognized as full partners in the nation and the war effort. Until the summer of 1862, federal law prohibited blacks from becoming soldiers, but when Congress repealed that law, blacks enlisted in the Union army.

Frederick Douglass explained why: "Once let the black man get upon his person the brass letters, *U. S.;* let him get an eagle on his button, and a musket on his shoulder and bullets in his pocket, and there is no

Parker Robbins served as sergeant-major of a Union cavalry regiment during the war. Later he was elected to the House of Representatives from North Carolina.

power on earth which can deny that he has earned the right to citizenship in the United States." By the end of the war 180,000 blacks had fought in the Union army and 29,000 in the navy.

Although they were allowed to enlist, black soldiers suffered discrimination. Their term of enlistment was longer than whites', and they were paid less. The army assigned them to all-black regiments mostly under the command of white officers. Medical care, bad enough even in the best circumstances, was even worse in the black units. The weapons black soldiers carried were often ones discarded by white troops. If taken prisoner by the Confederates, black soldiers (unlike white soldiers) faced enslavement or execution by hanging or firing squad.

In spite of such difficult conditions, the bravery of black soldiers under fire became well known. In the summer of 1863, for example, the all-black 54th Massachusetts Regiment led an assault on Fort Wagner in Charleston Harbor. Under heavy artillery barrage, nearly a hundred soldiers forced their way into the fort and engaged the Confederate troops in hand-to-hand combat. The

54th suffered great casualties in the battle, but such displays of courage won black soldiers a degree of acceptance among many white Americans.

For answers, see p. A 56.

Section Review

1. Define the following term: contraband.
2. What did President Lincoln believe was the primary reason for fighting the Civil War?
3. What were three sources of pressure on President Lincoln to end slavery?
4. Which areas of the nation were affected by the Emancipation Proclamation?
5. (a) What type of discrimination did black Americans face in the North when the war began? (b) What type of discrimination did black soldiers face in the Union army?

4 Behind the Lines

The war affected everyone, not just the troops on the front lines. Civilians behind the lines grew food crops and manufactured military equipment to support the war effort. They maintained transportation networks to move troops and supplies, and they tended the wounded. Governments in both the South and the North faced opposition to the war and the economic hardship it caused.

Discord in the North

The government of a nation at war counts on the loyalty and support of its citizens. Yet the Constitution of the United States guarantees Americans the right of free speech and open dissent. Did northerners who opposed Lincoln's handling of the war, then, have the right to speak out? At what point would political opposition to the war become treason? These were questions President Lincoln and his administration had to consider.

Throughout the North, a few citizens vocally supported the Confederacy. This was especially true in the Union border states and in sections of the Old Northwest originally settled by southerners. Other northerners simply opposed the war, demanding an armistice and peace negotiations. Loyal Republicans called opponents of the war *copperheads*, after the poisonous snake of the same name.

Lincoln believed that in time of war a President had special powers not available in peacetime. In order to preserve the Union, he felt justified in violating civil liberties guaranteed by the Constitution. At the beginning of the war, to prevent Maryland from seceding, he had denied habeas corpus to citizens of that state. On January 1, 1863, he denied habeas corpus to all persons who resisted the draft, discouraged enlistment, or were suspected of being "guilty of any disloyal practice affording aid and comfort to rebels."

Resistance to the draft was especially strong in large cities like New York, where many immigrant workers belonged to the Democratic party and had little sympathy for Republicans. Workers resented being drafted for what they considered to be a "rich man's war" when those who could afford to pay the exemption fee remained home. Some white workers resented competition from free blacks for jobs; consequently, they had little interest in fighting a war to free the slaves.

Resentment and frustration boiled over in July 1863, when a mob of workers in New York City attacked Union army recruiters. The mob then looted the homes of several wealthy citizens, burned a black orphanage, and lynched several blacks who were unfortunate enough to be caught in the vicinity. Federal troops were called in from Gettysburg to quell the disturbance.

Opposition to the draft and to the war continued until the war was over. Between 1863 and 1865 military authorities arrested and imprisoned more than 13,000 people for alleged disloyalty of one kind or another.

The Northern Economy

The Civil War stimulated economic growth in the North and accelerated the industrialization that had begun before the war. Between 1860 and 1865, for example, woolen mills producing uniforms for Union troops almost tripled their profits.

The war also spurred the growth of agriculture in the North. To meet the army's demands, farmers stepped up food production. Grain farmers purchased over 165,000 mechanical reapers during the war, simultaneously increasing grain supplies and freeing men for fighting.

Congress also came to the aid of farmers in 1862. The Homestead Act gave 160 acres (64 hectares) of western land to any citizen who agreed to occupy and improve it for five years. The Morrill Act gave states land grants to endow colleges of agriculture. To increase their support among midwestern farmers, Republicans worked for the creation of a cabinet-level Department of Agriculture, which Congress established in 1862.

Inflation accompanied the expansion of industry and agriculture. Wartime demand for goods increased prices by 50 percent between 1860 and 1862. Wages, however, failed to keep pace, increasing by only 10 percent. People could buy fewer goods with their weekly earnings than before the war. Thus, although the war stimulated the North's economy, individual citizens faced economic hardship.

Hardships in the South

Although life behind the lines was disrupted in the North, suffering in the South was far worse. Most of the fighting took place in the Confederacy, so the destruction of property and crops was greater. As the war progressed the Union blockade became increasingly effective, forcing many southerners to do without basic manufactured goods such as new clothing.

Factories in the North continued to supply Union armies with new equipment. But the South lacked the industrial capacity to carry on a long war. When locomotives broke down, they often could not be replaced or repaired because of a lack of parts. When track was destroyed, it could be replaced only by borrowing track from less important branch lines.

Shortages like these seriously hurt the war effort. Troops and supplies could not be moved, and food could not be distributed. In 1863, although Confederate farmers in the Shenandoah Valley had reaped good harvests, famine threatened Richmond and there were riots for bread.

Astronomical inflation was caused by the lack of a firm backing for Confederate currency. In 1863 a Confederate official noted that boots cost $200, coats $350, and shoes $125. Food was expensive, too, when it was available. Two chickens cost $30, potatoes $25 per bushel, and butter $15 per pound (0.45 kilogram). In 1863, flour sold for $275 a barrel; by the end of the war, that price had soared to $1,000.

Political Divisions in the Confederacy

The government of the Confederacy faced political as well as economic problems. Not all southerners supported the war. The draft, for example, was as unpopular in the Confederacy as in the Union. Small farmers, especially, objected to the exemptions for planters.

Pro-Union sentiment was widespread in the northern reaches of the South, the mountains, and the poorer sections of the Confederacy. In 1861 residents in the western sections of Virginia, who had traditionally opposed the eastern part of the state, organized a pro-Union government. In 1863, the area was formally admitted to the Union as the state of West Virginia.

President Davis, like Lincoln, attempted to suspend habeas corpus in order to deal with dissenters. Such efforts led some of Davis's critics to denounce him as a dictator. Yet others thought he was not decisive enough. Davis's most outspoken critic was his own Vice-President, Alexander H. Stephens. Stephens remained in his native state of Georgia for a substantial part of the war, refusing to serve in Richmond.

The unwillingness of some state governors to give up any authority to the central government also handicapped President Davis. For example, the governor of Alabama would not allow the central government to collect taxes in his state. Governor Joseph Brown of Georgia hindered the Confederate government at every turn. He even considered making a separate peace treaty with the Union.

Women in the War

Women, although not allowed to fight, nevertheless contributed greatly to the war effort. In the North and the South, women formed aid societies as soon as the war began. The Union's Sanitary Commission, for example, collected over $15 million worth of supplies. In the Confederacy, the Society of Center Ridge, Alabama, contributed "422 shirts, 551 pairs of drawers, 80 pairs of socks, 3 pairs of gloves, 6 boxes and a bale of hospital stores, 128 pounds of tapioca, and $18 for hospital use" in one month.

More informally, volunteer women operated "refreshment saloons" in the North, and "wayside homes" in the South, in which communities donated food, drink, and medical care to soldiers who were passing through. Women aided in the purchase of military hardware as well. "Ladies Gunboat Funds" were common in the Confederate states.

Women played an increased role in agriculture, especially in the South where labor was short. They often harvested crops and supervised the day-to-day operation of farms and plantations. In the North more and more women found employment in the federal government as clerical jobs were opened to them.

Nursing became an important activity for many women in both the South and the North. At first people did not consider nursing male soldiers proper work for women. The work was considered too unpleasant and difficult. Nevertheless, women stepped in to help.

In 1861 the Union government named Dorothea Dix superintendent of women nurses. She was efficient and warmhearted, but some men resented her skill as a tough administrator. Clara Barton, a school teacher, was not appointed to any official post, but she set immediately to work organizing care for the sick and wounded. She served behind Union lines and on the battlefields of some of the fiercest conflicts of the war.

Black women also took an active role in the northern war effort. They worked in hos-

Diary of a Confederate Nurse

Kate Cumming served the Confederate cause as a nurse, and she kept a diary of her experiences. In the excerpt below, she describes her first encounter with wounded soldiers after the battle of Shiloh.

April 11—Miss Booth and myself arrived at Corinth to-day. . . . My heart beat high with expectation as we neared Corinth. As I had never been where there was a large army, and had never seen a wounded man, except in the cars, as they passed, I could not help feeling a little nervous at the prospect of now seeing both. When within a few miles of the place, we could realize the condition of an army immediately after a battle. As it had been raining for days, water and mud abounded. Here and there were wagons hopelessly left to their fate, and men on horseback trying to wade through it. As far as the eye could reach, in the midst of all this slop and mud, the white tents of our brave army could be seen through the trees, making a picture suggestive of any thing but comfort. . . .

The crowd of men at the depot was so great that we found it impossible to get to our place of destination by ourselves. . . . I met Mr. George Redwood of Mobile, who kindly offered to pilot us. . . . We are at the Tishomingo Hotel, which, like every other large building, has been taken for a hospital. The yellow flag is flying from the top of each. Mrs. Ogden tried to prepare me for the scenes which I should witness upon entering the wards. But alas! nothing that I had ever heard or read had given me the faintest idea of the horrors witnessed here. . . . Certainly, none of the glories of the war were presented here. But I must not say that; for if uncomplaining endurance is glory, we had plenty of it. If it is that which makes the hero, here they were by scores. Gray-haired men—men in the pride of manhood—beardless boys—Federals and all, mutilated in every imaginable way, lying on the floor, just as they were taken from the battlefield; so close together that it was almost impossible to walk without stepping on them. I could not command my feelings enough to speak, but thoughts crowded upon me. O, if the authors of this cruel and unnatural war could but see what I saw there, they would try and put a stop to it! . . . What can be in the minds of our enemies, who are now arrayed against us, who have never harmed them in any way, but simply claim our own, and nothing more!

pitals and on battle lines, and they helped re-settle former slaves who had fled from the South. Sojourner Truth continued her effective public speaking, turning her oratory against all those copperheads who hoped to conclude peace without abolishing slavery. Charlotte Forten and Mary Peake taught former slaves to read and write. Harriet Tubman helped slaves to escape and acted as a spy behind Confederate lines. The work of women was indispensable to the war effort of both the South and the North.

For answers, see p. A 56.

Section Review

1. Identify the following: copperheads, Homestead Act, Morrill Act, Clara Barton.

2. What caused many northern workers to resent the draft?

3. What areas of the northern economy were stimulated by the war?

4. Why was there greater destruction of property in the South than in the North?

5. What areas of the South were pro-Union?

6. How did women contribute to the war effort?

During the Civil War, Susie King Taylor served with the Union army as a nurse and teacher. After the war she wrote memoirs describing her experiences.

5 An End to the War

As the war dragged on—longer than either side had expected—the North's superior resources began to make a difference on the battlefield. The Union's naval blockade squeezed tighter around the South, and the likelihood of southern victory became more and more remote. But still the Confederacy fought on.

Confederate Victories

After the battle of Antietam, General Lee's forces retreated through the Shenandoah Valley. Once again, General McClellan failed to pursue or attack; he encamped and sent requests for supplies. On November 7, 1862, President Lincoln removed McClellan from command and replaced him with General Ambrose E. Burnside.

Burnside was supposed to move on Richmond by way of Fredericksburg, Virginia. On December 13, he ordered his men to make six frontal assaults across open ground near Fredericksburg. Confederates under Lee pushed them back with withering fire.

The following spring the effective combination of Lee and Jackson outwitted Union General Joseph Hooker at Chancellorsville, Virginia. On May 3, 1863, Hooker tried to outflank the Confederates. But Lee and Jackson routed the Union forces in ten minutes. Although the Confederates won the battle, they suffered a severe loss. An edgy Confederate sentry fired into the night, hitting Stonewall Jackson twice in the arm. One of the Confederacy's ablest generals died the next day from a resulting blood clot.

Gettysburg

Victories at Fredericksburg and Chancellorsville inspired the Confederacy, but the Union showed no sign of giving up. General

Lee and President Davis hoped that another Confederate move into the North would break the Union's resolve. Thus Lee led his army into Pennsylvania and into the battle that would be the turning point of the war.

Fighting began unexpectedly at Gettysburg, Pennsylvania, when advance detachments of Lee's army met a cavalry division of the Union army commanded by General George Meade. On July 1 Confederates drove the Union forces out of the town, but Meade's army managed to set itself up on the strategically located Cemetery Ridge nearby. Lee's forces took up position across the way on Seminary Ridge.

The curve of Cemetery Ridge made it easy for Union troops to defend it along the crest. Lee's plan was to attack around both ends of the ridge and close in on the Union forces from behind. On July 2 Confederates led by General Richard S. Ewell took Culp's Hill, on the northern slope. But Union forces repelled the attack on the southern end at Little Round Top. If Confederates had occupied that hill, they could have directed their artillery fire up and down the main Union line. The next day Union forces drove Ewell off Culp's Hill.

Lee then decided to attack the Union forces at their center, but Meade anticipated this move. When 15,000 Confederates in three lines began their march across three quarters of a mile of open field, Union troops were ready and opened up a devastating fire. Still the Confederates pushed on. Through clouds of gunsmoke, General George Pickett led one last valiant attempt to storm the lines. About 100 Confederates actually breached the Union embankments temporarily, but Meade's forces held the ridge.

Lee had no choice but to take his exhausted and diminished army back south toward the Potomac. General Meade let him go, passing up an opportunity to pursue and capture the Confederates as they withdrew to Virginia. Nevertheless, the battle of Gettysburg marked the beginning of the end for the Confederacy.

Vicksburg and Port Hudson

At about the time that Lee was moving toward defeat at Gettysburg, General Ulysses S. Grant began a campaign to secure Union control of the Mississippi River between Vicksburg, Mississippi, and Port Hudson,

Louisiana. Vicksburg was situated on a heavily fortified bluff overlooking the Mississippi and the swamplands of the Yazoo River. Grant spent the first three months of 1863 unsuccessfully trying to outflank Confed-

■ *Following Confederate victories at Fredericksburg and Chancellorsville, General Lee marched into Pennsylvania, hoping to take the war to the North. At Gettysburg, however, the Confederate army suffered heavy losses in a battle that became a turning point of the war.*

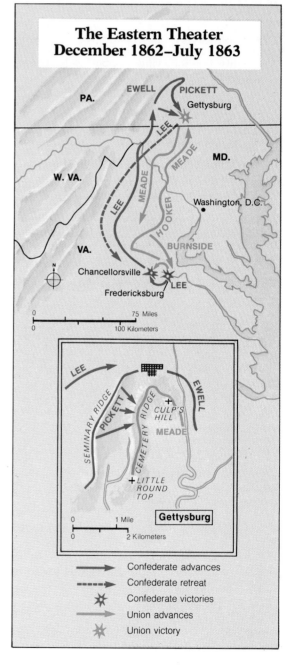

The Eastern Theater December 1862–July 1863

erate General John Pemberton in the Yazoo swamps. Failing to do so, Grant adopted a bolder strategy.

In April Union troops marched unnoticed south of Vicksburg while a fleet of Union gunboats floated silently downstream past Vicksburg, their engines and lights turned off. The gunboats then ferried the Union troops to the east bank of the Mississippi River.

Grant's men, carrying only four days' rations, marched east across Mississippi into enemy territory. After a series of small victories, they captured the state capital of Jackson on May 14. Grant then abruptly reversed his march and headed back to Vicksburg, arriving only 18 days after he had left. Union forces now surrounded Vicksburg. After a six-week siege the Confederates surrendered on July 4, 1863—the day after the Battle of Gettysburg ended.

On July 9 Port Hudson fell to Union forces. Two black regiments, spurred on by the heroism of Captain Andre Callious, were instrumental in the victory. The fall of Vicksburg and Port Hudson placed the entire Mississippi River in Union hands. The western grip of the anaconda was now firm. The Confederacy's position was becoming steadily more desperate.

Grant Takes Command

With the western front largely secure, Union troops moved to split the Confederacy even further by pushing eastward. In September Union armies under General William Rosecrans secured the strategic railroad center at Chattanooga, Tennessee. Mistakenly thinking that Confederate General Braxton Bragg's force was retreating to Atlanta, Rosecrans proceeded east and almost lost his entire army when Bragg's force counterattacked at Chickamauga on September 19 and 20. However, General George Thomas held off the Confederates long enough to allow Rosecrans to retreat to Chattanooga.

The next spring when Union forces began to march east again, Lincoln placed Grant in charge of all Union armies. Grant devised a three-pronged attack to destroy his opposition. One Union army would march into the fertile Shenandoah Valley, defeating enemy forces and laying waste to the land so that no crops would grow until after the war. General Philip E. Sheridan completed this

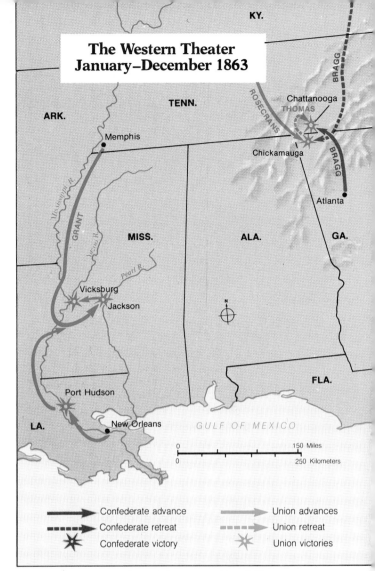

Union forces under General Grant moved to solidify Union control of the Mississippi River between Vicksburg and Port Hudson. In a swiftly executed maneuver, Grant sent ships and troops to surround Vicksburg. With the fall of Vicksburg and Port Hudson, the Union controlled the river.

mission in October 1864. Two other armies would be led by Grant himself and by General William Tecumseh Sherman.

Grant and Sherman were alike in several ways. Both men wore stubbly, short-cropped beards, dressed sloppily, and possessed an indomitable will to win. Both were willing to take any steps necessary to achieve victory. They intended to wage total war, defeating not only the opposing military forces but the civilian will to resist as well. Sherman's army was to march from Chattanooga to Atlanta, and Grant's was to march from Washington to Richmond.

339

Sherman's March to the Sea

General Sherman outfitted his 100,000 soldiers with only the most basic supplies. On May 6, 1864, they left Chattanooga. As the Union army proceeded it lived off the land, leaving destruction behind. General Sherman described the march: "We have devoured the land and our animals eat up the wheat and corn fields close. All the people retire before us and desolation is behind. To realize what war is one should follow our tracks."

Progress was slow, because Confederate forces under General Joseph Johnston and General John Hood opposed Sherman at every turn. Finally, on September 1, 1864, Sherman forced the Confederate army to abandon Atlanta.

Until the capture of Atlanta Lincoln had expected defeat in his bid for reelection because of public frustration over the war. The Democrats had adopted a platform calling for an armistice and had nominated General McClellan to oppose Lincoln. Even some Republicans had been urging immediate peace with the South. News of the fall of Atlanta rallied popular support for Lincoln and insured his reelection.

In mid-November General Sherman prepared to set out for Savannah, on the coast. Before leaving, he ordered his troops to set fire to Atlanta, destroying much of the city. Sherman's army arrived at Savannah on December 10, having left a path of devastation 60 miles (96 kilometers) wide. On December 21 Savannah fell.

Throughout the campaign Sherman's army had destroyed any supplies that might have been used to feed Confederate soldiers, wrecked railroad lines, and ruined cotton gins and mills. They dealt the South a devastating blow, which left southerners with bitter memories long afterward.

Capturing Richmond

Grant led the third part of his plan himself. Early in May 1864 troops under his command arrived in the Wilderness, a wild area near Fredericksburg, Virginia, where he began the first of three unsuccessful efforts to defeat Lee's much smaller army.

Both sides suffered heavy casualties over the next two months. Grant lost nearly 60,000 men, Lee nearly 30,000. Although Grant's casualties were greater, the Union had reserves to replace them. The Confederacy did not. Lee's army was forced to retreat to Petersburg, a few miles south of Richmond, where the Confederates dug a network of trenches, built heavy fortifications, and prepared for a siege.

Grant and Lee fought each other for nine more months. The siege of Petersburg lasted from the summer of 1864 through the winter of 1865. Faced with encirclement and cut off from his lines of supply, Lee finally withdrew his forces on the night of April 2, 1865. Grant pursued. With the battlements of Petersburg behind him, the Union commander moved into Richmond the next day and took the Confederate capital.

Appomattox: A Sad Peace

One week later, Lee's army was trapped near the small town of Appomattox Court House. Realizing that further resistance would lead

340

■ *General Sherman's "March to the Sea" left a wide path of destruction in Georgia. His army lived off the land, seizing the food and supplies it needed and destroying all others.*

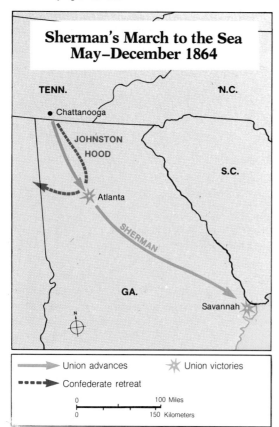

Sherman's March to the Sea
May–December 1864

TENN.

N.C.

● Chattanooga

JOHNSTON
HOOD

S.C.

Atlanta

SHERMAN

GA.

Savannah

Union advances ⟶   Union victories ✳

Confederate retreat ▸

0 — 100 Miles
0 — 150 Kilometers

only to greater loss of life among his troops, Lee sent a soldier carrying a white towel as a flag of truce to arrange a conference with General Grant.

On April 9, 1865, Lee and Grant met to discuss the terms of surrender. Robert E. Lee wore a full-dress uniform with ceremonial sash and sword. Ulysses S. Grant appeared, characteristically untidy, in a private's shirt, his collar unbuttoned. They talked about their days before the Civil War, when they had both served in the United States Army. Then Grant suggested generous terms of surrender:

> Officers and men paroled ... arms and material surrendered ... officers to keep their side arms, and let all the men who claim to own a horse or mule take the animals home with them to work their little farms.

One of Grant's aides recalled that General Lee "gazed sadly in the direction ... where his army lay—now an army of prisoners. He thrice smote the palm of his left hand slowly with his right fist in an absent sort of

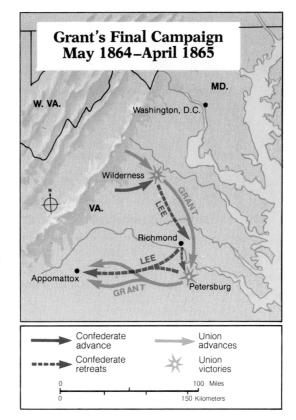

Grant's Final Campaign May 1864–April 1865

MD.

W. VA.

Washington, D.C.

VA.

Wilderness

GRANT

LEE

Richmond

LEE

Appomattox

GRANT

Petersburg

➡ Confederate advance	➡ Union advances
⇢ Confederate retreats	✴ Union victories

0   100 Miles
0   150 Kilometers

341

■ Union strategy in 1864 was to crush Confederate resistance between two fronts. While Sherman's troops marched through Georgia, Grant faced Lee in Virginia. Despite heavy losses at the Wilderness, Grant kept pressing the Confederate forces, and finally, at Appomattox, General Lee surrendered.

way." As the Union soldiers saw Lee mount and ride away toward his men, they began cheering. Grant immediately ordered them to stop. "The war is over," he told them, "the rebels are our countrymen again."

For answers, see p. A 57.

Section Review

1. Identify the following: William Tecumseh Sherman.

2. (a) What victories in late 1862 and early 1863 encouraged the Confederates? (b) What did Lee hope to accomplish by invading Pennsylvania?

3. What did the capture of Vicksburg and Port Hudson mean for the Union?

4. What were the three parts of General Grant's plan to bring down the Confederacy?

5. How did General Sherman try to destroy the Confederates' ability to resist?

6. What convinced Lee to surrender?

Major Events	
1861	Battle of Bull Run
1862	Battles of Fort Donelson, Fort Henry, Shiloh; Union capture of New Orleans; Confederacy passes draft law; battle of Fair Oaks; Department of Agriculture formed; Homestead Act; Morrill Act; Seven Days' Battle; Second Battle of Bull Run; battles of Antietam, Fredericksburg
1863	Emancipation Proclamation; National Bank Act; Union passes draft law; battle of Chancellorsville; West Virginia admitted as state; battles of Vicksburg, Port Hudson, Gettysburg, Chattanooga, Chickamauga
1864	Wilderness Campaign begins; siege of Petersburg begins; Sherman takes Atlanta; Lincoln reelected President; Sherman's March to the Sea
1865	Grant takes Richmond; Lee surrenders at Appomattox

At the end of the war, General Lee's troops had one final duty: to furl the Confederate flag for the last time. They returned to a homeland devastated by the long and bloody conflict.

★ ★ ★ ★ ★ ★ ★ ★ ★ ★ ★ ★ ★ ★ ★ ★ ★ ★ ★ ★

IN PERSPECTIVE   After the shelling of Fort Sumter both the United States of America and the Confederate States of America faced the task of preparing for war. The Union had important material advantages, but citizens of the Confederacy were ready to fight for their independence. Confederate troops won the first battle of the war, but by April 1862 General Grant had pushed as far south as Corinth, Mississippi, in the West. In the East General Lee repelled McClellan's attempt to take Richmond during the summer, but Lee's invasion of Maryland failed at Antietam Creek.

The Emancipation Proclamation, issued on January 1, 1863, changed the purpose of the war for many northerners. Although the proclamation did not directly affect free blacks or slaves in the Union, it did contribute to the struggle for greater rights.

The war affected all aspects of life. Confederate and Union governments were faced with opposition to the war and resentment over the draft, and both sides suffered from inflation. Yet economic growth was stimulated in the North while the Confederacy suffered greater hardships as the war progressed.

Confederate armies fought gallantly during the last two years of the war, but the superior numbers and supplies of the Union army gradually wore them down. Robert E. Lee finally surrendered to Ulysses S. Grant in April 1865. The war was over, but the task of reuniting the nation was just beginning.

For answers, see p. A 57.

Chapter Review

1. (a) What advantages did the Confederacy have as the war began? (b) What disadvantages did it have? (c) What advantages did the Union have? (d) What disadvantages did it have?

2. (a) Why did neither side rely completely on volunteers for their armies? (b) How were soldiers recruited? (c) Why did some people call the war "a rich man's war and a poor man's fight?" (d) Why was resistance to the draft especially strong in northern cities?

3. (a) Why did British support seem important to both the North and the South? (b) Which groups in Britain sympathized with the Union? (c) Which groups in Britain sympathized with the Confederacy? (d) What was Great Britain's official policy toward the war?

4. (a) Why did Congress establish a centralized banking system during the war? (b) How did the creation of the system help the Union finance the war? (c) What was the main way the South raised money for the war? (d) What problems did that cause?

5. (a) Describe General Scott's war strategy. (b) Why was it called the anaconda? (c) Was the strategy most successful in the West or in the East? (d) What impact did the blockade have on the Confederacy?

6. (a) Because the Confederates were mainly concerned with defending their homeland, what did General Lee hope to accomplish by invading the North in September 1862 and again in June 1863? (b) What was the result of each invasion?

7. (a) Why did President Lincoln handle the slavery issue cautiously early in the war? (b) Why did he finally decide to issue the Emancipation Proclamation? (c) Who was affected directly by the proclamation?

8. How did the status of black Americans in the North change during the Civil War?

9. (a) What type of discontent about the war existed in the North? (b) What type existed in the Confederacy? (c) How did Presidents Lincoln and Davis try to deal with discontent?

10. (a) What impact did the war have on the economy of the North? Why? (b) What impact did it have on the economy of the South? Why? (c) Why was Grant's and Sherman's policy of "total war" especially devastating to the southern economy?

11. (a) Describe General Grant's plan for defeating the Confederacy after Lincoln put him in charge of all Union armies. (b) Which part of his plan proved most difficult to achieve? (c) Why do you think this was the case?

For answers, see p. A 58.

For Further Thought

343

1. (a) Why do you think the question of remaining in the Union or joining the Confederacy was difficult for the border states? (b) Why was the status of Maryland, Missouri, and Kentucky especially important to the Union? (c) How might the course of the war have been different if any of those states had seceded? (d) Which state was probably the most crucial to the Union? Why?

2. (a) As you read, the North had more potential soldiers, more industry, and a more developed railroad system than the South. Yet the war lasted four long years. How might you explain the Union's inability to win sooner? (b) Why do you think it finally won? Give specific examples to support your answer.

3. (a) Why were there more casualties in the Civil War than in previous wars in North America? (b) What effect did new technology have?

4. (a) Why did many people think nursing was not a proper profession for women in 1861? (b) What developments in the first half of the nineteenth century may have increased the acceptance of women nurses?

For answers, see p. A 58.

Developing Basic Skills

1. *Comparing* Abraham Lincoln, Jefferson Davis, Ulysses S. Grant, George B. McClellan, Robert E. Lee, and Stonewall Jackson were important leaders during the Civil War. (a) What personal characteristics did each have that helped him be a good leader? (b) What personal characteristics did each have that weakened his leadership ability? (c) Which characteristics do you think are most important for leaders in wartime?

2. *Classifying* Make a chart with two columns, titled Western Theater and Eastern Theater; and three rows, titled Confederate Victory, Union Victory, and Neither. Write the name of each battle you read about in the appropriate box. Then answer the following questions: (a) Which side won the most battles in the eastern theater? (b) Which won the most battles in the western theater? (c) Which side won the largest total number of battles? (d) Does the chart help you explain the outcome of the Civil War? Why or why not? (e) Your text did not discuss all encounters between Confederate and Union troops. How might that affect the accuracy of your analysis?

See page 776 for suggested readings.

19

A Difficult Reunion

(1865–1877)

Ruins on Carey Street, Richmond, Virginia.

Chapter Outline

1 *Beginning of Reunion*

2 *Congress Takes Over*

3 *The Reconstruction South*

4 *Unfinished Business*

In 1865 both northerners and southerners could look back on the four years of civil war with mixed feelings of sadness and pride. Their nation had been ripped apart by the war, families had been separated, and many men and women had suffered hardship, injury, and death. But people on both sides had conducted themselves valiantly on the field of battle and behind the lines. Both could claim their share of heroes and tales of glory.

In contrast, the 12 years following the war were to produce few heroes. The truce at Appomattox led to a period of peace in which national leaders were determined to reunite the country. However, that task would prove to be a difficult one.

Although the Union had been preserved by the war, problems remained. The status of the former Confederate states had to be decided. Four million slaves had been freed, but they faced a difficult adjustment to freedom. The postwar period was called Reconstruction, but the scars of the war were slow to heal.

1 Beginning of Reunion

After four years of fighting, many Americans hoped to take up life where they left off before the war. But the war brought political, economic, and social changes in its wake, leaving great problems unsolved. The task of reunion would be a difficult one.

Effects of War

The human consequences of the war would haunt the nation for many years. Over 360,000 Union soldiers and 258,000 Confederate soldiers had lost their lives, as had many civilians. Thousands of veterans were permanently disabled. The war also left a legacy of bitterness and resentment. Confederates had lost their struggle for independence and seen much of their land laid waste by Union armies. Furthermore, many southerners feared retribution by the victorious North.

Beginning life anew was severely hindered by the economic dislocation caused by the war. The North had remained prosperous during the war, yet it faced serious problems in the postwar years. The Union dismissed 800,000 men from the army, and these men needed jobs. At the same time, factories that had been making arms and ammunition laid off many employees because the government canceled its orders. These abrupt changes produced a recession.

By the late 1860s manufacturers began to expand their factories and build new ones. Veterans found work as the demand for labor rose, and the northern population enjoyed a boom period that lasted until 1873. While disruptions in the North were temporary, the war had devastated the South. Union armies had destroyed factories and railroads, forcing banks to close and disrupting the structure of business. Atlanta, Charleston, Columbia, and Richmond were burned-out shells of cities. And the fighting had disrupted agriculture.

Some wealthy planters found their fortunes gone and their plantations destroyed. Small farmers and poor whites were even more severely affected. One traveler in Alabama reported, "I visited four families, within fifteen minutes' ride of town, who were living in the woods, with no shelter but pine boughs, and this in mid-winter."

Freedmen

The Civil War had begun as a war over the right of secession, but when it was over about 4 million slaves had been freed. To former slave owners, emancipation meant billion-dollar property losses. Moreover, it had a great impact on social relationships. In both the North and the South, white Americans were reluctant to accept blacks as equals. The Thirteenth Amendment to the Constitution, ratified in December 1865, abolished slavery, but it did not change people's attitudes. Few southern whites could think of blacks in any status other than as slaves, and many were afraid that newly freed slaves might seek revenge. Generous behavior on the part of most blacks did little to relieve such fears.

Former slaves, called *freedmen*, faced severe problems as the war ended. Since teaching slaves to read and write had been illegal in most states, few freedmen were literate. Although most were skilled in farming, they owned no land and had no money to buy any. Few people could afford to hire them, and in any case, going to work for a former master seemed too much like slavery.

In March 1865 Congress established the Freedmen's Bureau to aid freedmen and refugees. The bureau issued clothing and over 15 million rations of surplus army food to freed slaves and poverty-stricken whites. It provided over $5 million in educational funds and sent agents to organize schools for black children and adults. The agents sought work for the freedmen and attempted to prevent their exploitation by employers. The bureau also provided medical care for over a million people.

The Freedmen's Bureau was created to alleviate some of the immediate effects of the war, but the federal government had to face difficult questions concerning the legal status of the freedmen and of the former Confederate states.

Preliminary Steps of Reconstruction

Even before the end of the war, President Lincoln had begun to consider how to bring the seceded states back into the Union. From the beginning, the President had believed

Even before the war ended, the federal government set up the Freedmen's Bureau to help freed slaves adjust to their new lives. One of the main activities of the bureau was opening schools for people who as slaves had never been permitted to learn to read and write.

that states had no legal right to secede from the Union. When he first summoned troops after the fall of Fort Sumter, Lincoln treated the southern rebellion as an insurrection. The Confederacy, he argued, was only a group of individuals who were resisting federal authority, not states that had actually seceded. The Constitution gave the President, as commander-in-chief, power to quell insurrections; thus Lincoln believed it was his responsibility to restore harmonious relations with the South as soon as possible.

As early as December 1863 Lincoln had proclaimed a plan of reconstruction for those areas of the South that had come under Union control. He offered a pardon to Confederates on the condition that they swear an oath to support the Constitution and the Union. When 10 percent of the state's citizens who had voted in the 1860 election subscribed to the oath and formed a loyal government and when the state abolished slavery, the President promised to recognize its government and readmit it to the Union.

Lincoln believed that the process of reconstruction should work gradually and patiently because, he argued, "we shall sooner have the fowl by hatching the egg than by smashing it." By the spring of 1864 Louisiana and Arkansas had reorganized their governments according to Lincoln's 10-percent formula.

One group of Republicans in Congress, known as the Radicals, believed the President's plan treated the South far too leniently. Even moderate Republicans argued that Lincoln had overstepped his authority by issuing a plan of reconstruction without seeking the advice and consent of Congress.

In July 1864 moderate Republicans joined forces with the Radicals to pass a bill outlining their version of reconstruction. The Wade-Davis Bill stipulated that a majority of white males had to take an oath of allegiance before the state could be reorganized. Furthermore, those who wished to vote or take a more active role in the new governments would have to swear that they had never voluntarily supported the Confederacy. Finally, the Wade-Davis Bill required that southern state governments repudiate, or refuse to honor, old Confederate debts, abolish slavery, and repudiate their act of secession. Lincoln refused to sign the Wade-Davis Bill because he did not wish to place such severe restrictions on the seceded states.

The President Assassinated

Whether Lincoln's moderate plan could have succeeded is unknown. On April 14, 1865, little more than a month after his second inauguration, the President attended a play at Ford's Theater, seeking some relief from the strains of his office. During the play, an unstable former actor, John Wilkes Booth, crept into the President's box and fired a bullet into the back of his head. The President died next day. The nation was horrified. Rumors flashed across the country, and Confederate leaders were unjustly accused of masterminding the plot.

The army and Secret Service tracked Booth down and trapped him in a barn near Bowling Green, Virginia. When Booth refused to surrender, his pursuers set the barn on fire. Booth was shot, probably by himself, but, in any case, he did not escape. Authorities hung four alleged accomplices and imprisoned four others. Although the assassins were caught and rumors of wider conspiracy quieted, these actions could not compensate for the loss of Lincoln. His firm leadership and ability to compromise with so many groups within the Union would be sorely missed.

A New President, A New Plan

Vice-President Andrew Johnson, now thrust into the presidency, had been born in North Carolina and had moved to Tennessee as a young man. Johnson was a Democrat in the mold of Andrew Jackson, and he bore little love for the rich and aristocratic planters. He had been governor of Tennessee and had represented the state in both the House of Representatives and the Senate before the war broke out.

When Tennessee seceded in 1861, Johnson bitterly opposed the move. Consequently, President Lincoln appointed him military governor of the occupied areas of Tennessee during the war. In 1864 the Republicans offered Johnson the vice-presidential nomination. As a pro-Union Democrat from a state of the upper South, he attracted badly needed votes to help Lincoln win reelection.

As President, Johnson first appeared to take a harsh attitude toward the South. He promptly offered rewards for the capture of Jefferson Davis and other Confederate officials, vowing that "treason must be made infamous and traitors must be impoverished." Senator Benjamin Wade, a Radical Republican, rejoiced, "By the gods there will be no trouble now in running the government."

The Radical Republicans soon discovered, however, that Johnson's intentions differed from theirs. He quickly recognized the governments that had organized themselves according to Lincoln's plan. Then in May 1865 the President announced requirements for the readmission of the remaining states. These were stiffer than Lincoln's conditions but were more moderate than those of the Radical Republicans.

Johnson demanded that all former Confederate states disavow their acts of

Lincoln's Second Inaugural Address

When President Abraham Lincoln delivered his second inaugural address on March 4, 1865, Confederate armies still held out at Petersburg and Richmond. (See Chapter 18.) But Lincoln was already looking ahead to the difficult task of reuniting the nation, as you can see in the following excerpt.

. . . Fondly do we hope, fervently do we pray, that this mighty scourge of war may speedily pass away.

Yet, if God wills that it continue until all the wealth piled by the bondsman's 250 years of unrequited toil shall be sunk, and until every drop of blood drawn with the lash shall be paid by another drawn with the sword, as was said 3,000 years ago, to still it must be said, "The judgments of the Lord are true and righteous altogether."

With malice toward none, with charity for all, with firmness in the right as God gives us to see the right, let us strive on to finish the work we are in, to bind up the nation's wounds, to care for him who shall have borne the battle and for his widow and his orphan—to do all which may achieve and cherish a just and lasting peace among ourselves and with all nations.

Source: John G. Nicolay and John Hay, eds., *Complete Works of Abraham Lincoln* (New York: 1905) vol. 11, p. 47.

secession, repudiate their war debts, and ratify the Thirteenth Amendment. By the winter all the former Confederate states except Texas had moved to obtain Johnson's recognition. But some states were reluctant to fulfill all the President's terms. For example, several state legislatures repealed their acts of secession but would not condemn them. South Carolina refused to repudiate its war debt, and Mississippi refused to ratify the Thirteenth Amendment.

Even more troubling to many Republicans, southern legislatures indicated that they had no intention of giving freedmen equal rights. One state convention echoed the sentiments of many white southerners when it announced that theirs was a "Government of White People, made and to be perpetuated for the exclusive political benefit of the White Race" and that blacks ought not to be considered citizens.

President Johnson was eager to bring all the states back into the Union, however, and he recognized the new southern governments. The states immediately elected representatives to Congress, often selecting wartime leaders.

When Congress convened in December 1865, Johnson announced that his plan had worked, and he urged Congress to seat the southern representatives. Congress refused. Instead, a majority of Republicans, the moderate wing and the Radicals, voted to set up a Joint Committee on Reconstruction to determine if the southern states were truly "reconstructed." Soon Congress would challenge the President for control of Reconstruction.

For answers, see p. A 59.

Section Review

1. Identify the following: Freedmen's Bureau, Wade-Davis Bill, John Wilkes Booth, Andrew Johnson, Joint Committee on Reconstruction.
2. Define the following term: freedmen.
3. List one problem faced by the North and one problem faced by the South after the war.
4. What actions did the Freedmen's Bureau take to help former slaves and other southerners?
5. What was Lincoln's 10-percent plan for Reconstruction?
6. List three conditions that President Johnson established for readmitting former Confederate states to the Union.

2 Congress Takes Over

Andrew Johnson could direct the course of Reconstruction as long as the Radical Republicans in Congress did not have the two-thirds majority needed to override a veto. Gradually, however, many moderate Republicans joined the Radicals, and Congress took control of Reconstruction.

The Radical Position

Some Radical Republicans believed that the former Confederate states had forfeited their statehood when they seceded and had returned to the status of territories. As with new territories, the Radicals insisted, the southern states should be "under the exclusive jurisdiction of Congress." Therefore Congress, not the President, should decide when the states were ready to be readmitted to the Union. This argument was one basis for the Radical Republican opposition to the moderate plans of Lincoln and Johnson.

The Radicals' demand for a harsh policy toward the South also reflected their desire to retain a Republican majority in Congress. The newly elected representatives and senators from the southern states were mostly Democrats. If the Republicans agreed to seat them, the Republicans risked losing their majority and with it their power.

Furthermore, some Radical Republicans disapproved of Johnson's plan simply because they felt it was too lenient. Representative Thaddeus Stevens, one of the most outspoken Radicals, strongly protested presidential pardons of former Confederates. "Did any respectable Government ever before allow such high criminals to escape with such shameful impunity? . . . No sir; they have not been punished as they deserve. They have exchanged forgiveness with the President, and been sent on their way rejoicing." Stevens advocated confiscation of all plantations and division of the land among the freedmen.

Although hate and revenge played a part in the motivation of some Radical Republicans, not all were concerned with political gain or vengeance. Many had been fighting for the freedom of slaves long before abolitionism became popular and long before the Republican party came to dominate Congress.

These Radicals believed that unless black Americans received their full rights as citizens in the South and the North, every battle of the war had been fought in vain. "We must see to it that the man made free by the Constitution . . . is a freeman indeed," explained one Radical, "that he can go where he pleases; work when and for whom he pleases . . . and that he walks the earth, proud and erect in the conscious dignity of a free man."

The Black Codes

When the Joint Committee on Reconstruction (see page 348) met early in 1866, its members heard testimony about conditions in the South. This convinced many moderate Republicans that a more severe Reconstruction plan was needed. Among the most disturbing reports were those of laws designed to limit the activities of freedmen.

Such laws, known as Black Codes, were similar in many ways to former slave codes (see page 76), but they did provide freedmen with certain basic rights. They allowed blacks to sue and be sued and to buy and sell property. Ex-slaves who had been married informally could now make their marriages legal. The Black Codes also provided guidelines to protect young blacks who worked as apprentices. Employers were required to supply food, clothing, and training in a craft.

But the protection of certain rights could not hide the fact that the Black Codes explicitly limited the rights of black citizens by setting many restrictions. While the Constitution guaranteed the right to bear arms, the codes denied that privilege to black Americans. Blacks could not meet together after sunset. They could not marry whites. If any were found idle or unemployed, they were fined for vagrancy and faced imprisonment or hard labor for a year.

Southern state legislatures passed most of the Black Codes in the fall and winter of 1865 and 1866. Many southerners were still convinced that former slaves might rise in revolt or that, at best, they would be unable to contend with their sudden freedom.

Congress reacted to the Black Codes by trying to protect the rights of freedmen. In February 1866 it passed a bill to extend the work of the Freedmen's Bureau for an indefinite period and increase its authority. President Johnson vetoed the bill. He vetoed a second Freedmen's Bureau bill later in the year, but moderate Republicans joined the Radicals to override the veto.

In April Congress passed the Civil Rights Act, again over the President's veto. The act provided that blacks could become United States citizens and possess all the legal rights of citizens. Thus Radicals hoped to secure rights for black Americans even if state laws tried to abridge them.

A Guarantee of Citizenship

Like any law passed by Congress, the Civil Rights Act was subject to review by the Supreme Court. Since the Court had ruled in the Dred Scott case that blacks were not citizens (see page 313), Republicans feared that the Court might declare the Civil Rights Act unconstitutional. Congress therefore proposed a constitutional amendment guaranteeing citizenship to black Americans.

At the heart of the Fourteenth Amendment was the simple and direct statement that "All persons born or naturalized in the United States . . . are citizens." Any person who had held a national or state government position before the Civil War and who had given "aid or comfort" to the Confederate cause was forbidden to hold public office unless pardoned by Congress. In addition, all Confederate debts were cancelled, and no former slave owners could be reimbursed by any government, state or national, for the loss of their slaves by the act of emancipation.

Some Radicals wanted to include a provision guaranteeing all males, black and white, the right to vote. But many Republicans hesitated to go that far. At the time, only a few northern states permitted blacks to vote, and Republicans feared an angry reaction from their white constituents if blacks received the vote. The amendment did provide, however, that if southern states did not allow black males to vote, they would lose a proportionate number of seats in the House.

The Fourteenth Amendment was passed in June 1866 and sent to the states for ratification. By July 1868, enough states had approved the measure to make it part of the Constitution. Although the Fourteenth Amendment guaranteed citizenship to black Americans, they did not explicitly gain the right to vote in all states until the Fifteenth Amendment was ratified in 1870. The Fifteenth Amendment stated that no citizen could be denied the right to vote "on account of race, color, or previous condition of servitude."

The Beginning of Radical Reconstruction

When Republicans in Congress first proposed the Fourteenth Amendment in the summer of 1866, the split between them and President Johnson became irreparable. Johnson scorned the Fourteenth Amendment, urging southern legislatures to reject it as an invasion of states' rights.* To counter Radical influence, the President actively campaigned for candidates who supported his policies in the fall congressional elections. Unfortunately for Johnson, his speeches cost him support. When his audiences heckled him, he often lost his temper and responded with vulgar, vindictive language.

Outbreaks of racial violence in Memphis and New Orleans in which many blacks were killed reinforced the growing popular mood against the President. The riots convinced many northerners that Johnson's lenient policies had not worked and that stronger measures were needed to protect the freedmen.

The election results were a disaster for Johnson and a triumph for the Republicans. The Republican party won majorities in every northern state legislature, every northern governor's race, and over a two-thirds majority in both houses of Congress, assuring them of enough votes to override any presidential veto.

With control of Congress assured after the 1866 elections, Radical Republicans devised their own program for Reconstruction, passing the Reconstruction Act in March

---

*Every state government Johnson had recognized, except for the one in Tennessee, did reject the Fourteenth Amendment the first time it was considered.

1867. All former Confederate states except Tennessee, readmitted in July 1866 after it ratified the Fourteenth Amendment, had to meet a new set of requirements for readmission to the Union. Each state had to adopt a state constitution that disqualified former Confederate officials from holding office and granted black citizens the right to vote. The states also had to ratify the Fourteenth Amendment.

Until they were readmitted, the former Confederate states would be under military control. The Reconstruction Act divided the states into five military districts, each commanded by an army general. The commanders became responsible for organizing the state constitutional conventions and were required to register blacks and loyal whites to vote for convention delegates. In this way Congress tried to prevent state conventions from rejecting parts of the plan as Johnson had originally encouraged. The President vetoed the Reconstruction Act and several supplementary acts that followed it. But Congress easily overrode his vetoes, and Radical Reconstruction went into effect.

A Showdown Between the President and Congress

Although Congress had wrested control of Reconstruction from the President, it still feared that Johnson would try to execute as little of the plan as possible. Consequently Congress passed several laws that limited the President's freedom to act. One of these, the Tenure of Office Act, stated that any officeholder appointed by the President, with the advice and consent of the Senate, could not be dismissed without the Senate's consent. The Radicals hoped, thereby, to protect their sympathizers in the administration.

When Congress recessed in the summer of 1867, President Johnson decided to test the constitutionality of the act by removing Edwin Stanton, an ally of the Radicals, as Secretary of War. Stanton refused to leave, barricaded the doors of his office, and continued to issue orders. Johnson also angered Republicans by dismissing commanders of the military Reconstruction districts who sympathized too openly with Congress.

During 1867 many Radical Republicans came to believe that if Reconstruction were to succeed, Johnson would have to be removed from office. But the only way Congress could remove a President was to impeach and convict him for "high crimes and misdemeanors" committed while in office.* A congressional committee appointed to investigate the President's actions searched in vain for evidence of such crimes. Nevertheless, the Radicals proceeded with a plan of impeachment, claiming that Stanton's firing was serious enough to warrant action.

On February 24, 1868, the House of Representatives voted to impeach. President Andrew Johnson stood trial in the Senate from March 25 to May 26.

Much was at stake beyond the immediate issue of Reconstruction. Because Congress had no specific evidence to substantiate its charge of "high crimes and misdemeanors," it was essentially trying to dismiss a President simply because he disagreed with it. In the final tally 35 senators voted for conviction, 19 against, one vote short of removing the President from office.

Johnson served out his term, but the impeachment effort had undermined his power. Although Congress had not convicted him, it came close enough to demonstrate that it was determined to remain in absolute charge of Reconstruction.

---

* As you learned in Chapter 9, the House of Representatives can vote to impeach, or accuse, a President of committing "high crimes and misdemeanors." If a two-thirds majority of the Senate votes to convict a President, he or she is removed from office.

Facsimile of a ticket of admission to the impeachment trial of President Andrew Johnson.

For answers, see p. A 59.
Section Review

1. Identify the following: Thaddeus Stevens, Black Codes, Civil Rights Act, Reconstruction Act, Tenure of Office Act.

2. List four reasons why the Radical Republicans favored a harsh position toward former Confederate states.

3. (a) What rights did the Black Codes extend to black Americans? (b) What rights did they deny black Americans?

4. (a) What was the major provision of the Fourteenth Amendment? (b) What was the major provision of the Fifteenth Amendment?

5. What provisions did the Radicals establish in 1867 for readmitting former Confederate states?

6. What actions prompted Congress to begin impeachment proceedings against President Johnson?

3 The Reconstruction South

When the Radical Republicans imposed their own version of Reconstruction in 1867, citizens in southern states began the process of writing constitutions and electing state governments. Black voters participated for the first time in these elections. Republicans dominated the new state governments, which quickly fulfilled Congress's requirements for Reconstruction. Most former Confederate states had been readmitted by July 1868 and all had by 1871. But rebuilding the southern economy would prove more difficult.

The Difficulty of Rebuilding

The devastation caused by the war made southern economic recovery difficult. Efforts to rebuild were further handicapped by a lack of cash. Confederate money was worthless after the war, and United States currency did not filter into the South as rapidly as it was needed. Planters and small farmers who were deeply in debt at the end of the war looked for a way to borrow money and begin all over again. However, many found that difficult to do.

Since land was the chief item of value left in the South, many planters and farmers were forced to sell their land in order to survive. Others bought supplies on credit from merchants at high prices and high interest rates. Farmers promised to repay the loan when the crops were harvested. Each year, more planters and farmers found themselves going deeper into debt to the merchants.

Poor white and black farmers who owned no land of their own had to work on other people's lands either as tenants or as sharecroppers. *Tenants* rented land from a large landowner and supplied their own seed and supplies. Tenants might sell their crops and pay their rent in cash, but many paid "in kind" by giving the landowner a portion of the crop. *Sharecroppers* farmed a piece of land and shared the crops they raised with the landowners. Usually, one third of the crop would go to the landowner, one third to the sharecropper, and one third to whomever provided the seeds, fertilizer, mules, and other farming equipment.

Many freedmen became sharecroppers with the hope of being able to buy their own land one day. But few realized that dream. Instead, like many other southerners, they became locked into a system of debt that promised little more than year-to-year survival.

New Forces in Southern Politics

Politics in the South during Radical Reconstruction differed greatly from that of prewar days. The Fourteenth Amendment and congressional reconstruction acts had barred former Confederate officials from taking part in state governments and had opened up participation to black citizens. Two groups, which conservative southerners called carpetbaggers and scalawags, also influenced southern politics.

Carpetbaggers were those northerners who had settled in the South after the war and supported Radical Reconstruction. Southern whites viewed them as unscrupulous intruders from the North who were seeking only personal gain. All carpetbaggers, however, did not fit that description. Some were Union soldiers who had remained in the South after the war. Others had moved South to help freedmen face their new problems.

Scalawags were white southerners who supported Radical Reconstruction. Many had been southern Unionists during the war and continued their support for the Union. Although some southerners supported the Radicals in hopes of political or financial favor, many did so because they thought it was in the interest of the South. One such person

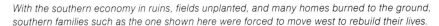

With the southern economy in ruins, fields unplanted, and many homes burned to the ground, southern families such as the one shown here were forced to move west to rebuild their lives.

A lawyer and a scholar, Robert Brown Elliot of South Carolina was a southern black leader elected to Congress after the Civil War. In this illustration he is shown arguing for a civil rights bill in the House of Representatives in 1874.

was James Longstreet, one of Lee's generals and a successful business leader after the war. He argued that in the long run it was best for the South to cooperate with the Radicals in order to regain economic stability.

The influence of carpetbaggers and scalawags varied from state to state. In Mississippi the carpetbaggers controlled politics. In Tennessee the scalawags did. In no state, however, did blacks control the government, although they played a part in all.

Black Americans held offices previously denied them, but their influence was far less than conservative whites claimed. Only in South Carolina did blacks win a majority in one house of a legislature, and in no state did they win the governorship. Hiram R. Revels and Blanche K. Bruce, both of Mississippi, were the only two black Americans elected to the United States Senate during the Re-

construction period. Like most blacks elected to office following the Civil War, they served with pride and dignity.

Actions of the Reconstruction Governments

The southern state governments during Radical Reconstruction achieved a number of genuine improvements for their states. Legislatures passed laws giving black citizens equal civil and political rights. For the first time, southern states established free public education for all children. New laws improved care in prisons and provided centers for the care of mentally and physically handicapped persons.

But the Radical Reconstruction governments faced many problems. Since most of

This cartoon illustrates southern resentment of Reconstruction. The South walks barefoot over sharp stones while federal soldiers wear shoes and walk on smooth ground. Furthermore, the South bears the burden of a heavy carpetbag full of weapons. The man riding the carpetbag is Ulysses S. Grant, President during much of the Reconstruction period.

Corruption also plagued the Reconstruction governments. One state legislature, for example, awarded $1,000 to the speaker of the house to cover a lost bet on a horse race; and billed the state for hams, perfume, clothing, champagne, and a coffin.

Although such corruption gave the Reconstruction governments a bad reputation, bribery and graft were characteristic of governments throughout the nation after the Civil War, as you will read in Chapter 22. But this was scant consolation to conservative white southerners. They resented northerners who came to the South and prospered while many southerners lost their land. As former Confederates, they were naturally bitter when they saw southern Unionists come to power in the new governments. And they reacted with fear and skepticism toward their former slaves, who now were voting and holding office in governments once controlled by the wealthy whites.

the South's experienced political leaders had been Confederates, the Reconstruction governments sometimes suffered from inexperience and incompetence. New officeholders often found it difficult to handle their jobs, since they had little preparation.*

_____
* In the years before the war, southern legislatures were dominated by wealthy planters who had denied educational and political opportunities to lower- and middle-class whites and to all blacks.

For answers, see p. A 60.

Section Review

1. Identify the following: Hiram R. Revels, Blanche K. Bruce.

2. Define the following terms: tenants, sharecroppers, carpetbaggers, scalawags.

3. What conditions contributed to a shortage of cash in the South?

4. What three groups were new forces in southern politics after the War?

5. What improvements did southern state governments make during Radical Reconstruction?

6. List two problems that plagued Reconstruction governments in the South.

4 Unfinished Business

With the passage of the Reconstruction Acts in 1867, the Radical Republicans reached the peak of their influence. They had defeated President Johnson's conservative Reconstruction program and neutralized his power by bringing impeachment proceedings. They had forced the southern states to call new constitutional conventions, elect new governments, and give black Americans the right to vote. But over the next ten years Radical Reconstruction steadily lost ground and finally collapsed completely.

A Changing Political Climate

Radical Reconstruction faltered in the South partly because the national leadership of the Republican party changed. Representative Thaddeus Stevens died in 1868, and Benjamin Wade lost his seat in the Senate in 1869. Other Radicals retired from public life.

Radical Republicans hoped to restore their falling influence by nominating General Ulysses S. Grant for President in 1868. In a close election, Grant defeated the Democratic nominee, Governor Horatio Seymour of New York. Once in office, however, President Grant proved much less sympathetic to the Radicals' cause than they had hoped. He was also ill prepared for the presidency.

As a military leader, the General had been hard driving, stubborn, and thorough. As a political leader, he lacked any real experience. Consequently, he often depended on the advice of others and rewarded many of his friends with appointments in the new administration. Several members of his cabinet swindled the government of millions of dollars.

By 1872 one group of Republicans, disillusioned with the corruption, split with the Grant administration. Calling themselves Liberal Republicans, they nominated New York Tribune editor Horace Greeley to run against Grant in his bid for reelection. The President, however, still retained much of his personal popularity and the worst of the scandals had not yet been exposed. Consequently, he won the 1872 election by a greater margin than he had in 1868.

The North's Declining Interest in Reconstruction

The war remained an important issue in the 1868 election and even in 1872. Republicans frequently reminded northern voters about the lives lost and money spent to win the war. But as the 1870s progressed, passions cooled. Northerners increasingly believed that the arguments and ill feelings of the past should be forgotten and that southerners should be allowed to run their own governments—even if that meant blacks might lose the rights they had so recently gained.

Furthermore, reports of corruption among carpetbaggers and scalawags shocked and disillusioned many Republicans who had supported the Reconstruction governments. They were also disheartened when some black officials, often through inexperience, became involved in the corruption. The longer Grant stayed in office, the more people focused their attention on the issue of corruption in government, both state and national. They grew less concerned with the older issues of Reconstruction.

Many northern business leaders argued for an end to Reconstruction. They believed that the Radical governments were preventing the South from expanding economically. Northern manufacturers wanted to invest in the South, but only if they could count on stable governments free from turmoil. "We have tried this Reconstruction long enough," concluded one business leader. "Now let the South alone."

Ending Radical Rule

A majority of white southerners had always resented the Republicans' attempt to reconstruct the South. Over the years they worked to regain control of the state governments from the Republicans. Some, particularly among the upper classes, believed that the best way to return to power was to accept the Radicals' changes, gain the goodwill of the new black voters, and woo them away from the Republicans into the Democratic party.

When Wade Hampton, a wealthy South Carolinian, ran for governor of his state in 1876, he campaigned among blacks, telling them, "We want your votes; we don't want you to be deprived of them. . . . if we are elected, as far as in us lies, we will observe, protect, and defend the rights of the colored man as quickly as any man in South Carolina."

But a large number of white southerners rejected this strategy. Poor white farmers, who were having trouble making a living in the war-torn South, feared economic competition from blacks. Blacks had been viewed as slaves for so many years that many white southerners, both rich and poor, resented the freedmen's right to vote and hold office. Consequently, these groups were determined to drive scalawags and carpetbaggers from office and to end the influence of blacks in elections.

Pressure and intimidation were among the tactics used. Newspapers might publish the names of southern whites sympathetic to Reconstruction, and the sympathizers were then snubbed by their neighbors. Landowners could pressure black tenant farmers to vote Democratic or not at all.

Other people resorted to force or the threat of it. In some areas, groups banded together in informal military groups or rifle clubs. They drilled conspicuously in areas where blacks lived or sent armed pickets to prevent blacks from registering to vote.

The Ku Klux Klan used floggings, hangings, and other acts of violence to intimidate blacks and their white supporters. This cartoon appeared in an Alabama newspaper as a warning to carpetbaggers of the fate awaiting them.

Secret organizations such as the Ku Klux Klan and the Knights of the White Camelia were formed with the purpose of ending Radical Republican rule in the South. The Klan tried to keep black and white Republican voters from the polls by burning houses and whipping, shooting, or hanging blacks and sympathetic whites. Dressed in white robes and hoods, the Klan often rode at night, breaking up Republican meetings. Moderate southerners condemned such violence and even some leaders of the Klan felt its organization had gone too far, but the Klan's campaign of intimidation kept many potential Republican voters away from the polls.

In 1870 and 1871 Congress passed the Force Act and Ku Klux Klan Act, outlawing the use of force to prevent people from voting, and authorized President Grant to use federal troops to enforce the laws. Under such pressure the Klan's activities diminished, but the threat of violence lingered. One by one, the southern states voted out the Radical Republican governments and replaced them with conservative ones. By 1876 only Louisiana, Florida, and South Carolina retained their Radical governments.

The Hayes-Tilden Compromise

The election year of 1876 found the Republicans in disarray. In 1874 southerners elected enough Democrats to Congress to give that party a majority in the House of Representa-

tives and a near-majority in the Senate. The Grant administration had been marred by scandal after scandal. With the issue of corruption so prominent, both parties nominated for President men with reputations as reformers. The Republicans chose Rutherford B. Hayes, an Ohio lawyer, and the Democrats selected Governor Samuel Tilden of New York.

In the election Tilden received 250,000 more popular votes than Hayes, but he was one vote short of the necessary 185 electoral votes. Hayes had only 165 electoral votes. The remaining 20 electoral votes, from the states of Florida, Louisiana, and South Carolina, plus one from Oregon, were claimed by both sides.

The Oregon vote eventually went to Hayes, but the decision in the other states was not easy. Florida, Louisiana, and South Carolina were the only states in the South still dominated by Republicans. Tilden had won a majority of the popular vote in each

Major Events	
1863	Lincoln proclaims 10-percent plan for Reconstruction
1864	Wade-Davis Bill proposed
1865	Congress establishes Freedmen's Bureau; Appomattox; Abraham Lincoln assassinated; Andrew Johnson becomes President; Thirteenth Amendment ratified
1866	Civil Rights Act passed; Fourteenth Amendment proposed
1867	Reconstruction Acts passed
1868	House of Representatives impeaches President Johnson; Fourteenth Amendment ratified; Ulysses S. Grant elected President
1870	Fifteenth Amendment ratified; Force Act passed
1871	Ku Klux Klan Act passed
1876	Rutherford B. Hayes elected President

state, but the Republican-controlled state election boards ruled that he had received his majority through fraud and intimidation of black voters. In the heat of the election dispute, rival Republican and Democratic electors claimed victory, voted for their candidate, and sent in their ballots.*

The nation now faced a terrible dilemma. Which electoral votes from these states should be counted? Congress finally named an electoral commission to decide the issue, consisting of seven Republicans, seven Democrats, and one independent. At the last minute, however, a Republican replaced the independent, and Hayes had the votes he needed to win the election.

---

*According to the Constitution, the electors of each state send a list of their votes to the President of the Senate, who counts the votes in the presence of both the House and the Senate.

Democrats were outraged, especially in the South. It seemed as if Hayes had stolen the election. Although there was some talk of a new civil war, conservative southerners in Congress negotiated a compromise with the Republicans. In return for their support, Hayes promised federal aid to construct new railroads and to control floods along the Mississippi River. Most important, he pledged to remove the last federal troops remaining in the South and to bring Reconstruction to a swift close.

357

The End of Reconstruction

Rutherford B. Hayes was inaugurated as President on March 5, 1877. In April the last federal troops withdrew from South Carolina and Louisiana, and Democratic governors replaced Republican incumbents. The

■ The election of 1876 was one of the closest in American history, and its results were fiercely disputed. As the table and graphs indicate, Tilden won the most popular votes. However, disputes over election irregularities in several states led both sides to claim victory in the electoral college. Eventually a compromise gave the disputed electoral votes to Hayes.

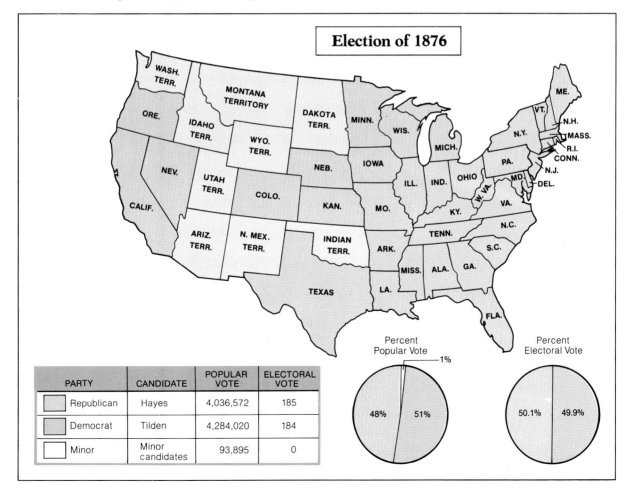

Election of 1876

PARTY	CANDIDATE	POPULAR VOTE	ELECTORAL VOTE
Republican	Hayes	4,036,572	185
Democrat	Tilden	4,284,020	184
Minor	Minor candidates	93,895	0

Percent Popular Vote: 48% / 51% / 1%

Percent Electoral Vote: 50.1% / 49.9%

Republican government in Florida had been defeated even before the inauguration.

Although Reconstruction was over, much of what it had started remained unfinished. The South had not recovered economically for blacks or whites. Neither civil nor political equality for black Americans was yet a reality in the South or North. In fact, in subsequent years many of the advances made in the early years after the war would be lost.

Nonetheless the postwar events had laid the foundation for change. The states had ratified two amendments, granting black Americans full rights of citizenship and the right to vote, at least in theory. Many years would pass before these rights would become a reality, but the amendments set standards toward which the country could aim. In later years, they would become levers for freedom.

358

For answers, see p. A 60.

Section Review

1. Identify the following: Ku Klux Klan, Force Act, Ku Klux Klan Act, Rutherford B. Hayes, Samuel Tilden.

2. How did the death of Thaddeus Stevens and the defeat of Senator Benjamin Wade affect Radical Reconstruction?

3. How did political corruption contribute to a declining interest in Reconstruction among northerners?

4. Why did northern business leaders seek an end to Reconstruction?

5. (a) What tactics were used to discourage blacks from voting? (b) Were they successful? Explain.

6. What did Hayes agree to in exchange for support from conservative southerners?

★ ★ ★ ★ ★ ★ ★ ★ ★ ★ ★ ★ ★ ★ ★ ★ ★ ★ ★ ★

IN PERSPECTIVE The Civil War had deeply divided the nation and left scars that remained for decades. Abraham Lincoln's dream of gradually bringing the Confederate states back into the Union died when he was assassinated. Andrew Johnson hoped to quickly recognize the governments of the Confederate states, but his program was challenged and eventually defeated by Congress.

The Radical Republicans considered Johnson's plans too lenient and many moderate Republicans came to agree with them. When the Radicals won a two-thirds majority in both houses of Congress in 1866, they were assured of the support needed to override any presidential veto. Their attempt to remove President Johnson from office failed, but it did seriously weaken his presidency.

Many black Americans voted for the first time in the elections of new state governments under the Radical Reconstruction program. Although the new governments were handicapped by inexperience and by the type of corruption common throughout the nation, they did institute important reform measures, such as funds for public schools.

Gradually the Radical Republicans lost support as the bitterness of the war faded and people became concerned with issues like corruption. Some southerners used intimidation and violence to prevent blacks and white Republicans from voting. Over the years more conservative state governments replaced the ones set up under Radical Reconstruction. In 1877, when President Hayes removed the last federal troops from the South, Reconstruction officially ended. Although the Fourteenth and Fifteenth Amendments guaranteed basic rights to black Americans, these rights were often ignored, as you will read. Reconstruction left many social, political, and economic problems to be faced by future generations.

For answers, see p. A 61.

Chapter Review

1. What factors made reunion of the North and South after the war especially difficult?

2. (a) What problems did former slaves face after the war? (b) How did the Freedmen's Bureau help former slaves adjust to their new life?

3. (a) Why did Lincoln believe it was his responsibility as President to reunite the nation? (b) Describe Lincoln's plan for Reconstruction. (c) Why did he favor a moderate approach?

4. (a) Why did the Radical Republicans believe that Johnson would be sympathetic to their position? (b) Were they right? Explain.

5. (a) Did the southern states completely fulfill Johnson's requirement for readmission? (b) Why did he recognize the new governments? (c) What was Congress's reaction when it convened in December 1865?

6. (a) What was the Radical Republicans' attitude toward the legal status of former Confederate states? (b) Why did they favor harsher requirements for readmission?

7. (a) What were the Black Codes? (b) Why did southern state legislatures pass them? (c) How did Congress react to the passage of the Black Codes?

8. (a) Why did Congress propose the Fourteenth Amendment to the Constitution? (b) What was its major provision? (c) What other provisions did it contain? (d) What was the major provision of the Fifteenth Amendment?

9. (a) Why were the 1866 congressional elections important for the Radical Republicans? (b) How did the impeachment of President Johnson strengthen the position of the Radical Republicans?

10. (a) Why did many planters and farmers go into debt after the war? (b) How did many poor whites and freedmen make a living after the war?

11. (a) How was politics in the Reconstruction South different from that of the prewar era? (b) How did white conservatives try to regain political influence? (c) Were they successful? Explain.

12. (a) What were the achievements of the Reconstruction governments in the South? (b) What problems did they have?

13. How did each of the following contribute to the collapse of Radical Reconstruction by 1876: (a) retirement of Radical leaders; (b) corruption in the Grant administration; (c) corruption in southern state governments; (d) desire for business expansion; (e) violence against blacks and sympathetic whites; (f) the Hayes-Tilden Compromise.

For answers, see p. A 61.

For Further Thought

1. Do you think the Radical Republicans believed in a strict or loose interpretation of the Constitution? Give specific examples to support your answer.

2. (a) Describe the process by which Congress can remove a President from office. (b) Why do you think the framers of the Constitution made it a difficult process? (c) Do you think the Radical Republicans had good reasons for trying to remove Andrew Johnson? Why or why not?

3. How might the history of Reconstruction have been different if President Lincoln had not been assassinated?

For answers, see p. A 61.

Developing Basic Skills

1. *Comparing* Make a chart with three columns. In one column list the provisions of Lincoln's Reconstruction policy. In column two list the provisions of Johnson's policy. In column three list the provisions imposed by the Radical Republicans. (a) Which policy seemed the least severe? (b) Which policy seemed the most severe? (c) Based on what you read, how would you explain the differences?

2. *Map Reading* Study the election map and graphs on page 357. (a) Which candidate received the most electoral votes? (b) Which candidate received the most popular votes? (c) In which states were the votes disputed? (d) Why do you think most southerners voted for the Democratic candidate?

See page 776 for suggested readings.

Unit Six

Transforming a Nation

20

The Western Frontier

(1865–1900)

Pioneer Woman, *by Harvey Dunn.*

Chapter Outline

1 *Visions of the West*

2 *Opening of the West*

3 *Tragedy for the Plains Indians*

4 *The Cattle Frontier*

5 *The Sodbusters' Frontier*

In July 1806 Zebulon Pike led an exploration party through what is now Kansas and eastern Colorado. Pike reported that he had seen enormous tracts "where the wind has thrown up the sand in all the fanciful forms of the ocean's rolling waves, and on which not a speck of vegetable matter existed." He argued that the land could not support farming and therefore should be left to the Indians. Fourteen years later Stephen Long explored the area that was to become Nebraska and Oklahoma and labeled it the "Great American Desert."

Until the 1860s that label stuck. Pioneers crossed the area to reach the lush lands of Oregon or the gold fields of California, but few stopped along the way. However, after the Civil War, a growing number of people began to settle the huge region between the Mississippi River and the Sierra Nevadas.

They came for various reasons. Prospectors sought gold and silver in the mountains. Cattle ranchers from Texas established vast grazing areas on the grasslands. Farmers devised new techniques to overcome the dry climate. The plans of the pioneers almost always conflicted with the cultures of the Native Americans living in the region. The history of the last western frontier is largely the story of how the new settlers changed the land and its people, how they tapped the resources of the region and molded it to their needs.

1 Visions of the West

The United States began as a nation with a frontier reaching along the Appalachians and into the Ohio Valley. Gradually the frontier line was pushed westward. By the Civil War American settlement had advanced west of the Mississippi River and into Texas, Iowa, and eastern Kansas and Nebraska. In these areas, with their rich soil and moderate rainfall, farming was profitable. But the Great Plains farther west provided new challenges.

Life on the Great Plains

The Great Plains stretch from about the 98th meridian to the Rocky Mountains. Less than 20 inches (50 centimeters) of rain falls on these vast plains each year, compared with up to 40 inches (100 centimeters) a year in the East. The land is treeless, except for occasional timber in the river bottoms.

West of Denver, Colorado, the Rockies spring abruptly out of the plains. Beyond the mountains extends the Great Basin, where Death Valley and the Mojave (moh HAH vee) Desert are located. The frontier of 1860 was bounded on the west by the high peaks of the Sierra Nevadas and the Cascades. Beyond these two ranges lay the rich valleys of California and Oregon, which were already being settled.

As you read in Chapter 1, before the arrival of European explorers many Plains peoples had been nomadic. On foot they hunted buffalo and other game. Horses had been extinct in the Americas for thousands of years, but early Spanish explorers and settlers brought their mounts from Europe. Over the years some horses had strayed and multiplied. Gradually herds of wild horses traveled north from Mexico onto the Great Plains. During the 1700s Plains Indians began to tame and ride horses, and by the 1780s most groups had become accomplished at riding.

The Kiowa, Sioux, Crow, Comanche, Cheyenne, Arapaho, Blackfeet, and other Indian nations could thus roam hundreds of miles on horseback to hunt buffalo. With more successful hunts, the Plains Indians prospered, and their population tripled, reaching about 150,000 by the mid-nineteenth century. Despite this growth, the vast plains remained sparsely settled. Most of the Indians hunted only enough buffalo to supply basic needs without destroying the herds.

These shaggy animals supplied most of the necessities of life. The carcass provided fresh meat. What excess meat could not be eaten was dried for use during winter. Women prepared buffalo hides to make teepees and clothing. Sinew was made into thread and bowstrings, bones into tools, and horns into eating utensils. Dried buffalo dung became fuel and the rough side of the tongue a hairbrush.

Native American Vision of the West

The Indians of the Great Plains believed that the natural world was in close harmony with the supernatural spirits who governed it. Only by maintaining a proper relationship with the many spirit-gods of the plains would the Indians be rewarded with success in hunting and in war. Accordingly, the purpose of Indian religious rituals was to bring the lives of the participants into harmony with the spiritual world.

Since they revered nature, the Plains Indians disturbed the land and its creatures as

For the Kiowa, as for other Plains people, vast buffalo herds provided food, clothing, and shelter. Kiowa warrior Two Hatchets, shown here, typifies the dignity of the Plains Indians.

little as possible. Any wasteful or harmful use of the natural environment disturbed their vision of a balanced world. But their way of life, resting on a precarious balance with nature, changed drastically with the arrival of immigrants from the East, immigrants who had a different vision of the West.

New Visions of the West

On the Fourth of July, 1868, William Gilpin, the first territorial governor of Colorado, stood up in the rough frontier town of Denver and delivered an enthusiastic oration on the future of the West. For Gilpin the Great Plains were not the Great American Desert, as some called them. He brushed aside the problem of limited rainfall by claiming that artesian wells, bored deep into the ground, would transform the plains into a garden.

Gilpin accepted the belief, common in his era, that once crops had been planted, the new vegetation would change the climate and encourage rain. As a booster of the West, Gilpin fancied that its resources were limitless, and he predicted that the land would eventually support over a billion people.

In the year after this address, a young man who was to reject Gilpin's vision began his own trek westward. John Wesley Powell was a rough. striking figure and a magnetic leader. Fighting as a volunteer in the Civil War, he had lost his right arm at the elbow in the battle of Shiloh. Undaunted, he returned to active service and rose to become a major.

In 1869, as a trained geologist, Powell was poised to lead a scientific expedition down the Colorado River through the Grand Canyon. He was not deterred by the frailty of his boats, the swirling canyon rapids, or the painful awkwardness created by his amputated arm. As he mapped the Grand Canyon and studied the surrounding areas, Powell built his own vision of how the land should be treated.

The West, he claimed, was a mixture of natural environments shaped by the amount of rainfall in each locality. One overriding fact remained: water was scarce throughout. While a farmer in the rainy East could make an adequate living on a farm of 160 acres (64 hectares), Powell predicted that in the arid West, over 1,200 acres (480 hectares) of unirrigated land would be needed.

With water so scarce, Powell foresaw the need for cooperation among western settlers. In the East a farmer had a legal right to do whatever he wanted with a river flowing through his property. In the West, Powell warned, the use of water would somehow have to be regulated and shared.

Beginning in 1860s the vision of the Native Americans would be challenged and then destroyed by miners, railroad builders, ranchers, and farmers who came west with their own dreams and hopes. Many of the first pioneers shared Gilpin's vision of unlimited resources, but gradually more settlers came to accept Powell's view that cooperation would be needed to overcome the hardships people would face.

For answers, see p. A 63.
Section Review

1. Identify the following: William Gilpin, John Wesley Powell.
2. List one climatic and one topographical feature of the Great Plains.
3. How did the Plains Indians make use of the buffalo?
4. How did the Indians of the plains treat the land? Why?
5. (a) What was the Native American view of the West? (b) What was Gilpin's vision? (c) What was Powell's vision?

2 Opening of the West

Before the 1860s the only American settlers to see the Great Plains, the Rocky Mountains, the Great Basin, and the Sierra Nevadas and Cascades beyond were traveling to California or Oregon. Those settlers considered the land worthless and crossed it as quickly as possible. But in the late 1850s and early 1860s new gold and silver strikes in the Rockies attracted a growing number of Americans to the West. The completion of a transcontinental railroad in 1869 made it easier for people to travel there.

The New Mining Frontier

Miners who had flocked to California during the Gold Rush of the late 1840s set out to find new strikes in the late 1850s. From California they pushed east into the Sierra Nevadas and the Rocky Mountains. Thus the mining frontier was unusual in American history, since it moved from the west coast eastward.

Most of the first strikes were made in the late 1850s and early 1860s. Nearest to the original California fields were the mines of western Nevada. In the next 20 years the Comstock Lode near Virginia City, Nevada, yielded over $300 million in gold and silver, the richest mining strike in history.

To the north, miners discovered valuable mineral deposits in the Columbia and Fraser river valleys. They also made strikes in Idaho and Montana along the Bitter Root and Salmon River mountain ranges. Farther east in Colorado, mining towns such as Denver, Boulder, and Colorado Springs grew up near gold strikes. (See the map on page 374.)

Even more than the earlier California mines, these deposits required large corporations to extract the mineral riches. In strikes like the Comstock Lode, the richest deposits lay well underground, trapped in quartz veins that could not be mined without costly tools. Only organized investors with large sums of money for rock-crushing machinery and drills that could bore down a thousand feet (300 meters) or more could take advantage of the new finds.

From Mining Camps to Towns and Cities

The discovery of mineral riches brought thousands of people to the West. Towns sprang up throughout the area as rumors of gold or silver strikes spread. If little gold and silver was found, people quickly left, leaving behind a ghost town of empty buildings.

Sometimes towns were built in anticipation of a big strike even before gold was discovered. In 1858 when Denver was founded along the South Platte River, only a few ounces of gold had been found in the Colorado streams. Yet farsighted planners had already bought up town space and begun laying out streets and erecting cabins. When rich deposits were found the following year, Denver prospered. By 1860 it had its own lending library, two newspapers, one theater,

a schoolteacher, and a barber who encouraged miners to "get your beards mowed."

Although most miners were men, enterprising women also profited from the new strikes. With only a few dollars to her name a woman could open a boardinghouse in a western boom town and make a tidy fortune. Cooking and baking jobs could bring rich rewards too. One ambitious baker reported that in less than a year she had baked and sold $18,000 worth of pies.

Frequently the rapid growth of towns led to disorder and lawlessness. Makeshift governments tried to establish order, but miners often organized *vigilante* committees, self-appointed enforcers of the law. Singling out the worst desperadoes and outlaws, vigilante groups gave them speedy trials and frequently lynched them.

Informal methods of government gradually gave way to more formal arrangements. In 1861 Colorado, Dakota, and Nevada were organized as territories; Idaho and Arizona followed in 1863 and Montana in 1864. Although boisterous mining towns would continue to spring up through the mid-1870s, the process of more permanent settlement had begun.

Transportation Opens the West

When news of gold strikes in Colorado first reached the East in 1859, transportation between the two regions was limited. Few railroads extended west of the Mississippi River. (See the map on page 374.) Without a good system of transportation linking West and East, the growth of the West would be severely limited.

In the 1850s the first stagecoach lines began offering service between East and West. John Butterfield's Overland Express looped south through Texas and New Mexico, then up the California coast. The firm of Russell, Majors, and Waddell followed a more central route along the Platte River and across the Rockies to San Francisco.

Travelers who could afford the $200 fee and were willing to wait 10 days to reserve a place on the stage could travel from Missouri to California in about 20 days. Passengers rode packed three abreast in an elegant coach complete with broad iron "tire" wheels that didn't sink in the sand. The bumpy ride nonetheless was exhausting and grimy.

Temporary lodging was available at the way stations where stage drivers changed horses, but few passengers cared to stop. The station huts offered only a few bunks covered with old rags and buffalo robes. The floors, grumbled one traveler, were "much like the ground outside, only not nearly so clean."

Mail service also improved. The Pony Express, established in 1860, delivered a letter from St. Louis to San Francisco in ten days at a cost of up to $10 an ounce. Eighty riders sped east and west along a route almost 2,000 miles (3,200 kilometers) long, working in relays to bring the mail through. But the Pony Express lasted less than two years. In 1862 wires had been strung across the plains, and messages could be transmitted instantly using the telegraph, invented by Samuel Morse in 1832.

Linking East and West by Rail

Observing the rapid growth of eastern railroads in the 1850s, many westerners concluded that their region would benefit greatly if rail service could be extended to the Pacific. A train could carry hundreds of passengers and large amounts of freight.

However, building a transcontinental railroad posed major problems. Most lines in the East were operated by small companies. The sums of money needed to build a railroad stretching across the nation were beyond the means of most private investors, especially since that route meant cutting through both the Sierra Nevadas and the Rocky Mountains.

In 1862 the government stepped in to encourage the railroad companies to build a transcontinental line. It offered railroad companies land in the West as an incentive. The United States government had acquired the western lands through treaties and purchases from Native Americans. (See the map on page 370.) Land that belongs to the nation and not to individuals is called *public domain*. For every mile (1.6 kilometers) of track laid, Congress granted the railroad companies 20 square miles (52 square kilometers) of land plus a 400-foot-wide (120-meter) right of way. In addition, Congress agreed to loan money for every mile of track completed.

The laying of the first section of track for the transcontinental railroad in 1863 started one of the great races in American history as two companies competed for the

For two years the riders of the Pony Express galloped across the West with 20-pound mail sacks. Stations were located every 10 to 20 miles along the 2,000-mile route. A rider would stop at a station just long enough to jump from the saddle of his exhausted horse to a fresh mount. This painting by Frederick Remington is titled The Coming and Going of the Pony Express.

By 1869 railroad tracks connected the west coast with the Midwest. Much of the back-breaking work of hacking out a railbed through the Sierra Nevadas was done by crews of Chinese workers. The workers in this painting cheer one of the first trains along a track they have built.

government grants and loans. Union Pacific crews laid their first tracks on Nebraska flatlands as they moved westward. Starting in Sacramento, California, and moving east, the workers of the Central Pacific had to break through the high Sierra Nevadas. In the first four years, the Central Pacific laid only about 100 miles (160 kilometers) of track.

Charles Crocker, in charge of the Central Pacific crews, was determined to conquer the difficult route. He supervised about 10,000 Chinese laborers who had been hired by the Central Pacific when few other workers were willing to take on the perilous task of bridging the mountains.

Facing solid granite walls, the Chinese workers had to cart away mounds of rubble, using only baskets and wheelbarrows. The work was so difficult that progress sometimes dwindled to a mere 8 inches (20 centimeters) a day. When winter came to the Sierra Nevadas, Crocker ordered his workers to dig tunnels through 40-foot (12-meter) snowdrifts in order to lay track on the frozen ground. Without the strength and endurance of the Chinese workers, the transcontinental railroad would have taken much longer to build.

To the east, the Union Pacific relied largely on Irish Americans, many of whom were Union veterans of the Civil War. Crossing the flat plains from Omaha, the work went quickly. As much as 3 miles (5 kilometers) of track might be laid between sunrise and sunset.

Every 60 miles (about 100 kilometers) the workers threw up a temporary town. As soon as the next stretch of track was complete, they pulled the buildings down, loaded the wood on a flatcar, and built a new town farther down the line. The towns included shacks for the men to live in as well as saloons, dance halls, and gambling tents for entertainment.

By 1868 the crews of both companies had reached the flat ground of the Utah plains, and the pace of laying track increased. Since each company was anxious to lay more track than the other, thereby receiving more government land and loans, the crews raced past each other without meeting. They continued putting down track until Congress ordered them to join at Promontory Point, Utah. When the last symbolic gold and silver spikes had been driven on May 10, 1869, the first transcontinental railroad was complete and the whole nation celebrated.

Settlement Follows the Rails

In time, five major railroads linked West and East. By 1893 the Southern Pacific railway ran from New Orleans across Texas and along the Mexican border into California. The Santa Fe connected Missouri with southern California. The Northern Pacific and the Great Northern spanned the upper Midwest to Washington and Oregon. (See the map on page 374.)

The railroad routes greatly influenced the course of development in the West. Towns grew quickly along the tracks. Railroads brought new settlers and insured them of supplies and a way to take their products to eastern markets. The largest towns and cities developed at the crossroads of major railroad lines. In southern California, for example, Los Angeles began its spectacular growth only after the Santa Fe and Southern Pacific railroads met there.

All across the West, the railroad signaled growth and prosperity for new settlements. With travel and transportation of goods made easier, it was not long before miners were followed by farmers and ranchers.

For answers, see p. A 63.

Section Review

1. Identify the following: Comstock Lode, Pony Express, Union Pacific Railroad, Central Pacific Railroad.
2. Define the following terms: vigilante, public domain.
3. Where were new discoveries of gold and silver made in the late 1850s and early 1860s?
4. List two disadvantages of travel by stagecoach.
5. What did the federal government offer railroad companies as an incentive for laying tracks in the West?
6. How did Chinese and Irish immigrants contribute to the completion of the first transcontinental railroad?

3 Tragedy for the Plains Indians

In 1830 when Andrew Jackson implemented his policy of removing all Native Americans to lands west of the Mississippi River, he expected conflict between the two cultures to end. But after 1840 the United States extended its boundaries to the Pacific. Wagon trains crossed the plains to reach Oregon and California. The mining frontier moved into Indian territory, and railroads crossed Native American hunting grounds. As more easterners recognized the value of the West, pressure on the Plains Indians increased.

Outbreak of Warfare on the Plains

In 1851 representatives of the United States government and the major Plains Indian nations met near Fort Laramie in Wyoming. They hoped to find a way for the Indians and the new settlers to live peacefully. In exchange for promises of yearly payments in money and goods, the Indian leaders agreed to confine their hunting to specified regions with definite borders.

By containing the Indians in certain areas, government representatives hoped to reduce the chances of conflict among Indian nations and between Indians and settlers. Government agents would also use the provision to negotiate with Native American nations individually.

The agreement of 1851 worked poorly because neither the United States government nor the Indian leaders could enforce it. The chiefs who signed the agreement could not prevent members of their nations from hunting where they wished, and arriving settlers consistently ignored Indian land claims.

When thousands of miners came to Colorado in the gold rush of 1859, the chance of conflict with Native Americans increased. Miners claimed land that less than a decade before had been promised "forever" to the Cheyenne and Arapaho nations. When United States agents forced Indian leaders to forfeit their land, many Indian nations declared war. In 1865 the Sioux went to war when the United States government announced it was going to build a road through Sioux hunting grounds to the mining towns of Bozeman and Virginia City.

The warfare was bitter. The Plains Indians were fighting for their homeland and their way of life against people who had consistently broken promises to them. Consequently, Indians attacked settlements and army supply trains. In 1866 Sioux in the Big Horn Mountains led a surprise attack on a detachment of troops led by Captain W. J. Fetterman, killing all 82 soldiers.

The new American miners and settlers believed that they had a right to the land. Most felt that they would make better use of its resources than Indian hunters had. Easterners were outraged by Indian ambushes, which they considered unfair, and were horrified by stories of Indians torturing captives.

United States government troops often struck back mercilessly at the Indians. In 1864, for example, Colonel John Chivington ordered his soldiers to slaughter 450 Cheyenne men, women, and children at Sand Creek, Colorado, after the Cheyenne had been guaranteed protection. "I have come to kill Indians," Chivington declared tersely, "and believe it is right and honorable to use any means under God's heaven to kill them."

Outcome of the Wars

The conflicts in the West convinced the government that a new Indian policy was needed. In 1867 and 1868 government agents demanded that the Plains nations give up even more land and move to *reservations*, areas specifically set aside for them, The Indians of the southern plains were expected to move to a poor, unproductive tract in Oklahoma. The northern nations were to be confined to the Black Hills area of the Dakota territory. Major Indian leaders agreed to the demands, but since many Indians did not, warfare on the plains continued.

Yet even the Indians who agreed to move to the reservations were not allowed to live peacefully. In 1874 miners discovered gold in the Black Hills. Thousands of prospectors rushed into the area to stake claims. The outraged Indians fought back. When Colonel George Custer led a detachment of 265 men into the heart of Sioux country in June 1876, he found himself outmaneuvered. Led by Crazy Horse, Sitting Bull, and Rain-in-the-Face, a Sioux force of 2,500 killed every one of Custer's men at Little Big Horn.

The Sioux had won the battle, but they lost the larger campaign. The U.S. Army could mount too many men with too many modern weapons for the Indians to withstand a prolonged war. In the autumn of 1876 the Sioux surrendered.

A few nations continued to resist in the following years but without real hope. In 1877 Chief Joseph led the Nez Percé (NEHZ puhr SAY) of Oregon and Idaho in a brilliant defensive campaign crossing a thousand miles (1,600 kilometers) before he was forced to surrender in Montana. The Apaches of

Fact and legend merge in the tales of Calamity Jane, a sharpshooter and frontier woman whose real name was Martha Jane Canary Burke. At one point during the Indian wars she worked as a scout for General George Crook.

Arizona, led by their determined chief, Geronimo, held out until 1886.

Individuals on both sides commented on the tragedy. Chief Joseph put aside his weapons wearily. "I am tired of fighting," he declared sadly.

> Our chiefs are killed. . . . The little children are freezing to death. My people, some of them, have run away to the hills and have no blankets, no food. . . . Hear me, my chiefs, I am tired; my heart is sick and sad. From where the sun now stands, I will fight no more forever.

General Philip Sheridan, the Civil War veteran who led many campaigns against the Indians after the war, was also aware of the injustice of the conflict. "We took away their country and their means of support, broke up their mode of living, their habits of life, introduced disease and decay among them, and it was for this and against this that they made war. Could anyone expect less?"

A Vanishing Way of Life

Sheridan had correctly perceived that the Indians had lost more than a few battles and a great deal of land. They were losing a whole way of life. One of the most devastating blows to the Plains nations was the destruction of the buffalo herds.

As you have read, the buffalo played a central role in Plains Indian culture. Beginning in the 1860s, however, the herds began to dwindle. As railroad crews laid tracks

■ *The United States government had promised large tracts of western land to Native American tribes. However, most of that land was ceded back to the government. By 1890 Indians were restricted to the reservations shown on this map.*

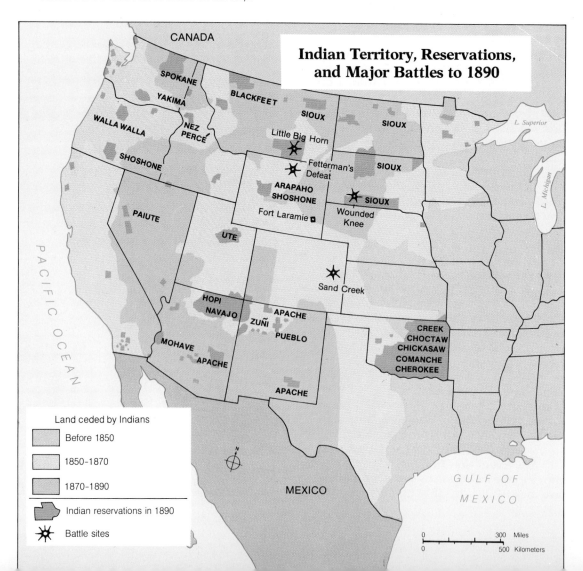

Indian Territory, Reservations, and Major Battles to 1890

Land ceded by Indians
- Before 1850
- 1850–1870
- 1870–1890
- Indian reservations in 1890
- ✶ Battle sites

across the prairie, thousands of animals were slaughtered to provide food. Buffalo hunting also became a fashionable sport for easterners, who would sometimes organize expeditions and shoot the herds from the comfort of train cars.

Then, in the 1870s, merchants discovered that buffalo hides could be sold in the East as fashionable robes or turned into belts to drive machinery. Commercial hunters shot thousands of the animals, skinned them right on the prairie, and hauled off the hides on large wagons. Out of the 13 million animals on the plains in 1860, only a few hundred remained by the end of the century.

With the buffalo nearly gone, Plains Indians could no longer support themselves as they had before. Driven onto reservations, they were forced to depend on the government for food. Unfortunately, the corruption that became widespread in government after the Civil War also affected Indian policy.

Money meant to purchase food supplies often went directly into the pockets of corrupt government agents. Food supplies that did find their destination were often spoiled. "No branch of the national government is so spotted with fraud, so tainted with corruption . . . as this Indian Bureau," concluded one member of the House of Representatives in 1869.

Calls for Reform

Others spoke out against the evils of the reservation system. Susette La Flesche, an Omaha Indian, campaigned vigorously on behalf of Native Americans. Her father had been chief of the Omaha when treaties had reduced his nation's hunting grounds to a small reservation on the Missouri River. In the 1870s, La Flesche drew attention to Indian grievances through her writing and by conducting lecture tours.

One of the people La Flesche influenced was Helen Hunt Jackson. Jackson was insensed by the Indians' plight, and she wrote a book, *A Century of Dishonor* (1881), which vividly outlined the history of broken treaties between the United States and the Indians.

Partly in response to such calls for reform, Congress passed the Dawes Act in 1887. The legislation was an attempt to bring Indians into the mainstream of American life by breaking up traditional Indian organizations. Reservation land was no longer to be held by the tribe in common but was parceled out in 160-acre (64-hectare) lots to families and individuals. Those Native Americans who accepted land became full citizens of the United States. Congress provided additional funds to support schools that would teach Indian children "the white man's way of life."

The creators of the Dawes Act failed to appreciate the strength of Indian traditions. Furthermore, white citizens eager for additional land often tricked Indians into selling their lots for a small price. The result was that once again Indian land ended up in white hands.

Reformers who supported the Dawes Act hoped the Indians would also give up their religion, but the Indians resisted. Looking back to their days of freedom, some of the Sioux on Dakota reservations began to practice a religious ritual known as the Ghost Dance. The dance celebrated the sacred customs of the past and hailed the time when the Sioux would return to the freedom of those days.

Settlers near the Sioux reservations feared that another uprising was in the making. In 1890 they summoned the cavalry. At Wounded Knee, South Dakota, the soldiers arrested a group of several hundred Indians

Both of these photographs are of Tom Torlino, a Navajo youth. At left is Torlino before he was sent to a school for Indians run by whites. At right, after attending the school for only a few months, all traces of his Navajo heritage seem to have vanished from his appearance.

and disarmed the men among them. In a moment of confusion a shot was fired, and the cavalry turned their machine guns on the defenseless Sioux. By the time the guns had ceased firing, over 290 men, women, and children had been killed or wounded.

For many Indians, the shootings at Wounded Knee symbolized the sad fate of their people. Although some Native Americans made the transition to "the white man's way of life," many others continued to cling with determination to the Indian vision of what the West should be. Unable to return to life on the plains as they had known it and unable or unwilling to adapt to a new culture, they had neither hope nor opportunity.

For answers, see p. A 63.

Section Review

1. Identify the following: Little Big Horn, Chief Joseph, Geronimo, Susette La Flesche, Helen Hunt Jackson, Dawes Act, Ghost Dance, Wounded Knee.

2. Define the following term: reservation.

3. (a) What was the purpose of the 1851 Fort Laramie agreement? (b) List two reasons it failed.

4. (a) What development led Plains Indians to declare war after 1859? (b) What development in 1874 led to new fighting?

5. List three ways buffalo herds were destroyed.

6. (a) What was the purpose of the Dawes Act? (b) List its major provisions.

4 The Cattle Frontier

As the mining frontier spread from the west coast eastward into the mountains, another wave of settlement, mainly from Texas, pushed northward onto the plains. The new settlers sought to take advantage of the prairie grass and public lands. Fortunes could be made there, not by panning gold, but by raising cattle.

The New Cattle Country

As you read in Chapter 14, the Mexicans and the Spanish before them had established cattle ranches in the Southwest. The countryside there had been so hospitable, in fact, that many cattle had thrived untended. A type of cattle known as the Texas longhorn roamed freely across the plains. By 1860 some 5 million longhorns grazed in Texas.

Despite the abundance of cattle, ranching developed slowly there. The Texas longhorn was a tough and ill-tempered creature, its wiry frame providing very little tender meat. In addition, few buyers existed. Texans could not sell outside of local areas since they had no way of transporting the beef to distant markets.

The railroads opened up those markets for Texas beef. As the population in the East grew, the demand for meat rose, and the railroads provided a quick way to ship it east. Cattle that could be purchased for $3 to $5 a head in Texas could be sold at the nearest railhead or shipping point for $30 to $50 each. A rancher who marketed a herd of 3,000 steers could make a profit of $100,000 in one year.

In 1866 the closest railheads lay over a thousand miles (1,600 kilometers) to the north, but that did not stop enterprising Texans. In the following years they drove their cattle north, looking for the best route across prairie country. Their successful search began the era of the "long drives" and the cattle boom. In 1867 the first herds reached the new depot of Abilene, Kansas. As the rails pushed west, new cattle centers sprang up at Ellsworth and Dodge City, Kansas. (See the map on page 374.)

The Long Drive

The men who drove the cattle along these trails soon earned a place in the folklore of the nation. The cowboys, as they were called, borrowed much of the Spanish vaquero's outfit; and the cowboy vocabulary incorporated many Spanish terms, including lariat, corral, hombre, and bronco. Vaquero even became translated as "buckeroo." Cattle drives attracted a large number of black and Mexican Americans. On the long drives, one out of every seven cowboys was black, and nearly one in five was Mexican.

Every year Texas ranchers drove their cattle to railheads hundreds of miles away. In the photo at left a cowhand keeps a wary eye on the herd. Herds were often on the trail for two or three months before reaching a rail depot. Many of the cowhands on the long drives were blacks or Mexican Americans. Yet in the folklore of the West, those cowhands were often ignored or forgotten.

Every spring, a rancher would select about 16 to 18 men to ride herd over some 3,000 cattle, about one cowboy for every 175 animals. A chuck wagon would follow with its cook and a wrangler who looked after the extra horses. For such demanding work, each cowboy had about eight mounts, so he would always have a fresh one. The horses had distinctive names such as Gold Dollar, Julius Caesar, Pop Corn, or Snakey.

The long drive often took two or three months to complete. Cattle walked in single file along the trail, with the cowboys spread out in pairs over the long line. Moving the men and animals at the required pace of 20 to 25 miles (32 to 40 kilometers) a day, the herd manager signaled his crew using arm motions borrowed from Plains Indian sign language. At night the herd would be gathered together along the side of the trail. Such work was hard indeed. Cowboys often sat in the saddle for 16 to 18 hours a day.

The Cattle Boom

The cattle business grew rapidly after 1867. Railheads became bustling centers where cattle were herded into yards and then shipped east, and where cowboys had a chance to let off steam after their grueling ride. In 1867, Abilene, Kansas, consisted of only a dozen log huts with dirt roofs. The town was so poor that the saloonkeeper tended a colony of prairie dogs that he sold to an occasional tourist. By 1870, when 300,000 cattle were shipped through Abilene, the town had become a bustling business center.

It was not long before cattle ranchers decided to expand their grazing range. As the buffalo vanished from the plains, ranchers began grazing cattle there. Routes like the Goodnight-Loving Trail opened up grazing areas in Colorado and Wyoming. (See the map on page 374.)

373

Ranchers let their cattle run wild across the prairie, identifying them with a distinctive mark, or brand. Twice a year the cattle were rounded up, and new calves were given the owner's brand mark with a hot iron.

By 1880 about 4.5 million cattle grazed on the plains from Kansas to Montana. The profits from ranching were so handsome that ranching became a field for speculation. Investors came from the East and as far away as Britain and other European nations. All of them viewed the cattle business as the latest bonanza, the newest way to get rich quick. But the bonanza was not to last.

From Boom to Bust

Several developments contributed to the end of the cattle bonanza. As the number of cattle multiplied, the plains were overgrazed

and the grasses died. Ranchers quarreled over land and water rights, often violently, and cattle rustlers, or thieves, proved to be a nagging problem.

Competition for grazing land led to other problems. Fencing had been limited on the plains as long as fencing materials—wood or stone—were scarce. When barbed wire was marketed in 1874, ranchers began stringing up fences to keep their cattle in. But ranchers were not the only people who found a use for barbed wire.

Conflict arose with other groups who wanted to use the land for their own purposes. Sheep ranchers brought their herds to the prairie, but sheep tended to crop the prairie grass so close to the ground that cattle could not eat it. Farmers also moved onto the plains and began fencing in land. Bitter range wars erupted over who had the

■ Railroads, mining, and cattle grazing helped open the Great Plains for later settlement, as indicated on this map.

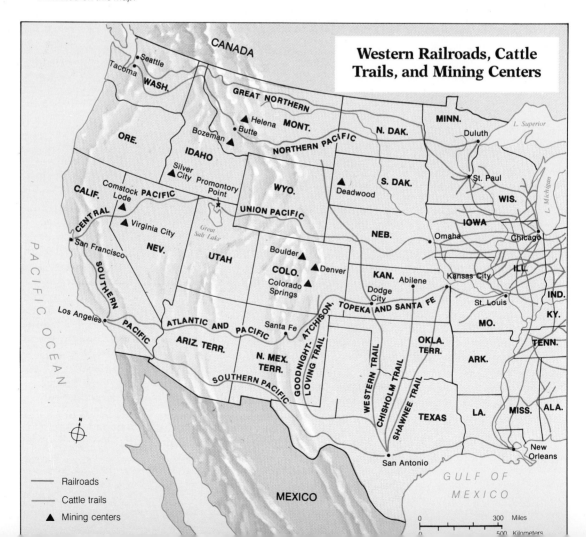

Spanish Roots of the American Cowboy

No other figure has so completely captured the American imagination as the cowboy. Thousands of novels and films describe this legendary figure. The freedom, independence, resourcefulness, and courage of the cowboy have become qualities that all Americans consider part of the American character. Yet the roots of the American cowboy go back to the Spanish settlers of present-day Mexico and the southwestern United States.

Between 1600 and 1845 the lands that became Texas, New Mexico, Arizona, and southern California were settled by Spaniards and later by Mexicans, who raised cattle on the open range. These settlers developed a unique way of life suited to the country in which they lived. This special way of life became the foundation for the traditions and character of the American cowboy.

Spanish words and customs were borrowed and adapted. The lands where livestock was raised, *ranchos* (RAN chohz) in Spanish, became American ranches. And the *vaqueros* (vah KEHR ohz), who tended the *vacas* (VAH cahz), or cows, became cowboys. The special saddle with a horn used by the vaquero became the "western" saddle of the cowboy. He draped his *riata* (ree AHT ah), or lariat, over the horn and tied the rope to it after throwing his *lazo* (lasso).

The American cowboy adopted the vaquero's clothing, which was superbly adapted for his work. He wore a wide-brimmed *sombrero* (sahm BREHR oh), in Spanish "a hat that provides shade," to protect his face and head from the hot sun. Special high-heeled, pointed-toe boots helped balance the cowboy when he used his lariat to throw and tie a calf during the roundup. The boots also kept his feet from slipping too far into the stirrups. The cowboy adopted the vaquero's leather *chaparrerjos* (CHAP ah RAY hohs), or chaps, around his legs to protect them from thorny chaparral bushes, and when he could afford it, he wore a buckskin jacket with silver buttons.

The vaqueros tested their skill in horsemanship, cattle roping, and branding at annual roundups, when the cattle were brought together from the open range for branding. The western rodeo of today has its roots in those roundup contests.

Vaqueros often sang and played the guitar in the evenings on the open trail. They sang for their own entertainment and to calm the cattle, who might be made nervous by the sounds of wild animals. Their songs were usually *corridos* (cohr REE dohz), or running accounts, of the adventures of the vaquero or people he knew. English-speaking cowboys adopted this custom and created their own ballads, many of which are still popular today.

---

right to use the land or control valuable water holes.

The weather delivered the biggest blow to the ranchers, however. The severe winter of 1885–1886 killed off large numbers of cattle. The following summer was extremely dry, and cattle suffered poor grazing. The winter of 1886–1887 whipped the plains with blizzards and subzero temperatures even more severe than the previous year. By the time warmth returned to the land 80 to 90 percent of all cattle lay dead.

Many ranchers and speculators were ruined. Those who survived the disaster discovered that the cattle business had changed. Many ranches went from individual ownership to management by large corporations such as the Union Cattle Company of Wyoming. Furthermore, with the spread of barbed wire, ranchers no longer let their animals roam free. Instead they purchased and fenced land, drilled wells to guard against dry weather, and provided hay for cattle during difficult winter months.

The cattle frontier had gone the way of the other boom economies. The days when individuals could make huge fortunes on the Great Plains had passed. Ranching remained an important part of the West, but it became more of a business and less of an adventure.

For answers, see p. A 64.
Section Review

1. Identify the following: Texas longhorn, long drives.
2. (a) How did railroads contribute to the growth of cattle ranching? (b) How did ranchers move cattle to the railhead?
3. List two ways competition for grazing land contributed to an end to the cattle bonanza.
4. What impact did weather have on the cattle bonanza?

5 The Sodbusters' Frontier

While miners and ranchers were staking their claims to the West, another group was not far behind: the farmers. The farming frontier expanded rapidly, especially after 1870. Rising prices on the world grain market lured farmers into the Dakotas, western Nebraska, Kansas, and western Texas. The first to arrive usually settled in the more fertile river valleys, but eventually other farmers tried their luck on the rolling plains.

Encouraging Settlement

In 1862 Congress passed the Homestead Act to encourage farmers to settle the West. The act provided that any citizen (or immigrant who intended to become a citizen) could purchase 160 acres (64 hectares) of public land for a small registration fee. By 1900, 600,000 farmers had claimed homesteads.

Despite government incentives, only about 20 percent of the homestead land was purchased directly by small farmers. Most was bought up by speculators who evaded the provisions of the Homestead Act. They purchased large parcels of land, then divided and resold the land to individual farmers at higher prices.

The Homestead Act was impractical in many areas. As John Wesley Powell had foreseen, a 160-acre (64-hectare) farm might be fine in the East, where rain was plentiful. However, in the West the costs and risks of farming were greater, and much larger tracts of land were needed to make a profit. Nonetheless, farmers came West. Many were encouraged by the Homestead Act. Others came in response to appeals from railroads.

As you read earlier, the government had given railroads large sections of land along their western routes. This land could not be bought under the Homestead Act, but the company executives knew that the success of their lines depended on attracting settlers. With more towns and farms in the West, passenger travel and freight shipping would increase. Consequently, the railroads advertised throughout the East, sold their land, and then provided transportation west.

The railroads advertised in Europe also. From the Scandinavian countries especially, thousands of families emigrated to areas of Minnesota and the Dakotas. Many German and Irish immigrants joined American settlers in Nebraska and the Dakotas.

When railroads worked together with the settlers to develop an area, both the region and the railroad prospered. One of the most successful and responsible attempts was led by James J. Hill, president of the Great Northern Railway. Towns and farms grew up quickly along his Dakota rail line.

Adapting to the Plains

Life on the dry, nearly treeless plains differed greatly from what the settlers had left behind in the East. They had to learn new skills to meet the challenges of their new land.

With little wood available, families relied on other materials to build houses. At first they used the land itself, tough sod held together by the tight weave of prairie-grass roots. Settlers cut bricks of sod, then arranged them into walls three feet (one meter) thick. The roof began with tarpaper, if available, then a layer of sod. Eventually sunflowers and grass might grow from the roof of the hut.

New techniques and inventions made farming the plains easier and more profitable. Among them were deep wells, dry farming, and improved machinery. Drilling deep wells allowed farmers to reach water several hundred feet into the ground. Windmills powered the pumps by harnessing the steady winds of the plains. Most wells supplied enough water to irrigate an acre near the house where the family could raise its own vegetables.

Dry farming enabled farmers to grow cash crops like wheat. Newly developed steel-tipped plows could cut through dense root networks that would have broken iron or wooden plows. With these plows, farmers were able to reach moisture lying deeper in the ground, which then rose gradually to the roots of the crops. The soil had to be broken up often to prevent the moisture from evaporating too quickly, especially after rains.

To make the large western farms profitable, farmers depended on machinery. Threshing machines were constantly being

To build a shelter on the often treeless Great Plains, early settlers carved out chunks of the earth itself. Tough prairie grass growing year after year undisturbed had created a thickly matted crust called sod. Squares of sod were cut, then used like bricks to make sod houses, or "soddies." The Kansas homesteaders in this photo have lined up the family and their prized possessions for a traveling photographer.

improved, and mechanical binders quickly tied wheat into bundles. Using improved machinery, a wheat farmer could harvest in three hours what originally took 61 hours to do. The time spent harvesting corn, oats, and hay also dropped dramatically.

Farm Life on the Plains

New farming techniques and labor-saving inventions made it possible for western farmers to survive, but life for most settlers still posed severe trials. Each season of the year held its special threat to the farmer.

Spring brought welcome warmth, but along with melting snow might come floods that washed away houses and livestock. In the summer temperatures soared over 100° Fahrenheit (39° Celsius) for weeks while hot winds blasted the plains. Moderate temperatures in the summer might mean grasshopper plagues. The grasshoppers ate everything: crops, food, clothing and even tree bark. The summer heat broke in autumn but by then the grasses were so dry that one spark could send thousands of acres into flames.

But the pioneers dreaded winter most. Cruel winds swept ice, dust, and snow across the plains. Settlers could awake to find their food frozen and snow on the furniture. Animals suffered even more.

Few of those who came to the plains could withstand the strains of farm life for long. Some moved on westward; others retreated back east. "From Kansas, where it rains grasshoppers, fire, and destruction," read the sign on one returning wagon.

Of course, life was not always so harsh, and many prairie farmers prospered. Still, farm families were isolated, living far from friends and neighbors. Under such conditions, all settlers pitched in to make life bear-

Major Events	
1851	Fort Laramie agreement
1860	Pony Express established
1862	Homestead Act passed
1863	Construction of transcontinental railroad begins
1867–68	Plains nations ordered onto reservations
1869	Wyoming grants women voting rights; first transcontinental railroad completed
1874	Barbed wire marketed
1876	Battle of Little Big Horn
1881	*A Century of Dishonor* published
1887	Dawes Act passed
1889	Oklahoma land rush

able. Women worked alongside men. Some, like Elinore Stewart from Wyoming, homesteaded their own farms. Women's contribution to life in the West was evidenced by the fact that 11 western states and territories, led by Wyoming in 1869 and Utah in 1870, granted women the vote before any states east of the Mississippi.

Almost from the start, churches and schools played an important part in western settlement. Church members joined together to recreate the patterns of community life left behind in the East or in Europe. Before the schools were built, most rural families relied on the churches and Bible reading to educate their children.

Soon, however, communities erected schools. These were usually one-room buildings with rows of hard benches where a teacher taught six to eight grades under one roof. Both the church and the school were centers of community life where farm families could gather and find relief from the isolation and hard work of life on the plains.

The Closing Frontier

As farmers spread across the plains, fewer areas remained to be settled. The last major land rush took place in central Oklahoma in 1889. This land had belonged to Cherokees, Creeks, Seminoles, and other southeastern nations since the 1830s, when Andrew Jackson's removal policy forced them from their eastern homes. In 1885 the United States, pressured by settlers, bought the land back.

The government made homesteads free to citizens, but these could be claimed only after noon on April 22, 1889. About 100,000 "boomers" lined up on the border in wagons, buggies, horses, and trains, waiting to rush in and stake claims. When the cavalry fired the official opening volley, all went charging in, only to find that others had gotten there sooner, having evaded the army border patrols. Between the "boomers" and "sooners," the entire district was parceled out in the space of a few hours.

The following year, the superintendent of the 1890 census announced that, for the first time in the history of the United States, settlements had spread so far that "there can hardly be said to be a frontier line."

One by one, the western territories became states: Nebraska in 1867; Colorado in 1876; North Dakota, South Dakota, Montana, and Washington in 1889; Idaho and Wyoming in 1890; Utah in 1896; Oklahoma in 1907; and New Mexico and Arizona in 1912.

For answers, see p. A 64.

Section Review

1. (a) What was the purpose of the Homestead Act? (b) What were the provisions of the act?
2. List one way railroad companies attracted settlers to the plains.
3. List three new techniques or inventions that made farming on the plains easier and more profitable.
4. How did schools and churches help provide the basis for community life on the plains?

★ ★

IN PERSPECTIVE   Indian nations had lived on the Great Plains for thousands of years. Few of the early European settlers to arrive in North America tried to make a permanent home on the open plains. After the Civil War, however, interest in the interior of the country grew. Discoveries of gold and silver deposits attracted miners eastward from California.

The growth of railroads further opened up the West. Cattle ranching became profitable because cattle could be shipped east by rail. New techniques and inventions enabled farmers and ranchers to adapt their methods to the harsh environment of the plains.

Most of the Plains Indians believed in a close relationship with nature. They hunted buffalo and other game without disrupting their environment. The influx of miners, cattle ranchers, and farmers destroyed the buffalo herds and led to conflict with the Indians. The United States government tried to confine Indian nations to reservations. When the Indians resisted, many years of warfare followed. Overwhelmed by the size and weaponry of the army, the Indians suffered defeat.

For answers, see p. A 64.

Chapter Review

1. (a) What are the Great Plains? (b) How did the introduction of horses in the 1700s affect the Plains Indians? (c) What role did the buffalo play in their lives?

2. (a) How did Native Americans view nature? (b) How did their way of life reflect this view?

3. (a) Describe William Gilpin's view of the West. (b) Describe John Powell's view of the West. (c) How did they differ from one another? (d) How did their attitudes differ from the Native American view of the West?

4. (a) Where was the new mining frontier of the 1850s and 1860s? (b) How did this frontier contribute to the growth of western towns and cities?

5. (a) Why was it necessary to establish a good transportation system before the West could be settled? (b) What improvements in transportation and communication were made during the 1850s and early 1860s?

6. (a) Why was building a transcontinental railroad difficult? (b) How were the difficulties overcome? (c) What effect did completion of the transcontinental railroad have on settlement of the West?

7. (a) How did the United States government try to find a way for settlers and Native Americans to live peacefully in 1851? (b) Was the attempt successful? Why or why not? (c) What new action did the government take in 1867 and 1868? (d) Was it successful? Why or why not?

8. (a) What efforts were made to improve the treatment of the Indians on reservations? (b) Were the efforts successful? Explain.

9. (a) What developments led to the cattle boom of the 1860s and 1870s? (b) What role did the long drive play in the growth of the cattle business?

10. Describe how each of the following contributed to the end of the cattle bonanza: (a) increased numbers of cattle; (b) barbed wire; (c) sheep ranches; (d) farmers; (e) climate.

For answers, see p. A 65.

For Further Thought

379

1. How did the disappearance of the buffalo symbolize the end of a way of life for the Plains Indians?

2. (a) Why was the warfare between the Plains Indians and new settlers so bitter? (b) How do you think these conflicts differed from earlier conflicts between Native Americans and settlers? (c) How were they similar?

3. How were the mining bonanzas and cattle bonanzas similar?

For answers, see p. A 65.

Developing Basic Skills

1. *Map Reading* Study the map on page 374. (a) What cities developed along railroad lines? (b) What cattle centers developed along railroad lines? (c) What major cattle trails led to these centers? (d) Based on what you have read, how did railroads contribute to the growth and prosperity of the West?

2. *Identifying Relationships* Make a list of the new states that entered the Union between 1860 and 1900. (See the chart on page 780.) Then study the map on page 374 and answer the following questions: (a) Which new states were located on the Great Plains. (b) In which new states were the sites of gold and silver discoveries during this period? (c) Which new states did cattle trails cross? (d) Which new states did transcontinental railroads cross? (e) What relationship can you identify between the "opening of the West" and the admission of new states between 1860 and 1900?

3. *Map Reading* Study the map on page 370. Then answer the following questions: (a) What lands did the Indians cede to the federal government between 1850 and 1870? (b) What lands did they cede to the government from 1870 to 1890? (c) Based on the information on this map and what you have read in this chapter, how would you describe what happened to Native Americans between 1860 and 1890?

See page 776 for suggested readings.

21

An Age of Industry

(1865–1900)

Fireworks at the opening of the Brooklyn Bridge in New York City.

Between 1865 and 1900 the United States was transformed from a largely rural nation to one of the leading industrial powers in the world. The Brooklyn Bridge, completed in 1883, symbolized the change. Its 16-inch steel cables supported a bridge 1,595 feet long, making it the longest suspension bridge in the world at that time.

Steel was one of the foundations of industrial development, and the discovery of an inexpensive way to produce it was a key to economic growth. Such growth was also fueled by other inventions and by innovations in business organization.

The impact of industry on the nation was uneven. Manufacturing was most common in the Northeast and Midwest, but industry also began to flourish in the South. While economic growth meant vast fortunes for some business leaders, factory workers faced long hours, hazardous conditions, and low pay. Consequently, workers began to organize to improve their lot. Throughout the last half of the nineteenth century, however, their efforts were to have limited success.

1 The Ties That Bind

As you read in Chapter 20, the transcontinental railroads and the telegraph helped open the West for settlement after the Civil War. Advances in transportation and communication also helped stimulate the nation's industrial growth.

Communication by Wire

In 1844, when Samuel Morse succeeded in sending coded messages over an electrical wire, he revolutionized communication. By 1860 telegraph wires connected the West with the East. The merger in 1866 of the Western Union Telegraph Company, which handled communications in the West, with the American Telegraph Company, which dominated eastern communications, created a nationwide telegraph network.

The telegraph greatly speeded the pace of business. For example, store owners and manufacturers could order supplies by telegraph almost instantaneously. But the telegraph did more than speed the delivery of messages. It provided a new source of employment for women, who were hired as telegraphers. It also helped make rail transportation safer and more efficient. The telegraph allowed stationmasters to coordinate the movement of trains. (The railroads had permitted Western Union to string wires parallel to their tracks in exchange for free telegraph service.)

More changes in communication were to come. In 1858 financier Cyrus Field and other investors spent $1.5 million to lay an underwater telegraph cable across the Atlantic. Although the cable broke shortly after the first few messages had been transmitted, Field did not give up. In 1866 he laid a new and improved cable, which provided almost instant communication across the Atlantic.

In 1876 Alexander Graham Bell, a Scotsman who taught speech to the deaf in Boston, transmitted the human voice over wires with his new "speaking telegraph." A year later, the first intercity phone conversation took place between Boston and New York, and that same year Bell organized the Bell Telephone Company.

Soon Bell Telephone was laying cable from business to business and from city to city. After 1885 American Telephone and Telegraph, which had been organized by the directors of Bell Telephone, combined 100 local telephone companies and provided business and government with long-distance service. By the mid-1880s over 300,000 of Bell's "electrical toys" were in use in the United States. Most of them were business phones, however. Not until rates were reduced in 1900 did many private households acquire telephones.

Transportation by Rail

Although advances in communication were important, they took a back seat to the achievements of railroad builders. Transportation was the key to industrialization. To succeed as an industrial nation, the United States needed to be able to quickly move freight and passengers to all parts of the country. In 1860, despite impressive progress since 1850, that could not be done.

The American rail system in 1860 consisted of about 30,000 miles (48,000 kilometers) of track. But much of it was in the East, and no railroad bridge yet crossed the Mississippi, Ohio, or Hudson rivers. Furthermore, a large number of small companies controlled various sections of track, which were often not interconnected. Richmond, Virginia, for example, was the last stop for six separate rail lines.

Even if local rail lines had been connected, one company's cars often would not have been able to travel on another company's track. No standard gauge, the distance between the rails, had been agreed upon, so the trains of one company did not fit on the track of another. Consequently, shippers who wished to send freight over a long distance had to have their freight loaded and unloaded all along the way. Each link in the journey required new freight charges, additional paperwork, and delay.

Consolidation of Railroads

After the Civil War, railroad builders took vigorous action to create a more efficient and economical system of rail transportation by *consolidating,* or combining, small lines. Owners of large lines often purchased smaller lines or tried to drive them out of business.

The development of the New York Central illustrates one method of consolidation. In 1866 the New York Central connected Albany and Buffalo. Other railroad lines ran east from Albany to Boston and New York City and west from Buffalo to Chicago. Commodore Cornelius Vanderbilt hoped to unite these lines into one company. He had already made a fortune with a steamship line on the Hudson River, hence his nautical title.

Vanderbilt quickly bought up most of the railroad lines linking New York and Chicago, but the strategically located New York Central held out. In the winter of 1867, to end the stalemate, Vanderbilt suddenly re-

Railroad tycoon Cornelius Vanderbilt is pictured in this cartoon as a modern colossus towering over his domain. But as the cartoon indicates, Vanderbilt was only one of several men who held the reins of the rapidly expanding rail network.

fused to let passengers and freight transfer from the New York Central line to his lines. With freight and passengers stranded, the New York Central vainly appealed to the New York State legislature for protection against Vanderbilt.

The New York Central finally surrendered, and Vanderbilt promptly went to work acquiring the feeder lines that joined his New York-to-Chicago trunk line. At the time of his death in 1877, he controlled 4,500 miles (7,200 kilometers) of integrated railroad connecting New York City and the Great Lakes region.

Progress Along the Rails

Consolidating small railroad lines often led to more efficient rail service despite the rough competition between railroad builders. The rail system also improved in other ways. By 1886 the railroads had adopted a standard gauge. Since trains were able to run longer distances without stopping, passengers and freight were moved more quickly.

Rates also decreased. By the end of the century, passenger fares had been cut in half, and freight rates dropped even more. Furthermore, rail companies had worked out arrangements allowing the freight cars of one line to use the tracks of another. Goods loaded on a car in Chicago, for example, stayed on the same car all the way to New York, and shippers paid only one fare for the whole distance.

Many railroads replaced iron rails with steel rails that could support the weight of new, more powerful locomotives. New signals along the track improved safety. Many major lines began to install a second set of tracks, so that traffic could move in both directions at the same time.

By 1883 efficient shipping had become so important to the nation's economic life that the American Railway Association divided the country into the four time zones that exist today: Eastern, Central, Mountain, and Pacific. Before the zones were created, each town kept its own time, which often varied by several minutes from the time kept in a neighboring town. These variations had made it difficult for the railroads to establish uniform schedules. The creation of the zone system simplified scheduling and improved efficiency.

The new railroads advertised heavily to attract riders. The Erie Railway, for instance, stressed the fabulous scenery at Niagara Falls.

Persistent Problems

Progress brought growing pains. Most of the railroads were heavily in debt. Constructing railroads required large amounts of money. To raise money, owners of railroad lines issued *bonds*, certificates that earn interest and are redeemed on a given date, and sold *stock certificates*, shares of ownership in a company.

Some of the stock certificates sold, however, were not actually backed by the companys' *assets*, that is, their property and cash. Such certificates were known as *watered stock* because selling them was similar to a trick used by some ranchers of having their cattle drink large amounts of water before being weighed for sale. Furthermore, railroad owners often did not have the money to pay the interest on bonds or to redeem them.

The burden of a large debt was complicated by cutthroat competition. Despite efforts to consolidate lines, in some areas many lines continued to compete for the same customers. A manufacturer wanting to ship freight from Atlanta to St. Louis, for example, could choose from 20 different carriers.

Rival railroad lines thus engaged in rate wars, even if they were forced to operate at a loss. Since owners had already paid for their tracks, engines, and freight cars, running at a loss seemed to be better than not running at all. The situation became so competitive that companies resorted to some illegal practices to solve their problems.

To attract a large volume of business, railroads secretly offered rebates to their largest customers. The *rebate* was a discount on the normal shipping charge. Because such reductions were not offered to all shippers, rebating was illegal. Small shippers complained, but the practice continued.

Where several railroads competed for business, *pooling* was sometimes practiced. Under a pooling arrangement, railroad managers from competing companies would agree that each line would carry a certain portion of the total volume of freight, thus assuring that they all could stay in business. They would also pledge not to cut prices in order to undersell their rivals.

Pooling, rebates, and other questionable practices, such as charging less per mile for a long haul than for a short haul, led state and federal governments to regulate railroads, as you will read in Chapter 22. In spite of the abuses, however, a nationwide rail system developed and became an essential part of the national economy. Improved communications and transportation strengthened the ties that bound the nation together.

For answers, see p. A 66.

Section Review

1. Identify the following: Samuel Morse, Alexander Graham Bell, Cornelius Vanderbilt.
2. Define the following terms: consolidate, bonds, stock certificates, assets, watered stock, rebates, pooling.
3. What impact did the telegraph have on business in the United States?
4. List two ways rail transportation in 1860 was inadequate.
5. What methods did Vanderbilt use to consolidate the railroads connecting New York City and the Great Lakes region?
6. List four ways railroads improved after the Civil War.
7. (a) How did railroad companies raise money? (b) What methods did they use to attract more business?

2 Innovations and Inventions

One reason for the tremendous growth of the American economy between 1865 and 1900 was the remarkable ability of industry to innovate. Some inventions, such as Bell's telephone, gave birth to whole new industries and radically changed American life. Others, like manufacturer Levi Strauss's use of rivets to strengthen the stress points of blue jeans, seemed small but proved to be of lasting importance. In the 1880s and 1890s Americans patented over 21,000 inventions a year—more than ten times the yearly average number during the 1850s. "America has become known the world around as the home of invention," observed the commissioner of the patent office.

Steel: A Foundation for Industry

No invention contributed more to the spread of industry in America than the discovery of how large quantities of steel could be made cheaply and easily. Steel is a form of purified iron. Long valued because it was stronger than iron, steel was difficult to make. Before the 1860s steel was made by heating iron to high temperatures that could be created only in small furnaces. The process was slow, required a large amount of coal to heat the furnace, and produced only a small amount of steel.

In 1859, however, Henry Bessemer, in England, and William Kelly, in the United States, independently discovered a better way to make steel. The *Bessemer process*, as it came to be known, began by heating iron in a large furnace. Blasts of cold air were then blown through the heated iron, causing the impurities to burn.

The "air boiling" technique invented by Bessemer and Kelly produced strong and durable steel. The Bessemer process reduced the amount of coal needed to produce one ton of steel from seven tons to one ton. It also speeded the manufacture of steel.

The process revolutionized industry. Before 1867, when the first Bessemer steel was produced, United States manufacturers were turning out fewer than 2,000 tons (1,820 metric tons) of steel a year. By the end of the nineteenth century, 7 million tons (6.4 million metric tons) were produced annually.

Much of the earliest Bessemer steel was rolled into train tracks, which lasted ten times longer than the old iron rails. But other industries soon began to discover uses for the cheap steel. New "skyscrapers," soaring 20 stories and more into the air, required steel girders to support their great weight. In 1879 plans for the Brooklyn Bridge called for the use of steel beams. Steel nails, screws, needles, pins, bolts, barrel hoops, and barbed wire were only a few of the everyday uses of steel.

Inventions Create New Industries

While the Bessemer process was reshaping many existing industries, other inventions made entirely new businesses possible. Alert business leaders rushed to take advantage of new technology.

The invention of the Bessemer process for refining iron into steel revolutionized industry. The use of Bessemer converters, shown above in a Pennsylvania plant, permitted the development of a large-scale steel industry. Because steel was stronger and more durable than iron, it spurred many other technical advances, such as the construction of steel bridges and steel-frame buildings.

For example, Gustavus Swift and Philip Armour introduced refrigeration to the meatpacking* industry in the late 1800s. They established firms in Chicago, midway between the cattle raised on the Great Plains and the cities of the East. Cattle were shipped from the West to the Chicago meatpacking plants, where they were slaughtered and cut into sides of beef. Refrigeration allowed Swift and Armour to store the beef in warehouses and to ship it East on railroad cars even in warm weather. This procedure, in effect by the 1880s, provided an efficient and inexpensive way to ship fresh meat.

The use of refrigeration in rail cars and meatpacking plants changed the national economy and the eating habits of many Americans. It made possible the marketing of the most perishable products and increased the availability of important sources of food. "Through the wages I disburse and the provisions I supply," boasted Armour, "I give more people food than any man living." The new packing facilities also provided thousands of jobs. Large, centralized facil-

ities took the place of small, local meat packers who could not compete.

Some new industries were created around inventions designed to improve rail travel. In 1864 George Pullman designed a sleeping car that eventually saw widespread

■ Americans—both native-born and immigrant—used what they called Yankee ingenuity to devise simpler, more efficient ways of making things. This chart shows the number of inventions filed with the United States Patent Office in the decades before 1900.

United States Patents Issued 1861–1900	
Five-Year Periods	**Number of Patents**
1861–1865	20,725
1866–1870	58,734
1871–1875	60,976
1876–1880	64,462
1881–1885	97,156
1886–1890	110,358
1891–1895	108,420
1896–1900	112,188

Source: *Historical Statistics of the United States*

---

*The term "meatpacking" was used in the days before refrigeration when beef was salted and packed in wooden barrels. Today meatpacking refers to the processing and distribution of fresh and frozen meat.

use. In 1868 George Westinghouse created a successful business by marketing his new air brake. The brake enabled locomotive engineers to stop all cars on a train simultaneously, eliminating the need for individual brakemen on each car. The results were increased passenger safety and comfort, as well as longer and faster trains.

Other inventions helped business prosper. Christopher Sholes, a printer, developed a typewriter that was first sold by the Remington Arms Company in 1875. The machine greatly improved business communication. In 1852 Elishu Otis developed the first passenger elevator. Frank Sprague, an engineer trained at the United States Naval Academy, helped to perfect the modern elevator, making movement from story to story in skyscrapers possible.

Thomas Edison's electrical inventions, especially the incandescent light bulb, opened the way for new industries. In 1882 the generators of the Edison Illuminating Company supplied enough power to light the New York Stock Exchange and several other large buildings in Manhattan. Both Edison's and George Westinghouse's companies worked to expand the electrical power industry. By 1900 local power companies were bringing electricity to many urban areas, and electric cars and trolleys had been introduced. Electrical machinery was beginning to replace steam-powered engines in many heavy industries.

A New Philosophy for Business

The innovations and inventions that sparked industrial growth allowed many business leaders to earn huge fortunes. By 1900 there were over 4,000 millionaires in the United States, compared with only a few before the Civil War.

The rich were not shy about displaying their wealth. Many of the new millionaires built large mansions and competed with each other to see who could sail the longest yachts, ride in the fanciest private railroad

Thomas Alva Edison: The Wizard of Menlo Park

Probably no other individual has contributed as much to the prosperity of United States industry or the comfort of the American people as Thomas Alva Edison. Born in Ohio in 1847 and basically self-taught, Edison was one of the leading figures in the technological development of the United States during the last two decades of the nineteenth century. At the time of his death, the former newsboy and telegraph operator held over 1,300 United States and foreign patents.

Edison's first inventions were connected with the telegraph industry. He devised a transmitter and receiver for the automatic telegraph, a system for transmitting four simultaneous messages, and an improved stock ticker system. He went on to invent the carbon telephone transmitter, which converted sound waves into electrical energy. This device was a forerunner of the microphone used today in radio, television, and recording systems.

Among his hundreds of other major inventions were the phonograph, the incandescent lamp and electrical power machinery to bring electricity to homes and factories, an experimental electrical railroad, the storage battery, synchronization of motion pictures and sound, the mimeograph machine, an ore separator, and an electric safety lantern.

Edison built and staffed a research laboratory in Menlo Park, New Jersey. This research laboratory, devoted entirely to inventive work, is considered by many to be his most important contribution to technology. Edison called his all-purpose research laboratory an "invention factory," and inventions poured from it in an unending stream. He made a business out of invention itself, hiring a staff of workers including distinguished physicists, engineers, clockmakers, and machinists. He boasted that he could turn out a minor invention every ten days and some "big job" every six months.

In the 1890s large industrial concerns began to follow Edison's lead and established their own research laboratories. Among the first and most important were the laboratories of Bell Telephone, Eastman Kodak, and General Electric. No longer did lone inventors pursue experiments at a workbench in some factory or barn. Modern research requires abundant good instruments, a group of expert helpers, and rigorous experimentation. Since the creation of Edison's "invention factory," United States corporations have generated a flood of technological developments that have transformed society.

cars, or purchase the fastest racehorses. Reports of spectacular parties became a regular feature of newspaper social pages. At one such affair the lobby of a hotel was turned into a small lake complete with gondolas. The emergence of a wealthy class of industrialists was accompanied by the development of theories to explain the success of those industrialists.

Andrew Carnegie, a millionaire steel mill owner (see page 389), vigorously defended the accumulation of wealth. The wealthy, Carnegie insisted in a magazine article written in 1889, had a right to make money and a responsibility to spend it properly. Carnegie argued that the millionaire should be a "trustee for his poorer brethren, bringing to their service his superior wisdom, experience, and ability to administer, doing for them better than they would or could do for themselves." This Gospel of Wealth, as Carnegie called it, commanded the wealthy to donate their money to worthy causes.

Some philosophers applied the theories of English biologist Charles Darwin to defend the accumulation of wealth. Darwin believed that there was a constant struggle in nature in which only the fittest members of a species survive. Thinkers who applied Darwin's concept of survival of the fittest to society became known as social Darwinists. Most influential among the social Darwinists was William G. Sumner, a professor of political and social science at Yale University.

Sumner and the other social Darwinists argued that the struggle for survival occurred in the business world and should not be checked by government regulation. Firms led by the "fittest" would drive their weak competitors out of business. As a result, the social Darwinists argued, society would find itself led by the strongest, wisest, and most able citizens.

Related to social Darwinist thought were the ideas of *laissez-faire economics*, a school of thought that rejected government involvement in the economy. Herbert Spencer, a social scientist from England whose ideas were well known in the United States, maintained that the economy worked best when it was free of government regulation. Government regulation, the supporters of laissez-faire argued, would upset the balance between supply and demand and plunge the economy into chaos.

The probusiness philosophy was accepted by rich and poor alike. Millions of people read the dime novels of Horatio Alger, which told over and over again the rags-to-riches stories of young men who worked hard in factories and then by "pluck and luck" got the breaks that brought them fame and fortune.

Thus the ideas of the late nineteenth and early twentieth centuries reflected the spirit of the age. Bessemer-produced steel, electric devices, and other inventions changed the patterns of day-to-day life. Americans found in the ideas of Carnegie, Sumner, Spencer, Alger, and others, a philosophy that explained and justified the change.

For answers, see p. A 66.
Section Review

1. Identify the following: Gustavus Swift, Philip Armour, George Pullman, George Westinghouse, Thomas Edison, Gospel of Wealth, social Darwinism.

2. Define the following terms: Bessemer process, laissez-faire economics.

3. How did the Bessemer process affect the production of steel?

4. What impact did the use of refrigeration have on the meatpacking industry?

5. List four inventions that helped create new industries in the nineteenth century.

6. What responsibility did Carnegie believe the wealthy had toward the poor?

3 New Ways of Doing Business

The size and production of industrial firms greatly increased in the years following the Civil War. For example, Pittsburgh steel mills that produced a maximum of 600 tons (546 metric tons) of steel per week in 1870 produced twice as much ten years later. United States industry produced $1.8 billion worth of goods in 1860 and almost $10 billion worth by 1890. Such growth required a new approach to business. Business leaders sought better organization and looked for ways to raise money and reduce competition.

The Rise of the Corporation

Before the Civil War, most businesses were owned and run by individual proprietors or by partners. Proprietorships and partnerships are well suited to small-scale operations in which a few employees produce simple goods or services. After the Civil War, as industries grew larger, such forms of business proved inadequate, and they were discarded in favor of the corporation.*

Several factors made the corporate form preferable to the proprietorship or partnership. One is the matter of responsibility for losses. Proprietors and partners are generally responsible for the debts of their business. Failure of the business could result in financial ruin for each investor.

Corporate organization eliminates this problem. A person who invests, or buys stock, in a corporation is responsible only for the amount he or she actually invests. The liability of the investor in the event of corporate failure is thus limited.

Other advantages of the corporation are its special legal status and its permanence. A corporation is recognized by a state government, which issues a charter defining the corporation's rights and activities. Unlike proprietorships and partnerships, the corporation is, for legal purposes, a "person" in its own right. A corporation may buy and sell property or sign contracts without directly involving its owners, the stockholders.

The survival of a corporation, unlike that of a proprietorship or partnership, does not hinge on the life of the owners. A corporation granted a charter by the state could "live" forever.

Because of such factors, corporations have less difficulty attracting investors and raising *capital*, or money used in a business, than do proprietorships and partnerships. Thus, after the Civil War, the executives of more and more companies decided to incorporate. The corporate form became common among manufacturers of iron, steel, brass, aluminum, textiles, and chemicals.

New Sources of Capital

With railroad construction booming, new industries springing up, and established manufacturers enlarging their operations,

business needed new sources of capital to finance and maintain a rapid rate of growth. Commercial and savings banks, which had been in existence before the Civil War, expanded to meet the demand. Between 1860 and 1900 the number of commercial banks in the United States rose from 1,500 to 12,000. Deposits in savings banks soared from about $600,000 to $6 million.

The money that people deposited was used to finance the construction of railroads and other businesses. In addition, banks spurred the growth of business by extending credit even when they did not have deposits on hand to cover all their loans. Life insurance companies provided another source of capital. By investing millions of dollars in railroad construction and by supplying mortgages to farmers, textile manufacturers, and other businesses, life insurance companies contributed extensively to economic expansion.

Gradually corporations raised additional capital by selling more and more shares of stock to the public. Although a corporation might be worth millions of dollars, the price of each of its shares of stock might be relatively low. Thus the average person could afford to invest in stocks. The widespread ownership of corporate stock increased the amount of investment capital available to business.

Seeking Better Organization

As corporations grew larger, the need for better internal organization became clear. Before the Civil War, large factories employing hundreds of workers had only a few executives to manage the bookkeeping and direct operations.

Gradually, however, corporations began to set up separate departments to handle each major activity: purchasing raw materials, manufacturing, marketing the finished product, and coordinating finances. An executive was put in charge of each department. The size and complexity of the corporate administration grew almost as quickly as the business itself.

As corporations expanded, they continued to search for ways to survive and prosper in the booming, competitive economy. Andrew Carnegie and John D. Rockefeller were two men who successfully pioneered new forms of business organization that helped make economic expansion possible.

---

*You read about early corporations in Chapter 12. See page 209.

The Incorruptible Cashier

Until the 1870s merchants had no way to figure their exact income or profit. Rather than keeping a detailed record of sales and receipts, clerks made change from their own pockets or from an open cashbox. The owner might request that clerks enter cash transactions into an account book, but carelessness, illiteracy, and dishonesty often stood in the way of accurately recorded income.

James Ritty, who ran a cafe in Dayton, Ohio, during the 1870s, was surprised that although business was brisk, he did not seem to be making a profit. Ritty suspected that it was because his employees were helping themselves to the open cash box. His health ruined by worries over his apparent losses in business, Ritty took a trip to Europe to recover. One day while visiting the ship's engine room, he noticed a machine that automatically recorded each revolution of the propeller shaft. He wondered whether a similar machine might record each sale in his cafe, and he rushed home to find out.

Ritty devised a simple cash register based on the principles he had discovered in the engine room and patented it in 1879. This first model machine was soon improved so that the amount could be displayed to both the clerk and the customer. Ritty believed that publicly showing the amount the clerk should put in the cash box would reduce the temptation to steal. He was so pleased to have found a machine that would keep clerks honest that he called his invention the "incorruptible cashier."

Later developments included a mechanism that recorded each day's transactions on a paper roll so that owner could check on the amount of money in the cash box and also check the number of transactions. Later still, a cash drawer and a bell that rang every time the drawer was opened were added. Now the clerk had to record the sale in order to have access to the cash drawer. At the same time all the transactions were added and recorded for the owner. And the bell announced to the public that a brisk business was being done.

As the cash register gained popularity, merchants became more conscious of statistics. Business people developed more complex methods of accounting, figuring inventories, and calculating profits and losses. In this way James Ritty's incorruptible cashier, devised to keep his clerks honest, helped develop modern merchandising methods.

Andrew Carnegie and the Vertical Integration of Steel

The career of Andrew Carnegie closely resembled Horatio Alger rags-to-riches stories. Born in Scotland in 1835, Carnegie came to America at age 13. He began working in a textile mill for $1.20 a week. Then he took a job as a telegram messenger. Carnegie worked long hours and studied Morse code at night. Soon Carnegie became a skilled telegrapher.

Luck favored Carnegie when Thomas Scott, superintendent of the Pennsylvania Railroad, hired the young man as his assistant. Scott introduced Carnegie to other industrial leaders and helped him invest the savings from his salary. Although Carnegie's annual salary was only $2,400, shrewd investments quickly made him a millionaire.

While traveling in England, Carnegie saw the revolutionary Bessemer process for making steel and realized its potential. Although the United States was in the midst of an economic depression in 1873, Carnegie began building the largest steel plant in the country, at Homestead, Pennsylvania, near Pittsburgh. Using the Bessemer process, Carnegie was able to produce steel rails inexpensively and sell them for half the price charged by his competitors.

But Carnegie was not satisfied with this initial success. In 1880 the steel and iron business was highly competitive, with over a thousand separate producers. Carnegie realized that his steel plant was vulnerable to people and forces he could not control. Carnegie's business depended on mining companies to remove iron ore from the ground. Ships and rail lines were needed to move the ore to a plant to be converted to pig iron. Other railroads then transported the pig iron to the Homestead plant for the production of steel.

To insure a steady supply of raw material and a dependable transportation network, Carnegie bought mining companies, rail lines, ore ships, and pig iron plants until he had a hand in each of the industries critical to steel making. The control of all the steps required to turn a raw material into a finished product is known as *vertical integration*. Vertical integration eliminated Carnegie's dependence on owners of independent mines, railroads, and shipping lines. This gave Carnegie an advantage in the competition with other steel companies.

John D. Rockefeller and the Standard Oil Trust

While Carnegie was vertically integrating his steel operation, John D. Rockefeller was trying to eliminate competition in the oil business. The first major oil drilling in the United States took place in 1859 near Titusville, Pennsylvania. At that time oil was valued because it could be used to make kerosene, an efficient and cheap fuel for lamps. When news of the first successful wells spread, a boom in oil drilling began.

Rockefeller correctly understood that oil was relatively valueless until it was re-

fined, or purified. Thus he concluded that the refinery business was the key to success in the industry. During the Civil War, Rockefeller entered the oil-refining business and in 1870 formed the Standard Oil Company.

Rockefeller believed that the savage competition of his era was wasteful and destructive. Unlike Carnegie, however, Rockefeller at first chose not to expand his business vertically. Instead of buying drilling companies, rail lines, and warehouses, Rockefeller concentrated on acquiring other refineries. Expansion in one area of production is known as *horizontal integration*.

Rockefeller often used ruthless methods to eliminate competition. Because the railroads needed Rockefeller's business, railroad executives agreed to give rebates to Standard Oil freight. Weakened by higher freight rates, rivals of Standard Oil were further hurt by Rockefeller's relentless price cutting. Standard Oil would lower oil prices to capture a competitor's customers and then raise prices after the competitor was driven out of business. As a result of Rocke-

After the first successful oil well was drilled at Titusville, Pennsylvania, in 1859, prospectors scrambled to locate more oil nearby. The hillside of Pioneer Run, Pennsylvania, in 1865 bristled with derricks and drillers' shanties.

feller's tough methods, Standard Oil controlled over 90 percent of American refining capacity by 1879.

To tighten his control over the industry, Rockefeller also accumulated the stock of other oil companies under trust agreements. In a *trust,* stockholders of independent companies agree to exchange their shares of stock for trust certificates issued by a giant firm such as Standard Oil. The holders of trust certificates receive *dividends,* or shares of the company's profit, but lose the right to participate in the management of the firm.

Eventually, Standard Oil embarked on a plan of vertical integration. It bought barrel companies and railroads and began to manufacture and install its own pipelines. By such methods Standard Oil acquired a virtual *monopoly* of the oil industry, that is, the company had almost total control of the market for oil.

Other large businesses quickly saw the advantage of operating as a trust and followed the example of Standard Oil. In the 1880s trusts appeared in such areas as sugar refining, whiskey distilling, and the manufacture of cottonseed and linseed oils.

Free Enterprise in an Age of Growth

Since the founding of the nation, the economy had been based on the idea of free enterprise. *Free enterprise* is a system in which private individuals make economic decisions such as what products to make, how much to produce, where to sell products, and what prices should be.

Some people in the late 1800s believed that leaders of the giant corporations were abusing the free enterprise system. These critics especially objected that the creation of monopolies eliminated competition, a central part of free enterprise. To end the abuses, critics began to demand government regulations, as you will read in the following chapter.

Historians and economists have continued to debate the consequences of the economic changes of the last half of the nineteenth century. Part of the debate centers on the character and aims of the business leaders of the period. Some historians, who label those business leaders robber barons, charge that men like Carnegie and Rockefeller ruthlessly drove small companies out of business and exploited workers.

Other historians use the term industrial statesmen to describe the leaders of American business. They believe that people such as Carnegie and Rockefeller should be praised for their innovative business methods as well as their generous financial support of hundreds of schools, libraries, and museums.

Another area of debate is the issue of the efficiency of the giant corporation. Critics of the large corporation charge that big firms discourage technological change rather than discard existing equipment. Some critics maintain that the big businesses that grew up after the Civil War polluted the environment and wasted raw materials.

The defenders of big business argue that large corporations invented and perfected technological breakthroughs that revolutionized American life. They maintain that the growth of giant corporations in the late 1800s brought lower production costs and prices, higher wages, and a better quality of life for millions of Americans.

Although the merits of post–Civil War business practices are still the subject of debate, there is no question that nineteenth-century business leaders transformed American life, taking the nation from the "horse and buggy" to the automobile age. Under their leadership Americans attained a standard of living higher than that of any other people on earth.

For answers, see p. A 67.

Section Review

1. Identify the following: John D. Rockefeller.

2. Define the following terms: capital, vertical integration, horizontal integration, trust, dividend, monopoly, free enterprise.

3. List three advantages of corporations over individual proprietorships and partnerships.

4. What sources of capital were available to business people in the last half of the nineteenth century?

5. How did vertical integration give Carnegie an edge over other steel companies?

6. What methods did Rockefeller use to eliminate competition in the oil industry?

7. (a) List one criticism of big business in the late nineteenth century. (b) List one defense of big business.

4 The Growth of Industry in the South

Before the Civil War, the southern economy was largely agricultural, and the South had relatively few factories. As the region struggled to recover from the devastation of war, many southerners believed that the way to prosperity lay with industry. They envisioned a "New South" economically similar to the industrial North. And indeed the South had many natural resources and agricultural products, including coal, iron ore, timber, sugar, and cotton, that could fuel industry.

The Rise of the "New South"

No one expressed the idea of the "New South" better than Henry Grady, editor of the Atlanta *Constitution.* In spreading the idea of southern industrialization, Grady liked to tell the story of a poor Georgia cotton farmer's funeral. The farmer had been buried in a pine forest in Georgia. His pine coffin, however, had been manufactured in Cincinnati. Although an iron mine stood not far from the cemetery, the coffin's iron nails were made in Pittsburgh. The cotton coat the farmer was buried in came from New York, his trousers from Chicago. Concluded Grady, the "South didn't furnish a thing on earth for that funeral but the corpse and the hole in the ground!"

Grady's story pinpointed the South's dilemma. Though rich in natural resources, the South produced few of the manufactured goods it consumed. Along with other southerners Grady argued that an important first step toward attracting industry was the improvement of the southern railroad network. Southern states encouraged northern financiers to invest in southern lines, offering free land as well as access to the natural resources of the region. As a result, southern railroads grew at a pace faster than the national average.

The South also had changed the gauge of its track to conform to the national standard. On one day at a prearranged signal, 8,000 workers for the Louisville and Nashville railroad moved the rails of over 2,000 miles (3,200 kilometers) of track 3 inches (7.5 centimeters) closer together. For the first time, rail freight was able to move directly between North and South.

Agricultural Industries

Many southerners realized that the best way to begin industrializing was to build plants geared to use agricultural goods, such as cotton and tobacco, that the South was already producing. After the war, a number of textile mills were built to weave cotton thread. The early mills were organized much like the old plantations. The factory owner provided the workers with housing, stores, churches, and schools, as well as jobs. Most of the textile workers were women and children. Wages were low, 75-hour work weeks were common, and decent housing was rare. But a small garden plot and a steady cash income put mill workers slightly ahead of most southern agricultural workers.

Nevertheless, by 1880 the entire South was still producing fewer textiles than the state of Massachusetts. During the 1880s the industry grew as southerners purchased the latest machinery for use in new textile factories. "Every little town wanted a mill," noted one observer. "If it couldn't get a big one, it would take a small one."

The American Cotton Oil Trust built factories in the South to extract oil from cotton seeds. Cottonseed oil was the essential ingredient in soap and cosmetics and was used as a substitute for butter and olive oil. The remaining cotton pulp was used for fertilizer and cattle feed.

The southern tobacco industry also grew rapidly after the Civil War. In 1865 Washington Duke returned from General Lee's army to his farm in North Carolina to find only one tobacco barn remaining. He and his son James soon began to market Duke's Mixture. Using innovative advertising techniques, James Duke sold cigarettes in the North as well as the South. He also purchased exclusive rights to the cigarette-rolling machine invented by James Bonsack, also a southerner.

With each machine turning out 100,000 cigarettes a day, Duke revolutionized the tobacco industry. Taking advantage of railroad rebates and lowered production costs, he bought out several competitors and in 1890 formed the American Tobacco Company. Like John D. Rockefeller, who served as his model, Duke established a mammoth trust

Within a decade of the Civil War, Charleston, South Carolina, had regained much of its prewar vitality. In the background of this 1872 painting are the masts of ships docked at the Charleston port. Many of the products of new southern industries were shipped to northern factories for the final steps of the manufacturing process.

that eventually controlled 90 percent of the nation's tobacco industry.

Mining and Lumbering

Southern industry was not restricted to the use of agricultural products. Mineral industries also grew. Local deposits of iron ore and coal made steel production cheaper in Alabama than in Pennsylvania. Pig iron was first produced in Birmingham, Alabama, in 1876. Steel production began in Birmingham in 1880, and by 1900 the population of the city had risen from 3,000 to 26,000.

Oil refining developed in Texas and West Virginia. Coal mining grew in West Virginia and Alabama, copper mining and granite and marble quarrying in Georgia and Tennessee. Forest-related industries also flourished. Many forests in the North had been depleted, and by 1895 the southern yellow pine was competing with the northwestern white pine in total production of

lumber. Some southern factories began to manufacture cypress shingles, and hardwood furniture was produced in High Point, North Carolina.

A Dependent Economy

By 1900 the South had made progress toward a more balanced economy. It had its own textile factories, consolidated railroads, and giant companies such as the tobacco trust. But the growth of the North and West had been even more spectacular. The South continued to lag behind. In fact, it had a lower percentage of the nation's factories in 1900 than it had in 1860.

Many factors contributed to this lag. To raise money, southerners often had to borrow from large northern banks. Consequently, northern bankers exerted control over many southern industries and reaped much of the profits. Furthermore, many of the industries in the South produced only raw materials. These were sent to factories in the North for final processing—and from final processing came the greatest profits.

When southern factories did produce finished goods, northern railroad owners charged them higher rates to ship the products. This made it difficult for southern products to compete with those made in the North. At the same time, the rates for shipping raw materials to the North were deliberately set low.

During the late 1800s, much of the wealth of the South went North. By 1900, Henry Grady's dream of a New South had begun to take shape, but years were to pass before the dream became a reality.

For answers, see p. A 67.

Section Review

1. Identify the following: Henry Grady, Washington Duke.
2. How did southern railroads improve after the Civil War?
3. List three ways southern industries used agricultural products grown in the South.
4. Give one reason why southern manufacturers found it difficult to compete with northern manufacturers.

5 Workers Organize

An expanding economy increased the need for factory workers. Many workers moved from rural areas to industrial cities like Chicago, Buffalo, and Pittsburgh. Large numbers of immigrants from Europe joined them. Low wages, long hours, dangerous factories, unhealthy working conditions, and periodic unemployment were common. To correct those problems, workers found it increasingly necessary to band together.

The Work Force

The industrial work force was made up of individuals from a variety of backgrounds. The majority of workers were white American men, many of whom had left the farm for the city hoping to better their lot. A small number of factory workers were black. When black Americans turned from rural labor to the urban factories, however, they were often turned away or given the hardest and lowest-paying jobs. Employers frequently hired blacks and immigrants to replace striking workers.

Women played an increasingly important role in the labor force. By 1890 approximately one million women were working in factories. They made up at least half of the work force in textile mills and tobacco factories and outnumbered men in the garment manufacturing trade. Women also worked in shoemaking, food processing, packaging, and other industries that did not require heavy physical labor. However, a few industries requiring heavy labor, such as tin plate mills and print shops, occasionally hired women. No matter what the work, women received less than half the wage of a man for the same job.

Between 1865 and 1900, over 13.5 million immigrants came to the United States. (See page 426.) Without their contribution to the work force, the national economy would never have expanded as rapidly and vigorously as it did. In 1870 about one third of all factory workers in America were foreign born. The immigrants tended to settle near and work with people of their own nationality. Thus different ethnic groups tended to specialize in different industries. Many Slavs, for example, took jobs in the steel mills of Gary, Indiana; Jews often worked in New York City's garment industry.

Because immigrants were new to the country and because their standard of living in Europe had often been lower than that of many Americans, they often accepted unpleasant, dangerous, and poorly paid jobs that Americans preferred to turn down. With immigrants so eager for work, employers found they could offer them less than the standard wage. In the steel industry, immigrants might expect to earn $12 a week, compared with $22 a week for white native-born workers.

Working Conditions

Working conditions varied from industry to industry, but most factories were badly lighted, poorly ventilated, and hazardous. Facing stiff competition, owners refused to pay for expensive safety features that would raise the price of their products. Textile workers inhaled the dust and fibers that filled the air in the mills. Workers in cigarette factories had to endure tremendous heat and the stench of tobacco. Coal miners deep underground faced the perils of explosions and cave-ins. Garment workers, who often did their work at home, crouched over tables in dimly lighted apartments, straining their eyes to see if the seams were properly sewn.

Among the most demanding and dangerous occupations were jobs in the steel mills. At Andrew Carnegie's Homestead plant, men toiled 12 hours a day, 6 days a week. In the furnace room Bessemer converters belched fire and sparks. The metal floors were so hot that when water was poured on them they sizzled. Men routinely worked close to molten steel, sometimes within inches of it. Inevitably, such conditions took their toll in human life. In one year during the late 1800s, industrial accidents killed 195 workers in the steel factories of Pittsburgh.

Wages and the Economy

Despite difficult working conditions, the economic situation of the average laborer improved between 1870 and 1900. Average wages rose more than 10 percent during that period. Buying power increased because consumer prices declined. This picture is somewhat deceptive, however. The statistical averages hide wide variations in pay among workers in different occupations and in different parts of the country. Even those whose wages increased found it difficult to support a family.

"A family of workers can always live well," commented a man familiar with the textile industry in Massachusetts, "but the man with a family of small children to support, unless his wife works also, has a small chance of living properly." Some families found their situation so desperate that they were forced to send their children to work. In Pennsylvania, for example, 10-year-old boys commonly worked in the mines. At the turn of the century, almost 2 million American children between the ages of 10 and 15 were at work.

Furthermore, workers' gains were subject to the uncertainties that plagued the industries. Competition was often fierce, and many companies went out of business suddenly, leaving workers without jobs. The depressions of 1873, 1882, and 1893, threw many people out of work. During 1873 and 1874 in New York City, for example, between one fourth and one third of the workers

New inventions often created new types of jobs, including jobs for women. Office clerks had traditionally been men. With the introduction of the typewriter, however, women began to replace men on office staffs. These typists worked for an insurance company.

396

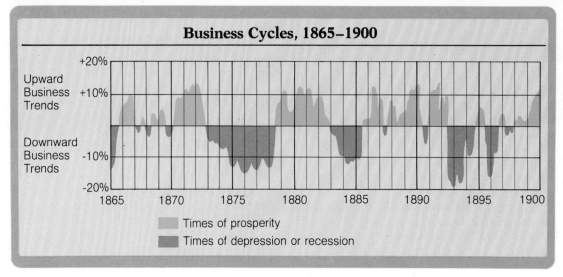

Business Cycles, 1865–1900

Upward Business Trends

Downward Business Trends

+20%
+10%
-10%
-20%

1865 1870 1875 1880 1885 1890 1895 1900

■ Times of prosperity
■ Times of depression or recession

■ *The ups and downs of the economy were felt more sharply as the nation industrialized and more people worked for wages. Which years were most prosperous? In which years did severe depressions strike?* For answers, see p. A 67.

were jobless. National unemployment figures soared from 4 percent in 1890 to 11.7 percent during the depression of 1893. Because there was no system of unemployment insurance, depressions were times of great distress.

The Knights of Labor

Low wages, periodic unemployment, illness, and accident threatened a worker's well being. Some workers escaped these misfortunes by moving on to better jobs. Others tried to band together to achieve common goals.

The organization known as the Knights of Labor was formed in 1869 as a secret brotherhood of skilled workers. Under the leadership of Uriah Stephens, a garment cutter, the society supported idealistic goals, chief among them the hope that all laborers would unite within "one big brotherhood." The Knights also advocated an eight-hour day for workers and equal pay for men and women.

In 1879 the Knights elected Terence V. Powderly as their leader. To strengthen his union, Powderly removed its veil of secrecy and opened its ranks to women, blacks, immigrants, and unskilled laborers. This was the first attempt to organize all workers.*

---

*Earlier unions had been restricted to skilled workers, as you read in Chapter 15. (See pages 269–270.)

Powderly tried to keep the organization free of politics, and he opposed the use of strikes, or work stoppages. He believed the Knights of Labor should campaign for social and economic reforms: the eight-hour day, improved safety in factories, and compensation for on-the-job injury. Under Powderly's leadership, membership increased from 9,000 in 1879 to approximately 115,000 by the end of 1884.

The Knights' greatest gains came in the following year. Despite Powderly's no-strike policy, railroad workers belonging to the Knights went on strike against tycoon Jay Gould's southwestern railroads to protest a pay cut. They forced Gould to restore the cut. Thousands of laborers, impressed by the successful railroad strike, joined the Knights of Labor. By mid-1886 membership had soared to a peak of 700,000.

The Haymarket Riot and the Decline of the Knights

Worker discontent, which had swelled the ranks of the Knights of Labor, led to an incident that, paradoxically, contributed to the downfall of the organization. In 1886, 80,000 Chicago workers went on strike in support of an eight-hour day. During the strike several workers were killed by the police in a disturbance near the McCormick Harvester Works. To protest these deaths, a group of *anarchists*, people who oppose all organized government, planned a rally for May 4.

Rain fell and a little more than a thousand people gathered in Haymarket Square to hear anarchist speakers denounce the police and the industrialists. When the police moved in to break up the meeting, a bomb was thrown, killing one police officer and six other people in the crowd. In the riot that followed, seven police officers and four civilians were killed.

Eight anarchists were convicted of conspiracy to commit murder in the bomb-throwing incident. Four were hanged, one committed suicide, and three were sentenced to long terms in prison.

The Haymarket riot turned the public sharply against labor organizations. Even though Terence Powderly and other officials of the Knights of Labor deplored the Haymarket bombing, their reputations were tarnished by it. Because the Knights and the anarchists both supported the eight-hour day, the two groups became linked in the mind of the public.

Weakened by the Haymarket incident and violence during an unsuccessful railroad strike in 1886, the Knights of Labor declined. By 1890 membership had dropped to 100,000. During the rest of the decade members either left the labor movement or joined the rising American Federation of Labor.

The American Federation of Labor

The American Federation of Labor (AFL) was founded in 1881. Its first president was a London-born cigarmaker named Samuel Gompers. Gompers believed that the Knights of Labor should not have tried to include unskilled workers in their unions. Membership in the AFL was restricted to skilled workers, who had special training. Unskilled workers, blacks, and women were not allowed to join. Recent immigrants, particularly those from Asia, were also excluded from AFL unions.

Workers did not join the American Federation of Labor directly. Individuals joined a local *craft union*, a union of persons practicing the same occupation. Each local union was affiliated with organizations on the state and national levels. The AFL was a federation of self-governing national unions. Each union was independent and had its own treasury but followed general AFL policies.

The AFL kept its goals specific and realistic. "Our organization does not consist of idealists," insisted one AFL leader. "We are going on from day to day. We are fighting only for immediate objects—objects that can be realized in a few years." The AFL favored the eight-hour day and worked for *collective bargaining*, the right of unions to represent workers as a group.

Unlike the Knights of Labor, the AFL regarded strikes as an acceptable tactic. And unlike anarchists and other radicals, the AFL rejected schemes to reorganize society. Its moderate philosophy attracted a growing number of workers. From 150,000 members in 1886, the AFL grew to 500,000 members by 1900 and reached more than a million by 1904.

Tension Between Labor and Management

Most company owners and managers were hostile to unions. Owners felt that they had the right to bargain with each worker individually. "If I wanted boiler iron," explained one railroad official, "I would go out on the

Terence Powderly opened the Knights of Labor to unskilled workers, blacks, immigrants, and women. In this drawing, Powderly (center) is introduced to the Knights' annual convention at Richmond, Virginia, by delegate Frank Farrell (left).

market and buy it where I could get it cheapest, and if I employ men, I would do the same." Unions, he argued, interfered with his rights.

For their part, union officials were skeptical of claims that employers had workers' best interests at heart. A few industrialists tried to provide their workers with such benefits as libraries and recreational facilities, but even those employers did not recognize the right of unions to exist. Consequently suspicion and distrust persisted on both sides.

With labor and management mutually antagonistic, violent strikes were not uncommon. The most serious strike erupted at Carnegie's Homestead steel plant in 1892. Angered by an unexpected wage cut, the Amalgamated Association of Iron and Steel Workers refused to accept the company's offer.

With a strike threatening, Henry Clay Frick, the plant manager, took action. He closed the plant, put up a wire fence around it, and hired 300 Pinkerton guards. When the Pinkerton guards rafted down the Monongahela River and tried to land at the plant, furious union workers attacked them. Gunfire erupted. Before the battle was over, seven Pinkerton men and nine workers lay dead.

In response to the violence, the Pennsylvania National Guard surrounded the plant and arrested the strikers. Gradually workers began to return to the steel mills, but no Amalgamated men were given their jobs back, and wages fell by about 50 percent.

Since the steel workers' union at Homestead had been the American Federation of Labor's largest union, the entire AFL suffered from this stunning defeat. The conflict set back the union movement in the steel industry for the next 20 years. The AFL continued to organize other industries, but the Homestead strike made it clear that unions faced a difficult battle for recognition.

Efforts to form labor organizations were slowed by public distrust of unions. In this 1886 cartoon, the Knights of Labor and trade unions are pictured careening toward lawless disorder. In the background, the less militant Brotherhood of Locomotive Engineers is shown, by contrast, as orderly and lawful.

Common Occupations in the Late 1800s

Occupation	Number of Males	Number of Females	Total
Farmers (self-employed, managerial)	5,055,130	226,427	5,281,557
Hired hands (farm)	2,556,958	447,104	3,004,062
Servants, waiters	238,152	1,216,639	1,454,791
Carpenters	618,044	198	618,242
Railroad workers	460,771	1,442	462,213
Miners	386,862	376	387,238
Wagon drivers, teamsters	368,265	234	368,499
Teachers, college professors	101,278	246,066	347,344
Dressmakers	836	292,668	293,504
Salespeople	205,943	58,451	264,394
Blacksmiths	209,521	60	209,581
Tailors	123,516	64,509	188,025
Bookkeepers, accountants	131,602	27,772	159,374
Physicians, surgeons	100,248	4,557	104,805
Lawyers	89,422	208	89,630
Clergy	87,060	1,143	88,203
Barbers, hairdressers	82,157	2,825	84,982
Sailors	76,823	51	76,874
Guards, police, detectives	74,350	279	74,629
Nursery workers, gardeners, florists	70,186	2,415	72,601

■ Women who joined the labor force in the late 1800s were concentrated in certain occupations, as can be seen on this table.

Reaction to Unions

Employers were not the only Americans who were unsympathetic to unions. Courts frequently issued *injunctions,* orders prohibiting a given action, to stop strikes. Furthermore, courts held that strikers could be held personally responsible for economic losses that employers suffered during a strike.

The press in many local communities sided with the employer during labor-management disputes. Newspaper publishers, who depended on local businesses for advertising revenue and who were employers themselves, often editorialized against what they saw as the unjustified demands of labor.

Furthermore, much of the public opposed unions. Despite the moderate positions of most American unions, people often considered them radical organizations. This belief was probably influenced by the activity of socialists in some European nations. Despite differing views, socialists believed that wealth derived from labor should be evenly distributed among the workers and that society as a whole, not profit-seeking individuals, should make economic decisions. In 1877 the Socialist Labor party was formed

Major Events

1844	Morse invents telegraph
1852	Otis invents passenger elevator
1859	Oil drilling begins in Pennsylvania; Bessemer process invented
1864	Pullman designs sleeping car
1869	Knights of Labor founded
1872	Westinghouse invents airbrake
1876	Bell invents telephone
1879	Edison invents incandescent light bulb
1881	American Federation of Labor founded
1883	Country divided into four time zones
1886	Haymarket riot
1892	Homestead strike

in the United States, but it remained small and had little influence.

The idea of collective bargaining also seemed foreign to many Americans. The tradition of individualism was strong, and people believed that individual effort was the way to advancement. The generally negative attitude of the public slowed the growth of unions.

For answers, see p. A 67.

Section Review

1. Identify the following: Knights of Labor, Terence Powderly, American Federation of Labor, Samuel Gompers.

2. Define the following: anarchists, craft union, collective bargaining, injunction.

3. (a) What dangerous conditions did American workers face in the late 1800s? (b) How did economic depressions affect workers?

4. (a) What were the goals of the Knights of Labor? (b) Which workers could join?

5. How did the Haymarket riot of 1886 affect the Knights of Labor?

6. (a) What were the goals of the American Federation of Labor? (b) Which workers could join?

7. How did much of the public react to unions in the late 1800s?

IN PERSPECTIVE   Many of the dramatic changes that transformed American life between 1865 and 1900 were the result of increasing industrialization. Corporate mergers and inventions in communication and transportation helped create a truly national economy. Increasingly, business people saw the entire nation as their market.

Nothing forged the nation together more than the railroads. Evolving from many independent lines to a more centralized system controlled by a few giant companies, the railroads brought consumers and producers closer together. The telegraph and later the telephone also put Americans in closer touch with each other.

These feats in transportation and communication paved the way for the consolidation of industry. Taking advantage of new inventions, enterprising industrialists expanded old businesses and created new ones. Many businesses, old and new, were consolidated into large, powerful units. Trusts, vertical integration, and horizontal integration served to make such large businesses more efficient and powerful.

Workers began to organize to improve working conditions and work for common goals. The Knights of Labor, which had enjoyed initial success, declined after the Haymarket riot of 1886. Although many Americans disapproved of labor unions, the American Federation of Labor, which stressed practical goals, grew during the late 1800s.

"The day of combination is here to stay," John D. Rockefeller concluded. Many people were convinced that he was right, but some also began to wonder whether the government had an obligation to regulate the new concentrations of industrial power, as you will read in Chapter 22.

For answers, see p. A 68.

Chapter Review

1. What technological developments in communication helped stimulate industrial growth?

2. (a) How was the post–Civil War railroad system inadequate? (b) What improvements were made?

3. (a) What problems were caused by the rapid growth of railroads between 1860 and 1900? (b) How did railroad owners try to solve these problems?

4. Explain how each of the following helped stimulate American industry: (a) Bessemer process; (b) refrigeration; (c) air brake; (d) typewriter; (e) incandescent light bulb.

5. Explain how each of the following contributed to a new philosophy for business: (a) Andrew Carnegie's Gospel of Wealth; (b) social Darwinism; (c) laissez-faire economics; (d) Horatio Alger's stories.

6. (a) Why did corporations have less difficulty raising capital than proprietorships and partnerships? (b) How did corporations raise capital?

7. (a) What is vertical integration? (b) How did it improve efficiency? (c) What is horizontal integration? (d) How did it reduce competition?

8. (a) Describe free enterprise. (b) Why did some critics of giant corporations believe that those corporations were abusing the free enterprise system? (c) Why do some people refer to the business leaders of the period as robber barons, while other people call them industrial statesmen?

9. (a) How did southern industries take advantage of the region's natural resources? (b) Why did the growing industry of the South fail to bring that region's economy up to the level of the northern economy?

10. (a) What conditions convinced many American workers to join unions in the late 1800s? (b) What attempts were made to create a national labor organization? (c) Were they successful? Explain.

11. (a) What was the reaction of industrialists to labor organizations? Why? (b) What was the reaction of the courts? (c) What was the reaction of much of the public? Why?

For answers, see p. A 69.

For Further Thought

1. Do you agree with John D. Rockefeller's observation that the United States was entering a period of combination? Cite specific examples to support your answer.

2. Review what you learned about the economy of the South before the Civil War. (See Chapter 15.) (a) How did Henry Grady's vision of the New South differ from conditions in the prewar South? (b) How was it similar? (c) Do you think a New South was being created in the late 1800s? (d) What evidence can you cite to support your answer?

3. Of all the inventions you read about in this chapter, which do you think had the greatest impact on the daily lives of Americans? Why?

For answers, see p. A 69.

Developing Basic Skills

1. *Comparing* Make a chart with two columns and four rows. Label one column Knights of Labor and the other American Federation of Labor. Label the rows Date Founded, Goals, Types of Members, and Approved Tactics.

   Use what you learned from this chapter to complete the chart. Then answer the following questions: (a) Which organization was founded earlier? (b) How did the membership of the organizations differ? Why do you think that was the case? (c) What goals did both organizations have in common? (d) What goals were different? (e) How did the approved tactics differ? (f) Do you think any of the factors you analyzed may have made the AFL more likely to succeed than the Knights of Labor? Explain.

2. *Comparing* Review the description of vertical and horizontal integration on page 390. Then answer the following questions: (a) What segments of an industry does a company control if it is vertically integrated? (b) What segments of an industry does a company control if it is horizontally integrated? (c) How might each make a company more efficient? (d) How might each give the company an edge over competition?

See page 776 for suggested readings.

22

Politics and Reform

(1867–1896)

The Lost Bet, *by Joseph Klir.*

Throughout much of the nineteenth century, American political campaigns had been colorful and exciting. The campaigns of the last half of the century were no exception. Despite the excitement, however, important political issues were far from the minds of most people.

One issue that did concern many Americans was the prevalence of corruption at all levels of government. Efforts to reform corrupt political practices began in earnest during the 1880s. Some people also demanded that government regulate the unfair business practices of the giant trusts that developed during the period.

A national political movement known as Populism drew on the reform spirit and on the discontent of farmers in the West and South. Since many farmers thought that they were not well represented by the two major political parties, they formed a third party. The Populist movement was short-lived, yet the Populists were to pave the way for later generations of reformers.

1 Political Corruption in a Gilded Age

The rapid industrialization of the years following the Civil War brought problems as well as material progress. The fortunes of industrialists gave them immense influence over many aspects of life, especially politics. Some industrialists, such as Andrew Carnegie, used their wealth to try to improve society, but others were mainly interested in increasing their fortunes and power.

Bribery and Politics

In 1877 Collis P. Huntington, builder of the Central Pacific Railroad and director of the Southern Pacific line, had a problem. His archrival, Thomas Scott of the Pennsylvania Railroad, had placed a bill before Congress that would break Huntington's control of rail routes to southern California. Huntington's solution was to bribe key members of Congress. "It costs money to fix things," he explained. To Huntington, bribery made good sense. "If [another] man has the power to do great evil, and won't do right unless he is bribed to do it," he said, "it is a man's duty to go up and bribe the judge."

Many industrialists openly showed their contempt for society and the law. Cornelius Vanderbilt, when told that some of his ac- tions were against the law, snorted, "Law! What do I care about the law? Haven't I got the power?" Indeed, with his huge private fortune and railroad empire, Vanderbilt did have the power.

The lure of power and riches tarnished Congress and the presidency. Votes, political favors, and political offices were bought and sold. Representatives of wealthy special interests bribed members of Congress to pass legislation that benefited those interests. Cabinet members and other high-ranking officials took advantage of their positions to make fortunes for themselves.

The climate of corruption also infected small businesses and governments at the state and local levels. The author Mark Twain believed that such corruption constituted the underside of public life, the brass under a thin layer of gold. He labeled the era the Gilded Age, and the nickname stuck.

Wheeling and Dealing in Congress

Congress itself helped confirm the popular notion that politicians were corrupt and interested only in enjoying the spoils of victory. Of the two houses of Congress, the

Giant trusts were popularly considered the ''bosses of the Senate,'' as this cartoon shows. What famous speech is parodied in the sign on the wall? For answer, see p. A 69.

Senate was by far the most powerful. In part, this was because senators faced reelection only every six years, unlike members of the House of Representatives, who faced it every two years. Some senators had been in office for several decades and had accumulated enormous reserves of power and influence. Many were political bosses in their home states, and they could reward supporters with a wide range of appointments and favors.

Many senators were also personally wealthy, so many in fact that the Senate became known as a "rich man's club." The country, remarked one prominent observer, had a "government of the people, by the people, for the benefit of the Senate."

The House of Representatives demonstrated less influence partly because it conveyed the impression of being a rather disorderly place. Representatives often sat with their feet propped on their desks, smoking cigars or spitting tobacco juice. Members might be seen reading newspapers or writing letters instead of attending to business. Representatives who wanted to listen to a speech had to crowd close to the podium in order to hear the proceedings. Nevertheless, some members emerged as effective legislators and prominent national figures.

Despite its tarnished reputation, Congress had a high opinion of itself. As you read in Chapter 19, the impeachment of President Andrew Johnson was a sign that Congress had decided to assert authority over the executive branch of the government. In the years after Reconstruction, the presidency remained weak and Congress became stronger. Congressional leaders firmly defended their responsibility to propose and make laws. The President, they believed, should only enforce laws passed by the legislative branch.

The Presidency During the Gilded Age

Acting under the shadow of the Congress, the Presidents who served during the Gilded Age did not achieve great distinction. Rather, the men who occupied the White House during the late 1800s tended to be colorless figures who were good politicians but not inspiring leaders. Although some of the Presidents during this period saw the need for reform and were often behind important changes, they basically agreed that the presidency was less powerful than the legislative branch.

Even if a President had wanted to lead vigorously, he would have found it difficult to do so. The executive staff was small. Without additional help, a President was in no position to take the initiative on legislative issues. Moreover, no President between 1865 and 1897 had the advantage of having his own party in control of both houses of Congress throughout his full term of office.

Finally, Presidents were thwarted by the widespread political corruption of the period. Although most of them were personally honest, they were often surrounded by unsavory politicians interested only in personal gain.

Scandals During Grant's Administration

The worst examples of corruption at the national level took place during the administration of Ulysses S. Grant (1869–1877). Grant was an honest, able military general, but loyalty to his friends led him to appoint people who eventually betrayed his trust.

The first major scandal came to light in 1872. A newspaper, the New York Sun, reported that officials of the Union Pacific Railroad had enriched themselves by creating a company called the Crédit Mobilier. The Crédit Mobilier was supposedly a construction company. As such, it received contracts from the Union Pacific to lay track on the transcontinental route. On the strength of these contracts, Crédit Mobilier raised additional money by selling shares of stock.

Much of the stock, which paid high dividends, was sold to members of Congress at bargain prices. In return, the stockholding legislators voted funds for Union Pacific construction. The Union Pacific then paid the Crédit Mobilier according to the contracts, but the firm never laid a foot of track. The company existed merely to make money.

Other investigations revealed that at least five members of Grant's cabinet had engaged in corrupt practices. The most serious offender was Secretary of War William Belknap, who was involved in many of the shady dealings used by white traders to cheat Native Americans who lived on reservations. (See page 371.)

When Grant's secretary of the treasury resigned over another scandal, his replacement uncovered what came to be known as the Whiskey Ring. The federal government was supposed to collect an excise tax on every bottle of whiskey sold. But hundreds of distillers had bribed treasury officials in order to avoid paying those taxes. Even the President's personal secretary was involved. Though Grant ordered investigators to "let no guilty man escape," the President protected his secretary from punishment.

The scandals of the Grant administration damaged the office of the presidency. Much of the public came to agree with Mark Twain that corruption in politics was indeed a hallmark of the Gilded Age. Yet the scandals also made some people more determined to reform political life, and the reformers were soon to gain prominence.

For answers, see p. A 70.

Section Review

1. Identify the following: Crédit Mobilier, Whiskey Ring.
2. What attitude did some wealthy industrialists, such as Collis P. Huntington and Cornelius Vanderbilt, have toward bribery?
3. (a) According to congressional leaders after Reconstruction, what were the legislators' two responsibilities? (b) In their opinion what was the President's job?
4. List three factors that prevented Presidents from leading vigorously during the Gilded Age.
5. What impact did scandals during Grant's administration have on the presidency?

2 Attempts at Reform

The widespread political corruption of the Gilded Age eventually convinced some Americans that reform was needed. The resulting reform efforts were not limited to attacks on bribery. Reformers also turned their attention to the abuse of power by giant railroads and trusts.

The Mugwumps

One strong movement for reform came from within the Republican party. These reform-minded Republicans were nicknamed Mugwumps, an Indian term meaning big chief. The Mugwumps believed in laissez-faire economics and clean politics. They opposed the "spoils system" that had begun under President Andrew Jackson. (See page 237.) The spoils—federal, state, and local offices—were being handed out, not for merit, but simply as rewards to loyal party workers. The Mugwumps argued that this *patronage system*, the practice of giving out government jobs as favors, should be replaced by a civil service in which job applicants would be tested to determine their fitness for particular jobs.

Among the Mugwumps were the editors of well-known journals: E. L. Godkin of *The Nation* and George W. Curtis of *Harper's Weekly*. They wrote editorials urging reform and exposés of corrupt political machines. One of the most effective publicists was *Har-per's* cartoonist Thomas Nast, whose caricatures of greedy trusts and wicked political bosses were popular throughout the nation.

The Mugwumps, however, were paid little attention by most politicians, who realized that the average American did not share the Mugwumps' distaste for the rough and tumble of politics. Nevertheless, the Mugwumps eventually achieved partial success in their crusade to clean up American politics.

Chipping Away at the Spoils System

Most Mugwumps would not have predicted that the three Republican Presidents who followed Ulysses S. Grant would advance the cause of reform. Yet Presidents Hayes (1877–1881), Garfield (1881), and Arthur (1881–1885) each took steps to reform the old patronage system.

As you read in Chapter 19, President Rutherford Hayes was elected to office in 1876 by a political deal. In that deal Republican politicians agreed to end Reconstruction in return for Democratic help in resolving the disputed presidential election. (See page 357.) But Hayes soon surprised Republican party leaders by appointing a noted reformer, Carl Schurz, to the cabinet as secretary of the interior. "Hayes has passed the Republican party to its worst enemies," grumbled one old-line Republican.

President Hayes also launched an investigation into the administration of the customs house in New York. The customs house, in charge of collecting duties on imports unloaded at the port of New York, had the reputation of being one of the most corrupt organizations in the nation. The investigation revealed that over 200 officials in the customs house were receiving salaries without doing any work. High officials were lining their pockets with some $1.5 million in duties each year. Although influential Republicans bitterly fought the investigation, the President dismissed two senior customs house employees.

Hayes's successor, James Garfield, no sooner assumed office in 1881 than he found himself in the middle of a spirited struggle over patronage between two rival factions of the Republican party. One group was the "Half-breeds," so called because of their half-hearted commitment to Reconstruction, and the other was the "Stalwarts," who had supported a tough policy of Reconstruction. Each tried to convince Garfield to reward their own loyal followers with the lion's share of political offices.

The efforts of the two groups ended abruptly on July 2, 1881 when a mentally unstable office seeker, Charles Guiteau, shot President Garfield. Guiteau was bitter because he had not received a government appointment. For nearly two months the President clung to life. His death in September left the nation shocked at the evils of the patronage system and eager to accept reform of some sort.

The Civil Service Act

When Vice-President Chester Arthur succeeded Garfield, few suspected that he would take any action toward reform. Arthur was an elegant, easy-going man with expensive tastes. He was also one of the customs house officials dismissed by President Hayes. Yet as President, Arthur rose to the demands of his new office and pushed for civil service legislation.

Reacting to public outcry, Congress passed the Civil Service Act in 1883, and President Arthur promptly signed it into law. The act classified approximately 15,000 federal jobs as civil service positions, to be given only to applicants who had passed a competitive examination administered by a Civil Service Commission. Furthermore, the act prohibited firing of civil service employees for political reasons.

Although the new legislation did not abolish the spoils system overnight, it was an important step. For the first time many federal employees did not hold office simply because they belonged to a certain political party. The Civil Service Act allowed Presidents to expand the list of civil service jobs. Over the years they did exactly that—not always out of idealism, but because it was a way to keep their appointees from being dismissed by a new President. By 1897 over half of the approximately 175,000 federal employees held civil service jobs.

Cleveland and Reform

The presidential election of 1884 offered a reformer to the public, but not Chester Arthur. Although Mugwumps had been surprised and delighted by Arthur's support for reform, old-line Republicans were angered. They refused to renominate him and instead chose James G. Blaine, a Maine senator who led the Half-breed faction of the party.

The reform candidate in 1884 was Grover Cleveland, the Democratic governor of New York. Cleveland had won a national reputation defying the political bosses in New York City, speaking his mind, and running an honest administration. During the campaign, each side blasted the other with accusations of dishonesty and immorality. Cleveland survived and went on to win the election. For the first time in 25 years, a Democratic President would be living in the White House.

President Cleveland's administration was often a stormy one. A man of principle, he worked diligently to satisfy the Mugwumps and appoint competent officeholders, but he angered many members of his own party who wanted their share of the spoils. In 1888 Cleveland lost a bid for reelection to Republican Benjamin Harrison, the grandson of President William Henry Harrison. When Harrison proved to be an undistinguished President, however, the voters reelected Cleveland to a second term in 1892.

Although Cleveland was interested primarily in reform of the civil service, perhaps the most significant piece of reform legislation passed during his first term concerned regulation of the railroads.

Regulating the Railroads

As you read in Chapter 21, cutthroat competition among railroads had resulted in practices such as rebates and pooling. (See page 383.) Small shippers complained that the railroads discriminated against them by giving their larger rivals lower rates. Often, too, railroads charged higher rates for hauling freight short distances than they did for long hauls.

As early as 1837, a few state governments had acted to regulate railroads, but not until the 1870s did many states establish regulatory commissions. Midwestern states, such as Iowa and Illinois, had strong commissions that enforced strict regulations. In other states, such as Massachusetts and Alabama, the commissions had only advisory power but were still influential.

The railroads did not accept regulation willingly. Their lawyers questioned whether states had the power under law to regulate the railroad business. In 1877, in the case of *Munn* v. *Illinois*, the Supreme Court ruled that the Constitution permitted state regulation of railroads. But the Court later reversed itself in the case of *Wabash, St. Louis, & Pacific Railway Company* v. *Illinois* in 1886. Only Congress, the justices stated, had the power to regulate commerce between the states. Railroad freight crossing state lines, the Court held, could not be regulated by state commissions.

Under the leadership of Representative John Reagan of Texas and Senator Shelby Cullom of Illinois, Congress responded to increased demands for reform by passing the Interstate Commerce Act in 1887. The act outlawed rebating and pooling. The railroads were ordered to establish "reasonable and just" rates and to refrain from charging short-haul customers higher rates than long-haul customers. A five-member Interstate Commerce Commission (ICC) was established to investigate complaints and take action by filing suit in the courts.

The Interstate Commerce Act proved difficult to enforce in the courts. Favored by skilled lawyers and judges who believed the government had limited regulatory power, the railroads were able to blunt the force of the act. Between 1887 and 1906 the ICC lost almost every railroad regulation case brought before the Supreme Court. Yet the Interstate Commerce Act set an important precedent. In the years ahead many federal commissions would be established to regulate other large industries; and as the Supreme Court became more sympathetic to the regulation of business in later years, the power of the ICC increased.

Attacking the Trusts

Pressure for reform also led Congress to curb the economic power of trusts. Although John D. Rockefeller had proclaimed that "the day of combination" had come to stay, many Americans viewed trusts with suspicion. They charged that the size and power of trusts gave them an unfair advantage, which hindered the operation of the free

Trusts were complicated legal arrangements that concentrated control of an industry, or several industries, in the hands of a few people. As this 1889 cartoon indicates, some people thought trusts were undermining traditional American individualism and liberties.

enterprise system. Large trusts could afford to drive smaller companies out of business by lowering prices and then raising them again. This enabled many to become monopolies, free to charge as high a price as they wanted for a product.

By ruthless use of monopoly power, trusts violated the public's sense of fair play. Cartoonists portrayed trusts as octopuses greedily grasping for still more economic control. In 1888 public demand for regulation of trusts had grown so great that both Republicans and Democrats endorsed the idea.

During President Benjamin Harrison's administration, Congress passed the Sherman Antitrust Act. The 1890 law prohibited monopolies, stating, "Every contract, combination in the form of trust or otherwise, or conspiracy in restraint of trade or commerce ... is hereby declared illegal." It thus became a crime for one corporation to eliminate all competition.

The Sherman Antitrust Act sounded uncompromising, but enforcing it proved difficult. To sidestep the law, corporations devised a substitute for the trust known as the *holding company*. Instead of merging separate companies into a trust, a holding company gained control of member companies by buying their stock. The "held" companies remained separate entities and business went on as usual, but the holding company controlled them just as effectively as a trust could. In the first five years after passage of the Sherman law, 25 new holding companies came into being.

Furthermore, government officials hesitated to challenge the powerful trusts, and no commission like the ICC existed to respond to complaints. Another blow was dealt to the effectiveness of the Sherman Act in 1895 when the Supreme Court narrowly interpreted the legislation in the case of *United States* v. *E. C. Knight Company*. This was the first Supreme Court case involving the act.

The suit against the E. C. Knight Company charged the company with furthering monopoly by selling out to the American Sugar Refining Company. With the purchase of Knight's sugar-refining facilities the American Sugar Refining Company became one of the strongest monopolies in the country. Yet the Court ruled that the sale did not violate the Sherman Antitrust Act because Knight refined all its sugar at plants within one state. The act, the Court held, prohibited the restraint of "trade or commerce." Since the E. C. Knight Company was not involved in shipping, it could not be prosecuted under the existing law.

With industry assured that the Supreme Court would interpret the antitrust legislation narrowly, the number of holding companies and monopolies continued to grow throughout the 1890s.

United States v. E. C. Knight Company

Reformers hoped that the Sherman Antitrust Act of 1890 would curb the power of giant trusts. In the case of *United States* v. *E. C. Knight Company*, however, the Supreme Court ruled that the act could be enforced only if a company were involved in trade between states or with foreign nations. The extract below, from the majority opinion of Chief Justice M. W. Fuller, states the Court's position.

It was in the light of well-settled principles that the act of July 2, 1890, [Sherman Antitrust Act] was framed. Congress did not attempt thereby to assert the power to deal with monopoly directly as such; or to limit and restrict the rights of corporations created by the states or the citizens of the states in the acquisition, control, or disposition of property; or to regulate or prescribe the price or prices at which such property or the products thereof should be sold. . . .

[W]hat the law struck at was combinations, contracts, and conspiracies to monopolize trade and commerce among the several states or with foreign nations; but the contracts and acts of the defendants related exclusively to the acquisition of the Philadelphia refineries and the business of sugar refining in Pennsylvania, and bore no direct relation to commerce between the states or with foreign nations. The object was manifestly private gain in the manufacture of the commodity, but not through the control of interstate or foreign commerce.

The Radical Reformers

Reform of the civil service, railroads, and trusts was achieved by politicians who wished to work within the established economic system. Even the Mugwumps accepted the basic idea of laissez-faire; but others during this period demanded more far-reaching reform.

One such reformer was Henry George, a self-taught economist whose book *Progress and Poverty* sold over 2 million copies. George believed that labor should be the basis of all wealth a person accumulated. Under the existing system, land rose in value simply because a railroad ran near it or a town sprang up. Land speculators thus made large profits without any labor. George proposed that Congress enact a single tax on land as a means of controlling what he considered illegitimate profits.

Edward Bellamy attracted considerable attention in 1888 with his novel *Looking Backward*. The novel pictured a utopia in 2000 A.D. in which the government ran all industry with great wisdom. Under such a system, Bellamy predicted, the "evils" of competition would no longer exist and people would live in harmony. Bellamy's followers urged that his proposals be enacted into law.

Henry Demarest Lloyd aroused public opinion against the trusts when he published *Wealth Against Commonwealth* in 1894. Lloyd concentrated his attack on Rockefeller's Standard Oil Company, marshaling facts and providing vivid examples of the trust's ruthless business practices.

These critics of American society were often widely read, but their proposed solutions were seldom accepted either by politicians or by most Americans. Still, the reformers focused public attention on problems that later political movements would deal with more effectively.

For answers, see p. A 70.

Section Review

1. Identify the following: Mugwumps; Civil Service Act; *Munn* v. *Illinois*; *Wabash, St. Louis, & Pacific Railway Company* v. *Illinois*; Interstate Commerce Act; Sherman Antitrust Act; *United States* v. *E. C. Knight Company*.

2. Define the following terms: patronage system, holding company.

3. According to the Mugwumps, how should government employees be selected?

4. In what way did the Civil Service Act make the hiring and firing of government employees less political?

5. (a) How did the railroads discriminate against small shippers? (b) How did they discriminate against short-haul shippers?

6. What important precedent was set by the Interstate Commerce Act?

7. What new form of organization did corporations create to sidestep the Sherman Antitrust Act?

3 Politics in the New South

The end of Reconstruction in 1877 brought significant political changes to the South. As you read in Chapter 19, Democrats had gradually gained control of southern state governments. (See page 356.) During the last part of the century, the Democratic party in the South achieved such strength that Republican opposition all but disappeared. At the same time, many of the gains made by black Americans during Reconstruction gradually eroded.

Conservatives in Control

The Democrats, also known as Conservatives, who came to dominate southern politics after the end of Reconstruction were not the same group of wealthy planters who had been in control before the Civil War. Many of the Conservatives were industrialists who strongly supported Henry Grady's vision of a New South.

Like most business leaders in the North and West, southern industrialists opposed interference with their business activities by either state or national government. But southerners had a special reason for supporting laissez-faire. They had just experienced Radical Reconstruction, which to them was the height of government interference. The Conservative leaders of the southern states thus framed new constitutions severely limiting the power of state governments to regulate economic affairs.

The Conservatives enjoyed widespread support, but they were not totally unopposed. Other southerners occasionally tried to vote them out of office, primarily because of scandals that rocked the Conservative governments from time to time. Graft and bribery flourished in the South as they did in the North. Whenever evidence of corruption came to light, independent candidates ran for office, and Republicans tried to win back southerners to their party.

Despite such attempts, Conservatives were seldom voted out of office. Republicans, tainted by the war and Reconstruction, would be politically crippled in the South for many years to come. The domination of the region's political affairs by Democrats gave rise to the expression the "solid South."

The Rise of Jim Crow

When President Hayes toured the South in 1877, he told black citizens that their "rights and interests would be safer" if southern whites were "let alone by the general government." Hayes was, in effect, advocating a laissez-faire policy toward race relations. The federal government would maintain that policy for the next 75 years.

For their own part, southern Conservatives adopted what they felt was a moderate policy toward black citizens. The white politicians did not regard former slaves as their equals but believed that blacks should have some limited rights, and they courted black political support.

Throughout the 1880s and early 1890s many blacks in the South continued to vote and hold minor political offices. They served as justices of the peace, constables, and occasionally as representatives in state legislatures. Southern blacks faced less social discrimination than blacks living in the North. Public transportation remained integrated, as did theaters, bars, soda fountains, parks, and cemeteries.

During the 1890s, however, southern state governments moved to deprive black Americans of their political rights and to segregate them from whites. Conservative politicians were partly responsible for the shift in policy. As you will read in the following section, many rural southern reformers challenged Conservative political dominance. To gain support from the reformers, the Conservatives abandoned their moderate racial

policy, and racial hatred became a major plank in Conservative platforms.

Difficult economic conditions also strained relations between whites and blacks. Falling farm prices and tightened credit during the depression of 1893 plunged white southern farmers into a desperate mood. Many turned their resentment toward blacks, demanding that they be segregated and denied the right to vote.

Although the Fifteenth Amendment to the Constitution guaranteed black Americans the right to vote, between 1890 and 1907 southern states one by one adopted laws making it all but impossible for black citizens to exercise that right. Rigid residency requirements for voting effectively *disenfranchised*, or denied the vote to, many sharecroppers who changed residences often. Literacy tests and *poll taxes*, fees paid in order to vote, further reduced the number of blacks who could vote, since many were unable to read or too poor to pay the tax.

However, these voting restrictions worked against poor whites as well as blacks. Consequently, many southern states adopted so-called *grandfather clauses*. These clauses allowed individuals to satisfy voting requirements if their father or grandfathers had been eligible to vote in 1867. Because blacks had not been allowed to vote at that time, they could not qualify under the grandfather clauses. (The Supreme Court declared such clauses unconstitutional in 1915.)

Southern legislatures also passed laws establishing strict social segregation. Blacks were forbidden to mingle with whites in railroad cars, buses, trolleys, passenger terminals, and other public facilities. Laws required blacks to drink from separate water fountains and sit in separate sections in theaters.

These Jim Crow* laws, as the segregation codes were called, received important support in 1896 when the Supreme Court decided the case of *Plessy* v. *Ferguson*. In that case, the Court ruled that segregation was legal as long as blacks were given "equal but separate" facilities. In other words, a state could require that blacks and whites sit in separate railroad cars if the railroad provided equal accommodations for members

---

*Jim Crow was a black stage character, created by a white song-and-dance man in 1830. The character conveyed an unfavorable impression of black people.

of both races. Despite the Court's ruling, however, the facilities for blacks, though separate, were rarely equal.

Sparked by racial hatred, lynch law and mob rule competed with justice in many parts of the United States. During the 1890's almost 200 people a year were lynched in the nation. Four fifths of the lynchings took place in the South, and most lynching victims in all areas of the country were black. Mark Twain, for one, was so shocked by the violence that he wrote an essay titled, "The United States of Lyncherdom."

The Black Response

Faced with segregation and violence, black Americans searched for a solution to their plight. Some looked to the West as a land of opportunity. In the years following 1877, approximately 200,000 blacks moved West, many homesteading in Kansas or Oklahoma.

Blacks who chose to remain in the South pursued a variety of occupations. The majority continued to be sharecroppers and tenant farmers. Others worked at skilled trades such as carpentry, masonry, plastering, and painting, but even fewer opportunities existed in these areas than before the war. A few blacks overcame the difficulties of raising capital and founded their own businesses. Most notable was the North Carolina Mutual Life Insurance Company,

organized in 1898. It soon became the largest black-owned business in the world.

Black Americans increasingly relied on each other for support in these difficult times. Black schools and churches, established during Reconstruction, continued to grow during the 1880s and 1890s. Fraternal lodges, mutual aid societies, and groups like the National Negro Business League, an association of black business people founded in 1900, all responded to the needs of black citizens.

Booker T. Washington and Practical Education

One of the most prominent black leaders during these years was Booker T. Washington. Born a slave, Washington was determined to improve his economic status after the war. He enrolled at Hampton Normal and Industrial Institute of Virginia, a school established by the Freedman's Bureau to help blacks learn trades, such as teaching and mechanics.

Washington decided to spread the Hampton ideal of practical education. In 1881 he founded the Tuskegee Institute in Alabama. Tuskegee attracted hundreds of young blacks seeking vocational training. Tuskegee also sponsored the research of the distinguished black scientist George Washington Carver. Carver, who began teaching

Thousands of blacks moved west in the late 1800s to escape racial segregation and violence. This family homesteaded a farm in Kansas in 1885.

Booker T. Washington attended the Hampton Institute in Virginia. The institute was founded after the Civil War to provide a practical education for newly freed blacks. Above, Hampton students work in a science laboratory.

at Tuskegee in 1896, discovered hundreds of uses for southern agricultural products.

Throughout his career, Booker T. Washington insisted that conditions in the South made political equality for blacks an impossible goal. He suggested that blacks ignore social equality and focus on achieving economic success. "Through the dairy farm, the truck garden, the trades, and commercial life . . . the negro is to find his way to the enjoyment of all his rights," he advised. Even without the vote, Washington noted, blacks had that "little green ballot," money, which could be deposited at the teller's window, where "no one will throw it out or refuse to count it."

Washington's message of conciliation and compromise found its fullest expression in a speech he gave before an Atlanta business convention in 1895. He assured white business and political leaders that blacks were loyal to the southern way of life. Because of that loyalty, Washington maintained, black citizens should have a chance to earn a decent living in the South. Washington's speech, in which he abandoned social and political equality and asked for prosperity, is often referred to as the Atlanta Compromise.

W.E.B. Du Bois Answers Washington

While Booker T. Washington advocated a policy of adjustment to segregated society, another black leader recommended vigorous protest against Jim Crow laws. William E. B. Du Bois grew up in Massachusetts and studied at Fisk and Harvard universities. He was the first black to graduate from Harvard with a Ph.D. degree. Du Bois began teaching economics and history at Atlanta University in 1896, about the time that Washington's views were receiving wide publicity.

The young Du Bois disagreed with Washington's advice to black Americans. Blacks, he argued, should fight for the right to vote and the right to enjoy equality of opportunity. In a book entitled *The Souls of Black Folks*, published in 1903, Du Bois attacked Washington for abandoning the goal of equal rights. "Negroes must insist continually," Du Bois maintained, "that voting is necessary to proper manhood, that color discrimination is barbarism, and that black boys need education as well as white boys."

Inspired by Washington, Du Bois, and others, southern blacks made slow but genuine economic progress. By 1900 one out of five owned a home, and the combined worth of black farms totaled almost $500 million. While less that 5 percent of blacks could read in 1865, approximately 56 percent were literate in 1900. By 1915 blacks in the South owned 30,000 businesses, including grocery and drug stores, dress shops, sawmills, banks, and insurance companies.

Yet there was no denying that the aspirations of black Americans in the South and the North were stifled by segregation and discrimination. The road to full political and social equality stretched far into the future.

For answers, see p. A 70.

Section Review

1. Identify the following: Conservatives, "solid South," Jim Crow laws, *Plessy* v. *Ferguson*, Booker T. Washington, Atlanta Compromise, W.E.B. Du Bois.

2. Define the following terms: disenfranchise, poll tax, grandfather clause.

3. What special reason did southerners have for supporting an economic policy of laissez-faire?

4. List three ways that southern blacks were discouraged from voting.

5. List four ways that Jim Crow laws discriminated against blacks in the South.

6. What kind of training was offered at Tuskegee Institute?

7. According to W.E.B. Du Bois, what rights should black Americans fight for?

4 The Populist Crusade

As long as the economy continued to prosper, reformers' demands for change had little appeal. In the mid-1880s, however, the economic problems of farmers in the West and the South sparked what came to be known as the Populist movement. Beginning as local alliances of farmers, it eventually grew into a nationwide third party that challenged the traditional two-party system.

Roots of Discontent

Farmers in the 1870s and 1880s found it increasingly difficult to make a living in the United States. Most were producing more than ever before, but the prices they received were declining. The increased production of American farmers was accompanied by a similar growth of agricultural production in Australia, South America, and Canada. With so much food on the world market, prices dropped. Some farmers realized that overproduction was a major cause of low prices. Mary Lease, a fiery Kansas reformer, expressed their frustration.

> We were told two years ago to go to work and raise a big crop, that was all we needed. We went to work and plowed and planted; the rains fell, the sun shone, nature smiled, and we raised the big crop they told us to; and what came of it? Eight-cent corn, ten-cent oats, two-cent beef, and no price at all for butter and eggs—that's what came of it.

Farmers suffered further when credit was hard to get, as it was during the 1880s and 1890s. They needed to borrow money to buy seed and machinery, then pay back their debts once crops were harvested and sold. A poor crop often meant farmers could not pay back their loans. In the West, especially, farmers had borrowed extensively to buy the large tracts of land needed to make farming profitable. Consequently, in all parts of the country farmers bore the burden of debt.

Being in debt was a special hardship during these years because the economy was experiencing *deflation*, that is, the price of goods and services was dropping. As a result, the dollar of 1886 bought more than that of 1876. Farmers who borrowed money one year and paid it back several years later found that the money they paid back was worth more than the money they had borrowed.

Furthermore, most farmers were angry at the railroads that shipped their grain to market. The farmers claimed, quite rightly in many cases, that the rates the railroads charged in the West, where they had a monopoly, were two or three times higher than rates charged in the East.

These hardships were aggravated by several natural disasters that struck during the late 1880s. Hard winters and summer droughts destroyed cattle and crops in the

All but the very young members of farm families worked from dawn to dusk to make ends meet. Several generations of women in the Alabama family shown here are spinning and weaving.

West. In the South floods in the lower Mississippi Valley ruined much land.

Organizing for Action

By the 1870s farmers had begun banding together to deal with their problems. In 1867 Oliver Kelley founded an association known as the Patrons of Husbandry, popularly called the Grange. Kelley's organization grew slowly at first, but by 1874 over 14,000 local grange associations had been started.

Kelley considered his organization a social one, designed to overcome the isolation and loneliness of rural life, but soon Grangers began to campaign for political causes. In midwestern states their influence helped to create state railroad commissions that came to regulate freight rates.

The Grange also acted to boost farm profits. Most farmers sold their harvested grain to distributors, who for a fee stored the grain in giant elevators and arranged to ship it to market. Grangers tried to eliminate the distributors by forming cooperatives. The cooperatives built their own grain elevators and marketed the grain themselves without charging a large fee for profit. Stores were established to buy farm machinery and sell it to members at low prices.

The Grange was strongest in the Midwest and in Kentucky and Missouri. But even in these areas, the organization became less active in the late 1870s as the economy recovered from the depression of 1873. As conditions worsened again in the mid-1880s, other protest organizations grew rapidly, especially in the South and the West.

The Northwestern Farmers' Alliance, established in 1880, represented farmers in the Midwest. Its largest membership was in the Dakotas and Kansas. Most prominent among the southern groups was the Southern Farmers' Alliance. The alliance had existed in Texas since 1875, but after 1886, under the direction of Charles W. Macune, an energetic Methodist preacher, it spread throughout the South. At its height, the alliance claimed as many as 3 million members, including small landowners and tenant farmers. At the same time, a separate Colored Farmers' National Alliance represented the interests of over a million black farmers.

The alliances adopted many of the Grangers' techniques. They organized cooperatives to purchase equipment and market crops. They began newspapers and lecture bureaus to spread their ideas. Increasingly, reformers in both the South and the West came to believe that if farmers were to prosper, political action was needed to change national policies.

The Ocala Platform

In 1889 a large part of the Northwestern Alliance joined with the Southern Alliance to form the National Farmers' Alliance. The following year, the organization met in a convention at Ocala, Florida, and created a program for political reform. The Ocala Platform, as it was called, outlined the reformers' major goals.

Chief among these was the demand that the government help the farmers out of their credit bind. Farmers had to sell their crops at harvest time in order to pay back loans for seed and machinery. If prices were low at that time, farmers could not make enough money to pay back the loans and their debts grew.

The Ocala Platform suggested that the government set up regional subtreasuries that would lend farmers up to 80 percent of the local market value of their crops. Thus farmers would receive the cash they needed and be able to store their agricultural products in warehouses or granaries until the market price rose.

The Ocala Platform advocated government action to discourage deflation. The government, it maintained, should increase the amount of money in circulation. It could do this in part by minting silver coins. The increase in the money supply would tend to inflate the currency and would work to the advantage of debtors.

The Ocala Platform also argued that government actions were unfairly burdening the farmer and landowner while aiding wealthy manufacturers. High tariffs protected domestic manufactured products from competition with cheaper European goods. Farmers then had to pay higher prices for the protected products. Yet they were forced to sell their agricultural products in the international market without any government protection similar to the tariff.

Furthermore, most government taxes were based on the amount of land a person owned. The Ocala Platform recommended that wealth, not land, be taxed. It proposed a *graduated personal income tax*, that is, the tax rate would be proportional to a person's income. Persons with higher incomes would pay a higher rate. Finally, the Ocala Platform

called for strict regulation of the railroads. If regulation failed to work, the National Farmers' Alliance recommended that the government take over the railroads and run them fairly.

Birth of the Populist Party

During the 1890 elections members of the National Farmers' Alliance worked to elect representatives to Congress. In the South, where the Democratic party dominated, farmers demanded that Democratic candidates publicly support reform measures in return for the farmers' votes. In the West many farmers decided to form their own independent parties.

Candidates sympathetic to agrarian reform enjoyed great success in the election of 1890. In the South the farmers' movement helped elect four governors, 44 representatives, and three senators. In the West, Kansas and South Dakota each elected a reform senator, and Nebraska and Kansas elected several reform representatives.

However, southern reformers were shocked to find that of all the "reform" Democrats they elected, only Tom Watson of Georgia continued to support agrarian reform once in office. Watson, a fiery rebel, left the Democratic party and formed his own "People's Party." A number of western reformers in Congress also backed Watson and began to put together a third-party national organization.

The Populist party, as the new party was generally called, met in Omaha, Nebraska, in 1892 to nominate a presidential ticket. This was no ordinary convention. From all over came farmers, cattle ranchers, miners, small-town newspaper editors—virtually anyone who was tired of the old parties and looking for change.

Many of the convention delegates appeared in broad-brimmed hats and dusty boots. Their leaders had nicknames like "Sockless Socrates" Simpson of Kansas, "Calamity" Weller of Iowa, and "Cyclone" Davis of Texas. But regardless of how rustic these people appeared to eastern reporters, their demands for action were clear.

The Populists finally agreed on two former Civil War generals as candidates, James B. Weaver of Iowa for President and James G. Field of Virginia for Vice-President. Throughout the campaign, the Populists

Kansas orator and author Mary Lease was among the most articulate spokespersons for the Populist cause. Populists represented a broad segment of American society, including farmers, small-town businesspeople, and others who felt squeezed by the power of large monopolies such as the railroads.

continued to support the platform formulated at Ocala.

Democrat Grover Cleveland won the election of 1892 and returned for a second term as President after being out of office four years. Yet the Populists did surprisingly well for a new party. Their national ticket received over a million popular votes and 22 electoral votes (from Kansas, Colorado, Idaho, Nevada, and North Dakota). As 1893 began, there were high hopes that the demand for reform would continue to grow.

For answers, see p. A 71.

Section Review

1. Identify the following: Grangers, National Farmers' Alliance, Ocala Platform, Populist party.

2. Define the following terms: deflation, graduated personal income tax.

3. List three problems faced by American farmers in the last half of the nineteenth century.

4. What actions did the Grangers take to aid farmers?

5. Name four reform goals outlined in the Ocala Platform.

6. How was the election of 1892 significant for the Populist party?

5 The Decline of Populism

The pressure for reform that surfaced in the 1892 elections grew even stronger when depression struck the nation the following year. The Populists looked forward to still greater success in the 1896 elections. Yet within five years of their surge in 1892, the Populist movement would exhaust itself.

The Depression of 1893

Within a few days of his inauguration in 1893, President Grover Cleveland found himself face to face with a financial collapse that sent the nation into the worst depression it had yet experienced. The collapse began when the Philadelphia and Reading Railroad went bankrupt. Panicked investors sold stock, and prices fell on the New York Stock Exchange. Worried bank officers demanded that loans be repaid, but companies were in no position to make good on their debts. One by one, other major railroads declared bankruptcy, including the Erie, the Union Pacific, and the Santa Fe.

The situation at the end of 1893 was grim. About 500 banks had failed and 1,500 businesses had gone bankrupt. Nearly 3 million workers were left unemployed by the business failures. Men and women who still had jobs had to accept drastic cuts in their wages.

President Cleveland strongly believed that the depression had been caused by allowing silver to circulate as part of the currency. Most economists today believe that government silver policies did little to either harm or benefit the economy, but Cleveland's belief and the actions he took provoked a political tempest.

Controversy Over Silver

The silver question had been the subject of heated debate for many years. Until 1873 the United States government had minted gold and silver coins and had printed paper money backed by gold and silver. In 1873 Congress passed the Coinage Act, which declared that henceforth gold alone would be minted and used to back paper money. The act effectively reduced the amount of money in circulation and thus contributed to the deflation of the period.

Farmers, as you have read, were hurt by deflation, and they demanded that silver be minted in order to increase the supply of money. Silver miners in the West also wanted to see the government buy silver for coins. This was especially true after discovery of new deposits in the 1870s drove down the price of silver.

In 1878 Congress responded to such demands by passing the Bland-Allison Act, which required the government to buy a set amount of silver each year to be minted into coins. Then in 1890, partly in reaction to pressure from the National Farmers' Alliance, Congress passed the Sherman Silver Purchase Act. The act increased the amount of silver that had to be purchased yearly and allowed the treasury to issue paper money backed by silver.

The Sherman Silver Purchase Act had a limited impact on the money supply, but Cleveland blamed its passage for the onset of depression in 1893. He believed that a currency based on both silver and gold, resulted in a decline in the value of gold. In his opinion, this decline in turn weakened the confidence of the business community, discouraged new investment, and created unemployment. Like many business people of the day, he maintained that a *gold standard,* or currency based solely on gold, was necessary for a healthy economic climate.

Consequently, President Cleveland wanted to do away with the Sherman Silver Purchase Act, which he once called a "dangerous and reckless experiment" in monetary reform. In 1893 Cleveland achieved his goal when Congress repealed the Sherman Act. Yet the depression continued.

Coxey's Army

As the depression deepened in 1894 with no relief in sight, more and more people blamed the President's policies. Among Cleveland's most vocal critics was an Ohio stone-quarry owner named Jacob Coxey. Over the years, Coxey had prospered, but now, like the Populists, he believed that something had to be done for the millions of unemployed. He proposed that the government begin a massive road-construction program to provide work relief. If the treasury issued $500 million in new money, Coxey argued, it would create inflation, stimulate the economy, and pay for the road construction.

Cleveland rejected all such schemes, as did Congress. Coxey angrily retorted that if Washington would not listen, he and his supporters would "send a petition to Washington with boots on." Over 500 followers

A hostile cartoonist in 1891 labeled the Populists "A Party of Patches." The cartoonist portrays the Populist party as a hastily stitched patchwork of dreamers and dangerous radicals. Several Populist leaders are shown floating along in the ramshackle balloon.

A PARTY OF PATCHES.
Grand Balloon Ascension—Cincinnati, May 20th, 1891.

marched from Massillon, Ohio, Coxey's home town, to Washington, D. C. Along the way, sympathetic crowds turned out to cheer the marchers, who became known as Coxey's Army.

When Coxey's Army arrived in Washington, it did not receive a pleasant welcome. The violence of labor strikes like the one at Carnegie's Homestead plant (see page 398) had led some government leaders to fear that revolution might be at hand. Although Coxey's intentions were peaceful, police arrested him along with other leaders and dispersed his followers.

The question of coining silver was to become a hotly contested issue at the Democratic presidential nominating convention of 1896. President Cleveland was committed to the gold standard, but western and southern Democrats demanded the unlimited coinage of silver. William Jennings Bryan of Nebraska warned against putting United States currency on a gold standard. "You shall . . . not crucify mankind upon a cross of gold," he declared. Cartoonists—both for and against Bryan—had a field day with the "cross of gold" image. This cartoon attacks Bryan for using a Biblical image to make his point.

THE SACRILEGIOUS CANDIDATE.

The Democrats Divide

Coxey's march demonstrated the depth of public discontent. President Cleveland also found growing opposition within his own party. Many southern and western Democrats disagreed with Cleveland's commitment to the gold standard. The President's low standing was reflected in the comment of Democratic Governor "Pitchfork" Ben Tillman of South Carolina: "I haven't got words to say what I think of that old bag of beef."

When the Democratic presidential nominating convention met in 1896, southern and western Democrats angrily outvoted Cleveland's eastern supporters. The party platform adopted many of the Populists' goals, including unlimited coinage of silver, a lower tariff, and an income tax.

In the midst of the debate on this issue, a dramatic orator from Nebraska, William Jennings Bryan, held the delegates spellbound. "We have petitioned and our petitions have been scorned; we have entreated, and our entreaties have been disregarded; we have begged, and they have mocked when our calamity came. We beg no longer; we entreat no more; we petition no more. We defy them!"

Referring to Cleveland's support of the gold standard, Bryan thundered, "You shall not press down upon the brow of labor this crown of thorns, you shall not crucify mankind upon a cross of gold!" The delegates roared their approval.

Bryan was nominated as the presidential candidate over the strong objections of Cleveland's supporters. Though only 36 years old, the Nebraskan was already well known throughout the South and West as the leading spokesman for the prosilver faction. He supported the Democratic party platform wholeheartedly.

The Populist party now faced a difficult choice. Many members had hoped to succeed as an independent third party, but the Democrats had stolen much of their thunder by nominating Bryan. Populist leaders wondered whether they too should support him. At their own convention, many Populists wanted to nominate a different candidate, but finally Tom Watson persuaded the delegates to place Bryan at the top of their ticket as the man most likely to have a chance against the Republicans. Thus Bryan was the candidate of two parties.

The Election of 1896

With the Democratic party divided, the Republicans sensed victory. They picked Senator William McKinley from Ohio as their presidential candidate. McKinley's first-ballot victory at the convention was the product of careful groundwork laid by Marcus "Mark" Hanna, a coal, iron, and shipping tycoon from Cleveland, Ohio.

The campaign that followed presented the voters with a dramatic contrast in style and policy. "Billy" Bryan moved at a hectic pace, traveling 18,000 miles (28,800 kilometers) to make over 600 speeches. He appeared before almost 5 million people. Always his themes reflected the Populist creed: regulate the railroads, curb the power of monopolies, and establish a currency backed by silver. The Bryan campaign gained the endorsements of reformers Henry George and Edward Bellamy, as well as labor leaders Eugene V. Debs of the Railway Union and Samuel Gompers of the AFL.

McKinley, for his part, remained in his home town of Canton, Ohio, throughout the campaign. Occasionally he read speeches from his front porch to admirers who came to town to hear him. Such speeches contained quiet assurances that the nation's economic system was sound and that the gold standard was best for the country.

Meanwhile, Mark Hanna worked hard behind the scenes to round up campaign contributions from the trusts, railroad owners, large banks, and industrialists. Hanna raised well over $3 million, ten times as much as Bryan's campaign had. With so much money at his disposal, Hanna sent Republican speakers across the country to stump for their candidate. He distributed some 250 million pieces of literature.

McKinley won the election by 600,000 popular votes. Bryan carried the South and most of the West, but McKinley took the populous Northeast. Bryan failed to capture the northern labor vote. Without support from the industrial sections of the country, the southern and western coalition had been unable to carry a presidential election.

The Populists' Fate

Bryan's defeat marked the end of the Populist movement. In part, the party declined because of a failure of morale. The agricultural reformers had done their best, carrying

Major Events	
1867	The Grange founded
1872	Crédit Mobilier scandal uncovered
1875	Southern Farmers' Alliance founded in Texas
1877	*Munn* v. *Illinois*
1878	Bland-Allison Act passed
1880	Northwestern Farmers' Alliance established
1881	President Garfield assassinated; Tuskegee Institute founded
1883	Civil Service Act passed
1886	*Wabash, St. Louis, & Pacific Railway Company* v. *Illinois*
1887	Interstate Commerce Act passed
1889	National Farmers' Alliance formed
1890	Sherman Antitrust Act passed; Sherman Silver Purchase Act passed
1892	Populist party formed
1893	Severe economic depression begins; Sherman Silver Purchase Act repealed
1894	Coxey's Army marches on Washington
1895	*United States* v. *E. C. Knight Co.*
1896	*Plessy* v. *Ferguson*

419

every state west of the Mississippi and in the South. Yet they had fallen short. Furthermore, the Democrats had lured many Populists back into the Democratic party.

Improved economic conditions also hurt the Populist movement. In the first three years of McKinley's term, prosperity slowly returned to the nation. A wheat crop failure abroad in 1897 stimulated demand for United States farm exports. Gold discoveries in Alaska helped expand the treasury's gold reserves. Ironically, the increase in the gold supply inflated the currency—which was exactly what the silver campaigners had been demanding. With conditions improving, the Populist drive lost its momentum.

Prosperity made McKinley's business principles appear sound. On the President's recommendation, Congress passed the Gold Standard Act of 1900 to put the nation back on the gold standard. The quiet acceptance of gold as the single basis of currency signaled the end of the long-standing controversy. Few people objected when Congress passed even higher tariff rates for industry in the Dingley Tariff Bill of 1897. In the next decade, other voices of reform would be raised, but by the time prosperity returned and the nineteenth century ended, the Populists' dramatic moment on the national scene had passed.

For answers, see p. A 71.

Section Review

1. Identify the following: Coinage Act, Bland-Allison Act, Sherman Silver Purchase Act, Coxey's Army, William Jennings Bryan, William McKinley, Mark Hanna.
2. Define the following terms: gold standard.
3. According to President Cleveland, what was the cause of the depression of 1893?
4. Name two groups that favored the coinage of silver.
5. Which two parties nominated William Jennings Bryan as their candidate in the election of 1896?
6. How did Mark Hanna help William McKinley's campaign for President?
7. What happened to the Populist movement after Bryan's defeat in 1896?

★ ★

IN PERSPECTIVE   The years after the Civil War were ones of political corruption in much of the nation, including Washington, D. C. The lure of great wealth tarnished the reputations of both Congress and the presidency. Scandals revealed during President Grant's administration, especially, weakened the presidency.

The abuses of power and wealth eventually led to attempts at reform. The Civil Service Act was passed to curb corruption in the national government by requiring applicants for certain government jobs to pass examinations before being hired. The Interstate Commerce Act tried to end abuses by the railroads, such as pooling and charging different rates for long and short hauls, and the Sherman Antitrust Act outlawed monopolies. The last two laws proved difficult to enforce, however. Both the railroads and the giant trusts found ways to evade the new regulations.

In the South the conservative Democrats consolidated their control of state governments. Although moderate at first, during the 1890s southern state governments began to pass laws to disenfranchise and socially segregate black Americans. In reaction thousands of blacks moved West to homestead. Others tried to improve their economic condition, as advocated by Booker T. Washington, and some believed like W.E.B. Du Bois that they should fight for their rights.

American farmers faced difficult economic problems during the late 1800s. They were burdened by debt and falling farm prices. They soon began to organize to improve their lives, first through the Grange and then through the National Farmers' Alliance. Eventually in 1892 farmers became part of a major third-party movement. The Populist party saw some success in the 1892 elections, and in 1896 many of their proposals were adopted by the Democrats. Although the movement was short-lived, many Populist political and economic goals were eventually accepted and became law.

For answers, see p. A 71.

Chapter Review

1. How did the concentration of wealth in the hands of industrialists contribute to political corruption during the late 1800s?

2. (a) What was the reputation of the Senate and the House of Representatives during the Gilded Age? (b) Why was Congress, with such a reputation, able to dominate the presidency? Give specific examples to support your answer.

3. (a) How were government jobs filled before the Civil Service Act of 1883? (b) What developments led many Americans to demand a change in this system? (c) How were some government jobs to be filled, according to the Civil Service Act?

4. (a) How did state governments try to regulate railroads in the 1870s? (b) What practices were they trying to control? (c) How did the Supreme Court rule on the states' power to regulate railroads in 1875? in 1886? (d) What were the major provisions of the Interstate Commerce Act?

5. (a) How were large corporations able to become monopolies? (b) What was the major provision of the Sherman Antitrust Act? (c) How were corporations able to sidestep the law? (d) How did the Supreme Court decision in *United States* v. *E. C. Knight Company* make the Sherman Act less effective?

6. (a) What actions did southern state governments take to disenfranchise black voters? (b) What were Jim Crow laws? (c) How did the Supreme Court decision in *Plessy* v. *Ferguson* strengthen Jim Crow laws?

7. (a) How did Booker T. Washington urge southern blacks to respond to segregation? Why did he favor this response? (b) What response did W.E.B. Du Bois recommend? Why did he favor such action?

8. (a) Why did farmers find it increasingly difficult to make a living in the late 1800s? (b) What organizations did they form to deal with their problems? (c) What methods did these organizations use to help farmers?

9. (a) What were the provisions of the Ocala Platform? (b) How would each plank improve conditions for farmers?

10. (a) Why did Tom Watson decide to form a "People's Party"? (b) How successful was the Populist party in the 1892 election?

11. (a) Why did farmers and miners favor the coinage of silver? (b) How did Congress react to pressure from the two groups? (c) Why did President Cleveland favor a gold standard?

12. (a) How did the Democratic party platform in 1896 reflect the goals of Populists? (b) What developments led to the decline of the Populists after 1896?

For answers, see p. A 72.

For Further Thought

1. (a) Why did Mark Twain label the decades after the Civil War the Gilded Age? (b) In what ways do you think it was a Gilded Age? Give specific examples to support your answer.

2. Why do you think the views of Booker T. Washington were more popular among white southerners than the views of W.E.B. Du Bois?

For answers, see p. A 73.

Developing Basic Skills

1. *Analyzing Political Cartoons* Political cartoons are valuable pieces of historical evidence. By analyzing them, you can learn more about the political issues of an historical period. Study the cartoon on page 407 and answer the following questions: (a) Which economic development is the cartoon illustrating? (b) What impact does the cartoonist think this development is having on the people of the United States? Which part of the cartoon reveals that information? (c) Do you think the cartoonist favors or opposes trusts? Why?

2. *Comparing* Make a chart with three columns. Label the first column Reform Actions. Label the second column Purpose and the third column Degree of Success. List the reform actions you learned about in this chapter in the first column. In the second column describe the problem the action was to solve. In the third column note how successful each of the actions was in the late 1800s. Then answer the following questions: (a) What problems were the reformers trying to solve? (b) How successful were they? (c) Why do you think this was the case?

See page 776 for suggested readings.

23

Toward an Urban Age

(1865–1900)

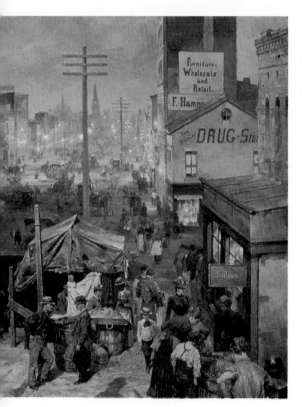

Washington St., Indianapolis, at Dusk, *by Theodore Groll.*

Chapter Outline

1 *Beginning of an Urban Age*

2 *Immigrants and Cities*

3 *An Urban Way of Life*

4 *A Changing Society: Problems and Prospects*

When Indianapolis became the capital of Indiana in 1825, its population was less than 1,000. With the completion of the National Road in 1830 and the construction of railroads during the 1850s, the population of the city grew, reaching over 18,000 by 1860.

Like many American cities, Indianapolis experienced its most dramatic growth during the last half of the nineteenth century. It served as a market for nearby farms and as a center of new industry. By 1900 nearly 170,000 people lived there.

Many American cities expanded rapidly during the late 1800s as the United States entered an urban age. Transportation, industry, and immigration were among the factors that contributed to urban growth. Developing cities were to provide jobs, entertainment, and excitement for millions of Americans. Yet they were also the source of new, often bewildering, social and political problems.

1 Beginning of an Urban Age

Although cities had played an important role in the development of the nation since colonial days, before the Civil War most Americans lived on farms or in villages. After the war, that pattern shifted so rapidly that bewildering new problems faced the nation.

The Rapid Growth of Cities

The explosive growth of cities was fueled by the expansion of industry in the late nineteenth century. Manufacturers built new plants in cities, where large numbers of workers could be found. Cities could provide transportation facilities needed to move raw materials and finished products. The additional jobs in turn drew increasing numbers of people to urban centers.

In 1880 less than 25 percent of all Americans were living in cities. Then between 1880 and 1900 the urban population doubled. New York City grew from less than 2 million residents in 1880 to nearly 3.5 million in 1900. The population of Chicago more than tripled, rising from 440,000 to 1.7 million. The tilt toward the cities was sharpest in the Northeast, as people left farms for city jobs. In the last 20 years of the nineteenth century, 60 percent of the rural townships of the Northeast lost population.

By 1900 nearly 40 percent of the 70 million people living in the United States resided in cities. Philadelphia had a population of more than a million. St. Louis, Boston, and Baltimore had populations exceeding 500,000. Smaller cities like San Francisco, Milwaukee, Cleveland, and Detroit were growing rapidly. The majority of Americans still lived in rural areas, but the trend was away from the country and toward cities. That trend would continue well into the twentieth century.

Urban growth was further spurred by the arrival of men and women from abroad. In the last half of the nineteenth century, immigrants poured into American cities. By 1890, 68 percent of Chicago's population were foreign born and another 10 percent were American-born children of immigrants. Indeed Chicago perhaps more than any other city symbolized the growth of an urban America.

Chicago: Symbol of the New Urban Age

Early in 1893, a crew of 7,000 workers led by architect Daniel Burnham labored around the clock through the rain, sleet, ice, and snow of a Chicago spring to meet a May 1 deadline. At times their workhorses floundered belly deep in mud. The hectic pace paid off, however, and on May 1, 1893, a fair marking the four-hundredth anniversary of Columbus's discovery of the New World was ready for the public.

Congress had awarded Chicago the honor of playing host to the Columbian Exposition, which was billed as a celebration of American progress and industry. The choice of Chicago was apt, for Chicago typified both the vitality and the problems of America's developing cities.

■ The total population of the United States grew rapidly in the late 1800s. As the graph indicates, the population of cities and towns grew faster in the 1880s and 1890s than did the population of rural areas.

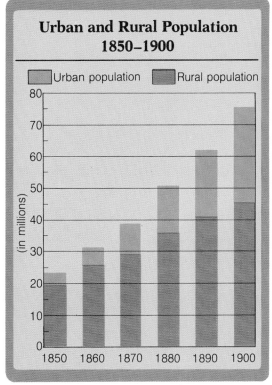

Urban and Rural Population 1850–1900

Urban population   Rural population

(in millions)

1850   1860   1870   1880   1890   1900

Source: *Historical Statistics of the United States*

For answers, see p. A 73.

Urban Growth: Interpreting Thematic Maps

As you learned in Chapter 5 (see page 89), maps are a valuable source of information for the study of American history. Many of the maps you have studied in this text have been general reference maps. They provide basic information such as the location of cities, rivers, mountains, or states. Other maps show the distribution of such things as population, rainfall, vegetation, or crop production. These special maps are called *thematic maps*. The legend is particularly important on a thematic map because it explains the meaning of the symbols used. To practice using thematic maps, study the maps below and on page 425. Then follow the steps outlined below.

1. **Decide what is shown on the maps.** Answer the following questions about the maps: (a) What is the topic of the two maps? (b) What do the different-sized circles represent? (c) What do the areas shaded orange represent?

2. **Read the information on the maps.** Answer the following questions based on these two maps: (a) How many cities appear on the 1860 map? (b) How many cities appear on the 1900 map? (c) Which cities had a population between 1 and 5 million in 1860? (d) Which cities had a population between 1 and 5 million in 1900? (e) Which of the cities that appear on both maps grew in population between 1860 and 1900? (f) Which areas of the country were industrialized in 1860? (g) To which areas had industry spread by 1900? (h) Which cities are located on important waterways?

3. **Draw conclusions about the historical period being studied.** Use what you learned in the text and the information on the maps to answer the following questions: (a) What relationship do the maps reveal between industry and urban growth? (b) What relationship can you see between the location of cities and important waterways? (c) In which areas of the country did cities develop between 1860 and 1900? (d) In which areas was there little urban growth? How might you explain this?

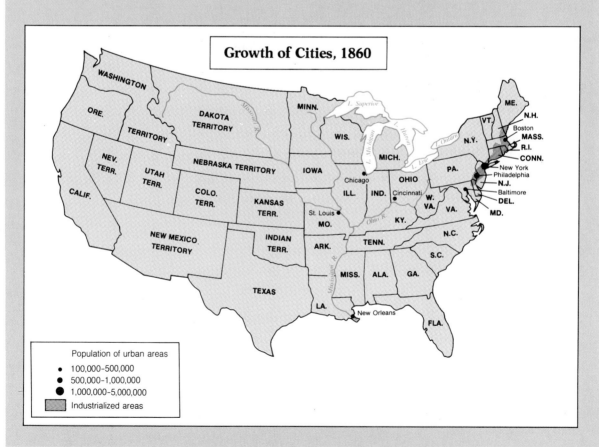

Growth of Cities, 1860

Population of urban areas
- • 100,000–500,000
- • 500,000–1,000,000
- ● 1,000,000–5,000,000
- ▨ Industrialized areas

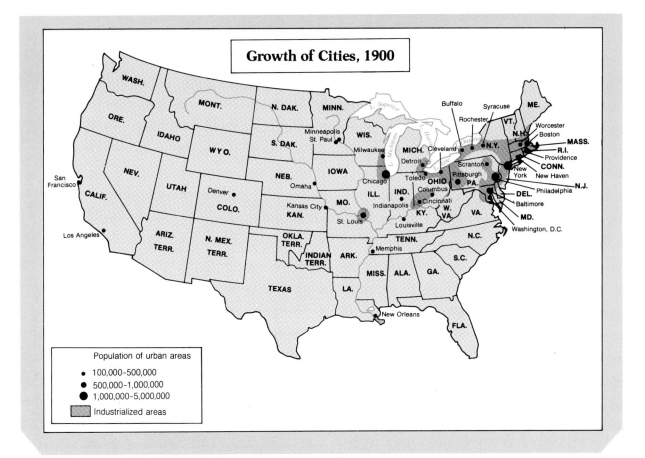

Growth of Cities, 1900

Population of urban areas
- 100,000–500,000
- 500,000–1,000,000
- 1,000,000–5,000,000

Industrialized areas

Chicago, located on the southern shore of Lake Michigan, had grown rapidly. A central geographic location had made the city a transportation hub. Railroads connected the city with the rest of the nation. Ships moved raw materials and finished products in and out of the port on Lake Michigan. The excellent transportation network and access to raw materials attracted industry. Each new industry in turn lured to the city manufacturers and people seeking jobs.

Pioneering industrialists and manufacturers in Chicago made fortunes in meatpacking, merchandising, and steel. More than 200 self-made millionaires lived in grand style in mansions lining the lake front.

Gradually manufacturing and industry pushed the city outward, and politicians began to annex nearby towns, extending the city boundaries. Communities that had been independent were absorbed into Chicago. When the city's transportation system reached these outlying areas, some wealthy residents and members of the small middle class moved out of the central city, leaving the downtown section to the poor and to commerce and industry.

Problems of a Growing City

Chicago's rapid growth created problems as well as fortunes. In contrast to the stately mansions on the lake front were the crowded tenements of the Chicago slums. There the poor citizens of the city lived in squalid conditions, often without even the most basic necessities, such as running water. Diseases like typhoid regularly raged through entire neighborhoods.

Tens of thousands of immigrants clustered in separate ethnic neighborhoods. Some sections became all Polish, some all Bohemian, Greek, Russian, or Chinese. Black Americans also moved to Chicago from the South and settled in neighborhoods of their own.

Rich and poor alike endured some of the problems created by the city's rapid growth. As late as 1890, only one third of Chicago's streets were paved with cobblestones. When rain fell or snow melted, the streets became quagmires of mud. The droppings of thousands of horses pulling wagons, trolleys, and carriages also fouled the city streets. Grease, sewage, and dead animals floated

425

Chicago, 1871

Area of city

Railroad lines

Brickton (Park Ridge)

• Elgin

• Evanston

LAKE MICHIGAN

Cicero

Chicago

• Aurora

South Chicago

0   20 Miles

0   30 Kilometers

Hammond

■ By 1871, the date of this map, Chicago was a boom town of 300,000 people. By 1900 it had become the major shipping and transfer point for the entire Midwest, and its population had surged to 1.7 million.

down the Chicago River. So many chemicals had to be dumped into the river to purify it that wealthy residents refused to drink from the city water supply.

Rapid urban growth also offered rich opportunity for corrupt politicians. Chicago, like most cities of the day, operated on graft and payoffs. (See page 437). A bribe bought a city contract. Chicagoans nicknamed the members of their city council the "gray wolves." In a popular vaudeville skit, a hostess looked at several city officials sleeping at her feet after an evening's partying. She asked her husband, "Will I wake them?" "Leave them be," he replied. "While they sleep the city's safe."

In 1893, when the Columbian Exposition was amazing 27 million visitors to Chicago, a concerted effort by Americans to deal with the problems of their cities seemed long overdue.

For answers, see p. A 74.

Section Review

1. Name two characteristics of cities that encouraged manufacturers to build plants in them.

2. In which part of the nation was urban growth the fastest?

3. What two means of transportation made Chicago a transportation hub?

4. List two problems Chicago faced as a growing city.

2 Immigrants and Cities

In 1886 France presented the United States with a statue to honor the American spirit of liberty. Joseph Pulitzer, an immigrant from Hungary, promptly launched a campaign in his newspaper to collect nickels and dimes from children and adults to build a base for the statue. Nearly 120,000 people contributed. For millions of immigrants the Statue of Liberty at the entrance to New York Harbor symbolized a welcome to a new life. Most newcomers began that life in America's cities.

The Pull of America

In the five decades after the Civil War a flood of immigrants reached the United States. From 1865 until the turn of the century, 13.5 million people arrived from abroad. Not until the 1920s, when Congress began setting immigration quotas, would the numbers dwindle.

Wars, famine, religious persecution, and overpopulation all prompted people to leave Europe and seek a better life in the United States. Some people left their homelands in search of political or religious freedom. Some left because, in spite of their skills or education, they were unable to find work. In many rural areas of Europe, small plots of land had been so often divided among children and grandchildren that the plots were too small to farm profitably. Younger sons and daughters had to look elsewhere if they wanted to farm their own land.

From the United States came letters that told of a better life. Friends and relatives who had already made the trip wrote home saying that work was available for all and that no one starved in America. One Polish immigrant wrote to relatives back in Europe, "We eat here every day what we get only for Easter in our country." But the passage to that new life was a difficult one.

Passage to the United States

Passage to the United States often cost a life savings. Hotel operators, railroad and steamship companies, and especially ticket agents sometimes cheated immigrants shamelessly. Most of the newcomers bought the cheapest steamship ticket for accommodations in steerage. That gave them space in the noisiest, least comfortable part of the ship, near the engines and the rudder. Packed in like cattle, steerage passengers had little to eat and endured filthy conditions. Consequently, outbreaks of disease were common.

The crowded steerage frequently contained a diverse group of people. Many were poor farmers. Some were schoolmasters unable to find work in Europe, skilled artisans looking for wider opportunities, or musicians and artists eager to see the world. Young men and women with a spirit of adventure were willing to risk traveling into the unknown. At journey's end, there was yet another ordeal to be overcome. A person could be shipped back if he or she failed to pass the medical inspection administered at the port of entry.

After 1890, Ellis Island in New York Harbor served as port of entry for most immigrants. The processing was a dehumanizing, humiliating experience for many. Long lines of people were tagged according to the language they spoke—one color for Greek, another for Italian, another for Armenian, Czech, and so on. Patiently, men, women, and children moved toward the dreaded moment before the immigration inspector.

With hundreds of immigrants to process daily, the overworked inspectors had just two minutes to ask 32 questions and to complete a medical inspection. A newcomer who was found to have a contagious disease would be detained and possibly shipped back home. Furthermore, a person whose last name was Bratkowski might emerge from the processing with the name Brown because the immigration official did not want to struggle with the foreign spelling.

The "New" Immigration

Before the 1880s most immigrants to the United States, some 85 percent, had arrived from Great Britain, Canada, Germany, and Scandinavia. Many of them had been Protestants, and a number spoke English. During the 1880s a dramatic shift occurred. In that decade an average of 500,000 immigrants arrived each year. The new immigrants came increasingly from southern and eastern Europe, from Italy, Poland, Russia, Hungary, and Bohemia.

Between 1865 and 1900, about 13.5 million immigrants arrived in the United States. Most traveled the cheapest way possible: on the steerage decks of jam-packed steamships. The deck of the S S Permland is shown here.

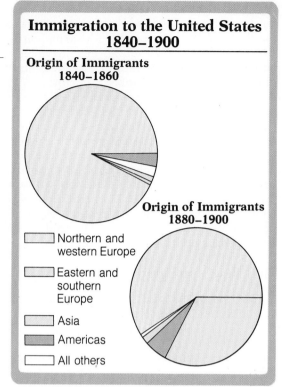

Immigration to the United States 1840–1900

Origin of Immigrants 1840–1860

Origin of Immigrants 1880–1900

- Northern and western Europe
- Eastern and southern Europe
- Asia
- Americas
- All others

Source: *Historical Statistics of the United States*

■ *Before 1880 nearly all immigrants to the United States came from the British Isles and northern Europe. These two circle graphs show the dramatic shift that began after 1880 as more immigrants began to arrive from eastern and southern Europe.*

People in this "new" immigration differed from Americans and from the "old" immigrants from northern and western Europe. The newcomers were often Catholic or Jewish. Their religion, language, and customs made them seem quite strange to many Americans.

The largest number came from Italy. Millions left the impoverished southern part of the country because of drought, economic disaster, and cholera. Three out of four were men whose families stayed behind. Some of these men planned to earn money in the United States and then return to Italy.

In the next largest group were Jews from eastern Europe, mainly Russia. More than 3 million arrived in the United States between 1880 and 1920. The Jewish arrivals fled Europe, not just because of economic hardships, but also to escape religious persecution. For 30 years Jews in Russia and Po-

land had been victims of *pogroms*, violent attacks against Jewish neighborhoods. A Russian Jew reflected on his past sufferings:

Sympathy for Russia? How ironical it sounds. Am I not despised? Am I not urged to leave? . . . Do I not rise daily with . . . fear lest the hungry mob attack me . . . It is impossible that a Jew should regret leaving Russia.

Jewish immigrants, unlike many Italian immigrants, did not plan to return home. Whole families came to America together.

More than a million Slavs from Russia, the Ukraine, Poland, Croatia, Serbia, Bulgaria, and Bohemia made up the third-largest group of immigrants. Other immigrants arrived from Greece, Portugal, Armenia, and Turkey, and from China and Japan.

Patterns of Settlement

Most of the new immigrants settled in American cities, especially the industrial centers and ports. By 1900 two thirds of the foreign-born people in the United States lived in cities. One third of the residents of Boston and one fourth of the residents of Philadelphia were immigrants. In New York City four out of five residents were either foreign-born or were the children of immigrants.

Italians often became subway workers in New York, stockyard workers in Chicago, miners in Illinois, Michigan, and Minnesota. Those who could afford to buy land often planted small gardens, orchards, or vineyards.

More than two thirds of the Jewish immigrants arrived as skilled workers. They entered New York's clothing industries by the thousands. By 1917, 70 percent of all the workers in the garment trades were Jewish. Other Jewish immigrants became bookbinders, teachers, and store owners.

Poles and other Slavs often moved to midwestern cities or to coal mining towns in Pennsylvania or the Midwest. Germans and Scandinavians frequently bought farms in Iowa, Nebraska, and the Dakotas. Chinese and Japanese immigrants settled on the west coast, usually in California. The influx of immigrants from eastern and southern Europe and from Asia in the late 1800s brought an outburst of nativism, or hatred of foreigners, which was similar in many ways to that of the 1840s. (See Chapter 15.)

Reaction Against Immigrants

Some native-born Americans feared and resented the new immigrants. Their languages, religions, and customs seemed especially strange to Americans who traced their heritage to northern and western Europe. The newcomers also competed for jobs. Desperate to find work, immigrants were often willing to accept lower wages and worse working conditions than American-born workers.

When economic conditions worsened, antiforeign feelings became stronger. Groups such as the American Protective Association urged Congress to bar immigration from certain countries. The American Protective Association, founded in 1887, attracted a million members and preached against Roman Catholic immigrants.

Immigrants faced attacks by some American newspapers. One editorial, for example, charged that the country was being

Emma Lazarus and *The New Colossus*

The campaign to raise money to build a pedestal for the Statue of Liberty, a gift from the French, seemed to reach a snag in 1883. The statue was almost completed and ready to be shipped from France, but the pedestal was not nearly finished. The Pedestal Fund Committee then organized a temporary art exhibition to raise funds. Prominent New Yorkers lent paintings, and a number of artists and writers contributed their drawings and letters to be auctioned. After some urging, Emma Lazarus produced a poem for the occasion.

Emma Lazarus, the daughter of a prominent New York Jewish family, was a crusader for ethnic tolerance. She had worked tirelessly to help the refugees who were streaming into New York City in ever-increasing numbers. Although she did not usually write patriotic works, to her, the Statue of Liberty, facing toward the Old World, held out a message of hope to all those uprooted from the land of their birth. Emma Lazarus called her poem "The New Colossus." (The brazen giant referred to in the first line is the Colossus of Rhodes, which once stood in the harbor of Rhodes and was known as one of the seven wonders of the ancient world.)

Not like the brazen giant of Greek fame,
With conquering limbs astride from land to land;
Here at our sea-washed, sunset gates shall stand
A mighty woman with a torch, whose flame
Is the imprisoned lightning, and her name
Mother of Exiles. From her beacon-hand
Glows world-wide welcome; her mild eyes command
The air-bridged harbor that twin cities frame.
"Keep, ancient lands, your storied pomp!" cries she

With silent lips. "Give me your tired, your poor,
Your huddled masses yearning to breathe free,
The wretched refuse of your teeming shore.
Send these, the homeless, tempest-tost to me,
I lift my lamp beside the golden door!"

The public showed little interest in the New Colossus after the unveiling in 1886. By that time, some Americans were increasingly alarmed by the thousands of immigrants flooding through the "golden door." Moreover the austere statue itself, designed to portray a different theme, did not itself suggest the idea of welcome. The statue had been intended as a symbol of political stability. The immigrants themselves, arriving year after year, gave the statue the meaning Lazarus attached to it. For the immigrants the statue became a symbol of a new land waiting for them, a land full of promise for a new beginning.

subjected to "an invasion of venomous reptiles . . . long-haired, wild-eyed, bad-smelling, atheistic, reckless foreign wretches, who never did a day's work in their lives."

New immigrants also encountered discrimination. Jewish immigrants, for example, were denied entrance to the nation's better universities, and it was difficult for Jews to get office jobs in New York City. In California, Chinese immigrants were subject to physical attacks. Gangs of ruffians routinely terrorized Chinese residents. In the summer of 1877 gangs burned 25 Chinese laundries in San Francisco. Congress yielded to the anti-Chinese feelings in 1882, passing an exclusion act that stopped immigration from China.

Contributions to American Society

Although much attacked, the new immigrants made valuable contributions to American life. They helped build and staff the booming new industries. They laid track, built roads, stitched clothing, made shoes, packed meat. Each group brought to America the traditions of homelands much older than the United States. They added a sparkling diversity to American life.

Immigrants brought to the cities their foods, their songs, their theater, and their literature. Foreign-language newspapers were published in many cities. The immigrants formed choral groups, literary societies, sewing clubs, theater groups, and sports clubs.

When the first attempts were made to start symphony orchestras and opera companies in the growing cities, most of the musicians and virtually all the conductors were foreign born. Italian, German, and Jewish immigrants filled the audiences to hear music they remembered from Europe. Immigrants helped shape the look and feel of nearly every city and made a lasting mark on the evolving urban culture.

For answers, see p. A 74.
Section Review

1. Define the following term: pogrom.
2. List three reasons many Europeans decided to immigrate to the United States in the years after the Civil War.
3. (a) Where did the largest group of new immigrants come from? (b) Who made up the second-largest group?
4. Where did most immigrants settle?
5. (a) How did bad economic conditions contribute to antiforeign feelings among some Americans? (b) What other factors contributed to those feelings?
6. What did the new immigrants contribute to the cultural life of cities?

3 An Urban Way of Life

"We cannot all live in cities," newspaper editor Horace Greeley commented, "yet nearly all seem determined to do so." Young people, he said, were looking for " 'hot and cold water,' baker's bread, the theatre, and the streetcars."

As Greeley noted, the city's lure was not just jobs. It included comforts like piped-in hot water and entertainment like vaudeville. There was always something new to marvel at and talk about: a new steel bridge, a skyscraper, or the latest crime reported in detail in the newspapers. New kinds of stores opened, new sports were played, and other activities unfolded in cities before spreading into rural areas.

Urban Transportation

The urban centers of the east coast had developed as "walking cities." Everything of importance was within walking distance of everything else. Only the rich rode to work in carriages. Everyone else walked. The horse trolley, the electric trolley, and finally the electric railway changed that way of life. With the new modes of transportation, cities began to expand.

The electric trolley, with its fixed overhead wire, could go twice as fast and carry three times as many passengers as the horse-drawn trolley. By 1895, 800 trolley lines were operating in the United States. The place-

Advent of the Streetcar

During the early part of the nineteenth century, movement in cities was largely restricted to the distance one could go on foot. Only those who could afford private carriages were able to travel much beyond the city's boundaries. Poorer citizens lived in crowded tenements within walking distance of their work. Then, about the time of the Civil War, omnibuses, large vehicles that anyone could board for a fee, came into use. The omnibuses, which had originated in Europe, were drawn by horses along rails set upon the cobblestone city streets. Americans, coining a new word, came to call them "streetcars."

Although an improvement, the horse-drawn streetcars were slow, and their range was limited to the power of the horse. Not until the invention of the electric motor by Thomas Edison and others did the streetcar really become an effective means of transportation.

One of the most important pioneers of the electric streetcar was Stephen Dudley Field, who had collaborated with Edison to provide an electric railway at the Chicago Railway Exposition in 1883. Field's most serious problem was how to transmit electricity from a central power station in a crowded city to a moving streetcar without endangering the lives of people in the streets. The problem was solved when a way was found to transmit power along a wire from an overhead trolley. Americans, again coining a new phrase, called the electric streetcars "trolleys."

The first extensive trolley system in the United States was built by Frank Julian Sprague in Richmond, Virginia, in 1888. It was an extraordinary feat of organization. Sprague had worked with Thomas Edison and had developed several electrical devices of his own. Leaving Edison, Sprague set up his own company and in 1887 contracted to establish an electric streetcar system in Richmond in only 90 days. Sprague had to build 80 motors, equip 40 cars, lay 12 miles (19 kilometers) of track, and install overhead trolley wires along the whole route—as well as build and equip an adequate central power plant. Incredibly, Sprague fulfilled his contract! Once the Richmond system was operating, he soon had contracts for a hundred other streetcar systems.

As new electric trolleys began to extend from cities in all directions, real estate developers went into action. They began promoting "streetcar suburbs" as part of the American way of life. The developers contrasted the crowded, tenement-filled cities of Europe with the promise of the new American suburbs. In the United States, they said, city workers could own their own houses. And they were right. The American dream of being a homeowner, publicized by the promoter, had been made possible by the electric streetcar.

ment of lines for trolleys and electrified railways affected the direction of a city's growth. Shops, housing, and businesses followed the transit lines out from the center of the city.

The new means of transportation did more then take workers to and from the job. People could now easily go for a picnic, to a library, or to the new department stores. With the electric trolley, urban working people gained greater mobility.

Department Stores

A new kind of store had emerged in American cities, the all-purpose department store where a shopper could browse and buy a wide variety of goods. Instead of keeping the best merchandise out of sight, to be brought out only for wealthy customers, these stores invited everyone to look, touch, and buy.

R. H. Macy in New York, John Wanamaker in Philadelphia, Jordan Marsh in Boston, and Marshall Field in Chicago pioneered such stores. They were widely copied elsewhere. The principle was to sell a larger volume of goods at slightly lower prices than smaller shops offered. Department stores also offered credit, free delivery, and a marked price. Shops of an earlier era often did not display prices. Instead customer and salesperson had dickered over the amount to be charged.

F. W. Woolworth took the single-price idea a step further. All goods in his store were marked with a fixed price, usually under a dime. His goods were so inexpensive that people were tempted to buy things they did not need. In Woolworth's new "five and tens" employees were kept busy stocking shelves with goods, rather than trying to sell customers a particular item.

Mass-Circulation Newspapers

Advertising from department stores helped pay for the mass-circulation newspapers that developed in the late nineteenth century. Such advertising brought in enough money to allow publishers to sell their papers cheaply. As circulations grew, advertisers were willing to pay well to reach a million or more readers with a single advertisement.

The mass-circulation newspapers attracted readers with news of crime, sports, and gossip. No paper was more flamboyant than Joseph Pulitzer's New York *World*. Pulitzer bought the newspaper in 1883 and promptly changed the tone and lowered the price. He called it a "people's paper" and charged two cents a copy. Pulitzer was master of devising stunts to attract more readers. Once he sent a reporter, Nellie Bly, on a race around the world and had readers guessing the exact number of days, hours, and minutes her journey would take.

Changing the Face of Cities

As more people and businesses moved to the cities the price of land rose sharply. Innovative architects built upward, gaining more usable space from small parcels of land. One of the first to do so was Louis Sullivan, a Chicago genius who began using steel as the skeleton for the tall buildings known as skyscrapers. (See Chapter 21.) In 1889 Sullivan designed the first all-steel skeleton building, the Auditorium Building in Chicago. A year later, the 26-story World Building was completed in New York. Other Sullivan buildings soon went up in St. Louis and Buffalo. The "race to the skies" in downtowns across the nation was on in earnest.

Retailers, too, sought a new kind of building in which to display their wares. The Cast Iron Palace in New York featured a huge first floor ideal for browsing. Patrons rode to upper floors on the newly invented elevator. Through plate-glass windows shoppers indulged in a new pastime, window-shopping.

Daniel Burnham was among the first to urge cities to plan their future growth. He spearheaded the development of a long-range plan for Chicago, setting aside park land on the lakefront. Other cities hurried to build parks before all downtown land was paved over. Frederick Law Olmstead designed Central Park in Manhattan and Prospect Park in Brooklyn. Olmstead's parks were laid out to give visitors a sense of being in the country. In this period, communities began to set aside land for botanical gardens, and several started zoos.

Music, Theater, and Art

With so many people, the cities could support leisure activities unavailable in most rural areas. Between 1862 and 1900, New York, Chicago, Pittsburgh, Cincinnati, and Philadelphia established symphony orchestras. In 1883 the Metropolitan Opera House opened in New York.

It was the heyday of vaudeville, with stand-up comedians, singers, dancers, and jugglers. Tickets to plays cost between 25 cents and $1.50, and people crowded the box offices. Plays ranged from fine Shakespearean works to popular but forgettable melodramas. Leading performers from Great Britain toured American cities to wild acclaim from audiences.

An increasingly literate public flocked to new public libraries. Over a period of years, Andrew Carnegie donated $60 million to establish libraries across the country. By 1900 there were about 9,000 public libraries in the United States. Many were in the small towns that still dominated much of the country. Several cities started museums of fine arts beginning in the 1870s. The new museums collected paintings and sculpture from all over the world.

Many of the best American artists, like James McNeill Whistler, preferred to live in Europe. At home, however, major talents were producing important works of art. In Maine, Winslow Homer painted scenes of the coastline, capturing the flickering of sunlight on water. Thomas Eakins, who taught at the Pennsylvania Academy of Art, painted realistic, often harsh, portraits of people and landscapes. His works, largely unsold in his lifetime, were vivid renderings of the new industrial age.

Eakins and some of the artists who followed him were called the American Realists because they portrayed the harsh life around them. This group and the American impressionist painters found few buyers in nineteenth-century America. In the early years of the twentieth century, however, their work began to draw international admiration.

Sports

The big-city newspapers, with their crisply written sports news, brought spectator sports such as baseball, football, and basketball into the mainstream of American life.

The exact origin of baseball is unknown, although popular myth credits Abner Doubleday with invention of the sport in Cooperstown, New York, in 1839. During the Civil War the game spread when Union soldiers from New York taught soldiers from other parts of the country how to play. At that time the pitcher threw the ball underhand, the catcher caught it on the first bounce, and none of the players wore gloves.

The first professional baseball team was the Cincinnati Red Stockings. In 1876 eight teams organized the National League of Professional Baseball Clubs. A rival American League was started some years later, and in 1903 the first World Series was held.

Basketball was invented in Springfield, Massachusetts, by Dr. James Naismith, who was looking for an indoor winter sport for young boys in his Young Men's Christian Association (YMCA). The first games in the United States were played in 1891 or 1892. Basketball became a popular sport and soon spread to other nations.

Games of football using various rules from British soccer and rugby had been played in North America since colonial days. College students began playing the game before the Civil War, and its popularity increased once the war was over. By the 1890s football games between Harvard, Yale, and Princeton were drawing huge crowds. In 1895 seven colleges in the Midwest began to organize what eventually became the Big Ten conference.

The wide variety of entertainment available in urban areas made them exciting for thousands of new residents. All the glitter, however, could not hide the problems that accompanied the rapid growth of the cities.

Boxing matches as well as football, baseball, and basketball games drew large crowds in the late nineteenth century. Thomas Eakins, who painted this scene, was a leader of the group of painters known as the American Realists.

For answers, see p. A 74.

Section Review

1. Identify the following: F. W. Woolworth, Joseph Pulitzer, Louis Sullivan, Winslow Homer, Thomas Eakins, American Realists, Abner Doubleday, James Naismith.

2. How did the building of electric trolley and electrified railway lines affect a city's growth?

3. List two ways department stores differed from the shops of earlier eras.

4. How did newspapers like the New York *World* try to attract more readers?

5. List three leisure activities that became popular in cities in the late nineteenth century.

433

4 A Changing Society: Problems and Prospects

Although there was much that was entertaining and exciting in the cities, there were also crushing problems. Nearly every city needed more sewers, better water systems, more roads, and more trolley lines. Disease and crime were widespread, and the cities lacked facilities to deal effectively with either. The cities also had to provide schools to educate a diverse group of children and deal with a dozen other urgent problems.

Exposing Urban Problems

Observers of life in American cities documented a wide range of urban problems, including street gangs, illiteracy, fire hazards, and unsanitary conditions giving rise to contagious diseases. Increasingly, reformers gathered facts and figures to bring to public attention. They believed that exposing terrible conditions was the first step in eliminating them.

Grim statistics were indeed revealed. For example, in one section of Chicago, in one year alone, 60 percent of all babies died before reaching 12 months of age. One New York social worker counted 1,231 people living in just 120 rooms in that city. Another was unable to locate a single bathtub in over 3 city blocks of tenements.

In 1890 *How the Other Half Lives*, written by a young New York reporter, Jacob Riis, was published. In the book Riis described in detail the wretched lives of people living in the city slums, including the horrid stench, everpresent filth, and blocked fire escapes. Reformers like Riis helped create a public demand for decent living conditions for all.

Jane Addams and the Settlement House Movement

In several cities, hardheaded idealists were already at work. They moved into slum neighborhoods and established settlement houses, community centers that offered a wide range of services to slum residents. The best known of the settlement houses was Hull House in Chicago, founded in 1889 by Jane Addams and a group of other young well-educated women.

On a trip to England, Addams had visited the founders of Toynbee House, a community center in the London slums. Impressed with the British achievements,

Reformers who visited crowded city slums were appalled at the conditions they found. To arouse the public to action, they published reports on disease, crowding, and other problems. Photos such as this one by Jacob Riis inspired public demand for stronger health laws and other reforms.

Addams spearheaded the purchase of a decaying mansion in one of the worst neighborhoods in Chicago and began Hull House.

Hull House provided a nursery and kindergarten for the children of working mothers. Adult education classes in English, nutrition, and health were offered. In time a gymnasium was added for young people. There was also a theater group.

The women of Hull House documented the urgent problems of the neighborhood. Then, armed with facts, the reformers worked to get new laws passed. Alice Hamilton, a physician working from Hull House, treated the neighborhood's sick. She soon realized that laws were needed to control the spread of disease, and she became an effective crusader for health legislation. Florence Kelley researched the harmful impact of industrial jobs on young children and became a national spokeswoman for effective child-labor laws. She also served briefly as chief factory inspector for Illinois.

By 1895 there were at least 50 settlement houses in American cities. The first settlement house operated by the Catholic church opened in 1898 in an Italian neighborhood of New York. Two years later Brownson House opened in a Mexican section of Los Angeles.

Settlement houses became testing grounds for ideas about how to improve urban living. The houses attracted a dedicated group of professional people. College professors and researchers came to visit and discuss ideas with social workers, teachers, and nurses. From the friendships and alliances forged there came the first effective group of urban reformers in the United States.

Despite their many successes, these reformers realized that private efforts were not enough. "Private beneficence," said Jane Addams, "is totally inadequate to deal with the vast numbers of the city's disinherited." Government action, the reformers believed, was necessary to correct harmful conditions.

Women: New Opportunities and the Struggle for Rights

Influenced by the settlement house movement, many college-educated women chose professions, such as teaching or social work, that enabled them to serve the poor. Opportunities in other professions, however, remained limited. For example, Iowa in 1869 was the first state to allow women to practice

The wistful eyes of this child underscore the task facing urban reformers. The dimly lighted slum in which he lived was overcrowded and probably lacked running water. Typically, the boy and his brothers and sisters could expect to begin working in a "sweatshop" in another year or two.

law, but it was not until 1920 that women could practice law in all states. Despite restrictions and discouragement, there were 1,000 women lawyers and 7,000 women physicians by the turn of the century.

Other opportunities also opened for women after the Civil War. Large numbers of clerical jobs were created by the invention of the typewriter, telegraph, and telephone. Women increasingly took such jobs, replacing men as office workers. The rise of department stores also created new jobs. By 1900 about 500,000 women worked in clerical and sales jobs.

By the turn of the century women had gained a firm position in the working world. The number of women who held jobs outside the home rose dramatically, from 4 million in 1890 to 8 million in 1910. Paralleling these developments were strides toward greater legal equality for women.

Increasingly in the late 1800s state legislatures passed laws giving married women control over their own property. Before 1900,

435

Born into a wealthy Illinois family, Jane Addams turned her enormous energies and talents to improving conditions in the Chicago slums. Hull House, which she helped found, became a model for other settlement houses. It offered education, medical care, English classes, sports, and other practical help for residents of the neighborhood in which it was located.

four western states—Wyoming, Colorado, Utah, and Idaho—had given women the right to vote in state elections. For most American women, however, the vote remained only a dream.

Turning that dream into reality continued to be a difficult struggle. Little headway had been made since the Seneca Falls Convention in 1848. (See page 293.) During the early twentieth century, women like Alice Paul and Carrie Chapman Catt would continue the struggle for women's suffrage, as you will read in Chapter 26.

The Growth of Public Education

For many Americans before 1870 education meant a one-room school and a *McGuffey's Reader*. The average adult in 1870 had at-

tended school for four years, and about one in five could not read or write. At the time there were only 160 public high schools in the entire nation.

In the period after the Civil War schools were built at a rapid rate. Dozens of new colleges and universities opened. The new graduates helped staff thousands of new classrooms. By 1900 the concept of free public schools for all citizens was widely accepted, and there were 6,000 public high schools in the United States.

In the cities, however, traditional methods of teaching, such as drills and memorizing, did not work for many children. A child who spoke no English could make little sense of what was happening in the classroom. A frequent visitor to Hull House, Professor John Dewey of the University of Chicago thought he had a solution.

Dewey urged schools to move away from the rote-learning routines. He and his wife, Harriet, tested their ideas at an experimental school at the university. Students in the school could work in a kitchen, a carpentry shop, or a sewing room, as well as in classrooms. Under Dewey's system, children actively participated in education.

Dewey's ideas were part of a broad movement to tailor education to fit the needs of the children being taught. The movement, often called progressive education, was part of a larger reform movement called progressivism. (You will read about progressivism in Chapters 25 and 26.)

Progressive teachers had three main goals. First, they believed that school programs should be widened to include teaching about health, jobs, family, and community life. Second, they wanted to apply new discoveries in science and psychology to classroom teaching. Third, they argued that teaching techniques should suit the kinds of children in the classroom. The reformers hoped to adapt and improve the education of children living in a more urban and industrial society than their parents had grown up in.

Other Humanitarian Efforts

As you read in Chapter 21, during the nineteenth century, many Americans argued that government had no right to interfere in their lives. This belief in laissez-faire extended to the area of social reform as well as economics. Religious leaders had usually shared this view. But late in the century the depth of social problems in the growing cities convinced some Christians that churches had to become actively committed to social reform.

These activist clergy developed what was called the Social Gospel. They argued that before churches could save souls, they had to improve the daily lives of the wretchedly poor. The Social Gospel was most prominent among Protestants.

Catholics also became more active in social reform. In 1889 an Italian nun, Frances Xavier Cabrini, arrived in the United States with a small group of nuns to work among Italian immigrants. Before her death in 1917, Mother Cabrini, as she was known, founded 70 hospitals throughout North and South America.

During the late 1800s a number of organizations were founded to deal with social problems in a systematic way. These included the Salvation Army and the Red Cross. William Booth, a Methodist minister, established the Salvation Army in London in 1878. Its purpose was to help house and feed the poor. An American branch of the Salvation Army was established a year later. Living in the poorest city slums, members of the Salvation Army established soup kitchens for the poor and homeless.

The Red Cross had been founded in Europe in 1859 originally to aid soldiers wounded in war. Clara Barton, who had served as a nurse during the Civil War, helped establish the National Society of the Red Cross in the United States in 1881. It provided needed social services in the growing urban areas.

Governing the Cities

In the late nineteenth century growing cities continued to be governed as they had been for over a century. Most had to have permission from state legislatures before passing important municipal laws. City governments, like state and national governments, suffered from the political corruption of the era. Andrew White, president of Cornell University, wrote, "With few exceptions, the city governments are the worst in Christendom—the most expensive, the most inefficient, and the most corrupt."

The governments White was describing were often run by a group of men known as political bosses. The bosses controlled what was called the "machine" or the "club." The machine offered city jobs and contracts to those who had the right connections. A well-placed bribe could win a company a contract to pave the streets, build schools, or operate trolley lines. "Boodle," payoffs in return for contracts or official favors, was a way of life in many cities.

Yet the machines did more than take bribes and offer favors. The politicians often

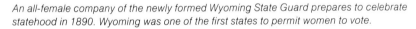

An all-female company of the newly formed Wyoming State Guard prepares to celebrate statehood in 1890. Wyoming was one of the first states to permit women to vote.

Major Events	
1883	Pulitzer buys New York *World;* Metropolitan Opera House opens in New York City
1889	Jane Addams founds Hull House; Hazen Pingree elected as reform mayor of Detroit
1890	Jacob Riis's *How the Other Half Lives* published
1893	Columbian Exposition opens in Chicago

provided important services for poor city residents. An unemployed slum dweller could turn to the boss or one of his "ward heelers" for help in finding a job or for a loan to pay the rent. The machine sometimes offered English lessons or legal advice to immigrants and helped them apply for citizenship. Food baskets were often given away on holidays. In return for such assistance, the boss was assured of the votes of most poor and immigrant city dwellers.

Perhaps the most notorious political boss of the era was William Marcy Tweed of New York City. Boss Tweed held no political office, but he controlled the Democratic political machine, popularly known as Tammany Hall. In three years, from 1868 to 1871, a group of Boss Tweed's associates, known as the Tweed Ring, robbed the city of over $20 million, perhaps as much as $200 million. Such pilfering provided more than enough money to keep the machine running "smoothly."

As cities grew larger during the last years of the century, many public-minded citizens came to realize that a better system of urban government was needed.

The Good-Government Movement

In city after city reformers like Jane Addams teamed up with honest business people in an attempt to make urban government more efficient and more honest. The reformers often began by tackling specific abuses such as undependable garbage collection. Each small success increased the reformers' authority and encouraged stronger drives for

better city government. Extension of water and sewer lines, improved building codes, better sanitation facilities, and more fire and police protection were all demanded. Essential to the reformers' goals was the destruction of the "invisible government" of the political machines.

Reformers scored a major victory when Detroit elected Hazen Pingree as mayor in 1889. Mayor Pingree forced the transit authority to lower streetcar fares. Under his leadership the city built more public parks and schools. When an economic depression struck, he started a relief program for the unemployed. Samuel M. "Golden Rule" Jones, Toledo's reform mayor, brought in professional city planners to help direct city operations. Cleveland elected Tom Johnson, called the "best mayor of the best-governed city in the United States."

Many of the reformers believed that cities should be run by professionals using business methods. They brought a new, well-educated group into city government, but the new officials sometimes overlooked the poor, whom the bosses had routinely "taken care of." Where the reformers succeeded, the middle and upper classes generally took control of the cities. Nevertheless, imperfect as it was, the reform movement at city level signaled the dawn of a major era of reform. The urban reformers led the way for the national progressive movement, which helped restore idealism to public life.

For answers, see p. A 74.
Section Review

1. Identify the following: Jacob Riis, Jane Addams, Hull House, John Dewey, Social Gospel, Frances Xavier Cabrini, William Booth, William Marcy Tweed.

2. Give four examples of urban problems that reformers like Jacob Riis helped bring to public attention.

3. List three services that were offered by Hull House.

4. (a) What types of job opportunities opened for women in the late nineteenth century? (b) In which states had women won the right to vote in state elections?

5. Name the three main goals of progressive education.

6. (a) What did political machines offer the urban poor? (b) What characteristics of the machines led reformers to demand a better system of urban government?

IN PERSPECTIVE   By 1900 the United States was becoming a nation of cities. Although most Americans continued to live in small towns or rural areas, cities grew dramatically between 1865 and 1900. They were the centers of the industrial development of the last half of the nineteenth century. Immigrants from Europe and Asia poured into the United States in the 1880s and 1890s. They were driven by difficult conditions in their homelands and attracted by the promise of a better life in America.

A new way of life was developing in the cities, characterized by electric trolleys, department stores, and skyscrapers. City dwellers could choose a wide variety of entertainment, from vaudeville to museums and baseball games. Yet despite the attractions, the growing cities suffered great problems.

Reformers like Jane Addams worked to improve such conditions. Settlement houses throughout the nation offered valuable services to urban dwellers. Other reformers sought to improve education and to clean up corrupt city governments. Although many problems remained, urban reformers introduced a new strain of idealism into American life that would lead to further reforms, as you will read in Chapter 25.

For answers, see p. A 75.

Chapter Review

1. What developments in the last half of the nineteenth century helped spark the growth of cities in the United States?

2. (a) What characteristics of the city attracted industry to Chicago? (b) What problems did Chicago face as a rapidly growing city?

3. (a) What attracted immigrants to the United States in the late 1800s? (b) How was their journey difficult?

4. (a) How did the "new" immigrants of the 1880s and 1890s differ from earlier immigrants to the United States? (b) How did these differences contribute to antiforeign feeling among some Americans?

5. Explain how each of the following affected life in the cities: (a) electric trolleys; (b) department stores; (c) mass-circulation newspapers.

6. (a) What types of problems arose in the new urban areas? (b) How did settlement houses attempt to solve these problems?

7. (a) How did the growth of industry and cities help create new job opportunities for women? (b) How did women's legal rights increase during this period?

8. (a) What role did political machines play in the government of many cities? (b) Why did reformers want to change city governments?

For answers, see p. A 75.

For Further Thought

1. (a) Why do you think many young people were attracted to city life in the late 1800s? (b) Would they probably be attracted by the same things today?

2. (a) How did humanitarian groups like the Salvation Army and the Red Cross try to improve the lives of city residents? (b) How do the activities of such groups reflect the American tradition of voluntary action to improve society?

For answers, see p. A 75.

Developing Basic Skills

1. *Relating Past to Present*   Make a list of the problems you read about in this chapter that faced the cities in the late 1800s. Using sources in your school or public library, decide whether each problem still exists in many cities today. Why do you think some have been solved and others not?

2. *Researching*   Visit the library to learn about the history of a city near where you live. Then answer the following questions: (a) Did the city grow rapidly during the late 1800s? Why or why not? (b) Did many "new" immigrants settle in the city? (c) If so, where did they come from?

See page 777 for suggested readings.

24

Becoming a World Power

(1865–1900)

Battle at Manila Bay, *by F. Fetherston.*

During the first half of the nineteenth century, the area of the United States doubled, stretching from the Atlantic Ocean to the Pacific. Although the nation bought Alaska from Russia in 1867, the decades after the Civil War were generally years of isolation from world affairs. Domestic concerns captured the energy and attention of most Americans.

Gradually, toward the end of the century, concern about international developments increased. The economic growth of the period fueled interest in new markets, and many Americans began to dream of territorial expansion. Such dreams, however, led to conflict with other nations and eventually to war with Spain.

When the United States acquired territory as a result of that war, the nation encountered the responsibilities of an overseas empire. Its response to those responsibilities was to have a major impact on future relations with nations in Latin America and Asia. Whether Americans favored an empire or not, most were aware that by 1900 the United States was becoming a world power.

1 The Dream of Expansion

In the years immediately following the Civil War, the attention of most Americans was focused on economic growth, settlement of the West, and the new entertainments of the Gilded Age. Most of the population had little interest in events beyond their shores. The New York *Sun* even suggested that the Department of State, which was responsible for foreign relations, had "outgrown its usefulness" and should be abolished.

With little concern about foreign relations, most Americans did not feel their country needed a large navy or army. The United States Navy had dwindled to a handful of rotting sailing ships following the Civil War. At the same time the European powers were building new steam-powered battleships. The powerful army of the Civil War was gradually reduced to only 25,000 soldiers. There were signs, though, that the United States was about to become a leading actor on the world stage.

Early Signs

William H. Seward, secretary of state under Presidents Lincoln and Johnson, believed that the United States should become the center of a vast *empire*, a system of territories governed by one nation. If the United States was to attain this goal, Seward decided, it had to prevent other nations from gaining influence in North America.

During the Civil War, France had set up a puppet government in Mexico backed by French soldiers. In 1866 Seward moved 50,000 United States troops to the Mexican border, making United States opposition to French intentions clear. The French eventually withdrew from Mexico.

Then, in 1867, Seward bought Alaska from Russia for just $7.2 million. Thereby he eliminated French and Russian influence in North America, and he acquired a huge territory for the United States. The secretary of state also hoped to buy the Virgin Islands. He negotiated a treaty with Denmark to buy the islands, but the Senate refused to ratify it. In 1867 most Americans, including members of Congress, were not interested in such ambitious overseas projects, so Seward dropped his plans.

During President Grant's administration a proposal to take over the island of Santo Domingo in the Caribbean and a scheme to annex Canada attracted little support. A Philadelphia newspaper expressed the popular mood when it stated, "The true interests of the American people will be better served ... by a thorough and complete development of the immense resources of our existing territory than by any rash attempts to increase it."

When it came to pressing financial claims, however, the United States showed determination. For example, the government demanded that Great Britain pay for about 100,000 tons (about 91,000 metric tons) of shipping destroyed during the Civil War by Confederate ships like the *Alabama* that were built in British shipyards. In 1871, after years of argument, the two countries signed

Before the discovery of gold in the Yukon, the purchase of Alaska from Russia in 1867 had been ridiculed by many as "Seward's Folly." However, by 1898, when this photograph was taken, prospectors were racing to Alaska. The two women prospectors in the photograph faced a hazardous journey over treacherous mountain passes to reach the Klondike. Their equipment had to be carried or hauled along.

the Treaty of Washington. Under that treaty, an arbitration court ordered the British to pay $15.5 million in damages for the so-called *Alabama* Claims.

During the 1880s the dream of empire began to surface again. The same economic growth that had preoccupied Americans since the Civil War inspired new dreams of overseas expansion. By 1880 the United States was producing more food and manufactured goods than could be used at home. As a result, Americans began to export more to other countries.

Exports increased from $450 million in 1870 to $853 million in 1880. By the early 1890s they exceeded $1 billion. Slowly but surely the United States began to penetrate world markets previously dominated by European nations. Such competition increased the likelihood of conflict with these nations.

A Rationale for Expansion

As Americans began to take a new interest in overseas markets and territories, three men offered reasons for such expansion: historian Frederick Jackson Turner, naval officer Alfred Thayer Mahan, and Congregationalist minister Josiah Strong.

Frederick Jackson Turner was a young professor of history at the University of Wisconsin during the 1890s. He maintained that the availability of free land in the West had enabled poor or restless Americans to move West and prosper. With the free land on the western frontier rapidly disappearing, he feared that Americans without much land might become rebellious. Indeed, labor unrest and political turmoil between 1870 and 1900 seemed to suggest that Turner was right.

The answer, according to Turner, was to channel the energies of Americans toward the expansion of trade abroad. Increased foreign trade would create jobs that might give ambitious people the same opportunity for success the frontier had once provided. Turner's ideas appealed to many Americans, including Theodore Roosevelt and Woodrow Wilson. As President, both Roosevelt and Wilson tried to expand American influence abroad, as you will read in Chapter 27.

Admiral Mahan also believed that the expanding industrial capacity of the United States required new markets abroad. Mahan preferred to see the expansion of trade rather than the acquisition of colonies. Even if the United States was not interested in more territory, he believed it needed a stronger navy. In Mahan's opinion, a powerful navy was essential to protect trade routes, especially since competition for trade might lead to conflicts with world powers.

Mahan urged the government to rebuild the navy and add modern steam-powered battleships. He also believed that the United States should build a canal across Central America and annex Hawaii. Hawaii would be an important naval base in the Pacific, and the canal would allow American ships to pass quickly between the Atlantic and Pacific oceans.

Josiah Strong envisioned an American Christian empire that would spread across the Pacific into Asia. He argued that the "white race," represented by the United States, had been divinely chosen to "civilize" the rest of the world. Strong had his own interpretation of Charles Darwin's theory of the "survival of the fittest." (See page 387.) In Strong's opinion, the white race was the "fittest" and thus the American empire would survive and prosper.

Strong stressed American territorial expansion, while Mahan and Turner were more interested in the expansion of trade. The ideas of all three influenced both the public and politicians as the United States took its first steps toward gaining greater influence in the Pacific.

A Foothold in the Pacific

Americans had traded with Asian nations since the eighteenth century. This trade had increased in the early 1800s. In 1844 the United States had signed a commercial treaty with China, and in 1858 Commodore Matthew Perry opened trade with Japan. (See page 267.) In 1882 the United States signed a treaty opening trade with Korea.

In the 1880s the United States began to show interest in the Pacific island of Samoa (sah MOH ah), where the fine harbor of Pago Pago (PAHNG oh PAHNG oh) could serve as a naval base and commercial harbor. Germany and Great Britain, however, also realized the value of the harbor. For several months in 1889 German and United States sailors eyed each other nervously from gunboats anchored at Pago Pago. A powerful storm sank the ships of both countries just as tensions were at their highest, and the threat of war soon eased.

Public sentiment in favor of expanding United States influence abroad was strong. In this proexpansion cartoon, McKinley appears to be fitting Uncle Sam for a larger set of clothes. Opponents of expansion, at left, try to convince Uncle Sam to take diet medicine.

Great Britain, the United States, and Germany finally agreed in 1899 to share control of Samoa, with the United States obtaining the harbor at Pago Pago. The events in Samoa had demonstrated the growing danger of conflicts with other powers.

Hawaii

Although agreeing to cooperate with the other powers in Samoa, the United States wanted sole control of Hawaii. Europeans and Americans had first learned of the Hawaiian Islands in 1778 after British sea captain James Cook had come ashore there for fresh water and to trade with the Hawaiians. The islands had originally been settled by visitors from the Polynesian islands in the Central and South Pacific 2,000 years before. The individual islands were ruled by local chiefs until 1795, when King Kamehameha (kah MAY hah MAY hah) unified Hawaii.

During the nineteenth century, Hawaii attracted traders from China, France, Spain, and the United States. Americans, especially, valued the islands as a stopover for the growing trade with China. Missionaries also settled in the islands. Many of their descendents became prosperous sugar growers who dominated the islands' economy and the government of King Kamehameha.

In 1891 Queen Liliuokalani (lih LEE oo oh kuh LAH nee), a strong nationalist, came to the throne. She tried to restore the power of the Hawaiian monarchy and reduce the privileges of foreign merchants, but the foreigners in Hawaii organized her overthrow in January 1893. With the help of a detachment of United States Marines, they then organized a new government.

President Benjamin Harrison supported an annexation treaty with the new Hawaiian government. However, Grover Cleveland, who succeeded Harrison in 1893, was outraged at the high-handed actions of the American sugar growers and the role of the marines in the revolt. Consequently, he withdrew the treaty from the Senate. Americans who favored annexation of Hawaii grew increasingly concerned that another nation might seize the islands. Finally, in 1898, during President McKinley's administration, Congress passed a joint resolution annexing Hawaii to the United States.

443

Queen Liliuokalani, who ruled from 1891 to 1893, was the last Hawaiian monarch. A strong nationalist, she tried to reduce the power of foreign merchants in the islands.

Latin America and the Caribbean

Since President James Monroe had issued the Monroe Doctrine in 1820, Americans had maintained a special interest in Latin America and the Caribbean. The Monroe Doctrine stated that the United States would oppose all European intervention in the affairs of independent nations in the Americas. (See page 222.)

Latin America became especially important in the late 1800s. Merchants and manufacturers valued the region's raw materials. Military leaders considered many areas to be strategically important. The navy was interested in Panama as a possible location for a canal across Central America. Such a canal could allow warships to pass between the Atlantic and Pacific without circling South America. It would also benefit the growing trade with Asia.

The French were the first to attempt to build a canal across Panama. In 1878 Ferdinand de Lesseps (leh SEHPS), a Frenchman who supervised the construction of the Suez Canal, announced plans to build a canal. Citing the Monroe Doctrine, President Hayes condemned the French plans. Despite the protest France went ahead with the canal project, which soon became a disaster. Malaria killed 20,000 of the canal workers, and financial problems plagued de Lesseps's company. Work on the canal stopped in 1889. (You will read about the eventual construction of the canal in Chapter 27.)

Meanwhile, south of Panama, a border dispute between Venezuela and the British colony of Guiana (gee AH nah) brought the United States close to war in 1895. The boundary between Venezuela and Guiana had long been contested. The discovery of gold in the disputed area increased the stakes and the tension. Britain rebuffed President Cleveland's offer to mediate the dispute. It also dismissed any claim that the Monroe Doctrine gave the United States the right to meddle in Britain's South American affairs.

Enraged by the insult to the Monroe Doctrine, President Cleveland threatened war if the British seized territory to which they had no right. Both sides seemed to be gearing up for a fight, but the British had more serious worries about German threats to their interests in Africa. As a result, the British wanted to avoid conflict with the United States. In 1897 after Great Britain agreed to have an independent commission settle the boundary dispute, the crisis ended. The events in Panama and Venezuela showed that Americans still considered the Monroe Doctrine a vital force in United States policy toward Latin America.

For answers, see p. A 75.

Section Review

1. Identify the following: William H. Seward, *Alabama* Claims, Frederick Jackson Turner, Alfred Thayer Mahan, Josiah Strong, Queen Liliuokalani.

2. Define the following term: empire.

3. How did Secretary of State Seward end Russian influence in North America?

4. According to Admiral Mahan, why was a strong navy essential?

5. According to Josiah Strong, what was the mission of the United States in the world?

6. (a) Which nations wanted to control Samoa? (b) What agreement was made regarding the island?

7. Who dominated the Hawaiian government before Queen Liliuokalani came to the throne?

8. What were the advantages of a canal across Central America?

2 The Spanish-American War

The United States had become increasingly involved in world affairs in the late 1800s, but it had not yet assumed a place among major world powers. The collapse of the Spanish empire in Latin America and Asia offered the United States the opportunity to develop an overseas empire. As the Spanish empire crumbled, expansionists in the United States were eager to pick up the pieces.

Moving Toward War

Although activity in foreign affairs during the 1880s and early 1890s had brought the United States close to war several times, actual battle had been avoided. The successful outcome of the disputes in Samoa, Venezuela, and Hawaii, along with growing naval strength, had made American citizens and their leaders confident.

This confidence in the nation's power, however, threatened to develop into *jingoism*, an intense national pride. Jingoists often advocated a more warlike foreign policy during the 1890s. In 1891 they demanded war with Chile after two United States sailors were killed and 17 injured during a riot in Valparaiso, Chile. President Harrison ordered the navy to prepare for war. Faced with American threats, the Chilean government offered compensation, and the crisis ended.

Near Florida, however, lay a trouble spot that eventually would lead to war: Cuba. Americans had invested money in Cuba since before the Civil War, mainly in the rich sugar plantations. There had even been talk of annexing the island, although it still belonged to Spain.

In 1895 Cuban hatred of Spanish rule and frustration with falling sugar prices led to a revolt. Choosing repression instead of reform, Spain sent a new governor, General Valeriano Weyler (WAY ee lair) to Cuba in 1896. He treated rebel prisoners brutally and imposed a policy of reconcentration on the Cuban people. *Reconcentration* meant that people in the towns and villages were marched into detention camps where they would be guarded by Weyler's soldiers. Inhuman conditions in the camps outraged Americans. Anti-Spanish feeling was fanned by a group of Cubans in New York who spread publicity for the rebel cause.

Rebel publicity was fed to two New York City newspapers, Joseph Pulitzer's *World* and William Randolph Hearst's *Journal*. In overstating Weyler's atrocities and playing down those of the rebels, these publishers gave birth to a new form of newspaper writing, called *yellow journalism*. They purposely tried to whip up the emotions of their readers. Paying little attention to the facts, the yellow press tried to sell newspapers by featuring screaming headlines and sensational stories, with Spain portrayed as the villain.

In the battle for readers in New York, Pulitzer and Hearst tried to outdo each other with more spectacular reports of Spanish

In the fierce competition for newspaper readers, popular dailies headlined sensational news and scandals. This cartoon satirizes the "mudslinging," or name calling, that was typical of the yellow journalism of the day. The tall figure is President McKinley.

Lola Rodríguez de Tió: Poet and Patriot

Lola Rodríguez de Tió was a true daughter of Cuba and Puerto Rico. Her poems and speeches inspired many Latin Americans seeking freedom from the despotic rule of Spain in the late nineteenth century. Born in the ancient town of San German, Puerto Rico, in 1843, Lola Rodríguez was educated by her father, who nourished her poetic skill and her independent spirit. She was the first Puerto Rican woman to deliver a public speech on the island and the first to join in the literary and political discussions that took place among the men of her native town.

After marrying Bonocio Tió Segarra, a journalist and poet, in 1865, Lola Rodríguez de Tió joined her husband in the struggle for Puerto Rican independence from Spain. In 1887, when a cruel Spanish governor unleashed a reign of violence and terror in Puerto Rico, the poet dared to appeal for help to the Spanish government. The tyrant was put out of office and the political prisoners were freed, but the Tió family was sent into exile.

They fled to Cuba, where their home became a meeting place for Cuban nationalists. But the family was forced to flee from Cuba after Lola Rodríguez de Tió recited her well-known poem, "A Cuba," in the glittering Teatro Tacon in Havana. The Spanish authorities considered the poem subversive. The Tiós then settled in New York. Lola Rodríguez continued to recite her patriotic poems and to work for Cuban independence from Spain. After the Spanish-American War, she returned to Havana, where she received a hero's welcome.

Lola Rodríguez de Tió published three books of verse. Her poems spoke of friendship, of patriotism, of her love for children, and of the natural wonders of the island of her birth. The works are praised as literary masterpieces throughout the Spanish-speaking world. The two verses, reproduced below in Spanish and English, are from *Mis Cantares*, her first book of poetry, published in 1876.

Es libre aquel que lo quiere,
Hombre llámese, o mujer,
Que aspirar puede al derecho
Quien reconoce el deber

Niega todo lo que quieras,
Si negar es tu desgracia,
Mas no me niegues tres cosas
El alma, Dios y la patria.

Freedom comes if you want it,
Be you called a man or woman,
If you can aspire to justice
If you can recognize duty.

Deny all that you like,
If denying is your misfortune,
But do not deny me three things:
Spirit, God and nation.

---

cruelty in Cuba. Hearst was so confident of his ability to sway public opinion that he told one photographer who was heading for Cuba, "You supply the pictures. I'll supply the war." Influenced by the yellow press, many Americans clamored for a war to liberate Cuba from Spanish rule. Sympathies might have been on the side of the rebels in any case, since the Cuban revolt could be compared to the Revolutionary War in the United States. Such natural sympathy, however, was intensified by the yellow press and jingoists calling for overseas expansion.

On the Brink of War

When riots erupted in Havana, the Cuban capital, in 1898, President McKinley ordered the battleship *Maine* into the harbor to protect United States citizens and property. On February 15, 1898, a huge explosion destroyed the battleship, killing 260 sailors. An investigation failed to reveal who had sunk the *Maine*, but people in the United States blamed Spain. An enraged public called for war. (See pages 448–449.)

After the sinking of the *Maine*, the United States wavered on the brink of declaring war for several months, but President McKinley opposed war. In March 1898 McKinley proposed a cease-fire to halt fighting between Spanish troops and Cuban rebels. He offered to mediate talks between Spain and Cuba but clearly indicated that the outcome should be Cuban independence. Spain rejected McKinley's peace plan.

War fever in the United States continued to run high. Expansionists, such as Admiral Mahan and Assistant Secretary of the Navy Theodore Roosevelt, foresaw a victory over Spain as the beginning of an empire for the United States. Many social reformers, labor leaders, and religious leaders favored a war as a moral crusade to improve conditions in Cuba. Millions of ordinary citizens, outraged by the sinking of the *Maine* and by Weyler's atrocities, also demanded war against Spain.

Most business leaders, on the other hand, except the few with large holdings in Cuba, opposed war. Industrialists believed that war would disrupt the United States economy, but they were not powerful enough to hold back the tide of war. In April 1898 Congress recognized Cuban independence from Spain. Spain responded by declaring war against the United States. The next day Congress declared war on Spain.

War in the Pacific

Fighting did not immediately break out in Cuba, however. The Spanish–American War began on the other side of the world, in the Philippine Islands, which were also controlled by Spain. The United States had begun preparations in the Philippines two months before the declaration of war. On February 25, Assistant Secretary of the Navy Theodore Roosevelt had sent a message to Commodore George Dewey, commander of the United States fleet based in Hong Kong. If war was declared, Roosevelt said, Dewey's mission would be to destroy the Spanish fleet at Manila Bay in the Philippines.

When war broke out, Dewey steamed out of Hong Kong toward Manila Bay. At dawn on May 1, Dewey's guns opened fire, sinking the entire Spanish fleet with just one American casualty. Having made contact with Filipino rebels led by Emilio Aguinaldo (AH gwee NAHL doh), Dewey asked for troops to conquer the Philippine Islands. McKinley sent 11,000 troops and additional naval support. On August 13, 1898, rebel and United States forces took Manila.

Even hardened antiexpansionists in the United States admired Dewey's victory. The expansionists were especially thrilled by the stunning naval performance in Manila Bay. Those who dreamed of empire believed that they were seeing the dawn of a new age of American expansion.

War in the Caribbean

While American forces were crushing the Spanish in the Philippines, preparations were under way for an invasion of Cuba. Anxious to fight in what Secretary of State John Hay called a "splendid little war," 200,000 men volunteered to join the army.

During the spring of 1898, 17,000 troops gathered at a military base in Tampa, Florida. The army, however, was not equipped to launch an invasion. Soldiers bound for Cuba were issued heavy woolen uniforms, while cavalry troops waited in vain for horses. Despite this confusion, the invasion force sailed on June 14. (See the map on page 451.)

Among these troops was the spirited Theodore Roosevelt. He had resigned his desk job in the Navy Department so that he could be second in command of a volunteer unit called the Rough Riders, filled with a motley crew of cowboys, college students, and adventurers. Roosevelt came to symbolize national enthusiasm for the fight against Spain.

■ *The sea battle between the United States and Spain ended quickly in the Pacific, when ships under Admiral George Dewey steamed south from Hong Kong to strike the Spanish at Manila. The Americans sank the Spanish fleet stationed in the Philippines.*

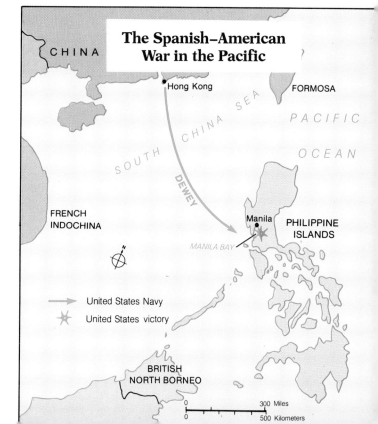

The Spanish–American War in the Pacific

CHINA

Hong Kong

FORMOSA

SOUTH CHINA SEA

PACIFIC OCEAN

DEWEY

FRENCH INDOCHINA

Manila

PHILIPPINE ISLANDS

MANILA BAY

United States Navy

United States victory

BRITISH NORTH BORNEO

0   300 Miles
0   500 Kilometers

For answers, see p. A 76.

Sinking of the *Maine:* Recognizing Propaganda

Propaganda is a deliberate attempt to manipulate the truth about people or events to further one's own cause or damage an opposing cause. Propaganda often includes many accurate facts, but the propagandist distorts the facts to fit the impression he or she wants to convey. This distortion can be done by supporting basic facts with hearsay evidence or half-truths, by presenting only one side of a story, or by supplementing facts with an emotional picture or description.

Many types of historical evidence may contain propaganda. Thus it is important to be able to recognize propaganda in order to understand historical events. Propaganda, for example, may have influenced the outbreak of the Spanish-American War. Two pieces of evidence about the sinking of the *Maine* are reproduced here and on page 449. One is the dispatch the captain of the *Maine* sent to the secretary of the navy immediately after the incident. The second is the front page of a newspaper account. Study both documents and follow the steps outlined below.

1. **Identify the facts.**   A fact is something that is true or that can be proven. An opinion is a judgment that reflects a person's feelings, beliefs, or attitudes. Read the message sent by Captain Sigsbee and the report printed in the *World*. (a) List the facts in Captain Sigsbee's message. (b) What opinions can you identify in his message? (c) List the facts in the *World* report. (d) Is any of the information in the report based on opinions? Give specific examples.

2. **Identify distortions of fact.**   Compare the two documents and answer the following questions: (a) What does Captain Sigsbee say in his message about the cause of the explosion? (b) What does the *World* imply about Sigsbee's opinion of the cause? (c) What does Captain Sigsbee say in his message about the reaction of the Span-

ish to the incident? (d) Does this information appear in the *World?* (e) How does the newspaper describe Captain Sigsbee's attitude toward the Spanish?

3. **Analyze the emotional appeal.**   (a) Does Captain Sigsbee seem interested in arousing public opinion against the Spanish? (b) What effect might the picture of the explosion in the *World* report have on the public? Why? (c) What impact might the use of the word enemy in the third headline have on the reader? (d) Find three other words that are likely to have an emotional appeal. What emotion is each word likely to arouse? Why?

4. **Reach conclusions.**   Use what you have learned from your text and the two documents to answer the following questions: (a) What overall message is conveyed by the author of the *World* report? (b) What feeling is aroused through the presentation of the evidence? (c) Why might the author want to present a distorted account of the incident? (d) What effect do you think reports such as the one in the *World* had on the outbreak of war between the United States and Spain?

Message From Captain Sigsbee to the Secretary of the Navy, February 15, 1898

Maine blown up in Havana Harbor at nine-forty tonight and destroyed. Many wounded and doubtless more killed or drowned. Wounded and others on board Spanish man-of-war and Ward Line steamer. Send lighthouse tenders from Key West for crew and the few pieces of equipment above water. No one has clothing other than that upon him. Public opinion should be suspended until further report. All officers believed to be saved. . . . Many Spanish officers, including representatives of General Blanco, now with me to express sympathy.

By the end of June, United States troops had established a beachhead near Santiago on the eastern tip of Cuba. Again inefficiency hindered the war effort. Many soldiers died from food poisoning after eating badly preserved meat. Finally, on July 1, troops engaged the Spanish defenders of Santiago. In a bloody fight the United States forces attacked the ridges surrounding the

city. Roosevelt's Rough Riders and black soldiers of the 9th Cavalry charged up San Juan Hill. Under withering fire, they suffered heavy casualties, losing over 1,500 men. The Spanish army, however, was demoralized and short of ammunition, and the Americans took the hill.

Then, on July 3, the United States Navy sank the Spanish fleet in a lopsided battle in

863,956
WORLDS CIRCULATED YESTERDAY
"Circulation Books Open to All."
VOL. XXXVIII. NO. 13,310.

The World.

863,956
WORLDS CIRCULATED YESTERDAY
"Circulation Books Open to All."

NEW YORK, THURSDAY, FEBRUARY 17, 1898.   PRICE

MAINE EXPLOSION CAUSED BY BOMB OR TORPEDO

Capt. Sigsbee and Consul-General Lee Are in Doubt---The World Has Sent a Special Tug, With Submarine Divers, to Havana to Find Out---Lee Asks for an Immediate Court of Inquiry---Capt. Sigsbee's Suspicions.

CAPT. SIGSBEE, IN A SUPPRESSED DESPATCH TO THE STATE DEPARTMENT, SAYS THE ACCIDENT WAS MADE POSSIBLE BY AN ENEMY.

Dr. E. C. Pendleton, Just Arrived from Havana, Says He Overheard Talk There of a Plot to Blow Up the Ship---Capt. Zalinski, the Dynamite Expert, and Other Experts Report to The World that the Wreck Was Not Accidental---Washington Officials Ready for Vigorous Action if Spanish Responsibility Can Be Shown---Divers to Be Sent Down to Make Careful Examinations.

Santiago Harbor. This blow ended Spanish resistance in Cuba.

With Spain dislodged from Cuba, the United States turned to the Spanish-held island of Puerto Rico. American troops landing in Puerto Rico during late July met little opposition and quickly conquered the island. On August 12, 1898, the defeated Spanish signed a truce.

Results of the War

In the peace treaty signed on December 10, 1898, the United States acquired Puerto Rico, the Philippines, and Guam, an island in the Pacific Ocean. Cuba became an independent nation. The United States Senate ratified the treaty in 1899. Although most Americans were pleased by the newly won

449

The 10th Cavalry was one of the regiments sent to fight the Spanish in Cuba in 1898. John J. Pershing, who may be one of the white officers in this painting, had served earlier as an officer with the black regiment on the western frontier. When war broke out with Spain, Lieutenant Pershing wrangled a transfer back to the 10th Cavalry. Pershing's nickname, "Black Jack," came from his years with the regiment.

status as a great power, they were soon to learn that power brought with it great, and sometimes troublesome, responsibilities.

For answers, see p. A 76.

Section Review

1. Identify the following: Valeriano Weyler, William Randolph Hearst, the *Maine*, George Dewey, Theodore Roosevelt.

2. Define the following terms: jingoism, reconcentration, yellow journalism.

3. What methods did the yellow press use to stir up hatred against Spain?

4. What effect did the sinking of the *Maine* have on American public opinion?

5. What effect did Dewey's victory in Manila Bay have on Americans?

6. Which battle ended Spanish resistance in Cuba?

7. (a) List the territories that the United States acquired as a result of the Spanish-American War. (b) What status did Cuba achieve as a result of the war?

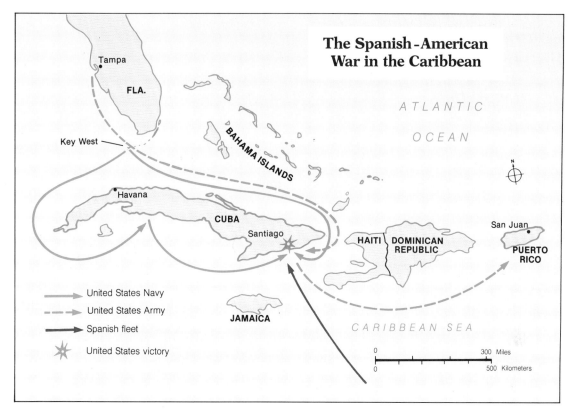

The Spanish-American War in the Caribbean

- → United States Navy
- --→ United States Army
- → Spanish fleet
- ✳ United States victory

0 — 300 Miles
0 — 500 Kilometers

■ *In the Caribbean the United States Navy sank a Spanish fleet in a one-sided battle. American ground troops met and defeated the Spanish in pitched battles in Cuba. Moving on to Puerto Rico, the Americans met little opposition from Spanish troops there.*

3 Responsibilities of Empire

The United States emerged from the Spanish-American War with far-flung overseas holdings. The nation now had colonies in the Pacific and Latin America, and its navy patrolled the waters of the Atlantic and Pacific. The easy victory over Spain made Americans confident that the United States could continue to expand. While some Americans were thrilled by the challenge of empire, others were troubled by the responsibilities.

The Cuban Problem

The conclusion of the war with Spain did not end United States involvement in Cuba. After the war, the island was in chaos: government was at a standstill, sanitation almost nonexistent, and disease rampant. In response to these conditions, President McKinley installed a military government to administer the island. Under the leadership of General Leonard Wood, the Americans worked to wipe out yellow fever and improve Cuban education and agriculture.

In 1900 Cubans began to draft a constitution, but President Theodore Roosevelt insisted that the Cubans include a document known as the Platt Amendment. Cuba would thereby agree not to make treaties or loans that might threaten its newly won independence. The United States would be allowed to establish two naval stations on the island. Finally, Cuba had to recognize the right of the United States to send troops to Cuba in order to preserve life, liberty, or property.

The United States pulled the army out of Cuba in 1904 but intervened again in 1906 and 1917. Cuba was at least technically an independent nation, but the United States had assumed control of the Philippines. This was to raise questions about the United States role as an imperial power.

Debate Over the Philippines

At the end of the Spanish-American War, President McKinley was not sure how the United States should treat the Philippines. He paced the floor of the White House night after night before deciding that the United States must rule the Philippines. The President argued that the Filipinos "were unfit for self-government" and that Americans had a duty to "uplift and civilize and Christianize them." He said this despite the fact that a majority of the population had been Christian for hundreds of years.

Most Americans probably shared McKinley's view that governing the Philippines was the responsibility of the United States. But some people insisted that colonialism was wrong. They maintained that the annexation of the Philippines violated Americans' belief in liberty. Some were also concerned that an overseas empire would drag the country into war with other powers. Other critics argued that the Constitution made no provision for governing colonies.

The American debate over annexation was complicated by a Filipino rebellion. Filipino nationalists had revolted against Spanish rule during the Spanish-American War. The revolutionaries led by Emilio Aguinaldo had hoped that an American victory over Spain would bring independence to the Philippines. But while the Senate debated the peace treaty ending the Spanish-American War, President McKinley had ordered American troops to occupy all the islands. Aguinaldo then rebelled against the United States.

The Senate ratified the treaty making the Philippines an American colony, but the war for independence continued. For three years Filipino nationalists fought a fierce battle against the foreign troops. Finally, in 1901, the United States declared that the Filipino revolt had been crushed. The war against Aguinaldo's rebels had lasted longer and cost more men and money than the original war against Spain in 1898. The long and bitter struggle showed that determining how

American power ought to be used was not going to be easy.

The Open Door Policy

United States interest in Asia, especially China, grew after the annexation of the Philippines and Guam. Americans saw these islands as stepping stones to China. Missionaries wanted the opportunity to convert the Chinese to Christianity, and merchants wanted to take part in the profitable China trade.

These hopes were threatened in the late 1800s by the great powers who sought to divide China into *spheres of influence,* or areas of control. Taking advantage of Chinese military weakness, Russia had seized Port Arthur in the north, Japan claimed the island of Formosa, Britain held Hong Kong off of China's southern coast, and Germany claimed the port of Kiachow. These spheres of influence restricted United States participation in the China market.

After the Spanish-American War the United States decided to try to open China to all nations on an equal basis. In 1899 Secretary of State John Hay sent letters, known as the Open Door notes, to the nations already involved in China.

Hay asked these powers to respect three principles: no power would prevent others from trading in a sphere of influence; tariffs in China would be collected by the Chinese, not by foreign nations; and no power would ask for harbor or railroad duties in its sphere that discriminated against the other powers. Most of the nations were neutral to the Open Door letters, but Hay announced that the Open Door policy was in effect since none of the nations had rejected it outright.

In the spring of 1900, a group of Chinese nationalists known as the Boxers rebelled against the Europeans, hoping to expel all foreigners from China. They killed more than 200 foreigners and attacked buildings owned by foreign governments in Peking. These hostilities, known as the Boxer Rebellion, lasted for more than a month until troops from several European countries and the United States arrived to repress the Boxer uprising.

After the siege of Peking ended, Hay sent another series of Open Door notes to the European powers and Japan. He hoped to prevent them from reducing China to a group of colonies as a reprisal for the Boxer Rebellion. This second series of notes not only upheld the principles of the first but stressed that the United States believed in maintaining an independent China.

Only Great Britain, France, and Germany accepted the second Open Door notes. However, the other powers, fearing that any attempt to divide China might lead to an open war, also observed Hay's policy. As a result, the United States gained access to trade with China.

The Fruits of Expansion

After 1900 the United States would annex few new territories, but it continued to extend its political and economic influence. Expansion had absorbed the national energy much as Frederick Jackson Turner had predicted. It provided new markets and sources of raw materials for American industry, which was rapidly becoming the largest and most efficient in the world. These markets and raw materials provided more jobs and investment opportunities for Americans. Expansion also increased United States involvement in international affairs.

In the meantime, another consequence of expansion became clear. The United States had been founded on the principle of self-government. Yet annexation often meant ruling without the consent of the governed. Expansionists justified colonial rule by insisting that the people who had been annexed were "not fit for self-government." But others maintained that colonialism was wrong because it violated the ideals of liberty and self-rule.

In some areas United States influence meant better education, improved health care, and more stable government than that which had prevailed before. The hard fact remained, however, that the United States had become a colonial power, like Great Britain at the time of the Revolutionary War.

Major European powers set up spheres of influence in a weak and divided China. When a group of Chinese militants called the Boxers tried to drive all foreigners out of China in 1900, the United States dispatched marines to rescue Americans trapped in Peking. Below, allied troops mass for an attack on the Boxers.

Major Events

1867	Purchase of Alaska from Russia
1871	The *Alabama* Claims
1889	Great Britain, United States, and Germany agree to share control of Samoa
1893	Queen Liliuokalani overthrown
1895	Venezuelan border dispute; Cuban revolt against Spain begins
1896	Weyler becomes Spanish governor of Cuba
1898	Sinking of the *Maine;* Spanish-American War begins; Dewey sinks Spanish fleet in Manila Bay; Battle of San Juan Hill; destruction of Spanish fleet in Santiago harbor; Hawaii annexed; treaty signed
1899	Filipino rebellion against United States; Hay sends Open Door notes
1900	Boxer Rebellion erupts

By 1900 the United States had taken its place among the international powers. One French diplomat observed, "The United States is seated at the table where the great game is played, and it cannot leave it." Indeed, Theodore Roosevelt and Admiral Mahan had no desire to see their nation abandon the contest. They could rejoice that in just over a century the United States had grown from a colony to a major world power.

For answers, see p. A 77.

Section Review

1. Identify the following: Platt Amendment, William McKinley, Emilio Aguinaldo, John Hay, Open Door notes, Boxer Rebellion.
2. Define the following term: spheres of influence.
3. List the rights that the Platt Amendment gave to the United States.
4. (a) What was the aim of the rebellion led by Emilio Aguinaldo in 1899? (b) Did he succeed? Explain.
5. (a) Which nations had spheres of influence in China? (b) What effect did the spheres of influence have on United States attempts to do business in China?
6. What was the purpose of Hay's second Open Door notes?

★ ★ ★ ★ ★ ★ ★ ★ ★ ★ ★ ★ ★ ★ ★ ★ ★ ★ ★

IN PERSPECTIVE   In the first years after the Civil War Americans had little interest in foreign affairs. Yet Secretary of State Seward's protest against French domination of Mexico and his purchase of Alaska from Russia were evidence of continued vigor in United States foreign policy. By the 1880s and 1890s American economic growth contributed to a renewed dream of expansion.

The United States had gained partial control of Samoa and annexed Hawaii by the 1890s. But it was the Spanish-American War that transformed the United States into a world power. Outraged by yellow-press reports of Spanish atrocities in the Cuban war for independence and angered by the sinking of the *Maine*, Americans clamored for war against the Spanish empire. After easily defeating Spain in 1898, the United States acquired Puerto Rico, Guam, and the Philippines. Cuba became free of Spanish rule but enjoyed limited independence under American protection.

Now a world power, the United States assumed huge responsibilities. Some Americans feared that being a colonial power would mean the sacrifice of liberty and the likelihood of frequent war. Aguinaldo's rebellion against United States rule in the Philippines showed that colonization carried with it grievous problems. But most Americans believed that expansion was good for the United States and good for the colonized people.

For answers, see p. A 77.

For answers, see p. A 78.

Chapter Review

For Further Thought

1. (a) What was the attitude of most Americans toward foreign affairs after the Civil War? (b) How did that attitude change by the 1880s? (c) What developments influenced the change?

2. The United States tried to enforce the Monroe Doctrine several times during the last half of the nineteenth century. Describe the actions taken in each of the following cases: (a) France in Mexico (1866); (b) France in Panama (1878); (c) Great Britain in Venezuela (1895).

3. (a) Why did Frederick Jackson Turner believe that the United States should expand its overseas markets? (b) Why did Admiral Mahan and Josiah Strong favor expansion?

4. (a) Why was the United States interested in the Hawaiian Islands during the 1800s? (b) Describe the events that led to annexation of Hawaii. (c) Why did President Grover Cleveland oppose the annexation?

5. Explain how each of the following contributed to the outbreak of the Spanish-American War: (a) jingoism; (b) appointment of General Weyler as governor of Cuba; (c) yellow journalism; (d) sinking of the *Maine.*

6. (a) Why did President McKinley install a governor in Cuba after the Spanish-American War? (b) What conditions did the Platt Amendment place on Cuban independence?

7. (a) Why were Americans interested in China during the late 1800s? (b) What prevented them from achieving their goals? (c) What action did Secretary of State Hay take to try to improve the United States position in China?

8. (a) What was the Boxer Rebellion? (b) Did it succeed? Explain.

1. William G. Sumner (see page 387) was one American who opposed the annexation of the Philippines. He argued that the notion of a civilizing mission was dangerous because it would lead the United States down the path of intervention and war. Do you think the developments in the Philippines between 1899 and 1901 tended to confirm or refute Sumner's argument? Cite specific evidence to support your answer.

2. (a) What reasons did President McKinley give for maintaining control of the Philippines after the Spanish-American War? (b) Do you think his rationale was justified? Why or why not?

For answers, see p. A 78.

Developing Basic Skills

1. *Relating Past to Present* Make a list of territories acquired by the United States between 1865 and 1901. (Include areas where the United States shared control with other nations or where the United States temporarily had control). Locate each area on the map of the world on pages 754–755. Then answer the following questions: (a) What is the present-day status of the area? (b) How does the present status differ from that of the late 1800s? (c) Choose one of the areas and research its history since 1900. Then write a report explaining how control of the area has changed.

2. *Ranking* Review the developments leading to the Spanish-American War. Then rank them according to which you think was most important in the eventual outbreak of the war. Explain why you ranked them in that order.

See page 777 for suggested readings.

Unit Seven

Entering a Modern Age

25

The Progressives

(1900–1909)

Theodore Roosevelt as portrayed in a political poster.

Chapter Outline

1 *Voices for Change*

2 *Reform of State and City Government*

3 *Theodore Roosevelt Takes Charge*

4 *The Square Deal in Action*

At the dawn of the twentieth century the United States was emerging from a period of phenomenal material growth. While many people did not share in the general prosperity, it was nevertheless a time of brimming national confidence and energy. Rapid change, however, had left parts of American society in disorder. In the cities, particularly, crowding, disease, illiteracy, and other ills proliferated. Political corruption was common.

As the century began, the reformers who had worked to establish settlement houses in the 1880s and to defeat corrupt city bosses in the 1890s joined in a broad crusade. Those reformers shared a belief that progress was possible, and from that belief came the label "progressive." The ideals and reform programs of the progressives dominated the politics of the early years of the twentieth century.

Most historians date the progressive era from 1901 to 1917, from the start of Theodore Roosevelt's presidency to the entry of the United States into World War I. In this period the progressives were to achieve major reforms in the economy and the politics of the nation.

1 Voices for Change

Although a few reform measures had been passed in the late nineteenth century, severe problems remained. Political corruption, monopolies, and poverty persisted, and many Americans continued to face political and economic inequality. By 1900 a new generation of reformers, known as progressives, resolved to right many of these wrongs.

Who Were the Progressives?

Kansas newspaper editor William Allen White joked that progressivism was simply Populism that had "shaved its whiskers, washed its shirt, put on a derby, and moved into the middle class." White correctly observed that progressivism was basically a middle-class movement. Progressive reformers were typically city dwellers and college-educated professionals. They sympathized with the downtrodden but were not among them.

Some progressives began their careers in the settlement houses. There social workers met with reform-minded reporters, professors, teachers, doctors, nurses, and business people. These middle-class individuals formed the core of the progressive movement.

Progressivism was a diverse movement. It included Democrats and Republicans, as well as members of smaller political parties. Some reformers were mainly concerned about corruption in government and the need to make government more responsive to the needs of the people. Many progressives worked to pass laws against unsafe working conditions, spoiled food, and slum housing. Others battled to pass legislation that would regulate the business practices of the powerful monopolies. But all progressives shared the belief that the United States needed to be reformed and the confidence that it could be.

The Muckrakers

The first step in reforming society was exposing the conditions that needed reform. Often that meant writing about grim details people would rather ignore. For example, Upton Sinclair charged in his book *The Jungle*, published in 1906, that the meatpacking industry slaughtered diseased cattle and injected the meat with dyes to disguise its color. Such reports disturbed many people, including President Theodore Roosevelt. In a Washington speech Roosevelt compared journalists like Sinclair to a man in a story who raked muck, or manure. That man, Roosevelt explained, was so intent on raking muck that he would not look up when he was offered a crown. Muckraking writers, declared Roosevelt, were similarly obsessed with wretched things.

Muckraking journalism had actually begun some years before Roosevelt labeled it. In 1902 Lincoln Steffens wrote a series of articles exposing corruption in city government. The articles were collected in a book and published in 1904 under the title *The Shame of the Cities*. In his article on Philadelphia, Steffens charged that voting lists in that city contained the names of "dead dogs, children, and non-existent persons," who voted for the party in power.

Muckraking journalists had a wide variety of concerns. John Spargo's book, *The Bitter Cry of Children* (1906), documented the poverty that resulted in hundreds of thousands of children going to school hungry. Ray Stannard Baker, who joined the staff of the muckraking *McClure's* magazine in 1897, wrote articles exposing the terror of lynching. Ida Tarbell's *History of the Standard Oil Company* (1903) cataloged the ruthless tactics John D. Rockefeller used to build his oil monopoly.

Although the muckrakers were not the first reformers to put their thoughts into print, they were the first to reach a vast American audience. Advances in printing and paper production made it possible for magazines to expand their circulation nationwide. Now the average American could read about corruption in high places and sickening conditions in meatpacking plants.

The muckrakers did not provide their readers with many solutions, but they did inform the public of urgent social and economic problems. Once aware, a growing number of Americans became involved in reform efforts, hoping to correct the evils the muckrakers had exposed.

Ida Tarbell was one of the most influential journalists of the progressive era. Her history of the Standard Oil Company, published in McClure's magazine, showed how the Rockefeller company had used rebates and price cuts to drive competitors out of business.

Organizing for Change

Despite their concern about injustice, many progressives were unconcerned about the plight of black Americans. A large number of progressives, like many white Americans of the period, believed that white people were superior to people with darker skin. Southern progressives often worked to strengthen Jim Crow laws. (See page 410.) Progressives in the North usually ignored the existence of segregation and discrimination.

But some progressives were outraged by the suffering inflicted on black Americans. After antiblack rioting erupted in Springfield, Illinois, in 1908, a group of progressives issued a declaration urging the creation of an organization to protect the rights of blacks. Among the signers of the declaration were the muckraking journalists Lincoln Steffens and Ray Stannard Baker, Jane Addams of Hull House, John Dewey, the founder of progressive education, and W.E.B. DuBois, an historian and outspoken advocate of black rights.

In 1909 this group of white and black reformers founded the National Association for the Advancement of Colored People (NAACP). DuBois edited the association's official journal, *The Crisis,* but most of the officers during the early years of the organization were white. Represented by lawyers

Historian and author W.E.B. DuBois was one of the founders of the National Association for the Advancement of Colored People in 1909. He is shown below in his office at the NAACP journal, The Crisis.

The Niagara Movement: A Declaration of Principles

In July 1905 a group of black teachers, ministers, lawyers, and other professionals met near Niagara Falls, New York, to protest discrimination against black Americans. Led by W.E.B. Du Bois, the group, which became known as the Niagara Movement, demanded political, economic, and social equality. The participants in the Niagara Movement were among those who founded the National Association for the Advancement of Colored People. A portion of the group's Declaration of Principles is printed below.

The members of the conference, known as the Niagara Movement, assembled in annual meeting at Buffalo, July 11, 12, and 13, 1905, congratulate the Negro Americans on certain undoubted evidences of progress in the last decade, . . . the buying of property, the checking of crime, the uplift in homelife, the advance in literature and art, and the demonstration of constructive and executive ability in the conduct of great religious, economic, and educational institutions.

At the same time, we believe that this class of American citizens should protest emphatically and continually against the curtailment of their political rights. We believe in manhood suffrage; we believe that no man is so good, intelligent, or wealthy as to be entrusted wholly with the welfare of his neighbor.

We believe also in protest against the curtailment of our civil rights. All American citizens have the right to equal treatment in places of public entertainment according to their behavior and deserts.

We especially complain against the denial of equal opportunities to us in economic life. . . . Common-school education should be free to all American children, and compulsory. High-school training should be adequately provided for all, and college training should be the monopoly of no class or race in any section of our common country. . . .

We demand upright judges in courts, juries selected without discrimination on account of color, and the same measure of punishment and the same efforts at reformation for black as for white offenders. . . .

We plead for health—for an opportunity to live in decent houses and localities, for a chance to rear our children in physical and moral cleanliness. . . .

We urge upon Congress the enactment of appropriate legislation for securing the proper enforcement of those articles of freedom, the Thirteenth, Fourteenth, and Fifteenth Amendments of the Constitution of the United States. . . .

Of the above grievances we do not hesitate to complain, and to complain loudly and insistently. To ignore, overlook, or apologize for these wrongs is to prove ourselves unworthy of freedom. Persistent, manly agitation is the way to liberty, and toward this goal the Niagara Movement has started and asks the cooperation of all men of all races.

At the same time we want to acknowledge with deep thankfulness the help of our fellowmen from the Abolitionist down to those who today still stand for equal opportunity and who have given and still give of their wealth and of their poverty for our advancement.

And while we are demanding, and ought to demand, and will continue to demand the rights enumerated above, God forbid that we should ever forget to urge corresponding duties upon our people:

The duty to vote.
The duty to respect the rights of others.
The duty to work.
The duty to obey the laws.
The duty to be clean and orderly.
The duty to send our children to school.
The duty to respect ourselves, even as we respect others.

This statement, complaint, and prayer we submit to the American people and to Almighty God.

Source: Cleveland *Gazette,* July 22, 1905.

who donated their time, the NAACP defended black citizens who had been arrested on questionable evidence. The organization investigated race riots and lynchings and fought for a federal antilynching law. By 1914 the NAACP had offices in 50 cities and a national membership of 6,000.

Advances for Workers

Workers endured hard conditions at the beginning of the twentieth century. In 1900 laborers in the steel industry worked 12 hours a day, 7 days a week. Textile workers, many of them women and children, worked from

60 to 84 hours a week. Unemployment insurance was unheard of, and workers injured on the job received no disability pay. Few employers offered retirement pensions. Child labor and unsafe machinery were common in many plants.

Labor unions had grown slowly since the 1880s. Only 3 percent of the workers belonged to unions in 1900. By 1910 the figure was just 5 percent. The American Federation of Labor (AFL), the nation's largest labor organization, consisted of skilled artisans such as printers, brewers, and carpenters. Unskilled workers were rarely organized in AFL unions. (See page 397.) Furthermore, longtime AFL president Samuel Gompers was suspicious of government efforts to improve labor conditions. If workers were well organized, Gompers argued, they would not need to be protected by government regulation.

The progressives entered the vacuum left by the AFL and fought with impressive

Muckraking journalists and progressive reformers drew public attention to the grim living conditions of workers in booming new industries. Pittsburgh steelworkers lived in the bleak and grimy neighborhood shown below.

results for legislation to protect working people. Between 1912 and 1917, 12 states passed minimum wage laws for women. Progressives also successfully pushed for state-sponsored insurance plans to cover industrial accidents. Thirty states had some kind of industrial accident insurance system by 1917. Laws that barred children from working at night were passed in many states. After a tragic fire at the Triangle Shirt Waist Factory in 1911 killed more than a hundred workers, a number of state legislatures tightened factory safety regulations.

Women in the Progressive Era

By 1910 women held nearly one fourth of all jobs in the United States. Although the majority of women working outside the home were employed as maids and cooks, more and more were moving into office jobs, factory work, and professions such as teaching and nursing.

The so-called New Woman who worked outside her home was most visible and vocal in the settlement houses. Many of these women became highly skilled organizers and advocates of reforms. Among the most successful was Florence Kelley, formerly of Hull House.

Kelley took over leadership of the National Consumers League, originally founded by a group of New York women in 1890. The league urged consumers to boycott companies that had unsafe working conditions and to buy only products that carried the league's white label. Members of the league and other progressive women campaigned for shorter working hours for women and children and for better working conditions. Oregon was the first state to pass a law limiting the working day for women to ten hours.

Although women could not vote in most states, they were involved in a wide range of political and economic issues. The General Federation of Women's Clubs, which had almost a million members in 1910, concerned itself with factory conditions, political corruption, and law enforcement. Many clubs limited their activity to discussing these problems, but some pressed for state and local reform. This helped broaden many women's political knowledge and experience and helped prepare them for the successful suffrage campaign you will read about in the following chapter.

For answers, see p. A 78.

Section Review

1. Identify the following: muckraker, Lincoln Steffens, John Spargo, Ray Stannard Baker, Ida Tarbell, NAACP, Florence Kelley.
2. Which groups of people formed the core of the progressive movement?
3. List three concerns of the progressives.
4. What were the major activities of the NAACP in its early years?
5. List four types of legislation passed to protect working people.
6. What action did the National Consumers League want consumers to take?

2 Reform of State and City Government

Appalled by the corruption and waste in city and state administration, most progressives believed that strong measures were necessary to save local government. One strategy they proposed was to make government more responsive to the will of the people. A second strategy was to employ experts, such as engineers and social workers, to make government more efficient. Greater democracy and efficiency emerged as two pillars of progressive reform.

Agenda for Government Reform

Progressives proposed several ways to make governments more responsive to the people. These included primary elections, the initiative, the referendum, and the recall election.

Until the beginning of the twentieth century political party leaders had traditionally chosen candidates for state and local government office. In some areas a political machine (see page 437) controlled the selection process. To make the process more democratic, progressives urged that *primary elections,* or elections to pick party candidates, be held before general elections. Voters would have a chance in the primary elections to choose among several candidates for the party nomination. Wisconsin adopted the primary in 1903. By 1916 all but three states had adopted the primary election.

Once voters elected members of a city council or a state legislature, the people had little influence on the government until the next election. Under established procedure only members of the legislature could introduce a bill, which meant that citizens could not submit their ideas to the legislature directly. To give voters a greater voice in law making, the progressives proposed a device called the *initiative.* It allowed citizens to initiate, or propose, a bill by collecting a required number of signatures from registered voters.

Progressives also thought voters should have a way to vote directly on some issues. In a vote called a *referendum,* proposals would appear on the ballot at an election. South Dakota, Utah, and Oregon adopted the initiative and referendum by 1902.

Another progressive proposal, the *recall election,* would allow voters to remove elected officials before they completed their terms. When a required number of voters signed a petition asking for a recall, a special election would be held to decide whether the official stayed in office. By 1914, 11 states had provided for recall elections.

Efficiency, as well as democracy, was an important consideration in progressive proposals for the reform of local government. One device for improving efficiency was the *city manager,* a professional administrator hired by an elected board of trustees to run a city government. Progressives believed that a professional manager with no political ambition would be more efficient than elected officials who had no training in municipal administration. The first city manager was hired in Staunton, Virginia, in 1908, and by 1914 the idea had spread to many cities.

La Follette and the Wisconsin Idea

Many cities and states experimented with progressive ideas for reform, but Wisconsin took the lead. When voters there chose Robert La Follette as governor in 1900, progressives had elected someone who would test their full program on a state-wide scale. Nicknamed "Battlin' Bob," La Follette was a tough-minded progressive who believed firmly in the need for greater democracy and

John Sloan was one of a group of painters that critics ridiculed as the "Ash Can School." Sloan painted the reality of urban life in the early 1900s, as seen in this view of New York City's Greenwich Village. Urban living conditions were among the concerns of progressive reformers.

efficiency in government. His far-reaching reforms of state government came to be known as the Wisconsin Idea.

Under La Follette's leadership the Wisconsin legislature established the direct primary in state elections. But Governor La Follette realized that good government needed more than a voting public. Complicated problems, he believed, needed to be solved by experts. Borrowing heavily from the University of Wisconsin faculty, La Follette recruited economists, engineers, and social workers to help him solve state problems.

La Follette's experts drafted legislation and sat on government commissions. His railroad rate commissions, for example, lowered rates and, as a result, increased the volume of freight traveling across the state. To the benefit of shippers and railroads alike, La Follette's experts made railroading more efficient.

The Wisconsin Idea was so successful that it became a national model, a so-called "laboratory for democracy." Several important progressive ideas became law in Wisconsin, including the creation of a tax system based on a person's ability to pay. The legislatures also passed laws strengthening the civil service and protecting natural resources. "Battlin' Bob" La Follette was elected to the United States Senate in 1906, where he continued as a major progressive spokesman.

Progressives in Other States

Although Wisconsin served as a model for progressive reform, progressives were active in every section of the country. In New Jersey, Woodrow Wilson, a former president of Princeton University, became a skillful reform governor. He won passage of laws establishing state regulation of railroads and utilities, the direct primary, and a system of industrial accident insurance.

California Governor Hiram Johnson successfully challenged powerful railroad interests who had controlled the state government. In New York Governor Charles Evans Hughes exposed corruption in the life insurance business. In the South Jeff Davis of Arkansas, Hoke Smith of Georgia, and "Pitchfork" Ben Tillman of South Carolina tried to weaken the influence of big business in state and local politics.

The progressives battled waste and corruption on many fronts. Robert La Follette crusaded for efficient government, while Hiram Johnson grappled with a railroad empire. But one man eventually captured the national imagination as a brash fighter for reform. He was the hero of San Juan Hill: Theodore Roosevelt.

First as governor of Wisconsin, then as a United States senator, Robert "Battlin' Bob" La Follette never backed away from the fight for progressive causes.

For answers, see p. A 78.

Section Review

1. Identify the following: Robert La Follette, the Wisconsin Idea, Woodrow Wilson.

2. Define the following terms: primary election, initiative, referendum, recall election, city manager.

3. What were two main pillars of progressive reform?

4. How did Governor La Follette try to make use of experts to solve state problems?

3 Theodore Roosevelt Takes Charge

On September 6, 1901, President William McKinley was shot while attending a reception in Buffalo, New York. When he died on September 15, Vice-President Theodore Roosevelt became President. As President Roosevelt made progressivism a national force. The White House, Roosevelt observed, was a "bully pulpit," from which he lectured the nation on the need for constructive political changes.

Roosevelt's Background

Theodore Roosevelt became President by accident, yet he was well qualified for the job. He had not only the necessary intelligence and the energy, he also had broad experience in government on the city, state, and national level. Roosevelt provided wonderful copy for the mass circulation newspapers of the day. Indeed, everything "Teddy" did seemed larger than life, whether he was leading a cavalry charge in the Spanish-American War or crusading as the New York City police commissioner.

This vigorous man began life as a sickly child suffering from asthma. His father, whom he admired greatly, urged young Teddy to overcome his physical weakness through exercise, to build his body to match his active mind. Shortly after graduation from Harvard University, Roosevelt began his political career as a member of the New York State legislature. Then tragedy struck. His young wife died in childbirth only hours after the death of his mother. At the end of his elected term, Roosevelt quit politics—he thought permanently. He bought two ranches in North Dakota, where he often worked on horseback for 12 hours a day.

465

Eventually, though, Roosevelt returned to public service, becoming a commissioner of the United States Civil Service, then commissioner of the New York City police force. He served as assistant secretary of the navy during President McKinley's first term. As the Spanish-American War loomed, Roosevelt recruited cowboys, polo players, mounted policemen, and college athletes into a cavalry troop nicknamed the Rough Riders.

Emerging from the war as a hero, Colonel Roosevelt was elected governor of New York. With typical gusto, he set out to reform the state. In fact, it was partly to get him out of New York that the state's Republican leaders engineered Roosevelt's nomination for the vice-presidency. They considered the position a powerless one. Mark Hanna, who dominated the Republican Party, was less than pleased. "Don't you realize there is but one heartbeat between the White House and this madman?" he exclaimed.

Prosecuting the Trusts

When Theodore Roosevelt succeeded to the presidency, many Republican leaders feared that he was a radical determined to remake society. In fact the President believed firmly in the free enterprise system. He welcomed the growth of industry, but he wanted government to have the authority to regulate the practices of giant corporations. He was called a trust buster, but Roosevelt opposed only what he called "bad" trusts: those that used ruthless competitive tactics. In his view, government had to protect the public from irresponsible elements in the business community.

The President's first opportunity to apply his ideas on the regulation of business came in 1902 when he confronted the Northern Securities Company. The Northern Securities Company had been created in 1901 by the merger of three railroads: the Great Northern; the Northern Pacific; and the Chicago, Burlington and Quincy. It monopolized a significant portion of the national railroad system.

In 1902 Roosevelt ordered the attorney general to bring suit against the Northern Securities Company, charging it with violating the Sherman Antitrust Act. (See page 408.) The act had been ineffective since the 1895 Supreme Court decision in *United States* v. *E. C. Knight Company*. The Northern Securities case was Roosevelt's invitation to the Court to revive the act.

In *Northern Securities Company* v. *United States* (1904) the Supreme Court ruled that the Northern Securities Company had violated the Sherman Antitrust Act, and it ordered the break-up of the company. Roosevelt's victory prompted him to move against other trusts. The beef, oil, and tobacco trusts were all prosecuted by the government during his presidency.

Despite these prosecutions, monopolies became more prevalent during the Roosevelt years. Robert La Follette questioned whether Roosevelt deserved to be called a trust buster. Roosevelt, La Follette charged, did not bust enough trusts, nor did he prevent new trusts from forming. In fact, although Roosevelt prosecuted more trusts than previous Presidents, the two Presidents who followed him were to prosecute even more.

The Supervision of Business

Roosevelt was not an enemy of big business. He accepted large businesses as an important part of the modern economy and thought that many combinations made good economic sense. However, the President did move against industrialists when he thought they acted irresponsibly, as in the 1902 strike by anthracite coal miners in Pennsylvania. The union asked for a shorter working day and better wages, but the coal operators flatly refused to negotiate.

Summer passed as coal supplies around the country dwindled. Schools and hospitals began to run out. Even after the union agreed to let an arbitrator settle the issues, the operators refused to negotiate. The arrogant attitude of the owners outraged both the President and the public.

The situation was ready-made for Roosevelt's drive to establish the government's right to control harmful business practices. He threatened to send troops in to run the mines if the coal owners refused to negotiate with the union. Other Presidents had used troops in labor disputes, but in support of employers, not workers. The coal mine operators backed down, and Roosevelt was hailed as a champion of working people.

In another effort to increase government supervision of business practices,

Roosevelt convinced Congress to establish the Department of Commerce and Labor in 1903. The department's first job was to assemble facts about American business. Within the department, the Bureau of Corporations publicized information about industry. Roosevelt believed that if the activities of an industry were open to public scrutiny, the business would stay honest.

In expanding government regulation of business, Roosevelt encountered strong opposition within the Republican party. "Old-guard" Republicans traditionally represented business interests. These politicians believed that government interference would weaken the free enterprise system. Thus Roosevelt moved somewhat cautiously in his first years as President, a job he had inherited rather than won on his own.

President in His Own Right

Although Roosevelt prosecuted several important trusts during his first term in office, he did not institute his overall program for reform. He wanted to win an election, to show popular support for his ideas. Roosevelt displayed all his political skills as he planned for the 1904 election. He used presidential appointments to gain supporters and consolidate his control over the party. The Republican convention nominated Roosevelt for President and Charles W. Fairbanks of Indiana for Vice-President.

Since the Republicans were running as reformers, the Democrats tried to attract conservative voters. They nominated Judge Alton B. Parker of New York. Parker's campaign was listless, and Roosevelt won by more popular votes than any previous President. He received 336 electoral votes, compared to Parker's 140, and took a stunning 2.5-million lead in the popular vote.

The election of 1904 made Roosevelt the unchallenged leader of his party. More im-

While some reformers wanted to ban all corporate trusts, Roosevelt made a distinction between "good trusts" and "bad trusts." He ordered the Department of Justice to bring suit against trusts he considered harmful. Roosevelt was the subject of many political cartoons, such as the one shown here.

portant, he and his programs received a clear vote of approval from the people. With typical energy, Roosevelt rushed to win passage of laws that would put his reform program into effect.

For answers, see p. A 79.

Section Review

1. Identify the following: *Northern Securities Company* v. *United States.*
2. What political experience did Theodore Roosevelt bring to the presidency?
3. Did President Roosevelt oppose all big business? Explain.
4. What action did Roosevelt take to settle the 1902 coal miners' strike?
5. What was the first task of the newly created Department of Commerce and Labor?

4 The Square Deal in Action

During the 1904 presidential election campaign, Theodore Roosevelt had promised, "I shall see to it that every man has a square deal, no less and no more." Roosevelt's plans for reform quickly became known as the Square Deal. With a combination of persuasion, patronage, and skillful use of public outrage, he prodded Congress to pass legislation increasing government authority to regulate business. The President won passage of laws on food, drugs, railroad rates, and the protection of natural resources.

Meat Inspection

"These rats were nuisances," Upton Sinclair wrote in *The Jungle*, "and the packers put out poisoned bread for them; they would die, and then rats, bread, and meat would go into the hoppers together.... The meat would be shoveled into carts, and the man who did the shoveling did not trouble to lift a rat out even when he saw one." Sinclair's book, published in 1906, generated enormous public support for laws requiring strict federal inspection of meatpacking plants.

One of the interested readers of *The Jungle* was the President. Although he regarded some of Sinclair's charges as unfounded, Roosevelt accepted the fact that unsanitary conditions existed in the meatpacking industry. He remembered that during the Spanish-American War hundreds of American soldiers had died from eating tainted meat. Consequently, he pressed Congress to pass a strong meat inspection law.

Albert Beveridge of Indiana piloted a rigorous bill through the Senate. The legislation gave the secretary of agriculture broad authority to settle disputes between government inspectors and meatpackers. It also outlawed misleading labels and dangerous chemical preservatives. The House of Representatives, however, proved friendlier to the meatpackers and passed a weaker bill. At that point Roosevelt stimulated public concern by publicizing a report supporting many of Sinclair's charges. The President encouraged the Republican leaders of the House and Senate to work out a compromise bill.

Reformers were not completely satisfied with the final meat inspection law. For example, it gave the courts, rather than the secretary of agriculture, final authority in disputes between inspectors and meatpackers. But the Meat Inspection Act of 1906 did provide for the enforcement of health and sanitary standards in all phases of the interstate meatpacking industry. Roosevelt thus achieved some but not all of what the reformers wanted. He also reasserted government authority to regulate an industry that ignored the public interest.

The Pure Food and Drug Act

Evidence of other harmful practices in the food and drug industries led to another major piece of legislation in 1906. Canned foods, argued Harvey Wiley of the Department of Agriculture, were being contaminated with dangerous chemical additives. Unfortunately for American consumers, the food industry had repeatedly blocked the passage of corrective legislation introduced up to that point.

While Wiley was exposing the dangers of canned food, Samuel Hopkins Adams was publishing muckraking accounts of misleading advertising in the nonprescription

The Need for "Pure" Food

By 1900 muckraking writers and government investigators began uncovering conditions in the food industry that threatened the health of Americans. Some of the problems resulted from a lack of sanitary standards or the greed of dishonest merchants, but many occurred because of the demands of a growing urban population for processed foods. For example, it was common knowledge in large cities that milk was diluted. All that dealers needed to boost two quarts of milk to a gallon of milk was access to a water pump. And to improve the color, they often added molasses, chalk, or plaster. Furthermore, milk from diseased cattle was distributed widely.

Some farmers bought garbage from city governments to feed to their cows. Distilleries often kept cows and fed them wastes from whiskey production. This "swill milk" was said to make babies tipsy. Butter and cheese were made from every imaginable part of the animal. Animal parts were blended with bleaches and other ingredients to resemble "Western butter." A popular jingle of the period described conditions.

Things are seldom what they seem;
Skim milk masquerades as cream;
Lard and soap we eat for cheese;
Butter is but axle-grease.

Rising concern led to the passage of laws in some states regulating the preparation of food products. Action on the national level came when Theodore Roosevelt sponsored the Meat Inspection and the Pure Food and Drug acts of 1906. Since then the federal government has continued to enforce standards for food production.

drug industry. Without any proof, companies often claimed that their products cured a wide variety of ailments. Finally, prodded by Roosevelt, Congress passed the Pure Food and Drug Act in 1906. The act barred the use of harmful additives in foods and forbade the use of misleading statements in the advertisement of drugs.

Controlling the Railroads

Farmers and owners of small businesses had long demanded new legislation to tighten government regulation of the railroads. The Interstate Commerce Commission, established in 1887, had been stripped of most of its power by a series of Supreme Court decisions. The Elkins Act, passed in 1903, barred rebates, but railroads were still free to set ruinous shipping rates.

Roosevelt and progressives in Congress proposed a bill that would give the Interstate Commerce Commission the power to nullify unreasonable freight rates. The House approved the measure, known as the Hepburn Bill, but conservatives in the Senate opposed it. President Roosevelt then threatened to lower import tariffs if the bill was not passed. Since the conservatives believed high tariffs were vital to industry, they voted for the bill.

The Hepburn Act, passed in 1906, gave the Interstate Commerce Commission the power to act on complaints from shippers by setting maximum freight rates. Although the railroads could challenge commission decisions in court, they had to charge the new rate while the issue was being decided. The act also placed other transportation facilities such as ferries and oil pipelines under the supervision of the Interstate Commerce Commission.

Conservation of Natural Resources

As an outdoorsman and one-time cattle rancher, President Roosevelt loved the American wilderness. Once in 1903 he camped out in a grove of giant sequoias with conservationist John Muir. "I stuffed him pretty well regarding the timber thieves, and the destructive work of the lumbermen, and other spoilers of the forest," said Muir. The next night, while the two camped out, four inches of snow fell. It was, proclaimed the exuberant Roosevelt, the "grandest day of

my life." Roosevelt took Muir's words to heart, lashing out at those who would "skin the land, and abandon it when impoverished . . . to the point of worthlessness."

Although Roosevelt loved the forest, he did not share Muir's belief that all the wilderness should be simply left alone. Roosevelt's views on conservation resembled those of Gifford Pinchot, chief of the United States Forest Service. Pinchot believed that forests could serve many purposes. They could be used for recreation, but they could also provide vital wood for lumber and wood products. Planned harvests of trees, Pinchot argued, would enable lumber companies to use the forests without destroying them.

The President urged a balanced conservation program. He supported the Forest Homestead Act in 1906, which allowed the secretary of the interior to open up certain forest lands for agricultural use. Then, in 1907, he slowed the destruction of American forests by barring the cutting of trees on 150 million acres (60 million hectares) of government timberland. Roosevelt also promoted conservation by creating five national wilderness areas.

Major Events	
1900	Robert La Follette elected governor of Wisconsin
1901	McKinley assassinated; Theodore Roosevelt becomes President
1902	Roosevelt intervenes in anthracite coal strike
1903	Congress creates Department of Commerce and Labor
1904	*The Shame of the Cities* published; Roosevelt elected for second term
1906	Upton Sinclair's *The Jungle* published; Hepburn Act passed; Meat Inspection Act passed; Pure Food and Drug Act passed
1908	William Howard Taft elected President
1909	NAACP founded

Agenda for Further Reform

"You have no idea," wrote progressive Senator Albert Beveridge in 1906, "how profound, intense, and permanent the feeling among the American people is that this great reform movement shall go on." President Roosevelt hoped to take advantage of the broad support.

In 1908 he created three groups to consider the problems of farmers and the need to protect national resources. Forty-four governors attended the National Conservation Congress and agreed that such meetings should be held regularly in the form of an annual governors' conference. The National Country Life Commission and the Inland Waterways Commission drafted documented reports, but their activity came to a standstill when Congress refused to provide funds. Many members of Congress feared that executive agencies had gained too much power under Roosevelt.

Roosevelt was discovering that a President whose term was drawing to a close had less influence than a newly elected chief executive. He was further handicapped by the onset of financial panic and depression in 1907. The split between Roosevelt and the conservative wing of his party deepened because conservatives blamed the panic on Roosevelt's antibusiness speeches and actions. They said his trust busting had destroyed confidence in American business.

In response, Roosevelt denounced the "malefactors [evildoers] of great wealth" and promised to continue his campaign against "speculation, corruption, and fraud." Executives of large companies, he said, had opposed "every measure for honesty in business that has been passed during the last six years."

In quick order Roosevelt proposed a series of reform measures that further alarmed conservative Republicans. In messages to Congress in December 1907 and January 1908, the President proposed inheritance and income taxes, more regulation of interstate commerce, and federal investigation of labor disputes. He called for an eight-hour work day and workers' compensation. He also suggested federal regulation of the selling and buying of stock.

Roosevelt's two speeches outlined an ambitious reform agenda for the future and further underscored the growing split between progressives and conservatives in the Republican party.

Passing the Reins to Taft

Following a tradition that began with George Washington, Roosevelt chose not to run for a third term. He did plan, however, to pick his successor. His choice was Secretary of War William Howard Taft. Taft had been a respected judge and had served admirably as governor-general of the Philippines. The Republican convention nominated Taft on the first ballot, with James S. Sherman of New York for Vice-President. The party platform had some progressive planks but was more conservative than Roosevelt or Taft would have liked.

The Democrats tried to regain the presidency by appealing to progressive sentiments. They nominated William Jennings Bryan, who ran a strongly antitrust and prolabor campaign. However, Bryan did not rekindle the fiery support he had received in his earlier races. In the end Taft won partially because people identified him with Roosevelt. He carried 52 percent of the popular vote and won in the electoral college by a vote of 321 to 162.

With the White House securely in Republican hands of his own choosing, Roosevelt embarked on a hunting safari in Africa that kept him out of the country for more than a year. He left behind a record of leadership and dynamism that set high standards for future Presidents. The presidency not only regained the prestige it had lost since the Civil War, but it was becoming the most powerful branch of the federal government. Furthermore, Theodore Roosevelt gave momentum to the progressive movement, which was to dominate the next decade of national politics.

For answers, see p. A 79.

Section Review

1. Identify the following: Upton Sinclair, Meat Inspection Act, Pure Food and Drug Act, Hepburn Act, John Muir, Gifford Pinchot, William Howard Taft.

2. How did President Theodore Roosevelt contribute to passage of the Meat Inspection Act?

3. How did Roosevelt convince Senate conservatives to vote for the Hepburn Act?

4. How did Pinchot's attitude toward the wilderness differ from Muir's?

5. What actions by Roosevelt in 1907 and 1908 contributed to a growing split between the progressive and conservative wings of the Republican Party?

471

IN PERSPECTIVE Progressivism was a reform movement that began around 1900. Political corruption, contaminated food, and unhealthy living and working conditions were among the concerns of the progressives. Crusading journalists known as muckrakers publicized scandalous practices, paving the way for reform.

Although many progressives were indifferent to the plight of black Americans, some helped organize the NAACP in 1909. Many progressives worked for the passage of minimum wage and factory safety laws. Women were active in the progressive movement even though they could not vote in most states. The progressives believed that government should be made more democratic and more efficient.

President Theodore Roosevelt brought progressivism to national government. He filed lawsuits against major trusts. During his second term in office, Congress passed laws establishing federal regulation of the meatpacking, drug, and railroad industries. Roosevelt also took steps to protect forests from destruction. Roosevelt chose William Howard Taft to succeed him. Taft easily won election in 1908.

For answers, see p. A 79.

Chapter Review

1. (a) What types of people became progressives? (b) What belief did most progressives share? (c) Did all progressives pursue the same reform goals? Explain.

2. (a) Who were the muckrakers? (b) How did they contribute to the growing reform efforts of the early 1900s?

3. (a) How did progressive attitudes toward the plight of black Americans differ? (b) What action did concerned progressives take to protect the rights of blacks?

4. (a) How did progressives try to improve conditions for workers? (b) Were they successful? Explain.

5. Describe how the progressives believed each of the following would make the political process more responsive to the people: (a) primary election; (b) initiative; (c) referendum; (d) recall election.

6. (a) What was Theodore Roosevelt's attitude toward big business? (b) How did he try to increase government supervision of business?

7. (a) Why did Americans feel there was a need to require federal inspection of meatpacking plants and guarantee the purity of processed food and drugs? (b) How did Congress respond to that need?

8. (a) What was Theodore Roosevelt's attitude toward the conservation of natural resources? (b) What actions did he take?

For answers, see p. A 80.

For Further Thought

1. (a) How did Theodore Roosevelt's actions as President increase the role of federal government in the national economy? (b) Do you think his actions were good for the country? Why or why not?

2. (a) Why do you think some people were angry about the muckrakers' activities? (b) Are there any journalists today whom you think might be called muckrakers? Explain.

For answers, see p. A 80.

Developing Basic Skills

1. *Relating Past to Present* Visit your local library to find out whether the initiative, referendum, or recall election is allowed in your state. If any of them are, write a report about their use. Include information about the number of times each has been used and what issues have been involved.

2. *Classifying* Make a chart with three columns. In the first column list the pieces of legislation you read about in this chapter. In the second column describe the problem or issue the law dealt with. In the third column describe how the law tried to solve the problem. When you have completed your chart, answer the following questions: (a) Which of the new laws reflected the concerns of the progressives? (b) Do you think progressives were satisfied with all the measures? Why or why not?

See page 777 for suggested readings.

26

Reform Continues

(1909–1919)

Portrait study of Woodrow Wilson.

Chapter Outline

1 *The Ordeal of William Howard Taft*

2 *Choosing a New President*

3 *Reform at High Tide*

4 *Amending the Constitution*

Launched nationally by Theodore Roosevelt and continued less enthusiastically by William Howard Taft, the progressive era reached its high point under President Woodrow Wilson. Even as the progressive tide ran strongest, cautious voices warned that government regulation and other progressive ideas could be dangerous.

Elihu Root, a former secretary of state and in 1913 a senator from New York, deplored the rapid pace of political change. He warned that "interference with individual liberty by government should be jealously watched and restrained." Root believed that the "habit of undue interference by government in private affairs breeds the habit of undue reliance upon government in private affairs at the expense of individual initiative, energy, enterprise, courage."

Despite conservative doubts, progressives continued to press for reform. They were instrumental in adding four amendments to the United States Constitution between 1913 and 1920. Although progressives did not achieve all their goals, they made fundamental changes in American government and politics. In the eyes of many, the progressives made politics respectable again.

1 The Ordeal of William Howard Taft

William Howard Taft faced many dilemmas. He was a conservative at heart but had been hand-picked for the Republican nomination by a progressive, Theodore Roosevelt. Taft had wanted to be a Supreme Court justice but had been pushed toward the presidency by his ambitious wife, Helen. As President, Taft hated the political deals that were part of his job. He was a quiet individual, serving in the shadow of the boisterous Roosevelt. While the presidency had been an exciting challenge for Roosevelt, it was somewhat of an ordeal for Taft.

Taft and the Tariff

Taft had consistently supported the reduction of tariffs on imported goods, an important part of the progressive program. As long as tariffs protected American products from foreign competition, manufacturers could charge high prices. Progressives considered this practice unfair to consumers. In his campaign Taft pledged to reduce the tariff, and upon taking office in 1909 he called a special session of Congress to do so.

During that session Republican Representative Sereno Payne sponsored a tariff-reduction bill, which the House passed. But the Payne bill ran into trouble in the Senate. There Senator Nelson Aldrich of Rhode Island added so many amendments to the bill that it actually raised the tariff on 500 frequently used items.

Instead of fighting to reverse the increases, Taft drifted into agreement with the Aldrich amendments. Thus the Payne-Aldrich Tariff Act of 1909 cut tariffs on a few items, but its main effect was to further insulate domestic manufacturers from foreign competition. When Taft called the tariff "the best bill that the Republican Party ever passed," progressives were dismayed. Progressive disaffection with Taft would soon extend to other issues.

The Fight Against Cannon

Throughout the first decade of the twentieth century and for many years before, the House of Representatives had been dominated by Representative Joseph G. Cannon of Illinois. As speaker of the house, Cannon made committee appointments, which were extremely important to representatives. If, for example, a representative from a farm state wanted to sit on a committee that drafted farm legislation, only Cannon could put him there.

Furthermore, under the rules of the House, the speaker had the right to appoint a majority of the members of the Rules Committee. That committee determined when bills would be debated by the entire House. Cannon, a conservative, had often used his power to block reform legislation.

Taft disliked Cannon personally and opposed his extreme conservative views. In 1909 when rebellious House Republicans proposed to strip Speaker Cannon of some of his power, Taft pledged to support them. Led by George Norris of Nebraska, House progressives began the struggle to change the rules of the House. They assumed that Taft would stand with them, but once again the President disappointed them.

Conservative Republicans promised to cooperate with Taft on other issues if he would support Cannon's reelection as speaker in 1910. The President agreed, but despite Taft's inaction, progressives from both parties were able to gather enough votes to pass rules limiting the speaker's power.

Conservation

Taft's action on the conservation of natural resources also disappointed many progressives. Although President Taft set aside more national park and forest land than Roosevelt had, he emerged as a villain to those who favored conservation.

The trouble began in 1910 when Taft's secretary of the interior, Richard A. Ballinger, issued an order allowing the government to sell certain wilderness areas in Wyoming and Montana. As a conservation measure these areas had been withdrawn from sale during the Roosevelt administration. Ballinger, who doubted the legality of Roosevelt's ban on the sale, repealed it.

Gifford Pinchot, the chief of the United States Forest Service, was enraged by the

Throughout his presidency, William Howard Taft worked under the shadow of Theodore Roosevelt. Comparisons between the two were made frequently. In this 1910 cartoon, Taft knits himself into a hopeless tangle of unsolved problems. Roosevelt turns a disapproving eye on the man he picked to succeed him.

repeal. He charged that Ballinger was trying to enrich corporations interested in exploiting the resources of the area. Angry at the attack on his administration, Taft fired Pinchot.

The Ballinger-Pinchot controversy was a political disaster for Taft. The public came to doubt the President's commitment to conservation. Popular outrage against Ballinger forced Taft to ask for his resignation. Theodore Roosevelt resented Taft's treatment of Pinchot and was impatient with the President's seeming indifference to conservation. The controversy widened a growing gap between Taft and Roosevelt supporters within the Republican party.

Continuation of Progressive Reform

President Taft's battles with Republican reformers obscured the achievements of his administration. He had supported several new conservation laws and had set aside more public lands for conservation than Roosevelt. Furthermore, although Roosevelt

was known as a trust buster, Taft's administration prosecuted more trusts.

President Taft was an unlikely opponent of trusts. As a judge he had a probusiness reputation, and as President he filled his cabinet with prosperous corporation lawyers. Yet Taft did not favor the trusts. Taft's attorney general filed 90 antitrust lawsuits, compared to 44 during the Roosevelt administration. Cases against Standard Oil and the American Tobacco Company resulted in the reorganization of those giant firms. Despite Taft's willingness to enforce antitrust laws, many progressives in Congress favored more far-reaching measures against monopolies.

President Taft took other progressive actions as well. He supported the Mann-Elkins Act of 1910, which allowed the Interstate Commerce Commission to regulate railroad rates on commission members' initiative even without complaints from shippers. The act also gave the ICC power to regulate telegraph companies.

The Department of Commerce and Labor was split into two separate departments under Taft, and Taft fulfilled another progressive objective by creating a Children's Bureau in the Labor Department. He also approved new safety regulations for mines and railroads. During his administration Congress established an eight-hour workday for government employees and increased the number of government jobs filled by the Civil Service, further limiting patronage positions. Yet Taft lacked the skill to turn these actions into political gains. Republican progressives saw Theodore Roosevelt as their leader.

Return of the Rough Rider

Progressive Republicans asked Roosevelt for support in the congressional elections of 1910. They felt that Taft and the conservatives were working to crush progressivism in the Republican party. Roosevelt, recently returned from his hunting trip in Africa, entered the fray.

In a speech at Osawatomie, Kansas, on August 31, 1910, Roosevelt advocated a New Nationalism. This program contained a full package of progressive reforms. It urged stringent federal regulation of business, the enactment of social welfare laws, and a curb on the power of courts to nullify regulatory legislation. Fired with enthusiasm, Roosevelt attacked "local selfishness" and championed

a strong national government committed to the public welfare.

Conservative Republicans shuddered at what sounded to them like a deeply radical program, and they deserted progressive Republican candidates in droves. With the Republicans badly split, the Democrats scored major gains in 1910. They won control of the House of Representatives for the first time in nearly 20 years. They also won many important governorships, including that of New Jersey, where Woodrow Wilson trounced the Republican opposition. Disunity would continue to plague the Republican party during the presidential election of 1912.

475

For answers, see p. A 80.

Section Review

1. Identify the following: Payne-Aldrich Tariff, Joseph Cannon, Richard Ballinger, Mann-Elkins Act, New Nationalism.
2. (a) Why did progressives oppose high tariffs? (b) How did they react to Taft's acceptance of the Payne-Aldrich Tariff?
3. What position made Joe Cannon powerful in the House of Representatives?
4. List three ways President Taft continued progressive reform.
5. What action by Theodore Roosevelt helped split the Republican party in 1910?

2 Choosing a New President

In March 1912 Theodore Roosevelt said of President Taft, "I have never been so disappointed in any man." Frustrated on the political sidelines, Roosevelt attempted to win the Republican nomination. His move further split the Republican party and helped put a Democrat in the White House for only the third time since the Civil War.

The Progressive Rebellion

As the 1912 election approached, Robert La Follette of Wisconsin challenged Taft for the Republican presidential nomination. La Follette drew strong support from Republican progressives. When La Follette's health failed, Roosevelt decided to take up the challenge. Taft refused to step aside for his for-

mer friend and sponsor, and the fight was on. Often the fight turned rowdy as Republican delegates at state conventions shouted, punched, and hurled chairs at each other.

President Taft controlled the Republican party apparatus that ran the national nominating convention held in June 1912. With skillful maneuvers, Taft filled the convention with loyal delegates. Roosevelt claimed fraud, and his supporters left the hall. The remaining delegates nominated Taft on the first ballot.

Roosevelt and his fellow progressives promptly launched a new political party, which they named the Progressive party. The new party held its own presidential nominating convention in Chicago in August. The delegates quickly nominated Roosevelt and greeted his fiery acceptance speech with thunderous applause. Roosevelt announced that he felt "as strong as a bull moose," so that animal became the party symbol. Now the Republican elephant and Democratic donkey had to contend with a fighting-mad bull moose.

The Progressive party platform called for the initiative and referendum (see page 463), women's suffrage, and direct presidential primaries. On the question of trusts, the Progressive party rejected suggestions that large monopolies be broken up. Instead the platform called for government regulation of the activities of large corporations. The party also urged passage of a minimum wage, unemployment insurance, and workers' compensation insurance. The platform clearly reflected the New Nationalism Roosevelt had outlined in 1910.

The point of this 1912 cartoon seems to be that the Progressive, or "Bull Moose," party was little more than a forum for Theodore Roosevelt. Yet the creation of the Progressive party did more than provide Roosevelt with a way to run for reelection. It also brought together leading reformers from both major political parties.

New Freedom Versus New Nationalism

Confident because of the split in Republican ranks, the Democrats looked forward to victory in 1912. The Democratic convention nominated Woodrow Wilson, a progressive who had been president of Princeton University and governor of New Jersey. Wilson was an attractive candidate, intelligent, honest, and dedicated to reform. It soon became apparent that the election was a two-way race between Wilson and Roosevelt. Taft had little chance for reelection.

Wilson championed what he called the New Freedom. The New Freedom demanded the break-up of the giant trusts because, Wilson believed, they choked off competition. He feared that increasing government regulation would make the government too powerful. In his opinion, competition was the best way to promote individual opportunity. Roosevelt, on the other hand, insisted that the federal government should be powerful enough to police even the largest trust. The issue of the trusts dominated the presidential campaign of 1912.

The Socialist Challenge

Taft, Wilson, and Roosevelt were not the only candidates running for the presidency in 1912. Eugene V. Debs, founder of the American Railroad Union, was the presidential candidate of the Socialist party.

The Socialist party was founded in 1901, with Debs as one of the prime architects. The party contained diverse elements. Moderate socialists, content with city-government ownership of the utility industries, were often called gas-and-water socialists. More radical socialists, including Debs, favored government ownership of all large-scale business. In this way Debs differed from Roosevelt, who believed that government should supervise monopolies, and Wilson, who believed they should be broken up.

The goal of government ownership of industry was too extreme for most Americans, but the Socialist party platform contained other planks that broadened its appeal. For example, it supported the right of workers to join labor unions.

Debs had first run for President in 1900. He ran again in 1904 and received four times as many votes as in 1900. In 1912 he made his most impressive showing: almost 900,000

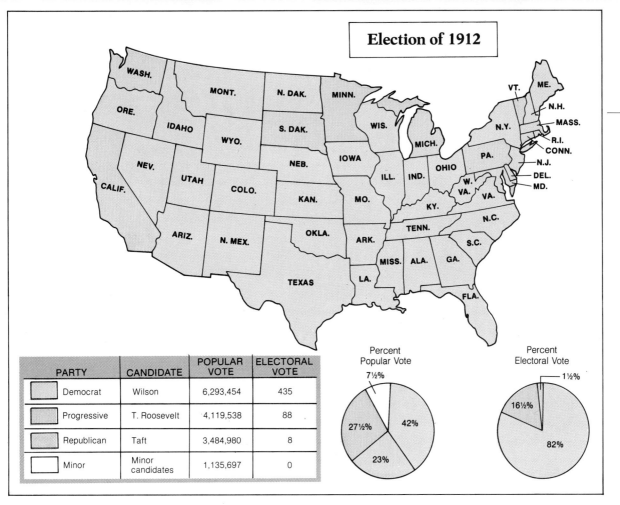

In the 1912 election Republican strength was split between party candidate William Howard Taft and ex-President Theodore Roosevelt, who ran as a Progressive. As the table and graph show, Democrat Woodrow Wilson won a stunning victory in the electoral college. The popular vote was much closer.

votes, or 6 percent of the total popular vote. Debs's increasing popularity was linked, in part, to the reform spirit of the period. Awakened to social injustices by journalists and other writers, much public dissatisfaction spilled over into support for the socialists. However, the Socialist party was unable to build on its gains in the 1912 election. By the 1920s its popular support had largely evaporated.

A Democratic Victory

Taft and Roosevelt split the Republican vote in the 1912 presidential election, and Woodrow Wilson won handily. He received only 42 percent of the popular vote but won a majority in the electoral college. (See the graphs above.) Democrats also won control of the House and the Senate and 21 governorships.

If the election of 1912 was a defeat for Roosevelt's Progressive party, it was not a defeat for reform. The three reform candidates—Wilson, Roosevelt, and Debs—received almost 11 million of the 15 million votes cast. Reform would be on the national agenda for the next four years.

For answers, see p. A 81.
Section Review

1. Identify the following: Progressive party, New Freedom, Eugene V. Debs, Socialist party.
2. What led Theodore Roosevelt to leave the Republican party in 1912?
3. How did the attitudes of Wilson and Roosevelt toward trusts differ?
4. What did Eugene V. Debs believe should be done about trusts?

3 Reform at High Tide

Many people looked skeptically at the scholarly professor elected President by less than half the voters. They wondered if a man who had spent most of his life in the academic world could withstand the demands of national politics.

Any such doubts soon vanished. In his own way Wilson was every bit as forceful as Roosevelt. An excellent leader, he knew how to inspire people. He believed that the President should be the voice of the highest national ideals. Of the President he said, "Let him once win the admiration and confidence of the country, and no single force can withstand him, no combination of forces can easily overpower him."

Tackling the Tariff

Progressives had been outraged over the Payne-Aldrich tariff passed under President Taft. They looked to Woodrow Wilson, who shared their goal of lowering tariffs. Wilson opposed high tariffs because he believed that American industry would become more efficient if it were faced with greater foreign competition. Competition would force American industrialists to improve their products and lower their prices. Wilson maintained that such actions would benefit the economy of the United States.

Soon after taking office in 1913 Wilson called Congress into special session to reduce tariff duties. To dramatize the moment, the President appeared in Congress to deliver his message personally. No President since John Adams had done so, and the action riveted public attention on the tariff issue.

Under strong pressure from Wilson, the House passed a bill removing the tariff from many items and lowering duties on others. But the Senate proved less cooperative. Lobbyists for such industries as lumber, steel, and wool, which would face greater competition under the proposed legislation, urged senators to vote against it. Probusiness newspapers supported the attacks on the tariff bill.

Wilson did not back away from the fight. As the hot Washington summer wore on, he kept up the pressure on wavering senators. Finally Wilson prevailed, and on October 3, 1913, he signed the Underwood-Simmons Tariff Act. The act substantially lowered the duty on imports for the first time since the Civil War, and many believed that it would lower the cost of living for the average citizen.

To replace revenues lost by cutting tariffs, the Underwood-Simmons Tariff Act included a provision that drew little debate at the time but would have a lasting effect on ordinary citizens. It enacted a *graduated income tax*, a system of taxing personal incomes by which people who had higher incomes paid proportionately higher taxes.

The Federal Reserve Act

After the passage of the Underwood-Simmons Tariff Act, Wilson pushed through other economic reforms. One such reform was the creation of the federal reserve system. The financial panic of 1907 had convinced many Americans that government action was needed to insure a reliable supply of credit. A small group of bankers seemed to control the national money supply, and they were often unable or unwilling to extend credit.

President Wilson believed that government should regulate the supply of credit. He declared that "control must be public, not private, [and] must be vested in government itself, so that the banks may be the instruments, not the masters, of business and individual enterprise and initiative." After a long struggle in Congress, Wilson's banking bill was passed.

The Federal Reserve Act, signed by Wilson on December 23, 1913, transformed the banking system. It divided the nation into 12 districts and established a federal reserve bank for each district. National banks within a district deposited monetary reserves in the federal reserve bank. This money could then be used to increase the credit supply.

The Federal Reserve Board, headquartered in Washington, D.C., controlled the system of banks. The board set interest rates on loans made by the federal reserve banks to member banks. By lowering interest rates, the Federal Reserve Board made loans easier to obtain, which thereby increased the money supply. By raising rates, the board, in turn, could tighten the money supply. President Wilson hoped that the Federal Reserve Act would increase competition in the business world by making it easier for investors to obtain credit.

Attacking the Trusts

As a candidate, Wilson seemed to favor the break-up of all large trusts. As President, he embarked on a more moderate course, but he did support two pieces of legislation that sought to control monopolies.

The Federal Trade Commission Act, passed in 1914, provided for the creation of the Federal Trade Commission (FTC). The purpose of the FTC was to preserve competition by preventing one firm from destroying another through unfair business practices. The commission would investigate complaints of unfair practices such as misleading advertising. If the commission found that a complaint was justified, a "cease and desist" order would be issued. Such an order would bar the firm from continuing the misleading advertising.

The Clayton Antitrust Act, also passed in 1914, was designed to strengthen the Sherman Antitrust Act. (See page 408.) The new law prohibited pricing policies that might destroy competition and outlawed the purchase of stock in competing firms. It also made the use of interlocking directorates illegal. The *interlocking directorate* was the practice of allowing the same individuals to serve on the boards of directors of various firms in the same industry. The practice had been used to create monopolies.

The Clayton Antitrust Act, unlike the Sherman Antitrust Act, stated that labor unions could not be prosecuted under antitrust laws. Furthermore, it recognized the right of workers to strike and picket. Samuel Gompers, president of the American Federation of Labor, considered the act a major victory for workers.

A Mixed Record on Social Issues

At the beginning of his administration Wilson was hesitant to foster social legislation. His main interest had been economic fairness. He had repeatedly opposed legislation that benefited only certain groups of people, but pressure from the progressive wing of his party made him more willing to support social-reform bills. These included the Seaman Act of 1915, establishing minimum standards for the treatment of merchant sailors, and the Adamson Act of 1916, establishing an eight-hour work day for railroad workers.

The elimination of child labor and a reduction in the long work week for all workers were key progressive goals. These young waterboys worked at the Homestead, Pennsylvania, steelworks. School ended at the eighth grade or earlier for many young people.

In 1913 department store owner Rodman Wanamaker financed an expedition to visit more than 200 Native American groups. The purpose of the expedition was to promote Native American citizenship and make a photographic record of Native American life. President Wilson recorded a speech to be played at ceremonies such as this one in Pauma, California.

Congress passed the Workingmen's Compensation Act in 1916. It provided financial assistance to federal civil service employees who became disabled. The Child Labor Act, signed by the President in 1916, banned from interstate commerce any goods produced by child labor. The President also signed the Farm Loan Act in 1916, which made it easier for farmers to get loans.

Wilson resisted pressure to increase restrictions on immigration even though many progressives favored the idea. Social workers, for example, wanted to restrict immigration because they believed it contributed to urban problems. Labor unions wanted to reduce the number of immigrants who competed for jobs. Twice the President vetoed bills that would have restricted immigration. But in 1917 Congress overrode his veto and passed a bill requiring immigrants to pass a literacy test.

As you read in Chapter 25, some progressives were concerned with the problems of black Americans, but many were not. During his campaign for President Woodrow Wilson had promised "absolute fair dealing" to black Americans. But when he took office his actions disappointed black leaders. For example, he approved the policy of official segregation in the federal government. According to this policy, black employees were forced to use separate rest rooms, and in some offices screens were placed between black and white employees.

In 1913 a group of black leaders went to the White House to talk to Wilson about segregation in government employment. After listening to their protest the President told them that "segregation is not humiliating but a benefit, and ought to be so regarded by you gentlemen." Throughout his presidency, Wilson did not change his attitude toward segregation in government.

For answers, see p. A 81.
Section Review

1. Identify the following: Underwood-Simmons Tariff Act, Federal Reserve Act, Federal Trade Commission, Clayton Antitrust Act.
2. Define the following terms: graduated income tax, interlocking directorate.
3. What impact did Woodrow Wilson believe lower tariffs would have on industry?
4. What action could the Federal Reserve Board take to increase the money supply?
5. Name two practices outlawed by the Clayton Antitrust Act.
6. Give three examples of social reform legislation passed during Wilson's administration.

4 Amending the Constitution

The framers of the United States Constitution purposely made the document difficult to change. To amend the Constitution both houses of Congress must pass a proposed amendment by a two-thirds majority. Although there are four ways to ratify an amendment, the most typical procedure is ratification by the legislatures in three fourths of the states. Since the first ten amendments, the Bill of Rights, were ratified in 1791, only five amendments had been added to the Constitution by 1912. Yet between 1913 and 1920 the Constitution was amended four times. The new constitutional amendments reflected the reform spirit of the progressive era.

The Income Tax

In 1895 the Supreme Court had ruled that an income tax was unconstitutional, but the progressives continued to push for one. An income tax would fulfill two of their goals. First, it would provide revenue to pay for progressive reforms. Second, a graduated income tax would place the greatest tax burden on those who had the highest incomes. The progressives believed that such a system would be fairest.

Many Americans opposed an income tax, however. Some believed that the government had no right to take away money that people earned. Others objected to the way the federal government spent tax revenues. They disapproved of such plans as workers' compensation insurance.

During President Taft's administration, progressives proposed an income tax to replace revenue lost by a reduction in tariffs. Taft favored an income tax, but he thought that the Supreme Court would again strike it down. Consequently, the only way to enact a federal income tax was to amend the Constitution.

In July 1909 Congress passed the Sixteenth Amendment, granting Congress the power to lay and collect taxes on incomes. By February 1913 three fourths of the states had ratified the amendment. Later that year the Underwood-Simmons Tariff Act imposed a graduated income tax.

Direct Election of Senators

Until 1913 voters did not choose United States senators directly. As specified in the Constitution, state legislatures elected the senators who represented the states in Congress. However, the election of senators by state legislatures was accompanied by many problems. Interest groups could "buy" seats in the Senate by bribing legislators. And political machines controlled some state legislatures, placing the election of senators in the hands of machine bosses.

Progressives believed that the direct election of senators would end these abuses and make the system more democratic. With people voting for senators directly, bribery would be eliminated. A special interest group might try to bribe a whole legislature, but it could not pay off the entire electorate.

Progressive efforts to change the constitutional procedure for electing senators met with rapid success. In May 1912 Congress passed the Seventeenth Amendment, requiring direct election of senators. A year later the required number of states had ratified the amendment, and it too became part of the Constitution.

Prohibition

The progressives favored the direct election of senators because they thought it would reduce corruption. A similar impulse aided the movement to outlaw liquor. Advocates of *prohibition*, the ban on the sale of alcoholic beverages, believed that liquor was a corrupting influence. They argued that excessive drinking ruined families and caused industrial accidents. Saloons were seen as centers of immorality and corruption.

The drive to eliminate alcoholic beverages from the United States had begun many years earlier as a moral crusade. The roots of prohibition reached far back into Protestant New England. As early as 1851, Maine had voted itself "dry," banning the sale of alcoholic beverages. (See page 288.) By 1917 there was 26 other dry states, although many permitted the sale of weaker beverages such as beer.

Spearheading the temperance crusade was the Women's Christian Temperance Union, headed by Frances Willard, and the Anti-Saloon League. Both groups urged a ban on the sale and manufacture of all alcoholic beverages. The prohibitionists helped create the moral climate that made prohibition possible, but many people believed a law against drinking would never succeed. Theodore Roosevelt, although sympathetic to temperance arguments, thought such a law would be unenforceable and would only lessen respect for laws in general.

The outbreak of war in Europe in 1914, however, strengthened the temperance movement. After the United States entered the war in 1917, prohibitionists argued that a ban on alcohol would increase industrial efficiency. Furthermore, they claimed that grain used for making alcohol could be used as food for soldiers instead. Congress passed the Eighteenth Amendment, prohibiting the manufacture, sale, and transportation of liquor, in December 1917. It was ratified in January 1919.

Women's Suffrage

As you read in Chapter 23, women at the turn of the century were entering the work force in greater numbers than ever before.

Women dominated the crusade to ban the use of alcoholic beverages. Saloons around the nation were shut down because of the prohibition amendment. For example, this former saloon at the Majestic Hotel in New York City became a library. Note the books on top of the "bar."

Carrie Chapman Catt: A Victory for Women

Carrie Chapman Catt, born in Wisconsin in 1859, was influenced by the frontier atmosphere of her youth. She developed a strong sense of independence and purpose. After graduating from Iowa State College in 1880, she had planned to enter law school but instead accepted a position as principal at a nearby high school. Within two years she had become superintendent of schools, an unusually responsible post for a woman at that time. Catt later worked for a year on a San Francisco newspaper before returning to Iowa, where she became active in the women's suffrage movement.

With her calm and logical delivery, commanding platform presence, and pleasing voice, Catt became an accomplished speaker for women's suffrage on both the state and national levels. She became president of the National American Woman Suffrage Association in 1900. In four years she built a nationwide organization with a healthy treasury and a foundation of administrative procedures unmatched in the 50-year history of the suffrage movement.

In 1916 the association adopted a strategy, proposed by Catt, that led to the passage of the Nineteenth Amendment. Association members worked to win women the right to vote in individual states. As a result of their efforts the number of so-called suffrage states increased dramatically in 1917 and 1918. These victories convinced President Wilson to actively support the amendment, which was passed by Congress in June 1919. Yet Catt's work was far from over. In the summer of 1920 she spent two months campaigning in Tennessee, the final state needed for ratification. The Tennessee legislature approved the amendment in August 1920, and women's suffrage was won.

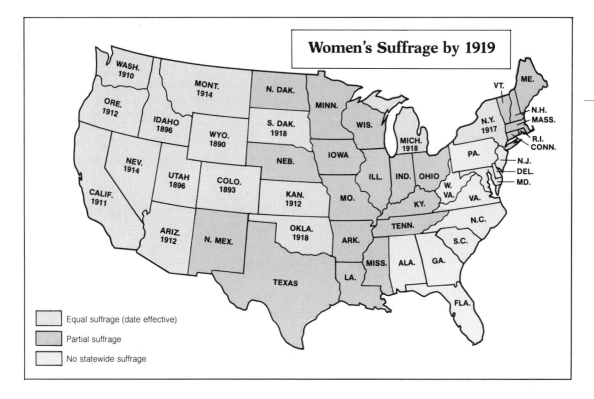

Women's Suffrage by 1919

WASH. 1910
ORE. 1912
IDAHO 1896
MONT. 1914
N. DAK.
MINN.
WIS.
VT.
ME.
N.H.
MASS.
N.Y. 1917
R.I.
CONN.
NEV. 1914
UTAH 1896
WYO. 1890
S. DAK. 1918
NEB.
IOWA
MICH. 1918
PA.
N.J.
DEL.
MD.
CALIF. 1911
COLO. 1893
KAN. 1912
MO.
ILL. IND. OHIO
W. VA.
KY.
VA.
ARIZ. 1912
N. MEX.
OKLA. 1918
ARK.
TENN.
N.C.
S.C.
TEXAS
LA.
MISS. ALA. GA.
FLA.

Equal suffrage (date effective)
Partial suffrage
No statewide suffrage

■ *By 1919 women in most states could vote in state and local elections. As the map shows, women had full suffrage in 15 states, mostly in the West. Only 11 states had no women's suffrage.*

Their growing economic independence nourished demands for political rights. Women's experience in state and national progressive reform movements also prompted them to demand the right to vote. Women reformers had learned that without the vote they lacked the power needed to bring about political change.

Some women believed that women should have the right to vote because they were morally superior to men. They argued that women in politics would raise the moral standards of public life. Suffragists asserted that without the right to vote, women were powerless against people who made and enforced laws affecting them.

By 1912 the impact of changed social roles and the general spirit of reform had allowed the suffrage movement to flourish. Two groups led this movement. One was the National American Woman Suffrage Association, headed by Carrie Chapman Catt. In state after state the association pressured legislatures to extend suffrage.

A young Quaker, Alice Paul, and the Woman's party she helped found introduced a more militant approach to the campaign for the right to vote. On the day of Wilson's inauguration, Paul organized a spectacular parade through Washington, D. C., to demonstrate support for women's suffrage. When Wilson refused to support a constitutional amendment granting women the right to vote, Alice Paul and the Woman's party began picketing the White House every day. She and other pickets were jailed and, when they went on a hunger strike, were force-fed. The resulting publicity dramatized the suffrage crusade.

While Congress stalled on suffrage, states in the West and Midwest voted it in one by one. By 1919, 15 states permitted full women's suffrage, and many other states allowed women to vote in local or state elections. Only 11 states, mostly in the East and South, did not allow women to vote at all. (See the map above.) After a major effort by both suffrage organizations, Congress passed the Nineteenth Amendment in 1919. It was ratified by the states in August 1920.

The Nineteenth Amendment marked the last major reform of the progressive era. During this period reformers had struggled to make politics less corrupt and more

Major Events

1909	Payne-Aldrich Tariff Act passed
1910	Ballinger-Pinchot controversy; Mann-Elkins Act passed
1912	Progressive party formed; Woodrow Wilson elected President
1913	Sixteenth Amendment, authorizing income tax, ratified; Seventeenth Amendment, establishing direct election of senators, ratified; Underwood-Simmons Tariff Act passed; Federal Reserve Act passed
1914	Federal Trade Commission established; Clayton Antitrust Act passed
1919	Eighteenth Amendment, prohibiting manufacture and sale of liquor, ratified
1920	Nineteenth Amendment, giving women right to vote, ratified

democratic. They had sought economic justice for workers, farmers, consumers, and owners of small businesses. Congress had accumulated an impressive record of legislation, and the Constitution had been changed in important ways. But by 1917, war loomed. Americans turned away from reform and paid closer attention to foreign affairs.

For answers, see p. A 82.

Section Review

1. Identify the following: Women's Christian Temperance Union, Anti-Saloon League, Carrie Chapman Catt, Alice Paul.
2. Define the following term: prohibition.
3. What two reasons did progressives have for favoring an income tax?
4. In the opinion of progressives, how would the direct election of senators reduce corruption?
5. (a) What reasons did advocates of prohibition give for banning the manufacture and sale of alcoholic beverages? (b) How did World War I help the prohibition movement succeed?
6. What tactics did Alice Paul use to bring attention to the suffrage movement?

★ ★

IN PERSPECTIVE William Howard Taft had been chosen for the Republican presidential nomination by the progressive-minded Roosevelt, but, as President, Taft disappointed many progressives. Although he instituted a number of reforms, Taft alienated progressives over issues such as the tariff and conservation.

Impatient with Taft's policies, Theodore Roosevelt tried to win the Republican nomination in 1912. When he failed, he founded his own political organization, the Progressive party. With the Republicans split, the Democratic candidate, Woodrow Wilson, won easily.

During Wilson's presidency, Congress continued to pass progressive legislation. It lowered the tariff, established federal control of the banking system, and strengthened antitrust laws. It also acted to improve working conditions.

Far-reaching constitutional changes occurred during the progressive era. Amendments were ratified authorizing an income tax, establishing the direct election of senators, extending suffrage to women, and banning the manufacture and sale of alcoholic beverages. By 1917, however, the attention of most Americans was turning from domestic reform to world affairs.

Chapter Review

For Further Thought

1. Explain how President Taft's actions in each of the following cases alienated the progressives: (a) Payne-Aldrich Tariff; (b) attempt to weaken power of Joseph Cannon; (c) Ballinger-Pinchot controversy.

2. In what ways did Taft continue progressive reform? Give specific examples.

3. (a) Why did Theodore Roosevelt decide to become involved in politics again in 1910? (b) What program did he propose? (c) What impact did his actions have on the Republican party?

4. (a) Why was the Progressive party founded? (b) What reform measures did the party platform call for?

5. (a) Why did President Wilson favor a reduction of tariffs? (b) What groups opposed such a reduction? Why? (c) What did the final tariff bill achieve?

6. (a) Why did many Americans believe that the banking system of the early 1900s needed to be reformed? (b) Describe the system established by the Federal Reserve Act. (c) How could the Federal Reserve Board control the amount of money in circulation?

7. (a) What two major pieces of legislation to control monopolies did President Wilson support? (b) Describe the major provisions of each.

8. (a) Why did Woodrow Wilson hesitate to promote social legislation? (b) What social reform measures were eventually passed during his administration? (c) What group was especially disappointed by Wilson?

9. (a) What four amendments to the Constitution were ratified between 1913 and 1920? (b) Describe the content of each.

10. (a) Why did the progressives support an income tax? (b) Why were many Americans opposed to an income tax?

1. Although the national political system has been dominated by two parties, other parties, like the Populists, have influenced the course of United States history. However, no third party had ever been as successful in a presidential race as the Progressive party in 1912. How might you explain that success?

2. Reform-minded women had demanded the right to vote since the 1840s, but they did not win suffrage until 1920. What developments between 1850 and 1920 do you think contributed to the eventual success of the women's suffrage movement?

3. Compare Wilson's New Freedom and Roosevelt's New Nationalism. Which of the two do you think was a better way to approach the giant trusts?

Developing Basic Skills

1. *Analyzing* Read the text of the Sixteenth, Seventeenth, Eighteenth, and Nineteenth amendments on pages 808–809. Then answer the following questions: (a) Which amendment or amendments changed part of the original Constitution? (b) Which constitutional clause or clauses were altered? (c) Which amendment was eventually repealed? Why do you think this was the case?

2. *Comparing* Make a chart with three columns. In column 1 list the actions of President Roosevelt that reflected progressive goals. (See Chapter 25.) In column 2 list the actions of President Taft that reflected progressive goals. In column 3 list the actions of President Wilson that reflected progressive goals. Based on your analysis, which President do you think best represented the progressive era?

See page 777 for suggested readings.

The United States in World Affairs

27

(1900–1916)

Detail from Across the Canal at Culebra, by Jonas Lie.

Chapter Outline

1 *The Growth of American Power Abroad*

2 *The Panama Canal*

3 *The United States and Asia*

4 *Woodrow Wilson and Moral Diplomacy*

By 1900 the United States had become an important actor in international affairs. American-held foreign territory included the Philippines, the Hawaiian Islands, Puerto Rico, and Guam. In addition, the United States exercised a protectorate over Cuba and was involved in the affairs of China. As the twentieth century dawned, Americans were beginning to realize that their nation had a vital role in world affairs.

In contrast to the nations of Europe, the United States had little experience in the complicated art of international diplomacy. It had asserted its power in Latin America under the provisions of the Monroe Doctrine, but challenging the power of Great Britain, France, Germany, Japan, and Russia would test American leaders.

Theodore Roosevelt gladly accepted the test. He wanted the United States to exercise authority in Latin America and Asia. The construction of the Panama Canal was symbolic of his efforts. Roosevelt's successors, William Howard Taft and Woodrow Wilson, based their actions on different theories, but they continued to pursue an active foreign policy.

1 The Growth of American Power Abroad

As President, Theodore Roosevelt pushed for greater American involvement in world affairs. He established policies that continued throughout the progressive era. Indeed, echoes of Roosevelt's foreign policy would be heard throughout most of the twentieth century. Roosevelt actively promoted commerce abroad. He championed the Monroe Doctrine and stood ready to meet any challenge to the national interest. He expressed his faith in action in 1900 when he said, "I have always been fond of the West African proverb, 'speak softly and carry a big stick, you will go far.'"

Advancing American Commerce

Americans needed new markets where they could sell their industrial and agricultural products, which were pouring forth in quantities never before seen anywhere in the world. The people of the United States lived in a country of extraordinary mineral wealth and vast fertile farmland. Those natural endowments, coupled with a great talent for inventing labor-saving machines and organizing businesses to produce on a grand scale, had given the United States the potential to become the richest nation on earth.

To realize this potential, businesses in the United States needed to be able to buy and sell goods abroad. President Roosevelt encouraged companies to sign contracts with buyers in Europe and Asia. To insure that American business would be able to compete successfully in the struggle for world markets and to safeguard national interests, the President prodded the navy to add new steam-powered warships to its growing fleet. United States merchant ships would be protected by modern, well-equipped naval vessels.

Policing the Western Hemisphere

Roosevelt's "big stick" policy expressed a view, held by many Americans, that it was the "mission" of "superior" countries such as the United States to carry out the "most regrettable but necessary international police duty which must be performed for the sake of the welfare of mankind." In 1902,

when British, German, and Italian warships blockaded Venezuela and fired on one of its seaports, the United States took the opportunity to initiate this "international police duty."

The situation in Venezuela was typical of that in a number of Latin American countries at the turn of the century. After overthrowing Spanish rule, Venezuela had been unable to establish a stable system of government. In an effort to advance their own interests, Great Britain, Germany, and Italy had loaned money to Venezuela. When the Venezuelans failed to repay the loan, the European powers decided to use force.

Venezuela asked the United States to intervene and settle the dispute. Germany and Great Britain in turn requested that President Roosevelt himself serve as mediator. Roosevelt accepted eagerly.

During the discussions, a German ship fired on a Venezuelan village. Roosevelt warned the Germans that he would not hesitate to use force to prevent them from seizing territory in Venezuela or anywhere else in the Caribbean. Roosevelt proposed that the issue be taken to the Permanent Court of Arbitration at The Hague in the Netherlands. Despite initial German opposition to the suggestion, the case was eventually decided at The Hague.

The Venezuelan incident was of great significance to the United States. It reinforced the Monroe Doctrine, since Great Britain, Germany, and Italy had followed the wishes of the United States. Interpreting the incident as a sign of the danger that could result from European intervention in the Western Hemisphere, Roosevelt began to formulate a new policy for the Caribbean.

Action in the Dominican Republic

The United States faced another problem in the Caribbean in 1903. Like Venezuela, the Dominican Republic had fallen into debt to European financiers. President Roosevelt was reluctant to get involved because, as he told Secretary of War Elihu Root, "If we intend to say 'Hands Off' to the powers of Europe, sooner or later we must keep order ourselves."

Nevertheless, Roosevelt believed that the Dominican Republic should honor its financial obligations. He also believed that the European powers would intervene if the United States did not. Still, the President claimed he had no plans to take on the Dominican Republic as a colony. "I have about the same desire to annex it as a gorged boa constrictor might have to swallow a porcupine wrong end to," he remarked.

In 1905 Roosevelt persuaded Dominican officials to submit to United States control of their national finances. Forty-five percent of Dominican customs revenues would be returned to the Dominican government for internal expenses. Fifty-five percent would go toward paying the foreign debts.

Roosevelt submitted his agreement to the Senate for ratification as a treaty. But the Senate was opposed to United States supervision of Dominican debts and refused to ratify the treaty. Roosevelt then signed an executive order, which did not require Senate approval, and put his financial plan into action.

The Roosevelt Corollary to the Monroe Doctrine

In December 1904 Roosevelt took advantage of the Dominican situation to announce a new Latin American policy known as the Roosevelt Corollary to the Monroe Doctrine. The President asserted the right of the United States to exercise "international police power" in Latin America.

The use of power by the United States had taken a new turn. Whereas the Monroe Doctrine had been designed to prevent European intervention in the Americas, the Roosevelt Corollary justified intervention by the United States. Countries such as Argentina, Brazil, and Chile, all strong enough to

Like many Americans of his time, Roosevelt believed that United States officials had a moral duty to act as "international police" for less-developed areas of the world. Would you say that the cartoonist of this 1905 cartoon agreed or disagreed with Roosevelt? For answer, see p. A 84.

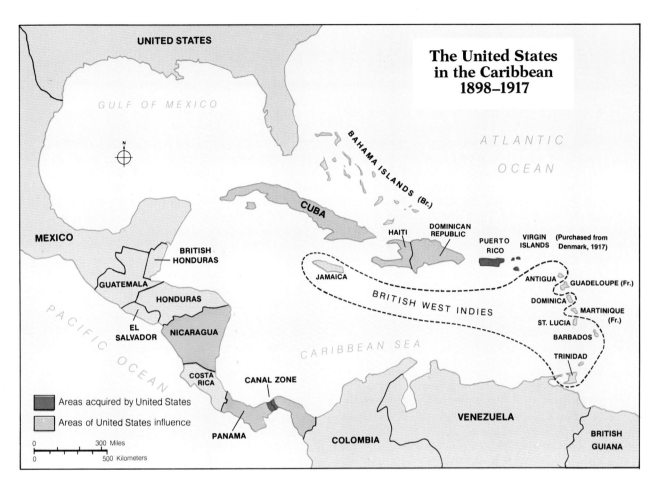

**The United States
in the Caribbean
1898–1917**

UNITED STATES

GULF OF MEXICO

ATLANTIC
OCEAN

BAHAMA ISLANDS (Br.)

CUBA

MEXICO

HAITI
DOMINICAN
REPUBLIC

PUERTO
RICO

VIRGIN
ISLANDS

(Purchased from
Denmark, 1917)

BRITISH
HONDURAS

JAMAICA

ANTIGUA
GUADELOUPE (Fr.)

GUATEMALA

HONDURAS

BRITISH WEST INDIES

DOMINICA

MARTINIQUE
(Fr.)

EL
SALVADOR

NICARAGUA

ST. LUCIA

BARBADOS

CARIBBEAN SEA

TRINIDAD

PACIFIC OCEAN

COSTA
RICA

CANAL ZONE

Areas acquired by United States

Areas of United States influence

VENEZUELA

BRITISH
GUIANA

0   300 Miles
0   500 Kilometers

PANAMA

COLOMBIA

■ *In 1904 Theodore Roosevelt asserted that the United States had the right to exercise
"international police power" over the neighboring Caribbean area. By 1917 the United
States controlled several areas, including Puerto Rico, part of the Virgin Islands, and the
Panama Canal Zone. The map also shows other areas of United States influence.*

take care of their own affairs, did not face intervention, but weaker nations did.

In 1906 a rebellion broke out in Cuba. Roosevelt sent Secretary of War William Howard Taft to stop the fighting and set up a new temporary government. Backed by 5,000 troops, American civilians governed Cuba for 28 months. Yet, Roosevelt said, "The United States wishes nothing of the Cubans save that they shall be able to preserve order among themselves and therefore to preserve their independence." When order returned, the Americans withdrew.

President Taft later used the Roosevelt Corollary to justify American intervention in Nicaragua and Honduras. Taft sent troops to impose civil order and used United States funds to pay debts owed European investors. He then forced the Nicaraguans and Hondurans to repay the United States. De-

spite claims by Roosevelt, and later by Taft, that United States intervention was in response to concern over European intentions, distrust of the United States grew steadily in Latin America.

For answers, see p. A 84.

Section Review

1. Identify the following: Roosevelt Corollary.

2. What role did the United States Navy play in American trade abroad?

3. (a) How did President Roosevelt help resolve the 1902 Venezuelan crisis? (b) What action did he take in the Dominican Republic in 1905?

4. How did the Roosevelt Corollary change the meaning of the original Monroe Doctrine?

5. How did the United States react to the 1906 rebellion in Cuba?

2 The Panama Canal

Ever since 1513 when Balboa sighted the Pacific Ocean from a mountain peak in Panama, Europeans and Americans had recognized the importance of the narrow strip of land, or isthmus, separating the Atlantic and Pacific oceans. American merchants and admirals alike yearned for a canal to be built across the Isthmus of Panama. By avoiding the trip around South America, ships could shorten the journey from New York to San Francisco by more than 7,500 miles (about 12,000 kilometers). A canal would reduce the cost of shipping and enable the United States to avoid the heavy expense of maintaining separate navies in the Atlantic and Pacific oceans.

Early Plans

As early as 1850, under the terms of the Clayton-Bulwer Treaty, the United States and Great Britain had agreed to joint control of a future canal in Panama or Nicaragua. Later the French made a separate agreement with Colombia, which controlled Panama. In 1882 a French company led by engineer Ferdinand de Lesseps began digging a canal in Panama. After eight years, however, de Lesseps gave up. His company lacked money and adequate tools, and many of his workers had died of tropical diseases.

In 1898 the Spanish-American War rekindled American interest in building a canal. The battleship *Oregon* had to steam from San Francisco all the way around South America to the fighting in Cuba. Congress then saw the strategic importance of an interocean canal, but the Clayton-Bulwer Treaty limited American ability to act.

"I Took the Canal Zone"

In 1901 President Roosevelt negotiated a new agreement with Great Britain, the Hay-Pauncefote Treaty. It gave the United States the sole right to build, operate, and fortify a canal across Panama or Nicaragua. A commission of experts recommended the Panama route. Congress authorized the President to negotiate with Colombia the purchase of the land for the canal.

When Colombia rejected the President's offer and demanded more money for the right to build, Roosevelt took his fight to the press. He called the Colombians "inefficient bandits" and the "blackmailers of Bogota." His comments encouraged Panamanian nationalists, who had revolted against Colombia 53 times in 57 years, according to Roosevelt's count.

From their rooms in the Waldorf-Astoria Hotel in New York City, a group of Panamanian conspirators plotted another revolt, with United States knowledge. The leader of the plot, a French citizen named Philippe Bunau-Varilla (byoo NOH vah REEL yah) met with Secretary of State John Hay and President Roosevelt. Roosevelt made no specific promises, but Bunau-Varilla left the meeting with the impression that the United States would not help Colombia suppress the Panamanian rebels and might even support the rebellion.

Not by coincidence, a United States warship, the USS *Nashville*, steamed into port in Panama on November 2, 1903. The Panamanians revolted the following day. United States troops blocked the advance of the Colombian army, and on November 3 Panama declared independence from Colombia. The United States officially recognized the new nation two days later.

Less than two weeks after that, the Panamanian government granted the United States a larger canal zone than the Colombians had proposed but on the same terms. Years later Roosevelt bragged, "I took the Canal Zone and let Congress debate."

Digging the Big Ditch

With the Canal Zone in hand, the United States set about completing the task undertaken by de Lesseps some 20 years earlier. British author James Bryce called the building of the Panama Canal "the greatest liberty Man has ever taken with Nature."

The operation began in 1904, when Colonel William C. Gorgas attacked the problem of disease in the isthmus. Gorgas, a physician, had wiped out yellow fever in Cuba after the Spanish-American War. Now he would try to destroy the mosquitoes that spread yellow fever and malaria and the rats that carried bubonic plague. Gorgas and his workers drained swamps, cut down brush, and destroyed grassy marshes where the mosquitoes bred. By 1906 his work was almost complete.

Roosevelt placed Colonel George W. Goethals, an army engineer, in charge of construction. In seven years, a work force of 43,400, including laborers from the West Indies, Italy, and Spain and clerical and construction workers from the United States, removed 211 million cubic yards (278 million cubic meters) of earth before finishing the "big ditch." Crews dug the Gaillard Cut, dammed the Chagres River to form Gatun Lake, and constructed three pairs of locks to lift and lower ships from one water level to another.

On August 5, 1914, the passenger-cargo ship SS *Ancon* made the first complete trip through the canal. The words on the official seal of the Canal Zone had at last come true: "The Land Divided, the World United." On July 12, 1915, President Woodrow Wilson formally proclaimed the opening of the Panama Canal. At a cost of thousands of lives and $400 million, the United States had provided its navy with easy access between the Atlantic and Pacific. As an emerging world power, the nation now had greater ability to extend its influence in Asia.

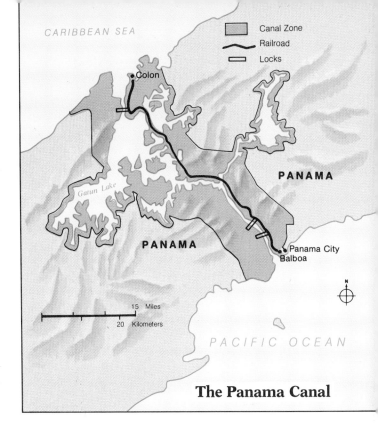

The Panama Canal

■ *Carving a canal through the dense jungles of Panama took about ten years and the work of about 43,000 laborers. A series of locks raised and lowered water levels for ships moving through the canal. The opening of the canal not only enabled shipping to move quickly from ocean to ocean, it also allowed the United States Navy to move more speedily between the Atlantic and the Pacific.*

491

Technological advances in medicine and industry made the building of the Panama Canal possible. Yellow fever had to be controlled, and swamps had to be drained. This photograph, taken at the Culebra Cut, shows the extent of the earth-moving task and the type of machinery used to accomplish it.

For answers, see p. A 84.

Section Review

1. Identify the following: Clayton-Bulwer Treaty, Hay-Pauncefote Treaty, Philippe Bunau-Varilla.

2. List two advantages to the United States of a canal across the Isthmus of Panama?

3. How did the Colombian government react to the United States offer to buy land for a canal?

4. What was the United States response to the revolt in Panama?

5. How did Colonel William C. Gorgas prepare the way for the digging of the Panama Canal?

3 The United States and Asia

President Roosevelt, like President McKinley before him, was not interested solely in Latin America and islands in the Pacific. He too looked beyond Hawaii and the Philippines to Asia. So did American businesses looking for markets and outlets for investment.

United States Interests in China

President Roosevelt did not think the United States had any vital interests in China, but he knew that the country had been previously involved there and might become so again. For example, John D. Rockefeller's Standard Oil Company had made huge investments in China, and the American China Development Company had engaged in railroad construction there. Roosevelt thus championed the Open Door policy, begun under President McKinley. (See page 452.) He believed that no nation seeking investment opportunities in China should be shut out.

Roosevelt hoped that competition between Japan and Russia for influence in China would keep China free of Russian domination. In that case, he thought, American businesses would be free to pursue their interests in China without direct involvement by the United States government. The rivalry between Japan and Russia, however, soon erupted into war.

■ Many foreign powers claimed territory in Asia. The map below shows the territorial possessions of Britain, France, the Netherlands, the United States, and Japan. In addition, several countries controlled trade in their "spheres of influence" in China.

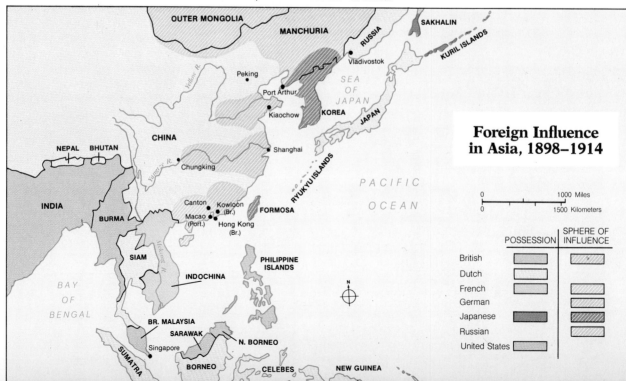

Foreign Influence in Asia, 1898–1914

In 1905 war between Russia and Japan flared over the control of the Chinese province of Manchuria. The personal intervention of President Theodore Roosevelt helped produce a peace treaty between the warring nations. This 1918 Japanese lithograph shows a Russian city in Manchuria.

The Russo-Japanese War

Japan, a densely populated island kingdom with few natural resources, needed raw materials to fuel its growing industry. Nearby Manchuria, in northern China, seemed the best source. However, Russia wanted to exclude Japan from China and seal off Manchuria for itself. Great Britain, long the most powerful European nation trading in Asia, attempted to maintain stability in China. In 1902 Britain signed a secret treaty with Japan, agreeing to cooperate in restricting Russian expansion into Manchuria.

For more than a year tensions between Russia and Japan ran high. Then, in February 1904, Japan launched a surprise torpedo attack on the Russian fleet anchored at Port Arthur in Manchuria. The Japanese followed their initial success with more victories. But by the spring of 1905, both nations were exhausted from the fighting and eager to make peace.

President Roosevelt invited Russia and Japan to send representatives to a peace conference at Portsmouth, New Hampshire. There, largely through Roosevelt's diplomatic efforts, the two nations worked out an agreement that ended the war.

The Treaty of Portsmouth, signed in September 1905, recognized the Japanese victory, the first for an Asian nation over a European power. Japan was awarded Port Arthur, the southern half of Sakhalin Island, control of the Manchurian railroads, and, in effect, control of Korea. In turn, Japan gave up its demand that Russia pay for war damages. Manchuria remained part of China.

To satisfy United States interests, Japan and Russia pledged that China would be kept open to trade with all nations. Through the Treaty of Portsmouth, the United States maintained the Open Door in China. Never before had an American president played a central role in an international crisis. Roosevelt won the Nobel Peace Prize for his efforts.

Japanese-American Relations

Roosevelt's efforts at Portsmouth impressed Europeans and Americans alike but won the friendship of neither the Russians nor the Japanese. The Russians blamed Roosevelt for their losses in the Treaty of Portsmouth. The Japanese still wanted Manchurian raw materials, and they feared that fewer of those resources would flow into Japanese factories as more nations took advantage of the Open Door policy.

Faced with these tensions, Roosevelt sent Secretary of War Taft to Japan. Taft exchanged full recognition of Japanese control over Korea for a pledge by the Japanese to leave the Philippine Islands under United States control.

Shortly after the Korea-Philippine agreement had been reached, agitation against Japanese immigrants flared up on the west coast of the United States. Many Americans resented the Asian newcomers because they competed for jobs and seemed so different. In 1906 the San Francisco Board of Education placed all Asian pupils in a special school. Japan sent a formal protest to the United States government, and Roosevelt intervened to soften what the Japanese regarded as a racial insult.

The President denounced the San Francisco school board action as a "wicked absurdity." He offered to bring the entire board to Washington to discuss the matter. A delegation of eight board members visited the White House and reached a compromise. The school board returned the Japanese children to their regular schools, and Roosevelt took steps to restrict further Japanese immigration.

During this crisis, nationalists on both sides of the Pacific called for war. Although the President had no intention of using military force, he wanted to make sure that no one interpreted his actions as a sign of weakness. Consequently, in 1907, Roosevelt undertook a dramatic demonstration of military strength.

The President sent the entire United States battle fleet on a cruise around the world. Congress objected to the expense of the voyage and questioned its value, but the fleet sailed on. When the Great White Fleet, as it was known, entered Japanese waters, leaders there were duly impressed by the second-largest navy in the world. Only the British had a larger fleet. Welcoming parties for the Americans seemed to be a sign of improved Japanese-American relations.

By the time the fleet returned to the United States in 1909, Secretary of State Elihu Root and Japanese Ambassador Takahira (tah kah HEE rah) signed a pledge settling most of the differences between the two countries. Both nations agreed to preserve stability in the Pacific, mutually respect territorial claims, maintain the Open Door in China, and use peaceful methods to protect Chinese independence.

Dollar Diplomacy in Asia

In 1909 William Howard Taft succeeded Roosevelt as President. He decided to modify Roosevelt's foreign policy by "substituting dollars for bullets." Taft tried to avoid military confrontations to further United States interests in Asia. Instead, he encouraged financial investments in China in the hope that an economic presence would "give the voice of the United States more authority in that country." President Taft was interested in commercial ventures that would advance United States foreign policy.

Taft's "dollar diplomacy" had little impact on Asian affairs, however. The United States did not make investments large enough to tip the balance of power there, and Taft would not resort to military intervention. Dollar diplomacy, however, did play a larger role in Latin America.

For answers, see p. A 85.

Section Review

1. Identify the following: Treaty of Portsmouth, "dollar diplomacy."
2. (a) What did Japan hope to find in Manchuria? (b) What was the Russian attitude toward Manchuria?
3. How did President Theodore Roosevelt help end the Russo-Japanese War?
4. What development in California led to increased friction between Japan and the United States?
5. How did President Taft hope to promote United States interests in Asia?

4 Woodrow Wilson and Moral Diplomacy

Woodrow Wilson, who was elected President in 1912, had little interest in world diplomacy. "It would be the irony of fate if my administration had to deal chiefly with foreign affairs," he remarked to a friend upon taking office. An unstable world order, indeed, forced Wilson to devote much of his energy to foreign affairs.

Instead of continuing the policies of Roosevelt and Taft, Wilson and his secretary of state, William Jennings Bryan, believed in a "moral diplomacy." They were determined to use negotiation and arbitration in dealings with other nations. They hoped that colonial empires would be replaced by independent nations with democratic governments. Stating that "the force of America is the force of moral principle," Wilson set out with missionary zeal to promote democracy, maintain the peace, and secure American economic interests abroad.

Moral Diplomacy in Action

In 1913 and 1914 Secretary of State Bryan set in motion a plan for achieving world peace through a series of "cooling-off" treaties. Under the terms of the treaties, 29 countries agreed to submit international disputes to a permanent international committee for investigation and arbitration. While the committee made its inquiry, the nations agreed to refrain from acts of war and from building up arms for a one-year period.

Bryan and humanitarian groups hailed the treaties as a great stride toward world peace. But Theodore Roosevelt and other proponents of military strength believed they were unenforceable and therefore meaningless.

In Asia Wilson pursued the policy of moral diplomacy by terminating United States participation in a China railway consortium organized by President Taft. A group of British, French, German, American, and later Russian and Japanese bankers had been formed to lend $125 million to China for construction of the Hukuang (hoo KWAHNG) Railroad. Sensing the threat to Chinese independence, President Wilson ordered United States bankers to withdraw.

Some suspected Wilson of ordering the bankers out for fear that Japan and Russia would dominate the consortium. Wilson's supporters endorsed the decision for preserving the Open Door policy, winning Chinese good will, and rejecting dollar diplomacy.

Moral Diplomacy Falters

Relations with Japan, in contrast, posed a number of problems for the concept of "moral diplomacy." In California, legislators seeking favor with local agriculture and labor groups had enacted a law prohibiting noncitizens from owning land in the state. Japanese immigrants were most specifically affected by the law, and they filed an angry protest in Washington.

President Wilson played down the issue and ignored the racist overtones of the California law. He thus failed to enforce national treaty obligations to treat Japanese immigrants fairly. Only after public outrage in Japan had risen to fever pitch did the President act. He dispatched the secretary of state to California, but Bryan could not persuade the state legislature and governor to discontinue their policy.

Japanese-American relations worsened in 1915. While the European powers were preoccupied with the war that had broken out in 1914, Japan presented 21 demands to China. In effect, by agreeing to the demands, China would become a Japanese protectorate. The United States objected to such a violation of the Open Door policy, however, and Japan eased its pressure on China, at least for the moment.

Reversals in Latin America

Although President Taft had not been able to make dollar diplomacy work in Asia, he was able to apply it more freely in Latin America. There, the United States faced little competition from the European nations that had long-standing interest in Asia.

Concern for the security of the Panama Canal undermined Woodrow Wilson's wish to abandon Taft's dollar diplomacy and promote democratic government in Latin America. Wilson and Bryan reasoned that to make the canal secure, the United States should encourage friendly relations with nearby countries. However, the instability of many of those countries frustrated such plans.

The outgoing Taft administration had drafted a treaty giving the United States a permanent option to build a second canal across Nicaragua. For this and other privileges, the United States was to pay Nicaragua the small sum of $3 million. Forsaking moral principles, Bryan not only supported the treaty but added a new provision authorizing the United States to intervene in Nicaraguan internal affairs.

In the Dominican Republic, Bryan began with moral principle. But when peaceful methods failed to end a civil war there, Wilson sent in the United States Marines. In 1916 the marines began a full-scale military occupation of Santo Domingo, the capital.

Events in Haiti turned out no better. In 1915 a series of revolutions and assassinations of high government officials rocked the country. In July 1915 United States Marines landed to restore order and to protect United States property and banking interests. The marines' efforts at "pacification" met with such stiff resistance from Haitian soldiers that a bloody war followed. To end the bloodshed the Haitian government signed a treaty in September establishing a United States protectorate over Haiti.

Although Wilson had hoped to aid the Latin American nations and prepare them for democracy, he failed. Instead, he created an "American lake" in the Caribbean and inspired hatred rather than friendship.

Civil War in Mexico

The United States maintained an interest in the affairs of all of Latin America, but interest in Mexico was especially strong. The two nations shared a common border, and the states of California, Arizona, Texas, and New Mexico had close cultural ties with Mexico dating back to Spanish settlement of the region some 400 years before. Yet political unrest in Mexico finally led Wilson to substitute military power for moral diplomacy.

In 1911 the dictatorial government of Mexico was overthrown. Two years later General Victoriano Huerta (WEHR tah) seized power from the new revolutionary government. A group led by Venustiano Carranza (kahr RAHN zah) opposed the Huerta regime. A bloody civil war raged in Mexico, and for a time Wilson adopted an attitude of "watchful waiting." He hoped that Mexico would adopt a constitutional government serving the needs of all Mexicans and that the new government would be friendly to the United States.

However, the civil war dragged on, and Huerta proclaimed himself military dictator of Mexico. First Wilson banned arms shipments to Mexico. Then he offered to mediate the dispute between Carranza and Huerta. Somewhat indiscreetly, he even offered to support the Carranza faction if it would guarantee the orderly establishment of constitutional government. Carranza refused.

In April 1914 Mexican soldiers in Tampico, Mexico, arrested members of the crew of the USS *Dolphin*. Although the sailors were promptly released with an apology, Wilson used the incident to push for United States entry into Mexican internal affairs.

Without waiting for congressional approval, the President ordered the navy to capture the port of Vera Cruz before a German ship could land a cargo of arms for Huerta's forces. The Mexicans resisted, and in the battle that followed, 126 "Huertistas" and 19 Americans died. The minor importance of the *Dolphin* arrests, contrasted with the severity of Wilson's reaction, brought outcries of horror from Huerta, his rival Carranza, and newspaper editors throughout the world.

Wilson and Bryan averted war by allowing Argentina, Brazil, and Chile to mediate the crisis. At a conference in Niagara Falls, New York, Carranza's delegation again resisted Wilson's attempt to direct the outcome of the Mexican struggle. In July 1914, a month before World War I began in Europe, Huerta accepted defeat. In August, Carranza took over the government in Mexico City.

United States Involvement

The dispute might have ended had not Francisco "Pancho" Villa (VEE yah), a Mexican revolutionary, led a revolt against Carranza. In October 1915 the United States recognized the Carranza government. Villa, in retaliation, began a series of anti-American raids. In January 1916 he removed 17 United States citizens from a train in Mexico and had them shot. In March, Villa and his band crossed the Rio Grande and set fires in Columbus, New Mexico, killing 19 Americans.

The Carranza government agreed to permit United States soldiers to enter Mexico to

Major Events	
1901	Hay-Pauncefote Treaty
1902	Venezuelan crisis
1903	Panama declares independence and grants canal zone to United States
1904	Construction of Panama Canal begins; Roosevelt Corollary to Monroe Doctrine issued
1905	United States supervises finances of Dominican Republic; Russo-Japanese War; Treaty of Portsmouth
1906	United States troops restore order in Cuba
1908	William Howard Taft elected President
1911	Mexican Revolution begins
1912	Woodrow Wilson elected President
1914	United States Navy captures Mexican port of Vera Cruz; Panama Canal opened to traffic
1915	United States Marines sent to Haiti
1916	United States troops enter Mexico to search for Pancho Villa; United States Marines sent to Dominican Republic

Pancho Villa's raids into the United States provoked a strong reaction in 1916. United States cavalry troops under General John Pershing pursued Villa and his followers for hundreds of miles across Mexico.

pursue Villa. The Wilson government organized a punitive expedition under Brigadier General John Pershing to capture Villa dead or alive. Far exceeding the spirit of the agreement, 6,000 troops pursued Villa over 300 miles (480 kilometers) into Mexico.

In April 1916 Carranza demanded an end to the United States "invasion." Wilson refused to recall the troops. Villa fueled growing war fever in the United States when he suddenly swung north to attack Glen Springs, Texas. Casualties on both sides and the capture of American troops posed a serious threat to peace.

Neither Carranza nor Wilson wanted war, however. Carranza had pressing domestic problems to deal with, and the war in Europe occupied the attention of Wilson. In July 1916 a joint commission was convened to resolve matters, and early the following year Wilson ordered American troops out of Mexico.

As the United States withdrew from Mexico, Americans turned their attention to the war that had begun in Europe in 1914.

They realized that their nation had undergone remarkable changes since 1898. United States troops and ships were stationed in Asia and Latin America. American business interests spanned the globe. The United States still sought peace, but it had become too much a part of the world community to ignore the outbreak of war in Europe.

For answers, see p. A 85.

Section Review

1. Identify the following: "moral diplomacy," Victoriano Huerta, Venustiano Carranza, Francisco "Pancho" Villa, John Pershing.

2. What was the purpose of the "cooling-off" treaties that Secretary of State Bryan negotiated in 1913 and 1914?

3. In which two Latin American countries did Bryan and Wilson resort to the use of troops during 1915 and 1916?

4. (a) How did the United States and Mexico avoid war in 1914? (b) What incidents led to American intervention in Mexico in 1916?

★ ★

IN PERSPECTIVE   The Spanish-American War marked the entrance of the United States onto the world stage. In the decades that followed, the nation took an increasingly active role in world affairs. President Theodore Roosevelt believed that the country had an international police duty, which he tried to carry out in Venezuela, the Dominican Republic, and Cuba. Roosevelt's assertion that the United States had a right to intervene in Latin America became known as the Roosevelt Corollary to the Monroe Doctrine. One benefit of the growing influence of the United States in Latin America was construction of the Panama Canal, which began under Roosevelt and was completed under Woodrow Wilson.

The United States had a less direct interest in Asia during the early twentieth century, but Roosevelt maintained the Open Door policy by helping negotiate an end to the Russo-Japanese War. Discrimination against Japanese immigrants in California disrupted relations between the United States and Japan under Roosevelt and Wilson, but both Presidents were able to preserve peace in the Pacific.

Woodrow Wilson and his secretary of state, William Jennings Bryan, brought moral zeal to American foreign policy. They wanted to maintain world peace and encourage the establishment of democratic governments for all people. Wilson also became involved in the affairs of Latin American nations. Soon the United States would look beyond the Western Hemisphere as a major war raged in Europe.

For answers, see p. A 85.

For answers, see p. A 86.

Chapter Review

For Further Thought

1. (a) Why did President Theodore Roosevelt believe the United States had an international police duty? (b) How did he perform that "duty" in Venezuela? (c) How did he perform that "duty" in the Dominican Republic?

2. (a) What was the Roosevelt Corollary to the Monroe Doctrine? (b) How did Roosevelt apply his corollary in Cuba? (c) How did Taft apply it in Nicaragua and Honduras?

3. (a) Why did the United States want to construct a canal across the Isthmus of Panama? (b) What steps did Theodore Roosevelt take to gain control of the canal zone for the United States? (c) How did the Panamanian revolt lead to United States control of the canal zone?

4. (a) What problems did the United States have to solve before work on the Panama Canal could begin? (b) How were these problems solved?

5. (a) Why did Russia and Japan go to war in 1905? (b) What was the outcome of the war? (c) What role did the United States play in ending the conflict? (d) What did the United States gain as a result of the peace treaty?

6. (a) Why were United States relations with Russia and Japan strained after the Russo-Japanese War? (b) What did President Roosevelt do in order to ease tensions with Japan? (c) What domestic events created more strains in United States-Japanese relations? (d) What was Roosevelt's reaction?

7. (a) What is the meaning of the term "dollar diplomacy"? (b) Was this policy successful in Asia? (c) Where was President Taft able to use it?

8. (a) What were the goals of Woodrow Wilson's "moral diplomacy"? (b) What steps did Wilson and Secretary of State Bryan take to put this diplomacy into action? (c) How did the policy falter in Japan?

9. (a) In what three Latin American countries were Wilson and Bryan unable to carry out their "moral diplomacy"? (b) What action did they take in each case?

10. (a) What was the purpose of Woodrow Wilson's "watchful waiting" in the Mexican civil war? (b) How did Wilson try to influence the outcome of that war? (c) Why did the United States send troops into Mexico in 1916?

1. American foreign policy went through three phases between 1900 and 1916: Roosevelt's "big stick," Taft's "dollar diplomacy," and Wilson's "moral diplomacy." (a) How did the *theory* behind each phase differ? (b) Based on what you learned in this chapter, do you think the policies differed in *action*? Explain. (c) Which foreign policy do you think was most appropriate in the early 1900s? Why? (d) How would you compare the government's foreign policy today with the foreign policies of the early 1900s?

2. Domestic events and foreign affairs have often influenced one another in United States history. Describe one example of this between 1900 and 1916.

3. Do you think the actions of the United States in world affairs between 1898 and 1916 are evidence that the nation had become a major world power? Why or why not?

4. When Woodrow Wilson took office in 1912, he remarked, "It would be the irony of fate if my administration had to deal chiefly with foreign affairs." (a) What did Wilson probably mean by that statement? (b) What issues do you think Wilson would rather have dealt with?

Developing Basic Skills

For answers, see p. A 86.

1. *Placing Events in Time* Review Chapter 24 and what you have read in this chapter. Then construct a time line of United States actions in world affairs from 1860 to 1916. When you have completed your time line, answer the following questions: (a) In which decades was there little activity? (b) In which decades did the United States acquire new territory? (c) In which decades did the United States intervene militarily in other nations? (d) What evidence can you find of growing United States power in the world?

2. *Map Reading* Study the map about foreign influence in Asia on page 492. Then answer the following questions: (a) Which nations claimed spheres of influence in China? (b) Which nations claimed territory in Asia? (c) What territory did the United States claim? (d) Based on the map, where might you expect conflict to occur?

See page 777 for suggested readings.

28

The World at War

(1914–1919)

Machine Gunner, *by Harvey Dunn.*

Europe had not experienced a major war since 1815, so Americans were shocked in the summer of 1914 when war broke out between Germany and Austria-Hungary on one side and Great Britain, France, and Russia on the other. "This dreadful conflict of the nations came to most of us as lightning out of a clear sky," Robert Page wrote his brother Walter, the American ambassador in London. "The horror of it all kept me awake for weeks, nor has the awfulness of it all deserted me."

Americans had reason to be horrified. This war was like no other. Modern technology had greatly enhanced the capacity of human beings to slaughter one another. Poison gasses, submarines, tanks, airplanes, machine guns, and long-range artillery were all part of modern arsenals. In 1915 alone—as Americans watched with increasing disbelief—France suffered 1.3 million casualties, Britain 313,000, and Germany 848,000. "We were not used to smelling blood from vast human slaughterhouses," wrote the despairing reformer William Allen White.

What would be the role of the United States as this tragedy unfolded? "Be ready," Walter Page wrote President Wilson from London, "for you will be called upon to compose their huge quarrel. I thank heaven for many things—first the Atlantic Ocean." Many Americans shared Page's hope that the broad Atlantic would keep the flames of war from their shores. Yet their hopes were in vain.

1 War in Europe

On June 28, 1914, in Bosnia, a province of Austria-Hungary, a young nationalist assassinated Archduke Francis Ferdinand of Austria. The young man belonged to a group that wanted to unite Bosnia with the independent nation of Serbia, now part of Yugoslavia. Few people expected a world war to result from this act.

War Begins

By 1914 the major powers of Europe had arranged themselves in competing alliances. On one side was the Triple Alliance of Austria-Hungary, Germany, and Italy. On the other side was the Triple Entente (ahn TAHNT) of France, Great Britain, and Russia. This system of alliances helped turn the archduke's assassination into a major war.

Austria-Hungary responded to the assassination by issuing a stiff ultimatum to Serbia. The Austrians claimed that the Serbs were behind the attack. Not satisfied with the Serbian reply and spurred on by Germany, Austria-Hungary declared war on Serbia. Russia, competing with Austria-Hungary for power in southeastern Europe, backed the Serbs and declared war on Germany. Russia's ally France supported this move. Then, on August 1, 1914, Germany declared war on Russia and two days later on France.

The Central Powers, as Austria-Hungary and Germany were called, anticipated a swift and total victory. They planned to march rapidly west to defeat France, then swing east to defeat Russia. The shortest route to France was through Belgium, a neutral nation. Germany requested permission to move troops through Belgium and offered King Albert payment for any resulting damages. The Belgian monarch refused the German request, stating, "Belgium is a nation, not a road."

Nevertheless on August 3, German forces invaded Belgium. The next day Britain, committed to defend Belgium, declared war on Germany. Within weeks Turkey joined the Central Powers, and Japan united with Britain, France, and Russia, which were known as the Allies.

A valiant defense by 200,000 Belgian soldiers failed to stop the Germans but delayed their progress long enough for the Allies to mobilize. The year 1914 ended with the German advance halted in France and a stalemate in the east. On both the eastern and the western battlefronts, opposing armies dug an extensive network of trenches from which enemy lines could be fired on. On both sides thousands of soldiers died to advance just a few yards.

Despite the slaughter early in the war, most European leaders expected quick and easy victories. They had no idea how costly the war would be or how long it would last.

American Neutrality

President Woodrow Wilson and most of his advisers favored the Allies. Wilson considered Germany a "lawless" nation. In

■ *Most European nations participated in the war as either Allied Powers or Central Powers. According to the map, which nations remained neutral?* For answer, see p. A 87.

Europe During the War

Allies
Central Powers
Neutral nations

addition, Germany had posed the greatest threat to United States interests in Latin America. But like most American policymakers, Wilson believed that the Allies could win without United States military involvement. Thus the President adopted a policy of formal neutrality. He urged Americans to be "impartial in thought as well as in action." He wanted the United States to shine as the light of reason in a world gone mad with violence and hate.

However, few Americans could remain calm, much less neutral. The United States was a nation of immigrants with strong emotional ties to the countries of their ancestors. The majority of Americans shared language and ancestry with the British. Traditional friendship with France also drew the United States to the cause of the Allies.

Many Americans, however, favored the Central Powers. Eight million German Americans viewed the war as a defense of German soil against French and Russian aggression. Some 4 million Irish Americans, bearing an ancient antagonism toward the British, generally sided with the Central Powers. Similarly, American Jews, harboring strong anti-Russian sentiments, tended to sympathize with the German cause.

Supporters of both the Central Powers and the Allies used propaganda to try to influence public opinion in the United States. Because most of the major newspapers backed the Allies, supporters of the Central Powers concentrated their efforts in German, Irish, and other immigrant newspapers. They tried to persuade Americans that the Allies had caused the war and that Germany was fighting to save Western Europe from a so-called "Slavic peril."

Allied propaganda probably had a greater impact on American thought. After the invasion of neutral Belgium, the British flooded the United States with stories of German atrocities against Belgian civilians. The Germans were more easily portrayed as aggressors, for most of the fighting was on Allied soil.

German experiments with such new weapons as submarines and poison gas struck Americans as brutal and immoral. Furthermore, many Americans believed that the Allies were fighting to defend civilization. They viewed the Germans as militaristic and authoritarian, believing in total obedience to authority rather than individual freedom.

Economic Impact

American economic ties to the Allies made strict neutrality unlikely. At first, war jolted the United States economy. For example, cotton exports to Germany and Austria stopped completely. But a deluge of war orders from the Allies soon created a boom.

Almost overnight a new munitions industry sprang up. Within three years, the United States sent $1 billion worth of arms and explosives to the Allies. Under the pressure of Allied orders, American steel, copper, oil, grain, and food production increased. Trade with the Allies grew from $500 million in 1914 to $3.5 billion in 1917.

At the same time a British naval blockade disrupted trade with the Central Powers. To make the blockade effective, the British navy mined the North Sea. The British also blocked United States trade with neutral Holland and Denmark and forced American ships into port for inspection. President Wilson protested these actions, but he could do little to make his protest effective.

The British, in turn, tried to soften the impact of the blockade on the United States economy. For example, they prevented a slump in the cotton market by purchasing the cotton that would normally have been sold to Germany. In light of such activities the Germans considered the United States a silent partner of the Allies. Wilson maintained, however, that the United States was not actively pursuing a pro-Ally policy and thus was not violating neutrality.

The Submarine Controversy

Although the American reaction to the British blockade was mild, the German use of a new weapon, the submarine or U-boat provoked outrage. In 1914 and 1915 while the German navy was bottled up in the North Sea by the British blockade, the Germans used submarines to attack Allied ships.

The submarine complicated the question of neutral rights in wartime. International law required that a ship give warning before an attack in order to allow the crew to escape. But submarines were slow on the surface and vulnerable to ramming, so they could not risk surfacing to warn their targets.

Early in 1915 the Germans warned that any ships entering a war zone around Great

Britain risked an attack without warning. However, President Wilson refused to compromise American honor or interrupt trade by declaring the zone off limits to shipping. When Americans began losing their lives in submarine attacks, the American public became incensed.

On March 28, 1915, a German torpedo sank the British liner *Falaba* in the Irish Sea, and one American was drowned. Then, six weeks later, on May 7, a German submarine torpedoed the *Lusitania*, a sleek British passenger ship. Among the 1,200 passengers who died were 128 Americans.

The United States was still officially a neutral nation in 1915 when a German submarine sank the British passenger liner Lusitania. *At bottom the flag-draped body of one of the 128 Americans who died in the attack is carried through the streets of Queenstown, Ireland, where temporary morgues were set up. Below is the front page of the New York* Times *report of the disaster.*

LUSITANIA SUNK BY A SUBMARINE, PROBABLY 1,260 DEAD; TWICE TORPEDOED OFF IRISH COAST; SINKS IN 15 MINUTES; CAPT. TURNER SAVED, FROHMAN AND VANDERBILT MISSING; WASHINGTON BELIEVES THAT A GRAVE CRISIS IS AT HAND

SHOCKS THE PRESIDENT

Washington Deeply Stirred by the Loss of American Lives.

BULLETINS AT WHITE HOUSE

Wilson Reads Them Closely, but Is Silent on the Nation's Course.

HINTS OF CONGRESS CALL

Loss of Lusitania Recalls Firm Tone of Our First Warning to Germany.

CAPITAL FULL OF RUMORS

Reports That Liner Was to be Sunk Were Heard Before Actual News Came.

The Lost Cunard Steamship Lusitania
X Where the First Torpedo Struck.   XX Where the Second Torpedo Struck.

SOME DEAD TAKEN ASHORE

Several Hundred Survivors at Queenstown and Kinsale.

STEWARD TELLS OF DISASTER

One Torpedo Crashes Into the Doomed Liner's Bow, Another Into the Engine Room.

SHIP LISTS OVER TO PORT

Makes It Impossible to Lower Many Boats, So Hundreds Must Have Gone Down.

ATTACKED IN BROAD DAY

Passengers at Luncheon—Warning Had Been Given by Germans Before the Ship Left New York.

Only 658 Were Saved, Few Cabin Passengers

QUEENSTOWN, Saturday, May 8, 4:20 A.M.—Survivors of the Lusitania who have arrived here estimate that only about 658 of

President Wilson demanded that the Germans end submarine attacks on unarmed ships. The Germans eventually apologized, but they continued their attacks. After the French steamer *Sussex* was torpedoed in March 1916, Wilson issued another protest to the Germans. The Germans did not want to push the United States into the war on the side of the Allies, so they agreed to suspend the unannounced submarine attacks.

Peace and the Election of 1916

Submarine warfare and the relationship of the United States to the European powers became a major political issue at home. Former President Theodore Roosevelt attacked President Wilson for his restraint in the face of German provocation and maintained that the United States should prepare the army and navy for a war.

Wilson disliked the prospect of a large standing army in peace time, and he resisted Roosevelt's efforts to marshall public opinion behind a major program of preparedness. Yet he could not ignore the possibility that the United States might become involved in the war. In 1916 the President doubled the size of the regular army and urged the construction of a "navy second to none."

As the presidential election of 1916 approached, however, the nation still seemed to favor peace. The Republicans nominated Charles Evans Hughes for President. Hughes was a respected justice of the Supreme Court and a former reform governor of New York.

Democrats labeled Hughes a "war candidate" in spite of his moderate position on the war. At the same time they portrayed Wilson as the candidate who would keep the nation out of the war. "Wilson and Peace with Honor, or Hughes with Roosevelt and War?" they asked the voters.

The election was close. Hughes went to bed election night convinced he had won, while glum Democrats awaited the final count. By morning, late returns from the South and West insured that Wilson would remain in the White House. He won 49.4 percent of the popular vote, compared to 46.2 percent for Hughes. The American desire for peace brought Wilson victory, but peace would not last long, for the tragedy in Europe was deepening.

The End of Neutrality

Wilson had long hoped to negotiate an end to the war in Europe. Twice he sent his trusted friend and adviser Colonel Edward House to mediate between the opposing sides, and twice House failed. In late 1916 Wilson once again hoped the senselessness of the slaughter might bring European leaders to the peace table.

In December the President worked on a diplomatic note pledging the United States to end the war and help keep the peace. Before he had finished his draft, the Germans announced they were ready to negotiate an end to the war. Confident of victory, they demanded territory from Belgium, France, and Luxembourg, in addition to concessions along the Baltic Sea and in Africa. Such demands were unacceptable to the Allies.

In January 1917 Germany unleashed its submarine fleet to sink all ships, enemy or neutral. German officers anticipated victory before the United States could enter the war. Wilson broke off diplomatic relations with Germany in response to these actions, but he hesitated to do more. However, the loss of American lives and ships to German submarine attacks moved the United States closer to war.

In early March news of a document known as the Zimmerman Telegram ended the President's reluctance. The government made public a note from German Foreign Minister Arthur Zimmerman to the German minister in Mexico instructing the minister to urge Mexico and Japan to join the Central Powers if the United States entered the war. With such a direct threat to United States security, Wilson knew the country could not remain neutral much longer.

Later the same month events in Russia removed Wilson's last doubts about entering the war. A revolution there overthrew the autocratic Czar and set up a constitutional government. Now the President could more easily claim that the Allied cause was more just. He asked Congress for a declaration of war on Germany, which it voted on April 6. The United States was officially at war.

For answers, see p. A 87.

Section Review

1. Identify the following: Central Powers, Allies, *Lusitania*, Charles Evans Hughes, Zimmerman Telegram.

2. What policy did President Wilson follow when war first broke out in Europe?

3. (a) How did the Central Powers and Allies try to influence American public opinion? (b) Which effort was more successful?

4. What impact did the war in Europe have on the United States economy?

5. (a) Why was it difficult for submarines to follow international law? (b) How did President Wilson react to German submarine attacks on unarmed ships? (c) What was the German response?

6. What three events eventually led to United States entry into the war?

2 The Home Front

When the United States declared war, President Wilson and his advisers had no idea how desperate the Allies were. Americans were shocked to learn that the Allies were down to their last reserves. Missions from the Allied countries begged for massive supplies of men and materials. To save the Allies, the United States devoted its resources and patriotic fervor to winning the war. The nation soon demonstrated that it had an abundance of both.

Raising an Army

Even before the United States entered the war, Congress had hotly debated the best way to raise an army. Should volunteers be recruited, or should all able-bodied men of a certain age be drafted? President Wilson favored the draft as the most rational and democratic means. Still, his selective-service bill triggered a long debate in Congress. Not until May 7, 1917, was Wilson able to sign the

Clubs for servicemen, called canteens, were set up in many cities as recreation centers for soldiers who would soon be leaving to fight in Europe. Women volunteers worked at canteens such as this one in Newark, New Jersey.

bill, which set the minimum age of draftees at 21.

Some officials feared the draft would lead to riots as it had during the Civil War, but patriotic appeals sparked a massive response among men eligible for the draft. By June 5, 1917, almost 10 million men between the ages of 21 and 31 had registered without protest of any kind. Through voluntary enlistments and the draft, the American military had almost 5 million soldiers under arms by November 1918.

Black Americans responded as enthusiastically as whites. Unfortunately, many of them encountered the same segregation and discrimination in the armed forces that they knew at home. Of the 371,000 black soldiers in uniform, only a few thousand ever went into combat. Those who did served in all-black units. The rest, also limited to segregated units, were restricted to menial duties.

For the black soldiers overseas, Europe proved a marked contrast to life at home. The French, for example, had no history of racial conflict. They treated black soldiers much like their white comrades. When a black regiment demonstrated great courage, the grateful French government awarded two of its members, Henry Johnson and Needham Roberts, the Croix de Guerre (CRAH duh GAIR), or War Cross, a high military honor.

Wartime Industry

The declaration of war caught the nation short of supplies. On hand were just 600,000 rifles, about 2,000 machine guns, and less than a thousand artillery pieces. The initial effort to increase production of military supplies was chaotic. American military leaders competed with the Allies and private industry to purchase equipment and material.

By the summer of 1917 President Wilson knew that bold action was necessary to create some order. He established the War Industries Board (WIB) to spur industrial production and coordinate activities. However, problems still remained. Soldiers in training lacked adequate clothing and shelter, rail transportation was snarled, and steel production was falling.

Then on March 4, 1918, the President appointed Wall Street genius Bernard Baruch as chairman of the WIB. Wilson gave Baruch sweeping powers to organize industry. The WIB established strict controls over scarce materials like steel, set prices, and standardized production.

Similar efforts brought order to the railroad and shipping industries. The energetic and resourceful Edward Hurley left the Federal Trade Commission to build an adequate merchant marine. The President appointed William Gibbs McAdoo, his son-in-law and an able lawyer, to head the United States Railroad Administration. McAdoo spent almost half a billion dollars to improve track and equipment and organized all the rail lines into a single national network.

The government supported the massive mobilization of citizens through increased taxes and bonds. Amidst fanfare, parades, and patriotic appeals, the government organized four Liberty Loan drives to sell war bonds. When citizens bought bonds, they were loaning the government money in exchange for a promise to repay the loan with interest at a future date.

Workers During the War

The effort and support of American workers was central to the successful mobilization of industry. In April 1918 President Wilson created the National War Labor Board to unify labor policies. The board served as an arbitrator of disputes between management and labor. The board sometimes sided with industrialists, but more often it favored workers. The mandatory mediation produced an unusual period of cooperation between employers and workers.

Wilson threw the full force of the federal government behind workers' rights, resulting in impressive gains for labor during the war. Active government support for the right of workers to organize and bargain collectively resulted in a jump in union membership. The American Federation of Labor grew from just over 2 million members in 1916 to nearly 3.3 million in 1920.

The federal government also worked to improve working conditions. In some cases it insisted on an eight-hour workday. It set standards for the employment of women and children, and it demanded that employers pay fair wages. Despite the rapid inflation of the war years, real income rose 14 percent in 1917 and 20 percent more in 1918.

Increased demand for workers to produce war materials opened up new economic opportunities for women. Many women found jobs in steel mills, and 100,000 worked in munitions factories. For the first time government agencies opened their doors to women lawyers and doctors.

Most of the new opportunities lasted only as long as the war. By 1920 the percentage of women who worked outside the home was lower than it had been in 1910. One union spokesman expressed the attitude of many when he declared that "the same patriotism that induced women to enter industry during the war should induce them to vacate their positions after the war."

Black Americans also found new job opportunities during the war. Blacks had been moving north in growing numbers since 1900. In the five years after 1914 the chance to find work in war industries attracted about 500,000 black Americans to northern cities. Yet the opportunities of wartime were short-lived. Once the war ended, many black workers were thrown out of work or had to accept lower-paying jobs.

Producing Food

When the United States entered the war, the people of France, Britain, and Italy,* along with their armies, were facing starvation. Thus increasing American food production became a top priority. To get the job done, President Wilson appointed Herbert Hoover, an engineer and self-made millionaire, as head of the Food Administration. Hoover was known worldwide as the man who had organized a massive food relief program to Belgium during the German invasion. The Lever Act, passed in August 1917, gave Hoover full authority over food production, distribution, and farm supplies.

The top food priorities were wheat, pork, and sugar. Poor harvests kept wheat supplies low, but voluntary restraints by Americans freed adequate supplies for the Allies. Meatless and breadless days brought the spirit of sacrifice home to the nation. "Victory gardens" in back yards stretched available produce.

The results were staggering. Without rationing or great sacrifice, the United States almost tripled the amount of food sent to the Allies. Before the war an average of 7 million tons (.63 million metric tons) of food crossed

*Italy entered the war on the side of the Allies in 1915.

The call to arms left thousands of jobs unfilled at home. Women stepped forward to do work previously considered suitable only for men. These young women are delivering ice, a daily necessity in an era before electric refrigeration. Other women worked in factories, mills, and offices.

the Atlantic each year. By 1919 the figure topped 18.6 million tons (16.9 million metric tons).

Influencing Public Opinion

President Wilson wanted Americans to know that they were fighting for a just cause. The President told the nation: "The world must be made safe for democracy. . . . We have no selfish ends to serve. We desire no conquest, no dominion." To solidify public support for the war effort, the President created the Committee on Public Information (CPI) and appointed journalist George Creel to head it.

Creel showed remarkable resourcefulness and zeal in converting any remaining

507

hostility to the war into patriotism. He enlisted over 150,000 lecturers, writers, actors, artists, and scholars in a gigantic propaganda campaign. Their message was that the war was being fought for freedom and democracy. They also warned that disloyalty, spying, and sabotage threatened the war effort.

The CPI successfully spurred the sale of Liberty Bonds, reduced job absenteeism, and raised morale, but it also stirred up fear and suspicion. German-Americans especially became the victims of hate campaigns. Schools banned the teaching of the German language. People renamed sauerkraut "liberty cabbage" and called German measles "liberty measles."

Critics of the war among pacifist and socialist ranks suffered verbal and physical abuse. Socialist leader Eugene V. Debs was imprisoned for criticizing the war in a speech. Dissent had become the same as treason.

Legislation passed during the war also stifled dissent. For example, the Espionage Act of 1917 imposed fines up to $10,000 and jail sentences up to 20 years for aiding the enemy or obstructing recruitment. The law

Backing the War Effort

During 1917 and 1918, as the trickle of American soldiers to the French battlefront became a flood, Congress established the Committee on Public Information to mobilize American support for the war effort. Artists, advertisers, poets, historians, photographers, educators, and actors were enlisted in the campaign. Key to that campaign were some 75,000 "four-minute" men, who stepped onto the stages of the nation's movie houses to encourage audiences to back the war effort. The "four-minute" men were local volunteers limited to speak for only four minutes at a time to try to fire their neighbors' enthusiasm for buying government bonds, conserving food and fuel, and any other actions needed to help win the war.

Four times during the course of the war, the government asked the American people to lend it billions of dollars, and the people responded. Pressure to buy Liberty Bonds was great. Neighbors knocked on doors to encourage each other to buy bonds. Those who bought bonds received Liberty Buttons, which they wore proudly on their lapels. Over $18 billion was raised through the sale of Liberty Bonds.

If to an adult "doing your bit for the country" meant buying a Liberty Bond, to a child it meant growing vegetables in the school playground and buying "thrift stamps" for a quarter each. Five million children joined the United States School Garden Army and turned school yards, public parks, and private estates into vegetable plots. By selling the vegetables, children earned money to buy thrift stamps. A filled thrift card bought a war savings stamp worth $5, and a filled war savings card bought a $50 Liberty Bond.

At home parents sang the same songs as their sons at the front. They showed their pride by hanging out a red and white service flag with a blue star sewn on it for each family member at

war. Occasionally one would see a flag with a gold star, for a son who died at the front. Rarely had the American people been so united in their dedication to sacrifice for a common goal: to make the world safe for democracy.

gave sweeping authority to the postmaster general to confiscate material considered disloyal. The Sedition Act passed in 1918 imposed punishment for any expression of disloyalty to the American government, flag, or military uniforms.

For answers, see p. A 87.

Section Review

1. Identify the following: War Industries Board, Bernard Baruch, William Gibbs McAdoo, National War Labor Board, Herbert Hoover, Committee on Public Information, George Creel.

2. How did the United States raise an army to fight in Europe?

3. What actions did the War Industries Board take to mobilize industry?

4. List two ways the government improved conditions for workers during the war.

5. How did the American public contribute to the increase of food production during the war?

6. What was the purpose of the Committee on Public Information?

3 The United States in the War

Because mobilization proceeded slowly at first, American troops were unable to rush to the aid of the battle-weary British and French armies. Although the United States officially entered the war in the spring of 1917, by March 1918 fewer than 300,000 American fighting men were in Europe. Reinforcements arrived more quickly after that, however, and the Germans felt the impact of the United States presence. At sea, the United States Navy provided vital help almost immediately.

War at Sea

The British navy dominated the surface of the oceans but was not very effective against German submarines, which continued to disrupt Allied shipping. Unescorted merchant vessels were easy targets for U-boats, even in areas patrolled by the British. U-boat attacks were destroying Allied ships faster than the shipbuilding industry could produce them. American fighting forces and war supplies would be of no value if they could not safely cross the Atlantic.

Admiral William S. Sims convinced the British to use the *convoy* to reduce the danger of submarine attack. In convoys, destroyers and other warships escorted merchant vessels across the ocean, providing some defense against U-boats. With the United States supplying many of the destroyers, the method proved effective. Convoys transported American soldiers to Europe without the loss of a single life. They also delivered supplies to the Allies and American

forces more quickly than had been anticipated, further strengthening the war effort.

American industry strained to produce warships, especially destroyers and sub chasers. The effort was so successful that by the end of the war, the United States Navy had grown to include over half a million sailors and 2,000 ships.

The American Expeditionary Force

President Wilson chose General John J. Pershing to lead American troops, known as the American Expeditionary Force. General Pershing angered Allied military leaders by insisting that American soldiers go through a period of training before heading for Europe. This delayed the arrival of large numbers of American combat troops until 1918.

Pershing also demanded that the American Expeditionary Force keep its own identity and not be used merely to reinforce the French and British armies. Allied leaders, desperately needing more troops, resented his attitude. Developments on the battlefield soon led to greater cooperation, however.

The first years of the conflict had consisted mostly of trench warfare. Both sides dug defensive trenches, often within a hundred yards of each other, maintained devastating artillery barrages, and mounted occasional infantry charges. The loss of life was great, with little territorial gain by either army. This situation changed in early 1918.

In November 1917 a second revolution within a year forced Russia to drop out of the war. As a result German officials focused their attention on the western front. In the spring of 1918 they launched an all-out attack on the Allied lines, breaking the defensive pattern of the war. Allied leaders appointed Field Marshall Ferdinand Foch of France commander of all Allied forces in Europe. Pershing quickly agreed to cooperate with Foch.

In May 1918 German troops moved to within 50 miles (80 kilometers) of Paris before Allied resistance stiffened. A combined force of French and American troops

■ For more than four years and at incredible loss of human life, fighting seesawed over the western front in Europe. Although the United States declared war in 1917, large numbers of United States troops did not reach France until 1918, when an Allied counteroffensive finally defeated the Central Powers.

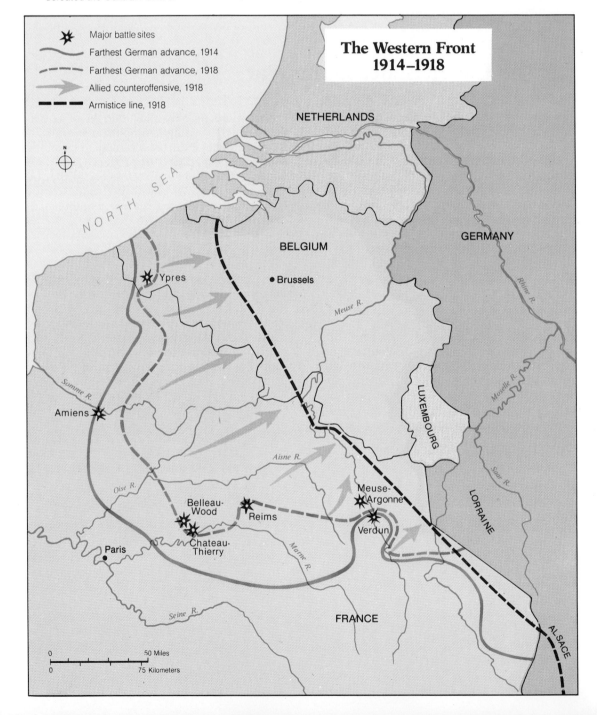

After Russia abandoned the war on the eastern front because of revolution at home, German armies massed their strength on the western front. At first Allied forces reeled backward. Then they began a massive counteroffensive. United States forces were assigned the section between Meuse and the Argonne Forest, shown above. One tenth of them were killed or wounded in the savage fighting.

stopped the Germans and drove them out of Belleau Wood. American troops also assisted the French army in stopping a German offensive near Rheims. By autumn, enough American soldiers had arrived to allow Pershing to control his own fighting force, the American First Army. He quickly mounted offensives against German lines in the south.

American successes in that sector allowed the British and French to gain control over the other areas of battle. By early November an Allied victory was assured. On November 11, 1918, German delegates met with Marshall Foch and signed an armistice. The war was over.

The arrival of American troops and supplies had helped turn the tide of battle. The "Yanks," as the American soldiers were known, not only provided the Allies with a numerical advantage but raised the spirits of the exhausted British and French soldiers. Although the United States effort had been vital and over 100,000 American soldiers had died, the other Allies had contributed even more. Britain lost nearly a million people, France 1.5 million, and Russia 1.7 million.

Diplomacy and War

As early as 1914 President Wilson had suggested the outlines for what he termed a "liberal" peace. He believed that disarmament would end the military competition among industrial powers and that public diplomacy would end the system of secret alliances that had contributed to the outbreak of war. Wilson urged rejection of territorial gains and payment of huge penalties, or *reparations*, by the losers. This policy, he claimed, would lead to a more permanent peace.

In 1916 Wilson explained that the United States wanted a peace treaty that guaranteed the *territorial integrity* of nations, that is, one that protected their boundaries. The peace should also guarantee the right to *self-determination*, or independence; freedom of the seas; and protection from aggression. These were grand ideas, but until the

511

Woodrow Wilson: A Proposal for Peace

In early 1917 President Wilson was still hopeful that peace could be negotiated between the Allies and the Central Powers. He outlined proposals for that peace in a speech to the Senate on January 22, 1917. The final part of Wilson's speech is printed below.

I am proposing, as it were, that the nations should with one accord adopt the doctrine of President Monroe as the doctrine of the world: that no nation should seek to extend its polity over any other nation or people, but that every people should be left free to determine its own polity, its own way of development—unhindered, unthreatened, unafraid, the little along with the great and powerful.

I am proposing that all nations henceforth avoid entangling alliances which would draw them into competitions of power, catch them in a net of intrigue and selfish rivalry, and disturb their own affairs with influences intruded from without. There is no entangling alliance in a concert of power. When all unite to act in the same sense and with the same purpose, all act in the common interest and are free to live their own lives under a common protection.

I am proposing government by the consent of the governed; that freedom of the seas which in international conference after conference representatives of the United States have urged with the eloquence of those who are the convinced disciples of liberty; and that moderation of armaments which makes of armies and navies a power for order merely, not an instrument of aggression or of selfish violence.

These are American principles, American policies. We could stand for no others. And they are also the principles and policies of forward-looking men and women everywhere, of every modern nation, of every enlightened community. They are the principles of mankind and must prevail.

United States entered the war, Wilson had little influence. The contribution of American troops and goods in ending the war strengthened the President's diplomatic position.

Early in 1918, with his country actively involved in the war, Wilson gave a speech in which he proposed a plan for peace called the Fourteen Points. The first five points called for open treaties, freedom of the seas, free trade, arms reductions, and impartial adjustment of colonial claims. Points six through thirteen dealt with national self-determination and the realignment of borders that had been changed during or prior to the war. The fourteenth point was essential to Wilson's personal vision of world peace. It called for the establishment of an international organization to settle disputes between nations and prevent future wars.

As the war neared an end, the President tried to guarantee a peace built around his Fourteen Points. Responding to pressure from Wilson, German Kaiser Wilhelm II stepped down on November 9. The Germans then established a democratic government in an attempt to win more lenient treatment from the victorious Allies. Now Wilson had to persuade Allied leaders, and many Americans, to accept his version of peace.

For answers, see p. A 87.

Section Review

1. Identify the following: Fourteen Points.
2. Define the following terms: convoy, reparation, territorial integrity, self-determination.
3. (a) What tactic did Admiral William S. Sims advocate for reducing the danger of submarine attack? (b) Was it successful? Explain.
4. What event in 1918 turned the tide of the war?
5. List three provisions of the "liberal" peace proposed by President Wilson.

4 Search for a "Just Peace"

When the fighting stopped, attention turned to negotiations for a peace treaty. Widespread enthusiasm for the Fourteen Points among the European people convinced Wilson that the delegates to the peace conference would use the plan as a guide. Although Allied leaders agreed with Wilson's overall ideas, they objected to specific details. They wanted to punish Germany and prevent it from ever becoming a major power again. Wilson also faced opposition in the United States.

Resistance at Home

Some of the domestic opposition to Wilson's plans for peace had political roots. The Republicans did not want the Democrats to use the peace to win votes in the upcoming election. Furthermore, many Americans questioned whether the United States should join a world organization, as called for in the fourteenth point. Avoiding involvement in European affairs had been a long-standing American tradition. People felt that now that the German threat was over, the United States should return to that tradition.

The President's own actions contributed to the growing opposition to his peace plan. President Wilson tried to increase popular support at home for his version of the peace by making the 1918 congressional elections a referendum on his policies. The effort backfired. Republicans gained control of both houses of Congress. Republican leaders insisted that the election results repudiated Wilson's foreign policy.

The President lost support in an already hostile Congress when he named the members of the negotiating team that would go to Paris. His appointees were all able men, experienced in diplomatic affairs, but he included no influential Republicans. Republi-

cans in Congress, therefore, looked on any treaty as a Democratic one, open to partisan attack.

Wilson also stirred up opposition when he decided to lead the delegation to Paris himself. No President had ever traveled abroad on a diplomatic mission. Many Americans felt that the President should stay home and help the nation deal with the problems of readjusting to peace.

A new difficulty arose when other countries at the conference demanded that the negotiations be secret. Secrecy alienated American reporters who were trying to keep their readers informed about the progress of the peace talks. Furthermore it seemed to violate the first of Wilson's Fourteen Points, which called for open agreements. Despite such concerns, President Wilson left for Europe in December 1918 with high hopes.

The Versailles Peace Conference

President Wilson visited several countries before the peace conference, which began in January 1919 at Versailles, near Paris. Wildly enthusiastic crowds greeted him in London, Paris, and Rome. Wilson considered his reception evidence of great popular support for his ideas among the people of Europe.

When the war officially ended on Armistice Day in 1918, Americans celebrated in the streets.
This impressionistic painting by Gifford Reynolds Beal captures the joyful spirit of the day.

For answers, see p. A 88.

An American Experience in the World War: Analyzing Fiction as Historical Evidence

Novels, short stories, and other works of fiction can be useful pieces of historical evidence. You would not read a novel to learn the basic facts of an historical period. However, a novel can bring an event to life. It can help you understand what it might have been like to live during another time.

An excerpt from *Three Soldiers,* a novel by John Dos Passos, is printed below. Dos Passos finished the novel in the spring of 1919, when memories of the war were fresh. Like a number of American writers, he had become disillusioned about the World War when the idealistic principles being fought for were tarnished by the harsh realities of modern warfare. Read the excerpt and use the following steps to analyze it as historical evidence.

1. **Identify the nature of the document.** Ask yourself the following questions: (a) What type of document is it? (b) Who wrote it? You may want to research the background of the author. (c) When was the document written?

2. **Analyze the document as an historical source.** Answer the following questions about the excerpt: (a) What was the author's attitude about the war? (b) Does that attitude seem to have influenced his description of the event? Explain. (c) Would you use this document as evidence about what every American soldier experienced during the war? Why or why not?

3. **Study the source to learn about an historical event.** Answer the following questions about the excerpt: (a) What can you learn about the war by reading this excerpt? (b) In what ways is the excerpt limited as historical evidence? (c) Look at the photograph on page 511. Do you think the soldiers shown there might have had experiences similar to Chrisfield's? Why or why not?

John Dos Passos

Chrisfield . . . looked at the stars in the black sky that seemed to be going along with the column on its march. Or was it that they and the stars were standing still while the trees moved away from them, waving their skinny shattered arms? He could hardly hear the tramp of feet on the road, so loud was the pandemonium of the guns ahead and behind. Every now and then a rocket would burst in front of them and its red and green lights would mingle for a moment with the stars. But it was only overhead he could see the stars. Everywhere else white and red glows rose and fell as if the horizon were on fire.

As they started down the slope, the trees suddenly broke away and they saw the valley between them full of the glare of guns and the white light of star shells. It was like looking into a stove full of glowing embers. The hillside that sloped away from them was full of crashing detonations and yellow tongues of flame. In a battery near the road, that seemed to crush their skulls each time a gun fired, they could see the dark forms of the artillerymen silhouetted in fantastic attitudes against the intermittent red glare. Stunned and blinded, they kept marching down the road. It seemed to Chrisfield that they were going to step any minute into the flaring muzzle of a gun.

Actually, few Europeans fully understood the American President's plan for peace. Rather, they saw him as a great leader, the head of the nation that had helped end the terrible war engulfing their countries. Their reception, however, only strengthened Wilson's determination to make the peace treaty fit his plan.

In Paris, Wilson encountered equally determined men. Prime Minister David Lloyd George of Britain, Premier George Clemenceau of France, and Prime Minister Vittorio Orlando of Italy all had clear ideas of what they wanted in the treaty. They sought to protect the interests of their own countries and punish Germany for the damages the Allies had suffered in the war. The Treaty of Versailles, which they forced Germany to sign on June 28, 1919, reflected these goals.

Austria-Hungary had collapsed, and the treaty recognized several new nations created out of the old empire. (See the map on page 515.) France acquired the province of Alsace-Lorraine from Germany, as well as mining rights in the Saar Valley and the right to occupy the Rhineland for 15 years. George, Clemenceau, and Orlando convinced Wilson to agree to demands that Germany pay huge reparations to France and Great Britain and that the treaty include a clause blaming Germany for the war.

Although much of the treaty seemed a violation of Wilson's original goals, he agreed to it because it included the Covenant, or constitution, of the League of Nations. Wilson believed that such an international body could prevent future wars through negotiation.

The President was aware, however, that a significant number of Republican senators opposed the idea of a League of Nations. In fact, during the negotiations, 39 Republican senators—enough to block ratification of a treaty—had signed a petition stating that the treaty was unacceptable. The senators, led by Henry Cabot Lodge of Massachusetts, especially objected to Article 10 of the Covenant of the League of Nations. That article guaranteed the territorial integrity of member states and called for possible economic and military sanctions against violators. These senators did not want an international body making foreign policy decisions for the United States.

Wilson negotiated changes in the original covenant in order to make it more acceptable to the Senate. In its final form, the covenant allowed voluntary withdrawal from the league, made participation in sanctions optional, and recognized the importance of the Monroe Doctrine in the Western Hemisphere. With the revised treaty in hand, the President returned to the United States to try to win ratification from the Senate, a step requiring the votes of two thirds of the 96-member body.

Defeat of the Treaty

On July 10, 1919, Woodrow Wilson personally delivered the 264-page Treaty of Versailles to the Senate. Democrats gave him a loud ovation. The Republican majority sat in silence.

Wilson's effort to revise the treaty failed to satisfy the Republicans. They resented the fact that Republicans had not participated in the negotiations, and some charged that Wilson was using the treaty to win a third term. Most Americans probably favored the treaty and American participation in the League of Nations although German and Irish Americans, along with many liberals, thought the treaty was too harsh on Germany.

In the Senate opposition and support for the treaty broke along party lines. All but 4 of the 47 Democrats stood loyally with Wilson. While some of the 49 Republican senators leaned toward the strict isolationist thinking of William Borah of Idaho and Hiram Johnson of California, most sup-

The map of Europe after the peace conference at Versailles looked very different from the map five years earlier. (See page 501.) Many new nations were created in eastern and central Europe as the old empires of Austria-Hungary and Russia collapsed.

ported a series of amendments to the treaty proposed by Henry Cabot Lodge.

Senator Lodge wanted to "Republicanize" the treaty so that the Democrats could not use it to their political advantage. More important, he believed that the League of Nations was a threat to the sovereignty of the United States. His goal was to prevent United States involvement in the internal affairs of other nations and to protect the authority of Congress to declare war.

Wilson refused to accept all but the mildest changes in the treaty. Failing to gain senatorial support, he decided to go directly to the American people. Early in September he embarked on a cross-country trip to explain the treaty. In Omaha, Nebraska, he warned, "I can predict with absolute certainty that within another generation there will be another world war if the nations of the world do not concert ... to prevent it." The crowds were friendly and enthusiastic, but the enthusiasm did not change Senate votes.

The trip destroyed the President's fragile health. On September 25 Wilson collapsed. A week later he suffered a stroke that paralyzed his left side. For weeks he lay near death, and for months he remained almost helpless in bed.

Major Events

1914	War begins in Europe
1915	German submarine sinks *Lusitania*
1916	Germany suspends unannounced submarine attacks
1917	Germany resumes submarine attacks; Zimmerman Telegram; United States enters war; Espionage Act passed
1918	Fourteen Points announced; War Industries Board created; National War Labor Board created; Sedition Act passed; Germany surrenders
1919	Treaty of Versailles signed
1920	Senate rejects treaty

In November 1919 the treaty, carrying Lodge's amendments, was defeated in the Senate. Wilson had ordered Democrats to vote against the treaty as long as it contained Lodge's amendments. In March 1920 another amended version of the treaty came before the Senate, and again it failed to pass. President Wilson was so opposed to Lodge's changes that he was willing to see the entire treaty defeated rather than accept them. By rejecting the Treaty of Versailles, the Senate dashed Woodrow Wilson's dream of a new world order. The League of Nations began its peacekeeping mission without the United States.

For answers, see p. A 88.

Section Review

1. Identify the following: Treaty of Versailles, League of Nations, Henry Cabot Lodge, Article 10.
2. List two actions by President Wilson that stirred up opposition to his plans for peace.
3. What part of the Treaty of Versailles disturbed Republican senators the most?
4. What did Wilson do to try to gain public support for the treaty?
5. What action did the Senate finally take concerning the Treaty of Versailles?

★ ★

IN PERSPECTIVE   When war broke out in Europe, President Wilson urged Americans to remain neutral, but neutrality was hard to achieve. A common heritage with Great Britain and skillful Allied propaganda influenced American attitudes toward the war. Even before the United States entered the war most Americans were friendly to the Allies. After a long series of provocations, Wilson asked Congress to declare war on Germany in April 1917.

The United States now turned its full attention to the war effort. Millions of men were drafted, and industry soared to unprecedented production heights. Congress created a War Industries Board to coordinate war production and a National War Labor Board to unify labor policy. Joining the Allied forces, the United States helped defeat Germany.

President Wilson did not want the victorious Allies to inflict a harsh peace settlement on Germany. But the European Allied leaders demanded a peace treaty that would punish Germany. The Treaty of Versailles deprived Germany of territory and forced the nation to make reparation payments to the victors. President Wilson agreed to the Treaty of Versailles because it contained a provision for the establishment of the League of Nations, but he was unable to persuade the Senate to ratify the treaty.

For answers, see p. A 88.

Chapter Review

1. (a) What policy did the United States government follow at the outbreak of war in Europe? (b) How did the heritage of many Americans and the propaganda of foreign governments work against that policy?

2. (a) Why did the United States trade more with Britain than with Germany during the early years of the war? (b) What effect did such trade have on the American economy?

3. (a) How did the German use of the submarine complicate the question of neutral rights? (b) How did Wilson react to the sinking of unarmed ships by German submarines? (c) Why did the Germans agree to stop unannounced attacks in 1916?

4. Explain how each of the following contributed to the United States entry into the war: (a) German resumption of submarine attacks; (b) Zimmerman Telegram; (c) Russian overthrow of the czar.

5. (a) How did the government try to mobilize industry to support the war effort? (b) What actions did the government take to win the effort and support of American workers?

6. (a) Why was increased food production important to the war effort? (b) How was the United States able to nearly triple the amount of food sent to the Allies?

7. (a) How did the government try to solidify public support for the war effort? (b) What negative impact did the efforts have?

8. How did the arrival of United States troops help the Allies win the war?

9. (a) Briefly describe President Wilson's Fourteen Points. (b) Which parts of the Treaty of Versailles seemed to contradict the Fourteen Points? (c) Why was Wilson willing to accept the treaty despite such contradictions?

10. (a) How did Wilson alienate many Americans even before the peace conference began? (b) Why did most Republican senators oppose the treaty? (c) What was the purpose of Senator Lodge's amendments to the treaty?

For answers, see p. A 89.

For Further Thought

1. (a) How did black Americans, women, and workers in general benefit during the war? (b) Why do you think this occurred during wartime and not earlier?

2. (a) What do you think the union official meant by his comment that "the same patriotism that induced women to enter industry during the war should induce them to vacate their positions after the war"? (b) Do you agree with him? Why or why not?

3. (a) What actions did President Wilson take to keep the United States neutral until 1917? (b) Which actions do you think were most effective? (c) Which do you think were least effective?

For answers, see p. A 89.

Developing Basic Skills

1. *Map Reading*   Compare the two maps on pages 501 and 515. Then answer the following questions: (a) Which new independent countries existed after the war? (b) Which nation no longer existed after the war? (c) Which nations lost territory as a result of the war? (d) Which nations gained territory? (e) Explain what was meant by the statement, "The map of Europe was transformed by the war."

2. *Using a Primary Source*   Read the excerpts from President Wilson's foreign policy speech on page 512. Then answer the following questions: (a) Why is this document a primary source? (b) What can you learn about Wilson's goals for peace by reading the document? (c) How does this primary source differ from a diary account?

3. *Using Visual Evidence*   Study the poster on page 508. Then answer the following questions: (a) What was the purpose of the poster? (b) How did it appeal to people's emotions? (c) What significance do you think the list of names on the right has? (d) Do you think the poster was probably effective? Why or why not?

See page 777 for suggested readings.

Unit Eight

The Roaring Twenties

A Search for Peace and Prosperity

29

(1919–1928)

Flag Day, *by Childe Hassan.*

Chapter Outline

1 *The Rocky Road to Peacetime*

2 *The Politics of Normalcy*

3 *Calvin Coolidge and the Business of America*

When the World War ended on November 11, 1918, Americans jubilantly looked forward to better times. After a period of fighting abroad and new government regulations at home, many yearned for calmer, more familiar times. Instead, they entered a decade of startling, bewildering change. The 1920s opened with labor unrest, social turmoil, and widespread panic about the possible effect of the Russian Revolution on the United States.

In such turbulent times, voters turned to politicians who promised calm and a return to prewar order. Business became the symbol of that order. Americans seemed worn out by crusades for peace abroad and reform at home. Many were far more concerned with gaining a bigger share of the "good life" for themselves.

Yet while newspapers wrote of rich movie stars and fancy new cars, many Americans struggled just to earn enough to eat. The prosperity of the Roaring Twenties masked underlying economic problems.

1 The Rocky Road to Peacetime

Before Americans could enjoy the fruits of victory, they had to solve the problems caused by war. Millions of veterans needed work. Factories had to switch from the production of war supplies and equipment to the production of consumer goods. The heated emotions of war needed time to cool.

Returning to Normal

When the war ended in 1918, President Woodrow Wilson asked for a rapid end to government ownership and operation of industries such as railroads, and Congress quickly agreed. However, the President concentrated his efforts on persuading the Senate to consent to the Versailles Treaty. (See page 515.) The country had no plan for easing soldiers and sailors back into civilian life or for avoiding economic dislocation.

The armed forces discharged 4 million men after the war. Hundreds of thousands of wartime employees were also cut from government payrolls. Soon thereafter many factories shut down to retool for peacetime production, so fewer jobs were available. Consequently unemployment climbed to almost 5 million in 1921.

Veterans who could not find work thought they deserved more help from the government. They demanded bonuses to make up for the wages they lost while in uniform. Some veterans received disability benefits, pensions, or hospitalization costs. However, Congress refused to grant the bonuses.

Consumers meanwhile went on a spending spree, buying goods that were unavailable during the war. Since the war began, prices had soared, doubling the cost of living between 1913 and 1920. Inflation pushed the retail price of a new Model T Ford from $360 in 1918 to $480 in 1920. Between 1920 and 1922 the country slid into a recession that was particularly hard on farmers. The price of wheat, for example, sank from a wartime high of $2.26 a bushel to less than $1 a bushel in 1922.

The end of the war also meant an end to peaceful relations between factory owners and workers. During the war the government had encouraged high wages and collective bargaining. In a spirit of patriotism, management and labor had worked to solve problems without strikes.

Rising prices and unemployment after the war fueled workers' demands for higher wages. Employers refused, and many unions went on strike. Workers in the clothing, textile, telegraph, and telephone industries won higher pay, but unions in other industries met with less success.

Some employers charged that union leaders were radicals who wanted to undermine the United States economy. Unions argued that factory owners were greedy and insensitive to the needs of workers. The nation was entering a period of industrial strife.

Postwar Labor Unrest

The first serious postwar confrontation between labor and management occurred in the steel industry. In 1892 the Homestead strike had temporarily ended attempts to unionize the steel industry. (See page 398.) After the war, the American Federation of Labor decided to launch a second organizing effort.

In September 1919 a newly formed steel workers' union demanded higher wages, one day's rest out of seven, and an end to the 12-hour work day. When steel mill owners refused to negotiate, the union called a strike. Within a week 365,000 workers across the country had walked out. When violence erupted, local police and state militia helped steel companies break the picket lines. Companies hired strikebreakers to replace the union workers. After 20 deaths and the loss of $100 million in wages, the union called off the strike on January 9, 1920. It had won no concessions.

A strike in the coal industry was more successful. The United Mine Workers, led by John L. Lewis, also went on strike in 1919. Attorney General A. Mitchell Palmer secured a court order against the strike. Lewis urged the miners to return to work, but they refused. Finally the government ordered a 14-percent wage increase, and the strike ended.

Two strikes in particular convinced many Americans that radical foreign forces might be causing the labor unrest: a general strike in Seattle, Washington, and a police strike in Boston, Massachusetts.

In 1919 the Central Labor Council of Seattle called a *general strike*, a strike of the members of all unions, in support of striking shipyard workers. The call for a strike by all union members, not just by workers in a single industry, alarmed many Americans. They considered the general strike a radical tactic imported from Europe. When Seattle Mayor Ole Hanson used troops to crush the strike, he became a national hero.

The strike by Boston police seemed even more alarming to most citizens. Police officers walked off the job in September 1919 after the police commissioner fired 19 officers who had tried to join the AFL. With no police protection, looting broke out despite efforts by volunteer groups to maintain order. Actual damage was small, but shock waves of fear rumbled across the nation. Massachusetts Governor Calvin Coolidge was widely admired for condemning the strike as a threat to public safety.

These strikes and hundreds of others hardened the public attitude toward unions. Union membership sank from more than 5 million in 1920 to about 3.6 million in 1923. Employee associations sponsored by management, called *company unions,* became more common, and collective bargaining became rarer.

The Red Scare

As you read in Chapter 28, after the November 1917 revolution Russia signed a ceasefire agreement with Germany. (See page 509.) The revolution had been led by the Bolsheviks, a group of radical communists. Communists believe in control of all property by the community as a whole or by the government. After the war the Russian Bolsheviks, called Reds, advocated worldwide revolution. To many people the labor unrest of the postwar years, typified by the strikes in Seattle and Boston, raised the threat of revolution in the United States.

Terrorist incidents created further anxiety. A package containing a bomb arrived in the Seattle mayor's office after the general strike. Similar packages—set aside for insufficient postage—were found in a New York post office addressed to known opponents of organized labor or immigration. One bomb sent to Senator Thomas Hartwick of Georgia exploded, injuring his maid. Another device exploded when a terrorist tried to plant it on Attorney General Palmer's front porch.

For many people those acts of terrorism, combined with labor unrest, confirmed the fear of communist revolution, and a period known as the Red Scare began. Many Americans could not see the difference between a few criminal terrorists and peaceful protestors or strikers. During 1919 and early 1920 socialists and other radicals were frequently harassed by individual citizens and local authorities. Immigrants, especially those from eastern Europe, were often the targets of such harassment. Some Americans believed these immigrants to be agents of the Russian Bolsheviks.

In response to public demands for action, Attorney General Palmer organized a series of raids to arrest suspected communists. In January 1920 over 6,000 people in 33 cities were seized. Almost none had committed any crime. Of those arrested, about 550 were deported. The raids revealed no plots to overthrow the government.

At first people responded enthusiastically to Palmer's actions, but eventually a growing number of Americans became concerned about violations of constitutional rights. Some public officials, such as former Supreme Court Justice Charles Evans Hughes, spoke out against Palmer's tactics. Furthermore, people lost their enthusiasm for such raids as it became obvious that no revolution had broken out. By late 1920 the Red Scare had faded.

Restrictions on Immigration

One of the underlying causes of the Red Scare had been a negative reaction to immigrants. As you read in Chapter 23, many Americans believed that the "new immigrants" from southern and eastern Europe and Asia would not fit into American society.

During the war, antiforeign feelings had been fueled by government warnings about foreign secret agents. Once the war had ended, a new flood of immigrants entered the country, causing further concern. Workers worried that immigrants would compete for jobs and drive wages down.

In the turbulent postwar period, antiforeign feelings erupted in a campaign to restrict immigration. The cartoonist whose work appears above clearly shared such sentiments. The "Black Hand" referred to in the cartoon was a European terrorist group.

In 1920 the Massachusetts trial of two Italian anarchists accused of murder during a payroll robbery revealed the depth of public concern. Nicola Sacco and Bartolomeo Vanzetti were convicted and sentenced to death even though the evidence against them was far from conclusive. Public opinion was split on the verdict. Many people, including several distinguished lawyers, believed the anarchists had been convicted because they were Italian and held unpopular political views. An equally vocal group argued that the executions would be a warning to other radicals. After many futile appeals, the two were put to death in 1927.

Congress responded to public demands for immigration restriction by passing the Emergency Quota Act of 1921. Annual immigration from Europe was restricted to a fixed quota, set at 3 percent of the population of a particular nationality living in the United States in 1910. When the Emergency Quota Act failed to reduce the flow of south-

ern and eastern European immigrants substantially, Congress passed the Immigration Act of 1924.

The new law lowered the quota from 3 to 2 percent and changed the base year from 1910 to 1890, when few southern and eastern Europeans were living in the United States. This provision substantially reduced the number of new immigrants from those regions. The act dealt even more harshly with the Japanese, barring them from the United States as "aliens ineligible to citizenship."

By 1929 Congress had reduced the annual quota of immigrants to about 152,000. Of this total, 132,000 were permitted from northern Europe and only about 20,000 from the rest of the world outside of the Western Hemisphere. Since the complicated quota system did not count black Americans, it effectively barred immigration from Africa. The new laws, however, did not limit immigration from the Western Hemisphere, which had increased sharply in the early 1900s.

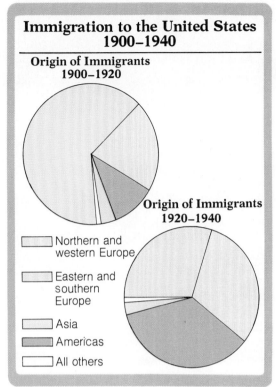

Immigration to the United States 1900–1940

Origin of Immigrants 1900–1920

Origin of Immigrants 1920–1940

- Northern and western Europe
- Eastern and southern Europe
- Asia
- Americas
- All others

Source: *Historical Statistics of the United States*

■ *New immigration laws drastically changed the pattern of immigration to the United States. The graph at top shows the percentage of immigrants from various areas before the new laws went into effect. While the new laws limited immigration from the rest of the world, they set no limit on newcomers from the Western Hemisphere. As the graph at bottom shows, more than one third of all immigrants between 1920 and 1940 came from Mexico, Canada, and other nations in the Americas.*

524

Disillusionment for Black Americans

The war had raised the aspirations of many black Americans as new job opportunities opened in war industries. Between 1917 and 1925 about 600,000 blacks migrated to northern industrial cities. Black veterans returned from Europe with a new sense of pride. Having served their country, they demanded better jobs and fair treatment.

The postwar years were a time of disillusionment for many blacks. They faced discrimination in northern cities and suffered greatly from the widespread unemployment of the period. White workers resented blacks competing for jobs. Tension between blacks and whites further increased in northern cities when blacks tried to move into all-white neighborhoods.

In 1919 racial tensions sparked riots in over 20 cities, including Washington, D. C.; Omaha, Nebraska; and Chicago, Illinois. The Chicago riot erupted when a black youngster swimming in a "white" area of Lake Michigan was attacked by a group of angry whites. Before the riot ended, over 500 people were injured and 38 were killed. In Washington, D. C., a mob outside the White House gates attacked black soldiers who were still in uniform.

The intolerance of the period was reflected by the revival of the Ku Klux Klan. The new Klan was formed in Georgia in 1915, and the organization spread quickly from the South to parts of the Midwest and West. While the original Klan, founded after the Civil War, had terrorized freed slaves and whites who sympathized with them, the

■ *The exodus of black Americans from the South, which began after the Civil War, picked up momentum around 1900. Most blacks moved north and west for better jobs. Some, however, left because of Jim Crow laws, enforcing segregation.*

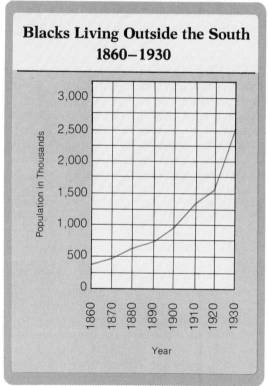

Blacks Living Outside the South 1860–1930

Population in Thousands

3,000
2,500
2,000
1,500
1,000
500
0

1860 1870 1880 1890 1900 1910 1920 1930

Year

Source: United States Bureau of the Census

After the World War, a revived Ku Klux Klan attacked blacks, Jews, Catholics, and immigrants, among others. Although the political strength of the Klan declined after 1924, the group staged a large parade down Pennsylvania Avenue in Washington, D.C., in 1925.

new Klan had a broader goal: to preserve the United States for white, native-born American Protestants. Consequently, the Klan attacked not only blacks, but also immigrants, Catholics, and Jews.

By 1923 the organization claimed 4 million members and had become a political force in Texas, Oregon, Georgia, Oklahoma, Alabama, and especially Indiana. Klan-supported candidates were elected to governorships in Oklahoma and Oregon. The political power of the Klan declined after 1924, however, as the corruption and illegal activities of many of its leaders became known.

For answers, see p. A 90.

Section Review

1. Identify the following: A. Mitchell Palmer, Calvin Coolidge, Bolsheviks, Red Scare.
2. Define the following terms: general strike, company union.
3. What two strikes convinced many Americans that radicals were causing labor unrest?
4. Which nationalities were affected by the new legislation restricting immigration?
5. Why were black veterans disillusioned?
6. How did the new Ku Klux Klan differ from the post–Civil War Klan?

2 The Politics of Normalcy

After the war years and the turbulent postwar period, Americans looked forward to a time of tranquility. Warren G. Harding, elected President in 1920, made popular a phrase that came to signify what the public wanted. He called it normalcy.

The Election of 1920

Republicans were confident of victory in the presidential election of 1920. With the Democratic party badly split over the Versailles Treaty, the Republicans thought that all they needed to win was an attractive candidate. Deciding on such an individual, however, proved to be difficult. The nominating convention, meeting in Chicago, was divided. Finally a group of party leaders gathered in a smoke-filled room at the Blackstone Hotel and chose Senator Warren G. Harding of Ohio. "This Harding's no world beater," they admitted, "but . . . he's the best of the bunch." The convention delegates agreed and selected Governor Calvin Coolidge of Massachusetts for Vice-President.

The Democratic presidential nominating convention took 44 ballots before choosing Governor James Cox of Ohio as their candidate. Franklin D. Roosevelt, Wilson's assistant secretary of the navy, was selected as the Democratic vice-presidential candidate.

In the first national election in which women had full suffrage, Harding polled a record 16 million votes, compared to Cox's 9 million. As one Democrat admitted, "It wasn't just a landslide, it was an earthquake." The President-elect urged the country to seek "not heroism but healing, not nostrums but normalcy." No one had heard the word "normalcy" before, but everyone knew what Harding meant.

The Harding Administration

Harding's inauguration began 12 years of Republican leadership. Throughout the 1920s Republicans controlled both the presidency and Congress.

The affable Harding fit the image of President. Distinguished, gray-haired, and handsome, he cut an impressive figure. Once a small-town politician and newspaper editor, he had risen to the United States Senate. But as President, Harding often felt the job was beyond him, and he nearly worked himself to death trying to meet the demands of the office. Unfortunately, he was probably correct when he said, "I knew this job would be too much for me." His problems often resulted from the questionable appointments of some of his poker-playing friends to major government positions.

During the election campaign Harding had promised to recruit the best minds in the country for his administration, and a few appointments did fulfill the promise. As secretary of state he named former Supreme Court Justice Charles Evans Hughes. Henry C. Wallace, the new secretary of agriculture, was a leader in the movement for farm reform. As secretary of commerce Harding appointed Herbert Hoover, an internationally admired engineer and humanitarian. The man who dominated Harding's administration, however, was Treasury Secretary Andrew Mellon, who had made a fortune as a banker and industrialist.

A Businesslike Economic Program

Andrew Mellon shared the probusiness orientation of the Harding administration. He favored a high tariff that would protect American business from foreign competition. Consistent with Mellon's views,

The great German physicist Albert Einstein was honored by President Harding on a visit to the United States. Einstein (at left) is shown in this photograph with his wife, Elsa Einstein, the President, and Dr. Charles Walcott, secretary of the Smithsonian Institution. In 1933 the Einsteins moved permanently to the United States.

Congress passed the Fordney-McCumber Act in 1922, raising tariffs to a new high.

Mellon also believed that taxes on large incomes should be reduced. If taxes were lowered, he argued, the wealthy would have more money to invest. More investment would create more jobs, which would mean more income for middle- and lower-income people. Mellon believed wealth would "trickle down" and improve the standard of living for everyone. A majority of Congress agreed with Mellon's reasoning. The Revenue Act of 1921 and other new tax laws slashed taxes on higher incomes.

In his drive to promote efficiency and economy in government, Mellon instituted a much-needed budgeting process for government departments. Working with the new budget director, Charles Dawes, Mellon reduced the national debt and balanced the budget. Government expenses fell from $6.4 billion in 1920 to $2.9 billion in 1927.

The determination to cut costs led to conflict with the American Legion and other veterans' groups. Congress had formed the Veterans Bureau in 1921 to handle claims for hospitalization and administer a program of veterans' insurance. Many veterans believed they deserved more government assistance and better medical treatment.

Twice Congress passed "bonus bills" to compensate veterans for the money they could have earned instead of serving at low pay in the armed forces. But President Harding vetoed the bills because he thought they were too expensive. In 1924 a bill giving the average veteran about $1,000 worth of life insurance was passed over President Coolidge's veto. However, the money was not to be paid for 20 years.

Corruption in Government

Although President Harding was honest, his administration was riddled with swindlers and corrupt officials. Attorney General Harry Dougherty and his friend Jesse Smith made fortunes selling government favors, immunities from prosecution, and pardons. The head of the Veterans Bureau, Charles Forbes, sold shipments of bandages, drugs, and bedding and pocketed the money while veterans lay in hospitals desperately short of supplies. Theft at the Veterans Bureau was just one scandal that shook President Harding's administration.

Who Says a Watched Pot Never Boils?

Dishonesty and corruption were common in the Harding administration. This 1924 cartoon refers to the Teapot Dome scandal, which involved the leasing of valuable government-owned oil fields.

In 1921 Secretary of the Interior Albert B. Fall convinced the secretary of the navy and President Harding to transfer control of oil reserves at Teapot Dome, Wyoming, and Elk Hills, California, from the Department of the Navy to the Department of the Interior. Once in control of the oil, Secretary Fall leased the reserves to two oil men, Harry F. Sinclair and Edward L. Doheny. In exchange for the oil reserves Sinclair and Doheny "loaned" Fall about $400,000.

Fall's sudden increase in wealth attracted attention. A Senate committee began an investigation in 1924, and a grand jury indicted Fall for bribery. He was eventually convicted, sentenced to one year in prison, and fined $100,000. Albert Fall was the first cabinet officer in history to be sent to prison. Doheny and Sinclair were acquitted on the bribery charge. Sinclair later went to jail for contempt of court and contempt of the Senate.

527

President Harding never learned the full extent of the corruption in his administration. He died of a heart attack on August 2, 1923. The task of restoring faith in government fell to Calvin Coolidge.

For answers, see p. A 90.

Section Review

1. Identify the following: Warren G. Harding, Andrew Mellon, Harry Dougherty, Albert Fall.

2. Define the following term: normalcy.

3. How did Andrew Mellon believe wealth would "trickle down" to middle- and lower-income people?

4. Name two ways Mellon tried to promote efficiency and economy in government.

5. What action led to Albert Fall's conviction for bribery?

3 Calvin Coolidge and the Business of America

Calvin Coolidge took the oath of office, administered by his father, a justice of the peace, in the living room of the Vermont farmhouse that five generations of Coolidges had called home. Because the new President rarely smiled and spoke little, he struck people as cold. Once a college student told Coolidge she had bet her roommate she could get him to say more than three words. "You lose," was the reply. Yet Coolidge proved able to restore national confidence in government.

No man was more committed to the business community. As the economy improved during the 1920s, Coolidge became more convinced that the United States should be guided by business principles. Thrilled by the prosperity that developed during his administration, Coolidge proudly proclaimed that "the business of America is business."

The Election of 1924

As the 1924 election neared, the Republicans nominated Coolidge without difficulty, but the Democrats battled for 17 days in a July heat wave before agreeing on a candidate and a platform. Millions of Americans listened on the radio to the struggle between the rural followers of William Jennings Bryan and the urban supporters of the Tammany Hall politicians from New York.

The most hotly contested issue at the Democratic convention was a proposed plank in the party platform condemning the Ku Klux Klan. The plank was defeated by just one vote out of more than a thousand cast. After 103 ballots the Democrats finally nominated John W. Davis, a corporate lawyer closely associated with Wall Street banking interests. Both parties thus chose candidates with a business orientation.

Farmers, social reformers, socialists, and progressives rallied behind the Progressive party candidacy of Robert La Follette of Wisconsin. La Follette supported government ownership of the railroads, the abolition of child labor, and the right of unions to organize and engage in collective bargaining. The Progressive party platform attacked "the control of government and industry by private monopoly."

Americans voted overwhelmingly to "keep cool with Coolidge," who won 35 states. Davis won 12 states, and La Follette won one: Wisconsin. A few progressive voices continued to argue for government regulation of the economy, but in the 1920s they fought lonely battles.

Business Under Coolidge

Coolidge did not disappoint those who wanted a President sympathetic to business interests. In 1925, for example, he appointed William E. Humphrey to chair the Federal Trade Commission. (See page 479.) The new chairman condemned the FTC as "an instrument of oppression" of the business community, and under his leadership the FTC systematically refused to investigate various monopolistic agreements.

Coolidge appointed other friends of business to run the Interstate Commerce Commission and the Federal Reserve Board, agencies that had been created to regulate business practices. (See pages 407 and 478.)

A View of Business in the 1920s

When President Calvin Coolidge proclaimed that "the business of America is business," he was expressing the opinion of many people. Seldom in American history had the business community been so admired as during the 1920s. The extent of that feeling can be seen in the following excerpts from an article written by Edward E. Purinton in 1921.

Among the nations of the earth today America stands for one idea: *Business*. . . . Through business, properly conceived, managed, and conducted, the human race is finally to be redeemed. . . .

What is the finest game? Business . . . The fullest education? Business. The fairest opportunity? Business . . . You may not agree. That is because you judge business by the crude, mean, stupid, false imitation of business that happens to be located near you.

The finest game is business. The rewards are for everybody, and all can win. There are no favorites—Providence always crowns the career of the man who is worthy. And in this game there is no "luck"—you have the fun of taking chances but the sobriety of guaranteeing certainties. The speed and size of your winnings are for you alone to determine; you needn't wait for the other fellow in the game—it is always your move. And your slogan is not "Down the Other Fellow!" but rather "Beat Your Own Record!" or "Do It Better Today!" or "Make Every Job a Masterpiece!" . . .

The fullest education is business. A proper blend of study, work, and life is essential to advancement. . . . In the school of business, moreover, you teach yourself and learn most from your own mistakes. What you learn here you live out, the only real test.

The fairest opportunity is business. You can find more, better, quicker chances to get ahead in a large business house than anywhere else on earth.

The President's appointments provoked progressive Senator George Norris of Nebraska to remark:

The effect of these appointments is to set the country back more than twenty-five years. It is an indirect but positive repeal of congressional enactments, which no administration, however powerful, would dare to bring about by any direct means. It is the nullification of federal law by a process of boring from within.

Critics charged that Coolidge's appointments were intended to destroy the effectiveness of the regulatory agencies.

The Revenue Act, signed by President Coolidge in 1926, was also favorable to business. The act drastically slashed tax rates on high incomes while making only modest rate cuts for middle incomes.

Coolidge's probusiness program appeared to be a great success as the nation enjoyed a period of dazzling prosperity. Between 1921 and 1929 the output of industry nearly doubled. Profits and wages grew, and unemployment was low. Not everyone became rich, but more people could afford to buy more products than ever before.

The Farm Problem

Farmers did not share in the general prosperity of the 1920s. They faced high expenses and low prices for farm products. During the war American farmers had increased the number of acres they planted in order to increase production. Prices soared because of the great demand from Europe. But when the war ended and European farmers returned to work, the demand for American produce fell and so did prices.

Prices rose gradually during the 1920s, but expenses rose faster. Railroad shipping rates, taxes, seed prices, and interest rates spiraled. Farmers bought expensive machinery and chemical fertilizer in order to increase production. Unfortunately for farmers, the resulting surplus of farm produce kept prices low. Increased harvests in nations such as Canada and Australia contributed to worldwide overproduction.

To improve their position, farmers banded together in farm bureaus, which in turn joined the American Farm Bureau Federation. Farmers also formed cooperatives to store, market, and ship their produce. But overproduction continued to glut the market, and prices continued to fall.

529

Major Events

1915	Ku Klux Klan reorganizes
1917	Bolsheviks take power in Russia
1918	War ends
1919	Strikes in steel industry and coal mines; Seattle general strike; Boston police strike
1919–1920	Red Scare
1920	Warren G. Harding elected President
1921	Emergency Quota Act passed
1923	President Harding dies; Vice-President Calvin Coolidge becomes President
1924	Immigration Act passed; Albert Fall indicted in Teapot Dome scandal; Coolidge elected President

Farmers also sought assistance from the federal government. Legislators from agricultural districts voted together as a "farm bloc" to promote measures that would help farmers. One such proposal was the McNary-Haugen bill.

The purpose of this legislation was to establish a government-supported two-price system for some farm products, such as wheat and corn. The farmer would receive a parity price regardless of the market price. *Parity* meant that a farmer's purchasing power would remain constant even if market prices dropped.

President Coolidge objected to this expansion of the government's role in the economy. He vetoed the McNary-Haugen bill in 1927 and again in 1928. The overall prosperity of the 1920s hid the severity of the farm problem as well as other flaws in the economy.

For answers, see p. A 90.

Section Review

1. Identify the following: McNary-Haugen bill.
2. Define the following term: parity.
3. What groups supported the Progressive party in the 1924 election?
4. What factors caused farm expenses to rise during the 1920s?

★ ★

IN PERSPECTIVE   Returning to normal after the war was not easy. High prices and unemployment contributed to a rising number of strikes. Partially because of these strikes and the successful Bolshevik revolution in Russia, many Americans began to fear a revolution in the United States. During the so-called Red Scare, many immigrants were arrested. Antiimmigrant feelings led to laws restricting immigration from southern and eastern Europe, Asia, and Africa. Black Americans also faced discrimination and violence during the postwar years.

By 1921 when Warren G. Harding was inaugurated, the heated emotions of wartime had cooled, and people looked forward to a time of peace and prosperity. Under both Harding and Coolidge, the government followed probusiness policies. Harding's administration was marred by scandals, but President Coolidge restored national confidence. He was encouraged by the general prosperity of the period, but, like many Americans, he overlooked the problems of farmers. As you will read in the following chapter, the prosperity of a growing number of people helped earn the new decade its nickname: the Roaring Twenties.

For answers, see p. A 90.

Chapter Review

1. (a) What economic problems did Americans face when the war ended? (b) How did these problems increase tension between employers and workers?

2. (a) What was the outcome of the steel strike in 1919? (b) What was the outcome of the coal strike? (c) Why did the Seattle general strike and the Boston police strike worry many Americans?

3. (a) How did the actions of terrorists contribute to the start of the Red Scare? (b) What actions did Attorney General A. Mitchell Palmer take in response to public concern about political radicals?

4. (a) What developments contributed to a rise in antiforeign feeling after the war? (b) How did Congress respond to that feeling? (c) What impact did the Emergency Quota Act of 1921 and the Immigration Act of 1924 have on the number of immigrants who came to the United States? (d) What impact did the legislation have on the source of immigration? (e) Which area of the world was indirectly affected by the immigration laws? Why?

5. (a) Why did black Americans expect a better life after the war? (b) What did they actually encounter?

6. How did Andrew Mellon reflect the probusiness orientation of the Harding administration? Give specific examples to support your answer.

7. (a) What major scandals came to light during Harding's presidency? (b) Why was Harding spared full knowledge of the scandals?

8. (a) How did President Coolidge help business during his administration? (b) How did progressives like George Norris react?

9. (a) Why were the 1920s a difficult time for American farmers? (b) What did farmers do to improve their situation? (c) Were they successful? Explain.

For answers, see p. A 91.

For Further Thought

531

1. List the actions taken during the administrations of Harding and Coolidge that would be considered probusiness. Describe how you think each action would help the growth of business and industry.

2. Review the description of the presidential campaign and election of 1924. (See page 528.) How might you use the election as evidence that the progressive era was over?

For answers, see p. A 91.

Developing Basic Skills

1. *Graph Reading* Study the graphs on immigration on page 524 and compare it with the graphs on page 428. Then answer the following questions: (a) From which region did the largest percentage of immigrants come between 1900 and 1920? (b) Which region showed the largest increase in immigration since the 1840s? (c) How would you describe the change in the origin of immigration to the United States since the 1840s?

2. *Comparing* You have read about a rise in antiforeign feelings during three periods of American history: during the 1840s (see pages 272 – 273); after 1880 (see pages 429 – 430); and during the 1920s. Review what you have learned and answer the following questions: (a) What groups were the objects of antiforeign feelings during each period? (b) What caused resentment among native-born Americans during each period? (c) What government action was taken? (d) In what ways were the three outbreaks of antiforeign feeling similar? (e) In what ways were they different? (f) How might you explain the similarities and differences?

See page 778 for suggested readings.

Life in the 1920s

(1920–1929)

A flapper on the cover of McClure's magazine.

Chapter Outline

1 A Decade of Material Progress

2 The Jazz Age

3 Behind the Facade

Life in the United States was never the same after the World War. Before the war people still hitched their horses to posts outside the general store, scrubbed their clothes over washboards, and read by flickering gaslights. After the war gas pumps replaced hitching posts, washing machines replaced scrub boards, and electric lights replaced gas flames. Farmers bought tractors to replace their workhorses. Women cut their hair short and abandoned the long, restrictive skirts they had worn before.

The 1920s was a breathless decade with many names: the Roaring Twenties, the Jazz Age, the Prosperity Decade, the Flapper Era, the Golden Twenties. Most of all it was a time of change—rapid and exciting change—as movies, radios, electricity, vacuum cleaners, and dozens of other inventions altered the patterns of everyday life.

One symbol of the decade was the automobile. Henry Ford's pioneering efforts to mass-produce a low-priced car allowed many Americans to buy one. The extensive use of private cars transformed American society.

1 A Decade of Material Progress

For many Americans, the 1920s meant a better life. Factories poured out a seemingly endless stream of goods, and more people than ever before could afford to buy them. Industrial innovations and improved technology increased productivity and added to the nation's material wealth.

A Surge of Electrical Power

The output of electricity soared after 1900 as a result of new production methods that allowed power plants to burn less coal while generating more power. Between 1902 and 1929 the production of electric power increased by 19 times. Before the war, 20 percent of American homes had electricity. By the end of the 1920s, 70 percent were equipped with electric power.

Abundant electricity allowed Americans to enjoy a wide range of electrically powered consumer goods. Electric refrigerators, vacuum cleaners, and electric stoves transformed American homes during the 1920s. Total sales of major household appliances more than doubled during the decade, while sales of portable appliances jumped from $71 million to $106 million. Electricity not only made home life more pleasant, it made industrial production more efficient.

More Efficient Industry

Although the number of industrial workers remained the same, production of goods in the United States increased 25 percent between 1921 and 1928. The growing use of electrically powered equipment was partially responsible. In 1914, 30 percent of American factory machinery was electrically powered. By 1929 that figure had risen to 70 percent. Electric power enabled a worker to do more in less time. Between 1920 and 1929 output per working hour went up 35 percent, twice the increase of the previous decade.

Scientific management also made industry more efficient. The leading advocate of scientific management was Frederick W. Taylor. He believed that employers should systematically study the performance of their workers in order to find ways to increase efficiency. As chief engineer at the Midvale Steel Company during the 1880s, Taylor studied the productivity of individual workers. He observed the number of steps a worker took and how often the worker picked up a particular tool.

Taylor conducted experiments to determine how much workers should be able to lift and carry. Then he devised plans to increase the efficiency of workers and machines. He might suggest the use of a smaller shovel or the repositioning of a machine control panel. At the Midvale plant Taylor was able to boost output by 300 percent with no increase in the work force.

News of Taylor's success spread rapidly, and many firms, including the Bethlehem Steel Company, sought his advice. Although

Improved technology and management methods combined to increase the productivity of business in the 1920s. The text of this 1925 advertisement noted that the product used "up-to-date machinery so located that every manufacturing process follows in logical order."

Taylor died in 1915, other "efficiency experts" emerged to continue his work. By the 1920s Taylor's methods were widely practiced in American industry.

Henry Ford

Henry Ford was one industrialist who learned Taylor's lessons well. After working as chief engineer for the Edison Illuminating Company, Ford turned his attention to the manufacturing of cars. After he organized the Ford Motor Company in 1903, he revolutionized the automobile industry. Ford applied electric power and scientific management to the production of an item the public wanted to buy.

In 1914 Ford introduced an electrically powered assembly line at his Highland Park, Michigan, plant. On the *assembly line* workers stood at their work stations while unfinished cars moved past them on a conveyor belt. Each worker performed one simple task on each car as it moved by. Ford's efficiency experts determined what each individual task should be and how long

it should take. The Model T, Ford's first car, rolled off the new assembly line in record numbers.

Before the introduction of the assembly line, each car had taken 14 hours to build. But in Ford's new Highland Park plant a car could be assembled in an hour and a half. As other automobile manufactuers instituted Ford's techniques, the industry prospered. The number of cars produced annually soared from 4,000 in 1900 to 4.8 million in 1929.

Ford knew how to sell cars. He believed that more people would buy a car if the price was low. With his efficient assembly lines, Ford could produce cars inexpensively. In 1914 a new Model T sold for $400. A decade later Ford had reduced the price to $260. Although the Model T came in only one color—black—people flocked to Ford showrooms.

The Impact of the Automobile

About 9 million automobiles were registered in the United States in 1920. By 1930 registra-

Dozens of new products appeared on the market in the 1920s, but none was more sought after than the automobile. By 1928, when this photo was taken in Maryland, a new phenomenon had entered the American scene: the traffic jam.

tions had more than tripled. The millions of new cars created new demands. In 1920 highways were often nothing more than rutted dirt roads, and driving was often hazardous. Congress passed the Federal Highway Act of 1921 to encourage road building. State governments imposed taxes on gasoline to raise money for highway construction. Between 1921 and 1929 surfaced road mileage in the United States almost doubled. When the Bronx River Parkway opened in New York in 1927, visitors came from Europe to study it. The parkway was an American innovation in highway construction: a limited-access road that wound through a parklike setting.

With good roads, car owners no longer found it necessary to live close to their jobs in the city. The new mobility caused a boom in the growth of suburbs. During the 1920s the population of Shaker Heights, a suburb of Cleveland, increased tenfold. The population of Scarsdale, a New York City suburb, almost tripled during that same period.

The effects of growing suburbs rippled through the economy. Homes, schools, churches, libraries, and post offices had to be built to meet the needs of suburban residents. New construction provided work for many thousands of carpenters, bricklayers, masons, and other skilled workers.

Automobile production generated economic growth in other fields. New jobs opened up in industries that supplied materials used to build cars. These included the rubber, steel, and glass industries. Roadside food stands and motels were built to serve motorists. By 1930 one out of nine workers had a job related to the automobile industry. Each new industry generated jobs, providing more money to spend on goods such as sewing machines, refrigerators, and, of course, cars.

Scientific Breakthroughs

Although the automobile industry was the most spectacular sign of progress during the 1920s, technological breakthroughs affected hundreds of other industries. Many new inventions transformed American life.

During the war, shortages of natural fibers had forced Americans to rely on *synthetics*, or chemically produced fibers. Research in chemistry during the 1920s created additional synthetic fibers. Celanese was developed as an alternative to silk and rayon, an earlier silk substitute. Synthetics wrinkled less easily than natural fibers and were thus popular among busy people who had little time for ironing. A new plastic called cellophane was developed as an alternative to wrapping paper.

Telephoto, a process for sending pictures by wire, was invented during the 1920s, and the first transcontinental photo was sent in 1925. The first transatlantic telephone service between New York and London also began during the decade. Although commercial television was not available in the United States until the late 1940s, researchers performed successful experiments with television during the 1920s. The first televised transmission of pictures occurred in 1927. The following year researchers broadcast the first drama on television.

Advances were also made in medicine. Improvements in anesthesia made surgery safer and less painful. Phenobarbital, a sedative, was first used for the control of epileptic seizures. In 1928 the iron lung was developed to help polio patients breath. A year later a British researcher, Dr. Alexander Fleming, discovered penicillin.

The life expectancy of Americans increased from 49 to 59 years between 1910 and 1930. Infant mortality dropped by two thirds. Deadly diseases such as tuberculosis, diptheria, and smallpox were brought under control. Advances in science and medicine combined with major technological breakthroughs to improve the quality of life for many Americans.

For answers, see p. A 92.

Section Review

1. Identify the following: Frederick W. Taylor, Henry Ford.
2. Define the following terms: scientific management, assembly line, synthetics, telephoto.
3. What impact did Frederick Taylor's studies have on output at the Midvale Steel plant?
4. How was Ford able to keep the prices of his Model T low?
5. Name three other industries that prospered from the growth of the automobile industry.
6. List three scientific advances that occurred during the 1920s.

2 The Jazz Age

Novelist F. Scott Fitzgerald called the period between the war and 1929 the Jazz Age. "My candle burns at both ends," wrote poet Edna St. Vincent Millay, offering an image that captured the restless spirit of the 1920s. This was the decade in which American jazz captured world acclaim and Hollywood became the international film capital. American playwrights, novelists, and poets created enduring works esteemed on both sides of the Atlantic. Americans searched for fun and escape—and many thought they found it.

The American Sound

Of all the music that poured from the new radios, none was more uniquely American, more original, or more typical of the 1920s than jazz. Born in the South, perhaps in New Orleans, jazz blended West African rhythms, black work songs and spirituals, minstrel songs, and European harmonies. Jazz also had roots in the ragtime rhythms of composers such as Scott Joplin and in another kind of music created in the United States, the blues. Musicians improvised on a theme to make jazz what it was: flexible, alive, and everchanging.

The first great jazz musicians were black. They included composer "Jelly Roll" Morton, singer Bessie Smith, and trumpet player, singer, and great improviser Louis Armstrong. Jazz transcended color, however, and musicians of all backgrounds adopted it, adding to the repertoire. In 1917 the all-white Original Dixieland Jazz Band became the first jazz group to make recordings with a large record company.

The Harlem Renaissance

Jazz spread from New Orleans to Chicago to the area of New York City known as Harlem. There Duke Ellington led a jazz band that performed in the well-known Cotton Club. Harlem was home to many black musicians, poets, and novelists. During the 1920s, their work produced a flowering of creativity that became known as the Harlem Renaissance.

Much of the poetry of the Harlem Renaissance protested the prejudice of the era. Langston Hughes, probably the best-known figure of the Harlem Renaissance, proudly reminded his readers of black Americans' African heritage.

Poet Countee Cullen was a Harvard graduate and New York City schoolteacher. One of his earliest poems, "A Song of Praise" (1925), was filled with black pride. Pride was also an important theme in the poetry of Claude McKay. Although McKay lived in Europe during much of the Harlem Renaissance, his powerful verse cast a penetrating light on the problem of discrimination in the United States.

Other figures of the Harlem Renaissance wrote scholarly books and articles about black Americans. Carter G. Woodson, a pioneer in the field of black history, established the *Journal of Negro History* in 1916. The *Journal* published articles on every aspect of black life and history. W.E.B. DuBois (see page 412) wrote about the history of black people and advanced the idea that the fate of blacks in America and Africa was linked.

Marcus Garvey, who came to New York from Jamaica in 1916, drew widespread attention when he urged American blacks to return to Africa to establish a nation there. Garvey's weekly paper, *Negro World*, spread the message of racial pride and tried to popularize the idea of returning to Africa. Although he attracted a large following, Garvey never established an American black community in Africa. His plans collapsed after the failure of several business ventures.

The Movies

The motion picture became a popular pastime during the 1920s. Movie theaters began to appear as early as 1903. After the war Hollywood, a suburb of Los Angeles, emerged as the movie capital of the world.

Early films did not identify the actors, but movie studios soon discovered that the public had clear favorites and would buy tickets to see them again. The age of the movie star had begun, as Clara Bow, John Barrymore, Mary Pickford, Charlie Chaplin, and Lilian Gish became celebrities. With Barrymore or Gish on the marquee, a studio could be almost certain of success.

Izzy and Moe: Prohibition Agents

The doorman at a New York speakeasy, or illegal nightclub, peered through his peek hole. Outside, a fat man clutched a pail of dill pickles. Though the doorman did not recognize the fellow, he opened the door. Who could suspect a person carrying pickles? The pickle salesman, however, was a federal prohibition agent. As such, he was charged with enforcing the Eighteenth Amendment to the Constitution, which prohibited the manufacturing, buying, and selling of alcoholic beverages.

Isadore "Izzy" Einstein stood five feet, five inches tall and weighed 225 pounds. His partner, Moe Smith, was a bit taller and heavier. They were imaginative and flamboyant and frequently made newspaper headlines as the zaniest and most effective prohibition agents in the country.

Izzy, particularly, was a master of disguise. He could move through New York's diverse neighborhoods easily, for he spoke five languages well, four others not so well. On the waterfront he would dress as a fisherman, lugging along a string of fish.

Once, to trap the owner of a "soda fountain" into serving alcohol, Izzy and ten other hefty agents suited up in muddy football uniforms. Then they thundered into the place, whooping that they had just won the last game of the season. "Would any saloon keeper refuse drinks to a bunch of football players in that state of mind?" asked Izzy.

Between them, Izzy and Moe made more than 4,000 arrests. In their five-year career they seized $15-million worth of alcohol and much equipment for making alcohol. Few agents could approach their record of success.

By the mid-1920s, bootlegging, the illegal manufacture and sale of alcohol, was a billion-dollar-a-year business. About half a million people were involved in bootleg operations. Fleets of boats brought alcohol across the Great Lakes from Canada. Rumrunners from Cuba landed easily on the long coastline of Florida. Cars with "booze" hidden in false bottoms crossed the Mexican border. Thousands of homemade stills turned out home-brewed concoctions. Fifteen hundred federal prohibition agents were charged with shutting down these diverse operations. They were expected to patrol the entire country.

Because they were so effective, Izzy and Moe were often sent to other cities to help with important cases. On the road, Izzy timed how long it took a stranger (himself) newly arrived in town to find and buy an illegal drink. His report: New Orleans, 35 seconds; Pittsburgh, 11 minutes; Atlanta, 17 minutes; Washington, D.C., one hour. His experience was just one more indication that while Americans may have voted for Prohibition, millions did not want it applied to their own lives. When Izzy wrote a book about his exploits, he dedicated it "to the 4,392 persons I arrested, hoping they bear me no grudge for having done my duty."

Until 1927 movies were silent; that is, they had no sound track. Audiences read subtitles to follow the plot, and a theater organ or piano provided background music. Americans roared with laughter at the antics of Laurel and Hardy. They thrilled to the fearless exploits of Douglas Fairbanks in *The Three Musketeers* (1921) and adored the romantic Rudolf Valentino in *The Sheik* (1921). The "western" achieved popularity early in the silent era. Actors such as Tom Mix and William S. Hart played tight-lipped heroic cowboys who outsmarted and outfought outlaws.

Despite early popularity, attendance at the silent films began to taper off by the mid-1920s. People were listening to the radio instead. Then, on October 6, 1927, the first talking movie was released, *The Jazz Singer,* starring Al Jolson. The great success of *The Jazz Singer* signaled the end of the silent era. Charlie Chaplin's *City Lights,* made in 1931, was among the last of the great silent movies. Audiences delighted in the new "talkies." Attendance at the movies rose from 60 million paid admissions per week in 1927 to 110 million per week in 1929. Even so, the movies did not dim the popularity of the radio.

Radio

Experimental radio stations had begun to broadcast around 1915, but before 1920 radio was mainly limited to "ham operators" with earphones and crystal sets. The first commercial broadcasting station, WWJ in Detroit, went on the air on August 20, 1920.

The first radios were cumbersome devices. Sounds could be heard only through earphones attached to wires. Rapid technological advances soon modified radio design, however. Within a few years of this photograph, radios had become common in millions of American homes.

On November 2, 1920, KDKA in Pittsburgh broadcast the presidential election returns. But few heard the news of Harding's election on the radio, which was still a novelty in American homes.

By 1921 the new invention had attracted enough interest to fill Madison Square Garden in New York with people listening to radio reports from Arlington National Cemetery on the burial of the "unknown soldier" from the war. Also in 1921, those who had sets could hear blow-by-blow accounts of the heavyweight fight between Jack Dempsey and the French war hero Georges Carpentier. A year later listeners were tuning in to a radio broadcast of the World Series.

President Harding had a radio installed in the White House. Millions listened to the 1924 Democratic convention and the heated debates over candidates and whether to condemn the Ku Klux Klan.

The popularity of radio spread across the United States with stunning speed. Two years after the first commercial broadcast, annual sales of radios totalled $60 million. In 1929 Americans spent $843 million on radios. By 1930 one home in three had a radio. The government began assigning wavelengths to stations in 1927.

A new style of life developed as families clustered around the radio after dinner to listen to their favorite programs. Classical music was a mainstay of early radio programming, which also included comedy series, popular music, news reports, and broadcasts of sports events.

A Time for Heroes and Fads

Bringing nearly immediate reports of news into millions of homes, radio helped create instant heroes and fads. After Gertrude Ederle became the first woman to swim the English Channel in 1926, New York City, her home town, gave her a ticker tape* parade. A year later Charles A. Lindbergh received an even larger parade.

In May 1927 Lindbergh flew from New York to Paris in 33 hours, making the first solo nonstop flight across the Atlantic. Presi-

*Offices in the Wall Street area were equipped with ticker tape machines, devices that record telegraphed stock quotations on strips of paper or tape. During a ticker tape parade, office workers would throw shreds of ticker tape out of windows.

Charles Lindbergh's solo flight across the Atlantic to Paris made the modest young captain an instant hero. This tickertape parade in New York City was one of several parades in his honor.

dent Coolidge sent a warship to bring the pilot and his plane home. When Lindbergh returned to New York City he received a tumultuous welcome. Newspapers estimated that street cleaners swept up 1,800 tons (about 1,600 metric tons) of paper after Lindbergh's ticker tape parade. Lindbergh was widely regarded as a hero, since his feat combined bravery and skill. To many he embodied the values of courage and modesty.

Other heroes emerged from the movies, as millions felt they personally knew glamorous stars like Greta Garbo, Mary Pickford, and Douglas Fairbanks. Comedians Buster Keaton and Charlie Chaplin, in their gentle satires of the newly mechanized society, touched the lives of thousands. Young people tried to copy the dress, hairstyles, and mannerisms of the stars. Sports greats such as auto racer Barney Oldfield, tennis player Helen Wills, and boxer Jack Dempsey achieved glory and captured the imaginations of many.

In 1926 fans listened to their radios breathlessly as Babe Ruth hit one homerun after another to set a record of 60 homers in one season. Fans filled major league baseball stadiums to see Ruth, Ty Cobb, and other stars. College football, with stars like Red Grange, also drew thousands of spectators. Sports events of all kinds, from horse and auto racing to tennis, enjoyed rising attendance. The number of golf courses tripled in the decade.

Magazines, newspapers, and radio stations looked for amusing stories and publicized dozens of fads from sitting on flagpoles for days to playing the Chinese game Mah Jong. Crossword puzzles also became a rage. Golfers studied the *Psychology of Golf* while insurance salespeople pored over the *Psychology of Selling Life Insurance*. A Frenchman, Emile Coué (ay MEEL koo AY), filled auditoriums with his lectures on how to find contentment. His formula, simplified, consisted of repeating, "Day by day in every way I am getting better and better."

A Modern Kind of Art

On February 17, 1913, a huge art show opened at the Sixty-ninth Regimental Armory in New York City. The Armory Show was organized by the Association of Painters

The Flapper: A Symbol of the Roaring Twenties

A popular song described her as having "turned-up nose" and "turned-down hose." She was, the singer said, a "flapper, yes sir, one of those." And then he asked wistfully, "Has anybody seen my gal?" If there was a single symbol of the Roaring Twenties, it was the flapper, the restless young woman who always liked to be moving on and trying something new. She shocked her elders in a dozen ways, with her clothes, her slang, her dances, and her refusal to follow traditional rules.

Clothes were the outward expression of her defiance of tradition. Compare a young flapper to the young woman of ten years earlier. The older girl dressed in skirts to her ankles over several layers of petticoats. Under all that she wore a rigid corset to achieve an "hourglass" figure. Her sleeves were long and her neckline high. Her long hair was caught up modestly in braids or a bun.

The flapper refused to wear petticoats or to squeeze into a corset. She shortened her skirts right up to the knee, revealing, not traditional dark cotton stockings, but flesh-colored silk hosiery. Frequently, she rolled the stockings down to her knees. She "bobbed" her hair short for comfort and simplicity. And, while the well-bred woman of an earlier generation rarely "painted" her face, the flapper wore bright red lipstick.

Yet the flapper was more than just a giddy symbol of the jazz age. She also symbolized the new social freedom of women. A 1922 letter to the *Daily Illini*, a college newspaper, noted:

> The word flapper to us means, not a female atrocity who smokes, swears, delights in pictures like *The Sheik*, and kisses her gentlemen friends good night. . . . We always think of the flapper as the independent . . . young woman, a typical American product. . . . Any real girl . . . who feels pugilistically inclined [ready to fight] when called the "weaker sex" . . . and who wants to get into things herself, is a flapper.

The most common image of the flapper, however, was that of a zany young woman such as the one shown below, being serenaded by musicians at the Washington Zoo. Just about everyone knew what a flapper should look like, for week after week sketches of flappers appeared on the covers of popular magazines. From such pictures, young women who were not quite sure how to achieve the proper style could pick up pointers.

and Sculptors and had for its motto "The New Spirit." The exhibition was the first major display of modern art in the United States.

While traditional European and American artists tried to represent reality in a fairly photographic way, modern artists did not let realism limit what they put on the canvas. Much of modern art was abstract. For example, Pablo Picasso, a Spanish artist, painted his figures in geometric shapes: cubes, spheres, and cones. The new styles provoked howls of protest. An abstract painting by Marcel Duchamp titled *Nude Descending the Staircase* became the object of endless jokes. One skeptic parodied Duchamp's work by painting *The Rude Descending a Staircase*, a rather jumbled picture of the New York subway at rush hour.

Although modern art remained controversial, during the 1920s many American artists and critics began to accept the new form. In 1929 the Museum of Modern Art opened in New York City. Under the direction of Alfred H. Barr, Jr., the museum began to bridge the gap between European and American art. It displayed not only paintings and sculpture but also the work of architects, designers, photographers, and filmmakers. It thus helped the public understand that these fields too were "art."

While the museum tried to define trends in art, individual painters pursued their own private visions, sometimes far outside the "modern" framework. Edward Hopper's landscapes captured both the isolation of rural farmhouses and the lonely anonymity of industrial cities. Grant Wood also painted scenes of rural America, including his memorable portrait of a somber farm couple, *American Gothic* (1930). Georgia O'Keefe celebrated urban landscapes of skyscrapers in her early paintings and later turned to southwestern themes.

The variety of entertainment Americans enjoyed during the 1920s reflected the restless spirit of the decade. Movies and radio made use of new technology, and many musicians and painters tried to capture the mood of the growing cities. Yet the world of entertainment and fads was only part of life during the Roaring Twenties.

For answers, see p. A 92.

Section Review

1. Identify the following: Harlem Renaissance, Langston Hughes, Marcus Garvey, Gertrude Ederle, Charles Lindbergh, Museum of Modern Art.
2. What types of music provided the roots of jazz?
3. What two new forms of entertainment became popular during the 1920s?
4. What characteristics helped make Charles Lindbergh a hero to many Americans?
5. What type of art was exhibited at the Armory Show of 1913?

3 Behind the Facade

The glamor of the Roaring Twenties shone from movie screens and blared from radio speakers. However, not all Americans were caught up in the excitement. Many rejected the glitter and the changing values, defending a more traditional way of life. Large numbers of Americans were bypassed by the material prosperity of the decade. One group of disillusioned American writers saw conformity and corruption behind a facade of material progress.

In Defense of Traditional Values

Millions of Americans, especially those living in small towns and rural areas, believed that the rapid social and economic changes of the Roaring Twenties were destroying a way of life. To counteract what they considered an immoral force, these people worked to strengthen and defend their own values.

Church membership grew throughout the 1920s, and books on religion multiplied. Revival meetings attracted large audiences. All over the nation people went to church socials, rodeos, and country fairs—pastimes far removed from city speakeasies, private clubs where alcohol was sold illegally.*

---

*As you read in Chapter 26, the Eighteenth Amendment had banned the manufacture, sale, and transportation of alcoholic beverages. The amendment was in effect throughout the 1920s, but it was frequently ignored even by otherwise law-abiding citizens.

The fads and fancies of the Jazz Age attracted publicity, but the traditional life of much of rural America continued with little outward change. Painter Grant Wood captured the serenity and prosperity of the countryside in this painting, entitled Stone City, Iowa.

To many Americans, Henry Ford represented the strength of traditional values. He was widely admired for his rise from modest origins, his organizational ability, and his vast fortune. Because Ford championed the values of honesty and thrift, he was a hero to many Americans.

Changes for Women

Henry Ford praised the 1920s as a time of great opportunity. Yet that opportunity was more a promise than a reality for American women. Women had won the right to vote with the ratification of the Nineteenth Amendment in 1920. (See page 483.) Many reformers believed that this victory would usher in an age of complete equality, but they were wrong. Women did not concentrate their political efforts on women's rights causes or candidates. The League of Women Voters, for example, supported a wide range of reform measures, not just "women's" issues.

Some young women expressed a new sense of social freedom by cutting their hair short and wearing loose-fitting, comfortable clothes. Homemakers also found some of their tasks simplified by new electrical appliances and by a trend to smaller houses and apartments. However, few women achieved economic independence in the 1920s. Although more women were working outside the home, they received far from equal treatment in the job market. Most women held jobs with low pay and little prestige.

Those Prosperity Missed

Although prosperity was symbolic of the 1920s, not all Americans enjoyed economic well-being. As you read in Chapter 29, farmers found it increasingly difficult to make a living after the war. Southern agriculture was particularly hard hit. The boll weevil destroyed millions of acres of cotton. New synthetic fabrics decreased the demand for cotton and lowered cotton prices. Black sharecroppers* suffered terribly during these years.

Because of the depressed economy and rigid racial segregation in the South, almost a million blacks fled to the North during the 1920s. Yet few found greater prosperity in northern cities. Black workers were excluded from most labor unions and often limited to the lowest-paying jobs when they could find them.

Native Americans and Mexican immigrants were also deprived of the prosperity of the 1920s. The authors of the Dawes Act, passed in 1887, had hoped to see Indians assimilated into the general population. (See page 371.) Reservation land was to be divided up among individual Indians to encourage farming.

In actuality, however, Native Americans lost over 60 percent of the land they had owned before 1887, and what acreage remained was often unsuitable for farming. Furthermore, the Dawes Act had weakened Indian culture and traditions. A 1926 report on conditions among Native Americans revealed that a majority were "extremely poor" and that they suffered from poor health and inadequate education.

In 1900 there were about 100,000 people of Mexican birth living in the Southwest. From 1911 to 1920, the Mexican Revolution disrupted the Mexican economy and sparked an exodus to the United States. By 1930 more than a million Mexicans had crossed the border.

Mexicans were attracted to the United States by the availability of jobs in the vegetable fields and orchards of the Southwest. As the area became industrialized, the immigrants took factory jobs. By 1930, 180,000 Mexican-Americans worked in agriculture while 150,000 were employed in industry.

Mexican agricultural workers lived under difficult conditions. As *migrant workers,* they traveled from farm to farm, employed by farmers only as long as necessary to bring in a crop. Migrant workers usually received low wages and could find only squalid hous-

---

*As you read in Chapter 19, sharecroppers farmed a piece of land and shared the crops they raised with the landowners.

ing. In the cities Mexican Americans were crowded into dilapidated, poverty-stricken districts. Like most blacks and Native Americans, Mexican Americans shared little of the material wealth of the 1920s.

The Lost Generation

Some of the best writers of the 1920s took a critical look at prosperity and material progress. In books, plays, and poetry, this Lost Generation, as they were known, described a society that congratulated itself on progress while stifling dissent and creativity.

No writer was more scathing than Sinclair Lewis, author of *Main Street* and *Babbitt,* novels about fictitious Midwestern communities. George Babbitt, the main character of the second novel, illustrated all the traits Lewis disliked. Babbitt was boorish, smug, and determined to make everyone else think and act as he did. When Lewis won the Nobel Prize for Literature in 1930, however, he remarked that it should have gone instead to another American writer, Willa Cather. Cather, a former magazine editor, wrote novels stressing the importance of moral values. She had won a Pulitzer Prize in 1922 for *One of Ours.*

F. Scott Fitzgerald, author of *The Great Gatsby* and *This Side of Paradise,* attacked the transparent values of the period and

Major Events	
1913	Armory Show of modern art
1914	Henry Ford introduces assembly line
1920	First radio broadcasting station goes on the air
1926	Gertrude Ederle swims English Channel
1927	Charles Lindbergh flies Atlantic Ocean; first televised transmission of pictures; *Jazz Singer* is first talking movie
1928	Iron lung developed
1929	Museum of Modern Art opens in New York City

spent a great deal of his career in Paris. There he mingled with other talented American *expatriates*, people who had given up their homeland to live abroad, such as Ernest Hemingway. In his books Hemingway explored the disillusionment of people who had believed the war had been fought for the betterment of humanity.

The brilliant American poet T. S. Eliot moved permanently to London, where he wrote, but for some years he had to earn a living as a bank clerk. Others of the Lost Generation remaining in the United States often clustered in places where conformity was not expected, such as Greenwich Village in New York City. Wherever they lived, talented Americans produced enduring literature during this period. Eugene O'Neill wrote 18 plays during the 1920s. Theodore Dreiser wrote *An American Tragedy*. Eliot produced *The Waste Land*, and John Dos Passos wrote *Manhattan Transfer*.

Most of the great writers of the period were deeply concerned about the quality of American life. They believed that Americans had become obsessed with wealth and material progress. These writers believed that conformity was burying the tradition of individualism. They saw vitality in American life but believed that Americans were wasting their energies on frivolous, meaningless pursuits. Some great literature was produced in reaction to the new values of the Roaring Twenties.

For answers, see p. A 92.

Section Review

1. Identify the following: Sinclair Lewis, Willa Cather, F. Scott Fitzgerald, Ernest Hemingway, T. S. Eliot.

2. Define the following terms: migrant worker, expatriate.

3. Did achieving the right to vote usher in an age of equality for women? Explain.

4. What groups missed the prosperity of the 1920s?

5. What did the name Babbitt come to mean as a result of Sinclair Lewis's novel *Babbitt*?

★ ★

IN PERSPECTIVE   The 1920s were years of impressive material progress. The use of electricity grew rapidly, and industry became more efficient. Productivity increased, especially in the automobile industry, in which Henry Ford introduced the assembly line and efficient manufacturing methods. The period saw the beginning of the automobile age, leading to the rapid growth of suburbs and of industries that supplied materials for automobile manufacture.

Jazz, a uniquely American music, flourished and gave the decade its flavor. The period also saw a flowering of black culture known as the Harlem Renaissance. By the end of the 1920s silent movies, popular early in the decade, were being replaced by "talkies." Radio was a novelty in 1920, but by 1930 it had become a major part of American life. The new form of mass communication helped popularize heroes and fads.

Not everyone participated in the social changes of the Roaring Twenties, however. Millions of Americans continued to believe in traditional values and traditional ways of life. Many people were also denied the prosperity of the decade. Farmers, blacks, Native Americans, and Mexican Americans frequently suffered economic hardship. Some of the best American writers of the 1920s were critical of the materialism they saw in American society. As you will read in the following chapter, their pessimistic visions became reality for much of the nation as the decade drew to a close.

For answers, see p. A 92.

Chapter Review

1. (a) How did the use of electricity change between 1900 and 1930? (b) How did that change affect American home life? (c) How did it affect industry?

2. (a) How did Frederick Taylor try to make industry more efficient? (b) Was he successful? Explain.

3. (a) What new techniques did Henry Ford introduce into the manufacture of automobiles? (b) What impact did such techniques have on the industry?

4. (a) How did the growth of the automobile industry affect American society? (b) What impact did it have on other industries?

5. What were the themes of much of the writing of the Harlem Renaissance?

6. (a) How did motion pictures change during the 1920s? (b) What impact did radio have on people's lives?

7. (a) How did the "modern art" at the Armory Show in 1913 differ from traditional art? (b) What impact did the Museum of Modern Art have on the public attitude toward art?

8. (a) Why did winning the right to vote not usher in an era of complete equality for women? (b) How did the lives of some American homemakers change during the 1920s? (c) What was the status of women who worked outside the home during that decade?

9. Explain how each of the following missed the prosperity of the 1920s: (a) black Americans; (b) Native Americans; (c) Mexican Americans.

For answers, see p. A 93.

For Further Thought

1. (a) How did the writers of the Lost Generation describe American society? (b) What do you think influenced these writers' opinions? (c) Do you think most Americans agreed with them? Explain.

2. (a) How might you explain the stunning growth in the popularity of radio during the 1920s? (b) What evidence of that growth can you cite?

For answers, see p. A 93.

Developing Basic Skills

1. *Using Primary Sources* Works of art and literature can be important sources of information about an historical period. Studying a painting or a poem, for example, can help you understand the artist's view of the time in which he or she lived. Choose an artist or writer who was active during the 1920s and study one of his or her works. Write a report in which you explain what you learned about the 1920s from the work.

2. *Relating Past to Present* Consider the role that television plays in contemporary society. (a) In what ways do you think radio played a similar role in the 1920s? (b) How has the role of radio in American society changed since the 1920s?

See page 778 for suggested readings.

31

From Prosperity to Despair

(1928–1932)

A cover from Vanity Fair *magazine.*

For many Americans the 1920s seemed a decade of unending prosperity. Yet in the fall of 1929 the United States plunged into a prolonged economic depression that shattered the lives of millions of Americans. The depression continued throughout the 1930s and did not end completely until the United States entered a second world war in 1941.

Before 1929 most Americans believed that with an education, hard work, and a little luck, they could get ahead. At the very least, their children could get ahead. However, the long, bleak years of depression dimmed that optimism.

Millions of people eager for work were unable to find jobs. Feet shuffling with embarrassment, they stood in endless lines for bread and soup. They begged for work—any work, at any salary. By 1932, the worst year of the Great Depression, one in four Americans in the labor force was jobless.

1 The Bubble Bursts

The glitter of the Roaring Twenties hid economic problems that lay beneath the surface of general prosperity. Workers were finding it more difficult to make a decent living. Farmers were suffering from low prices. More and more people were borrowing money to finance get-rich-quick schemes. Signs of these problems were evident by 1927, but few observers noticed.

Signs of a Slowdown

Although the wages of industrial workers grew during the 1920s, they did not keep up with rising prices or the rising production of goods. Thus workers found it increasingly difficult to buy the very products they made. As a result, demand for some goods began to decline, and production slowed down. Manufacturers invested less money in new plants and equipment. As factories cut back production, workers were laid off. The cutbacks lowered workers' income still further. In 1929 a study of working families in Muncie, Indiana, revealed that in 40 percent of the families, a worker had been laid off at least one month that year.

Some industries, such as textiles and soft-coal mining, had been in a state of decline for many years. For workers in those industries, the prosperity of the 1920s was just something they read about in the newspapers. The words on a tombstone in a Pennsylvania mining town lament the plight of many workers:

> For forty years beneath the sod
> With pick and spade I did my task
> The coal king's slave, but now, thank God,
> I'm free at last.

Even in prosperous industries there were signs of economic slowdown. By 1929 construction was growing at a slower pace than earlier in the decade. Production in the automobile industry, which had been one of the fastest-growing industries of the decade, began to decline. Conditions in agriculture were even more disturbing.

One third of American families lived on farms during the 1920s, and they faced grim economic conditions throughout much of the decade. It was becoming increasingly expensive to run a farm. Like most Americans, farm families wanted modern appliances and a car. But their expenses rose much faster than the prices they received for their products. The very efficiency of the farmers contributed to their financial problems, since overproduction kept prices low. (See page 529.)

As the 1928 presidential election neared, most people saw the farm problem as the one major economic difficulty facing the country. They had not yet noticed the other warning signals.

The Election of 1928

Had he run for reelection, Calvin Coolidge might have won easily. However, he surprised nearly everyone by announcing in his typically concise fashion, "I do not choose to run for President in 1928."

Republicans had little difficulty choosing Herbert Hoover to replace Coolidge. Secretary of Commerce Hoover had the popularity, the experience, and the confidence of party leaders. He had made a fortune as a consulting engineer on projects all over the world. Hoover had also directed a massive famine-relief program in Europe in the wake of the war. Through his efforts, millions of people were fed. As secretary of commerce for eight years, he had actively promoted the development of United States business. To many Americans, Hoover represented several ideals: he was a self-made man of wealth, an efficiency expert, and a humanitarian.

At their convention in Houston, Texas, Democrats picked a candidate who offered a vivid contrast to the businesslike, restrained Hoover. They chose the outspoken four-time governor of New York, Al Smith. The son of Irish immigrant parents, Smith grew up in New York City. He differed from Hoover in his background, style, and beliefs.

Smith's initial rise in politics had been through the New York City Tammany Hall political machine. A Roman Catholic, he attracted the support of many of the "new immigrants" from southern Europe who had settled in cities. In contrast, Hoover, born in West Branch, Iowa, seemed to represent traditional small-town Protestant America.

The positions of the two candidates were also quite different. Hoover believed in what he called the "rugged individualism" of Americans. He recognized that farmers were suffering, but he felt that their problems could be solved by their own efforts and through cooperation. Government, he claimed, should not meddle in farmers' problems. Hoover also opposed government interference in business.

By contrast, Al Smith stood for public ownership of some electric power companies. Furthermore, the Democratic platform urged strong government action to help farmers. As the first Roman Catholic to be nominated for the presidency by either party, Smith became the focus of a savage anti-Catholic campaign. His pledge to end Prohibition also drew fierce attacks from "dry" forces who wanted it continued.

On election day the popular Hoover swept 40 of the 48 states, including Smith's own New York. Hoover's victory reflected the voters' belief that the nation was healthy and, in general, prosperous. During the campaign, Hoover capitalized on this belief when he declared, "We in America today are nearer to the final triumph over poverty than ever before in the history of any land."

Get-Rich-Quick Fever

When people made quick fortunes during the 1920s, newspapers told their stories. Soon many people who read these stories believed that they too might stumble onto a pot of gold. They thought that the quickest way to get rich was to speculate in land or stocks.* The object was to buy a piece of land or a stock at a low price, wait for the price to rise, and then sell the stock or property for a handsome profit.

People speculated in land all across the country as the building of suburbs drove land prices skyward. But nowhere was the land boom as big as in Florida. The suitability of the warm Florida climate for vacation resorts attracted many speculators. People bought any land available, including swamps, in the hopes of making a big profit. And indeed the value of Florida land soared. Those who had bought early made huge profits. But a devastating hurricane roared through Florida in 1926, ending the land boom there.

If investing in land seemed too risky, speculators could always turn to the stock market. Only a small percentage of the population actually bought stocks during the 1920s. One estimate put the number of investors at about 1.5 million. However, their success stories fascinated people everywhere. Investors often paid little attention to what the companies issuing the stocks actually earned. Inexperienced investors assumed that prices would simply keep rising no matter how well the companies did.

To attract investors, many brokers sold shares of stock *on margin*. That is, the investor paid only part of the selling price in cash and borrowed the rest on margin from the stock broker. The broker in turn borrowed money from banks and corporations in order to cover loans made to investors. If the investor could not repay the loan, the

Among the many get-rich-quick schemes of the 1920s was speculation in Florida land. This 1925 drawing for the cover of Life *magazine mocks a couple who bought Florida land sight unseen, only to learn that their "land" was in a swamp.*

---

*As you learned in Chapter 21, stocks are shares of ownership in a corporation.

broker took the stock. Investors had to pay interest on the loan, but if the price of the stock went up, the buyer could repay the loan and the interest and still make a profit. By 1929 some 600,000 investors were buying on margin.

The Crash

For a while, the system seemed to work. Stock prices rose steadily during the 1920s. In March 1928 prices began to soar, and the number of shares traded rose sharply. There seemed little reason for the upswing since business profits and prices of goods had leveled off the year before. But the boom continued through the summer of 1929.

By September stock prices were 400 percent higher than they had been five years earlier. Some cautious investors began to sell their stocks. There were fewer buyers, and prices edged downward. In early October, prices slid badly as orders to sell outnumbered orders to buy.

A flood of sell orders hit the New York Stock Exchange on October 24. Prices tumbled. Brokers put out *margin calls* to cover loans. That is, the brokers asked investors who had bought on margin to put up more money to cover their loans on stocks that were now worth less. Some investors were unable to put up the extra money and lost their stocks. The margin calls produced more selling as investors tried desperately to raise money. Banks and other creditors, meanwhile, called in their loans to brokers.

On October 29 orders to sell at any price swamped the stock market. There were almost no buyers. The value of stocks crashed downward on the worst day in stock market history. Fortunes made during the boom years vanished in hours.

Business leaders and bankers met hurriedly to find ways to avert a panic. In an attempt to restore public confidence in the economy, John D. Rockefeller announced, "My son and I have for some days been purchasing some common stocks." When he heard this, comedian Eddie Cantor replied, "Sure, who else has any money left?"

549

For answers, see p. A 93.

Section Review

1. Identify the following: Al Smith.
2. Define the following terms: on margin, margin calls.
3. What was one sign of economic slowdown during the 1920s?
4. Name three characteristics of Herbert Hoover that made him a popular presidential candidate in 1928.
5. How did Herbert Hoover and Al Smith differ on the question of government action to help farmers?
6. What two types of investment attracted many speculators during the 1920s?

The Nation's Marketplace

The New York Stock Exchange is often called the nation's marketplace because it is the largest center in the world for buying and selling stock in American and foreign businesses. It was organized in 1792 on Wall Street in New York City. Each year investors trade billions of shares of stock through the New York exchange and other stock exchanges in major cities throughout the United States.

Corporations sell stock to raise money. When investors buy stock, they are entitled to a share in the profits of the corporation and a voice in how the business is run. To buy stock a person places an order with a stockbroker, who handles the transaction. The broker relays the order to a partner working on the floor of the stock exchange, a large open area where purchases and sales are negotiated. The partner buys the stock for the investor at the market price. The transaction is recorded and relayed to brokerage firms through a nationwide communications network.

Stock prices often reflect the state of the economy. If business conditions are good, stock prices tend to rise, creating a bull market. If conditions are poor, stock prices tend to drop, creating a bear market. During the bull market of the 1920s stock prices rose so high that they no longer reflected the state of the economy or the value of the corporations in which stockholders were investing. Much of the stock had been bought on margin, and when brokers began to demand repayment of the loans, investors had to sell at a big loss. The resulting panic led to the great stock market crash of 1929.

2 The Grim Years Begin

The stock market crash did not cause the depression that followed, but it did mark the end of the apparent prosperity of the 1920s. Few escaped the effects of the economic collapse. For major corporations and millions of individuals, fear and failure became as commonplace as optimism and prosperity had been only a short time earlier.

The Causes of the Depression

Many factors contributed to the onset of a wide-ranging economic depression. One cause was a sharp imbalance between supply and demand. For a free enterprise system to operate effectively, the supply of products should equal the demand for those products. But demand had begun to fall during the late 1920s.

American industry had mastered mass production techniques and was supplying a growing number of products. Yet demand was not growing as rapidly as supply. As you read earlier in this chapter, workers' wages had not kept up with prices. Consequently, workers could not afford to buy the goods being produced. The continued weakness of agriculture also meant that farm families could afford to buy few products.

Furthermore many of the items produced in such abundance were durable goods. *Durable goods* are products designed to last several years before being replaced, such as automobiles, refrigerators, stoves, and tractors. By 1929 many people either owned the goods they wanted or could not afford to buy any more, even on credit. Thus the demand for such goods decreased.

Business inventories, or lists of unsold goods on hand, crept upward in 1928 and 1929. In response factories cut back production and laid off some workers. Each person laid off represented another family unable to buy durable goods that year. Job layoffs therefore cut consumer demand still further.

The frailty of the banking system also contributed to the economic collapse. Despite the federal reserve system (see page 478), many individual banks were unable to survive the economic slowdown. Banks had loaned large amounts of money to speculators. In the wake of the stock market crash, some banks failed when borrowers could not pay back their loans. Each bank closing shook the confidence of depositors in other banks, and people began withdrawing their money. Each withdrawal further decreased the money supply. Nearly 5,000 banks failed between 1929 and 1932.

The onset of depression in the United States had international repercussions. Faced with harsh economic troubles of their own, European investors withdrew their money from the United States. A key Vienna bank failed in 1931, indicating a worldwide economic breakdown. The collapse of the German economy came next. The Great Depression had begun.

The ripple effects of economic collapse wiped out many fortunes. Fred Bell, who had been rich before the depression, was photographed selling apples on a San Francisco corner in 1931. The image of a once-prosperous person peddling apples became an enduring symbol of the Great Depression.

Economic Collapse

The spread of depression in the United States was swift and relentless. In 1930, 26,355 businesses failed. Two million fewer cars rolled off the assembly lines than in 1929. Industrial areas suffered first, as payrolls dropped by one third. Employers tried to save money by reducing the work week. They cut the work week to three days, then two, then one. Finally, they laid workers off.

The unemployed workers bought little more than necessary food. Old clothes were patched, mended, or darned. Families fell behind on credit payments for radios, cars, and homes. In time, many lost their cars and houses. People who fell behind on rent were evicted. Construction of new housing came to a halt, throwing still more people out of work.

Bank failures wiped out the savings of hundreds of thousands of individuals who thought they had provided for emergencies. People who had deposited money in savings accounts throughout their entire careers found that their banks had closed. Frequently their money was gone.

For those who were poor when the depression began, life became much more desperate. Poet Langston Hughes noted that the depression took everyone down a peg or two, but that blacks had fewer pegs to fall.

Impact of the Collapse

The United States had experienced depressions before, but the Great Depression seemed to be the worst. For the first time in history, newspapers, magazines, and radio, carried the images of joblessness and homelessness to every corner of the nation. Furthermore, during earlier depressions, more people had lived on farms, where they could at least grow some of their own food. But in

Painter Isaac Soyer captured the soul-crushing despair of being out of work and out of hope in this painting, entitled Employment Agency.

Index of Common Stock Prices
1920–1932

Price Index

28
27
26
25
24
23
22
21
20
19
18
17
16
15
14
13
12
11
10
9
8
7
6
5
4
3
2
1
0

1920 1921 1922 1923 1924 1925 1926 1927 1928 1929 1930 1931 1932

Year

Source: *Historical Statistics of the United States*

■ *There are many ways to measure and chart the changes of a national economy. The graph above and the three that follow reveal pieces of the economic pattern between 1920 and 1932. This graph traces the dizzying climb in the price index of common stocks in the 1920s, the sharp break in 1929, and the plummet after the crash. An index is a method for measuring economic change. The index of common stocks is a weighted average of the prices of selected stocks. The numbers along the vertical axis of the graph are not dollar amounts, but benchmarks for measuring price movements.*

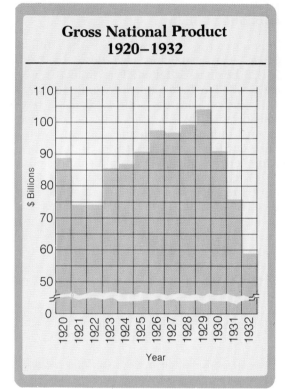

Gross National Product
1920–1932

$ Billions

110
100
90
80
70
60
50
0

1920 1921 1922 1923 1924 1925 1926 1927 1928 1929 1930 1931 1932

Year

Source: *Historical Statistics of the United States*

■ *The gross national product, or GNP, is the total dollar value of all goods and services produced by a country in one year. It is therefore considered a good measure of overall economic health.*

1930 millions depended on industrial jobs for their livelihood. When the factories closed there was no job, no food, and no land on which to grow any.

The depression did not just undercut people's standard of living. It also sapped their sense of personal worth. Americans traditionally valued hard work and believed that the individual was responsible for his or her own welfare. By 1930, 4 million Americans were out of work. By 1932 the figure had risen to 12 million, almost a quarter of the work force.

But such statistics tell little of the misery of broken people looking hopelessly for a job. Men and women lost their identities as carpenters, masons, secretaries, bookkeepers, or auto workers. Whole families scavenged at the city dump and in restaurant garbage cans. Many men, unable to find work, left their families to roam the land seeking work.

New suburban houses built during the boom years stood empty while thousands of families were homeless. People moved into condemned buildings, took over abandoned railroad boxcars, built shacks of tin, cardboard, or orange crates. Everywhere there were lines—lines of people waiting to apply for a job, lines of people waiting for free soup, lines of people waiting for donated clothing.

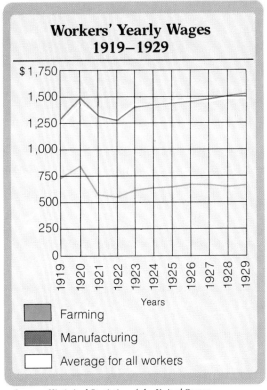

Workers' Yearly Wages 1919–1929

Farming

Manufacturing

Average for all workers

Source: *Historical Statistics of the United States*

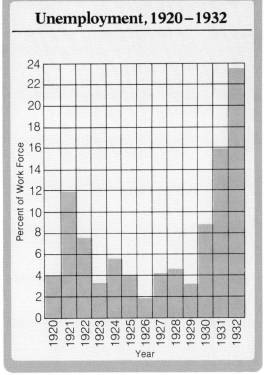

Unemployment, 1920–1932

Source: *Historical Statistics of the United States*

■ *Most workers drew larger pay checks as the 1920s progressed. However, farmers did not share this increased prosperity because of falling world prices for agricultural products. Farm workers earned less in 1929 than they had ten years earlier. Another way of measuring a nation's economic health is to look at the percentage of people who cannot find work. Note the rise and fall in unemployment in the 1920s, then the steep jump in unemployment in 1930, 1931, and 1932. By 1932 nearly one out of every four workers was jobless.*

For answers, see p. A 94.

Section Review

1. Define the following terms: durable goods, business inventories.

2. How were supply and demand imbalanced in the late 1920s?

3. What impact did the stock market crash have on banks?

4. Give two examples of how the onset of the depression affected people's lives.

3 Failure of Traditional Remedies

In the first years of the depression, President Hoover believed he should provide moral leadership and bolster public confidence in the economic system. He stood steadfastly by his belief that government should not intervene directly in the economy. Government-sponsored relief programs, in the President's opinion, would undermine people's self-reliance.

An Initial "Hands-Off" Policy

The President's advisers believed that depression was an inevitable part of the economic cycle and so was recovery. Thus they urged Hoover to allow the depression to proceed without government intervention. Andrew Mellon believed that the depression was a good thing. "People will work harder,

For answers, see p. A 94.

The Economy of the Roaring Twenties: Synthesizing Pieces of Evidence

Throughout this book, you have read, analyzed, and interpreted various kinds of evidence. In order to make the best use of historical evidence, however, you must be able to synthesize, that is, put pieces of evidence together to form a whole.

You will use four pieces of evidence to practice the skill of synthesizing: the graph of the index of common stock prices on page 552; the graph of workers' average yearly wages on page 553; the picture on page 548; and the quotation printed at right from an article by Leonard P. Ayres published in 1927. After studying the pieces of evidence and synthesizing the information they contain, you should have a better understanding of the economy of the 1920s. Follow the steps described below:

1. **Analyze each piece of evidence.** Use the following questions to study the four pieces of evidence: (a) According to the graph on page 552, what was the index of common stock prices in 1925? (b) How had it changed by 1929? (c) According to the graph on page 553, how did the average yearly income of farm workers change between 1922 and 1929? (d) Which group of workers had the largest increase in yearly wages between 1921 and 1929? (e) What economic development is portrayed in the picture on page 548? (f) What did Leonard Ayres think would happen to abrupt changes in the business cycle?

2. **Compare the pieces of evidence.** Answer the following questions: (a) If you looked only at the graph of stock prices between 1925 and 1929, what would you conclude about the economy of the 1920s? (b) Would the data about the wages of farm workers confirm that conclusion or conflict with it? (c) Does the picture give you the same impression of the economy of the 1920s as the quotation does? Explain. (d) How might the picture and what you learned in your text help explain what happened to the stock market after 1929?

3. **Synthesize the evidence in order to draw conclusions.** Review the pieces of evidence and what you read in your text. Then answer the following questions: (a) Would you agree or disagree with the statement that the 1920s was generally a period of economic prosperity? Explain. (b) What economic problems can you identify? (c) Write a paragraph in which you describe the economy of the 1920s in your own words. Cite specific pieces of evidence to support your conclusions.

From "This Prosperity"

Business has attained a degree of stability in this country that is quite beyond any previous precedent. It is wholly probable that the old abrupt business cycles, with their rapid ascents from depression, to recovery, and on up to prosperity in about two years, and their still more rapid descents through general decline back down to depression again in about another year, are things of the past. The country is now too wealthy, and our credit supplies are too ably administered through the Federal Reserve System, to permit a return of those . . . recurring conditions.

live a more moral life, . . . and enterprising people will pick up the wrecks from less competent people."

Despite such advice, President Hoover did try to turn the economy around. He realized that many people had lost confidence in the economy, and he wanted to restore public morale. Hoover tried to convince Americans that conditions were improving. In May 1930 he stated, "We have now passed the worst, and with continued unity of effort we shall rapidly recover." A month later the President announced that the "depression is over."

In another effort to bolster confidence, Hoover invited business leaders to the White House for a series of economic conferences. He urged businesses to expand rather than cut back. Hoover obtained a promise from those who attended the conferences that they would not reduce wages and prices. However, such agreements failed to survive worsening conditions. By September 1931 most major industries had begun to cut wages in order to maintain profits.

The President also suggested spending public funds on public-works projects such as dams and highways. Such projects, he argued, would increase employment and put money back into the economy. By the end of Hoover's presidency, the federal government was spending $500 million more a year on public works than it had in 1928.

Hoover urged state and local governments to spend more money on public works as well. However, the depression had sharply cut revenue from state and local taxes. Thus few governments had extra money for public-works projects. President Hoover insisted that federal public-works projects be funded only to the extent that there was cash to pay for them. He rejected the advice of some experts that the government should borrow money to pay for projects that would create jobs.

Believing that the business cycle would correct itself, Hoover maintained a "hands-off" policy in the beginning of the depression. But the public did not share the President's faith in the economy. In the 1930 elections, voter discontent returned the Democrats to control in the House of Representatives for the first time since 1916.

The Reconstruction Finance Corporation

Pressures for more government action mounted, and Hoover responded in late 1931 by proposing a government agency that could stop bank failures and business closings. Congress created the Reconstruction Finance Corporation (RFC) in 1932. The RFC had power to make loans to banks, railroads, and insurance companies. In addition, Congress went beyond the President's intentions and gave the RFC the right to lend money to local communities for public-works programs.

The RFC did not work the way the President or Congress had hoped. RFC officials were reluctant to loan the money that Congress had given the agency. Banks that did receive loans often used the funds to strengthen their own finances rather than extend credit to the community. The RFC virtually ignored the congressional goal of financing public works.

The creation and operation of the RFC reflected Andrew Mellon's "trickle-down" theory. If the problems of business and industry were solved, the theory held, then benefits would trickle down to ordinary people. But there was little time for the "trickle-down" theory to work as conditions rapidly worsened.

The winter of 1931–1932 was the third winter of depression. "Men are sitting in the parks all day long and all night long, hundreds and thousands of them, muttering to themselves, out of work, seeking work," said William Green, a labor leader from Detroit.

In New York hundreds of homeless people rode the subways all night long that winter because it was warmer than sleeping on a park bench.

By December 1931, 800,000 were jobless in New York City. In Detroit some 223,000 people had no jobs. In Chicago 40 percent of all workers were jobless. Social workers tried valiantly to find money to feed the unemployed and to force government to act. "Have you ever seen the uncontrolled trembling of parents who have gone half starved for weeks so the children may have food?" demanded Lillian Wald of the Henry Street Settlement House in New York.

A Question of Relief

Although President Hoover opposed any direct relief action by the federal government, he urged a massive effort to provide relief through private, voluntary agencies. Organizations such as settlement houses, the Salvation Army, the YMCA, community chests, church groups, and others worked relentlessly to feed and shelter the jobless millions. But sheer numbers of unemployed overwhelmed the effort.

The system of public relief that existed in the first years of the depression was strictly on a local level. Neither the states nor the federal government took part. In rural areas and in some cities and towns, no public relief was available at all. Local poverty relief had been designed to take care of small numbers of people who were unable to work. The system had not been intended to handle the needs of millions.

Furthermore, just when communities needed more money for relief, income from taxes was shrinking. Some cities responded by reducing the amount of relief per family. By the winter of 1931–1932, for example, New York City was able to give each family on relief just $2.39 a week. Many areas did not have even that much to offer.

After more than two years of depression, many city treasuries were empty. By 1932 about 100 cities had run out of funds. In that year only about one in four unemployed received any kind of relief. What they did receive was primarily food. Yet 12 million Americans were jobless, and the number was growing monthly. Those who did have jobs sometimes worked for five or six cents an hour.

At a national conference of social workers in Milwaukee, Wisconsin, Jacob Billikopf, executive director of the Federation of Jewish Charities, warned that private efforts, however valiant, were failing. Government, he said, "will be compelled, by the cruel events ahead of us, to step into the situation and bring relief on a large scale."

The Bonus Army

As the cry for government action increased, jobless veterans took to the road to dramatize their demands. After the war Congress had voted veterans a bonus to be paid in 1941. In 1931 Congress voted to let veterans borrow up to 50 percent of the value of their bonuses, but President Hoover vetoed the bill.

In protest a group of veterans from Oregon set out on a widely publicized journey to Washington, D. C., to demand their bonuses immediately. As they traveled eastward, hundreds and then thousands of other veter-

ans joined them. About 17,000 reached the capital city in the spring of 1932. Most camped in makeshift tents or shacks on the Anacostia Flats, a swampy area near the Potomac River. Some set up camp in abandoned warehouses and government buildings nearby. Wives and children joined many of the veterans.

The House of Representatives voted to give the veterans their bonuses immediately, but the Senate overwhelmingly rejected the bill. Discouraged, some of the "bonus marchers" returned home, but thousands decided to stay in Washington. They vowed to camp there until the government gave them their money.

The presence of such a large group of protestors did little to improve the image of the Hoover administration. Despite the fears of Hoover and his advisers, the veterans were largely peaceful. Much of the calm could be attributed to the tireless actions of Washington Police Chief Pelham Glassford, a former brigadier general. Some of the vet-

Across the United States men, women, and children stood in lines. They stood in lines at factories or employment offices, hoping to get a job. Like the people in this rural soup line, they stood in line for food. Most early relief efforts were private, church-sponsored, or run by local government.

Many jobless veterans hoped that the federal government would make early payment of long-promised World War bonuses. When President Hoover vetoed a bonus bill, thousands of veterans joined a "March on Washington." The signs and placards of these Pennsylvania veterans tell their story.

erans had served under Glassford in the war, and he still considered them "his boys." Daily he rode through the bonus camp on his motorcycle, helping people locate food, shelter, and medicine. When food ran out, he spent his own money to buy more.

President Hoover refused to meet with march leaders. When a fight broke out between marchers and local police, the President ordered the army to tear down the veterans' camp. Under the command of General Douglas MacArthur, cavalry troops used tear gas to clear out the veterans and their families. Newspaper and magazine photos and movie newsreels of the event shocked the public. The scene convinced many that the Hoover administration was incapable of handling the spreading misery of the depression.

The Election of 1932

President Hoover had taken more government action to try to alleviate economic problems than Presidents had in any pre-vious depression. Yet because of the widespread misery in 1932, Hoover became the object of anger and scorn. People living in shanty towns called their communities Hoovervilles. Empty pockets turned inside out were called Hoover flags. Day-old newspapers were known as Hoover blankets.

The President became gloomier as time went on. One observer noted, "If you put a

Major Events

1926	Hurricane hits Florida
1928	Herbert Hoover elected President
1929	Stock market crashes
1932	Reconstruction Finance Corporation created; Bonus Army arrives in Washington, D. C.; Franklin D. Roosevelt elected President

Presidential Election Results, 1928 and 1932

	Party	Candidate	Popular Vote	Percent of Popular Vote	Electoral Vote
1928	Republican	Herbert Hoover	21,391,993	59	444
	Democrat	Alfred Smith	15,016,116	41	87
1932	Republican	Herbert Hoover	15,758,901	40	59
	Democrat	Franklin Roosevelt	22,809,638	58	472
	Minor	Minor candidates	881,951	2	0

■ *The decline of Herbert Hoover's popularity can be seen clearly in this table comparing the 1928 and 1932 presidential elections. In 1928, with the nation enjoying unparalleled prosperity, Hoover swamped his Democratic opponent. Four years later, with joblessness and bank failures at all-time highs, Hoover's bid for reelection was buried in a landslide of votes for Franklin Roosevelt.*

rose in Hoover's hand, it would wilt." The delegates to the Republican nominating convention knew that Hoover's reelection would be almost impossible, but they stood by him and renominated him for a second term.

Democrats at their convention in Chicago had little doubt that Hoover could be defeated, and several well-known leaders sought the nomination. By the fourth ballot the delegates had agreed on the governor of New York, Franklin Delano Roosevelt. A distant cousin of Theodore Roosevelt, the candidate bore a name recognized by most Americans.

A popular and progressive governor, Roosevelt had acted quickly and compassionately when the depression hit. New York was the first state to set up a relief plan for the unemployed. Roosevelt initiated a program that created jobs on land conservation projects, and he proposed a plan for unemployment insurance.

Once nominated, Roosevelt broke tradition by flying to the convention to deliver an acceptance speech in person. "I pledge myself," he told the delegates, "to a new deal for the American people."

During the election campaign, Hoover was dreary and pessimistic while Roosevelt radiated charm and confidence. Roosevelt did not outline a specific program, but he insisted that something needed to be done:

The country needs bold, persistent experimentation. It is common sense to take a method and try it. If it fails, admit it frankly and try another. But above all, try something.

A majority of Americans agreed with him. Roosevelt won the election by a landslide, with 57 percent of the popular vote. Hoover carried only six states, all in the Northeast.

Roosevelt's support had come from city dwellers, immigrants, workers, and farmers. As the Democratic candidate, he also won the "solid South," where Democrats had been in control since the end of Reconstruction. These groups began to form a coalition of voters that would make the Democrats a majority party for the first time since the Civil War.

For answers, see p. A 94.

Section Review

1. Identify the following: Reconstruction Finance Corporation, Bonus Army, Franklin Delano Roosevelt.

2. What did President Herbert Hoover think his main responsibility should be at the onset of the depression?

3. How did Congress go beyond Hoover's intentions when it created the RFC?

4. Give one reason why local relief agencies were unable to provide enough relief during the early years of the depression.

5. What did the Bonus Army want from the federal government?

6. What was Hoover's attitude during the election campaign of 1932?

IN PERSPECTIVE   By the late 1920s the economy showed signs of imbalance, especially in agriculture, but few people were aware of them. Most Americans looked forward to a bright and prosperous future when they overwhelmingly elected Herbert Hoover President in 1928. Speculation in land or stock seemed an easy way of assuring that future. However, such speculation also contributed to the end of prosperity. When stock prices began to fall in late 1929, the flood of orders to sell led to a stock market crash. The economy of the United States slipped into a deep depression. Businesses and banks closed, and people lost their jobs, their cars, and even their homes.

President Hoover opposed federal government interference in the economy, but he did propose the Reconstruction Finance Corporation to halt business and bank failures. He also urged local agencies to provide relief, but the problem was too severe for their meager resources. As the depression deepened without any sign of ending, more and more people blamed Hoover and demanded government action. In 1932, 57 percent of the voters cast their ballots for Franklin D. Roosevelt.

For answers, see p. A 95.

Chapter Review

1. What were the signs of economic problems underlying the prosperity of the 1920s?

2. Describe the personal and political differences between Herbert Hoover and Al Smith, the presidential candidates in 1928.

3. (a) How did speculators try to "get rich quick" during the 1920s? (b) What ended the Florida land boom? (c) How were investors able to buy stock without paying the full price?

4. Describe how each of the following contributed to the onset of depression: (a) imbalance of supply and demand; (b) production of more durable goods; (c) rising business inventories; (d) bank closings.

5. (a) How did the onset of the depression affect many people? (b) Why did this depression seem worse than earlier depressions?

6. (a) What did President Hoover's advisers urge him to do? Why? (b) How did Hoover try to restore public confidence? (c) What type of public-works programs did he support?

7. (a) What powers did Congress grant the Reconstruction Finance Corporation? (b) How did it carry out those powers?

8. (a) Who did Hoover think should be responsible for providing relief? (b) Why were private agencies and local governments unable to provide enough relief?

9. (a) What was the Bonus Army? (b) What did it hope to accomplish?

For answers, see p. A 95.

For Further Thought

1. (a) How was the Reconstruction Finance Corporation an example of Andrew Mellon's "trickle-down" theory? (b) Based on what you have learned about Herbert Hoover, why do you think he supported that theory?

2. Why do you think almost 60 percent of American voters cast their ballots for Franklin Roosevelt in 1932?

For answers, see p. A 95.

Developing Basic Skills

1. *Using Primary Sources*   Visit your local library and look at copies of a newspaper from October 1929. What evidence can you find that the stock market was collapsing?

2. *Using Statistics*   Study the table on page 558 and answer the following questions: (a) How many electoral votes did the Democratic candidate receive in 1932? (b) How many popular votes did the Democratic candidate receive in 1932? (c) How many more popular votes did Hoover receive in 1928 than in 1932? (d) How many more electoral votes did the Democratic candidate receive in 1932 than in 1928? (e) How might you explain this change?

See page 778 for suggested readings.

Unit Nine

A Time of Trial

A New Deal

(1933–1935)

Franklin Delano Roosevelt, *by Ellen Emmet Rand.*

Chapter Outline

1 *The Roots of the New Deal*

2 *The First Hundred Days*

3 *Critics of the New Deal*

4 *The Second New Deal*

When Franklin D. Roosevelt took the oath of office in March 1933, the nation's situation could not have been bleaker. The banking system was near collapse. After three years of depression, the number of unemployed had grown to 13 million. One quarter of the population had virtually no income, and their desperation was frightening.

In January 1933 several hundred jobless people surrounded a restaurant in New York City, demanding to be fed free of charge. In February 5,000 unemployed people besieged the County-City Building in Seattle, demanding help for themselves and their families. Over one million Americans, one quarter of them under age 21, roamed the country looking for work. Wherever they went, they found signs reading: "Move on. We can't take care of our own."

In his acceptance speech at the Democratic nominating convention, Franklin Roosevelt had promised "a new deal for the American people." Now he and his administration faced the overwhelming prospect of implementing that new deal to revive the stricken country.

1 The Roots of the New Deal

The policies and programs that comprised the New Deal reflected the diversity of the people who framed it. A new breed of government workers streamed into Washington as the Hoover administration drew to a close. Social workers, sociologists, economists, political scientists, and lawyers came with highly varied learning, experience, and plans for action. Their goal was to pull the nation out of economic crisis, and their leader was President-elect Franklin D. Roosevelt.

The Shaping of Franklin D. Roosevelt

Like his distant cousin Theodore, Franklin Roosevelt came from a background unusual for a professional politician. As a boy, Franklin grew up in the genteel atmosphere of Hyde Park, New York, amid the rolling country estates lining the Hudson River. There his strong-willed mother taught him that the wealthy and privileged had an obligation to help those less fortunate than themselves.

Roosevelt studied history and government at Harvard College and law at Columbia University. In 1905 he married Anna Eleanor Roosevelt, niece of then President Theodore Roosevelt.

Bored with the idea of a Wall Street law practice, the young Roosevelt was attracted to a potentially more exciting career: politics. In quick succession, he became a New York State senator, assistant secretary of the navy during the war, and Democratic candidate for Vice-President in 1920. After the Democrats lost the 1920 election, Roosevelt returned to private life.

The following summer, as the family vacationed at Campobello in New Brunswick, Canada, Franklin Roosevelt was stricken with polio. At the age of 39, his legs paralyzed, he thought his political career was over.

Eleanor Roosevelt and her husband's devoted political adviser Louis Howe thought differently. They convinced Roosevelt not to give up his active life. Buoyed by their faith in him and his own courage, Roosevelt worked to overcome his physical limitations. After years of grueling exercise and therapy, he was able to walk with the help of heavy metal braces clamped to his nearly useless legs.

In 1928 Franklin Roosevelt ran for governor of New York at the request of Democratic presidential candidate Al Smith. Roosevelt won, even though the national Democratic ticket was defeated. The stock market crashed during his first year in office. As governor Roosevelt saw all too clearly the human suffering caused by the Great Depression. He believed that the government should do what it could to end the depression and relieve the suffering.

Roosevelt had learned early that his wealth obliged him to help others. His illness gave him a sense of compassion for victims of adversity. Those experiences and his belief that government should aid people in need all shaped his political philosophy. That philosophy was one of the bases of the New Deal.

Ideas for Action

In politics, Roosevelt was above all an activist. Although he had no specific program, he had promised a "new deal" during the 1932 campaign. (See page 558.) Once elected, Roosevelt sought bold ideas for action. Many of the ideas on which the New Deal was based were not new. They reflected the aims of progressives early in the century: conserving natural resources, breaking down monopolies, regulating business, and improving working conditions. Like the progressives, the architects of the New Deal wanted to preserve democracy and the free enterprise system.

The lessons learned during the World War also influenced the development of the New Deal. To fight the war, government planning agencies had worked with business and agriculture to coordinate the efficient production of food and manufactured goods. (See page 506.) Many of Roosevelt's advisers thought that similar federal agencies should be set up to fight the war against economic depression.

Still more ideas came from a group of advisers called Roosevelt's brain trust, so named because several of them had taught at universities. These professors of economics, social planning, and law, led by Raymond Moley and Rexford Tugwell, helped Roosevelt chart the course of the early New Deal. They stressed the value of centralized planning to avoid overproduction and wasteful competition.

Roosevelt's cabinet members also contributed to the New Deal programs. The new secretary of the interior, Harold Ickes, had been a progressive Republican and a leader of reform politics in Chicago. Henry A. Wallace, another progressive Republican, led the fight for new farm programs as secretary of agriculture. Roosevelt called on Frances Perkins, a labor relations specialist, to take the post of secretary of labor, making her the first woman ever to hold a cabinet position.

Frances Perkins, the first woman cabinet officer, served as secretary of labor through the Roosevelt years. Previously, as chairwoman of the New York State Industrial Board, she had won reduction of the work week for women in New York from 54 to 48 hours. Here, the secretary of labor greets workers.

Although Roosevelt began the New Deal with few concrete plans, he had a wealth of ideas from which to choose. Furthermore the goals of the new President and his administration were clear: to provide relief for the unemployed as quickly as possible, to help bring about the recovery of the nation's weakened economic structure, and to enact reforms to correct the conditions that had contributed to the economic crisis.

A New Beginning

On inauguration day, March 4, 1933, Herbert Hoover and Franklin Roosevelt rode together in an open car down Pennsylvania Avenue toward the Capitol. The months since the November election had strained relations between the two men. Hoover had asked Roosevelt for a pledge to carry out certain policies that the Republican President thought essential. Roosevelt, who rejected his predecessor's economic policies, had refused. As they rode along, they barely spoke to each other.

When they spoke to the country at large that day, they expressed opposite points of view. Upon leaving office, Hoover had lamented privately, "We are at the end of our rope. There is nothing more we can do."

Roosevelt, on the other hand, voiced confidence, optimism, and promise for the country in his inaugural address. "First of all," he began, "let me assert my firm belief that the only thing we have to fear is fear itself—nameless, unreasoning, unjustified terror which paralyzes needed efforts to convert retreat into advance." Promising a dramatic change in economic policy, the President concluded, "The nation asks for action and action now. We must act and act quickly."

For answers, see p. A 96.
Section Review

1. Identify the following: brain trust, Harold Ickes, Henry A. Wallace, Frances Perkins.
2. How did Franklin Roosevelt's being stricken with polio probably affect his attitude toward fighting the Great Depression?
3. List several sources of ideas for the New Deal.
4. How did the moods of Hoover and Roosevelt differ on Inauguration Day in 1933?

2 The First Hundred Days

The Roosevelt family had barely moved into the White House when the new President plunged into action. He knew that he had to move quickly to convince the American people that their nation could indeed be saved from total economic disaster. During the first three months of his administration Roosevelt drafted and convinced Congress to pass 15 major pieces of legislation. The new laws established agencies to fight every aspect of the Great Depression. This period of frenzied action came to be called "the hundred days."

Relieving the Banking Crisis

During the four months between Roosevelt's election and his inauguration the national banking system neared total collapse. Fearful of repeated bank failures, people withdrew their money and hoarded it in mattresses, under floorboards—anywhere but in the banks. As the money flowed out, the banks failed. The governor of Michigan had ordered all the banks in Detroit closed in an attempt to save them. Similar action was planned in the major banking centers of Chicago and New York.

Roosevelt decided that his first step must be to halt the crippling bank failures. Within hours of his inauguration he declared a national "bank holiday." With this action he closed all the banks in the country for an indefinite period. This "holiday," he believed, would stop people from withdrawing their money and thus prevent still more bank failures.

At the same time, the President ordered his secretary of the treasury to draft an emergency banking bill to save the banking system. Five days later the bill was read to a special session of Congress, called by the new President. With shouts of approval, Congress passed the Emergency Banking Relief Act almost unanimously.

The new law allowed the reopening of banks that had sufficient funds to satisfy depositors' withdrawal requests. Essentially sound banks would be allowed to borrow federal funds to reopen. Those banks judged unsound would remain closed.

A few nights later Roosevelt went on nationwide radio with the first of many *fireside chats*, informal talks he made to the American people. In clear and convincing terms he described the measures the Emergency Banking Relief Act provided. He urged his listeners to return their money to the reopened banks. "I can assure you," he said, "it is safer to keep your money in a reopened bank than under the mattress."

During those first days Roosevelt presented other proposals to Congress. He sent the legislature a government economy bill that would reduce the salaries of all federal employees and cut veterans' pensions. Two days later Congress passed the bill despite the vehement opposition of veterans. The President also submitted a proposal to legalize the sale of beer and light wines. Again Congress agreed, this time over the opposition of the prohibitionists.*

The speed with which the new administration converted proposals into action excited many Americans. Will Rogers, the popular humorist, summed up Roosevelt's first week in office: "The whole country is with him, just so he does something."

Relieving the Employment Crisis

Over 13 million people were out of work in 1933. Those unemployed desperately needed money for the barest essentials of food, clothing, and shelter. During the first months of the new administration Congress passed two major acts to provide financial assistance and jobs.

The first was the Civilian Conservation Reforestation Relief Act. It had the dual aims of conserving natural resources and putting young people to work. The act set up the Civilian Conservation Corps (CCC), which enlisted unemployed single men between the ages of 18 and 25. In forestry camps all over the nation the new work force planted trees, dug reservoirs, built bridges, and developed parks. The federal

---

*Later in 1933, the Twenty-first Amendment to the Constitution, repealing the earlier prohibition amendment, was ratified.

One of the most successful New Deal programs was the Civilian Conservation Corps, which provided jobs and training for men between the ages of 18 and 25. Members of the CCC planted 17 million acres of forests, built dams, and created parks and other recreational facilities. At the same time, the CCC offered medical care and valuable training for its members. This corpsman is learning the use of an engineer's transit.

government paid for the men's housing, clothes, and food, so part of their salary could be sent home to help their families. By the end of the 1930s, more than 2.5 million young men had served in the CCC.

Next Congress passed the Federal Emergency Relief Act (FERA) to provide immediate "relief" payments to the unemployed. The FERA allocated money to local and state welfare agencies, which distributed it to the unemployed.

Roosevelt appointed Harry Hopkins, who had administered a New York State relief program, to head the FERA. Hopkins moved to Washington, D.C., set up a desk in a federal office building, and distributed $5 million in his first two hours on the job. But in spite of his energetic efforts, Hopkins felt that the program was inadequate. He be-

lieved that to rebuild their lives and self-respect, the unemployed needed jobs, not handouts.

President Roosevelt agreed with Hopkins that the major task of the government was to get Americans back to work. As a result Roosevelt authorized Hopkins to establish the Civil Works Administration (CWA). The CWA offered jobs rather than relief. Within a few months it employed over 4 million people.

Hopkins displayed a genius for creating jobs. Working for the CWA, construction crews built roads, athletic fields, and airports. Opera singers toured rural areas giving concerts, and archaeologists excavated prehistoric mounds. Despite such achievements, the CWA drew a great deal of criticism. Some people accused the agency of spending funds on unnecessary "make-work." Concerned that the country might grow overly dependent on the CWA, the President ended the program early in 1934.

Planning for Agricultural Recovery

Depression, unfortunately, was not unfamiliar to American farmers. As you read in Chapter 31, farm profits had fallen steadily throughout the 1920s. Much of the problem resulted from chronic surpluses of such crops as wheat, corn, and cotton. As farm prices fell, farm costs rose. Farmers planted more crops to try to cover costs, creating larger surpluses and going further into debt to buy seed and machinery.

The Roosevelt administration decided that something extraordinary had to be done to break the vicious cycle of production surpluses, falling prices, and decreasing farm income. The President's economic advisers thought that if the size of major crops could be reduced, their prices would rise. The administration proposed that farmers reduce their production to specified levels.

In return for the farmers' cooperation, the government would pay them for the crops they did not plant. The money for those payments would come from a special tax collected from the mills and packing houses that prepared agricultural products for the consumer.

By April 1933 the Department of Agriculture had prepared a draft of these proposals for Congress. There was little time to waste. Farmers were growing desperate as more and more faced bank foreclosures of the mortgages on their farms. In Iowa a group of farmers had forced their way into a courtroom and nearly lynched a judge who had authorized banks to foreclose the farmers' mortgages. Moreover, spring had come and farmers were beginning to plant their crops. As one Agriculture Department official put it, "We were racing against the sun."

Even so, it was May before Congress passed the Agricultural Adjustment Act, forming the Agricultural Adjustment Administration (AAA). By that time over 40 million acres (16 million hectares) of cotton had been planted. Another surplus was expected.

Roosevelt and Congress decided to pay the farmers to plow under, and thus destroy, part of their crops. Agriculture agents traveled across the South in the late spring and summer of 1933, convincing farmers to sign up for the plow-under campaign. One of the biggest difficulties was convincing the mules. They had been taught to walk between rows of cotton; now they had to learn to trample the cotton plants.

Since there was also a surplus of pork, the AAA bought and destroyed 5 million pigs. It was bitterly ironic that sources of food and clothing were destroyed while thousands of Americans were hungry and poorly clothed. Secretary of Agriculture Henry Wallace, himself a farmer, regretfully pointed out that "to destroy a standing crop goes against the soundest instincts of human nature." Yet the plan seems to have worked—for the farmers at least. In later years farmers limited production as planned. Bad weather also reduced production. As a result prices and farm income rose.

Planning for Industrial Recovery

Like agriculture, industry was also trapped in a downward economic spiral. One fourth of the labor force had no jobs at all. Those fortunate enough to be employed found their wages steadily reduced as employers cut costs to lower prices. Competition for sales was fierce since a growing number of people could not afford to buy manufactured products. Falling consumer purchasing power further decreased the demand for goods, which lowered production, which caused still more unemployment, which further reduced buying power. There seemed no end to the plunge.

The administration decided to take major action, as it had with agriculture. Several members of the brain trust urged that government and industry cooperate to provide overall planning of industrial production. They suggested that the War Industries Board, which had set priorities and production quotas during the World War, be used as a model.

In June 1933 Congress passed the National Industrial Recovery Act to establish a similar agency to fight the depression. The major provision of the act established trade associations in each industry to draft codes regulating production, prices, and working conditions within the industry. Section 7A of the act forbade employers to interfere with attempts by workers to organize unions. It also guaranteed labor unions the right to bargain with employers about wages, hours, and working conditions.

The administration hoped that cooperative action would stabilize production, end the price cutting that forced business to cut wages and lay off workers, and establish decent standards of wages and working hours. The National Recovery Administration (NRA) was created to enforce the codes.

The National Industrial Recovery Act also established the Public Works Administration (PWA), headed by Secretary of the Interior Harold Ickes. Like the CWA, the new agency tried to stimulate employment by spending large sums of money on public works projects. The PWA started slowly, but PWA workers eventually built a municipal auditorium in Kansas City; the Triborough Bridge in New York City; a water supply system in Denver; a deep-water port for Brownsville, Texas; new schools in Los Angeles; and two aircraft carriers for the navy.

With all the fanfare of a national crusade, the NRA, under the colorful leadership of former army general Hugh Johnson, began functioning during the summer of 1933. The agency emblem was a Blue Eagle over the slogan "We Do Our Part." To show they were following NRA codes, business people stamped the symbol on their products and posted it in store windows, on factory doors, and on delivery trucks.

Huge parades were held in several cities to dramatize the Blue Eagle crusade and to urge Americans to buy only products stamped with the symbol. In New York City a quarter of a million people, ranging from

The Fireside Chats

When Franklin D. Roosevelt was inaugurated in March 1933, the American people were ready to welcome a friendly voice. In the depths of what seemed to be an endless economic depression, people throughout the country were seeking assurance that something could be done to set the nation back on its feet.

To Franklin Roosevelt, radio broadcasts seemed ready-made for this purpose. Before the advent of radio, public figures made formal addresses to live audiences. Newspapers then published the speeches for people to read. But by 1933, the President of the United States could sit in his study and speak to citizens in their homes. He could give "fireside chats" that explained government policies to Americans everywhere. Secretary of Labor Frances Perkins described the President's fireside chats in these words:

> When he talked on the radio, he saw them [the people] gathered in the little parlor, listening with their neighbors. He was conscious of their faces and hands, their clothes and homes. His voice and his facial expression as he spoke were those of an intimate friend. After he became President, I often was at the White House

when he broadcast, and I realized how unconscious he was of the twenty or thirty of us in that room and how clearly his mind was focused on the people listening at the other end. As he talked his head would nod and his hands would move in simple, natural, comfortable gestures. His face would smile and light up as though he were actually sitting on the front porch or in the parlor with them. People felt this, and it bound them to him in affection.

> I have sat in those little parlors and on those porches myself during some of the speeches, and I have seen men and women gathered around the radio, even those who didn't like him or were opposed to him politically, listening with a pleasant, happy feeling of friendship. The exchange between them and him through the medium of the radio was very real. I have seen tears come to their eyes as he told them of some tragic episode. . . . I have also seen them laugh. . . . [T]he laughter of those gathered around radios of the country was a natural, sincere, and affectionate reaching out to this man.

Roosevelt's fireside chats gave the American people new hope. The broadcasts created the impression that the head of a vast and powerful nation had the people's interests at heart and was working to improve their lives.

factory workers to stock brokers to actors, marched down Fifth Avenue behind the NRA Blue Eagle.

But the NRA needed more than fanfare to succeed. Before long, problems appeared. The extension of NRA regulation resulted in codes for the production of hair tonic,

shoulder pads, dog leashes, and musical comedies. More important, many businesses simply ignored the codes. Industrialist Henry Ford had refused to cooperate with the NRA from the start. Labor leaders complained that the NRA kept wages too low. The NRA had helped to stop the price-cutting, wage-cutting cycle in large industries, but enforcing its numerous codes became increasingly difficult.

Remaking a Region: TVA

In a time of bold experimentation perhaps no program was more daring than the Tennessee Valley Authority (TVA), which Congress authorized during the frantic first hundred days of Roosevelt's presidency. The TVA was to transform the entire Tennessee River Valley from a backwater of poor farms into a rich and productive region. Never before had a nation embarked upon a conservation and social planning effort on such a grand scale.

The area, extending over parts of seven states, had been victimized by careless use of resources resulting in frequent flooding. Loggers had cut down most of the trees in the area, loosening the soil and causing massive erosion. Heavy rainfall regularly swelled the Tennessee River, which flooded crops. Such conditions made farming difficult. Personal income in the region was half the national average, and living conditions were abysmal.

The TVA changed the face of the area. Engineers built a series of dams along the length of the Tennessee River and its tributaries. Then the TVA constructed hydroelectric power plants to supply electricity to homes and farms in the valley and to attract industry and new jobs. The dams also helped control flooding and conserve water for future use. (See the map on page 570.)

The TVA channeled some of the newly created power into the manufacture of fertilizer, selling it to farmers at cost. With fertilizers, farmers improved the land and were able to increase harvests. The TVA also planted millions of trees in the valley to stop erosion. Finally, the authority introduced many educational, recreational, and health services into the region to improve economic and social conditions.

The TVA was the subject of heated controversy. Power companies in the area objected to government production and sale of power. The companies argued that such government competition was unfair. Other critics objected to "social planning" by the TVA. They maintained that the federal government had no right to interfere in the region and that problems there were matters of state and local concern. Despite such criti-

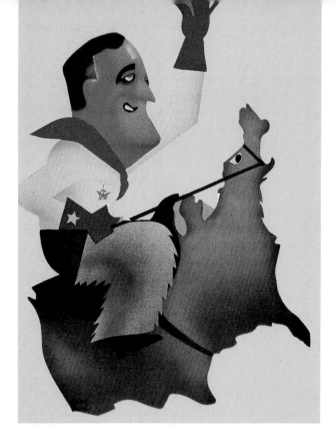

The whirlwind creation of new agencies and programs during "the hundred days" aroused deep fears among those who believed the President was destroying traditional values and institutions. This illustration for the February 1934 cover of Vanity Fair *magazine shows Roosevelt wearing the symbol of the National Recovery Administration, the Blue Eagle, and riding roughshod over the nation. Many people thought that such New Deal programs as the NRA gave government too much power over private business.*

cism, the mammoth project transformed the region and continues in operation today.

Other Hundred Days Measures

The legislation passed during the first hundred days of Roosevelt's administration was not part of a unified plan for recovery. Rather, each law passed or agency created represented an attempt to solve a particular problem or to change a particular condition plaguing the depression-ridden nation.

The Truth-in-Securities Act tried to end the wild stock market speculation that had helped bring on the crash. This law required full public disclosure of all relevant financial information about corporation stocks. Misrepresenting such information became a criminal offense.

The Glass-Steagall Banking Act reformed the national banking system. It

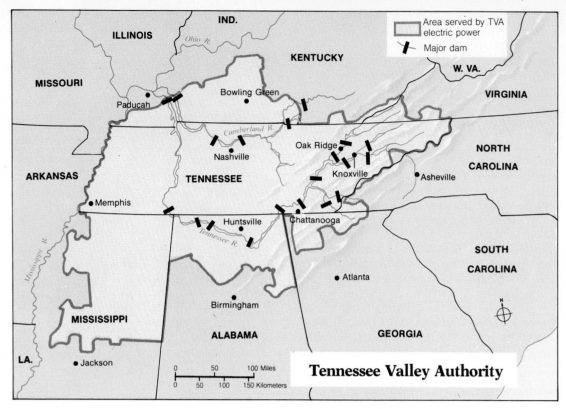

Tennessee Valley Authority

■ *The vast Tennessee Valley Authority project affected seven states, harnessing the power of the Tennessee River and others nearby. In addition to electricity, TVA dams created lakes that spurred recreational development in the region. The map shows the location of major TVA dams and the total area provided with electric power by the authority.*

created the Federal Deposit Insurance Corporation (FDIC), which to this day insures savings accounts against bank failure. The law provided that in the event an FDIC-insured bank failed, the government would reimburse the depositors. Depositors began to put money back into banks instead of taking it out.

The Farm Credit Administration (FCA) was established to provide low-interest loans for farmers, to enable them to pay their debts and keep their farms. During the mid-1930s the FCA helped as many as 300 farmers a day save their farms from foreclosure and bankruptcy.

The Home Owners' Loan Corporation (HOLC) performed a similar service for home owners. It provided owners with low-interest loans that could be repaid over a long period of time, thus reducing monthly payments. The HOLC helped almost 1,000 families a day keep their homes during the mid-1930s.

The hundred days ended in the early hours of June 16 as Congress adjourned. The weary legislators expressed the hope that their efforts would bring the depression to a swift conclusion. But the nation was mired in an economic crisis that would not be easily solved.

For answers, see p. A 96.

Section Review

1. Identify the following: Harry Hopkins, Blue Eagle.
2. Define the following term: fireside chat.
3. What two actions did President Franklin Roosevelt take to relieve the banking crisis?
4. What were the two aims of the Civilian Conservation Reforestation Relief Act?
5. (a) What was the purpose of the Federal Emergency Relief Act? (b) How did the purpose of the Civil Works Administration differ from that of the FERA?
6. How did the Agriculture Adjustment Act try to reduce farm surpluses?
7. (a) What was the main provision of the National Industrial Recovery Act? (b) What was the main purpose of the Public Works Administration?
8. List three actions of the Tennessee Valley Authority.

The Tennessee Valley Authority was created to revitalize an entire seven-state area. Through the building of a series of dams such as the Fontana Dam, above, the TVA generated electrical power, provided jobs, and helped attract new industry to the economically depressed region.

3 Critics of the New Deal

A noted political writer, Walter Lippman, praised the first hundred days of the New Deal: "At the end of February, we were a [collection] of disorderly panic-stricken mobs and factions. In the hundred days from March to June we became again an organized nation confident of our power to provide for our own security and to control our own destiny."

But not all Americans shared Lippman's enthusiasm for the New Deal. Some critics firmly believed that the government was interferring too much in people's lives. Others believed that the administration should take more drastic steps to aid the American people. Many critics had originally supported Roosevelt. Now they spoke against the New Deal in growing numbers.

Demands for Stronger Action

One of the first of Roosevelt's earlier supporters to attack the New Deal was Senator Huey Long of Louisiana. The Kingfish, as he was called, felt that Roosevelt's New Deal had done nothing to redistribute the nation's wealth more evenly. He proposed his own plan for the future, expressed in the motto "Share Our Wealth."

Long suggested that the government confiscate "the swollen fortunes" of the rich and tax 100 percent of all income over $1 million a year. The senator wanted the money redistributed to provide every American family with a house, a car, education for the children, a pension for the elderly, and an income of $2,000 to $3,000 a year. Long's idea attracted millions, especially among the poor. He decided to challenge Roosevelt for the presidency, but in 1935 he was shot and killed by a young man, for reasons never clearly understood.

Another vocal critic of Roosevelt and the New Deal was Father Charles Coughlin, known as the radio priest. Each week he told at least 10 million radio listeners that the depression was the fault of an international conspiracy of bankers. Before the 1932 election, Coughlin backed Roosevelt, telling his listeners that they could choose "Roosevelt or ruin." Eventually, however, Coughlin lost his enthusiasm for the New Deal, believing that stronger actions should be taken against "banking and money interests." Soon he was using his radio programs to attack Roosevelt and his programs.

Dr. Francis E. Townsend, a retired California physician, wanted the government to help older citizens. He proposed that the government pay every person over age 60 a monthly pension of $200. In return, the recipient would agree to retire, freeing a job for someone else. The pensioner would also agree to spend the entire $200 within the month, thereby further stimulating the economy. Like Long and Coughlin, Townsend had many supporters, and Townsend Clubs sprang up all over the country.

Roosevelt and his advisers knew that they could not ignore the supporters of such

Cartoonists and critics often made fun of the many "alphabet agencies" created by the New Deal. In his first campaign, Roosevelt had promised to try new remedies to end the depression. If those remedies failed, he said he would abandon them and try others. Can you supply the full names of the programs labeled by letters in this cartoon? For answers, see p. A 96.

critics as Long, Coughlin, and Townsend. "In normal times, the radio and other appeals by them would not be effective," said Roosevelt, "However, these are not normal times; the people are jumpy and very ready to run after strange gods." Furthermore, the rise of dictators in Italy and Germany (see page 597) had shown to what extremes nations might go. Consequently, the planners of the New Deal began to reconsider their positions regarding taxation, banking, and aid to the elderly.

Conservative Reaction to the New Deal

While Long, Coughlin, and Townsend wanted the government to do more, many critics wanted it to do less. These conservatives were convinced that the new laws were a threat to individual liberty. Many business people, especially, thought they were being paralyzed by excessive taxes and regulations. They argued that the government had no right to tell them how to run their businesses. Raymond Moley, who had been a member of Roosevelt's brain trust, bitterly criticized administration policies that he thought undermined the free-enterprise system.

In 1934 two prominent Democrats helped to found the American Liberty League because of their objections to some aspects of the New Deal. Members of the league believed that the government had a duty to encourage private enterprise and to protect private ownership and use of property. They charged that New Deal programs were undermining private enterprise with heavy taxation and government planning and regulation. Among the many well-known members of the American Liberty League was Roosevelt's one-time political ally, Al Smith.

Attack by the Supreme Court

Administration officials had based the legislation of the first hundred days on the view that the depression was a national emergency, similar to war, which justified an expansion of government power. They believed the government should use that power to revitalize the nation's economic and social well-being.

From the outset, however, many of Roosevelt's advisers worried that the Supreme Court might find the expansion of federal power unconstitutional. Their concerns proved justified. On May 27, 1935, the Supreme Court handed down a decision involving a Brooklyn, New York, chicken processor who had been convicted of violating an NRA code. In *Schechter* v. *United States,* the Court declared unanimously that since the federal government had no power to regulate intrastate* commerce, the National Industrial Recovery Act was unconstitutional.

In 1936, the Court struck down the Agricultural Adjustment Act. The Court ruled that Congress had violated the Constitution when it levied a tax to pay farmers for cutting back production because it had taken "money from one group for the benefit of another."

In the same session the Court declared three other New Deal laws unconstitutional. In each case the Court ruled that under the

---

*intrastate: within the boundaries of one state.

New Deal the federal government had gone beyond the limits of constitutional authority. Roosevelt complained that the Supreme Court decisions reflected a "horse and buggy," or old-fashioned, definition of what the Constitution allowed, but the decisions stood.

For answers, see p. A 96.
Section Review

1. Identify the following: Huey Long, Charles Coughlin, Francis E. Townsend, American Liberty League, *Schechter* v. *United States.*
2. According to Huey Long, what should the government do with tax money collected from the rich?
3. What group of people was Francis Townsend especially concerned about?
4. What government actions did conservatives consider a threat to private enterprise?
5. List two New Deal laws the Supreme Court declared unconstitutional.

4 The Second New Deal

The Supreme Court decisions striking down key legislation ended the period known as the first New Deal. During that time, relief and recovery measures were uppermost among administration priorities. Some reform measures had been passed—the Truth-in-Securities Act and the Glass-Steagall Banking Act, for example—but the main emphasis had been on relief and recovery.

Roosevelt believed that to achieve national economic health, the causes as well as the symptoms of the depression had to be treated. In this spirit, he and Congress launched a "second hundred days" of legislative action. From July into September 1935, Congress passed a series of far-reaching reform acts, but it did not end efforts to provide relief.

The Works Progress Administration

As the New Deal entered its third year, widespread unemployment continued to resist solution. Twenty million people still relied on public assistance and welfare to survive. Roosevelt decided that only a massive public

works program could provide the jobs needed to bring about economic recovery. Yet Congress had grown more cautious about passing New Deal programs Roosevelt proposed. After some pressure from the administration, it passed the Emergency Relief Appropriations Act, which created the Works Progress Administration (WPA).

Roosevelt named Harry Hopkins, former head of the Civil Works Administration, to head the new agency. Hopkins distributed huge sums of money to provide jobs and get money into circulation. As with the CWA, Hopkins was accused of creating "make-work" projects that would not benefit the country in the long run. "People don't eat in the long run," Hopkins replied with exasperation. "They eat today."

The WPA immediately put people to work on a wide variety of construction projects. WPA workers built or improved 2,500 hospitals, 5,000 schools, 13,000 parks and playgrounds, and 1,000 airports. But such projects employed only construction workers. Hopkins set about providing jobs for other workers as well.

573

Soon the WPA established several projects for people in the arts. The Federal Theatre Project hired actors, actresses, and directors to put on plays, vaudeville shows, and circuses across the country. Entertainers often traveled to remote rural areas where people had never seen a theater production. The Federal Writers Project employed authors to write historical and geographical guides for every state in the nation. The Federal Art Project hired artists to paint murals in public buildings.

Despite providing work for nearly 3 million people, the WPA fell far short of meeting the goal of providing work for all the able-bodied unemployed. Nearly 3 million families were still on relief, and youngsters in such households often had to quit school to look for a job. In so doing, young people lost the opportunity for an education and more often than not wound up on the unemployment rolls.

An extension of the WPA, the National Youth Administration (NYA) attacked that problem. The NYA offered young people a way to stay in school and earn money by providing part-time jobs in and around their schools. The agency helped 600,000 students work their way through college and another 1.5 million stay in high school.

Reforming Labor Relations

Organized labor had won a victory when Congress passed the National Industrial Recovery Act. Section 7A of that law had banned interference with union organizing. It had had guaranteed collective bargaining. When the law was declared unconstitutional, section 7A was struck down with it.

Senator Robert F. Wagner of New York had become the leading advocate for workers in Congress. In 1935 he introduced a new bill to guarantee workers' rights to organize and bargain collectively. The bill also banned as unfair certain practices employers used to discourage employees from organizing. Such practices included firing

Mary McLeod Bethune

Soon after his inauguration, President Franklin Roosevelt called together a group of black Americans to advise him on programs and policies. Among the members of this so-called Black Cabinet were Robert C. Weaver, who later served as secretary of the Department of Housing and Urban Development; Robert L. Vann, a special assistant to the attorney general; William Hastie, assistant solicitor in the Department of the Interior; and Ralph Bunche, who later won a Nobel Peace Prize. Mary McLeod Bethune, a well-known educator, also served in the Black Cabinet.

Bethune had been an adviser to President Coolidge. Impressed with her abilities, Roosevelt asked Bethune to serve on the committee that helped establish the National Youth Administration (NYA) in 1934. The NYA made it possible for thousands of hard-pressed high school and college students to continue their educations. In 1936, when the Division of Negro Affairs of the NYA was established, Bethune was appointed to direct it. She was the first black American to head a government agency.

Bethune served as director of the NYA from 1936 to 1944. In 1945 she served as a consultant on interracial understanding at the San Francisco Conference of the United Nations. Mary McLeod Bethune worked tirelessly in government service and education. She received many honors, including in 1935 the Spingarn Medal for outstanding achievement, awarded annually by the NAACP. She is pictured below in the 1950s.

workers who joined unions or infiltrating unions with company spies.

Many business people opposed the bill vehemently, insisting that it defined unfair action by management but said nothing about unfair action by labor. Nevertheless Congress passed the National Labor Relations Act in July 1935. The Wagner Act, as it was known, established the National Labor Relations Board (NLRB) to administer the law. The NLRB had the authority to determine when enough workers in an industry desired union representation. In such matters the business community often accused the NLRB of consistently favoring labor over management.

Regulating the Utilities

The Roosevelt administration had watched with growing concern the increasing monopoly of the utility companies. By the 1930s, gigantic holding companies had taken complete control of gas and electricity distribution in various sections of the country. The holding companies could effectively close out competition in those areas. Thus they could set rates at any level, knowing that customers had nowhere else to go for power.

To break this monopoly and lower customer rates, Roosevelt urged Congress to pass the Public Utilities Holding Company Act. Under this act, the government could forbid holding companies from owning more than one utility company in any one part of the country. The government could dissolve any holding company that could not prove that it was servicing a local area efficiently.

When the legislation was introduced, the powerful utilities mounted a million-dollar campaign to defeat it. But Congress passed it nonetheless. The Public Utilities Holding Company Act ended most of the large empires and put the rest under direct supervision of government agencies.

Providing Social Security

For Secretary of Labor Frances Perkins, providing security against poverty in old age and against wage loss during unemployment was a top priority. In fact, Perkins was so

concerned that she had refused to take her cabinet post until Roosevelt accepted her ideas for a program of old age and unemployment insurance. Once in office, she mobilized support for the program and, with the help of Senator Wagner, guided the legislation through Congress.

In September 1935 Congress passed the last piece of legislation of the second hundred days: the Social Security Act. The act created a national system of pensions for the elderly, supported by payments from employers, employees, and the federal government. It also established state-run insurance programs to provide unemployment compensation for people who lost their jobs. Finally, the act granted states money to provide support for the handicapped and dependent children.

Criticism of the Social Security Act was varied. Some people thought the bill did not go far enough in providing for the unemployed or the elderly. They argued that too many workers were not eligible to take part. Other people were alarmed by the idea of a public rather than a private insurance

Major Events	
1932	Franklin Roosevelt elected President
1933	National bank holiday ordered; Emergency Banking Relief Act, Civilian Conservation Reforestation Relief Act, Federal Emergency Relief Act, Agricultural Adjustment Act, and National Industrial Recovery Act passed; Tennessee Valley Authority formed
1934	American Liberty League formed
1935	Supreme Court declares National Industrial Recovery Act unconstitutional; Works Progress Administration formed; National Labor Relations Act, Public Utilities Holding Company Act, and Social Security Act passed
1936	Supreme Court declares Agricultural Adjustment Act unconstitutional

The Social Security Act created a separate fund in the federal treasury for old age and disability benefits. Critics said that Social Security was the first step toward socialism. To some, the idea of issuing a number to identify each United States citizen was an attack on the American tradition of individualism.

program. One business leader believed it would ruin the nation "by destroying initiative, discouraging thrift, and stifling individual responsibility." Despite the criticism, the Social Security Act went into effect and continues as law today.

For answers, see p. A 97.
Section Review

1. Identify the following: Robert F. Wagner.
2. Define the following term: utility company.
3. (a) What problem led to creation of the Works Progress Administration in 1935? (b) How did the WPA try to solve that problem?
4. What did the National Youth Administration accomplish?
5. What rights did the Wagner Act guarantee to workers?
6. (a) What was the purpose of the Public Utilities Holding Company Act? (b) What did it accomplish?
7. (a) What groups of people were affected by the Social Security Act of 1935? (b) Describe the major provisions of the act.

IN PERSPECTIVE   During the presidential campaign of 1932, Franklin Roosevelt promised the American people action. He did not have a specific plan for action, but he had a wealth of ideas, experiences, and advisers on which to rely. During the first hundred days the administration produced a flood of legislation aimed at providing immediate relief and recovery from the Great Depression. These laws were designed to end bank closings, distribute money for food and clothing, and provide jobs for millions of unemployed. The AAA and NRA were created to further the recovery of agriculture and industry.

The early New Deal encountered considerable opposition. Some critics thought the programs did not do enough to help the American people. Others argued that the actions of the government threatened the free-enterprise economic system. In 1935 the Supreme Court ruled several New Deal laws unconstitutional.

Legislation passed during the second hundred days primarily concerned reforms, although the Works Progress Administration was another attempt to relieve widespread unemployment. Organized labor won important rights in the Wagner Act. The elderly and unemployed gained some protection from financial ruin through the Social Security Act. The government had acted as Roosevelt had promised in 1932, but whether its actions would end the Great Depression remained to be seen.

For answers, see p. A 97.

Chapter Review

1. How did Franklin Roosevelt's experiences before he was elected President help shape his policies?

2. Explain how each of the following contributed to the ideas of the New Deal: (a) progressivism, (b) lessons from the world war, (c) the brain trust, (d) cabinet members.

3. (a) Describe the banking crisis Roosevelt faced when he took office. (b) How did he try to solve that crisis?

4. (a) What two pieces of legislation did Congress pass during the first hundred days to provide immediate relief to the unemployed? (b) Describe the provisions of each act. (c) Why did Roosevelt agree to the creation of the Civil Works Administration?

5. (a) What was the purpose of the Agricultural Adjustment Act? (b) How was it to work? (c) What extraordinary actions did the government take to implement the act in 1933? (d) Why were those actions ironic?

6. (a) How did the National Industrial Recovery Act try to stop the downward economic spiral in industry? (b) What problems were encountered in implementing the act?

7. (a) What was the purpose of the Tennessee Valley Authority? (b) Why was there heated opposition to the TVA?

8. Explain why each of the following criticized the New Deal: (a) Huey Long, (b) Charles Coughlin, (c) Francis E. Townsend, (d) Raymond Moley, (e) American Liberty League.

9. (a) Why did the Supreme Court rule the National Industrial Recovery Act unconstitutional? (b) Why did the Supreme Court rule the Agricultural Adjustment Act unconstitutional?

10. (a) What legislation made up the second hundred days? (b) What was the main purpose of that legislation?

For answers, see p. A 98.

For Further Thought

1. Some historians believe that Franklin Roosevelt generated the hope and enthusiasm the American people needed in 1933. (a) What actions and attitudes contributed to Roosevelt's impact? (b) Why do you think hope and enthusiasm were important in 1933?

2. (a) What advances did organized labor make during the New Deal? (b) How did those advances compare with the situation of labor during the early 1920s? (See Chapter 29.) (c) How might you explain the difference?

3. (a) Why did some critics fear that the New Deal programs would undermine the free-enterprise system? (b) Do you think their concern was justified? Explain.

For answers, see p. A 98.

Developing Basic Skills

1. *Classifying* Make a chart with three columns. In the first column list the New Deal laws described in this chapter. In the second column describe the problem or problems each law tried to solve. In the third column list the groups of people each law affected.

   After completing your chart, answer the following questions: (a) Which problem generated the largest number of laws? (b) What groups of people were affected by New Deal legislation? (c) Which group was probably affected most? (d) Can you identify a relationship between your answers to questions a and c? Explain.

2. *Relating Past to Present* Find out whether the Work Projects Administration sponsored any projects near where you live. (You may be able to learn about WPA projects from the local chamber of commerce or local historical society.) How do you think the WPA contributed to your community?

See page 778 for suggested readings.

The New Deal Continues

(1936–1939)

Years of Dust, *by Ben Shahn.*

Chapter Outline

1 *New Deal Gains and Losses*

2 *Further Reform*

3 *Life During the New Deal Years*

The situation in the United States seemed brighter in 1936 than it had in 1933. The bread lines had disappeared, as had the apple sellers in the streets. The flood of bank closings had slowed to a trickle. Six million jobs had reopened in private industry, relieving unemployment to a degree. Farm income had increased. Nevertheless, 10 million American workers were still unemployed, and nearly 4 million more remained on government relief.

By 1936 the feeling of hopelessness and panic that had contributed to Franklin Roosevelt's election in 1932 had subsided. So had Congress's willingness to pass whatever legislation President Roosevelt sent it. When Roosevelt was first inaugurated in March 1933, one leading senator had said, "Whatever laws the President thinks he may need to end the depression, Congress will jump through a hoop to put through."

Now, three eventful years later, Congress was through hoop jumping. Roosevelt would meet more resistance to his New Deal in the years to come. Yet the New Deal was to continue, especially in the area of reform.

1 New Deal Gains and Losses

In November 1936 the New Deal faced a nationwide test at the polls. Voters would have a chance to register their approval or disapproval of New Deal programs. In 1934 state and congressional elections had indicated approval. The Democrats had gained 20 new seats in the Senate and 18 in the House. Roosevelt and his administration seemed to have little cause for worry as the 1936 election approached. But support for the New Deal faltered in the months following the election.

The Election of 1936

The Republican party chose Governor Alfred M. Landon of Kansas to oppose Roosevelt in the election. Landon had an impressive political record. In 1934, when Democrats won widespread victories in state and congressional elections, he had been the only Republican governor in the nation to win reelection.

Landon represented the moderate wing of the Republican party, which accepted many of the New Deal efforts to use government power to fight the Great Depression. However, Landon's campaign attracted those who shared the strong anti-Roosevelt feeling held by some members of the business community. Such critics thought that Roosevelt's programs threatened the free-enterprise system. The family of millionaire J. P. Morgan, Jr., for example, asked visitors not to mention the President's name in Morgan's presence, fearing that his blood pressure would rise dangerously.

Roosevelt met such antagonism head on. At a campaign speech in Madison Square Garden in New York, he lashed out against his critics in business and financial circles. "Never before in all our history have these forces been so united against one candidate as they stand today," he told the cheering crowd. "They are unanimous in their hate for me—and I welcome their hatred."

When Landon opened his campaign, his criticism of the New Deal was moderate. He did not call for an end to Roosevelt's programs. Instead, he argued that Republicans could manage those programs more effectively, waste less money, and achieve longer-lasting results. But when this strategy brought little support, Landon stepped up his attack. By November, he was denouncing the Social Security Act as "unjust, unworkable, stupidly drafted, and wastefully financed."

The day before the election, Roosevelt's campaign manager accurately predicted that the President would carry every state except Maine and Vermont. Roosevelt won 61 percent of the popular vote, Landon 37 percent. The Union party, formed by followers of Father Coughlin, Dr. Townsend, and the late Huey Long, won 2 percent of the popular vote. Roosevelt and the New Deal seemed to have received an overwhelming vote of confidence from the people.

The Roosevelt Coalition

Much of the success the New Deal enjoyed at the polls stemmed from the Democratic coalition Roosevelt had carefully built since his election in 1932. Each group in the coalition had its own reasons for backing the Democratic party.

Before 1936 the Democrats had been the smaller of the two major parties. They drew membership from two very different sources. One source was the "solid South," where distaste for the Republican party remained since the Civil War and Reconstruction. The other source was the political machines of many big eastern and midwestern cities. Those party organizations could deliver votes for Democratic candidates with the regularity of well-oiled machinery. The votes came mainly from the immigrant groups that had most recently settled in the cities.

To that base Roosevelt added organized labor. The Wagner Act (see page 575) had given workers the right to organize without opposition from management. Consequently, organized labor not only voted Democratic in strength, but also became a major source of campaign funds.

Roosevelt and the New Deal were also able to attract black Americans to the Democratic party. Abraham Lincoln had issued the Emancipation Proclamation, and for years black voters had remained loyal to the Republicans, "the party of Lincoln." However, under the New Deal, the government began taking an active interest in the conditions of black life. Eleanor Roosevelt, especially, tried to see that New Deal programs did not discriminate against black Americans. Blacks were also brought into important government positions. (See page 574.)

Finally, Roosevelt attracted scholars to the Democratic party. Their number may have been small, but they had significant influence. As teachers, university professors, and writers, they helped mold public opinion by publicizing and popularizing Democratic party ideas and candidates. The coalition, first formed in 1936, was to strengthen the Democratic party and make it the majority party for decades to come.

An Attack on the Supreme Court

Roosevelt opened his second term as President with a spectacular announcement. In February 1937 he asked Congress to redesign the federal judiciary. He argued that there were too few federal judges, resulting in long delays before cases could be heard. Therefore he wanted more judges appointed.

The heart of the problem, Roosevelt said, was the Supreme Court. He believed the Court needed not only more justices but also younger ones. He recommended that the President have the power to appoint one additional justice for every justice on the Supreme Court aged 70 or over who refused to retire. The maximum number of justices on the Supreme Court would be increased from nine to fifteen.

Unfortunately for Roosevelt, his plan was recognized as an attack on the Supreme Court. As you have read, the Supreme Court had struck down several key pieces of early New Deal legislation. (See page 572.) The President feared that the Social Security Act and the Wagner Act might also fail to survive a court test.

The Court loomed as a major roadblock to the administration's plans. Four justices usually supported New Deal measures, but they were neutralized by the "Four Horsemen," as the conservative justices were known. The fate of most cases rested with Justice Owen Roberts, who often voted with the conservatives. Roosevelt thought the appointment of additional justices would create a sympathetic majority.

Roosevelt's political instincts had failed him, however. He was accused of trying to

Roosevelt's plan to increase the number of justices on the Supreme Court was widely seen as an attack on the Court itself. Critics believed the idea would weaken the Court. This cartoon shows Roosevelt asking Secretary of the Interior Harold Ickes for money from the Public Works Administration (PWA) to carry out his plan.

"pack" the Court, and opposition came from all sides. Critics of the New Deal who had worried all along that Roosevelt was out to destroy constitutional government in the United States saw their suspicions confirmed. Even supporters of Roosevelt on other issues began to desert him on this one. Upon hearing of Roosevelt's court plan, one supporter of the New Deal in Congress turned to reporters and said, "Boys, here's where I cash in my chips."

Few people believed the President's claim that he sought only to improve the Court's efficiency. Chief Justice Charles Evans Hughes pointed out that there was no significant delay in cases coming before the Court. He insisted that an increase in the number of justices might actually delay decisions. After a six-month battle, Roosevelt finally accepted defeat and withdrew his proposal for court reform.

The Supreme Court fight cost the President congressional and public support and badly divided the Democratic party. At the same time, however, there were two unexpected results. First, the Court suddenly began upholding New Deal legislation. Justice Roberts voted with the President's supporters to uphold all the key provisions of the Social Security Act as well as the Wagner Act and a minimum-wage law in the state of Washington.

Second, the retirement of one of the conservative justices gave Roosevelt the opportunity to make his first appointment, without the need for reorganization. By the end of his presidency, the President had appointed a total of eight associate justices and one chief justice. Looking back on the court fight of 1937, Roosevelt always claimed that although he had lost the battle, he had won the war.

The Economy Takes Another Plunge

The turmoil over court reform had barely begun to subside when the Roosevelt administration found itself deep in another crisis. During 1935 and 1936, the economy had slowly but steadily improved. By early 1937 several of Roosevelt's key advisers believed that many of the New Deal programs to stimulate economic recovery could wind down.

Those advisers believed that the government should reduce heavy expenditures in public works and employment programs. Now it was time to allow private enterprise to complete the recovery without federal aid. As Secretary of the Treasury Henry Morgenthau, Jr., later said, "this was the moment . . . to strip off the bandages, throw away the crutches, and see if American private enterprise could stand on its own feet." The President agreed that the time was right to cut government spending. Congress drastically reduced WPA programs and allocated no funds for new programs.

Meanwhile two other developments reduced the total amount of private spending in the economy. First, the Federal Reserve Board had raised interest rates, increasing the cost of loans for new factories and equipment. Thus, companies began to cut back. Second, new social security taxes on employers and employees left less money for business and consumer spending.

The combination of reduced government spending and the inability of private business to take up the slack resulted in a se-

vere economic recession in the fall and winter of 1937–1938. Unemployment increased by 4 million in a seven-month period. Large inventories piled up in warehouses as reduced wages and loss of jobs decreased consumer spending. Across the nation, the economic collapse was actually sharper than in the first months of the Great Depression. Nearly all of the gains in employment and production were wiped out.

Despite the severe conditions, Roosevelt at first hesitated to act. He hoped private business could reverse the downward trend of the economy without the stimulus of renewed government spending for jobs and relief. By March 1938, however, the President decided that the government had to resort to deficit spending in order to stimulate the economy. *Deficit spending* is the practice of spending more money than is taken in

581

■ *This chart of the percentage of people out of work between 1932 and 1945 shows a rise in employment between 1933 to 1937. It seemed for a time that the end of the Great Depression was in sight. However, with another economic recession in 1937 and 1938, joblessness rose again. How did World War II affect unemployment?* For answer, see p. A 98.

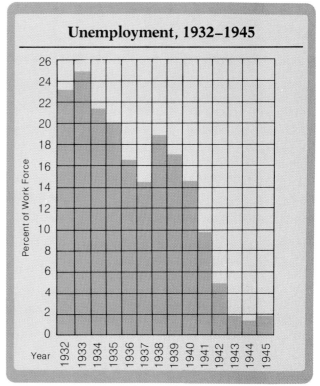

Source: *Historical Statistics of the United States*

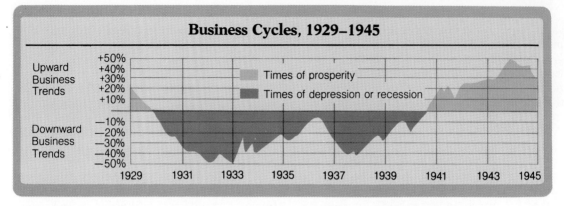

Business Cycles, 1929–1945

Upward Business Trends: +50%, +40%, +30%, +20%, +10%

Downward Business Trends: −10%, −20%, −30%, −40%, −50%

Times of prosperity
Times of depression or recession

1929 1931 1933 1935 1937 1939 1941 1943 1945

■ *This chart traces fluctuations in the business cycle between the stock market crash of 1929 and the end of World War II in 1945. Economic recovery from the Great Depression seemed near in 1936, but the deep slump of 1937–1938 signaled a new recession. As the chart shows, the depression did not finally end until the United States geared up for war production in 1941.*

from taxes. The recession of 1937–1938 showed the extent to which the New Deal policies of the previous five years had failed to bring about full recovery.

For answers, see p. A 98.
Section Review

1. Identify the following: Alfred M. Landon.
2. Define the following term: deficit spending.
3. What was Alfred Landon's original attitude toward the New Deal?
4. List the groups that made up the Democratic coalition in 1936.
5. How did President Roosevelt want to increase the size of the Supreme Court?
6. What happened to the economy in the fall and winter of 1937–1938?

2 Further Reform

As Roosevelt entered his second term, he continued to press for reform. The intended beneficiaries of such reform were primarily those hardest hit by the Great Depression: workers, farmers, and the poor.

The Growth of Organized Labor

The passage of the Wagner Act in 1935 was taken as a clear signal by labor unions to go ahead with further organization. The American Federation of Labor began a massive drive to recruit a million more workers into labor unions and thus increase its bargaining power.

For some union leaders in the AFL, the recruiting drive did not move fast enough. Furthermore, they thought that the AFL was concentrating too much on unions for skilled workers such as pipe fitters, machinists, and printers. Those leaders wanted to form unions in large industries—such as steel, textile, and automobile manufacturing—which employed great numbers of unskilled laborers.

At the head of that faction was John L. Lewis, president of the United Mine Workers. At the 1935 AFL convention, he argued in favor of *industrial unions,* unions that would represent every worker in an entire industry, not just workers in skilled crafts. Many AFL leaders opposed this idea. In the heated debate that followed, Lewis punched William "Big Bill" Hutcheson of the Carpenters' Union and knocked him down. Lewis may have won the fist fight, but he did not win AFL support for his plan. As a result he and several other AFL union leaders formed a rival group of unions, later called the Congress of Industrial Organizations (CIO).

The CIO proceeded to organize workers in whole industries, as Lewis had demanded.

The organizers came into conflict with employers who resisted labor unions in spite of the Wagner Act. In response to such resistance, workers in the Goodyear tire factory in Akron, Ohio, developed a new type of action, the *sitdown strike*. One night at exactly 2:00 A.M., the workers stopped the production line. Then they sat down next to the idle machines and refused to leave the factory until their employers recognized the union. The employers chose not to use force to remove the workers because of the potential destruction of factory property.

Soon sitdown strikes spread to other industries. A common tactic of plant managers was to turn off the heat to force sitdown strikers out of the factory. Often the workers sang, danced, and roller-skated to keep warm. Even gravediggers in Kansas City and Chicago used the new sitdown tactic.

Strikes began to achieve success in the automobile industry. In 1937 a six-week sitdown strike closed several General Motors plants in Flint, Michigan. The company called in the police and the National Guard, but the union held out. Eventually General Motors recognized the United Automobile Workers as the employees' union, the first in the industry.

The steel industry proved even more difficult. Union organizers recalled the bloody battles of the early 1920s, when the steel industry had defeated several strikes for better working conditions. Unexpectedly, in 1937 the huge U.S. Steel Corporation agreed to recognize the Steel Workers Organizing Committee of the CIO. Other steel companies refused to follow that example, however, and violence resulted. In what became known as the Memorial Day Massacre, police shot and killed ten strikers at the Republic Steel Plant in Chicago. The National Labor Relations Board then stepped in and forced the steel industry to negotiate with the union.

Total union membership grew from fewer than 3 million in 1933 to nearly 9 million in 1939. Organized labor had clearly attained more economic and political power under the New Deal than ever before in history.

The Fair Labor Standards Act

Large numbers of workers were still unorganized by the union movement. For millions of laborers working conditions remained dismal. Shoe factory workers in New

Passage of the Wagner Act in 1935 opened the way to more aggressive labor organizing techniques. Unions made major efforts to organize automotive workers on an industry-wide basis. In 1937 auto workers used a new technique in labor-management relations, the sitdown strike. The strike closed General Motors for six weeks before the company agreed to recognize the United Auto Workers as its employee union.

England earned only $853 per year. Cotton factory workers in the South averaged less than 40 cents an hour. Most worked 12 hours a day, six days a week throughout the year.

In 1937 Roosevelt urged Congress to pass a bill to improve wages and conditions for all workers in the country. He wanted a federal wages-and-hours law that would "put a floor below which wages shall not fall, and a ceiling beyond which the hours of industrial labor shall not rise."

Such a bill met with strong opposition, especially from business owners who felt that government was once again threatening private enterprise. Farmers also objected because they felt they could not pay workers as much as industries did. Only by agreeing to exclude a wide range of workers, such as agricultural laborers and domestic servants, did the supporters of the bill save it.

Finally, in June 1938, Congress passed the Fair Labor Standards Act. The act established minimum wages and maximum hours of work in a number of industries whose products were shipped across state lines. It also banned child labor under age 16 in industries engaged in interstate commerce. Furthermore, the act established a precedent for federal legislation to improve working conditions.

The Dust Bowl

Suffering severe hardships since the end of the World War, many farmers found it nearly impossible to survive the Great Depression. Then, in the midst of the economic disaster, large sections of the Midwest from Texas to the Dakotas suffered a .drought from 1932 to 1936. Vast stretches of grassland and crops lay scorched and withered. The skies darkened as clouds of dust, thousands of feet across, arose from the sun-dried land, giving the area a new name, the Dust Bowl.

The clouds blew across the plains, so thick that train engineers were unable to read signal lights. Winds dropped trails of grit and dirt everywhere. As far east as Cleveland and Memphis, people had to mask their faces with handkerchiefs to protect themselves from the "black blizzards." Red snow fell on New England, and sailors in the Atlantic found traces of Nebraska soil.

Many midwestern farmers watched helplessly as their land was blown away and what was left of their farms was taken over by banks and land companies. Thousands of families sadly loaded their possessions into old cars or trucks and headed west.

Over a million "Okies" or "Arkies," so named because they came from Oklahoma and Arkansas, made the weary trek along Highway 66 toward the Pacific coast. They sought work in the orchards, orange groves, and lettuce fields of Washington, Oregon, and California. For many, however, the end of the journey brought, not work, but eviction by sheriffs and self-appointed vigilantes of western towns. Westerners had their own unemployment problems and wanted no outside competition.

Tenant Farming and Sharecropping

The poverty of the Okies and the Arkies was matched by that of another farming group: the tenant farmers and sharecroppers of the southern cotton belt. Too poor to buy land of their own, these farmers rented a few acres, from which they struggled to obtain a meager living. Each spring they borrowed enough money from a bank or the landowner to plant a crop, usually cotton, in the field. When the crop was harvested in the fall, the farmers used it to pay off the loan, keeping what was left over for themselves. With worsening economic conditions, there was almost nothing left. Each year the farmers were driven deeper into debt.

The early farm policies of the New Deal actually worsened the plight of tenants and sharecroppers. By reducing the number of acres in production in order to cut surpluses, the Agricultural Adjustment Act forced these people off the land they worked. Unlike the landowners, who were paid for agreeing not to produce, the tenants and sharecroppers received nothing in return.

Agricultural Reforms

The Roosevelt administration grew increasingly aware of the problems of rural poverty and searched for new ways to overcome it. One attempt had been the Resettlement Administration (RA), established in 1935 to resettle poor farmers on good land and provide sufficient equipment and advice for them to make a fresh start. But the program received little support and was hampered by lack of funds. As a result the RA resettled only 4,441 families, compared to the projected goal of 500,000.

In 1937 the Farm Security Administration (FSA) replaced the Resettlement Administration. The FSA extended loans to help tenants and sharecroppers buy farms and equipment. By 1940 short-term loans were made to more than 800,000 farm families and long-term farm-purchase loans to another 13,600. One other New Deal action helped ease the drudgery of life for many farmers. The Rural Electrification Administration loaned money for building electric power lines, thus extending electricity to isolated rural areas.

Soil conservation became another New Deal priority. The President himself inspired one way to attack drought. At his urging, the Forest Service planted a "shelter belt" of trees across the open plains. These trees blocked wind, held moisture and soil, and provided a refuge for animals.

In 1936 President Roosevelt signed the Soil Conservation and Domestic Allotment Act. Provisions of the act encouraged farmers to stop growing soil-depleting crops like corn, tobacco, cotton, and wheat on part of their land. They were to substitute soil-enriching land cover such as grass and soybeans to revive the fertility of the soil. In addition, farmers would receive payments from the government to compensate them for lost crops.

A New Agricultural Adjustment Act

When the Supreme Court struck down the Agricultural Adjustment Act in 1936, the government lost a way of limiting farm surpluses. As the four-year drought ended, surpluses began to reappear, threatening the gains farm prices had made earlier. Secretary of Agriculture Henry Wallace ironically complained that if there was a good harvest "we would be sunk." To solve the new farm problem and help alleviate future difficulties, Congress passed the second Agricultural Adjustment Act in 1938.

Under the new act the government could once again call on farmers to limit their crops. But payments for such limitations could not come from the processing tax that had caused the first Agricultural Adjustment Act to be struck down. Money would come instead from congressional appropriations. Crop production could be limited either through crop allotments—set amounts that each farmer was allowed to grow—or by taking land out of production

for soil conservation. The second Agriculture Adjustment Act also insured wheat farmers against drought losses.

Finally, the act put into practice Wallace's plan for an "ever-normal granary." Under this plan, crop surpluses would not be sold on the open market. Instead the government would buy the crops and store them for use in times of poor harvests. In this way farm products would be available in steady supply.

Other New Deal Reforms

In Roosevelt's second inaugural speech he had stated that one third of the nation was still "ill-housed, ill-clad, and ill-nourished." The National Housing Act was passed in 1937 to do something for the ill-housed. The act provided loans to stimulate the construction industry to provide new housing for low-income families in rural and urban communities. It also created the United States Housing Authority, which in only a few years helped fund more than 150,000 new housing units.

To give consumers better protection in the marketplace, Congress passed the Food, Drug, and Cosmetic Act in 1938. It was a much stronger piece of legislation than the 1906 Pure Food and Drug Act. For the first time manufacturers were ordered to list the ingredients of certain products on the package. The new law also required that new drugs be rigidly tested before they could be sold.

In 1939 Congress passed the Hatch Act to prevent abuses of power by government officials. The need for such an act came to light as a result of scandals connected with the WPA. Some officials had granted people relief payments only in return for promises to vote for Democratic candidates. One series of newspaper stories charged that a Kentucky senator's reelection had been "bought with WPA votes." The Hatch Act forbade government employees, except those in policy-making positions, from actively participating in political campaigns.

One reform few people noticed at the time was to have far-reaching consequences in later years. In 1939, in response to the growing demands on the presidency, Roosevelt issued Executive Order 8248, by which he created the Executive Office of the President. The new office included administrative assistants, press secretaries, budget officers,

The FSA Photographs: Faces of Rural America

Crops froze in the California pea fields in the spring of 1936. Photographer Dorothea Lange recalled the scene:

> I saw and approached the hungry and desperate mother as if drawn by a magnet. . . . She asked me no questions. . . . I did not ask her name. . . . She said that they had been living on frozen vegetables from the surrounding fields, and birds that the children had killed. She had just sold the tires from the car to buy food.

The photograph Lange took of that mother and her children (below) is one of the best known in an extraordinary collection. Lange and ten other photographers worked for the Historical Section of the Farm Security Administration (FSA). Their assignment was to create a pictorial record of life in rural America during the Great Depression.

Dorothea Lange, Walker Evans, and Ben Shahn, better known as a graphic artist and painter (his lithograph *Years of Dust* appears on page 578), were among the first individuals hired for the project. Their work set a standard of excellence for the eight other photographers who joined the FSA project between 1935 and 1943.

FSA photographers shot pictures during frigid New England winters, when their cameras sometimes froze. They recorded cotton pickers in Mississippi, the laughter of an elderly midwestern couple, and a thousand other scenes of rural life. Yet it was the stark images of sharecroppers in wretched shacks, of dusty migrant families, and of the haunted eyes of fathers and mothers unable to feed their children that left the strongest impressions on viewers. These photographs, available free to newspapers and magazines, helped awaken city people and Congress to the urgency of rural suffering. In an era before television, the FSA collection brought home to more fortunate people the grinding reality of desperate poverty.

Arthur Rothstein

Dorothea Lange

Dorothea Lange

legal counsels, and other assistants. Later Presidents were to add more positions, and the Executive Office became an important part of the executive branch of government.

For answers, see p. A 98.

Section Review

1. Identify the following: John L. Lewis, Congress of Industrial Organizations, Farm Security Administration, second Agricultural Adjustment Act.

2. Define the following terms: industrial union, sitdown strike.

3. What type of workers did John L. Lewis want to organize?

4. What were the two major provisions of the Fair Labor Standards Act?

5. What two disasters affected many farmers in the Midwest during the 1930s?

6. How did the second Agricultural Adjustment Act differ from the first?

3 Life During the New Deal Years

Nearly everyone who lived through the Great Depression would carry vivid memories of the hardships for the rest of their lives. Those memories would be passed down to children and grandchildren in the form of advice about family budgets, borrowing and spending money, and the importance of financial security.

The depression upset traditional ideas about the "American dream." People who had worked hard all their lives and saved their money to provide a secure future lost everything when a bank closed or a business failed. Hard-working people lived in poverty because of forces over which they had no control. Children watched as shock and helplessness overpowered their parents. "I remember how, after dinner, my father would just lie on the couch in utter despair, night after night for hours," recalled one adult many years later.

The Search for Entertainment

Americans everywhere needed diversion from daily worries. Talking pictures and radio were popular sources of entertainment. Many people could afford a radio. Movie theaters charged only 25 cents and gave away free dishes one night a week.

The 1930s were the golden years of the American film industry, and Hollywood, California, was its headquarters. Before the New Deal, many movies questioned traditional values. Gangsters were frequently movie heroes. In films such as *Little Caesar*, *Public Enemy*, and *Scarface*, gangsters combined ambition, hard work, and loyalty in order to get ahead in a chaotic world. Those

This 1937 mural, entitled Comedy, *was painted in Westport, Connecticut, by John Steuart Curry. Curry included familiar faces from movies and cartoons as well as portraits of popular radio personalities. Will Rogers appears in the cowboy hat.*

who were normally expected to uphold law and order, including police, lawyers, and politicians, were often shown as dishonest and corrupt. Social disorder was even the subject of movie comedies such as the Marx Brothers' *Duck Soup* and Mae West's *She Done Him Wrong*.

With the coming of the New Deal, Hollywood moved in a new direction. Comedies with stars like Cary Grant, Katherine Hepburn, and Irene Dunne showed how even when the world seemed totally confused, the social order still worked. New dramas made heroes of federal government agents who relentlessly stalked criminals. Lavish musicals, film versions of the classics of literature, and huge epics such as Margaret Mitchell's Civil War story *Gone With the Wind* gave audiences a chance to escape, for a few hours at least, from the troubles of the real world.

The Great Depression had badly shaken Americans' faith in their society. Many Hollywood directors and producers set out to restore that faith and rebuild confidence in the value of hard work, perseverance, and moderation. Walt Disney's cartoon character Mickey Mouse embodied the ideals of initiative and enterprise. In the *Three Little Pigs*, Disney used an old story that captured the purposeful spirit of the New Deal. When the pigs in the cartoon sang "Who's Afraid of the Big, Bad Wolf?" many in the audience recognized the big, bad wolf as a symbol of the depression.

Director Frank Capra introduced Americans to populist-style heroes in *Mr. Smith Goes to Washington*, starring James Stewart, and in *Mr. Deeds Goes to Town* and *Meet John Doe*, starring Gary Cooper. Capra's heroes struggled against corrupt power. They met humiliation and frustration, but with the help of "ordinary" people, they accomplished their missions.

Like the movie industry, the radio broadcasting industry thrived during hard times. As the depression forced vaudeville theaters to close, talent flooded the airwaves. Such stars as George Burns, Gracie Allen, Jack Benny, Mary Livingston, Ed Wynn, and Fred Allen offered listeners comic relief. With so many people out of work and at home, daytime radio serials drew large audiences. These popular shows were called soap operas because soap companies often sponsored them.

Art Reflects the Times

The cruelty of the depression years was powerfully portrayed by American artists and writers. One of the best-known novels of the 1930s was John Steinbeck's *Grapes of Wrath*. In it the author traced the painful and heartbreaking migration of Okies and Arkies westward to California.

Dorothea Lange captured pitiful Dust Bowl scenes in photographs later published in *An American Exodus*. Photographer Margaret Bourke-White vividly portrayed rural poverty in the South in *You Have Seen Their Faces*, as did photographer Walker Evans and writer James Agee in *Let Us Now Praise Famous Men*. Richard Wright's novels *Uncle Tom's Children* and *Native Son* opened many Americans' eyes to what it meant to grow up as a black youth during the Great Depression.

Because of WPA-supported projects in literature, painting, and sculpture, many writers and artists were able to carry on their work. Often the work reflected the search for common themes that could bind the country together.

The past was given new emphasis as writers compiled histories of each state and wrote biographies of figures such as Benjamin Franklin and Abraham Lincoln. Painters used walls of public buildings for giant murals of farmers at work in the countryside and construction workers erecting huge projects in the cities. Federal funds enabled the sculptor Gutzon Borglum to continue carving the massive heads of Washington, Jefferson, Lincoln, and Theodore Roosevelt on Mount Rushmore in the Black Hills of South Dakota.

Black Americans and the New Deal

For black Americans the depression worsened an already intolerable situation. They continued to be victims of racial discrimination in both the North and the South. Many could live only in segregated areas, and most were paid less for their work than whites were paid.

Blacks who had jobs in industries in the North found themselves the objects of the "last hired, first fired" employment policy. They were often the first to be laid off in any cutback. Black tenant farmers and sharecroppers in the South frequently lost their

In the process of creating jobs, the Works Progress Administration (WPA) became a patron of the arts on a grand scale. The WPA gave jobs to writers, photographers, sculptors, and painters. This mural by William Gropper captures the monumental scope of such WPA projects as dam building.

land as a result of surplus reduction policies. (See page 584.) Furthermore, lynching of blacks increased during the tense early years of the depression. Over 60 blacks lost their lives to lynch mobs between 1930 and 1934.

President Franklin Roosevelt denounced the lynchings as "collective murder," but he refused to encourage a bill in Congress that would have made lynching a federal crime. Southern legislators controlled key committees in the House and Senate, and the President needed their support for his economic programs. "I did not choose the tools with which I must work," he told black leaders who urged him to support the bill. "If I come out for an anti-lynching bill now, they will block every bill I ask Congress to pass, to keep America from collapsing. I just can't take that risk."

Black Americans witnessed some improvement during the New Deal, however. As you have read, Eleanor Roosevelt, as well as Harry Hopkins and Harold Ickes, tried to prevent discrimination against blacks in the relief and job programs of the New Deal. Thousands of young black men received the opportunity to learn a trade through the Civilian Conservation Corps. More blacks than ever before were appointed to impor-

tant government positions during the New Deal. Although no legislation was passed to protect civil rights or end discrimination, the New Deal offered black Americans greater hope for political and social improvement than they had had before.

Attempts to Improve Life for Native Americans

During the 1930s John Collier directed the Bureau of Indian Affairs. Collier was deeply committed to assisting Native Americans in the West and Southwest. With the support of President Roosevelt, he worked to extend the benefits of New Deal relief and job programs to Indians.

Under Collier's leadership, the sale of land originally granted to Indians was stopped. In addition, a special Indian Emergency Conservation Work group was established under the CCC. The group employed Indians in programs of soil erosion control, irrigation, and land development.

By improving agriculture, Collier helped to improve Native Americans' economic position in their local communities. The Indian Reorganization Act of 1934 was a further effort to better Native American life. Funds were set up to provide scholarships for promising students and to help Indians set up their own businesses.

Expulsion of Mexican Americans

As you read earlier, hundreds of thousands of Mexicans had been migrating to California and the Southwest since the early 1900s. (See page 543.) Most of these people labored as migrant workers or found jobs in local industries or in coal and copper mines. As much of the country became the Dust Bowl and as factories and mines closed during the depression, many Americans who had been happy about the influx of cheap labor now saw the Mexican workers as serious competition for the few remaining jobs.

Popular unrest in the region convinced government officials to adopt a deportation policy whereby thousands of families were uprooted and sent back to Mexico. The majority of those families had children born in the United States. The children were therefore American citizens, but the government refused to honor their rights.

Small Gains for Women

During the 1920s women had made some economic gains, entering the work force in greater numbers and holding jobs with higher status and incomes. But when depression struck, women were often forced out of their jobs, and men were hired to replace

Eleanor Roosevelt was a niece of Theodore Roosevelt and a distant cousin of her husband, Franklin. She became an outspoken advocate for the jobless, the disadvantaged, and minorities. A tireless traveler, Roosevelt is shown here speaking at a Resettlement Administration project in Tennessee.

them. It was argued that since men were the "breadwinners" in the average family, they should have what jobs were available. Many companies refused to hire a woman if her husband had a job.

In 1932 Franklin Roosevelt appointed Mary Dewson, an officer of a national consumers' organization, to coordinate women's activities in the presidential campaign and later in the administration. She urged Roosevelt to support the rights of women in two ways. First, Dewson persuaded the President to appoint women to important posts in the administration. The most notable was Secretary of Labor Frances Perkins. Roosevelt also appointed the first women to serve as minister to a foreign nation, as director of the United States mint, and as judge in a circuit court of appeals. Mary Dewson also worked for equal treatment of women in New Deal programs.

Eleanor Roosevelt was the most visible champion of women's rights during the New Deal. After her husband was elected President, she began holding her own press conferences—for women reporters only. Since her activities and statements frequently became front-page news, her press conferences gave women reporters a chance to publish major stories before male reporters. The First Lady had her own syndicated newspaper column, called "My Day," and her own radio program. She was also active in the League of Women Voters and the Women's Trade Union League.

The efforts of such women as Mary Dewson, Frances Perkins, and Eleanor Roosevelt showed American women that they might gain more political, social, and economic equality by supporting the New Deal.

Impact of the New Deal

After 1938 the New Deal lost most of its momentum. Americans began to turn their attention to events in Europe and Asia that were propelling the world toward war. The depression seemed to be under control, but it had not ended. Six million Americans were still unemployed.

Yet the New Deal had profoundly affected American life and government. For one thing, Franklin Roosevelt had shown Americans that a democratic republic could survive a severe crisis without becoming a dictatorship. Through the New Deal, the government had taken a moderate course. It had preserved the free enterprise system by reforming it.

New Deal programs had greatly increased the size and scope of the federal government. The government had assumed a much larger role in the economy. Government regulation of big business and the control of monopoly did not originate with the New Deal, but the banking, securities, and public utility legislation of the period expanded the concept. For the first time, in the United States at least, the government had acted as an employer of the unemployed and a sponsor of work projects.

People's views about the responsibility of government had also changed during the New Deal. Before the 1930s, most people viewed government assistance to the needy as charity, something that humiliated those forced to accept it. But the New Deal fostered the idea that people were entitled to public assistance when they became victims of economic conditions over which they had no control.

For answers, see p. A 99.

A View of the New Deal: Analyzing Oral Evidence

As the study of history approaches more recent times, historians have access to a new source of evidence: oral accounts. They no longer need to rely on written or visual evidence but can talk directly with people who lived during the period being studied. An oral history is prepared by tape-recording interviews with individuals. Often the tape recording is then transcribed, that is, a written copy is made.

An oral account of an event can be a valuable historical document. It can help you understand how historical events affect people and can give you insight into what it was like to live during a specific time. An oral account should be analyzed as is any historical document. An extract from an oral history is printed at right. It is part of an interview with David Kennedy in the late 1960s. Kennedy had served on the Federal Reserve Board during the New Deal. At the time of the interview he was the chairman of the board of a major company. Follow the steps below to analyze the document.

1. **Identify the source of the document.** Answer the following questions: (a) Who was interviewed? (b) When did the interview take place?

2. **Decide how reliable the evidence is.** Use the following questions to judge the reliability of the document: (a) What was the person's role in the events being described? How might his role affect his interpretation? (b) How long after the event did the interview take place? How might that affect his account? (c) How might the person's position at the time of the interview affect his account?

3. **Study the evidence to learn more about an historical event.** Read the document carefully. Use it and what you have read in your text to answer the following questions: (a) How does the person think President Roosevelt may have helped the nation early in the New Deal? (b) How did his attitude toward Roosevelt change? Why? (c) What can you learn about the effect of the New Deal from this document?

David Kennedy

Roosevelt gave us quite a bit of hope early. He probably saved us from complete collapse in that sense. But he did not answer the things. Many of his programs were turned on and off, started and stopped . . . shifting gears. Because we had never been in anything like this.

Planning had not been done. So they'd go out and sweep the mountains and clean up the debris, and then the wind comes along and blows it back again. It gave some work. But the people that got the money in some ways were benefited and in other ways were hurt. They didn't like to see the waste. . . . They had mixed reactions. . . .

I was enthusiastic when Roosevelt came in. I thought: We're in serious trouble. Something has to be done, and here's a man that's going to do it. I voted for him his first term and his second. After that, I voted against him. It wasn't just on the two-term basis, although that was important. The packing of the Supreme Court and the fact that we were not making the progress I thought our country was capable of making . . . I became terribly disenchanted.

He was a dramatic leader. He had charm, personality, poise, and so on. He could inspire people. But to me, he lacked the stick-to-it-iveness to carry a program through.

Source: Studs Terkel, *Hard Times* (New York: Avon, 1970).

Before 1933 most Americans considered the federal government remote from their lives. By 1939 it was hard to find anyone who did not have a friend or relative who owed a job, house, farm, education, or some other benefit to a New Deal program. Defenders of the New Deal pointed to that fact with pride. Never before, they argued, had people had security against old age or unemployment.

However, critics charged that the growth of the federal government threatened American values and traditions. The ideals of individual initiative and free enterprise, they argued, were being undermined by government intervention and control.

Debate about whether the changes brought about by the New Deal were good for the nation has continued. Yet few people deny that the New Deal had a major effect on government, the economy, and society.

Major Events	
1935	Congress of Industrial Organizations founded
1936	Roosevelt elected for second term
1937	Roosevelt proposes redesign of judiciary; Farm Security Administration established; National Housing Act passed; severe recession begins
1938	Second Agricultural Adjustment Act; Food, Drug, and Cosmetic Act; and Fair Labor Standards Act passed
1939	Hatch Act passed; Executive Order 8248 issued

For answers, see p. A 100.

Section Review

1. Identify the following: John Steinbeck, Dorothea Lange, Margaret Bourke-White, Walker Evans, James Agee, Richard Wright, John Collier, Mary Dewson.
2. What sources of entertainment helped Americans forget their troubles during the Great Depression?
3. List two ways black Americans were affected by the New Deal.
4. What was the main activity of the Indian Emergency Conservation Work group?
5. What impact did the depression have on Mexican workers in the United States?
6. What important government posts did women hold in Roosevelt's administration?

★ ★ ★ ★ ★ ★ ★ ★ ★ ★ ★ ★ ★ ★ ★ ★ ★ ★ ★ ★

IN PERSPECTIVE   In 1936 over 60 percent of American voters indicated their support for Franklin Roosevelt by electing him to a second term. Soon, however, even some of his strongest supporters questioned his attempt to "pack" the Supreme Court. A severe recession in 1937 and 1938 revealed that although New Deal programs had temporarily relieved unemployment, the problems underlying the Depression had not been solved.

During his second term, Roosevelt continued to support reform measures that benefited workers and farmers. The Congress of Industrial Organizations helped unskilled workers organize for the first time. Farmers were especially hard hit during the 1930s because of a severe drought, but several new laws were designed to improve conditions for them.

The Great Depression devastated the lives of millions of Americans, and many sought escape through movies and radio. Artists documented the effect of the depression, and many chose themes that would encourage economic recovery. In some ways the reform spirit of the New Deal improved conditions for black Americans, women, and Native Americans, but many Mexican workers were forced to return to Mexico. Although the New Deal did not end the depression, it did result in rapid growth in the size and influence of the federal government.

For answers, see p. A 100.

Chapter Review

1. (a) How did Alfred Landon's views on the New Deal change during the 1936 election campaign? Why? (b) How did Roosevelt respond to anti–New Deal feelings?

2. (a) What groups comprised Roosevelt's coalition in the 1936 election? (b) How had the Democrats won the support of organized labor and black Americans?

3. (a) What did Roosevelt hope to accomplish by redesigning the Supreme Court? (b) Was he successful? Explain.

4. (a) What developments led to a severe recession in 1937–1938? (b) Why did Roosevelt hesitate to increase government spending?

5. (a) What types of workers were represented by the Congress of Industrial Organizations? (b) What new tactic did workers use? (c) Was that tactic successful? Explain. (d) What did workers gain from the Fair Labor Standards Act?

6. (a) How did drought from 1932 through 1936 affect midwestern farmers? (b) What actions did the Roosevelt administration take to try to alleviate the problems of farmers?

7. (a) Why was the Great Depression an especially difficult time for many black Americans? (b) In what ways did the situation for blacks improve during the New Deal?

8. (a) How did John Collier try to improve the conditions under which Native Americans lived? (b) What did the Indian Reorganization Act of 1934 offer?

9. (a) How did the onset of depression affect women working outside the home? (b) How did Mary Dewson try to improve women's position?

For answers, see p. A 101.

For Further Thought

593

1. (a) How did movies and radio help Americans cope with the effects of the Great Depression? (b) What values did many movies try to reinforce? (c) What impact do you think the efforts of filmmakers had on people at the time?

2. (a) What lasting impact did the New Deal have on the federal government? (b) In what other ways do you think the New Deal affected American life? (c) Do you think the New Deal was good for the nation in the 1930s? (d) Do you think its long term effect has been positive or negative?

3. Many observers believed that President Roosevelt's plan to add justices to the Supreme Court would have upset the system of checks and balances. Do you agree or disagree with that view? Why?

For answers, see p. A 101.

Developing Basic Skills

1. *Using Visual Evidence* The painting on page 589 was done as a WPA project. (a) What is shown in the painting? (b) How does the painting reflect the goals of the New Deal? (c) What message do you think the artist was trying to convey to people living during the Great Depression? (d) What can you learn about the period from the painting?

2. *Collecting Evidence* In this chapter you have read about oral history. (See page 591.) Talk with someone you know who lived during the 1930s and ask what life was like during the Great Depression. Write a report about what you learned.

See page 778 for suggested readings.

Prelude to Another World Conflict

34

(1920–1941)

The front page of the New York Times, *September 1, 1939, as war begins in Europe.*

Chapter Outline

1 *American Diplomacy From Harding to Hoover*

2 *International Challenges During the 1930s*

3 *The Threat of War*

4 *Between Peace and War*

Between 1920 and 1941 most Americans were pre-occupied with events at home. The horrors of the world war that ended in 1919 convinced many people that the United States should avoid becoming involved in any new world conflicts. During the Roaring Twenties the desire to "get rich quick" and to take part in the gaiety of the age seemed more important than distant events in Europe and Asia.

During the Great Depression of the 1930s, millions of Americans had to concentrate on simply surviving from day to day. They read about political turmoil in Germany, but such developments seemed far removed from the burdens of their own lives.

Japanese aggression in Asia and the rise of dictatorships in Italy and Germany threatened world peace. Yet even after war broke out in Europe in 1939, Americans still hoped to avoid the conflict. Eventually, however, actions by Japan were to end American isolationism.

1 American Diplomacy From Harding to Hoover

Americans were weary of foreign involvements after the World War, and the Presidents they elected during the 1920s shared those feelings. President Harding shunned a major American role in world affairs. He remained true to his promise that "normalcy" would be restored during his administration. His successors in the White House, Calvin Coolidge and Herbert Hoover, were also hesitant to plunge the United States into the complexities of world affairs.

Despite a deep distrust in foreign affairs, the American people did accept some policies requiring cooperation with other nations. Limited cooperation emerged as a major theme of United States foreign policy during the 1920s.

Isolation Versus World Cooperation

During the 1920s most government officials and many citizens were *isolationists*, that is, they believed that the United States should avoid alliances and entangling agreements with other nations. Isolationism kept the United States from joining the League of Nations. (See page 516.) Rather than sign the Treaty of Versailles, which contained a provision for league membership, the United States negotiated a separate peace treaty with Germany in 1921.

President Harding was also hostile to membership in the League of Nations. The United States, Harding declared in 1923, "does not propose to enter [the league] now by the side door, or the back door, or the cellar door."

No matter how strong the isolationist mood, the United States could not stand aloof from world affairs. After the World War, Japan had begun building a powerful navy to support its goal of creating a Pacific empire. Great Britain and the United States opposed such actions. As a result all three nations became involved in a naval arms race, competing to build more battleships and cruisers.

In 1921 President Harding asked representatives of nine Asian and European nations to meet in Washington to discuss ways to ease tensions in the Pacific. American

Secretary of State Charles Evans Hughes startled the delegates when he proposed a limit on construction of large warships for ten years. The delegates to the Washington Naval Conference finally agreed that for every five large ships the United States or Britain owned, Japan could have three, and France and Italy could have one and three fourths.

Japan resented its inferior position under the new treaty. Therefore the United States, Britain, and France offered a Four Power Treaty. Along with Japan, they agreed to respect each others' rights in the Pacific and to refer any future disputes to a conference. The delegates also signed a Nine Power Treaty in which they formally accepted the Open Door policy toward China.

The Washington Naval Conference seemed to be an important step toward peace. It eased the arms race and tensions in the Pacific. Soon, however, all the agreements came undone. Nations avoided them by building smaller warships and submarines. Japan also continued to strive for a Pacific empire.

As international tensions increased in the late 1920s, United States Secretary of State Frank B. Kellogg and French Foreign Minister Aristide Briand proposed a pact to try to guarantee peace. In 1928, 15 nations signed the Kellogg-Briand Pact, outlawing war except in cases of self-defense. Eventually, most other nations joined the pact, but there was no military or political organization to enforce it. Senator Carter Glass of Virginia said the treaty was worth no more than a postage stamp, but he voted with 84 other senators to consent to it.

During the 1920s the United States also participated in many League of Nations conferences on international trade, communications, and transportation. Still, United States tariff policy showed the strength of isolationist sentiments. The Fordney-McCumber Act of 1922 had raised most tariff rates. During the first years of the Great Depression, the Hawley-Smoot Act of 1931 raised rates even more. Those highly protective tariffs disrupted world trade and made the depression worse for all nations.

The United States in the World Economy

The United States took a direct role in the world economy in 1923 when Germany, devastated by wild inflation, failed to make reparation payments to France.* In reaction French troops occupied the Ruhr region of Germany, threatening the delicate balance of power. In 1924, to help Germany pay reparations to France, the United States proposed the Dawes Plan, named after banker Charles G. Dawes.

According to the plan, the United States would lend money to Germany. Germany would then use the loan to pay reparations to France and the other Allies. The Allies, in turn, would be able to repay their wartime debts to the United States by drawing on the reparations received from Germany. The Dawes Plan rescued Germany from economic ruin and enabled the Allies to repay the United States.

Despite isolationist sentiment and high tariffs, the 1920s was a period of growing international trade and investment for the United States. The nation emerged from the World War with a strong economy. Many factories and farms in Europe had been destroyed during the war, but United States industry and agriculture was undamaged.

Exports soared in 1919 and 1920 and then slackened as the national economies of Europe recovered. Nonetheless, in 1925 the volume of United States exports was almost double what it had been in 1913. Investment abroad also grew as American companies built manufacturing plants in Europe and established an interest in Middle Eastern oil fields.

United States Policy in Latin America

United States policy toward Latin America was not one of isolationism. Unstable conditions in several Latin American nations prompted the United States to send in troops to restore order. During the early 1920s United States soldiers were stationed in Panama, the Dominican Republic, and Honduras. The marines, in Nicaragua since 1912, withdrew in 1925. But when civil war broke

---

*As you read in Chapter 28, reparations were penalty payments that Germany was to make to the Allies for war damages.

out in 1928, the marines were sent back to Nicaragua to fight antigovernment forces and enforce a free election.

By the end of the decade, the pattern of military intervention was coming to an end. Under fire from progressives in his own party, President Coolidge placed less emphasis on armed intervention in Latin America. Developments in Mexico tested Coolidge's ability to deal with a Latin American neighbor without resorting to force.

In 1927 the Mexican congress passed a law limiting United States ownership of Mexican oil resources to 50 years. President Coolidge appointed Dwight W. Morrow, a prominent banker, to negotiate with the Mexican government. Morrow was instructed "to keep us out of war." The resulting agreement allowed United States corporations to retain oil properties acquired before 1917. Morrow's success encouraged the United States to continue this more peaceful approach to Latin American affairs.

In 1928 Undersecretary of State J. Reuben Clark drew up a memorandum stating that the United States did not have a right to intervene militarily in the affairs of Latin American nations. Officially released by the Hoover Administration in 1930, the Clark Memorandum was warmly received throughout Latin America. Within a short time President Hoover demonstrated that he meant to honor the principle of nonintervention. He refrained from sending troops to El Salvador in 1932 when that country failed to repay some debts. He also agreed to withdraw troops from Haiti.

War in Asia

Developments in Asia threatened world peace when, in 1931, Japanese troops began to occupy the northern Chinese province of Manchuria. China petitioned the League of Nations for help. The league considered an economic boycott against Japan and asked the United States to participate. The Hoover administration refused, and the league took no action. Manchuria fell in January 1932, and Japan set up a "puppet" state, that is, one controlled by Japan. In February the Japanese air force bombed Shanghai, killing many civilians.

Japanese aggression outraged Americans, but the United States did not want to become involved in a war on the other side of the world. Unable to make even mild threats, Secretary of State Henry L. Stimson issued a statement, known as the Stimson Doctrine. He declared that the United States would refuse to recognize Japanese territorial gains in China. Although the Stimson Doctrine was a declaration of American opposition to Japanese aggression, no proposals for concrete action against Japan were included.

Most Americans, fearing that the United States would be drawn into an Asian war, supported President Hoover's cautious policy toward Japan. Only a minority of the population, known as *internationalists*, wanted the United States to abandon the policy of isolation and take a more active role in world affairs. They warned that American inaction would encourage hostile acts by aggressive powers.

For answers, see p. A 101.

Section Review

1. Identify the following: Kellogg-Briand Pact, Dawes Plan, Clark Memorandum, Stimson Doctrine.
2. Define the following: isolationist, internationalist.
3. What was President Harding's response to suggestions that the United States join the League of Nations?
4. What were two results of the Dawes Plan?
5. What agreement did Dwight Morrow and the Mexican government work out with respect to oil rights in Mexico?

2 International Challenges During the 1930s

The Great Depression dominated the lives of nearly all Americans during the 1930s. People concentrated on immediate problems such as jobs, food, clothing, and shelter. They paid little attention to international events. But aggressive acts by Germany, Italy, and Japan eventually forced the United States to become involved in world affairs.

Rise of Totalitarian Dictatorships

By the mid-1930s dictators had established totalitarian governments in Italy and Germany. In a *totalitarian state* the government is supreme and individuals have few rights. All constitutional representation and political opposition is forbidden.

Benito Mussolini had established himself as dictator of Italy in 1922. His followers, known as Fascists, suspended elections and crushed all opposition. Mussolini put the Italian economy under strict government supervision and began to modernize the armed forces. To his people, he held out the promise that Italy would become a great power in the Mediterranean region and in Africa.

The military gradually assumed control of Japan after 1930, and Emperor Hirohito became little more than a figurehead. The aggression in Manchuria was only the beginning of an effort to secure markets and raw materials essential to a powerful empire.

Adolf Hitler and his National Socialist, or Nazi, party came to power in Germany in 1933. The Nazis had grown increasingly popular during the 1920s and early 1930s because of Hitler's fierce attacks on the Treaty of Versailles. He expressed the feelings of many Germans who believed that Germany had been unfairly punished by the treaty. Other Germans supported Hitler because he promised to keep the communists out of power.

Once in power Hitler and the Nazis established totalitarian control of Germany. One of their earliest actions was to secretly begin building up the German military in preparation for aggressive expansion.

Economic Issues

Totalitarian dictatorships won much support during the 1930s because of the worldwide depression. Industry was virtually at a standstill. Many nations had erected high tariff barriers to protect their failing businesses from foreign competition. But the collapse of international trade only made the depression worse.

President Roosevelt and Secretary of State Cordell Hull believed that the depression in the United States and the rest of the world could be eased by reviving international trade. American exports had

By 1933 Adolph Hitler's totalitarian Nazi party controlled the German government. This German poster shows Hitler holding a flag depicting the Nazi symbol, the swastika.

dropped 50 percent between 1929 and 1933. Roosevelt and Hull wanted to reverse the trend as quickly as possible.

One strategy was to *devalue* the currency, that is, to reduce the value of the dollar in relation to other currencies. As a result, American products would be less expensive on the world market. In the hopes of stimulating exports, the President began a policy of devaluing the dollar in 1933, but the devaluation had little impact on trade.

In another attempt to improve foreign trade, Roosevelt pressed for lower tariffs. Congress responded by passing the Trade Agreements Act in 1934. Under the act the President had the power to lower existing tariffs as much as 50 percent for nations agreeing to lower import taxes on United States goods.

Roosevelt had hoped that lower tariffs abroad would enable the United States to increase exports. If exports increased significantly, economists argued, industrial production would rise and unemployment would fall. But because of the worldwide depression, there was little demand for American products, and exports increased only modestly.

Economic considerations also played a part in the decision to grant diplomatic recognition to the Soviet Union in 1933. The United States had refused to recognize the Bolshevik government after the revolution in 1917. Some Americans believed that recognition of the Soviet Union would result in greatly increased trade with that country. The expectations of vigorous trade, however, did not materialize.

The worldwide depression also affected the repayment of wartime debts. During the war the Allies had borrowed almost $10 billion from the United States. According to the Dawes Plan of 1924 the Allies paid their debts to the United States by collecting reparation payments from Germany. The reparation payments, as you have read, were partly financed by United States loans to Germany. When the depression struck, the United States stopped aid to Germany, and Germany slowed its reparations payments to the Allies. The Allies consequently found themselves unable to pay their debts to the United States.

In 1931 President Hoover suspended all debt payment for a year. But when payments again came due, many of the debtor nations were still unable to fulfill their obligations. The United States eventually collected about one quarter of the money owed by the Allies. Americans resented the Allies for not paying for their full share of the war effort. (Only Finland met its obligations.) This resentment helped strengthen isolationist sentiment during the 1930s.

The Isolationist Impulse

United States foreign policy continued to be dominated by isolationism during the 1930s. From 1934 to 1936 Senator Gerald Nye of North Dakota chaired a congressional committee investigating the United States entry into the World War in 1917. The committee's findings strengthened isolationist feelings and influenced foreign policy.

Nye claimed that the United States had been drawn into the war in Europe by international bankers. They feared that France and Britain would be unable to repay bank loans because of the expense of the war. The Nye committee charged that the bankers lobbied powerfully for the United States to enter the war. The committee further alleged that, anticipating increased profits, munitions industries also pressed for American entry into the war. With each new allegation more people were won over by the isolationists.

Taking advantage of the growing isolationist feeling in the country, congressional isolationists introduced legislation banning arms sales and loans to nations at war. The Neutrality Act of 1935 authorized the President to bar arms sales to warring nations. President Roosevelt soon invoked the act, refusing to sell arms to Italy or Ethiopia. The two nations were at war following the Italian invasion of Ethiopia earlier in 1935. However, Italy was in a stronger military position and was able to continue purchasing food and gasoline, which were not covered by the act. Consequently the act worked against Ethiopia.

In 1936 Congress extended the neutrality legislation to include loans to belligerents. However, developments in Spain soon tested the policy of neutrality. In 1936 civil war broke out between supporters of the republican government and fascists led by Francisco Franco. Franco received military support from Germany and Italy, while the republicans received aid from the Soviet Union. Despite widespread American sympathy for the republican government, President Roosevelt asked for strict neutrality. A joint resolution of Congress in January 1937 banned United States aid to either side.

In 1937 isolationists extended presidential authority to bar shipment of nonmilitary goods. The new law also banned travel by Americans on the ships of belligerents. Thus a powerful isolationist impulse shaped the foreign policy of the United States during the 1930s. As Germany, Italy, and Japan became more aggressive, however, that policy was to be challenged.

The Good Neighbor Policy

Faced with aggressive dictatorships in Europe and Asia, President Roosevelt tried to secure the friendship of the Latin American nations. In his inauguration speech in March 1933, Roosevelt proclaimed that the United States would follow "the policy of the good neighbor."

In late 1933 Secretary of State Cordell Hull attended the Seventh Pan-American Conference in Montevideo, Uruguay. At the conference Hull supported the principle that "no state has the right to intervene in the internal or external affairs of another." In 1934 Roosevelt implemented the "good neighbor" policy by withdrawing the marines from Haiti and nullifying the Platt Amendment, which had restricted Cuban independence.

The "good neighbor" policy benefited the United States. In 1936 when President Roosevelt traveled to Buenos Aires, Argentina, to attend the Inter-American Conference for the Maintenance of Peace, he received an enthusiastic welcome. In his address to the conference Roosevelt stressed the unity of the United States and Latin America. He informed his listeners that nations outside the Western Hemisphere seeking "to commit acts of aggression against us will find a hemisphere wholly prepared to consult together for our mutual safety and our mutual good." The friendship of Latin American nations proved to be important for the United States when war broke out.

As the threat of war in Europe grew, most Americans hoped the United States would not become involved in the conflict. As this 1938 cartoon indicates, many Americans recalled the battle casualties of World War I. Others were critical of European nations for failure to repay World War I debts to the United States.

The Good Neighbor Policy

Latin American nations had long been critical of United States military intervention in the region. Resentment was still strong in the early 1930s even though Presidents Coolidge and Hoover had reduced the United States' military role there. President Roosevelt announced the "good neighbor policy" in his first inaugural address. In 1936 in a speech at Chautauqua, New York, he spoke of the success of that policy:

> We seek no conquest: we stand for peace. In the whole of the Western Hemisphere our good neighbor policy has produced results that are especially heartening. . . .

> Throughout the Americas the spirit of the good neighbor is a practical and living fact. The twenty-one American republics are not only living together in friendship and in peace—they are united in the determination so to remain.

> To give substance to this determination a conference will meet on December 1, 1936, at the capital of our great southern neighbor Argentina, and it is, I know, the hope of all chiefs of state of the Americas that this will result in measures which will banish wars forever from this vast portion of the earth.

> Peace, like charity, begins at home; that is why we have begun at home. But peace in the Western world is not all that we seek.

> It is our hope that knowledge of the practical application of the good neighbor policy in this hemisphere will be borne home to our neighbors across the seas.

For answers, see p. A 101.

Section Review

1. Identify the following: Benito Mussolini, Adolf Hitler, Nye committee, "good neighbor" policy.
2. Define the following: totalitarian state, devalue.
3. What issue helped Hitler gain popularity in Germany?
4. What did Roosevelt hope to accomplish by devaluing the dollar?
5. According to the Nye committee, which economic groups tried to push the United States into World War I?
6. List two ways that President Roosevelt implemented the "good neighbor" policy.

3 The Threat of War

The League of Nations, the treaties signed at the Washington Naval Conference, and the Kellogg-Briand Pact had all been designed to promote peace and cooperation. But they did not prevent aggressive acts by Italy, Japan, and Germany. Italy invaded and conquered Ethiopia in 1935 and 1936, and Japan conquered much of northern and eastern China in 1937. In the meantime Germany began to expand into central Europe.

Japanese Militarism in Asia

United States policy toward Japanese aggression in Asia changed little after Franklin Roosevelt was inaugurated. In 1934 Congress passed the Tydings-McDuffy Act, promising the Philippine Islands complete independence within a decade.* The United States appeared ready to withdraw from a military or political role in Asian affairs.

Japan renewed attacks on China in 1937, seizing Peking, Shanghai, and other cities. Because of American sympathy for China, President Roosevelt did not invoke the Neutrality acts, which meant that both sides could buy arms from the United States. Although the President hoped his action would help China, the Japanese were able to acquire more war materials because they had more merchant ships to carry arms.

---

*As you read in Chapter 24, the United States had taken control of the Philippines after the Spanish-American War.

In 1931 Japan invaded and captured the Chinese province of Manchuria. In 1937 the Japanese attacked China again, overwhelming the ancient capital of Peking and the port city of Shanghai, where this photograph of Japanese troops was taken.

In a major speech in Chicago in 1937 the President warned Americans that unless nations acted positively "to preserve world peace," armed conflict anywhere in the world would affect all nations. Comparing war to a highly contagious disease, Roosevelt urged a "quarantine" of armed conflict wherever it might break out.

Despite Roosevelt's efforts to alter isolationist sentiments in the country, events two months later demonstrated that he had not succeeded. On December 12, 1937, Japanese bombers attacked and sank the American gunboat *Panay,* on patrol on the Yangtze River in China. Two crew members were killed in the *Panay* incident. The United States took no action. Instead the government accepted a Japanese apology and payment of $2 million for damages.

So many Americans feared that a similar incident would lead the country into war that many supported the Ludlow Amendment to the Constitution. That amendment would have required a national vote before the United States could enter a war, except in case of invasion. The proposed amendment failed by a narrow margin in Congress. The near passage of the amendment was evidence of a strong desire to avoid war.

Germany on the March

Once, when an adviser suggested to Adolf Hitler that he not anger other European powers, Hitler boasted that they would "never act! They'll just protest. And they will always be too late." Events proved Hitler correct. Throughout the 1930s he accelerated military preparations for expansion.

In 1936 German soldiers marched into the Rhineland, German territory located between the Rhine River and the French and Belgian borders. In so doing, Germany violated the Versailles Treaty. The French viewed the German troops as a threat but did not want to start a war over the Rhineland. Therefore, France offered no resistance, and the German army remained.

The policy of meeting Hitler's demands became known as *appeasement.* To avoid war, Britain and France allowed Germany to acquire new territory in Europe. Sooner or later, the European leaders believed, Hitler would gain enough and end his conquests.

In 1938 Germany annexed Austria to the Third Reich* without resistance from the

---

*The Third Reich was the name of the German state under the Nazis.

Austrians or the rest of Europe. Later that year Hitler demanded that Germany take possession of the Sudetenland, the western section of Czechoslovakia. He argued that the Sudetenland should be part of Germany because 3 million Germans lived there.

At a conference in Munich, Germany, in 1938, British Prime Minister Neville Chamberlain claimed he had found a formula for "peace with honor" and "peace for our time." The French and British agreed to allow Germany to take the Sudetenland. Italy and Germany in turn joined Britain and France in a pledge that none of the four would ever make war on the others. Czechoslovakia protested vigorously at the loss of its territory but was powerless to resist the German action.

At Munich Hitler had assured Chamberlain that he had no interest in more territory in Czechoslovakia or anywhere else in Europe. Yet in 1939 Hitler annexed the remainder of Czechoslovakia without resistance. In the same year Italy conquered Albania.

Hitler had decided that if he was to continue seizing European land, he would have

The appeasement policy of European leaders at Munich cost Czechoslovakia land the Germans wanted. This cartoon, showing Hitler as the taxi passenger, appeared in 1938.

TAKE ME TO CZECHOSLOVAKIA, DRIVER

YES SIR!

TAXI

to protect Germany from a war with the Soviet Union. In August 1939 the foreign ministers of the Soviet Union and Germany signed a nonaggression agreement. The Molotov-Ribbentrop Pact, named after the foreign minister of each nation, proclaimed that neither side would make war on the other. Secret provisions divided Poland between the two nations and guaranteed that Germany would not interfere if the Soviet Union invaded Finland.

Early Preparations in the United States

Chamberlain may have forecast peace, but Britain and other European countries had begun preparing for war. The United States, meanwhile, had almost no military force. Following the end of war in 1918, Congress had ordered drastic reductions in the size of the armed forces. Hitler had such disdain for United States military might that he mocked, "The inferiority and decadence of this allegedly new world power is evident in its military inefficiency."

The United States did make some attempts to expand the army and navy in the mid- and late 1930s. For example, President Roosevelt authorized the construction of additional cruisers and aircraft carriers. And in 1935 Congress increased the size of the army to 165,000 personnel. Despite such actions, however, the United States remained unprepared for war.

President Roosevelt was more concerned with diplomacy than with weapons. After the Munich Conference with Hitler, he searched for ways to alter the neutrality acts so the United States could aid allies in case of war. Roosevelt especially urged Congress to repeal the restrictions on selling arms. "I've fired my last shot," Roosevelt told Senate leaders in 1939. "I think I ought to have another round in my belt." But Congress refused to honor the President's request, and the neutrality legislation remained in effect.

The War Begins

At dawn on the morning of September 1, 1939, German airplanes, tanks, and infantry invaded Poland. Britain and France had committed themselves to the defense of Poland following the German occupation of Czechoslovakia. Thus, two days after the invasion of Poland they declared war on

Aggression in Europe 1935–1939

■ *In 1935 Italy under Mussolini invaded Ethiopia. Then between 1936 and 1939 Hitler dispatched the formidable German army to claim control of several areas bordering Germany. Said Hitler of the other European powers: "They'll just protest. And they will always be·too late." The areas shown in yellow on the map were occupied by Germany before war officially began on September 1, 1939, when Germany invaded Poland.*

Germany. After several weeks of German Blitzkrieg, or lightning war, Poland surrendered on October 6, 1939. Meanwhile, Soviet troops had invaded eastern Poland. The two nations then divided Poland into German and Soviet zones. One month later the Soviet Union invaded Finland, an act that especially outraged Americans since Finland had been the one nation that had continued to repay its previous war debts.

An overwhelming majority of Americans sympathized with the Poles, Finns, British, and French. A public opinion poll in the fall of 1939 showed that 84 percent of Ameri-

cans supported the Allies, as Britain and France were called. Only 2 percent supported Germany. Roosevelt issued a proclamation of neutrality two days after the outbreak of war but commented that Americans need not "remain neutral in thought."

Even while declaring neutrality, Roosevelt made further efforts to repeal restrictions on arms sales to nations at war. Isolationists in Congress fought the proposal. Finally, a compromise called cash-and-carry allowed the United States to sell arms to the Allies as long as they paid cash and transported the materials on their own ships. At the same time, Roosevelt assured isolationists that there was not "the remotest possibility of sending the boys of American mothers to fight on the battlefields of Europe."

German Victories

After the occupation of Poland, there was a lull in the fighting. Newspapers in the United States began to write about the "phony war." However, in April 1940 the Germans attacked and overran Norway and Denmark. One month later, German forces invaded neutral Belgium and the Netherlands before pushing on to France. Mussolini entered the war by attacking France from the south. "The hand that held the dagger," said Roosevelt, "has struck it into the back of his neighbor."

French forces and British support troops buckled before the crushing Nazi Blitzkrieg. Retreating to the coast of France, the British Army was just saved from destruction at Dunkirk. Hundreds of small boats rushed across the English Channel to evacuate the exhausted forces from the beaches. France surrendered to Germany on June 22, 1940.

Britain now stood alone. Neville Chamberlain, the prime minister who had carried out the ill-fated policy of appeasing Hitler, resigned. Winston Churchill, a longtime critic of appeasement, succeeded him. As Britain braced itself for attack, Churchill told his people he could only offer them the prospect of "blood, toil, sweat and tears." He inspired the British and won the admiration of Americans by pledging "to wage war, by sea, land and air, with all our might and with all the strength God can give us."

In the United States, preparations for war began in earnest. Congress authorized huge sums of money to modernize the army and navy. Within five months over $17 billion was appropriated for defense.

In 1940 Prime Minister Churchill pleaded with Roosevelt for ships to reinforce the British Navy. Roosevelt at first hesitated. But in September, as German submarine attacks on British shipping continued, he agreed to a deal. In exchange for a 99-year lease on naval and air bases in Newfoundland and the Caribbean, the United States transferred 50 old but usable destroyers to the British fleet. Roosevelt called the destroyer agreement "the most important action in the reinforcement of our national defense that has been taken since the Louisiana Purchase."

For answers, see p. A 102.

Section Review

1. Identify the following: *Panay* incident, Ludlow Amendment, Neville Chamberlain, Winston Churchill.
2. Define the following: appeasement, Blitzkrieg.
3. In what way did the United States help China after the Japanese attack in 1937?
4. (a) What promise did Hitler make to Britain and France at the Munich Conference? (b) Did he keep the promise? Explain.
5. List three steps the United States took to prepare for the possibility of war in 1939 and 1940.

4 Between Peace and War

Night after night during the summer of 1940, German planes rained bombs on British cities. The British evacuated thousands of children to the northern parts of the island nation. Those who remained in London spent long nights in the subway stations below the streets to escape the bombs. The armed forces prepared for a German invasion. The Royal Air Force took to the skies to defend the country and, at a terrible cost of life and aircraft, managed to fight off the German planes. In the United States people listened to nightly radio broadcasts by Edward R. Murrow and other war correspondents reporting directly from London. Americans wondered how much longer the United States could stay out of the war.

A Third Term for Roosevelt

Meanwhile a presidential campaign had begun in the United States. The Republicans nominated Wendell Willkie, a corporate executive from Indiana. Willkie had come to national attention during the early years of the New Deal. As president of Commonwealth and Southern, a public utilities holding company, he had led the fight against the policies of the Tennessee Valley Authority regarding electrical power.

Franklin Roosevelt had dominated the Democratic party for the previous eight years. No successor to his leadership had emerged, and the President seemed the likely choice to oppose Willkie in the election. Yet the "third-term issue" bothered some Democrats. Never before had a President served more than two terms. Roosevelt, citing the crisis in Europe and his established relations with European leaders, had announced his decision to run again. By the summer of 1940 the international situation overshadowed the third-term issue, and the Democrats renominated Roosevelt. He chose Secretary of Agriculture Henry Wallace as his running mate.

Willkie opposed many aspects of the New Deal, but he was an internationalist who approved of many of Roosevelt's foreign policy actions. He supported increased aid to Britain, including Roosevelt's destroyer deal. (See page 604.) Willkie also approved of the Selective Service Act, which instituted the first peacetime draft of young American men. The act went into effect in the fall of 1940. As the presidential campaign continued through the fall, Willkie had increasing trouble finding an issue on which to challenge Roosevelt.

Late in the campaign, Willkie began accusing Roosevelt of maneuvering the country into war. The President responded with his old promise. He told an audience in Boston, "I have said this before, but I shall say it again and again: Your boys are not going to be sent into any foreign wars." Roosevelt easily won election to an unprecedented third term with 54 percent of the popular vote.

Lend-Lease

During 1940 Britain had been buying supplies from the United States under the cash-and-carry arrangement, but by the end of the year the British treasury was running out of money. Despite sympathy for Britain, many Americans, including members of Congress, hesitated to support loans of money. They hoped that Hitler's aggression could be stopped without dragging the United States into war.

Shortly after the election, President Roosevelt proposed a solution: the United States would lend Britain whatever supplies it needed to wage war against Germany. He compared his idea to that of helping neighbors whose house was on fire. If the neighbors needed your garden hose to put out the fire, Roosevelt pointed out, you would not waste time arguing about the cost of the hose or how it would be paid for. You would simply give your neighbors the hose and tell them to return it after the fire.

In early 1941 Congress passed the Lend-Lease Act by a large margin. The act gave the President the authority to sell, exchange, lend, or lease war materials to any country whose defense he deemed vital to the defense of the United States. Roosevelt told the

605

By 1940 all of England's allies had been crushed by the German war machine. Poland, Denmark, Norway, Luxembourg, the Netherlands, and France—all had fallen. Hitler assumed that Britain too would yield quickly. But Prime Minister Winston Churchill vowed, "We shall fight on the beaches . . . and in the streets. . . . We shall never surrender." Between September 1940 and May 1941 German planes bombed London nightly. Below, Churchill inspects the wreckage of the House of Commons.

country that the United States must now become the "arsenal of democracy."

During 1941 a growing volume of war supplies left Atlantic coast ports for Britain. But getting the supplies across the ocean proved difficult. "Wolf packs" of German submarines sank many ships throughout the spring of 1941. Some advisers urged Roosevelt to order navy destroyers to escort and protect the British ships as they made the dangerous voyage across the Atlantic. But the President rejected such a drastic step. Instead, he extended the area of the Atlantic in which United States Navy ships would cruise on patrol.

However, in July 1941, faced with continued German attacks on vessels carrying lend-lease supplies, Roosevelt announced that United States warships would accompany British freighters as far as Iceland. At Iceland the British Navy would take responsibility for escorting the merchant vessels to British ports. Soon an undeclared naval war had erupted on the Atlantic. During September and October German submarines attacked the American destroyers *Reuben James* and *Kearny*. The United States was on the brink of war.

End of Isolationism

In May 1940, when the German Blitzkrieg struck France, Roosevelt had proclaimed that the European conflict created an "unlimited national emergency" for the United States. The President urged an all-out effort to strengthen national defense. Internationalist groups, which had long believed that the country should prepare for war, were pleased by the proclamation.

A vocal group of isolationists, however, continued to mount vigorous arguments against involvement in foreign military and political affairs. The America First Committee led the opposition to the Lend-Lease Act and all other aid to the Allies. As events worsened in Europe, the isolationist position became increasingly unpopular.

Most Americans wanted to see Germany defeated but without direct United States participation. Thus policy makers continued to seek a middle road between isolationism and war. However, international events soon engulfed the ongoing debate. In June 1941 Germany launched a surprise attack on the Soviet Union. German troops pushed deep into Soviet territory. They soon held Stalingrad and Leningrad under siege and were threatening Moscow.

The United States immediately extended the Lend-Lease Act to include the Soviet Union. Roosevelt and Churchill agreed that even if Stalin's government was in many ways as oppressive as that of Hitler, it was nonetheless essential to help the Soviet Union ward off the German invasion.

Britain and the United States continued to move toward an alliance, although the United States remained officially neutral. Military leaders of the two countries met secretly in Washington, D.C., to plan a joint strategy to be followed if the United States did enter the fighting. In August 1941 Roosevelt and Churchill met aboard a warship off the coast of Newfoundland. They talked extensively about the crises in Europe and Asia. Roosevelt still refused to commit fighting forces, but he and Churchill did agree on a statement of "certain common principles" on which they based "their hopes for a better future for the world."

In this statement, the Atlantic Charter, the United States and Britain agreed to seek no territorial gain and supported "the right of all peoples to choose the form of government under which they will live." The United States and Great Britain urged all nations to cooperate economically to raise the general standard of living in the world. They also proposed the disarmament of all aggressor nations after the defeat of Nazism and "the establishment of a wide and permanent system of general security." But while Roosevelt and Churchill met, the danger of a wider war in Asia grew.

Embargo Against Japan

Relations between Japan and the United States had worsened steadily since 1937. (See page 601.) Despite American support for China, Japan continued to import 90 percent of its scrap metal and 60 percent of its oil from the United States. President Roosevelt hesitated to cut off the trade for fear that Japan would invade Southeast Asia in order to obtain supplies there.

When France and the Netherlands fell to Germany in the spring of 1940, their Asian colonies were open to Japanese attack. In September Secretary of State Cordell Hull informed Japan that the United States would not tolerate Japanese military presence in European colonies in Asia. However, before the month ended, Japan had established military bases in French Indochina (now the nations of Vietnam, Cambodia, and Laos). The United States responded on September 26 by placing an embargo on the export of scrap metal, oil, and aviation fuel to Japan. The following day Japan announced that it had formed a military alliance with Germany and Italy.

Thereafter the United States increased aid to China in the hope of stemming Japanese aggression. War loomed closer in the summer of 1941. On July 25 Japan established more bases in French Indochina. The next day the United States froze all Japanese bank accounts in American banks, preventing Japan from buying any goods from the United States.

In November 1941 Secretary of State Hull met in Washington, D.C., with Japanese diplomats. The Japanese asked the United States to end aid to China and restore full economic relations with Japan. Hull countered with a proposal that Japan withdraw its troops from China and Indochina. In exchange the United States would end the economic embargo on Japan. The talks continued without agreement.

While their diplomats met with Hull, the Japanese prepared for an attack against the United States. On November 25 Japanese aircraft carriers set out for Pearl Harbor, the American naval base in Hawaii.

Pearl Harbor

On Sunday, December 7, 1941, Japanese carrier-based airplanes attacked the United States fleet at Pearl Harbor. The United States Navy was taken by surprise. Despite many warnings, military leaders had believed that Japan would attack southeast Asia rather than Pearl Harbor. Thus no special precautions had been taken. Most of the fleet was caught at anchor. Among the large ships based at Pearl Harbor, only the aircraft carriers were not docked at the time of the attack.

The attack on Pearl Harbor was a catastrophe for the United States. Fifteen ships, including light battleships, sank or suffered severe damage. Japanese planes destroyed over 150 aircraft still on the ground. Nearly 2,000 American soldiers and sailors died.

The next day, a visibly grim and shaken President addressed a special joint session of Congress. The hall was silent as Roosevelt described the "sudden and deliberate attack" on United States forces by Japanese airplanes on a day "which will live in infamy." Roosevelt asked Congress to declare that a state of war had existed between the United States and Japan since the hour of the attack. Congress passed a declaration of war with only one negative vote. Several days later Germany and Italy declared war on the United States. Congress immediately passed a declaration of war against the two European powers.

Major Events	
1921	Washington Naval Conference
1922	Mussolini seizes power in Italy
1924	Dawes Plan
1928	Kellogg-Briand Pact
1930	Hawley-Smoot Act; Clark Memorandum
1931	Japan invades China
1932	Stimson Doctrine
1933	Hitler seizes power in Germany; Roosevelt announces Good Neighbor Policy
1935	First Neutrality Act passed
1936	Germany occupies Rhineland; Spanish Civil War begins
1938	Munich Conference
1939	Molotov-Ribbentrop Pact; Germany invades Poland; World War II begins
1940	Bases-for-destroyers agreement with Britain; Roosevelt elected to third term
1941	Lend-Lease Act; United States embargo on supplies to Japan; Japan attacks Pearl Harbor; United States enters World War II

On Sunday morning, December 7, 1941, a surprise Japanese air raid destroyed the United States fleet at Pearl Harbor in Hawaii. Fifteen ships, including vital battleships, were put out of commission or sunk, and over 150 planes were wrecked. Fortunately, the aircraft carriers normally stationed at Pearl Harbor were not in port. The United States immediately declared war on Japan.

For answers, see p. A 102.

Section Review

1. Identify the following: Wendell Willkie, Lend-Lease Act, Atlantic Charter.

2. In what way were the positions of Roosevelt and Willkie on foreign policy similar?

3. What development led Roosevelt to propose the policy of "lend-lease"?

4. How did the United States react to the German invasion of the Soviet Union in 1941?

5. Why was trade with the United States important to Japan?

6. Where did United States military leaders think the Japanese would attack?

★ ★ ★ ★ ★ ★ ★ ★ ★ ★ ★ ★ ★ ★ ★ ★ ★ ★ ★ ★

IN PERSPECTIVE   During the 1920s most of the American public and elected officials shared isolationist feelings. Yet the United States participated in many international conferences and signed the Kellogg-Briand Pact. During the 1930s the nation tried to insulate itself from a troubled world by passing a series of neutrality acts.

When war broke out in Europe in September 1939, the United States stayed out of the fighting but began building up the army and navy. Germany quickly conquered much of Europe, and soon Britain stood alone against the onslaught. President Roosevelt increased aid to Britain, and later the United States Navy was deployed as far as Iceland to protect British ships carrying lend-lease supplies.

In the Pacific, Japan was waging war on China and extending its influence in Asia. The United States futilely tried to halt Japanese aggression by imposing an economic embargo. Tensions between the two nations increased during 1941, and on December 7, 1941, Japan bombed the United States naval base at Pearl Harbor, Hawaii. The United States was now engaged in a second world war.

For answers, see p. A 102

Chapter Review

1. (a) How did the policies of President Harding reflect the isolationist mood of many Americans in the early 1920s? (b) What economic measures also reflected that spirit?

2. (a) How did the United States show a willingness to support world cooperation during the 1920s? (b) How did the country become directly involved in the world economy in 1924?

3. (a) Was United States policy toward Latin America isolationist? Explain. (b) How did the policy toward Latin American change under Presidents Coolidge and Hoover? (c) What was Franklin Roosevelt's policy toward Latin America?

4. (a) How did the worldwide depression affect international trade? (b) How did President Roosevelt try to improve foreign trade? (c) Did he succeed? Explain.

5. (a) How did the Nye committee investigation contribute to feelings of isolationism during the mid-1930s? (b) Describe the legislation passed as a result of the isolationism of the period.

6. (a) What actions by Japan between 1930 and 1937 alarmed the United States? (b) How did the Hoover administration react? (c) How did Franklin Roosevelt react? (d) Was Roosevelt able to counter the isolationist mood of the country at that time? Explain.

7. (a) How did Britain and France react to the movement of German soldiers into the Rhineland? (b) Where did Germany expand in 1938? (c) How did war begin in 1939?

8. (a) What was the reaction of the American public to the outbreak of war in Europe? (b) What was the initial response of the United States government?

9. (a) What was the Lend-Lease Act? (b) How did it allow the United States to help Britain?

10. (a) What economic actions did the United States take to stop Japanese aggression? (b) What finally led the United States to declare war on Japan?

For answers, see p. A 103.

For Further Thought

1. How do you think the mood of the Roaring Twenties (see Chapters 29 and 30) may have contributed to the feeling of isolationism during that decade?

2. No President had ever served more than two terms, yet Franklin Roosevelt was elected for a third term in 1940. Why do you think that happened? Cite specific evidence to support your answer.

For answers, see p. A 103.

Developing Basic Skills

1. *Comparing* Review the events that led to United States entry into the World War in 1917. (See Chapter 28.) How did entry into World War II differ? Were there any similarities? Explain.

2. *Analyzing Political Cartoons* Study the cartoon on page 599. Then answer the following questions: (a) What is the subject of the cartoon? (b) The cartoon is titled "A Good Time for Reflection." What do you think Uncle Sam is reflecting on? (c) Based on the cartoon, how do you think the cartoonist viewed the threat of war in Europe? (d) Would you consider this cartoon isolationist, internationalist, or neither? Explain.

3. *Classifying* Construct a chart with two columns and two rows. Label the first column Isolationist and the second column Internationalist. Label one row 1920s, and the other row 1930s. Classify the events of each decade as isolationist or internationalist and write them in the appropriate box. Based on your chart, in which decade does the United States appear to have been more isolationist? Explain.

See page 778 for suggested readings.

609

35

The Second World War

(1941–1945)

Detail of Tank Breakthrough at St. Lo, *by Ogden Pleissner.*

Rarely had Americans faced a crisis so united in spirit and purpose as during the months following the Japanese attack on Pearl Harbor. The four years of war that followed demanded the full energy of United States military forces, the American economy, and the American people. Few escaped its impact.

The United States and its allies encountered defeat and disappointment in the first year after Pearl Harbor. But by 1943 they seemed to have stemmed the tide of German and Japanese advances. For the first time they sensed victory.

But the Allies faced two more years of brutal fighting on Pacific Islands, in eastern Europe, in Sicily and Italy, in France and Germany. Millions of soldiers, sailors, and civilians would lose their lives. The cost in money and supplies was staggering. The effect of the war would be felt for decades to come.

610

1 A World War

No war in history covered as much of the earth, cost as many lives, or caused as much destruction as World War II. Over 50 nations took part before the war ended.

The Allies Against the Axis Powers

Early in the war 26 nations, calling themselves the United Nations or Allies, had joined forces to fight the Axis powers. The Axis powers included Germany, Italy, Japan, and four other nations. The major powers among the Allies were the United States, Great Britain, and the Soviet Union. By the end of the war the Allies numbered 49 nations. (See the chart below.)

Because of the vast distance between the Pacific and Europe, World War II was actually two separate wars. In the Pacific war the United States, Great Britain, Australia, and New Zealand were pitted against Japan. The fighting stretched for 5,000 miles (8,000 kilometers) from Alaska in the north to Java in the south, and for 7,000 miles (about 11,000 kilometers) from Hawaii in the east to India in the west.

The war in Europe and Africa consisted of three major fronts, or battle zones. Savage fighting took place on the eastern front, where the Soviet Union faced Germany, Bulgaria, Finland, Hungary, and Romania. On the southern front United States, British, and

■ *Few nations remained neutral in World War II, as this chart shows. The date in parentheses after a country's name is the year in which it entered the war.*

Allies and Axis Powers

Allies

Argentina (1945)	Ethiopia (1942)	New Zealand (1939)
Australia (1939)	France (1939)	Nicaragua (1941)
Belgium (1940)	Great Britain (1939)	Norway (1940)
Bolivia (1943)	Greece (1940)	Panama (1941)
Brazil (1942)	Guatemala (1941)	Paraguay (1945)
Canada (1939)	Haiti (1941)	Peru (1945)
Chile (1945)	Honduras (1941)	Poland (1939)
China (1941)	India (1939)	San Marino (1944)
Colombia (1943)	Iran (1941)	Saudi Arabia (1945)
Costa Rica (1941)	Iraq (1943)	South Africa (1939)
Cuba (1941)	Lebanon (1945)	Syria (1941)
Czechoslovakia (1941)	Liberia (1944)	Turkey (1945)
Denmark (1940)	Luxembourg (1940)	U.S.S.R. (1941)
Dominican Republic (1941)	Mexico (1942)	United States (1941)
Ecuador (1945)	Mongolian People's	Uruguay (1945)
Egypt (1945)	Republic (1945)	Venezuela (1945)
El Salvador (1941)	Netherlands (1940)	Yugoslavia (1941)

Axis Powers

Albania (1940)	Italy (1940)
Bulgaria (1941)	Japan (1941)
Finland (1941)	Romania (1940)
Germany (1939)	Thailand (1942)
Hungary (1940)	

Neutral Nations

Eire (Ireland)
Portugal
Spain
Sweden
Switzerland

Australian troops fought the Germans and Italians in North Africa and Italy. On the western front, the greatest air-sea-land military operation in history involved 3 million people to plan and carry out an invasion of Europe across the English Channel.

Dark Days of 1942

After the Japanese attack on Pearl Harbor, Admiral Ernest King and General Douglas MacArthur proposed that the United States concentrate its armed forces to defeat Japan. But President Roosevelt had already accepted the British view that the Allies must defeat Germany and Italy first.

The United States entered the war short of almost all critical war materials. Some early military training was conducted with broom handles for rifles and airplanes made of plywood. German and Japanese submarines were sinking ships faster than the Allies could build them.

Furthermore, in the first years of the war, the Japanese had conquered many of the islands in the western Pacific and a considerable area of eastern and southern Asia. By early 1942 Chinese resistance was severely strained, India was threatened from east and west, and Australia was preparing for a Japanese invasion.

The war in the Pacific seemed nearly lost, and the Allies found little cause for optimism in Europe. Germany had conquered most of western and eastern Europe before the attack on Pearl Harbor. In the spring of 1942, Hitler's armies renewed their onslaught against the Soviet Union. They drove deep into Soviet territory, threatening oil fields in the south and advancing on the capital, Moscow. Moreover, the British defense of Egypt was near collapse. Germany and Italy were close to controlling North Africa, the Suez Canal, and the oil fields of the Middle East.

The War in North Africa

In 1942 American Generals George C. Marshall and Dwight D. Eisenhower urged the Allies to undertake an invasion of France across the English Channel no later than the spring of 1943. They were afraid the Soviet Union might be driven from the war. The Soviets were enthusiastic, hoping that such an invasion would force Hitler to divert some of his troops from the eastern to the western front. The British agreed reluctantly, but as the Allies suffered defeat after defeat, Prime Minister Winston Churchill proposed an alternative strategy: an invasion of North Africa, followed by advances into the Mediterranean area. The strategy was named Operation Torch.

In November 1942 combined British and United States forces under the command of General Eisenhower landed on the coast of French North Africa in Morocco and Algeria. The troops easily defeated soldiers of Vichy (VEE shee), France,* who were stationed in North Africa. Reaching Tunisia, the Allies met stiff resistance from the German Afrika Korps, led by Field Marshall Erwin Rommel. After initial setbacks, the Allied troops drove the Germans north toward the Mediterranean Sea. In May 1943 the greatly outnumbered Axis forces in North Africa surrendered.

Allied victory in North Africa opened the Mediterranean Sea to Allied shipping and made an invasion of southern Europe possible. Even more important, for the first time the Allied countries heard good news about the war. Though the Allies had suffered 70,000 casualties, the Germans and Italians had lost over 250,000 soldiers and much valuable equipment.

A Holding Action in the Pacific

The Japanese had followed the attack on Pearl Harbor with what seemed an endless string of victories. Guam, Wake Island, and Hong Kong fell within three weeks. Singapore fell two months later. In May 1942 American and Filipino defenders surrendered the Philippine Islands. General Douglas MacArthur led the defense of Bataan and Corregidor, but when the situation became hopeless he was evacuated. Before he left, however, he promised the people of the Philippines, "I shall return." Meanwhile, Japanese forces advanced from Indochina into Burma, threatening India to the west and Australia and New Zealand to the south.

The adoption of a "beat Hitler first" strategy did not mean abandoning the Pacific theater. Fortunately, the United States aircraft carriers then stationed in the Pacific had survived the attack on Pearl Harbor.

---

*After France fell to Germany in 1940, some French officials decided to cooperate with the Germans. They formed a government at Vichy, in southern France.

The war in North Africa was often fought in blistering desert heat. Here, officers of a tank destroyer battalion consult their maps in Tunisia. American forces launched highly successful hit-and-run attacks with half-track personnel carriers such as the one in the photo. The speedy half-tracks waited until enemy tanks were near, fired off a barrage, then raced away faster than the lumbering German tanks could follow.

Relying on the aircraft carriers, a naval task force engaged a Japanese fleet in the Coral Sea near Java in early May 1942. After a three-day battle the Japanese fleet fled northward, but only after severely damaging the aircraft carrier *Lexington* and sinking two other American ships.

One month later, the United States Navy won a major victory at Midway Island in the central Pacific. The navy destroyed four Japanese carriers, several smaller ships, and 253 planes. It lost the carrier *Yorktown*, a destroyer, and 150 planes. Later that summer United States Marines began a hard-fought struggle for control of Guadalcanal in the Solomon Islands. The island was secured by February 1943.

By early 1943 United States forces had stopped Japanese advances through the Pacific and Southeast Asia. Allied troops had driven the Axis powers out of North Africa.

Finally, Soviet soldiers and civilians, aided by one of the worst winters in history, had halted the German advance into their country. For the first time in the war the Allies sensed eventual victory. But almost three years of bloody fighting still lay ahead.

For answers, see p. A 103.

Section Review

1. Identify the following: Allies, Axis powers, Operation Torch, Dwight D. Eisenhower, Douglas MacArthur.

2. In what two areas was most of World War II fought?

3. What developments made the Allied situation in the Pacific desperate in early 1942?

4. List two reasons why the Allied victory in North Africa was significant.

5. What battles helped stop the Japanese advance in the Pacific?

2 On the Home Front

The Japanese attack on Pearl Harbor united the American people as nothing had before. Although no fighting took place in the United States after Pearl Harbor, the war became a fact of life for everyone. Most families had a father, brother, sister, or other relative in the armed services. News of the war filled newspaper headlines and radio waves. Industries idled by the Great Depression sprang back to life, and economic prosperity returned. The war would demand sacrifices, but Americans faced the struggle united.

Building the Armed Forces

After declaring war, Congress swiftly set out to build up United States fighting forces. Six million men and women volunteered for service. Almost 10 million men were drafted. Women enlisted in the Women's Auxiliary Army Corps, the Women Appointed for Voluntary Emergency Service in the Navy, the Women's Auxiliary Ferrying Squadron, the Women's Reserve of the Coast Guard Reserves, and the Women Reserve of Marine Corps.

Training took place at posts and bases across the nation. At one time the army alone had to provide housing for over 5 million personnel. Training for a worldwide war was not easy. Soldiers might have to fight in jungles on Pacific islands, in African deserts, or in European countryside. To meet this challenge, the armed forces were soon providing soldiers with a wide variety of equipment, clothing, and combat training.

Organizing for Wartime Production

The war had to be won as much on the production lines of industry as on the battlefields. President Roosevelt announced staggering production goals for 1942: 60,000 airplanes, 45,000 tanks, 20,000 antiaircraft guns, and 8 million tons (7.3 million metric tons) of merchant shipping. United States industry and workers met the demands and sometimes surpassed them. Even higher goals were achieved in 1943 and 1944.

To manage and control the economy, Roosevelt created the War Production Board. The first task of the board was to supervise conversion from a peacetime to wartime economy. Factories that had manufactured shirts redesigned assembly lines to make mosquito netting. Model-train producers made bomb fuses. Metal weather-stripping factories switched to producing mortar shells. Kitchen sink assembly lines were retooled to produce cartridge cases. After 1942 all manufacture of civilian automobiles halted as auto makers changed to full-time production of tanks, trucks, armored personnel carriers, and aircraft.

In an attempt to control inflation, Roosevelt established the Office of Price Administration (OPA). The OPA set price ceilings on most items, including rents, since housing was scarce throughout the war. The agency also supervised a rationing system for such items as gasoline, tires, coffee, canned food, and meat by allotting a certain number of coupons per item per family.

By 1943 industry was fully mobilized for war. Under James Byrnes, the Office of War Mobilization coordinated the activities of all wartime agencies. The War Manpower Commission made the critical determination of where in the economy workers were most needed. The problem of peace between labor and management occupied the War Labor Board. The board contributed to the growth of union membership by enforcing the provisions of the Wagner Act. (See page 575.) The board allowed wage increases to offset rising prices and at the same time tried to limit inflation. The wages of most Americans climbed steadily from 1941 to 1945.

To pay for the war, the government raised taxes, especially on the incomes of high-salaried workers. In addition, it borrowed huge amounts of money by selling war bonds. Spectacular drives employing movie stars and comic book heroes such as Batman and Dick Tracy were mounted to sell bonds and bolster patriotic spirit.

The Return of Prosperity

The improvements in the United States economy during the war were staggering. Between 1939 and 1945 the gross national product rose from $91.1 billion to $213.6 billion. During 1942 alone, war production rose over 300 percent. The United States produced more than Germany, Italy, and Japan combined. In 1939 American aircraft manufacturers employed about 47,000 workers to make 5,900 planes. Five years later, 2.1 million workers were producing almost 100,000 planes annually. The output of the shipbuilding industry grew from one million tons (.91 million metric tons) in 1941 to 19 million tons (17.3 million metric tons) in 1943.

Not only was such production crucial to the Allied war effort, it also ended the depression as demand for manufactured goods skyrocketed. As industries geared up, unemployment decreased dramatically. Growing demand for agricultural products also brought farmers a level of price stability and prosperity they had not experienced since 1919. Between 1940 and 1945 crop prices doubled. Production increased even though farm population and acreage declined.

Resisting Government Controls

Various groups in the labor force believed that the controls set by the War Labor Board were unfair. In January 1943 miners in Alabama struck. John L. Lewis, president of the United Mine Workers, asked union members to return to the coal fields while he negotiated with the War Labor Board. Negotiations continually broke down, and the miners called further strikes.

In May the President seized the mines. He threatened to send soldiers to replace the miners and warned that he would draft the striking miners. The miners, however, refused to be intimidated. By November negotiations had broken down again, and a fourth strike had taken 530,000 men out of the mines. The government was forced to agree to some of the union's demands. The 11-month struggle won the miners a pay raise of $1.50 per day.

Other challenges came from business. Montgomery Ward, a large mail-order firm, refused to recognize its workers' union. When the workers went on strike, the War Labor Board ordered Sewell Avery, the company president, to negotiate with the union. Avery ignored the order. President Roosevelt then invoked the wartime Smith-Connally Act, which gave him power to seize any strike-bound plant necessary to the war effort. Newspapers across the country ran a front-page picture of two soldiers carrying Avery out of his office after he refused to leave. For the rest of the war, the government ran the company.

Changes in Daily Life

Family separation, frequent movement from one place to another, and worry about men and women fighting overseas were concerns shared by most Americans during World War II. Such experiences gave Americans a common sense of purpose. The "V for Victory" became a familiar symbol. It was displayed on buildings, sketched in store windows, and broadcast in Morse code as the sign-on and sign-off signal used by radio stations. Back yards became "victory gardens" to stretch the food supply. Scrap-rubber and scrap-iron collection drives were held to bring in scarce materials.

Americans grew accustomed to saving ration coupons and standing in long lines to buy scarce items. Newspaper, magazine, and radio advertisements urged Americans to sacrifice luxuries and make do with less, all for the war effort. Instead of urging people to buy more, industries mounted campaigns explaining that certain purchases would best be put off until after the war. One tire manufacturer asked consumers to conserve rubber by driving less, using the slogan, "Hitler smiles when you waste miles."

The role of women changed dramatically during the war, though in many cases only temporarily. Women joined the various military services by the hundreds of thousands. They piloted bombers across the Atlantic Ocean to bases in Europe, repaired airplanes and land vehicles, drove trucks, operated radios, and did clerical and technical work of all kinds.

As the demand for workers rose, women joined the civilian work force in record numbers. By the end of the war, one out of every three workers in industry and business was a woman. Traditional barriers against the employment of women in such industries as steel and shipbuilding fell before the ever-increasing demand for more workers. Songs and stories praised the women who kept American production lines moving.

As factories worked around the clock to produce the ships, planes, uniforms, ammunition, and hundreds of other items needed for war, women assumed jobs formerly open to men only. Below, a woman works on a bomber in California. One aircraft company popularized a mythical worker called "Rosie the Riveter" to symbolize the women doing factory work as part of the war effort.

Changes in clothing, appearance, and hair styles reflected new work roles. More basic, however, was the impact on how people felt and thought. Many women began to believe that they could pursue a career and have a family at the same time. Women became more aware of the wide range of roles available to them.

Black Americans During the War

The war years produced a mixed record in the long struggle of black Americans for economic, political, and social equality. The increase in war production provided black Americans good jobs in unprecedented numbers. Some 2 million blacks worked in aircraft factories, steel mills, and shipyards. In both North and South blacks experienced improved levels of social acceptance and economic well-being. Lynchings stopped almost completely. Black and white leaders joined to form the Southern Regional Council to fight prejudice and misunderstanding.

The need for workers in expanded war industries opened jobs to groups that often had been excluded: blacks, migrants, teenagers, senior citizens, and the handicapped. The number of black women in industry, for example, rose 11.3 percent during the war. The woman in this photo is stitching a parachute.

Yet discrimination and racial tension had not disappeared. In 1941, before the United States entered the war, A. Philip Randolph, head of the Brotherhood of Sleeping Car Porters, threatened to lead a march on Washington, D.C., to protest prejudice against black workers. In response President Roosevelt issued Executive Order 8802. The order banned discrimination in all government agencies, in job training programs, and in all companies doing business with the federal government. It also established the Fair Employment Practices Committee to insure equal treatment for blacks and other minorities in war industries.

During much of the war, however, official policy established all-black units of soldiers or sailors commanded by white officers. In the navy most blacks were designated as porters. In huge training camps in the South, black soldiers on leave had to contend with segregated eating places, movie houses, and recreational facilities.

In the North increased migration of southern blacks to northern industrial cities aggravated housing shortages. White workers continued to resent black competition for jobs. In one instance street car workers in Philadelphia went on strike to protest the upgrading of black workers to motormen. The President sent in army troops to maintain operation of vital war industries in the city.

Sometimes resentment flared into violence. In Detroit efforts to move blacks into a federal housing project named after Sojourner Truth, the black abolitionist, aroused anger among whites. In the summer of 1943 isolated violent incidents erupted into a riot. Before police and federal troops restored order, 25 blacks and 9 whites lay dead.

Other Victims of Discrimination

Mexican Americans continued to face discrimination, especially in the cities of the Southwest. Like many recent immigrants before them, Mexican Americans were frequently crowded into run-down urban areas, suffered high unemployment rates, and met hostility from long-time residents.

Young Mexican Americans became the object of frequent violent attacks in Los Angeles. During the early 1940s, young Mexican American men adopted a flamboyant style of dress, sporting "zoot" suits and wearing their hair long and slicked back into "duck tails." In July 1943 groups of sailors and soldiers home on leave roamed the streets, beating up the "zooters," tearing their clothes, and cutting their hair.

Newspaper and radio reports blamed the violence on the zooters. However, a citizens' committee appointed by California Governor Earl Warren revealed the truth about the riot and the need for improved housing for Mexican Americans.

Italian Americans and German Americans also felt the sting of discrimination from fellow citizens during the war. Some of them changed their names to conceal their families' country of origin. Yet the problems suffered by the European immigrants were not nearly as severe as those experienced by Japanese Americans.

Japanese Americans Lose Their Liberties

Because of the attack on Pearl Harbor, Japanese Americans were the target of great bitterness. Since most of them lived on the Pacific coast, in small, easily identifiable communities, they were especially vulnerable to systematic discrimination.

In February 1942 defense officials labeled Japanese Americans living on the Pacific coast "a menace which had to be dealt with." Military leaders insisted that Japanese Americans be moved away from the coastal areas where, officials warned, acts of sabotage could be committed. President Roosevelt and the Justice Department supported this demand and granted the War Department full authority to relocate thousands of innocent people.

With little or no warning, Japanese Americans were moved to huge inland internment camps. Two thirds of those evacuated were American-born citizens. They had to sell their homes, businesses, household goods, and most of their personal possessions for whatever prices they could get. For most of the war, the Japanese Americans were detained in the isolated camps. Home was a wooden barracks, with but one room per family.

In 1944 the Supreme Court upheld the forced relocation of the Japanese Americans as a justifiable wartime measure. The following year, when Allied victory appeared certain, the people were allowed to return to their communities to rebuild their shattered lives.

After the surprise attack on Pearl Harbor, many people feared a similar attack on the west coast of the continental United States. In this atmosphere of fear, Americans of Japanese descent on the Pacific Coast were labeled a menace to national security. In the spring of 1942, the government uprooted 112,000 Japanese Americans and moved them to temporary camps inland, where they were forced to remain for three years.

For answers, see p. A 103.
Section Review

1. Identify the following: War Production Board, Office of Price Administration, Office of War Mobilization, War Manpower Commission, War Labor Board, A. Philip Randolph, Executive Order 8802.

2. Give two examples of how industry converted from peacetime to wartime production.

3. How did conditions for workers improve during the war?

4. What type of work opened up to women as a result of the war?

5. (a) Give one example of how opportunities for black Americans increased as a result of the war effort. (b) Give one example of problems blacks continued to face.

6. What fear led to the relocation of Japanese Americans during the war?

3 The Allies on the Offensive

During 1942 and early 1943 the Allies had worked to stop the advances of the Axis powers in Europe and the Pacific. Meanwhile the Allies developed strategies for counterattack and the mobilization of people and industry in support of the war effort. In 1943 the Allies were prepared to take the offensive against Italy and Germany in Europe and against Japan in the Pacific.

The Invasion of Italy

As you have read, the United States commanders had originally wanted to attack Europe by crossing the English Channel into France. (See page 612.) But they finally agreed with the British that Italy was the weakest point in the Axis empire. While continuing air attacks on German cities,* the Allies began an invasion of Italy.

In July 1943 paratroopers of the 82nd Airborne Division parachuted into Sicily in

---

*Allied air attacks on German cities began in the summer of 1942 from bases in Britain. The attacks increased in intensity during 1943 and 1944. By 1945 the Allied air war had nearly paralyzed German transportation and destroyed many vital war industries. Yet German war production increased until almost the end of the war. The Allies lost over 158,000 pilots and crew members and over 40,000 planes in the air war over Germany.

■ By the time the United States entered the war at the end of 1941, Axis powers controlled virtually all of western Europe and North Africa. Arrows indicate the important Allied campaigns between 1942 and 1945. By 1943 Soviet troops were attacking the Axis powers from the east. The vast invasion along the coast of Normandy in 1944 was the beginning of the final assault on Germany.

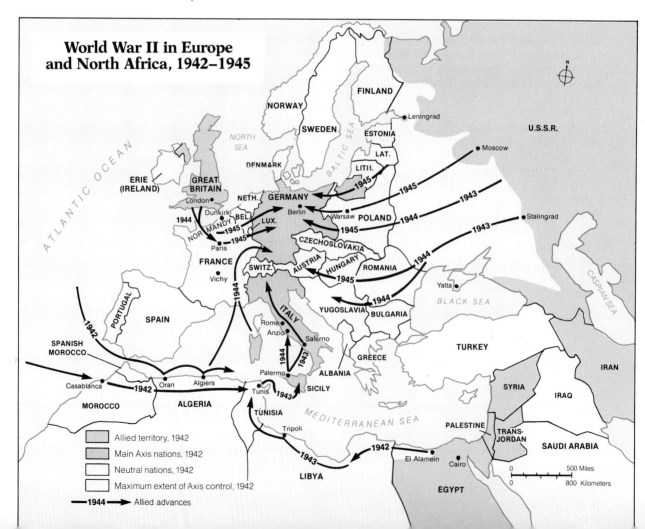

World War II in Europe and North Africa, 1942–1945

Legend:
- Allied territory, 1942
- Main Axis nations, 1942
- Neutral nations, 1942
- Maximum extent of Axis control, 1942
- ——1944——➤ Allied advances

the first large-scale Allied airborne assault of the war. The attack suffered from bad weather and poor coordination between army assault forces and naval bombardments of the island. However, the invasion of paratroopers and forces landed from seaborne transports succeeded.

From Sicily, Allied forces pushed on to the Italian mainland, assaulting Salerno in September 1943. In the face of the successful Allied invasion, Mussolini was overthrown. The new Italian government surrendered to the Allies and offered to join in the fight against Germany.

The actual conquest of Italy, however, proved long and difficult. Hitler ordered German troops in Italy not to surrender. Bitter and costly fighting marked almost every mile up the Italian peninsula. At Monte Cassino, in central Italy, the Germans stopped the Allied advance. The Allies responded with another amphibious landing in January 1944 at Anzio, near Rome. It took six months of fighting before Rome finally fell to the Allies. The Allies then continued north, but German forces in Italy did not surrender until the war had nearly ended.

The Eastern Front

For almost three years the most bitter fighting of the war took place in the Soviet Union on the eastern front. To help his embattled nation survive the German onslaught, Soviet Premier Joseph Stalin had asked for three things from his allies: massive supplies, recognition of his territorial demands in eastern Europe, and the establishment of a second front in western Europe. He had been disappointed on all three.

Churchill and Roosevelt feared that the Soviet Union might make a separate peace with the Axis powers. But during the winter of 1941–1942 Soviet troops halted the German advance outside Moscow. A year later they ended the 900-day German siege of Leningrad.

The Allies meanwhile had found a way to deliver critical supplies to the Soviet Union. German submarines had made it impossible to send ships to the northern Soviet port of Archangel. Consequently, the United States and Great Britain shifted their supply operations to a much longer but safer route that went north through the Persian Gulf and across Iran.

By the summer of 1943 the Red Army, as the army of the Soviet Union is known, had gone on the offensive. It soon recaptured the Ukraine, the Crimean peninsula, White Russia, and eastern Poland. By capturing Romania, Bulgaria, and Hungary during a four-month period in 1944, the Soviets forced Hitler's Balkan allies to surrender. The Soviet offensive helped the British and Americans launch the largest single military operation in history. With the opening of a successful second front and the supply operations, only Stalin's territorial demands threatened to drive the Allies apart.

The Cross-Channel Invasion

In early 1944 the Supreme Allied Command made final plans for the long-awaited cross-channel invasion from England into France. General Eisenhower, summoned from the Italian front, was appointed supreme allied commander of the European theater of operations. The attack, code-named Operation Overlord, was scheduled for the late spring of 1944.

The success of Overlord depended on three conditions. First, the Allies had to build up an enormous reserve of supplies for the invasion: ammunition, trucks, food, construction equipment, medical supplies, tanks, artillery, and countless other items. Complete artificial harbors, constructed out of concrete, had to be towed across the channel and used for the landing and for unloading supplies. The second condition was secrecy. The Germans expected an attack but did not know when or where it might come. The third condition was clear weather. An unexpected storm or fog would make paratroop landings behind German lines and amphibious landings on the beaches all but impossible.

At 6:30 A.M. on June 6, 1944, the largest amphibious invasion in history began. Nearly 6,000 Allied ships ferried 60,000 men and their supplies across the channel and onto beachheads in northern France. The invaders met with heavy resistance. At one beachhead, American casualties in the first assault groups on the beach were 60 percent.

Six weeks passed before landing areas were fully secured. By that time, other Allied troops had moved into northern France and captured the port of Cherbourg, which would serve as a major receiving point of

On June 6, 1944, American, Canadian, and British forces stormed ashore along the French coast. Despite heavy bombarding to weaken German positions before the amphibious landing, Allied losses in the first waves were staggering. At left, the First Infantry wades ashore at Omaha Beach in Normandy. At right, a French farmer offers prayers and flowers beside the body of an American soldier killed in 1944.

supplies for the rest of the war. On August 25 the rapidly advancing Allied armies liberated Paris after four years of German occupation.

General Eisenhower did not believe the Allies had sufficient supplies to launch a single drive into the heart of Germany. Instead he decided to move along a broad front. In August he ordered an invasion across the Mediterranean into southern France. As the winter of 1944–1945 approached, Eisenhower's armies had recaptured most of western Europe. Now they planned the final assault on Germany.

Taking the Offensive in the Pacific

While the Allies attacked Europe from the south, the east, and the west, an equally important war raged in the Pacific. There, Allied forces were under the command of General MacArthur and Admiral Chester Nimitz. The two men disagreed on the best "road to Tokyo." MacArthur preferred a South Pacific route, pushing northward from Australia through New Guinea and the Phil-

ippines and on to Japan. Nimitz favored an advance toward Japan via the islands of the central Pacific.

The military commanders finally decided to follow both strategies. They succeeded with a *leapfrogging* technique. Rather than take Japanese-held islands one by one, the Allies decided to invade a few strategically placed islands, bypassing others. The theory was that the Japanese would not be able to supply their forces on islands that the Allies had leapfrogged. Isolated, these islands would have to surrender.

In 1943 and 1944 the United States Marine Corps, with naval support, assaulted the islands of Tarawa (tuh RAH wuh), Kwajalein (KWAHJ uh lihn), Wake, and Guam in the central Pacific. Meanwhile, MacArthur's troops captured New Guinea in the south. Fierce Japanese resistance resulted in heavy Allied casualties. At Tarawa, for example, casualties in some marine units reached 50 percent. But the technique of amphibious landings—requiring close coordination among air bombings, naval support, and troop movements—steadily improved.

In October 1944 General MacArthur's forces began an invasion of the Philippine Islands. MacArthur himself landed on the island of Leyte (LAY tee), where he proclaimed, "People of the Philippines, I have returned." In the battle of Leyte Gulf, which followed, the United States Navy sank an entire Japanese fleet. By late 1944, United States bombers had begun steady aerial attacks on the islands of Japan itself.

■ By 1942 the situation in the Pacific seemed desperate. Japan controlled much of China, the nations of eastern and southern Asia, and a string of Pacific islands that cut through Australian and United States supply lines. Although neither side realized it at the time, the Battle of Midway in 1942 was a turning point. At Midway the United States Navy, crippled by the destruction of much of the fleet at Pearl Harbor, nevertheless stopped the Japanese fleet. For the next two years Allied forces attacked Japanese-held islands in a "leapfrog" pattern. At times casualties in the difficult amphibious landings numbered as many as half the troops involved.

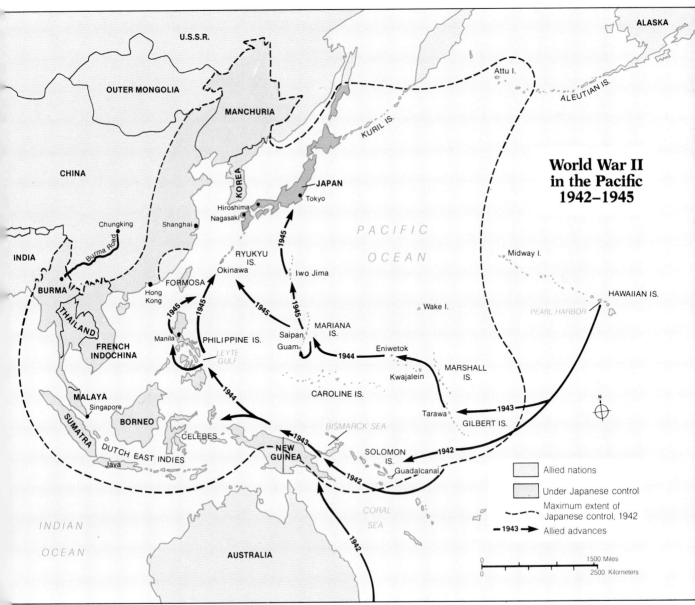

World War II in the Pacific 1942–1945

622

In the Pacific, the war was fought inch by inch, island by island, often against Japanese snipers who were prepared to die rather than surrender. Besides the Japanese, there were other enemies: savage heat, jungle fevers, malaria, fungus infections. Above, Americans storm a beach in the Solomon Islands in June 1943.

For answers, see p. A 104.

Section Review

1. Identify the following: Joseph Stalin, Operation Overlord, Cherbourg, Chester Nimitz.
2. Define the following term: leapfrogging.
3. What events led to the overthrow of Benito Mussolini in Italy?
4. When did the Red Army begin an offensive against Germany?
5. List the three conditions necessary for the success of Operation Overlord.
6. What strategy did the Allies follow in the Pacific in 1943 and 1944?

The Code That Was Never Broken

One of the most important weapons of a nation during wartime is a good communications system. Information on deployment of troops and instructions to commanders in the field must be transmitted quickly and efficiently. To maintain secrecy, military messages are sent in code. But there is always a risk that the enemy will break the code.

During World War II, the United States military used a code system that was virtually foolproof. The Marine Corps recruited a group of Navajos to work as code talkers, using their own language instead of an artificial code. Because Navajo was still an unwritten language, few people other than the Navajo themselves were able to speak it. It was also extremely difficult to learn.

About 350 Navajo code talkers worked in the Pacific theater during the war. They were a familiar sight in command posts or huddled over radio sets in combat zones, transmitting messages. The code talkers assigned the names of birds, fish, and animals to military terms and then transmitted the code words in Navajo. A member of the team on the receiving end translated the Navajo words into English. Calls to headquarters for airplanes or artillery were thus transmitted rapidly and accurately in complete secrecy. The Japanese were unable to break the Navajo "code," which helped Allied forces advance from the Solomons to Okinawa and achieve eventual victory over Japan.

4 Wartime Diplomacy and Politics

During the war, Allied leaders conferred frequently through correspondence and occasionally in person. They made broad policy decisions, which were relayed to military officers around the world. At home politics continued. In 1944 presidential elections took place against the backdrop of war.

The Big Three Confer

By the fall of 1943 the Allies were confident that they would win the war. Therefore, they began planning for the postwar period. The foreign ministers of Britain, the Soviet Union, and the United States met in Moscow in October 1943. They discussed plans for the creation of a new organization of nations to maintain international peace and security. Membership in the organization was to be open to all nations, no matter how large or small.

In November 1943 Roosevelt boarded the battleship *Iowa* for a long journey to Cairo, Egypt. There he and Churchill met with Chinese President Chiang Kai-shek (jyahng ky SHEHK) to discuss plans for supply lines through Burma and a new Chinese military offensive against Japan. Stalin did not attend because the Soviet Union was not at war with Japan.

From Cairo, Roosevelt and Churchill flew to Teheran, capital of Iran, for their first face-to-face meeting with Soviet Premier Joseph Stalin. Although the Big Three, as the leaders of the United States, Britain, and the Soviet Union were known, made only tentative plans, the Teheran Conference influenced the shape of the postwar world.

Discussions began on the strategy for final defeat of the Axis powers. Stalin and Roosevelt insisted on final commitment to Overlord. Stalin, in turn, promised a spring offensive to coincide with the cross-channel landing. Furthermore, he promised to enter the Pacific war once Germany surrendered. The three leaders also discussed the planned international organization and the postwar fate of Germany.

At the end of the conference, the three leaders declared, "We leave here, friends in fact, in spirit, and in purpose." The Teheran meeting represented the high point of Allied good will. A troubled road lay ahead.

Diplomatic discussions after the Teheran Conference continued to focus on postwar settlements. Economic ministers meeting in Bretton Woods, New Hampshire, in 1944 drew up plans for the International Monetary Fund and the International Bank. These organizations were designed to aid in postwar recovery and to finance long-range improvements in nonindustrial and war-ravaged countries. At Dumbarton Oaks, in Washington, D.C., delegates from the United States, Britain, China, and the Soviet Union made further plans for the creation of an international peace-keeping organization, to be known as the United Nations.

The Election of 1944

At the height of the war, Americans began to ask if their President would seek a fourth term in office. "All that is within me cries to go back to my home on the Hudson," Roosevelt told reporters in the summer of 1944. Nevertheless, citing the need for continuity in leadership during the war, Roosevelt decided to run again.

The President had almost no opposition within his party. However, the Democrats did have some difficulty selecting a candidate for Vice-President. After rejecting Henry Wallace as too liberal and several other candidates as too conservative, the nominating convention settled on Senator Harry S. Truman of Missouri.

The Republicans selected New York Governor Thomas E. Dewey, who had come to prominence as a strong district attorney, to oppose Roosevelt. Dewey chose to avoid international issues in the campaign. Instead he focused on the failure of Democratic economic policies. Only the war, he charged, had ended the depression. A peacetime economy would require better management than a Democratic administration could provide, Dewey told American voters.

Although the strain of his years in office had aged Roosevelt noticeably, the President made special efforts during the campaign to show he was still in good health. At one point he spent an entire day in New York City campaigning from an open car during a rain storm. Roosevelt's popularity remained high, and a majority of voters did not want to change leaders during the war. As a result, Roosevelt won election to an unprecedented fourth term as President with 54 percent of the popular vote and 432 of 531 votes in the electoral college.

The Meeting in Yalta

In February 1945 Roosevelt, Churchill, and Stalin met for the second and last time at the winter resort of Yalta in the Soviet Union. They continued their discussions of strategy in Asia, postwar settlements in Europe, and plans for the United Nations. Above all Roosevelt wanted a firm commitment from Stalin to enter the war against Japan. The island campaigns in the Pacific had made clear that many hundreds of thousands of Americans would be killed or wounded in an assault on Japan.

At Yalta, Stalin again agreed to declare war on Japan three months after the surrender of Germany. In return, Roosevelt and Churchill agreed to Stalin's demands for postwar control of the Kurile Islands and southern Sakhalin Island, Japanese territories off the Pacific coast of the Soviet Union. The Soviet Union would retain control of the province of Outer Mongolia in northern China. It would also maintain ship-

ping rights in the harbor of Port Arthur and control over railroads in Manchuria.

The leaders agreed that free elections should be held as soon as possible in the countries that Germany had occupied during the war. Germany would be divided into four zones of occupation, governed by American, British, French, and Soviet forces. April 1945 was set as the month for a conference of the United Nations in San Francisco. There the nations of the world were to draw up a charter for a permanent peace-keeping organization.

By April 1945 the Red Army already occupied much of eastern Europe as it prepared for the final attack on Germany. (See page 619.) Roosevelt's and Churchill's vision of world peace rested on the hope that Stalin would honor the spirit of the Yalta agreements and allow free elections in the occupied nations. Churchill would later comment, "Our hopeful assumptions were soon to be falsified. Still, they were the only ones possible at the time."

For answers, see p. A 104.

Section Review

1. Identify the following: Chiang Kai-shek, the Big Three, United Nations, Harry S. Truman, Thomas E. Dewey.
2. List the topics the Big Three discussed at Teheran in 1943.
3. What issue did Dewey emphasize in the election of 1944?
4. What did the Big Three decide at Yalta about the fate of Germany after the war?

5 Victory

In the final year of the war in both Europe and the Pacific, Allied forces drove steadily toward victory over Germany and Japan. Allied armies battled across France and into Germany. Allied airplanes bombed major cities in the enemy's homeland. Naval and marine forces inched closer to Japan. By 1945, as the United States entered its fourth year of war, victory seemed near. But neither Germany nor Japan was willing to sue for peace. It was clear that the price of victory would be high indeed.

Ending the War in Europe

In December 1944 German troops launched one last counteroffensive in the Ardennes Forest along the border of Belgium and Luxembourg. In the Battle of the Bulge, the Germans, with the advantage of surprise, broke through Allied lines and surrounded American soldiers at the small town of Bastogne. Despite heavy casualties and what appeared to be certain defeat, when asked to surrender, Brigadier General Anthony C.

McAuliffe replied, "Nuts." The Allies stopped the German advance although the Battle of the Bulge slowed the Allied invasion of Germany by six weeks.

The German war machine was disintegrating. In the east the Soviets pushed across Poland, Czechoslovakia, and Hungary into Germany. Allied bombers pounded Berlin, Hamburg, and other German cities. One particularly severe fire bombing leveled the entire center of the city of Dresden. In March a small American force captured a key bridge across the Rhine River. Soon Allied armies crossed the Rhine and began the final conquest of Germany.

At that point General Eisenhower had to decide whether to concentrate his forces for a swift advance across Germany to meet the Red Army near Berlin or to spread his armies out to pursue German troops in the southern provinces. Churchill urged Eisenhower to push on to Berlin. The British prime minister did not trust Stalin's promise for free elections in postwar Europe. He wanted the United States and Britain to occupy as much of Germany and eastern Europe as possible before the war ended.

However, Eisenhower believed that the military goal of defeating Germany as completely as possible should outweigh postwar political considerations. The general permitted his field commanders to move slowly but thoroughly as they conquered Germany. Shortly before the war ended, American and Russian troops met at the Elbe River, nearly 100 miles (160 kilometers) west of Berlin.

The Third Reich was now in almost total ruin. The Nazi dictator had committed suicide in Berlin on April 30. One week later, on May 7, General Eisenhower accepted Germany's unconditional surrender, effective the next day, thereafter known as V-E Day.

The joy accompanying the end of the war in Europe was clouded. As Allied troops moved across Europe, they liberated huge concentration camps at Buchenwald, Dachau, Bergen-Belsen, and Auschwitz. Within these horrible camps, the Nazis had carried out their policy of genocide against European Jews. *Genocide* is the systematic destruction of a race of people. The Nazis had starved, tortured, and murdered about 12 million civilians in the concentration camps, including over 6 million Jews. One third of the Jewish population of Europe perished under the Nazi regime.

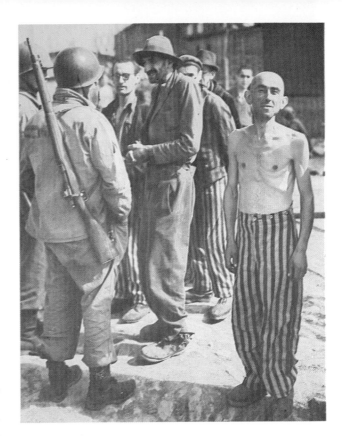

No rumors of the horrors of Nazi concentration camps could match the scenes Americans found when they liberated the prisoners. Above, at the Buchenwald concentration camp in Germany, United States troops talk to newly freed prisoners. The gaunt man at right was healthier than many of the starving prisoners who managed to survive the camps.

President Truman Takes Office

On April 12, less than one month before the Germans surrendered, President Roosevelt died at his vacation resort in Warm Springs, Georgia. Americans mourned his loss with the greatest outpouring of grief since the death of Abraham Lincoln.

On the afternoon of April 12, Eleanor Roosevelt informed Vice-President Harry S. Truman that her husband had died. Shocked, Truman asked if there was anything he could do for her. "Is there anything we can do for *you*?" she replied. "For you are the one in need of help now."

Certainly Truman had not been prepared for the responsibilities of the office he now assumed. He had no information about the atomic bomb that American scientists were developing. Truman knew little of the Yalta agreements, and he had never been in the secret map room of the White House.

"I felt," Truman admitted, "like the moon, the stars, and all the planets had fallen on me." Nevertheless, Truman, a veteran of Missouri and national politics, moved quickly to take up the unfinished business of Roosevelt's administration.

One of Truman's first acts was to announce that the United States would participate in the United Nations conference in San Francisco later that month, as planned. With Truman's approval, the conference drafted and adopted the Charter of the United Nations. Congress consented to United States membership in the world organization in July 1945.

Meanwhile, planning of the final offensive against the Japanese continued. Hard-won battles on the islands of Iwo Jima (EE woh JEE muh) and Okinawa (OH kuh NAH wuh) brought United States forces within striking distance of Japan. The final assault on the home islands promised to be bitter and bloody, with heavy casualties almost certain. At Iwo Jima and Okinawa, Japanese fighter pilots had employed *kamikaze* tactics, sacrificing their lives by deliberately crashing their planes into Allied ships. There was every reason to think the Japanese would put up an even more desperate struggle if the United States were to invade Japan.

A New Weapon

In July 1945 President Truman went to Potsdam, near Berlin, for a final meeting of the Big Three to discuss postwar settlements in Europe and to plan the final attack on Japan. While at Potsdam, Truman received word that American scientists had successfully detonated an atomic device. On July 16, a blinding light illuminated the early morning sky over the New Mexico desert. Windows cracked over 75 miles (about 120 kilometers) away.

The explosion of the atomic device in New Mexico was the result of a massive research effort known as the Manhattan Project. Between 1942 and 1945, the United

Large American aircraft carriers could launch 300 airplanes—planes that sometimes flew bombing raids over Tokyo. The carriers were therefore prime targets for hundreds of Japanese kamikaze pilots flying suicide missions. A kamikaze pilot would dive straight at a ship, firing as his plane zoomed to its inevitable crash. In this painting by Dwight Shepler, a kamikaze plane is hit before it can strike the carrier Hornet. *About one in four kamikaze pilots hit their targets.*

The city of Hiroshima, Japan, was leveled when an American bomber dropped the first atomic bomb ever used in warfare. A second bomb was dropped on Nagasaki before the Japanese agreed to unconditional surrender.

States government had spent over $2 billion to design and build three atomic bombs. The project required 37 factories and laboratories in 19 states and Canada. It employed over 120,000 people, including many of the most respected nuclear physicists from the United States, Britain, and Canada as well as scientists from throughout Europe who had fled Nazi tyranny.

For President Truman, news of the successful nuclear test came as a great relief. The discussions with Stalin over Poland, Germany, and other difficult postwar problems now seemed less pressing. American leaders had tried to compromise with Stalin because they believed the United States would need Soviet help to defeat Japan. Now that the United States had the atomic bomb, Soviet help became less crucial.

Truman told Stalin about an unspecified new American weapon, and Stalin encouraged him to use it. In the declaration that emerged from the Potsdam Conference, the Allies warned the Japanese that they faced complete destruction if they did not agree to unconditional surrender. Unaware of what the warning really meant, the Japanese ignored it.

On August 6, 1945, the *Enola Gay*, a specially fitted B-29 bomber, dropped an atomic bomb on Hiroshima, Japan, leveling the city. Three days later a second atomic bomb was dropped on Nagasaki. Over 150,000 Japanese died in the two explosions. Thousands more civilians were injured by the radiation from the bomb. In the face of these disasters and the Soviet entry into the war on August 8, the Japanese surrendered on August 14.

The Legacy of World War II

World War II brought unequaled destruction to the nations of the world. Over 55 million civilians and soldiers died in the conflict, nearly 30 million in the Soviet Union alone. About 290,000 Americans died, and 670,000 were wounded. Three military dictatorships had been defeated, but a terrible price had been paid.

The war also changed the map of the world. Former colonial powers, such as France, the Netherlands, Germany, Italy, Japan, and Great Britain, found their empires in ruin. Nations formerly under imperial rule in Asia and Africa were seeking independence and would soon enter the world community as free states. The Soviet Union had become the dominant power in Europe and a powerful force in the rest of the world. The United States had demonstrated that it had the most powerful military force in the world.

World War II revealed the enormous potential of science and technology to either advance civilization or destroy it. The mushroom clouds over Hiroshima and Nagasaki would linger in memory as the dreaded symbols of a new age. But if put to peaceful use, science and technology could improve the

628

Major Events

1941	Executive Order 8802 issued
1942	War Department relocates Japanese Americans; Battle of Coral Sea; Battle of Midway; Operation Torch begins
1943	Siege of Leningrad ends; Allies secure Guadalcanal; Axis forces in North Africa surrender; Allies invade Italy; Teheran Conference
1944	Allies begin cross-channel invasion of Europe; United States invades Philippines; Roosevelt elected for fourth term; bombing of Japan begins; Battle of the Bulge
1945	Yalta Conference; Roosevelt dies; Truman becomes President; United Nations founded; Germany surrenders; Potsdam Conference; United States drops atomic bomb on Hiroshima and Nagaski; Japan surrenders

human condition. Better communication and transportation systems could be used either to control people or to liberate and enlighten them.

Americans entered the postwar era hopeful that their arsenal of weapons and their good will could serve the cause of peace. These hopes were soon tested. Questions about boundaries and free elections that had divided the Allies during the war threatened the peace they had struggled so painfully to achieve. A new era of confrontation was dawning.

For answers, see p. A 104.

Section Review

1. Identify the following: Manhattan Project.
2. Define the following terms: genocide, kamikaze.
3. What did Germany accomplish in the Battle of the Bulge?
4. What did General Eisenhower think the most important Allied goal was in 1945?
5. What discovery clouded the joy over German surrender?

IN PERSPECTIVE When the United States entered World War II, the future appeared bleak for the Allies. The German army was driving deep into the Soviet Union, and the Japanese were nearly in control of the Pacific and eastern Asia. Allied victories in North Africa and a United States holding action in the Pacific gave the Allies some hope by early 1943.

The American effort on the home front was crucial to ultimate success in the war. Industrial production increased dramatically, and the Great Depression came to an end. The war affected the lives of all Americans. Women assumed a larger role in the civilian labor market. Black Americans also found new opportunities in industry, but black civilians and soldiers continued to face discrimination. Because of fear of sabotage, Japanese Americans living on the Pacific coast were removed from their homes and jobs and relocated at inland camps.

By 1943 the Allies had begun to take the offensive against the Axis powers. United States and British troops invaded Italy, and Soviet forces moved into eastern Europe. In June 1944 the Allies began the cross-channel invasion of France. The Japanese suffered and inflicted heavy casualties as they relinquished control of Pacific islands. A final German counter-offensive failed, and in early 1945 the Allies marched into Germany. By May the Germans had surrendered, but the war in the Pacific continued until the United States dropped atomic bombs on Hiroshima and Nagasaki in August, ending the war in the Pacific.

For answers, see p. A 104.

Chapter Review

1. (a) Why was 1942 a dark year for the Allies? (b) How did Operation Torch improve the Allied situation in Europe? (c) Why did the Allied position in the Pacific improve by early 1943?

2. Explain how each of the following helped mobilize American industry in support of the war effort: (a) War Production Board, (b) Office of Price Administration, (c) Office of War Mobilization, (d) War Manpower Commission, (e) War Labor Board.

3. What impact did the war have on the American economy? Give specific evidence to support your answer.

4. Explain how the war affected each of the following groups: (a) organized labor, (b) women, (c) black Americans, (d) Mexican Americans, (e) Italian and German Americans, (f) Japanese Americans.

5. (a) Why did the Allies decide to invade Italy? (b) Were they successful? Explain.

6. (a) Describe Operation Overlord. (b) Was it successful? Explain.

7. (a) What strategies did MacArthur and Nimitz propose to defeat Japan? (b) How did the technique of leapfrogging help them succeed? (c) What other Allied technique was important in attacks on Pacific islands?

8. (a) Where did diplomatic conferences between Allied leaders take place during the war? (b) What topics did the Big Three discuss at these conferences? (c) What agreements did they reach at Yalta?

9. (a) What was the Battle of the Bulge? (b) What did it mean for the Allies?

10. (a) Why did American leaders believe the final assault on Japan would be very costly? (b) What impact did that belief have on American willingness to compromise with Stalin?

For answers, see p. A 105.

For Further Thought

1. The war that lasted from 1914 to 1918 is usually called World War I, while the war that lasted from 1939 to 1945 is called World War II. Would you agree that World War II was actually more "worldwide" than World War I? Explain.

2. (a) How were Japanese Americans treated during World War II? (b) How does their treatment compare to the way German Americans were treated during World War I? (c) How might you explain the difference?

For answers, see p. A 105.

Developing Basic Skills

1. *Comparing* Review how the government mobilized industry during World War I. (See Chapter 28.) (a) In what way was the effort during World War II similar? (b) In what way was it different? (c) How might you explain the similarities and differences?

2. *Analyzing Fiction as Historical Evidence* World War II has been the topic of many fictional stories in novels, movies, and television shows. Review the steps for analyzing fiction on page 514. Then write a report about a story you have read or seen about the war. Be sure to answer the following questions in your report: (a) What type of source did you use? (b) When was it written or produced? (c) What do you know about the author or creators? (d) What can you learn about World War II by using this source? (e) How is the source limited as historical evidence?

See page 779 for suggested readings.

Unit Ten
The United States in a Changing World

631

The Postwar International Scene

36

(1945–1960)

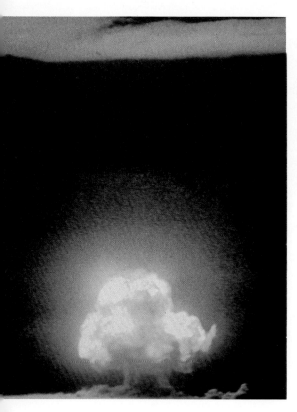

A 1946 atomic bomb test in New Mexico.

At 7:00 P.M. on August 14, 1945, President Harry Truman announced the unconditional surrender of Japan. Across the nation millions of Americans poured into the streets to celebrate. Two million people danced and cheered in Times Square in New York City, where the celebration lasted until dawn. In St. Louis people knelt quietly at 2:00 A.M. for a prayer service. Rain in Salt Lake City did not dampen the enthusiasm of crowds there. Celebrants swarmed down Hollywood Boulevard in Los Angeles singing and dancing. Everyone rejoiced that the war was over.

Behind the outpouring of joy, however, hung doubts about the future. The explosions of atom bombs at Hiroshima and Nagasaki cast a shadow over the victory celebration. Incredible destruction in Japan and many European nations created concern about · their future. Americans grew increasingly worried about the intentions of the Soviet Union. Diplomats and private citizens alike wondered whether the Soviets would live up to their wartime promises.

1 The Postwar World

After World War I, the United States had tried to withdraw from foreign affairs. At the end of World War II, however, the nation was a major world power with awesome responsibilities. Both allies and enemies had been devastated by the war, leaving only the Soviet Union and the United States to compete for world leadership.

Roots of Conflict in Europe

From the moment the Bolsheviks seized power in 1917, most Americans had viewed the Soviet Union with a mixture of mistrust and fear. World War II had brought the Soviet Union and the United States together as Allies, but deep suspicions lingered on both sides.

Soviet Premier Joseph Stalin had doubted his allies' willingness to assist the Soviet Union during the war. He believed that the British and Americans had purposely delayed the cross-channel invasion in order to prolong the Soviet struggle against Germany. He was also angered by their refusal to acknowledge that the Soviet Union needed a buffer zone of friendly states near its borders to protect it against future German attack.

Many Americans, including some officials in the Department of State, doubted that the United States could trust the Soviet Union. Some believed that the Soviets had a plan for worldwide revolution and unlimited territorial expansion. Soviet actions after the war seemed to justify such concern.

In 1944 and 1945 the Red Army had driven German troops out of Soviet territory and continued to pursue them west. (See page 619.) As a result the Soviet Union emerged from the war in control of much of eastern Europe. During the wartime conferences, Stalin had agreed to allow free elections in Poland once the war was over. Instead, the Soviets installed a communist-dominated government and crushed all opposition. A similar fate befell other eastern European nations over the next three years. The Red Army maintained order, and Soviet-backed communists organized governments.

Another conflict arose over the future of Germany. During the war Britain, France, the United States, and the Soviet Union had agreed to divide Germany into four zones. (See the map below.) The capital city, Berlin, was similarly divided into four sectors. But Berlin itself was located deep in the Soviet zone, and the agreement among the Allies did not guarantee free access to Berlin through Soviet-controlled territory. Soviet actions in Berlin and the rest of eastern Europe were soon to emerge as major points of conflict between the United States and the Soviet Union.

The United Nations

The Allies knew that the end of the war would not result in an end to international conflict. Even as war raged they had planned

■ *At the end of World War II, the Allied powers—the United States, France, Great Britain, and the Soviet Union—divided Germany into four zones of occupation. Although the German capital, Berlin, was in the Soviet-occupied zone, all four Allies shared control of the city.*

The Occupation of Germany

United States
Great Britain
France
Soviet Union

DENMARK

NETHERLANDS

BELGIUM

LUX.

GERMANY

Berlin

INTERNATIONAL ZONE

POLAND

CZECHOSLOVAKIA

FRANCE

AUSTRIA

SWITZERLAND

100 Miles
200 Kilometers

for an international peace-keeping organization. (See page 623.) In April 1945 representatives of 50 nations met in San Francisco and adopted a charter for such an organization, the United Nations (UN). Member states pledged to seek peaceful solutions to international disputes. The UN would try to prevent wars and try to stop those that did break out. UN members also pledged to work together to eliminate hunger, disease, and illiteracy.

According to the UN charter, six major bodies make up the United Nations. (See the diagram below.) All member nations belong to the General Assembly, which discusses world problems and recommends action to members or other UN organizations.

The Security Council is the UN body most directly responsible for maintaining world peace. Originally representatives of 11 nations made up the Security Council, but that number has since grown to 15. Five major powers—the United States, Great Britain, France, the Soviet Union, and China—have permanent seats on the council. The remaining members are elected for two-year terms by the General Assembly.

The Security Council investigates conflicts between nations and recommends solutions. It can organize a peace-keeping force made up of troops from member nations. However, the council has no power to enforce its decisions. Furthermore, any permanent member of the Security Council can veto council resolutions. The Soviet Union used the veto frequently during the early postwar years.

UN Action in the Middle East

The first case to come before the Security Council involved a confrontation between the Soviet Union and the United States over Iran. During the war, Soviet, British, and American troops had occupied Iran to guard its vital oil fields and protect the main supply route to the Soviet Union. When the war ended, the Soviets encouraged rebellion in

■ *Representatives of 50 nations met in San Francisco in 1945 to adopt the Charter of the United Nations. The diagram shows the six major bodies of the United Nations, which has its headquarters in New York City.*

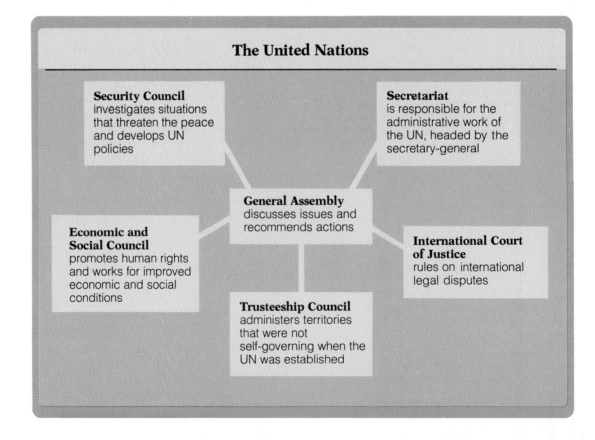

The United Nations

Security Council
investigates situations
that threaten the peace
and develops UN
policies

Secretariat
is responsible for the
administrative work of
the UN, headed by the
secretary-general

General Assembly
discusses issues and
recommends actions

**Economic and
Social Council**
promotes human rights
and works for improved
economic and social
conditions

**International Court
of Justice**
rules on international
legal disputes

Trusteeship Council
administers territories
that were not
self-governing when the
UN was established

Iran, and Soviet troops prevented the Iranian government from restoring order.

With strong support from the United States, Iran brought a complaint before the UN Security Council. As the council debated, the Soviet Union refused to remove its troops even though Britain and the United States had already done so. Finally, in April 1946, after forcing an oil concession from the Iranians, the Soviets withdrew and the crisis ended.

The UN also tried to settle a crisis in Palestine, a territory administered by Great Britain since World War I. British rule became increasingly unpopular after World War II, both among the Arabs, who made up a majority of the population, and among resident Jews. Many European Jews had settled in Palestine during the 1930s as a result of Nazi persecution.

In 1947 a UN commission recommended that Palestine be divided into an Arab and a Jewish state. In 1948 the British withdrew, and the Jewish residents of Palestine proclaimed the nation of Israel. President Truman immediately recognized Israel. But neighboring states vowed to resist, and war broke out. The UN eventually arranged an armistice in 1949, which restored an uneasy peace to the area.

Turmoil in Southern Europe

World War II plunged much of southern Europe into political and economic turmoil. After the Allies drove the Nazis out of Greece in late 1944, a bitter civil war erupted between supporters and opponents of the Greek monarchy. A truce in January 1945 ended the fighting temporarily, but civil war broke out again in 1946. Meanwhile the Greek economy was in ruin, and starvation was widespread.

Major opponents of the Greek monarchy were communists who received aid from Yugoslavia, a communist nation bordering Greece. The Greek monarchy received aid from Britain. Fear on the part of United States officials that communists might seize power in Greece was heightened when it became apparent that Britain could not continue to aid the Greek government for long.

Communists also became a political force in Italy after World War II. Difficult economic conditions made many Italians desperate for reform, and some turned to the Communist party. In the 1946 parliamentary elections the Communist party won 104 of 556 seats.

East Asia Transformed

The end of the war brought dramatic changes to East Asia, especially Japan, Korea, and China. After the war, the United States Army, under the command of General Douglas MacArthur, occupied Japan. General MacArthur drafted a constitution for Japan that called for representative government and left the emperor powerless. Traditional educational practices, family-controlled land trusts, state-supported religion, and the large standing army were abolished. MacArthur intended to demilitarize Japan, that is, to end the influence of the military on Japanese society and government.

Japan had been the most powerful nation in Asia for decades. The defeat and demilitarization of Japan left a power vacuum in East Asia. As a result, the United States and the Soviet Union competed for influence there. Korea, which had been under Japanese control since 1910, became a major area of conflict. A wartime agreement between the United States and the Soviet Union provided that Korea would be divided along the 38th parallel. The Soviet Union was to disarm Japanese troops in the northern zone, and the United States was to do the same in the southern sector. The two powers agreed that national elections would be held to unify the country.

After the war the Soviet Union installed a communist government in its zone and refused to cooperate in national elections. An American-born Korean, Syngman Rhee (SIHNG muhn REE), was elected president in the south. In effect, by 1948 Korea had become two nations: North Korea backed by the Soviet Union and South Korea backed by the United States. The stage was set for further conflict.

Civil war had raged in China since the early 1930s. Mao Tse-tung (MOW zuh DUNG) led communist forces against the nationalist government of Chiang Kai-shek. During World War II, Chiang had used his best troops against the communists rather than concentrating on Japan. Once the war was over, the civil war became more bitter. The communists had an army of 500,000 troops, less than one fourth the strength of the nationalist army. The nationalist army was also more modern, largely trained and equipped by the United States. However, the government of Chiang Kai-shek was plagued by widespread corruption. That weakened the nationalists' ability to fight and drove many Chinese to support the communists.

In December 1945 President Harry Truman sent General George C. Marshall to China to work for the unification of China under a government acceptable to both sides. Shortly after Marshall's arrival a cease-fire was declared, and negotiations between the nationalists and the communists began. But neither side was willing to compromise. The civil war continued, and Marshall returned to the United States in January 1947.

For answers, see p. A 106.

Section Review

1. Identify the following: United Nations, Security Council, General Assembly, Mao Tse-tung, Syngman Rhee.

2. What agreement did the Allies reach about the fate of Germany after the war?

3. What nations have permanent seats on the UN Security Council?

4. What role did the UN play in the creation of Israel?

5. What development left a power vacuum in East Asia after the war?

6. What were the two opposing forces in the Chinese civil war?

2 A Cold War Begins

The events of the early postwar years in eastern and southern Europe and in East Asia contributed to growing tension between the United States and the Soviet Union. In 1946 Bernard Baruch, an elder statesman and presidential adviser, used the term "cold war" to describe that tension. That same year in a speech in Fulton, Missouri, Winston Churchill described an "iron curtain" that had fallen between the nations of western and eastern Europe.

The Truman Doctrine

United States policy toward the Soviet Union after World War II drew on the ideas of George Kennan. Kennan had served as a diplomatic officer in the United States embassy in Moscow and had become a leading expert on the Soviet Union. His wartime dispatches from Moscow contained many warnings about Soviet ambitions.

Kennan attributed Soviet actions largely to Stalin's fear that "hostile capitalist" nations would encircle the Soviet Union. In Stalin's view, Kennan continued, the Soviet Union would have to overthrow all western governments to prevent such encirclement. Kennan argued that the United States should "contain" aggressive Soviet actions by applying counterforce at strategic political and geographic locations.

Events in Greece and Turkey soon gave the Truman administration an opportunity to apply such a "containment" policy. In February 1947 the British informed the United States they could no longer afford to assist the Greek monarchy. As you have read, Greece was in the midst of a civil war. (See page 635.) President Truman feared that British withdrawal would mean victory for the communist forces. Political unrest in neighboring Turkey made that nation desperate for foreign assistance as well. Furthermore the Soviet Union was demanding part of Turkish territory.

Encouraged by Under Secretary of State Dean Acheson, Truman decided to ask Congress for $400 million in aid to Greece and Turkey. In what became known as the Truman Doctrine the President declared before a joint session of Congress that "it must be the policy of the United States to support free peoples who are resisting attempted subjugation." In his speech Truman formally recognized a cold war between democratic nations and those under communist domination. Economic and military aid, he said, would be the major weapons of the United States.

George Kennan objected to the administration's application of containment. The unrest in Turkey was not caused by communists, he argued, and military aid might be

The Truman Doctrine

On March 12, 1947, President Harry S. Truman went before a joint session of Congress to seek aid for Greece and Turkey. United States military experts had told the President that the Greek government might fall to communist revolutionaries if it did not receive assistance. Turkey was facing territorial demands by the Soviet Union. A portion of Truman's speech is printed below. The policy he proposed became known as the Truman Doctrine.

I believe that it must be the policy of the United States to support free peoples who are resisting attempted subjugation by armed minorities or by outside pressures. I believe that we must assist free peoples to work out their own destinies in their own way. I believe that our help should be primarily through economic and financial aid, which is essential to economic stability and orderly political processes. . . .

It would be an unspeakable tragedy if these countries, which have struggled so long against overwhelming odds, should lose that victory for which they sacrificed so much. Collapse of free institutions and loss of independence would be disastrous not only for them but for the world. Discouragement and possibly failure would quickly be the lot of neighboring peoples striving to maintain their freedom and independence.

Should we fail to aid Greece and Turkey in this fateful hour, the effect will be far-reaching to the West as well as to the East. We must take immediate and resolute action. . . .

The seeds of totalitarian regimes are nurtured by misery and wants. They spread and grow in the evil soil of poverty and strife. They reach their full growth when the hope of a people for a better life has died. We must keep that hope alive. The free peoples of the world look to us for support in maintaining their freedoms. If we falter in our leadership, we may endanger the peace of the world—and we shall surely endanger the welfare of our own nation.

Great responsibilities have been placed upon us by the swift movement of events. I am confident that the Congress will face these responsibilities squarely.

---

unnecessarily provocative. However, Truman and Acheson disagreed with Kennan because they were eager to take a forceful stance in the growing cold war. The Truman Doctrine proved to be effective in both Greece and Turkey. Bolstered by American aid, the Greek monarchy defeated the uprising against the government, and order was restored in Turkey.

The Marshall Plan

In 1947 Secretary of State George C. Marshall returned from a trip to Europe greatly concerned. He had seen nations and people badly in need of economic and material assistance. "The patient is sinking while the doctors deliberate," he warned.

With its attention now focused on western Europe, the Truman administration moved quickly. The Europeans needed financial assistance to rebuild their devastated economies. Marshall urged European leaders to draw up a plan for recovery. He purposely did not exclude the Soviet Union or the eastern European nations, which had become known as the Soviet bloc.

In June 1947 a Soviet delegation arrived in Paris to meet with delegations from Great Britain and France. Three days later the Soviets left, refusing to accept the French and British plan for a program for recovery in Europe as a whole. Within a week the Soviet Union had devised a plan to create an economic bloc in eastern Europe. Meanwhile, representatives from 16 other nations met in Paris to work out a recovery program, which was completed by September. They requested $16 billion in American aid over a period of four years.

In presenting the program to Congress, President Truman pointed out that such aid would have many benefits for the United States. Stronger economies would help the nations of western Europe resist any domestic communist threat. Economic recovery would also strengthen their military capacity. Furthermore, Truman noted that the demand for American exports would increase, thereby improving the United States economy.

For the United States, the key to the European Recovery Plan, or Marshall Plan, as it was known, was the economic recovery of Germany. "Without a revival of German production," Marshall told Congress, "there can be no revival of Europe's economy." Though fearful of a strong Germany, other European nations agreed, since they would also benefit from the aid. In four years over $12 billion went into rebuilding western Europe.

The Marshall Plan became the crowning achievement of the containment policy. As prosperity returned to Europe, the likelihood of communist victories subsided. But the decision to help rebuild western Germany was to lead to conflict with the Soviet Union.

The Berlin Blockade

Germany, as you have read, had been divided into four zones of Allied occupation after the war. (See page 633.) Britain, France, and the United States worked closely in the administration of the western sectors of the country, while the Soviet government administered the eastern section. By June 1948, after fruitless discussions with the Soviet Union over the unification of Germany, the United States, Britain, and France decided to merge the western zones and establish the area as an independent nation. The unified zones would become the German Federal Republic, known today as West Germany.

On June 24, 1948, the Soviet Union responded to the division of Germany by denying all road, rail, and river access to West Berlin, thereby cutting off supplies to more than 2 million residents. Berlin, located in the Soviet zone, was highly vulnerable to a blockade. The Soviets hoped that the blockade would drive the other Allies out of Berlin and lay the basis for the unification of Germany under Soviet influence.

President Truman reacted strongly to the Soviet challenge in Berlin, ordering a massive airlift to supply West Berlin during the blockade. Each day for 321 days, the Berlin airlift delivered thousands of tons of supplies to the western sector of the city. In May 1949, convinced of American determination to preserve the independence of West Berlin, the Soviet Union ended the blockade.

Growing Commitment

In March 1948 Britain, France, Belgium, the Netherlands, and Luxembourg had signed the Brussels Treaty, stating that if any of the five was the victim of military attack, the others would offer assistance. Although originally opposed to a military alliance with European nations, many members of the United States Congress changed their minds

When the Soviet Union closed off all road, rail, and river traffic to West Berlin in 1948, the United States launched an airlift to supply the encircled city. An American cargo plane delivering food and other vital supplies to West Berlin is seen here above the walls of Berlin buildings bombed during World War II.

after the Berlin blockade. They saw that such a union would be of political as well as military benefit.

In April 1949 representatives of the Brussels Treaty nations, joined by Denmark, Norway, Portugal, Italy, Iceland, Canada, and the United States, signed a mutual defense treaty creating the North Atlantic Treaty Organization (NATO).* The treaty stated that an attack on any one of the NATO nations would be considered an attack on all of them. The Soviet Union later formed an opposing alliance, the Warsaw Pact, with Albania, Bulgaria, Czechoslovakia, East Germany, Hungary, Poland, and Romania. (See the map on page 640.)

United States membership in NATO represented a break with an isolationist past. It was the first time that the United States had joined a peacetime alliance committing the country to the defense of Europe. Possession of nuclear weapons made the United States the most important member of the alliance. As a result, the commander of NATO military forces was always an American general.

A successful foreign policy contributed to Truman's reelection in 1948. In his inaugural address, however, he tried to balance public concern about military issues by announcing a "bold new program" to provide economic aid to newly independent nations. After 18 months of debate Congress agreed to provide $27 million in aid. The aid program thereafter was modest, but it had some effect. For example, American assistance helped the Iranians wipe out malaria.

1949: Challenges to Postwar Confidence

Two events in late 1949 underscored the realization among Americans that the tension of the cold war was to dominate international affairs for years to come. The first of these occurred in China. Each month of 1949 brought news of another victory of Mao Tse-tung's communist forces over the nationalist armies of Chiang Kai-shek. By the end of the year, the communists had taken control of mainland China and established the People's Republic of China. The nationalists had retreated to the island of Formosa, now known as Taiwan.

European concern about Soviet aggression after World War II was a major reason for the founding of NATO. This French poster shows the Soviet military threatening Europe. The figures in the background are Soviet citizens being sent to Siberia. The letters URSS on the planes are French for USSR. Stalin is the small figure in the center.

Mao's victory provoked a storm of criticism against the Truman administration. Critics charged that Truman had "lost" China by concentrating military and economic aid to Europe. More aid to the nationalists, some Americans insisted, would have saved Chiang's regime. The defeat of the Nationalist Army weakened American confidence in the way President Truman was applying the policy of containment.

Truman refused to recognize the communist government on mainland China. Instead the United States government recognized the nationalists on Taiwan as the legitimate government of China. In 1950 the United States began providing military protection for Taiwan.

Another event in 1949 dampened American hopes for a quick end to the cold war. In September, President Truman announced that the Soviet Union had successfully tested an atomic device. United States monopoly on atomic power was over. As Senator Arthur Vandenberg of Michigan grimly put it, "This is now a different world."

639

---

*Turkey and Greece joined NATO in 1952, West Germany in 1955.

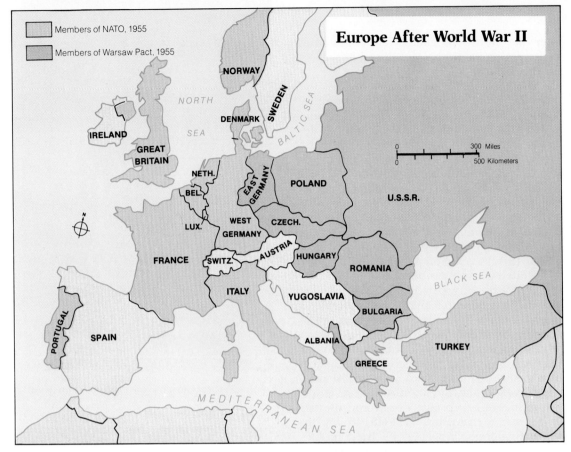

Europe After World War II

Members of NATO, 1955

Members of Warsaw Pact, 1955

NORWAY

NORTH SEA

SWEDEN

DENMARK

BALTIC SEA

IRELAND

GREAT BRITAIN

NETH.

BEL.

EAST GERMANY

POLAND

U.S.S.R.

LUX.

WEST GERMANY

CZECH.

FRANCE

SWITZ.

AUSTRIA

HUNGARY

ROMANIA

BLACK SEA

ITALY

YUGOSLAVIA

BULGARIA

PORTUGAL

SPAIN

ALBANIA

GREECE

TURKEY

MEDITERRANEAN SEA

300 Miles

500 Kilometers

■ *The United States joined with nations of western Europe in 1949 to create the North Atlantic Treaty Organization. NATO countries agreed that an attack on one was an attack on all. Countries under Soviet influence later formed the Warsaw Pact. As the map shows, few countries in Europe remained outside the two alliances. Compare this map with the map of Europe after World War I on page 515. What countries existed independently in 1918 but not in the 1950s? What happened to them?* For answers, see p. A 106.

Responding to criticism at home and to the Soviet nuclear test, President Truman authorized full-scale work on the development of the even more powerful hydrogen bomb. Over the next two years the United States began rebuilding its conventional, or nonatomic, forces, such as land armies, weapons, and air power. All of them had been greatly reduced after World War II. Many of the rebuilt forces were committed to the NATO command in Europe.

President Truman further authorized the National Security Council, which consisted of the heads of defense and intelligence agencies, to undertake a full examination of possible foreign policy strategies. In 1950 the council produced the classified document NSC 68. It described the future of the world as "an indefinite period of tension and danger." The authors of NSC 68 argued that the United States must com-

mit itself to whatever military steps necessary to protect the noncommunist world and to meet "each fresh challenge promptly and unequivocally." NSC 68 provided the basis for United States foreign policy through much of the 1950s and 1960s.

For answers, see p. A 106.

Section Review

1. Identify the following: Truman Doctrine, Marshall Plan, NATO.

2. Define the following term: containment.

3. What led President Truman to decide to aid Greece?

4. According to General Marshall, what was the main purpose of the Marshall Plan?

5. How did the United States react to the Berlin blockade?

6. What two events in 1949 increased cold war tension?

3 The Korean War

In the midst of President Truman's re-examination of cold war policies after the events of 1949, the United States faced a major crisis in Asia. A communist invasion of South Korea tested American commitment to the policy of containment.

The War Begins

As you have read, after World War II Korea was divided into a northern zone dominated by the Soviet Union and a southern zone tied to the United States. Negotiations on the unification of Korea had been unsuccessful. On June 11, 1950, the South Korean government arrested several delegates from the north. And on June 25, 1950, North Korea invaded South Korea.

An emergency meeting of the United Nations Security Council later that day passed a resolution condemning the invasion and demanding immediate withdrawal of North Korean forces. Two days later, the council recommended United Nations action to aid South Korea. Both votes in the Security Council passed because the Soviet

representative was not present to veto the resolutions. The Soviet Union was boycotting the council to protest the failure of the UN to grant membership to the People's Republic of China.

On the same day that the UN voted to provide military aid to South Korea, President Truman ordered United States planes and ships to back up the South Korean army. Three days later, on June 30, Truman ordered United States troops into the Korean fighting. A week later the UN voted to establish a joint UN fighting force under the command of a general chosen by the President of the United States. Truman selected General Douglas MacArthur. About four fifths of the UN force under MacArthur consisted of United States troops.

The goal of the United Nations action, as described by President Truman, was to drive the North Koreans out of South Korea. But United States troops rushed in from bases in Japan were poorly prepared to fight, and the South Koreans lacked vital equipment. Consequently, Soviet-supplied North Korean troops pushed farther south. By August 1950

When North Korea attacked South Korea in 1950, the United Nations condemned the action. The United States and other UN countries sent troops to help the South Koreans. Here, North Korean prisoners under American guard file through a Korean field.

the North Koreans had captured virtually all of South Korea. In September, however, MacArthur directed a surprise landing at Inchon, behind North Korean lines. Within two weeks, UN forces had recaptured almost all of South Korea.

According to the original objectives of the war, the United Nations–United States mission was complete. But the momentum of MacArthur's assault now began to take over. In October, under MacArthur's orders and with the approval of both Truman and the UN General Assembly, UN forces crossed the 38th parallel into North Korea. As MacArthur pushed north, the UN revised

■ *War in Korea began in 1950 when North Korean troops attacked South Korea. A United Nations force came to the assistance of the South Koreans. A strong North Korean advance drove deep into South Korea. Then UN troops under General Douglas MacArthur landed at Inchon, far behind North Korean lines. From there they recaptured most of South Korea. When the forces continued north across the 38th parallel, however, the People's Republic of China entered the war in support of North Korea.*

The Korean War

| Line of farthest North Korean advance, September 1950 |
| Line of farthest UN advance, November 1950 |
| Line of farthest North Korean–Chinese advance, January 1951 |
| Armistice line |

its aims, calling for "the establishment of a unified, independent, and democratic Korea."

The invasion of North Korea brought disastrous consequences. Communist China had warned that it would not "sit back with folded hands" if United States troops marched into North Korea. American leaders paid little attention to such warnings, believing that China would never intervene. The American leaders were wrong. In late November hundreds of thousands of Chinese soldiers crossed the Yalu River into North Korea and forced United Nations troops to retreat with heavy losses across the 38th parallel.

A Clash Between Truman and MacArthur

The Korean conflict was now, in General MacArthur's words, "an entirely new war." How that war should be fought became the focus of a controversy between General MacArthur and President Truman. Truman and most of his advisers decided to revive the original objectives of the war: restoring the boundary between North and South Korea. They now supported the strategy of limited war. In a *limited war* the United States would seek specific objectives rather than total victory over North Korea. Limited war also meant that nuclear weapons would not be used.

Truman reasoned that a major land war in Asia to defeat North Korea and China might provoke Soviet retaliation in Europe or elsewhere in Asia. MacArthur, however, did not accept the concept of limited war. In war, he declared, "there is no substitute for victory." He believed that political decisions made in Washington hampered his ability to conduct the war. MacArthur wanted to extend the war into China by bombing bases in Manchuria.

Relations between MacArthur and Truman grew steadily worse. By March 1951, after United Nations forces had recovered most of South Korea, Truman was ready to seek a negotiated peace. MacArthur, however, wanted to advance into North Korea again. Ignoring the President, MacArthur issued a public statement demanding total North Korean surrender. The statement undercut Truman's attempt at negotiations. Because of MacArthur's insubordination, President Truman removed the general from command and ordered him back to the United States.

MacArthur returned home to a hero's welcome, and he received a standing ovation when he addressed a joint session of Congress. A congressional committee began investigating Truman's dismissal of MacArthur. For a time, feelings ran high in support of the general, but Truman successfully defended his decision. The long-standing tradition of civilian control of the military in the United States was reaffirmed.

Cease-Fire

Negotiations to work out a cease-fire in Korea began in July 1951. They continued for the next two years while the fighting went on. During the presidential election campaign of 1952, the Republican candidate, General Dwight D. Eisenhower, pledged that if elected he would personally go to Korea and get the stalled peace negotiations moving again.

Eisenhower won the election and visited Korea within a few weeks of his victory. By then both sides were eager for a cease-fire. Only the problem of what to do about prisoners of war remained. The two sides finally agreed to turn the prisoner-of-war issue over to an international commission.

A cease-fire ending the hostilities in Korea was signed on July 27, 1953. The agreement restored the 38th parallel as the boundary between North and South Korea and provided for a demilitarized zone along that boundary. Relations between North and South Korea remained tense, with periodic conflicts in the demilitarized zone, but these incidents never erupted into war. Over 54,000 Americans and 3,000 soldiers from other United Nations countries had lost their lives in the Korean War. The UN force had successfully repelled the invasion of South

Dismissed as commander in Korea by President Truman, General Douglas MacArthur returned to a hero's welcome in New York City. The President and MacArthur bitterly disagreed over the issue of fighting a limited war in Korea.

Korea, and the United States government had demonstrated its determination to stop armed aggression.

For answers, see p. A 106.

Section Review

1. Identify the following: 38th parallel.
2. Define the following term: limited war.
3. What action did the UN Security Council take when North Korea invaded South Korea?
4. (a) What was the original goal of the UN and the United States in the Korean War? (b) How did that goal change in October 1950?
5. What issue led to conflict between President Truman and General MacArthur?

4 New Directions in Foreign Policy

With the end of the Korean conflict, the cold war continued under new leadership in both the United States and the Soviet Union. In the United States, a new President, Dwight Eisenhower, began his term by rejecting many of the policies of his predecessor. Two months after Eisenhower took office Soviet Premier Joseph Stalin died. After an intense political struggle, Nikita Khrushchev (nuh KEET uh kroosh CHAWF) emerged as premier of the Soviet Union. New leadership offered the opportunity to reduce tension between the United States and the Soviet Union.

643

A Different Approach

John Foster Dulles was secretary of state under President Eisenhower. Dulles believed that communism was an immoral system of government. He rejected the containment policy of the Truman administration because that policy tolerated Soviet power where it already existed. The secretary of state believed the object of United States foreign policy should be not merely to contain communism but to destroy it.

Dulles's foreign policy was guided by two principles. First, he believed that the United States should encourage the "liberation of the captive peoples" in eastern Europe by widespread use of political pressure and propaganda. Radio broadcasts to eastern European countries by the Voice of America and Radio Free Europe urged people in those nations to overthrow their communist governments.

Second, Dulles proposed a new military strategy of *massive retaliation*. Instead of merely supporting local efforts to fight aggression, as in Korea, Dulles believed that the United States should make clear its determination to retaliate directly against the Soviet Union or China with nuclear weapons if necessary. During the 1950s the United States and the Soviet Union began an *arms race* to accumulate sophisticated nuclear arsenals. However, neither the policies of Dulles nor the arms race prevented efforts to reduce tensions by the late 1950s.

A "Thaw" in the Cold War

After the death of Stalin in 1953, Soviet policy underwent several changes. First, Soviet leaders began to concentrate on improving living conditions within the Soviet Union. They hoped to impress nations in Asia, Africa, and Latin America with the superiority of communism as an economic system. In addition, the Soviet leadership now stated that war between the Soviet Union and the West* was unnecessary. In their opinion peaceful competition between the two

would demonstrate the superiority of the Soviet system.

New directions in Soviet policy offered an opportunity for a "thaw" in the cold war. President Eisenhower resisted the advice of those who condemned any negotiations with the Soviets. Cautiously he moved to relax tensions between the two powers.

The first indication of the thaw was a summit conference held in Geneva, Switzerland, in 1955. President Eisenhower met with the leaders of the Soviet Union, Britain, and France to begin discussions about European security and disarmament. The western powers wanted Germany to be reunited. The Soviets resisted, fearing the threat of a powerful reunited Germany, especially if it was allied with the West.

There was some agreement on the issue of disarmament, however. Both East and West had come to realize the terrible danger of nuclear destruction that threatened the entire world as long as the arms race continued. Thus, discussions of banning the testing of nuclear weapons continued after the Geneva meeting. In 1958 the Soviet Union, the United States, and Britain suspended the testing of nuclear weapons as efforts continued for a permanent halt to the arms race.

The high point of the thaw in American-Soviet relations came in the summer of 1959 when Nikita Khrushchev made a two-week visit to the United States. The Soviet leader toured factories, attended a midwestern barbecue, discussed raising corn with an Iowa farmer, and visited Hollywood.

Khrushchev concluded his tour with a lengthy series of talks with President Eisenhower at Camp David, the presidential retreat outside Washington. The two leaders agreed to hold a summit meeting the following year. Hopes for a further relaxation of tensions ran high as the "spirit of Camp David" warmed Soviet-American relations.

A Setback to Peaceful Relations

The spirit of Camp David was soon destroyed by what became known as the U-2 incident. A U-2 is a high-altitude plane specially equipped to take photographs of ground activities. For example, U-2 planes could take pictures of convoys of Soviet troops and missile locations. American U-2s began making flights over the Soviet Union in 1956.

*The United States, nations of western Europe, and other nations opposed to Soviet expansion were often referred to as the "West" or the "western powers." The Soviet Union and its allies became known as the "East" or the "eastern powers."

In 1960, ten days before the planned Paris summit conference, Khrushchev announced that a U-2 had been shot down over the Soviet Union. The pilot had been captured and had admitted that his job was to photograph Soviet military facilities. Several days later President Eisenhower stated that he had authorized the U-2 flights in the interest of national security.

In an effort to save the summit conference, Eisenhower announced that he had suspended U-2 flights, but Khrushchev was not satisfied. The Soviet leader arrived in Paris and demanded an apology. Eisenhower refused, and the summit collapsed.

For answers, see p. A 106.

Section Review

1. Identify the following: Nikita Khrushchev, John Foster Dulles.
2. Define the following terms: massive retaliation, arms race.
3. How did Dulles think the United States should encourage the people of eastern Europe to revolt against the Soviet Union?
4. What was the high point of the thaw in the cold war in the late 1950s?
5. What effect did the U-2 incident have on the thaw?

645

5 The Challenge of Nationalism

Nationalism emerged as a powerful force during the 1950s. In Africa, the Middle East, and Asia nationalist groups sought to free their nations from the colonial rule of the British, French, and Dutch. Many of those colonies did win independence. Throughout the postwar period the United States and the Soviet Union competed for influence in the newly independent nations.

The United States and the Soviet Union also faced growing nationalism in neighboring countries. The Soviets were challenged by the people of eastern Europe who were unhappy living under foreign domination. In Latin America resentment of the United States exploded in violence and revolution.

The Hungarian Uprising

In 1956 anti-Soviet nationalism erupted in two eastern European nations. Relaxation of some political and economic controls within the Soviet Union encouraged the people of eastern Europe to demand more freedom for themselves. In Poland workers rioted against Soviet rule and won greater control of their own government.

Encouraged by the Polish example, Hungarian nationalists demanded that pro-Soviet Hungarian officials be replaced, that Soviet troops be withdrawn, and that noncommunist political parties be legalized. Hungarian students and workers organized huge demonstrations in support of these demands.

Soviet tanks and troops moved swiftly into Hungary to crush the uprising. The western powers provided refuge for those Hungarians who escaped, but they sent no direct aid. Some Americans regarded the inability of the United States to help the Hungarians as proof that Secretary of State Dulles's demand for the "liberation" of eastern Europe was not a practical policy.

War in Southeast Asia

After the defeat of Japan, the French returned to their colonial territories of Vietnam, Cambodia, and Laos in Southeast Asia. But Vietnamese forces led by Ho Chi Minh (hoh chee mihn) continued the long and costly war for independence that they had been waging since the 1930s.

By the late 1940s the French considered withdrawing from Southeast Asia. Since Ho Chi Minh was a communist as well as a nationalist, however, the United States urged France to continue the war. For almost five years the United States contributed money and supplies to the French war effort. But even with the aid, France was unable to defeat Ho's guerrilla forces.

Meanwhile Ho's armies continued to grow in strength and popular support. In May 1954, after a month-long siege, the

In small groups and large, Europeans by the millions eluded border guards to flee communist-controlled eastern Europe. After Soviet troops crushed a 1956 revolt in Hungary, some 200,000 Hungarians fled the country. The Hungarians above escaped across a river into Austria by a makeshift bridge consisting of a log and a guiderope.

remaining French force surrendered at Dien Bien Phu (dyehn byehn foo). President Eisenhower, fearing another land war in Asia like the Korean conflict, refused to commit United States troops to the fighting. He also rejected Dulles's advice to use nuclear weapons against the Vietnamese. Instead, an international conference in Geneva in 1954 divided Vietnam into two regions, with the promise that elections to reunify the country would be held later.

A communist government led by Ho Chi Minh took control of North Vietnam. In South Vietnam the United States supported the government of Ngo Dinh Diem (noh din ZEE em). Diem resisted holding elections to unify the two Vietnams, and the country remained divided.

The United States replaced France as the leading western power in Southeast Asia. Many justified American presence there by what became known as the domino theory. According to this theory, if one nation accepted communism, neighboring nations would topple like a set of falling dominoes. United States policy was to prevent the first domino from falling.

To prevent communist expansion in Asia, the United States sponsored the creation of the Southeast Asia Treaty Organization (SEATO).* Under the terms of this alliance the United States pledged to aid nations threatened by aggression. Furthermore, in 1955 the United States began to send military advisers to help train the South Vietnamese armed forces. The United States also pledged to come to the aid of Taiwan if it were attacked by mainland China.

The Middle East

Gamal Abdel Nasser, who became president of Egypt in 1956, was a strong nationalist. Like other Arab nationalists, Nasser opposed the existence of Israel. (See page 635.) In the first year of Nasser's leadership, the United States withdrew support from construction of a dam it had offered to build in Egypt. Nasser reacted by seizing control of the Suez Canal, which was important for western economic and military interests. Britain and France threatened military action against Egypt, expecting the United States to join them. Dulles and Eisenhower opposed such action.

In the midst of the Suez crisis, Israel, in reaction to frequent Arab raids along its border, attacked Egypt. With the outbreak of war, Britain and France began bombing Egyptian targets, claiming that they were protecting the canal. The United States

---

*The original members of SEATO included the United States, Great Britain, France, Australia, New Zealand, Thailand, Pakistan, and the Philippines.

pressed Britain and France to stop the fighting before the war became a larger conflict. In the United Nations, the United States sponsored a resolution condemning the attack on Egypt. Faced with combined UN and United States pressure, Israel and its allies ended their invasion. Eventually the Suez Canal reopened under Egyptian control.

Although the Soviet Union had not been directly involved in the Suez Crisis, it had offered military and economic aid to Egypt. The threat of further Soviet activity in the Middle East could not be ruled out. To cope with that threat, President Eisenhower announced that the United States would offer financial support to Middle East countries that requested help against communist aggression. This policy became known as the Eisenhower Doctrine. In 1958 the Eisenhower Doctrine was used to justify the landing of United States marines in Lebanon as a show of force to end civil war there.

Revolution in Latin America

By the 1950s dictators had taken power in many Latin American countries. The United States government had maintained friendly relations with those dictators in the hopes that they would provide a strong defense against the possibility of revolution. Many Latin Americans resented the dictatorial rule of their leaders and believed that the dictators had been installed to protect the investments of United States corporations.

In 1958 a visit by Vice-President Richard Nixon to Peru and Venezuela revealed the depth of anti-American feeling. Angry mobs threw stones and eggs at the Vice-President and attacked his limousine. United States marines were alerted for possible intervention, but the Vice-President returned to Washington before serious violence occurred.

In 1959 a young lawyer named Fidel Castro led a successful revolution against the dictatorial regime of Fulgencio Batista (bah TEES tah). President Eisenhower recognized the new government a week after Castro took power. During the following months, however, Castro's policies resulted in increasingly tense relations with the United States. The Cuban economy was heavily dependent on the United States. For example,

Americans owned 80 percent of the Cuban utilities industry, 40 percent of its sugar plantations, and 90 percent of its mineral resources.

Castro believed that any attempt to strengthen the Cuban economy would have to begin by lessening the control of American private enterprise. In June 1960 the Cuban government seized several American- and British-owned oil refineries. President Eisenhower retaliated by reducing the quota of Cuban sugar exports to the United States. Relations worsened during the summer and fall of 1960, when the Cuban government seized more American businesses. In October President Eisenhower placed an embargo on trade with Cuba.

Major Events	
1945	United Nations founded
1947	Truman Doctrine and Marshall Plan announced
1948	State of Israel proclaimed; Soviet Union blockades Berlin
1949	NATO founded; Berlin blockade ends; Soviet Union tests atomic device; communists win civil war in China
1950	Korean War begins
1952	Dwight D. Eisenhower elected President
1953	Cease-fire in Korean War
1955	Summit conference in Geneva
1956	Hungarian uprising; Suez crisis begins
1959	Cuban revolution; Khrushchev visits the United States
1960	U-2 incident
1961	United States breaks off relations with Cuba

During this period Cuba was establishing close ties with the Soviet Union. In July 1960 Premier Khrushchev proclaimed that the Soviet Union would protect Cuba from any military attack by the United States. The Soviets began to supply Cuba with growing amounts of economic and military aid. By the end of 1960 Cuba was clearly moving into the Soviet camp. President Eisenhower broke off diplomatic relations with Cuba on January 3, 1961, 17 days before his term of office ended.

Between 1945 and 1960 the United States had strengthened its relationship with the industrialized nations of Europe and Asia. However, in the competition with the Soviet Union for the allegiance of other nations, the results were less certain. Furthermore, the arms race between the two powers continued to threaten the peace and security of the entire world.

For answers, see p. A 107.

Section Review

1. Identify the following: Ho Chi Minh, Dien Bien Phu, domino theory, SEATO, Gamal Abdel Nasser, Eisenhower Doctrine, Fidel Castro.

2. What did Hungarian nationalists demand during their uprising in 1956?

3. What led the United States to encourage France to stay in Vietnam?

4. What action did France and Britain take when Israel invaded Egypt in 1956?

5. What actions by Castro disrupted relations between the United States and Cuba?

IN PERSPECTIVE   International developments after World War II presented many challenges to the United States. Eastern Europe had fallen under Soviet influence, and communist movements in Greece and Italy challenged the governments in those countries. In China communist forces were struggling to seize power. By 1946 a cold war had broken out in Europe. President Truman declared that the United States would block further communist expansion. To enforce the policy of containment, the United States sponsored the Marshall Plan, organized the Berlin airlift, and joined NATO.

In Asia, the policy of containment was tested when North Korea invaded South Korea in 1950. After early defeats, the combined United Nations–United States force drove back the invaders. In 1953 a cease-fire restored the prewar border between North and South Korea. Dwight D. Eisenhower became President shortly before the end of the Korean War. During his administration, tensions between the United States and the Soviet Union relaxed until the U-2 incident.

Nationalism became an important international force during the 1950s. It contributed to a Hungarian uprising against Soviet control and the continuation of the Vietnamese war against France. Soviet influence increased in Egypt and Cuba as nationalists in those nations reacted against the western powers. Competition between the United States and the Soviet Union was to continue both in developing nations and in other parts of the world as you will read in Chapter 38.

Chapter Review

1. (a) What developments during World War II contributed to postwar tensions between the Soviet Union and the United States? (b) How did the Soviet Union defend its actions in eastern Europe? (c) What was the United States reaction to that defense?

2. (a) What were the goals of the United Nations? (b) What was the main responsibility of the Security Council? (c) What action could the council take to achieve that goal? (d) How were its actions limited?

3. Describe the postwar conditions that contributed to the cold war in each of the following areas: (a) Greece, (b) Italy, (c) Korea, (d) China.

4. (a) What was the Truman Doctrine? (b) Why did Truman implement it? (c) Was it successful? Explain.

5. (a) What was the Marshall Plan? (b) In what way was it a part of the policy of containment? (c) Was it successful? Explain.

6. (a) Why did the Soviet Union blockade Berlin? (b) How did the United States break the blockade?

7. (a) How did President Truman react to Mao's victory in China? (b) What was the American reaction to the Soviet test of an atomic bomb?

8. (a) How did the United States react to the North Korean invasion of South Korea? (b) Why did the goal of the UN and the United States change in October 1950? (c) What was the consequence of the invasion of North Korea?

9. (a) What led to a "thaw" in the cold war during the late 1950s? (b) What resulted from the 1955 summit conference between Khrushchev and Eisenhower? (c) What ended the thaw?

10. (a) Why did Nasser seize the Suez Canal in 1956? (b) How did Britain and France react? Why? (c) What role did the Soviet Union play in the war?

11. (a) What was the first reaction of the United States to the revolution led by Fidel Castro in Cuba? (b) Why did the American attitude toward Castro change?

For Further Thought

1. Would you agree with Senator Vandenberg that after the Soviets exploded their first atomic weapon, it was "now a different world"? Why or why not?

2. The United States had tried to stay out of European affairs since the nation was founded. However, in 1949 it entered into a military alliance with ten European nations. What developments contributed to the change in the long tradition of isolationism?

3. American aid was important for the political and economic recovery of many European nations after World War II. (a) Why was the United States in a position to offer such assistance? (b) Where do you think the aid was most important? Why? (c) What do you think might have happened if the United States had not been able to provide aid to Europe?

4. Do you think the policy of containment was generally successful between 1947 and 1960? Why or why not?

For answers, see p. A 108.

Developing Basic Skills

1. *Map Reading*   Locate the original members of the NATO alliance on the map on page 640. (Include the nations that joined in 1952 and 1954.) Then locate the members of the Warsaw Pact. (a) Where are the NATO nations located? (b) Where are the Warsaw Pact nations located? (c) How do you think that alignment of nations contributed to the fact that nations opposed to Soviet expansion are often called the West and pro-Soviet nations are called the East?

2. *Using Visual Evidence*   Study the photograph on page 643. Then answer the following questions: (a) What is being shown in the photograph? (b) How might a supporter of General MacArthur interpret the meaning of the photograph? (c) What issue led to a dispute between President Truman and MacArthur? (d) How was the dispute resolved? (e) What constitutional provision was reinforced by that outcome?

See page 779 for suggested readings.

A Search for Stability

(1945–1960)

The Kansas City Spirit, *by Norman Rockwell.*

Chapter Outline

1 *From War to Peace*

2 *The Cold War at Home*

3 *Stability Under Eisenhower*

4 *A Deceptive Calm*

American entry into World War II ended the Great Depression as orders for munitions and other war supplies revitalized industry. Yet no one was certain whether the return to peace would mean continued prosperity. The spirit of hard work and sacrifice displayed by Americans during the war years would be needed in the years ahead as well.

Once the war ended, Americans sought greater stability, as they had after World War I. Economic and political concerns plagued the early postwar years. The Cold War intruded upon American life and fed suspicions that some Americans were disloyal to their country. But by the mid-1950s many Americans thought they had found stability under President Dwight Eisenhower.

Despite the outward calm, the 1950s proved to be a time of important social change. Black Americans' demands for full equality were to grow during the period. Furthermore, a reevaluation of the educational system would lead to greater emphasis on science and mathematics in American schools.

1 From War to Peace

When World War II ended on August 14, 1945, Americans burst into demonstrations of joy and relief. But clouds loomed on the horizon. What could Americans expect from their new President? Would he follow the path of Franklin Roosevelt and extend New Deal benefits? Or would he end the reforms, as many Roosevelt critics urged? Above all, Americans feared that the end of wartime spending might mean a return to the high unemployment of the depression years.

Economic Issues

During World War II unemployment fell to an extreme low of 1.9 percent. The war brought high wages, but there were few consumer products to buy. Americans had saved a total of $44 billion during the war, and now they were eager to spend.

Such anticipation would turn to frustration, however. Throughout the war the government had established ceilings to keep prices and rents reasonable. As soon as Congress lifted the controls, rapid inflation struck. Prices soared upward as customers bought goods in short supply. Many people were willing to pay an extra dollar to get a scarce steak or offer an extra month's rent for an apartment. By 1948 prices were 48 percent higher than in 1945.

An almost unending string of strikes slowed the conversion from war to peace. As inflation cut into buying power, workers demanded large wage increases. When employers resisted their demands, the workers went out on strike. In January 1946 the steel, automobile, meatpacking, and electrical appliance industries were idled by strikes. Even gravediggers walked out. The nation seemed almost paralyzed.

Truman was especially angered when railroad workers walked off their jobs in May 1946. "What decent American would pull a strike at a time like this?" the President asked. Truman's efforts to resolve the dispute between railroad workers and management failed to produce a settlement. He then stunned the nation by asking a joint session of Congress for emergency power "to draft into the armed forces of the United States all workers who are on strike against their government."

Under that pressure the union quickly came to an agreement to end the strike. Liberals and conservatives alike condemned the President's abuse of the draft system. Senator Robert Taft of Ohio called the threat an offense against the Constitution, and labor leaders never quite forgave Truman.

Yet Truman had worked hard to smooth the conversion to peacetime. In 1944 Congress had passed the Servicemen's Readjustment Act, sometimes called the GI* Bill of Rights. It granted veterans a variety of benefits. A year of unemployment insurance provided income for veterans unable to find work. Those who attended college after the war received financial aid. The act also entitled veterans to government loans for building homes and starting businesses.

In the spirit of the New Deal, President Truman asked Congress to make "maximum employment, production, and purchasing power" a formal government responsibility. Conservative members of Congress opposed the request as an attempt to revive New Deal spending programs. As a result, the Employment Act passed in 1946 did little to spur employment. It did, however, make full employment a national goal. The act also established a Council of Economic Advisors to guide the President on economic matters. Unemployment rose to about 6 percent during the late 1940s but did not return to the levels of the Great Depression.

The Eightieth Congress

By the 1946 congressional elections, many voters were tired of inflation, shortages, and strikes. They blamed the President for their problems. One critic joked, "To err is Truman." Republicans referred to the President's problems in their campaign slogan, "Had enough?" and won a majority in both houses of Congress.

Most members of the Eightieth Congress, which convened in January 1947, believed that much of the New Deal legislation had undermined personal initiative and private enterprise. As a result, Truman faced a

---

*GI refers to a member of the United States armed forces. The term originated in soldiers' jokes that they, like their equipment, were "government issue."

hostile Congress. The legislature refused to pass bills to provide federal funds for public housing or education and rejected a federally financed medical insurance plan.

The most far-reaching action of the Eightieth Congress was passage of the Taft-Hartley Act. Enacted in 1947 over Truman's veto, the act reflected antiunion feeling generated by the epidemic of postwar strikes. According to the act, the attorney general could apply for a court order to delay for 80 days any strike endangering health or safety. Other provisions banned union contributions to political campaigns and the *closed shop*, in which all workers are required to be union members. Sponsors of the bill believed that closed shops denied workers the right to work without joining a union.

The Election of 1948

The Republicans expected victory in the presidential election of 1948. Their stunning gains in the 1946 congressional elections and Truman's sagging popularity indicated that the President could be defeated easily. The Republicans again nominated Governor Thomas E. Dewey of New York. Truman won the Democratic nomination.

Truman's candidacy was badly hampered by a split within his party. Southern Democrats, angry at Truman's support for civil rights legislation (see next column), broke with the Democratic party and established the States' Rights party. They nominated Governor Strom Thurmond of South Carolina for President. Meanwhile, other Democrats, unhappy with Truman's containment policy, formed a new Progressive party. The Progressives turned to Henry Wallace, Vice-President during Franklin Roosevelt's third term. Truman supporters feared that the candidacies of Thurmond and Wallace would draw Democratic voters away from the President.

Yet Truman refused to give up. In a vigorous campaign, he traveled over 20,000 miles (32,000 kilometers) and made nearly 300 speeches in eight weeks. He attacked what he called the "do-nothing" and "good-for-nothing" Eightieth Congress. Condemning that Congress as the "worst in history," Truman lashed out at the Republicans for opposing his social legislation.

On election day few doubted that Dewey would be the next President. Into the night Dewey supporters celebrated the anticipated victory. A Chicago *Daily Tribune* headline proclaimed, "Dewey Defeats Truman." But when all the votes were counted, Truman emerged as the victor with 49.5 percent of the popular vote compared to 45 percent for Dewey. He had managed the political upset of the century.

The Fair Deal

After the election the President declared, "Every segment of our population and every individual has the right to expect from his government a fair deal."

The Fair Deal Truman proposed would have extended the New Deal with a broad package of reform. He successfully worked for the passage of the National Housing Act of 1949, a measure that helped finance low-income housing. Also in 1949 Congress passed an amendment to the Fair Labor Standards Act (see page 584), raising the minimum hourly wage from 40 cents to 75 cents. The most important piece of Fair Deal legislation was probably the Social Security Act of 1950. That law increased the number of people covered under the old-age insurance provisions of the Social Security Act of 1935.

But Truman failed to accomplish some major objectives. Congress refused to repeal the Taft-Hartley Act and again rejected bills to provide federal aid to education and establish federally financed health insurance. Bills to ban the poll tax* and discrimination in employment were also defeated.

Extending Civil Rights

Although Truman was unable to persuade Congress to pass civil rights legislation, he did try to use his influence as chief executive to lessen discrimination against black Americans. Racial segregation persisted after World War II. In the North there was much *de facto segregation*, that is, segregation that existed in fact if not in law. In the South, Jim Crow laws separated black and white public facilities. Blacks could not sit at the counters in most coffee shops. They attended segregated schools and movie theaters and were

---

*As you read in Chapter 22, poll taxes were fees a person had to pay in order to vote. They had been used to prevent poor blacks from voting.

Jackie Robinson was the first black baseball player on a major league team. He played infield for the Brooklyn Dodgers.

restricted to separate sections on buses and in other public facilities.

Yet some change was apparent. In 1947, for example, Jackie Robinson became the first black man to play on a major league baseball team. Blacks had previously been allowed to play only in all-black leagues. During and after the war there were also some public demonstrations against segregation in dining and recreational facilities.

In September 1946 representatives from an antilynching organization visited the President to protest violence against blacks. The President publicly condemned lynchings, declaring that Americans could not tolerate "acts of intimidation and violence in our . . . communities."

Truman also created the President's Committee on Civil Rights. In 1947 the committee issued a report entitled *To Secure These Rights.* The report called for "the elimination of segregation from American life." Although the committee had no authority to enforce its suggestions, it did inform the public of the injustice of segregation.

In 1948 Truman issued a directive banning segregation in the armed forces. The executive order proclaimed that it was "the policy of the President that there shall be equality of treatment and opportunity for all persons in the armed services." Desegregation of the military proceeded slowly during the late 1940s, but by 1951 most units in the Korean War were integrated.

In order to reduce discrimination in employment Truman reaffirmed Franklin Roosevelt's executive order banning discrimination in firms doing business with the federal government. Early in 1952 the President created the Committee on Contracts Compliance to investigate instances in which employers receiving government contracts had discriminated against minorities. The committee, however, lacked enforcement powers, and it proved ineffective in curbing discrimination. Nonetheless, President Truman's actions in support of greater civil rights contributed to a movement that would grow stronger in the 1950s and 1960s, as you will read later in this chapter and the next.

For answers, see p. A 108.

Section Review

1. Identify the following: Taft-Hartley Act, Thomas E. Dewey, States' Rights party, Progressive party.

2. Define the following terms: closed shop, de facto segregation.

3. How did American workers react to postwar inflation?

4. What were the major provisions of the GI Bill of Rights?

5. What was the attitude of the Eightieth Congress to social welfare legislation?

6. List three measures that were part of Truman's Fair Deal.

7. What actions did President Truman take to reduce racial discrimination in employment?

2 The Cold War at Home

The cold war that developed between the United States and the Soviet Union after World War II divided much of the world into opposing blocs. It also began to divide Americans at home. Many people resented the New Deal, the strikes by labor unions, and other dislocations caused by the war. Some blamed national problems on people they considered subversive or disloyal to the country.

A Question of Loyalty

As the cold war intensified, many Americans grew increasingly intolerant of anyone who was sympathetic toward communism or the Soviet Union. Although the Communist party in the United States was small and had little influence, people worried that it might harbor Soviet spies.

In 1947 President Truman recognized public concern about communism and created the Loyalty Review Board. The purpose of the board was to guarantee the "unswerving loyalty" of all employees of the federal government. Truman created the board even though he personally did not believe that any government employees were disloyal to the nation. When the board revealed that some people of "doubtful loyalty" were on the federal payroll, critics charged that Truman had been unmindful of the dangers of communism.

Other investigations increased public concern about the potential influence of communists in the United States. The House of Representatives had created the Un-American Activities Committee (HUAC) in 1938 to investigate possible subversive activity by fascists or communists. After the war it focused on communist activity. The committee held hearings on alleged communist activity in the movie industry in 1947. Although there was rarely any solid evidence, the hearings tarnished the reputations of a number of writers, producers, and performers. The committee also pressed filmmakers to adopt a "blacklist" barring employment to anyone suspected of being a communist.

In 1948 HUAC began an investigation of disloyalty in government. Whittaker Chambers, a former member of the Communist party, testified that a state department official, Alger Hiss, had belonged to the party during the 1930s. Chambers also charged that Hiss had given him official state department documents to pass on to Soviet agents. Chambers then led investigators to his farm, where he had hidden microfilmed documents in a pumpkin.

In 1950 Hiss was convicted of perjury, or lying under oath, because he had denied to the committee that he knew Chambers. Hiss's conviction convinced many Americans that President Truman had been too hasty when he had dismissed claims that communists had infiltrated the government.

But nothing generated more concern about internal security than the charge that some Americans had secretly helped the Soviets build an atomic bomb. Dr. Klaus Fuchs, a British subject, had been a member of the research team that developed the atomic bomb at Los Alamos, New Mexico. In February 1950 British authorities arrested Fuchs and charged him with sending atomic secrets to the Soviet Union. Fuchs pleaded guilty and agreed to reveal the workings of the Los Alamos spy ring.

The Fuchs case led to the arrest of Ethel and Julius Rosenberg, both American citizens, in the summer of 1950. The Rosenbergs were charged with passing atomic secrets to

Soviet agents. A jury found them guilty of spying, and they were executed in 1953. The widely publicized cases of Hiss and the Rosenbergs increased public anxiety and contributed to the rise to prominence of a Republican senator from Wisconsin.

McCarthyism

Senator Joseph R. McCarthy of Wisconsin seized on American fear about disloyalty in government and almost overnight became the most controversial senator in the nation.

Much of the controversy surrounding McCarthy stemmed from the scope of his accusations. In a speech delivered February 9, 1950, in Wheeling, West Virginia, McCarthy claimed that he had the names of 205 state department employees who were members of the Communist party. The charge provoked a furor. Later McCarthy said he meant there were "205 bad security risks" in the department. Then he claimed that 57 employees were communists. In subsequent speeches he used different numbers. It was impossible for the state department to refute such a variety of accusations.

For four years Senator McCarthy continued to denounce his enemies. He charged that the Democratic party had been guilty of "twenty years of treason." He called for

Truman's impeachment, maintained that General George C. Marshall had been "an instrument of the Soviet conspiracy," and hinted that President Eisenhower was not sufficiently anticommunist.

McCarthy's influence was so great during the early 1950s that people came to use the term "McCarthyism" to refer to his technique of making sweeping accusations, frequently without evidence. Although his investigations revealed little anti-American activity, he persuaded millions that he was protecting national security. Even though he was unable to prove most of his accusations, the publicity he created ruined the reputations of many scholars and other public figures for years to come.

McCarthy's Fall

McCarthy's recklessness, which had been his source of strength, eventually caused his downfall. When his assistant, David Schine, was drafted into the army in 1954, McCarthy allowed his top aide, Roy Cohn, to press the army to make Schine an officer. The army rebuffed Cohn's efforts. Soon a major controversy developed over the Schine case. In April 1954 the Senate held hearings to air the differences between McCarthy and the army. The Army-McCarthy hearings were

Senator Joseph McCarthy (with map) charged that communists had infiltrated many areas of American life. In 1954 he accused the United States Army of misconduct. In this photograph McCarthy testifies before the Senate in the Army-McCarthy hearings. At left is the army counsel, Joseph Welch. The televised hearings diminished McCarthy's popularity, and in December 1954 the Senate censured him for "conduct unbecoming a member."

televised and ran for a total of 187 hours. On some days as many as 20 million people watched the hearings.

McCarthy claimed that there were many communists at the Fort Monmouth, New Jersey, army base. He charged that the army was holding Schine as a "hostage" to discourage an investigation of Fort Monmouth. This time McCarthy had gone too far. Television cameras focused on McCarthy's abrasive manner. The army's lawyer, Joseph Welch, subjected the senator's case to intense examination. For many Americans, McCarthy emerged from the hearing as a bully, not a hero.

In December 1954 the Senate passed a resolution condemning McCarthy for "conduct unbecoming a member." The censure resolution eroded McCarthy's popular appeal, and he soon ceased to be a national political force.

For answers, see p. A 109.

Section Review

1. Identify the following: House Un-American Activities Committee, Joseph R. McCarthy, McCarthyism.
2. What was the purpose of the Loyalty Review Board?
3. List two developments that helped heighten public concern about communist activity in the United States.
4. How did Joseph McCarthy rise to national prominence?
5. What event led to McCarthy's decline?

3 Stability Under Eisenhower

Senator McCarthy's accusations of treason in high places and the seemingly endless war in Korea undermined President Truman's popularity. He decided not to run again in 1952. Voters wanted someone who could bring stability, prosperity, and peace to the nation.

Victory for the Republicans

In 1952 the Democratic party nominated Governor Adlai E. Stevenson of Illinois for President and Senator John J. Sparkman of Alabama for Vice-President. The Republicans chose Dwight D. Eisenhower as their presidential candidate and Senator Richard M. Nixon of California as his running mate.

The race was uneven from the start. Stevenson was virtually unknown outside Illinois, and the public considered him too intellectual. Opponents labeled Stevenson an "egghead." Eisenhower, on the other hand, was a national hero. He had commanded the United States forces in Europe during World War II and the American occupation forces in Germany after the war. From 1948 to 1951, Eisenhower served as president of Columbia University. He also possessed great personal appeal.

The Republicans, who had not won a presidential election since 1928, fought a hard campaign. They reminded voters that Truman had once scoffed at the charge that communists filled important posts in the federal government. They also blamed the Democrats for the stalemate in Korea. Eisenhower promised to break the deadlock by going to Korea personally.

Eisenhower won by a landslide, receiving nearly 34 million votes compared to 27 million for Stevenson. Four years later, in 1956, Eisenhower ran against Stevenson again and beat him by an even larger margin.

As President, Eisenhower took a moderate political course. He condemned two of McCarthy's assistants, but he refused to denounce McCarthy personally until the Wisconsin senator had passed the height of his power. While Eisenhower resisted demands to dismantle New Deal programs, he also refused to work for new social legislation.

Government and the Economy

President Eisenhower and the Republican-controlled Congress tried to reduce the government's role in the economy. Congress limited federal aid for public housing and ended the wage and price controls established by the Truman administration. Furthermore, Congress transferred offshore oil fields, previously under federal control, to state control. The secretary of agriculture reduced federal aid to farmers.

The American people generally prospered during the Eisenhower years. Unemployment hovered at about 5 percent. Industrial wages increased somewhat, but inflation lowered purchasing power. Nonetheless, inflation was not as serious as in the years immediately following the war. The gross national product, the total of goods and services produced during a given year, climbed upward until 1957, when the economy was hit by a serious recession, or economic downturn.

Eisenhower's handling of the 1957–1958 recession reflected his belief that the government should not control the economy. When unemployment reached 6.8 percent in 1958, the Democrats called for New Deal–style public works projects to stimulate the economy. But Eisenhower refused to aid the economy with federal money.

In a 1958 speech, delivered after economic recovery had begun, the President declared that it was wrong to believe "that when the economy starts to slow up, only a vast outpouring of . . . tax dollars will pump us out of trouble." He maintained that increased federal spending would create a false prosperity and increase inflation. "Huge programs," he argued, "would have only enfeebled the economy." Eisenhower survived Democratic criticism as the economy slowly recovered. By 1959 unemployment had returned to 5 percent.

Life in the 1950s

One of the most profound social changes in the 1950s was the rapid growth of suburbs. Several factors encouraged that growth. A postwar "baby boom" created a need for new housing, while the prosperity of the period enabled many people to buy their own homes. The GI Bill of Rights also provided federal aid for veterans seeking home-loan mortgages. Furthermore, a massive postwar road-building program linked suburban homes to city jobs.

During the 1950s the suburbs became increasingly self-contained. While suburban residents of the 1920s had depended on the city for entertainment and shopping, the postwar suburban dweller could find a vast array of goods and services in nearby shopping plazas.

After the war, most of the women who had entered the work force returned to being homemakers. Managing a home in the

Presidential candidate Dwight David Eisenhower, the five-star general who had commanded United States armies in Europe during the war, accepts the cheers of the 1952 Republican convention. Nominated as his running mate was a young California congressman, Richard Nixon (at left). Americans were weary of the drawn-out Korean War, and Eisenhower promised to go to Korea to end it.

suburbs and raising a family became the goal of many women during the 1950s. The popular culture of the period reinforced their view of women's role in society. Some commentators argued that women could not compete with men in the business world. Others blamed a rise in crime among young people on the fact that more mothers were working outside the home.

Newspapers, magazines, and especially television had an impact on the perception of women's role in society. Since the beginning of national network broadcasting in 1946, the popularity of television had risen dramatically. During the 1950s almost 7 million television sets were sold each year. Most commercials showed only women doing domestic tasks. Popular programs such as *Father Knows Best* seldom portrayed them with other careers. The view that women should only be homemakers was reinforced through the decade.

Religion played an especially important part in American life during the 1950s. Church membership grew twice as fast as the population. The Reverend Norman Vincent Peale wrote a best seller, *The Power of*

657

After two decades of depression and war, the United States went on a building binge in the 1950s. In the surging postwar prosperity, millions of new homes were built, spilling suburban development into former farmlands. Techniques of mass production helped produce suburbs like Levittown, New York, shown here. Levittown had 17,477 low-priced houses, all with the same floor plan. With the GI bill, veterans could buy such homes with low down payments that allowed millions to become homeowners.

658

During the Battle of Britain in World War II, nightly radio reports by Edward R. Murrow had brought the sounds of the war to Americans. With the rapid spread of television in the 1950s, Murrow emerged as one of the most respected television reporters. He was among the first to make television documentaries that reported in depth on American life.

Positive Thinking, which stressed the need for religion in a successful life. Religion on television was also influential. For example, Bishop Fulton J. Sheen hosted a popular program, and the Reverend Billy Graham led a television crusade that gave his ministry national attention.

The growing religious feeling among many Americans was one indication of their search for stability and peace. Religious faith became closely linked with patriotism. As President Eisenhower stated, "our government makes no sense unless it is founded in a deeply felt religious faith." In 1954 Congress added the words "under God" to the Pledge of Allegiance to the Flag.

For answers, see p. A 109.

Section Review

1. Identify the following: Adlai E. Stevenson.
2. List two advantages Dwight Eisenhower had in the election of 1952.
3. What was President Eisenhower's attitude toward the government's role in the economy?
4. List two factors that encouraged the growth of suburbs after World War II.
5. What was the goal of many American women during the 1950s?

4 A Deceptive Calm

For most Americans the 1950s was a period of general stability. Yet beneath the surface calm, developments were occurring that would greatly affect the future. Black Americans increased their demands for civil rights. Young people adopted a new music that shocked many parents. Social critics lamented the national emphasis on conformity. And an impatient public demanded a more rigorous education for American youth.

Early Steps Against Segregation

In the 1896 case of *Plessy* v. *Ferguson* the Supreme Court had ruled that "separate but equal" facilities for blacks and whites were constitutional. (See page 410.) That decision had provided the legal basis for segregation. During the 1940s the National Association for the Advancement of Colored People had begun to attack the "separate but equal" principle by suing segregated colleges and universities. As a result the University of Texas and the University of Oklahoma as well as several other southern colleges admitted black students. However, elementary and secondary schools remained segregated.

In the early 1950s the NAACP filed suit against the Board of Education of Topeka, Kansas, on behalf of Linda Brown. The board had denied Brown admission to an all-white school. The case reached the Supreme Court in 1954.

Brown's lawyer, Thurgood Marshall, charged that public school segregation violated the "equal protection" clause of the Fourteenth Amendment to the Constitution. He maintained that segregation deprived black children of an equal educational opportunity. Separate could not be equal, the NAACP argued, because segregation in itself lowered the morale and motivation of black students.

In *Brown* v. *Board of Education of Topeka*, the Supreme Court ruled that "separate educational facilities are inherently unequal." "The doctrine of 'separate but equal,'" it held, "has no place in public education." A year later the Court ordered school integration to proceed "with all deliberate speed."

The Court's decision sparked an angry reaction among many southern officials who considered the ruling a threat to state and local authority. President Eisenhower believed

Brown v. Board of Education of Topeka

In 1954 the Supreme Court reversed the 1896 ruling in *Plessy* v. *Ferguson*, which had stated that separate facilities for blacks and whites were legal if they were equal. In *Brown* v. *Board of Education of Topeka* the Court ruled unanimously that "separate but equal" facilities were unconstitutional. In the excerpt from the decision printed below, Chief Justice Earl Warren describes the importance of education in American society.

Today, education is perhaps the most important function of state and local governments. Compulsory school-attendance laws and the great expenditures for education both demonstrate our recognition of the importance of education to our democratic society. It is required in the performance of our most basic public responsibilities, even service in the armed forces. It is the very foundation of good citizenship. Today it is a principal instrument in awakening the child to cultural values, in preparing him for later professional training, and in helping him to adjust normally to his environment. In these days, it is doubtful that any child may reasonably be expected to succeed in life if he is denied the opportunity of an education. Such an opportunity, where the state has undertaken to provide it, is a right which must be made available to all on equal terms.

We come then to the question presented: Does segregation of children in public schools solely on the basis of race, even though the physical facilities and other "tangible" factors may be equal, deprive the children of the minority group of equal educational opportunities? We believe that it does.

that the government should not try to force integration, but in 1957 he decided he had to intervene.

The governor of Arkansas had called in the National Guard to prevent a group of black students from attending Little Rock Central High School. In reaction to the governor's open defiance of federal authority, President Eisenhower sent troops to Little Rock, and the students entered the school. Resistance to school integration remained strong in some parts of the country, but the Supreme Court ruling was a significant step toward greater equality.

Black citizens also increased their use of organized public protest against continued segregation. In December 1955 Rosa Parks, a

In 1957 black students tried to enroll in formerly all-white public schools in Little Rock, Arkansas, but the governor called out the National Guard to stop them. In response, President Eisenhower sent federal troops to protect the students. Below, federal troops are shown guarding the first black students (on bottom stairs at left) to attend Central High.

Under segregation laws, blacks had to sit in the back of public buses if whites needed a seat. One day in 1955 Rosa Parks refused a bus driver's order to give up her seat to a white person. She was promptly arrested. The arrest led to a year-long boycott of the bus system by black citizens in Montgomery, Alabama. In 1956, after the United States Supreme Court ruled against segregation on public transportation, Rosa Parks, shown above, sat in the front of a Montgomery bus.

black woman, was arrested for refusing to move from the "white" section of a bus in Montgomery, Alabama. Black citizens quickly organized a boycott of the bus line. The Reverend Martin Luther King, Jr., led the year-long boycott. He advocated *civil disobedience*, that is, nonviolent protest against an unjust law or condition, as the best way to fight segregation.

The bus company finally agreed to integrate the buses and hire black drivers after the Supreme Court ruled that bus segregation violated the Constitution. Early on the morning of December 21, 1956, Reverend King signaled the end of the boycott by boarding one of Montgomery's newly integrated buses.

Protest against segregation grew as Eisenhower's term drew to a close. On February 1, 1960, a group of black college students were denied service at a department store lunch counter in Greensboro, North Carolina. The students refused to leave their seats at the lunch counter until closing time.

After several months of such "sit-ins," the lunch counter agreed to serve blacks and whites equally. Sit-ins spread to many southern communities. Within 18 months of the Greensboro protest, 70,000 people had participated in sit-ins throughout the South. Integrated eating facilities were won in a hundred communities. The sit-in movement drew national attention to the problem of segregation, as you will read in Chapter 38.

A Crisis in Education

In October 1957 the Soviet Union launched the first satellite into orbit around the earth. Americans had long believed that superior technology would keep the United States ahead of the Soviet Union. The successful *Sputnik I* flight undermined that confidence. National confidence was shaken further when the first American attempts to launch a satellite failed. In January 1958 the United States put a satellite, *Explorer I*, into orbit.

Concerned Americans charged that the nation had fallen behind in space technology because of weaknesses in education. Several months after the Sputnik launch, *Life*, a popular weekly magazine, featured a series of articles called "The Crisis in Education." The articles reported that American educational standards were "shockingly low." Many parents agreed that the schools had failed to challenge young people. Critics demanded a rigorous curriculum with heavy emphasis on science and mathematics. These subjects, it was argued, held the key to victory in the new "space race."

Congress responded to the criticism by passing the National Defense Education Act in 1958. The act provided federal aid to schools and colleges, especially for projects designed to improve instruction in science and math. Congress also increased the budget of the National Science Foundation, which provided research grants to scientists and funded curriculum projects.

New Forms in the Arts

During the 1930s and 1940s popular music had been dominated by the sentimental melodies of such "crooners" as Bing Crosby and Frank Sinatra and by the "big band" sound of such musicians as Glenn Miller and Duke Ellington. In the early 1950s a new type of popular music came into being. Rock 'n' roll, as the new music was called, was a uniquely American sound. It blended elements from country-and-western music with rhythm and blues. American teenagers liked the strong beat, repeated harmonies, and loud volume.

However, some people objected to the hair styles, clothing, and dance styles of rock stars like Elvis Presley, Chuck Berry, and Buddy Holly. Some complained about the volume of the music and the lyrics, which they could not understand. Others actually thought that rock music would contribute to teenage crime. A 1955 movie, *Blackboard Jungle* reinforced such concern. The film portrayed delinquent teenagers in a tough city high school and included the song "Rock Around the Clock," recorded by Bill Haley and the Comets.

Despite such objections, rock became the music of American youth. Rock stars became internationally famous, and rock 'n' roll

The new sound of the 1950s was rock 'n' roll. Like jazz, rock 'n' roll was an American music form that appealed to people around the world. One of its originators was Buddy Holly (shown with guitar). A plane crash in 1959 cut short his career.

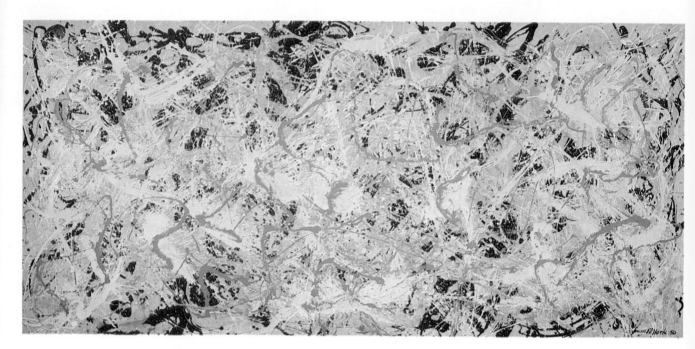

By the 1950s a group of American painters called abstract expressionists had become a major force in world art. Because many of them worked or exhibited their art in New York City, they were also known as the New York School. Foremost among them was Jackson Pollock. In his finest paintings , such as this one, entitled Number 27, *he applied swirling lines of color with the drip and splash technique that he originated.*

still fills the air waves today. In the 1950s the driving beat of rock stood in sharp contrast to the quiet tone of much of the Eisenhower era.

After the war the visual arts underwent a minor revolution. American artists led an international movement away from realistic representation to a form known as abstract expressionism. Visitors to museums and galleries were often puzzled by what appeared to be little more than paint randomly splashed on canvasses. But the abstract expressionists were serious artists. Some, such as Jackson Pollock, used swirling colors to absorb the viewer in emotion. Other painters offered engaging repetitions of colors and lines.

While abstract expressionism led the viewer away from conventional representations of reality, "pop art" portrayed objects with cameralike precision. Pop art, which emerged during the late 1950s, made common items like soup cans and soda bottles the subject of art. Andy Warhol and Roy Lichtenstein emerged as leading figures of the pop art movement during the 1960s.

A Sense of Disillusionment

Although most people seemed content with American society during the 1950s, a few criticized the established order. One group, labeled "beatniks," refused to conform to accepted ways of dressing, thinking, and acting. Conformity, they insisted, stifled individualism. They ridiculed American attachment to material success and lived in voluntary poverty. The "beatniks" displayed their differences from American society by informal dress and colorful jargon.

Some social scientists wrote scholarly critiques of American society. William H. Whyte argued in his book *The Organization Man* (1956) that bureaucratic organizations tended to discourage creativity and individualism. In *The Lonely Crowd* (1950), David Riesman charged that many Americans cared too much about pleasing others. Riesman also lamented the power of advertising to mold public tastes.

Economist John Kenneth Galbraith argued that unplanned economic growth had resulted in great private fortunes but had left the public sector impoverished. In his book *The Affluent Society* (1958), Galbraith called for more resources to be invested in schools, theaters, and other public facilities.

In 1959 a scandal on a television quiz show convinced some critics that their concerns about American society were well founded. Charles Van Doren, a Columbia University instructor, revealed that the show's producers had given him the correct answers enabling him to win thousands of dollars.

Some Americans saw signs of national decline in the misconduct of Van Doren and the television executives. Novelist John Steinbeck claimed, "on all levels American society is rigged. . . . I am troubled by the cynical immorality of my country. It cannot survive on this basis." An article in the magazine *Look* lamented the emergence of "the freedom to chisel." Such feelings of disillusionment became a campaign issue in the presidential election of 1960.

The Election of 1960

In 1960 the Republicans nominated Vice-President Richard M. Nixon as their presidential candidate. Henry Cabot Lodge, Jr., of Massachusetts won the Republican nomination for Vice-President. The Democratic party nominated John F. Kennedy, a young senator from Massachusetts, for President and chose Senator Lyndon B. Johnson of Texas as his running mate.

Kennedy focused his campaign on the vague sense that the country was drifting under Eisenhower. The senator took advantage of his strong public image and promised to "get America moving again." In nationally publicized televised debates between Kennedy and Nixon, Kennedy seemed confident and vigorous while Nixon appeared nervous and unsure of himself.

During the campaign, Kennedy argued that the Republicans had allowed the Soviet Union to achieve nuclear superiority over the United States. He charged that there was a "missile gap," which he would close if elected President. Nixon campaigned on Eisenhower's record, stressing the peace and prosperity the United States had enjoyed under the Republicans. Although neither candidate made an issue of the fact that Kennedy was Catholic, his religion probably gained him votes in eastern cities and hurt his candidacy in rural areas and in the West.

The election was close. Kennedy received 34,227,096 popular votes to Nixon's

Televised debates between Richard Nixon (left) and John Kennedy (right) in 1960 marked a first in presidential elections. For the first time, millions of voters could watch and compare the candidates as they discussed the same points.

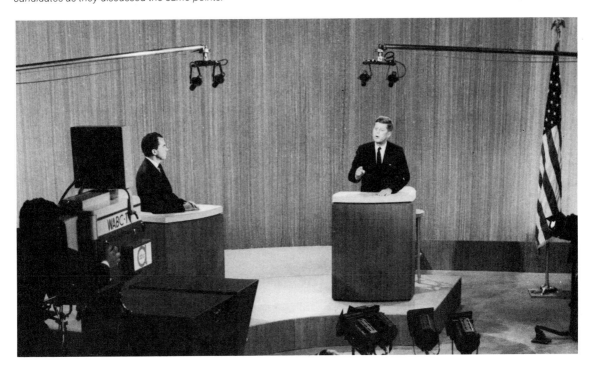

Major Events

1944	GI Bill of Rights passed
1947	Taft-Hartley Act passed
1948	Truman orders end to segregation in armed forces; Truman reelected
1950	McCarthy charges there are communists in government
1952	Dwight D. Eisenhower elected President
1954	Army-McCarthy hearings; *Brown v. Board of Education of Topeka*
1955	Montgomery bus boycott
1957	Eisenhower orders troops to Little Rock; *Sputnik I* launched
1958	National Defense Education Act passed
1960	Sit-in movement begins; John F. Kennedy elected President

34,108,546, but in the electoral college Kennedy won by 303 to 219. At 43 years of age, Kennedy was the youngest person and first Catholic to be elected President of the United States.

For answers, see p. A 109.

Section Review

1. Identify the following: Rosa Parks, Martin Luther King, Jr., *Sputnik I*, rock 'n' roll, beatniks, Richard M. Nixon, John F. Kennedy.
2. Define the following term: civil disobedience.
3. (a) What did the Supreme Court rule in *Brown v. Board of Education of Topeka?* (b) What action did President Eisenhower take to enforce the Court ruling in Little Rock, Arkansas?
4. What two tactics did black Americans begin to use against segregation during the 1950s?
5. How did Congress react to public outcry about the launch of *Sputnik I*?
6. Give two examples of new art forms that developed during the 1950s.
7. (a) List two issues John Kennedy campaigned on in 1960. (b) What issues did Richard Nixon campaign on?

★ ★ ★ ★ ★ ★ ★ ★ ★ ★ ★ ★ ★ ★ ★ ★ ★ ★ ★ ★

IN PERSPECTIVE The transition from war to peace was troubled by unemployment, inflation, and strikes. Discontent over these problems led many to believe that President Truman would be beaten easily in the election of 1948. However, Truman won and began to institute his Fair Deal program. He also used presidential authority to reduce discrimination against black Americans.

The Cold War contributed to anxieties about the potential threat of communism at home. The discovery of a few cases of disloyal activity fed such fears, and Senator Joseph McCarthy charged that many communists were active in high levels of government. McCarthy's investigations uncovered little evidence of such activity, and his popularity declined after the televised Army-McCarthy hearings.

Dwight D. Eisenhower, who easily won the election in 1952, pursued a moderate course. Although he resisted demands to use government action to end the recession of 1957–1958, he did not dismantle any New Deal programs. The Eisenhower years were generally viewed as a time of stability, but there were some significant social changes. The Supreme Court ruled that segregation in public schools was unconstitutional, and black citizens increased protest against segregation. The Soviet launching of *Sputnik I* shocked Americans into demanding a more rigorous educational system. In the 1960 presidential election, John F. Kennedy promised "to get America moving again."

For answers, see p. A 110.

Chapter Review

1. (a) What economic problems confronted the nation after World War II? (b) What were the basic causes of those problems? (c) What actions did the government take to try to solve them?

2. (a) Why did the Republicans win a majority in both houses of Congress in 1946? (b) What impact did the Eightieth Congress have on Truman's legislative program? (c) What parts of Truman's Fair Deal did Congress pass after the 1948 election? (d) What parts of the Fair Deal failed to pass?

3. (a) How did segregation differ in the North and the South? (b) Describe how President Truman advanced the civil rights of black Americans.

4. Why did the American public become increasingly concerned about the potential danger of communist activity at home? Give specific examples to support your answer.

5. (a) What type of charges did Senator Joseph McCarthy make? (b) What effect did he have? (c) Why did he eventually cease to be a political force?

6. (a) Describe general economic conditions during President Eisenhower's administration. (b) How did Eisenhower react to the recession of 1957–1958? Why?

7. (a) Why did suburbs grow dramatically during the 1950s? (b) How were they different from the suburbs of the 1920s?

8. (a) How did the Supreme Court decision in *Brown* v. *Board of Education of Topeka* differ from the 1896 Court decision on racial segregation? (b) What arguments did the NAACP lawyer make against "separate but equal" facilities? (c) Why did President Eisenhower decide to send troops to Little Rock?

9. (a) Why was the launching of *Sputnik I* by the Soviet Union a shock to most Americans? (b) What did many people blame for that development?

10. Why were some people disillusioned by American society during the 1950s? Give specific examples to support your answer.

For answers, see p. A 111.

For Further Thought

1. Review what you learned about the attitude of the United States toward the Soviet Union after World War II. (See Chapter 36.) What relationship do you see between foreign policy and the domestic politics you studied in this chapter?

2. (a) How do you think McCarthyism was similar to the Red Scare of 1920? (See page 522.) (b) How was it different?

3. How did President Eisenhower's attitude toward government activity in the economy differ from President Truman's?

4. Why do you think some people objected to the rock music of the 1950s?

For answers, see p. A 111.

Developing Basic Skills

1. *Using Visual Evidence* A popular song in 1962 described suburban homes as little boxes that all looked the same. Study the photograph of Levitown, New York, on page 658. (a) Using that picture as evidence, do you think the words of the song accurately describe the suburb shown? (b) In what way is the evidence limited? (c) Find out if there are any suburbs that grew up in the 1950s near where you live. Does the song accurately describe those suburbs?

2. *Relating Past to Present* Observe how women are portrayed in television commercials today. (a) How does the view presented of women's roles in society differ from that presented in 1950s commercials? (b) How are the views similar?

3. *Collecting Evidence* Interview a friend or relative who lived during the 1950s. Ask the person what he or she remembers about the following topics: McCarthyism, television programs, the launching of Sputnik, the beginning of rock 'n' roll. Compare the person's recollections with what you have read in the text. (a) How are they similar? (b) How are they different? (c) What did you learn about life in the 1950s through your interview?

See page 779 for suggested readings.

38

A Turbulent Decade

(1960–1969)

The launching of a space flight.

The decade of the 1960s dawned with promise for the American people. The youthful confidence of John F. Kennedy, the nation's youngest President, reflected the hopes of many citizens for an era of economic, social, and technological progress. Such goals as human space flight, the elimination of poverty, and the achievement of social justice appeared within reach.

Yet the decade progressed differently than most Americans could have guessed. Blacks, Hispanics, Native Americans, and women pressed for an equal share of economic and social opportunities. On college campuses, students joined protest movements. In many cities, the desperation of Americans living in ghettos erupted in riots.

Foreign affairs contributed to the growing turmoil. The United States gradually became more deeply involved in the affairs of a small country thousands of miles away. By the end of the decade, over 500,000 Americans had been sent to fight in Vietnam. What began as student opposition to the war spread through the nation as a whole. Genuine progress was made in technology, the war on poverty, and the fight for civil rights during the 1960s. But debate over how to achieve the goals shared by most Americans left the nation divided.

1 Increased World Tension

When John Kennedy took office in January 1961 the cold war still dominated relations between the Soviet Union and the United States. During President Kennedy's administration, a series of international crises threatened to erupt into actual warfare between the two nations.

The Kennedy Team

John Fitzgerald Kennedy brought to the White House a combination of youth, intelligence, and ideals, tempered by an eye for practical politics. He had used his charisma, family wealth, and organizational skills to achieve political success. However, Kennedy recognized that as President, his youth might be viewed as a liability. Consequently he chose his cabinet and advisers carefully. He appointed respected experts from the academic world and former military leaders, including a few Republicans.

The man who most symbolized the dynamism of the new administration was Secretary of Defense Robert McNamara. McNamara had been part of a young group of administrators known as the "whiz kids," who had helped save the Ford Motor Company from bankruptcy during the 1950s. McNamara was eventually appointed company president before coming to Washington to serve under President Kennedy.

A Shift in Foreign Relations

Despite President Eisenhower's military background, he had pursued a moderate defense policy. In the years following the Sputnik launching, for example, government expenditures on military weapons rose only 2 percent. When Eisenhower left office, he warned against the "unwarranted influence" that could come to be exerted by what he labeled "the military-industrial complex." However, during the 1960 campaign, John Kennedy spoke of a "missile gap." He claimed that the Soviet Union had a superior arsenal of military weapons, especially long-range missiles. Consequently he stepped up military spending once in office.

In the wake of the Cuban revolution, President Kennedy also wanted the armed forces to be prepared to combat possible Soviet-supported revolutions around the world. Premier Khrushchev had pledged Soviet support for such "wars of liberation."

To counter potential uprisings, the Kennedy administration began to develop *strategic forces*, that is, specially trained units that could be moved quickly to any part of the world. At Fort Bragg, North Carolina, and in the American-controlled Panama Canal Zone, the armed forces established jungle warfare schools to teach guerrilla fighting techniques.

Kennedy did not limit American response to the Soviet challenge to military measures. He also proposed a new type of foreign aid through the Peace Corps. The Peace Corps was to be composed of Americans volunteering to teach or to contribute technical advice in developing countries. Such foreign aid was designed to build

The youngest person ever elected President, John Kennedy, shown here, held a special appeal for young people. In his inaugural speech, he struck a responsive chord in young and old alike as he said, "Ask not what your country can do for you. Ask what you can do for your country."

friendship with countries in Africa, Asia, and South America. Further, President Kennedy hoped that such aid would persuade neutral nations that western-style democracy offered the best way to achieve peace, stability, and economic growth.

In 1961 the administration moved to improve relations with Latin American countries by organizing the Alliance for Progress. The United States pledged approximately $20 billion in aid to Latin American countries over a ten-year period. Latin American nations were to invest some $80 billion of their own funds in economic development.

Members of the alliance were required to reform unjust land or tax policies in order to develop more democratic economic systems and thereby reduce the chances of violent revolution. President Kennedy warned that, "those who make peaceful revolution impossible will make violent revolution inevitable." Although few governments were eager to comply with the reform provisions of the Alliance for Progress, its creation did improve the image of the United States among Latin American nations.

Trouble in the Bay of Pigs

Whatever goodwill the United States won through the Alliance for Progress was soon undermined when the Kennedy administration attempted to overthrow the government of Cuba. By the end of the Eisenhower administration the Central Intelligence Agency (CIA) had begun training anti-Castro Cuban exiles for such a task.

President Kennedy was briefed on the plan and told that with United States air support, success was likely. A secret invasion force trained in Guatemala was to land at the Bay of Pigs in Cuba. The assault group was to join up with anti-Castro forces in the mountains and march on Havana, the capital.

Convinced that Castro lacked support from the Cuban people, Kennedy allowed the invasion to begin on April 17, 1961. It was a disaster. The Cubans were well prepared. The "secret" training activities in Guatemala had been reported in the New York *Times*, and Cuban intelligence officials had apparently briefed the military about the invasion. The promised air strike, which was to destroy the six-plane Cuban air force, never took place. Furthermore, expected Cuban support for the invaders did not materialize. Castro's forces cleared the beach at the Bay of Pigs in four days and captured some 1,200 attackers.

Initially President Kennedy denied United States involvement in the invasion, but eventually he assumed full responsibility. "All my life, I've known better than to depend on the experts," Kennedy remarked privately. "How could I have been so stupid, to let them go ahead?" The failure at the Bay of Pigs demonstrated the difficulties of using military tactics to achieve broad political goals.

Growing Tension in Europe

In June 1961 President Kennedy traveled to Vienna, Austria, to meet with Premier Nikita Khrushchev. The Soviet Union wanted NATO forces withdrawn from West Germany. The Soviet leader also voiced his concern over the increasing flow of East German youth, intellectuals, and technicians defecting to West Berlin.

Premier Khrushchev may have considered the President weak in light of the Bay of Pigs. Khrushchev threatened to sign a defense treaty with East Germany if NATO troops were not withdrawn by December. Kennedy refused to discuss a withdrawal.

On August 13 the East Germans suddenly erected a wall between East and West Berlin. The wall effectively cut off the flow of defectors, but it proved to be a valuable propaganda weapon for the western powers. It appeared to them that the communist governments of eastern Europe had to use force to keep their people from fleeing.

In 1963 the President visited West Berlin and was greeted by enormous crowds who heard him declare, *"Ich bin ein Berliner"* ("I am a Berliner"). With that statement he assured the residents of West Berlin that the United States would maintain its support of the city.

After the Berlin crisis, the Soviet Union and the United States increased efforts to strengthen their military capabilities. In September 1961 the Soviet Union broke the three-year moratorium on nuclear tests with a series of above-ground explosions. The United States began tests the following spring. President Kennedy also launched a program to build fallout shelters in case of a nuclear attack.

In 1961 East German authorities tried to stop East Berliners from fleeing into West Berlin by building a wall between the two sections of the city. To underscore American support for the free people of West Berlin, President Kennedy stood before the Berlin Wall in 1963 and declared in German to cheering thousands, "Ich bin ein Berliner" ("I am a Berliner").

The Cuban Missile Crisis

In the midst of heightened tension, the President learned that Premier Khrushchev had placed offensive weapons in Cuba. Aerial photographs revealed missile launch pads under construction there. The insignia on the equipment were Soviet.

The President immediately convened a group of his advisers chaired by his brother Robert, the attorney general. For six days, while the advisers weighed alternatives, the President carried on public business as if nothing had happened. The President's advisers then proposed two options: a naval blockade of Cuba or an air strike against the missile sites.

On October 22, 1962, President Kennedy announced the presence of the Soviet missile launch pads to a shocked nation. Kennedy informed the public that a naval blockade would prevent further entry of offensive weapons to Cuba. As Soviet ships steamed toward Cuba, Kennedy placed the armed forces on full alert.

Tensions mounted as work continued on the Cuban bases and Soviet ships approached the blockade. Then the ships stopped. "We're eyeball to eyeball," reported Secretary of State Dean Rusk at the height of the crisis, "and I think the other fellow just blinked." Convinced of American determination, Premier Khrushchev ordered the ships to turn back and the bases to be dismantled.

The crisis was over, but the prospect of a nuclear war had been sobering indeed. American and Soviet leaders established a direct telephone link, known as the "hot line," between Washington and Moscow. The missile crisis also contributed to a new desire to limit the testing of nuclear weapons.

The Soviet Union was willing to limit nuclear tests because it wanted to devote more resources to improve its domestic economy. In addition, American public opinion strongly favored steps to reduce the radioactive fallout from nuclear tests. President Kennedy pronounced:

> If we cannot end now all our differences, at least we can help make the world safe for diversity. For . . . we all inhabit this small planet. We all breathe the same air. We all cherish our children's future. And we are all mortal.

In July 1963 the two powers concluded a treaty banning nuclear tests in the atmosphere, although underground tests were still permitted. In addition to the United States and the Soviet Union, Great Britain also ratified the treaty. The test-ban treaty proved to be a significant step in easing the international tensions that had played so great a part in the history of the previous two decades.

For answers, see p. A 111.

Section Review

1. Identify the following: Robert McNamara, Peace Corps, Alliance for Progress.

2. Define the following term: strategic forces.

3. (a) What was the purpose of the Peace Corps? (b) What was the purpose of the Alliance for Progress?

4. What event undermined the goodwill of the United States in Latin America?

5. In what way did the Berlin wall prove to be a valuable propaganda weapon for the western powers?

6. What two options did President Kennedy's advisers offer in reaction to Khrushchev's decision to build missile bases in Cuba?

2 The New Frontier

During the Democratic nominating convention of 1960, John F. Kennedy had spoken of the frontiers Americans had conquered in the past. He had challenged the nation to turn to a "new frontier": those national goals that remained unfulfilled. As President, Kennedy tried to advance his New Frontier in the areas of economic development, civil rights, and the exploration of space.

The Frontier of Space

In the race to explore the new frontier of outer space, the Soviet Union had already proven its abilities with numerous satellite launches. It made further progress in April 1961, when Yuri Gagarin (YOO ree guh GAHR uhn) became the first person to orbit the earth. One month later United States Navy Commander Alan Shepard, Jr., rode a tiny Mercury capsule in a suborbital flight of 300 miles (about 500 kilometers). Shortly afterward President Kennedy pledged that the United States would put an American on the moon before 1970.

On February 20, 1962, Lieutenant Colonel John Glenn was launched into orbit from Cape Canaveral, Florida. Unlike the practice in the Soviet Union, the National Aeronautics and Space Administration (NASA) permitted live press coverage of the manned flights. Millions of Americans heard the slow countdown, watched the rocket's takeoff, and followed Glenn's conversations with ground control at Cape Canaveral. Glenn orbited the earth three times and returned home safely in what he called a "fireball of a ride."

Other manned and unmanned launches followed. Telstar, a commercial communications satellite, orbited the earth relaying live television broadcasts over long distances. The Mariner series of space probes came within 21,000 miles (about 34,000 kilometers) of the planet Venus and radioed back information.

Economic Policies

During the last years of President Eisenhower's administration, economic growth had slowed, yet the rate of inflation had steadily increased. President Kennedy hoped to stimulate economic growth while controlling inflation. An alliance of Republicans and conservative Democrats resisted the President's attempts to increase government spending, but Congress did raise the minimum wage. It also began debate on a tax cut. Many economists argued that a reduction in taxes would stimulate the economy by leaving the taxpayer more money to spend on consumer products.

President Kennedy urged Congress to pass several programs designed to reduce poverty, especially in urban slums and poor rural areas such as Appalachia, the hilly country stretching south from Pennsylvania through West Virginia, Kentucky, Tennessee, and Alabama. The programs were geared to involve local citizens in planning economic programs suited to local needs.

In an attempt to control inflation, the President established an informal standard of "wage-price guideposts" that he hoped business and labor would follow. He was particularly concerned about wages and prices in the steel industry. Steel was used in many industries, and a rise in steel costs would affect the entire economy.

In April 1962 the administration convinced steel workers to accept a contract with moderate wage increases. The union agreed with the understanding that the steel companies would not raise steel prices. But U.S. Steel and other major producers surprised the President by announcing a steep price increase. In a press conference Kennedy condemned the steel companies' actions. The Defense Department then announced it would purchase steel only from those companies that had not raised prices.

Inland Steel and many smaller companies kept their prices down, which forced the other producers to return to the old price levels. The President had won a major battle against inflation, but his attack on the steel companies damaged administration relations with big business.

Civil Rights

Because Kennedy had long advocated civil rights legislation, he received support from black Americans during the 1960 election. Once in office, Kennedy moved cautiously because he needed the backing of southern Democrats in Congress for his other programs. However, he did support a voting rights bill and the Twenty-fourth Amendment to the Constitution, prohibiting poll taxes. The Twenty-fourth Amendment was passed by Congress in August 1962 and ratified in 1964. (See page 780.) Kennedy also appointed blacks to key positions in government, including Robert Weaver as Home Finance administrator and Thurgood Marshall as a federal judge.

Attorney General Robert Kennedy dealt firmly with violations of civil rights. In 1961 he sent federal troops to Alabama to protect blacks trying to integrate buses and trains. Robert Kennedy personally supervised the case of James Meredith, a black Air Force veteran who attempted to enroll at the all-white University of Mississippi. When Meredith registered for classes in 1962, rioting erupted, and the President sent federal marshals to the campus to back the National Guard. Several hundred soldiers remained there until Meredith graduated.

In Alabama, Governor George Wallace gained national attention by temporarily halting federal marshals as they escorted black student Autherine Lucy to the formerly all-white University of Alabama. Lucy also continued her education with the protection of the National Guard.

In 1963 President Kennedy presented Congress with a comprehensive civil rights legislative package that would ban discrimination in employment and voting and in state programs receiving federal aid. The laws would also guarantee all Americans access to public accommodations. In a television message, the President asked:

> Are we to say to the world—and much more importantly, to each other—that this is the land of the free except for the Negroes; that we have no second-class citizens, except Negroes; that we have no class or caste system, no ghettos, no master race, except with respect to Negroes?

Tragedy in Dallas

On November 22, 1963, President Kennedy arrived in Dallas, Texas, on a political tour. As the presidential motorcade proceeded from the airport to the center of the city, the crowd was friendly and enthusiastic, and the President waved and smiled warmly in response.

Suddenly rifle shots rang out. The President lurched, then slumped in his seat. The limousine sped to Parkland Memorial Hospital, but the President was fatally wounded and could not be revived. That afternoon aboard an Air Force jet bound for Washington, Vice-President Lyndon Johnson was sworn in as the thirty-sixth President of the United States.

The nation and the world viewed the events of that November weekend with horror and grief. Lee Harvey Oswald was arrested and charged with the assassination. Millions watched television in disbelief as they saw Oswald, while being escorted by police, shot to death by Jack Ruby, a local nightclub operator.

From around the world the White House received expressions of grief and loss. Americans wept with the Kennedy family and a host of somber world leaders as television cameras followed the flag-draped casket carrying the President's body to Arlington National Cemetery. Although President Kennedy had not been in office long enough to test fully the measure of his leadership, his vigor and idealism had shaped the first years of the decade.

On the plane carrying the coffin of John Kennedy from Dallas to Washington, Lyndon Baines Johnson was sworn in as President. Shown here, from left, are federal Judge Sarah T. Hughes administering the oath, Lady Byrd Johnson, the new President, and Jacqueline Kennedy.

For answers, see p. A 112.

Section Review

1. Identify the following: Alan Shepard, John Glenn, Telstar, James Meredith, George Wallace.

2. What goal did President Kennedy set for the exploration of space?

3. (a) What action did Kennedy take to try to control inflation? (b) What industry was he especially concerned about?

4. List two actions President Kennedy took in support of civil rights.

3 Building the Great Society

The outpouring of grief for the slain President brought with it an equal measure of support for his successor, Lyndon Johnson. In the first years of his administration, Johnson dedicated himself to fulfilling the Kennedy program, building what the new President called the Great Society. The Great Society, asserted Johnson, "asks not only how much, but how good; not only how to create wealth, but how to use it; not only how fast we are going, but where we are headed."

The Great Society Begins

When Lyndon Johnson arrived in Washington on November 22, 1963, he said simply, "I'll do my best. That's all I can do." Although he became President unexpectedly, few leaders in Washington had more experience for the job than Lyndon Johnson. He had first been elected to the House of Representatives from Texas in 1937. In 1948 he won a Senate post by 87 votes in a disputed election that earned him the nickname "Landslide Lyndon." By 1953 he was the Democratic minority leader in the Senate.

Johnson's success resulted from shrewd political sense and the ability to convince fellow senators to vote for legislation he favored. His vigorous persuasion became known as the "Johnson treatment." Senator George Smathers of Florida recalled the treatment as being like "a great overpowering thunderstorm that consumed you as it closed in around you." In 1958 when Johnson became majority leader of the Senate, he was perhaps the most influential politician on Capitol Hill.

As President, Johnson immediately urged Congress to pass the major bills of the Kennedy administration. He won over opponents to the tax cut proposal by promising a more efficient federal budget. Congress passed Kennedy's civil rights package as the Civil Rights Act of 1964. President Johnson also expanded government efforts to help the poor.

In 1964 approximately 30 million Americans (16 percent of the population) lived in families with incomes below the "poverty line," as defined by the government. The keystone to what Johnson called his War on Poverty was the Economic Opportunity Act of 1964. The act provided for job training programs for the poor, loans to encourage rural farm cooperatives and urban businesses, and aid to migrant laborers. It also created VISTA, Volunteers in Service to America, a domestic Peace Corps.

A Democratic Landslide

Johnson's active first year in office assured his nomination as the Democratic presidential candidate in 1964. As his running mate, he chose Hubert H. Humphrey, a well-known senator from Minnesota.

The Republicans were divided between New York Governor Nelson Rockefeller and Senator Barry Goldwater of Arizona. Rockefeller represented the moderate wing of the Republican party, with its strength in the Northeast. Goldwater represented the conservative wing of the party. He was a strong supporter of states' rights. Goldwater's rise to prominence also indicated the growing strength of the Southwest in United States politics.

Goldwater won the nomination and chose William Miller, a New York congress-

man, as his running mate. In accepting the nomination, Goldwater squarely faced the charge that his views were too extreme. "Extremism in the defense of liberty is no vice," he said. "Moderation in pursuit of justice is no virtue."

During the campaign Johnson and Humphrey portrayed themselves as moderate alternatives to Goldwater. Democratic political advertisements emphasized statements and positions that made Goldwater seem "dangerous" to many Americans. The tactic worked. Lyndon Johnson enjoyed the biggest victory since Franklin D. Roosevelt in 1936. Johnson received 61 percent of the popular vote compared to 39 percent for Goldwater.

Twenty-eight Democratic senators and 37 new representatives were also voted into office, giving the Democrats a large majority in both houses. President Johnson thus had the votes he needed to enact a long list of legislative bills.

A Flood of Legislation

During the election campaign, Lyndon Johnson summarized the goals he believed most Americans sought. "They want education for their children and an improving life for their families. They want to protect liberty and pursue peace. They expect justice for themselves and are willing to grant it to others." To meet these goals Johnson set before Congress an ambitious slate of social legislation, much of which was passed in 1965.

One of the most far-reaching pieces of legislation was the Medicare Act. It provided hospital coverage for citizens over 65 and allowed them to participate in a program that shared the cost of other medical expenses. In addition a Medicaid program provided funds for states to assist poor people of all ages who were not covered by Medicare. In passing Medicare, the federal government for the first time sought to guarantee a minimum level of health care for Americans.

President Johnson pressed for further civil rights legislation after the Reverend James J. Reeb, a black civil rights worker, was shot during a voter registration campaign in Selma, Alabama. The Voting Rights Act of 1965 authorized federal officials to register voters in states where state officials continued to discriminate on the basis of race. The enforcement of this law in Selma and throughout the country resulted in the

In 1965 black and white civil rights marchers from all over the nation joined the Reverend Martin Luther King, Jr., in a "freedom march." They walked the 65 miles from Selma, Alabama, to the state capital of Montgomery to demand voting rights.

registration of a million new black voters by the 1968 election.

The Immigration Act eliminated quotas that had limited immigration from certain parts of the world since the 1920s. (See page 523.) The Housing Act provided federal funds for constructing low- and middle-income housing. Congress created the Department of Housing and Urban Development (HUD), and President Johnson named Robert Weaver to head the department, making him the first black to serve in a presidential cabinet. Congress also expanded social security benefits, provided aid to higher education, began efforts to curb water pollution, and created the National Foundation for the Arts and Humanities.

In October 1965, after Congress had adjourned for the year, the President presented a display case of 50 pens to members of the White House press. The inscription read, "With these fifty pens President Lyndon B. Johnson signed into law the foundations of the Great Society, which was passed by the historical and fabulous first session of the Eighty-ninth Congress."

For answers, see p. A 112.

Section Review

1. Identify the following: VISTA, Hubert H. Humphrey, Barry Goldwater.
2. Name two characteristics that contributed to Lyndon Johnson's political rise?
3. List two provisions of the Economic Opportunity Act of 1964.
4. What did the Medicare Act provide?
5. What was the result of the Voting Rights Act of 1965?

4 A Struggle for Equal Rights for Black Americans

In his appeal for the creation of the Great Society, President Johnson envisioned a nation in which economic and spiritual needs would be fully satisfied. Yet, as he himself recognized, not all citizens were able to share equally in that dream. The civil rights movement begun by black Americans in the 1950s would grow throughout the 1960s.

Tactics of Nonviolence

During the early 1960s advocates of greater civil rights generally used the nonviolent tactics followed by the Reverend Martin Luther King, Jr. His organization, the Southern Christian Leadership Conference, was joined by others, including the Congress of Racial

Equality (CORE) and the Student Non-violent Coordinating Committee (SNCC). The National Association for the Advancement of Colored People continued to work for equality through the courts, where it filed suits against acts of discrimination.

As you read in Chapter 37, a movement against the segregation of public facilities in the South began when a group of young blacks refused to leave an all-white lunch counter in 1960. Soon the tactic was adopted by black and white civil rights workers. "Freedom riders" quietly but firmly refused to be segregated on buses and trains or in depots, stations, or rest rooms. Groups marched in protest when voting rights were denied, or staged "sit-ins" at restaurant counters labeled "for whites only." Other protesters led campaigns to desegregate schools.

The response to such tactics was often violent. Angry mobs attacked buses of freedom riders. Police sometimes dispersed protesters with water hoses, police dogs, or electric cattle prods. Civil rights workers were frequently imprisoned and fined. Often they sought arrest to bring national attention to their cause. In the North advocates of civil rights organized rent strikes to protest poor housing conditions and boycotted stores that refused to hire blacks.

In 1963 over 200,000 blacks and whites gathered in Washington, D.C., to demand racial equality. Civil rights leaders addressed the crowd, and Martin Luther King proclaimed in a ringing speech of hope: "I have a dream!" The protests had their effect as local communities began to repeal segregation laws. The federal government passed further civil rights legislation calling for an end to discrimination in public establishments and at polling places. Yet others were demanding more radical action.

A More Militant Movement

After 1963 a growing number of black leaders came to believe that King's philosophy of nonviolence was not bringing equality quickly enough. These radical leaders were especially concerned with the problems

675

I Have a Dream

On August 28, 1963, over 200,000 people from all walks of life joined a public demonstration for racial equality at the Lincoln Memorial in Washington, D.C. The marchers both black and white urged Congress to deal with the problems of racial discrimination and poverty in the United States. Martin Luther King, Jr., was among ten speakers to address the crowd. A portion of his stirring speech is printed below.

I say to you today, my friends, that in spite of the difficulties and frustrations of the moment I still have a dream. It is a dream deeply rooted in the American dream.

I have a dream that one day this nation will rise up and live out the true meaning of its creed: "We hold these truths to be self-evident; that all men are created equal." . . .

I have a dream that my four little children will one day live in a nation where they will not be judged by the color of their skin but by the content of their character. . . .

When we let freedom ring, when we let it ring from every village and every hamlet, from every state and every city, we will be able to speed up that day when all of God's children, black men and white men, Jews and Gentiles, Protestants and Catholics, will be able to join hands and sing in the words of the old Negro spiritual, "Free at last! Free at last! Thank God Almighty, we are free at last!"

faced by northern blacks. Over the previous 50 years, blacks had moved in increasing numbers to northern cities.

Life in northern cities was hard and frustrating for most blacks. Although segregation laws did not exist in the North, widespread discrimination did. De facto segregation kept most blacks in rundown ghettos, where many lived in decayed buildings, often with inadequate plumbing and heating. Although the average income of black workers had risen since 1950, it remained much lower than the average income of whites. Unemployment was also higher among blacks than whites.

Radicals demanded immediate action to correct such conditions. One radical group was the Black Muslims, led by Elijah Muhammed. The Muslims believed that blacks would succeed only if they separated completely from white society. Founded in 1930, the movement received little national attention until its views were spread by Malcolm Little, an energetic Muslim minister who adopted the name Malcolm X.

By 1964 Malcolm X had rejected Elijah Muhammed's separatist ideas in favor of creating "a society in which there could exist honest white-black brotherhood." In February 1965 Malcolm X was shot and killed, presumably as the result of his dispute with the Black Muslims. His ideas, expressed in the *Autobiography of Malcolm X*, have remained influential.

Malcolm X and other blacks warned that frustration and despair in black ghettos might lead to violence. In 1964 and 1965 those warnings proved accurate. Harlem and Rochester, New York, were the sites of riots in the summer of 1964. In August 1965 even greater turmoil broke out in the Los Angeles ghetto known as Watts. For five days Watts was plagued by looting, rioting, and arson. The governor sent 14,000 National Guardsmen to restore order. By the time calm returned, 34 people were dead, 4,000 had been arrested, and $35 million worth of property had been destroyed or damaged.

In 1966 and 1967 riots erupted in other major cities, including Newark, Cincinnati, Atlanta, and Detroit. Although different incidents set off each riot, the violence and turmoil appeared to have spread because of the anger and frustration widely shared by blacks living in ghetto areas across the nation.

Black Power

During the late 1960s militant black leaders such as Stokely Carmichael and Floyd McKissick rejected cooperation with sympathetic whites and put forth a philosophy of "black power." Blacks, they argued, should take control of the economic and political aspects of their lives even if it required a violent revolution to do so. One radical group, the Black Panthers, urged blacks to arm themselves and fight for their rights when necessary.

Moderate black leaders stressed that black power should be expressed as self-reliance and pride, not as violence. Opinion polls revealed that most black Americans preferred the goals of integration and the more moderate interpretation of black power. However, the more violent rhetoric attracted widespread attention.

The mood of tension and violence increased in April 1968 when Dr. Martin Luther King, Jr., went to Memphis, Tennessee, to support a strike called by black sanitation workers. Having received many threats on his life, King told his followers, "I've seen the Promised Land. I may not get there with you. But I want you to know tonight that we as a people will get to the Promised Land." The next day, April 4, a sniper's bullets killed Dr. King, bringing sorrow and rage to the nation.

Riots broke out in over 170 cities across the nation. Amid the violence the body of Dr. King, the man who had won the Nobel Peace Prize "for the furtherance of brotherhood among men," was laid to rest at Morehouse College in Atlanta, Georgia. Inscribed on his gravestone are the words, "Free at last, free at last, thank God Almightly I'm free at last."

A Warning and Cautious Hope

The mixture of cautious hope and frustration that characterized most of the civil rights struggle was reflected in a report issued shortly before Martin Luther King's death. The Kerner Commission, appointed by President Johnson and headed by Illinois Governor Otto Kerner, spent six months studying the causes and consequences of the civil disorders that had swept the nation.

The commission report noted that black Americans had made significant progress in some areas. Freedom riders had largely succeeded in desegregating public places, and millions of blacks were voting. The Civil Rights Act of 1968 for the first time declared that no person could be denied housing on account of race. The only housing units not covered by the act were owner-occupied houses sold directly by the owners.

The Kerner report also stressed that more remained to be done. "Our nation is moving toward two societies," the commission warned, "one black, one white—separate but unequal." Despite the new laws, blacks still faced discrimination in housing, employment, and education. According to the report, only "a commitment to national

action—compassionate, massive, and sustained" could bring equality for all.

For answers, see p. A 112.

Section Review

1. Identify the following: Black Muslims, Malcolm X, Kerner Commission.
2. List three tactics black Americans used against segregation in the early 1960s.
3. Give two examples of conditions that led some black leaders to demand more radical action.
4. What goal did Malcolm X come to support before his death?
5. How did moderate black leaders believe black power should be expressed?

5 A Continuing Struggle for Equality

The struggle for equal rights among black Americans during the 1960s sparked other groups to demand their rights. The reform spirit of the decade especially affected Hispanics, Native Americans, and women.

Hispanic Americans

As the black civil rights movement grew, Hispanic groups also began to work more actively to overcome inequalities they faced. Such efforts were often more regional than national, however, because Hispanic groups with various heritages lived in different parts of the nation.

During the 1600s small groups of Spanish farmers had settled in what is now the southwestern United States. Many of their descendants, known as Hispanos, continued to live in the rural uplands and mountains of New Mexico and Colorado. The majority of the Hispanos raised sheep or tended small farms, as their ancestors had done.

A much larger Hispanic minority were the descendants of Mexicans who had lived in the Southwest when the United States annexed the territory in the Mexican War. Mexicans continued to migrate to the United States, especially after 1910. (See page 543.) By 1960 approximately 3.5 million Mexican Americans lived in the Southwest.

In the eastern United States most Hispanic immigrants came from Puerto Rico. The United States had annexed the island in

1898, and in 1917 Congress granted American citizenship to residents there. In 1952 the United States Congress and the citizens of Puerto Rico agreed to a commonwealth status for the island. Puerto Ricans drafted their own constitution and elected a governor and a legislature. At the same time, they retained the rights of United States citizens, were protected militarily by the United States, and came under the jurisdiction of federal agencies such as the post office and the customs service. Puerto Ricans could also immigrate to the United States and travel freely within its borders.

Before World War II, only about 70,000 Puerto Ricans had moved to the mainland, most of them settling in New York City. After the war, as the Puerto Rican population expanded rapidly, the number of emigrants increased. By 1960 some 600,000 had come to the mainland. Many continued to settle in New York, but some moved to other cities, including Chicago, San Francisco, and Bridgeport, Connecticut.

When Fidel Castro began setting up a communist state in Cuba in the early 1960s, thousands of Cubans sought to leave their country. Between 1961 and 1970 over 200,000 Cubans immigrated to the United States. Some fled the island in small boats. Most Cuban immigrants settled in southern Florida. Many resumed careers in medicine, law, and teaching. Miami, the city with the largest number of Cuban immigrants, acquired a new appearance. Shop windows displayed signs in Spanish. Cuban restaurants were built to cater to the new immigrants. Spanish-language radio stations began broadcasting. As their numbers grew, Cuban Americans became an increasingly powerful force in southern Florida.

The Problems of Discrimination

Hispanos, Mexican Americans, and Puerto Ricans faced many forms of discrimination. They lived in a land in which the dominant culture was English, while theirs was Spanish. Few schools had programs to teach English to students whose first language was Spanish. Consequently Hispanic students found themselves at a disadvantage. The lack of a good education in turn made it more difficult to obtain good jobs. But even well-educated Hispanics encountered discrimination among employers.

A government program started in the 1950s created special problems for Mexican American migrant workers. Under that program, Mexicans could obtain temporary permits to work in the United States. *Braceros*, as the Mexican workers were known, were willing to work for very low wages. Consequently migrant workers had to accept lower wages in order to compete with the braceros. The program was halted in 1965.

Hispanics who sought to correct the heritage of discrimination used a variety of tactics. In 1962 Cesar Chavez (SAY zahr CHAH vays) began a movement to unionize California grape pickers. The majority of grape pickers were Mexican Americans, or Chicanos, as younger activists were coming to call themselves. Chavez believed that a strong union would help migrant workers gain higher wages and better working conditions. Chavez adopted a nonviolent strategy similar to Martin Luther King's. He sought wide support by organizing sit-ins and protest demonstrations. During the late 1960s Chavez organized a nationwide boycott of table grapes that forced an increasing number of growers to accept the union by 1970.

In southwestern Texas, José Ángel Gutiérrez (hoh SAY AHN hehl goo TYEHR rehs) sought power for his people through political action. "Mexicanos need to be in control of their destiny," argued Gutiérrez. "We have been complacent for too long." His political party, La Raza Unida, called for bilingual education in public school systems, improved public services in Chicano neighborhoods, and an end to job discrimination.

In urban areas, more radical Chicano groups formed organizations such as the Brown Berets in Los Angeles and La Comunidad Latina in Chicago. Like the Black Panthers, such groups stressed militant self-defense and also sponsored health clinics and breakfast programs for schoolchildren.

By the end of the 1960s Hispanic groups had made definite gains. Cesar Chavez's efforts to unionize migrant workers spread to other fruit and vegetable industries, and a growing number of Americans of Spanish heritage gained access to better jobs. Some school districts had become more sensitive to their needs. Yet large numbers of Hispanics continued to face economic hardship and discrimination. Much remained to be done.

Native Americans

Toward the end of the 1960s Native Americans also adopted the techniques of protest. In addition to the problems of discrimination faced by other minorities, Native Americans were embittered by the government's long history of contradictory and changing policies.

As you read in Chapter 20, the Dawes Act of 1887 proposed a policy that sought to break up the old tribal system and divide reservation lands among individual Native Americans. In 1934 the government reversed that policy. The Indian Reorganization Act encouraged Native Americans to govern themselves through tribal arrangements.

The National Congress of American Indians was founded in 1940 in reaction to many years of discrimination and the confusion of government policy. The National Congress regularly petitioned Congress for greater recognition of Indian rights. During the 1950s government officials shifted policy again, recommending that the federal government turn the programs over to the states. Such inconsistancy brought sharp protests from the National Congress and other Indian groups.

In the 1960s the federal government once again encouraged a return to a tribal system. But by then the Indian population was becoming increasingly urban. By 1969 an estimated 75 percent of all Native Americans lived in urban areas, most in the East. City life weakened traditional tribal ties and customs. In reaction many urban youth, especially, began to take a great pride in their heritage and make more radical demands for Indian rights. One group, led by Dennis Banks and Clyde Bellecourt, organized the militant American Indian Movement (AIM) in 1968.

A major confrontation between AIM members and federal authorities occurred at Wounded Knee, South Dakota, site of a massacre of Indians by the United States Army in 1890. (See page 371.) In March 1973 AIM members seized the trading post at Wounded Knee. The government responded by surrounding the area with federal law officers. The militants' position was weakened when other Native Americans did not support their demands, and they were forced to leave Wounded Knee.

Like the movements led by Hispanics and blacks, the Native American protests signaled a new attitude among minority groups. Native Americans demonstrated increasing pride in their heritage, confidence in their ability to contribute to the diversity of American society, and willingness to act to achieve their goals.

In 1973 members of the American Indian Movement seized a trading post and church at Wounded Knee, South Dakota. They demanded Senate hearings on United States treaties with Indian groups.

The Women's Rights Movement

Throughout the 1960s women had been active in urging social reform, as they had during the reform years of the 1830s and 1840s and during the progressive era of the early twentieth century. Although women in the 1960s had full political rights and many worked outside the home, some women argued that they continued to be victims of discrimination.

Betty Friedan presented that argument in her book *The Feminine Mystique*, published in 1963. Friedan argued that after World War II, society had forced women to retreat from the job market and from their careers back into the home. The business world continued to be dominated by men, she pointed out. Women's jobs were limited primarily to a few professions, such as nursing, teaching, and secretarial work. When women did perform the same jobs as men, women's salaries were consistently lower.

In 1966 Friedan founded the National Organization for Women (NOW) to press for legislation that would give women greater freedom and equality. The organization campaigned in favor of equal pay for equal work and the opening of opportunities for women at all levels of employment. It also worked to provide day care facilities for the children of mothers who worked outside the home.

Through the women's rights movement, women began to assume more diverse roles during the 1960s. The Equal Pay Act of 1963 guaranteed equal pay for equal work, and the Civil Rights Act of 1964 banned job discrimination on the basis of sex as well as race or ethnic origin. Although those acts were not always vigorously enforced, they provided a legal basis for greater equality. In the late 1960s and early 1970s women entered the work force in record numbers. Many companies made special efforts to promote women to management positions.

Despite such efforts much inequality remained. In 1970 only 2.8 percent of all lawyers and 9 percent of medical students were women. Only 7 percent of women working outside the home earned more than $10,000 a year, compared with 40 percent of working men. A California study in 1974 revealed that while more women were employed, their salaries were even farther behind men's in 1974 than they had been in 1960.

Median Income of Men and Women 1950–1970

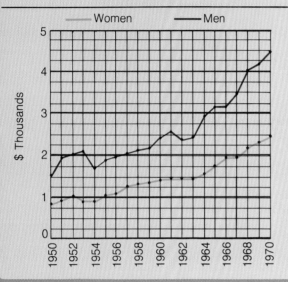

$ Thousands

— Women   — Men

Source: *Historical Statistics of the United States*

■ *Incomes of women continued to lag far behind those of men. The chart shows the median incomes of men and women in a 20-year period ending in 1970. Although women's incomes rose, men's incomes rose even faster. ("Median income" means that half of all incomes are lower and half are higher than the figure named.)*

680

A proposed constitutional amendment forbidding discrimination by sex was passed by Congress in 1972. The Equal Rights Amendment, as it became known, encountered strong opposition from men and women who believed that it would undermine certain traditional values. Opponents of the amendment also argued that women already had equal rights. The amendment was defeated when it was not ratified by June 1982. Like other groups, women were to continue their campaign for greater equality into the 1970s and 1980s.

For answers, see p. A 112.

Section Review

1. Identify the following: Cesar Chavez, National Congress of American Indians, Dennis Banks, Clyde Bellecourt, American Indian Movement, Betty Friedan, National Organization for Women, Equal Rights Amendment.
2. Define the following term: bracero.
3. What status did Puerto Rico have after 1952?
4. List two tactics Cesar Chavez used to gain support for his union.
5. How did Native American groups react to the government decision to turn Indian programs over to the states?
6. What two pieces of legislation provided a legal basis for greater economic equality of men and women?

The Equal Rights Amendment proposed by Congress in 1972 created great controversy. Opponents and proponents often demonstrated to convince state legislatures to vote their way.

6 Growing Involvement in World Affairs

President Johnson had begun his administration with the hope of building a Great Society. The struggle for equality by minorities and women reflected the aspirations of millions of Americans. Increasingly, however, national attention turned to a growing conflict in Southeast Asia. The war in Vietnam was to divide the nation. It also raised the question of what policy the United States should adopt toward nonindustrial, or developing, nations.

The United States and the Third World

By the 1960s the developing nations of Asia, Africa, and Latin America had become known as the Third World. (The other two "worlds" were the United States and its allies, and the Soviet Union and the communist bloc.) The Soviet Union and the United States frequently competed for the friendship of many of the nations that had become independent since World War II. Such competition contributed to a number of conflicts during the 1960s.

In 1960 the Belgian Congo became the independent Congo. (It is now Zaire.) Soon a civil war broke out between groups wanting to control the new government. President Kennedy decided to aid a pro-American faction. American assistance helped that faction win the civil war. Consequently many Africans resented American involvement, especially since white mercenaries from South Africa also took part.

For many years the governments of South Africa and Rhodesia (now Zimbabwe) practiced *apartheid* (ah PAHR tīd), a policy of racial separation by law. Although the majority of the population was black, the governments were controlled by the white descendants of European colonists.

For the United States, to oppose the white regimes was to risk the loss of valuable economic resources and strategic naval bases in South Africa. But to endorse the governments would violate principles of justice, as well as alienate newly independent black nations. For a while the United States compromised by publicly condemning apartheid while trading with South Africa and Rhodesia for important resources.

In Latin America civil war erupted in the Dominican Republic in the early 1960s. Juan Bosch, elected in 1962 as the country's first democratic leader, was ousted by the military seven months later. Reluctantly the United States recognized the new regime. In April 1965 Bosch and his followers attempted to overthrow the military leaders. They had nearly succeeded when President Johnson, fearing instability in the region, landed 23,000 marines in the Dominican Republic and called for a cease-fire. United States influence allowed the Dominican military to remain in power.

The United States had intervened, Johnson explained, to protect American civilians in the Dominican Republic and to prevent communists from taking over Bosch's revolution. Critics, however, claimed that the communist threat was more imagined than real. Bosch, an advocate of democratic reform, was bitter. "This was a democratic revolution smashed by the leading democracy in the world," he lamented.

In the Middle East the United States balanced massive Soviet aid to Egypt by sending military aid to Israel. In 1967 Israel drove Egyptian forces out of the Sinai Desert and across the Suez Canal during a six-day war. Israeli troops also routed Syrian forces from the Golan Heights and seized all of Jerusalem and lands on the West Bank of the Jordan River.

During the crisis American and Soviet leaders used the Moscow-Washington telephone hot line for the first time. They assured each other that they would not intervene in the conflict. However, continuing hostilities between Egypt and Israel insured that the Middle East would remain an area of concern for future administrations.

Growing Involvement in Vietnam

Southeast Asia represented another area of growing United States involvement. As you read in Chapter 36, when France withdrew from Vietnam in 1954, the country had been divided into two regions. North Vietnam was led by the communist government of Ho Chi Minh and South Vietnam by the government of President Ngo Dinh Diem. When Diem refused to hold the elections that had been proposed at the peace negotiations, the followers of Ho Chi Minh began a campaign to overthrow him.

The anti-Diem rebels were known as the National Liberation Front, or the Viet Cong. Using guerrilla warfare tactics, they killed village officials supporting Diem and tried to replace them with their own "shadow government." Viet Cong influence spread throughout South Vietnam, in part because of disciplined tactics and in part because Diem's government was unpopular. When Diem began widespread imprisonment of Buddhists who opposed his government, opposition to his regime grew.

In 1962 President Kennedy provided the South Vietnamese army of 150,000 men with United States military advisers and equip-

■ The long war in Vietnam eventually affected most of Southeast Asia. The Ho Chi Minh Trail, shown on this map, was a main supply line from North Vietnam to Viet Cong guerrillas. American supplies, by contrast, had to travel thousands of miles by sea or air.

Southeast Asia

ment. Still the South Vietnamese forces were unable to combat the estimated 15,000 Viet Cong. In 1963 the unpopular Diem was assassinated by military officers, but the situation did not improve. When President Johnson took office in 1963 approximately 16,000 United States troops were serving in Vietnam as advisers.

Escalation at the Gulf of Tonkin

During the early stages of the war, most Viet Cong guerrillas were South Vietnamese. North Vietnam had sent supplies and a few guerrilla fighters south. As American involvement grew, North Vietnam increased support to the Viet Cong. In 1964, 7,000 northern guerrillas traveled to the South.

Then, in August 1964, North Vietnamese torpedo boats attacked the United States destroyers *Maddox* and *Turner Joy* not far from the North Vietnamese coast. The destroyers were patrolling the Gulf of Tonkin while South Vietnamese ships attacked North Vietnamese islands in the gulf. North Vietnam claimed that it was rightfully chasing attackers from its territorial waters, but President Johnson argued that the attack was unprovoked. He ordered retaliatory air strikes against North Vietnam.

The President asked Congress for the authority to take "all necessary steps" to "prevent further aggression" by the North Vietnamese. The Gulf of Tonkin resolution, granting this far-reaching power, passed the House by a vote of 416 to 0 and the Senate by a vote of 88 to 2. Later in 1964 American involvement in Vietnam began to increase dramatically.

The United States initiated a bombing campaign called Rolling Thunder. The campaign was aimed at cutting the flow of supplies from North Vietnam to the Viet Cong. Beginning in February 1965, United States planes regularly flew missions over North Vietnam.

In April President Johnson ordered 20,000 American combat troops into Vietnam. By June General William Westmoreland, commander of United States forces in Vietnam, asked for an additional 200,000 troops. American forces grew to 385,000 by the end of 1966 and 536,000 by the end of 1968.

Escalation of the war was interrupted periodically as President Johnson sought

In 1965 President Johnson ordered United States combat troops into Vietnam. The Viet Cong frequently proved to be difficult to find because they seemed to melt away into jungles and villages. In this 1965 photograph American soldiers wade waist deep in water during a mission to "search and destroy" enemy forces.

peace through negotiation with North Vietnam. Neither side, however, could agree on conditions for peace. North Vietnam demanded a place for the National Liberation Front in any postwar government. The United States refused to negotiate on such terms. So the fighting continued.

Opposition at Home

Although President Johnson had received overwhelming support for the Gulf of Tonkin resolution in Congress, American opposition to the war increased as more American troops were sent to Vietnam. The costs of the war, both material and spiritual, were staggering. In 1967 the government spent $20 billion on the war. More important, by the end of 1968 over 25,000 Americans had been killed. The air war was destroying the Vietnamese countryside. Approximately 3.2 million tons (about 3 million metric tons) of explosive were dropped—50 percent more than all the explosives dropped on Europe and Asia during World War II.

In February 1968 American perception of the war began to change. During the Vietnamese holiday of Tet, the lunar new year, the Viet Cong launched attacks on major cities throughout South Vietnam. Although eventually repulsed by American and South Vietnamese forces and suffering major losses, the Viet Cong won a strategic victory by demonstrating that no part of Vietnam was safe, despite the massive American troop commitment.

In the United States thousands of college students protesting the war held "teach-ins" and marched on the Pentagon. The student protests against United States involvement in Vietnam were part of a spirit of political activism that characterized the decade. Young people were actively involved in the reform movements of the period, and college campuses were the scenes of numerous protest demonstrations. Student demands included greater participation in school administration and an end to military training and research. Increasingly, student protests centered on the war.

As the war escalated, so did protests against it. In 1967 some 35,000 antiwar protesters marched on the Pentagon. Met by the raised rifles of military police, one protester began silently placing carnations in their rifle barrels.

As casualties increased and the drafting of young men not in college continued, opposition to the war spread. The war became a major issue in the 1968 presidential election campaign. Democratic Senator Eugene McCarthy, an opponent of the war, ran a surprisingly strong race in the New Hampshire presidential primary. President Johnson won the primary by only a narrow margin. Growing antiwar sentiment put increasing pressure on the President.

In February 1968 General Westmoreland asked for an additional 200,000 troops. Even strong administration supporters of the war reluctantly concluded that the United States could not win using traditional military tactics. President Johnson refused Westmoreland's request. On March 31 the President announced that he was suspending the bombing of North Vietnam and that he would not run for reelection. North Vietnam responded by agreeing to enter negotiations, which were set in Paris.

The Election of 1968

When President Johnson withdrew from the race, Robert Kennedy and Vice-President Hubert Humphrey entered the presidential campaign. Humphrey cautiously supported administration policies in Vietnam. Although Kennedy had at first supported American intervention in Vietnam, by 1968 he was speaking out against the war. His energetic campaign produced an impressive string of victories over McCarthy and Humphrey. The greatest of those came in the important California primary of June 1968.

But on the evening of Kennedy's victory speech in Los Angeles, a young Palestinian named Sirhan Sirhan, angered by Kennedy's support of Israel, shot and killed him. The nation, still recovering from Martin Luther King's assassination, mourned another leader.

Robert Kennedy's death left Hubert Humphrey in the lead for the presidential nomination as the Democrats prepared for their convention in Chicago. Antiwar activists from around the country gathered in Chicago to protest the convention and Humphrey's support of the war. As Chicago police patrolled outside the convention hall, violence broke out.

Demonstrators assaulted the police with obscenities, bricks, bottles, and garbage. The police reacted with surprising force. Numerous police officers and demonstrators were injured. In addition, 49 reporters were arrested, beaten, or sprayed with mace, a caustic chemical designed for crowd control. Inside the hall the convention delegates nominated Humphrey, who chose Senator Edmund Muskie of Maine as his running mate.

Reacting to the antiwar movement and to urban riots, Alabama Governor George Wallace became a third-party candidate for President. He campaigned on the pledge to restore "law and order" to the nation.

In Miami the Republicans turned again to Richard Nixon as their candidate. His nomination was the result of a remarkable political comeback. Defeated as the Republican presidential candidate in 1960 and as a candidate for governor of California in 1962, Nixon had spent the following six years repairing his personal and political fortunes.

The Music of Protest and Change

Popular music reflected the diverse moods and movements of the 1960s. Folk singers with political messages found a large and receptive audience. With songs such as "Where Have All the Flowers Gone?" and "What Have They Done to the Rain?" folk singers protested war and radioactive fallout. Bob Dylan became the leader of folk protest. His musical poetry spoke out against war, bigotry, and injustice.

Dylan and other folk singers expressed the sentiments of a "counterculture." Participants in the counterculture rejected what they considered "dehumanizing" careers with large corporations and sought other paths to personal fulfillment. They believed that the "establishment" had too much influence on American life. In the tradition of rugged individualism, some moved to the countryside, grew their own food, and tried to become self-sufficient. Others established isolated rural communes where everyone shared the work.

Rock music underwent a type of revolution in the early 1960s when the Beatles and other British rock groups, such as the Rolling Stones and the Who, took the United States by storm. Thousands of screaming fans greeted the Beatles in February 1964 when they made their first national appearance on the *Ed Sullivan Show*. The Beatles were not simply another fad. Their 1967 album, *Sergeant Pepper's Lonely Hearts Club Band*, demonstrated their growing talent and opened the door to experimental rock music. From the west coast American groups such as the Jefferson Airplane and the Grateful Dead also contributed to experimental rock.

Dance crazes like the Twist, the Monkey, the Mashed Potato, and the Frug spawned musical styles of their own. The Beachboys kept alive the California "surf" sound they had introduced in the early 1960s. From Detroit came the "Motown" rhythms that introduced wide audiences to black stars. Such performers as the Temptations, the Four Tops, Martha and the Vandellas, Stevie Wonder, and the Supremes consistently topped the pop music charts.

A three-day outdoor rock festival in August 1969 brought the music of the 1960s to a climax. Over 300,000 people—most of them under age 30—gathered near Bethel, New York, for the Woodstock Music and Art Fair. Woodstock offered the nation a glimpse of the counterculture and became the symbol of the youth solidarity of the 1960s.

Bob Dylan.

Major Events

1961	Peace Corps and Alliance for Progress created; Bay of Pigs invasion
1962	Cuban missile crisis
1963	President Kennedy assassinated; Lyndon B. Johnson becomes President
1964	Civil Rights Act, Gulf of Tonkin resolution, and Economic Opportunity Act passed; Johnson elected President
1965	Regular bombing missions over North Vietnam begin; Medicare Act, Voting Rights Act, Housing Act, and Immigration Act passed
1967	Six-Day War between Israel and Egypt
1968	Tet offensive begins; Martin Luther King, Jr., assassinated; Robert Kennedy assassinated; Richard M. Nixon elected President

With his running mate, Spiro Agnew, governor of Maryland, Nixon narrowly won the election with 43.4 percent of the popular vote. Humphrey won 42.7 percent of the popular vote, Wallace 13.5 percent. The election results underscored the divisions in American society. Those divisions were to challenge Nixon's campaign promise to "bring us together."

For answers, see p. A 113.

Section Review

1. Identify the following: Third World, Viet Cong, William Westmoreland, Eugene McCarthy.

2. Define the following term: apartheid.

3. What was United States policy regarding the governments of South Africa and Rhodesia?

4. What authority did President Johnson ask for after the Gulf of Tonkin incident?

5. What was the main purpose of the Rolling Thunder campaign?

6. What two actions did Johnson take in March 1968 in reaction to growing opposition to the war?

★ ★ ★ ★ ★ ★ ★ ★ ★ ★ ★ ★ ★ ★ ★ ★ ★ ★ ★ ★

IN PERSPECTIVE   In contrast to the 1950s, the decade of the 1960s was a turbulent one. The Bay of Pigs invasion, construction of the Berlin Wall, and the Cuban missile crisis increased tensions between the United States and the Soviet Union. On the home front the decade began with high hopes. President John Kennedy urged Americans to turn to new frontiers, but his efforts were cut short by his assassination in November 1963. President Johnson continued Kennedy's programs and convinced Congress to pass legislation to create what he called the Great Society.

The movement among black Americans to gain equal rights grew dramatically during the 1960s. Many civil rights leaders adopted the nonviolent methods of Martin Luther King, Jr., but others demanded more radical action. Growing anger and frustration contributed to riots in many American cities in the mid-1960s. Hispanic Americans and Native Americans also began to organize to end discrimination. The women's rights movement of the 1960s contributed to a growing consciousness of the roles women could play in society.

By the end of the decade, the war in Vietnam overshadowed the struggle for equality. American involvement in the war grew after the Gulf of Tonkin incident. Opposition to the war grew also. In 1968 President Johnson withdrew from the presidential race and announced an end to the bombing of North Vietnam. The task of carrying out peace talks fell to the winner of the 1968 election, Richard Nixon.

Chapter Review

1. (a) What military actions did President Kennedy take in reaction to Khrushchev's pledge to support anti-American "wars of liberation"? (b) What actions did Kennedy take to try to win the friendship of Third World nations?

2. (a) What was the purpose of the Bay of Pigs invasion? (b) What was the outcome? Why?

3. (a) What developments increased tensions between the United States and the Soviet Union in 1961 and 1962? (b) Why were both sides willing to limit nuclear tests by 1963?

4. Describe John Kennedy's New Frontier goals in each of the following areas: (a) space exploration, (b) the economy, (c) civil rights. How did he begin to move toward those goals?

5. (a) What did President Johnson mean by the "Great Society"? (b) Describe the major pieces of legislation Congress passed as part of the Great Society.

6. (a) What tactics did black Americans use against segregation in the early 1960s? (b) Why did some black leaders demand more radical tactics? (c) What did black power mean to militant blacks? (d) What did it mean to moderate black leaders?

7. (a) What special problems of discrimination did Hispanic Americans face by the 1960s? (b) How did Cesar Chavez try to improve conditions for migrant workers? (c) What other actions did some Hispanic leaders propose to fight discrimination?

8. (a) How had government policy toward Native Americans changed since the 1880s? (b) Why did some Indians begin to make more militant demands for Indian rights?

9. (a) How did Betty Friedan describe the condition of women in her book *The Feminine Mystique*? (b) How did that condition change during the 1960s? (c) In what ways did it stay the same?

10. (a) What type of military assistance did President Kennedy provide South Vietnam? (b) What led to increased American involvement in 1964?

11. (a) What factors contributed to growing opposition to the war? (b) What impact did that opposition have on the 1968 presidential election?

For Further Thought

1. President Truman was unable to implement many of his ideas for social and economic reform, yet President Johnson was able to institute an extensive program. Why do you think there was such a difference?

2. Would you agree that the report of the Kerner Commission offered both warning and cautious hope? Explain.

3. (a) Why do you think President Johnson was able to implement so many parts of his Great Society program in 1964 and 1965? (b) Which pieces of legislation do you think had the most impact in the mid-1960s? (c) Which do you think have had the greatest long-term effect on life in the United States? (d) Do you think the long-term effect has been mainly positive or negative? Why?

4. (a) How did United States involvement in the Vietnam War differ from United States involvement in the Korean War? (b) How did it differ from involvement in World War II? (c) How do you think those differences affected public attitude toward the war? Why? (d) How did each war affect the Presidents who were in office? (e) How might you explain the differences?

Developing Basic Skills

1. *Placing Events in Time* Construct a time line of major developments in the struggle of black Americans for greater equality. Your time line should cover the years 1930 to 1968. Then answer the following questions: (a) In which period were there the most developments? Why do you think that is the case? (b) In which period was there the most government activity? (c) Can you identify any trends from studying the time line?

2. *Graph Reading* Study the graph on page 680 and answer the following questions: (a) How did the income of women change between 1950 and 1970? (b) How did the income of men change between 1950 and 1970? (c) How did the difference between the median income of men and the median income of women change between 1950 and 1970? (d) Based on the information on this graph and what you have read in this chapter, how would you describe the change in the economic position of women during that period?

See page 779 for suggested readings.

Challenges at Home and Abroad 39

(1969–1976)

The 1976 bicentennial celebration in New York Harbor.

In 1976 the United States was to celebrate its bicentennial, the two-hundredth anniversary of the Declaration of Independence. Yet as Richard Nixon took office in January 1969, an anniversary celebration was far from the minds of most Americans. Urban violence, assassinations, and growing antiwar protest seriously divided the nation. During his election campaign, Nixon had promised to bring Americans together, but that pledge proved difficult to fulfill. The very process of reducing United States commitment in Vietnam was to lead to new protests and violence.

For a time, there was evidence of increased stability. President Nixon pursued a policy of improving relations with the Soviet Union and the People's Republic of China. His appointments to the Supreme Court were to make the Court more conservative. A landing on the moon marked the culmination of a successful space program.

Yet Nixon's presidency ended early, with his resignation. To his successor, Gerald R. Ford, fell the task of healing the wounds dividing the nation. President Ford faced continuing political, economic, and foreign policy challenges as the nation prepared to celebrate its bicentennial.

1 A Balance of Power

Richard M. Nixon brought over two decades of political experience to the presidency. He had devoted much of his career to conservative Republican policies and strong anticommunism. As President, however, he surprised many of his supporters by pursuing a foreign policy that called for improved relations with the People's Republic of China and the Soviet Union. At the same time he worked to disengage the United States from Vietnam.

The New President

With his election as President in 1968, Richard Nixon capped a long political career. He had been elected to the House of Representatives from California in 1946, and in 1950 he went on to win a seat in the Senate. From 1953 to 1961, Nixon served as Vice-President under President Eisenhower.

In the first major defeat of his political career, Nixon narrowly lost the 1960 presidential election to John F. Kennedy. In 1962 he experienced a second bitter defeat when he ran for governor of California and lost. His political career seemed at an end. Throughout the 1960s, however, Nixon remained active in Republican party politics, and in 1968 the party chose him as its presidential candidate. (See page 685.) With Nixon's victory in that election, the nation had its first President from California.

Views on Foreign Affairs

Richard Nixon brought to the presidency a keen interest in foreign affairs. As Vice-President under Eisenhower, he had traveled to many nations and gained experience in the daily conduct of foreign affairs. As President, Nixon chose an expert in foreign affairs, Henry Kissinger, to be his national security adviser.

Kissinger was an analyst of diplomatic history. He had written extensively about international relations while a professor at Harvard University. Born in Germany, Kissinger and his family had fled to the United States in 1938 to escape the Nazis. He served in the United States Army during World War II. After the war, Kissinger took up his university studies and earned a doctorate degree.

Kissinger shared Nixon's view that the world had changed over the previous decade and that United States foreign policy had to change too. Nixon and Kissinger believed that the world could no longer be seen as two blocs, one communist and one noncommunist. Rather, there were many centers of world power—including Europe, Japan, the People's Republic of China, the Soviet Union, the Middle East, and the United States. Each of these centers of power had different interests and spheres of influence. Thus, in Kissinger's opinion, a foreign policy should seek a balance of world powers.

Within this framework, Nixon and Kissinger concluded that the United States had overextended itself militarily. The new administration moved to reduce obligations abroad, while maintaining a position of "strength and honor." According to Nixon:

> The United States will participate in the defense and development of allies and friends, but cannot—and will not—conceive *all* the plans, design *all* the programs, execute *all* the decisions and undertake *all* the defense of the free nations of the world. We will help where it will make a real difference and is considered in our interest.

The War in Vietnam

Over 540,000 American troops were in Vietnam when Richard Nixon took office. The President considered the Vietnam War a drain on vital American resources. Therefore, he wanted to reduce the commitment of troops and materials. Thus in 1969 he announced a policy of "Vietnamization." Under Vietnamization South Vietnam would take increased responsibility for fighting the war.

The new policy presented problems, however. Nixon ordered a resumption of the bombing of North Vietnam in order to give the South Vietnamese support while American troops withdrew. The bombing was unpopular among those Americans who wanted to see the war end immediately. In May 1970 the President ordered 32,000

United States troops to join the South Vietnamese in an invasion of Cambodia. Nixon said the move was necessary to stop the flow of supplies to the Vietcong. Critics charged that he was widening the war, and opposition to the war increased.

An incident at Kent State University in Kent, Ohio, four days after the invasion of Cambodia, symbolized the strong emotion generated by the war. A large number of Kent State students had gathered on campus to protest the war. They carried signs, sang protest songs, and chanted slogans. Troops from the Ohio National Guard were sent to maintain order. In the confusion, they fired their weapons into the crowd, killing four demonstrators and injuring nine. At Jackson State College in Mississippi, a similar incident left two students dead and twelve injured.

The deaths outraged many Americans. On May 5, 1970, the day after the killings at Kent State, the President announced that he would withdraw the troops from Cambodia within two months. But demonstrations against the war continued. Almost 100,000 protestors assembled in Washington, D.C., on May 9 to demonstrate opposition to the war. In December 1970 Congress voted to repeal the Gulf of Tonkin Resolution, which had provided the legal basis for the conduct of the war. However, Nixon argued that his position as commander in chief gave him the authority to keep troops in Vietnam.

Although the war continued, the policy of Vietnamization brought American troops home. By September 1972 only 60,000 remained in Vietnam. In the meantime, the President had increased the bombing of North Vietnam, hoping to force the North Vietnamese to make concessions at the Paris peace talks, which had stalled.

In October 1972, on the eve of the presidential election, Henry Kissinger announced that a tentative cease-fire had been agreed upon in Paris. "Peace is at hand," he promised, but negotiations faltered again. Finally, in January 1973, a cease-fire called an "Agreement on Ending the War and Restoring Peace in Vietnam" was signed. American troops were withdrawn over the next few months, and an uncertain calm settled over the two Vietnams.

This ended the direct involvement of United States troops in Vietnam. In the longest war in the nation's history, over 57,000 Americans lost their lives. More than 300,000 soldiers came home wounded. The economic costs of the war were enormous, amounting to about $150 billion. Furthermore, the war in Vietnam seriously divided the nation. For many years to come, Americans would debate the causes of the war and how such conflicts might be avoided in the future.

Members of Congress were especially troubled by the fact that a President had sent troops into battle without a formal declaration of war. A declaration of war would have required congressional approval. In November 1973 Congress passed the War Powers Act over President Nixon's veto. The act declared that a President could not send United States military forces into action for longer than 60 days unless authorized to do so by Congress.

Visits to the People's Republic of China and the Soviet Union

Few Americans expected Richard Nixon, long a strong opponent of communism, to improve American relations with the People's Republic of China and the Soviet Union. However, Kissinger and Nixon believed that the rift between China and the Soviet Union would allow the United States to make diplomatic gains.

In July 1971 Kissinger secretly traveled to China. He prepared the ground for President Nixon to visit China in February 1972. After 20 years the wall of suspicion that had separated China and the United States was coming down. The President was cordially received by Chinese leaders during his one-week visit. A large number of American television and newspaper reporters followed him as he toured the ancient Great Wall of China, attended banquets, and met with Mao Tse-tung.

Chinese and American leaders agreed to allow scientific, cultural, and journalistic exchanges between the two countries. They also announced an interest in increasing trade. A year after Nixon's visit, China and the United States established diplomatic offices in one another's capitals.

Soviet leaders also seemed willing to ease tensions. In May 1972 Richard Nixon became the first President to visit the Soviet Union since World War II. His trip marked the flowering of an era of *détente* (day TAHNT), a relaxation of tension between the United States and the Soviet Union.

Following the communist victory in China, there was no direct contact between the People's Republic of China and the United States for more than 20 years. When relations between the two countries thawed during the early 1970s, some of the first visitors to China were American teenagers. They were part of the United States table tennis team, which toured China. Part of the group is shown here with interpreters, visiting the Great Wall of China.

While in Moscow the President and Soviet leaders signed an arms control agreement. The Strategic Arms Limitation Talks (SALT) restricted the types and numbers of nuclear warheads and missiles that each country could deploy. Nixon also negotiated agreements that provided for increased trade and scientific cooperation.

President Nixon's visits to China and the Soviet Union opened new avenues of international cooperation. It was hoped that increased trade would benefit the American economy. Farmers in particular welcomed the higher grain prices that wheat sales to the Soviet Union brought. However, American consumers complained that such sales meant a rise in domestic food prices. Nevertheless, most Americans approved of détente. They were eager to diminish international tensions and the possibility of nuclear war.

For answers, see p. A 115.
Section Review

1. Identify the following: Henry Kissinger, SALT.
2. Define the following term: détente.
3. What centers of world power did Henry Kissinger identify?
4. What did President Nixon hope to accomplish with the policy of Vietnamization?
5. How did United States military involvement in Vietnam end?
6. What was the major provision of the War Powers Act?
7. What agreement did President Nixon reach with Chinese leaders during his 1972 visit?

2 The Politics of Stability

During the presidential election campaign of 1968, Richard Nixon had won the support of those Americans who felt that the protest and reform movements of the 1960s had gone too far. His supporters, Nixon claimed, were the "silent majority" of Americans. He believed that the demonstrators were only a vocal minority. Once elected, Nixon promised, he would bring unity and stability to the nation.

A Lunar Triumph

One of the high points of the early years of the Nixon administration occurred when the United States made the first manned landing on the moon. In 1961 President Kennedy had vowed to send astronauts to the moon by 1970, and the American space program forged ahead. Tragedy struck in 1967 when a flash fire during launch practice killed three astronauts. But by 1968 a manned Apollo spacecraft had circled the moon, taken detailed pictures, and returned to earth.

In July 1969 Commander Neil Armstrong led the three-man mission that orbited the moon and then descended to its surface in a lunar module. Millions watched on television as Armstrong carefully stepped into a thin layer of lunar dust and said, "That's one small step for a man, one giant leap for mankind." Two other lunar landings followed in November 1969 and December 1972.

The space program brought many benefits beyond the excitement of exploration. Satellites improved communications, naviga-tion, and weather forecasting on earth. The need for small computers aboard space capsules stimulated the new industry of micro-electronics. Other space research led to the production of materials that insulated homes more efficiently, devices that generated solar energy, and freeze-dried foods for the supermarket.

Not everyone agreed that the achievements in space were worth the $24-billion cost. Critics of the space program thought the money could have been better spent to solve pressing problems such as poverty and disease. The dramatic moon landing temporarily overwhelmed critics. Further unmanned space probes such as the Viking missions to Mars in 1971 and 1976 radioed back valuable information at a much lower cost than the manned missions.

The Supreme Court and Crime

Nixon had stressed law enforcement throughout his campaign for the presidency. Once elected he supported a bill that granted federal funds to local police departments.

In 1969 United States astronauts Neil Armstrong and Edwin "Buzz" Aldrin landed on the moon and set up television cameras. Millions on earth watched on live television as the first humans hopped around in the moon's light gravity, collecting rock and soil samples.

The Apollo-Soyuz Mission: Détente in Space

In July 1975 millions of spectators in the United States and the Soviet Union watched on television as three Americans and two Russians lived, worked, and ate together in their joined space-craft. The successful Apollo-Soyuz mission, as it was called, represented the willingness of the two superpowers to put aside cold war issues for a cooperative venture in space. The agreement to conduct the joint mission was signed in May 1972, when détente between the two nations was at its height.

For three years working groups from both countries met frequently to iron out technical and political difficulties. To solve the communication problem, each crew learned the other's language.

Finally, on July 15, 1975, the two spacecraft were launched—an Apollo from the United States and a Soyuz from the Soviet Union. Two days later the two craft successfully docked using equipment supplied by the United States. Four crew exchanges were made through the docking device. Millions of people watched, captivated, as the two crews joined in live, televised press conferences.

In all, the Apollo crew conducted 27 experiments in space. Of these, 5 were conducted jointly with the Soyuz crew. One experiment allowed the Soyuz crew to photograph the outermost fringe of the sun. This view was made possible by the Apollo spacecraft's blocking out the sun's bright center as the two spacecraft moved apart. Later planned joint missions were scrapped as relations between the two nations cooled.

His most lasting influence on the legal system probably resulted from the four appointments he made to the Supreme Court.

During the 1960s, under Chief Justice Earl Warren, the Supreme Court had handed down several rulings protecting the rights of people accused of crimes. In *Gideon* v. *Wainwright* (1963), for example, the Warren Court held that the states had to provide free legal representation for defendants who could not afford to hire lawyers.

Other Warren Court decisions restricted the tactics police could use to gain evidence against suspected criminals. In *Mapp* v. *Ohio* (1961) the Supreme Court ruled that items illegally seized by police could not be used as evidence against the accused. In *Miranda* v. *Arizona* (1966) the Supreme Court held that, before questioning accused persons, police were required to inform them of their rights to remain silent and to be represented by a lawyer.

Reaction to the Warren Court

Many Americans believed that the Warren Court rulings unreasonably restricted the power of the police. Such rulings, critics argued, protected the rights of accused persons at the expense of victims and society as a whole. President Nixon agreed with this criticism.

In 1969 Chief Justice Warren resigned from the Court because of poor health. President Nixon then appointed Warren Burger, a respected judge from Minnesota, to replace him. The Senate confirmed Burger's appointment with little opposition. Burger shared the President's concern that the Supreme Court had been too liberal in protecting criminal suspects.

When Nixon had an opportunity to appoint a second justice, he nominated Judge Clement Haynsworth. But the Senate rejected Haynsworth because it discovered that as a judge he had ruled on cases involving corporations in which he owned stock. (Judges are required to disqualify themselves in cases in which they have a personal interest.)

The President then nominated Judge G. Harrold Carswell. Once again the Senate refused to approve the appointment because Carswell's record as a federal appeals judge had been unimpressive and because of his hostility to civil rights for blacks. Finally the President nominated Judge Harry Blackmun of Minnesota, whom the Senate quickly confirmed. President Nixon later filled two more vacancies on the Court, selecting Lewis F. Powell of Virginia and William H. Rehnquist of Arizona. Neither nominee encountered serious difficulty in his confirmation hearings.

Nixon's four appointments made the Supreme Court more conservative. The Burger Court did not reverse the landmark criminal procedure decisions handed down during the 1960s. But it did limit their scope. For example, the Supreme Court held that even if police violated the *Miranda* rule in obtaining a pretrial confession, that confession could still be used to discredit trial testimony of the defendant. The Burger Court also narrowed the scope of the *Mapp* decision by ruling that questions based on illegally seized evidence could be asked at a grand jury hearing, even if they could not be asked in a jury trial.

Domestic Policies

President Nixon's appointments to the Supreme Court were only one example of his concern with law-and-order issues in domestic policies. He supported strong anticrime measures that increased the power of law enforcement officials to deal with criminal suspects. Nixon's statements on law and order reflected the deep concern of many Americans about the rapid rise of crime, urban violence, and campus disorder.

Nixon opposed many of the programs established under Lyndon Johnson's Great Society. He closed the Office of Economic Opportunity, which had directed Johnson's War on Poverty, and he hoped to cut back other programs. But support for the Great Society remained strong in Congress. Nixon vetoed several major bills that provided funds for social programs, and Congress overrode some of the vetoes. In 1973 President Nixon began to *impound*, or refuse to spend, funds that had been appropriated by Congress.

Despite such actions, federal spending on social programs continued to rise during the Nixon years. For example, the federal contribution to Medicaid almost doubled between 1970 and 1974. However, aid to elementary and secondary education increased only slightly.

To many Americans, Nixon appeared to be far less interested in the rights of minorities than his predecessor was. His administration publicly opposed the extension of the Voting Rights Act of 1965. President Nixon also spoke out against court-ordered busing to achieve racial integration. And the White House loosened guidelines governing school desegregation in the North and South.

President Nixon's main goal for black Americans was to increase the number of jobs for skilled black workers and to develop programs to assist black-owned businesses. In these areas the administration had some success. During the Nixon years, for example, the number of small businesses owned by black Americans increased. The majority of blacks, however, considered the Nixon record disappointing.

The Problem of Stagflation

The war in Vietnam contributed to economic problems in the early 1970s. Huge military expenditures pushed the annual inflation rate to 5 percent in 1970. At the same time, recession slowed economic growth. Economists labeled the economic slump *stagflation*, a combination of stagnation and inflation. As more Vietnam veterans returned home and entered the job market, unemployment increased to over 6 percent.

As a conservative, President Nixon disliked government interference in the economy. Nevertheless, with inflation rising, Nixon ordered a 90-day freeze on wages, prices, and rents on August 15, 1971. The first part of the President's anti-inflation program was called Phase I.

In Phase II, which began on November 14, 1971, Nixon substituted broad price controls for the freeze. The Cost of Living Council was charged with monitoring prices and blocking unreasonable price hikes.

President Nixon urged Congress to cut taxes. He also lowered interest rates and increased government spending. Those measures encouraged consumer spending and lowered unemployment. By the end of 1972 stagflation seemed to be beaten. When the Phase II controls were lifted in early 1973, however, prices jumped at a record rate.

The Election of 1972

Nixon seemed assured of reelection in 1972. The economy appeared stable, and the President's trips to China and the Soviet Union were popular. Furthermore, Kissinger's first announcement of a breakthrough in the Paris peace talks came shortly before the election. (See page 690.)

The Democratic party, on the other hand, was badly split. A series of bitter primary elections had shown the party's deep divisions. Senator George McGovern of South Dakota won the nomination, but many Democrats felt he was too liberal. McGovern's problems mounted when reporters discovered that his running mate, Senator Thomas Eagleton of Missouri, had once suffered an emotional illness. With growing public concern about Eagleton's health, McGovern was forced to replace him with Sargent Shriver, former director of the Peace Corps and a brother-in-law of John and Robert Kennedy.

Meanwhile, President Nixon based a well-organized and well-financed campaign on his image as a statesman working in the White House. Nixon boasted about the strength of the economy and the progress in the Vietnam peace negotiations. He also promised stricter law enforcement. Not even the arrest of burglars who were publicly linked to the White House, at Democratic party headquarters in June 1972, detracted from the President's strength. He was widely seen as decisive and competent by the American people.

Nixon won the election in a landslide. He carried every state but Massachusetts and won almost 61 percent of the vote. In the electoral college, the margin was even more lopsided: 521 to 17 votes. Nixon began his second term with a strong national mandate. Few could have predicted that within two years his long political career would end in disgrace.

An Oil Embargo

Early in his second term President Nixon faced a new international crisis. In October 1973 Egyptian and Syrian troops launched a surprise attack on Israel on the Jewish holiday of Yom Kippur. Fighting raged for more than two weeks until a fragile peace was arranged by the United Nations.

In the tense days following the war, Henry Kissinger helped negotiate a cease-fire agreement between Egypt and Israel. (Kissinger had become secretary of state earlier in 1973.) In the spring of 1974 he shuttled back and forth between capitals in the Middle East, trying to work out a formal cease-fire between Israel and Syria. As a result of Kissinger's "shuttle diplomacy," the two countries signed a cease-fire agreement in May 1974.

The United States had been a strong supporter of Israel for many years. And it had provided military aid to Israel during the October War. Arab nations resented this American support of Israel. In reaction, on October 17 they ordered an embargo on oil shipments to the United States. Because Americans imported about 25 percent of the oil they used, the embargo soon disrupted life.

Americans found themselves waiting in long lines to buy gasoline—if they could get any at all. They wondered whether enough oil would be available to heat their homes during the coming winter. The oil embargo contributed to higher inflation. The price of

The oil embargo that began in October 1973 caused chaos at gas stations such as these in Chicago. By January 1974 many gas stations were closing early to conserve fuel. Other stations had closed down because they had run completely out of fuel.

fuel and thousands of other petroleum-based products, such as plastics, medicines, and fertilizers, soared. Consumer prices rose by 6 percent in 1973 and jumped by 11 percent the next year.

President Nixon reacted to the energy crisis by encouraging Americans to conserve energy. He asked the states to lower their highway speed limits to 55 miles per hour. In an effort to increase the production of domestic oil, he signed the Alaskan Pipeline Act. This act authorized construction of an oil pipeline across Alaska and Canada. Finally, in March 1974, the Arab nations lifted the oil embargo. The immediate energy crisis had passed, but the lesson was clear: Americans needed to take a closer look at the way they used energy.

For answers, see p. A 115.
Section Review

1. Identify the following: Neil Armstrong, Earl Warren, Warren Burger, George McGovern.
2. Define the following terms: impound, stagflation.
3. List two benefits of the space program.
4. What did the Supreme Court rule in *Miranda* v. *Arizona*?
5. Describe two ways President Nixon tried to weaken Lyndon Johnson's Great Society.
6. What was Phase I of President Nixon's plan to slow inflation?
7. List three factors that contributed to President Nixon's reelection in 1972.
8. What role did Henry Kissinger play after the October War of 1973?

3 A Crisis in the Presidency

President Nixon and Vice-President Agnew had won a decisive victory in the 1972 election. Yet within two years, Agnew was to resign in disgrace, and Nixon was to become the first President to resign under the threat of impeachment and removal from office.

Behind the crisis in the executive branch lay a scandal that at first seemed to involve only a few minor officials of the President's reelection campaign. Further investigation revealed that higher officials and greater issues were involved.

A Puzzling Burglary

At 2:30 A.M. on June 17, 1972, Washington, D.C., police arrested five men who had broken into the headquarters of the Democratic National Committee, located in the Watergate apartment complex. The men were not ordinary burglars. They wore business suits and rubber surgical gloves. And they carried a walkie-talkie, 40 rolls of unexposed film, two cameras, lock picks, two pen-sized tear gas guns, and several bugging devices.

One of the Watergate burglars, James McCord, was a former CIA agent. McCord had been more recently employed as a security consultant to President Nixon's reelection committee. An address book carried by the burglars contained the name of another former CIA agent, E. Howard Hunt, a White House employee. Despite those links to the President, White House Press Secretary Ronald Ziegler called the break-in "a third-rate burglary attempt." He claimed that "certain elements may try to stretch this beyond what it is."

During the following months other disturbing facts came to light, many of them uncovered by Washington *Post* reporters Carl Bernstein and Bob Woodward. For example, one of the burglars had a checking account containing $89,000 from the Committee to Reelect the President (CREEP).

Reports pointed to the existence of a $350,000 cash "slush fund" controlled by CREEP to finance undercover projects designed to hinder Democratic party rivals. Former Nixon cabinet members Maurice Stans and John Mitchell knew of the fund, the reports suggested, and might have even approved the illegal activities.

Despite those reports, the Watergate break-in did not become a major issue in the 1972 presidential campaign. The President announced in August that White House counsel John Dean had conducted an investigation of the burglary and that "no one on the White House staff . . . was involved in this very bizarre situation."

After a lengthy inquiry by the Federal Bureau of Investigation (FBI), the five Watergate burglars, Howard Hunt, and G. Gordon Liddy, a lawyer for CREEP, were prosecuted. In January 1973 two defendants were found guilty, and five pleaded guilty. On March 23 the trial judge, John Sirica, sentenced all the defendants to prison terms.

On the day the sentences were imposed, Judge Sirica made public a letter he had received from James McCord. McCord charged that witnesses had committed perjury and that certain high officials had pressed the burglars to plead guilty so the trial would be concluded quickly. McCord's accusations heightened suspicions about the link between the burglars and the White House.

The Cover-up Unravels

McCord's revelations suggested that the White House was trying to hide the truth about the Watergate burglary. Further investigation linked high-level officials to the cover-up, including John Mitchell and Maurice Stans as well as President Nixon's two closest personal aides, H. R. Haldeman and John Ehrlichman. By April 1973 events forced President Nixon to accept the resignations of Haldeman and Ehrlichman.

Then in May a special committee set up by the Senate convened to hear testimony about Watergate. The Senate Select Committee on Presidential Campaign Activities was composed of seven senators and chaired by Senator Sam Ervin of North Carolina. Ervin was noted for his knowledge of constitutional law. He was determined to discover what the President knew about the Watergate burglary and cover-up. The committee hearings were televised for three

The televised Senate Watergate hearings showed the process of the American constitutional system in a time of crisis. The historic hearings were chaired by Senator Samuel Ervin of North Carolina (left), shown listening to chief counsel for the committee, Sam Dash.

months, giving the public a close look at the Watergate investigation.

Witnesses testified that Attorney General John Mitchell, the highest law enforcement officer in the country, had been present when Gordon Liddy outlined proposals for the Watergate burglary and other espionage activities.

The most astonishing testimony came from John Dean, who had been fired from his post as White House counsel in April. In a quiet voice Dean methodically confirmed much previous testimony and then went further. As recently as April, Haldeman, Ehrlichman, Mitchell—even President Nixon himself, Dean claimed—had continued to suppress information about the Watergate activities. Dean charged that the President had approved plans to pay the Watergate burglars "hush money" to remain silent.

Of all the witnesses, only Dean claimed that the President had tried to suppress information linking the Watergate burglary and the White House. Then, on July 16, 1973, Alexander Butterfield, an assistant to H. R. Haldeman, stunned committee members by revealing that a secret White House tape recording system had been in existence for years. All conversations with the President had been routinely taped. Investigators immediately requested the tapes as a potential source of evidence.

Agnew's Undoing

While the Watergate affair was under investigation, another inquiry into unrelated matters was in progress. Officials charged that Vice-President Agnew, while governor of Maryland and even while Vice-President, had accepted bribes from construction companies doing business with the state.

Faced with a strong case against him and the prospect of going to prison, Agnew decided to resign as Vice-President on October 10, 1973. He also pleaded no contest, the equivalent of pleading guilty, to a single charge of federal income tax evasion. In exchange, the prosecutors dropped the other charges against him. The court fined him $10,000 and sentenced him to three years on probation.

According to the Twenty-fifth Amendment, the President must select a new Vice-President when that office becomes vacant. President Nixon chose Representative Gerald Ford of Michigan and submitted his name to Congress for confirmation. Congress confirmed Ford's appointment on October 12.

The Investigation Continues

In order to dispel charges that he was obstructing the Watergate investigation, President Nixon instructed his new attorney general, Elliot Richardson, to appoint a special Watergate prosecutor. Richardson chose Archibald Cox, a respected Harvard University law professor. When Butterfield disclosed the existence of the White House taping system, Cox moved to obtain the tapes.

On July 23 Cox requested a subpoena, a legally binding order, directing the President to turn over nine tapes to the special prosecutor's office. Judge Sirica granted the request. President Nixon appealed the decision. He claimed that "executive privilege" allowed him to retain the tapes for reasons of national security. But in October the United States Court of Appeals upheld Judge Sirica's ruling. In an attempt to prevent the release of the tapes, Nixon ordered Richardson to fire Cox.

Richardson refused and promptly resigned, as did his immediate subordinate, William Ruckelshaus. The solicitor general finally carried out the order, and on Saturday, October 20, Cox was removed. Reporters dubbed the resignations and firing the Saturday Night Massacre. Letters of protest poured into Congress. Sixteen separate bills calling for impeachment of the President were introduced. The House Judiciary Committee, under Chairman Peter Rodino of New Jersey, began deliberations.*

Under these pressures, President Nixon appointed a new special prosecutor, Leon Jaworski of Texas. The President also released the tapes to Judge Sirica. But embarrassed White House lawyers were forced to tell the court that some of the subpoenaed tapes were missing. Even worse, an apparently crucial 18½-minute segment had been erased from one tape. Experts testified that the erasures were most probably deliberate.

The crisis deepened in March 1974 when the grand jury investigating Watergate matters indicted Mitchell, Haldeman, Ehrlichman, and several other Nixon aides for perjury and obstruction of justice. The grand jury named the President as an unindicted co-conspirator.

In April, Special Prosecutor Jaworski and the House Judiciary Committee requested additional tapes. The President refused to submit them, but by the end of the month he agreed to supply edited transcripts. White House secretaries produced over 1,200 pages, which the President made public. The transcripts revealed the President discussing the Watergate cover-up.

Neither the Judiciary Committee nor Jaworski was satisfied with edited transcripts of the tapes. At the end of May, Jaworski obtained an order from Judge Sirica directing the President to turn over the Watergate tapes. Nixon appealed to the Supreme Court, but the Court upheld Sirica's order.

Late in July the Juidiciary Committee passed three articles of impeachment against President Nixon. The articles claimed that the President had obstructed justice, misused his presidential powers, and refused to comply with the committee's request for evidence.

At the insistence of his lawyers, the President then released transcripts of taped conversations recorded June 23, 1972, only a few days after the Watergate burglary. The transcripts demonstrated beyond all doubt that he had known of the burglars' connection to the White House and had acted to limit the FBI investigation. Even the President's staunchest supporters in Congress refused to defend him. Impeachment by the House seemed certain.

On August 8, 1974, President Richard M. Nixon appeared on national television and announced his resignation. He became the first President in the history of the republic to take such an action. Gerald Ford then became President.

In a televised speech to the nation on August 8, 1974, Richard Nixon became the first President in American history to resign from office.

---

*As you have read, the House of Representatives can impeach, or accuse, a President of high crimes and misdemeanors. The Senate then tries the case, and if it votes to convict, the President is removed from office.

The Imperial Presidency

Even before Watergate, some critics had charged that President Nixon was creating an "imperial presidency" by assuming too much power. During the Nixon years, the White House staff grew to 500 persons, more than double the size of any previous President's staff. Members of the White House staff did not have to be confirmed by the Senate, as cabinet members did. Thus, influential staff members, such as H. R. Haldeman and John Ehrlichman, were not responsible to anyone but the President.

Nixon's presidential style contributed to the uneasiness many Americans felt about the growing powers of the presidency. He would go for months without holding a press conference, and he often spent many hours during the day alone. This behavior created an image in many people's minds of a remote and secretive chief executive.

Furthermore, critics objected to policies they believed exceeded the President's authority. Nixon had defied the Democratic-controlled Congress by impounding funds Congress had appropriated. He also angered members of Congress when he claimed that he had the right as President to refuse to allow members of the executive branch to testify before congressional committees.

Richard Nixon had not created the powerful presidency. The executive branch of the federal government had been growing in size and authority since the 1930s. The events of Watergate, however, focused attention on the powers of the President and brought demands for reform.

Congress responded with several new laws. The Congressional Budget and Impoundment Act of 1974 revised congressional budget-making practices and forbade a President to impound funds appropriated by Congress. Congress strengthened the 1966 Freedom of Information Act, giving the public greater access to information on government decisions and activities.

In addition, the Federal Campaign Reform Act of 1974 provided tax funds to candidates for federal office who met certain qualifications. The act also placed limits on private campaign contributions. This was an effort to prevent the sort of misuse of funds that had occurred in the 1972 election. However, critics argued that even stronger laws were needed.

Watergate in Retrospect

The Watergate crisis was a traumatic experience for the United States. There had been other governmental scandals in American history, but a President had never resigned from office. The Watergate crisis shook the confidence of some Americans in their government. However, for many people, the crisis demonstrated the strength of the federal system of checks and balances. Congress and the Supreme Court had successfully checked the power of the President when he appeared to be abusing that power. The balance of powers as outlined in the Constitution had been maintained, and the transition from one administration to the next had been smooth.

With the presidency of the United States comes enormous power. The President is both the commander in chief of the armed forces and the principal designer of domestic and foreign policies. Watergate revealed the dangers of an imperial presidency, but it also demonstrated that no President is above the law. As Gerald Ford commented upon assuming the office of President, "Our great republic is a government of laws and not of men." That no President can ignore the laws of the United States seems to be one enduring lesson of the Watergate experience.

To some observers, the real end of the turbulent decade of the 1960s came with Nixon's resignation in August 1974. Strong feelings about the war in Vietnam and Watergate had sharply divided the nation. It was now up to Gerald Ford, the first President to assume the office without having been elected President or Vice-President, to try to heal the nation's wounds. He would also face a host of difficult challenges as the nation entered its third century.

For answers, see p. A 116.

Section Review

1. Identify the following: John Sirica, Sam Ervin, John Mitchell, John Dean, Archibald Cox, Leon Jaworski.

2. What did James McCord charge in the letter he wrote to Judge Sirica?

3. What led to Vice-President Agnew's resignation in October 1973?

4. What was the Saturday Night Massacre?

5. What three charges did the House Judiciary Committee make against President Nixon?

4 A New Start

After taking the oath of office, President Gerald R. Ford proclaimed, "The Constitution works. . . . Our long national nightmare is over." Indeed, after the turmoil of Vietnam and Watergate, the public desperately wanted a return to stability.

The Unexpected President

Gerald Ford had served his congressional district in Michigan for 25 years, earning a reputation for hard work and dependability. From 1965 to 1973, he served as minority leader in the House of Representatives. His colleagues in the House liked him, and they had warmly supported his selection as Vice-President when Spiro Agnew resigned in October 1973.

After the disillusionment caused by the Watergate affair, Ford seemed an ideal person to hold the presidency. People saw him as outgoing and scrupulously honest. They responded to his simple lifestyle. Ford's pledge of "openness and candor" for his presidency drew wide praise. So too did his promise to hold regular news conferences and to make himself available to the nation.

Ford moved quickly to assure stability and to restore confidence in government. He selected Nelson Rockefeller, a former governor of New York, as his Vice-President. In foreign affairs, he announced that Henry Kissinger would be retained as secretary of state. Furthermore, he promised to follow the foreign policy guidelines established during the Nixon administration.

With a popular new President in the White House, the nation looked forward to a time of quiet healing. Early in the Ford presidency, however, new revelations ignited controversy.

New Controversies

Only a month after taking office, President Ford issued a blanket pardon to Richard Nixon that freed Nixon from prosecution for any crimes he might have committed while in office. Ford stated that he wanted to spare the country the agony of putting a former President on trial.

Some Americans supported the pardon because they agreed with President Ford that Richard Nixon had suffered enough. However, polls showed that the majority of Americans opposed the action. They questioned the justice of allowing Nixon to escape punishment while many of his subordinates had gone to jail.

The White House was flooded with phone calls and telegrams critical of the pardon. There were many charges that Ford's pardon was the result of a deal between Ford and Nixon. President Ford strongly denied that there had been any deal. Nevertheless, his popularity declined dramatically. He would never entirely regain the good will and support he had when he first took office.

Disclosures of misconduct in the CIA and FBI also startled the nation. In December 1974 the press revealed that the CIA had

Nixon's resignation brought Vice-President Gerald Ford to the White House. Ford had a reputation for being down-to-earth. The new President is shown here making breakfast in the family dining room.

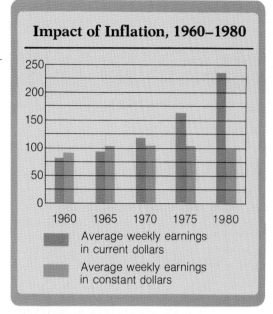

Impact of Inflation, 1960–1980

Average weekly earnings in current dollars

Average weekly earnings in constant dollars

Source: *Statistical Abstract of the United States*

■ One of the most troubling problems of the modern economy has been persistent inflation. During an inflationary period it costs more dollars to buy the same goods and services. To make comparisons between years when the dollar had different values, economists use a concept called "constant dollars." That is, they choose a specific year, then use the amount of goods and services a dollar would buy in that year as a yardstick. On this graph, the "constant dollar" used is that of 1967. You can see that although wages have increased dramatically, people's buying power has not.

kept files on American citizens, in direct violation of the agency's charter. It also came to light in February 1975 that J. Edgar Hoover, the longtime head of the FBI, had maintained secret files on prominent Americans.

President Ford appointed a high-level commission under the leadership of Vice-President Nelson Rockefeller to investigate the charges against the CIA. At the same time, Congress set up special committees to investigate the CIA and FBI and moved to restrict the undercover activities of the two agencies.

Ford sparked another heated controversy when he offered amnesty, or pardon, to those who had illegally avoided military service during the Vietnam War. The President said he wanted to heal the social divisions caused by the war. However, critics charged that Ford's plan was too lenient on people who had refused to fight for their country. Few people took advantage of the offer of amnesty in any case. Some refused because they thought the requirement of alternative national service was an admission that resistance to military service had been wrong.

Troubled Economy

Serious economic challenges also faced the Ford administration. Soon after taking office, Ford targeted inflation as the nation's main economic problem. Following the 1973 oil embargo, steep increases in the price of oil had fueled a sharp jump in the rate of inflation. To counter rising prices, Ford began a voluntary program of controlling prices and wages called WIN (Whip Inflation Now), but he saw no success.

Instead of improving, the economy took a turn for the worse, moving into the worst recession since the 1930s. Factories closed down and consumer demand for goods dropped sharply. The rate of unemployment rose steadily, reaching about 9 percent by late 1975.

To stimulate the stagnant economy, Ford persuaded Congress to approve a tax cut. While the cut contributed to a modest economic recovery, it also stimulated a new round of inflation. The economy seemed to be stalled in a pattern, swinging between periods of recession and growing inflation. President Ford tried to curb inflation by cutting government spending. He vetoed a number of spending bills passed by the Democratic-controlled Congress. Despite such actions, inflation continued to plague the nation.

Continuity in Foreign Policy

In foreign affairs, President Ford continued the policies developed during the Nixon administration. With his secretary of state, Henry Kissinger, he promoted détente. Ford visited the Soviet Union in November 1974 and met with Soviet President Leonid Brezhnev to discuss a new treaty to limit nuclear arms.

The following year the President traveled to Helsinki, Finland, where he signed an agreement with the Soviet Union, Canada, and 32 nations in western and eastern Eu-

Henry Kissinger relished the art of diplomatic negotiations. Once he described himself as a "Lone Ranger"–style diplomat. He rode into town when there was trouble, solved the crisis, and rode out again in search of other crises. He is shown here visiting Israeli Prime Minister Golda Meir as part of his shuttle diplomacy following the 1973 October War.

rope. The agreement, known as the Helsinki Accords, fixed the national boundaries established after World War II. It also spelled out human rights standards that the signing nations pledged to observe.

Despite these examples of cooperation, by 1976 relations with the Soviet Union had begun to cool. Critics of détente charged that the Soviet Union had cheated on nuclear arms agreements and had steadily increased its arsenal of weapons. They believed that the Soviet Union had encouraged Egypt to attack Israel in 1973 and that it was arming other countries in the Third World. Some Americans cautioned that the Soviet Union should be viewed as an adversary rather than as a partner in détente.

In the Middle East, Ford and Kissinger could point to some success. Kissinger continued the shuttle diplomacy he had begun after the October War. As a result of his efforts, Israel agreed to withdraw from some of the territory it had occupied in the western Sinai Peninsula. The Middle East was just one area where Kissinger took an active role in foreign affairs. In all, he traveled about 650,000 miles as secretary of state.

The Fall of South Vietnam

The cease-fire signed in January 1973 brought about the withdrawal of American forces from Vietnam, but it did not bring peace to the region. The cease-fire soon broke down, and the war between South Vietnam and the Vietcong and North Vietnam resumed. Without aid from the United States, the South Vietnamese army crumbled. In April 1975 it surrendered. On May 1 North Vietnamese forces entered Saigon. North and South Vietnam were reunited, and the former South Vietnamese capital was renamed Ho Chi Minh City.

At about the same time, the pro-American government in Cambodia collapsed and was replaced by a communist regime led by Pol Pot. Cambodia's new regime seized the American merchant ship *Mayaguez* after the ship had entered Cambodian waters. President Ford reacted forcefully. He sent a naval force and about 2,000 marines to free the crew of 39. Some Americans criticized the operation because it cost the United States 15 dead and 50 wounded, but most Americans supported President Ford.

Celebrating the Anniversary of the Nation's Birth

On July 4, 1976, in small towns and big cities all across the nation, millions of Americans celebrated the two-hundredth anniversary of the Declaration of Independence. Many towns sponsored firework displays and parades. In Seward, Nebraska, a time capsule containing such items as a 1976 car and letters from townspeople was sealed. Italian Americans in Rome, New York, planned one of the biggest spaghetti dinners ever held, preparing 600 pounds of pasta for a crowd of 3,000. In Newport, Rhode Island, citizens planted a buttonwood Liberty Tree next to one planted in 1876 in honor of the one-hundredth anniversary of the nation's birth.

Special events in large cities drew enormous crowds. In Washington, D.C., the Declaration of Independence, the Constitution, and the Bill of Rights were on display for 76 consecutive hours to accommodate the thousands of tourists visiting the nation's capital. And in New York City hundreds of thousands of people were treated to a spectacular sight as a flotilla of 225 majestic sailing ships from 30 nations entered New York Harbor.

An occasion stirring national pride, the bicentennial reflected another celebration a century earlier. Philadelphia had been made the focal point of the 1876 centennial because of the city's important role in the founding of the nation. On July 4, 1876, a crowd of 200,000 gathered at Independence Hall in Philadelphia to hear a reading of the Declaration of Independence. Celebrations in all regions of the country marked the occasion. With the country still suffering the aftershocks of the Civil War, the South's participation in the centennial was considered an important step in reuniting the nation.

In 1976 the nation was again suffering from the memory of a recent and divisive war, the conflict in Vietnam. However, celebration of the nation's birthday was a time for drawing together and for renewing the spirit of independence and freedom created two centuries earlier.

At the Republican national convention President Ford was challenged by the conservative wing of the Republican party. The conservative Republicans backed Ronald Reagan, who had served as governor of California in the late 1960s and early 1970s. Despite spirited support from many convention delegates, Reagan's challenge was narrowly defeated.

Although the long years of fighting in Vietnam had finally ended, the effects of the war would be felt for years to come. More than 100,000 South Vietnamese left their country immediately after the communist takeover. Most of these people settled in the United States. Thousands later fled in small boats, some of which capsized in the open seas. When neighboring countries refused to accept the flood of South Vietnamese refugees, the problem became a serious international issue.

In Cambodia, the suffering brought about by a radical communist regime was devastating. The full extent of the tragedy may never be known, but more than 1 million people are believed to have starved or been executed under the Pol Pot regime.

The 1976 Election

The Ford administration had little time to forge its own policies, but the President's honesty and goodwill helped the nation recover from the atmosphere of Watergate. Most Americans welcomed the positive

mood as they celebrated the nation's bicentennial anniversary on July 4, 1976.

Nonetheless, President Ford faced a strong challenge for the 1976 Republican presidential nomination. Ronald W. Reagan, former governor of California, had the support of the conservative wing of the Republican party. Ford won a narrow victory at the party convention, but the Watergate scandal damaged the Republicans' chances in the general election.

Former Georgia governor Jimmy Carter carried the Democratic banner. Carter had seemed an unlikely presidential candidate two years earlier, but his effective campaigning among the people won him the nomination. Carter's strong civil rights record as governor brought him overwhelming support from black voters. Labor also rallied behind him.

The primary issues during the election campaign were inflation, unemployment, and energy shortages, but neither candidate offered well-defined programs on those issues. Carter stressed humanitarian concerns in foreign policy and in all his dealings. "I

Major Events	
1969	American astronauts make first manned lunar landing; Vietnamization begins
1970	United States and South Vietnamese forces invade Cambodia; Congress repeals Gulf of Tonkin Resolution
1972	Nixon visits the People's Republic of China and Soviet Union; Nixon reelected
1973	Vietnam cease-fire signed; Watergate investigation begins; October War in Middle East; Ford appointed Vice-President; Arab oil embargo
1974	Nixon resigns; Gerald R. Ford becomes President
1975	Saigon falls to North Vietnam; *Mayaguez* seized by Cambodians; Helsinki Accords signed
1976	Bicentennial celebration; Jimmy Carter elected President

will never lie to you," he promised the American people. Jimmy Carter won a slim popular majority, with 40.8 million popular votes compared to 39.1 million for Ford. In the electoral college, Carter won 297 votes compared to 241 for Ford.

For answers, see p. A 116.

Section Review

1. Identify the following: Nelson Rockefeller, WIN, Helsinki Accords, Jimmy Carter.
2. Describe the conflicting points of view about President Ford's pardon of Richard Nixon.
3. What revelations about the CIA and FBI startled the nation in 1974?
4. (a) How did President Ford try to stimulate the economy? (b) What effect did this measure have?
5. On what grounds did some Americans criticize the policy of détente during the mid-1960s?
6. (a) What happened to the cease-fire in Vietnam after the withdrawal of United States forces? (b) What was the result of this development?
7. What action did President Ford take when Cambodian forces seized the *Mayaguez*?
8. What were the main issues in the 1976 elections?

IN PERSPECTIVE   Under President Nixon the United States began to disengage from the war in Vietnam. Nixon worked to improve relations with China and the Soviet Union, with the hope of contributing to a more stable world. He also sought to increase stability at home. The nation, however, continued to be troubled by inflation, which was aggravated by the rapid rise of oil prices after 1973.

In 1974 the Watergate crisis led to President Nixon's resignation. The nation was shaken by the events of Watergate, but the crisis also demonstrated that the system of checks and balances worked. Gerald Ford, a man known for his honesty, seemed to be the President the nation needed in 1974. However, President Ford was plagued by economic problems and by criticism of his pardon of Richard Nixon. In the 1976 presidential election, Ford lost to Democrat Jimmy Carter.

For answers, see p. A 116.

Chapter Review

1. How did the foreign policy of Henry Kissinger and President Nixon differ from American foreign policy during the 1950s and 1960s?

2. (a) How did Vietnamization reduce American involvement in the Vietnam War? (b) What action by President Nixon in May 1970 created greater opposition to the war? (c) How did Congress try to limit the authority of the President in the war?

3. How did President Nixon reduce tensions with China and the Soviet Union in 1972?

4. (a) Describe the decisions of the Warren Court that extended the rights of people accused of crimes. (b) Why did many people object to those decisions? (c) How did the Burger Court limit the scope of those decisions?

5. (a) Why did Arab nations impose a boycott on oil shipments to the United States in 1973? (b) What impact did the boycott have on American life? Why?

6. (a) Why did the House Judiciary Committee begin hearings on the impeachment of President Nixon? (b) What did the committee decide? (c) What was Nixon's reaction?

7. (a) What is meant by the term "imperial presidency"? (b) Why did some critics charge that President Nixon created an "imperial presidency"? (c) After the Watergate crisis, how did Congress try to prevent a President from becoming too powerful?

8. (a) What strengths did Gerald Ford bring to the presidency? (b) How did those strengths help the nation recover from the trauma of Watergate?

9. (a) What economic problems faced the nation during the Nixon-Ford years? (b) What policies were implemented to deal with those problems? (c) To what extent were those policies successful?

For answers, see p. A 117.

For Further Thought

1. Why do you think it was probably easier for President Nixon to improve relations with China and the Soviet Union than it would have been for a person without a strong anticommunist background?

2. Explain why each of the following groups may have been dissatisfied with the Nixon presidency: (a) opponents of the Vietnam War, (b) opponents of the communist government in China, (c) supporters of the Great Society, (d) critics of the "imperial presidency."

3. Review the system of checks and balances set up in the Constitution. (See page 161.) (a) How did the system work during the Watergate crisis? Cite specific actions in your answer. (b) Do you think the presidency had become too powerful by 1974? Why or why not? (c) Does the presidency seem as powerful today as it was before the Watergate crisis? Explain your answer.

4. (a) How might a trial of Richard Nixon after he resigned as President have harmed the nation? (b) How might such a trial have benefited the nation? (c) Do you think President Ford was right to pardon Richard Nixon? Why or why not?

For answers, see p. A 117.

Developing Basic Skills

1. *Writing a Report*   Investigate one or more of the products you use that was developed through space technology. (You could begin with the products described on page 692, but there are many others.) Write a report in which you describe how the product was used in the space program and how it was adapted for everyday use.

2. *Graph Reading*   Study the graph on page 702 and answer the following questions: (a) What were the average weekly earnings of American workers in current dollars in 1960? in 1980? (b) What were the average weekly earnings in constant dollars in 1960 and in 1980? (c) How did the relationship between current dollars and constant dollars change between 1960 and 1980? (d) How do you think the average American worker was affected by this development?

See page 779 for suggested readings.

Beginning the Nation's Third Century

40

(1977–Present)

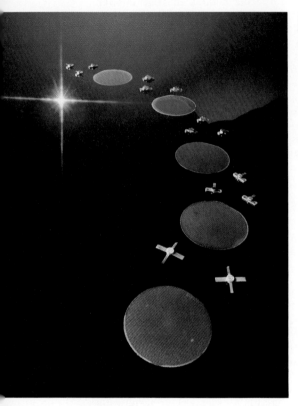

Silicon wafers used in computers.

Computers became a symbol of progress in the late 1970s and the 1980s. They became a common tool of office and factory workers, and computer games became a popular leisure activity for millions of Americans. Doctors began to rely on computers for fast, accurate diagnoses, and economists used computers to forecast the outcomes of various policies.

Despite such progress, however, solving the nation's economic problems would prove to be a difficult task for President Carter and President Reagan. The energy crisis of the early 1970s reappeared later in the decade, and inflation continued to plague the economy. Both President Carter and President Reagan took steps to guarantee a stable energy supply for the nation and to reduce inflation.

In foreign affairs, the United States faced challenges in many parts of the world. American involvement in Vietnam had ended, but growing tensions in regions such as the Middle East and Central America threatened to draw the nation into new conflicts.

1 The Carter White House

During the presidential campaign of 1976, Jimmy Carter reminded voters that he had few ties to official Washington. His administration, he promised, would bring new faces and ideas to national government. However, as an "outsider" Carter had to convince the traditional leadership in Washington to enact his programs. This task was a difficult one in light of growing inflation and recession at home and mounting world tensions, particularly in the Middle East.

New Leadership in Washington

When James Earl Carter announced that he would seek the Democratic nomination for President, few people thought he could win. Carter had served as governor of Georgia, but he had little experience in national or international politics. No candidate from the deep South had won the presidency since before the Civil War. And Carter did not have much support from the leaders of the Democratic party. However, Carter proved to have wide appeal among rank-and-file Democrats.

He later described his political style as "a southern peanut farmer populist type." He promised honest government to a nation still struggling to forget the Watergate scandals. Many Americans welcomed his low-key, folksy manner and deep religious convictions. They thought that such a President would surely bring government in Washington back into touch with the people.

Previous Presidents had drawn many of their advisors from top New York City law firms, major corporations, big states like New York, Texas, and California, or from the government itself. Carter planned to appoint people to his administration who were new to Washington and national government.

Jimmy Carter brought other unusual qualities to the presidency. Not since Herbert Hoover had an occupant of the White House been so familiar with science and technology. Carter had worked on nuclear submarines after graduating from the United States Naval Academy. He left his Navy career when his father's death forced him back home to Plains, Georgia, to run the family peanut warehouse business.

Carter showed at his inauguration that he intended to transplant much of the simple, down-home style of Plains to Washington. Rather than ride in the presidential limousine, he walked down Pennsylvania Avenue. He substituted a business suit for the formal attire Presidents usually wore for the ceremony. And when Carter was sworn in, the Chief Justice of the Supreme Court used his nickname, "Jimmy," rather than his given name, James Earl.

Jimmy Carter tried to bring the informality of his inaugural walk to his term in office. He discouraged the use of lavish ceremonies and often appeared in public in casual clothing. When he visited his home in Plains, Georgia, the President was often photographed playing softball with members of his staff and reporters.

A Stalemate With Congress

Carter faced problems that would have taxed any President. After Vietnam and Watergate, Congress had tried to limit the authority of the executive branch to reduce the danger of an "imperial presidency." Inflation, the energy crisis, and other domestic issues called for solutions that promised to be painful and unpopular. Efforts to improve relations with the People's Republic of China or the Soviet Union always provoked controversy. Furthermore, such issues as arms control seldom have broad popular appeal.

The new President's style sometimes made this difficult situation even worse. As an outsider, he did not have close ties with the Democratic leadership in the House and Senate. Many of his advisors were equally new to Washington. It took the administration a long time to master the intricacies of running the national government. Furthermore, Carter did not always work effectively behind the scenes to build support for his programs.

Carter's critics charged that the President became so involved with details that he did not emphasize broad goals for his administration. Even his supporters never knew which measures were most important for the administration's program.

In his first year in office Carter presented Congress with almost a dozen major bills. The legislative program covered tax reform, social security, energy, and a host of other pressing matters. It immediately ran into strong opposition. As a result, no bill passed without major alterations. For example, the President proposed an ambitious plan for tax reform. He asked Congress to pass a bill lowering income taxes for the poor and closing certain "loopholes" in current tax laws. Such loopholes allowed many people to avoid paying taxes no matter how much money they made.

Congress undermined much of the President's tax reform proposal. The bill that passed did lower some taxes. But it raised the social security tax, which increased the tax bill for most people. At the same time Congress reduced the taxes of some high-income people by cutting the rates they paid for capital gains, the increased value of assets such as stock and property. Critics pointed to such failures as evidence that Carter had not displayed effective leadership.

Controversy in Foreign Policy

In his inauguration speech, Jimmy Carter made the idea of human rights* a central part of his foreign policy. "Our commitment to human rights must be absolute," he told the nation. "Because we are free we can never be indifferent to the fate of freedom elsewhere."

In practice, Carter found a human rights policy easier to adopt than to enforce. He required the State Department to use the protection of human rights as a criterion for receiving aid from the United States. His administration suspended military aid to several nations guilty of severe violation of rights.

Yet, some of the United States' most loyal allies had the poorest records of political abuses. For example, the shah of Iran, Mohammed Reza Pahlavi, was an enthusiastic supporter of the United States in the Persian Gulf region. However, he ruled through a military dictatorship that became increasingly corrupt. His secret police, Savak, became synonymous with the use of torture to silence political opponents. President Carter might quietly urge the shah to improve his record on human rights, but he did not want to embarrass a loyal ally. As a result, critics charged that the policy was unfairly enforced. Nations less important to the United States were held to stricter standards.

The application of Carter's human rights policy did lead to a more active American role in Africa. Encouraged by UN Ambassador Andrew Young, the Carter administration condemned the apartheid policies of South Africa and Rhodesia. At times Young's candid remarks embarrassed the President. Young's opponents called him irresponsible and demanded that Carter restrict his comments. But Young was eager to forge new ties between the United States and black African nations. He participated in negotiations between representatives of the white minority and the black majority in Rhodesia.

---

*"Human rights" refers to the opportunities of people to make political choices, to express their beliefs without the threat of persecution or violence, and to own personal property. Traditionally, governments in democratic countries such as Great Britain, Sweden, Japan, and the United States respect human rights more than do military dictatorships or governments in Soviet bloc nations.

As a result of the negotiations, Rhodesia became Zimbabwe and majority rule was established.

Two other foreign policy issues sparked heated debate during the Carter administration—the Panama Canal treaties and diplomatic recognition of the People's Republic of China. In 1978 President Carter agreed to a series of treaties granting Panama control over the Canal Zone by the year 2000. Many critics did not recognize that the United States had never actually owned the Panama Canal. They charged that Carter was giving away American property.

President Carter saw the treaties as an important step toward improving the image of the United States in Latin America. Besides, he believed that the danger of sabotage would be reduced if the Panamanians gained control. The Senate voted its approval of the treaties in March 1978.

President Nixon had encouraged a thaw in United States relations with the People's Republic of China after his historic trip in February 1972. (See page 690.) Trade and diplomatic talks had continued since then. In 1979 Jimmy Carter decided the time had come to renew the tradition of friendship between the two nations. He concluded a series of agreements that included formal diplomatic recognition and increased opportunities for trade.

Even though most Americans supported the President, diplomatic recognition led to considerable controversy. The Peking government had insisted that the United States withdraw its recognition of the nationalist government in Taiwan as the official government of China. Conservative Republicans had long made support for the nationalists a cornerstone of their foreign policy. They accused Carter of abandoning a long-time ally of the United States.

The Camp David Summit

One of President Carter's successes in foreign affairs resulted from his efforts to settle the disputes between Israel and Egypt. In the years following the October War of 1973, Egyptian President Anwar el-Sadat began to develop closer ties with the United States. In 1975 Egypt canceled a treaty of friendship signed with the Soviet Union in 1971.

In November 1977 President Sadat visited Israel, becoming the first Arab head of state to do so. Sadat held cordial talks with Israeli Prime Minister Menachem Begin. Both sides agreed to work toward a peaceful settlement of their differences.

Such a settlement did not come easily, however. Israel still held the Sinai Peninsula it had captured from Egypt in 1967. Furthermore, Sadat insisted that Begin provide self-rule to Palestinians under Israeli jurisdiction. Israel in turn insisted that Egypt recognize Israel's right to survive as a nation. Begin also refused any settlement that did not guarantee his country's security.

When negotiations faltered, President Carter invited Begin and Sadat to the United States to discuss their differences. For 12

■ Israel gained territory in each of three wars fought in the Middle East—in 1948, 1967, and 1973. In a 1978 agreement reached at Camp David, Maryland, the leaders of Egypt and Israel agreed to initial steps toward resolving the long Middle East dispute. Israel agreed to withdraw from the Sinai Peninsula, the Gaza Strip, and part of Jordan over a five-year period. The withdrawal from the Sinai was completed in May 1982, as this map shows.

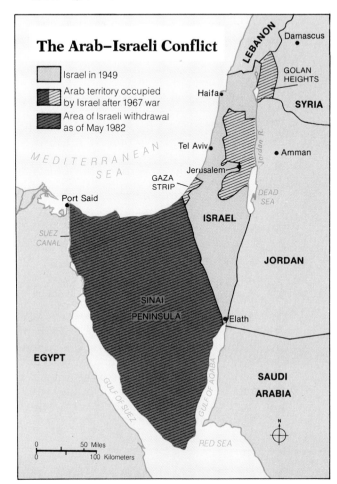

The Arab–Israeli Conflict

Israel in 1949

Arab territory occupied by Israel after 1967 war

Area of Israeli withdrawal as of May 1982

MEDITERRANEAN SEA

LEBANON
Damascus
GOLAN HEIGHTS
Haifa
SYRIA
Tel Aviv
Jordan R.
Amman
Jerusalem
GAZA STRIP
DEAD SEA
Port Said
ISRAEL
SUEZ CANAL
JORDAN
SINAI PENINSULA
Elath
EGYPT
GULF OF SUEZ
GULF OF AQABA
SAUDI ARABIA
RED SEA

0   50 Miles
0   100 Kilometers

In 1978 President Jimmy Carter brought together President Anwar el-Sadat of Egypt (left) and Prime Minister Menachem Begin of Israel (right) for private talks on the Middle East. At Camp David, Maryland, they agreed to the "Framework for Peace in the Middle East," a possible first step to peace in that region.

days the three leaders met at the President's Camp David retreat in the mountains of Maryland. For the President it was a bold gamble. If the talks broke down, many people would blame him.

In September 1978 the tired but elated heads of state returned to Washington to sign the "Framework for Peace in the Middle East." The document proposed a five-year plan under which Israel, Jordan, and the Palestinians could work out a formula for Palestinian self-rule. It also laid the groundwork for a peace treaty between Egypt and Israel that would return the Sinai territory to Egypt.

Changing Relations with the Soviet Union

President Carter took office anxious to conclude a new arms agreement with the Soviet Union. Negotiations for such an agreement had begun during the Ford administration. American and Soviet negotiators had met regularly in Vienna, Austria. They sought a formula to extend the limits on nuclear missiles agreed to in 1972 under SALT I. In June 1979 President Carter flew to Vienna to meet Soviet President Leonid Brezhnev. After a round of talks, the two men signed SALT II.

Carter found it easier to reach agreement with Brezhnev than with his own opponents in the Senate. Critics of SALT II unleashed a barrage of criticism. They argued that the agreement would give the Soviets a dangerous advantage in warheads and missiles. For ten years, they pointed out, the Soviet Union had been outspending the United States on defense. Carter's supporters did not deny that the treaty posed some risks. Still, they thought it was an important and necessary step toward reducing the danger of nuclear war.

Any chance of ratifying SALT II ended in December 1979 when the Soviet Union invaded Afghanistan. Soviet troops quickly seized major cities in an effort to suppress a rebellion against the pro-Soviet government there. The international community generally condemned the Soviet action. President Carter spoke for many when he angrily declared, "The Soviet Union must pay a concrete price for its aggression."

Carter ordered a series of economic and political measures against the Soviet Union. He banned the sale of such high-technology equipment as computer hardware and oil drilling equipment. In a move that provoked an outcry from midwestern farmers, he severely limited grain sales to the Soviet Union.* In an even more controversial step Carter ordered United States athletes to boycott the summer Olympics scheduled for Moscow in 1980. Many people thought the President had been unfair in asking athletes and farmers to pay the price of showing American opposition to the invasion.

The Soviet action in Afghanistan showed clearly the vulnerability of vast oil fields in countries bordering the Persian Gulf. Every 20 minutes a huge tanker left the gulf loaded with the oil that fueled the economies of the world. If the Soviet Union tried to establish a foothold on the gulf, those supplies might be lost to western powers.

As a result, after the Soviet invasion of Afghanistan, President Carter warned that the United States would fight if the Soviets made any military move toward the Persian Gulf. He also announced that he would increase the military budget over the next five years and that the United States would install new nuclear weapons in western Europe. The cold war threatened to heat up again.

Crisis in Iran

No sooner had Americans become concerned with events in Afghanistan than their attention was drawn to Iran. In 1979 right-wing Islamic fundamentalists overthrew the regime of the shah. They objected to what they saw as the material and spiritual corruption of Iran under the shah. Their religious leader, the Ayatollah Khomeini (i uh TOH luh hoh MEH nee), assumed the leadership of Iran when the shah fled the country.

In November 1979 the Carter administration allowed the exiled shah to enter the United States for medical treatment. When the United States refused to return the shah to Iran for trial, militant Iranians stormed the American embassy in Teheran, the capital of Iran. They took more than 50 American hostages and vowed not to release them until the United States returned the shah.

---

*Each year the Soviets made large purchases of American wheat and corn to make up for the low output of Soviet farms.

For six months after the capture of the American hostages, diplomatic efforts and economic sanctions aimed at their release had little effect.

Then, on April 24, 1980, specially trained United States forces attempted a daring rescue mission. But mechanical difficulties forced the cancellation of the mission. During the withdrawal from the desert landing site, a United States helicopter collided with a transport plane. Eight Americans died in the fiery crash. Later that year, the shah's death and the outbreak of war between Iran and Iraq did little to change the situation.

The hostage crisis dominated newspaper headlines and weighed heavily on the minds of Americans throughout 1980. Many thought the President had not shown sound judgment or strong leadership during the crisis. Yet there seemed little he could do without creating a grave threat to the hostages' lives. Until the last hours of his presidency Jimmy Carter devoted his energies to freeing the hostages.

713

The Soviet invasion of Afghanistan in December 1980 disrupted relations between the Soviet Union and the United States. As this cartoon shows, many Americans considered the action another example of Soviet agression toward neighboring countries.

A Weakening Economy

The revolution in Iran did more than weaken the strategic position of the United States in the Persian Gulf region. Iran's oil exports dropped to practically nothing. The resulting shortage helped drive the price of oil from about $13 per barrel in 1978 to over $31 in 1980. Only Saudi Arabia's willingness to make up Iran's lost oil supplies spared the United States from an even worse crisis.

The cost of oil contributed to a sharp increase in the rate of inflation. In 1976 the United States had spent $31 billion on imported oil. By 1980 the bill for oil was $62 billion. Inflation in 1979 soared to 11.3 percent, and in 1980 the prices consumers paid for goods rose by 13.5 percent.

At the same time interest rates on loans rose. Americans found it more difficult to borrow money for major purchases such as cars and homes. Auto sales went into a severe slump. New home sales, an important indicator of the state of the economy, dropped significantly. Businesses could not easily afford to borrow money for new investments in plants and equipment. Unemployment jumped from 5.8 percent in 1979 to 7.1 percent in 1980. Black Americans were particularly hard hit as their unemployment rate reached over 13 percent. As a result, Americans faced the 1980 election worried about the health of the economy.

The 1980 Election

The combination of economic distress and the long, drawn-out hostage crisis undermined President Carter's popularity. In July 1981 just 21 percent of the people polled approved of Jimmy Carter's performance in office. Many Democrats were so certain he would lose the election that they persuaded Senator Edward Kennedy to seek the nomination. Nonetheless, when the Democratic convention met, Carter easily won renomination.

The Republican party had been divided badly in the 1976 election. Moderate Republicans backing Gerald Ford resented the attacks of conservative supporters of Ronald Reagan. However, in 1980 the party rallied behind Reagan and his running mate, George Bush of Texas. Only the defection of John Anderson of Illinois, who ran for President as an independent, marred GOP unity.

Ronald Reagan made the economy and the hostage crisis major issues of his campaign. He asked voters to consider whether they were better off in 1980 than when

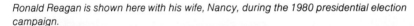

Ronald Reagan is shown here with his wife, Nancy, during the 1980 presidential election campaign.

Jimmy Carter had taken office in 1977. Double-digit inflation and high interest rates forced many Americans to agree with Reagan's charge that Carter did not have a sound economic program. In addition, Reagan stressed his determination to reduce the role of the federal government in the lives of Americans and to strengthen national defense.

Jimmy Carter did little active campaigning, although he agreed to television debates with Reagan. Reagan's skill as a public speaker helped persuade much of the television audience that he was the stronger candidate. While Carter stayed in Washington to work on the hostage crisis, other Democrats campaigned. They argued that Reagan's promise to lower the cost of government while greatly increasing defense spending did not make sense.

As election day drew near, public opinion polls and political commentators predicted a close election. However, the voters proved them wrong. Ronald Reagan won 51 percent of the popular vote compared to 41 percent for President Carter and 7 percent for John Anderson. In the electoral college, Reagan won 489 electoral votes and Carter won 49.

Furthermore, for the first time in 26 years the Republicans gained a majority in the Senate, winning 53 seats compared to 41 in the 1978 mid-term election. In the House of Representatives they remained a minority, but they claimed 191 seats compared to 159 in 1978. Many traditional Democratic voters in labor unions, large cities, and the South had shifted to the Republicans.

Ronald Reagan described the election as a mandate for his program of lower taxes, reduced government spending, less government regulation, and stronger defense. Later Jimmy Carter would write, "I hope history will deal kindly with me. But I am at peace with the knowledge I did the best I could."

For answers, see p. A 118.

Section Review

1. Identify the following: Anwar el-Sadat, Menachem Begin, Mohammed Reza Pahlavi.

2. (a) Describe President Carter's tax reform plan. (b) How did the tax bill passed by Congress compare with Carter's plan?

3. How did President Carter try to make concern for human rights an important part of United States foreign policy?

4. What were the results of the Camp David summit?

5. (a) What agreement was reached with the Soviet Union in June 1979? (b) Why was this agreement not ratified by the Senate?

6. How did economic conditions affect the outcome of the 1980 presidential election?

2 The Reagan Years

Ronald Reagan's election in 1980 brought a major shift in political direction for the United States. At home, Reagan wanted to cut government spending on social programs and reduce government regulation. In foreign affairs, he saw the need to increase military spending to counter Soviet power. "We have every right to dream heroic dreams," he boldly proclaimed on inauguration day in 1981. The President achieved remarkable success in getting much of his program passed during his first two years in office. However, the program had some economic results he had not expected.

The New President

Ronald Reagan had spent most of his adult life as a film and television actor. During many of those years, he was a registered Democrat and a firm supporter of labor unions. In the 1960s both Reagan's career and politics changed. In 1962 he joined the Republican party. Four years later he was elected governor of California, his first public office. During his two terms as governor, Reagan emerged as a leader of the conservative wing of his adopted party.

Before Reagan won the Republican nomination in 1980, many political observers considered him an unlikely presidential candidate. They thought his positions were too conservative to appeal to most middle-of-the-road voters. Some argued that his film career and his cowboy image on television's popular *Death Valley Days* made him an inappropriate candidate. But Reagan handily defeated Jimmy Carter—and by a wide

On September 25, 1981, Sandra Day O'Connor was sworn in as an associate justice of the Supreme Court by Chief Justice Warren Burger. She took the oath of office on two family Bibles held by her husband, John J. O'Connor.

margin. He saw his victory as a mandate from the American people to put his conservative plans into practice.

In fact, Ronald Reagan's background in films proved to be an asset. As an effective public speaker, he managed to clearly explain his administration's direction to the American people. This contrasted strongly with President Carter's problems in communicating a clear sense of direction. Reagan also differed from Carter in that he appeared less interested in the details of day-to-day administration. These tasks he delegated to his aides. What remained to be seen was whether his genial ways and conservative program would have the results he intended.

An Eventful First Year

The very first day of the Reagan administration was one of high drama and suspense. While the nation held its breath, intense negotiations in the final hours of the Carter administration produced agreement to free the American hostages in Iran. Just minutes after Ronald Reagan took the oath of office, word came of the hostages' release. The 52 Americans held captive for 444 days in the United States Embassy in Teheran returned home to a joyous welcome.

Two months later an assassination attempt nearly ended the new President's life. Shots fired by a lone gunman outside a Washington, D.C., hotel wounded the President, his press secretary, and two security officials. President Reagan spent almost two weeks in the hospital and then a period in the White House recovering from his injuries.

Later that year a presidential appointment marked an historic milestone. In July 1981 President Reagan announced the nomination of Sandra Day O'Connor to fill a vacancy on the United States Supreme Court. O'Connor had been the first woman to serve as majority leader of a state legislature. Since 1979 she had been a judge on the Arizona Court of Appeals. She developed a reputation as a scholarly jurist whose opinions were well-researched and well-written. Her nomination was confirmed in the Senate by a vote of 99 to 0.

Reaganomics

Throughout the 1980 election campaign, President Reagan had stressed that his first priority would be to cure the nation's economic ills. He listed five economic problems: excessive government spending, high taxes, inflation, high interest rates, and unemployment. His economic program for dealing with these problems called for major alterations in the nation's economic course. The program came to be known as Reaganomics.

Reagan believed that excessive spending by the federal government was to blame for many economic problems. Year after year, the government had spent more than it took in from tax revenues. This practice had created large budget deficits that in turn fueled inflation. Reagan promised to curb federal spending in order to reduce budget deficits. He also pledged to cut back the size of the federal government by reducing government regulation.

Reagan believed that high taxes had hurt the economy. He proposed a cut in personal income taxes. If people had more money in their pockets, he argued, they would start new businesses, build more factories, and buy additional goods. This increased business activity would produce enough new revenue to make up for money lost through tax cuts. New businesses would also spur economic growth.

These economic proposals were hotly debated in the new Congress. But through skillful lobbying the President got his program through. In 1981 Congress approved a three-year cut in federal income taxes and a $35-billion cut in the amount budgeted for several social programs including food stamps, Medicaid, Medicare, and the school lunch program.

President Reagan predicted that these measures would produce an economic recovery by the end of 1981. Instead, the economy moved into a deep recession, partly caused by continuing high interest rates. People found it too expensive to borrow money to start new businesses and to buy homes, cars, and other goods. Thus, new tax revenue from economic growth was not produced, and the federal deficit continued to grow.

A serious consequence of the recession was the steep jump in the rate of unemployment, which climbed to almost 11 percent by 1983. This was the highest unemployment rate since the Great Depression. Workers in the construction and automobile industries were especially hard hit.

Because of the deepening recession and projected federal budget deficits approaching $200 billion, many Americans urged the President to change his policies. But Reagan remained convinced that his program would produce economic recovery. As evidence of progress, he pointed to a significant drop in inflation and interest rates. (See the graph below.) There were no "quick fixes" for long-standing problems, Reagan argued. He urged the country to have patience and allow more time for his programs to work.

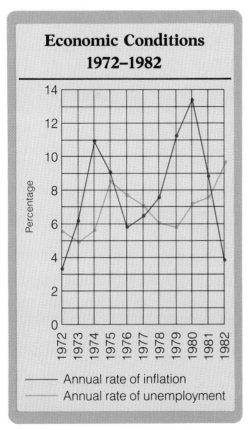

■ *A high rate of inflation was a problem during much of the 1970s. The rate of inflation dropped dramatically in the early 1980s, but, as this graph shows, unemployment rose as the result of a deep recession. In 1983 there were indications of a recovery, but unemployment remained high.*

Economic Conditions 1972–1982

—— Annual rate of inflation
—— Annual rate of unemployment

Source: *Statistical Abstract of the United States*

717

A Tough Stand

President Reagan entered the White House as a vocal critic of the policy of détente begun by Richard Nixon. (See page 690.) "So far, détente's been a one-way street the Soviet Union has used to pursue its own aims," he told the nation in his first press conference, on January 29, 1981. Reagan believed that a buildup of Soviet conventional and nuclear forces threatened the security of the United States. To counter the Soviet buildup, Reagan promised large increases in United States defense spending.

With harsh language reminiscent of the cold war years, Reagan regularly criticized Soviet behavior. He spoke out against the continuing Soviet occupation of Afghanistan and Soviet policies of repression at home. The Soviet Union assumes the right "to commit any crime, to lie, to cheat to attain its ends," he said in January 1981.

Developments in Poland further strained relations with the Soviet Union. An independent trade union known as Solidarity had organized strikes and demonstrations for greater political freedom in Poland and for economic reform. In December 1981 the Polish government imposed martial law and outlawed the union. United States officials were convinced that the Soviet Union had pressured the Polish government into taking these actions. As a result, the Reagan administration imposed trade and political sanctions against the Soviet Union.

In November 1982 the death of Leonid Brezhnev, the Soviet leader for 18 years, added new uncertainty to United States–Soviet relations. Immediately after Brezhnev's death, President Reagan pledged that his administration would work with the new Soviet leader, Yuri Andropov, to improve relations between the two nations. But he pointed out that the Soviets would have to match friendly words with deeds.

Although taking a tougher stand against the Soviets, the President expressed a commitment to arms control. He claimed that the Russians had achieved a position of nuclear superiority. It would be impossible to negotiate with them successfully, he argued, unless the United States spent more for defense. With stronger defense, the country could bargain from a position of strength.

The President's policy triggered a harsh response from critics. Some defense experts argued that it was inaccurate to say that the Soviets had achieved superiority. While the Soviet Union had more land-based nuclear warheads than the United States, the United States defense system relied more heavily on airborne and undersea missiles. In a larger sense, many critics were disturbed by the Reagan administration's hard-line foreign policy. They feared a return to the cold war tensions of the 1950s. If a new arms race began, they warned, it might end in a devastating nuclear war.

Other Foreign Policy Challenges

Strained relations with the Soviet Union affected ties between the United States and its allies in western Europe. Since the beginning of détente, trade with the Soviet bloc had become important to western European nations. Therefore, many European nations were reluctant to join the Carter and Reagan administrations in applying economic pressure on the Soviets in response to events in Afghanistan and Poland.

Europeans also feared that if a limited nuclear war broke out between the United States and the Soviet Union, their territory would be the battleground. They pressed the Reagan administration to move more vigorously in arms control talks. As a result, President Reagan tried to balance his tough stance against the Soviet Union with policies that satisfied European allies.

The Middle East was another area of concern. Since the mid-1970s the Palestine Liberation Organization (PLO) had used southern Lebanon as a base for raids into Israel. In the summer of 1982, Israel sent 60,000 soldiers into Lebanon to clear out the PLO.

Most of the international community, including the United States, criticized Israel's action. Israel maintained that the action was necessary for its security. After a cease-fire agreement was reached, United States Marines joined an international peacekeeping force stationed in Lebanon. The purpose of the peacekeeping force was to help the Lebanese government maintain order.

The Reagan administration's actions in another trouble spot, Central America, created controversy at home. In 1979 leftist

Economic problems were a frequent topic of discussion between President Reagan and other world leaders. The President is shown here at a 1982 economic summit in France with leaders from Japan, Great Britain, France, and West Germany.

guerrillas had toppled the military government of Nicaragua. By the early 1980s rebel forces were threatening the governments of other Central American nations, especially El Salvador.

President Reagan favored sending military aid to the government of El Salvador. He argued that the rebels were supported by Cuba. Opponents objected to sending aid to what they considered to be a repressive and corrupt government. Late in 1982 President Reagan traveled to several countries in Latin America, including Brazil and Colombia. He hoped to improve relations between the United States and its southern neighbors.

The Election of 1982

By the mid-term elections of 1982, it remained unclear whether President Reagan's bold changes in policy would accomplish his goals. In part this was because several aspects of the President's policies had unexpected effects.

In domestic affairs Reagan had wanted to stimulate the economy with a tax cut while sharply reducing government spending. In the 1980 campaign, he had criticized Jimmy Carter for allowing budget deficits of almost $60 billion. But by 1982, government economists were predicting that Reagan's deficit would rise to over $200 billion, more than four times the size of Carter's.

This huge deficit occurred even though the President cut spending in several social programs. One cause of the deficit was a sharp increase in defense spending. In addition, because of the President's large tax cut and the recession, the government was taking in much less revenue than it had under the Carter administration.

In the 1982 election campaign, Reagan and his supporters maintained that he had inherited many longstanding problems that could not be solved overnight. Opponents claimed that high unemployment and recession could not be cured unless the President altered his policies. To lower the deficit, they suggested, military spending should not be increased so drastically, and some of the tax cuts should be eliminated.

The election results reflected the nation's mixed views of Reaganomics. The Republicans kept their majority in the Senate, but the Democrats won 26 new seats in the House. The Democratic party also picked up seven additional governorships and won majorities in several state legislatures.

The changed complexion of the House meant that the President would find it more difficult to win congressional approval for his legislative program. How to close budget gaps, what should be done for the unemployed, and how to make further budget cuts would continue to be subjects of much congressional and public debate. The discussion of government priorities promised to occupy national political life for the remainder of the decade.

For answers, see p. A 118.

Section Review

1. Identify the following: Sandra Day O'Connor, Reaganomics, Solidarity.

2. (a) According to President Reagan, what had caused the economic problems facing the nation as he took office? (b) What elements of Reagan's economic program were enacted by Congress in 1981?

3. How did the economy worsen in 1981 and 1982?

4. Why were United States Marines sent to Lebanon in 1982?

5. What issues were important in the 1982 midterm elections?

3 Science and Technology in the 1980s

Americans have long looked to science and technology to improve the quality of life. Throughout the 1980s further advances in medical research, computer technology, and communications will continue to affect the way Americans live and work. The factories, offices, and homes of the future may be increasingly operated by machines. New video and computer devices will link Americans to vast networks of information, news, and entertainment as the home becomes a center for both work and recreation.

Toward a Healthier Life

Throughout the twentieth century improvements in nutrition, public sanitation, and medical care have extended life expectancy. Americans born in 1920 could expect to live about 54 years. Americans born in 1980 can reasonably hope to live about 74 years.

Medical researchers have contributed to this trend by finding ways to control or prevent many devastating diseases. Smallpox, once a great killer, has been virtually eliminated around the world. Vaccines have reduced the incidence of such childhood menaces as polio and measles. Antibiotics offer doctors additional weapons to combat many types of infections. However, overuse of some antibiotics has created superstrains of bacteria resistant to treatment.

Genetic engineering promises major advances for medicine and industry. Microbiologists are now able to identify the genetic codes of cells. Increasingly scientists are able to alter the codes to eliminate

■ Medical advances such as the development of penicillin and vaccines to prevent diseases have increased the number of years most Americans live. In 1900 the average person lived to age 47. Today average life expectancy is about 74 years of age. One result of this trend is a rising percentage of older people in the population.

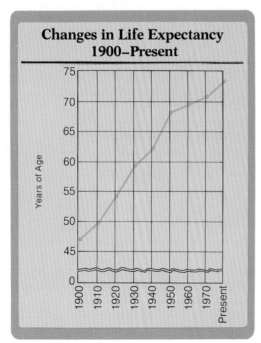

Changes in Life Expectancy 1900–Present

diseases or produce new materials. For example, they have inserted human genes into bacteria to produce insulin, needed by millions of diabetics to control the level of sugar in their blood. Future genetic research may provide keys to eliminating diabetes and other diseases.

Advances in technology have also affected medical treatment. Microsurgery is now used successfully to reattach severed limbs. The development of nylon thread so fine that it can pierce a human hair is expected to speed the spread of microsurgery.

Lasers and computers (see page 723) have become essential tools of medical research and treatment. Lasers are so precise they can burn away diseased tissue without harming the healthy tissue around it. Their high heat seals off incisions with a minimum of bleeding. Advances in computer-assisted X-ray scanning have provided valuable tools to diagnose illnesses. With such procedures doctors can create pictures of areas inside the brain and other organs with small risk. The use of computers to help paraplegics gain muscular control is in the experimental stage.

Electronic devices have been developed to assist or substitute for the body's own organs. For example, pacemakers regulate the rhythm of irregular heartbeats. Dialysis machines cleanse the blood of patients whose kidneys have failed.

Synthetic materials such as plastic and stainless steel are now widely used to repair damaged parts of the body. Doctors can replace knees, hips, and other joints crippled by arthritis. In December 1982 surgeons implanted an artificial heart in Barney Clark, who was dying from heart failure. With the artificial heart, Clark lived until March 1983.

Such advances have contributed to rising medical costs. In 1963 a patient could expect to pay about $35 for each day in a hospital. By the early 1980s that cost had soared over 700 percent to $250 a day. Americans found that a growing part of their income was going to pay medical costs.

The Computer Age

In the past American families reminisced about when they got their first telephone, first car, or first television. The generation of the 1980s will most likely ask, "Remember when we got our first computer?" As computers become smaller, less expensive, and

Computers have a wide variety of uses today. At left, computer-operated robots weld auto bodies in an assembly plant in Illinois. The student at right uses the computer to display a visual image of a football player.

more adaptable, they will become as common as televisions in American homes.

Computers are electronic machines that do calculations such as simple addition and computations involving complex numbers and logic. They are also used to assemble, store, process, and reproduce information. Computer programmers design programs that instruct the machines how to code or decode the information the user requests.

When computers first appeared on the market in the 1950s, they were bulky and slow by today's standards. Such machines might fill several large rooms, require separate air conditioning systems, and cost millions of dollars. By using transistors and tiny silicon circuit chips instead of vacuum tubes, engineers made computers smaller, cheaper, and faster. Some personal computers that sold for under $10,000 in the early 1980s were more powerful than the million-dollar machines of 20 years earlier.

Miniaturization has vastly expanded the use of computers. Video games, wristwatches, automatic features on appliances, automobile engines, and calculators have all been refined through the use of small computers. In many homes, personal computers have taken their place alongside telephones, televisions, and radios for communications, entertainment, and record keeping. Consumers of the future may never have to leave home to go shopping. Letters and newspapers may be sent and received through computer networks.

In the 1980s a generation of computers for home and office was designed to be "user friendly." The machines could teach their operators how to make them work. This development would spark an even more explosive growth in the application of computers.

The uses of computer-based technology in factories and offices are extensive. By the early 1980s factories were in operation in which computer-controlled robots did almost all the manufacturing. Computers ordered and shipped parts automatically. Computers also perform office tasks such as record keeping, inventory control, payroll accounting, and billing.

In areas where the work is repetitive or dangerous, computers have been a real benefit. This means, however, that machines do jobs people once performed. Today's worker must adjust to a job market in which computers play an increasingly important role. Factory and office workers must know how to make computers do their jobs properly.

The Challenge of the Computer Age

Despite the many benefits of computers, many people view the computer age uneasily. Some fear that artificial intelligence in machines may someday make people less important. Certainly computers will eliminate many jobs and require much of the work force to acquire more technical skills.

Without advances in computer technology the United States could not have sent satellites or people into space. Yet those same advances have made modern weapons far more accurate and destructive than any before them. And as more businesses and banks perform financial transactions with computers, a new generation of robbers has

721

emerged. A far cry from the masked desperadoes of old, these criminals use computers to steal money. Advertisers use computerized systems to bombard homes with huge quantities of unsolicited junk mail. Machines can automatically dial phone numbers and play prerecorded messages.

Computers strike many people as a serious threat to privacy. More and more information about people's personal lives is stored in computers. That information could be used to help or hurt people. In an emergency a doctor would have immediate access to a patient's medical history. But that same information in the wrong hands could be abused. Spies, for example, might invade computers to steal vital national secrets.

The computer age is just dawning. No one can say how far the computer revolution will go or what its long-term consequences may be. Sociologist Daniel Bell has argued that the new machines of the 1800s, such as the railroad and telephone, changed lives far

more than the computer will. However, one of the pioneers of the computer revolution argues that computers, like many innovations, offer "unbounded possibilities for good and for evil."

Space Technology

The development of computer technology has made a crucial contribution to the success of the American space program. Computers helped design almost all the equipment and then allowed the engineers to make sure it worked properly.

The reusable space shuttle *Columbia* has become the centerpiece of the American space program for the 1980s. By 1982 the *Columbia* had made five successful round trip voyages into space. On the fifth trip the huge investment of almost $11 billion began to pay returns. Two private communications corporations paid to have their satellites launched from the space shuttle's enormous cargo bay.

To launch their communications satellites, private companies have booked space on all future scheduled flights of *Columbia*. They can save millions of dollars they would have spent on disposable rockets. The shuttle astronauts will also be able to repair damaged satellites during their space voyages.

The communications satellites launched by *Columbia* will transmit television signals around the globe. Satellites to be launched in the future will locate natural resources on land and under the sea more accurately than can be done today. Still other satellites will be used for defense purposes.

A space telescope launched in 1983 will permit scientists to scan parts of the universe previously beyond human vision. Two unmanned Voyager spacecraft launched in 1977 are also providing a glimpse of the far reaches of the solar system by sending back pictures of the outer planets. *Voyager 1* came within 78,000 miles of Saturn in November 1980 and sent back clear pictures of the planet's rings. *Voyager 2* came even closer to the planet, passing within 63,000 miles in August 1981. The spacecraft took photographs and gathered information about Saturn, its moons, and its breathtaking series of rings.

Voyager 2 will travel by Uranus in 1986 and Neptune in 1989. After passing the outlying planets, *Voyager 2*, which is carrying ar-

The space shuttle Columbia *is shown here landing at the White Sands Missile Range in New Mexico. In 1983* Columbia, *the first reusable spacecraft, made its fifth round trip into space. A second shuttle,* Challenger, *made its first trip the same year.*

tifacts representing life on Earth, will leave the solar system to visit unknown parts of the universe.

Laser Technology

In the 1930s and 1940s science fiction writers described such future weapons as ray guns. These weapons would shoot beams of light rather than bullets. Today, the laser has brought that vision close to reality. The term was coined in 1957 when scientist Gordon Gould created a device for Light Amplification by Stimulated Emission of Radiation (LASER). Lasers create intense light of a narrow range of wavelengths.

Lasers, like computers, have the potential for "good and evil." You have read about the role of lasers in medicine. Lasers can also be used in warfare. Both the United States and Soviet Union are experimenting with many military applications. Some scientists talk of placing laser guns on satellites orbiting the earth. Weapons using laser beams to destroy distant targets had been developed by the early 1980s.

In fact, lasers are widely used today. Most people are familiar with the black bar code on many packages. Lasers connected to computers read those codes to provide cashiers with the price and inventory number. In modern factories, gas torches have given way to cleaner and more powerful lasers that cut and weld metals.

The use of lasers promises to revolutionize entertainment. The newest stereo equipment uses lasers rather than a needle or stylus to play records. Video discs for television operate on a similar system. Lasers can be used to create stunning visual effects, as in the popular movie *Star Wars*.

Lasers also have great potential use in the field of communications. Electronic messages can be sent by amplified light over flexible glass fiber wires called fiber-optic cables. These cables have many advantages over copper wires. They are far cheaper to make and install. Since they are much thinner, many more messages can be carried.

In the future lasers will be tied in to computer-based communications systems. Fiber optics will make it practical to transmit the vast amounts of data stored by computer systems. Eventually, fiber optics may be used within computers themselves. The result would be machines that are even smaller, faster, and more powerful than those in use today.

The Information Age

Advances in computer technology and satellite communications have helped create a new age of information. By the late 1980s, many homes will be equipped to serve as information centers. Since the mid-1970s, cable television systems have been set up in many parts of the country to provide viewers with a greater variety of programs than ever before. Subscribers can choose from movies, sports, children's programs, stock information, and other types of programming.

Some cable systems carry local government meetings and telephone talk shows that permit viewers to question their elected officials. Others contain special hookups that allow viewers to respond to questions posed over the air. Some have referred to this device as an electronic town meeting. In the future, cable systems will increasingly include means for two-way communication so that viewers can take part in television programs as well as receive them.

New technology has also revolutionized the way information is gathered. Many news organizations and other corporations are linked electronically to their offices around the world. News and information are spread almost instantaneously across the country and around the globe.

The electronic age has also affected the way newspapers, magazines, and books are produced. Once type was set by hand. Today, computers do much of the typesetting more quickly and efficiently than in the past. In the future, many families will be able to read newspapers, magazines, and books on home computer screens.

For answers, see p. A 118.

Section Review

1. Identify the following: *Columbia, Voyager 1, Voyager 2*, laser.
2. Describe three recent medical advances?
3. How are computers changing office work?
4. How are private companies making use of the space shuttle?
5. How is new technology transforming the way news and information are distributed?

The Making of *Star Wars*

The making of *Star Wars*, a fantasy film about a faraway galaxy, involved a blend of creativity and sophisticated computer technology. The result, for those who have seen *Star Wars* and its sequel, *The Empire Strikes Back*, is a lifelike creation of a world inhabited by strange-looking creatures and technologically advanced machines. The sound, the light, the action sequences—all represent significant achievements for the filmmakers and the standard against which future action films will be judged.

For the memorable battle sequences in *Star Wars*, especially the final attack on the Death Star, the film crew created a special camera linked to a computer that recorded and memorized every shot. The camera thus had the ability to remember all its previous moves. By consulting the camera's memory, new elements could be added to each scene.

To create the realistic look of many spacecraft swooping around each other, George Lucas, the director of *Star Wars*, spliced together footage of old war movies. He studied this film carefully. Then, using the special camera with computer memory, Lucas superimposed as many as twelve different pieces of film on one another to capture the right look. Editing the ten-minute sequence of the attack on the Death Star took eight weeks.

With the money he earned from *Star Wars*, Lucas built one of the world's largest sound stages and a state-of-the-art special effects studio. His studio invented a $500,000 machine called a quad printer that contains four projectors each holding a separate piece of film. For *The Empire Strikes Back* the quad printer was used to film the voyage of the *Milennium Falcon*, Han Solo's spacecraft, through an asteroid field. One of the projectors showed film of the *Falcon*, another showed the asteroids, another showed the stars, and the fourth showed shadows and laser beams. All four separate bits of film were projected through a prism that combined them into one seamless piece. The synchronization of the four film sequences was accomplished by computer.

Techniques such as those used in *Star Wars* and *The Empire Strikes Back* are revolutionizing filmmaking. Many of the techniques are finding their way into other movies and even into television commercials.

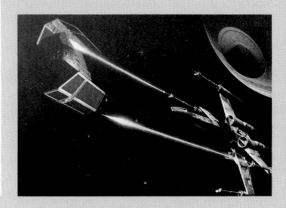

4 Energy in the 1980s

Energy is vital to modern civilization and to the continued growth of the American economy. Until the 1970s it was so plentiful it was almost taken for granted. Throughout the first half of the twentieth century, the United States relied on large domestic oil reserves to satisfy growing energy needs. Little noticed was a growing dependence on imported foreign oil.

The energy shocks of the 1970s alerted Americans to the dangers of this growing dependence. At the same time, many Americans became more aware of the limited supplies of oil and other key natural resources. Such limits challenge American industry and consumers to use resources more efficiently and to find substitutes for resources that are in short supply.

The Age of Oil

In the late 1800s a major invention—the oil-burning internal combustion engine—helped usher in the age of oil. This invention transformed transportation and industry. Automobiles, trucks, buses, airplanes, and ships increased the mobility of the American people. By the 1940s oil had replaced coal as the major fuel of industry.

As the use of oil grew, the demand began to exceed supply. The United States began to import oil from abroad. Importing oil was often cheaper than producing it at home. By 1970, 24 percent of the oil used in the United States was imported. That percentage increased after 1973, when President Nixon removed quotas restricting the amount of foreign oil that could be imported. The risks of this dependence on foreign oil was brought home to Americans by the energy crises of the 1970s.

The Role of OPEC

As domestic oil production decreased, the United States increasingly turned to the oil fields of the Middle East, Latin America, Asia, and Africa to supply its energy needs. In many cases, discovery of oil in those countries was made by American oil companies. Those companies had been able to control production of this oil and set the price. In 1960 the major oil exporting nations formed the Organization of Petroleum Exporting Countries (OPEC). OPEC demanded a voice in setting prices and in controlling the amount of oil produced.

The 13 OPEC nations met with little success until the Arab oil embargo of 1973. By then oil had become so scarce that buyers were willing to bid the price up. Oil that had sold for only $1.20 a barrel in 1969 brought about $10 a barrel in 1974. In 1979, when the revolution in Iran disrupted oil exports, prices soared to over $20 a barrel.

Soaring oil prices contributed to higher inflation rates in the United States and other nations. Some developing nations were forced to borrow large amounts of money to pay higher oil bills. Rising fuel prices also hurt the economies of industrialized nations, where it had become more costly to buy fuel for vehicles and power plants. It also cost more to produce products, such as vinyl and synthetic fabrics, in which oil is a key component. A slowdown in industrial production led to a worldwide recession in the late 1970s.

The global economic slowdown created differences of opinion among OPEC members. Some OPEC members argued that higher oil prices could hurt their own economies in two ways. First, high oil prices raised the prices of goods they purchased from industrialized nations. Second, because of the

recession, the demand for oil had dropped. Thus, some OPEC nations pressed for a suspension of price increases for OPEC oil.

Other OPEC members disagreed with this position and urged further increases in the price of oil. As a result of this disagreement, in December 1979 the idea of maintaining a uniform price for OPEC oil was abandoned. Instead, a range of prices was instituted. In 1979 prices ranged from $24 a barrel for Saudi Arabian oil to $30 a barrel for Libyan oil.

During the early 1980s a world surplus of oil developed. Demand continued to fall as a result of the recession in the world economy. In addition, some new oil producers such as Norway and Britain were not subject to OPEC restrictions on production. New discoveries of oil in countries such as Venezuela and Mexico also added to the oil surplus. The growing surplus intensified disagreements among OPEC members and led some political observers to speculate about OPEC's future.

■ *OPEC oil prices rose steadily between 1973 and 1981, as this graph shows. However, a world surplus of oil began to bring oil prices down during 1982. In the spring of 1983, OPEC members agreed to a crude oil price of $29 a barrel.*

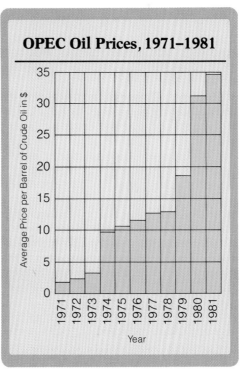

Source: Conoco, Inc.

Meeting the Energy Crises

The energy crises of the 1970s forced American leaders to search for a way to reduce dependence on foreign oil. When the Arab oil boycott of 1973 produced long lines of angry motorists at gas stations, President Nixon proclaimed Project Independence. His goal was to make the United States self-sufficient in energy by 1980. He planned to do this by encouraging conservation and increasing domestic production. Within a few weeks of the President's proclamation, however, the embargo was lifted, and oil was again available, although at a higher price. While more Americans were now aware of the dangers of energy dependence, the sense of urgency to solve the problem was gone.

As Jimmy Carter was preparing to assume the presidency, a new energy crisis loomed large. The winter of 1976–1977 was an especially bitter one in parts of the United States. Shortages of natural gas and other fuels caused school and factory closings, business losses, and layoffs for many American workers. Energy policy thus became a major priority for the Carter administration.

In April 1977 Carter sent his National Energy Plan to Congress. The bill included high taxes on crude oil, which would increase the price of petroleum products. Carter hoped that higher prices would convince more people to conserve energy. The revenue raised would be used for mass public transportation. The energy bill passed the House with only minor changes. But by the time it passed the Senate, few of the President's ideas were left.

However, Congress did take some steps toward creating an energy policy. Later in 1977, at the President's request, Congress created a new Cabinet office, the Department of Energy. Other measures provided tax credits to encourage conservation and the use of solar energy in homes and businesses. In 1979 President Carter authorized $100 million for solar energy research. Later that year Congress passed Carter's synthetic fuels program to provide government financing for the development of synthetic fuels and other alternative energy sources.

Lifting Controls on Production

President Carter believed that the most effective way to limit energy demands would be to end price controls on domestic oil. Those controls had kept the price of domestic oil low and had thus discouraged exploration. If the price of domestic oil was allowed to rise to world levels, he thought, both production and conservation would be encouraged. As a result, Carter decided to phase out controls on the price of domestic crude oil.

By 1980 the results of Carter's action had begun to show. Higher prices led to a boom in exploration and domestic drilling. They also produced a decline in oil consumption as both individuals and industries tried to conserve the more expensive fuel. In 1980 there was a record drop in oil imports. Eighteen percent less crude oil was imported in 1980 than in 1979. By 1981 imports had dropped to the lowest point since 1975.

President Reagan agreed with his predecessor's policy of removing price controls on domestic oil. Shortly after taking office in January 1981, he signed an executive order abolishing price controls on most domestic crude oil and its byproducts. When controls were removed, the price of oil surged at first.

Higher prices were expected to encourage more domestic production. But the world oil glut discouraged many companies from investing in expensive new oil drilling.

Major Events	
1977	Panama Canal treaties signed
1978	Camp David summit agreement signed
1979	United States recognizes People's Republic of China; SALT II signed; Iranians seize American hostages; Soviet Union invades Afghanistan
1980	Ronald Reagan elected President
1981	American hostages released from Iran; Reagan shot in assassination attempt; Sandra Day O'Connor appointed to Supreme Court
1982	Marines join international peacekeeping force in Lebanon; successful artificial heart implant

726

Alternative Energy Sources

Until the 1970s oil was an increasingly popular, inexpensive, and plentiful fuel for electric power plants, heating, transportation, and the manufacture of plastics. However, heavy consumption, rising costs, and the danger of a cutoff of imported oil supplies led to an emphasis on energy conservation and to a reevaluation of energy sources for the future. During the 1970s Americans began to curb their use of electricity and gasoline. Researchers explored nuclear energy, coal, solar energy, synthetic fuels, and other alternatives to oil.

The production of electricity from nuclear power has been beset by problems. Many people became alarmed about the potential danger of nuclear energy in March 1979 following an accident at a nuclear power plant on Three Mile Island, in Pennsylvania. In that incident a faulty valve in the reactor's cooling system allowed nuclear fuel rods to heat to dangerously high temperatures. The situation was brought under control without a major catastrophe, but public concern was aroused. Disposing of harmful radioactive wastes from nuclear plants remains a problem. Furthermore, the production of nuclear energy has become increasingly expensive.

The cost of building a nuclear reactor has risen dramatically in recent years, and the cost of the uranium used as fuel in nuclear plants soared from $8 a pound in 1972 to over $50 in 1980. Experts expect nuclear power to continue to provide a portion of national energy needs, but the industry has not grown as rapidly as once expected.

The use of coal will probably increase as industries and utilities try to reduce their use of oil. The supply of coal in the United States is plentiful, perhaps enough to last over 300 years. Yet the use of coal also presents problems. Deep coal mining is dangerous, and many people worry about the environmental impact of strip mining.

In the past burning coal to produce energy had been a major source of air pollution. Scrubbers can be installed to remove sulphur and other impurities, but that is an expensive process. Furthermore, many of the coal reserves are in the West. The nation does not yet have the transportation facilities needed to ship western coal to power plants across the country. In spite of those difficulties, coal will probably be one of the main alternatives to oil in the future.

The use of solar energy spread during the 1970s and 1980s as a growing number of individuals, businesses, and even the White House installed solar heating units on roofs. Such units use sun rays to heat water. A newer development, the photovoltaic cell, can turn sunlight directly into electric current. The equipment needed to produce solar energy has remained expensive. Except for a few areas such as the Southwest, solar energy has not become competitive with other energy sources. Interest in solar energy, however, remains high, and many large corporations are entering the field. Future developments may put solar power within financial reach of the average consumer.

The search for alternative sources of energy has led in various directions. Many communities are burning garbage and other biological waste products to produce electricity. Waste products can also be converted to gases or oil. In addition to providing energy, such processes are an efficient way to dispose of wastes.

Experimental work is being done to derive synthetic fuels from coal, oil shale, and coal tars. But to date, that process has proven very expensive. Other experiments are under way to harness wind power with giant windmills. Wind power generators are being tested in various parts of the country. (See the picture below.) Geothermal power, heat from the earth, is also being tested. In addition the use of gasohol—a mixture of alcohol and gasoline—as automobile fuel began in the late 1970s.

Some experts expect utility companies to revive hydroelectric power. Fifty years ago hydroelectric power provided one third of the electricity used in the United States, but today it supplies only 4 percent. The oceans are another potential source of energy. Scientists are studying ways to convert the energy of ocean currents, tides, and waves to electricity. Experiments are also under way to make use of temperature differences in ocean water to produce energy.

A NASA wind energy experiment.

The glut also discouraged the creation of expensive synthetic fuels programs. Many major corporations canceled their alternative energy projects. In addition, as part of his program to cut government spending, President Reagan reduced spending on solar energy and synthetic fuels.

Even though lower prices made oil practical in the short run, Americans realized that they must find alternatives. At current rates of use, supplies will eventually run out, and new crises could deny the United States access to Middle Eastern oil.

Heavy use of fossil fuels* such as oil and coal also poses serious environmental risks. Scientists have recently discovered that high concentrations of acids in rainfall have killed much plant and fish life in the Adirondack Mountains of New York. Acid rain in upstate New York and nearby Canada is caused by emissions from oil- and coal-burning plants in the Ohio River Valley. The possible destruction of agriculture, forests, and water supplies from acid rain is one of the major environmental issues of the 1980s.

_____
*Fossil fuels are those obtained from the earth.

The search goes on for clean and plentiful new sources of energy. Scientists at Princeton University recently tested a machine that promises to harness fusion energy—the same process that generates the sun's energy. Still, practical fusion energy is at best decades away. Planning for the nation's short- and long-term energy needs remains one of the most pressing unsolved problems for the future.

For answers, see p. A 118.

Section Review

1. Identify the following: OPEC, Project Independence.
2. How did some OPEC members create an energy crisis in late 1973?
3. How did rising oil prices affect the economies of the oil importing nations?
4. Why did oil prices decline during the early 1980s?
5. (a) Describe two parts of the Carter administration's energy program. (b) What action did President Reagan take to increase domestic exploration and drilling?
6. What environmental risks are posed by the heavy use of fossil fuels?

★ ★

IN PERSPECTIVE When Jimmy Carter became President in January 1977, he had high hopes that he could bring a fresh approach to the problems facing the nation. However, his position as an outsider made it difficult for him to work with Congress. Carter did play an important role in the successful conclusion of the Camp David agreement. Other parts of his foreign policy, however, created great controversy. The worsening economy and the hostage crisis in Iran contributed to Carter's defeat by Ronald Reagan in 1980.

During his first years in office, President Reagan introduced an economic program known as Reaganomics. Despite a deepening recession, Reagan urged Congress and the American people to give his program time to work. In foreign affairs, Reagan took a firm stand in relations with the Soviet Union.

Advances in science and technology made significant contributions to many fields, including medicine and communications. Computers revolutionized both the work place and leisure time for many Americans. Satellites helped locate deposits of scarce resources such as oil. The oil crises of the 1970s convinced most Americans that a long-term solution to energy needs had to be found.

For answers, see p. A 119.

Chapter Review

1. (a) Describe President Carter's relationship with Congress. (b) Why did this relationship develop? (c) What were the consequences of this relationship?

2. Describe the controversies surrounding each of the following aspects of Jimmy Carter's foreign policy: (a) human rights, (b) Panama Canal treaties, (c) recognition of the People's Republic of China, (d) ratification of SALT II.

3. How did the revolution in Iran affect the United States?

4. Compare the presidential styles of Jimmy Carter and Ronald Reagan.

5. (a) What economic problems did President Reagan face? (b) How did those problems compare with the economic problems Jimmy Carter faced? (c) How did Reagan propose to solve the nation's economic problems?

6. (a) What actions by the Soviet Union concerned President Reagan? (b) How did he respond to those actions?

7. How have medical advances increased the life expectancy of Americans?

8. Why is the 1980s being called the computer age?

9. Describe the two main components of the space program in the 1980s.

10. Why was the United States less vulnerable to OPEC policies in the 1980s than it was in the 1970s?

For answers, see p. A 119.

For Further Thought

1. Some observers have speculated that Jimmy Carter might have won the election of 1980 if the hostages in Iran had been freed before election day. Others argued that his record doomed any chance for reelection. Which argument do you think is stronger? Explain.

2. Compare Ronald Reagan's response to the recession of the early 1980s with Franklin D. Roosevelt's response to the Great Depression of the early 1930s. (See Chapters 32 and 33.) (a) How did the basic approach of the two Presidents differ? (b) What developments of the past 50 years might help explain why their approaches were different?

3. Few aspects of life are unaffected by computers today. How do you think computers will directly affect your life during the next ten years?

For answers, see p. A 120.

Developing Basic Skills

1. *Graph Reading* Study the graph on page 717 and answer the following questions: (a) What was the unemployment rate in 1974? (b) In what year was the unemployment rate the lowest? (c) In what year was the inflation rate the highest? (d) During what periods did the United States suffer from rising unemployment and rising inflation? (e) What generalization about the economy between 1980 and 1982 can you draw from the information on the graph?

2. *Relating Past to Present* Make a list of the foreign policy problems faced by the United States during the 1970s and 1980s. Compare these problems with the issues facing the United States after World War II. (See pages 633–648.) What are the similarities and differences between the two periods?

3. *Analyzing a Cartoon* Study the cartoon on page 713. Then answer the following questions: (a) What event is portrayed in the cartoon? (b) What do the names on the tank represent? (c) What nations does the cartoonist indicate are in danger? (d) How would you describe the cartoonist's attitude toward Soviet foreign policy?

See page 779 for suggested readings.

The United States: 41
Yesterday and Tomorrow

A view of the earth from an Apollo flight.

As the Apollo astronauts viewed the earth from their ship, they were awed by its beauty against the deep background of space. Photographs of that view inspired millions of Americans. After hundreds of years of history the United States had crossed the threshold of outer space.

The mobility of the American people had changed the face of the nation over hundreds of years. Millions of immigrants from all parts of the world had helped create a unique and varied cultural heritage. As the nation expanded, its government and economy grew.

Over the course of the nation's history, an increasing proportion of Americans gained access to political rights and economic opportunities. The history of United States relations with other nations had been one of growing involvement. At home and abroad, economic, social, and political changes would continue to challenge American ingenuity.

1 The American People

The United States has been populated by adventurous people from all over the earth. Since the 1500s millions of people have left behind the life they had known to seek a better life on American shores. They have brought their hopes and dreams, their talents and beliefs. All have contributed to the creation of an American people.

A Land of Immigrants

Since the earliest peoples crossed the Bering Strait thousands of years ago, the Americas have been a land of immigrants. The many diverse cultures of the first Americans were joined by the Spanish and later by the French, English, Dutch, Swedish, Africans, and others.

Most early immigrants to the British colonies in North America were English, but there were also many Germans and Scotch-Irish as well as other Europeans. Africans, most of them brought to the colonies as slaves, also contributed to colonial American culture.

In the 1840s and 1850s large numbers of Germans and Irish immigrated to the United States. That wave of settlers added to the ethnic and religious diversity of the young nation. Since colonial times, American immigrants had been predominantly Protestant, but most of the Irish and many of the Germans were Catholic.

The origin of immigrants shifted in the late nineteenth and early twentieth centuries. Between 1880 and 1920 a growing number of people from southern and eastern Europe sought greater opportunity in the United States. These new immigrants included large numbers of Catholics as well as many Jews seeking refuge from persecution.

In the 1920s Congress restricted immigration from eastern and southern Europe and from Asia, but people continued to arrive from Canada, Mexico, and other Latin American nations. The restrictions imposed in the 1920s were lifted in 1965, and the nature of immigration to the United States shifted again.

Immigration from Asia grew dramatically during the 1970s. In the 1960s, 13 percent of the people who immigrated to the United States came from Asia. The figure jumped to 34 percent in the 1970s. At the same time, immigration from Europe slowed—from 33 percent in the 1960s to 18 percent in the 1970s. Immigration from Latin America continues to increase.

Each year a quota is set for the number of new immigrants who will be allowed to enter the country. In 1980, 654,000 people came to the United States, the highest number since World War II. A large share of these newcomers were from Cuba and Haiti.

■ *Since the 1960s immigrants to the United States have come increasingly from the nations of the Western Hemisphere and Asia. In the aftermath of the Vietnam War, large numbers of refugees from Vietnam and Cambodia settled in the United States. After Castro's revolution in 1959, and again in 1980, large numbers of Cuban refugees joined the ranks of immigrants.*

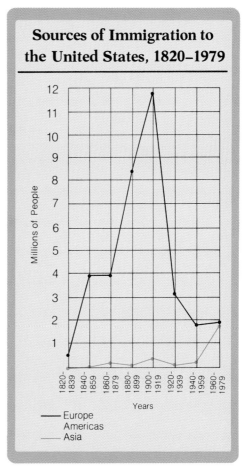

Sources of Immigration to the United States, 1820–1979

Millions of People

Years

—— Europe
Americas
—— Asia

Sources: *Statistical Abstract of the United States* and *Historical Statistics of the United States*

In addition to legal immigrants, hundreds of thousands of people each year enter the United States illegally. Some slip over borders. Others overstay tourist visas. Many Americans are concerned about this growing flow of illegal newcomers. They argue that illegal immigrants take jobs from Americans, particularly a problem during times of high unemployment. How the United States will resolve the issue of illegal immigration is an important concern for the 1980s.

Cultural Diversity

For many years, historians wrote about the United States as a melting pot where different cultures merged into one. More recently, some observers have described the United States as a pluralistic society where many different cultures exist side by side. Whether a melting pot or a pluralistic society, the United States has always had a rich cultural heritage because of the diverse traditions immigrants have brought from their homelands. These traditions can be seen in many aspects of life: in the names of families, towns, and cities; in the variety of food and

Fine arts such as ballet and opera have attracted many talented people to the United States. For example, the Italian opera star Luciano Pavarotti has made opera popular among millions of Americans.

clothing; and in the diversity of religious worship and traditional festivals held across the country.

The diversity of the nation's population has presented problems. New immigrants have often been met with suspicion and hostility from some Americans. Many immigrants have also faced a language barrier and unfamiliar customs that seemed to threaten their cherished traditions. The children of immigrants who do not speak English face many difficulties when they enter school. Schools have tried to meet the needs of these children by introducing bilingual education. In bilingual education programs, students take courses partly in English and partly in their native language.

Bilingual programs have provoked much controversy. Critics say they do not encourage children to learn English and are too expensive. Supporters counter that teaching children in their native languages until they have the chance to learn English eases the transition to a new society. Eventually, most new immigrants—old and young—learn English and adapt to American ways of life. The traditions they keep, however, have contributed to a unique American culture.

A Changing Population

If current trends continue, the nature of the country's population will be much different in the 1990s than it is today. One trend is slower population growth. Americans are

Americans cherish the food, music, dances, and traditions of the homelands of their ancestors. Across the country there are Puerto Rican parades, Chinese New Year feasts, Jewish holidays, Yugoslav and Italian festivals, and a dozen other salutes to the many heritages of Americans.

Major Religious Bodies in the United States

Eastern Churches of America	⛪
Jewish Congregations	🕍 🕍
Roman Catholic	♜♜♜♜♜♜♜♜♜♜♜
Protestant	⛪⛪⛪⛪⛪⛪⛪⛪⛪⛪⛪⛪⛪
Other	🏠

One symbol represents 5 million members

Source: *Statistical Abstract of the United States*

■ *One evidence of cultural diversity in the United States is the variety of religions. This graph shows the main religious groups in the United States. Most of the large categories contain dozens of smaller religious denominations.*

marrying later and having fewer children. Throughout the 1970s the population increased by less than 1 percent a year. Some experts predict that by the year 2050 the United States will reach zero population growth. In other words, the population will stop increasing. The number of children born will equal the number of people who die in a given year.

In addition to growing more slowly, the population is becoming older. As fewer babies are born, there are fewer young people in the population. During the 1970s the number of children 14 years old and younger dropped by 11.5 percent. Experts predict that during the 1980s, teenagers will make up less than 30 percent of the population for the first time ever.

At the same time, the number of older people is growing as improved health care extends human life. (See the graph on page 720.) In 1970 the median age of the population was about 28. That is, half of the population was older than 28 and half was younger. In 1979 the median age was 30. By

■ *This graph is called a population pyramid. By studying it, you can learn a great deal about the population of the country. It shows the percentage of men and women in various age groups. At what age do males outnumber females? How will the shape of the pyramid change as the number of older people increases?* For answers, see p. A 120.

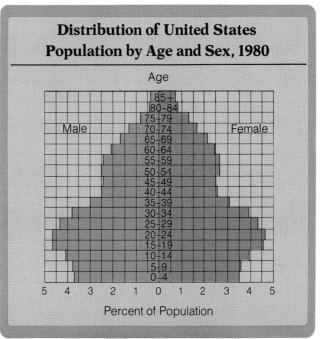

Source: United States Bureau of the Census

Sun City, Arizona, is a new kind of community designed for older people whose children are grown. Such retirement communities, with golf courses and other recreational facilities, have become very popular.

A Mobile People

Americans, it seems, have always been on the move. People pushed farther and farther west from the earliest English settlements on the east coast of the continent. Pioneers searched for fertile farm land, and some sought adventure. By the 1850s they had settled much of the land east of the Mississippi River. During the last half of the nineteenth century prospectors opened up the far West while ranchers and farmers moved onto the Great Plains.

By the end of the 1800s an increasing number of Americans were moving to the rapidly growing cities of the Northeast and Midwest. That movement continued throughout the first half of the 1900s. The United States, which had begun as a rural nation, became an urban one.

While some people were moving to cities, others began moving out of cities into suburbs. The advent of an inexpensive automobile in the 1920s sparked the growth of suburban areas because people could easily commute between jobs in the city and

1990 it may be as high as 32 or 33. In addition, by 1990 it is predicted that one out of every eight Americans will be 65 years of age or older.

This aging of the population will have significant economic and social effects. If more people are in their thirties and forties, advertisers will aim their products at those age groups rather than at people in their teens or twenties. Eventually the proportion of people of working age will decline and the number of retired persons will increase more rapidly. This will put more pressure on the social security system, which was nearly bankrupt by the early 1980s.

Significant changes in the ethnic and racial composition of the population occurred during the 1970s. The number of black Americans increased by 17 percent. The Hispanic population grew even faster. In the 1970 census 9.1 million Americans, or 4.5 percent of the population, listed themselves as of "Spanish origin." Ten years later 14.6 million people, or 6.5 percent, placed themselves in that category. This trend is expected to continue throughout the 1980s. By the end of the decade, some experts predict, Hispanics will pass blacks as the largest minority group in the United States.

734

■ *The desire to own a single-family home produced an explosive growth of suburbs after World War II, but that growth has slowed in recent years. The percentage of people living in rural areas rose dramatically during the 1970s.*

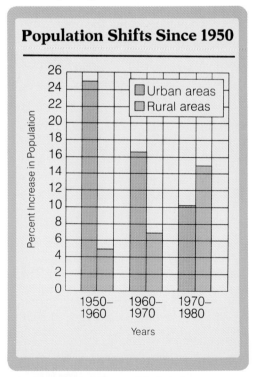

Source: *Statistical Abstract of the United States*

Americans have moved south and west by the millions. Southern and western cities such as Houston have grown dramatically. One lure has been warmer winters, which mean more time outdoors and lower fuel bills. Another lure has been more jobs, for industry has grown much faster in the sunbelt than in other parts of the country.

homes outside it. After World War II the suburbs mushroomed. During the 1960s the population of suburbs increased by 27 percent while the population of cities grew by only 6 percent. By 1970 more Americans lived in suburbs than in cities and rural areas.

During the 1970s a major shift in population movement occurred. For the first time since 1820, rural areas and small towns grew faster than metropolitan centers. This trend is expected to continue throughout the 1980s and beyond, as many Americans leave cities hoping to find jobs and a better quality of life.

Suburbs grew in the 1970s, but a smaller proportion of the population lived in them. In the 1980s suburbs will continue to grow but at an even slower rate than in the 1970s. Part of suburban growth is due to an influx of growing numbers of black Americans. In 1970 less than 16 percent of Americans living in suburbs were black. By 1980 that figure had jumped to 23 percent.

The population of large cities, especially those in the Northeast and Midwest, declined in the 1970s. For over 20 years, large cities have been plagued with rising unemployment as businesses and factories moved elsewhere. Poverty, decay, and crime have become characteristic of many urban areas that are losing middle-class residents. The

1980 census showed that cities now have a higher poverty rate than rural areas.

Despite these problems, there is evidence of a rebirth of cities. One cause of the rebirth is the rising cost of gasoline, which has made commuting from distant suburbs by car increasingly expensive. Another cause is the massive face lift many cities are undergoing as businesses and families seek an alternative to suburbs. Billions of dollars are being poured into cities for construction of new office towers, shopping plazas, hotels, and apartments. Factory lofts, waterfront warehouses, and old houses are being renovated. As a result, more people are considering a move back to the cities.

Larimer Square in Denver, Georgetown in Washington, D.C., and the Upper West Side of Manhattan in New York City are only a few examples of city neighborhoods that residents are rebuilding. A new generation of urban pioneers is repairing homes in once blighted areas. Although they are experiencing a population decline, American cities may be on the threshold of a rebirth.

The Sunbelt

Many of the people who leave northern metropolitan areas are moving to the *sunbelt*, that is, the states of the Southeast and Southwest known for their warm, sunny

735

weather. The westward movement is a continuation of a historic trend.

The population of the western states has grown steadily since the Civil War. The population of the southern states had generally decreased until the 1970s, when it grew dramatically. While the Northeast and Midwest lost over 1 million people between 1970 and 1975, the South gained almost 2 million. During the 1970s the population of the West and South grew by 24 percent and 20 percent, which is almost twice the rate of growth of the country as a whole.

Forty percent of the national population growth since 1970 has occurred in three states: Texas, California, and Florida. (See the map below.) Five sunbelt cities—Los Angeles, Dallas, San Diego, Houston, and San Antonio—now rank among the nation's ten largest cities. As a result of the move to the sunbelt, northeastern and midwestern states lost 17 congressional seats in 1982 to states in the South and West.

Life in the sunbelt is attracting Americans for many reasons. A growing number of manufacturing firms have been moving plants to the South. The prospect of good jobs keeps local residents from leaving the area and attracts people from other regions. The mild winters appeal to many people from northern states, especially to the growing number of retired. Retirement communities are prominent in Florida, California, and Arizona. They will probably continue to grow, since retired people represent an increasing portion of the population.

■ On this map you can see the distribution of population growth between 1970 and 1980. Which states lost population during this period? Explain why the map is titled "Move to the Sunbelt." Can you think of reasons why Alaska, which is outside the sunbelt, grew more than 30 percent in population during the period? For answers, see p. A 120.

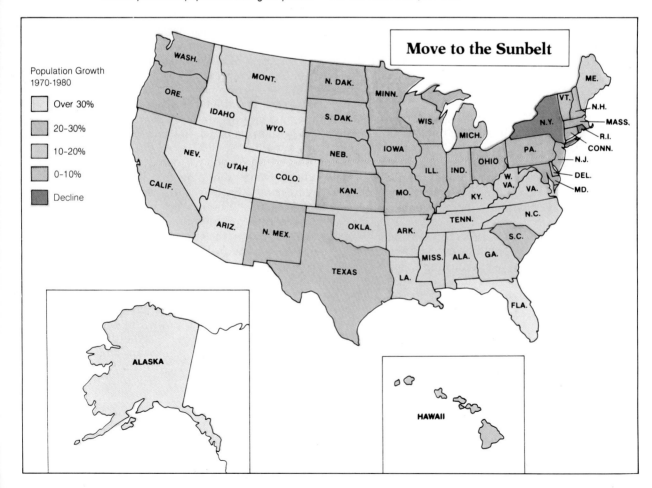

Move to the Sunbelt

Population Growth 1970-1980

- Over 30%
- 20-30%
- 10-20%
- 0-10%
- Decline

For answers, see p. A 120.

Section Review

1. Define the following term: sunbelt.
2. How did the immigrants of the 1840s and 1850s add to religious diversity in the United States?
3. From what two areas did increasing numbers of immigrants come to the United States during the 1970s?
4. What is the difference between a melting pot and pluralistic society?
5. How are current trends affecting (a) population growth and (b) the age of the population?
6. (a) What development during the 1920s contributed to the growth of the suburbs? (b) What happened to suburban growth during the late 1970s? (c) What factors have contributed to the decline of major cities?
7. List two reasons more people are moving to the sunbelt.

2 Governing a Growing Nation

From 13 states on the east coast, the United States has grown to 50 states that span a continent and extend into the Pacific. The population of the country has expanded from about 4 million to over 200 million. The government of the nation has also grown. Today government employs more people, spends more money, and touches more lives than ever before. The people's role in government has also grown since the nation was founded.

Extending the Right to Vote

In most of the colonies the right to vote was restricted to white male Protestant property owners. When the Constitution was ratified in 1789, the barriers of religion and property began to fall. By the 1830s most states had extended the vote to all adult white males.

The Fifteenth Amendment to the Constitution, ratified in 1870, stated that citizens could not be denied the right to vote on the basis of race. However, by the 1880s southern states were using devices to keep black citizens from voting. A series of voting rights legislation in the 1960s finally guaranteed the right to vote to all black Americans. The Twenty-fourth Amendment, ratified in 1964, outlawed the poll tax.

The long struggle for women's suffrage ended in 1920 when the states ratified the Nineteenth Amendment. The Twenty-sixth Amendment, ratified in 1971, guaranteed the right to vote to persons 18 years of age or older.

Although a growing proportion of Americans has gained the right to vote, the percentage of eligible voters who take advantage of that right has declined. For example, in the 1964 presidential election 62 percent of the electorate voted, while in 1980 only 53 percent went to the polls. Even fewer people participated in congressional elections: 45 percent in 1966 compared to 35 percent in 1978. However, in the 1982 congressional elections this trend was reversed when 41 percent of voting age Americans went to the polls.

■ *As you can see on this graph, more people vote in presidential elections than in off-year elections, when only members of Congress are being chosen.*

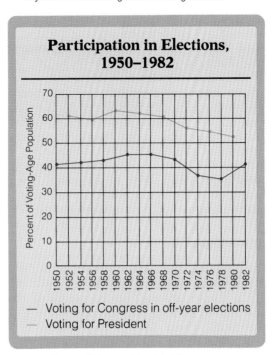

Participation in Elections, 1950–1982

— Voting for Congress in off-year elections
— Voting for President

Source: *Statistical Abstract of the United States*

A More Direct Voice

As the right to vote has been extended, Americans have gained a more direct role in their government. The nation's founders limited the direct influence of the people. They believed that most people did not have the information or background needed to govern directly. Today books, radio, television, newspapers, and magazines provide a constant supply of information to American citizens.

In some states citizens can propose legislation in an initiative and vote on it directly in a referendum. In 1980 voters in 18 states and the District of Columbia placed a total of 42 issues on the ballot through an initiative. In 1978 the passage in California of a referendum called Proposition 13 had nationwide impact. Adoption of this referendum slashed property taxes for California residents. It was publicized around the nation and was widely interpreted as a sign of voter discontent with rising taxes. In addition, voters in some states can remove officials from office by a recall election.

The initiative, referendum, and recall were introduced early in this century during the progressive era. That era also witnessed ratification of the Seventeenth Amendment to the Constitution, which called for the direct election of senators by the voters of each state. Today about half the states hold primary elections to select delegates to party nominating conventions, giving voters a more direct voice in selecting presidential candidates.

Although the direct influence of voters has increased during the past 100 years, Presidents continue to be chosen by the electoral college. Some people have proposed the direct election of the President, but opponents of the idea contend that such a method would give too much influence to densely populated areas of the nation. Continuation of the electoral college helps protect the interests of less populous areas.

Expansion of Government

The federal government has experienced dramatic growth over the course of the nation's history. During the first years of the new nation, federal expenditures were just over $4,000 a year. In 1979 they were an estimated $531 billion, and in 1980 that figure in-

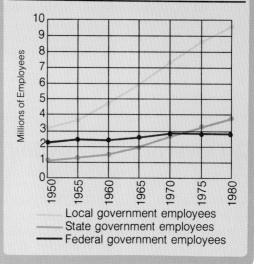

Number of Government Employees, 1950–1980

Millions of Employees

Local government employees
State government employees
Federal government employees

Source: *Statistical Abstract of the United States*

■ *Since World War II the total number of government jobs has increased dramatically. As the chart shows, the increase has been sharpest in local government employment.*

creased to an estimated $663 billion. In other words, the federal government spends money at the rate of over $1.8 billion a day.

As the role of government in people's lives has increased, expenditures have kept pace. The founders of the nation envisioned a limited national government with only a few functions, such as delivering the mail, collecting import duties, maintaining an army, and enforcing a rather small body of laws.

Over the years, however, the activities of government have grown. The first and second national banks of the early 1800s were among the earliest examples of government participation in the national economy. The rapid expansion of industry and the development of giant corporations in the late nineteenth century brought demands for more government regulation. The first regulatory agency, the Interstate Commerce Commission, was created in 1887 to prevent abuses of economic power in the railroad industry. Other agencies followed.

Today hundreds of government agencies oversee and regulate some aspect of the national economy. Government regulations affect nearly every aspect of American life, from the content of hot dogs to the air quality in textile mills. The regulations affect the food Americans eat, the clothes they wear, the cars they drive, and their work environment. Industry often passes on the costs of following regulations to consumers by raising prices.

During the late 1970s some of the regulatory agencies increasingly came under attack. Critics cited the existence of millions of regulations that required vast amounts of time, money, and paper work to administer. While many people believe that some regulation is necessary to protect the public interest, they argue that the benefits of many regulations do not justify the expense of meeting their requirements.

During the past 50 years Americans have come to expect many services from their governments at the local, state, and na-

tional levels. For example, unemployment insurance protects people who lose their jobs. Social Security provides a guaranteed income for retired workers and their families. Governments build and maintain roads, mass transit systems, water purification plants, and airports.

Many such services were once provided only by private agencies and local governments. Until the 1930s few people believed the federal government should play a major role in providing social services. However, since then its role has grown tremendously. In 1929 the federal government spent $625 million on social programs. By 1939 that figure had grown to $3 billion, and in 1976 federal expenditures on social services amounted to $109 billion. In 1982 over $340 billion was spent for federal benefits. From 1967 to 1982 the price tag of federal benefits programs increased from about 27 percent of the total federal budget to an estimated 49

■ *These graphs show two ways of looking at federal spending. The circle graph at left shows how federal funds were allocated in 1981. The bar graph at right traces the increase in federal expenditures from 1930 to 1980. The Vietnam War and inflation were major reasons for the steep increase in the 1970s.*

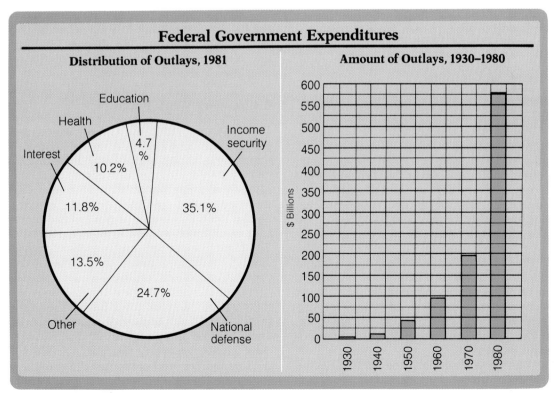

Source: *Historical Statistics of the United States* and *Statistical Abstract of the United States*

percent. In addition to funding its own programs, the federal government pays about one quarter of all expenditures by state and local governments.

740

Many Americans have become increasingly concerned about the cost of government in the United States. Some groups have organized successful protests against rising state taxes. Such actions have resulted in cuts in state budgets and services. Nationally, a proposed constitutional amendment requiring a balanced budget has gained some support. Such an amendment, its supporters say, would restrict congressional spending and taxation powers.

For answers, see p. A 120.

Section Review

1. What group of Americans gained the right to vote by the Twenty-sixth Amendment to the Constitution?
2. How has the percentage of eligible voters who vote in presidential elections changed since 1964?
3. List three ways voters have gained a more direct role in government.
4. What was the purpose of the first federal regulatory agency?
5. Give two examples of services that governments provide.

3 A Land of Opportunity

The rich natural resources of North America and the industriousness of the American people have combined to create an economy of abundance unmatched in the rest of the world. Yet today, more Americans than ever are seeking a share of that abundance. Furthermore, other nations are competing vigorously for their own share of the world's business. These changing conditions are prompting new responses from the American people.

A Growing Economy

Explorers of the 1500s sought gold and silver in North America. They found little, but later settlers discovered other valuable resources: fertile soil and vast forests. Forest products and agriculture were central to the American economy until the advent of the industrial revolution in the 1800s. Then the nation relied on rich deposits of coal and iron ore; long, navigable rivers; and supplies of oil and natural gas to transform it into an industrial giant.

By 1900 the United States had become one of the great economic powers of the world. Although devastated by the Great Depression, the American economy emerged from World War II strong and vibrant, making the United States the world's leading economic power.

The gross national product (GNP), the total dollar value of goods and services, has grown throughout the nation's history. From 1890 to 1970 the productivity of American workers more than quadrupled. In other words, a worker in 1970 produced four times as much dollar value per hour as did a worker in 1890.

As the variety and number of products available to Americans has increased, so has their income. From 1930 to 1980 the average real income of Americans tripled. From 1950 to 1980 the number of automobiles sold in the United States tripled. Today over 80 percent of American families own at least one car. Nearly all American families own a refrigerator and a television set.

A Changing Work Force

Until the late 1800s the United States was chiefly a farming nation. After the Civil War the manufacturing sector grew dramatically, and by 1900 a majority of workers were employed in areas other than farming. This trend continued into the twentieth century. By the 1980s less than 4 percent of the American work force was involved in agriculture. Yet farm production has increased significantly, partly as a result of the use of improved equipment, fertilizers, and pesticides.

Over the past 50 years, the fastest-growing parts of the work force have been in the professional fields and the service industries. These areas employ workers who do not produce goods. Lawyers, teachers, secretaries, doctors, nurses, and computer programmers are examples of such workers. Today about nine out of every ten new jobs created are service or technical in nature. The need for

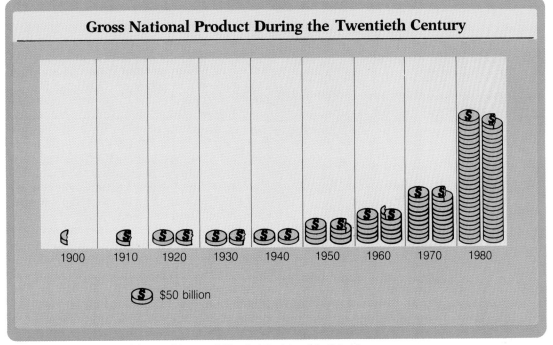

Gross National Product During the Twentieth Century

1900 1910 1920 1930 1940 1950 1960 1970 1980

$ = $50 billion

Source: *Statistical Abstract of the United States* and *Historical Statistics of the United States*

■ *The United States emerged from World War II with the world's strongest economy. One measure of economic strength is the gross national product (GNP). The GNP is the total dollar value of goods and services produced in a year. The growth of the GNP of the United States in the twentieth century is shown clearly on this graph.*

people to service new sophisticated machinery has also created an important area of growth.

The shift of jobs from manufacturing to service industries has created new places for highly skilled people. Computers and other technological advances have transformed many jobs in the office and on the assembly line. Government, industry, and educational institutions have been spending about $40 billion a year to retrain workers to adapt to changes in their jobs. Many experts believe more job training programs will be necessary to prepare the labor force for the changing nature of work in the United States.

One of the biggest changes in the American economy during the past three decades has been an influx of women into the wage-earning work force. Today two thirds of new workers are women. An increasing percentage of married women now work outside the home—51 percent in 1980 compared to 34 percent in 1950. Among women with school-age children, six out of ten now work outside the home.

■ *Membership in labor unions has not grown as fast as the labor force. In fact, the percentage of the work force in unions has dropped in recent years, as this graph shows.*

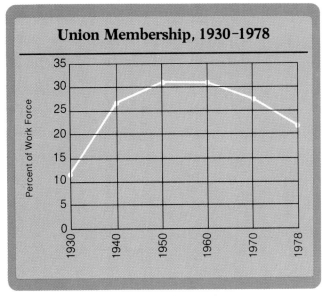

Union Membership, 1930–1978

Percent of Work Force

35
30
25
20
15
10
5
0

1930 1940 1950 1960 1970 1978

Source: *Statistical Abstract of the United States* and *Historical Statistics of the United States*

In the 1970s the number of women in medicine and the sciences increased dramatically. This researcher works in the San Diego Zoo.

A majority of women continues to work in such traditional female occupations as secretary, sales clerk, teacher, and registered nurse. However, women have made significant inroads in other professions. For example, the percentage of women graduates of engineering schools rose from .8 percent in 1971 to 10.4 percent in 1981. Similar increases have occurred in law, medicine, and business. Furthermore, the number of women managers doubled during the 1970s. Despite these changes, women still earn significantly less than men. In 1981, women earned an average of 65 percent of men's salaries.

Black Americans have also entered new areas of the job market. The percentage of blacks in professional and technical jobs almost tripled between 1960 and 1980, and the number of blacks in managerial positions doubled. Yet the median family income* of black Americans remains between 50 and 60 percent of the median family income of whites. Unemployment is also higher among

*Half of all family incomes are higher than the median family income and half are lower.

■ *Compare these two circle graphs showing the kinds of work done by men and women. In the 1960s and 1970s women entered the work force in unprecedented numbers, and many more women took professional or managerial jobs. Despite these changes, the graphs show that women still far outnumber men in lower-paying service and clerical jobs.*

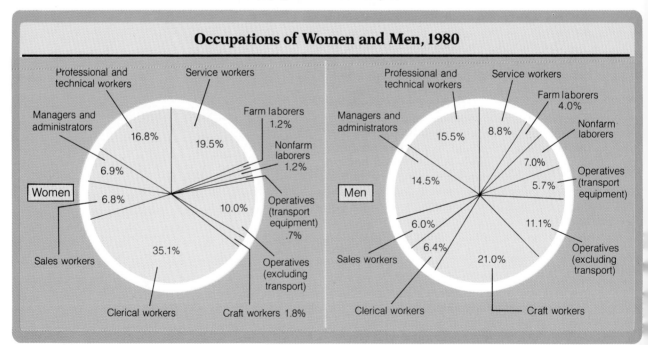

Occupations of Women and Men, 1980

Women
- Professional and technical workers: 16.8%
- Service workers: 19.5%
- Farm laborers: 1.2%
- Nonfarm laborers: 1.2%
- Managers and administrators: 6.9%
- Operatives (transport equipment): .7%
- Sales workers: 6.8%
- Operatives (excluding transport): 10.0%
- Clerical workers: 35.1%
- Craft workers: 1.8%

Men
- Professional and technical workers: 15.5%
- Service workers: 8.8%
- Farm laborers: 4.0%
- Nonfarm laborers: 7.0%
- Managers and administrators: 14.5%
- Operatives (transport equipment): 5.7%
- Sales workers: 6.0%
- Operatives (excluding transport): 11.1%
- Clerical workers: 6.4%
- Craft workers: 21.0%

Source: *Statistical Abstract of the United States*

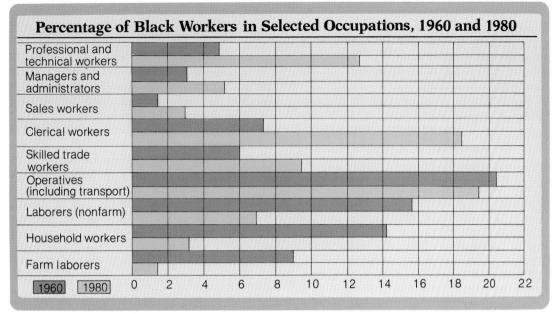

Percentage of Black Workers in Selected Occupations, 1960 and 1980

Occupation	1960	1980
Professional and technical workers		
Managers and administrators		
Sales workers		
Clerical workers		
Skilled trade workers		
Operatives (including transport)		
Laborers (nonfarm)		
Household workers		
Farm laborers		

Source: *Statistical Abstract of the United States*

■ In the past two decades the percentage of black Americans in white collar jobs has almost tripled, growing to 39 percent in 1980. On the chart, these jobs are labeled Professional and technical workers, Managers and administrators, Sales workers, and Clerical workers. Despite such advances, incomes of blacks continue to trail those paid whites.

black Americans, especially among black youth. In some large cities, more than 40 percent of black teenagers were unemployed in 1982. Some businesses are designing programs to help employ black youth by providing training programs and jobs.

Another group of Americans seeking to enter the labor force in greater numbers is the handicapped. In recent years, the trend has been to equip public buildings with facilities designed to meet the needs of handicapped Americans. For example, elevators often have Braille numbers to designate the floors. And ramps provide access to buildings for people in wheelchairs. Many cities are also exploring ways to accommodate the handicapped on public transportation and in parking facilities. Like other minorities in the United States, the handicapped have formed organizations to press for these and other rights.

Continuing Challenges

Despite widespread abundance, many Americans live in poverty. In 1978, 11.4 percent of Americans had incomes below the poverty line established by the government. In 1981

During the 1970s and 1980s many people with physical handicaps have fought for their right to take advantage of the economic opportunities available to Americans. Special buses such as the one shown here enable people in wheelchairs to take public transportation to and from work.

this figure rose to 14 percent, the result of a deep recession. Some families are able to stay above the poverty line only because husband and wife both work outside the home.

Single-parent families often face severe economic strain. Such families have one wage earner at most. Often a single parent must care for children and thus is unable to work.

Another group facing hard economic times is the unemployed. In 1982 more than 10 million people in the United States were out of work. Much of this unemployment was the direct result of the recession. As the demand for products dropped, many plants closed and workers were laid off.

Even with recovery, some experts predict that segments of the economy such as the automobile and steel industries will never employ as many people as they once did. Demand for some American-made products has declined as cheaper foreign products become available. Computers and robots are also replacing some workers. One of the economic tasks of the future will be to devise new approaches to match workers with available jobs, including training programs for high-technology jobs.

Inflation during the 1970s and early 1980s reduced the buying power of wage earners at all levels. For example, although average hourly wages rose 73 percent between 1967 and 1975, workers could buy only 7 percent more.

Inflation has been a factor in the American economy since the end of World War II. A dollar, which bought 100 cents' worth of goods in 1945, bought 60 cents' worth in 1961 and less than 24 cents' worth in 1980. The rate of inflation declined in 1982, but the decline was accompanied by a deep recession. (See page 717.) Few experts think that a permanent solution to the problem of inflation has been found.

According to many economists, one key to strengthening the American economy is to increase productivity. *Productivity* is output per hour of work. Greater productivity means that goods can be produced more efficiently and thus can be sold for a lower price.

Although American productivity is increasing, the rate of increase has been slower than the rate of increase in Japan and some European countries. For example, productivity in Japan increased by 29.4 percent between 1977 and 1981. It increased by 14.5 percent in France and by 12.8 percent in West Germany. However, during the same period productivity in the United States increased by only 4.5 percent. The smaller increase in productivity has helped make American products less competitive on the world market.

Some American companies have tried to increase productivity by investing in new plants and equipment. Giving workers a larger role in solving on-the-job problems has increased productivity in some factories. Plant managers have found that as workers gain more responsibility they are less likely to be absent from their jobs. Businesses are also experimenting with more flexible working schedules, including job sharing, longer vacations, and a four-day work week.

Foreign Competition

Cars made in Japan and West Germany are a common sight on American streets. Many of the sweaters you find in department stores were made in the People's Republic of China. Foreign companies sell not only cars and clothing but other consumer goods such as television sets, radios, and calculators and materials such as steel in the United States.

As you have read, foreign competition is threatening the future of some major American industries. As people buy less-expensive foreign products, the demand for American products falls. As a result, factories close and workers are laid off.

Many factors have contributed to the ability of foreign companies to sell their products for a lower price than American-made products. In some cases, foreign companies sell their products at a lower price in the United States than in their own country. This practice is known as dumping. The United States government has tried to discourage dumping by monitoring the prices charged by foreign companies.

In most cases, however, the products can be produced more cheaply in the foreign country than in the United States. Often, lower wages and production costs keep prices low. In some countries, the government subsidizes key industries, allowing companies to sell without making a profit. Growing productivity in countries such as Japan and West Germany also reduces the cost of producing goods.

In addition, American industries are often hampered by old factories and equipment. Most of the major factories in Japan and parts of western Europe were rebuilt after World War II. Many American factories, however, date from the early 1900s.

To reduce the impact of foreign competition, many American companies are trying to increase productivity and update equipment. In addition, the United States government has tried to reach agreement with foreign governments to restrict the quantity of foreign products that can be sold in the United States. Sterner measures have also been proposed. Some politicians favor imposing tariffs on imported goods to raise their prices. Another proposal would require foreign cars sold in this country to have a specific percentage of American-made parts.

Such proposals have sparked heated public debate.

A Healthy Living and Working Environment

One of the tasks facing Americans in the nation's third century is to maintain a balance between a healthy living environment and a healthy economy. The very abundance of American life has made that difficult.

Millions of automobiles clog the roads and emit fumes that are harmful when inhaled in sufficient quantities. Communities must find ways to dispose of billions of tons of garbage and wastes, including radioactive wastes from nuclear power plants. New scientific discoveries have had unexpected side effects. Some newly created chemicals, for

Women in Sports

A widely publicized incident during the 1967 Boston Marathon involved an angry race official chasing Katherine Switzer in an attempt to remove her from the event. At that time, women were not allowed to run in the Boston Marathon. Only by registering as "K. Switzer" had Switzer been able to obtain an official number. After eluding the irate official, she became the first woman with an official number to finish the race.

Besides the inspiration of athletes like Switzer, the fitness boom of the 1970s and 1980s has contributed to women's increased interest in sports. On any given day, some 70 million Americans—almost one half of the adult population—do some form of exercise. In 1971, 233 ran the New York Marathon. Ten years later 25,000 runners applied for the 16,000 places available.

Today there are an estimated 15 million women runners, many of whom participate in marathons, including the one in Boston. For 1984 a women's marathon was added to the Olympic games, a fitting symbol of the great strides taken by women athletes during the past decade.

Women have improved their performances in many sports. Amateur athletes have shaved seconds off existing records in track-and-field events, swimming, and other sports. One reason for this is the growing number of women who participate in high school and college athletics. In 1970, 7 percent of high school athletes and 2 per-

cent of college athletes were women. By the early 1980s, women constituted 35 percent of high school athletes and 30 percent of college athletes.

In addition, professional women athletes have seen a dramatic increase in prize money. For example, women golfers on the pro tour earned a total of $6.4 million in 1982, compared with $1.2 million in 1975. Women tennis pros, such as Chris Evert Lloyd, once earned purses far smaller than those of their male counterparts, but today they are paid at comparable levels for their efforts.

For exercise, for fun, and to save gas, more Americans are using bicycles. In some places, roads and parkways close at special times to permit bicyclists like this family to enjoy a ride without dodging cars. Recently, however, bicyclists have been competing for road space with a new and growing group—roller skaters.

As American society has become more complicated and technological, many people have turned to the outdoors for a change of pace. Sales of camping gear have soared in the past two decades.

example, have been linked to cancer and nerve disorders. Fumes, wastes, and chemicals can contaminate the air people breathe, the water they drink, and the food they eat.

The search for a balance between the economic needs of a community and the need for a healthy environment has been a difficult one. Some environmentalists have demanded that factories be required to follow strict antipollution requirements in order to protect the health of workers and local residents.

Plant owners point to the measures already taken to protect the environment. They charge that further regulations will not significantly improve environmental conditions but will add to operating expenses. That in turn, they argue, could increase the prices consumers pay for products and might even force plants to close. Consequently, some workers also oppose regulations they consider too strict.

The continued growth of the American economy has depended on abundant natural resources. However, people are coming to realize that the supply of many resources is limited. The oil crises of the 1970s made this clear to many Americans. Practical limits require American industry and consumers to use resources efficiently and to find substitutes for those that are scarce.

For answers, see p. A 120.

Section Review

1. Define the following term: productivity.
2. Name two natural resources that contributed to the growth of American industry.
3. Which parts of the work force have grown the fastest over the past 50 years?
4. How did the percentage of women working outside the home change between 1950 and 1980?
5. How did the value of a dollar change between 1945 and the present?
6. (a) Why is productivity an economic concern in the United States? (b) What efforts have been made to improve productivity?
7. (a) How has abundance contributed to environmental problems? (b) Why is it often difficult to find a balance between a healthy living environment and a healthy economy?

4 The United States and the World

Americans hear about world developments every day. Events thousands of miles away can affect the price Americans pay for sugar or oil, and events in the United States can affect the lives of people all over the world. This was not always the case, but the history of relations between the United States and the world has been one of growing involvement.

A Cautious New Nation

As part of the British Empire, the American colonies were closely tied to Europe. They could not avoid conflicts such as the French and Indian War. After 1783, however, the new nation hoped to stay out of European disputes. The early Presidents urged neutrality, but in 1812 the United States was drawn into a war with Great Britain. Following the war, the nation returned to its goal of avoiding involvement in European affairs.

The young republic was far from isolated, however. It expanded to the Pacific by treaties with France, Spain, and Britain and through a war with Mexico. Alaska was purchased from Russia. The United States also participated in world trade.

During the first half of the nineteenth century, the nation imported mostly manufactured goods and exported raw materials such as cotton and wood products. In 1830, for example, it exported $40 million worth of raw materials and only $5 million worth of manufactured products. That same year the United States imported $36 million worth of manufactured goods.

Toward World Leadership

Rapid industrialization after the Civil War contributed to a new world status for the United States. The country became a major producer of iron and steel, and it expanded its markets overseas. The value of United States exports rose from $845 million in 1890 to $2.3 billion in 1914. Almost one third of all exports in 1914 were manufactured goods.

American involvement in world politics also had increased by the end of the 1800s. President McKinley and his successors worked to protect American interests in Latin America, Asia, and Europe. The United States acquired an overseas empire, annexing Hawaii in 1898 and assuming control of several Spanish colonies after the Spanish-American War.

The United States reluctantly entered World War I in 1917 after attempts to remain neutral had failed. Following the war, Americans sought a return to peace, and for many that meant isolation from world events. However, aggression by Germany and Japan during the 1930s convinced national leaders to aid China and Britain. The United States entered World War II after the Japanese attack on Pearl Harbor in 1941 and emerged from the war as the most powerful nation—economically and militarily—in the world.

A Changing World Scene

For many years after World War II, American leaders were primarily concerned with containing the growing power of the Soviet Union. They sent vast amounts of aid to western Europe and Japan to help rebuild their economies and eventually extended aid to many Third World nations. Alliances such as NATO also aimed at containing Soviet power. By the 1980s, however, most Americans had come to realize that the world economic and political balance was becoming increasingly complex.

Policy makers have found that classifying nations as pro-Soviet or pro-American is not as easy as it once was. Major powers such as China are pursuing independent courses, as are many smaller nations in Africa, Asia, and Latin America. Traditional American allies such as France and West Germany no longer automatically support American positions.

The complexity of world politics is matched by the economic situation. As Japan and the nations of western Europe recovered from World War II, they entered a period of rapid economic growth. By the 1960s and 1970s they were competing with the United States for world markets. In 1959 about 20 percent of all world exports originated in the United States. By 1980 that figure had fallen to about 10 percent. Nevertheless, the United States remains unrivaled

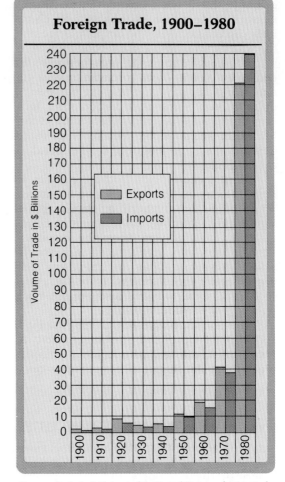

Source: *Statistical Abstract of the United States* and *Historical Statistics of the United States*

■ *From the time of its emergence as a major industrial power, the United States has usually sold more goods to foreign countries than it has bought. On this chart you can trace imports and exports from 1900 to 1980. Note how the pattern shifted around 1970. As oil prices rose and the United States imported more petroleum, the cost of imports rose to record levels. At the same time, the surging economies of Japan and western Europe provided more competition for American companies trying to sell products overseas.*

in the world for its output of goods and services. In 1980 the United States, with only 5.1 percent of the world's population, produced 21.3 percent of the world's output.

The economies of the United States and other industrialized nations are increasingly affected by developments in other parts of the world. For example, during the 1970s

For answers, see p. A 121.

Trends in American History: Forecasting Alternative Futures

In this chapter you have reviewed several trends in American history. But what lies ahead for the United States? Will immigrants continue to add to the diversity of American culture? Will the national government continue to expand, or will its growth slow down? Will the American people find a solution to the energy crisis? These are just a few of the questions you might ask about the future.

While no one can predict exactly what will happen, you can forecast, or suggest, possible developments. Such forecasts can influence your decisions and actions in the present. For example, if you forecast that energy costs will continue to rise, you may decide to buy an energy-efficient automobile or a solar-heated house. Use the steps below to practice the skill of forecasting.

1. **Identify a trend.** Review this chapter and select one of the trends discussed. Write a paragraph in which you describe the trend in your own words.

2. **Project alternative future developments.** Use the following questions to project future developments for the trend you are studying: (a) What might happen if the trend continues? (b) What type of future events might change the trend? (c) How might the trend be affected by each of those events?

3. **Determine the likelihood of possible developments.** To complete this step you should research background material about the trend. Current news magazines, newspapers, and books are important sources. After researching the possible developments, decide which is most likely to occur and which is least likely to occur. Write a report explaining your conclusions about possible future developments.

OPEC's decision to raise the price of oil had far-reaching effects on American life.

Higher prices for oil and other imports also affected the United States *balance of trade*, the difference in value between imports and exports. (If the value of imports exceeds the value of exports, a nation has a *trade deficit*. If the value of exports exceeds that of imports, it has a *trade surplus*.) In 1960 the United States had a trade surplus of $4.6 billion, but in 1982 the trade deficit was about $44 billion.

Oil prices began to decline in the 1980s, but the United States continues to have a large trade deficit. Competition from foreign manufacturers contributes to this deficit. In addition, worldwide recession has lowered demand for American products in other countries.

The worldwide recession also affects the United States in another way. Many Third World nations were hard hit by higher oil prices in the 1970s. They borrowed large amounts of money from governments and from banks in Europe and the United States. The recession has lowered demand for the minerals, metals, and farm products these nations export. Thus, they are finding it difficult to pay their debts. If a nation *defaults*, or

fails to pay its debt, the soundness of some banks could be threatened. Economists worry that the failure of an important bank could trigger a worldwide financial panic.

Close economic ties throughout the world mean that Americans—from government policy makers to business leaders to individual citizens—cannot ignore the larger world around them. Decisions made on all levels of government and business can affect the future economic and political role of the United States in world affairs.

For answers, see p. A 121.

Section Review

1. Define the following terms: balance of trade, trade deficit, trade surplus, default.

2. (a) What type of goods did the United States export in the early 1800s? (b) How did the value of American exports change between 1890 and 1914?

3. What was the primary concern of American leaders after World War II?

4. How did the world political scene become more complex between the 1950s and the 1980s?

5. How did the United States balance of trade change between 1960 and 1982?

749

IN PERSPECTIVE Immigrants from many lands have brought rich cultural traditions to American shores. Such traditions have helped make Americans a diverse people. In addition, the population has always seemed to be on the move, first from rural areas to cities and then to suburbs. Americans have migrated steadily westward, and more are moving south.

Over the years a growing proportion of the American population has gained the right to vote and acquired a more direct voice in government. The government itself has grown and become more involved in the economy and in the everyday lives of its citizens. The American economy of abundance is being challenged by inflation and limited resources and by the need to balance economic growth and a healthy environment.

The United States' role in world affairs has grown since the birth of the nation, despite strong sympathy for isolation during much of the nineteenth and part of the twentieth centuries. By the end of World War II the nation had become a major world power, and today it faces an increasingly complex world.

For answers, see p. A 121.

Chapter Review

1. Describe the nature of immigration to the United States during each of the following periods: (a) 1840s and 1850s, (b) 1880 to 1920, (c) late 1960s and 1970s.

2. (a) How did changes in immigration contribute to religious and cultural diversity in the United States? (b) What challenges has such diversity presented?

3. (a) In what way is the movement to the sunbelt a continuation of a traditional movement? (b) How has it reversed previous trends?

4. (a) How has the right to vote been extended since colonial days? (b) How have Americans gained a more direct role in government?

5. (a) How has the role of government in people's lives changed since the late 1800s? (b) Why do some Americans object to that change? (c) How has President Reagan tried to change the role of the federal government?

6. (a) What occupation did a majority of Americans follow before the late 1800s? (b) How has the work force changed over the past 50 years?

7. (a) How does inflation affect buying power? (b) What challenges do limited natural resources present to Americans?

8. How have world economic developments affected the United States economy?

For answers, see p. A 121.

For Further Thought

1. (a) How does the federal government affect your daily life? (b) Do you agree with people who believe that government in the United States has grown too large? Why or why not?

2. (a) Why do some people insist on strict anti-pollution regulations? (b) Why do others oppose such regulations? (c) With which position do you agree? Why?

For answers, see p. A 122.

Developing Basic Skills

1. *Reading Graphs* Study the circle graphs on page 742. Then answer the following questions: (a) What information is shown on the graphs? (b) What percentage of women in the work force are clerical workers? (c) What percentage of men in the work force are clerical workers? (d) How do the percentages of men and women in professional fields differ? (e) Use the graph to cite one reason why working women as a whole make lower salaries than working men?

2. *Writing a Report* Gather evidence of cultural diversity in your community. List the types of churches and restaurants. Research the origins of the names of rivers, lakes, and streets. Then write a report describing the results of your investigation.

3. *Ranking* List the challenges facing the United States during the 1980s and rank them according to which you think are most important. Then write an essay explaining your ranking and describing the possible consequences of not successfully meeting the challenge you ranked as most important.

See page 779 for suggested readings.

Reference Section

752

Seattle
Spokane
WASHINGTON
1889
Olympia
CASCADE RANGE
Portland
Columbia
Salem
Eugene
OREGON
1859

Great Falls
Missouri R.
Helena
ROCK
MONTANA
1889
Billings

IDAHO
1890
Boise
Snake R.
Pocatello

GREAT

SIERRA NEVADA
Reno
Sacramento
Carson City
San Francisco
Oakland
San Jose
NEVADA
1864
BASIN

Ogden
Great Salt Lake
Salt Lake City
UTAH
1896
Green R.

WYOMING
1890
Casper

MOUNTAINS
Cheyenne
Denver
Colorado Springs
COLORADO
1876

Minot
Grand Forks
NORTH DAKOTA
1889
Bismarck

SOUTH DAKOTA
1889
Rapid City
Pierre
Sioux Fall

GREAT
Platte R.
NEBRASKA
1867
Lincoln

PLAINS
KANSAS
1861
Arkansas
Wichita

CALIFORNIA
1850
Las Vegas

Los Angeles
Long Beach
Salton Sea
San Diego

Colorado R.
ARIZONA
1912
Gila R.
Phoenix
Tucson
San Pedro R.

Santa Fe
Albuquerque
NEW MEXICO
1912
Las Cruces
El Paso

LLANO
ESTACADO

OKLAHOM
1907
Oklahoma City

Ft. Worth

TEXAS
1845
Austin
San Antonio
Rio Grande

MT. WAIALEALE
Honolulu
HAWAII
1959

0   50   100 Miles
0 50 100 150 Kilometers

BROOKS RANGE
Yukon R.
Fairbanks
ALASKA
1959
RANGE
ALASKA
Anchorage

Juneau

0   200   400 Miles
0   200   400   600 Kilometers

Lake of the Woods

Lake Superior

Duluth

MINNESOTA
1858

Minneapolis • St. Paul

Green Bay

Lake Michigan

Lake Huron

WISCONSIN
1848

Milwaukee
Madison

MICHIGAN
1837

Grand Rapids
Lansing Detroit

Lake Ontario

Rochester Albany

Buffalo

NEW YORK
1788

Lake Erie

Cleveland

Akron

Hudson R.

Burlington
Montpelier
VT.
1791
N.H.
1788

Concord
Manchester

MASS.
1788

Boston

Hartford
CONN.
1788

Providence

R.I.
1790

ioux City

IOWA
1846

Omaha • Des Moines

Chicago

Gary
Fort Wayne

ILLINOIS
1818

Peoria

INDIANA
1816

Indianapolis
Springfield

Toledo

OHIO
1803

Columbus

Cincinnati

PENNSYLVANIA
1787

Pittsburgh
Harrisburg

Newark
New York
Jersey City
NEW JERSEY
1787

Trenton
Philadelphia

Wilmington
DEL. 1787
Dover

MD.
1788
Baltimore
Washington

Annapolis

WEST
VIRGINIA
1863

Charleston
Huntington

eka

Kansas City
Jefferson
City
St. Louis

MISSOURI
1821

Springfield

Tulsa

Fort Smith

OUACHITA MTS.

ARKANSAS
1836

Little Rock

Ohio R.

Louisville
Frankfort
Lexington

KENTUCKY
1792

Knoxville
Nashville

TENNESSEE
1796

Memphis

Mississippi R.

Tennessee R.

Winston-Salem

VIRGINIA
1788

MOUNTAINS

Richmond

Norfolk

Greensboro
Raleigh

NORTH CAROLINA
1789

Charlotte

APPALACHIAN

Columbia

SOUTH
CAROLINA
1788

Charleston

llas

Shreveport

LOUISIANA
1812

Jackson

MISSISSIPPI
1817

ALABAMA
1819

Montgomery

Birmingham

Atlanta
Macon

Columbus

GEORGIA
1788

Savannah

Houston

Baton Rouge
Lake
Pontchartrain

New Orleans

Mobile

Pensacola

Tallahassee

Jacksonville

FLORIDA
1845

Tampa

Lake
Okeechobee

Miami

N

The United States

★ Capital city

• Other city

1787 Year of admission
to the Union

0   100   200   300 Miles

0   100   200   300   400 Kilometers

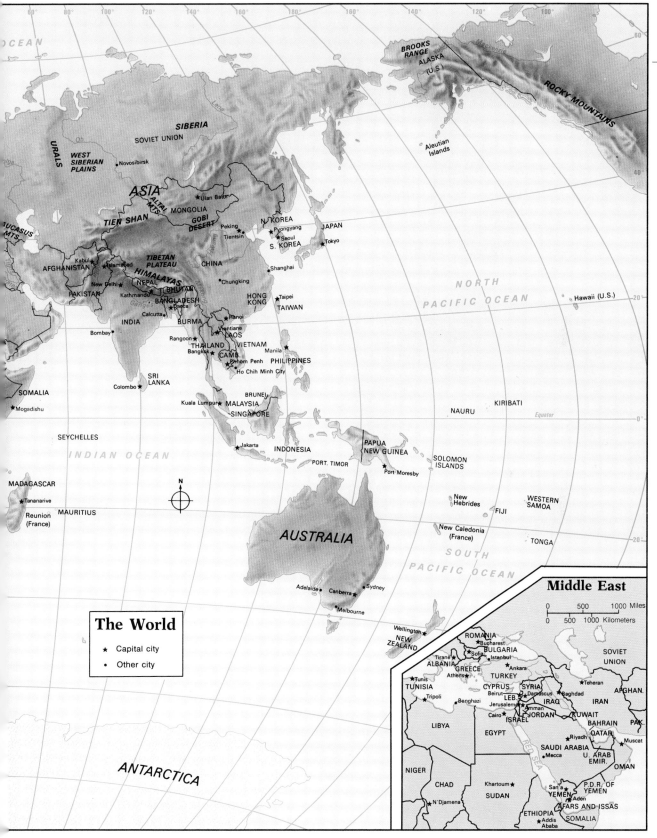

755

The World

★ Capital city
• Other city

Middle East

| 0 | 500 | 1000 Miles |
| 0 | 500 | 1000 Kilometers |

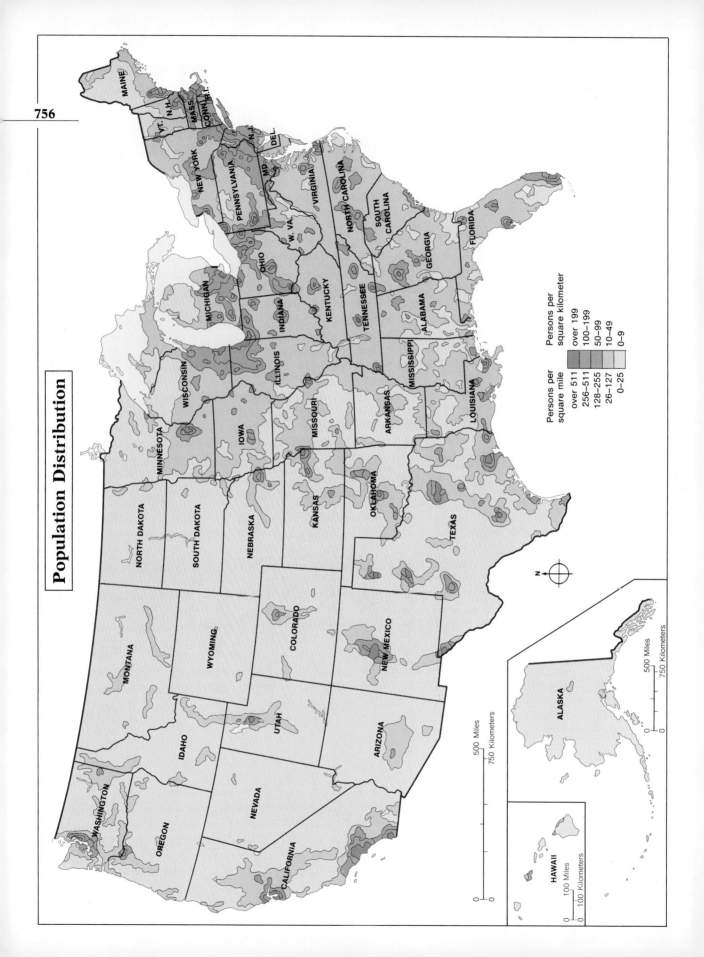

Population Distribution

Persons per
square mile
- over 511
- 256–511
- 128–255
- 26–127
- 0–25

Persons per
square kilometer
- over 199
- 100–199
- 50–99
- 10–49
- 0–9

500 Miles
750 Kilometers

ALASKA

500 Miles
750 Kilometers

HAWAII

100 Miles
100 Kilometers

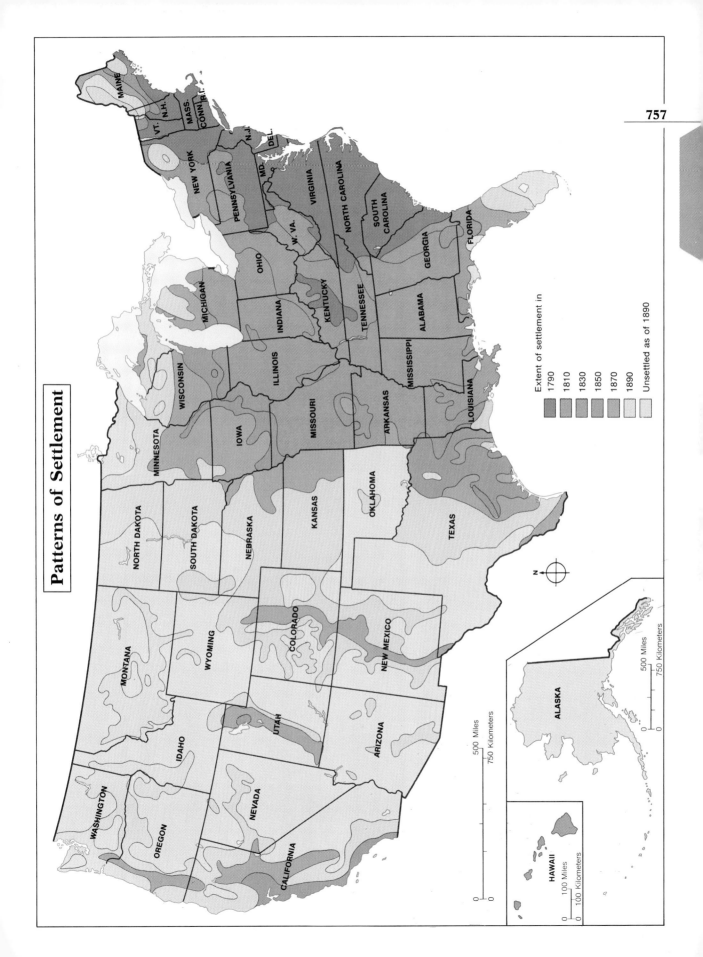

Patterns of Settlement

Extent of settlement in

1790
1810
1830
1850
1870
1890
Unsettled as of 1890

MAINE
N.H.
VT.
MASS.
CONN. R.I.
N.Y.
N.J.
DEL.
NEW YORK
PENNSYLVANIA
MD.
VIRGINIA
NORTH CAROLINA
SOUTH CAROLINA
W. VA.
OHIO
KENTUCKY
TENNESSEE
GEORGIA
FLORIDA
MICHIGAN
INDIANA
ALABAMA
WISCONSIN
ILLINOIS
MISSISSIPPI
LOUISIANA
MINNESOTA
IOWA
MISSOURI
ARKANSAS
NORTH DAKOTA
SOUTH DAKOTA
NEBRASKA
KANSAS
OKLAHOMA
TEXAS
MONTANA
WYOMING
COLORADO
NEW MEXICO
IDAHO
UTAH
ARIZONA
WASHINGTON
OREGON
NEVADA
CALIFORNIA

N

500 Miles
750 Kilometers

ALASKA

500 Miles
750 Kilometers

HAWAII

100 Miles
100 Kilometers

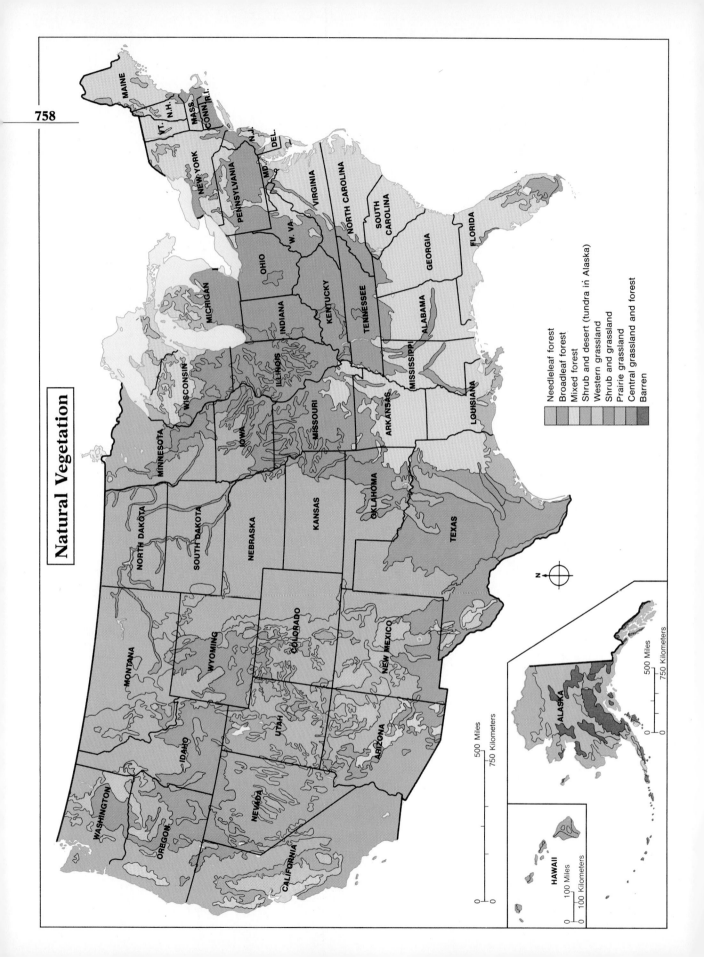

Natural Vegetation

Needleleaf forest
Broadleaf forest
Mixed forest
Shrub and desert (tundra in Alaska)
Western grassland
Shrub and grassland
Prairie grassland
Central grassland and forest
Barren

Agriculture

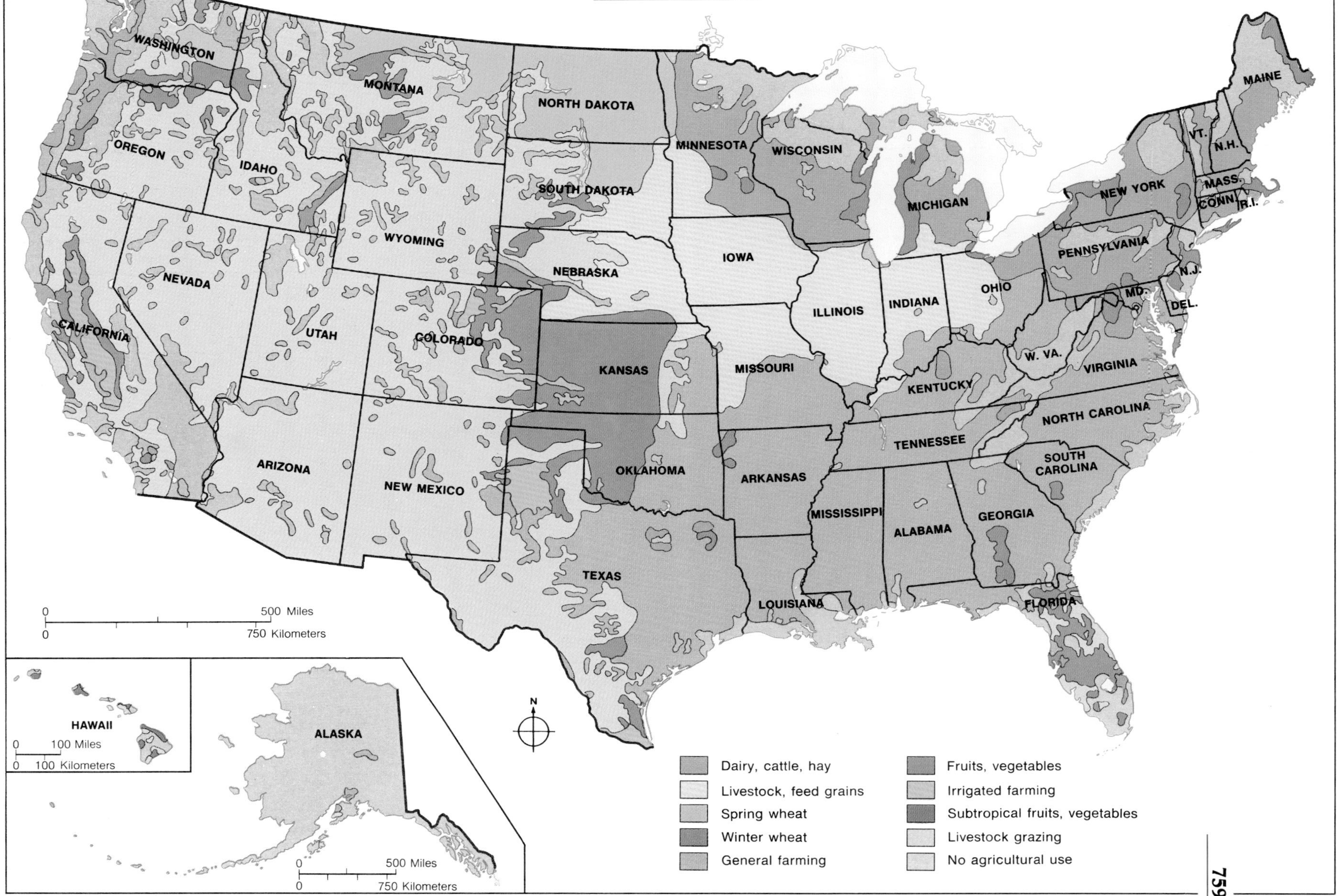

Legend:

- Dairy, cattle, hay
- Livestock, feed grains
- Spring wheat
- Winter wheat
- General farming
- Fruits, vegetables
- Irrigated farming
- Subtropical fruits, vegetables
- Livestock grazing
- No agricultural use

MAINE, VT., N.H., MASS., CONN., R.I., NEW YORK, N.J., PENNSYLVANIA, DEL., MD., W. VA., VIRGINIA, NORTH CAROLINA, SOUTH CAROLINA, GEORGIA, FLORIDA, OHIO, INDIANA, ILLINOIS, MICHIGAN, WISCONSIN, MINNESOTA, IOWA, MISSOURI, KENTUCKY, TENNESSEE, ALABAMA, MISSISSIPPI, ARKANSAS, LOUISIANA, OKLAHOMA, KANSAS, TEXAS, NEBRASKA, SOUTH DAKOTA, NORTH DAKOTA, MONTANA, WYOMING, COLORADO, NEW MEXICO, UTAH, ARIZONA, IDAHO, NEVADA, OREGON, WASHINGTON, CALIFORNIA

ALASKA

HAWAII

500 Miles
750 Kilometers

100 Miles
100 Kilometers

N

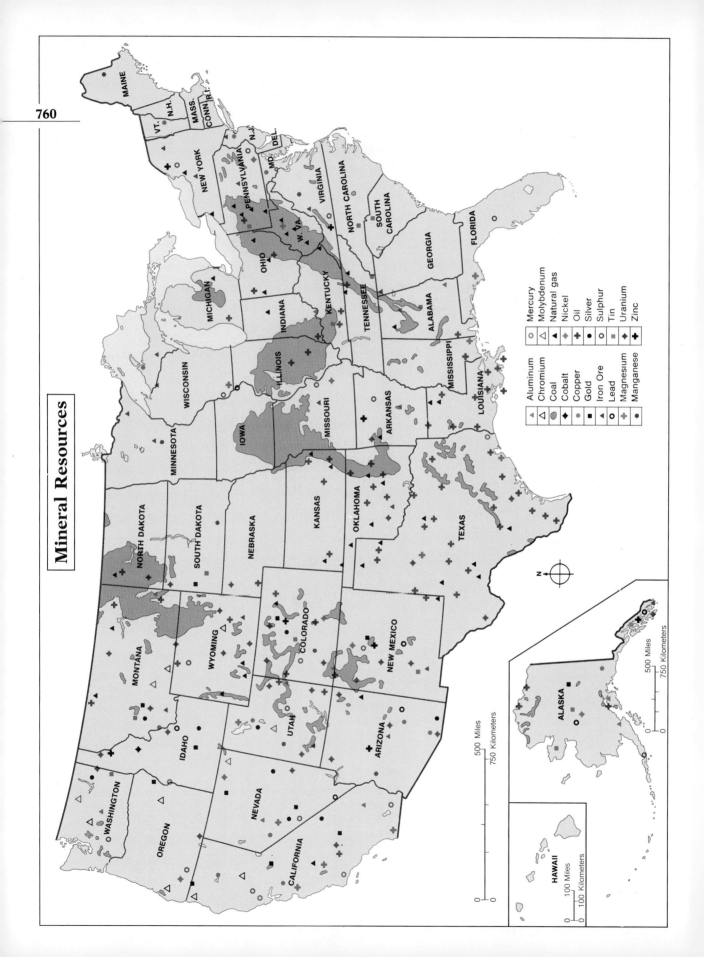

Mineral Resources

Legend

Aluminum	Mercury
Chromium	Molybdenum
Coal	Natural gas
Cobalt	Nickel
Copper	Oil
Gold	Silver
Iron Ore	Sulphur
Lead	Tin
Magnesium	Uranium
Manganese	Zinc

MAINE
N.H.
VT.
MASS.
CONN. R.I.
NEW YORK
N.J.
PENNSYLVANIA
MD. DEL.
OHIO
W. VA.
VIRGINIA
NORTH CAROLINA
SOUTH CAROLINA
KENTUCKY
TENNESSEE
GEORGIA
FLORIDA
ALABAMA
MISSISSIPPI
LOUISIANA
MICHIGAN
INDIANA
ILLINOIS
WISCONSIN
MINNESOTA
IOWA
MISSOURI
ARKANSAS
NORTH DAKOTA
SOUTH DAKOTA
NEBRASKA
KANSAS
OKLAHOMA
TEXAS
MONTANA
WYOMING
COLORADO
NEW MEXICO
IDAHO
UTAH
ARIZONA
NEVADA
CALIFORNIA
OREGON
WASHINGTON

ALASKA

HAWAII

500 Miles
750 Kilometers

100 Miles
100 Kilometers

500 Miles
750 Kilometers

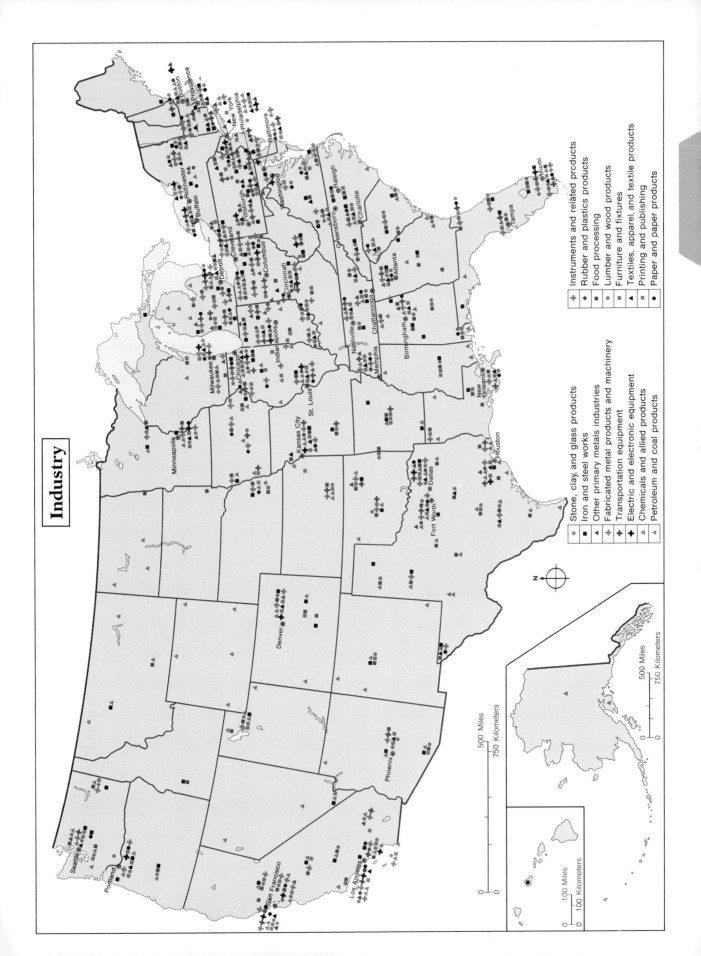

Industry

Instruments and related products +
Rubber and plastics products ●
Food processing ■
Lumber and wood products ●
Furniture and fixtures ■
Textiles, apparel, and textile products ▲
Printing and publishing ▲
Paper and paper products ●

Stone, clay, and glass products ●
Iron and steel works ■
Other primary metals industries ▲
Fabricated metal products and machinery +
Transportation equipment +
Electric and electronic equipment +
Chemicals and allied products ▲
Petroleum and coal products ▲

500 Miles

750 Kilometers

100 Miles

100 Kilometers

500 Miles

750 Kilometers

Seattle
Portland
San Francisco
Los Angeles
Phoenix
Denver
Fort Worth
Dallas
Houston
Kansas City
St. Louis
Minneapolis
Milwaukee
Chicago
Indianapolis
Cincinnati
Columbus
Detroit
Cleveland
Pittsburgh
Buffalo
Rochester
Boston
Providence
New York
Philadelphia
Baltimore
Washington
Greensboro
Raleigh
Charlotte
Atlanta
Chattanooga
Nashville
Memphis
Birmingham
New Orleans
Tampa
Miami

A Chronology of American History

This chronology includes some of the most important events and developments in American history. It can be used to trace developments in politics and government, exploration and innovation, society and economics, and culture and religion. The number following each entry refers to the chapter in which the event or development is discussed in the text.

	Politics and Government	Exploration and Innovation
Prehistory–1499	Mayan Empire reaches its height 1 Crusades for Holy Land begin 1 Aztecs establish empire in Mexico 1 Strong monarchies develop in Europe 1 Incas establish empire in South America 1	Mayas predict eclipses of sun 1 Aztecs develop system of mathematics 1 Marco Polo travels to China 1 Columbus sails to America 2 Vasco da Gama reaches India 1
1500–1599	Cortés defeats Aztecs 2 Pizarro captures Inca capital 2 Spanish enact Laws of the Indies 2 English colony established at Roanoke 2 English defeat Spanish Armada 2	Spanish explore North America 2 Magellan's expedition circles the globe 2 Cartier sails up St. Lawrence River 2 Drake sails around the world 2

1600–1649	House of Burgesses set up in Virginia 3
	Mayflower Compact signed 3
	Massachusetts Bay colony founded 3
	Maryland becomes first proprietary
	   colony 3
		English joint stock companies sponsor
		   settlement in North America 3
		Champlain founds Quebec 5
		Spanish found Santa Fe 5
		West Indian tobacco adapted to Virginia 3

1650–1699	Town meetings held in New England 4 Restoration of Charles II in England 3 Royal colonies develop 3 France claims Louisiana 5 Glorious Revolution in England 3	Spanish explore Pacific coast 5 Joliet and Marquette explore Mississippi River 5 La Salle reaches Mississippi Delta 5
1700–1749	Georgia founded 3 Molasses Act passed 4 English settlers move into Ohio Valley 5	Indigo developed as cash crop 4 Benjamin Franklin develops scientific approach to medicine 4
1750–1799	French and Indian War 5 Intolerable Acts passed 6 Declaration of Independence signed 6 Revolutionary War 7 Articles of Confederation ratified 8 Constitution ratified 9	Watt patents steam engine 12 Fitch launches first steam-powered boat 12 Slater sets up textile mills in New England 12 Eli Whitney invents cotton gin 12

Society and Economics

Culture and Religion

Society and Economics	Culture and Religion	
Agriculture develops in Americas 1 Rise of merchants and bankers in Europe 1 Trade between Europe and Asia expands 1 Incas develop diverse economy 1	Mayas develop system of writing 1 Aztecs build Tenochtitlán 1 Renaissance begins in Europe 1 Incas construct great cities 1	**Prehistory–1499**
Native American population of Spanish America declines 2 Slave trade begins in Americas 2 French develop fishing and fur trading in North America 2	Spanish try to convert Native Americans to Christianity 2 Universities open in Spanish America 2 John White paints watercolors of life in North America 2	**1500–1599**
John Smith organizes life in Jamestown 3 Slavery introduced in Virginia 3 Bible Commonwealth in Massachusetts 3	Persecution of Puritans in England 3 Harvard founded 4 Public school law passed in Massachusetts 3 Religious tolerance granted in Maryland 3	**1600–1649**
New England becomes shipbuilding center 4 Navigation Acts passed 5 Royal African Company established 4 Bacon's Rebellion 4	Quakers seek religious freedom in Pennsylvania 3 Spanish missions in Southwest 5 Religious freedom granted in Massachusetts 4 College of William and Mary founded 4	**1650–1699**
Triangular trade flourishes 5 Immigration to Middle Colonies grows 4 Plantations expand in Southern Colonies 4 Growth of port cities 4	Yale College founded 4 First regular newspaper in colonies founded 4 John Peter Zenger arrested for libel 4	**1700–1749**
Proclamation of 1763 6 Parliament passes Sugar, Quartering, Stamp, Currency, and Townsend acts 6 Colonies boycott British goods 6 Northern states abolish slavery 8 Northwest Ordinance takes effect 8	American literature reflects nationalism 8 Southern states disestablish Episcopal Church 8 Noah Webster promotes an American language 8 National capital designed and built 10	**1750–1799**

	Politics and Government	Exploration and Innovation
1800–1824	Louisiana Purchase 11 War of 1812 11 Missouri Compromise passed 17 Monroe Doctrine 12	Lewis and Clark expedition 11 Steamboats improved 12 Steam-powered locomotives developed 15
1825–1849	Jacksonian democracy 13 Indian Removal Act passed 13 Texas wins independence 14 Oregon divided along 49th parallel 14 Mexican War 14	Erie Canal opened 12 Mechanical reaper, steel plow, and telegraph developed 15 First commercial railroads in use 15 Gold discovered at Sutter's Mill 14
1850–1874	Compromise of 1850 17 Kansas-Nebraska Act passed 17 Civil War 18 Reconstruction 19 Alaska purchased from Russia 24 Warfare on the Great Plains 20	Passenger elevator, sleeping car, and air brake invented 21 Bessemer process developed 21 Pony Express founded 20 Ironclad ships used in Civil War 17 Transcontinental railroad completed 20

1875–1899	Battle of Little Big Horn 20
	Populist movement 22
	ICC created 22
	Sherman Antitrust Act passed 22
	Spanish-American War 24
		Refrigeration in meatpacking
		  developed 21
		Telephone, phonograph, incandescent
		  light bulb invented 21
		First skyscraper built 23

1900–1924	Progressive era 25, 26 Roosevelt Corollary 27 World War I 28 Fourteen Points 28 Treaty of Versailles rejected 28 Red Scare 29	Panama Canal built 27 Assembly line introduced 30 Scientific management introduced 30 Synthetic fibers developed 30 Electric appliances become widespread 30
1925–1949	Bonus Army 31 New Deal 32, 33 World War II 34, 35 Truman Doctrine and Marshall Plan 36 NATO created 36	Transatlantic telephone service begins 30 First television pictures broadcast 30 Lindbergh flies across Atlantic 30 Iron lung developed 30 Atomic bomb developed 35
1950–1974	Korean War 36 McCarthyism 37 Cuban missile crisis 38 Vietnam War 38, 39 Watergate crisis 39	*Explorer I* launched into orbit 37 Computers marketed commercially 40 American astronauts land on moon 39 Viking probe of Mars 39

1975–Present	Diplomatic recognition of China 40
	Camp David agreement on Middle East 40
	Hostage crisis in Iran 40
	Sandra Day O'Conner appointed to
	  Supreme Court 40
		Genetic engineering, computers, lasers,
		  and artificial joints and organs
		  advance medicine 41
		Flights of *Columbia* 41
		Voyager expeditions pass Saturn 41

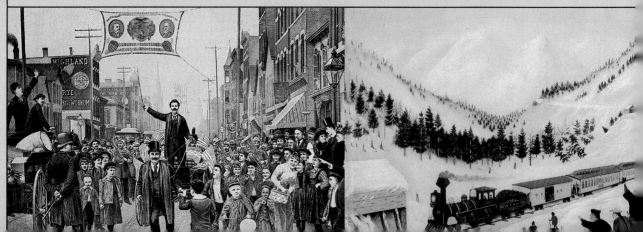

765

Pronunciation Key

When difficult terms or names first appear in the text, they are respelled to aid pronunciation. A syllable in LARGE CAPITAL LETTERS receives the most stress. Syllables with a secondary stress appear in SMALL CAPITAL LETTERS. The key below lists the letters used for respelling. It includes examples of words using each sound and shows how they would be respelled.

Symbol	Example	Respelling
a	hat	(hat)
ay	pay, late	(pay), (layt)
ah	star, hot	(stahr), (haht)
ai	air, dare	(air), (dair)
aw	law, all	(law), (awl)
eh	met	(meht)
ee	bee, eat	(bee), (eet)
er	learn, sir, fur	(lern), (ser), (fer)
ih	fit	(fiht)
ī	mile	(mīl)
ir	ear	(ir)
oh	no	(noh)
oi	soil, boy	(soil), (boi)
oo	root, rule	(root), (rool)
or	born, door	(born), (dor)
ow	plow, out	(plow), (owt)
u	put, book	(put), (buk)
uh	fun	(fuhn)
yoo	few, use	(fyoo), (yooz)
ch	chill, reach	(chihl), (reech)
g	go, dig	(goh), (dihg)
j	jet, gently, bridge	(jeht), (JEHNT-lee), (brihj)
k	kite, cup	(kīt), (kuhp)
ks	mix	(mihks)
kw	quick	(kwihk)
ng	bring	(brihng)
s	say, cent	(say), (sehnt)
sh	she, crash	(shee), (krash)
th	three	(three)
th	then, breathe	(thehn), (breeth)
y	yet, onion	(yeht), (UHN-yuhn)
z	zip, always	(zihp), (AWL-wayz)
zh	treasure	(TREH-zher)

Glossary

This glossary defines many important historical terms and phrases. Most of the entries appear in italics the first time they are used in the text. The page number following each definition refers to the page on which the term or phrase is first discussed in the text.

amendment a revision or change; an addition to the Constitution, proposed by Congress or a national convention and ratified by the states (page 165)

appeasement a policy of giving in to the demands of a hostile power to prevent conflict; specifically, the policy followed by European leaders in the 1930s of granting Hitler's demands for more territory in order to avoid a second world war (page 601)

arms race the competition between the United States and the Soviet Union since 1949 to develop the most powerful nuclear arsenal (page 644)

assembly line a grouping of machines and workers in which work passes from one worker to another, each performing one task in the production of an item (page 534)

assets the property and cash of a business or individual (page 383)

balance of trade the difference in value between a nation's imports and exports (page 749)

bank note paper money backed by a bank's reserves of gold or silver (page 215)

bicameral legislature a legislature that has two chambers, or houses (page 144)

bill of attainder a legislative act that prescribes punishment for a person even though he or she has not been found guilty by a court (page 166)

Blitzkrieg in German, "lightning warfare"; a sudden, swift, large-scale offensive intended to win a quick victory; used by Germany during World War II (page 603)

bond a certificate issued to a person who lends money to a business or a unit of government; the certificate earns interest and is redeemed for cash on a given date (page 383)

bounty a sum paid to a recruit for signing up for military service; used by the Union during the Civil War (page 325)

bracero a Mexican worker who, under a government program started in the 1950s, obtained a temporary permit to work in the United States; program ended in 1965 (page 678)

brain trust a group of scholars and technical experts who advised President Franklin Roosevelt during the New Deal (page 563)

capital money invested in a business (page 209)

carpetbagger a northerner who settled in the South after the Civil War and supported Radical Reconstruction (page 352)

cash crop a crop grown to be sold at a profit rather than to be consumed by the farmer (page 73)

checks and balances a system established under the Constitution by which each branch of government can check or control the power of the other branches (page 161)

city manager a professional administrator hired by an elected board of trustees of a city to manage the city government (page 463)

civil disobedience a form of nonviolent protest in which the protester violates the law but is willing to accept the penalties arising from his or her acts (page 660)

closed shop a business in which union membership is a requirement for employment (page 652)

collective bargaining the process by which a union represents a group of workers in negotiations with management (page 397)

company union an employee association sponsored by management (page 522)

compulsory education the requirement that every child attend school until a certain age (page 289)

concurrent powers powers shared by the national and state governments (page 160)

confederation an alliance of independent states (page 145)

consolidate to combine into a single unit, as to combine smaller companies into a larger one (page 382)

containment foreign policy first outlined in 1947 stating that the United States would contain, or hold, Soviet influence within its existing limits (page 636)

convoy a protective escort provided by navy warships for merchant vessels crossing the ocean during wartime (page 509)

craft union a union in which all members practice the same occupation (page 397)

de facto segregation segregation that exists in fact, although not by law (page 652)

default to fail to pay a debt (page 749)

deficit spending a spending plan in which government spending exceeds tax revenues (page 581)

deflation an economic condition in which the price of goods and services declines (page 413)

delegated powers powers given by the Constitution exclusively to the national government and forbidden to the states (page 159)

depression an economic condition marked by a drastic decline in production and sales and a severe increase in unemployment (page 240)

détente a relaxation of tensions between the United States and the Soviet Union beginning in the early 1970s (page 690)

disenfranchise to take away the right to vote (page 410)

dividend a share of a company's profits issued to stockholders on a periodic basis (page 391)

dollar diplomacy a term describing President William Howard Taft's policy of encouraging financial investments in Asia as a means of increasing United States power there (page 495)

domino theory the idea, prevalent during the Vietnam War, that if one Asian nation became communist, neighboring nations would follow (page 646)

due process protection that guarantees individuals accused of crimes a fair, standardized, and open legal process (page 167)

electoral college an assembly elected by voters to formally elect the President and Vice-President of the United States (page 162)

embargo a ban on trade with another nation (page 196)

empire a system of territories governed by one nation (page 441)

ex post facto law a law that makes an act a crime after it has been committed (page 166)

factory system a system for organizing labor in which all workers in the manufacturing process are brought together to work under one roof (page 209)

federalism a system of government in which authority is divided between national and state governments (page 159)

feudalism the political and social system of Europe during the Middle Ages, characterized by self-sufficient manors, decentralized political control, and obligations of service and loyalty among classes (page 27)

freedman a former slave freed as a result of the Civil War (page 345)

free enterprise a system in which individuals make economic decisions, such as what products to make, how much to produce, and how to set prices (page 391)

free soiler a person who opposed the expansion of slavery into United States territories during the 1850s; many joined the newly formed Republican party (page 312)

free state a state in which slavery was not permitted before the Civil War (page 305)

gang system a system of field work in which slaves worked together in gangs under an overseer (page 279)

general strike a strike of the members of all unions in a particular location (page 522)

gold standard a system in which a nation's currency is based on the value of gold (page 417)

graduated personal income tax a system in which the tax rate is proportionate to a person's income (page 415)

grandfather clause voting regulation adopted by a number of southern states after Reconstruction; it allowed a man to satisfy voting requirements if his father or grandfather had been eligible to vote in 1867 (page 410)

Grange an organization of farmers founded in 1867 for social reasons; later campaigned for state regulation of railroads and other reforms (page 414)

holding company a company that gains control of other companies by buying their stock (page 408)

horizontal integration a form of business organization in which a corporation acquires rival companies for the purpose of eliminating competition (page 390)

impeachment the process by which the House of Representatives makes an accusation of wrongdoing against the President or other high federal official (page 162)

impound to refuse to spend appropriated funds (page 694)

impressment British practice of forcing American sailors to serve in the British navy during the early 1800s (page 196)

inalienable rights natural rights that governments cannot take away from citizens (page 144)

indentured servant a person from Europe or Africa who agreed to work for an employer in colonial America for a specified period of time in return for the cost of passage (page 75)

industrial union a union in which members work at various jobs in a single industry (page 582)

inflation an economic condition in which prices rise substantially over a significant period of time (page 129)

initiative a procedure that allows citizens to propose a bill by collecting a specific number of signatures from registered voters (page 463)

injunction a court order prohibiting a given action; used frequently against workers in nineteenth-century labor-management disputes (page 399)

interchangeable parts identical component parts that can be used in place of one another in the manufacturing process (page 210)

interlocking directorate a system under which the same people serve on the boards of directors of several firms within the same industry (page 479)

internationalism the belief, held by some Americans in the 1930s, that the United States should aid the victims of international aggression (page 597)

isolationism the belief, widely held during the 1920s and 1930s, that the United States should minimize its involvement in foreign affairs (page 595)

jingoism intense national pride particularly widespread in the United States before and during the Spanish-American War (page 445)

joint stock company a form of business organization devised around 1600 by European nations to finance business ventures and exploration; it pooled the funds of many investors by selling shares in the company (page 51)

judicial review the power of the Supreme Court to determine the constitutionality of acts of the legislative and executive branches of the government (page 190)

laissez-faire noninterference; has come to mean a policy by which the government minimizes its regulation of industry and the economy (page 190)

lame duck an elected official who has been defeated at the polls but whose term of office has not yet expired (page 317)

limited liability refers to a situation in which an investor's personal responsibility for the debts of a business does not exceed his or her initial investment (page 209)

limited war a war in which specific objectives are sought, rather than total victory over the enemy; became a major issue during the Korean War (page 642)

literacy rate the proportion of the population that can read and write (page 79)

localism the tendency of states or areas to act independently and not as part of a unified nation (page 127)

long drive a cattle drive during the mid-1800s in which a large herd was moved across hundreds or thousands of miles to a railhead, from which the cattle could be shipped to market (page 372)

loose construction an interpretation of the Constitution holding that the federal government has broad powers implied by its delegated powers (page 176)

manifest destiny a commonly held belief in the first half of the nineteenth century that the United States had a mission to expand its borders to incorporate all land between the Atlantic and Pacific Oceans (page 255)

mercantilism an economic system prevalent in Europe after the Middle Ages in which each nation attempted to export more than it imported in order to strengthen its economy (page 85)

migrant worker an agricultural worker who travels from place to place doing seasonal work (page 543)

monopoly complete control of a product or service in a particular market by a single company (page 391)

moral diplomacy term describing President Woodrow Wilson's approach to foreign policy, which emphasized the use of negotiation and arbitration rather than force to settle international disputes (page 495)

muckrakers early twentieth-century American journalists who tried to improve society by exposing political corruption, health hazards, and other social problems (page 459)

mugwumps reformers within the Republican party who crusaded to end political corruption during the late 1800s (page 405)

naturalization the process by which a citizen of one country becomes a citizen of another (page 196)

normalcy President Warren G. Harding's term for the return to peace after World War I (page 525)

nullify to declare a law invalid and therefore unenforceable (page 185)

on margin refers to the practice of buying stock by which the buyer uses some of his or her own money and borrows the rest from a broker (page 548)

parity a system in which the government supports the price of certain farm products in order to maintain the purchasing power of farmers (page 530)

party platform a political party's declaration of its principles and programs (page 230)

patronage system the practice of giving out government jobs as favors to loyal party workers (page 405)

piedmont region region of rolling hills; in the South, the piedmont lies between the Appalachian Mountains and the tidewater region (page 73)

planter a powerful plantation owner who planted cash crops and employed a large number of slaves (page 73)

poll tax a fee that had to be paid in order to vote; instituted in the South after the Civil War to prevent blacks from voting; rendered unconstitutional by the Twenty-fourth Amendment (page 410)

pooling an agreement among railroad administrators to divide the total volume of freight among their lines (page 383)

popular sovereignty the method suggested by Stephen Douglas in the 1850s by which the voters of a territory would decide whether to allow slavery within the territory (page 306)

primary election an election held before the general election to choose candidates for office (page 463)

productivity the output per hour of work (page 744)

prohibition the ban on the sale and manufacture of alcoholic beverages resulting from ratification of the Eighteenth Amendment in 1919 (page 481)

proprietor an individual who received colonial land in America from the king of England and who was expected to administer that land in accordance with the laws of England (page 59)

protective tariff a tax on imports designed to discourage their sale and to favor the development of domestic industry (page 176)

public domain land that belongs to the nation rather than to individuals or corporations (page 366)

ratification the process of officially approving a proposal (page 146)

rebate a discount; in the nineteenth century some railroads offered rebates on shipping charges to attract business (page 383)

recall election a special election that allows voters to remove an elected official before the completion of his or her term (page 463)

recession an economic condition characterized by a mild increase in unemployment and a moderate decline in production and sales (page 396)

referendum the process by which people can vote directly on a bill (page 463)

reparations payments made by nations defeated in war as compensation for the damage they caused (page 511)

reservation an area of land specifically set aside by the federal government for Native Americans (page 369)

reserved powers powers retained by the states because they are not expressly given to the federal government nor denied to the states (page 159)

royal colony an American colony in which the governor and council were appointed by the king (page 63)

scalawag a white southerner who supported Radical Reconstruction (page 352)

scientific management the systematic study of the performance of workers and machines for the purpose of increasing efficiency (page 533)

sea dogs English sailors who pirated Spanish ships carrying precious minerals from the New World back to Spain (page 45)

secede to withdraw from a large political body (page 191)

segregation the practice of separating people on a racial basis (page 140)

self-determination the freedom of a country to determine its own future and form of government (page 511)

separation of powers a system in which the branches of government exercise distinct powers (page 160)

sharecropper an agricultural worker who works part of another person's land, receives supplies and equipment from the landowner, and in return gives the landowner part of the harvest (page 352)

sitdown strike a strike in which workers sit down on the job and refuse to leave the work place until their demands are met (page 583)

slave codes laws regulating the conduct of slaves before the Civil War (page 76)

slave state a state in which slavery was permitted before the Civil War (page 305)

sovereignty the source of a government's power or authority (page 159)

spoils system the practice of dismissing government job holders affiliated with a defeated party and replacing them with supporters of the victorious party (page 237)

squatter a person who settles on land without a legal right to do so (page 148)

stagflation an economic condition characterized by both inflation and recession (page 695)

stock certificate a document stating that the holder owns a share of a corporation (page 383)

strategic forces specially trained armed forces units that can be moved quickly to any part of the world (page 667)

strict construction a literal interpretation of the Constitution, holding that the federal government has only those powers explicitly delegated to it in the Constitution (page 176)

strike an organized work stoppage by employees, conducted for the purpose of improving pay or working conditions (page 269)

subsistence farming a level of farming at which farmers produce just enough to feed their families (page 67)

sunbelt a term referring to southeastern and southwestern states known for their mild climates and expanding economies (page 735)

task system a system by which individual slaves were assigned specific jobs each day (page 279)

temperance movement a campaign against the consumption of alcohol (page 288)

tenant farmer an agricultural worker who rents land from another person and pays the rent either in cash or by giving the landowner a portion of the crop; tenants provide their own seed and supplies (page 352)

territorial integrity condition in which a nation's borders are guaranteed against disturbance by other nations (page 511)

tidewater region a flat coastal plain where the land is so low that rivers crossing it flow backwards with incoming tides (page 73)

totalitarian state a country in which the government is supreme and individuals have few rights (page 597)

trade deficit a situation in which the value of a nation's imports exceeds the value of its exports (page 749)

trade surplus a situation in which the value of a nation's exports exceeds the value of its imports (page 749)

triangular trade the pattern of trade during the colonial era in which merchant ships traveled a triangular route, stopping in New England, Africa, and the West Indies (page 87)

trust a form of business organization, widespread during the late 1800s, in which investors in rival corporations exchanged their stock certificates and voice in management for trust certificates issued by a giant firm (page 391)

unconstitutional refers to a legislative act or executive action that violates the Constitution (page 162)

underground railroad the network of people who helped slaves escape to the northern states or to Canada (page 296)

union an association of workers formed to improve wages and working conditions (page 269)

vertical integration a form of business organization in which a manufacturing corporation acquires firms that contribute to the completion of a finished product (page 390)

veto an action by which a chief executive rejects a bill submitted to him or her by the legislature (page 144)

writ of habeas corpus a court order directing authorities to bring a prisoner to court to explain the basis for his or her detention (page 166)

writ of assistance a document issued by British authorities during the colonial period that allowed officials to conduct unrestricted searches (page 106)

Suggested Readings

General Works

Commager, Henry Steele, ed. *Documents of American History*. Appleton-Century-Crofts. A large selection of government documents.

Ferrell, Robert H. *American Diplomacy*. Norton. A general history of American diplomacy.

Franklin, John Hope. *From Slavery to Freedom: A History of American Negroes*. Knopf. A standard history of black people in America.

Handlin, Oscar and Mary F. *The Wealth of the American People*. McGraw-Hill. A history of the growth of the American economy since colonial times.

Josephy, Alvin. *The Indian Heritage of America*. Knopf. One of the most complete and accurate treatments of Native Americans in North, Central, and South America from prehistoric times to the present.

Malone, Dumas, ed. *Dictionary of American Biography*. Scribner. A multivolume work useful to the student who wants to compare the backgrounds of people who participated in an historical event.

Moquin, Wayne, and Van Doren, Charles, eds. *A Documentary History of the Mexican Americans*. Praeger. A collection of documents that trace the history of Mexican Americans from the 1500s to the late 1960s.

Morris, Richard B. *Encyclopedia of American History*. Harper & Row. A well-organized guide to American history.

O'Neill, William L. *Everyone Was Brave: A History of Feminism in America*. Quadrangle. A history of the women's rights movement from its mid-nineteenth-century origins to the late 1960s.

Unit One The Americas

Chapter 1

Cheyney, E.P. *The European Background of American History, 1300–1600*. Scholarly Press. A discussion of the social, political, and economic developments in Europe that led to the discovery of the New World.

Davies, Nigel. *The Aztecs*. Putnam. A political history of the Aztec civilization; contains illustrations of Aztec art and architecture.

Hyams, Edward, and Ordish, George. *The Last of the Incas*. Simon & Schuster. A comprehensive, illustrated account of Inca rulers and accomplishments.

Terrell, John Upton. *Pueblos, Gods and Spaniards*. Dial. A history of the Pueblo after the arrival of the Spanish; good general reading.

Thompson, J. Eric. *The Rise and Fall of Maya Civilization*. University of Oklahoma. A classic account of Maya cultural, political, and social patterns.

Chapter 2

Builders of America. Funk & Wagnalls. Biographies of early American explorers and colonial leaders.

Cumming, W.P.; Skelton, R.A., and Quinn, D.B. *The Discovery of North America*. McGraw-Hill. A fascinating collection of original paintings, engraved maps, and primary source narratives of French, Spanish, and English exploration of the New World.

Horgan, Paul. *Conquistadores in North American History*. Farrar, Straus. A fast-reading book about Spanish exploration in North America, focusing on individual conquistadores.

Marshall, James V. *The Wind at Morning*. Morrow. An historical novel based on Magellan's journey around the world.

Morison, Samuel Eliot. *The European Discovery of America*. Oxford University. An illustrated history of European explorations in North and South America.

Chapter 3

Covey, Cyclone. *The Gentle Radical: A Biography of Roger Williams*. Macmillan. Williams's life provides the focus for historical events and life in seventeenth-century New England.

Morgan, Edmund S. *The Puritan Dilemma: The Story of John Winthrop*. Little, Brown. A clear but sophisticated analysis of Puritan thought.

Peare, Catherine Owens. *William Penn*. Holt. A comprehensive account of the life of William Penn and his devotion to the founding of Pennsylvania.

Vaughan, Alden. *American Genesis: Captain John Smith and the Founding of Virginia*. Little, Brown. A biography of Smith that explores the problems of organizing a distant overseas colony.

Chapter 4

Hofstadter, Richard. *America at 1750: A Social Portrait*. Knopf. A descriptive portrait of American culture, economics, and society in the mid-1700s.

Land, Aubrey C., ed. *Letters From America*. Harvard University. Letters of William Eddis to a friend in England; provide valuable insight into the life of the planter class in the Southern Colonies.

Nash, Gary B. *Red, White, and Black: The Peoples of Early America.* Prentice-Hall. An account of the interaction of European, African, and Native American cultures before the Revolutionary War.

Sandburg, Carl. *Remembrance Rock.* Harcourt. A novel about life in New England from Puritan days to the dawn of the Revolutionary War.

Williams, Selma R. *Demeter's Daughters: The Women Who Founded America, 1587–1792.* Atheneum. A discussion of the roles, rights, and responsibilities of colonial women; includes biographical sketches of prominent women.

Wright, L.B., ed. *The American Heritage History of the Thirteen Colonies.* American Heritage. An illustrated history of colonial life.

Chapter 5

Chidsey, Donald Barr. *The French and Indian Wars: An Informal History.* Crown. A history of the rivalry between England and France in the New World; includes information about the roles of Native Americans and English colonists.

Cooper, James Fenimore. *The Last of the Mohicans.* Scribner. A classic novel about events in upper New York during the French and Indian War, despite the inaccurate description of Native Americans.

Lawson, Don. *The Colonial Wars.* Abelard. A fast-reading account of the Spanish, French, and British struggle for supremacy in North America.

Segal, Charles M., and Stineback, David. *Puritans, Indians, and Manifest Destiny.* Putnam. An examination of relations between Puritans and Native Americans in the 1600s; set around the theme of conflict between different cultures.

Unit Two Creating a Republic

Chapter 6

Acheson, Patricia C. *America's Colonial Heritage.* Dodd, Mead. A discussion of the ideas and events contributing to the movement toward independence.

Allen, Harvey. *The City in the Dawn.* Rinehart. A novel about the life of a Native American before, during, and after the American Revolutionary War, set in Ohio and Pennsylvania.

Chidsey, Donald Barr. *The World of Samuel Adams.* Thomas Nelson. An account of Adams's activities as a politician and patriot.

Freeman, Douglas Southall. *George Washington,* vol. 3, *Planter and Patriot.* Scribner. An enjoyable account of George Washington's transformation from farmer to leader of the American revolution.

Gipson, Lawrence Henry. *The Coming of the Revolution, 1763–1775.* Harper & Row. An in-depth examination of the causes of the American Revolution.

Chapter 7

Booth, Sally Smith. *Women of '76.* Hastings House. Information about colonial, Native American, and European women of the revolutionary period.

Canfield, Cass. *Samuel Adams's Revolution, 1765–1776.* Harper & Row. A description of the causes, events, and heroes of the American Revolution; enjoyable reading.

Catton, Bruce, ed. *The American Heritage Book of the Revolution.* Simon & Schuster. An illustrated History of the Revolutionary War.

Cooper, James Fenimore. *The Pilot.* Dodd, Mead. A classic novel inspired by the adventures of John Paul Jones.

Smith, Page. *A New Age Now Begins: A People's History of the American Revolution.* McGraw-Hill. A history of the Revolutionary War that makes good use of anecdotes.

Vaughan, Alden T., ed. *Chronicles of the American Revolution.* Grosset & Dunlap. A collection of articles, speeches, sketches, journals, and illustrations from the Revolutionary War period.

Whitney, Janet. *Abigail Adams.* Little, Brown. A fast-reading biography of Abigail Adams during the American revolution. One of the few biographies about a woman of the revolutionary period.

Chapter 8

Jensen, Merrill. *The New Nation: A History of the United States During the Confederation, 1781–1789.* Random House. A classic account of political developments during the 1780s.

Morgan, Edmund S. *The Birth of the Republic, 1763–1789.* University of Chicago. An historical account that emphasizes the development of a common heritage in the colonies and the new republic.

Nye, Russell B. *The Cultural Life of the New Nation, 1776–1830.* Harper & Row. Interesting material on education, literature, and religion in the newly established nation.

Chapter 9

Chidsey, Donald Barr. *The Birth of the Constitution.* Crown. An informal history of the issues and individuals that created the Constitution.

Hamilton, Alexander; Jay, John; and Madison, James. *The Federalist.* Random House. A collection of essays written in support of ratification of the Constitution.

Kenyon, Cecelia, ed. *The Antifederalists.* Bobbs-Merrill. A collection of letters, pamphlets, and documents written by opponents of ratification of the Constitution.

Rossiter, Clinton. *1787: The Grand Convention.* Macmillan. A detailed and thorough description of the people, setting, and consequences of the Constitutional Convention.

Unit Three **An Emerging Nation**

Chapter 10

Cunliffe, Marcus. *The Nation Takes Shape, 1789–1837.* University of Chicago. An interesting analysis of conflicting forces in the early years of the nation.

Hendrickson, Robert. *Hamilton,* vol. 2, *1789–1804.* Mason/Charter. An absorbing biography of Washington's secretary of the treasury.

Hofstadter, Richard. *The Idea of a Party System.* University of California. An account of how early political leaders came to accept a party system.

Smith, Page. *John Adams,* vol. 1, *1735–1784.* Greenwood. A scholarly description of Adams's public and private life.

Chapter 11

Brodie, Fawn M. *Thomas Jefferson: An Intimate History.* Norton. A biography revealing Jefferson's personal and public life.

Chidsey, Donald Barr. *Lewis and Clark: The Great Adventure.* Crown. A popular history that uses entries from the explorers' original diaries to highlight adventurous episodes.

Gerson, Noel B. *Mr. Madison's War: 1812, the Second War for Independence.* Julian Messner. A vivid examination of the issues and personalities involved in the bitter struggle between the United States and Great Britain.

Smith, Page. *Jefferson: A Revealing Biography.* McGraw-Hill. An illustrated biography of Thomas Jefferson; interesting reading.

Vidal, Gore. *Burr: A Novel.* Random House. A biographical novel based on the life of Aaron Burr.

Chapter 12

Ammon, Harry. *James Monroe: The Quest for National Identity.* McGraw-Hill. A biography of Monroe; reveals the political and private life of the fifth President.

Billington, Ray A. *Westward Expansion: A History of the American Frontier.* Macmillan. A comprehensive treatment of westward growth in the United States.

Dangerfield, George. *The Awakening of American Nationalism, 1815–1828.* Harper & Row. An exploration of economic and political nationalism in the early nineteenth century.

Garraty, John A., ed. *Quarrels That Have Shaped the Constitution.* Harper & Row. An account of landmark Supreme Court cases, including

an absorbing account of the Court under John Marshall.

Unit Four **An Era of Expansion**

Chapter 13

Bartlett, Irving H. *Daniel Webster.* Norton. A recent biography of this charismatic symbol of American nationalism.

Jahoda, Gloria. *The Trail of Tears.* Holt. A moving account of the removals of American Indians from 1813 to 1855.

Schlesinger, Arthur M., Jr. *The Age of Jackson.* Little, Brown. A wide-ranging, favorable account of Jackson's presidency.

Taylor, George Rogers, ed. *Jackson vs. Biddle's Bank.* D.C. Heath. A history of the dispute over the second Bank of the United States.

Chapter 14

Chidsey, Donald Barr. *The War With Mexico.* Crown. A clear description of the causes, events, heroes, and villains of the Mexican War.

Egan, Ferol. *Frémont.* Doubleday. An exciting biography of John Frémont, who epitomizes the era of expansion.

Parkman, Francis. *The Oregon Trail.* New American Library. A record of Parkman's adventurous journey west in the 1840s.

Webb, Todd. *The Gold Rush Trail and the Road to Oregon.* Doubleday. A photographic record of the way west; includes excerpts from letters and diaries.

Chapter 15

Eaton, Clement. *The Growth of Southern Civilization, 1790–1860.* Harper & Row. A widely respected history of the pre–Civil War South.

Groner, Alex. *The American Heritage History of American Business and Industry.* American Heritage. An illustrated history of business and industry in the United States.

Litwack, Leon. *North of Slavery.* University of Chicago. An analysis of the position of free blacks in the North before the Civil War.

Rayback, Joseph G. *A History of American Labor.* Macmillan. A comprehensive overview that includes a discussion of early trade unions and labor parties.

Stampp, Kenneth M. *The Peculiar Institution: Slavery in the Ante-Bellum South.* Knopf. A searching and critical examination of American slavery; valuable for its portrayal of daily life on the plantation.

Chapter 16

The Beauty of America in Great American Art. Morrow. Full-color reproductions of American paintings accompanied by selections from poets and authors.

Mabee, Carleton. *Black Freedom*. Macmillan. An historical account that focuses on the abolitionist movement from 1830 through the Civil War.

Miller, Douglas. *Then Was the Future*. Knopf. A social history of the North from 1815 to 1850 as portrayed in letters, diaries, songs, speeches, and art.

Thomas, John R. *The Liberator: William Lloyd Garrison*. Little, Brown. A biography of Garrison portraying him as a controversial and moralistic individualist.

Unit Five A Nation Torn Apart

Chapter 17

Catton, Bruce. *The Coming Fury*. Doubleday. An historical account that traces the split between the North and South from the election of 1860 through the first battle of Bull Run.

Nevins, Allan. *The Emergence of Lincoln*, vol. 2. Scribner. A political history of people and events from 1857 to 1861.

Nevins, Allan. *Ordeal of the Union*, vol. 2, *A House Dividing, 1852–1857*. Scribner. Classic work on the conflicts that divided North and South from 1852 to 1857.

Truman, Nelson. *The Old Man: John Brown at Harpers Ferry*. Holt. A biography of John Brown, focusing on his later years.

Chapter 18

Crane, Stephen. *The Red Badge of Courage*. Norton. A classic Civil War novel about the feelings of a Union soldier in the face of enemy fire; originally published in 1895.

Eaton, Clement. *Jefferson Davis*. Free Press. A biography of the President of the Confederacy.

Ketchum, Richard, ed. *The American Heritage Picture History of the Civil War*. American Heritage. A large collection of photographs, sketches, paintings, drawings, and maps of the Civil War; both North and South are covered.

Luthin, Reinhard H. *The Real Abraham Lincoln*. Prentice-Hall. A scholarly biography of Lincoln's adult years.

Nevins, Allan. *The War for the Union*. Scribner. An account of the Civil War that emphasizes the problems of a war-torn nation rather than a series of military engagements.

Quarles, Benjamin. *The Negro in the Civil War*. Little, Brown. An absorbing account of the role of black Americans in the Civil War.

Wheeler, Richard. *Voices of the Civil War*. Crowell. A collection of eyewitness accounts of the Civil War by foot soldiers, generals, and civilians.

Young, Agatha. *The Women and the Crisis*. McDowell, Obolensky. A history of women in the North during the Civil War.

Chapter 19

Carter, Hodding. *The Angry Scar: The Story of Reconstruction*. Greenwood. An account of southerners' reactions to Reconstruction.

Fast, Howard. *Freedom Road*. Crown. A novel about a black congressman during Reconstruction.

Franklin, John Hope. *Reconstruction After the Civil War*. University of Chicago. A sympathetic treatment of congressional efforts to reconstruct the old Confederacy.

Stampp, Kenneth M. *Era of Reconstruction: 1865–1877*. Random House. A scholarly reexamination of Reconstruction.

Unit Six Transforming a Nation

Chapter 20

Beebe, Lucius, and Clegg, Charles. *The American West: The Pictorial Epic of a Continent*. Dutton. The Old West in pictures including introductions to people and events.

Brown, Dee. *The Gentle Tamers*. Bantam. Easily read, entertaining social history of women in the West.

Cather, Willa. *O Pioneers!* Houghton Mifflin. A major American author's fast-reading novel about immigrants to the Midwest and their struggles against adversity.

Haines, Francis. *The Plains Indians*. Crowell. A recent study of the Plains Indians, including their confrontation with white society.

Katz, William Loren. *The Black West*. Doubleday. A collection of rare documents and photographs of black Americans on the frontier.

Chapter 21

Allen, Frederick Lewis. *The Lords of Creation*. Quadrangle. A history of the corporations and industrialists prominent in American economic expansion during the late 1800s and early 1900s.

Maddow, Ben. *A Sunday Between Wars*. Norton. An illustrated history of the building of American industry and the human costs of that progress; good general reading.

Norris, Frank. *The Octopus*. Airmont. Readable novel about California farmers and their struggle with railroad injustices.

Weisberger, Bernard, and Nevins, Allan. *Captains of Industry*. American Heritage. A fast-moving description of industrial leaders including contemporary illustrations.

Chapter 22

Boardman, Fon W., Jr. *America and the Gilded Age, 1876–1900*. Henry Z. Walck. A brief portrait of a period of rapid changes.

Hicks, John D. *The Populist Revolt: A History of the Farmer's Alliance and the People's Party*. University of Nebraska. A comprehensive treatment of the origins of the populist movement.

Twain, Mark. *The Gilded Age.* Bobbs-Merrill. A readable novel portraying the materialism and corruption of the post–Civil War period.

Washington, Booker T.; Johnson, James Weldon; and DuBois, William E.B. *Three Negro Classics.* Avon. Includes DuBois's *Souls of Black Folk* and Washington's *Up From Slavery;* particularly interesting for DuBois's appraisal of Washington.

Woodward, C. Vann. *The Strange Career of Jim Crow.* Oxford University. Discussion of race relations in the South after the Civil War.

Chapter 23

Beard, Annie E. *Our Foreign Born Citizens.* Crowell. A compilation of short biographies of 23 distinguished immigrants.

Davis, Allen F. *American Heroine: The Life and Legend of Jane Addams.* Oxford University. A detailed biography of Jane Addams; explores her motivations and accomplishments.

McKelvey, Blake. *The Urbanization of America, 1860–1915.* Rutgers University. A detailed book about the growth of American cities in the late 1800s and early 1900s.

Riis, Jacob August. *How the Other Half Lives.* Peter Smith. An illustrated study of tenements in New York City at the turn of the century by a contemporary reporter.

Chapter 24

Azoy, Colonel A.C.M. *Charge!* Longman. Entertaining description of the battle of San Juan Hill.

Chidsey, Donald Barr. *The Spanish-American War.* Crown. Popularized behind-the-scenes account of the Spanish-American War.

Pratt, Julius W. *America's Colonial Experiment.* Peter Smith. An account of how the United States gained and governed a widespread colonial empire.

Weems, John Edward. *The Fate of the* Maine. Holt. An enjoyable description of the ship and the crew, based on original documents and interviews with survivors.

Unit Seven Entering a Modern Age

Chapter 25

Goldman, Eric. *Rendezvous With Destiny.* Knopf. Contains interesting descriptions of the politics and personalities of the progressive era.

Morris, Edmond. *The Rise of Theodore Roosevelt.* Coward, McCann & Geoghegan. Recent biography of Roosevelt focusing on the many facets of his life and career.

Pinchot, Gifford. *Breaking New Ground.* University of Washington. The story of American forestry and conservation.

Reiger, C.C. *The Era of the Muckrakers.* Peter Smith. Discussion of the role of muckraking journalism during the first decade of the twentieth century.

Sinclair, Upton. *The Jungle.* New American Library. A classic contemporary attack on unsanitary practices and conditions in the meatpacking industry.

Chapter 26

Anthony, Susan B.; Stanton, Elizabeth Cady; et al., eds. *History of Woman Suffrage.* Arno. A collection of documents from the leaders of the women's rights movement in the late 1800s and early 1900s.

Faulkner, Harold V. *The Decline of Laissez-Faire, 1897–1917.* M. E. Sharpe. Account of the growth of federal regulatory power during the progressive era.

Link, Arthur. *Woodrow Wilson and the Progressive Era, 1910–1917.* Harper & Row. A scholarly account of the politics of progressivism by Wilson's leading biographer.

Scott, Anne Firor, and Scott, Andrew M. *One Half the People: The Fight for Women's Suffrage.* Lippincott. A brisk, lively analysis of the suffrage movement in the United States; includes documents.

Stein, Leon. *The Triangle Fire.* Lippincott. An interesting recreation of the Triangle Shirt Waist Company fire, based on original documents and interviews with survivors.

Chapter 27

Beale, Howard K. *Theodore Roosevelt and the Rise of America to World Power.* Johns Hopkins University. A detailed, scholarly account of American expansion under Roosevelt.

Kennan, George F. *American Diplomacy, 1900–1950.* New American Library. The early chapters present a concise history of early twentieth-century foreign policy.

Mason, Herbert Molloy, Jr. *The Great Pursuit.* Random House. An illustrated account of Pershing's expedition into Mexico in search of Pancho Villa.

McCullough, David. *The Path Between the Seas.* Simon & Schuster. The exciting account of the people, nations, and money behind the construction of the Panama Canal.

Chapter 28

Barbeau, Arthur E., and Henri, Florette. *The Unknown Soldiers.* Temple University. A history of black American troops in World War I.

Hemingway, Ernest. *A Farewell to Arms.* Scribner. A classic American novel about fighting on the Italian front.

Hoehling, A.A. *The Great War at Sea.* Crowell. Fast-reading discussion of American naval action between 1914 and 1918.

Leckie, Robert. *The Story of World War I.*

Random House. A lavishly illustrated history of the first world war.

Sinclair, Upton. *World's End*. Viking. A novel about the role of munitions makers during the war.

Unit Eight **The Roaring Twenties**

Chapter 29

Hicks, John D. *Republican Ascendancy, 1921–1933*. Harper & Row. A thorough political history of the era.

Lathem, Edward Connery, ed. *Meet Calvin Coolidge*. Stephen Greene. An enjoyable description of how Coolidge was seen by family, friends, neighbors, and colleagues.

Murray, R.K. *Red Scare: A Study in National Hysteria*. University of Minnesota. The roots, major events, and effects of the Red Scare.

Sinclair, Andrew. *The Available Man*. Quadrangle. A description of Warren G. Harding's political and personal life.

Chapter 30

Allen, Frederick Lewis. *Only Yesterday*. Harper & Row. Popular, lively social history of the 1920s.

Dodds, John W. *Everyday Life in Twentieth Century America*. Putnam. A social history of the 1920s.

Fitzgerald, F. Scott. *The Great Gatsby*. Scribner. A classic American novel about jazz-age society on Long Island in the 1920s.

Huggins, Nathan Irvin. *Harlem Renaissance*. Oxford University. An account of the flowering of black culture during the 1920s.

Morrden, Ethan. *That Jazz*. Putnam. Entertaining look at jazz as the symbol of the times.

This Fabulous Century, vol. 3, *The Twenties*. Time-Life. Fascinating collection of photographs of the people, places, and events of the 1920s.

Chapter 31

Bernstein, Irving. *The Lean Years. A History of the American Worker, 1920–1933*. Houghton Mifflin. A discussion of the growth of the labor movement during the prosperous twenties and the early years of the Great Depression.

Emery, Anne. *American Friend: Herbert Hoover*. Rand McNally. The last chapters of this sympathetic biography tell the story of the early years of the Great Depression.

Galbraith, John. *The Great Crash, Nineteen Twenty-Nine*. Houghton Mifflin. Easy-to-understand economic history of the causes and effects of the stock market crash.

Schlesinger, Arthur M., and Fox, Dixon R., eds. *The Age of the Great Depression, 1929–1941*. Franklin Watts. Discussion of popular reactions and moods during the depression.

Unit Nine **A Time of Trial**

Chapter 32

Deal, Bordon. *Dunbar's Cove*. Scribner. Novel based on a family's fight with the Tennessee Valley Authority over the condemnation of their land for a dam.

Graff, Robert D.; Ginna, Emmett; and Butterfield, Roger. *FDR*. Harper & Row. A pictorial account of Roosevelt's life and politics integrated with interesting text.

Gunther, John. *Roosevelt in Retrospect*. Harper & Row. Fast-reading anecdotal biography of Franklin Roosevelt.

Hurd, Charles. *When the New Deal Was Young and Gay*. Hawthorn. A nostalgic look at Roosevelt's first four years in office.

Chapter 33

Allen, Frederick Lewis. *Since Yesterday*. Harper & Row. Popularized social history of the 1930s, including an account of the Great Depression.

Bourke-White, Margaret, and Caldwell, Erskine, eds. *You Have Seen Their Faces*. Arno. Day-to-day existence of black and white rural poor in the South during the 1930s portrayed in poignant photographs with sensitive text.

Einaudi, Mario. *The Roosevelt Revolution*. Greenwood. Analysis of the permanent changes in American life and thought brought on by the New Deal.

Ellison, Ralph. *Invisible Man*. Random House. Discussion of relations between blacks and whites during the depression years.

Flynn, John T. *Country Squire in the White House*. Da Capo. A highly critical view of Roosevelt and the New Deal.

Steinbeck, John. *Grapes of Wrath*. Penguin. Classic American novel about Oklahoma Dust Bowl families who become migrant fruit pickers to survive.

Chapter 34

Ferrell, Robert H. *American Diplomacy in the Great Depression: Hoover-Stimson Foreign Policy, 1929–1933*. Norton. Detailed, scholarly study of President Hoover's foreign policy.

Rauch, Basil. *Roosevelt: From Munich to Pearl Harbor*. Da Capo. Detailed but readable political study of the era.

Sinclair, Upton. *Presidential Agent*. Curtis. Novel about an American secret agent during the late 1930s.

Williams, Ben Ames. *Time of Peace*. Houghton Mifflin. Exploration of the changing reactions of Americans to the threat of war.

Chapter 35

Beach, Edward. *Run Silent, Run Deep*. Holt. A novel about submarine warfare in the Pacific.

Buchanan, A. Russell. *The United States and World War II*. Harper & Row. Excellent survey of the military history of World War II, including discussion of diplomacy and the home front.

Conrat, Maisie and Richard. *Executive Order 9066*. Massachusetts Institute of Technology. Sensitive photographic study of Japanese internment in the United States during World War II.

Hoehling, A.A. *Homefront U.S.A.* Crowell. Illustrated story of the public and private citizens who fought the war at home.

Motley, Mary Penick, ed. *The Invisible Soldier*. Wayne State University. Anthology of 55 oral histories of the experiences of black American soldiers in World War II.

Unit Ten **The United States in a Changing World**

Chapter 36

Agar, Herbert. *The Price of Power: America Since 1945*. University of Chicago. Fast-moving history of the decade after World War II.

Jones, Joseph M. *The Fifteen Weeks*. Harcourt. Detailed account of people and events from the inception of the Truman Doctrine to the launching of the Marshall Plan.

Michener, James A. *The Bridges at Toko-ri*. Random House. Novel about a United States naval task force assigned to bomb enemy supply lines during the Korean War.

Chapter 37

Archer, Jules. *Battlefield President: Dwight D. Eisenhower*. Julian Messner. Readable biography of President Eisenhower stressing the military and political aspects of his career.

Handlin, Oscar. *Fire-Bell in the Night: Crisis in Civil Rights*. Little, Brown. A study of the racial crises of the 1950s.

Hayman, Leroy. *Harry S. Truman: A Biography*. Crowell. Easy-to-read account of Truman's personal and political life.

Keylin, Arleen, ed. *The Fabulous Fifties as Reported by the New York* Times. Arno. Excellent coverage of the era, with photographs of television shows, movies, musicians, and other aspects of social life juxtaposed with front pages of the *Times*.

Chapter 38

Browne, Malcolm. *The New Face of War*. Bobbs-Merrill. Inside look at the Vietnam War by a newspaper reporter.

Burns, James MacGregor. *John Kennedy: A Political Profile*. Harcourt. Comprehensive biography of Kennedy based on the author's access to Kennedy's files, family records, and letters.

Deloria, Vine, Jr. *Custer Died for Your Sins: An Indian Manifesto*. Macmillan. Biting, witty indictment of white actions toward Native

Americans and description of the situation in the 1960s by a member of the Sioux tribe.

Friedan, Betty. *The Feminine Mystique*. Dell. A critique of post–World War II inequities and discrimination against women.

Harwood, Richard, and Johnson, Haynes. *Lyndon*. Praeger. Somewhat sentimental portrait of Lyndon Johnson illustrated with over 100 photographs.

King, Martin Luther, Jr. *Stride Toward Freedom: The Montgomery Story*. Harper & Row. Account of the struggle of black citizens against segregation in Montgomery, Alabama.

O'Neill, William C. *Coming Apart: An Informal History of America in the 1960s*. Quadrangle. A lively treatment of politics and protest during the 1960s.

Chapter 39

Ford, Gerald. *A Time to Heal*. Harper & Row. The former President's autobiography, with special emphasis on his White House years.

Kalb, Bernard and Kalb, Marvin. *Kissinger*. Little, Brown. A richly detailed biography of the former secretary of state.

White, Theodore. *Breach of Faith: Fall of Richard Nixon*. Atheneum. The Watergate story, by one of America's most distinguished journalists.

Chapter 40

Evans, Christopher. *The Making of the Micro: A History of the Computer*. Van Nostrand Reinhold. A brief history of electronic computing.

Evans, Rowland and Novak, Robert. *The Reagan Revolution*. Dutton. A sympathetic account of Ronald Reagan's political and economic ideas.

Friedman, S. David. *Energy: The New Era*. Random House. A scholarly discussion of America's energy policies and prospects.

Lasky, Victor. *Jimmy Carter: The Man and the Myth*. Richard Marek. An analysis of Carter's rise to the presidency, the problems he confronted, and the questions raised during his administration.

Chapter 41

Drucker, Peter F. *The Age of Discontinuity: Guidelines to Our Changing Society*. Harper & Row. A critic of government regulation of the economy presents an optimistic view of America's ability to meet coming economic challenges.

Olson, James Stuart. *The Ethnic Dimension in American History*. St. Martin's. Discusses the role of ethnic identity in American history.

Sale, Kirkpatrick. *Power Shift: The Rise of the Southern Rim and Its Challenge to the Eastern Establishment*. Random House. Discussion of the causes of the rise of the sun belt and its political consequences.

The Fifty States

State	Capital	Date of Entry to Union (Order of Entry)	Area in Square Miles	Population (1980 Census)	Number of Representatives in House
Alabama	Montgomery	1819 (22)	51,609	3,890,061	7
Alaska	Juneau	1959 (49)	586,412	400,481	1
Arizona	Phoenix	1912 (48)	113,909	2,717,866	5
Arkansas	Little Rock	1836 (25)	53,104	2,285,513	4
California	Sacramento	1850 (31)	158,693	23,668,562	45
Colorado	Denver	1876 (38)	104,247	2,888,834	6
Connecticut	Hartford	1788 (5)	5,009	3,107,576	6
Delaware	Dover	1787 (1)	2,057	595,225	1
Florida	Tallahassee	1845 (27)	58,560	9,739,992	19
Georgia	Atlanta	1788 (4)	58,876	5,464,265	10
Hawaii	Honolulu	1959 (50)	6,450	965,000	2
Idaho	Boise	1890 (43)	83,557	943,935	2
Illinois	Springfield	1818 (21)	56,400	11,418,461	22
Indiana	Indianapolis	1816 (19)	36,291	5,490,179	10
Iowa	Des Moines	1846 (29)	56,290	2,913,387	6
Kansas	Topeka	1861 (34)	82,264	2,363,208	5
Kentucky	Frankfort	1792 (15)	40,395	3,661,433	7
Louisiana	Baton Rouge	1812 (18)	48,523	4,203,972	8
Maine	Augusta	1820 (23)	33,215	1,124,660	2
Maryland	Annapolis	1788 (7)	10,577	4,216,446	8
Massachusetts	Boston	1788 (6)	8,257	5,737,037	11
Michigan	Lansing	1837 (26)	58,216	9,258,344	18
Minnesota	St. Paul	1858 (32)	84,068	4,077,148	8
Mississippi	Jackson	1817 (20)	47,716	2,520,638	5
Missouri	Jefferson City	1821 (24)	69,686	4,917,444	9
Montana	Helena	1889 (41)	147,138	786,690	2
Nebraska	Lincoln	1867 (37)	77,227	1,570,006	3
Nevada	Carson City	1864 (36)	110,540	799,184	2
New Hampshire	Concord	1788 (9)	9,304	920,610	2
New Jersey	Trenton	1787 (3)	7,836	7,364,158	14
New Mexico	Santa Fe	1912 (47)	121,666	1,299,968	3
New York	Albany	1788 (11)	49,576	17,557,288	34
North Carolina	Raleigh	1789 (12)	52,586	5,874,429	11
North Dakota	Bismarck	1889 (39)	70,665	652,695	1
Ohio	Columbus	1803 (17)	41,222	10,797,419	21
Oklahoma	Oklahoma City	1907 (46)	69,919	3,025,266	6
Oregon	Salem	1859 (33)	96,981	2,632,663	5
Pennsylvania	Harrisburg	1787 (2)	45,333	11,866,728	23
Rhode Island	Providence	1790 (13)	1,214	947,154	2
South Carolina	Columbia	1788 (8)	31,055	3,119,208	6
South Dakota	Pierre	1889 (40)	77,047	690,178	1
Tennessee	Nashville	1796 (16)	42,244	4,590,750	9
Texas	Austin	1845 (28)	267,338	14,228,383	27
Utah	Salt Lake City	1896 (45)	84,916	1,461,037	3
Vermont	Montpelier	1791 (14)	9,609	511,456	1
Virginia	Richmond	1788 (10)	40,817	5,346,279	10
Washington	Olympia	1889 (42)	68,192	4,130,163	8
West Virginia	Charleston	1863 (35)	24,181	1,949,644	4
Wisconsin	Madison	1848 (30)	56,154	4,705,335	9
Wyoming	Cheyenne	1890 (44)	97,914	470,816	1
District of Columbia			67	637,651	1 (nonvoting)

Presidents and Vice-Presidents of the United States

President	Term(s) Served	Political Party	Vice-President	Term(s) Served
1. **George Washington** (b. 1732, d. 1799)	1789–1797	None	John Adams	1789–1797
2. **John Adams** (b. 1735, d. 1826)	1797–1801	Federalist	Thomas Jefferson	1797–1801
3. **Thomas Jefferson** (b. 1743, d. 1826)	1801–1809	Dem.-Rep.	Aaron Burr	1801–1805
			George Clinton	1805–1809
4. **James Madison** (b. 1751, d. 1836)	1809–1817	Dem.-Rep.	George Clinton	1809–1812
			Elbridge Gerry	1813–1814
5. **James Monroe** (b. 1758, d. 1831)	1817–1825	Dem.-Rep.	Daniel D. Tompkins	1817–1825
6. **John Quincy Adams** (b. 1767, d. 1848)	1825–1829	Dem.-Rep.	John C. Calhoun	1825–1829
7. **Andrew Jackson** (b. 1767, d. 1845)	1829–1837	Democrat	John C. Calhoun	1829–1832
			Martin Van Buren	1833–1837
8. **Martin Van Buren** (b. 1782, d. 1862)	1837–1841	Democrat	Richard M. Johnson	1837–1841
9. **William H. Harrison** (b. 1773, d. 1841)	1841	Whig	John Tyler	1841
10. **John Tyler** (b. 1790, d. 1862)	1841–1845	Whig	*	
11. **James K. Polk** (b. 1795, d. 1849)	1845–1849	Democrat	George M. Dallas	1845–1849
12. **Zachary Taylor** (b. 1784, d. 1850)	1849–1850	Whig	Millard Fillmore	1849–1850
13. **Millard Fillmore** (b. 1800, d. 1874)	1850–1853	Whig	*	
14. **Franklin Pierce** (b. 1804, d. 1869)	1853–1857	Democrat	William R. King	1853
15. **James Buchanan** (b. 1791, d. 1868)	1857–1861	Democrat	John C. Breckinridge	1857–1861
16. **Abraham Lincoln** (b. 1809, d. 1865)	1861–1865	Republican	Hannibal Hamlin	1861–1865
			Andrew Johnson	1865
17. **Andrew Johnson** (b. 1808, d. 1875)	1865–1869	Republican	*	
18. **Ulysses S. Grant** (b. 1822, d. 1885)	1869–1877	Republican	Schuyler Colfax	1869–1873
			Henry Wilson	1873–1875
19. **Rutherford B. Hayes** (b. 1822, d. 1893)	1877–1881	Republican	William A. Wheeler	1877–1881
20. **James A. Garfield** (b. 1831, d. 1881)	1881	Republican	Chester A. Arthur	1881
21. **Chester A. Arthur** (b. 1829, d. 1886)	1881–1885	Republican	*	
22. **Grover Cleveland** (b. 1837, d. 1908)	1885–1889	Democrat	Thomas A. Hendricks	1885
23. **Benjamin Harrison** (b. 1833, d. 1901)	1889–1893	Republican	Levi P. Morton	1889–1893
24. **Grover Cleveland** (b. 1837, d. 1908)	1893–1897	Democrat	Adlai E. Stevenson	1893–1897
25. **William McKinley** (b. 1843, d. 1901)	1897–1901	Republican	Garret A. Hobart	1897–1899
			Theodore Roosevelt	1901
26. **Theodore Roosevelt** (b. 1858, d. 1919)	1901–1909	Republican	Charles W. Fairbanks	1905–1909
27. **William H. Taft** (b. 1857, d. 1930)	1909–1913	Republican	James S. Sherman	1909–1912
28. **Woodrow Wilson** (b. 1856, d. 1924)	1913–1921	Democrat	Thomas R. Marshall	1913–1921
29. **Warren G. Harding** (b. 1865, d. 1923)	1921–1923	Republican	Calvin Coolidge	1921–1923
30. **Calvin Coolidge** (b. 1872, d. 1933)	1923–1929	Republican	Charles G. Dawes	1925–1929
31. **Herbert C. Hoover** (b. 1874, d. 1964)	1929–1933	Republican	Charles Curtis	1929–1933
32. **Franklin D. Roosevelt** (b. 1882, d. 1945)	1933–1945	Democrat	John N. Garner	1933–1941
			Henry A. Wallace	1941–1945
			Harry S. Truman	1945
33. **Harry S. Truman** (b. 1884, d. 1972)	1945–1953	Democrat	Alben W. Barkley	1949–1953
34. **Dwight D. Eisenhower** (b. 1890, d. 1969)	1953–1961	Republican	Richard M. Nixon	1953–1961
35. **John F. Kennedy** (b. 1917, d. 1963)	1961–1963	Democrat	Lyndon B. Johnson	1961–1963
36. **Lyndon B. Johnson** (b. 1908, d. 1973)	1963–1969	Democrat	Hubert H. Humphrey	1965–1969
37. **Richard M. Nixon** (b. 1913)	1969–1974	Republican	Spiro T. Agnew	1969–1973
			Gerald R. Ford	1973–1974
38. **Gerald R. Ford**† (b. 1913)	1974–1977	Republican	Nelson A. Rockefeller	1974–1977
39. **Jimmy Carter** (b. 1924)	1977–1981	Democrat	Walter F. Mondale	1977–1981
40. **Ronald Reagan** (b. 1911)	1981–	Republican	George Bush	1981–

* Prior to ratification of the Twenty-fifth Amendment in 1967, there was no constitutional provision for replacing a Vice-President if that office became vacant.

† Inaugurated August 9, 1974, to replace Nixon, who resigned the same day.

The Declaration of Independence

When in the course of human events it becomes necessary for one people to dissolve the political bands which have connected them with another and to assume, among the powers of the earth, the separate and equal station to which the laws of nature and of nature's God entitle them, a decent respect to the opinions of mankind requires that they should declare the causes which impel them to the separation.

We hold these truths to be self-evident, that all men are created equal; that they are endowed by their Creator with certain unalienable rights; that among these are life, liberty, and the pursuit of happiness. That, to secure these rights, governments are instituted among men, deriving their just powers from the consent of the governed; that, whenever any form of government becomes destructive of these ends, it is the right of the people to alter or to abolish it, and to institute a new government, laying its foundation on such principles, and organizing its powers in such form, as to them shall seem most likely to effect their safety and happiness. Prudence, indeed, will dictate that governments long established should not be changed for light and transient causes; and, accordingly, all experience hath shown that mankind are more disposed to suffer, while evils are sufferable, than to right themselves by abolishing the forms to which they are accustomed. But when a long train of abuses and usurpations, pursuing invariably the same object, evinces a design to reduce them under absolute despotism, it is their right, it is their duty, to throw off such government and to provide new guards for their future security. Such has been the patient sufferance of these colonies, and such is now the necessity which constrains them to alter their former systems of government. The history of the present King of Great Britain is a history of repeated injuries and usurpations, all having, in direct object, the establishment of an absolute tyranny over these States. To prove this, let facts be submitted to a candid world:

He has refused his assent to laws the most wholesome and necessary for the public good.

He has forbidden his governors to pass laws of immediate and pressing importance, unless suspended in their operation till his assent should be obtained; and, when so suspended, he has utterly neglected to attend to them.

He has refused to pass other laws for the accommodation of the large districts of people, unless those people would relinquish the right of representation in the legislature: a right inestimable to them and formidable to tyrants only.

He has called together legislative bodies at places unusual, uncomfortable, and distant from the depository of their public records, for the sole purpose of fatiguing them into compliance with his measures.

He has dissolved representative houses, repeatedly for opposing, with manly firmness, his invasions on the rights of the people.

He has refused, for a long time after such dissolutions, to cause others to be elected: whereby the legislative powers, incapable of annihilation, have returned to the people at large for their exercise; the state remaining, in the meantime, exposed to all the danger of invasion from without and convulsions within.

He has endeavored to prevent the population of these States; for that purpose, obstructing the laws for naturalization of foreigners, refusing to pass others to encourage their migration hither, and raising the conditions of new appropriations of lands.

He has obstructed the administration of justice by refusing his assent to laws for establishing judiciary powers.

He has made judges dependent on his will alone for the tenure of their offices and the amount and payment of their salaries.

He has erected a multitude of new offices and sent hither swarms of officers to harass our people and eat out their substance.

He has kept among us, in time of peace, standing armies, without the consent of our legislatures.

He has affected to render the military independent of, and superior to, the civil power.

He has combined with others to subject us to a jurisdiction foreign to our Constitution and unacknowledged by our laws, giving his assent to their acts of pretended legislation—

For quartering large bodies of armed troops among us;

For protecting them by a mock trial from punishment for any murders which they should commit on the inhabitants of these States;

For cutting off our trade with all parts of the world;

For imposing taxes on us without our consent;

For depriving us, in many cases, of the benefit of trial by jury;

For transporting us beyond seas to be tried for pretended offences;

For abolishing the free system of English laws in a neighboring province, establishing therein an arbitrary government, and enlarging its boundaries, so as to render it at once an example and fit instrument for introducing the same absolute rule into these colonies;

For taking away our charters, abolishing our most valuable laws, and altering, fundamentally, the powers of our governments;

For suspending our own legislatures and declaring themselves invested with power to legislate for us in all cases whatsoever.

He has abdicated government here by declaring us out of his protection and waging war against us.

He has plundered our seas, ravaged our coasts, burnt our towns, and destroyed the lives of our people.

He is, at this time, transporting large armies of foreign mercenaries to complete the works of death, desolation, and tyranny already begun with circumstances of cruelty and perfidy scarcely paralleled in the most barbarous ages, and totally unworthy, the head of a civilized nation.

He has constrained our fellow citizens, taken captive on the high seas, to bear arms against their country, to become the executioners of their friends and brethren, or to fall themselves by their hands.

He has excited domestic insurrections amongst us and has endeavored to bring on the inhabitants of our frontiers, the merciless Indian savages, whose known rule of warfare is an undistinguished destruction of all ages, sexes, and conditions.

In every stage of these oppressions, we have petitioned for redress in the most humble terms; our repeated petitions have been answered only by repeated injury. A prince whose character is thus marked by every act which may define a tyrant is unfit to be the ruler of a free people.

Nor have we been wanting in attention to our British brethren. We have warned them, from time to time, of attempts made by their legislature to extend an unwarrantable jurisdiction over us. We have reminded them of the circumstances of our emigration and settlement here. We have appealed to their native justice and magnanimity, and we have conjured them, by the ties of our common kindred, to disavow these usurpations, which would inevitably interrupt our connections and correspondence. They, too, have been deaf to the voice of justice and consanguinity. We must, therefore, acquiesce in the necessity which denounces our separation, and hold them, as we hold the rest of mankind, enemies in war, in peace, friends.

We, therefore, the representatives of the United States of America, in general Congress assembled, appealing to the Supreme Judge of the world for the rectitude of our intentions, do, in the name and by the authority of the good people of these colonies, solemnly publish and declare, that these united colonies are, and of right ought to be, free and independent states: that they are absolved from all allegiance to the British Crown, and that all political connection between them and the state of Great Britain is, and ought to be, totally dissolved; and that, as free and independent states, they have full power to levy war, conclude peace, contract alliances, establish commerce, and to do all other acts and things which independent states may of right do. And, for the support of this declaration, with a firm reliance on the protection of Divine Providence, we mutually pledge to each other our lives, our fortunes, and our sacred honor.

The Constitution of the United States of America

The text of the Constitution is printed in black. Annotations are printed in blue. The titles of articles, sections, and clauses have been added for clarity. They are not part of the original document. The portions of the Constitution in brackets have been changed by amendments or no longer apply. Page numbers in the annotations refer to relevant material in your textbook. Difficult terms in the Constitution are italicized and defined in the annotations.

Preamble

We, the people of the United States, in order to form a more perfect Union, establish justice, insure domestic tranquillity, provide for the common defense, promote the general welfare, and secure the blessings of liberty to ourselves and our posterity, do ordain and establish this Constitution for the United States of America.

The Preamble introduces the purposes of the government established by the Constitution. It does not have the force of law. Therefore, parties to lawsuits cannot base claims on the provisions contained in the Preamble.

Article 1. The Legislative Branch

Legislative powers refers to the power to make law. The Senate and the House of Representatives make up the federal government's legislative branch.

Section 1. A Two-House Legislature

All legislative powers herein granted shall be vested in a Congress of the United States, which shall consist of a Senate and House of Representatives.

Through custom other branches of the federal government also possess law-making power. When judges interpret the Constitution, they are, in effect, making law (page 208). Furthermore, such regulatory agencies as the Federal Trade Commission can make rules that have the effect of law. The powers of the federal regulatory agencies, however, are subject to the control of Congress.

Section 2. House of Representatives

1. Election of Members The House of Representatives shall be composed of members chosen every second year by the people of the several states, and the electors in each state shall have the qualifications requisite for electors of the most numerous branch of the state legislature.

Clause 1 *Electors* refers to voters. Members of the House run for election every two years. The original Constitution does not specify voting qualifications. It provides that people qualified to vote in elections for the largest house of the state legislature must be allowed to vote in elections for the House of Representatives. Four amendments to the Constitution—the Fifteenth, Nineteenth, Twenty-fourth, and Twenty-sixth—have restricted state power to limit the right to vote.

2. Qualifications No person shall be a Representative who shall not have attained to the age of twenty-five years, and been seven years a citizen of the United States, and who shall not, when elected, be an inhabitant of that state in which he shall be chosen.

Clause 2 A member of the House must live in the state he or she represents, but members need not be legal residents of the district they represent. Tradition, however, dictates that candidates run for election in the districts in which they legally reside.

3. Determining Representation Representatives [and direct taxes] shall be apportioned among the several states which may be

Clause 3 *Persons bound to service* refers to indentured servants, while *all other persons* refers to the slave population. The *enumeration* that will be made every ten years refers to a census.

This holiday give them a gift that makes a difference all year long.

Think teens are tough to buy for? Not anymore! This holiday you can give your favorite teen something he or she will enjoy all year—a gift subscription to *Guideposts for Teens*. Written just for teens, *Guideposts for Teens'* faith-building true stories are real so teens can relate. Plus, each issue includes a dynamic pullout poster— an added bonus, FREE!

With each gift subscription you give, the teen in your life will receive the *Guideposts for Teens* 2001 Wall Calendar, filled with amazing graphics and powerful quotes.

FREE with each gift

SEND BILL TO:

Your Name   (please print)
_____

Address   Apt. No.
_____

City   State   ZIP
_____

☐ **YES,** send a full year (6 bi-monthly issues) of *Guideposts for Teens* for only $19.95 ($28.95 outside the U.S.) to the teen(s) listed here. Your teen(s) will also receive a *Guideposts for Teens* 2001 Wall Calendar absolutely FREE. Gift subscriptions start with the December/January 2001 issue. Satisfaction is unconditionally guaranteed or you'll refund my money for any unmailed issues.

SEND A GIFT SUBSCRIPTION AND GIFT ANNOUNCEMENT CARD TO:

Name
_____

Address   Apt. No.
_____

City   State   ZIP
_____

Name
_____

Address   Apt. No.
_____

City   State   ZIP
_____

04-201554108

**SEND NO
MONEY NOW!**

BUSINESS REPLY MAIL

FIRST-CLASS MAIL   PERMIT NO. 13   VERNON CT

POSTAGE WILL BE PAID BY ADDRESSEE

Guideposts for
Teens

PO BOX 1813
VERNON CT 06066-9883

included within this Union, according to their respective numbers [which shall be determined by adding to the whole number of free persons, including those bound to service for a term of years, and excluding Indians not taxed, three-fifths of all other persons]. The actual enumeration shall be made within three years after the first meeting of the Congress of the United States, and within every subsequent term of ten years, in such manner as they shall by law direct. The number of Representatives shall not exceed one for every 30,000, but each state shall have at least one Representative; [and until such enumeration shall be made, the state of New Hampshire shall be entitled to choose three; Massachusetts, eight; Rhode Island and Providence Plantations, one; Connecticut, five; New York, six; New Jersey, four; Pennsylvania, eight; Delaware, one; Maryland, six; Virginia, ten; North Carolina, five; South Carolina, five; and Georgia, three.]

4. Filling Vacancies When vacancies happen in the representation from any state, the executive authority thereof shall issue writs of election to fill such vacancies.

5. Selection of Officers; Power of Impeachment The House of Representatives shall choose their Speaker and other officers; and shall have the sole power of impeachment.

Section 3. The Senate

1. Selection of Members The Senate of the United States shall be composed of two Senators from each state [chosen by the legislature thereof], for six years, and each Senator shall have one vote.

2. Alternating Terms; Filling Vacancies Immediately after they shall be assembled in consequence of the first election, they shall be divided as equally as may be into three classes. [The seats of the Senators of the first class shall be vacated at the expiration of the second year, of the second class at the expiration of the fourth year, and of the third class at the expiration of the sixth year,] so that one-third may be chosen every second year; [and if vacancies happen by resignation, or otherwise, during the recess of the legislature

A state's representation in the House is based on its population. According to the original clause, the state's entire free population is counted for the purpose of representation, but only three fifths of the slaves were to be counted. This arrangement resulted from a compromise at the Constitutional Convention (page 157). The so-called three-fifths clause became meaningless when the Thirteenth Amendment, which freed the slaves, was added to the Constitution. An act of Congress has fixed the number of members in the House at 435.

Clause 4 *Executive authority* refers to the governor of a state. A *writ of election* is an order to hold an election. When a member of the House leaves office prior to the end of his or her term, the governor must fill that vacancy by calling a special election.

Clause 5 The *speaker of the House* is a member who acts as its presiding officer. By modern practice, the speaker is chosen by the party that has a majority in the House. The speaker applies House rules and determines when members will be allowed to address the House. *Impeachment* is an accusation of misconduct that can be made against the President and Vice-President, federal judges, and other high federal officials. Impeachment and removal from office are discussed in Section 3.

Clause 1 According to the original clause, the legislature of each state was to elect two senators. This clause was nullified by the Seventeenth Amendment, ratified in 1913.

Clause 2 Unlike the House, in which the terms of all members expire at the same time, the terms of only one third of the senators expire in any congressional election year. Thus every two years one third of the Senate stands for reelection. Normally only one of a state's senators would run in any election year. The election of the Senate by thirds insures that the body will not be totally transformed in any one election.

This clause allows the governor, the *executive*, to fill vacancies that occur between elections by making temporary appointments if the state legislature is not in session. Under this clause, when the legislature reconvenes it has the power to fill any existing vacancies. The method for filling vacancies was changed by the Seventeenth Amendment.

of any state, the executive thereof may make temporary appointments until the next meeting of the legislature, which shall then fill such vacancies.]

3. Qualifications No person shall be a Senator who shall not have attained to the age of thirty years, and been nine years a citizen of the United States, and who shall not, when elected, be an inhabitant of that state for which he shall be chosen.

Clause 3 The qualifications for membership in the Senate are more restrictive than qualifications for membership in the House. The age qualifications must be met at the time the oath of office is taken.

4. President of the Senate The Vice-President of the United States shall be president of the Senate, but shall have no vote, unless they be equally divided.

Clause 4 The Vice-President of the United States is the president of the Senate. As presiding officer, he or she applies the rules of the Senate. The president of the Senate may vote only to break a tie. The first Vice-President, John Adams, cast 20 votes during his term in office. Besides filling a vacancy created by the President's death or resignation, these are the only powers the Constitution assigns to the Vice-President.

5. Election of Senate Officers The Senate shall choose their other officers, and also a president *pro tempore*, in the absence of the Vice-President, or when he shall exercise the office of the President of the United States.

Clause 5 *Pro tempore* means temporary. The president pro tempore must be a member of the Senate. He or she presides over the Senate in the absence of the Vice-President. Under the Presidential Succession Act of 1947, the president pro tempore of the Senate follows the Vice-President and the speaker of the House in the line of succession if the office of President becomes vacant.

6. Impeachment Trials The Senate shall have the sole power to try all impeachments. When sitting for that purpose, they shall be on oath or affirmation. When the President of the United States is tried, the Chief Justice shall preside; and no person shall be convicted without the concurrence of two-thirds of the members present.

Clause 6 The *Chief Justice* refers to the Chief Justice of the Supreme Court. By a majority vote the House may impeach the President and Vice-President, federal judges, and cabinet officers for "treason, bribery, or other high crimes and misdemeanors." (See Article 2, Section 4).

The Senate acts as a jury in impeachment cases. A two-thirds vote against the accused results in conviction. Although several federal judges have been convicted by the Senate, no President has ever been convicted. The House impeached President Andrew Johnson in 1868, but the Senate acquitted him of the charges (page 351). President Richard Nixon faced the possibility of impeachment and conviction, but his resignation ended the impeachment proceedings in progress (page 699).

7. Penalties Upon Conviction Judgment in cases of impeachment shall not extend further than to removal from office, and disqualification to hold and enjoy any office of honor, trust, or profit under the United States; but the party convicted shall nevertheless be liable and subject to indictment, trial, judgment, and punishment, according to law.

Clause 7 *Judgment* in this clause means conviction by the Senate. Government officials convicted in impeachment proceedings are removed from office and barred from holding office in the future. The Senate does not have the power to impose any other penalty on convicted officials. However, they may be tried subsequently in criminal courts.

Section 4. Times of Elections and Meetings

1. Election of Congress The times, places, and manner of holding elections for Senators and Representatives shall be prescribed in

Clause 1 Under this clause the state legislatures are free to determine the time and manner of congressional elections unless Congress acts. Prior to 1842 Congress allowed the states to regulate congressional elections. In

each state by the legislature thereof; but the Congress may at any time by law make or alter such regulations, except as to the places of choosing Senators.

2. Annual Sessions The Congress shall assemble at least once in every year, [and such meeting shall be on the first Monday in December, unless they shall by law appoint a different day.]

Section 5. Rules for the Conduct of Business

1. Organization Each house shall be the judge of the elections, returns, and qualifications of its own members, and a majority of each shall constitute a quorum to do business; but a smaller number may adjourn from day to day, and may be authorized to compel the attendance of absent members, in such manner, and under such penalties, as each house may provide.

2. Procedures Each house may determine the rules of its proceedings, punish its members for disorderly behavior, and with the concurrence of two-thirds, expel a member.

3. A Written Record Each house shall keep a journal of its proceedings, and from time to time publish the same, excepting such parts as may in their judgment require secrecy; and the yeas and nays of the members of either house on any question shall, at the desire of one-fifth of those present, be entered on the journal.

4. Rules for Adjournment Neither house, during the session of Congress, shall, without the consent of the other, adjourn for more than three days, nor to any other place than that in which the two houses shall be sitting.

some states members of the House were chosen on a state-wide basis. In 1842 Congress required the states to create congressional districts. One representative was to be elected from each district. In 1872 Congress provided that congressional elections be held in every state on the same date in even-numbered years.

Clause 2 The Twentieth Amendment changed the date for the beginning of each congressional session to January 3 unless Congress resolves to meet on another day.

Clause 1 A *quorum* is the minimum number of members required to be present for the conduct of business. Each house of Congress has the right to decide the qualifications of its members. Until 1969 it was generally held that Congress could impose qualifications not specified in the Constitution. Thus some members have been barred from Congress because they were found to have engaged in misconduct.

For example, in 1967 the House of Representatives refused to seat Adam Clayton Powell of New York because of "gross misconduct." When Powell's suit challenging his exclusion reached the Supreme Court, the Court held that the Constitution does not permit Congress to exclude legally elected members who have met all the requirements specified in Article 1, Section 2.

Clause 2 This clause gives both houses of Congress wide power to conduct their business. The Senate, for example, has established rules for debate that allow *filibustering*, the practice of giving lengthy speeches for the purpose of obstructing pending legislation. In 1917 the Senate passed a *cloture* rule, a rule allowing the Senate to vote to stop a filibuster. The right to filibuster does not exist in the House.

Clause 3 The *Congressional Record*, published daily, prints all speeches made on the floor of the House and the Senate. It also records the votes cast.

Clause 4 Neither the House nor the Senate can adjourn for more than three days without the approval of the other body. This clause requires the two houses of Congress to meet in the same place. For example, the House cannot adjourn its session in Washington, D.C., and reconvene in another place.

Article 2, Section 3 gives the President the power to adjourn both houses of Congress if they cannot agree on a time to adjourn. To date the President has never exercised this power.

Section 6. Privileges and Restrictions

1. Salaries and Immunities The Senators and Representatives shall receive a compensation for their services, to be ascertained by law and paid out of the Treasury of the United States. They shall in all cases, except treason, felony, and breach of the peace, be privileged from arrest during their attendance at the session of their respective houses, and in going to and returning from the same; and for any speech or debate in either house, they shall not be questioned in any other place.

Clause 1 The salary for members of Congress is set by an act of Congress. Members with special responsibilities, such as the speaker of the House, receive larger salaries.

This clause provides that when Congress is in session its members shall enjoy an immunity from arrest in civil cases. Thus the clause protects members of Congress from imprisonment for debt. The clause does not provide immunity from arrest in state or federal criminal cases.

A member of Congress is protected from libel and slander suits for things he or she says in Congress while it is in session. This provision also protects members of Congress from lawsuits concerning their written words. Immunity under the speech and debate provision does not extend to words spoken outside Congress.

2. Restrictions on Other Employment No Senator or Representative shall, during the time for which he was elected, be appointed to any civil office under the authority of the United States, which shall have been created, or the emoluments whereof shall have been increased, during such time; and no person holding any office under the United States shall be a member of either house during his continuance in office.

Clause 2 *Emolument* means salary. The first part of this clause bars a member of Congress from holding a federal office that was created or the salary of which was increased during his or her term in Congress. The second part of the clause prevents officeholders in the executive and judicial branches from serving in Congress. This provision strengthens the separation of powers.

Section 7. Law-Making Process

1. Tax Bills All bills for raising revenue shall originate in the House of Representatives; but the Senate may propose or concur with amendments as on other bills.

Clause 1 *Revenue* is income raised by a unit of government through taxation. Under this clause, federal revenue bills must originate in the House. This was a democratic measure because when the Constitution was written, the House was the only branch of government elected directly by the people. The Senate can amend revenue legislation. By custom, bills authorizing the expenditure of federal money also originate in the House.

2. How a Bill Becomes a Law Every bill which shall have passed the House of Representatives and the Senate shall, before it become a law, be presented to the President of the United States; if he approve, he shall sign it, but if not, he shall return it, with his objections, to that house in which it shall have originated, who shall enter the objections at large on their journal, and proceed to reconsider it. If after such reconsideration two-thirds of that house shall agree to pass the bill, it shall be sent, together with the objections, to the other house, by which it shall likewise be reconsidered, and, if approved by two-thirds of that house, it shall become a law. But in all such cases the votes of both houses shall be determined by yeas and nays, and the names of the persons voting for and against the bill shall be entered on the journal of each house

Clause 2 A *bill* is a proposal for a law. Bills passed by a majority of the House and Senate are presented to the President. If the President signs the bill it becomes law. A bill can also become law without the President's signature. The President can refuse to act on a bill. If Congress is in session at the time, the bill becomes law ten days after the President receives it.

The President can *veto*, or reject, a bill in two ways. He or she can veto it by sending it back to the house where it originated or by refusing to take any action on it. If the President withholds action and Congress adjourns within ten days of the President's receipt of the bill, the bill is dead. This method of killing a bill without taking action is known as the *pocket veto*.

A bill vetoed by the President can still become law if it is passed again by a two-thirds vote in each house of Congress. This clause is an important part of the system of checks and balances established by the Constitution (pages 161–162).

respectively. If any bill shall not be returned by the President within ten days (Sundays excepted) after it shall have been presented to him, the same bill shall be a law, in like manner as if he had signed it, unless the Congress by their adjournment prevent its return, in which case it shall not be a law.

3. Resolutions Passed by Congress Every order, resolution, or vote to which the concurrence of the Senate and House of Representatives may be necessary (except on a question of adjournment) shall be presented to the President of the United States; and before the same shall take effect, shall be approved by him, or being disapproved by him, shall be repassed by two-thirds of the Senate and House of Representatives, according to the rules and limitations prescribed in the case of a bill.

Clause 3 This clause was inserted to prevent Congress from bypassing the President by calling pieces of legislation resolutions rather than bills. *Joint resolutions* go through the same process as bills and have the force of law. Such resolutions are passed when there is no need for prolonged examination of a measure before Congress. For example, proposals to renew an existing piece of legislation sometimes take the form of a joint resolution.

Concurrent resolutions are the expression of the will of Congress. They are not submitted to the President and do not have the force of law. Changes in rules of legislative procedure typically take the form of concurrent resolutions. Congressional resolutions proposing constitutional amendments are not presented to the President.

Section 8. Powers Delegated to Congress
The Congress shall have power

1. To lay and collect taxes, duties, imposts, and excises, to pay the debts and provide for the common defense and general welfare of the United States; but all duties, imposts, and excises shall be uniform throughout the United States;

Clause 1 *Duties* are tariffs, and *excises* are taxes on the production or sale of particular goods. *Imposts* refers to taxes generally. This clause gives Congress the power to tax and to spend tax revenues.

The clause does not give Congress unlimited taxation power. For example, Congress may not tax exports (see Section 9, Clause 5) or the activities of state governments. Until the ratification of the Sixteenth Amendment in 1913, Congress could not impose an income tax unless the tax was apportioned among the states according to population. Taxes under this clause must be imposed uniformly.

2. To borrow money on the credit of the United States;

Clause 2 Congress may authorize the sale of bonds to the public to raise money for the operation of the government. The government thus borrows money from the bond holders. People and banks invest in bonds on the assumption that the government will meet its obligations to creditors. The Constitution sets no limit on the total indebtedness of the federal government.

3. To regulate commerce with foreign nations, and among the several states, and with the Indian tribes;

Clause 3 This clause gives the federal government exclusive power to regulate foreign and interstate trade. For example, only the federal government may impose tariffs on foreign goods or regulate the freight rates of railroads crossing state lines. The so-called commerce clause provided the constitutional basis for the Interstate Commerce Act (page 407), the Sherman Antitrust Act (page 408), as well as other federal regulatory legislation.

4. To establish a uniform rule of naturalization, and uniform laws on the subject of bankruptcies throughout the United States;

Clause 4 *Naturalization* is the process by which a citizen of one country becomes a citizen of another country. This clause requires that the naturalization process be the same throughout the United States. A business or individual is *bankrupt* when it is unable to pay its debts. The clause empowers Congress to pass laws to supervise the collection of debts from bankrupt businesses or individuals.

5. To coin money, regulate the value thereof, and of foreign coin, and fix the standard of weights and measures;

Clause 5 Under this clause Congress is authorized to coin metallic currency. The clause also provides the legal basis for the printing of paper currency by the government. The government determines the metallic content of coins and the amount of gold and silver that backs printed currency. It also has the power to adjust the value of the dollar in relation to foreign currencies.

6. To provide for the punishment of counterfeiting the securities and current coin of the United States;

Clause 6 *Counterfeiting* is the act of making an unauthorized copy of United States currency for the purpose of using it as legal tender. Law enforcement agents from the Treasury Department investigate this crime.

7. To establish post offices and post roads;

Clause 7 By virtue of this clause Congress has the power to establish a government monopoly over delivery of mail.

8. To promote the progress of science and useful arts by securing for limited times to authors and inventors the exclusive right to their respective writings and discoveries;

Clause 8 Under this clause Congress may pass *copyright* laws that enable a person to register his or her work in the United States Copyright Office. Once copyrighted, a work may not be used or copied without the author's permission. A copyright registered prior to January 1978 lasts for 28 years and may be renewed for an additional 28 years. A copyright registered after January 1978 lasts for the author's lifetime plus 50 years.

The clause also allows Congress to enact legislation to protect the work of inventors. The government issues *patents* to people who invent new goods or manufacturing processes. An invention registered with the Patent Office may not be manufactured and sold without the permission of the patent holder. Patents for inventions last for 17 years.

9. To constitute tribunals inferior to the Supreme Court;

Clause 9 Article 3, Section 1, establishes the Supreme Court. This clause gives Congress the power to create *inferior,* or lower, federal courts.

10. To define and punish piracies and felonies committed on the high seas and offenses against the law of nations;

Clause 10 *Piracy* is robbery of ships on the high seas. Under this clause United States courts have jurisdiction over piracy cases even though the crime may have been committed outside national territorial limits.

11. To declare war, [grant letters of marque and reprisal,] and make rules concerning captures on land and water;

Clause 11 *Letters of marque and reprisal* are documents issued by the government authorizing an armed merchant vessel to attack ships of an enemy nation.

Congress has the exclusive power to declare war. Declarations of war are granted upon request of the President. This procedure was followed in the War of 1812, the Spanish-American War, and the two world wars. But the United States has engaged in armed conflict without a congressional declaration of war, as in Korea and Vietnam (page 690). The legal basis of a war fought without congressional declaration is the President's authority as commander-in-chief (Article 2, Section 2, Clause 1) to order American forces into action. During the late 1960s and early 1970s the Supreme Court refused to review claims that challenged the constitutionality of the Vietnam War. The War Powers Act of

1973 placed restrictions on the President's power to engage American forces without an official declaration of war (page 690).

12. To raise and support armies, but no appropriation of money to that use shall be for a longer term than two years;

13. To provide and maintain a navy;

14. To make rules for the government and regulation of the land and naval forces;

15. To provide for calling forth the militia to execute the laws of the Union, suppress insurrections, and repel invasions;

16. To provide for organizing, arming, and disciplining the militia, and for governing such part of them as may be employed in the service of the United States, reserving to the states, respectively, the appointment of the officers, and the authority of training the militia according to the discipline prescribed by Congress;

17. To exercise exclusive legislation in all cases whatsoever, over such district (not exceeding ten miles square) as may, by cession of particular states, and the acceptance of Congress, become the seat of government of the United States, and to exercise like authority over all places purchased by the consent of the legislature of the state in which the same shall be, for the erection of forts, magazines, arsenals, dock-yards, and other needful buildings;—and

18. To make all laws which shall be necessary and proper for carrying into execution the foregoing powers, and all other powers vested by this Constitution in the government of the United States, or in any department or officer thereof.

Section 9. Powers Denied to the Federal Government

1. The Slave Trade [The migration or importation of such persons as any of the states now existing shall think proper to admit shall not be prohibited by the Congress prior to the year 1808; but a tax or duty may be imposed on such importation, not exceeding $10 for each person.]

Clauses 12, 13, 14 These clauses subordinate the military to the control of Congress. Congress determines the level of funding for the army and navy, and it has the power to fix the size of the armed forces. Although these clauses do not mention a military draft, the power "to raise and support armies" suggests the authority to establish a draft. Clause 14 empowers Congress to write a code governing military discipline.

Clauses 15, 16 *Militia* refers to the various state militias. The militia exists to protect the United States from insurrection and foreign invasion. Although the militia, now called the National Guard, is organized along state lines and is under the command of the governor of each state, it can be placed under the command of the President. President Eisenhower placed the Arkansas National Guard under federal control during the Little Rock school integration crisis (page 660).

Clause 17 This clause provides that the site of the nation's capital be outside the jurisdiction of any state. It calls upon the federal government to exercise full control over the district in which the capital is located. In 1790, after much discussion, Congress made Washington, D.C., the nation's capital (page 174). Congress has the power to legislate for Washington, D.C., but in 1973 it gave the district's residents the right to elect local officials.

Clause 18 The first 17 clauses in this section list the powers that the Constitution specifically delegates to Congress (page 159). The framers of the Constitution realized that Congress could not deal with the changing needs of the nation if it was limited to only those powers explicitly listed. They therefore added this clause. Under the clause Congress may pass legislation that is "necessary and proper" for implementing its delegated powers. It is sometimes called the elastic clause because it allows Congress to stretch the meaning of its delegated powers.

Clause 1 This clause, which deals with the importation of slaves, was the result of a compromise between supporters and defenders of the slave trade (page 157). To satisfy slave owners, the Constitution barred Congress from immediately prohibiting the importation of slaves. But the Constitution did provide that Congress could prohibit the slave trade after 1808. The $10 import tax was never imposed. This clause is now obsolete.

2. Writ of Habeas Corpus The privilege of the writ of *habeas corpus* shall not be suspended, unless when in cases of rebellion or invasion the public safety may require it.

Clause 2 A *writ* is a court order directing an action. A *writ of habeas corpus* is a court order directing government officials to bring a prisoner to court and explain why he or she is being held. The writ of habeas corpus is an important safeguard against unlawful imprisonment. A judge can order the release of a prisoner if he or she finds that there are insufficient grounds for the prisoner's detention.

The clause allows for the suspension of the writ of habeas corpus in times of rebellion or invasion. But it does not state which branch of government has the power to suspend the writ. In 1861, in the case of *ex parte Merryman*, Chief Justice of the Supreme Court Roger B. Taney ruled that Congress, not the President, has the power to suspend the writ of habeas corpus. Congress subsequently passed legislation authorizing the President to suspend the writ. President Abraham Lincoln suspended the writ of habeas corpus during the Civil War.

3. Bills of Attainder and Ex Post Facto Laws No bill of attainder or *ex post facto* law shall be passed.

Clause 3 A *bill of attainder* is a legislative act declaring that a person is guilty of a particular crime. *Ex post facto* laws impose penalties on acts that were committed when the conduct was not forbidden by law.

Bills of attainder punish the accused without giving him or her the benefit of a trial by jury. For example, during World War II Congress prohibited the payment of salaries to three government officials accused of being unpatriotic. In 1946 the Supreme Court nullified the act, holding that the legislation constituted a bill of attainder. Legislation requiring communists to register with the government, however, has been held not to constitute a bill of attainder.

There have been many court decisions explaining what constitutes an ex post facto law. For example, in 1972 a United States district court held that a law barring the payment of government pensions to persons previously found guilty of *perjury*, or lying under oath, in national security matters constituted an ex post facto law and thus could not be enforced. In this case the people claiming the pensions had not been federal employees at the time the pension law was passed.

4. Apportionment of Direct Taxes [No capitation or other direct tax shall be laid, unless in proportion to the census or enumeration herein before directed to be taken.]

Clause 4 A *capitation tax* is a tax levied directly on each person. Direct taxes, according to this clause, can be imposed only if they are divided among the states according to population. The Sixteenth Amendment gives Congress the right to establish an income tax without regard to the population of the states.

5. Taxes on Exports No tax or duty shall be laid on articles exported from any state.

Clause 5 Congress is explicitly barred from taxing exports. The clause was inserted at the insistence of southern states, since their economies depended on exporting agricultural products (page 157).

6. Special Preference for Trade No preference shall be given any regulation of commerce or revenue to the ports of one state over those of another; nor shall vessels bound to, or from, one state, be obliged to enter, clear, or pay duties in another.

Clause 6 To *enter* means to report to the customs house. A vessel is *cleared* when it obtains the proper documents at the customs house. The clause bars Congress from passing legislation that would promote the commerce of one state to the disadvantage of others. It also prohibits states from imposing tariffs on interstate commerce.

7. Spending No money shall be drawn from the Treasury, but in consequence of appropriations made by law; and a regular statement and account of the receipts and expenditures of all public money shall be published from time to time.

793

Clause 7 The federal government may not spend any money unless Congress has authorized its expenditure. Thus the President is prohibited from drawing money from the treasury for programs that have not been approved by Congress. This power provides Congress with an important check on the President.

Whether the President must spend money authorized by Congress is unclear. For example, President Lyndon Johnson refused to release federal aid for highway funds to the states, and President Richard Nixon refused to spend food stamp money appropriated by Congress. The refusal of the President to spend money authorized by Congress is called *impoundment.*

8. Creation of Titles of Nobility No title of nobility shall be granted by the United States; and no person holding any office of profit or trust under them, shall, without the consent of the Congress, accept of any present, emolument, office, or title, of any kind whatever, from any king, prince, or foreign state.

Clause 8 Meeting at a time when feeling against monarchy ran high, the framers inserted a clause prohibiting the government from awarding titles of nobility. American citizens are not allowed to accept titles of nobility from foreign governments without the consent of Congress. Consistent with the provisions of this clause, Congress has passed legislation permitting government officials to receive small gifts from foreign officials. But gifts that exceed "minimal value" must be accepted in behalf of the United States and become the property of the nation.

Section 10. Powers Denied to the States

1. Unconditional Prohibitions No state shall enter into any treaty, alliance, or confederation; grant letters of marque and reprisal; coin money; emit bills of credit; make anything but gold and silver coin a tender in payment of debts; pass any bill of attainder, *ex post facto* law, or law impairing the obligation of contracts, or grant any title of nobility.

Clause 1 See Article 1, Section 8, Clause 11, for letters of marque and reprisal. Some of the powers denied to the states are similarly denied to the federal government. The prohibition against bills of attainder, ex post facto laws, and the creation of titles of nobility fall into this category.

Other prohibitions apply only to the states. For example, the states are barred from making treaties and coining money. The framers of the Constitution feared the prospect of a nation divided by conflicting diplomatic obligations and separate currencies. The obligations of contracts provision bars a state from nullifying valid contracts, that is, from declaring them void.

The prohibitions listed in this clause are unconditional. Congress cannot pass a law granting these powers to the states.

2. Powers Conditionally Denied No state shall, without the consent of the Congress, lay any imposts or duties on imports or exports, except what may be absolutely necessary for executing its inspection laws; and the net produce of all duties and imposts, laid by any state on imports or exports, shall be for the use of the Treasury of the United States; and all such laws shall be subject to the revision and control of the Congress.

Clauses 2, 3 Powers listed in Clauses 2 and 3 are denied to the states, but Congress can lift the prohibitions by passing appropriate legislation.

Clause 2 bars the states from taxing imports and exports unless permitted by Congress. The clause allows the states to charge inspection fees on goods entering the states if approved by Congress. Fees collected by the states must be turned over to the United States Treasury.

Tonnage refers to the carrying capacity of a ship. A duty on tonnage would be based on a ship's cargo capacity. States may not impose tonnage taxes unless authorized by Congress.

Clause 3 forbids the states to maintain an army and navy without the consent of Congress. The states are similarly barred from entering into agreements with foreign nations or engaging in war unless the threat of invasion is imminent.

3. Other Denied Powers No state shall, without the consent of Congress, lay any duty of tonnage, keep troops, or ships of war in time of peace, enter into any agreement or compact with another state, or with a foreign power, or engage in war, unless actually invaded, or in such imminent danger as will not admit of delay.

Article 2. The Executive Branch

Section 1. President and Vice-President

1. Chief Executive The executive power shall be vested in a President of the United States of America. He shall hold his office during the term of four years, and together with the Vice-President, chosen for the same term, be elected as follows:

2. Selection of Electors Each state shall appoint, in such manner as the legislature thereof may direct, a number of electors, equal to the whole number of Senators and Representatives to which the state may be entitled in the Congress; but no Senator or Representative, or person holding an office or trust or profit under the United States, shall be appointed an elector.

3. Electoral College Procedures [The electors shall meet in their respective states, and vote by ballot for two persons, of whom one at least shall not be an inhabitant of the same state with themselves. And they shall make a list of all the persons voted for, and of the number of votes for each; which list they shall sign and certify, and transmit sealed to the seat of the government of the United States, directed to the president of the Senate. The president of the Senate shall, in the presence of the Senate and House of Representatives, open all the certificates, and the votes shall then be counted. The person having the greatest number of votes shall be the President, if such number be a majority of the whole number of electors appointed; and if there be more than one who have such majority, and have an equal number of votes, then the House of Representatives shall immediately choose by ballot one of them for President; and if no person have a majority, then from the five highest on the list the said House shall in like manner choose the President. But in choosing the President the votes shall be taken by states, the representation from each state having one vote. A quorum for this purpose shall consist of a member or members from two-thirds of the states, and a majority of all the states shall be necessary to a choice. In every case, after the choice of the President, the person having the greatest number of votes of the electors shall be the Vice-President. But if there should remain two

Clause 1 As chief executive the President is responsible for enforcing laws passed by Congress. Whether the President has additional power as chief executive has been a matter of dispute. President Theodore Roosevelt believed that the President could do "anything that the needs of the nation demanded unless such action was forbidden by the Constitution and the law." Others have argued that the authority of the chief executive should be limited to enforcing the law. See Article 2, Section 3, for a further discussion of the powers of the President.

Clauses 2, 3 Some of the framers of the Constitution feared allowing the people to elect the President directly (page 162). Consequently, the Constitutional Convention established the electoral college. According to Clause 2 each state's electoral vote is to equal its combined number of senators and representatives. The states may decide the procedure for selecting electors. Members of Congress and federal officeholders are barred from serving as electors. This much of the original electoral college system is still in effect.

Clause 3 called upon each elector to vote for two candidates without designating one for President and one for Vice-President. The candidate who received the most electoral votes (provided it was a majority) would become President. In cases in which no candidate won a majority of the electoral vote, the House would choose the President, and the Senate would choose the Vice-President.

The election of 1800 revealed a defect in the original electoral college system (page 186). Thomas Jefferson was the presidential candidate of the Republican party, and Aaron Burr was the vice-presidential candidate. But since the vote ended in a tie, either could have become President. The House finally elected Jefferson. The Twelfth Amendment altered electoral college procedures.

or more who have equal votes, the Senate shall choose from them by ballot the Vice-President.]

4. Time of Elections
The Congress may determine the time of choosing the electors, and the day on which they shall give their votes; which day shall be the same throughout the United States.

Clause 4 According to legislation passed in 1792 electors are chosen on the Tuesday following the first Monday of November every four years. Congress has required that the electors of each state meet to cast their ballots on the first Monday after the second Wednesday in December, following the election in November. The votes of the electoral college are counted in the House of Representatives on January 6.

Today voters in each state cast ballots for slates of electors pledged to presidential candidates. The candidate receiving most of a state's popular vote wins that state's electoral vote. Neither the Constitution nor federal law requires electors to vote for the candidate to whom they are pledged. However, according to custom, electors nearly always do so. Thus the general election in November settles the issue of who will be the next President, and the balloting in December attracts little interest.

5. Qualifications for President
No person except a natural-born citizen [or a citizen of the United States, at the time of the adoption of this Constitution], shall be eligible to the office of the President; neither shall any person be eligible to that office who shall not have attained to the age of thirty-five years, and been fourteen years a resident within the United States.

Clause 5 The first seven Presidents of the United States could not claim to be natural-born citizens of the United States, because they were born subjects of the British crown. But they qualified for the presidency because they were citizens "of the United States at the time of the adoption of this Constitution."

Although the issue has never been resolved by the courts, scholarly opinion suggests that the children of American citizens born abroad meet the citizenship requirements of this clause. Note that natural-born and native-born are not identical terms. A child of American parents who is born abroad is a natural- but not a native-born citizen of the United States.

6. Presidential Succession
In case of the removal of the President from office, or of his death, resignation, or inability to discharge the powers and duties of the said office, the same shall devolve on the Vice-President, and the Congress may by law provide for the case of removal, death, resignation, or inability, both of the President and Vice-President, declaring what officer shall then act as President, and such officer shall act accordingly, until the disability be removed, or a President shall be elected.

Clause 6 This clause states that the powers of the President shall pass to the Vice-President if the President leaves office or is unable to discharge the duties of the office. The language of this clause caused confusion the first time a President died in office. When President William Henry Harrison died, it was uncertain whether Vice-President John Tyler should remain Vice-President and simply act as President or actually be sworn in as President. Tyler persuaded a federal judge to swear him in, and the precedent was created that the Vice-President assumes the office of President when that office becomes vacant. The Twenty-fifth Amendment superseded this clause.

7. Salary
The President shall, at stated times, receive for his services, a compensation, which shall neither be increased nor diminished during the period for which he shall have been elected, and he shall not receive within that period any other emolument from the United States, or any of them.

Clause 7 In 1983 the President received a salary of $200,000. The Constitution prohibits the salary from being increased or decreased during a President's term. This clause bars the President from accepting any other federal or state position during his or her term in office.

8. The Oath of Office
Before he enter on the execution of his office, he shall take the following oath or affirmation:—"I do solemnly swear (or affirm) that I will faithfully execute

Clause 8 By custom the presidential oath is administered by the Chief Justice of the Supreme Court. But this has not always been the case. After President John Kennedy's assassination, Vice-President Lyndon Johnson was sworn in by a federal district judge.

the office of President of the United States, and will to the best of my ability, preserve, protect, and defend the Constitution of the United States."

Section 2. Powers of the President

1. Commander in Chief of the Armed Forces The President shall be Commander in Chief of the Army and Navy of the United States, and of the militia of the several states, when called into the actual service of the United States; he may require the option, in writing, of the principal officer in each of the executive departments, upon any subject relating to the duties of their respective offices, and he shall have power to grant reprieves and pardons for offenses against the United States, except in cases of impeachment.

Clause 1 This clause, combined with the provisions outlining congressional control over the military (see Article 1, Section 8, Clauses 11–15), established the principle of civilian control of the armed forces. Although the President may not serve in the armed forces while in office, he or she occupies the highest position in the military chain of command. President Harry Truman exercised the principle of civilian control of the military during the Korean War. He relieved General Douglas MacArthur of his command after MacArthur criticized Truman's handling of the war (page 642).

Since President Lincoln's administration, the definition of the commander-in-chief's powers has expanded beyond narrowly military actions. For example, Lincoln based his issuance of the Emancipation Proclamation on this power (page 332). During World War II President Franklin Roosevelt supervised labor relations, claiming that his power as commander-in-chief enabled him to impose sanctions on employers and employees who threatened industrial peace.

A *reprieve* suspends punishment prescribed by law. A *pardon* issued before trial bars prosecution. If a pardon is issued after conviction, it wipes out the judgment of the court. The President may not issue pardons in impeachment cases. President Gerald Ford's pardon of Richard Nixon barred the government from prosecuting the former President for possible criminal offenses (page 698). Because Nixon had already resigned from office, impeachment was no longer an issue.

2. Making Treaties and Nominations He shall have power, by and with the advice and consent of the Senate, to make treaties, provided two-thirds of the Senators present concur; and he shall nominate, and by and with the advice and consent of the Senate, shall appoint ambassadors, other public ministers and consuls, judges of the Supreme Court, and all other officers of the United States, whose appointments are not herein otherwise provided for, and which shall be established by law; but the Congress may by law vest the appointment of such inferior officers, as they think proper, in the President alone, in the courts of law, or in the heads of departments.

Clause 2 As part of the system of checks and balances, this clause requires that treaties negotiated by the President be approved by two thirds of the Senate. The Senate defeat of the Versailles Treaty in 1919 illustrates the President's dependence on the consent of the Senate (page 516).

Executive agreements made with foreign heads of state are not subject to Senate approval. For example, President Franklin Roosevelt bypassed the Senate in the 1940 bases-for-destroyers deal with Britain. Roosevelt declared that his power as commander-in-chief enabled him to execute that agreement. The Supreme Court has sanctioned executive agreements as a valid exercise of presidential power.

This clause also requires that the President's appointments to high public office be confirmed by the Senate. Most presidential appointments are routinely confirmed, but the Senate refused to confirm two of President Nixon's nominations to the Supreme Court (page 694).

3. Temporary Appointments The President shall have power to fill up all vacancies that may happen during the recess of the Senate, by granting commissions which shall expire at the end of their next session.

Clause 3 If the Senate is recessed, the President may fill high government posts with temporary appointments.

Section 3. Duties

He shall from time to time give to the Congress information of the state of the Union, and recommend to their consideration such measures as he shall judge necessary and expedient; he may, on extraordinary occasions, convene both houses, or either of them, and in case of disagreement between them, with respect to the time of adjournment, he may adjourn them to such time as he shall think proper; he shall receive ambassadors and other public ministers; he shall take care that the laws be faithfully executed, and shall commission all the officers of the United States.

797

This section has helped make the President a legislative leader. The President has the power to recommend the enactment of legislation. Section 3 requires the President to give a state of the union address to Congress. This address is given in January, and since 1913 it has been delivered in person by the President.

The provision empowering the President to receive ambassadors and other public ministers, together with the powers to command the armed forces and negotiate treaties, gives him or her a predominant role in shaping foreign policy.

This section also requires that the President "take care that the laws be faithfully executed." President Dwight Eisenhower's dispatch of troops to Little Rock, Arkansas, during the 1957 school integration crisis was an application of this principle (page 660). Administration of programs created by Congress are primary examples of the President's execution of the law.

Section 4. Impeachment and Removal From Office

The President, Vice-President, and all civil officers of the United States, shall be removed from office on impeachment for, and conviction of, treason, bribery, or other high crimes and misdemeanors.

Civil officers include federal judges and members of the cabinet. The role of Congress in the impeachment and removal process is discussed in Article 1, Section 2, Clauses 6 and 7.

The term *high crimes and misdemeanors* is ambiguous. When applied to the impeachment of judges, the phrase has included violations of particular laws as well as general noncriminal misconduct. Because only one President—Andrew Johnson—has been impeached, the courts have not had occasion to decide whether "high crimes and misdemeanors" must include violations of law when applied to impeachment of a President. During the Watergate affair President Nixon's lawyers insisted that impeachable offenses must be violations of law. But some members of the House argued that noncriminal misconduct could provide the basis for impeachment.

Article 3. The Judicial Branch

Section 1. Federal Courts

The judicial power of the United States shall be vested in one Supreme Court, and in such inferior courts as the Congress may from time to time ordain and establish. The judges, both of the Supreme and inferior courts, shall hold their offices during good behavior, and shall, at stated times, receive for their services a compensation, which shall not be diminished during their continuance in office.

Judicial refers to the courts. The Constitution created the Supreme Court, but it does not specify the size of the Court, nor does it establish additional federal courts. The framers left these tasks to Congress. This section does provide, however, that all federal judges shall serve for life, dependent upon good behavior.

According to the Judiciary Act of 1789 the membership of the Supreme Court was fixed at six (nine justices now sit on the Court), and a system of lower courts was established (page 173). Congress created 13 district courts and three courts of appeals. Today there are 94 district courts and 13 courts of appeals.

District courts conduct trials of criminal and civil cases. Courts of appeals hear claims that a district court committed errors in the conduct of a trial or pretrial proceedings. While the Congress may abolish the district courts or courts of appeals, it may not abolish the Supreme Court.

Section 2. Jurisdiction of Federal Courts

1. Scope of Judicial Power The judicial power shall extend to all cases, in law and equity, arising under this Constitution, the laws of the United States, and treaties made or

Clause 1 *Jurisdiction* refers to the right of a court to hear a case. The distinction between courts of law and courts of equity is now largely obsolete. Federal courts can decide only cases brought by parties to a lawsuit. Federal courts cannot make rules of law when no lawsuit exists.

which shall be made, under their authority; to all cases affecting ambassadors, other public ministers and consuls; to all cases of admiralty and maritime jurisdiction; to controversies to which the United States shall be a party; to controversies between two or more states; [between a state and citizens of another state;] between citizens of the same state claiming lands under grants of different states, and between a state or the citizens thereof, and foreign states, citizens, or subjects.

2. The Supreme Court In all cases affecting ambassadors, other public ministers and consuls, and those in which a state shall be a party, the Supreme Court shall have original jurisdiction. In all the other cases before mentioned, the Supreme Court shall have appellate jurisdiction, both as to law and fact, with such exceptions, and under such regulations as the Congress shall make.

3. Trial by Jury The trial of all crimes, except in cases of impeachment, shall be by jury; and such trial shall be held in the state where the said crimes shall have been committed; but when not committed within any state, the trial shall be at such place or places as the Congress may by law have directed.

Section 3. Treason
1. Definition Treason against the United States shall consist only in levying war against them, or in adhering to their enemies, giving them aid and comfort. No person shall be convicted of treason unless on the testimony of two witnesses to the same overt act, or on confession in open court.

2. Punishment The Congress shall have power to declare the punishment of treason, but no attainder of treason shall work corruption of blood or forfeiture except during the life of the person attainted.

Federal courts are empowered to hear cases *under this Constitution*. This means that the federal judiciary can determine the constitutionality of acts of Congress and state legislatures as well as of actions of the President and other government officials.

The right of a court to rule on the constitutionality of laws and official acts is known as *judicial review*. Already exercised by the state courts, the doctrine was reaffirmed in *Marbury* v. *Madison* (page 190), when the Supreme Court held that "a legislative act, contrary to the Constitution, is not law." Federal courts also have jurisdiction in cases involving ambassadors and cases in which the United States is a party. The provision allowing federal jurisdiction in cases "between a State and citizens of another State" has been modified by the Eleventh Amendment.

Clause 2 *Original jurisdiction* refers to the power of a court to hear a case when it originates. Typically courts of original jurisdiction find the facts of a case and determine the issue of guilt or liability. Courts of *appellate jurisdiction* do not decide the question of guilt or liability. They review claims that a lower court judge made legal errors in conducting the trial or pretrial proceedings.

Under this clause the Supreme Court exercises original jurisdiction over a narrow range of cases: disputes in which a state is involved and cases involving ambassadors or public ministers. In recent times the Supreme Court has exercised its original jurisdiction infrequently. Instead it functions almost exclusively as an appellate court.

Clause 3 This clause does not guarantee trial by jury in *civil cases*, legal disputes that do not involve allegations of criminal wrongdoing. Nor does it require the states to provide jury trials. The clause applies to federal criminal prosecutions. See the Sixth Amendment for a more extended discussion of the right to trial by jury.

Clause 1 An *overt act* refers to a concrete action, not merely a state of mind.

Clause 2 This clause allows Congress to punish traitors, but it forbids punishment of the traitor's children for the crime of the parent. *Attainder* refers to the loss of rights that accompanies conviction for a serious crime. Under English law attainder of treason was transmitted to the children of traitors. In England *corruption of blood* meant that the children of criminals could not inherit or retain property owned by the parents. Such a punishment is prohibited by this clause, and it has been abolished in England.

Article 4. Relations Among the States and Between States and Federal Government

Section 1. Official Records and Acts

Full faith and credit shall be given in each state to the public acts, records, and judicial proceedings of every other state. And the Congress may by general laws prescribe the manner in which such acts, records, and proceedings shall be proved, and the effect thereof.

The purpose of this section is to guarantee that the official records and acts of one state are recognized by the other states. For example, the section requires a state to recognize valid marriage certificates issued by another state.

Section 2. Privileges and Rights of Citizens

1. Privileges The citizens of each state shall be entitled to all privileges and immunities of citizens in the several states.

Clause 1 Despite this clause, the Constitution, as interpreted by the courts, does not forbid state residence requirements for lower tuition rates, hunting, fishing, and professional licenses.

2. Extradition A person charged in any state with treason, felony, or other crime, who shall flee from justice, and be found in another state, shall on demand of the executive authority of the state from which he fled, be delivered up, to be removed to the state having jurisdiction of the crime.

Clause 2 *Extradition* is the process of returning an alleged criminal or fugitive found in one state to the state in which he or she is sought. The Supreme Court has ruled that federal courts are powerless to order a governor to extradite a fugitive from justice. The Court interpreted this clause to mean that governors may deliver an escaped criminal to the authorities of another state but are not required to do so.

3. Return of Fugitive Slaves [No person held to service or labor in one state, under the laws thereof, escaping into another, shall in consequence of any law or regulation therein, be discharged from such service or labor, but shall be delivered up on claim of the party to whom such service or labor may be due.]

Clause 3 *Persons held to service or labor* refers to slaves and indentured servants. This clause required states to return runaway slaves to their owners. See pages 308–310 for a discussion of the fugitive slave controversy. The Thirteenth Amendment nullified this clause.

Section 3. Admission of States and Governing Territories

1. New States New states may be admitted by the Congress into this Union; but no new state shall be formed or erected within the jurisdiction of any other state; nor any state be formed by the junction of two or more states, or parts of states, without the consent of the legislatures of the states concerned as well as of the Congress.

Clause 1 This clause gives Congress the power to admit new states. However, Congress does not have unrestricted authority to set conditions for admission. For example, when Oklahoma applied for admission to the Union, Congress made the location of the state capital a condition for admission. In *Coyle* v. *Smith* (1911) the Supreme Court held that Congress may not set admission requirements in areas exclusively under state control.

2. Federal Lands The Congress shall have power to dispose of and make all needful rules and regulations respecting the territory or other property belonging to the United States; and nothing in this Constitution shall be so construed as to prejudice any claims of the United States, or of any particular state.

Clause 2 Congress can make rules for the administration of land owned by the United States. This includes territories not organized into states and federal land located within a state. See page 148 for a description of how Congress administered the Northwest Territory. The Supreme Court has prohibited states from taxing federal property.

Section 4. Guarantees to the States

The United States shall guarantee to every state in this Union a republican form of government, and shall protect each of them against invasion; and on application of the legislature, or of the executive (when the legislature cannot be convened) against domestic violence.

A *republic* is a form of government in which the voters have supreme authority and power is exercised by elected representatives. According to this section the United States government must protect the existence of a republican form of government in every state. The federal government must also protect the states from foreign invasion and supply armed forces to suppress disorder when asked to do so by a state. The President may also, on his or her own initiative, send troops to a state to enforce the laws and preserve order. See Article 2, Section 2, Clause 1.

Article 5. Amendment of the Constitution

The Congress, whenever two-thirds of both houses shall deem it necessary, shall propose amendments to this Constitution, or, on the application of the legislatures of two-thirds of the several states, shall call a convention for proposing amendments, which, in either case, shall be valid to all intents and purposes, as part of this Constitution, when ratified by the legislatures of three-fourths of the several states, or by conventions in three-fourths thereof, as the one or the other mode of ratification may be proposed by the Congress; provided that [no amendments which may be made prior to the year 1808 shall in any manner affect the first and fourth clauses in the Ninth Section of the First Article; and that] no state, without its consent, shall be deprived of its equal suffrage in the Senate.

This article provides that amendments to the Constitution can be proposed by a two-thirds vote of both houses of Congress or by a national convention called by Congress at the request of two thirds of the state legislatures. No amendment has ever been proposed by the latter method. Proposed constitutional amendments can be ratified either by the legislatures of three fourths of the states or by three fourths of special state conventions. The latter method has been used only once. Congress determines by which method a proposed amendment will be ratified.

The Constitution does not specify the period of time in which a proposed amendment must be ratified. However, Congress may establish a time limit for ratification. Since the passage of the Twentieth Amendment, Congress has provided that proposed amendments will be void unless ratified within seven years. Such a limitation has been upheld by the Supreme Court.

In October 1978 Congress extended the ratification deadline for the proposed Equal Rights Amendment. The constitutionality of that resolution is the subject of debate. The question of whether a state may rescind, or withdraw, its ratification of an amendment is also disputed. Several state legislatures rescinded their approval of the proposed Equal Rights Amendment, but the legality of that action has not yet been determined by the Supreme Court.

Article 6. Other Provisions

Section 1. Prior Public Debts

All debts contracted and engagements entered into, before the adoption of this Constitution, shall be as valid against the United States under this Constitution, as under the Confederation.

According to this clause the United States government agreed to pay debts incurred prior to the adoption of the Constitution.

Section 2. Supreme Law of the Land

This Constitution, and the laws of the United States which shall be made in pursuance thereof, and all treaties made, or which shall be made, under the authority of the United States, shall be the supreme law of the land; and the judges in every state shall be bound thereby, anything in the constitution or

This section makes the Constitution, acts of Congress, and treaties ratified by the Senate the "supreme law of the land." The Supreme Court has held that a state may not regulate the operation of any federal activity. For example, a state may not examine the qualifications of federal mail truck drivers, nor may it impose dietary standards in federal institutions.

The section requires state judges to strike down state laws that conflict with the Constitution or an act of

laws of any state to the contrary notwith-
standing.

Section 3. Oaths to Support the Constitution

The Senators and Representatives before mentioned, and the members of the several state legislatures, and all executive and judicial officers, both of the United States and of the several states, shall be bound by oath or affirmation, to support this Constitution; but no religious test shall ever be required as a qualification to any office or public trust under the United States.

Article 7. Ratification

The ratification of the convention of nine states shall be sufficient for the establishment of the Constitution between the states so ratifying the same.

Done in Convention, by the unanimous consent of the states present, the seventeenth day of September, in the year of our Lord one thousand seven hundred and eighty-seven, and of the independence of the United States of America the twelfth. *In Witness* whereof, we have hereunto subscribed our names.

Attest:

William Jackson,
Secretary

George Washington,
President and Deputy from Virginia

New Hampshire
John Langdon
Nicholas Gilman

Massachusetts
Nathaniel Gorham
Rufus King

Connecticut
William Samuel Johnson
Roger Sherman

New York
Alexander Hamilton

New Jersey
William Livingston
David Brearley
William Paterson
Jonathan Dayton

Pennsylvania
Benjamin Franklin
Thomas Mifflin
Robert Morris
George Clymer
Thomas Fitzsimons
Jared Ingersoll
James Wilson
Gouverneur Morris

Delaware
George Read
Gunning Bedford, Jr.
John Dickinson
Richard Bassett
Jacob Broom

Maryland
James McHenry
Dan of St. Thomas Jennifer
Daniel Carroll

Virginia
John Blair
James Madison, Jr.

North Carolina
William Blount
Richard Dobbs Spaight
Hugh Williamson

South Carolina
John Rutledge
Charles Cotesworth Pinckney
Charles Pinckney
Pierce Butler

Georgia
William Few
Abraham Baldwin

Amendments to the Constitution

The first ten amendments, which were added to the Constitution in 1791, are called the Bill of Rights. Originally the Bill of Rights applied only to actions of the federal government. However, the Supreme Court has used the due process clause of the Fourteenth Amendment to extend many of the rights to protect individuals against action by the states.

Amendment 1. Freedoms of Religion, Speech, Press, Assembly, and Petition

Congress shall make no law respecting an establishment of religion, or prohibiting the free exercise thereof; or abridging the freedom of speech, or of the press; or the right of the people peaceably to assemble, and to petition the government for a redress of grievances.

Amendment 2. Right to Bear Arms

A well-regulated militia, being necessary to the security of a free state, the right of the people to keep and bear arms shall not be infringed.

Amendment 3. Lodging Troops in Private Homes

No soldier shall, in time of peace, be quartered in any house, without the consent of the owner; nor in time of war, but in a manner to be prescribed by law.

Amendment 4. Search and Seizure

The right of the people to be secure in their persons, houses, papers, and effects, against unreasonable searches and seizures, shall not be violated; and no warrants shall issue but upon probable cause, supported by oath or affirmation, and particularly describing the place to be searched, and the persons or things to be seized.

Amendment 5. Rights of the Accused

No person shall be held to answer for a capital, or otherwise infamous, crime, unless on a presentment or indictment of a grand jury, except in cases arising in the land or naval forces, or in the militia, when in actual service in time of war or public danger; nor shall any person be subject for the same offense to be twice put in jeopardy of life and limb; nor shall be compelled, in any criminal case, to be a witness against himself; nor be deprived of life, liberty, or property, without due process of law; nor shall private property be taken for public use, without just compensation.

Amendment 6. Right to Speedy Trial by Jury

In all criminal prosecutions, the accused shall enjoy the right to a speedy and public trial, by an impartial jury of the state and district wherein the crime shall have been committed, which district shall have been pre-

viously ascertained by law, and to be
informed of the nature and cause of the accusation; to be confronted with the witnesses

against him; to have compulsory process for
obtaining witnesses in his favor, and to have
the assistance of counsel for his defense.

Amendment 7. Jury Trial in Civil Cases

In suits at common law, where the value
in controversy shall exceed $20, the right of
trial by jury shall be preserved, and no fact
tried by a jury shall be otherwise re-examined
in any court of the United States than according to the rules of the common law.

Amendment 8. Bail and Punishment

Excessive bail shall not be required, nor
excessive fines imposed, nor cruel and unusual punishments inflicted.

Amendment 9. Powers Reserved to the People

The enumeration in the Constitution, of
certain rights, shall not be construed to deny
or disparage others retained by the people.

Amendment 10. Powers Reserved to the States

The powers not delegated to the United States by the Constitution, nor prohibited by it to the states, are reserved to the states respectively, or to the people.

Amendment 11. Suits Against States

Passed by Congress on March 4, 1794. Ratified on January 23, 1795.

The judicial power of the United States shall not be construed to extend to any suit in law or equity, commenced or prosecuted against one of the United States, by citizens of another state, or by citizens or subjects of any foreign state.

Amendment 12. Election of President and Vice-President

Passed by Congress on December 9, 1803. Ratified on June 15, 1804.

The electors shall meet in their respective states, and vote by ballot for President and Vice-President, one of whom, at least, shall not be an inhabitant of the same state with themselves; they shall name in their ballots the person voted for as President, and in distinct ballots the person voted for as Vice-President, and they shall make distinct lists of all persons voted for as President, and of all persons voted for as Vice-President, and of the number of votes for each, which lists they shall sign and certify, and transmit, sealed, to the seat of government of the United States, directed to the President of the Senate; the President of the Senate shall, in the presence of the Senate and House of Representatives, open all the certificates and the votes shall then be counted; the person having the greatest number of votes for President shall be the President, if such number be a majority of the whole number of electors appointed; and if no person have such majority, then from the persons having the highest numbers not exceeding three on the list of those voted for as President, the House of Representatives shall choose immediately, by ballot, the President. But in choosing the President, the votes shall be taken by states, the representation from each state having one vote; a quorum for this purpose shall consist of a member or members from two-thirds of the states, and a majority of all the states shall be necessary to a choice. And if the House of Representatives shall not choose a President whenever the right of choice shall devolve upon them, [before the fourth day of March next following,] then the Vice-President shall act as President, as in the case of the death or other constitutional disability of the President. The person having the greatest number of votes as Vice-President, shall be the Vice-President, if such number be a majority of the whole number of electors appointed, and if no person have a majority, then, from the two highest numbers on the list, the Senate shall choose the Vice-President; a quorum for the purpose shall consist of two-thirds of the whole number of Senators, and a majority of the whole number shall be necessary to a choice. But no person constitutionally ineligible to the office of President shall be eligible to that of Vice-President of the United States.

Amendment 13. Abolition of Slavery

Passed by Congress on January 31, 1865. Ratified on December 6, 1865.

Section 1. Neither slavery nor involuntary servitude, except as a punishment for crime whereof the party shall have been duly convicted, shall exist within the United States, or any place subject to their jurisdiction.

Section 2. Congress shall have power to enforce this article by appropriate legislation.

Amendment 14. Rights of Citizens

Passed by Congress on June 13, 1866. Ratified on July 9, 1868.

Section 1. Citizenship All persons born or naturalized in the United States and subject to the jurisdiction thereof, are citizens of the United States and of the state wherein they reside. No state shall make or enforce any law which shall abridge the privileges or immunities of citizens of the United States; nor shall any state deprive any person of life, liberty, or property, without due process of law; nor deny to any person within its jurisdiction the equal protection of the laws.

Section 2. Apportionment of Representatives Representatives shall be apportioned among the several states according to their respective numbers, counting the whole number of persons in each state, excluding Indians not taxed. But when the right to vote at any election for the choice of electors for President and Vice-President of the United States, Representatives in Congress, the executive and judicial officers of a state, or the members of the legislature thereof, is denied to any of the male inhabitants of such state, being twenty-one years of age and citizens of the United States, or in any way abridged, except for participation in rebellion, or other crime, the basis of representation therein shall be reduced in the proportion which the number of such male citizens shall bear to the whole number of male citizens twenty-one years of age in such state.

Section 3. Former Confederate Officials No person shall be a Senator or Representative in Congress, or elector of President and Vice-President, or hold any office, civil or military, under the United States, or under any state, who, having previously taken an oath, as a member of Congress, or as an officer of the United States, or as a member of any state legislature, or as an executive or judicial officer of any state, to support the Constitution of the United States, shall have engaged in insurrection or rebellion against the same, or given aid or comfort to the enemies thereof. But Congress may, by vote of two-thirds of each house, remove such disability.

Section 4. Government Debt The validity of the public debt of the United States, authorized by law, including debts incurred for payment of pensions and bounties for services in suppressing insurrection or rebellion, shall not be questioned. But neither the United States nor any state shall assume or pay any debt or obligation incurred in aid of insurrection or rebellion against the United States or any claim for the loss or emancipation of any slave; but all such debts, obligations, and claims shall be held illegal and void.

Section 5. Enforcing the Amendment The Congress shall have power to enforce, by appropriate legislation, the provisions of this article.

Amendment 15. Right of Suffrage

Passed by Congress on February 26, 1869. Ratified on February 2, 1870.

Section 1. Extending the Right to Vote The right of citizens of the United States to vote shall not be denied or abridged by the United States or any state on account of race, color, or previous condition of servitude.

Section 2. Enforcement The Congress shall have power to enforce this article by appropriate legislation.

Amendment 16. The Income Tax

Passed by Congress on July 12, 1909. Ratified on February 3, 1913.

The Congress shall have power to lay and collect taxes on incomes, from whatever source derived, without apportionment among the several states, and without regard to any census or enumeration.

Amendment 17. The Election of Senators

Passed by Congress on May 13, 1912. Ratified on April 8, 1913.

Section 1. Method of election The Senate of the United States shall be composed of two Senators from each state, elected by the people thereof, for six years; and each Senator shall have one vote. The electors in each state shall have the qualifications requisite for electors of the most numerous branch of the state legislatures.

Section 2. Vacancies When vacancies happen in the representation of any state in the Senate, the executive authority of such state shall issue writs of election to fill such vacancies: *Provided* that the legislature of any state may empower the executive thereof to make temporary appointments until the people fill the vacancies by election as the legislature may direct.

[**Section 3. Those Elected Under Previous Procedure** This amendment shall not be so construed as to affect the election or term of any Senator chosen before it becomes valid as part of the Constitution.]

Amendment 18. Prohibition of Alcoholic Beverages

Passed by Congress on December 18, 1917. Ratified on January 16, 1919.

[**Section 1. Ban on Alcohol** After one year from the ratification of this article the manufacture, sale, or transportation of intoxicating liquors within, the importation thereof into, or the exportation thereof from, the United States and all territory subject to the jurisdiction thereof for beverage purposes is hereby prohibited.

Section 2. Enforcement The Congress and the several states shall have concurrent power to enforce this article by appropriate legislation.

Section 3. Method of Ratification This article shall be inoperative unless it shall have been ratified as an amendment to the Constitution by the legislatures of the several states, as provided in the Constitution, within seven years from the date of the submission hereof to the states by the Congress.]

Amendment 19. Women's Suffrage

Passed by Congress on June 4, 1919. Ratified on August 18, 1920.

Section 1. The Right to Vote The right of citizens of the United States to vote shall not be denied or abridged by the United States or by any state on account of sex.

Section 2. Enforcement Congress shall have power to enforce this article by appropriate legislation.

Amendment 20. Presidential Terms; Sessions of Congress

Passed by Congress on March 2, 1932. Ratified on January 23, 1933.

Section 1. Beginning of Term The terms of the President and Vice-President shall end at noon on the 20th day of January, and the terms of Senators and Representatives at noon on the 3rd day of January, of the years in which such terms would have ended if this article had not been ratified; and the terms of their successors shall then begin.

Section 2. Congressional Sessions The Congress shall assemble at least once in every year, and such meeting shall begin at noon on the 3d day of January, unless they shall by law appoint a different day.

Section 3. Presidential Succession If at the time fixed for the beginning of the term of the President, the President-elect shall have died, the Vice-President-elect shall become President. If a President shall not have been chosen before the time fixed for the beginning of his term, or if the President-elect shall have failed to qualify, then the Vice-President-elect shall act as President until a President shall have qualified; and the Congress may by law provide for the case wherein neither a President-elect nor a Vice-President-elect shall have qualified, declaring who shall then act as President, or the manner in which one who is to act shall be selected, and such person shall act accordingly until a President or Vice-President shall have qualified.

Section 4. Elections Decided by Congress The Congress may by law provide for the case of the death of any of the persons from whom the House of Representatives may choose a President whenever the right of choice shall have devolved upon them, and for the case of the death of any of the persons from whom the Senate may choose a Vice-President whenever the right of choice shall have devolved upon them.

[Section 5. Date of Implementation Sections 1 and 2 shall take effect on the 15th day of October following the ratification of this article.

Section 6. Ratification Period This article shall be inoperative unless it shall have been ratified as an amendment to the Constitution by the legislatures of three-fourths of the several states within seven years from the date of its submission.]

Amendment 21. Repeal of Prohibition

Passed by Congress on February 20, 1933. Ratified on December 5, 1933.

Section 1. Repeal of National Prohibition
The eighteenth article of amendment to the Constitution of the United States is hereby repealed.

Section 2. State Laws The transportation or importation into any state, territory, or possession of the United States for delivery or use therein of intoxicating liquors, in violation of the laws thereof, is hereby prohibited.

[**Section 3. Ratification Period** This article shall be inoperative unless it shall have been ratified as an amendment to the Constitution by conventions in the several states, as provided in the Constitution, within seven years from the date of the submission hereof to the states by the Congress.]

Amendment 22. Limit on Number of President's Terms

Passed by Congress on March 12, 1947. Ratified on March 1, 1951.

Section 1. Two-Term Limit No person shall be elected to the office of the President more than twice, and no person who has held the office of President, or acted as President, for more than two years of a term to which some other person was elected President shall be elected to the office of the President more than once. [But this Article shall not apply to any person holding the office of President when this Article was proposed by the Congress, and shall not prevent any person who may be holding the office of President, or acting as President, during the term within which this Article becomes operative from holding the office of President or acting as President during the remainder of such term.]

[**Section 2. Ratification Period** This Article shall be inoperative unless it shall have been ratified as an amendment to the Constitution by the legislatures of three-fourths of the several states within seven years from the date of its submission to the states by the Congress.]

Amendment 23. Presidential Electors for District of Columbia

Passed by Congress on June 16, 1960. Ratified on April 3, 1961.

Section 1. Determining the Number of Electors The District constituting the seat of Government of the United States shall appoint in such manner as the Congress may direct:

A number of electors of President and Vice-President equal to the whole number of Senators and Representatives in Congress to which the District would be entitled if it were a State, but in no event more than the least populous State; they shall be in addition to those appointed by the States, but they shall be considered, for the purposes of the election of President and Vice-President, to be electors appointed by a State; and they shall meet in the District and perform such duties as provided by the twelfth article of amendment.

Section 2. Enforcement The Congress shall have power to enforce this article by appropriate legislation.

Amendment 24. Abolition of Poll Tax in National Elections

Passed by Congress on August 27, 1962. Ratified on January 23, 1964.

Section 1. Poll Tax Banned The right of citizens of the United States to vote in any primary or other election for President or Vice-President, for electors for President or Vice-President, or for Senator or Representative in Congress, shall not be denied or abridged by the United States or any state by reason of failure to pay any poll tax or other tax.

Section 2. Enforcement The Congress shall have the power to enforce this article by appropriate legislation.

Amendment 25. Presidential Succession and Disability

Passed by Congress on July 6, 1965. Ratified on February 11, 1967.

Section 1. President's Death or Resignation In case of the removal of the President from office or his death or resignation, the Vice-President shall become President.

Section 2. Vacancies in Vice-Presidency Whenever there is a vacancy in the office of the Vice-President, the President shall nominate a Vice-President who shall take the office upon confirmation by a majority vote of both houses of Congress.

Section 3. Disability of the President

Whenever the President transmits to the President pro tempore of the Senate and the Speaker of the House of Representatives his written declaration that he is unable to discharge the powers and duties of his office, and until he transmits to them a written declaration to the contrary, such powers and duties shall be discharged by the Vice-President as Acting President.

Section 4. Whenever the Vice-President and a majority of either the principal officers of the executive departments or of such other body as Congress may by law provide, transmit to the President pro tempore of the Senate and the Speaker of the House of Representatives their written declaration that the President is unable to discharge the powers and duties of his office, the Vice-President shall immediately assume the powers and duties of the office as Acting President.

Thereafter, when the President transmits to the President pro tempore of the Senate and the Speaker of the House of Representatives his written declaration that no inability exists, he shall resume the powers and duties of his office unless the Vice-President and a majority of either the principal officers of the executive department or of such other body as Congress may by law provide, transmit within four days to the President pro tempore of the Senate and the Speaker of the House of Representatives their written declaration that the President is unable to discharge the powers and duties of his office. Thereupon Congress shall decide the issue, assembling within 48 hours for that purpose if not in session. If the Congress, within 21 days after receipt of the latter written declaration, or, if Congress is not in session, within 21 days after Congress is required to assemble, determines by two-thirds vote of both houses that the President is unable to discharge the powers and duties of his office, the Vice-President shall continue to discharge the same as Acting President; otherwise, the President shall assume the powers and duties of his office.

Amendment 26. Suffrage for Persons 18 Years or Older

Passed by Congress on March 23, 1971. Ratified on July 1, 1971.

Section 1. Lowering of Voting Age The right of citizens of the United States, who are 18 years of age or older, to vote shall not be denied or abridged by the United States or any state on account of age.

Section 2. Enforcement The Congress shall have the power to enforce this article by appropriate legislation.

Proposed Amendment. Representation for the Capital District

Passed by Congress on August 27, 1978.

Section 1. District Treated as a State For purposes of representation in the Congress, election of the President and Vice-President, and Article V of this Constitution, the District constituting the seat of government of the United States shall be treated as though it were a State.

Section 2. Enforcement The exercise of the rights and powers conferred under this article shall be by the people of the District constituting the seat of government, and as shall be provided by the Congress.

Section 3. Effect on the Twenty-third Amendment The twenty-third article of amendment to the Constitution of the United States is hereby repealed.

Index

Italicized page numbers refer to illustrations. The *m*, *c*, or *p* preceding the number refers to a map (*m*), chart (*c*), or picture (*p*) on that page. An *n* following a page number refers to a footnote.

820

829

Illustration Credits   *(continued from page 4)*

Fraunces Tavern Museum; **128** *l* Chicago Historical Society, *r* Anne S.K. Brown Military Collection, Brown University Library; **131** NYPL; **138** Peale Museum; **140** Bettmann Archive, Inc.; **141** Museum of Art, Rhode Island School of Design, gift of Miss Lucy T. Aldrich; **147** NYHS; **149** Peabody Museum, Salem, Mass.; **151** Filson Club; **154** Mystic Seaport Museum, Mystic, Conn.; **156** Independence National Historic Park; **164** NYHS; **166** Boatman's National Bank of St. Louis.

UNIT THREE Pages 170–171 Chicago Historical Society; **172** NG, gift of Edgar William and Bernice Chrysler Garbisch; **174** LC; **175** NYHS; **177** MMA, gift of Edgar William and Bernice Chrysler Garbisch; **183** NYSHA; **184** NYPL, I.N. Phelps Stokes Collection of American Historical Prints; **188** NYHS; **195** NYPL, Rare Book Division; **196** British Museum; **200** Field Museum of Natural History, Chicago; **203** New Orleans Museum of Art; **206** MMA (detail); **208** Library of the Boston Athenaeum; **210** SI; **211** MFA, M. and M. Karolik Collection; **214** Henry Clay Memorial Foundation; **218** MFA; **220** NYHS.

UNIT FOUR Pages 226–227 St. Louis Art Museum, loaned by Arthur Ziern, Jr.; **228** NG; **232** NYPL, Prints Division; **233** Museum of Art, Rhode Island School of Design; **234** LC; **236** Michal Heron, courtesy of Cherokee Museum; **239** Boston Public Library; **241** NYHS; **244** C.R. Smith Collection, University Art Museum, University of Texas at Austin; **246** Thomas Gilcrease Institute of American History and Art, Tulsa, Okla.; **248** Oregon Historical Society; **252** LC; **254** Institute of Texan Cultures; **260** California Historical Society, San Francisco; **264** Kennedy Galleries, Inc., New York; **267** SI; **269** Newark Museum, gift of William F. LaPort, 1925; **276** Musee de Pau; **278** Louisiana State Museum; **280** Missouri Historical Society; **281** LC; **286** St. Louis Art Museum (detail); **291** by permission of Houghton Library, Harvard University; **292** NYHS; **293** LC; **294** Vassar College Library; **297** LC; **299** MMA, gift of Mrs. Russell Sage, 1908.

UNIT FIVE Pages 302–303 University of North Carolina; **304** Cincinnati Art Museum (detail), purchased from the Webber estate by a popular subscription fund; **309** NYPL; **314** (both) LC; **316** Pennsylvania Academy of Fine Arts; **322** LC; **327** LC; **330** *l* LC, *r* NA; **333** State of North Carolina Division of Archives and History; **337** NYPL; **342** West Point Museum; **344** LC; **346** LC; **351** LC; **352** LC; **353** Chicago Historical Society; **354** NYPL; **356** Alabama Department of Archives and History.

UNIT SIX Pages 360–361 Taft Museum, Cincinnati, Ohio; **362** City Library, DeSmet, S.Dak. (detail); **363** SI; **366** Thomas Gilcrease Institute of American History and Art, Tulsa, Okla.; **367** Thomas Gilcrease Institute of American History and Art, Tulsa, Okla.; **369** LC; **371** SI; **373** *l* LC, *r* Granger Collection; **377** Western History Collections, University of Oklahoma Library; **380** MCNY, J. Clarence Davies Collection; **382** Newberry Library; **383** Coverdale and Colpitts; **385** Bethlehem Steel Corporation; **390** American Petroleum Institute; **393** Abby Aldrich Rockefeller Folk Art Center, Colonial Williamsburg Foundation; **395** Metropolitan Life Insurance Co.; **397** LC; **398** NYPL; **402** Chicago Historical Society, Solomon D. Butcher Collection; **403** Newberry Library; **407** NYPL; **411** Nebraska State Historical Society; **412** LC; **414**, U.S. Department of Agriculture; **416** Kansas State Historical Society; **417** LC; **418** LC; **422** Indianapolis Museum of Art, gift of a Couple of Old Hoosiers (detail); **427** LC; **429** George Hall/Woodfin Camp and Assoc.; **433** Philadelphia Museum of Art; **434** MCNY, photograph by Jacob A. Riis, Jacob A. Riis Collection; **435** International Museum of Photography at George Eastman House; **436** LC; **437** Wyoming State Archives, Museums and Historical Department; **440** LC; **441** LC; **443** LC; **444** LC; **445** LC; **449** Granger Collection; **450** LC; **453** LC.

UNIT SEVEN Pages 456–457 MCNY; **458** J. Doyle De Witt Collection, University of Hartford; **460** *t* LC, *b* NAACP; **462**

UPI; **464** Phillips Collection, Whitney Museum of American Art; **465** LC; **467** LC; **472** National Portrait Gallery, Washington, D.C.; **474** Theodore Roosevelt Collection, Harvard Library; **476** LC; **479** LC; **480** AMNH; **482** UPI; **486** U.S. Military Academy at West Point; **488** LC; **491** LC; **493** LC; **497** NA; **500** SI; **503** *t* WW, *b* NA; **505** NA; **507** NA; **508** New Jersey Historical Society; **511** NA; **513** NA.

UNIT EIGHT Pages 518–519 New School for Social Research, New York; **520** White House Historical Association; **523** LC; **525** LC; **526** LC; **527** LC; **532** LC; **533** LC; **534** Culver Pictures, Inc.; **537** Bettmann Archive, Inc.; **538** Westinghouse Electrical Corporation; **539** Culver Pictures, Inc.; **540** LC; **542** Joslyn Art Museum; **546** LC; **548** LC; **550** WW; **551** Collection of the Whitney Museum of American Art; **556** NA; **557** LC.

UNIT NINE Pages 560–561 courtesy of the Bronx General Post Office, photograph by John Serafin; **562** courtesy of the Franklin D. Roosevelt Library; **564** LC; **566** NA; **568** *t* LC, Farm Security Administration, *b* UPI; **569** LC; **571** U.S. Department of Agriculture; **572** LC; **574** Bettmann Archive, Inc.; **576** LC; **578** LC; **580** LC; **583** LC; **586** (all) LC, Farm Security Administration; **587** King's Highway Elementary School, Westport, Conn.; **589** National Collection of Fine Art, SI; **590** LC; **594** Bettmann Archive, Inc.; **598** The Pentagon; **599** LC; **601** LC; **602** LC; **605** Thomson Organization; **608** NA; **610** Civic Center Department, City of Detroit; **613** U.S. Army photograph; **615** LC; **616** LC; **617** LC; **620** *l* LC, *r* U.S. Army photograph; **622** NA; **625** LC; **626** Navy Combat Art Collection; **627** U.S. Army photograph.

UNIT TEN Pages 630–631 MMA; **632** LC; **638** Fenno Jacobs/Black Star; **639** LC; **641** U.S. Department of Defense photograph, U.S. Marine Corps; **643** UPI; **646** NA; **650** Hallmark Cards, Inc.; **653** UPI; **655** UPI; **657** UPI; **658** *t* UPI, *b* WW; **660** (both) UPI; **661** Michael Ochs Archives; **662** Collection of the Whitney Museum of American Art; **663** American Broadcasting Company; **666** National Aeronautics and Space Administration; **667** NA; **669** LC; **672** LC; **674** James H. Karales/Design Photographers International; **675** Flip Schulke/Black Star; **679** Michael Abramson/Black Star; **680** *l* Frank Johnston/Black Star, *r* Owen Franken/Stock Boston; **683** LC; **684** Paul Conklin for Time, Inc.; **685** John Launois/Black Star; **688** Dan Budnik/Woodfin Camp and Assoc.; **691** Frank Fishbeck for *Life* magazine, © 1971 Time, Inc.; **692** NASA; **693** NASA; **696** UPI; **698** UPI; **699** Fred Ward / Black Star; **701** WW; **703** David Rubinger / Black Star; **704** *l* Don Holway / Contact Press Images, *rt* Tiziou/Sygma, *rb* Sygma; **705** Franken/Liaison Agency; **708** David Madison/Bruce Coleman, Inc.; **709** Naythons/Gamma-Liaison; **712** D.B. Owen/ Black Star; **713** From *Herblock On All Fronts*, New American Library, 1980; **714** Owen Franken/Woodfin Camp and Assoc.; **716** Breese/Gamma-Liaison; **718** Kennerly/Gamma-Liaison; **721** *l* Arnold Zann/Black Star, *r* David Madison/Bruce Coleman, Inc.; **722** NASA; **727** Energy Research and Development Administration; **730** NASA; **732** *b* Nick Sapicha/ Stock Boston; *t* Riccardi / Gamma-Liaison; **734** John Running / Stock Boston; **735** Wally McNamee / Woodfin Camp and Assoc.; **742** Michal Heron; **743** Glen Donahue/ Globe Photos; **745** Globe Photos, Inc.; **746** *t* Lee Lockwood/ Black Star, *b* Michal Heron.

REFERENCE SECTION   Page 762 *l* Independence National Historical Park. *r* Peale Museum; **763** *l, r* Colonial Williamsburg Foundation; **764** *l* Chicago Historical Society, Solomon D. Butcher Collection, *r* Thomas Gilcrease Institute of American History and Art, Tulsa, Okla; **765** *l* Bethlehem Steel Corporation, *r* Joslyn Art Museum.

Photo coordinator: Michal Heron
Photo research assistants: Shirley Green, Julia Moran, Reyna Chewiwi
Text maps, graphs, and charts: Lee Ames & Zak, Ltd.
Reference maps: R. R. Donnelley & Sons Company